7 MYSTERIES SOLVED

7 Issues that Touch the Heart of Mankind

"A man will turn over
half a library
to make one book."

—DR. SAMUEL JOHNSON

7

MYSTERIES SOLVED

7 Issues that Touch the Heart of Mankind

HOWARD A. PETH

Investigating the classic questions of faith

SECOND EDITION, REVISED

HART BOOKS
A MINISTRY OF HART RESEARCH CENTER
FALLBROOK, CALIFORNIA

7 MYSTERIES SOLVED —
7 ISSUES THAT TOUCH THE HEART OF MANKIND

Cover art direction and design: Ed Guthero
Cover illustrations: Robert Hunt
    Darrell Tank
Cover photos: John Baker
    Tiffany Yost
    Ed Guthero
Typeset: 11.5/13.5 Minion Condensed

Unless otherwise noted, all Scripture references are from the King James Version of the Bible (KJV). Other versions cited are as follows:

Amplified Bible: published by Zondervan, © 1993, The Lockman Foundation.
Living Bible: Paraphrased, published by Tyndale House Publishers, © 1971.
NASB: New American Standard Bible, © 1973, The Lockman Foundation.
NEB: New English Bible, © 1970, Oxford & Cambridge University Presses.
NIV: New International Version, published by Zondervan, © 1989.
NKJV: New King James Version, published by Thomas Nelson Publishers, © 1982.
NRSV: New Revised Standard Version, published by Zondervan, © 1990.
Phillips: The New Testament in Modern English, Macmillan, © 1958, J. B. Phillips.
REB: Revised English Bible, © 1989, Oxford & Cambridge University Presses.
RSV: Revised Standard Version, published by Thomas Nelson, © 1952.
TEV: Today's English Version, Good News Bible, © 1976, American Bible Society.

HART RESEARCH CENTER

The author assumes responsibility for the accuracy of all facts and quotations as cited in this book.

ISBN 1-878046-50-0

Printed in the United States of America

This book is dedicated to

DIANE

my darling wife and best friend

whose helpful advice and patient understanding

made this volume possible.

"Rather than love,
than money,
than fame,
give me TRUTH."
—HENRY DAVID THOREAU,
WALDEN, XVIII, Conclusion

TABLE OF CONTENTS

LIST OF ILLUSTRATIONS

Foreword by Mark Finley

A bewildering array of voices calls for our attention today. So many declare that they have some special message for us. The average person is confused with a multitude of doorways to "truth." Can anyone be certain of what truth really is? Almost two millennia ago Pilate asked Jesus the question, "What is truth?" Unfortunately, the Roman governor never waited for Jesus' answer.

There is an answer. It is possible to discover truth in our day. Amidst the confusion, there is a certain voice. God's Word speaks. Its message is certain. Its answers to our most perplexing questions are solid.

Howard Peth brilliantly unfolds God's message for today. Howard is an experienced college teacher who has shared Biblical truths on a secular California campus for over 30 years. His clear, articulate way of communicating Biblical values for this generation is powerful.

As you read these pages, read them with a prayer that the same Spirit that inspired the Bible will touch your heart. I'm encouraged that the message of this book will make a dramatic difference in your life. Prophecies of the Bible unfold answers to the complexity of modern life. This is a book to be read, studied, re-read and studied again.

May God bless you on your journey for truth. For, "It is written, man shall not live by bread alone, but by every word that proceeds out of the mouth of God," Matthew 4:4.

Mark A. Finley
Speaker / Director
It Is Written Television

"**D**ECLARE YE AMONG THE NATIONS, AND PUBLISH.... **PUBLISH**, AND **CONCEAL NOT.**" —J**EREMIAH** 50:2

Author's Preface

W E'RE CREATURES OF CURIOSITY, with minds that seek for answers. Like insatiably inquisitive children, we're intrigued by riddles, fascinated by puzzles, entertained by quiz shows. But "inquiring minds want to know" more than the latest gossip of sensational tabloids like the *National Enquirer.* We like to apply our minds to some of the more worthwhile questions of life which perplex us all in our more thoughtful moments.

You hold in your hands a rare book—one that addresses the great, ultimate, eternal questions. It opens with the basic question of God's existence, examines the claims of evolutionary theory and the deity of Christ, and investigates the final mystery of death.

It proceeds to probe the issue of Christian days of worship to determine their Biblical validity. Then the panorama of prophecy is scrutinized to find what the future holds. Finally the Beast power is revealed as we unmask Antichrist in "a theological thriller."

You'll find real-life mysteries like these will prove more fascinating than fiction as you examine point after point of evidence and track down every clue. Once you "connect all the dots," you'll see the whole picture emerge very clearly.

This book does not take the conventional, "party line" approach to its subject for fear of being different. For instance, it differs from most religious books in that it does not assume the reader begins by believing in God, in Christ, in divine Creation, *etc.* It meets the reader where he is and leads him to logical solutions for seven of the most puzzling mysteries ever to confront mankind.

Provocative? Yes. Controversial? Perhaps. But the answers uncovered by this book are unquestionably sound and satisfying, based as they are on solid research and documentation—over 2100 footnote references cite authorities in history, science, religion, *etc.*

7 MYSTERIES SOLVED is as suspenseful as a good thriller, culminating in the most vitally important manhunt of all time—that of the Antichrist/Beast. Fictional detective stories are popular in books and other media, but no imagination could concoct mysteries more challenging—or more worthy of our best efforts to solve—than the seven presented here.

People are hungry for Truth. Their natural appetite for it has been stimulated by a meager menu of cover-ups, evasive answers, and downright deception. As intelligent beings, they're tired of being offered a daily diet of flavorless falsehoods they can hardly swallow even with a grain of salt.

We needn't be scientific professionals to welcome the latest advances in research which push back the frontiers of scientific truth. And we needn't be religious fanatics to deplore the distortions which masquerade as Bible truth today.

Take a cool, dispassionate look at the religious scene today, and you'll find that many things have been "swept under the rug." We shouldn't need the skills of an investigative reporter to dig out the facts contained in this book. They should be preached from pulpits everywhere. The fact that they're not is not always the fault of individual ministers. Heaven knows the great majority of overworked and underpaid pastors and priests in God's work are honest-hearted.

But the religious establishment has brainwashed many of them by seminary teaching based more on myth than Scripture. And the system, in generation after generation, perpetuates itself and fails to come to grips with this problem.

Readers often call this book "an eye-opener." I hope that it is. Fourteen years of my life have been devoted to researching, writing, and re-writing. When I began, I had no idea it would take this long or grow to this size. But it's been a labor of love. My study was fascinating and thrilling—I pray you'll also find it so.

I don't believe people want to hear simply what I or any other man thinks. The world is already overpopulated by self-appointed experts. We need a higher authority, a more dependable standard, and that—to me—is the Bible. That's why I've tried to prove each point I make from God's Word, making these chapters truly "lessons from heaven."

My wife and I like to hear from our readers. We pray for each one of you and wish it were possible to know you all personally. God bless you in your study!

✦ ✦ ✦

7 MYSTERIES SOLVED first appeared twelve years ago, in 1988, printed at that time in two volumes. Readers of that edition will note that the material has been updated and revised in many instances. Chapter 11, "Solving the Mystery of Death—Part II," has been added, as have two appendixes.

This Second Edition also includes new discoveries in the fields of biochemistry and molecular biology. These disciplines continually reveal hitherto unknown COMPLEXITY in living cells and organisms—all of which baffles evolutionists in their atheistic attempts to account for the miracle of LIFE by purely natural means. Yet we've retained many older statements and admissions by leading scientists—including Darwin—for truth remains true till shown to be false, and evolution has not been able to produce new evidence on behalf of its cause.

- The back of the book offers eleven *Appendixes,* designated A through K, containing supplemental information you'll find valuable and pertinent.

- References to the Bible are from the *King James Version* unless otherwise noted.

- Titles and pronouns referring to DEITY are capitalized, even in quotations where they were not so printed.

- Emphasis is supplied, even in quotations, to telegraph meaning for instant intelligibility. Subtle nuances are thus made so clear that one can almost hear the author's voice.

- Contractions are freely used to achieve a lighter, more conversational tone in what might otherwise be heavy and bookish. Popular nonfiction presents scholarly facts to the masses, but a serious subject needn't be a solemn one!

- At the end of each chapter you'll find references documenting every claim. Keep a bookmark there so you can easily flip back and forth as you read, for many notes found there illuminate the main text. As a teacher, I want you to be able to close this book with the satisfied feeling that you did indeed learn something new!

H. A. P.
San Diego, California
April, 2001

"HOW MANY A MAN
HAS DATED A NEW ERA IN
HIS LIFE FROM THE READING
OF A GOOD BOOK."
—HENRY DAVID THOREAU

MYSTERY #1
God's Existence

Does God exist? How can we know
there really is a Divine Being?

"Ask, and
it shall be given you;
seek, and
ye shall find. . . ."
—Matthew 7:7

~

CHAPTER ONE

THE FOLLY OF ATHEISM

W HAT CAN WE BELIEVE about the realm of religion? Is prayer mere
mumbo-jumbo? Is faith simply superstition? Did God create man,
as the Bible says, or did man create God as a figment of his own imagination? We've all asked ourselves questions like these:

Does God EXIST?
Where did I COME from?
Why am I HERE?
Where am I GOING?
Is there any MEANING or PURPOSE in life?

These questions are not unanswerable—though I didn't always feel this
way. In college I took some courses that made me doubt God's existence, but
I was willing to investigate these basic questions of life, and God supplied
answers that gave me a deep and satisfying personal faith.

I don't pretend to have all the answers. But I write with the firm conviction that answers ARE available and that truth is revealed to all who earnestly seek it. The words of Jesus apply here: "Ask, and it shall be given you;
seek, and ye shall find. . . ."[1]

WHAT TO DO WITH DOUBT

Did you know the Bible approves a certain kind of doubt? It encourages
questions and invites investigation. God is willing to run the risk of honest
inquiry. The Apostle John advised, "Beloved, do not believe every spirit, but
test the spirits whether they be of God; because many false prophets have
gone out into the world."[2] And Paul wrote, "Prove all things; hold fast that
which is good."[3]

You see, sincere doubt seeks not to reject truth but to find it. Even the
best thinkers have been subjected to the agony of mental struggle in order
to reach certainty in the realm of truth. So we need not suppress doubt on

the basis that it's wrong in itself, and we mustn't construe a reasonable doubt as a denial of faith.

As Lord Alfred Tennyson wrote:
"There lives more faith in honest doubt,
Believe me, than in half the creeds."[4]

And poet P. J. Bailey echoed, "He who never doubted, never half believed." In fact, honest doubt may well be an important step toward faith, for it can spur us on to study these important questions. And we must be willing to study. Simply to raise a doubt or question and then neglect to search diligently for the answer is unfair and unwise. A tragic sight is someone whose mind has gone out of business as far as spiritual values are concerned. Our minds must be actively aroused on these matters, and God may use uneasy feelings of doubt to accomplish this.

But we must also understand that God condemns doubt of another kind. Preoccupation with doubt is a form of spiritual sickness. Some even use their doubts as an excuse for shedding personal responsibility to the claims of God in their lives.[5] When doubt represses a genuine conviction, our spiritual nature is undermined, for stifling the truth destroys our capacity for it. A confirmed habit of doubt is spiritual suicide.

THE DEVIL'S TARGET: YOUR MIND

This deadly habit of doubt is what Satan seeks to plant in your mind. There's nothing he wants more than to destroy confidence in God and His Word—and to a large extent he's been successful. It's become fashionable to doubt. Many distrust the Word of God for the same reason they reject its Author—because it condemns sin. "This is the condemnation, that light is come into the world, and men loved darkness rather than light, because their deeds were evil," said Jesus.[6] This class of doubter raises questions as a substitute for commitment. He claims the reason for his doubt is lack of evidence, when the real reason is an obstinate will.

Another class of doubter feels he can gain intellectual distinction simply by stating that he doesn't believe. He thinks it a virtue, a mark of intelligence, to question and quibble. But those who in their pride of mind choose to remain in doubt rather than make a firm commitment for belief in God have, by their very attitude, condemned themselves. We are responsible for the use of our minds when confronted with the truth of God.

Yet some are reluctant to give up this habit of doubt. Perhaps this is because, having openly expressed unbelief, they feel they must maintain their position. But why should they resign themselves to being assailed by dismal doubts? How frustrating, how utterly unsatisfying it must be to go through life and never encounter the ultimate Answer!

CAN WE LOVE GOD WITH THE MIND?

Can we be both religiously devout and intellectually honest? Or must we abdicate our sense of reason in order to believe in a Supreme Being? Are believers gullible, naive persons playing a solemn game of "Let's Pretend"? Some label religion a crutch, a delusion, a hang-up, an escape from reality. But it certainly wasn't an "escape" for the early Christians—when following the Lord meant being thrown to Caesar's lions! God isn't an escape: He's a direct encounter with Reality.

Christ doesn't ask us to leave our mind on the doorstep when we enter into a Christian experience. Since the mind is our supreme possession, it's reasonable that we *use* it in our worship of God. In fact, the mind gives us our capacity to worship—it distinguishes us from the lower animals.

Can we love God with the mind? God Himself actually commands us to do so when He says: "Thou shalt love the Lord thy God . . . with all thy mind."[7]

But some may say, "I can't love something or someone I've never even seen, and I can't believe in anything I can't see, either." Can't you, really? Think about this:

THE UNSEEN PRESENCE

We're surrounded this moment—and have been since we were born—by the substance most vital to our very existence. It's not only around us but within us and part of us. If separated from it, we'd lose consciousness in five minutes, experience brain damage in eight minutes, and be dead in fifteen minutes.

This substance is the most abundant element on earth. It's nearly equal in quantity to all the other elements put together. But in spite of its abundance and importance, it was unknown to man till just two hundred years ago, when Joseph Priestley, an English scientist, demonstrated the existence of oxygen.

Since the beginning of time oxygen had surrounded man; yet he'd been unaware of it. This is not too surprising, for oxygen cannot be directly perceived through the senses. We can't see it or smell it or taste it.

Thus the man who accepts nothing but what his own feeble senses can verify is severely limited even in the scientific world. (For instance, no one has ever seen the atomic particle called an electron, yet scientists have no doubt of its existence. A few examples of other things which are invisible yet factually real are gravitational force, magnetic force—and your own thoughts!) And this type of shortsighted skeptic is even more limited in the spiritual realm, for as Shakespeare's Hamlet said to his friend:

> "There are more things in heaven and earth, Horatio,
> Than are dreamt of in your philosophy."[8]

Yes, there's much more to life than meets the eye! For it's in the *mind's* eye that the heavenly vision is seen. This doesn't mean we should go around imagining things. It simply means we should keep our spiritual eyes open. American philosopher Ralph Waldo Emerson said, "All I have seen teaches me to trust the Creator for all I have NOT seen." And Jesus told His doubting disciple, "Thomas, because you have seen Me, you have believed. Blessed are those who have not seen and yet have believed."[9]

As the great Apostle Paul put it: "We look not at the things which are seen, but at the things which are not seen: for the things which are seen are temporal; but the things which are not seen are eternal."[10] How true! Material things which are seen, like buildings and monuments of the past, soon crumble into dust and are quite temporary compared to spiritual things that endure through time, like faith and hope and love.

No, my friend, our belief must not be limited only to those things we perceive through our senses or those things we fully comprehend. Blaise Pascal, the famous French mathematician, jotted some thoughts in his *Pensées* that are pertinent here: "The last step of a reasoning mind is the recognition that there are an infinite number of things which are beyond it. . . . If natural things are beyond it, what are we to say about supernatural things?"[11] Remember also the truth expressed in these words of Pascal: "Everything that is incomprehensible does not cease to exist."[12]

THREE VARIETIES OF RELIGIOUS EXPERIENCE

Yet apparently it's not easy for everyone to have the same measure of faith—or even to believe at all. Many who inherently want to believe confess they have serious reservations. Because of this, it's possible to delineate at least three categories of religious experience: the *atheist,* the *agnostic,* and the *believer.* Let's examine each of these.

1. THE ATHEIST

Strictly speaking, atheism is the absence of a "religious experience," for it's the belief that there is no God. An atheist rejects all religious beliefs and absolutely denies God's existence. But one clergyman, the late Bishop Fulton

J. Sheen, observed that atheists "talk an awful lot about God. They find it hard to stop talking about Him; they seem to meet Him at every turn and around every corner." One man who found fault with today's religion exclaimed: "Thank God I'm an atheist!"

And one of my college students gave a talk in which she set out to prove that God is indeed in the life of even an atheist. Among other points made was that she would ask the atheist, "Do you swear? Do you ever say, 'God damn it!'? Many atheists do, but why? Why does a man who claims he doesn't believe in God call on this supposedly non-existent God to damn something for him? God IS in the life of even the atheist, you see—or there's a strange inconsistency here."

Both this student speaker and Bishop Sheen touched upon something Sir Francis Bacon commented on four hundred years ago in his essay "Of Atheism" when he declared:

"The Scripture saith, 'The fool hath said in his heart, There is no God';[13] it is not said, 'The fool hath thought in his heart'; [it's] as if he rather said it by rote to himself than that he can thoroughly believe it, or be persuaded of it. . . . Atheism is rather in the lip than in the heart of man."

In other words, though man may deny God at the top of his voice, he still believes in Him at the bottom of his heart.

Atheistic thoughts are really a psychological "set" of mind, a mind closed to the possibilities and ignoring the probabilities of God. The atheist is like a blind man refusing to believe in the sun and claiming its warmth comes from some other source.

Louis Nizer, the brilliant trial lawyer, states: "The best reply to an atheist is to give him a good dinner and ask him if he believes there's a cook." Yet the chances are that such a question will merely bring an amused smile to the lips of the unbeliever and a comment that the question is "irrelevant."

But the remarkable fact is that man—and I mean all mankind, including the atheist—is inescapably religious. This fact is amply demonstrated by the late Dr. Harry Emerson Fosdick, renowned minister at New York City's Riverside Church. In his sermon on "The Impossibility of Being Irreligious," Dr. Fosdick builds a convincing case to support his contention that religion is inescapable and inevitable in the life of everyone. He begins by observing an obvious fact in the ancient world—the universality of religion. Then he goes on to say:

"In our modern world many suppose that situation to be outgrown. . . . Yet look at our world today! Were the Nazis irreligious? On the contrary, they saw that they could never do what they were determined to do on the basis of the Jewish-Christian faith, so they set themselves to find a substitute religion. They said they wanted 'no God but Germany'; they put the Fuehrer in the place of Christ; they glorified this religion in impressive ritual, confirmed it in a fanatical fellowship, and gave it a devotion that makes us Christians wish we could match it in our loyalty to Him whom we call Lord. Hitler never could have done what he did had he not made of his cause a religion."[14]

Fosdick goes on, exploring the fact that:

"A man's real religion is what he puts his faith in and gives his devotion to. The consequence of that, however, at once confronts us. Faith is a capacity in human nature that we cannot get rid of; we exercise it all the time on something or other. One man in our New York community we would naturally call irreligious. He certainly doesn't believe in God. 'I am,' he writes contemptuously, 'for all religions equally, as all impress me as being equally hollow.' But just at the point where we begin to think, Here is really an irreligious man, he says this: 'To me, pleasure and my own personal happiness . . . are all I deem worth a hoot.' So *that* is what he has faith in! He does have an inner shrine where he worships—himself. He does have an altar—not to an unknown god but to his own ego, put first in this whole universe as all he deems worth a hoot. That is his religion.

"All through this congregation are folk, I suspect, who habitually think of religion as a matter of their free election; they can be religious or not, as they choose. But that is a delusion. Every last man and woman of us puts faith in something, gives devotion to something, is coerced by a psychological necessity to make a religion of something. Isn't the conclusion urgent? Thus compelled to be religious—with momentous consequence to ourselves and to our influence in the world—let's get the best religion we can find, the very best!"[15]

In this way Dr. Fosdick drives home his point that all men—atheist or believer, conformist or "hippy"—put their faith in something (though not all have their confidence equally well placed!). Therefore, if we cannot give up religion any more than we can give up eating, if by our deepest nature we're made for religion, then we're faced with this unavoidable choice:

> not, Will we HAVE any religion at all?
> but, What KIND of religion will we have?

When you make your own choice, ask yourself quite candidly: What does atheism have to offer? Some famous—or infamous!—examples of men who didn't believe in God were Adolf Hitler and Karl Marx. (It was Marx who said, "Religion . . . is the opium of the people."[16]) Pertinent here are Jesus' words, "By their fruits you shall know them."[17] How many leper colonies have been founded by atheists? Is this the kind of work they're known for? On the contrary, no one is amazed when an infidel indulges in wickedness and debauchery. Instead, the usual reaction is, What else could we expect?

As author and illustrator Don Herold put it: "Atheists may be pretty smart fellows, but you don't find them doing any great organized good in the world. You never hear of an Atheists' Hospital or an Atheists' Committee for the Relief of Starving Whoosis Tribes. Atheists don't even have their own glee clubs, picnics or bowling teams. It seems to take some kind of faith to get people together to do some good or even to have some fun."

Yes, atheists may be pretty smart fellows—but rather shortsighted ones. The skeptic's dilemma is the PARADOX that, though he doubts all religion and is skeptical about philosophy and may even take pleasure in doubting EVERYTHING right down to the ground, there's one thing he doesn't doubt: He doesn't doubt DOUBTING—he fails to doubt the wisdom of being a skeptic. Perhaps clergyman Samuel McCrea Cavert was right when he said, "The worst moment for an atheist is when he feels grateful and has no one to thank."

2. THE AGNOSTIC

The agnostic is not so bold as the atheist. He doesn't come right out and say, "There is no God," as the atheist does. No, the agnostic simply says, "I don't know if God exists; He may or He may not."

The word *agnostic* comes from the Greek language and literally means "not known." So an agnostic thinks it's impossible to know whether or not there is a God, or a future life, or anything beyond physical phenomena.

At first glance, agnosticism seems different from atheism, and agnostics may feel offended if told there is no essential difference between their position and that of the atheist. Agnostics see themselves as being simply un-committed—and that's vastly different from the outright skepticism of atheists, isn't it? After all, agnostics have taken a comfortable middle-of-the-road position: They're neither fish nor fowl, neither atheist nor believer. (Perhaps that's why poet Robert Frost said, "Don't be an agnostic. Be something."[18])

But there's no refuge, no safety in agnosticism. God is patient, yet He cannot permit us to waver in indecision forever—we MUST decide one way or the other. As free moral agents, we have freedom OF choice but not free-dom FROM choice. The need to choose, the responsibility to decide, "comes with the territory"—it's a part of life we can't escape. "And Elijah came unto all the people, and said, How long halt ye between two opinions? If the Lord be God, follow Him: but if Baal, then follow Him."[19] You see, there's no neutrality in this war—God expects us to stand up and be counted.

So, as Harvard theologian Harvey Cox points out, "Not to decide is to decide." He means: Not to decide to believe in God is to decide NOT TO. No fence-sitting is allowed. Jesus decisively declared: "He that is not with Me is against Me."[20] Therefore Joshua urges us, "Choose you this day whom ye will serve. . . . As for me and my house, we will serve the Lord."[21]

I like the way Dr. Fosdick shows that there's an ISSUE to be faced here:

> "Consider, in the first place, that we indeed must choose. I know all about agnosticism, and how it seems a place of neutral retreat. We neither believe in God, nor disbelieve, men say; we do not know. But that is a DECEPTIVE NEUTRALITY. Real faith in God is a positive matter—you either have it or you don't. . . . If a man is an atheist, he hasn't got it, but if a man is an agnostic he hasn't got it either. Positive faith in God is something we either have, or have not. . . .
>
> "Like it or not, life is full of forced decisions. A man can love and trust his wife, and deepening with the years such love and trust can be a glorious experience. A man either has that experience or he hasn't. If, as the alternative, he distrusts his wife, he has missed it. And if he tries to be agnostic about his wife, saying, 'I neither trust her nor distrust her; I suspend judgment as to whether she is trustworthy or not,' he has missed it too. In all such vital matters there is no escape into neutrality. Life presents us with forced decisions."[22]

But if the choice is a forced one, it need not be a painful one. The classic words of Pascal still ring true in his analogy of "The Wager":

> "This much is certain, either God is, or He is not; there is no middle ground. But to which view shall we be inclined? Think of a coin being spun which will come down either heads or tails. How will you wager? Reason can't make you choose either, reason can't prove either wrong in advance. . . . But you must wager, for you are already committed to life, and not to wager that God is, is to wager that He is not. Which side, then, do you take?
>
> "Let's weigh the gain or loss involved in calling heads that God exists: If you WIN you win everything, if you LOSE you lose nothing. Don't hesitate then; wager that He does exist. For there is an infinity of infinitely happy life to be won, and what you're staking is finite. That leaves no choice. Since you are obliged to play, you must be renouncing reason if you hoard your life rather than risk it for an infinite gain which is just as likely to occur as a loss amounting to nothing."[23]

English poet Lord Byron agrees: "The Christian has greatly the advantage over the unbeliever, having everything to gain and nothing to lose."

If you find it hard to believe in God, remember that no mere mortal can ever comprehend ALL of the great God of the universe. A god small enough for our minds wouldn't be big enough for our needs. Believe in as much of God as you can—that's the way to start.

3. The BELIEVER

The believer, we say, has "faith." But what does that term mean? A small boy once defined faith as "believin' whatcha know ain't so." That's a good definition of what faith is NOT, for no one—in either sacred or secular affairs—has ever been so credulous as to believe something he knew wasn't true.

Furthermore, we've already learned from Fosdick's sermon on "The Impossibility of Being Irreligious" that even atheists put their "faith" in something. If both the atheist and the believer exercise some kind of faith, then where does the difference lie? What's the virtue in being a "believer"? Hannah W. Smith supplies the answer in her book *The Christian's Secret of a Happy Life:*

> "The virtue does not lie in your believing, but in the thing you believe. If you believe the truth, you are saved; if you believe a lie, you are lost. The act of believing in both cases is the same: the things believed are exactly opposite, and it is this which makes the mighty difference. Your salvation comes, not because your faith saves you, but because it LINKS you to the Savior who saves; and your believing is really nothing but the link."[24]

Implicit in those words is the thought that study is important, study that helps us know the difference between "the truth" and "a lie." Bible study will help us here, for the Good Book says, "Faith cometh . . . by the Word of God."[25] And this same Word of God defines faith with these inspired words: "Faith is the substance of things hoped for, the evidence of things NOT seen."[26]

Let's keep this Biblical definition in mind as we think about the question "Does God exist?" For faith, by its very nature, cannot deduce proof—if it could, it would be something other than faith. Faith is always "the evidence of things NOT [yet] seen." And that brings us to our next point.

God's Existence Cannot Be PROVED
— *or* DISPROVED

The candid admission that man cannot prove God exists may come as a surprise to some, but why should it seem surprising? After all, to say that we can't use science or logic to prove the existence of the supernatural is simply to recognize the limitations of science and logic: these have their proper sphere within which they function quite effectively—but the world of the spirit transcends them both.

As world-famous physician Sir William Osler wrote: "Nothing in life is more wonderful than FAITH—the one great moving force we can neither weigh in the balance nor test in the crucible."[27]

These thoughts have been echoed by many, such as W. T. Stace, philosophy professor at Princeton University. We may summarize a portion of his book *Time and Eternity*[28] as follows:

> "Religious consciousness lies in a region forever beyond all proof or disproof. If God does not lie at the end of any telescope, neither does He lie at the end of any line of logic. We can never, starting from the natural order, prove the divine order. Proof of the divine must somehow lie within itself and be its own witness. But if, for these reasons, God can never be proved by arguments that take natural facts for their premises, for the very same reason He can never be disproved by such arguments.
>
> "Nevertheless God is not without witness. Nor is His existence any less certain. God is 'in the heart.' It's in the heart, then, that the witness of Him, the proof of Him, must lie, and not in any external circumstance of the natural order. God is known only by intuition, not by the logical intellect. Exactly the same situation exists in regard to the aesthetic consciousness by which we perceive art. For artistic values are incapable of being proved except by aesthetic intuitions."

Stace draws a striking analogy between art and religion when he says that asking for proof of the existence of God is on a par with asking for proof of the existence of beauty. It's exactly as absurd, and for identical reasons. Either you directly perceive beauty, or you don't. And either you directly perceive God in intuition, or you don't. Both the beautiful and the divine are matters of direct experience. No LOGIC will bring you a sense of the beauty of a poem or symphony, if you don't feel it. A skillful critic may tell you where to look, what other people have found beautiful, what elements in the work of art are those in which the artistic may be found. Such a process may lead you to see beauty where you did not see it before. But in the end you must SEE it for yourself; that is, you must recognize it intuitively. Just as it would be absurd to accuse artistic judgments of being "irrational," it's unfair for unbelievers to level that charge against religious truths.

Along this same line, you may remember *A Man Called Peter*, the best-selling biography by Catherine Marshall about her late husband, who became an extraordinary minister and served as Chaplain of the United States Senate. She wrote:

> "Peter's favorite thought was that 'spiritual reality is a matter of perception, not of proof. . . . There are some things that never can be proved. Can you prove—by logic—that something is lovely? Could you prove that a sunset is beautiful? . . . Either we see beauty—or we do not.'"[29]

Both Stace's book and Marshall's book were published in the 1950's, but what they said was expressed long ago by an ancient prophet: "Can you fathom the mysteries of God? Can you probe the limits of the Almighty? They are higher than the heavens—what can you do? They are deeper than the depths of the grave—what can you know? Their measure is longer than the earth and wider than the sea."[30]

In other words, God can't be searched out scientifically or proved logically. But faith is not concerned with proofs—it dares to plunge beyond sight. Centuries ago Augustine, a great thinker and theologian, said: "Faith is to believe what we do not see, and the REWARD of faith is to see what we believe."

This is not to say that Christian faith is irrational, illogical, or unscientific! Our next chapter, for instance, will present strong arguments, composed of logical reasons and persuasive evidence, answering the question "Does God exist?" You'll find that God has given sufficient evidence on which to base an intelligent faith if you WISH to believe.

What Do You Stand to LOSE?

Many years ago this story came out of Russia, long before the Communist regime began:

It seems that a certain atheist was parading up and down the countryside, pouring out his verbiage against the very thought of God, and ridiculing all those who believed in God.

On one occasion he addressed a group gathered in a large hall. He stirred them to a high pitch and then hurled a challenge to God, that IF there BE a God, He reveal it by striking him dead. Of course, God did not, so the atheist turned to his audience and sneered: "See, there is no God."

Whereupon a little Russian peasant woman with a shawl about her head arose to speak. She addressed her remarks to the speaker and said:

"Sir, I cannot answer your arguments. Your wisdom is beyond me. You are an educated man—I'm just a peasant woman. With your superior intelligence will you answer me one question?

"I've been a believer in Christ for many years. I've rejoiced in His salvation, and I've enjoyed my Bible. His comfort has been a tremendous joy. If when I die I learn that there is no God, that Jesus is not His Son, that the Bible is not true, and that there is no salvation and no heaven—pray, sir, what have I lost by believing in Christ during this life?"

The room was very still. The audience grasped the woman's logic, and then they turned to the atheist, who by that time was swayed by the woman's simplicity.

In quiet tones he replied: "Madam, you haven't lost a thing."

The peasant woman smiled, "You've been kind and answered my question. Permit me to ask another. If, when it comes your time to die, you discover that the Bible IS true, that there IS a God, that Jesus IS His Son, and that there IS a heaven AND a hell—pray, sir, what will YOU stand to lose?"

The atheist had no answer.

THE WILL TO BELIEVE [31]

People who do not believe in God are usually those who will not believe in Him. Unbelievers choose NOT to believe in God. The problem lies not in the MIND but in the WILL. Those willing to know God will find Him—and will find the evidence for His existence satisfying and abundant. The atheist or agnostic, by closing his eyes to the very real evidence of God's existence, is playing a game he cannot win.

The trouble is, man's head has overshadowed his heart: He has knowledge without wisdom, facts without faith, logic without love. But while the agnostic is adrift on a sea of uncertainty, the believer has anchored his faith in the pages of God's Word. While some people want an affidavit from God certifying that He really exists, Faith sees the invisible, believes the incredible, and receives the impossible.

The unbeliever, not willing to accept God for a Father, becomes a lonely orphan in an alien universe. Unlike believers who feel "Heaven is our home," he's like "The Man Without a Country." Paul describes such people as "without Christ . . . aliens . . . strangers . . . having no hope, and without God in the world." [32]

Perhaps that's why Henry David Thoreau observed that "The mass of men lead lives of quiet desperation." [33] Because uncertainty breeds unhappiness, J. Alfred Prufrock lamented his "hundred indecisions," unhappily admitting: "I have measured out my life with coffee spoons." [34] And we ourselves become so caught up in daily living—measuring out our lives in coffee spoons and cocktail glasses, in income-tax forms and insurance policies, in triumphs and tragedies—that we rarely pause to ask the great questions of life!

You'll find that having faith in God can help not only you yourself but others—your family and friends. For atheism and agnosticism are in fact COMMUNICABLE DISEASES. If you habitually display an attitude of doubt and continually voice words of skepticism, you may infect young minds of loved ones with the malignancy called disbelief—sometimes with fatal results.

But you need not succumb to atheism. You need not submit to the agony of religious doubt. You can free your mind from the shackles of unbelief. Your faith in God will grow as you continue to seek Him. For God Himself tells us:

> "Ye shall seek Me, and FIND Me,
> when ye shall search for Me
> with all your heart."[35]

～

Notes to Chapter 1

1. Matthew 7:7 and Luke 11:9.
2. 1 John 4:1, NKJV.
3. 1 Thessalonians 5:21.
4. Lord Alfred Tennyson, *In Memoriam*, Part XCVI, Stanza 3.
5. Denying God's existence is an escape mechanism often resorted to by those who want to deny moral accountability for their actions. They don't like to be told that certain things are right or wrong, so they "erase" God from their philosophy—and they think that takes care of the whole matter. John Bunyan, author of the classic *Pilgrim's Progress*, explained it this way: "When wicked persons have gone on in a course of sin, and find they have reason to fear the just judgment of God for their sins, they begin at first to wish that there were no God to punish them; then by degrees they persuade themselves that there is none; and then they set themselves to study for arguments to back their opinion."
6. John 3:19.
7. Matthew 22:37, Mark 12:30, & Luke 10:27. Cited from Deuteronomy 6:5.
8. William Shakespeare, *Hamlet, Prince of Denmark*, Act I, Scene v, lines 166-167.
9. John 20:29, NKJV.
10. 2 Corinthians 4:18.
11. Blaise Pascal, *Pensées [Thoughts]*, translated by A. J. Krailsheimer (Harmondsworth, England: Penguin Books, Ltd., c. 1966), p. 85, #188.
12. Pascal, *Pensées*, translated by Krailsheimer, p. 101, #230.
13. Psalms 14:1 and 53:1. Reinforcing the thought expressed in those Bible verses, a bumper sticker proudly proclaims that now atheists even have their own National Holiday! It's April 1st.
14. Dr. Harry Emerson Fosdick, "The Impossibility of Being Irreligious," in his *On Being Fit to Live With*, (New York: Harper & Brothers, 1946), pp. 79-80.
15. *Ibid.*, pp. 80-81.
16. Karl Marx, *Introduction to A Critique of the Hegelian Philosophy of Right* (1844). To show what kind of person Karl Marx was, he also said: "There are no morals in politics; there is only expediency." Furthermore, he said: "PROMISES are like PIE-CRUST—made to be broken."
17. Matthew 7:20, NKJV.
18. Robert Frost, in "A Walk with Robert Frost," *Reader's Digest* (April 1960), p. 79.
19. 1 Kings 18:21.
20. Matthew 12:30 and Luke 11:23.
21. Joshua 24:15.
22. Harry Emerson Fosdick, "Why We Believe in God," in his *On Being a Real Person*, (New York: Harper & Brothers, 1943), pp. 29-90.
23. Pascal, *Pensées*, translated by Krailsheimer, #418.
24. Hannah W. Smith, *The Christian's Secret of a Happy Life* (New York: Fleming H. Revell Company, c. 1883), p. 70. In other words, we must have faith not in faith itself but in Jesus Christ, the Savior.

25. Romans 10:17.

26. Hebrews 11:1.

27. Sir William Osler, quoted in Harvey Cushing, *The Life of Sir William Osler* (Oxford: The Clarendon Press, 1925), Volume I, Chapter 30.

28. Walter Terence Stace, *Time and Eternity* (Princeton, New Jersey: Princeton University Press, 1952), pp. 136-144.

29. Catherine Marshall, *A Man Called Peter* (New York: McGraw-Hill Book Company, 1951), pp. 43-44.

30. Job 11:7-9, NIV.

31. Professor William James of Harvard, the American pioneer in psychology, gave an important lecture in 1896 called "The Will to Believe" which he described as "an essay in justification of faith, a defence of our right to adopt a believing attitude in religious matters."

32. Ephesians 2:12. French writer Jean Paul Sartre promoted *existentialism*, his atheistic philosophy of despair which asserts the *meaninglessness* of life. He said: "Life is an empty bubble floating on the sea of nothingness"! But atheists certainly don't need Sartre to find their forlorn existence meaningless. Belief in the saving power of God is needed to make sense out of an otherwise senseless world.

33. Henry David Thoreau, *Walden* (New York: New American Library, 1957), p. 10.

34. T. S. Eliot's poem, "The Love Song of J. Alfred Prufrock."

35. Jeremiah 29:13.

No God—no peace.
Know God—know peace.

"Acquaint thyself now
with Him,
and be at peace:
thereby good
shall come unto thee."

—Job 22:21

CHAPTER TWO

~

DOES GOD EXIST?

WHEN NAPOLEON BONAPARTE was sailing down the Mediterranean to Egypt with his great military force, the officers, most of whom were skeptics, were standing under the glittering stars on the ship's deck expressing their atheistic theories. After a while Napoleon grew tired of it all and said: "Your arguments are all very clever, sirs—but who made all these stars?" A heavy silence followed as Napoleon walked away to his sleeping quarters and left the perplexed men gazing up at the dazzling majesty of the heavens.

Yes, that's the question: How do we explain the existence of the universe? We live in a world of unfailing cause-and-effect relationships. Nothing happens in and of itself—it invariably results from one or more causes. In science, causality is always a basic assumption. In fact, this assumption is so obviously true that it's called the Law of Cause and Effect. Now this law, as we'll see in a moment, provides potent evidence of God's existence.[1] In fact, the evidence for the existence of God is overwhelming. But we may still be unimpressed by it unless we're willing to believe.

THE PRIMARY REQUIREMENT:
A WILLING MIND

When we embark on an inquiry like this, we must be willing to re-educate our minds and re-groove our thinking out of the ruts of worldly skepticism, to seek what James calls "the wisdom that is from above."[2]

Our chapter on "The Folly of Atheism" stated that it's impossible to prove the existence of God. Now, don't misunderstand—there's plenty of evidence that God exists, but no absolute proof. The evidence is reasonable and ample, but those who reject God do so, not because the evidence is weak, but because they've already chosen not to believe in God, for other reasons. Belief in God rests on abundant, logical evidence, but the possibility of doubt always remains.

Some may wonder, Why doesn't God send proof? Well, the time is coming when God WILL prove to everyone that He exists. Proof will then make unbelievers non-existent. But for the present, God has left room for doubt in order to make room for faith.

The reality of God's existence can be sustained by exceedingly strong arguments, but God never FORCES the will. No argument will ever convince someone who doesn't want to submit to God. Even if he's completely overpowered and silenced by the arguments, he'll still be of an unbelieving heart, and that's what really counts. As the poet said:

> "A man convinced against his will
> Is of the same opinion still."

To experience the illumination God is eager to give us, we need a certain frame of mind. We need a receptive attitude toward truth. We need to be open-minded. One man said, "Minds are like parachutes: They function only when open." But some minds are like concrete—all mixed up and permanently set! The person who's willing to believe has already taken the first step toward a satisfying faith. The importance of this willingness, this open-mindedness, cannot be overemphasized. For all who desire to believe, all who are open and willing to believe, the evidence is persuasive.

CLUES TO UNRAVEL THE MYSTERY

The Bible says, "No one has seen God at any time."[3] But the fact that God is hidden or invisible is not the whole story, for God provides signs of His presence and activity. However, God discloses Himself when and where He chooses and not as man might want. So although God is a mystery, He gives clues to help us unravel part of that mystery. These clues to reality are pointers, indicators, evidences of the existence of God. They provide reasons for rational belief in the invisible God.

Now we come to the crux of our investigation: What specific reasons are there for believing in God? Man's inquiring mind has long sought such reasons—as long ago as the 13th century Thomas Aquinas systematized some of the reasons for believing in God's existence. You'll find there's not just one but in fact several compelling reasons for that belief.

CLUE #1:
PHYSICAL MATTER

The inexorable Law of Cause and Effect teaches that things don't just "happen"—they must be brought about by a cause that precedes the effect and that's sufficient to produce it. We can explain a puddle in the road by talking of a spring shower, but it's impossible to explain the ocean that way, for great effects call for great causes.

The existence of PHYSICAL MATTER is a reality beyond all dispute. Yet where did it come from? You see, in a universe governed by the Law of Cause and Effect, it's impossible to account for the origin of matter by natural means. *Ex nihilo nihil fit* is a Latin phrase meaning "out of nothing comes nothing" or "nothing is made from nothing." This phrase enunciates not only a common-sense fact we know in our hearts but also a sound scientific principle, for the Law of Conservation of Mass states: "Matter cannot be created."[4]

Some scientists reject the Bible account: "In the beginning God created the heaven and the earth."[5] But they have nothing to put in its place! Evolutionary theories sometimes speculate about this, but they're hardly worthy of being called theories of *origin,* for they don't account for beginnings. They always assume the pre-existence of matter in some state, speaking of "primeval dust" or "gaseous matter" solidifying to form our little planet—but no man-made theory even pretends to explain how this whole universe with its unnumbered worlds and stars first came into existence! Instead of accepting the Biblical concept that God is the Creator and Sustainer of all things, the theory of evolution teaches that:

No One   +   Nothing   X   Blind Chance   =   EVERYTHING!

If we cannot explain the origin of the universe by NATURAL causes, then we must look to the existence and action of a SUPERNATURAL Cause for its origin.

"The heavens declare the glory of God," said the Psalmist.[6] God challenges us to "Lift up your eyes on high, and behold who hath created these things."[7] The fact that matter exists is a clue, a pointer to the existence of the God who made it. The existence of even one single ATOM is a mighty argument for God as Creator.[8] The evidence of God's existence is all around us, from the tiny grain of sand to the majestic mountain looming on the horizon.

Matter—whether solid, liquid, or gas—had to have a beginning. It makes no difference what we consider the first step in creation, or how far back into prehistoric time we push the event. There must have been a Creator to bring the universe into being. The believer maintains that without God there is no answer; to him God is the glorious First Cause.

CLUE #2:
MOTION & KINETIC ENERGY

An Arab camel driver, when asked how he knew there's a God, replied by asking another question: "How do I know whether a camel or a man passed by my tent last night? By their footprints in the sand." So, from the most minute molecule to the most remote galaxy, all the universe reveals the footprints of its Maker.

We've just seen that one of the footprints of God is the existence of matter, but another is the presence of MOTION in the universe. In order to have motion (of the earth and other heavenly bodies) there must be a moving force. The laws of physics teach that things don't set themselves in motion—they stay at rest until moved by some other moving object. If we set a book on the table, it will stay there forever unless and until it's acted upon by some outside force. If we see a ball suddenly roll across the floor, we naturally turn to see who or what started it rolling. Instinctively we realize that motion is not natural to inanimate objects.

Yet we see great masses of matter hurtling through space at tremendous speeds![9] Countless worlds ceaselessly circle the boundless realms of space. Think of planets in their orbits and the march of constellations—what started them moving? What great force provided the initial impetus? Whence came such colossal energy? Motion without a mover is as impossible as creation without a Creator. Here again the only explanation that meets the demands of fact is that God not only created the world, but He also set it in motion. The believer sees God as the great Prime Mover.

CLUE #3:
LIFE

The unbeliever, leaving God out of the picture, finds it hard enough to account for the existence of MATTER and MOTION in our universe, but he also faces the insurmountable task of explaining the origin of LIFE itself. And there's a tremendous difference—a vast gulf—between the living and the non-living, between organic and inorganic matter. A small seed looks tiny beside a boulder, but the seed has within it a promise and potency that the inert boulder entirely lacks. The marvelous nerves and tissues of pulsing, living creatures—both plants and animals—must be accounted for.

How did this vital force originate? Where did that first spark of life come from? Men may speculate and propose theories, but no one really knows. Some believe nature is self-activating; they think nature possesses in itself some "vital principle." But this is not true—nature is not self-activating.

No less a scientist than Louis Pasteur himself, the father of microbiology, exploded the theory of spontaneous generation by proving it false in a series of classic experiments in the mid-1800's. Pasteur showed that microbes, like other forms of life, arise only from pre-existing, similar living things. *Only life begets life.* More will be said on this point in Chapter 4, when we discuss evolution.

Perhaps you can see the magnitude of the problem confronting the atheist, for there's not one chance in billions that life on our planet is an accident. Professor Edwin Conklin, biologist at Princeton University, has often said, "The probability of life originating from accident is comparable to the probability of the Unabridged Dictionary resulting from an explosion in a printing shop!"[10]

The existence of even "simple" forms of life demands a Lifegiver, the living God.

Clue #4:
DESIGN & ORDER

So far we've seen that God is a MUST: any rational explanation of the MATTER and MOTION and LIFE we see all around us presupposes the necessary existence of God. As a matter of fact, even Voltaire, the famous French skeptic, had to admit: "If there were no God, it would be necessary to invent Him." Believers, of course, have no more "invented" God than they've invented or imagined the physical evidence we've just examined as manifestations of His creative power, but they see the logical necessity of His existence.

A fourth clue pointing to the reality of God is the presence of order, purpose, and DESIGN. All through nature there's variety, yet order and beauty. Every leaf on a tree is different from every other leaf, yet they all serve the same purpose—of producing food from the air and sunshine, and of providing beauty and shade for man. Fish are designed to live in the sea, as animals are designed for the dry land.

If the world came into existence as a result of blind chance, without a divine Intelligence, it could have been a chaos with no law or order. The fact that earth is not in a chaotic state calls for explanation. Albert Einstein, seeing a sense of order in the universal laws of nature, said: "The most incomprehensible thing about the world is that it IS comprehensible."[11]

Astrophysicists recognize an amazing precision in the mathematical order of the universe!

So many exacting conditions are necessary for life on earth that they couldn't possibly exist in proper relationship by chance. The earth rotates on its axis 1000 miles an hour at the equator; if it turned at only 100 miles an hour, our days and nights would be ten times as long as now, and the hot sun would likely scorch our vegetation each day, while in the long night any surviving sprout might well freeze.

Furthermore, the sun has a surface temperature of 10,000 degrees Fahrenheit, and our earth is just far enough away so this ball of fire warms us just enough and not too much! If the sun gave off only one-half its present radiation, we'd freeze, and if it gave half as much more, we'd roast. But God "set the thermostat" just right! Did you know that if the polar ice caps melted away, New York, Tokyo, and London would be under water?

It's a cynical put-down to call this planet the "3rd ROCK from the Sun." For the earth is a MIRACLE of careful—and hospitable—design. Our atmosphere of life-supporting gases is sufficiently high and dense to blanket the earth against the deadly impact of twenty million meteors that daily enter it at speeds of about thirty miles-per-second. Among its many other functions, the atmosphere also maintains the temperature within safe limits for life, and carries the vital supply of fresh water-vapor far inland from the oceans to irrigate the land, which otherwise would become a barren desert.

If the earth were as small as the moon (one-fourth its present diameter), the force of gravity would be only one-sixth as strong and would fail to hold both atmosphere and water, so temperatures would be fatally extreme. If the moon were only 50,000 miles away instead of its actual distance (240,000 miles), our tides would be so enormous that twice a day all continents would be submerged, and even the mountains could soon be eroded away.[12]

According to *Rare Earth,* a new book by two prominent scientists, modern science is showing that conditions on Planet Earth are so rare this may be the only place for complex life forms.[13] Professor Ward, a paleontologist at the University of Washington, states: "We have finally said out loud what so many have thought for so long—that complex life, at least, is rare. And to us, complex life may be a flatworm." Professor Brownlee, a noted astronomer and chief scientist of NASA's Stardust Mission, adds: "Almost all environments in the universe are terrible for life. It's only Garden-of-Eden places like Earth where it can exist."[14]

You may have heard the oft-told account of how Sir Isaac Newton had a skilled craftsman build him a scale model of our solar system which was then displayed on a large table in Newton's home. Not only did the excellent workmanship simulate the various sizes of the planets and their relative proximities, but it was a working model in which everything rotated and orbited when a crank was turned.

One day while Newton was reading in his study, a friend came by who happened to be an atheistic scientist. Examining the model with enthusiastic admiration, he exclaimed: "My! What an exquisite thing this is! Who made it?" Without looking up from his book, Sir Isaac answered, "Nobody."

Stopping his inspection, the visitor turned and said: "Evidently you misunderstood my question. I asked who made this."

Newton, no doubt enjoying the chance to teach his friend a lesson, replied in a serious tone, "Nobody. What you see here just happened to assume the form it now has."

"You must think I'm a fool!" retorted the visitor. "Of course somebody made it, and he's a genius. I want to know who he is."

Laying his book aside, Newton arose and laid a hand on his friend's shoulder, saying:

"This thing is but a puny imitation of a much grander system whose laws you know, and I am not able to convince you that this mere toy is without a designer and maker; yet you profess to believe that the great original from which the design is taken has come into being without either designer or maker! Now tell me by what sort of reasoning do you reach such an incongruous conclusion?"[15]

Many other examples could be cited showing the critical adjustments of design we take for granted. Dr. Wernher von Braun, former German rocket expert who headed the American space effort that took man to the moon, had a bad word for scientists who believe in unseen electrons but reject an unseen Deity. He said: "One cannot be exposed to the order and beauty of the universe without conceding there must be a divine intent behind it."

Observe the delicate design of a flower. Take a microscopic look at the human eye—hardly bigger than a marble, yet with complete photographic equipment and marvelous features man cannot duplicate. Consider the ear,[16] with its minute bones and sensitive nerves—all these point to an intelligent Designer. The human brain—seat of perception, memory, imagination—is another amazing example of intelligent design. It can do all and more than a heavy, cumbersome computer can do, yet it weighs only a few ounces. Who hasn't marvelled at the wonders of the human body with all its interacting systems—or even at the unique designs of snowflakes?

From the minutest atom to the greatest world, all things, animate and inanimate, declare that the Hand that made them is divine. To propose that the intricately designed organs mentioned above arose spontaneously from nothing, or perhaps from chaos, by pure chance or accident, is somewhat uncomplimentary to a man's reason. That would be a greater miracle by far than the work of Creation by divine decree, and requires much more faith— or gullibility—than to believe in God.

The existence of a watch demands a watchmaker. Dozens of additional examples could be cited, but suffice it to say that design demands a designer. For the believer, the undeniable fact of ever-present order and design leads to God as Intelligent Designer.

CLUE #5:
THE MIRACLE OF MIND OVER MATTER

The evidence we've already considered lies in the objective, physical world that's largely outside of man. Yet there are still other reasons for believing in God as the only credible explanation for the universe. Some of these clues the Creator has placed within man himself—in man's very nature—and these we must consider now.

Just for a moment, consider the marvelous MIND of man! We speculate in vain about how the brain works. The mysteries and miracles of the mind intrigue us, fascinate us, yet elude us even as we stretch our minds to the task of explaining the origin of thoughts, memories, feelings.

After all, the brain is made up of mere matter—molecules following the laws of physics and chemistry. So . . .

● How can a mental molecule inside our heads produce new ideas? How can it comprehend, understand, or know anything? Or develop and grow intellectually through learning?

● How can an atom awake to an alert awareness of itself? How can it happily recall nostalgic memories? Or dream—either awake or sleeping?

● How can the material stuff of our brain experience love or hate, joy or sadness, outrage or delight? How can it philosophize and puzzle over a problem? Or appreciate artistry and enjoy contemplating beauty?

● How can mere flesh and blood possibly give rise to thought? How can it make a reasoned judgment? Or discern meaning and make sense of things?

● How can brain tissue be convinced by an argument or amused by a joke? How can it find an idea intriguing or feel intellectual curiosity? Or give birth to ingenious inventions?

● How can the gray matter of our cerebral cortex verify truth? How can it display the unique power of creative imagination? Or compose a speech or symphony?

Those are good questions—challenging questions indeed for any who leave God, our divine Creator, out of the picture!

Those who minimize the miracle must still account somehow for the million marvels of the mind. Atheists tell themselves (and try to convince others) that everything in the universe, including man's mind, "just happened"—coming about by natural means with no thanks due to God. But how ridiculous it is to contend that man's marvelous mental processes can be accounted for on a purely physical level—as if life is pure chemistry, our brain just a piece of meat, and our conscious awareness merely the random firing of networking neurons! [17]

Yet anyone able to grasp the implications of the thoughts expressed on this page knows it's not as simple as that. No one has ever been able to blueprint the architecture of intelligence. We can't explain even the nature of thought on a physical level. Consciousness, the key function of human brains, cannot be duplicated by computers, which is one reason computers cannot truly "think," despite playing a game of chess. The world inside our skulls—equally as vast as that outside—remains a marvelous mystery. For the believer, the infinite inventiveness of the human mind is a great gift from God.

CLUE #6

MAN'S IRREPRESSIBLE RELIGIOUS IMPULSE

A sixth clue to God's existence is the universality of man's religious impulse. We are not gods, nor have we ever seen God. Then how did we get the idea that there is a God? Why did even the pagan Greeks erect an altar "To the Unknown God"?[18] Men everywhere seem to have come to the conclusion that there is a supreme God, though they know little about Him.

Religion is one of man's oldest institutions. One authority says: "History is unable to show us any age in which man lived without religion; even in the earliest periods of which we have any record man was a religious being, and the question concerning the origin of religion, history is unable to answer."[19]

What we may call "the Idea of God" has been tenaciously persistent throughout man's history. Thousands of years of idolatry dimmed man's knowledge of the one true God, yet never submerged it. Cultural anthropologists are kept busy studying the religions of all peoples in all ages, for there seems to be an undying need to worship something, a restless conviction that some Power of Mind lies beyond ourselves.

Distinguished Oxford professor Max Müller observed, "Man is an incurably religious animal." Müller was right: man IS by nature religious. To deny religion is to deny our very humanity, for man is more than an animal, more than a chance organism of space and time. Man, the seeker, is a child of God. He can come to terms with himself only when he realizes what he is and what he might be. Augustine put it quite well in these lines:

"Bless Thee, Lord, that we are restless
Till our souls find rest in Thee!"

The basic stuff of our humanity simply demands something to worship. Human beings have a compelling need to worship a god. But though this seems universally true, like a common denominator among the races of MAN, there's no evidence that this restless religious impulse is exhibited among the lower animals. An animal sees the same earth and sky as we do but never discerns the invisible God. All the researches of science haven't uncovered a single instance of any ANIMAL erecting an altar for worship. Man's need to worship could not possibly have evolved from animals—it's a unique characteristic appearing only in human beings.

The great psychoanalyst Dr. Carl Jung declared that "There is in every man *a God-shaped vacuum* which can be filled only by the divine." The inner life of man, with the deep issues of life's purpose and destiny, evokes in man a sense of the holy and leads him to worship. These facts aren't private fancies of the individual but experiences shared among vast numbers of men and women. This consciousness is too universal and constant to be accounted for by imagination and self-delusion. Even Socrates, who knew not the God of the Bible, regarded the knowledge of God as natural to man. [20]

For man lives not by calories alone: There's a soul hunger only God can satisfy. If we could glimpse what lies within the human heart, we'd see some sordidness and selfishness—but we'd also see a hunger after divine things: what theologian Karl Barth called "the Godsickness of the human heart," for God is a longing that lodges in the heart.

This eternal attraction to the eternal God arises because men and women are created BY God—FOR God. So people need God. They need His Word. They need His assurance. Though not all are church-goers, all feel this spiritual hunger to some degree. And many discover the satisfying solution to their heart craving by reading the Bible or literature on vital Biblical themes. After all, where else can they turn? For the Lord says: "I am God, and there is none else; I am God, and there is none like Me." [21]

Religion, meeting a deeply-felt human need, provides an inner experience missing from many lives today. A survey reported in the November 1974 issue of *Psychology Today* Magazine testifies to this fact. Forty thousand replies to the *Psychology Today* religion questionnaire reveal that Americans "still *ache* to believe . . . there is something beyond our personal and collective reach." Editors were surprised at both the number of responses and the pervasive religious sentiment among readers of this sophisticated, secular magazine.

Today many young people seek ultimate answers to the profound questions of life. The young exhibit this universal need to worship, for the young person wants, needs, is in fact desperate to believe in something. He's in constant search of it—in astrology, in love, in radicalism, in mind-bending drugs—in anything he feels might satisfy his spiritual hunger.

The seed of faith God plants in every man's soul [22] may be dwarfed, may have feeble roots, but it comes to fruition somehow, even in the parched lives of apparent unbelievers. The fact that all people have a universal concept of a Supreme Being, and have some form of worship, is a strong argument for God's existence. It certainly harmonizes with the Biblical record of Creation, which declares God created man in His own image. Those who deny God's personal existence have no argument to equal it in support of their theory.

Why does man alone have this "God consciousness"? Why is he "wired for God"? Is this innate, instinctive urge in man a mere accident? Far from it: The believer is convinced that here we see another evidence of God implanted by the Creator in man's very nature.

Clue #7:
The MORAL Argument

In 1781 German philosopher Immanuel Kant published his *Critique of Pure Reason* and initiated this line of moral argument, holding that reflection upon man as a moral being can lead us to the idea of God. In his conclusion Kant wrote: "Two things fill me with constantly increasing admiration and awe the longer and more earnestly I reflect upon them—the starry heavens without and the moral law within."

Many besides Kant have recognized man's moral sense as another pointer to the reality of God. Among those was the late C. S. Lewis of Cambridge University who wrote *The Case for Christianity* in which he considers the moral experience of men. His Book One, called "Right and Wrong as a Clue to the Meaning of the Universe," begins as follows:

> "Everyone has heard people quarrelling. Sometimes it sounds funny and sometimes it sounds merely unpleasant; but however it sounds, we can learn something very important from listening to the things they say. They say things like this: 'That's my seat, I was there first'—'Give me a bit of your orange, I gave you a bit of mine'—'Come on, you promised.' People say things like that every day, educated people as well as uneducated, and children as well as grown-ups." [23]

What interests Lewis about these remarks is that the man who makes them isn't just saying that the other man's behavior doesn't happen to please him. He's appealing to some standard of behavior he expects the other man to know about. And the other man very seldom replies, "To hell with your standard." Nearly always he tries to prove that what he's been doing doesn't really go against the standard, or that if it does, there's some special excuse, some special reason in this particular case why the person who took the seat first should not keep it, or that things were quite different when he was given the bit of orange, or that something has turned up which lets him off keeping his promise. In fact, it looks as if both parties had in mind some Law or Rule of fair play or decent behavior or morality or whatever you like to call it, about which they really agreed. And they have. If they hadn't, they might fight like animals, but they couldn't quarrel in the human sense of the word. Quarrelling means trying to show that the other man's in the wrong. And there'd be no sense in trying to do that unless you and he had some agreement as to what Right and Wrong are. [24]

So the Moral Law God put into our minds is another bit of evidence pointing to His existence. Believers and unbelievers alike recognize *obligation* and *guilt* as facts of experience. All know the sense of "ought," but not all recognize its profound significance. For the atheist, it's "just one of those things," a mysterious power that creates feelings of guilt if resisted. For the believer, the duty to do what's right and the obligation to pursue what's good are neither a mystery nor simple human policy for the sake of society. If the moral law were mere policy, guilt would lack its power to shame us.

You see, if God doesn't exist, neither does an objective standard of Good and Evil. For if it's not God who condemns murder, then we have no way of declaring murder evil. All we can say is that we don't happen to like it. If moral standards don't come from a Higher Source, then each of us is his own source of morality. Each becomes "a law unto himself," and Right and Wrong become matters of purely personal taste: "What you think is good is good for you, and what I think is good is good for me." If ethics are not based on God but become "a do-it-yourself project," then the morality of Attila the Hun or Hitler is every bit as valid as that of St. Paul or Mother Teresa.

Man's moral sense, our innate recognition of "goodness," means that no matter how far we personally fall short, we automatically respect such things as honesty, sincerity, kindness, fairness, and other things we consider good while we denounce deceit, corruption, brutality, treachery and other things we consider evil. This universal recognition of "good" is another significant pointer to the reality of God. For the believer, man's inherent sense of Moral Law demands a Lawgiver.

CLUE #8:
FULFILLMENT OF PROPHECY

The remarkable fulfillment of Bible prophecies gives yet another convincing clue to the existence of God—but this must be dealt with in a future chapter, Chapter 15, to do justice to this important subject. Only a divine, all-intelligent Being can know the future. Men may make "educated guesses," but it's only by chance if they occasionally succeed in being correct.

When we study fascinating Bible prophecies and trace their unmistakable fulfillment, we'll see God's hand on the helm of history—we'll see, too, that the validity of the Bible and the reality of God go hand in hand.

CLUE #9:
GOD'S SELF-PORTRAIT

No discussion of the evidence of God's existence would be complete without mention of Jesus Christ, who has been called "God's Self-portrait." The prophet Isaiah spoke truth when he said, "You are a God who hides Himself."[25] But God has seen fit to reveal Himself in three important ways:

- In the beauty and majesty of NATURE,
  through His creative power;
- In the pages of His written Word, the BIBLE;
  and
- In the Person of His Son, the Lord JESUS CHRIST,
  who veiled His divinity in humanity.

The evidence for Christ's deity and resurrection is presented in Chapters 7, 8 and 9, but Christian believers know that the supreme Proof of God's existence occurred when the Emperor of the Universe walked the dusty roads of Galilee, living among men and revealing His love by dying for them. Every kind word He said, every loving act He did was another BRUSH STROKE on Jesus' portrait of His Father, giving us a perfect picture of God.[26]

WHO MADE GOD?
DID GOD HAVE A BEGINNING?

Some may ask, "But where did *God* come from? How did *He* begin?" The fact is that God is ETERNAL—without beginning of days or end of years. He stands beyond the dimensions of TIME. Time, measured by the movement of the planets and the rotation of the earth, is ever-present in our earth-bound existence. But time as we know it may not exist at all in the heavenly New Earth—we're told that "there shall be no night there."[27] The simple truth is:

> Just as God will have an infinite existence
> in the FUTURE, without END,
> He has had an infinite existence
> in the PAST, without BEGINNING.

The Bible declares that God "inhabits eternity."[28] He comfortably dwells in what we might think of as beginningless and endless time. Both Genesis 1:1 and John 1:1, by stating "In the beginning God . . ." show that at whatever point in the past we wish to consider as the beginning—no matter how far back we try to stretch our finite minds—God already existed. So where did God come from? He didn't "come from" anywhere. He was always there!

Time-oriented humans may find this concept new and strange. It IS rather difficult to comprehend. But that's just another proof of the fact that FINITE minds cannot comprehend the INFINITE. In a world where nations rise and fall, where mountains crumble and governments collapse, we need to stretch our minds to comprehend the Psalmist's sublime thought: "FROM everlasting TO everlasting, Thou art God."[29] We mortals think in terms of beginnings and endings, but God is eternal: "The same yesterday, and today, and for ever."[30] The unchanging heavenly Father, "with whom is no variableness, neither shadow of turning,"[31] declares: "I am the Lord, I change not."[32] Like a PERFECT CIRCLE, there's no BEGINNING and no ENDING to "The mighty God, the *EVERLASTING* Father."[33]

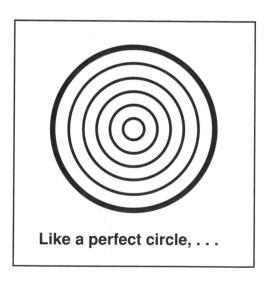

Like a perfect circle, . . .

CONCLUSION: GOD *DOES* EXIST!

As we survey the landscape of ideas, we see peaks and valleys, plains and mountains. But towering above all trivial facts and mundane concepts is the most remarkable fact of all time—the timeless thought that GOD EXISTS! The reality of a loving, personal God who's interested in all details of our lives is a tall, majestic peak that intrigues us and beckons us on to explore the heights of Truth.

We've seen many evidences of God's existence. Some are external clues that lie in the objective world of reality beyond man (such as the existence of physical matter, motion and energy, life itself, and orderly design). Some are internal clues that lie within man himself (such as man's mind, his religious impulse, and his moral sense).

As I said at the beginning, I don't insist that these clues are absolute proofs—but they are pointers whose cumulative testimony is impressive. The atheist must explain the origin or existence of each of the nine clues discussed above. To explain even one of these apart from God is something that science and worldly philosophy have never been able to do—but all nine must be explained before God, the Creator, can be taken out of the picture!

Paul tells us that "spiritual things . . . are spiritually discerned."[34] If we open our minds—if we lay aside our pride and prejudice—we'll understand and admit that the existence of God is a basic reality of life. The universe is not a cosmic accident but a masterpiece designed by a Master Architect and engineered and built by a Master Craftsman. Faith in God is not "a leap in the dark" but a conviction and commitment intelligently based upon more than adequate evidence of the living, loving God who made us all.

> "Now acquaint yourself with Him,
> and be at peace;
> thereby good will come to you."[35]

Notes to Chapter 2

1. English poet William Cowper said, "*Nature* is but a name for an EFFECT whose CAUSE is God." Fredrich von Schelling declared that "The chief business of all philosophy consists in solving the problem of the *existence* of the *world*," in his *Philosophical Letters on Dogmatism and Criticism,* quoted in Frederick Copleston, S. J., *History of Philosophy, volume VII: Modern Philosophy—From the Post Kantian Idealists to Marx, Kirkegaard, and Nietzsche* (New York: Image Books, 1994), p. 100.

2. James 3:17.

3. John 1:18, NKJV.

4. "Law of Conservation," *Encyclopedia Britannica*® (CD 98 Standard Edition: Encyclopedia Britannica, © 1994-1998).

5. Genesis 1:1. The word "created" in this verse is translated from the Hebrew word *bara,* which appears in the Old Testament almost fifty times. This word appears only in the context of DIVINE activity: it denotes the work of God alone. *Bara* "is a special verb in the OT [Old Testament]. It *always* has God as its subject; it is *never* used of human activity. You and I may make, form, or fashion, but only God CREATES."—Ronald F. Youngblood, *The Book of Genesis* (Grand Rapids, Mich.: Baker Book House, 1991), p. 23. The *Theological Dictionary of the Old Testament* states that "As a special theological term, *bara* is used to express the incomparability of the creative work of God in contrast to all secondary products and likenesses made from already existing material by man."

6. Psalm 19:1.

7. Isaiah 40:26.

8. Often such evidence is taken for granted and passed by without notice. But Ralph Waldo Emerson said, "If the STARS should appear just *one night* in a thousand years, how men would believe and adore!"

9. A renowned astronomer asks us to "Reflect on how many ways you are now *moving* through space. In England you have a speed of about 700 miles an hour round the Solar axis of the Earth. You are rushing with the Earth at about 70,000 miles an hour along its pathway round the Sun. . . . On top of all this, you have the huge speed of about 500,000 miles per hour due to your motion around the Galaxy."—Sir Fred Hoyle, *The Nature of the Universe* (New York: Harper & Row, 1960), pp. 67-68.

10. Edwin Conklin, quoted in *The Evidence of God in an Expanding Universe,* edited by John Clover Monsma (New York: G. P. Putnam's Sons, 1958), p. 174. This excellent book contains the affirmative religious views of forty American scientists.

11. Albert Einstein, quoted in Philipp Frank, *Einstein: His Life and Times,* translated by George Rosen (New York: Alfred A. Knopf, Inc., 1947), p. v.

12. A. Cressy Morrison, "Seven Reasons Why a Scientist Believes in God," *Reader's Digest,* October 1960, pp. 71-72, and Frank Allen, "The Origin of the World—by Chance or Design?" in *The Evidence of God in an Expanding Universe,* pp. 21-22.

13. Peter Douglas Ward and Donald C. Brownlee, *Rare Earth: Why Complex Life Is Uncommon in the Universe* (Springer-Verlag: Copernicus Books, c. 2000).

14. Science writer William J. Broad interviewed Ward and Brownlee for his *New York Times* News Service article "Maybe We Are Alone, After All," in the *San Diego Union-Tribune*, Section E, page 4, February 16, 2000.
15. "Who Made It?" *Minnesota Technolog* XXXVIII (October 1957), p. 11. English author G. K. Chesterton said: "An atheist must see the universe as the most EXQUISITE mechanism ever constructed by NOBODY."
16. "The *hearing ear* and the *seeing eye*, the Lord has made them both." Proverbs 20:12, RSV. The study of anatomy could convert many an atheist.
17. Paul Davies—professor of mathematical physics at the University of Adelaide who is *not* a Biblical creationist—wrote, "I cannot believe that our existence in this universe is a mere quirk of fate, an accident of history, an incidental blip in the great cosmic drama. . . . The existence of MIND in some organism on some planet in the universe is surely a fact of fundamental significance. Through *conscious beings* the universe has generated self-awareness. This can be no trivial detail, no minor byproduct of mindless, purposeless forces. We are truly *meant* to be here."
18. Acts 17:22-23.
19. Herman Bavinck, *The Doctrine of God*, (Grand Rapids, Michigan: Wm. B. Eerdmans Publishing Company, 1951), p. 76.
20. Socrates, see *Plato, The Republic*, translated by W. H. Gillespie, p. 273, and *Works of Plato*, Volume IV, translated by George Burges, pp. 375 ff.
21. Isaiah 46:9.
22. The Bible says, "God hath dealt to EVERY MAN the measure of faith." Romans 12:3.
23. C. S. Lewis, *The Case for Christianity*, in *Mere Christianity* (New York: The Macmillan Company, 1960), p. 17.
24. Lewis, *op. cit.*, pp. 17-18.
25. Isaiah 45:15, NIV.
26. When Philip asked, "Lord, show us the Father," Jesus replied, "He who has seen *Me* has *seen* the Father." See John 14:8-9.
27. Revelation 21:25.
28. Isaiah 57:15, NKJV.
29. Psalms 90:2.
30. Hebrews 13:8, NKJV.
31. James 1:17. Latest manuscript discoveries show that the end of this verse should be translated: "no turning [or shifting] of the shadow," as on a SUNDIAL. So the text means that God is both *changeless* and *timeless*.
32. Malachi 3:6.
33. Isaiah 9:6. After all, what does the word *infinite* mean? Can something that is really "infinite" *have* a beginning—or an ending?
34. 1 Corinthians 2:14. The following lines, I believe, are from Franz Werfel, author of *The Song of Bernadette:*
    "For those who do *not* believe in God, there *is* no explanation.
    For those who *do* believe in God, no explanation is *needed*."
35. Job 22:21, NKJV.

An eminent scientist wisely observed:

"This universe EXISTS,
and by *that one impossible fact*
declares itself a MIRACLE . . .
the one *unquestioned* miracle we know,
implying every attribute of God."

—SIR ISAAC NEWTON

MYSTERY #2
Evolution

Is evolutionary theory
a valid explanation
for the nature of things?

"Professing themselves
to be WISE,
they became FOOLS."
—Romans 1:22

CHAPTER THREE

~

THE THEORY OF
EVOLUTION:
WEIGHED AND FOUND WANTING
PART I.

"THE FIRST POINT TO MAKE about Darwin's theory is that it is no longer a theory, but a fact. No serious scientist would deny the fact that evolution has occurred, just as he would not deny the fact that the earth goes around the sun." [1]

This bold declaration was made on a television panel celebrating the centennial of Charles Darwin's book *Origin of Species* by famous British biologist Sir Julian Huxley, who has exerted a profound influence on 20th century thought even as his grandfather, Thomas Henry Huxley, did in the 19th century.

Of course, Huxley was a rather rash advocate for evolution, and his assertions are often pervaded by a spirit of missionary fervor. Even so, the quotation found above is not an isolated statement, but typical of evolutionary pronouncements. For years we've been bombarded by assertions geared to gain our acceptance of evolution as one of "the facts of life." Militant evolutionists make dogmatic declarations that sometimes go far beyond the facts of science. Let's look at a few of these statements:

Richard B. Goldschmidt, Professor at the University of California at Berkeley, emphatically stated that "Evolution of the animal and plant world is considered by all those entitled to judgment to be a fact for which no further proof is needed." [2]

Theodosius Dobzhansky, geneticist and well-known evolutionist, Professor at Columbia University, has said that "Among the present generation no informed person entertains any doubt of the validity of the evolutionary theory in the sense that evolution has occurred." [3]

And H. H. Newman, Professor Emeritus at the University of Chicago, minced no words in declaring, "There is no rival hypothesis [to evolution] except the outworn and completely refuted one of special creation, now retained only by the ignorant, the dogmatic, and the prejudiced." [4]

To quote just one more biologist, Dr. Richard Lull, Professor of Paleontology at Yale:

> "Since Darwin's day, Evolution has been more and more generally accepted, until now in the minds of informed, thinking men there is no doubt that it is the only logical way whereby the creation can be interpreted and understood. We are not so sure, however, as to the *modus operandi*, but we may rest assured that the great process has been in accordance with great natural laws, some of which are as yet unknown, perhaps unknowable." [5]

Commenting on this statement, chemist Anthony Standen said, "And so biologists continue to 'rest assured.' But one may be tempted to ask, IF some of the great natural laws are as yet unknown, how do we know that they are there? And if some are perhaps unknowable, how do we know that they are 'logical'?" [6]

In the light of these strong statements by such eminent scientists, anyone trying to refute the teachings of evolutionists must feel like David approaching Goliath! But remember that young David didn't win the battle in his own strength, and in this case truth will be determined not by me or any other man but by the facts themselves.

The assertions of the evolutionists quoted above, if in fact true, would definitely tip the scales of Truth in favor of the evolutionary theory. But let's weigh in the balance some other statements, equally forceful and made by equally eminent men of science.

ADMISSIONS MADE BY EVOLUTIONARY SCIENTISTS

We've already seen that Horatio H. Newman felt that any alternative to evolution can be held "only by the ignorant, the dogmatic, and the prejudiced." But in another book Newman was candid enough to write: "Reluctant as he may be to admit it, honesty compels the evolutionist to admit that there is NO absolute proof of organic evolution." [7]

Professor Ernst Mayr of Harvard, a heavyweight among evolutionists, confessed: "The fact that the synthetic [evolutionary] theory is now so universally accepted is NOT in itself proof of its CORRECTNESS. . . . The basic theory is in many instances hardly more than a postulate." [8] (A postulate, by the way, is defined by Webster as "a position or supposition assumed without proof.")

Some time ago Oxford University Press published a book entitled *A Short History of Science*, by Charles Singer. The author frankly confessed to his faith in the evolutionary theory. Despite this, he declared: "Evolution is perhaps unique among major scientific theories in that the appeal for its acceptance is NOT that there is EVIDENCE for it, but that any other proposed interpretation is wholly incredible." [9] Statements like this betray a non-scientific bias which is devastating to any search for truth.

And Thomas Hunt Morgan, founder of the Morganian school of genetics and esteemed Professor at both Columbia and Caltech, frankly declared: "Within the period of human history we do not know of a SINGLE instance of the transmutation of one species into another one. . . . Therefore it may be claimed that the theory of descent is LACKING in the most essential feature that it *needs* to place the theory on a scientific basis. This MUST be admitted." [10]

Paul Ehrlich and Richard Holm, biologists at Stanford University, criticize the dogmatic assumptions of those like Huxley in saying: "Perpetuation of today's theory as dogma will not encourage progress toward more satisfactory explanations of observed phenomena." [11]

Wistar Institute in Philadelphia published a Symposium Monograph in 1967 entitled, *Mathematical Challenges to the Neo-Darwinian Interpretation of Evolution.* [12] And in a company publication, *Scientific Research*, McGraw-Hill, Inc., published two such articles: "Heresy in the Halls of Biology: Mathematicians Question Darwinism" [13] and "Thinking the Unthinkable: Are Evolutionists Wrong?" [14]

W. R. Thompson, for many years Director of the Commonwealth Institute of Biological Control at Ottawa, Canada, is a world-renowned entomologist. Dr. Thompson was chosen to write the Foreword to the new edition of Darwin's *Origin of Species* published in the Darwinian Centennial Year as part of the *Everyman's Library Series*. His entire Foreword is a devastating indictment and refutation of Darwinian evolution and perhaps even more so of the *scientific morality* of evolutionists! Note the following excerpts:

> "As we know, there is a great divergence of opinion among biologists, not only about the causes of evolution but even about the actual process. This divergence exists because the evidence is unsatisfactory and does NOT permit any certain conclusion. It is therefore right and proper to draw the attention of the non-scientific public to the dis-

agreements about evolution. But some recent remarks of evolutionists show that they think this unreasonable. This situation, where men rally to the defense of a doctrine they are unable to define scientifically, much less demonstrate with scientific rigor, attempting to maintain its credit with the public by the suppression of criticism and the elimination of difficulties, is *abnormal* and *undesirable* in science." [15]

G. A. Kerkut, Professor of Physiology and Biochemistry at the University of Southampton, England, is an evolutionist but is critical enough and honest enough as a scientist to admit: "The evidence that supports it [the theory of evolution] is NOT sufficiently strong to allow us to consider it as anything more than a working hypothesis." [16]

Thus Kerkut concluded his book written to expose the weaknesses and fallacies in the evidence used to support evolutionary theory. But the REVIEW of Kerkut's book, written by John T. Bonner, one of the nation's leading biologists and Professor at Princeton University, was as startling as the book itself—note Dr. Bonner's words:

> "This is a book with a disturbing message; it points to some unseemly cracks in the foundations. One is disturbed because what is said gives us the uneasy feeling that we knew it for a long time deep down but were never willing to admit it even to ourselves. It is another of those cold and uncompromising situations where the naked truth and human nature travel in different directions. The particular truth is simply that we have NO reliable evidence as to the evolutionary sequence of invertebrate phyla. . . . We have all been telling our students for years not to accept any statement on its face value but to examine the evidence, and, therefore, it is rather a shock to discover that we have FAILED to follow our own sound advice." [17]

Is Evolution SCIENTIFIC?

What criteria must be met for a theory to be considered scientific? George Gaylord Simpson, Professor at Harvard and perhaps the foremost writer on evolution, has stated that "It is inherent in any definition of science that statements that cannot be checked by OBSERVATION are not . . . science." [18]

A definition of science given by the monumental *Oxford English Dictionary* is: "A branch of study which is concerned either with a connected body of DEMONSTRATED truths or with OBSERVED facts systematically classified."

Note that SCIENCE deals with "demonstrated . . . observed" data arrived at by experimenting in a laboratory or observing in the real world of nature. But evolution cannot be studied in a laboratory or seen in nature, since its assumed mechanisms operate so slowly as to require millions of years for demonstrable results. This fact is admitted by David Kitts in *Evolution* Magazine: "Evolution, at least in the sense that Darwin speaks of it, cannot be detected within the lifetime of a single observer." [19]

As a matter of fact, the whole question of ORIGINS (whether by creation OR evolution) is really outside the limits of science, not being subject to scientific experimentation and analysis. Both creationists and evolutionists alike agree that no human observer witnessed the origin of our earth and its life, so the observational aspect of scientific investigation is automatically ruled out in any consideration of origins.

Another limitation of a scientific theory is that it must be capable of FALSIFICATION. That is, it must be possible to conceive some experiment the failure of which would disprove the theory, for in order to be sure a theory is right, there must be some way of proving it wrong. Francisco Ayala, of Rockefeller University, wrote: "A hypothesis or theory which cannot be, at least in principle, FALSIFIED by empirical observations and experiments does not belong in the realm of science." [20] Yet evolutionists consider everything in the world a verification of their theory!

Nobel Prize-winner Peter Medawar, a leading biologist at Oxford University, admits: "It is too difficult to imagine or envisage an evolutionary episode which could NOT be explained by the formulae of neo-Darwinism." [21] This is true because even when evolutionists are forced to admit that evolution is impossible NOW, they invoke long ages of time during which, they say, anything can happen—and who is to prove them wrong?

But Sir Karl Popper, Professor of Logic and Scientific Method at the London School of Economics, is a connoisseur of the scientific method who says: "A theory which is not REFUTABLE by any conceivable event is NON-scientific. Irrefutability is not a virtue (as people often think) but a vice." [22]

This is why Paul Ehrlich and L. C. Birch, Professors of Biology at Stanford University, say quite candidly: "Our theory of evolution . . . is thus 'outside of empirical science.' . . . No one can think of ways in which to TEST it. Ideas, either without basis or based on a few laboratory experiments carried out in extremely simplified systems, have attained currency far beyond their validity. They have become part of an evolutionary DOGMA accepted by most of us as part of our training." [23] But *dogma* is a RELIGIOUS term, not a scientific one!

Actually, much of evolutionistic thinking lies more in the realm of RELIGION or PHILOSOPHY than SCIENCE. Belief in evolution obviously requires a tremendous exercise of faith, faith in an assumption. (Assumptions are proper working tools, but never forget that they *are* assumptions!) Some evolutionists freely acknowledge this need for faith to bridge the gap between evidence and proof. For instance, Dr. Louis T. More, Dean of the Graduate School at the University of Cincinnati and a staunch evolutionist, delivered a series of lectures at Princeton University which were then published in his book *The Dogma of Evolution,* in which he says:

> "The more one studies paleontology, the more certain one becomes that evolution is based on FAITH alone, exactly the same sort of faith which it is necessary to have when one encounters the great mysteries of RELIGION." [24]

Dr. More's conclusion had been reached earlier by none other than Thomas Henry Huxley, who frankly declared:

> "To say, therefore, in the admitted absence of evidence, that I have any belief as to the mode in which the existing forms of life have originated would be using words in a wrong sense. . . . I have no right to call my opinion anything but an act of philosophical FAITH." [25]

Remember that T. H. Huxley was the one man more responsible for the acceptance of evolution than Darwin himself. Darwin was a rather retiring person who had no heart to be at the forefront of controversy. But Huxley, as the foremost champion of evolution, became "Darwin's bulldog." Thomas Henry Huxley became a brilliant press agent and enthusiastic salesman for the theory—debating, defending, promoting it with untiring voice and pen.

How strange, then, that in 1896—many decades AFTER *Origin of Species* was published in 1859, AFTER Darwinism had triumphantly risen to full flower, AFTER Darwin lay buried in Westminster Abbey among the honored of England for fourteen years—Huxley admits the "*absence* of *evidence*" for the evolution of living protoplasm from nonliving matter and says, "I have no right to call my opinion anything but an act of philosophical FAITH"!

Evolutionary theory is no LESS religious and no MORE scientific than the doctrine of special creation. Throughout the rest of this study we'll see that the evidence for evolution is circumstantial at best and contradictory at worst. Now let's turn to a candid examination of the facts—for after all, one FACT is worth a thousand THEORIES.

I. VARIATION Only *Within* KINDS

Variation among living things is a most obvious fact. Unless born an identical twin, each human being is unique, different from all others. The same seems true of all plants and animals.

There can be no argument about the fact that change takes place in all nature. Some things have changed a great deal since creation. The difference between the theory of evolution and the doctrine of creation is NOT that one accepts the fact of change and the other doesn't, for change is obvious to and admitted by ALL. The difference lies in the AMPLITUDE of change, the DEGREE of change produced by natural processes. The evolutionist claims that these processes know no bounds in producing change. The creationist maintains that all variation lies within clearly defined limits.

Darwin mistakenly thought change was without limit, that the lid was off, as it were: "Slow though the process of selection may be . . . I can see NO LIMIT to the amount of change." [26] So Darwin gave free rein to his imagination. He cherished the idea that variation could proceed endlessly. Thus his closing sentence in *Origin of Species* declared: "From so simple a beginning ENDLESS FORMS most beautiful and most wonderful have been, and are being, evolved." [27] And the majority of scientists today, like Darwin, speak unjustifiably of unlimited variation.

It's understandable that evolutionists take this attitude, for they realize that unless change can proceed to the point of producing NEW KINDS of living things, evolution is impossible. Limited change of life already created does not fulfill the requirements of the theory of evolution. So there's a difference between mere variation and actual evolution. The term "evolution," when used as the theory demands, means the ultimate changing of one kind of plant or animal into another basic type.

Let me underscore the fact that evolution does NOT simply mean CHANGE. This is important, for the evidence cited by most writers in favor of their claim that evolution is a "fact" is simply evidence of change. But true evolution in the Darwinian sense would be a certain KIND of change, a high DEGREE of change not seen in the world of reality.

To describe degrees of variation, let's use the terms "micro" for small changes and "macro" for large ones. Members of the dog family have undergone many micro changes of color, size, *etc.,* so that there are many varieties of dogs in the world today—but they're all unmistakably DOGS! The same may be said of cats, horses, and all other animals as well as plants. They may vary within their basic kinds but horses remain horses, cows remain cows, and wheat remains wheat.

Creationists recognize that "micro-evolution"—change WITHIN basic kinds—has occurred. But evolutionists are eagerly searching for mechanisms that will provide for macro-evolution of organisms from one basic type into another basic kind. No one has ever seen a macro change take place, either in the living world or among the fossils.

At no time has a laboratory experimenter or field investigator shown that any plant or animal has changed into another basic kind. Changes always take place within a charmed circle, within the circumscribed limits of the basic kinds. This is a FUNDAMENTAL LAW of all living things, both plants and animals.

In view of these facts, since Darwin saw only different varieties within a given species, he should have given his book NOT the overly-ambitious title of *The Origin of Species* but simply and more accurately *The Origin of Varieties*.

Read this devastating admission by Richard Goldschmidt, evolutionary biologist from the University of California at Berkeley:

> "Microevolution does NOT lead beyond the confines of the species, and the typical products of microevolution, the geographic races, are NOT incipient species. There is no such category as incipient species." [28]

Incipient, of course, refers to "the early, initial stages of something new." Goldschmidt also said:

> "Microevolution by accumulation of micro-mutations . . . leads to diversification strictly WITHIN the species. . . . Subspecies are actually, therefore, neither incipient species nor models for the origin of species. They are more or less diversified blind alleys within the species. The decisive step in evolution, the first step toward macroevolution, the step from one SPECIES to another, requires another evolutionary method than that of sheer accumulation of micro-mutations." [29]

EXTRAPOLATING—for Fun and Profit

Unfortunately, not all evolutionists are this frank. They know that what Goldschmidt says is true, but their allegiance to the theory leads them to say, "Maybe evolution doesn't create new living things today, but just give it time, and you'll get a new kind"—but that is philosophy, not science. Their faith in the theory also leads them to EXTRAPOLATE. Extrapolating (estimating beyond the known range) is a dangerous procedure, warns Dr. Norman Macbeth:

> "If you have a broad base of sound observations, you can extend a little at the ends without too much risk; but if the base is short or insecure, extension can lead to grotesque errors. Thus if you observe the growth of a baby during its first months, extrapolation into the future will show that the child will be eight feet tall when six years old. Therefore all statisticians recommend caution in extrapolating. Darwin, however, plunged in with no caution at all." [30]

Note Mark Twain's whimsical views on extrapolation:

> "In the space of 176 years the Lower Mississippi has shortened itself 242 miles. That is an average of a trifle over a mile and a third

per year. Therefore any calm person who is not blind or idiotic can see that . . . 742 years from now the Lower Mississippi will be only a mile and three-quarters long, and Cairo [Illinois] and New Orleans will have joined their streets together and be plodding along comfortably under a single mayor and a mutual board of aldermen. There is something fascinating about science. One gets such wholesale returns of conjecture out of such a trifling investment of fact." [31]

DISCONTINUITY Among Kinds

The fact of discontinuity is as obvious as the fact of variation. We find the different kinds of living things distinctly separated—cats, dogs, and elephants; palm trees, clover, and tumbleweed. The same clear-cut discontinuity occurs among the fossils (which we'll consider in the next chapter).

So even though there are many varieties or breeds of horses, and the same is true of cows, there exists between horses and cows a clear-cut gap. There are unbridgeable gaps between ALL the different kinds, and no amount of variation has even made a start at crossing these gaps. But if evolution were true, the GAPS shouldn't BE there at ALL. For if all organisms really descended from a common ancestor, they'd be all interconnected by imperceptible gradations.

This crucial fact is admitted by no less an evolutionist than Professor Dobzhansky of Columbia University when he says:

> "If we assemble as many individuals living at a given time as we can, we notice at once that the observed variation does NOT form any kind of continuous distribution. Instead, a multitude of separate, discrete distributions are found. The living world is NOT a single array in which any two variants are connected by an unbroken series of intergrades, but an array of more or less distinctly separate arrays, intermediates between which are absent or at least rare." [32]

So everywhere we look in the world of nature, we see clusters, families, or distinct groups of living things which make up the basic kinds. And these families cannot be cross-bred. Dogs may cross-breed with dogs but can never successfully mate with cats or other animals to produce offspring. Only LIKE KINDS can reproduce.

George Gaylord Simpson, an evolutionist with impressive credentials, freely admits: "CROSS BREEDING . . . is almost never satisfactorily possible at the level of the genera, and absolutely never above that level." [33]

And evolutionist Gavin De Beer puts it very plainly in his book on Darwin: ". . . one species does not grow from the seed of another species." [34]

Hybrids, of course, may be produced. Hybridization is simply the crossing of two organisms diverse enough to constitute at least different varieties of a single kind, such as red sunflowers and yellow sunflowers or wolf and coyote. But the variability is still limited within a basic kind. For instance, farmers have succeeded in raising high-yield hybrid corn. Yet no matter what was done to that corn, it always stayed CORN. It did not, and can not, change into some other kind of plant.

Furthermore, the offspring of hybrids are often sterile and require constant hybridizing. A horse, for example, may mate with a donkey and produce the hybrid we call a MULE. But mules have reached the limits of variability and cannot reproduce themselves as a permanent species. Note this illuminating statement from Professor Goldschmidt: "Nowhere have the limits of the species been transgressed, and these limits are separated from the limits of the next good species by the unbridged gap, which also includes sterility." [35]

DARWIN'S TRAGEDY

While working on his yet-unpublished book, Darwin wrote a significant letter to his friend and confidant the botanist Joseph Hooker, in which he said: "I am almost convinced (quite contrary to the opinion I started with) that species are not (it is like confessing a murder) immutable." [36] WHY should Darwin feel that saying species are not unchangeable "is like confessing a murder"?

Darwin's tragedy was his misunderstanding of the teaching of Genesis in the Bible. He permitted men who were poor scholars of the Bible to tell him what the Bible taught. You see, the church in Darwin's day held a narrow view on origins, especially on the fixity of species. The great church universities taught (and young Charles Darwin had studied theology at Cambridge) that the offspring of any plant or animal were as alike as coins from the mint—that there could be NO change whatever. Apparently without studying Genesis for himself, Darwin believed that it said "no variation." Yet he looked on the earth and saw variation, and his theory attempted to account for it. Darwin undoubtedly believed he had proved the Bible wrong, but he proved only the misinterpretation of it wrong.

Actually, the erroneous assumption that the Bible required rigid fixity led many to reject the Bible entirely. But the old idea of "fixity of species" is NOT part of the Biblical concept of special creation. That would be an impossibly narrow and inaccurate conception of special creation. For the Bible speaks of mankind having originated from a single pair, yet recognizes the difference between a Jew and an Ethiopian [37] and between normal men and giants. [38]

Other texts suggest that CHANGE was to be EXPECTED: The fact that the serpent was cursed "above" all cattle and wild animals suggests a general curse that would change those living things, and the fact that "thorns . . . and thistles" were to spring up suggests that the cursed PLANT world would also change. [39]

Thus the old argument that ANY change in living things refutes the Bible is without support. Many evolutionists today think that if a Christian opposes the theory of evolution it's because he supports the idea of "fixity of species." But the Bible doesn't even use the word "species." It simply says God created living things "after their kind." For example, the Bible mentions "the owl . . . after his kind." [40] But the owl is NOT just a species—the owl is an entire "order" (Strigiformes), so the term "kind" can obviously include several species.

Kind is an old word with roots in the word *kin*. TEN TIMES in the first chapter of Genesis we're told that the created forms, both plant and animal, were to bring forth "after their kind"—not after some other kinds. [41] The Biblical idea of "kind" is not to be confused with the modern term "species," for NO ONE KNOWS what a species is. The *Encyclopedia Britannica* informs us that:

> "The nature of species is a question of considerable importance in general biology . . . but despite its wide use its definition remains ELUSIVE. . . . An exact definition of the species concept has given zoologists MUCH TROUBLE." [42]

So creationists DO believe in "fixity"—but not in the fixity of so-called "species." Exactly what constitutes a species is largely a matter of opinion of the authority who classifies and names it. Large groups are often split into smaller "species," varying from each other in minor points such as color. Many of the modern supposed "species" have developed right before our eyes, not taking millions of years but only a few generations. But these variations are merely strains of a common stock. We start with pigeons and end with pigeons. No evolution of new kinds is occurring.

Creationists don't shut their eyes or close their ears to the evidence. Variation within permanently fixed basic kinds is a fact open to the observation of all, scientist and layman alike. That is, living things DO vary, but they vary only within certain fixed limits. And variation within the kind is NOT THE TYPE of evolution that could possibly build our modern organic world from a few one-celled forms, as Darwin theorized.

LIKE always begets LIKE: a cow always gives birth to a calf, not an ostrich; and if you plant an acorn, only an oak will grow. One basic kind may produce many varieties, but it never changes into another basic kind. This is always true in the REAL world—as opposed to the hypothetical world of evolutionary speculation and the imaginary world of children's fairy tales, where pumpkins turn into coaches and mice into men.

We've seen that the fact of change and variation in living things is certainly no proof that Darwin's theory is right and the Bible is wrong. We've also seen that the discontinuity evident everywhere, with gaps among different kinds, is much more in harmony with the doctrine of creation than with the assumptions of evolution. In other words, defenders of the theory are wrong when they say evolution HAS taken place. Now let's consider what they say about HOW it supposedly takes place.

II. LAMARCKISM WAS NOT THE ANSWER

In the early 1800's those who believed in evolution accepted the idea that characteristics acquired by an organism during its lifetime could be transmitted to its offspring. The doctrine of the inheritance of acquired characteristics came to be known as "Lamarckism," after a French zoologist named Jean Baptiste Lamarck. But Lamarck himself was by no means the only evolutionist who taught this idea.

Darwin, for instance, "believed that any variation acquired by the body can, sooner or later, impress itself in the germ cells [sex cells of reproduction] and become an inherent variation (inheritance of acquired characteristics). Therefore, he did not mind accepting the idea that certain variations of the Lamarckian type—variations determined by use, by activity—might play an evolutionary role." [43] A book called *The Evidence of Evolution* quotes Darwin as admitting his agreement with Lamarck: "The conclusions I am led to are not widely different from his." [44]

Darwin, Lamarck, and others reasoned that use and disuse, exercise and activity could affect one's body and those effects could be PASSED ON to one's offspring. Thus giraffes got long necks because they ran out of vegetation and had to stretch their necks to reach higher leaves. In this way, each generation passed on to its offspring a slightly longer neck. (No one has ever seen evidence, either living or fossilized, of giraffes with short necks, but no matter!) By the same logic, birds probably developed wings by flying so much.

If Lamarck's theory were correct, cats would be able to operate a can opener by now, and all mothers would have twelve hands! But Lamarckism is simply not true and has been utterly disproved both by experiments and by our growing knowledge of genetics. Characteristics acquired by the individual during his life may affect his body but cannot bring about a corresponding change in his reproductive cells, which carry all hereditary information. If you lose a finger in an accident, your children will still be born with a full set. Though Chinese women kept their feet small by tight binding for many centuries, modern Chinese women still have feet of normal size.

Herbert Spencer, an influential evolutionist contemporary with Darwin, was so convinced about Lamarckism that he wrote, "Close contemplation of the facts impresses me more strongly than ever with two alternatives—either there HAS BEEN inheritance of ACQUIRED characters or there has been NO EVOLUTION." [45]

But others, like August Weismann, could not accept Lamarckism. Weismann was one of the first German scientists to support Darwin's theory but also one of the first to demonstrate the falsity of the inheritance of acquired characteristics. In one experiment he cut off the tails of mice for many generations, but the young mice were always born with tails as long as ever. "His critique on this point is authoritative and has never been refuted." [46] But doesn't evolution NEED Lamarck's idea? "To this, Weismann answered that it is unworthy of the scientific mind to make a case for an unlikely and unproved phenomenon because a theory needs bolstering." [47]

Still, pet theories die hard, and Ernst Haeckel, a notorious evolutionist born in Germany the same year as Weismann, wrote: "Belief in the inheritance of acquired characters is a NECESSARY axiom. . . . Rather than agree with Weismann in denying the inheritance of acquired characters, it would be better to accept a mysterious creation of all the species as described in the Mosaic account [of the Bible]." [48]

Today we know that inheritance is controlled by the genes found only in the sex cells. Only alterations in the genes of the reproductive cells are inheritable. Acquired traits play no part in evolution, and Lamarckism today exists only on the "lunatic fringe" of biology, now and then catching the fancy of some speculative thinker.

III. MUTATIONS ARE NOT THE ANSWER

The new science of genetics (of which Darwin knew nothing, since it emerged after his time) has found four causes of variation in living things: (1) recombinations, (2) hybridization, (3) chromosome changes, and (4) gene mutations. The first of these, RECOMBINATIONS of genes, is the ordinary cause of change. It's always present when sexual reproduction takes place and accounts for virtually all the variation seen in nature today. It simply combines, in one individual, traits of two parents—as we say, "He's got his mother's eyes and his father's chin."

Recombination works like this: Inside the nucleus of every plant or animal cell are tiny rod-shaped bodies called chromosomes. The chromosomes always come in pairs—one member of each pair has come from one parent and one from the other. When reproduction takes place, it's by means of sex cells: sperm in the male and eggs in the female. But these sex cells differ from ordinary cells in that their chromosomes are not in pairs, but are single. (This is because a reduction division occurred when the sex cells were formed, and the PAIRS of chromosomes SPLIT. In the male, one member of a chromosome pair goes into one sperm and the other goes into another. In the female, when the egg cell is formed, it receives one chromosome member and discards the other.)

Thus, because the sperm and egg each carry only half of each pair of chromosomes, when fertilization occurs and the sperm joins the egg, the full chromosome number is restored. This process is known as "recombination," and in every generation there is a reduction and a recombination of chromosomes.

Since the chromosomes contain genes that determine such characteristics as color, size, shape, etc., and since we never know exactly how the parents' genetic factors will recombine in new offspring, recombination is a potent force for change. Obviously, God PLANNED for variety, for the number of possible gene combinations is astronomical, since virtually everyone except identical twins has a gene combination different from any other individual that ever lived!

However, as the term itself implies, recombination of genes does not introduce anything new but only rearranges factors already present. Recombination cannot produce new basic types, because it consists merely of a new grouping, a different assortment, a reshuffling of genes already on hand.

As Dr. Burns explains in his book *The Science of Genetics: An Introduction to Heredity,* "Recombination . . . merely redistributes existing genetic material among different individuals; it makes no CHANGE in it." [49] It's clear, then, that this process has little to do with evolution.

HYBRIDIZATION, too, offers little hope to the evolutionist in his search for a mechanism of evolutionary change. For hybrids, as we know, are nearly always sterile. More importantly, it's obvious that hybridization is merely another form of recombination, with nothing present in the hybrid form that wasn't already present in one or both of the parents.

CHROMOSOME CHANGES, called ploidy (heteroploidy, polyploidy), result when the number of chromosomes is sometimes doubled or tripled, *etc.* But polyploidy, in the first place, hardly ever exists among animals and is quite rare even among plants. In the second place, it often produces feeble offspring with lowered viability and consequent loss of competitive power. Polyploids, therefore, when they do occur among plants, offer no promising material for progressive evolution. And finally, polyploidy does not add new kinds of genes to the plants, for the doubled chromosomes contain the same variety of genes as appeared in the race before the doubling or tripling. So this method has been rejected as a mechanism of evolution, because nothing new is added.

This brings us to MUTATIONS, a term coming from a Latin word meaning "to change." Mutations are due to actual changes in the genes themselves. It was Dutch botanist Hugo De Vries who, around 1901, first theorized that the evolutionary formation of species was due not to gradual changes but to sudden mutations. It's true that mutations offer more promise than Lamarckism (which is powerless to change the genes in the sex cells) and recombination (which cannot add anything new). Mutations are a very real occurrence in nature and are responsible for hornless cattle, seedless grapes, and navel oranges.

But some evolutionists think of mutation as an Aladdin's lamp that will create the changes needed to bridge the evolutionary gaps. Both Sir Julian Huxley and Dobzhansky of Columbia University say that mutation provides "the raw material of evolution." [50] And Ernst Mayr, Professor of Zoology at Harvard and a leading authority on the subject, agrees: "It must not be forgotten that mutation is the ultimate source of ALL genetic variation found in natural populations and the ONLY raw material available for natural selection to work on." [51]

The desperation of the evolutionists' search for a mechanism to produce evolution is shown by the fact that they've been forced to select mutation. They selected mutation not because it offered a good logical possibility but because those means which had seemed to offer really good possibilities had all been eliminated. One by one, it was shown that these could NOT have operated to produce evolution, because they added nothing new but just reshuffled those characteristics already present in the mechanism of heredity. Mutations may constitute the last best hope on earth for an evolutionary mechanism—but, unfortunately for evolutionists, mutations pose more problems than possibilities. Let's look at THREE of those problems right now.

1 – Most Mutations Are Very SMALL

The effect of any one mutation is now believed too small to have any significant evolutionary value. To quote Professor Mayr again (in a statement which practically contradicts his words quoted two paragraphs above): "We now believe that mutations do not guide evolution; the effect of a mutation is very often far too SMALL to be visible." [52]

Evolutionists know that mutations with slight effects are much more common than those with marked effects, and they contend that mutations with NO visible effects are the most common of all (though there is some nonsense in this, for if we can't see a mutation or in some way detect it—how can anyone say it exists at all?!).

"After observing mutations in fruit flies for many years, Professor Goldschmidt fell into despair. The changes, he lamented, were so hopelessly MICRO that if a thousand mutations were combined in ONE specimen, there would still be no new species." [53] But Goldschmidt, the respected geneticist from the University of California, perhaps found the only way out for evolutionists. His unique solution? A BIG mutation; one that didn't accumulate gradually; one that violated all the gene theories; one that would be fatal under normal circumstances. He named it "The Hopeful Monster." It would simply happen that something laid an egg—and something ELSE got born! [54]

But many even among evolutionists believe Goldschmidt is the one who laid the egg, since there's not a shred of evidence to support his "hopeful monster" hypothesis. As Dobzhansky puts it: "Systemic mutations [large mutations which transform one species at once into another] have NEVER been observed, and it is extremely improbable that species are formed in so abrupt a manner." [55]

2 – Mutations Are Very, Very RARE

Mutations are not only small but also exceedingly rare. The lucky combination of favorable mutations required to produce even a fruit fly, let alone a man, is so much rarer still that the odds against it would be expressed by a number containing as many *zeros* as there are *letters* in an average novel, "a number greater than that of all the electrons and protons in the visible universe," to quote Sir Julian Huxley. [56]

Huxley's statement is true because mutations are so rare that they simply don't accumulate in any organism. Even *single* mutations are rare. In *Science Today* evolutionist C. H. Waddington, Professor of Animal Genetics at Edinburgh University, says a mutation "happens RARELY, perhaps once in a million animals or once in a million lifetimes." [57] To say that mutations are few and far between is classic understatement!

Because mutations are so rare, scientists have used as a laboratory subject the common fruit fly. Thomas Hunt Morgan and his colleagues at Columbia University subjected the fruit fly *Drosophila melanogaster* ("black-bellied lover of dew") to genetic experiments for more than one thousand generations, since fruit flies can go through at least 26 generations in a year. Also, Professor Hermann J. Müller found that bombarding *Drosophila* with x-rays would increase the mutation rate one hundred and fifty times.

So they x-rayed the daylights out of those fruit flies—and did succeed in causing mutations. The eyes changed color, the wings changed this way and that, and the number of body bristles changed within certain limits. But the mutant flies that survived were STILL fruit flies. They never changed into a mosquito or anything else.

Since single mutations are so rare, multiple, simultaneous mutations are impossible. Professor George Gaylord Simpson, an ardent evolutionist, faces this fact: "Obviously," he concludes, "such a process [of multiple mutations] has played no part whatever in evolution." He explains that even under the most favorable circumstances, "The chances of multiple, simultaneous mutation seem to be . . . indeed negligible." He estimates that the probability of even FIVE mutations in the same nucleus would be:

$$.000000000000000000001$$

(that's a decimal point with 21 zeros between it and the number ONE)! Simpson explains: "With an average effective breeding population of 100 million individuals and an average length of generation of one day, again extremely favorable postulates, such an event [of five mutations in one organism] would be expected only once in about 274 BILLION YEARS, or about a hundred times the probable age of the earth. Obviously, . . . such a process has played NO part whatever in evolution." [58]

3 – MUTATIONS ARE USUALLY HARMFUL
AND SOMETIMES LETHAL

It's a good thing that mutations are as rare as they are, for they're nearly always harmful. In the experiments with fruit flies, most of the mutations were lethal. Lethal changes may cause death at any stage of development from fertilized egg to adult.

Even Sir Julian Huxley admits: ". . . the great majority of mutant genes are HARMFUL in their effects on the organism." [59] Dr. Ernst Mayr echoes his words: "It can hardly be questioned that most visible mutations are deleterious." [60] And Professor Hermann J. Müller, the geneticist who received the

NOBEL PRIZE in 1946 for his work with fruit flies, declared flatly: "In MORE than 99 per cent of cases the mutation of a gene produces some kind of harmful effect, some disturbance of function." [61]

Again, Müller stated: "Most mutations are bad. In fact, good ones are so rare that we can consider them ALL as bad." [62]

Gene mutations are most often caused by bombardment with RADIATION or by CHEMICAL agents. The atomic bombs that exploded over Japan in 1945 caused many mutations, resulting in damage, deformity, or death. That's why research workers take great precautions to protect themselves from radiation. Chemicals like the tranquilizer drug thalidomide also caused harmful mutations, producing horribly deformed babies, some without arms or legs. Chance mutations have also produced albino men and other albino animals, mental disorders, blood-clotting problems (hemophilia), and other harmful effects. Most mutants are simply considered monstrosities or freaks of nature: two-headed fish, one-eyed fish, and Siamese twins.

So a change in a gene is usually a change for the WORSE. Practically all mutations—like ACCIDENTS in the genetic machinery of living things—are degenerative, and when they're extensive, the organism is usually destroyed.

John J. Fried, in his book *The Mystery of Heredity*, speaks of the true character of mutations:

> "We have to face one particular fact, one so peculiar that in the opinion of some people it makes nonsense of the whole theory of evolution: Although the biological theory calls for incorporating BENEFICIAL variants in the living populations, a vast majority of mutants observed in any organism are DETRIMENTAL to its welfare." [63]

This paradox forces Dobzhansky to admit: "A majority of mutations, both those arising in laboratories and those stored in natural populations, produce DETERIORATIONS of the viability, hereditary DISEASES, and MONSTROSITIES. Such changes, it would seem, can HARDLY serve as evolutionary building blocks." [64]

And in his book *Progress and Decline* Professor Hugh Miller speaks of "The relative RARITY of these . . . mutant changes" and says their effect upon development is "more often than not LETHAL. . . . The great importance currently attached to gene-mutations as a factor in evolutionary history is in part the result of erroneous expectations initially aroused by their discovery." [65] Thus we can understand Professor Hooton of Harvard when he confesses: "Now I am afraid that many anthropologists (including myself) have sinned against genetic science and are leaning upon a broken reed when they depend upon mutations." [66]

Finally, it's well to remember that in all the thousands of mutations studied, mutational change has never accomplished more than to produce a new variety of an organism already in existence. No new basic types arose among the mutants. Dr. Maurice Caullery was an honorary professor at the Sorbonne in Paris when he observed that mutation, as a mechanism of evolutionary change, fails miserably and totally, for: "Out of the 400 mutations that have been provided by *Drosophila melanogaster*, there is NOT ONE that can be called a new species. It does NOT seem, therefore, that the central problem of evolution can be solved by mutations." [67]

IV. "NATURAL SELECTION" OR "THE SURVIVAL OF THE FITTEST"

Now we come to the heart of Darwin's theory. Natural selection was his *modus operandi*, his answer to how and why evolution takes place. Darwin even went so far as to entitle his book *On the Origin of Species BY MEANS OF Natural Selection.* "Without natural selection, Darwin declared, the theory of descent was unintelligible and unprovable." [68]

Darwin's idea here is based on the simple fact that living things produce more offspring than survive the struggle for life and that any favorable advantage individuals have over others will give them the best chance to survive and reproduce their kind. But this idea was not really original with Darwin. George Gaylord Simpson, a convinced evolutionist and perhaps the leading writer on the theory, admits that ". . . there is practically nothing in Darwin's theories that had not been expressed by others long before him." [69]

For example, Darwin titled his chapter on this subject: "Natural Selection; or the Survival of the Fittest." The second part of that title was borrowed from Herbert Spencer, who coined this phrase and published his ideas on biological evolution before the views of Darwin were known. And the title of another key chapter, "Struggle for Existence," Darwin borrowed from Thomas Malthus, after having read his *Essay on the Principle of Population.*

Malthus was an economist, not a biologist, who stated that LIFE tends to increase faster than FOOD, resulting in over-population and a struggle for existence. Though Darwin praised Malthus extravagantly, he should have recognized that there can be no distinction between life and food since food IS living things (or substances provided by living things) and that plants and small animals, serving as food for larger animals, reproduce faster than the large animals. Himmelfarb calls our attention to:

> "the basic fallacy of Malthus . . . the internal contradiction in Malthus' theory which Darwin, like so many others, failed to recognize.

... For if human beings tended to increase geometrically, so did animals and plants—and perhaps even more than geometrically, their natural rate of reproduction being, if anything, higher than that of man." [70]

The fact that this central idea in Darwin's theory was not original is not important IF natural selection still holds some value in helping science unlock the secrets of nature. Obviously Darwin thought it was a valuable idea, or he would not have made it basic to his theory. And some modern evolutionists like Julian Huxley still argue that natural selection is the sole factor in evolution:

> "The discovery of the principle of natural selection . . . has rendered all other explanations of evolution untenable. So far as we now know, not only is natural selection inevitable, not only is it AN effective agency of evolution, but it is THE ONLY effective agency of evolution." [71]

Sir Gavin De Beer, eminent British zoologist, sides with Huxley: ". . . so only natural selection is left, and it is selection, not mutation, that controls evolution." [72]

But their enthusiasm for natural selection is RARE among evolutionists today. As confirmed evolutionist Sir James Gray, Professor of Zoology at Cambridge University, put it:

> "All biologists are not equally satisfied. . . . We have either to accept natural selection as the only available guide to the mechanism of evolution, and be prepared to admit that it involves a considerable element of speculation, or feel it in our bones that natural selection, operating on the random mutations, leaves too much to chance. . . . But, your guess is as good as mine." [73]

Ernst Mayr, an eminent evolutionist, states: "Natural selection is no longer regarded as an all-or-none process but rather as a purely statistical concept." [74] And does evolutionary biologist Jean Rostand feel natural selection is an adequate explanation?

> "No, decidedly, I cannot make myself think that these 'slips' of heredity [mutations] have been ABLE, even with the cooperation of natural selection, even with the advantage of the immense periods of time in which evolution works on life, to BUILD the entire world. . . . I cannot persuade myself that the eye, the ear, the human brain have been formed in this way. . . . Should a person say he is convinced when he is not? For whatever my denial is worth, I cannot change it to assent." [75]

And no less an evolutionist than George Gaylord Simpson says of natural selection that ". . . the theory is quite unsubstantiated and has status only as a speculation." [76]

Finally, even Darwin himself, in a remarkable confession found in his second major book, *The Descent of Man*, explained that he formerly *erred* in giving too much prominence to natural selection: "I now admit . . . that in the earlier editions of my *Origin of Species* I probably attributed TOO MUCH to the action of natural selection or the survival of the fittest."[77]

WHY such a startling reappraisal of the value of this crucial point? It's because natural selection falls short in two ways. As we shall now see, natural selection is both

(1) POWERLESS as a *mechanism* for evolutionary change

and

(2) MEANINGLESS as a *statement* for scientific explanation.

1 – WHAT NATURAL SELECTION **CANNOT** DO

Himmelfarb reports that:

"A growing number of scientists . . . have come to question the truth and adequacy of natural selection. And these are neither religious nor philosophical malcontents. So unexceptional a devotee of science and scientific method as Bertrand Russell has said that 'the particular mechanism of "natural selection" is no longer regarded by biologists as adequate.' " [78]

The old war cry of "natural selection" has lost most of its popularity because all who have thought carefully on the subject know that mere selection cannot possibly originate anything. Selection—either by man or nature—cannot create anything new but only make more of a certain type already existing. Natural selection fails as a causative agent because the mere sifting out of the fit by exterminating unfavored forms cannot initiate *new* variations. So as an originator of favorable variations, natural selection is completely impotent and never explains the real ORIGIN of anything at all. Someone has said that natural selection may explain the SURVIVAL of the fittest—but it can never explain the ARRIVAL of the fittest!

2 – "A ROSE IS A ROSE IS A ROSE . . . "

Gertrude Stein's thought quoted above may be adequate as a poetic comment, but it's hardly illuminating as a scientific statement—and neither is the evolutionary idea of natural selection. The reason is that natural selection or the survival of the fittest is a *tautology* (needless repetition of a single idea, as if more than one idea were being expressed). For example, it doesn't explain much to say, "Your deafness is caused by the impairment of your hearing." The statement is a meaningless tautology.

Dr. Norman Macbeth, a Harvard-trained lawyer who wrote a devastating indictment of evolution and evolutionistic thinking in his penetrating book, *Darwin Retried*, focuses on this inherent weakness, this inability of the theory to explain the HOW of evolution. He points out that some species have multiplied while others have remained stable and still others have dwindled or died out. This obvious fact is conceded by all and needs no further demonstration. The problem is to EXPLAIN why and how this happens. Note Macbeth's reasoning:

> "Thus we have as QUESTION: Why do some multiply, while others remain stable, dwindle, or die out? To which is offered as ANSWER: Because some multiply, while others remain stable, dwindle, or die out. The two sides of the equation are the same. We have a tautology. The definition is meaningless." [79]

For instance, Professor Simpson says, "I . . . define *selection*, a technical term in evolutionary studies, as anything tending to produce systematic, heritable CHANGE in population between one generation and the next." [80] And Macbeth asks, "But is such a broad definition of any use? We are trying to explain what produces change. Simpson's explanation is natural selection, which he *defines* as what produces change. Both sides of the equation are again the same; again we have a tautology. . . . If selection is anything tending to produce change, he is merely saying that change is caused by what causes change. . . . The net explanation is nil." [81]

When evolutionists are asked how we determine who are the fittest, they inform us that we determine this by the test of survival—there is no other criterion. But this means that a species *survives* because it is the *fittest* and is the *fittest* because it *survives*, which is CIRCULAR REASONING and is equivalent to saying that whatever IS, is FIT. Nothing has been explained; it's a meaningless tautology.

Surprisingly enough, some leading evolutionists like C. H. Waddington recognize this shortcoming and still do not object to it! He said:

> "Natural selection, which was at first considered as though it were a hypothesis in need of experimental or observational confirmation, turns out on closer inspection to be a TAUTOLOGY. . . . It states that the fittest individuals in a population (defined as those which leave most offspring) will leave most offspring. . . . This fact in no way reduces the MAGNITUDE of Darwin's achievement . . . biologists realize the ENORMOUS POWER of the principle as a weapon of EXPLANATION"!! [82]

Others like J. B. S. Haldane recognize the problem but try to minimize it by saying, ". . . the phrase, 'survival of the fittest,' IS something of a TAU-

TOLOGY. . . . There is no harm in stating the same truth in two different ways." [83]

But Macbeth points out that:

"This is extremely misleading. There is no harm in stating the same truth in two different ways, if one shows what one is doing by connecting the two statements with a phrase such as *in other words*. But if one connects them with *because*, which is the earmark of the tautology, one deceives either the reader or oneself or both; and there IS ample harm in this. The simplest case, where one is informed that *a cat is black because it is black,* may be harmless, though irritating and useless; but the actual cases are always HARDER TO DETECT than this, and may darken counsel for a long time."[84]

Decades ago Professor E. W. MacBride, in the leading English scientific journal *Nature*, declared:

"Of one thing, however, I am certain, and that is that 'natural selection' affords no explanation of mimicry or of any other form of evolution. It means nothing more than 'the survivors survive.' Why do certain individuals survive? Because they are the fittest. How do we know they are the fittest? Because they survive." [85]

It's noteworthy that many of the world's leading scientific minds can find only this amount of real thought in that slogan which for so long was hailed by millions as the very essence of scientific wisdom!

Proving NATURAL Selection— by *ARTIFICIAL* Selection?

Evolutionist Loren Eiseley makes this candid admission:

"It would appear that careful domestic BREEDING, whatever it may do to improve the quality of race horses or cabbages, is not actually in itself the road to the endless biological deviation which is evolution. There is great irony in this situation, for more than almost any other single factor, domestic breeding has been used as an argument for the reality of evolution." [86]

Eiseley's statement as a whole is a strong indictment against evolution. But note that Darwinism's use of "domestic breeding . . . as an argument for the reality of evolution" is itself based on a false and misleading analogy. For artificial selection used in domestic breeding is basically NOT the same thing as natural selection in supposed evolution but rather something fundamentally DIFFERENT. You see, plant and animal breeders use intelligence and specialized knowledge (1) to *select* breeding stock carefully and purposely, and (2) to *protect* their stock from natural dangers. In the words of Douglas Futuyma:

> "When Darwin wrote *The Origin of Species,* he could offer no good cases of NATURAL selection because no one had looked for them. He drew instead an ANALOGY with the ARTIFICIAL selection that animal and plant breeders use to improve domesticated varieties of animals and plants. By breeding only from the woolliest sheep, the most fertile chickens, and so on, breeders have been spectacularly successful in altering almost every imaginable characteristic of our domesticated animals and plants to the point where most of them differ from their wild ancestors." [87]

However, Darwin's theory was supposed to establish that random, purposeless NATURAL processes can substitute for intelligent design. "That he made that point by citing the accomplishments of intelligent designers [that is, domestic breeders] proves only that the receptive audience for his theory was highly uncritical." [88]

For breeding of domestic animals has produced NO new species! That's why the eminent French zoologist Pierre Grassé concludes that the results of artificial selection provide powerful testimony AGAINST Darwin's theory:

> "In spite of the intense pressure generated by ARTIFICIAL selection (eliminating any parent not answering the criteria of choice) over whole millennia, NO new species are born. . . . This is not a matter of opinion or subjective classification, but a measurable reality. The fact is that selection . . . does not constitute an INNOVATIVE evolutionary process." [89]

In his book review, evolutionist Theodosius Dobzhansky paid Grassé this tribute:

> "The book of Pierre P. Grassé is a frontal attack on all kinds of 'Darwinism.' Its purpose is 'to destroy the MYTH of evolution, as a simple, understood, explained phenomenon.' . . . One can disagree with Grassé but not ignore him. He is the most distinguished of French zoologists, the editor of the 28 volumes of *Traite de Zoologie,* author of numerous original investigations, and ex-president of the Academie des Sciences. His knowledge of the living world is encyclopedic." [90]

The stance taken by Grassé shows that it is indeed possible for a person in complete command of the facts to come to the conclusion that Darwinism is a "myth."

The LIGHT & the DARK of the Peppered Moth

Darwin's claims for natural selection received no experimental support till a century elapsed—and then results were bleak indeed. Most biology students since the 1950's were taught about the PEPPERED MOTH in England and how it changed color from LIGHT to DARK! It was hailed as a classic demonstration of the power of natural selection.

Unfortunately for evolutionists, and for Oxford zoologist Bernard Kettlewell who announced the discovery,[91] it's a very unconvincing "proof." Here's what happened: A hundred or more years ago, there were both light and dark varieties of peppered moths. Passing the day at rest on light-colored tree trunks and rocks, the light-colored moths blended with their background, escaped detection, and survived better than the dark-colored ones, most of whom would be devoured by their major predator—birds.

But as the Industrial Revolution came to England and smoke and soot from factories gradually darkened the tree trunks and rocks in urban surroundings, the situation slowly changed. After a while the light-colored moths, who stood out clearly against the darker tree bark, were picked off by the birds while the dark moths were better camouflaged and survived.

However, this observation by Kettlewell—as now everyone agrees—"is NOT an example of evolutionary change from light-colored to dark-colored moths, because both kinds were already in the population . . . but [it is] one that is often misrepresented in textbooks."[92] In other words, there were light and dark moths before Industrialization, and light and dark moths afterward. Only the LOCAL POPULATION RATIOS of one variety to the other changed. This has nothing to do with the origin of any species, or even of any variety, because dark and light moths were present throughout.

HAS EVOLUTION PRODUCED DRUG-RESISTANT MICROBES?

Evolutionists make similar claims in regard to certain MICROBES—germs that over time have developed a resistance to antibiotics. For instance, penicillin is generally now less effective than before. Stronger drugs have replaced ones that formerly did the job, yet some "super germs" make treatment difficult.

We may ask, have these drug-resistant microbes "evolved"? As is frequently the case, we must distinguish between microevolution (variation, adaptation, and recombination of EXISTING traits) and macroevolution (the rise of NEW and different genes, body parts, and traits). Since each species of germ remained that same species and nothing new was produced, we understand that macroevolution did NOT occur. This acquired resistance to antibiotics is due simply to a population shift.

Here's how it works: When a colony of billions of bacteria is exposed to an antibiotic, most of the microbes die. But some, through a lucky genetic recombination, are resistant to the antibiotic. They're the only ones to survive and reproduce, and their descendants inherit the same genetic resistance. Over time, virtually all possess this resistance. Thus—as in the case of the peppered moth—there were microbes susceptible to the drug and microbes resistant to it both before and after it was introduced. Only their POPULATION RATIOS changed. No new genetic information was produced—in fact, genetic information was *lost*, with the many microbes that were wiped out by the drug. [93]

Also, it has been proven that resistance to many modern antibiotics was present DECADES BEFORE their discovery. In 1845, sailors on an ill-fated Arctic expedition were buried in the permafrost and remained deeply frozen till their bodies were exhumed in 1986. Preservation was so complete that six strains of nineteenth-century bacteria found dormant in the contents of the sailors' intestines were able to be revived! When tested, these bacteria were found to possess resistance to several modern-day antibiotics, including penicillin. Such traits were obviously present prior to penicillin's discovery, and thus could NOT be an evolutionary development. [94]

Thus Natural Selection—once Darwinism's mighty PILLAR—does not support the theory but crumbles under its own inherent weakness.

V. CLASSIFICATION & COMPARATIVE ANATOMY

The arguments for evolution from classification and comparative anatomy are so intimately connected that they can best be considered together. The argument from CLASSIFICATION is short and easily stated. It's that the modern system of naming and classifying plants and animals, besides being a convenient system, also shows their true blood relationship to one another.

But today's system of classification has largely been made by evolutionists for the purpose of illustrating the supposed evolutionary heritage of living things (that's like cutting the pattern to fit the cloth!). This is admitted by Sir Julian Huxley himself. [95] Thus classification is not an independent witness for evolution. It has been in collusion with the defendant and has been coached to testify. Even so, its evidence can still be interpreted much more reasonably in favor of creation and against evolution, as we'll see.

The field of classification is also called "taxonomy" or "systematics." Notice what Earnest Albert Hooton, evolutionary anthropologist at Harvard for more than forty years, says about it:

> "The business of taxonomy, or zoological classification (pigeon-holing), works well enough for coarse categories, such as classes . . . orders . . . and families. Like big business in the commercial world, it

masquerades under a guise of efficiency and accuracy which proves to be illusive under closer examination. Formerly I was under the impression that taxonomic indiscretions were peculiar to anthropologists, but now I am convinced that a zoological classificationist may be as dissolute and irresponsible as a lightning-rod salesman. Further, the more I inspect the family trees of man, so facilely constructed by students of human paleontology, including myself, the more I am inclined to agree with the poet that 'only God can make a tree.'" [96]

Professor Hooton is justified in his indictment of taxonomists because classification is so highly subjective. It's often true that subjective opinion, not objective fact, is what chiefly decides the degree of supposed evolutionary relationship. The pigeon-holes used by classifiers are often a matter of opinion. E. W. MacBride, of London University, deplores "to what an enormous extent the PERSONAL EQUATION enters in the determination of these questions." [97]

And Paul Weatherwax, Professor of Botany at Indiana University, says: "Botanists still disagree widely on the proper grouping of many plants, but this is because they do not agree in their theories as to the ORIGIN of the differences which separate the groups." [98]

We've already seen how taxonomists have found great difficulty in defining a basic, crucial term like "species." This difficulty is by no means imaginary. As Dr. Ernst Mayr says: "It may not be exaggeration if I say that there are probably as many species concepts as there are thinking systematists and students of speciation." [99] Sir Julian Huxley concurs: "Even competent systematists do not always agree as to the delimitation of species." [100] In other words, by no means do all biologists speak the same language when they use the word *species*.

Another dispute in the ranks of taxonomists is between the "splitters" and the "lumpers." The "splitters" like to elevate mere varieties into new, full-fledged species and therefore divide one species into several. The "lumpers," on the other hand, prefer large species and tend to combine several old species into a larger one. This may seem like a joke to the uninitiated, but Sir Julian solemnly informs us that "the battle of the 'splitters' and the 'lumpers' still continues." [101] Thus we see that classification (which sounds grandly awesome with its Latin names and seems quite "scientific" to the average person) is simply man-made and often rests at bottom on mere opinion.

Speaking of the chaos that exists in taxonomy of PRIMATES [the highest order of animals, including man, apes, monkeys, *etc.*], Harvard paleontologist and taxonomist George Gaylord Simpson declares: "A major reason for this confusion is that much of the work on primates has been done by students who had no experience in taxonomy and who were completely incompetent to enter this field, however competent they may have been in other respects."[102] No wonder, then, that specimens which one investigator groups as a "family" may, in the opinion of another, deserve no more than "genus" rank!

So at best, the system of classification is man-made and may or may not have any real meaning in itself. Assuming that it does show some real relationship, the relationship may well be that of a common Designer instead of a common ancestor. Does resemblance among CARS like Mustang II, Thunderbird, and Lincoln show that they "evolved" from the Galaxie—or simply that they were all designed and built by Ford Motor Company? Likewise, a fish and a submarine have roughly similar shapes, but no one claims they're blood brothers. Similarity may imply not common relationship but only a common design.

Professor W. R. Thompson, in his Foreword to the Centennial Edition of Darwin's *Origin of Species,* warned fellow evolutionists against ASSUMING an evolutionary relationship in the classification of living things. He makes plain that not all things that can be classified have a parent-child relationship:

> "The arrangement of the chemical elements . . . is a true classification and so is the arrangement of geometric forms; yet no genealogical considerations are involved. . . . If we wish to erect a genealogical classification . . . we must discover through what forms the existing organisms have actually descended. IF these historical facts cannot be ascertained, then it is useless to seek for substitutes, and from the fact that a classification IS possible we certainly cannot infer that it is genealogical and is in any sense a proof of evolution." [103]

As a matter of fact, the very possibility of a classification is strong evidence AGAINST evolution. For example, organisms are neatly categorized in terms of species, genus, family, order, class, phylum, and kingdom. But the ease with which we can "pigeon-hole" basic kinds—with clear-cut gaps between—does NOT indicate an evolutionary relationship. Just the OPPOSITE is indicated, for *if* all organisms arose by slow descent from a common ancestor, there should be a continuous *blending* from one kind into another. It should be impossible to tell where one species stops and another begins, so that any system of classification would be quite impossible.

Yet Dr. Goldschmidt says: "It is not difficult to show that between them [species] exist the 'bridgeless gaps' which we are discussing." [104] Because this is true, very little experience is needed to distinguish a birch from a beech tree, a flying squirrel from a bat, or humans from chimpanzees.

Scientists should use our classification system merely as a convenient device to avoid confusion in naming plants and animals—and should cease to maintain that it provides a picture of evolutionary heritage.

Now let's look at COMPARATIVE ANATOMY, also called *morphology*. Here's what evolutionists say about it: "Morphology deals with the FORM and STRUCTURE of organisms, and it affords some of the strongest evidence of organic evolution."[105] If this evidence constitutes "some of the strongest" that evolutionists can find, it's unfortunate for the theory because here again the so-called "evidence" rests on subjective opinion, not objective fact.

Of course, anyone who compares anatomical structures is impressed with certain similarities among various creatures. For instance, the forelimbs of all limbed vertebrates have the same three bones—humerus, radius, and ulna. Many also have what are called pentadactyl limbs—that is, limbs with five fingers and toes. Those are the FACTS, but what do they MEAN? Well, here the evidence ends and speculation begins. Evolutionists begin at this point and speculate that such agreement in bones can mean only descent from a common ancestor. The creationist believes that such similarities actually result from the fact that creation is based on the master plan of the Master Planner. Where similar functions were required, God used similar structures, merely modifying these structures to meet the individual requirements of each organism.

Always remember that the FACTS of SCIENCE are one thing, but the CONCLUSIONS of SCIENTISTS may be quite another. There's a difference between observing certain facts and drawing conclusions from those facts. Darwin saw the similarities and jumped to the conclusion of evolution.

But similarity of form cannot in any way prove ORIGIN. One can show similarities of form all day long and not even approach the question of origin. Such similarities by themselves prove nothing about origins—yet the question of origin is what it's all about, isn't it? You see, the fact that certain plants and animals resemble each other does not supply the information that evolutionists so earnestly seek, which is where the plants and animals came from. By arranging his BOOKS on a shelf in a graded system (depending on their size or complexity), a student could just as well prove their "evolution." You can see the absurdity of such an argument, for it assumes the very thing which needs to be proved.

This "evidence" is largely circumstantial and therefore quite unsatisfactory. None of us would wish to be sentenced to life imprisonment or the gas chamber on nothing but circumstantial evidence. The fact that we were in a house at the time a murder was committed in it would not prove we had any part in the murder. And the argument for evolution in this case rests on the same kind of unsatisfactory evidence. Far from providing "clear proof" of evolution, the common patterns of design point just as well to common origin from the one Architect, Engineer, or Designer.

Genesis informs us that God created ALL the original types of life, from the simple forms to those more complex. But in making more complex forms, WHY shouldn't He employ certain rules of structure for all of them—for example, a backbone for a whole category of animals? If the backbone is good for one, why is it not good for another? It's nonsense to suppose that because the Creator had once used a good plan, He must never again utilize it in creating other animals with this plan only slightly modified. Must every kind of creature be so completely different from all others that we can detect no resemblance between any two? Inevitably, then, as we survey the wonderful variety of living things, we'll find similarities.

What's the DIFFERENCE?

But it's amazing that evolutionists seem unable to give proper weight to the dissimilarities between man and animals. We read that "The comparative anatomist finds that physically man is bone for bone, muscle for muscle, nerve for nerve, in striking agreement with the higher apes." [106] But what about the differences? Though evolutionists may try to minimize the fact, there are vast differences between man and even the "highest" animal forms.

For instance, man differs from the apes in his efficiency as a ground-dwelling BIPED whereas the ape is basically a tree-dwelling QUADRUPED. Only man walks upright on two feet. Apes are called "knuckle-walkers" because, contrary to popular belief, they seldom walk on their hind legs and usually move about on all fours. Except for a few birds like the ostrich, man is the only creature that moves exclusively on two feet.

Man has a nose with a prominent bridge and elongated tip, while the ape's nose lacks both of these. Man has red lips formed by an extension of the mucous membrane from inside his mouth, whereas apes don't have lips of this nature. The skull in man is perfectly balanced on the upper end of the spinal column, but the curvature of the spinal column in apes is convex (humped) toward the back. The arms of man are shorter than his legs, yet all apes have elongated forelimbs. The human foot is constructed for walking and running, having a well-formed arch and the big toe in line with the others. All four feet in apes are HAND-LIKE with an opposable "thumb" which may grasp objects.

Other differences along this line could be mentioned, such as features of man's skin and the sparsity and distribution of his hair. But perhaps we should turn to man's great power of INTELLECT. It's this tremendous difference between animal brain and human mind that lifts man above any classification with the beasts. Only man is teachable; you can train an animal such as an ape, but you cannot teach him to exercise independent judgment as human beings can. At times animals may draw simple inferences, but even apes and monkeys possess little or no capacity for abstract thought or conceptual reasoning. A monkey can look at the starry heavens, but only man can ponder their meaning.

The proportional size of the brain compared to the body is unquestionably an indicator of intelligence. When comparable body weight is considered, the gulf between man's brain size and that of the anthropoid apes is enormous. Think of man's capacity for articulate speech—far beyond the whines and growls of the brute creation. And man alone can also use written language, as you now prove by perusing these black marks on white paper! Man designs, constructs, and uses complex tools and machines of which animals know nothing. Only man can appreciate truth, beauty, and moral values. Only man is self-conscious and possessed of the ability to understand the difference between right and wrong. Human beings are the only creatures who weep as an emotional response.

Many other characteristics might be considered, such as man's spiritual nature and elements of man's culture, which are never exhibited in the animal world. But we can't explain man's mental machinery simply in terms of physics and chemistry. The science of biology misses the point if it feels anatomy alone constitutes the creature. It becomes a science of dead remains if it feels man can be explained on the basis of his dissected body.

No, man did not evolve by slow degrees from lower forms of animal or vegetable life but came into being as a son of God, formed by the Creator in His own image. To some extent Darwin acknowledged man's noble qualities, but his closing words in *The Descent of Man* are: "Man still bears in his bodily frame the indelible stamp of his LOWLY origin." We may with greater truth reply: Man's inner being, his MIND, gives unmistakable proof that his origin was a high and noble one.

VI. "VESTIGIAL" Organs

Thus the arguments offered for evolution by classification and comparative anatomy are greatly weakened by subjective whim and wishful thinking. Closely related to comparative anatomy is the subject of VESTIGIAL ORGANS, which evolutionists say are the last vestiges of organs that once had a use but are no longer needed because of man's advance up the evolutionary ladder. Believers in evolution often cite these as "sufficient to show that the human body cannot be considered as a perfect final work of creation but rather the ultimate product of eons of evolutionary change, resulting in a very imperfect being from the physical point of view—a veritable museum of antiquities!" [107]

But the supposed presence of so-called "vestigial" organs in man gives less and less proof for evolution as time goes by, for our list of "useless" organs decreases as our knowledge of anatomy and physiology increases. Evolutionists at one time listed about 180 organs in the human body considered "useless relics of the past" that were useful in man's animal ancestors. With increasing knowledge, however, this list has steadily shrunk till the number has been reduced to practically zero.

For instance, this list once included such organs or structures as the appendix, the adrenal glands, the tonsils, the coccyx (the lower end of man's spinal column), the thymus gland, and others all said to be vestigial—so much "excess baggage" we carry around. But note what a report in the November 1966 *Reader's Digest*, entitled "The 'Useless' Gland That Guards Our Health," states:

> "For at least 2000 years, doctors have puzzled over the function of . . . the THYMUS gland. . . . Modern physicians came to regard it, like the appendix, as a useless, vestigial organ which had lost its original purpose, if indeed it ever had one. In the last few years, however, . . . men have proved that, far from being useless, the thymus is really the master gland that regulates the intricate immunity system which protects us against infectious diseases. . . . Recent experiments have led researchers to believe that the appendix, tonsils and adenoids may also figure in the antibody responses." [108]

The *Encyclopedia Britannica* also declared: "Many of the so-called vestigial organs are now known to fulfill important functions." [109]

The COCCYX (composed of several terminal vertabrae) is often cited as a functionless remnant of a TAIL in man, but it serves as the anchor for important muscles of elimination (its removal would interfere with defecation). It also helps support the pelvic cavity, furnishes a surface for attachment of a portion of the large gluteal muscle which extends and rotates the thigh, and encloses the terminal portion of the spinal cord. Furthermore, one cannot sit comfortably following removal of the coccyx.

The APPENDIX is possibly the only organ still on the vestigial list, but scientists are no longer so sure. Professor William Straus, an anatomy expert, states that "there is no longer any justification for regarding the vermiform appendix as a vestigial structure." [110] It should be noted that the higher apes (gorilla, chimpanzee, *etc.*) possess an appendix, whereas their immediate relatives, the lower apes, do not; but it appears again among the still lower mammals such as the opossum. How does the evolutionist account for this?

Furthermore, the absurdity of calling the appendix "vestigial" in man is apparent from this fact: that its function is unknown not only in MAN but also in every other species of animal that possess it. Tonsils were once almost routinely removed, but removal of the tonsils and appendix is now believed to increase susceptibility to Hodgkin's disease.[111] Finally, these so-called vestigial organs prove nothing in favor of evolution, for EVEN IF man's appendix had a clear and obvious function, even if he possessed fully functional wisdom teeth, *etc.*, he would still be a MAN and would not thereby become a new basic type of animal.

Evolutionary biologist Douglas Futuyma cites the "rudimentary eyes of cave animals; the tiny, useless legs of many snakelike lizards; [and] the vestiges of the pelvis in pythons" as evidence that evolution has occurred.[112] But because we haven't yet discovered a use for a structure does not mean that none exists. A python pelvis might be doing something useful of which we're ignorant. Besides, biochemistry professor Michael Behe perceptively points out that:

> "Futuyma never explains how a REAL pelvis or eye developed in the first place, so as to be able to give rise to a VESTIGIAL organ later on, yet BOTH the functioning organ and the vestigial organ require explanation."[113]

And the whole suggestion of vestigial structures possessing any evolutionary significance is open to serious question when we realize that they're entirely absent from PLANTS. IF plants evolved from simpler forms, why don't they display the same sort of vestigial FORGET-ME-NOTS that animals are supposed to show?

Remember that even if an organ could be identified as a useless vestige of a once-useful organ, this would constitute evidence NOT of evolution, but of deterioration, and would thus prove the wrong thing. Truly vestigial organs fit better into a pattern of regressive change and DEGENERATION than of progressive change and IMPROVEMENT. What evolution NEEDS is rudimentary or nascent organs in various stages of development, on their way toward the fully-formed state. But the entire LACK of such hopeful structures pointing toward NEW organs must be disappointing to even the most avid evolutionists.

The absence of developing, rudimentary organs poses such a problem for evolutionists that they seldom mention it. Darwin admitted:

"If it could be demonstrated that any complex organ existed, which could not possibly have been formed by numerous, successive, slight modifications, my theory would absolutely BREAK DOWN." [114]

And he was right, of course; Darwin's theory does break down on this very point. Take as an example some organ such as the EYE. The eye is an enormously complex mechanism and poses a tremendous challenge to evolutionary theory. Darwin himself said:

"To suppose that the EYE, with all its inimitable contrivances for adjusting the focus to different distances, for admitting different amounts of light, and for the correction of spherical and chromatic aberration, could have been formed by natural selection, seems, I freely confess, absurd in the highest degree." [115]

And other evolutionary scientists agree with him. Professor Ernst Mayr says: "It must be admitted, however, that it is a considerable strain on one's credulity to assume that finely balanced systems such as certain sense organs (the EYE of vertebrates . . .) could be improved by random mutations." [116] George Gaylord Simpson of Harvard is forced to the same conclusion: "Evolution in the mutationist world is not merely AIMLESS but DIRECTIONLESS. The origin of such an organ as an EYE, for example, entirely at random seems almost infinitely improbable." [117]

That's the reason why, in a letter to American botanist Asa Gray dated April 3, 1860, Darwin said: "I remember well the time when the thought of the EYE made me cold all over." [118] But obviously he wasn't the only evolutionist who shudders at the thought. Dr. Garrett Hardin, Professor of Biology at the University of California at Berkeley, asks:

"How then are we to account for the evolution of such a complicated organ as the EYE? . . . If even the slightest thing is wrong—if the retina is missing, or the lens opaque, or the dimensions in error—the eye fails to form a recognizable image and is consequently useless. Since it must be either PERFECT, or perfectly USELESS, HOW could it have evolved by small, successive, Darwinian steps?" [119]

Hardin must have been burdened by the magnitude of the problem, for he returns to it later in his book, saying:

". . . That DAMNED EYE—the human eye . . . which Darwin freely conceded to constitute a severe strain on his theory of evolution. Is so simple a principle as natural selection equal to explaining so complex a structure as the image-producing eye? Can the step-by-step process of Darwinian evolution carry adaptation so far? Competent opinion has wavered on this point." [120]

These evolutionary scientists are so candid because they have no choice. How could an EYELESS creature begin a million-year project of forming an eye that would be of no use until the million years were over? Why would this rudimentary organ be retained before it would work? (For it must be complete or it won't function, and partially-formed, non-functioning organs would be a DISadvantage and be eliminated by natural selection.) Could an organ on-its-way-to-becoming-an-eye give any advantage in the struggle for survival? And if it would give some advantage, why are there not now MANY of these developing organs?

So the old argument of "vestigial organs" has no demonstrative value. On the contrary, that argument itself requires demonstration.

Our discussion of evolution will be concluded in **PART II**,
which follows. There we'll consider such matters as

the origin of LIFE,
the origin of SEX,
ENTROPY,
the FOSSIL record,
EARLY MAN,
MOLECULAR biology,
and other vital issues.

Notes to Chapter 3

1. Sir Julian Huxley, "At Random: A Television Preview," in Sol Tax, editor, *Issues in Evolution*, Volume 3 of *Evolution After Darwin* (Chicago: The University of Chicago Press, 1960), p. 41.

2. Richard B. Goldschmidt, *American Scientist*, Volume 40 (1952), p. 84.

3. Theodosius Dobzhansky, *Genetics and the Origin of Species*, Second Edition (New York: Columbia University Press, 1941), p. 8.

4. Horatio H. Newman, *Outlines of General Zoology*, (New York: The Macmillan Company, 1924), p. 407.

5. Richard Swann Lull, *Organic Evolution* (New York: The Macmillan Company, 1948), p. 15.

6. Anthony Standen, *Science Is a Sacred Cow* (New York: E. P. Dutton & Company, 1950), p. 106.

7. Horatio H. Newman, *Evolution, Genetics, and Eugenics*, Third Edition (Chicago: University of Chicago Press, 1932), p. 57.

8. Ernst Mayr, *Animal Species and Evolution* (Cambridge, Massachusetts: Harvard University Press, 1963), pp. 7-8.

9. Charles Singer, *A Short History of Science* (New York: Oxford University Press, 1946), p. 387.

10. Thomas Hunt Morgan, *Evolution and Adaptation* (New York: The Macmillan Company, 1903), p. 43.

11. Paul R. Ehrlich and Richard W. Holm, "Patterns and Populations," *Science*, Volume 137 (August 31, 1962), p. 656.

12. Paul S. Moorhead and Martin M. Kaplan, editors, *Mathematical Challenges to the Neo-Darwinian Interpretation of Evolution*, Symposium Monograph No. 5 (Philadelphia: The Wistar Institute Press, 1967).

13. Robert Bernhard, "Heresy in the Halls of Biology: Mathematicians Question Darwinism," *Scientific Research*, Volume 2, No. 11 (November, 1967).

14. Robert Bernhard, "Thinking the Unthinkable: Are Evolutionists Wrong?" *Scientific Research*, Volume 4, No. 18 (September, 1969).

15. W. R. Thompson, "Introduction" to *The Origin of Species* by Charles Darwin (New York: E. P. Dutton & Company, Everyman's Library, 1956). Thompson's Introduction has also been reprinted in the *Journal of the American Scientific Affiliation*, Volume 12 (March, 1960), pp. 2-9.

16. G. A. Kerkut, *Implications of Evolution* (New York: Pergamon Press, 1960), p. 157.

17. John T. Bonner, Review of Kerkut's book, *American Scientist*, Volume 49, No. 2 (June, 1961), p. 240.

18. George Gaylord Simpson, *Science*, Volume 143 (1964), p. 769.

19. David G. Kitts, "Paleontology and Evolutionary Theory," *Evolution*, Volume 28 (September, 1974), p. 466.

20. Francisco J. Ayala, "Biological Evolution: Natural Selection or Random Walk?" *American Scientist*, Volume 62 (November-December, 1974), p. 700.

21. Peter Medawar, quoted in Moorhead and Kaplan, editors, *Mathematical Challenges to the Neo-Darwinian Interpretation of Evolution*, Symposium Monograph No. 5 (Philadelphia: The Wistar Institute Press, 1967), p. xi.

22. Sir Karl R. Popper, *Conjectures and Refutations* (London: Routledge and Kegan Paul, 1963), pp. 33-37. In another book, he stated, "Darwinism is not a TESTABLE scientific theory, but a METAPHYSICAL research programme."—Karl Popper, *Unended Quest: An Intellectual Autobiography* (La Salle, Illinois: Open Court, © 1976).

23. Paul R. Ehrlich and L. C. Birch, "Evolutionary History and Population Biology," *Nature*, Volume 214 (April 22, 1967), p. 352.

24. Louis Trenchard More, *The Dogma of Evolution* (Princeton, New Jersey: Princeton University Press, 1925).

25. Thomas Henry Huxley, *Discourses Biological and Geological* (1896 edition), pp. 256-257.

26. Charles Darwin, *On the Origin of Species: A Facsimile of the First Edition* (Cambridge, Massachusetts: Harvard University Press, 1964), p. 109.

27. *Ibid.*, p. 490.

28. Richard B. Goldschmidt, *The Material Basis of Evolution* (Paterson, New Jersey: Pageant Books, Inc., 1960), p. 396.

29. *Ibid.*, p. 183.

30. Norman Macbeth, *Darwin Retried* (New York: Dell Publishing Company, 1971), p. 31.

31. Mark Twain, quoted in Macbeth, *op. cit.*, pp. 37-38.

32. Theodosius Dobzhansky, *Genetics and the Origin of Species*, Third Edition, Revised (New York: Columbia University Press, 1951), p. 4.

33. George Gaylord Simpson, *The Major Features of Evolution* (New York: Columbia University Press, 1953), p. 340. *Genera* is the plural of *genus*, the biological class one step above a basic species.

34. Sir Gavin De Beer, *Charles Darwin: Evolution by Natural Selection* (Garden City, New York: Doubleday and Company, 1964), p. 1.

35. Richard B. Goldschmidt, *The Material Basis of Evolution* (Paterson, New Jersey: Pageant Books, Inc., 1960), p. 168.

36. Letter from Darwin to Joseph Hooker, January 11, 1844, in *The Life and Letters of Charles Darwin*, edited by his son Francis Darwin, (New York: D. Appleton and Company, 1896 [Reprinted 1972]), Volume I, p. 384.

37. See Numbers 12:1 and Jeremiah 13:23.

38. Genesis 6:4.

39. See Genesis 3:14-19.

40. Leviticus 11:16.

41. See Genesis 1, verses 11, 12, 21, 24, and 25.

42. *Encyclopedia Britannica* (1967 edition), Volume 20, p. 1149, Article "Species" and Volume 23, p. 1006, Article "Zoology."

43. Jean Rostand, *The Orion Book of Evolution* (New York: The Orion Press, 1960), p. 61.

44. Charles Darwin, quoted in Nicholas Hotton III, *The Evidence of Evolution* (Garden

City, New York: Doubleday and Company, 1962), p. 138.

45. Herbert Spencer, *Contemporary Review*, February and March, 1893.

46. Jean Rostand, *The Orion Book of Evolution* (New York: The Orion Press, 1960), p. 62.

47. *Ibid.*, p. 64.

48. Ernst Haeckel, quoted in J. A. Thompson, *Heredity*, Fifth Edition (New York: Coleman, 1926), p. 190.

49. George W. Burns, *The Science of Genetics: An Introduction to Heredity* (New York: The Macmillan Company, 1969), p. 291.

50. Sir Julian Huxley, *Evolution in Action* (New York: Harper & Brothers, 1953), p. 38, and Theodosius Dobzhansky, *The Biological Basis of Human Freedom* (New York: Columbia University Press, 1956), p. 56.

51. Ernst Mayr, *Animal Species and Evolution* (Cambridge, Massachusetts: Harvard University Press, 1963), p. 176.

52. *Ibid.*, p. 7.

53. Norman Macbeth, *Darwin Retried* (New York: Dell Publishing Company, 1971), p. 33.

54. Richard Goldschmidt, *The Material Basis of Evolution* (Paterson, New Jersey: Pageant Books, Inc., 1960), pp. 390-392.

55. Theodosius Dobzhansky, *Genetics and the Origin of Species*, Second Edition (New York: Columbia University Press, 1941), p. 80.

56. Sir Julian Huxley, in Huxley, Hardy, and Ford, editors, *Evolution As a Process* (London: 1954), p. 5.

57. *Science Today*, chapter entitled "EVOLUTION: The Appearance of Design in Living Things," by C. H. Waddington (New York: Criterion Books, First American edition, 1961), p. 36.

58. George Gaylord Simpson, *The Major Features of Evolution* (New York: Columbia University Press, 1953), p. 96.

59. Sir Julian Huxley, *Evolution in Action* (New York: Harper & Brothers, 1953), p. 39.

60. Ernst Mayr, *Animal Species and Evolution* (Cambridge, Massachusetts: Harvard University Press, 1953), p. 174.

61. Hermann J. Müller, "Radiation and Human Mutation," *Scientific American* (November, 1955), p. 58.

62. Hermann J. Müller, in "Gloomy Nobelman," *Time* (November 11, 1946), p. 96.

63. John J. Fried, *The Mystery of Heredity* (New York: The John Day Company, 1971, p. 135.

64. Theodosius Dobzhansky, *Genetics and the Origin of Species*, Third Edition, Revised (New York: Columbia University Press, 1951), p. 73.

65. Hugh Miller, *Progress and Decline* (New York: 1963), p. 38.

66. Earnest Albert Hooton, *Apes, Men, and Morons* (Freeport, New York: Books for Libraries Press, 1970), p. 118.

67. Maurice Caullery, *Genetics and Heredity* (New York: Walker and Company, 1964), p. 119.

68. Gertrude Himmelfarb, *Darwin and the Darwinian Revolution* (Garden City, New

York: Doubleday and Company, 1962), p. 312.

69. George Gaylord Simpson, *Life of the Past: An Introduction to Paleontology* (New Haven: Yale University Press, 1953), p. 142.

70. Gertrude Himmelfarb, *Darwin and the Darwinian Revolution* (Garden City, New York: Doubleday and Company, 1962), p. 164. This is not the place to enter into an extended discussion of Malthus, but for a good critique, see Himmelfarb's article on Malthus in *Encounter*, V (1955), pp. 53-60.

71. Sir Julian Huxley, *Evolution in Action* (New York: Harper & Brothers, 1953), p. 36. The capitalized words are emphasized by Huxley in the original.

72. Sir Gavin De Beer, *Charles Darwin: Evolution by Natural Selection* (Garden City, New York: Doubleday and Company, 1964), p. 192.

73. *Science Today*, chapter entitled "The Science of Life," by Sir James Gray (New York: Criterion Books, First American edition, 1961), pp. 29-30.

74. Ernst Mayr, *Animal Species and Evolution* (Cambridge, Massachusetts: Harvard University Press, 1963), p. 7.

75. Jean Rostand, *The Orion Book of Evolution* (New York: The Orion Press 1960), p. 79.

76. George Gaylord Simpson, *The Major Features of Evolution* (New York: Columbia University Press, 1953), pp. 118-119.

77. Charles Darwin, *The Descent of Man*, First Edition (London: 1871), Volume I, p. 152.

78. Gertrude Himmelfarb, *Darwin and the Darwinian Revolution* (Garden City, New York: Doubleday and Company, 1962), p. 445. Her Bertrand Russell quotation is taken from Russell's book *The Scientific Outlook* (London, 1931), pp. 43-44.

79. Norman Macbeth, *Darwin Retried* (New York: Dell Publishing Company, 1971), p. 47.

80. George Gaylord Simpson, *The Major Features of Evolution* (New York: Columbia University Press, 1953), p. 138.

81. Norman Macbeth, *Darwin Retried* (New York: Dell Publishing Company, 1971), p. 49.

82. C. H. Waddington, "Evolutionary Adaptation," in Sol Tax, editor, *The Evolution of Life*, Volume 1 of *Evolution After Darwin* (Chicago: The University of Chicago Press, 1960), p. 385. Phillip Johnson observes Waddington's comment "was not an offhand statement, but a considered judgment published in a paper presented at the great convocation at the University of Chicago in 1959 celebrating the hundredth anniversary of the publication of *The Origin of Species*. Apparently, none of the distinguished authorities present told Waddington that a tautology does not explain anything."—*Darwin on Trial*, Second Edition (Downers Grove, Illinois: InterVarsity Press, © 1993), p. 22. Johnson is Professor of Law at the University of California at Berkeley specializing in the logic of arguments.

83. J. B. S. Haldane, "Darwinism Under Revision," *Rationalist Annual* (1935), p. 24.

84. Norman Macbeth, *Darwin Retried* (New York: Dell Publishing Company, 1971), p. 63.

85. E. W. MacBride, *Nature* (May 11, 1929), p. 713.

86. Loren Eiseley, *The Immense Journey* (New York: Vintage Books, 1958), p. 223.

87. Douglas J. Futuyma, *Science on Trial: The Case for Evolution* (New York: Pantheon Books, © 1983), Chapter Six. Futuyma is the author of one of the leading college textbooks on evolution and an internationally recognized authority.

88. Phillip E. Johnson, *Darwin on Trial,* Second Edition (Downers Grove, Illinois: InterVarsity Press, © 1993), p. 18. It has been pointed out that the very name Darwin gave to his brain child—"natural selection"—is in itself contradictory: "natural" indicating pure naturalistic chance, and "selection" referring to intelligent choice. One cannot have it both ways. (See William A. Dembski, *"The Act of Creation: Bridging Transcendence and Immanence,"* p. 11:1.)

89. Pierre P. Grassé, *The Evolution of Living Organisms* (New York: Academic Press, 1977 [English translation of *L'Evolution du Vivant,* originally published in France in 1973]), pp. 124-125.

90. Theodosius Dobzhansky, Review of Grassé's book *Evolution of Living Organisms,* quoted in Phillip E. Johnson, *Darwin on Trial,* Second Edition (Downers Grove, Illinois: InterVarsity Press, © 1993), p. 174.

91. H. B. D. Kettlewell, "Darwin's Missing Evidence," *Scientific American* Volume 200, No. 3 (March, 1959), pp. 48-53, see p. 49.

92. The *Science Framework* published by the California State Board of Education (1990) to guide textbook publishers, p. 103. For much of this information on peppered moths, the author is indebted to Phillip E. Johnson, *Darwin on Trial,* Second Edition (Downers Grove, Illinois: InterVarsity Press, © 1993), pp. 27-28, and to Michael Denton, *Evolution: A Theory in Crisis* (Bethesda, Maryland: Adler & Adler, © 1986), pp. 79-80.

93. John D. Morris, "Do Bacteria 'Evolve' Resistant to Antibiotics?' *Back to Genesis Newsletter,* No. 118 (October 1998), p. 4. Published free by INSTITUTE FOR CREATION RESEARCH, P. O. Box 2667, El Cajon, CA 92021.

94. *Medical Tribune* (December 29, 1988), pp. 1 & 23, cited in Morris, *loc. cit.*

95. Sir Julian Huxley, *Evolution: The Modern Synthesis* (New York: Harper & Brothers, 1943), p. 391.

96. Earnest Albert Hooton, *Apes, Men, and Morons* (Freeport, New York: Books for Libraries Press, 1970), pp. 115-116.

97. E. W. MacBride, *Cambridge Natural History,* Volume 1, p. 460.

98. Paul Weatherwax, *Plant Biology* (Philadelphia: W. B. Saunders, Second Edition, 1947), p. 257.

99. Ernst Mayr, *Systematics and the Origin of Species* (New York: Columbia University Press, 1942), p. 115.

100. Sir Julian Huxley, *Evolution: The Modern Synthesis* (New York: Harper & Brothers, 1943), p. 157.

101. *Ibid.,* p. 402.

102. George Gaylord Simpson, "The Principles of Classification and a Classification of Mammals," *Bulletin of the American Museum of Natural History,* Volume 85 (1945), p. 181.

103. W. R. Thompson, "Introduction" to *The Origin of Species* by Charles Darwin (New York: E. P. Dutton & Company, Everyman's Library, 1956). This quote is from the

reprint of Thompson's Introduction in the *Journal of the American Scientific Affiliation*, Volume 12 (March, 1960), p. 146.

104. Richard Goldschmidt, *The Material Basis of Evolution* (Paterson, New Jersey: Pageant Books, Inc., 1960), p. 145.

105. Nathan Fasten, *Introduction to General Zoology* (Boston: Ginn and Company, 1941), p. 640.

106. M. F. Guyer, *Animal Biology*, Third Edition (New York: Harper & Brothers, 1941), p. 517.

107. Richard Swann Lull, *Organic Evolution*, Revised Edition (New York: The Macmillan Company, 1945), p. 669.

108. "The 'Useless' Gland That Guards Our Health," *Reader's Digest* (November, 1966), pp. 229, 235.

109. *Encyclopedia Britannica* (1946 edition), Volume 8, p. 926.

110. William Straus, *Quarterly Review of Biology*, 1947, p. 149. Dr. Straus was an anatomist at John Hopkins University.

111. See *Science News*, March 20, 1971.

112. Douglas Futuyma, *Science on Trial* (New York: Pantheon Books, 1982), p. 207.

113. Michael J. Behe, *Darwin's Black Box: The Biochemical Challenge to Evolution* (New York: The Free Press, © 1996), p. 226.

114. Charles Darwin, *On the Origin of Species: A Facsimile of the First Edition* (Cambridge, Massachusetts: Harvard University Press, 1964), p. 189.

115. *Ibid.*, p. 186.

116. Ernst Mayr, *Systematics and the Origin of Species* (New York: Columbia University Press, 1942), p. 296.

117. George Gaylord Simpson, *This View of Life* (New York: Harcourt, Brace & World, 1964), p. 18.

118. Letter from Darwin to Asa Gray, April 3, 1860, in *The Life and Letters of Charles Darwin*, edited by his son Francis Darwin (New York: D. Appleton and Company, 1896 [Reprinted 1972]), Volume II, p. 90.

119. Garrett Hardin, *Nature and Man's Fate* (New York: Mentor Books, 1961), p. 71.

120. *Ibid.*, p. 224.

✦ ✦ ✦

"Extraordinary CLAIMS require extraordinary PROOF."
—CARL SAGAN

~

CHAPTER FOUR

THE THEORY OF EVOLUTION:
WEIGHED AND FOUND WANTING
PART II.

VII. THE ORIGIN OF LIFE

ANOTHER IMPORTANT FACT challenges the evolutionist: his failure to offer any satisfactory explanation for the origin of LIFE. People wonder, Where did we come from? The birth process cannot account for us. For all the human body does is transmit life it did not produce! To say that *life comes only from existing life* is to state a fact of science as firmly established as the Law of Gravitation.

Until the 1860's, many men believed the theory of "spontaneous generation"—that is, that life (particularly lower forms of life) can arise or be generated spontaneously (from characteristics within the substance itself, as in spontaneous combustion). Perhaps no view has ever seemed more self-evident, more safely beyond debate. After all, didn't WORMS spring from mud, and MAGGOTS from spoiled meat? If one left rags in the corner, MICE would appear. FROGS were created spontaneously in pond water. And wheat would generate RATS. Even Sir Francis Bacon (1561-1626) believed that INSECTS were "creatures bred from putrefaction," LICE were "bred by sweat close kept," and FLEAS "principally of straw and mats, where there hath been little moisture."[1]

Then came the great scientist Louis Pasteur, who with a series of brilliant experiments concluded in 1864 disproved once and for all the idea of spontaneous generation. Pasteur's experiments, which involved a procedure of sterilization, showed that any substance kept free from infection or contamination would never allow the anticipated creatures (such as maggots from decaying meat) to develop. Pasteur was a convinced creationist, and from his day to the present moment virtually NO educated person has given credence to the idea of spontaneous generation.

But the spontaneous generation of life is the first LINK in the CHAIN of evolution. Obviously, if that link cannot be forged, the whole evolutionary theory is hopelessly weakened. There must be LIFE before there can be DIVERSITY of life. So it's quite necessary for the evolutionist to insist on some form of spontaneous generation, as that's the only way life can be accounted for apart from a Creator.

Note the way Dr. George Wald, Professor of Biology at Harvard, puts it in an article in the *Scientific American*. He first traces the history of the collapse of the old idea of spontaneous generation as a result of Pasteur's experiments, then adds immediately:

> "We tell this story [of Pasteur's great work] to beginning students of biology as though it represents a triumph of reason over mysticism. In fact it is very nearly the opposite. The reasonable view was to believe in spontaneous generation; the only alternative, to believe in a single, primary act of supernatural creation. There is no third position. For this reason many scientists a century ago chose to regard the belief in spontaneous generation as a 'philosophical necessity.' It is a symptom of the philosophical poverty of our time that this necessity is no longer appreciated. Most modern biologists, having reviewed with satisfaction the downfall of the spontaneous generation hypothesis, yet unwilling to accept the alternative belief in special creation, are left with nothing." [2]

AN EXHIBIT IN **BLIND FAITH**

Dr. Wald goes on to show how infinitely impossible would be the CHANCE combination of proper elements to produce life, but draws this remarkable conclusion: "One has only to contemplate the magnitude of this task to concede that the spontaneous generation of a living organism is IMPOSSIBLE. Yet here we are—as a result, I believe, of spontaneous generation." [3]

Professor Wald may be admired for his refreshing frankness but pitied for his slavish adherence to a theory. How much "science" is involved in believing something totally disproved by all scientific experiments? Wald and those who agree with him hold this position not because of any scientific evidence for spontaneous generation, but because of their pre-conceived ideas, personal prejudice, or disbelief in God.

Some evolutionists try to dodge the issue by saying that life must have originated on earth by coming from another world, perhaps via a meteorite or similar object. But this answer is neither scientific nor satisfactory. It's not *scientific* because we know of no natural way in which protoplasm could bridge the deadly celestial gap. If the cold temperatures and absence of oxygen in interstellar space did not destroy it, the heat generated by the vehicle (meteors become incandescent through friction as they strike our atmosphere) would most certainly kill it. And it's not a *satisfactory* answer, for even if we grant that life could have been brought here from another planet, we haven't solved the problem of the origin of life; we've simply transferred the problem to another world. Though the problem is moved a great distance away, it nevertheless is still entirely unsolved!

It's also certain that IF one little speck of protoplasm were started alone in the world—from whatever source—it would live only long enough to STARVE to death. For there must be a balance of life, a web of life, to enable any living things to maintain their existence. That's why God created ALL living things, plants and animals as well as man, during a few days of creation week. (See Chapter 6, "How Long Were the Days of Creation?" for more information on this point.)

You can see that the problem is not an easy one to solve within the framework of atheistic evolution. I appreciate the honesty of evolutionist John Tyler Bonner, Professor of Biology at Princeton University, when he admits in his book *The Ideas of Biology*: "The study of early evolution really amounts to EDUCATED GUESSWORK." [4]

Of course, cherished ideas and pet theories die hard, so scientists sometimes try to create life in the laboratory. You may have read some press release purporting to announce the "creation of life in a test tube." Careful reading reveals that such claims are exaggerated and misleading. Most reports the average person encounters are mere rumors or hearsay. The next time an evolution enthusiast tells you he's "sure that science has produced life in the laboratory," ask him the name of the wonder-worker. He won't be able to tell you, despite the fact that the one who creates LIFE would automatically become much more famous than Thomas Edison or Jonas Salk.

It's interesting that A. R. Moore found that if the plasmodium of slime mold is allowed to *flow* through a sieve, even a very fine one, it will accomplish the feat unharmed. However, if *forced* through even a moderately fine sieve, it will be found on the other side apparently unchanged physically and chemically, but dead.[5] The individual who can explain the results of this simple experiment will be able to explain the difference between living and nonliving systems.

But until man is able to take the dead slime mold, which was alive only a moment before and which seemingly has all its chemical elements and substances present, and make it alive again, he stands no chance whatever of synthesizing living protoplasm by mingling substances from the bottles in his laboratory.

WHERE IS THE "SIMPLE" CELL?

Discovery of the world of viruses has led some evolutionists to speculate that perhaps here are entities resembling primitive life or pre-life—a link, a step between lifeless chemicals and the simplest cells. Viruses are extremely small, much smaller than true cells. It's been calculated that a single average-sized human cell could hold more than 60 MILLION polio viruses![6]

But our knowledge of the virus eliminates it as a candidate for the first life. Though it's simpler than the simplest cell, the virus presents too many problems. In the first place, its only "food" is living cells. This fact alone is sufficient to disqualify it from being the first life. Also, because viruses cannot function and reproduce apart from living cells or cell substance, many virologists feel that they are NOT actually LIVING bodies, but only agents that modify the activities of living cells which they infect or parasitize. Viruses don't have the basic components to carry on LIFE processes independently.[7]

Most believers in evolution now agree that the single CELL rather than the virus must have been the first life from which other forms evolved. But the time is long gone when scientists viewed the living cell as a mere "blob" of jellylike protoplasm. Scientists are just beginning to understand how fantastically COMPLEX the so-called "simple" cell is. Each year produces newly-discovered complications of which Darwin knew nothing. Even George Wald, whose credulous faith in spontaneous generation we noted above, admits:

> "The most complex machine man has devised—say an electronic brain—is child's play compared with the simplest of living organisms. The especially trying thing is that complexity here involves such SMALL dimensions. It is on the molecular level; it consists of a detailed fitting of molecule to molecule such as no chemist can attempt."[8]

THE REVOLUTION IN MOLECULAR BIOLOGY

Let's take a quick look at a bit of history: In order to advance in knowledge, biology had to wait for a series of technological breakthroughs. The first was the MICROSCOPE, that optical instrument that opened—to some degree—the world of small marvels beyond our range of vision. Galileo used one of the first microscopes and was amazed to discover the compound eyes of insects. Leeuwenhoek was the first person ever to see a bacterial cell.

But the cell itself was a mystery to Darwin and to every other scientist of his time. Its mystery could not be fathomed without further technological developments, the next one of which was the ELECTRON MICROSCOPE. Since the wavelength of the electron is shorter than the wavelength of visible light, much smaller objects can be examined if they're "illuminated" with electrons.

Electron microscopy came into its own after World War II. New sub-cellular structures were discovered. The same cell that looked so simple under a light or optical microscope now looked much different. The COMPLEX STRUCTURES revealed by the electron microscope were themselves made of smaller components!

X-RAY CRYSTALLOGRAPHY also began to be used to determine the structures of small molecules. Crystallography involves the strenuous application of mathematics, but it can indicate the position of each and every ATOM in the molecule. It's a tremendous amount of hard work, but it yields results never before seen. [9]

The decade of the 1950's brought with it an explosion of fundamental knowledge in biochemistry. Before 1950 hardly anything was known of the molecular basis of life. Yet the next ten years brought a succession of dramatic discoveries which opened new horizons and totally transformed our understanding of life.

It was as a result of X-ray work that Watson and Crick in 1953 made their momentous discovery of the double helical structure of DNA. And J. C. Kendrew, after decades of work, determined the 3-D structure of the protein myoglobin in 1958. For the first time, biochemists actually knew the shapes of the molecules they were working on. Scientists began close study of the tiny components of life and wondered: What were those components? What did they look like? How did they work? The answers to those questions take us out of the realm of biology and into chemistry. The beginning of modern BIOCHEMISTRY, which has progressed at a breakneck pace since, can be dated from that time.

Authority Michael Behe gives us this definition: "Biochemistry is the study of the very basis of life: the MOLECULES that make up cells and tissues, that catalyze the chemical reactions of digestion, photosynthesis, immunity, and more." [10]

Thus the mystery of the cell was opened to reveal *molecules*—the bedrock of nature. The biochemical knowledge about living systems that has accumulated in the last few decades has provided a vast body of information by which to TEST evolutionary claims. Modern biochemistry enables us to look at the rock-bottom level of life.

Behe, Associate Professor of Biochemistry at Lehigh University in Pennsylvania, has written an important book called *Darwin's Black Box: The Biochemical Challenge to Evolution.* It's a volume which may become as much a landmark as Darwin's *Origin of Species.* Michael Behe is not a creationist but a scientist who argues persuasively that biochemical machines must have been DESIGNED—either by God, or by some other higher intelligence.

The impact of biochemistry on evolutionary theory is enormous: evolution now must be argued at the MOLECULAR level. However, Behe points out that:

> "If you search the scientific literature on evolution, and if you focus your search on the question of how molecular machines—the basis of life—developed, you find an EERIE and COMPLETE SILENCE. The COMPLEXITY of life's foundation has PARALYZED science's attempt to account for it; molecular machines raise an as-yet-impenetrable barrier to Darwinism's universal reach." [11]

When we see the mind-boggling complexity of these marvelous molecules, we doubt that they can EVER be explained by random mutation/natural selection.

Consider this evaluation made in 1971 by Garret Vanderkooi, Professor at the University of Wisconsin. Vanderkooi is a scientist who studies enzymes, the chemical "workmen" in body cells so vital for life. He says:

> "In the past, evolutionists were confident that the problem of the origin of life would be solved by the new science of BIOCHEMISTRY. To their dismay, the converse has occurred. The more that is learned about the chemical structure and organization of living matter, the more difficult it becomes even to speculate on how it could have developed from lower forms by natural processes. . . . [In fact,] from the scientific point of view, evolution may have been a plausible hypothesis in Darwin's day, but it has now become UNTENABLE, as a result of fairly recent developments in molecular biology." [12]

Formerly it was thought that a cell was composed of a nucleus and a few other parts in a "sea" of cytoplasm, with large spaces in the cell unoccupied. Now it's known that a cell literally "swarms," that is, is packed full of important, functioning units necessary to the life of the cell and the body containing it. The theory of evolution assumes life developed from a "simple" cell—

which seemed hardly more than a blob of jelly—but science today demonstrates that there's NO SUCH THING as a simple cell!

Emphasizing the enormous gap between lifeless molecules and living cells, Vanderkooi quotes from a recent book by two prominent biochemists, Dr. D. E. Green and Dr. R. F. Goldberger, entitled *Molecular Insights into the Living Process*:

> "There is one step [in evolution] that far outweighs the others in enormity: the step from macro-molecules to cells. All the other steps can be accounted for on theoretical grounds—if not correctly, at least elegantly. However, the macro-molecule to cell transition is a jump of fantastic dimensions, which lies beyond the range of testable hypothesis. In this area, all is conjecture." [13]

In other words, the REAL "missing link" in the evolutionary chain is not a half-monkey, half-man. Neither is it a half-fish, half-animal. It's an intermediate stage (or a THOUSAND intermediate stages) between a lifeless molecule and a living cell—"a jump of fantastic dimensions. . . . In this area, all is conjecture."

LOOK Magazine was understating the enormous complexity when it declared: "The cell is as complicated as New York City." [14] And evolutionist Loren Eiseley quotes German biologist Von Bertalanffy as stating: "To grasp in detail the physico-chemical organization of the simplest cell is FAR beyond our capacity." [15]

Still, much has been learned since the early 1950's when James Watson and Francis Crick discovered the structure of the DNA (deoxyribonucleic acid) molecule, for which work they won the 1962 Nobel Prize. DNA is incredibly tiny, [16] residing within the chromosomes which are found within the nucleus which is found within each and every living cell. But DNA is the marvelous molecule that contains the secret of heredity. It "spells out" an incredibly complex coded message that transmits to the offspring all instructions needed for every genetic trait.

The LIFE Science Library volume on *The Cell* says that it's the particular make-up of "DNA molecules that make a horse give birth to a horse instead of a giraffe, an oyster or a fern—that determine color of eyes, texture of hair, shape of fingers." [17] (And as shown in the preceding chapter, it's DNA which guarantees that all variations remain WITHIN the basic kind.)

The amount of information coded in the DNA of an organism is amazing. The information in a single cell of human DNA is estimated as equivalent to 1,000 printed volumes, with 600 pages per volume and 500 words per page! The staggering complexity of the supposedly "simple" cell is absolutely mind-boggling! Instead of evolution's search being a converging one where we're finding all the answers, biochemistry and molecular biology have made it a diverging one where we're raising more questions. For instead of simplicity emerging from investigation, we find increasing complexity.

That's why Sir James Gray, Professor of Zoology at Cambridge University, says: "A bacterium is FAR MORE COMPLEX than ANY inanimate system known to man. There is not a laboratory in the world which can compete with the biochemical activity of the smallest living organism." [18] Within a single bacterial cell *(Escherichia coli)* are an estimated 1,000,000 to 3,000,000 protein molecules, including 2,000 to 10,000 different kinds of enzymes—all in a space 1/25,000 of an inch in diameter and 3/25,000 of an inch long. A single liver cell *(hepatocyte)* contains an estimated 53,000,000 protein molecules, which would probably include tens of thousands of different kinds of enzymes, all organized into a smoothly-running cellular "machine."

So next time you hear an evolutionist theorizing about how "Life originated in a simple cell," tell him that the idea of a "simple" cell went out with World War II.

Evolution's Stumbling-block: IRREDUCIBLE COMPLEXITY

Behe's book is outstanding and illuminating—but very challenging to the reader in its technical details. He recognizes this and apologizes for it, but he refuses to water-down his scientific message because he's describing the overwhelming complexity of living systems, and he says: "complexity must be EXPERIENCED to be APPRECIATED." [19]

Yet some of his ideas are easy to grasp, one of which I'd like to share with you now. He quotes from Darwin a statement we met in our last chapter: "If it could be demonstrated that any complex organ existed, which could not possibly have been formed by numerous, successive, slight modifications, my theory would absolutely BREAK DOWN." [20]

Michael Behe then asks, "What type of biological system could not be formed by 'numerous, successive, slight modifications'? Well, for starters, a system that is irreducibly complex. By *irreducibly complex* I mean a single system composed of several well-matched, interacting parts that contribute to the basic function, wherein the REMOVAL of any ONE of the parts causes the system to effectively CEASE functioning." [21]

A humble MOUSETRAP is a good example.

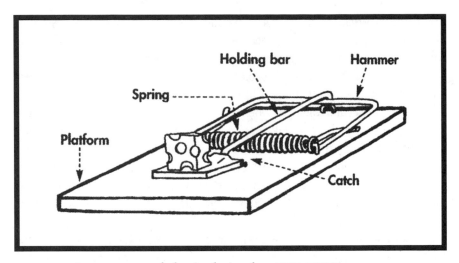

--A mousetrap of classic design has FIVE PARTS:

1. A PLATFORM to act as a base.
2. A metal HAMMER to crush the mouse.
3. A SPRING with extended ends to power the hammer.
4. A HOLDING BAR that locks the hammer back.
5. A sensitive CATCH that releases under the slightest pressure.

To determine if a system is IRREDUCIBLY COMPLEX, ask if all its components are REQUIRED for its function. In the mousetrap, the answer is clearly YES: If the platform were missing, there'd be nothing to hold the pieces together. If the hammer were missing, there'd be nothing to catch and crush the mouse. If the spring were missing, the hammer would lie useless and impotent. If the holding bar were missing, the hammer could not be loaded in readiness. And if the catch were missing, the mouse could dance on the cheese all night long.

The point is that the mousetrap is an irreducibly complex system that won't accomplish its purpose if any one part is missing—as Behe says: "the REMOVAL of any ONE of the parts causes the system to effectively CEASE functioning." It won't function with one, two, three, or even four components. You have to have all five working together. And NOT just TOGETHER—but with the right materials, the right shapes, and the right placement to make successful functioning possible. [22]

Professor Behe shows that within the body there are millions—no, billions—of systems which are irreducibly complex but on a much higher level than the elementary example of the mousetrap. Darwin recognized the problem of the EYE because its outward anatomy (gross anatomy) was known in his day. That organ of sight—as an irreducibly complex system—was complicated enough! But it's no longer enough for evolutionary "explanation" to consider only the anatomical structures of WHOLE EYES. Instead of what has been called "fact-free science," evolutionists now must consider the tiniest levels of biology—the chemical life of the cell.

It took molecular biologists of our day to learn precisely how the eye's infinitely-minute and intricately-shaped molecular STRUCTURES interact and function—in short, how they WORK. Biochemists now know that our cells work because of PROTEINS. Most of us think of proteins as something to eat. But in the body of a living animal or plant they play very active roles as the *machines* within living tissue that build the structures and carry out the chemical reactions necessary for life.

I don't want to go into the technical terms Behe uses in discussing the BIOCHEMISTRY of vision and other functions—like *rhodopsin, trans-retinal, guanylate cyclase, phosphodiesterase, etc.* But I must say that readers of his book will gain a fresh perspective and a new appreciation for the MIRACLE of LIFE. After inspecting God's INGENIOUS BLUEPRINTS for our intricately-designed bodies, they'll understand as never before the truth of the Psalmist's words: "I am fearfully and wonderfully made: MARVELOUS are Thy works"! [23]

Let me close this discussion of irreducible complexity by quoting Behe's inescapable conclusions about evolutionists' unwillingness even to consider non-Darwinian explanations:

> "Imagine a room in which a body lies crushed, flat as a pancake. A dozen detectives crawl around, examining the floor with magnifying glasses for any clue to the identity of the perpetrator. In the middle of the room, next to the body, stands a large, gray ELEPHANT. The detectives carefully avoid bumping into the pachyderm's legs as they crawl, and never even glance at it. . . .
>
> "There is an elephant in the roomful of scientists who are trying to explain the development of LIFE. The elephant is labeled 'INTELLIGENT DESIGN.' To a person who does not feel obliged to restrict his search to UNintelligent causes, the straightforward conclusion is that many biochemical systems were DESIGNED. They were designed not by the laws of nature, not by chance and necessity; rather, they were planned. The designer knew what the systems would look like when they were completed, then took steps to bring the systems about. Life on earth at its most fundamental level, in its most critical components, is the product of INTELLIGENT activity. . . .
>
> "The IMPOTENCE of Darwinian theory in accounting for the molecular basis of life is evident . . . from the COMPLETE ABSENCE in the professional scientific literature of any detailed models by which com-

plex biochemical systems could have been produced. . . . In the face of the enormous complexity that modern biochemistry has uncovered in the cell, the scientific community is PARALYZED. No one at Harvard University, no one at the National Institutes of Health, no member of the National Academy of Sciences, no Nobel Prize winner—no one at all can give any detailed account of how the cilium, or vision, or blood clotting [all of which Behe explains and illuminates in his book], or any complex biochemical process might have developed in a Darwinian fashion. But we are here. Plants and animals are here. The complex systems are here. All these things got here somehow: if not in a Darwinian fashion, then HOW?" [24]

The STATISTICAL IMPOSSIBILITY of Evolution

From all this and much more besides, it's increasingly clear that it would be easier for science to show that evolution is impossible than to explain how it happened. One branch of mathematics deals with STATISTICAL PROBABILITY—the chance that undirected, accidental events will occur. For instance, since a coin has two faces, the probability of tossing a *head* is therefore 1 in 2. One of a pair of dice has six faces; therefore the probability of throwing a *four* would be 1 in 6. To figure the chance of throwing *two* fours in a row we'd multiply the probability of the first event, which is 1/6, by the probability of the second event, also 1/6, and find the answer to be 1 in 36.

Obviously, the probability is much less when the number of possibilities is increased. Mathematicians found that a person wishing to throw the same number *ten times in succession* would have only one chance in about *sixty million* tosses of the lone dice. And if the dice—like a living cell—were made of a FRAGILE material that lasts for only a few hundred tosses, the chances of getting the same number ten times in a row would be greatly reduced—so much that it would be virtually impossible.

Scientists and mathematicians have spent much time computing the possibility that LIFE could have started by chance. Lecomte du Nouy, a French scientist, has done a great deal of work on this. His book, *Human Destiny*, tells of these investigations. [25] Lecomte du Nouy consulted Professor Charles Eugene Guye, a Swiss mathematician, as to the possibilities of a single protein molecule being formed by chance. The protein molecule contains the elements carbon, hydrogen, nitrogen, and oxygen—plus a trace of one of the metallic elements such as iron, copper, or sulphur. Most scientists agree that this molecule represents the SIMPLEST, MOST BASIC form of living matter. But even so, note the complexity of a molecule of insulin, one of the smallest and simplest of the proteins: Like all proteins, insulin consists of complicated chains of amino acids. The insulin molecule has **51** amino acid units, in two chains, one having **21** units, the other **30**. EACH UNIT (of the fifty-one) has **254** carbon atoms, **377** hydrogen atoms, **65** of nitrogen, **75** of oxygen, and **6** of sulphur—a total of **777** atoms in EXACT combination!

To simplify the problem as much as possible, Professor Guye considered a hypothetical molecule containing only TWO elements instead of the usual five. The first conclusion was that there was not enough matter in existence to provide an opportunity for such a molecule to form by chance combination. According to Professor Guye, it would take a mass of material millions of times GREATER than all the known universe, including the farthest galaxies. [26]

To form even a simplified protein molecule, it would be necessary for a great number of atoms to combine, under exactly the right conditions. Taking into consideration the great complexity of the atoms concerned, the chance that such a protein molecule could have formed is almost nothing. Not only is there not enough MATTER in the universe for such a complex combination to take place, there is also not enough TIME. Even if the material of this huge mass were shaken together at many times per second, it would still require billions and billions of years to provide one opportunity for this protein molecule to be formed by chance. So even supposing the earth has existed for the evolutionary estimate of 4.5 billion years, not nearly enough time has elapsed for this one chance to appear.

Of course, those figures concern the formation of only a single MOLECULE of protein matter, very much simplified at that. The same mathematician states that if we tried to express the chance formation of a CELL, "the preceding figures would seem negligible." [27] In other words, the time necessary for the formation of a cell is so fantastically greater than the earth's age that it may be considered mathematically impossible. With these facts in mind we can well understand the statement of Lecomte du Nouy:

> "It was impossible to explain, or to account for, not only the birth of LIFE but even the appearance of the SUBSTANCES which seem to be required to build life, namely, highly dissymmetrical molecules."[28]

Thus we see that Darwin was right about one thing: The apostle of evolution himself admitted, "The BIRTH both of the species and of the individual are equally parts of that grand sequence of events which our minds REFUSE to accept as the result of blind chance. The understanding REVOLTS at such a conclusion." [29]

For a frog to turn into a handsome prince in an instant is an act of MAGIC found only in children's fairy tales. Evolutionists pretend that for the same thing to happen over a billion years is SCIENCE. TIME becomes the fairy's magic wand. Stripping us of both our divine origin and heavenly destiny, evolution is a GRIM fairy tale indeed! Evolutionists pay lip service to science but postulate the creation of life spontaneously, magically. Creationists are accused of resorting to magic when they accept God's supernatural act of creation. But creationists, unlike evolutionists, don't disguise magic behind high-sounding words intended to sound scientific. Faith in evolutionary theory is faith, not in a scientific fact, but in a mathematical impossibility.

VIII. THE ORIGIN OF SEX

When it comes to an "explanation" for the origin of life, evolution is a blind alley leading nowhere. But aside from the origin of life, another question evolution cannot answer is: Where did not only Adam but EVE come from? How did the TWO SEXES originate?

Evolutionists teach that life evolved from the simple, lower forms of life to the complex, higher forms. But what do we see when we look at the lower forms of life? There are NO male or female protozoa, no masculine or feminine amoebas! One-celled organisms like the amoeba reproduce asexually (that is, without sex) by cell division, simply dividing in two to form a duplicate. IF asexual reproduction was satisfactory—and it was, for such organisms survive today, multiplying in exactly the same way—then WHY should sexual reproduction arise?

Evolutionists like J. William Schopf, Paleontologist and Geologist at UCLA, contend that sex apparently did not exist on earth for the first two thirds of biological history (this would be for the first 3 BILLION of the estimated 4.7 billion years of the earth's age). But scientists are BAFFLED by the question of how sex got started. There's no need for breeding or mating among the simple forms of life, for they're asexual. Then, why sex? WHERE did it originate? HOW did it develop?

Males and females are so very different that we even give them different names within the same species: man and woman, rooster and hen, stallion and mare, *etc.* These differences must be accounted for if things "just happened" by chance.

But males and females are not only very different, they're also obviously inter-dependent: a group of males or a group of females by themselves spell DOOM for any species. But HOW could male and female sex organs that perfectly complement each other arise gradually, paralleling each other, yet remaining useless until completed?

If the female mammary glands came about by slow evolution, HOW did females feed their young in the meantime? (Remember that the mother must have a perfectly functioning lactation system or the baby—who can't chew—DIES.) If they already HAD another way to feed them, why develop breasts? And if breasts developed because they were a superior way of feeding, then why do we still have animals that feed otherwise and survive just as well? Also, how did the marvelous WOMB develop in female mammals?

The February 1984 issue of science magazine *Discover* carried a provocative article entitled "WHY SEX?" The authors quote Dr. Graham Bell, a geneticist at Montreal's McGill University, as saying: "Nobody's got very far with the problem of how sex began." [30]

They explain the riddle of sex in these words:

> "Sex is an inefficient, risky way for an organism to reproduce itself. . . . It contradicts a basic biological tenet: that the main goal of an organism is to transmit as many of its GENES as possible to the next generation. In fact, sex dictates that a parent can pass on only HALF its genes to each of its progeny. Asexual reproduction (without sex) seems a likelier choice for nature to make. It is faster and more efficient, and it allows a creature to replicate itself without the bother of mating, and to produce offspring that carry all of its genes. . . . Says George Williams, a population biologist of the State University of New York at Stony Brook, 'At first glance, and second, and third, it appears that sex shouldn't have evolved.'" [31]

The authors sum up the question "Why Sex?" by admitting: "It is evolution's single most important and most perplexing riddle." [32]

In contrast to extremely speculative theories—or complete silence—about the origin of sex, the Bible tells plainly where Adam and Eve came from. The very first chapter of Genesis tells about the creation of mankind: "MALE and FEMALE He created them." [33] Yes, God Himself—knowing that "one is a lonely number"—gave Adam a companion, creating woman from a rib of man. She was made not from his HEAD to top him or control him, nor from his FEET to be trampled upon as an inferior, but from a rib of his SIDE to stand by his side as an equal, under his arm to be protected, and near his heart to be loved. A part of man—bone of his bone and flesh of his flesh—she was his second self, showing the close union and affection that should exist in this relationship. [34] So, in addition to all His other wonders of creation, God invented sex.

IX. ENTROPY *versus* EVOLUTION

There's an important law in science known as the Second Law of Thermodynamics which is diametrically opposed to the basic idea of evolution. This law, sometimes called the principle of ENTROPY, did not arise from speculation. It's firmly founded on countless thousands of experiments on systems ranging in size from the nuclear to the astronomic—and there's never been an exception to it observed.

Sir Arthur Eddington showed insight when he called this law 'time's arrow,' for it helps illustrate nature's time sense—the one-wayness of events. When events take place, they do so in a way that serves to distinguish between backwards and forwards. The ancients even made lists of events which never take place in reverse: Rivers do not flow uphill, plants and men do not grow backwards, forest fires do not turn ashes into fully grown trees.

Only in a world of magic or dreams can we imagine a different, backward trend of events; a world where food, already eaten, emerges whole, or Niagara Falls tumbles up the mountainside in reverse, or an atomic bomb explodes and turns gigantic piles of rubble into houses, streets, and crowds of people. In the world of reality, the world of science, events go in only one direction—a direction in which disorder increases and order is destroyed.

Entropy is a measure of this loss of order, this loss of available energy. It's based on the observation that there's a continuous flow of HEAT from warmer to colder bodies and never spontaneously in the reverse direction. Place a hot object, such as an electric iron, in a room and unplug it. After a time the iron has cooled, the air has warmed, and all objects in the room approach the same uniform temperature—the heat energy tends to be evenly distributed but less available.

The iron in the room is like the sun in the sky. Energy from the sun tends to dissipate and be distributed throughout the universe. The Second Law of Thermodynamics or entropy indicates that the universe is "running down" to a condition when all bodies will be at the same extremely low temperature and no energy will be available. This burning out or running down has been called HEAT DEATH and will certainly occur if present processes continue indefinitely (that is, if God doesn't intervene as Christians believe He will).

The words of Sir James H. Jeans, eminent English astronomer and physicist, are still as true as when written some years ago:

> "The universe is like a clock which is running down, a clock which, so far as science knows, no one ever winds up, which cannot wind itself up, and so must stop in time. It is at present a partially wound-up clock, which MUST, at some time in the past, have been wound up in some manner unknown to us."[35]

This sober man of science goes on to say:

> "Everything points with overwhelming force to a definite event, or series of events, of creation at some time or times not infinitely remote.

The universe can NOT have originated by chance out of its present in-gredients, and neither can it have been always the same as now."[36]

You see, the existence of MATTER—physical matter throughout the universe—has always been an embarrassing problem for evolutionists be-cause they cannot explain its origin. Realizing the truth of the dictum *ex nihilo nihil fit* (out of nothing, nothing is made) they're left with only two alternatives to account for the reality of matter: Either it was CREATED or it has ALWAYS EXISTED. Not willing to accept the former possibility, atheistic evolutionists lean toward the latter explanation, saying: "Matter isn't hard to account for, because it's possible that matter is eternal. For all we know, the universe has always existed."

This explanation may have sounded plausible or at least possible before scientists understood the principle of ENTROPY. But the fact of entropy is absolutely devastating to this argument AND to the theory of evolution in general! Matter cannot possibly be eternal—the universe cannot possibly have always existed—IF the available energy is decreasing, as we know it is.

Nature, you see, points definitely to a beginning of things. Science clearly shows that the universe could NOT have existed from all eternity, or it would have run out of useful energy and ground to a halt long ago. For instance, radium, uranium, and other radioactive elements are constantly emitting radiation and are constantly losing weight as they slowly change to other elements until at last the element we call *lead* remains. In a universe that had no beginning but had always existed, NO radioactive elements would remain.

In any system, some energy is lost for future use. When we burn wood, chemical energy is converted into heat; this can be used in an engine to do work, but a certain amount of energy is never available again, being de-graded into non-usable heat energy by friction. This principle of entropy makes it obvious that ultimately ALL energy in the universe will be unavail-able energy. If the universe were infinitely old, if it had always existed, this state of absolute entropy would already have happened. The fact that the universe has not yet "died" in this fashion proves, as certainly as science can prove anything, that the universe had a beginning. A supposedly eternal universe can therefore be eliminated from consideration.

DISINTEGRATION A FIXED LAW

But the principle of entropy does more than demolish atheistic theories on the eternity of matter. The Second Law of Thermodynamics says that time causes DECAY. This is easy to understand, as every material thing within our experience verifies the Second Law: Houses decay, trees decay, people decay. Even pyramids decay. Of course, this innate tendency toward decay may be temporarily offset in the growth a child, the formation of a crystal, or the raising of a building. But that child or crystal or building or anything else will eventually start to grow old or wear out or decay. Everywhere there's an innate, universal tendency toward disorder and disintegration, NOT growth and development.

Popular scientific writer Isaac Asimov, in an article in the *Smithsonian Institute Journal*, interestingly expresses the idea of entropy as follows:

> "Another way of stating the Second Law then is: 'The universe is getting more disorderly!' Viewed that way, we can see the Second Law all about us. We have to work hard to straighten up a room, but left to itself it becomes a mess again very quickly and very easily. Even if we never enter it, it becomes dusty and musty. How difficult to maintain houses, and machinery, and our own bodies in perfect working order; how easy to let them deteriorate. In fact, all we have to do is nothing, and EVERYTHING collapses, breaks down, wears out, all by itself, and that is what the Second Law is all about." [37]

But this is the REVERSE of evolution. Actually, as Dr. Henry M. Morris puts it,

> "It would hardly be possible to conceive of two more completely OPPOSITE principles than this principle of entropy increase and the principle of evolution. Each is precisely the converse of the other. As Huxley defined it, evolution involves a continual INCREASE of order, of organization, of size, of complexity. The entropy principle involves a continual DECREASE of order, of organization, of size, of complexity. It seems axiomatic that both cannot possibly be true. But there is no question whatever that the Second Law of Thermodynamics is true!" [38]

So entropy and evolution are "two DIAMETRICALLY OPPOSED systems. They are alike in only one respect, in that both involve a continual change. But one is a change UP—the other is a change DOWN. One is development, the other deterioration; one growth, the other decay." [39]

Evolutionists, seeing the insurmountable problem this poses for their theory, sometimes say that the principle of entropy applies only in the physical realm, not in the biological realm of living things. But entropy seems to be everywhere: Physical systems, left to themselves, run down and stop; biological systems grow old and die. And evolutionist Harold F. Blum, in his book *Time's Arrow and Evolution*, admits the parallel between living and non-living systems: "Like any other MACHINE, the living system must have a supply of energy for its operation. If it does external work as, for example, in bodily movement or in the expulsion of waste products, free energy must be expended." [40]

But just for the sake of argument, let's assume that entropy does apply only to inanimate matter. The Second Law of Thermodynamics would STILL work against the build-up of amino acids and proteins needed before that original spark of life could develop on the earth. How could complex molecules organize themselves BY themselves when the universal trend is NOT toward organization but toward disorder and disintegration? Even Dr. Wald of Harvard, noted before as perhaps the world's lone believer in spontaneous generation, admits that forces of "spontaneous dissolution" make "the spontaneous generation of a living organism . . . IMPOSSIBLE." For, he explains,

> "In the vast majority of the processes in which we are interested the point of equilibrium lies far over toward the side of dissolution. That is to say, spontaneous dissolution is much more probable, and hence proceeds much more rapidly, than spontaneous synthesis. For example, the spontaneous union, step by step, of amino acid units to form a protein has a certain small probability, and hence might occur over a long stretch of time. But the dissolution . . . is much more probable, and hence will go ever so much more rapidly. The situation we must face is that of patient Penelope waiting for Odysseus, yet much worse: each night she undid the weaving of the preceding day, but here a night could readily undo the work of a year or a century." [41]

Wald states immediately that living organisms in our present-day world are able to synthesize or put together these complex organic compounds in spite of the forces of dissolution. Thus they're able to live and grow. He observes that "a living organism is an intricate MACHINE for performing exactly this function" of combining, synthesizing, building organic compounds. A cow, for instance, can build amino acids and proteins into the milk it gives—but a cow is a living milk factory. LIFELESS elements of matter cannot so combine to create the building blocks of life. This leads Wald to confess: "What we ask here is to synthesize organic molecules without such a machine. I believe this to be the most STUBBORN problem that confronts us— the WEAKEST LINK in our argument." [42]

How devoted to a theory can a man become? But that's not a scientist speaking—it's a special pleader for a cause displaying a WILL to believe.

One last point that might be made here is that MUTATIONS offer a perfect illustration of the Second Law of Thermodynamics among living things. For the Second Law says that the natural tendency of all change is toward a greater degree of disorder. Thus the overall direction of change is deteriorative rather than developmental. And that's exactly what mutations are—degenerative changes which are harmful and often deadly to the organism that suffers them. Even those rare mutations which may seem rather desirable as a convenience to man, such as the seedless navel orange, offer no real benefit to the plant itself.

The universe was to maintain itself in perfect running order—until man fell into sin and ruined God's creation. At that point man began to die, animals began to die, and the universe started to run down. I believe the CURSE that fell upon man as a result of sin included the degenerative effect of the Second Law of Thermodynamics—one of the best-proved and most universal laws known to science.

There's no such thing as the evolution of NOTHING into matter and of MATTER into life—the trend is all in the other direction. The FACT of entropy and the THEORY of evolution are contradictory principles which are forever incompatible and irreconcilable.

X. FOSSILS—THE RECORD OF THE ROCKS

In many ways the crust of the earth is like a giant layer cake. Over vast areas layer upon layer of sedimentary rocks are found to contain fossils. This special study lies in the fields of GEOLOGY—the study of the earth itself—and PALEONTOLOGY—the study of ancient things, especially the study of ancient life as preserved in fossils.

It's no mere play on words to say that the rocks are viewed by evolutionists as the real foundation of their theory. W. E. Le Gros Clark, the well-known British evolutionist, has said: "The really crucial evidence for evolution must be provided by the paleontologist whose business it is to study the evidence of the fossil record." [43] Thomas Hunt Morgan also declares that this evidence from the earth's strata is "by all odds the strongest evidence of the theory of evolution." [44] And Yale geologist Carl O. Dunbar says: "Although the comparative study of living animals and plants may give very convincing circumstantial evidence, FOSSILS provide the ONLY historical, documentary evidence that life has evolved from simpler to more and more complex forms." [45] So fossils supposedly furnish the only real proof for evolution.

It's true that the only evidence (apart from divine revelation, which evolutionists refuse to accept) concerning prehistoric life on earth is that which can be deduced from the fossil remains of creatures buried in rocks of the earth's crust. As W. R. Thompson puts it,

> "Evolution, if it has occurred, can in a rather loose sense be called a historical process; and therefore, to show that it has occurred, histori-

cal evidence is required. . . . The ONLY evidence available is that provided by the fossils." [46]

But contrary to common evolutionary claims—like those above—the fossil record constitutes one of the most telling arguments AGAINST evolutionary assumptions possible! As a matter of fact, geology strongly contradicts
evolution, providing compelling evidence against the theory. Historian Himmelfarb, in her landmark [47] book, states: "Geology, however, has been notably
UNforthcoming, and instead of being the chief support of Darwin's theory, it
is one of its most serious weaknesses." [48] Interestingly enough, Darwin himself didn't think fossils gave much support for his theory of evolution. The
weaknesses inherent in the record of the rocks were of such concern to him
that he wrote an entire chapter in *The Origin of Species* entitled, "On the
IMPERFECTION of the Geological Record."

We cannot take time here to explore all the geological and fossil evidence that allegedly supports evolution. Your attention is called simply to
THREE MAIN POINTS regarding this fossil evidence in an attempt to determine
how valid it really is.

1. THE **SUDDEN** APPEARANCE OF LIFE

Geologists have given names to the various layers, or strata, of rock in
the earth's crust. One of the lower layers is called the CAMBRIAN layer. Though
it is by no means the lowest layer or "basement level" of rock, it is the first
that contains fossils of living things, or the lowest "fossiliferous" strata. This
fact directly contradicts the evolutionary theory, which says that life originated during the PRE-Cambrian era. Noteworthy is the fact that EVERY major
invertebrate form of life is found in Cambrian strata—in fact, billions and
billions of fossils are found in Cambrian strata. Yet not a single fossil (other
than alleged fossil micro-organisms) has ever been found in Pre-Cambrian
rock!

Even Darwin recognized this problem. He wrote:

> "There is another and allied difficulty, which is much more serious.
> I allude to the manner in which species belonging to several of the
> main divisions of the animal kingdom SUDDENLY appear in the lowest
> known fossiliferous rocks. . . . IF the theory be true, it is indisputable
> that before the lowest Cambrian stratum was deposited long periods
> elapsed, as long as, or probably far longer than, the whole interval from
> the Cambrian age to the present, day; and that during these vast peri-
> ods the world swarmed with living creatures. Here we encounter a for-
> midable objection. . . . To the question why we do not find rich fossil-
> iferous deposits belonging to these assumed earliest periods prior to

the Cambrian system, I can give NO satisfactory answer. . . . The difficulty of assigning any good reason for the absence of vast piles of strata rich in fossils beneath the Cambrian system is very great. . . . The case at present must remain inexplicable; and may be truly urged as a valid argument AGAINST the views here entertained." [49]

Darwin wrote those words well over a century ago. TREMENDOUS amounts of sedimentary rock were laid down before the Cambrian, yet they contain NO fossils. So the SUDDEN OUTBURST of life in the Cambrian period is a real puzzle, when there should be billions of years of evolution shown before this. In recent years George Gaylord Simpson conceded that the absence of Pre-Cambrian fossils is the "MAJOR MYSTERY of the history of life." [50] Bear in mind that Dr. Simpson, a paleontologist at Harvard University, was formerly Professor of Vertebrate Paleontology at Columbia University. Before that he was long associated with the American Museum of Natural History in New York City where he was Curator of Fossil Mammals and Birds. He's a world-renowned paleontologist and ardent evolutionist.

Simpson honestly admits:

"Fossils are abundant only from the Cambrian onward, which is probably not more than one-fourth of the whole history of life. . . . Then, with the beginning of the Cambrian, unquestionable, abundant, and quite varied fossil animals appear . . . the change is great and abrupt. This is not only the most PUZZLING feature of the whole fossil record but also its greatest INADEQUACY." [51]

Note this illuminating statement from the geology textbook by Kay and Colbert:

"The introduction of a variety of organisms in the early Cambrian, including such complex forms of the arthropods as the trilobites, is surprising. . . . The introduction of abundant organisms in the record would not be so surprising IF they were simple. Why should such complex organic forms be in rocks about six hundred million years old and be absent or unrecognized in the records of the preceding two billion years? . . . IF there has been evolution of life, the absence of the requisite fossils in the rocks older than the Cambrian is PUZZLING." [52]

The World We Live In, one of the attractively illustrated books by the editorial staff of *LIFE*, puts it this way: "For at least three-quarters of the book of ages engraved in the earth's crust, the pages are BLANK." [53] Note also what *Scientific American* Magazine says:

"Both the sudden appearance and the remarkable composition of the animal life characteristic of Cambrian times are sometimes explained away or overlooked by biologists. Yet recent paleontological research has made the puzzle of this sudden proliferation of living organisms increasingly difficult for anyone to evade. . . . Neither can the general failure to find Pre-Cambrian animal fossils be charged to any lack of trying." [54]

Evolutionists attempting explanation usually say:

(1) "Wait. This apparent lack of Pre-Cambrian fossils is due to insufficient collecting—give us time to do more searching."

(2) "Perhaps the earlier fossils were destroyed by metamorphism —heat and pressure in the rock."

(3) "The earlier forms of life must have been soft-bodied types not likely to be preserved as fossils."

But none of these supposed explanations holds up well under careful scrutiny. Let's let Dr. Norman D. Newell, Paleontologist at Columbia University, deal with the three attempts at explanation listed above:

(1) A CENTURY of intensive search for fossils in the Pre-Cambrian rocks has thrown very little light on this problem.

(2) Early theories that these rocks were dominantly non-marine or that once-contained-fossils have been destroyed by heat and pressure have been abandoned because the Pre-Cambrian rocks of many districts are very SIMILAR to younger rocks in all respects EXCEPT that they rarely contain any records whatsoever of past life. . . .

(3) Unequivocal fossils of soft-bodied invertebrates, although by no means common, are known in many places and should have turned up in Pre-Cambrian rocks by now. [55] Although such localities are rare, in a single Cambrian locality in the Canadian Rockies, C. D. Walcott collected thousands of specimens of more than 130 species of delicately preserved soft-bodied animals. [56]

Finally, Dr. Daniel I. Axelrod, Professor of Geology at the University of California at Los Angeles, sums up the problem facing evolutionists:

"One of the MAJOR unsolved problems of geology and evolution is the occurrence of diversified, multicellular, marine invertebrates in Lower CAMBRIAN rocks on ALL the continents. . . . However, when we turn to examine the Pre-Cambrian rocks for the forerunners of these Early Cambrian fossils, they are nowhere to be found. Many THICK (over

5,000 feet) sections of sedimentary rock are now known to lie in unbroken succession below strata containing the earliest Cambrian fossils. These sediments apparently were suitable for the preservation of fossils, because they often are identical with overlying rocks which are fossiliferous, yet NO FOSSILS ARE FOUND IN THEM. Clearly, a significant but unrecorded chapter in the history of life is missing from the rocks of Pre-Cambrian time." [57]

2. The "Missing Link" Is STILL Missing!

So the fossil record does not support the evolutionary assumption in at least one major respect—if the evolutionary ancestors of the Cambrian fossils ever existed, they've certainly never been found. But a much worse, almost insurmountable, problem exists in the fossil record—the problem of MISSING LINKS.

You see, the very essence of evolutionary thinking is slow change. So according to the theory there should be a continuous array of living forms, an unbroken chain of gradations, with all groups imperceptibly merging. There should be NO missing links or gaps between phyla, classes, orders, *etc*. Therefore, if evolutionary theory is ever to have any scientific basis, gradual transitions of fossils must be found.

But such is not the case. If we look closely at the fantastic idea of evolution as reflected in the fossil record, we note SO MANY "missing links" it's impossible to enumerate them. Countless numbers of connecting links are needed to bridge the gaps that separate EVERY major group from its supposed neighbors. The study of fossils reveals the complete lack of intermediate stages of evolution which would link one stage of life with another.

Here's how Darwin himself described the difficulty:

"WHY, if species have descended from other species by fine gradations, do we not everywhere see innumerable transitional forms? ... As by this theory innumerable transitional forms must have existed, WHY do we not FIND them embedded in countless numbers in the crust of the earth? ... Why then is not every geological formation and every stratum FULL of such intermediate links? Geology assuredly does NOT reveal any such finely-graduated organic chain; and this, perhaps, is the most OBVIOUS and SERIOUS objection which can be urged against the theory. ... What geological research has NOT revealed, is the former existence of infinitely numerous gradations, as fine as existing varieties, connecting together nearly ALL existing and extinct species. ... The absence of innumerable transitional links between the species which lived at the commencement and close of each formation, pressed so hardly on my theory. The ABRUPT manner in which whole groups of species SUDDENLY appear in certain formations, has been urged by several paleontologists . . . as a FATAL objection to the belief in the transmutation [evolution] of species. If numerous species, belonging to the same genera or families, have really STARTED INTO LIFE AT ONCE, the fact would be FATAL to the theory of evolution through natural selection. For the development by this means of a group of forms, all of which are descended from some one progenitor, MUST have been an extremely slow process; and the progenitors must have lived long before their modified descendants. . . . Geological research . . . does not yield the infinitely many fine gradations between past and present species required by the theory; and this is the most OBVIOUS of the MANY objections which may be urged against it." [58]

Of course, Darwin tried to take refuge in what he called "the extreme imperfection of the geological record" and "the poorness of paleontological collections." [59] He and his enthusiastic early followers were optimistic that the prominent gaps would soon be filled in. They argued that much of the earth was still unexplored and that such transitional forms would yet be found. But they were doomed to bitter disappointment. After more than a CENTURY of intensive search, such links between diverse groups have yet to be unearthed. Scientific historian Charles Singer states: "It has now LONG been apparent that such 'links' are, in fact, conspicuous by their absence." [60] And Professor Newell of Columbia University notes "the systematic discontinuity" (missing links) in the fossil record and admits: "Many of the discontinuities tend to be more and more EMPHASIZED with increased collecting" over the years. [61]

Thus Darwin recognized the seriousness of this difficulty—and more than ONE HUNDRED FORTY YEARS of research has in no way lessened the validity of this objection. But he's by no means the only one who's noticed this fatal flaw in the evolutionary theory. Many scientists have expressed wonder over the fact that NO connecting links are found between the supposed stages of evolution.

For example, Dr. Alfred S. Romer, Professor of Zoology and Curator of Vertebrate Paleontology at the Museum of Comparative Zoology of Harvard University, makes this startling admission: "'Links' are missing just where we most fervently desire them, and it is all too probable that many 'links' will continue to be missing." [62]

Professor G. G. Simpson, also of Harvard, confesses that "transitional sequences are not merely RARE, but are virtually ABSENT. . . . Their absence is so nearly UNIVERSAL that it cannot, offhand, be imputed entirely to chance. . . ."[63] In another book Simpson says: "It remains true, as every paleontologist knows, that most new species... appear in the record suddenly and are NOT led up to by known, gradual, completely continuous transitional sequences."[64]

If Dr. Simpson were not the world's foremost evolutionary paleontologist, his words might not carry so much weight—though facts are facts no matter who states them. In a book written to commemorate the centennial anniversary of the publication of Darwin's *Origin of Species*, Simpson tells us:

> "It is a feature of the known fossil record that most taxa [kinds of plants and animals] appear abruptly. They are NOT, as a rule, led up to by a sequence of almost imperceptibly changing forerunners such as Darwin believed should be usual in evolution. . . . GAPS among known orders, classes, and phyla are systematic and almost always large."[65]

Here is a very important statement by this specialist. Simpson says the gaps are "systematic"—throughout the whole system! But this is precisely what cannot be allowed if the theory is to be supported scientifically.

IF evolution were a universal law of nature, as evolutionists claim, then there should be abundant evidence of CONTINUITY and TRANSITION between all the kinds of organisms—both in the present world and in the fossil record. Instead, we find GREAT GAPS between all the basic kinds. And essentially the same clear-cut discontinuity seen in the LIVING world today—between dog and cat, horse and cow, *etc.*—is found in the FOSSIL record of the past.

Even if the intermediates *once* lived but are now extinct, at least a few of them should be preserved as fossils. But except for a few extinct species such as dinosaurs (which I believe did not enter Noah's Ark and thus perished in the Genesis Flood), we're left without a solution. Is it plausible that "blind fate" or "chance" would always miss recording such transitions between groups and yet preserve abundant remains of the stable basic types? The more natural explanation is that the missing links never existed.

And that's exactly what was stated some years ago by Austin H. Clark, in his book *The New Evolution*. Clark, a famous biologist on the staff of the Smithsonian Institution and himself an evolutionist, states:

> "Since we have not the slightest evidence, either among the living or the fossil animals, of any intergrading types following the major groups, it is a fair supposition that there NEVER HAVE BEEN any such intergrading types."[66]

Elsewhere in the same book Dr. Clark asserts that

> "from the very earliest times, from the very first beginnings of the fossil record, the broader aspects of animal life upon the earth have

remained UNCHANGED. When we examine a series of fossils of any age we may pick one out and say with confidence, 'This is a crustacean'— or a starfish, or a brachiopod, or an annelid, or any other type of creature as the case may be. . . . If they are sufficiently well preserved we have no difficulty in recognizing at once the group to which each and every fossil animal belongs. . . . Since all the fossils are determinable as members of their respective groups . . . it follows that throughout the fossil record these major groups have remained essentially unchanged. This means that the interrelationships between them likewise have remained unchanged." [67]

All these statements, honestly made by evolutionists themselves, are diametrically opposed to the theory of slow evolutionary change. Sir Julian Huxley was quite right when he made the following assertion in a superbly illustrated children's book, *The Wonderful World of Life*: "IF evolution is TRUE, fossil history will reveal a branching plan for the advance of life, with each branch showing gradual improvement for its particular mode of existence." [68] At the top of the page is a diagram showing various land animals branching off from a common ancestor. Each branch illustrated has broad connections with the trunk. The amoeba-to-man theory demands such connections. But they do NOT, in fact, exist!

The first sponges are complex sponges; the first starfish are unquestionably starfish; the first whales, plainly whales; the first turtles, clearly turtles; and so on through the animal kingdom. If fish evolved into amphibia, WHERE are the transitional forms? How did gills change to become lungs? How did fins change into feet and legs? And if reptiles gave rise to birds, where are those transitional forms? How did scales change into feathers? How did heavy reptilian bones become hollow bones for birds?

W. E. Swinton, an evolutionist expert on birds at London's British Museum of Natural History, states: "The origin of birds is largely a matter of deduction. There is NO fossil evidence of the stages through which the remarkable change from reptile to bird was achieved." [69]

WHY is it always the same story—that the transitions, the links between major groups of plants and animals, are MISSING? And PLANTS, incidentally, do present the same picture. Evolutionist E. J. H. Corner, Professor of Botany at England's Cambridge University, frankly admits that the fossil record of plants gives no support for evolution, but "to the unprejudiced, the fossil record of plants is in favor of special creation." [70]

In the light of these statements and many others which may be brought to bear on this question, we see that W. R. Thompson was correct in stating: ". . . that Darwin in the *Origin* was NOT able to produce paleontological evidence sufficient to prove his views but that the evidence he DID produce was adverse to them; and I may note that the position is not notably different today."[71]

Therefore, if there's no real evidence, PAST or PRESENT, that there ever was a continuous series of forms from the most simple to the most complex, then how can any scientist justify the assumption that all organisms have evolved from simpler forms? Such an assumption is not in keeping with the facts—and, as stated above, one fact is worth a thousand theories.

Both of these problems, (1) the absence of fossils in Pre-Cambrian strata, and (2) the absence of connecting links between kinds of organisms, are enormous difficulties for evolutionists—and are more in favor of special creation! If either or both of these problems cannot be solved—and they've remained unsolved for a hundred and forty years—then the theory of progressive evolution must be considered inadequate.

3. Reasoning in a Circle

So not only is the first three-quarters of the evolutionary record entirely missing, but the fossils fail to supply connecting links even in the last quarter of the evolutionary chain! The weight of evidence the fossils give against evolution is already crushing, but let's briefly consider a third point.

Circular logic is used in dating the rocks and the fossils: The assumed age of each is used to prove the age of the other. The fossil is dated by the rock in which it is found, and the rock is dated by the fossil it contains. Let me illustrate:

> If a paleontologist finds a DINOSAUR bone, he'll announce that it is 70 million years old because of the ROCK STRATA in which it's found. Obviously anything found buried in rock laid down 70 million years ago had to be buried when that rock was formed and would have to be 70 million years old also. But how do we KNOW that certain ROCK STRATA are really 70 million years old? Simply because DINOSAURS are found in it!

This is a glaring example of the fallacy called reasoning in a circle. Each element is used to "prove" the other. But after a scientist has used the FOSSILS to tell the ages of the ROCKS, why should he be allowed to turn around and use such rock formations to tell the age of the fossils? AROUND and AROUND we go! One can prove ANYTHING if he starts with his conclusion and then reasons in a circle.

When I first learned this fact, the revelation came as quite a shock to me. I had assumed that rocks were usually dated by their mineral or lithographic nature, but such is not the case. Professor Henry Shaler Williams, whom Dana picked to succeed himself at Yale, tells us:

> "The character of the rocks themselves, their composition, or their mineral contents have NOTHING to do with settling the question as to the particular system [or age-level] to which the new rocks belong. The fossils ALONE are the means of correlation." [72]

Other recognized authorities in geology say the same thing, as for instance Grabau in *Principles of Stratigraphy:* "The primary divisions of the geological timescale are, as we have just seen, based on changes in LIFE, with the result that fossils ALONE determine whether a formation belongs to one or the other of these great divisions." [73]

E. M. Spieker, Professor of Geology at Ohio State University, emphasizes that the geologic time-scale is based predominantly on paleontological evidence (fossil sequences) rather than on any physical evidence such as the nature of the rocks themselves or their relative position in terms of vertical layers, *etc.*:

> "And what *is* this actual time-scale? On what criteria does it rest? When all is winnowed out and the grain reclaimed from the chaff, it is certain that the grain in the product is mainly the paleontological record [the fossils] and highly likely that the physical evidence is the chaff." [74]

And one of the most prominent European paleontologists declares: "The ONLY chronometric scale applicable . . . for dating geologic events exactly is furnished by the FOSSILS." [75]

You see, "the geologic ages are identified and dated BY the FOSSILS contained in the sedimentary rocks. The fossil record also provides the chief evidence for the theory of evolution, which in turn is the basic philosophy upon which the sequence of geologic ages has been erected. The evolution–fossil–geologic age system is thus a CLOSED CIRCLE which comprises one interlocking package. Each goes with the other two." [76]

Evolution ASSUMES that older rocks contain fossils of animals that are more simple whereas younger rocks contain fossils of animals that are more complex. THEN it determines the age of rocks by the fossils found in them, so rocks containing fossils of simpler animals are considered older, and those containing fossils of more complex animals are considered younger. With a system like this, it would seem that evolutionists couldn't miss!

Resorting to this MERRY-GO-ROUND type of reasoning embarrasses evolutionists, so they don't talk about it much. But R. H. Rastall, of Cambridge University, admits it in the *Encyclopedia Britannica:*

"It cannot be denied that from a strictly philosophical standpoint geologists are here ARGUING in a CIRCLE. The succession of organisms has been determined by a study of their [fossil] remains buried in the rocks, and the relative ages of the ROCKS are determined by the [fossil] remains of organisms that they contain." [77]

To me, this is a FATAL admission, for I have my doubts about theories that involve the fallacy of reasoning in a circle. But perhaps even this circular logic wouldn't be so bad IF it were fully consistent—that is, if the fossils and the rock layers containing them were always found in the assumed order. But countless contradictions and inconsistencies are found everywhere! In many places—in every mountainous region on every continent—are many examples of strata with fossils which are LESS complex on top of MORE complex fossils.

We'd naturally think that strata on top are more RECENT than those underneath, but if they contain "less evolved" fossils, they're called OLDER. It's as if some giant took a huge pancake turner, scooped up thousands of square miles, and flipped them over upside down so that the layers are reversed.

The problem of how rocks laid down earlier could climb on top of rocks laid down later is so serious for evolutionists that, to resolve it, they say that the rocks on top did not form there by sedimentation but came from other places. This might be plausible if it were limited to small amounts of rock, but as it is, countless MILLIONS of TONS of rock would have to be moved, sometimes for hundreds of miles, to find themselves on top of "more recent" strata. Even this might occasionally be possible if we were dealing with gravel or boulders, but it's often layers which are even and smooth—in many cases thousands of square miles in area.

This problem has necessitated building theory upon theory upon theory. We hear of "displaced geological beds" and "overthrust" theories, but they can account for only small shifts at the most. Yet some of these "displaced" beds cover an immense expanse. For instance, the Lewis Overthrust in the area of Montana is 6 miles thick and 135 to 350 miles long, weighing approximately 800,000 BILLION TONS! Its rock layers are in reverse order to that demanded by the theory of evolution, but there's no real physical evidence of a thrust fault—no evidence of sliding, grinding, or abrasive action between the layers, not to mention the problem of the source of the tremendous ENERGY required to move such gigantic blocks of rock.

But these out-of-order strata are quite common. In the strange world of geologic dating, any combination of geologic ages can occur in ANY vertical order. ANY age may be present or absent, in normal chronological order or inverted, with supposedly "ancient" rock formations resting on top of supposedly "young" formations. This is exactly contrary to the requirements of BOTH evolution and common sense, which would require the oldest rocks at the bottom.

Thus the record of the rocks, as interpreted by evolutionary geologists, provides a very SHAKY foundation for the theory of evolution. In fact, Robin S. Allen, a geologist of some importance, made this startling statement:

> "Because of the sterility of its concepts, historical geology, which includes paleontology and stratigraphy, has become static and unproductive. Current methods . . . of establishing chronology are of dubious validity. Worse than that, the criteria of correlation—the attempt to equate in time, or synchronize the geological history of one area with that of another—are logically vulnerable. The findings of historical geology are SUSPECT because the PRINCIPLES upon which they are based are either inadequate, in which case they should be reformulated, or false, in which case they should be discarded. Most of us REFUSE to discard or reformulate, and the result is the present DEPLORABLE state of our discipline."[78]

EXHIBIT A: THE HORSE

The classic example which convinces many people of the supposed truth of evolution, is the fossil record of ancient horses. The development of the horse is allegedly one of the most CONCRETE examples of evolution. But how valid, really, is this example?

1.   Textbook illustrations and museum displays impress the casual observer with the apparent stages in the so-called horse "series" of development. But the fact is that this succession is entirely MAN-MADE and has been assembled from several localities. The bones of fossil horses were gathered from different parts of the world and deliberately arranged in evolutionary sequence. In not even one place can this order be found in the actual rocks. The only reason for arranging the fossils in this order (from the most "primitive" to the modern horse) is the ASSUMPTION that evolution has taken place. Thus after artificially arranging the fossils to tell the story of evolution, evolutionists turn around and offer the same as proof of evolution!

Scientist Theodosius Dobzhansky frankly states:

> "Many textbooks and popular accounts of biology represent the evolution of the horse family as starting with *eohippus* [the primitive "dawn horse"] and progressing in a direct line towards the modern horse, *Equus*. This evolutionary progress involved, allegedly, the animals getting steadily larger and larger, while their feet were losing toe after

toe, until just a single hoof was left. According to Simpson, this OVER-SIMPLIFICATION really amounts to a FALSIFICATION." [79]

Here one eminent evolutionist quotes another to tell us that what is commonly taught about the supposed evolution of the horse is an "oversimplification . . . a falsification"! And anthropologist Ashley Montagu, a leader in his field, deplores the misleading charts shown in evolutionary textbooks to illustrate the assumed development of the horse. Such a diagram, he says, "puts the chart before the horse"! [80]

2. Even in this famous horse "series," transitional links between the major stages are missing. Evolutionist Lecomte du Nouy, speaking of the horse family, admits: "The known forms remain separated like the piers of a ruined bridge. . . . The continuity we surmise may never be established by FACTS." [81]

Professor Goldschmidt echoes du Nouy's statement: "Within the slowly evolving series, like the famous horse series, the decisive steps are abrupt WITHOUT transition." [82] So here again the "links" are missing!

3. As for the assumed increase in SIZE, that, too, "is subjective and NOT supported by the data," says evolutionist George Gaylord Simpson. He adds, "The diagrams of steady increase in size [of fossil horses] are made by *selecting* species that FIT this PRECONCEIVED idea." [83]

Furthermore, many fossil horses have been found in many regions, fully as large and sometimes larger than the modern horse. Besides, there's a great range in size among LIVING horses today: On the one hand we see huge draft horses like the Clydesdale or Percheron, and yet "A miniature type of pony bred in England often grows no taller than 28 inches." [84] So differences in size are certainly no proof of evolution.

4. There's an interesting discrepancy in the skeletal development of this series—the anatomy of the various models does not compare. For example, the RIB COUNT VARIES back and forth from 15 to 19: *Eohippus* had 18 pairs of ribs; *Orohippus* had only 15 pairs; then *Pliohippus* jumped to 19; and *Equus scotti* is back to 18. Also, the LUMBARS of the BACKBONE vary back and forth from 6 to 8. Therefore, many eminent scientists disagree on the theoretical chain of fossil horses.

5. Finally, consider the CHANGE in the number of toes. The evidence for a gradual change from four toes on the front legs and three on the back to just one toe on each is presented as a proof of evolution. But it really proves the wrong thing, because it moves from the COMPLEX to the SIMPLE—from more toes to fewer! Evolution demands an increase in complexity which proponents of the theory say has brought us from the simple cell to life as we know it today. Losing toes makes an animal more simple, not more complex. That process carried to an absolute extreme could reduce the horse to a one-celled organism, but it could never evolve a one-celled creature into a horse. At the most, the horse "series" demonstrates DEGENERATION rather than PROGRESSIVE evolution.

How much credence can we place in a theory based on this kind of evidence as its strongest "proof"?

XI. MAN—from the APES, or NOT?

Over the years, I've had occasion to discuss Darwin's brainchild with many evolutionists. In these discussions I've encountered an extremely interesting, though inexplicable, reaction. Whenever I voice my disbelief in the idea that human beings descended from apes, the evolutionist smiles indulgently and replies in a very predictable way: He patiently explains that the evolutionary development of man from apes is a popular misconception—he asserts that Darwin never taught such a thing, that evolutionists today do not teach it, and he suggests in a kindly way that I should get my facts straight.

Often he'll go on to say that evolution merely states that both apes and men have evolved from some unknown ancestor. So he concludes that I'm guilty of slander against evolution when I erroneously impute ideas to the theory which it never taught.

Naturally, after encountering this reaction I began to wonder where people ever got the idea that, according to evolution, man came from the apes. Here's a little of what I found:

Darwin really DID say man evolved from monkeys. In the conclusion of Chapter VI in his book *The Descent of Man,* the apostle of evolution declared:

> "The Simiadae then branched off into two great stems, the New World and Old World MONKEYS; and FROM the latter, at a remote period, Man, the wonder and glory of the Universe, proceeded." [85]

Modern evolutionists perpetuate this idea almost as a ceaseless refrain. Professor Earnest Albert Hooton, Harvard anthropologist, puts it this way: "Fossil man invented the first tools and discovered the use of fire; he was probably the originator of articulate speech. He made HIMSELF FROM AN APE and created human culture." [86]

Let's look at a few key chapters among the beautifully illustrated (and, unfortunately, widely influential) books in the Life Nature Library put out by TIME-LIFE Books. One volume is called *Early Man* and contains a chapter entitled "Back Beyond the APES" and another significantly called "Forward from the APES." Another of their volumes, on *The Primates,* has a concluding chapter entitled "From APE Toward MAN."

Early Man contains a five-page foldout chart showing APES in a straight line of development leading to modern MAN. This full-color chart has been reproduced in countless magazine advertisements for the books. Under one of the APES pictured (*Ramapithecus*), we're told that some experts believe that beast to be "the oldest of MAN'S ancestors in a direct line." [87]

The public is further misled by deliberately depicting the apes WALKING UPRIGHT on two feet like a man, though apes always are "knuckle-walkers," shuffling about on all fours. This misrepresentation of posture supposedly is done "for purposes of comparison," but the average reader is left with the erroneous impression that the evolution of MAN from APE is very plausible.

Those books, thoroughly steeped in evolutionary philosophy, represent one of the greatest publishing ventures ever undertaken. And Desmond Morris wrote a popular book about man called *The Naked APE.* Subtitled *A Zoologist's Study of the Human Animal,* Dr. Morris's book was given wide circulation as a BOOK-OF-THE-MONTH CLUB SELECTION. There he calmly declares that

> "There are one hundred and ninety-*three* living species of monkeys and apes. One hundred and ninety-*two* of them are covered with hair. The exception is a naked APE self-named *Homo sapiens* [that is, THINK-ING MAN]. . . . He is proud that he has the biggest brain of all the primates, but . . . in becoming so erudite, *Homo sapiens* has remained a naked APE nonetheless." [88]

Perhaps the popular idea connecting MAN'S supposed evolution with APES is not so much of a misconception after all! For it's not just popular books put out for public consumption like those mentioned above which teach the APE/MAN connection—it's scholarly TEXTbooks used by the college students of our nation which make one wonder: Is there a MONKEY in your family tree? Is man a miracle?—or a mutation? Did man come from *GOD*— or *GORILLA?*

An example of such a textbook (used at the college where I taught and at countless others across the country) is one edited by famed evolutionary anthropologist Louis Leakey entitled *Adam, or Ape: A Sourcebook of Discoveries About Early Man.* [89] When impressionable college freshmen are presented with the "Adam or APE" alternative by instructors who themselves have been brain-washed by evolutionary dogma, you can guess to which side they'll lean.

Before we can accept the contention that evolution does not teach that "Man came from apes," the evolutionists are going to have to get their STORIES STRAIGHT!

BONES OF CONTENTION: "EARLY MAN" FOSSILS

For years, evolutionists have tried to link man to lower forms of life. Their efforts are doomed to failure, since man did not originate that way. But millions of young boys and girls in school have been exposed to pictures and stories of "cave men" which promote evolutionary concepts. No doubt men did live in caves many years ago—in some parts of the world they still do. Some isolated tribes can be found living under extremely primitive conditions today, and future generations could dig up their remains and judge them to be thousands of years older than other societies also living today.

The discovery of "primitive" human remains, evolutionists say, proves that man has evolved from ape-like creatures. To clinch their argument, they show a series of effigies of the more notorious human fossils—a regular "rogues' gallery" of fossil men, such as NEANDERTHAL Man, CRO-MAGNON Man, JAVA Man, PEKING Man, NEBRASKA Man, PILTDOWN Man, etc., ending with a representation of MODERN man.

Schools often have students visit museums displaying such evolutionary exhibits. But Thomas Hunt Morgan, himself an evolutionist, deplores this practice and says:

> "I have never known such a course to fail of its intention. In fact I know that the student often becomes so thoroughly convinced that he RESENTS any such attempt as that which I am about to make to point out that the evidence for his conviction is NOT above criticism." [90]

In the first place, the evidence provided by fossils to ANTHROPOLOGY (the study of man) is extremely limited. Discussing the recent discovery of a bone fragment purportedly human, *Newsweek* Magazine reports:

> "The evidence for man's evolution could hardly be more TENUOUS: a collection of a few hundred fossilized skulls, teeth, jawbones and other fragments. Physical anthropologists, however, have been ingenious at reading this record—perhaps too ingenious, for there are almost as many versions of man's early history as there are anthropologists to propose them. There are only a few facts on which all the scientists have agreed." [91]

Though the fossil evidence for human evolution is scarce and sketchy, and though early man is long dead, he's still a live issue among evolutionists. Let's examine his supposed evolutionary history briefly.

NEANDERTHAL MAN

In 1856 portions of a skeleton were dug out of a cave in the Neander Valley near Dusseldorf, Germany. Fourteen pieces of bone were found, but only the skull-cap was of much diagnostic value. Darwin's followers claimed this find was a "link" between man and ape, and in 1856 it was classified as *Homo* (man) *neanderthalensis*. Partial remains of three similar skeletons were discovered in 1886 in Belgium, and a few other finds have also been made.

Evolution-minded scientists of the day depicted Neanderthal Man as a SQUAT, STOOPING, APE-LIKE creature. In an article called "Upgrading Neanderthal Man," *Time* Magazine explained:

> "Neanderthal's APISH image was further enforced by the writings early in this century of the respected French paleontologist Pierre Marcellin Boule. His portrait of Neanderthal as a stunted, beetle-browed creature who walked with bent knees and arms dangling in front of him served as the MODEL for several generations of artists and cartoonists." [92]

Boule's prestige as Director of the French Institute of Human Paleontology was great, and his work on Neanderthal Man was considered the final authority. The only trouble was, Boule was mistaken—and many other evolutionary scientists perpetuated his error over the years before the truth was discovered. It's now known that Boule based his conclusions on a poor specimen: because the skeleton he studied had curvature of the spine, he felt this was good evidence that man did not always walk upright.

But later Neanderthal discoveries brought forth skeletons that stood perfectly upright. Subsequently the Boule specimen with curvature of the spine was re-examined and found to have suffered from a form of arthritis. Two anatomists, Dr. W. L. Straus of Johns Hopkins University and Dr. A. J. E. Cave of St. Bartholomew's Hospital Medical College in London, have published a thorough study on the POSTURE of Neanderthal Man that shows the supposed ape-like features are mistaken interpretations without foundation in fact. Concerning the fossil remains they write:

> "We were somewhat unprepared for the fragmentary nature of the skeleton itself and for the consequent extent of restoration required. Nor were we prepared for the severity of the *osteoarthritis deformans* affecting the vertebral column. . . . There is thus no valid reason for the assumption that the posture of Neanderthal Man . . . differed significantly from that of present-day men. . . . There is NOTHING in this total morphological pattern to justify the common assumption that Neanderthal Man was other than a fully erect biped when standing and walking. It may be that the arthritic [specimen used by Boule] . . . of Neanderthal Man did actually stand and walk with something of a pathological kyphosis [curvature of the spine]; but, if so, he has his counterparts in modern men similarly afflicted with spinal osteoarthritis. He

cannot, in view of his manifest pathology, be used to provide us with a reliable picture of a healthy, normal Neanderthalian. Notwithstanding, IF he could be reincarnated and placed in a New York subway—provided that he were bathed, shaved, and dressed in modern clothing—it is doubtful whether he would attract any more attention than some of its other denizens." [93]

It's true that Neanderthal fossils do possess certain characteristics, particularly in the shape of the skull and face, which differ from the average modern man. But scientists believe this was due to the pituitary disorder known as *acromegaly*. In his book *Up from the Ape*, Harvard evolutionist Earnest Albert Hooton informs us that

> "ACROMEGALY, a disease . . . of the pituitary gland, produces in its victims an elongation of the face and jaws and an enlargement of the brow-ridges and increase in the forehead slope. . . . It is possible that the great brow-ridges, deep jaws, and other features common to . . . the Neanderthal type have been developed through some hyperfunctioning of the pituitary. . . ." [94]

While much is made of the fact that some fossil men had brains somewhat smaller than those of modern man (a fact which could easily be explained by their being degenerate strains), it's remarkable that Neanderthal's brain chamber was LARGER than the average for men today. Modern man has a brain capacity somewhere between **1200** and **1500** cc., but in *Up from the Ape* evolutionary anthropologist Hooton tells us that Boule's specimen of Neanderthal Man "had a cranial capacity of about **1600** cc., which is far above the average of male Europeans today. In the gross size of the brain, the Neanderthal ancients were quite up to the level of modern man." [95]

And, far from being the barbaric brutes that fictionized science paints them to be, Neanderthal Man made cave paintings, cultivated flowers, and buried his dead. A book on the Neanderthals calls them "the first flower people" and reports that an archeological expedition found that at least one of the nine Neanderthal skeletons uncovered in the Shanidar cave was buried with flowers. [96] Comments Dr. Carleton S. Coon, anthropologist at the University of Pennsylvania and past president of the American Association of Physical Anthropologists: "On the ground of behavior alone, the Shanidar folk merit the title of *Homo sapiens* [that is, fully human, "thinking" man]." [97]

Finally, referring to the "Many misconceptions . . . found in popular books, even textbooks," concerning the "BRUTISH Neanderthals," French prehistorian François Bordes declares: "Reconstructions show him as only a little better off than the big apes, and his tools are described as 'crude' by people who would not, to save their lives, be able to make them. The TRUTH is, indeed, quite different." [98]

CRO-MAGNON MAN

Named for a cave in southwestern France where the remains of these men were found in 1868, Cro-Magnon Man was skilled in working with both bone and stone. Dr. William C. Putnam, Professor of Geology at UCLA, reports that the Cro-Magnons "developed the technique of fashioning stone tools and weapons to a degree of perfection never equalled since." [99]

Also, these people were a highly *artistic* race. Objects of art include a variety of ivory carvings, and on the walls of their caves are drawings and colored paintings of many of the animals they hunted. Portraits or caricatures include human faces, some of which are bearded and others clean-shaven. These drawings, of SUPERB artistic quality, are "vibrantly life-like." [100]

Cro-Magnon Man, like his Neanderthal brother, had learned to make and use FIRE. He also buried his dead. Professor Hooton reports the discovery of one Cro-Magnon family "buried with tombstones at their heads and at their feet." [101]

And the Cro-Magnon race was known to have been superior to modern man, in both physical size and brain capacity. They were tall and well-proportioned, the men often reaching more than six feet in height. As to cranial capacity, it averaged larger than that of either Neanderthal or modern man. Note how Dr. Hooton speaks of

> ". . . the SKULL of the Cro-Magnon man that is supposed to define the type. It is a MASSIVE skull, large in every dimension. . . . The brain-case of this old man is estimated to have contained **1660** cc., which is roughly **150** cc. ABOVE the modern European average [and the modern European average is larger than the average for other living races of the world]." [102]

As the *Science Digest* puts it: "Since the Cro-Magnon man . . . the human brain has been decreasing in size." [103] This indicates degeneration, not evolution. In fact, modern man himself may be a somewhat deteriorated descendant of these ancestors.

JAVA MAN

The discovery called Java Man fills an important niche in the evolutionary Hall of Fame. It was made in 1891 by Eugene Dubois, a Dutch army doctor. Dubois had gone to the island of Java with the announced purpose of discovering primitive man, and there, on the bank of the Solo River, he unearthed two teeth and a piece of a skull-cap. The teeth were found separated from the skull-cap, lying several feet away. A year later, and at a distance more than fifteen yards from the place where he had found the skull-cap, Dubois uncovered a thigh bone. [104] Despite the fact that the thigh bone and skull-cap were so widely scattered, Dubois asserted that "both of them, and the teeth as well, belonged to ONE skeleton"! [105]

Pictures and reconstructions in museums of Java Man (complete even to the hair) give the unsuspecting public the impression that the specimen must have been quite intact. But as you can see, the scattered remains were very meager. In 1894 Dubois returned from Java and published his scientific report on the famous "missing link." *Evolution*, a volume in the *Life Nature Library*, says, "Deliberately and almost provocatively, Dubois NAMED this creature he had materialized from the past *Pithecanthropus erectus*"[106]—"ERECT APE-MAN," from the Greek *pithekos* for APE, and *anthropos* for MAN. Dubois unhesitatingly declared that his find "represents a so-called transition form between MAN and APES . . . the immediate progenitor of the human race." [107]

Naturally, his assertions caused quite a controversy in society, even among the scientists of his day. Then Dubois, annoyed at the skepticism and criticism that greeted his discovery, "became increasingly suspicious and eccentric." [108] "In 1895 he LOCKED the fossils in a strongbox . . . and permitted no one to see them for the next 28 years." [109]

It was not until 1923, after Dr. Henry Fairfield Osborn, head of the American Museum of Natural History, appealed to the president of the Dutch Academy of Sciences, that Dubois opened his strong-box and again allowed scientists to see the original bones. So there is some basis for questioning the integrity and judgment of Dubois. He considered anyone who opposed his ideas a personal enemy. FOR THIRTY YEARS he refused to allow his finds to be studied by other scientists. "If anyone came to his door in whom he scented a colleague, he was simply not at home." On other occasions, "he was stated to be ill." [110]

Dubois estimated the cranial capacity of Java Man to be about **900** cc., about two thirds of that for modern man—but it's impossible to determine cranial capacity from a skull-CAP alone. Furthermore, Dubois concealed the fact that he had also discovered at nearby Wadjak, and at approximately the same level, TWO HUMAN SKULLS (known as the Wadjak skulls) with a cranial capacity of about **1550-1650** cc., somewhat above the present human average. To have revealed this fact at that time (1890's) would have made it difficult, if not impossible, for his Java Man to have been accepted as a "missing link."

It wasn't until 1920, when a similar discovery was about to be announced, that Dubois revealed the fact that he had possessed the Wadjak skulls FOR THIRTY YEARS. (Apparently such concealment of evidence that did not conform to the theory was not a rare or isolated practice. Evolutionary anthropologist Hooton, for instance, brings this candid indictment: "Heretical and non-conforming fossil men were BANISHED to the limbo of dark museum cupboards, FORGOTTEN or even DESTROYED." [111])

Puzzlingly enough, evolutionists report that "Dubois became, as it were, his own opponent. Having discovered the earliest man, he fought doggedly throughout the rest of his life to maintain that *Pithecanthropus* was NOT an early MAN but a giant man-like APE." [112] The work of Dubois on Java was continued by German paleontologist G. H. R. von Koenigswald, who also informs us that Dubois finally decided that his *Pithecanthropus* bones belonged to a larger gibbonlike ape. [113] Von Koenigswald concludes:

"It therefore becomes manifest on what shaky ground Dubois erected his hypothetical building, and we can only WONDER at the boldness and tenacity with which he defended his *Pithecanthropus*." [114]

PEKING MAN

Near Peking, China, in 1927, Davidson Black found a lower molar tooth. From this single tooth he created a new genus and named it *Sinanthropus pekinensis* ("Chinese man of Peking"). Two years later, further digging at this site led to the discovery of some fourteen skull-caps, portions of facial bones, many teeth, and a few limb bones. By comparing pieces and combining information from all fourteen skull-caps or parts, it still was not possible to restore one complete skull. Professor Hooton explains:

"It appears that these skulls were TROPHIES of head hunters, and, furthermore, that said hunters usually bashed in the bases of the skulls when fresh, presumably to eat the brains therein contained. Many crania show that their owners met their deaths as a result of skull fractures induced by heavy blows." [115]

Thus the evidence given by Peking Man was always sparse—but NOW it's non-existent, for it was lost when the Japanese advanced on Peking in December, 1941. All that existed of Peking Man has disappeared, never to be seen again.[116] To this day no record has come to light of the unhappy fate of Peking Man.

"PUT NOT YOUR FAITH IN RECONSTRUCTIONS"

Fossil evidence of man's evolution is, therefore, extremely scarce. Paleontologist G. H. R. von Koenigswald, who spent much of his earlier life search-

ing for human fossils, calculated in 1956 that if ALL the then-known fragments of *Homo erectus* were gathered together they could be comfortably
displayed on a medium-sized table. [117]

But this scarcity has not hindered evolutionists from "reconstructing"
fragmentary fossils into full-fledged individuals. How precarious a business
this restoration of a fossil specimen can be is seen from Dr. Hooton's words:

> "No anthropologist is justified in reconstructing the entire skeleton
> of an unfamiliar type of fossil man from parts of the skull-cap, one or
> two teeth, and perhaps a few oddments of mandible [jaw] and long
> bones. . . . Inferences concerning the missing parts are very precarious,
> unless more complete skeletons of other individuals of the same type
> are available to support the reconstruction." [118]

A reconstruction is nothing more than an INTERPRETATION by the scientist making it, and entering into such an interpretation will inevitably be his
subjective opinion and personal prejudice.

> "When a scientist finds a SINGLE bone or tooth which supposedly
> dates back a few hundred thousand years, on what basis of measure-
> ment can he draw a picture of the WHOLE creature? When the first
> fossil bones were discovered many years ago, there were no other bones
> with which to compare them, no other measurements by which to judge
> them, so the first drawings of ancient men were the products of IMAGI-
> NATION. The men who drew the first pictures IMAGINED man as rather
> ape-like in appearance, so they drew him with the facial features of a
> creature sort of half-way between a man and an ape. They gave him a
> slightly crouching stance, a long face with huge jaws, and a look of
> doubtful intelligence. This [misleading] picture has stayed with us down
> through the years." [119]

Harvard anthropologist Earnest Albert Hooton warns us, "Put NOT your
faith in reconstructions," for scientists can't tell what the EYES, EARS, NOSE,
and LIPS looked like. They don't know what the SKIN COLOR was or the HAIR
COLOR or TEXTURE, or whether there was a LIGHT or HEAVY BEARD or NO BEARD
at all. In fact, a Neanderthal skull can be made to look very modern or very
primitive.

Professor Hooton concludes with this penetrating statement:

> "Some anatomists model reconstructions of fossil skulls by build-
> ing up the SOFT parts of the head and face upon a skull cast and thus
> produce a bust purporting to represent the appearance of the fossil
> man in life. When, however, we recall the fragmentary condition of
> most of the skulls, the faces usually being missing, we can readily see
> that even the reconstruction of the facial skeleton, leaves room for a

good deal of DOUBT as to details. To attempt to restore the soft parts is an even MORE hazardous undertaking. The LIPS, the EYES, the EARS, and the NASAL TIP leave no clues on the underlying bony parts. You can, with equal facility, model on a Neanderthaloid skull the features of a CHIMPANZEE or the lineaments of a PHILOSOPHER. These alleged restorations of ancient types of man have very little, if any, scientific value and are likely only to mislead the public." [120]

Evolutionists, proceeding as they do on the basis of such flimsy evidence, are bound to make some embarrassing mistakes. One such fiasco was the case of . . .

NEBRASKA MAN

Nebraska Man was actually nothing more than a TOOTH, a single rather worn molar tooth found in Nebraska by an individual named Harold Cook in 1922. Cook mailed the tooth to the famous paleontologist Henry Fairfield Osborn, director of the American Museum of Natural History in New York City. Fascinated with such a find, Osborn immediately compared the specimen with "all the books, all the casts, and all the drawings" and consulted with three other scientists, two of whom were eminent specialists on fossil primates. Here, they felt, was the first PROOF of early man on the North American continent. They wrote an article for a scientific journal announcing the discovery, stating:

> "It is hard to believe that a *single* water-worn *tooth* . . . can signalize the arrival of the anthropoid primates in North America. . . . We have been eagerly anticipating some discovery of this kind, but were not prepared for such CONVINCING EVIDENCE . . ."! [121]

Osborn and his colleagues couldn't quite decide whether the original owner of this tooth should be classed as an ape-like MAN or a man-like APE. He was given the important-sounding scientific name of *Hesperopithecus haroldcookii* ("Harold Cook's Western Ape") and become popularly known as Nebraska Man. The London *Daily Illustrated News* displayed a full-page spread on Nebraska Man. They reconstructed this creature from his tooth alone, exhibiting his exact shape, even to the prominent brow ridges and broad shoulders. [122]

As a matter of fact, in 1925 the *Hesperopithecus* tooth was even introduced as "evidence" by the EXPERT TESTIMONY of evolutionists in the famous Scopes "monkey trial" in Tennessee.

But two years later, Nebraska Man's career came to an abrupt halt. It turned out that he was NOT a man. He was not EVEN an ape!

Evolutionist Le Gros Clark explains: "As is well known, the tooth proved later to be that of a fossil peccary" [123]—a small animal resembling a PIG! Dr. Duane Gish says, "This is a case in which a PIG made a MONKEY out of an evolutionist!" [124]

SKULL DUGGERY!

Experiences like this tend to keep most scientists humble and cautious. Professor Clark goes on to say that "there can be few paleontologists who have not erred in this way at some time or another!" [125] But mistakes, of course, are understandable. Less acceptable is outright fraud, such as we see in the case of Charles Dawson's Piltdown Man.

PILTDOWN Man

The extent to which some evolutionists have stooped to manufacture the facts so sorely needed for their theory is well illustrated in the case of the "earliest Englishman," as Piltdown Man was frequently dubbed. Early in 1912, Charles Dawson, an amateur fossil hunter, brought some specimens to Dr. Arthur Smith Woodward, the Director of the British Museum. Dawson said he'd found them in a gravel pit near Piltdown, south of London.

Soon the world was informed of the discovery of most of one side of a lower jaw, with the first and second molar teeth still in place, and part of a skull. The SKULL seemed human, but the JAW was clearly ape-like. Yet surfaces of the teeth were flat—and only a human jaw, with its free-swinging motion, could have worn them down to that flat-top shape. Thus the find appeared to be a "missing link" in human evolution. Prehistoric animal remains found in the same gravel pit made this fossil the earliest known human. In honor of the discoverer, Woodward named it *Eoanthropus dawsoni* ("Dawson's Dawn Man"), more commonly called PILTDOWN MAN.

Controversy existed among scientists, some of whom claimed that the human cranium and ape-like jaw did not match, but most evolutionists used Piltdown Man to their advantage. Pictures and plaster casts of the Piltdown reconstruction were widely displayed in books and museums, and the *Encyclopedia Britannica* called Piltdown Man the second most important of the fossils in showing the evolution of man, adding authoritatively: "Amongst British authorities there is now agreement that the skull and jaw are parts of the same individual." [126] For more than forty years Piltdown Man did his work as a cardinal member of the evolutionary Hall of Fame.

Then it was learned that Piltdown Man was a careful, cunning forgery— a complete FAKE! In 1953 three scientists (Dr. Kenneth Oakley, a British Museum geologist; Dr. J. S. Weiner, Oxford University anthropologist; and Dr.

Le Gros Clark, professor of anatomy at Oxford University) proved that the fossils comprising Piltdown Man were a clever but shameful HOAX. Using sophisticated new instruments as modern as X-ray spectrograph and Geiger counter, they subjected the hallowed Piltdown fragments to the most searching and critical examination they had ever received. Instead of being half a million years old as originally estimated, the skull was closer to several thousand—and the jawbone wasn't fossilized at all! An improved chemical dating test clearly showed that the jaw wasn't much older than the year of its discovery.

The jaw had come from a modern ape, probably an orangutan. But the jaw and the non-human teeth had been cunningly "fossilized" by staining them with chemicals to give them the appearance of age. Moreover, telltale scratches on the molars showed beyond doubt that the teeth had been artificially filed down. In plaster casts of the Piltdown jaw studied the world over, these details were lost, but they were only too clear in the original specimens examined by these scientists in the British Museum. As stated in the *Reader's Digest* article on "The Great Piltdown Hoax": "Every important piece proved a forgery. Piltdown Man was a fraud from start to finish!" [127]

While this story shows that modern methods have improved over those of earlier years, it also shows that scientists can be fooled in examining and dating fossils. The whole fantastic story was published in *The Piltdown Forgery*, a fascinating, real-life "whodunit" by Dr. J. S. Weiner, "chief detective" in the case. [128] Although "all circumstantial evidence points to Dawson as the author of the hoax," [129] Weiner will not flatly accuse him in the absence of absolute proof. The curious Mr. Dawson died in 1916 at the age of 52 and at the height of his fame. If his motive in perpetrating the infamous hoax was to achieve recognition, then he died happy, for "he did win fame in his own time as the fossil was named for him—*Eoanthropus dawsoni*"! [130]

Yes, Charles Dawson, like Charles Darwin, is dead—but unfortunately their legacy lives on. For we read:

> "Today the statues of Piltdown Man have been removed from their places in the museums and his pictures from the books, though the HARM he has done in destroying people's faith in God's creation of man lives on in the lives of many. It is unfortunate that greater reserve is not used in teaching as facts to school children things recognized by reputable scientists as being questionable." [131]

XII. WHY IS EVOLUTION ACCEPTED?

In closing this chapter, we may well inquire, Why do people believe in evolution? For despite the reckless boasts about evolution made by a few over-zealous supporters, we've seen that the theory contains FATAL FLAWS. Evolutionary theory is not only destitute of proof but is positively disproved by every test we can presently apply to it. We seek in vain for a single SHRED of direct evidence to support it. So how can we explain the fact that millions of people today accept the evolutionary philosophy?

In the first place, Darwin presented his theory NOT to a hostile world but to a very receptive one, a world waiting and longing for just such a theory. True, a few ardent theologians stood up against it, but they were an exception. The world in 1859 was ready for Darwin's book, and it sold remarkably well. The first edition was completely sold out on the very day of publication! Historian Himmelfarb is not overstating the case when she says: "The sale of the *Origin* was beyond everyone's expectations. . . . As works of science went— and such sober works of science—the *Origin* was a popular success." [132]

You see, "up to then, those who had turned away from organized religion had done so primarily as a reaction against the corruption, intolerance, and often cruelty of the [Roman Catholic] Church, defects often equalled in the 16th through 19th centuries by the Protestants. Thus, out of reaction against the rigidity of the Church, and fortified by science in their doubts relating to church dogma, many were ripe indeed for 'the book that shook the world.'" [133]

Especially ripe were many scientists of the day who still chafed under the extreme bondage to authority in which all scientists were chained during the Dark Ages. They remembered how GALILEO had been forced by the power in authority, the Roman Catholic Church, to RECANT his scientific opinion— an opinion now known to be the truth. The oppression of science by narrow-minded individuals led scientists to look for a way of escape, and Darwin pointed toward an attractive exit. The reaction of scientists was natural enough and quite understandable. And they, like Darwin himself, believed that the evidence needed to fill in gaps in the theory would come in the course of time.

For more than a century, biological phenomena have largely been described according to evolutionary premises. If one looks at the world through Darwinian spectacles, if science is viewed in an evolutionary perspective, then certain answers—for example, anything involving the supernatural— will automatically be ruled out.

Furthermore, evolution has become a well-publicized philosophy and as such has gained adherents rapidly among both scientists and laymen. Thomas Henry Huxley, for instance, was a very good salesman! Other important spokesmen from all fields of thought have given their stamp of approval to evolution. Today we live in a society saturated with evolutionary dogma. Evolution is the modern, *fashionable* theory that seems to be "in" today, and many unthinking people accept it simply because it's widely accepted. They're cowed into accepting it out of fear of being called ignorant.

Probably most educated people believe in evolution simply because they've been told that most educated people believe in evolution! CONFORMITY is a powerful motivating force. Ask any teenager: If there's anything he fears, it's to be different from the crowd. But we need not be seduced by the constant refrain that "All intelligent persons agree that evolution is a fact." We should realize that many scientists and laymen of our day resist the regimentation attempted by evolutionists—and have the moral courage to stand by their convictions.

Perhaps others accept evolution because they want to believe it, they prefer to believe in a godless universe. For if evolution is not true, then the only alternative is divine creation—and some are very uncomfortable when made to realize that God has a direct concern with this world and with their own personal lives. So they seek by every means available, consciously or subconsciously, to relegate God to as inconspicuous a role as possible. These people eagerly embrace any philosophy that dispenses with the necessity of God and gladly accept Darwinism as an escape hatch. Human nature being what it is, most people believe what they WANT to believe, regardless of its truth or falsity. When people have an apparent compulsion to reject the idea of God, they welcome even unproved and unprovable "scientific" notions.

The desire to be free from one's responsibility to his Maker has turned many to evolution and atheism. For example, Aldous Huxley (Sir Julian's brother and a popular novelist) gives this frank account in a magazine article called "CONFESSIONS OF A PROFESSED ATHEIST: Aldous Huxley":

> "I had MOTIVES for not wanting the world to have meaning; consequently assumed that it had none, and was able without any difficulty to find satisfying reasons for this assumption. . . . For myself, as, no doubt, for most of my contemporaries, the philosophy of meaninglessness was essentially an instrument of liberation. The liberation we desired was . . . liberation from a certain system of morality. We objected to the morality because it interfered with our SEXUAL FREEDOM." [134]

It's sad but true that our fallen natures resist the demands of God's Word, just as it's true that "the god of this world [Satan] has BLINDED the minds of the unbelieving." [135]

But undoubtedly the main reason most of us end up believing in evolution is that we've been TAUGHT the theory so well. For several generations now, Darwin's brainchild has been force-fed on us and our children. We've been "brain-washed" by the theory of evolution so effectively that we accept it as surely as 2 + 2 = 4. Before graduating from high school nearly all students are exposed to and indoctrinated with the current evolutionary theories on the origin of man—but those theories are taught as fact.

The education of a lifetime is not without effect. Most people believe what they're taught—whether it's true or false. Man may pride himself on being "the thinking animal," but we often fail to act as rational beings. Our reluctance to investigate may lead us to accept the words of some "authority." People believe in evolution not because of the weight of EVIDENCE—for most have never examined that! They believe in it because of the weight of AUTHORITY, and we live in an age that worships authority.

Science itself has many worshipers. It has become a virtual religion, a new faith—SCIENTISTS are its priests (dressed not in black robes but in white coats), their PRONOUNCEMENTS are its gospel (which must be believed and accepted), and the LABORATORY is its temple. How, then, is the average person, with little or no special knowledge of the various sciences, to challenge the authorities? It's natural to accept what "experts" say—and most people do. [136]

So our minds have been programmed, our thinking has been conditioned, our children have been indoctrinated with the DOGMA of evolution. We accept in good faith the assertions of scientists who teach the evolutionary theory. After all, if evolution is in the textbooks and in the superbly illustrated books published by Time-Life, it must be true.

Thus there are many understandable reasons why evolution has come to be so universally accepted that it permeates much of man's thinking today. Yet one marvels in dismay that many intelligent people could permit themselves to be led so far astray from the facts of science.

CONCLUSION

What's wrong with the theory of evolution? Only everything. Our investigation in these two chapters has shown every assumption of evolutionists to be TRANSPARENTLY FALSE. The general theory of evolution has been accepted without the critical analysis it must have. Too much has been taken for granted, too much has been assumed to be true. Any scientific theory must harmonize with all known FACTS. If it be negated by as much as one of these facts, it's a faulty theory. In this regard I like the words of Thomas Henry Huxley:

> "Men of science do not pledge themselves to creeds; they are bound
> by articles of no sort: there is not a single belief that it is not a bounden
> duty with them to hold with a LIGHT hand and to PART WITH cheer-

fully, the moment it is really proved to be contrary to ANY fact, great or small." [137]

I submit not only that evolution is seen to be contrary to MANY facts, but that *it's unproved, unprovable, untestable, unreasonable, and impossible!* Recent research in molecular biology has made the evolutionary theory a bankrupt hypothesis. The pillars supposedly supporting the evolutionary structure are seen to be weak or nonexistent. The evolutionists' case for man's development from a nonhuman ancestor is in complete disarray—for man is more than a biological accident, more than the end product of germ, mollusk, and ape. [138]

Neither Darwin nor anyone else has PROVED the theory of evolution. The only thing Darwin proved is that it's dangerous even to THINK without God. If we leave God out of the picture, our speculations will ever be unwise, unfruitful, and unsafe.

Notes to Chapter 4

1. Sir Francis Bacon, quoted in Ernest E. Stanford, *Man and the Living World*, Second Edition (New York: The Macmillan Company, 1940), p. 34.
2. George Wald, "The Origin of Life," *Scientific American*, Volume 191, No. 2 (August, 1954), p. 46.
3. *Ibid.*
4. John Tyler Bonner, *The Ideas of Biology* (New York: Harper & Brothers, 1962), p. 18.
5. A. R. Moore, "On the Cytoplasmic Framework of the Plasmodium," *Science Reports*, Tohoku Imperial University, Japan, 4th series, Volume 8 (December, 1933), pp. 189-191.
6. John Pfeiffer and the Editors of Time-Life Books, *The Cell* (New York: Time-Life Books, 1972), p. 171.
7. Two attributes are generally regarded as essential for a cell or an organism to possess "life": (1) the ability to maintain its own metabolism—as CELLS do—and (2) the ability to REPRODUCE. The basic unit of life is the cell; *i.e.*, if there is no cell, there is no life. Viruses do not consist of cells and cannot reproduce without pirating the metabolism of another living cell; therefore they do not possess "life."
8. George Wald, "The Origin of Life," *Scientific American*, Volume 191, No. 2 (August, 1954), p. 46.
9. Another important technique for determining structure is called *nuclear magnetic resonance* (NMR). With NMR a molecule can be studied while in solution—it doesn't have to be tediously crystallized. For much of this information the author is indebted to Michael Behe, *Darwin's Black Box: The Biochemical Challenge to Evolution* (New York: The Free Press, © 1996), pp. 8-12.
10. Michael Behe, *Darwin's Black Box: The Biochemical Challenge to Evolution* (New York: The Free Press, © 1996), p. 3.
11. *Ibid.*, p. 5.
12. Garret Vanderkooi, "Evolution as a Scientific Theory," *Christianity Today* (May 7, 1971), p. 13.
13. D. E. Green and R. F. Goldberger, *Molecular Insights into the Living Process*, quoted in Vanderkooi, *op. cit.*, p. 14.
14. *Look* Magazine (January 16, 1962), p. 46.
15. Von Bertalanffy, quoted in Loren Eiseley, *The Immense Journey* (New York: Random House Modern Library Paperback, 1957), p. 206.
16. My son majored in biochemistry as preparation for medical school. He told me that molecular biologists—who study the marvels of nature at the *sub*-microscopic level—have a saying: "If you need a microscope to see it, it's TOO BIG!"
17. John Pfeiffer and the Editors of Time-Life Books, *The Cell* (New York: Time-Life Books, 1972), p. 68.
18. *Science Today*, chapter entitled "The Science of Life" by Sir James Gray (New York: Criterion Books, First American edition, 1961), p. 21.
19. Michael Behe, *Darwin's Black Box*, "Preface," p. xii.

20. Charles Darwin, *On the Origin of Species: A Facsimile of the First Edition* (Cambridge, Massachusetts: Harvard University Press, 1964), p. 189.

21. Behe, *op. cit.,* p. 39.

22. The writer also found very helpful here Dwight K. Nelson's book, *Built to Last: A Thoughtful Look at the Evidence that a Master Designer Created Our Planet* (Nampa, ID: Pacific Press, © 1998), pp. 37-38.

23. Psalms 139:14.

24. Behe, *op. cit.,* pp. 192-193, 187.

25. Pierre Lecomte du Nouy, *Human Destiny* (New York: Longmans, Green & Co., Inc., 1947), p. 30.

26. Charles Eugene Guye, cited in Lecomte du Nouy, *op. cit.,* p. 35.

27. *Ibid.,* p. 36.

28. Pierre Lecomte du Nouy, *Human Destiny* (New York: Longmans, Green & Co., Inc., 1947), p. 39.

29. Charles Darwin, *The Descent of Man*, Second Edition in One Volume (Philadelphia: David McKay, 1901), Chapter XXI, p. 637.

30. Graham Bell, quoted in Gina Maranto and Shannon Brownlee, "Why Sex?" *Discover*, Volume 5, Number 2 (February, 1984), p. 28.

31. George Williams, quoted in Maranto and Brownlee, "Why Sex?" *Discover*, Volume 5, Number 2 (February, 1984), p. 24.

32. Gina Maranto and Shannon Brownlee, "Why Sex?" *Discover*, Volume 5, Number 2 (February, 1984), p. 24.

33. Genesis 1:27, NKJV. God, with loving concern for Adam, said: "It is *not good* for the man to be *alone.* I will make a helper suitable for him."—Genesis 2:18, NIV.

34. See Genesis 2:20-23.

35. Sir James Jeans, *Eos, or the Wider Aspects of Cosmogony* (London: 1928), p. 52.

36. *Ibid.,* p. 55.

37. Isaac Asimov, "In the Game of Energy and Thermodynamics You Can't Break Even," *Smithsonian Institute Journal* (June, 1970), p. 10.

38. Henry M. Morris, *The Twilight of Evolution* (Ann Arbor, Michigan: Baker Book House Company, 1963), p. 35. (Note: The author has found this book and others by Dr. Morris to be particularly valuable.)

39. Morris, *op. cit.,* p. 41.

40. Harold F. Blum, *Time's Arrow and Evolution* (Princeton, New Jersey: Princeton University Press, 1951), p. 87.

41. George Wald, "The Origin of Life," *Scientific American*, Volume 191, No. 2 (August, 1954), p. 49.

42. Wald, *op. cit.,* p. 50.

43. W. E. Le Gros Clark, *Discovery* (January, 1955), p. 7.

44. Thomas Hunt Morgan, *A Critique of the Theory of Evolution* (Princeton, New Jersey: Princeton University Press, 1916), p. 24.

45. Carl O. Dunbar, *Historical Geology*, Second Edition (New York: John Wiley and Sons, Inc., 1961), p. 47.

46. W. R. Thompson, "Introduction" to *The Origin of Species* by Charles Darwin (New

York: E. P. Dutton & Company, Everyman's Library, 1956). This quote is from the reprint of Thompson's Introduction in the *Journal of the American Scientific Affiliation*, Volume 12 (March, 1960), p. 6.

47. Historian Gertrude Himmelfarb (Mrs. Irving Kristol) worked under grants from the American Philosophical Society and the John Simon Guggenheim Memorial Foundation to produce this well-documented book that was studied and commended by scholars even before its publication. As Ronald Good puts it in *The Listener:* "The reason why her study is so valuable is, paradoxically, that she is not a biologist but a historian, and so she has the inestimable advantage of being able to view her subject free from professional partisanship."

48. Gertrude Himmelfarb, *Darwin and the Darwinian Revolution* (Garden City, New York: Doubleday and Company, 1962), p. 330.

49. Charles Darwin, *The Origin of Species*, Sixth Edition (New York: P. F. Collier & Son, 1909), Chapter X, pp. 359-361.

50. George Gaylord Simpson, *The Meaning of Evolution*, Revised Edition (New Haven, Connecticut: Yale University Press, 1967), p. 20.

51. George Gaylord Simpson, "The History of Life," in Sol Tax, editor, *The Evolution of Life*, Volume 1 of *Evolution After Darwin* (Chicago: University of Chicago Press, 1960), pp. 143-144.

52. Marshall Kay and Edwin H. Colbert, *Stratigraphy and Life History* (New York: John Wiley and Sons, 1965), pp. 102-103.

53. Lincoln Barnett and the Editors of Time-Life Books, *The World We Live In* (New York: Time-Life Books, 1955), p. 93.

54. *Scientific American* Magazine (August, 1964), pp. 34-36.

55. Norman D. Newell, "The Nature of the Fossil Record," *Proceedings of the American Philosophical Society*, Volume 103, No. 2 (April, 1959), p. 269.

56. See Richard M. Ritland, *A Search for Meaning in Nature* (Boise, Idaho: Pacific Press Publishing Association, 1970), p. 141.

57. Daniel I. Axelrod, "Early Cambrian Marine Fauna," *Science*, Volume 128 (3314) (1958), pp. 7-9.

58. Charles Darwin, *The Origin of Species*, Sixth Edition (New York: P. F. Collier & Son, 1909), pp. 178, 179, 334, 352, 354-355, 503.

59. *Ibid.*, pp. 334 and 340.

60. Charles Singer, *A History of Biology*, Third Revised Edition (London and New York: Abelard-Schuman, 1959), p. 277.

61. Norman D. Newell, "The Nature of the Fossil Record," *Proceedings of the American Philosophical Society*, Volume 103, No. 2 (April, 1959), p. 267.

62. Alfred S. Romer, "Time Series and Trends in Animal Evolution," in Glenn L. Jepson, Ernst Mayr, and George Gaylord Simpson, editors, *Genetics, Paleontology and Evolution* (Princeton, New Jersey: Princeton University Press, 1963), p. 114.

63. George Gaylord Simpson, *Tempo and Mode in Evolution* (New York: Columbia University Press, 1944), pp. 105-106.

64. George Gaylord Simpson, *The Major Features of Evolution* (New York: Columbia University Press, 1953), p. 360.

65. George Gaylord Simpson, "The History of Life," in Sol Tax, editor, *The Evolution of Life*, Volume 1 of *Evolution After Darwin* (Chicago: The University of Chicago Press, 1960), p. 149.

66. Austin H. Clark, *The New Evolution: Zoogenesis* (Baltimore: Williams and Wilkins, 1930), p. 196.

67. *Ibid.*, pp. 100-101.

68. Sir Julian Huxley, *The Wonderful World of Life* (New York: Garden City Books, 1958), p. 12.

69. W. E. Swinton, in A. J. Marshall, editor, *The Biology and Comparative Physiology of Birds* (New York: Academic Press, 1960), Volume 1, p. 1.

70. E. J. H. Corner, in A. M. MacLeod and L. S. Cobley, editors, *Contemporary Botanical Thought* (Chicago: Quadrangle Books, 1961), p. 97.

71. W. R. Thompson, "Introduction" to *The Origin of Species* by Charles Darwin (New York: E. P. Dutton & Co., Everyman's Library, 1956). This quote is from the reprint of Thompson's Introduction in the *Journal of the American Scientific Affiliation*, Volume 12 (March, 1960), p. 7.

72. Henry Shaler Williams, *Geological Biology* (New York: Henry Holt and Company, 1895), p. 38.

73. Amadeus William Grabau, *Principles of Stratigraphy*, Second Edition (New York: A. G. Seiler, 1924), p. 1103.

74. E. M. Spieker, "Mountain-Building Chronology and the Nature of the Geologic Time-Scale," *Bulletin, American Association of Petroleum Geologists*, Volume 40 (August, 1956), p. 1806.

75. O. H. Schindewolf, "Comments on Some Stratigraphic Terms," *American Journal of Science*, Volume 255 (June, 1957), p. 394.

76. Henry M. Morris, *The Remarkable Birth of Planet Earth* (San Diego: Institute for Creation Research, 1972), pp. 76-77.

77. Robert H. Rastall, *Encyclopedia Britannica*, Fourteenth Edition (1956), Volume 10, p. 168, article "Geology."

78. Robin S. Allen, "Geological Correlation and Paleoecology," *Bulletin of the Geological Society of America*, Volume 59 (January, 1948), p. 2.

79. Theodosius Dobzhansky, *Evolution, Genetics, and Man* (New York: John Wiley & Sons, Inc., 1955), p. 302.

80. M. F. Ashley Montagu, *An Introduction to Physical Anthropology*, Third Edition (Springfield, Illinois: Charles C. Thomas, Publisher, 1960), p. 267.

81. Lecomte du Nouy, *Human Destiny* (New York: Longmans, Green & Co., Inc., 1947), p. 95.

82. Richard B. Goldschmidt, *American Scientist*, Volume 40 (1952), p. 97.

83. George Gaylord Simpson, *Tempo and Mode in Evolution* (New York: Columbia University Press, 1944), p. 160.

84. *World Book Encyclopedia* (1964 edition), Volume 13, p. 311.

85. Charles Darwin, *The Descent of Man*, Second Edition in One Volume (Philadelphia: David McKay, 1901), Chapter VI, p. 181.

86. Earnest Albert Hooton, *Apes, Men, and Morons* (Freeport, New York: Books for Libraries Press, 1970), p. 105.

87. F. Clark Howell and the Editors of Time-Life Books, *Early Man* (New York: Time-Life Books, 1970), p. 42.

88. Desmond Morris, *The Naked Ape: A Zoologist's Study of the Human Animal* (New York: McGraw-Hill Book Company, 1967), p. 9.

89. Louis S. B. Leakey, editor, *Adam, or Ape: A Sourcebook of Discoveries About Early Man* (Cambridge, Massachusetts: Schenkman Publishing Company, 1971).

90. Thomas Hunt Morgan, *A Critique of the Theory of Evolution* (Princeton, New Jersey: Princeton University Press, 1916), p. 9.

91. "Bones of Contention," *Newsweek* Magazine (February 13, 1967), p. 101.

92. "Upgrading Neanderthal Man," *Time* Magazine (May 17, 1971), p. 76.

93. William L. Straus, Jr., and A. J. E. Cave, "Pathology and the Posture of Neanderthal Man," *Quarterly Review of Biology,* Volume 32, No. 4 (December, 1957), pp. 348-363.

94. Earnest Albert Hooton, *Up from the Ape*, Revised Edition (New York: The Macmillan Company, 1946), p. 346.

95. *Ibid.*, p. 329.

96. Ralph S. Solecki, *Shanidar: The First Flower People* (New York: Alfred A. Knopf, 1971).

97. Carleton S. Coon, quoted in "Upgrading Neanderthal Man," *Time* Magazine (May 17, 1971), p. 75.

98. Francois Bordes, "Mousterian Cultures in France," *Science*, Volume 134 (September 22, 1961), p. 803.

99. William C. Putnam, *Geology* (New York: Oxford University Press, 1964), p. 463.

100. *Ibid.*

101. Earnest Albert Hooton, *Up from the Ape*, Revised Edition (New York: The Macmillan Company, 1946), p. 371.

102. *Ibid.*, pp. 367-368.

103. *Science Digest* (April 1951), p. 33.

104. Eugene Dubois, *"Pithecanthropus erectus*—a Form from the Ancestral Stock of Mankind," in Louis S. B. Leakey, editor, *Adam, or Ape: A Sourcebook of Discoveries About Early Man* (Cambridge, Massachusetts: Schenkman Publishing Company, 1971), p. 167.

105. *Ibid.*, p. 175.

106. Ruth Moore and the Editors of LIFE, *Evolution* (New York: Time Incorporated, 1962), p. 131.

107. Eugene Dubois, quoted in Louis S. B. Leakey, *op. cit.,* p. 175.

108. F. Clark Howell and the Editors of Time-Life Books, *Early Man* (New York: Time-Life Books, 1970), p. 13.

109. Ruth Moore and the Editors of LIFE, *Evolution* (New York: Time Incorporated, 1962), p. 132.

110. Richard M. Ritland, *A Search for Meaning in Nature* (Boise, Idaho: Pacific Press Publishing Association, 1970), footnote on p. 250.

111. Earnest Albert Hooton, *Apes, Men, and Morons* (Freeport, New York: Books for Libraries Press, 1970), p. 107.

112. Marcellin Boule and Henry V. Vallois, *Fossil Men* (New York: The Dryden Press, 1957), p. 3.

113. G. H. R. von Koenigswald, *Meeting Prehistoric Man* (New York: Harper & Brothers, 1956), p. 55. Also, on page 147 of *Man's Evolution*, by C. L. Brace and M. F. Ashley Montagu (Toronto, Ontario: The Macmillan Company), we read that "Strangest of all, however, was the view of Dubois himself when he once again began to publish on his discoveries. His revised opinion was that *Pithecanthropus* had been a giant gibbon and quite unrelated to the human line of development."

114. Von Koenigswald, *op. cit.*, p. 34.

115. Earnest Albert Hooton, *Up from the Ape*, Revised Edition (New York: The Macmillan Company, 1946), p. 304.

116. Ruth Moore and the Editors of LIFE, *Evolution* (New York: Time Incorporated, 1962), p. 136. See also James Stewart-Gordon, "The Mystery of the Missing Bones," *Reader's Digest* (September, 1976), pp. 177-186.

117. G.H.R. von Koenigswald, *Meeting Prehistoric Man* (New York: Harper & Brothers, 1956), p. 18.

118. Earnest Albert Hooton, *Apes, Man and Morons* (Freeport, New York: Books for Libraries Press, 1970), p. 115.

119. David D. Riegle, *Creation or Evolution?* (Grand Rapids, Michigan: Zondervan Publishing House, 1971), pp. 47-48.

120. Earnest Albert Hooton, *Up from the Ape*, Revised Edition (New York: The Macmillan Company, 1946), p. 329.

121. Henry Fairfield Osborn, *"Hesperopithecus*, the First Anthropoid Primate Found in America," *American Museum Novitates*, No. 37 (April, 1922), pp. 1-5.

122. London *Daily Illustrated News,* June 24, 1922.

123. W. E. Le Gros Clark, *The Fossil Evidence for Human Evolution* (Chicago: The University of Chicago Press, 1955), p. 25.

124. Duane T. Gish, *Evolution—The Fossils Say NO!* (San Diego: ICR Publishing Company, 1973), p. 91. (*Note*: This is an excellent book.)

125. W. E. Le Gros Clark, *The Fossil Evidence for Human Evolution* (Chicago: The University of Chicago Press, 1955), p. 25.

126. *Encyclopedia Britannica* (1946 edition), Volume 14, p. 763.

127. Alden P. Armagnac, "The Great Piltdown Hoax," *Reader's Digest* (October, 1956), p. 182.

128. J. S. Weiner, *The Piltdown Forgery* (New York: Oxford University Press, 1955. See also William L. Straus, Jr., "The Great Piltdown Hoax," *Science*, Volume 119 (February 26, 1954).

129. Alden P. Armagnac, "The Great Piltdown Hoax," *Reader's Digest* (October, 1956), p. 182.

130. Robert Silverberg, *Scientists and Scoundrels: A Book of Hoaxes* (New York: Thomas Y. Crowell Company, 1965), p. 232. See also C. L. Brace and M. F. Ashley Montagu, *Man's Evolution* (Toronto, Ontario: The Macmillan Company), p. 171.

131. Thomas F. Heinze, *The Creation vs. Evolution Handbook* (Grand Rapids, Michigan: Baker Book House, 1970), pp. 39-40. (Excellent book.)

132. Gertrude Himmelfarb, *Darwin and the Darwinian Revolution* (Garden City, New York: Doubleday & Company, 1962), pp. 253-254.

133. Marshall Hall and Sandra Hall, *The TRUTH: God or Evolution?* (The Craig Press, 1974), p. 122. (Another excellent book.)

134. Aldous Huxley, "Confessions of a Professed Atheist: Aldous Huxley," *Report* (June, 1966), p. 19.

135. 2 Corinthians 4:4, NASB.

136. Unfortunately, many make the same mistake in the realm of RELIGION, accepting without question what some authority figure says, instead of studying for themselves.

137. Thomas Henry Huxley, *Darwiniana*, 1893 edition (printed in the U.S. by Appleton, 1901), pp. 468-469.

138. As a brief addendum to this chapter, see *Appendix A: "A Physician's View of Evolution,"* at the back of this book.

CHAPTER FIVE

~

THEISTIC EVOLUTION: UNWISE CHRISTIAN COMPROMISE

MOST CHRISTIANS simply cannot accept the theory of evolution for reasons outlined in the preceding chapters. But, as the saying goes, "The Devil has a soup for every taste," and he's cooked up an alternative which some believers find rather appetizing. His diabolical recipe calls for mixing evolution and Christianity in the same philosophical pot, well seasoned with skepticism.

Theistic evolution—as opposed to the Godless, atheistic variety—is man's attempt to harmonize the Bible and evolutionary theory. It's a kind of halfway house midway between atheism and the settled faith of those honoring God as Creator. It's a philosophy which says there IS a God and He IS the Creator—but He uses evolution as His tool or method. Theistic evolutionists think the Bible tells us WHO created, and evolution tells us HOW.

History does not record the name of the person who, when faced with the choice between atheistic evolution and divine Creation, first asked: "Why does it have to be *either/or*—why can't it be BOTH?" Men thus try to WED the Bible doctrine of divine Creation to the godless theory of evolution in an unholy alliance called "theistic evolution." But the miserable marriage is doomed to fail because too many irreconcilable differences exist between the two!

The two concepts are mutually exclusive, as we'll see, and the attempt to reconcile Scripture with atheistic science is not acceptable either to Bible believers or to mainline evolutionists. This UNWISE COMPROMISE offers no real safety and no satisfying answers as a middle ground, just as agnosticism offers no safe harbor to those adrift between belief and atheism.[1]

Unfortunately, such "harmonizing" efforts usually end up by accepting EVOLUTION lock, stock, and barrel, and relegating the GENESIS record to the realm of myth.

The great tragedy is that the Christian church, in large measure, has surrendered to the doctrine of evolution! Theistic evolution is accepted today not only by the liberal Protestant churches but also by the Roman Catholic Church. Neither Darwin's *Origin of Species* nor his *Descent of Man* was ever included on the Catholic Church's INDEX of unapproved or condemned books. In fact, the *New Catholic Encyclopedia* goes so far as to state: "The evolution of man from lower forms, as Darwin and Wallace agreed, does not at all imply that man is a mere animal."[2]

A perfect illustration of the inroads made by theistic evolution is the fact that official Catholic doctrine, enunciated by Pope Pius XII in his 1950 encyclical *Humani Generis* and by Pope John Paul II in his 1996 pronouncement to the Pontifical Academy of Sciences, PERMITS the belief and teaching of evolution in the church. *Time* Magazine reported that "The statement by John Paul reflects the church's acceptance of evolution,"[3] provided that man's soul is still recognized as a divine creation. This is theistic evolution, pure and simple.

Some may find this alternate theory appealing because the average person hates to argue and take sides. And the theistic evolutionist, with a foot in both camps, doesn't have to argue with anyone. He can just smile and agree with both sides. But has he read the "fine print" in the Devil's contract so he's aware HOW MUCH such harmony costs? Has he compromised the Truth to such an extent that he's sold his own soul?

Satan wants us to believe "we can have our cake and eat it, too." But *theistic evolution* is an oxymoron, a contradiction in terms, like "wise fool."

This variant concept seeks to put a HALO around evolutionary theory, but remember that theistic evolution is STILL evolution—cleverly camouflaged and sugar-coated, but evolution just the same.

From the scientific point of view, theistic evolution is not a satisfactory compromise. It's merely an alternate form of evolution with no scientific distinction, vulnerable to all the objections (such as GAPS in the fossil record, *etc.,* outlined in Chapters 3 and 4) for evolution in general.

Since theistic evolution attempts to bring God into the picture as an evolutionary agent, let's focus on the theological implications of this theory, answering such questions as: Should a Christian believe in evolution? Can one be a true Christian and still open the door to evolutionary theory? We'll find that just as SCIENTIFIC evidence won't support the atheistic version of evolution, SCRIPTURAL evidence won't support the theistic version. The closer we look at this theory, the more clearly we see that it's a monstrous blasphemy on the character of God—a horrid libel on the wise and loving Creator the Bible reveals.

Let's briefly examine some of the reasons why Christians can never accept this man-made compromise.

REASON #1:
IT ATTACKS & UNDERMINES THE SCRIPTURES

The Bible speaks out on Creation from PAGE ONE. That's why Bible scholar Louis Berkhof says this about theistic evolution: "In a word, it is a theory that is absolutely subversive of Scripture truth." [4]

Far from being only a slight variation on orthodox Christian belief, this theory actually calls in question the entire Bible account of origins. All that follows in Holy Scripture can be rightly understood only against the backdrop of Genesis. Yet evolution labels as "legends" those foundational chapters. As *Time* Magazine reports, "Evolution suggests that *Homo sapiens* is descended not from one set of parents but from many, thus making a literal Adam and Eve quite unlikely." [5]

Theistic evolutionists feel that Science has delivered us from having to believe the Bible story of Creation. But the rest of Scripture—especially the New Testament—frequently quotes from and alludes to the Book of Genesis, including its earliest chapters. Though many today consider the Genesis record to be only allegory, a mere myth, it was NOT considered so by the inspired Bible writers!

While proclaiming their belief in God, theistic evolutionists attack His Word—the only objective standard by which we may know the truth He has revealed.

REASON #2:
ITS INFLUENCE IS OPPOSED TO CHRISTIAN SOCIETY

In His immortal Sermon on the Mount, Jesus taught that "the meek"— not the aggressive—"shall inherit the earth." [6] A follower of Christ struck on one cheek by an aggressor will "turn to him the other also." [7] But evolutionary doctrine is diametrically opposed to such noble teaching. In harmony with evolution's idea of the "survival of the fittest" in "the struggle for existence," German philosopher Friedrich Nietzsche (1844-1900) directed that "Man shall be trained for war and woman for the recreation of the warrior; all else is folly." [8] According to Nietzsche, the Germans were the "master race" of Supermen (*Uber-mensch*) and best fitted to survive and dominate the world. Adolf Hitler was a devoted disciple of Nietzsche, whose ideas were eagerly exploited by the Nazis in their ruthless rise to power. The bloody result is one of the saddest chapters in history.

The two philosophies of Christ and Nietzsche can never be made to harmonize. For there's a basic contradiction between Jesus' Golden Rule of "Do unto others as you would have them do unto you" [9] and evolution's survival-of-the-fittest idea that "might makes right."

Reason #3:
It Attributes to NATURAL Causes
Our Creator's SUPERNATURAL Works

One goal of Satan has always been to rob Christ of His glory as Creator. [10] The basic theory of evolution, being completely atheistic, is an outright denial of God. Theistic evolution is more subtle, more indirect in its denial, but it nevertheless places severe limitations on God's power and ability, putting Him in the position of a mere "overseer."

Yet Bible writers throughout the Scriptures accept the literal story of Creation as pure history. If Genesis is not historically true, then the other Bible writers, and Christ Himself, were guilty of either ignorance or deliberate misrepresentation when they cited the events of Creation as inspired truths. Either conclusion is unthinkable to the consistent Christian. Note the following unequivocal statements:

- The "wise man" **SOLOMON** declared: "Lo, this only have I found, that God hath made man UPRIGHT; but they have sought out many inventions." [11]

- The Apostle **PAUL** accepted the origin of man by special creation: "It is written, The first man Adam was made a living soul. . . . Man was not made from woman; but woman from man. . . . For Adam was formed first, then Eve." [12] Paul also wrote of "God, who commanded the light to shine out of darkness," [13] clearly referring to Genesis 1:3, when God commanded: "Let there be light."

- **JUDE,** in his New Testament letter, describes the faithful patriarch Enoch as "the seventh from Adam."[14] But why refer to a man as "the seventh" in ancestral line IF the starting point for that line is only a myth?

- If the Genesis account of Creation is a myth, we must throw out the testimony of Gospel writer **LUKE,** who traces Jesus' ancestry all the way back to "Seth, who was the son of Adam, who was the son of God."[15] Linking Adam directly to the Creator puts Luke in perfect harmony with the Genesis record and in direct opposition to ANY evolutionary theory.

- The Apostle **JAMES** also testifies on the side of divine Creation when he writes of "men, who have been made in the likeness of God."[16]

- The Apostle **PETER** supports the inspired Record of Genesis when he writes of "Noah . . . building the ark. Yet only eight persons were saved from drowning in that terrible flood."[17]

- The Apostle **JOHN,** in writing the Book of Revelation, corroborates Genesis (3:1-6) when he writes of "that serpent of old, called the Devil, and Satan, who deceives the whole world."[18] Furthermore, John promises that when the earth is made new, "there shall be no more curse,"[19] again echoing Genesis (3:17).

- Though evolutionists scoff at the idea of God's creation of Adam and Eve and the Flood of Noah's day, the Lord **JESUS** endorsed them both. In speaking of the special Creation of Adam and Eve as a historical fact, Christ declared: "Have you not read that He who made them at the beginning made them male and female?"[20] This clearly refers to the account of Man's creation in Genesis 1:27—"Male and female He created them." Jesus also put His stamp of approval on the Bible account of the Flood in these words: "In the days before the Flood, they were eating and drinking, marrying and giving in marriage, until the day that Noah entered the ark."[21] Can conscientious Christians dismiss Genesis as mere myth or legend when Christ Himself acknowledged its accuracy?

The Bible states that after Adam was created, there was found in all the animal kingdom NO "help meet for him [that is, no companion or helper suitable for him]."[22] This shows that Adam was NOT related to the animals and had nothing in common with them. That's why God specially formed Eve to be Adam's wife.

Since the Scriptures speak out on Creation from PAGE ONE, those who believe the Bible is the Word of God can't regard the Creation record as

merely figurative language when inspired Bible writers—and the Lord Himself—considered it literal and authoritative.

REASON #4:

ITS BRUTAL METHOD IS UNWORTHY OF A GOD OF LOVE

Advocates for this theory assert that evolution is simply God's way of
working. However, the question is not whether God COULD use evolutionary
processes as a means of creating our world and its inhabitants but whether
He WOULD employ those processes. What about the moral aspects of this
theistic theory? Would a good God use PAIN and DEATH to carry out His
design for making a perfect world?

You see, the METHOD attributed to God by this theory is unworthy of
Him and raises serious questions regarding God's character.

As two graduate students discussed theistic evolution and Creation, the
more liberal fellow asked: "Why is it important to fuss over HOW it happened
as long as it DID happen and we believe God was involved?" The other replied, "Creation, like all of God's acts, is primarily revelation. It tells us something about God's character. So it matters what we say about Creation because ultimately it reflects upon our understanding of God." He concluded by
saying, "Since the WAY a thing is made tells us something about its maker,
we should be careful about the METHODS we ascribe to our Maker." [23]

The method which theistic evolution supposes was used in Creation would
be, to quote the poet Tennyson,

> "As if some lesser god had made the world,
> But had not force to shape it as he would." [24]

The god postulated by theistic evolution is not the same majestic, all
powerful God of the Bible. Instead, he's a bungling deity who perpetrates age
upon age of bloodshed, stumbling through a slow process, making millions
of mistakes in trial-and-error attempts to perfect his created organisms. That's
why one man said, "I grant that the evolution theory may indeed permit
belief in a god, but *what a god!*" [25]

Evolution's bloody reign of tooth and claw for millions of years to eliminate the unfit is utterly incompatible with the Bible's portrayal of origins.
The two concepts are as far from each other as the east is from the west.
God's perfect work of Creation was beautiful to behold and worthy of its
omnipotent Author.

"The evolutionary process depends partly on destruction of the weak by
the strong. Theistic evolution makes GOD responsible for all of this, whereas

the Biblical concept of a perfect creation and a subsequent fall makes SATAN responsible for the destructive side of nature." [26]

Harvard's illustrious professor of zoology, Louis Agassiz, protested against the idea that God used evolution as His method of Creation in these words: "The resources of the Deity cannot be so meager, that in order to create a human being endowed with reason, He must change a monkey into a man." [27]

REASON #5:
IT CONTRADICTS SCRIPTURE'S "FINISHED" CREATION

Creation was not merely BEGUN at that time spoken of in the opening chapters of Genesis. The inspired Record states that it was FINISHED, and the seventh day was set apart as a special day to commemorate the COMPLETION of God's great work.

Evolution postulates an ongoing creative process continuing over millions of eons, whereas Scripture declares God's work of Creation to have been COMPLETED, at least as regards this earth: "The works were FINISHED from the foundation of the world." [28]

The Apostle Paul states the fact of a completed Creation when he says: "By Him were all things created." [29] Note that the verb phrase "were . . . created" is in the PAST TENSE. Therefore, Creation is not going on at present, which would be true if evolution were an ongoing creative process.

The inspired Record explicitly states that at the end of Creation week, after God had brought into being the earth with all its varied forms of plant and animal life, including Man, God's creative work was a COMPLETED act. Please note: "Thus the heavens and the earth were FINISHED, and all the host of them. And on the seventh day God ENDED His work which He had made; and He rested on the seventh day from all His work which He had made." [30]

This same thought of Creation's completed work is echoed and re-echoed throughout the Bible in such passages as the following:

- **Exodus 20:11, NIV** — "For in six days the Lord made the heavens and the earth, the sea, and ALL that is in them, but He rested on the seventh day. Therefore the Lord blessed the Sabbath day and made it holy."

- **Psalm 33:6 & 9** — "By the word of the Lord were the heavens made; and all the host of them by the breath of His mouth. . . . For He spake, and it was DONE; He commanded, and it stood fast."

- **Hebrew 4:10** — "For he that is entered into His rest, he also hath ceased from his own works, as God did from His."

REASON #6:
IT THEORIZES THAT DEATH CAME AT THE WRONG TIME

In the closing paragraphs of his book *The Origin of Species,* Darwin wrote that "the production of the higher animals" was brought about by "the WAR of nature, from famine and DEATH." In the first place, ask yourself: Does "the war of nature, from famine and death" sound like the means GOD would use to create a world He pronounced all "very good"?[31]

In the second place, recognize that evolution's claim that death was the causative factor in producing the higher animals contradicts the Bible teaching on the cause of death. The Scriptures plainly teach that there was no suffering and death in the world before Adam sinned. Death entered the world as a direct result of Man's sin:

- **Romans 5:12** — "By one man [Adam] sin entered into the world, and death by sin; and so death passed upon all men, for that all have sinned."
- **1 Corinthians 15:21** — "By man came death."

But if evolutionary theory were correct, there would have been BILLIONS of deaths before the first man ever existed! Theistic evolution asks us to believe that suffering and death existed for long ages in a SINLESS world made by a wise and holy God!

REASON #7:
IT OVERLOOKS OR IGNORES THE FALL OF MAN

The theme of the Bible is "the Fall of Man" into sin and his need of a Savior. Note the unmistakable sequence of Man's creation, fall, and subsequent salvation:

1. Beginning with a PERFECT Creation,
    there follows
2. Man's DEgeneration (the Fall of Adam & Eve),
    and then
3. Man's REgeneration (the Plan of Salvation).

But theistic evolution is totally unacceptable to all who know and believe the Bible, because it does away with our need of Jesus Christ as Savior. The only "Fall" allowed in evolution is a fall UPWARD, for underlying evolutionary thought is the basic idea of PROGRESS. And if the assumption of progress is correct—if Man began from lower forms of life and is on the upgrade, constantly climbing, he's

- not a FALLEN creature in need of a Savior
- but a DEVELOPING organism on the road to perfection.

Instead of being condemned for his mythical "fall" from grace, Man should be congratulated on the progress he's made! Evolutionary theory and Bible theology postulate quite different trends—trends which are polar opposites!

That's why it's more consistent to be an out-and-out ATHEIST than a theistic evolutionist! Evolution—providing for no "fall," hence needing no Savior—is decidedly anti-Christian.

Ask yourself: Is the story of man's fall in Genesis *history* [32] or *myth?* Is man a civilized ape or a fallen sinner? Evolution sees man as a glorified beast, a creature who never fell but has always climbed higher and higher. Such an origin makes the death of Christ of no effect in man's behalf, as we see from the following chain of logic:

- If there was NO FALL, then there's NO SIN.

- If there's NO SIN, then there's NO NEED of a Savior from Sin.

- Therefore, Christ died in vain.

So this teaching robs Christ of His divine role as Redeemer. His sacrifice redeems the fallen members of God's family—and there can be redemption only of that which was once possessed but forfeited. Man is not an upward-evolving animal but a lost sinner condemned to death. Christ gave His life to save a fallen man, NOT a noble beast!

Many who haven't really studied the subject feel they can believe in evolution and still believe all of the Bible except a small part at the beginning of Genesis. But God's great act of Creation is too pervasive a subject to be confined to Chapter One of Genesis or even limited to the Old Testament. Its spiritual implications are so broad and far-reaching that Jesus plainly said: "If ye believe not HIS [Moses'] writings, how shall ye believe MY words?" [33]

Evolution of ANY kind rejects the Bible account of how God directly created man. And Satan knows it's impossible to dismiss the Genesis record of Creation by calling it a "myth" or "allegory" without simultaneously undermining our faith in the rest of the Bible.

A theistic evolutionist must fight not only against facts of science which nullify evolutionary theory but also against texts of Scripture which reveal how God created the world. As Thomas F. Heinze put it, "He is following a religion which he himself has made up." [34]

On the other hand, there's no conflict, no contradiction between God's book of nature and His written Word, for the Author of nature is the Author of the Bible. Creation and Christianity have one God.

REASON #8:

IT USES DEISM TO ROB GOD OF HIS ROLE AS SUSTAINER

Theistic evolution is only a step away from the unorthodox religious concept of deism, which teaches that God—like an ABSENTEE LANDLORD—originally created Planet Earth and its primitive life forms, then concerned Himself with other business. He may occasionally stop by to see how things are going, but most of the time He lets things manage themselves in the same way we wind up a clock and leave it to run itself. In the mechanistic view of deism, our Creator is a very IMPERSONAL God. Theistic evolution, too, implies that God has little or no regular contact with the earth and mankind.

But God is NOT "an absentee landlord" as some suggest. In fact, the Bible teaches that He's "not far from every one of us: For in Him we live, and move, and have our being." [35] It's only due to God's sustaining power that we live day by day and moment by moment: "He giveth to all life, and breath, and all things." [36] Every pulsing beat of the heart is an evidence of God's loving care.

Deism and theistic evolution would have us believe that God created the universe but then went off and left it to evolve by itself. In contrast, the Bible teaches that God upholds and sustains every part of His creation. The pen of Inspiration writes of God's dear Son "upholding all things by the word of His power." [37] "Thou has MADE heaven, the heaven of heavens, with all their host, the earth, and all things that are therein, the seas, and all that is therein, and Thou PRESERVEST them all." [38] Here the prophet is saying that God is both the CREATOR and SUSTAINER, the MAKER and MAINTAINER of all things.

For instance, one fascinating phenomenon is seen in the basic building block of matter, the atom. Tiny as it is, the atom is made up of still tinier sub-atomic particles: electrons, protons, and neutrons. Electrons have a negative charge, protons have a positive charge, and neutrons are neutral, having no charge. The central core or nucleus of the atom is made up of a cluster of protons [39] and neutrons around which electrons orbit, just as planets orbit around the sun—except that electrons revolve around the nucleus billions of times every millionth of a second!

Scientists know that opposites attract, so the opposite charges of positive protons and negative electrons keep the orbiting electrons from flying off into space—just as the gravitational pull between the earth and moon keeps the moon anchored in its earth-centered orbit. But LIKE charges repel, so two positive or two negative charges are strongly repulsive to each other. Now here's the really REMARKABLE thing: inside an atom's tightly-packed nucleus are protons which all carry the SAME positive charge, yet snugly cohere together rather than being powerfully repelled![40] Who can explain this mystery revealed inside the atom? Who reversed the law of electrical charges within the nucleus, so that positive charges attract positive charges among the protons?--

Paul, inspired by the Holy Spirit, declares of Christ that "all things were created by Him, and for Him: and He is before all things, and by Him all things consist."[41] That word *consist* means all things "cohere, are held together," as the Amplified Bible puts it. Other modern versions like the Revised Standard Version, the New Revised Standard Version, the New English Bible, the Living Bible, the New American Standard Bible, and the New International Version make clear that Jesus "holds everything together" as the Sustainer or "upholding principle"[42] of the universe. The hand that holds the atom's nucleus together, the hand that holds the worlds in space, is the hand that was nailed to the cross for us!

CONCLUSION

Those who wish to compromise God's vital role in Creation must face the fact that the first chapter of Genesis mentions the name of "God" 31 times—count 'em, 31! That's a LOT for one single chapter—mentioning God in every verse, on the average, to emphasize His active involvement in each step of Creation. Yet some people still close their eyes to the facts.

The divine Record is so plain, there's no excuse for wrong conclusions. "God said, 'Let Us make man in Our image, according to Our likeness. . . . So GOD CREATED MAN in His own image; . . . male and female He created them."[43] There's no ground here to suppose that man evolved by slow degrees from lower forms of life. Man is a child of God, our heavenly Father—not an orphan of the apes!

The Bible cannot be simply a "good book." It cannot be a good book if it's a book of lies. Either it's true—or it's not. Either it's the inspired Word of the living God—as it claims to be—or it's not. One or the other.

Man's hope and destiny are determined by the quality of his faith. Can we as Christians safely accept any theory which undermines our faith in the Bible? Can we accept a teaching which makes God out to be a liar? Can we afford to accept the confused theories of evolution—theistic or otherwise? If we're willing to admit into our thinking the existence of a Creator God, why should we want to limit His power and explain away the plain statements of His Word?

As intelligent Christians, we'll neither ignore science nor try to explain away Genesis. Those who reject the Genesis account may not realize that by so doing they reject Christianity. For evolution and Christianity are incompatible and irreconcilable. If evolution is true, then the whole fabric of Christian faith is a mass of error. Theistic evolution is a man-made compromise theory forever opposed to the Bible.

Notes to Chapter 5

1. See Chapter 1, above, for an analysis of atheism, agnosticism, and belief in God.
2. *New Catholic Encyclopedia* (1967 edition), Volume 4, p. 428, article "Creation of Man."
3. "Vatican Thinking Evolves," *Time Magazine* (November 4, 1996), p. 85. See also syndicated columnist Cal Thomas, "The Misguided Evolution of the Pope," *Los Angeles Times* (October 29, 1996), p. B7. Then under the headline that a Catholic "Bishop Offers Another View of Adam and Eve," the Associated Press reported: "Adam and Eve may have been created in 'some other form' than human and it is possible that the first living creature was a 'lower animal,' [New York] Cardinal John O'Connor has told worshipers at St. Patrick's Cathedral."—*Los Angeles Times* (November 30, 1996), p. B5.
4. Louis Berkhof, *Systematic Theology* (Grand Rapids, Michigan: Eerdmans, 1941), p. 163.
5. "The Sin of Everyman," *Time* Magazine (March 21, 1969), p. 67.
6. Matthew 5:5.
7. Matthew 5:39.
8. Friedrich Nietzsche, *Complete Works of Nietzsche*, edited by Oscar Levy (6th edition, 1930), Volume II, p. 75.
9. See Matthew 7:12 and Luke 6:31.
10. Please see pages 372-373, below, for the section showing *"Christ Is the Creator."*
11. Ecclesiastes 7:29.
12. 1 Corinthians 15:45; 11:8, RSV; and 1 Timothy 2:13, RSV.
13. 2 Corinthians 4:6.
14. Jude 14.
15. Luke 3:38, Phillips Translation.
16. James 3:9, NASB.
17. 1 Peter 3:20, The Living Bible. Other support for the Biblical historicity of the Flood is found in 2 Peter 2:5 and 3:3-7.
18. Revelation 12:9, NKJV.
19. Revelation 22:3.
20. Matthew 19:4, NKJV.
21. Matthew 24:38, NKJV. And Hebrews 11:7, NASB reads: "By faith Noah, being warned by God about things not yet seen, in reverence prepared an ark for the salvation of his household."
22. Genesis 2:20.
23. Donald John, "The Creation Story," *INSIGHT* Magazine (October 11, 1977), p. 21.
24. Lord Tennyson, *Idylls of the King: The Passing of Arthur*, lines 14-15.
25. Francis D. Nichol, *God and Evolution* (Washington, D.C.: Review and Herald Publishing Association, 1965), p. 56.
26. Leonard Brand, "Faith and the Flood," *Ministry* Magazine (February 1980), p. 80.

27. Louis Agassiz, *Methods of Study in Natural History* (Boston: © 1863; reprinted in New York: Arno Press, 1970), p. iv.
28. Hebrews 4:3.
29. Colossians 1:16.
30. Genesis 2:1-2.
31. Genesis 1:31. See also Dr. Gary Parker, "From Evolution to Creation: A Personal Testimony," *ICR Impact Series* (San Diego: Institute for Creation Research) No. 49, July 1977, p. ii.
32. The Apostle Paul obviously accepted it as literal history, writing under inspiration that "the serpent deceived Eve through his craftiness." 2 Corinthians 11:3, NKJV.
33. John 5:47. God's inspired penman for the Creation account in the Book of Genesis was Moses.
34. Thomas F. Heinze, *The Creation vs. Evolution Handbook* (Grand Rapids, Michigan: Baker Book House, 1970), p. 51.
35. Acts 17:27-28.
36. Acts 17:25.
37. Hebrews 1:1-3.
38. Nehemiah 9:6.
39. All atoms have MULTIPLE protons in their nucleus—except hydrogen, the lightest element, which has only one. Helium has *two,* oxygen has *eight,* iron has *twenty-six,* on up to uranium which has *ninety-two.* This is what gives each element its "atomic number" or atomic weight.
40. This miraculous phenomenon is all the more remarkable when we realize that we're talking about absolutely ENORMOUS repulsive forces which are incomparably stronger than gravity or ordinary electromagnetic attraction. So powerful is this force that scientists had to devise a new name for it: atomic physicists officially call it "the STRONG nuclear force."
41. Colossians 1:16-17.
42. Phillips translation of Colossians 1:17.
43. Genesis 1:26-27, NKJV.

✦　✦　✦

CHAPTER SIX

~

How Long Were
The Days of Creation?

A WIDESPREAD TEACHING TODAY holds that each day of Creation Week wasn't a twenty-four-hour day but a long period of time, perhaps millions of years long, covering vast geologic ages.

This "day-age theory" is taught by many who profess to believe the Bible, for they feel it solves one of the many problems faced by advocates of theistic evolution.[1] But the Bible resoundingly refutes the day-age concept. Let's look at the evidence drawn not only from God's Word but also from language, science, and logic—evidence that clearly shows why we cannot accept this theory.

CLUE #1
EACH DAY WAS A PERIOD OF DARKNESS & LIGHT

When the Lord declares He made the world in six days and rested on the seventh, He makes it plain He means a day of twenty-four hours, for He says, "the evening and the morning were the first day . . . the evening and the morning were the second day . . . the evening and the morning were the third day," and so on.[2] No other language could have made God's thought more explicit than these words. No other terms in the Hebrew language express the idea of literal days more forcefully than the words here employed. The literal rendering of the Hebrew is, "There was evening, there was morning, day one"; "There was evening, there was morning, day two," and so on.

Thus the designation of days in Creation Week conforms exactly with the method of recording time throughout the Bible, for God taught His people that each day begins with sunset and ends with the following sunset.[3] To describe each of the six days as an evening and a morning certainly gives evidence that these were days just like all others that followed since the dawn of history. As Ralph Waldo Emerson observed: "God had infinite time to give us; but how did He give it? In one immense tract of lazy millenniums? No, He cut it up into a neat succession of new mornings." A complete day of twenty-four hours is composed of a period of darkness and a period of light. Such were the original days of creation, and such are the days of earth now— darkness and light, darkness and light, as the earth spins on its axis. God leaves no room for philosophic speculation here: "the evening and the morning" are still the component parts of each earthly day.

CLUE #2
HOW DID THE SEVEN-DAY WEEK ORIGINATE?

The seven-day week, an institution as old as history, has no basis in the world of nature. Every other period of time or grouping of days is marked by some movement of the heavenly bodies:

- The twenty-four-hour DAY is determined by the rotation of the earth on its axis.

- The MONTH is marked off by the revolution of the moon around the earth.

- The three-hundred-sixty-five-day YEAR is measured by the time it takes the earth to complete one circuit of the sun.

But from WHAT comes the seven-day WEEK? Nothing in nature accounts for it. God Himself measured off the first week as a sample for all successive weeks to the close of time. Like every other week, it consists of seven literal days.

As the *Encyclopedia Britannica* states in its article "Calendar": "WEEK NOT ASTRONOMICAL. — The week is a period of seven days, having no reference whatever to the celestial motions, a circumstance to which it owes its unalterable uniformity. . . . It has been employed from time immemorial in almost all Eastern countries; and as it forms neither an aliquot [evenly divisible] part of the year nor of the lunar month, those who reject the Mosaic recital will be at a loss to assign to it an origin having much semblance of probability." [4]

So you see, the week, composed of seven days, is itself another proof that the days of creation were seven literal days as we have them now. It owes its origin to the creation of the world in six literal days and the Creator's rest on the seventh. If not, how did the week ever get started? How is that in virtually every land the week of seven days is known and recognized? The universal recognition of the week from earliest times fits perfectly with the Bible record but does NOT fit any long series of so-called geologic ages.

CLUE #3
GOD'S SABBATH COMMAND IMPLIES 24-HOUR DAYS

In the heart of the Ten Commandments is God's command to keep holy the seventh day. But the wording of the Fourth Commandment can be harmonized with the demands of logic only when the days of Creation Week are considered as solar days, for the Lord asks US to work six days and rest on the seventh day, because HE made the earth in six days and rested on the seventh. [5] This Commandment shows that the six creation days were the same kind He allocates for our affairs each week. And remember, this parallel between the events of Creation and our present week was set up not by theologians or other well-intentioned persons but by God Himself.

The reason God gives for this command—pointing back to His own example of working and then resting during Creation Week—appears beautiful and forceful when we understand the days of Creation to be literal. But the unwarranted assumption that the events of the first week required thousands or millions of years strikes directly at the foundation of the Fourth Commandment and makes it something less than the reasonable requirement of a reasonable God! It represents the Creator as commanding men to observe literal days to commemorate vast, indefinite periods. It makes obscure what God has made very plain. It also implies God is a liar. The first six days of each week are given to man for labor, because God employed the same period of the first week in His great work of Creation; on the seventh day man is to refrain from labor, to commemorate the Creator's rest.

CLUE #4
THE FIRST SABBATH WAS NOT A GEOLOGIC PERIOD

The duration of the seventh day of Creation Week is determined by the length of the other six. If we assume that those days were long geologic periods, then, to be consistent, we must likewise assume that the Creator's day of rest was also a period of a million years. But in that case God is still resting, because Bible chronology indicates that only about six thousand years have elapsed since the creation of Adam. And if God is still in His seventh day, and resting, then it's difficult to explain Jesus' statement: "My Father is working still, and I am working." [6] Christians know that God has been very active in human affairs in providing for man's salvation.

Another dilemma for those who wish to believe in evolution without giving up faith in the Bible is this: Adam, according to the Bible, did not die till long after the first Sabbath. But if that Sabbath is not yet ended, what about Adam? No one claims that he is still living! Furthermore, God blessed the seventh day *because* that in it He HAD rested from all His work." [7] How could He bless the day after He had rested on it, if that day were millions of years long and has not yet ended? These facts are just a few more of many that refute the day-age theory.

Clue #5
The Age of Adam Poses a Problem

How anyone who accepts the Bible record as true history could think of the days of Creation as long, indefinite periods, millions of years in length, is hard to understand. For the Bible declares that Adam was created on the sixth day. [8] Thus the first two days of his life were two of the original seven days—but if we believe the day-age theory, they were millions of years in length! Even if Adam died as early as the first day of the second week, he still would have lived through one entire "period" and parts of two others. How old would that have made him, according to the theory? Well, a modest estimate would require several million years! But Genesis 5:5 states that Adam lived 930 years and died. So the day-age theory contradicts the Bible and leaves no way to compute the age of Adam. Men may choose to believe one or the other of these accounts. But there's no way to harmonize them.

Clue #6
Would God Call Sin "Very Good"?

Suppose someone wanted to accept the Biblically-stated age of Adam as literal but still hold the day-age theory for Creation Week in general. Adam was created on the sixth day and lived 930 years. Long before those years were finished he had sinned, been driven from Eden, and in his sinful state reared a family. According to the supposition stated above, Adam must have lived his whole life—and sinned—within the span of that sixth "day," for 930 years is but a small part of a period measured in millions of years.

Now here's the point: when God finished His great work of those six days, we're told, "God saw every thing that He had made, and, behold, it was VERY GOOD." [9] But if Adam had already sinned, had already succumbed to the devil's temptations, would God say that "every thing . . . was very good"? No! Adam fell into sin later. And when God rested on the seventh day and looked back over Creation Week, He blessed that day as a fitting climax to a perfect work. Therefore, no sin had yet entered to mar the earth.

Clue #7

Hebrew Language Scholars Reject the Theory

We've already considered some of the BIBLICAL evidence against the assumptions made by the day-age theory. Now let's look at a few LINGUISTIC points. Actually, the idea that the Hebrew word *yom* ("day"—as in *Yom Kippur*, the Jewish "Day of Atonement") means a period of time longer than twenty-four hours finds no support in reputable Hebrew dictionaries, such as the following:

- Frants Buhl – *Gesenius' Handwoerterbuch ueher das alte Testament*
- Brown, Driver, & Briggs – *A Hebrew and English* Lexicon of the Old Testament
- Eduard Koenig – *Woerterbuch zum Alten Testament*

Hebrew dictionaries are our primary source of reliable information concerning Hebrew words, but these standard sources know nothing of the notion that *yom* means an indefinite period millions of years long.

And Bible commentators decidedly state that *yom* when used to refer to one of the periods of creation can only mean a 24-hour day. For instance, John Skinner remarks in his *International Critical Commentary (Genesis)*: "The interpretation of *yom* as *aeon*, a favorite resource of harmonists of science and revelation, is opposed to the plain sense of the passage and has no warrant in Hebrew usage."[10]

Clue #8

YOM with a Definite Numeral ALWAYS Means 24 Hours

The book of Genesis was written by Moses, and of course Moses did not write in English. In fact, he didn't use the word *day* at all, but employed instead the Hebrew word *yom*. This word *yom* is found 1,480 times in the Scriptures. On rare occasions it's translated by some term other than "day," but in the overwhelming number of cases its usual translated meaning is "day." Note that Genesis 1:5 uses *yom* in two different senses: "Day" (*yom*) when used with "night" (*layelah*) refers to the light part of the day, roughly twelve hours; and when the Bible says that "the first *day*" is ended, the same word (*yom*) is also used to mean a twenty-four-hour period.

Now some skeptical friend may say, "Well, since the Hebrew word *yom* doesn't always mean the same specific period, you can't be certain that *yom* in the first chapter of Genesis means a twenty-four-hour day." But there are two reasons why we can be certain.

First of all, when the Hebrew word *yom* means anything but a solar day, it's stated or plainly implied in the context. For example, Genesis 4:3 states:

"And *in process of time* it came to pass, that Cain brought of the fruit of the ground an offering unto the Lord." This is clearly an indefinite period of time. Any intelligent child reading this would so understand it, for the context makes it clear. It doesn't mean an age, an eon, an era of a hundred or a million years. It means not a specific 24-hour day, but an indefinite period after which Cain brought his offering to the Lord. This shows how the context makes it plain that here *yom* doesn't refer to a solar day of 24 hours.

Secondly, note the following fact: In Hebrew manuscripts, in every instance where *yom* is accompanied by a definite NUMERAL, it means a solar day of twenty-four hours. Without fail we have *the second yom* of the feast, *the third yom* of the journey, *the seventh yom* of the week, *the fifteenth yom* of the month, and so on—all meaning regular *days!* There's not one single exception to this rule in the whole Bible. If we apply this fact to the days of Creation Week, we note that a definite number is used with each of these periods from one to seven. This leaves only one valid conclusion: those days were 24-hour days, and the translators were correct in their English wording.

CLUE #9
SOUND INTERPRETATION DEMANDS THE MOST OBVIOUS MEANING

One basic principle of Biblical interpretation is that students of Scripture should stick to the original and literal meaning of a word unless there's a compelling reason for adopting a derived or figurative meaning. And the whole Creation account is written as simple narrative—there's nothing in the Record to suggest that the words should not be understood in their ordinary meanings.

A good question is: If it REALLY took five billion years for God to make all things, WHY did He TELL us it took only six days? There's every reason to believe that Moses, the inspired penman of Genesis, understood those days to mean (and intended his readers to understand them to mean) literal days. He certainly gave no hint of anything like the ideas suggested by evolutionists.

Since the Scripture Record contains no suggestion that the days of Creation were anything but literal, 24-hour days, the burden of proof is definitely on those who try to twist the simple, clearly-worded Genesis account to mean long ages of time!

CLUE #10
GOD DIFFERENTIATED BETWEEN DAYS & YEARS

How can one seriously maintain that the days of creation were long geological ages lasting millions of years, when the Bible makes clear that God knows the difference between days and years? In Genesis 1:14 we read: "And God said, Let there be lights in the firmament of the heaven to divide the day from the night; and let them be for signs, and for seasons, and for DAYS, and YEARS." With this distinction set forth in the very Bible chapter under consideration, aren't those who contend that *seven days* means *countless years* taking undue liberties with God's Word?

Furthermore, a quick comparison of Genesis 7:11 & 24 with Genesis 8:3 & 4 shows that a record was kept of the years, months, and days in Noah's time. Each month was composed of 30 days, and the Flood lasted 150 days or five months exactly. So the Bible states that the Flood began on the seventeenth day of the second month and ended on the seventeenth day of the seventh month. The record is precise and definite, and it shows that Genesis clearly differentiates among these units of time. If God had MEANT years rather than days, He would have SAID years—for He certainly knew the difference!

CLUE #11

INSTANTANEOUS ACCOMPLISHMENT IS IMPLIED

Another linguistic point is this—the very wording of the Scripture narrative indicates a short time involved, a fact diametrically opposed to the evolutionary theory. To illustrate, in Genesis 1:3 we read that God said, "Let there be light," or, as it is in the Hebrew, *Ye-hi-or* —"Let light be!" Then follow the words, *Wa-ye-hi-or* — "And light was." The response was instantaneous. When God spoke, it was so—light existed. He didn't have to wait a million years for it to appear.

When succeeding verses record the creative words of God, in every case— without exception—the thing created was instantly there in its perfection. Other portions of Scripture bear the same consistent testimony. For instance, in Psalm 33:6 & 9 we read: "By the word of the Lord were the heavens made; and all the host of them by the breath of His mouth. . . . For He spake, and it was done; He commanded, and it stood fast." Nothing in Scripture indicates that eons or long periods of time were involved. The phraseology indicates instantaneous action.

God's NEW creation will also be instantaneous, just like the FIRST Creation. When Jesus returns, we'll be changed to immortality "in a moment, in the twinkling of an eye." [11] No eons of time will be required to transform these old bodies into glorious new ones!

✦　✦　✦

CLUE #12

LONG PERIODS WERE NOT NEEDED BY THE CREATOR

Aside from the clear wording of the inspired Book denoting instantaneous accomplishment, it's obvious that, if we accept God Almighty as the Creator at all, we need not insist on long, indefinite periods for the accomplishment of His creative work. If we accept the Scripture that tells us "He spake, and it was done," [12] we needn't pretend that God had to do a lot of speaking over ages of time.

After all, if God is able to perform His colossal miracle of Creation in 500 million years, common-sense logic tells us He can do it in one year, one day, one second! God didn't need to take even six days to create the world, but He chose to do so—six literal days according to the Bible record, and on the seventh day He rested.

CLUE #13

IDENTICAL PHRASES SUGGEST UNIFORM TIME PERIODS

Some proponents of the day-age theory make much of the fact that the sun and moon weren't spoken into existence till the fourth day of Creation Week, so they say no one can tell just how long the preceding "days" were. But remember, on the very first day of creation LIGHT had shone out of darkness. We're not told the source of this light at the beginning, except that God provided it—and in God's manifestation to His people, light has always symbolized His presence.[13] When this light appeared, the succession of night and day began, for the Bible speaks of "the evening and the morning" of even those first three days.

On the fourth day "God made two great lights; the greater light to rule the day, and the lesser light to rule the night." [14] Not only are the words *day* and *night* obviously used here as we use them today, but note also the IDENTICAL statement: "And the *evening* and the *morning* were the fourth day." [15] Hence the question that day-age theorists must answer is: IF on the fourth day and onward "the evening and the morning" means ordinary days measured by sun and moon, WHY should the identical phrase used earlier in the same narrative by the same writer mean something entirely different?

CLUE #14

CONSIDER PLANTS AND THE DARK PERIOD OF EACH DAY

We've already considered some BIBLICAL arguments and LINGUISTIC evidence against the day-age theory. Now let's turn to the field of SCIENCE.

On the third day of Creation Week, God created all plant life, and on the fourth day He made the sun to shine upon the earth. Now just suppose those two days were periods of 100 million years each. How long would the dark part of each day have been? Why, 50 million years, of course. And this alternation of light and darkness took place during each of the six days. Can you imagine shrubs and flowers, grass and trees growing for 50 million years in utter DARKNESS? If they did, we're confronted with a more amazing miracle than Genesis was thought to contain—the plant kingdom flourishing for long ages without sunlight!

Aside from the fact that plants need LIGHT to survive and grow, think of the terrible COLD that would settle down on the earth in a month of total darkness. Temperatures fluctuate considerably even in a 12-hour period. That's why the weatherman predicts: "Low tonight, 64. High tomorrow, 82." Gradually the frozen death of the South Pole would creep over the earth, at last approaching even the terrible cold of outer space—50 million years of infernal darkness and unbroken frost, with coldness penetrating thousands of feet into the earth! All life would vanish long before the first ten years had passed—not to mention the first thousand, or hundred thousand, or million years of the 50-million years of darkness.

CLUE #15
CONSIDER **PLANTS** AND THE **LIGHT** PERIOD OF EACH DAY

Then would follow 50 million years of blazing, unceasing sunlight, with the heat rising up to unheard-of levels.[16] Plants would dry up and wither from the scorching rays of the sun. And what we've said here about PLANTS freezing to death or burning to a crisp applies just as well to ANIMAL life on the fifth, sixth, and seventh days of Creation Week if "the evening and the morning" were as long as the time demanded by day-age theorists. In any case, animal life depends on plants for its existence. How could any life—vegetable, animal, or human—exist under such conditions? It couldn't, of course. And these facts forever disprove the theory that the days of Creation were long periods of time.

CLUE #16
PLANTS **DEPEND** UPON THE **ANIMAL** KINGDOM

In our ecological system, animals depend on vegetable life for nutrition and also for the oxygen released by plants during photosynthesis. But the converse is also true: Many plants are dependent on the animal kingdom. The Bible says that plants, including flowering kinds, were created on the

THIRD day, but no animal life was formed until the FIFTH and SIXTH days. Now, the *interdependence* of plants and animals is a very conspicuous fact in the world of living things. In the matter of pollination alone, multitudes of plants could not carry on from generation to generation without insects. For example, bees are so important as insect pollinators that the National Geographic Society estimates their agricultural value—aside from honey and wax production—at hundreds of millions of dollars each year.

And entomologist Ronald Ribbands states in *Scientific American* Magazine: "When we think of bees, we are apt to associate them first with honey and secondly, perhaps, with their sting. Actually it would be more appropriate to think of them first of all as the great pollinators, without whom many of the plants upon which mankind depends would DISAPPEAR from the earth." [17]

Yet the divine Record states that seed-bearing plants flourished from the very start. [18] This would have been impossible if insects didn't appear till millions of years later, as would be the case if the days were geologic periods.

Clue #17
Earth Was Created "To Be INHABITED"

Isaiah 45:18 tells us that God created the earth "not in vain," but "He formed it to be inhabited." Would God's purpose have been realized if the earth were UNinhabited by any higher beings for millions upon millions of years? "To be inhabited" cannot mean by ANIMALS, because a land in which "the beasts of the field multiply" unchecked is said to be "desolate" according to Exodus 23:29. Thus construing a "day" as untold ages rather than as twenty-four hours means the earth must be considered as created "in vain" during those supposed eons when earth was an uninhabited wasteland—for man, the crowning achievement of Creation, was formed only at the end of God's wonderful work.

Clue #18
Day-Age Theory FAILS to Close Bible-Evolution GAP

Besides all the preceding arguments against the day-age theory, it's clear that interpreting *yom* as a long period of time still fails to bring about the harmony between evolution and the Bible which is so much sought by theistic evolutionists. For geology does not teach the evolution of the world in SIX geologic periods. In the geologic time scale, three or four ERAS are divided into at least eleven PERIODS, some of which in turn are subdivided into several EPOCHS.

Furthermore, the ORDER of events in Genesis does not conform to those of the evolutionary scheme. So merely conceiving the six days of Creation as long periods fails to harmonize Genesis with evolutionary geology—the two systems lack important basic parallels.[19]

CLUE #19

2 PETER 3:8 DOES NOT SUPPORT DAY-AGE THEORY

Supporters of the day-age theory usually are content merely to assert its validity without offering much in the way of Scripture texts or other evidence as proof. However, one text they're fond of citing is 2 Peter 3:8 — "One day is with the Lord AS a thousand years, and a thousand years AS one day." In considering this text, THREE THINGS must be borne in mind.

First of all, Peter is not literally equating one day and a thousand years. The text is clearly figurative, employing a figure of speech known as a SIMILE and using the word AS—the way we might say, "His heart's as big as all outdoors." A similar text is Psalm 90:4, which says: "A thousand years in Thy sight are but *as* yesterday when it is past, and *as* a watch in the night." Now are we to understand that "yesterday" and "a thousand years" are actually and literally the same? Of course not! The Psalmist here is simply using a figure of speech. Taking literally a statement intended to be figurative does violence to the meaning.

Secondly, the main point Peter is trying to make here is simply this: Time means nothing to the ETERNAL God. As "the high and lofty One that inhabiteth eternity,"[20] God does not wear a wristwatch—He's not on the same time-frame as we are. "The eternal God,"[21] "the everlasting Father,"[22] is above and beyond the passage of time, and the Bible repeatedly asserts this fact. In the verse under question, Peter is explaining NOT the duration of a DAY but the timelessness of GOD.

Thirdly, let's ask: In what setting or context was this verse written? We must be careful not to take verses out of context,[23] lest we be among those who twist the Scriptures "unto their own destruction" as Peter himself puts it in the same chapter.[24] Look at the verses before and after the text in question, and you'll understand Peter's purpose in writing this verse. In this chapter Peter is discussing Christ's Second Coming, and in verses 3 and 4 he specifically replies to "scoffers" who walk after their own lusts, saying, "Where is the promise of His coming?" In the verse under consideration Peter answers these impatient scoffers by reminding them that God is untouched by time, yet he adds: "The Lord is not slack concerning His promise, as some count slackness, but is longsuffering toward us, not willing that any should perish but that all should come to repentance. But the day of the Lord will come as a thief in the night." [25] In other words, Peter's purpose in this passage is simply to show that we should be patient in waiting for the Lord's return, for time means nothing to our eternal God, and if Christ seems to be delaying His coming it's only out of mercy for those who have not yet "come to repentance."

These three reasons effectively refute the claims of those who use this verse for much-needed proof of the day-age theory.

CONCLUSION

Some would have us believe that the "days" of Creation were vast geological ages. Others contend that they were literal 24-hour periods, the same as days today. Obviously, both views can't be right. Yet Christians need not prove that the days of Creation were 24 hours long—that's already established by the fact that we HAVE 24-hour days! The burden of proof really rests on those who contend that those "days" were long ages. To them I say, "Since all days we know about have always been 24 hours [26] long, you must prove to ME that the days of Creation were DIFFERENT."

We've looked at this question from several points of view:

Biblically,
    linguistically,
        scientifically,
            and logically.

The nineteen clues we've considered provide REASONS why we can safely conclude the days of Creation were not indefinite periods eons long but regular, literal days of 24 hours' duration. In contrast to these sound reasons which strengthen our faith in God's Word, the arguments used by day-age theorists are nothing but speculation which careful scrutiny proves false. [27]

❧

Notes to Chapter 6

1. The preceding chapter discusses the compromise theory called "theistic evolution."
2. See Genesis 1, verses 5, 8, 13, 19, 23, and 31.
3. See Leviticus 23:32 and Deuteronomy 16:6.
4. *Encyclopedia Britannica* (11th edition), Volume 4, p. 988, article "Calendar."
5. Exodus 20:8-11.
6. John 5:17, RSV.
7. Genesis 2:3.
8. Genesis 1:26-31.
9. Genesis 1:31.
10. John Skinner, *International Critical Commentary* , Volume 1, p. 21, on *Genesis.*
11. 1 Corinthians 15:52.
12. Psalm 33:9.
13. Critics of the Bible sometimes say, "Moses made a mistake when he wrote that God said, 'Let there be light' on the FIRST day—then he turned around and wrote that God didn't create the sun till the FOURTH day! That's a direct contradiction." But almighty God is NOT dependent on the sun for light. The supposed "problem" on the Bible's first page disappears when we look at its last page, which speaks of the NEW creation of God: "And the city had no need of the sun, neither of the moon, to shine in it: for the glory of God did lighten it, and the Lamb [Jesus] is the light thereof. . . . And there shall be no night there; and they need no . . . light of the sun; for the Lord God giveth them light." Revelation 21:23 and 22:5.
14. Genesis 1:16.
15. Genesis 1:19.
16. To illustrate this with an example from the real world, consider the MOON, which rotates almost 30 times more slowly than the earth, making its days that much longer than ours. Thermal variations on the moon are consequently much greater, with the difference in temperature between the lunar night (dark side) and lunar day (bright side) being about $450°$ Fahrenheit.
17. Ronald Ribbands, "The Honeybee," *Scientific American* (August 1955), p. 52.
18. Genesis 1:11-12.
19. Over a dozen discrepancies and contradictions have been pointed out in many books. See, for example, the brief tabulation in *The Young Earth* by John D. Morris (Green Forest, Ark.: Master Books, 1994), p. 33.
20. Isaiah 57:15.
21. Deuteronomy 33:27.
22. Isaiah 9:6.
23. It's been well said that "A text without a CONtext is a PREtext!"
24. 2 Peter 3:16.
25. 2 Peter 3:9-10.
26. Each day is 23 hours, 56 minutes, 4.09 seconds, to be exact.
27. The reader is directed to *Appendix B* at the back of this volume for some thoughts on the harmony between "Science and the Scriptures." ✦ ✦ ✦

SOMEONE HAS SAID THAT
THE WORD **BIBLE**

IS AN *ACRONYM*.
IT STANDS FOR:

B - BASIC
I - INSTRUCTION
B - BEFORE
L - LEAVING
E - EARTH

MYSTERY #3
The DEITY of CHRIST

Was Jesus Christ divine?
Was the humble Carpenter of Nazareth
really the holy Son of God?
What can we believe about His resurrection?

"How shall we ESCAPE,
if we NEGLECT
so great salvation?"
—HEBREWS 2:3

"We have found Him,
of whom Moses . . . and
the prophets, did write,
Jesus of Nazareth."
—JOHN 1:45

~

CHAPTER SEVEN

JESUS MEETS EVERY TEST

THE GREATEST AMBASSADOR FOR CHRIST the world has ever known was probably the Apostle Paul, who "preached Christ in the synagogues, that He is the Son of God . . . and confounded the Jews who dwelt in Damascus, PROVING that this Jesus is the Christ [that is, the Messiah]." [1]

Thoughtful people today may wonder how Paul was able to PROVE to skeptics the divinity of our Lord. The Book tells us how: "For he mightily convinced the Jews . . . showing by the SCRIPTURES that Jesus was Christ." [2]

Yes, Paul reasoned with men from the sacred pages of God's own Word, giving Scriptural evidence on which to base their beliefs. "Paul, as his custom was, went in to them, and three Sabbaths reasoned with them from the SCRIPTURES . . . [that] 'This Jesus . . . is the Christ.'" [3]

ONLY JESUS FITS ALL THE SPECIFICATIONS

Jesus' life was measured by the great PROPHETIC BLUEPRINT outlined by God in the Scriptures. Men were drawn to Christ as they compared Him with the prophetic statements of the Old Testament. His disciples unhesitatingly announced: "We have found Him, of whom Moses . . . and the prophets, did write, Jesus of Nazareth." [4]

After His resurrection, Jesus reviewed with His doubting disciples the stipulations of the prophetic Word regarding Himself: "Then He said unto them, O fools, and slow of heart to believe all that the prophets have spoken. . . . And beginning at Moses and ALL the prophets, He expounded unto them in ALL the Scriptures the things concerning Himself." [5]

The late Alfred E. Smith, in his 1928 Presidential campaign, was fond of saying, "Let's look at the record." That's exactly what we'll do now: take a candid look at the Bible record to see for ourselves how closely Jesus fits the DIVINE BLUEPRINT. Listed below are dozens of specific promises and prophecies from the Old Testament which pointed forward to Christ, the Messiah. Each is followed by its unique fulfillment as recorded in the New Testament.

> "These are written, that ye might BELIEVE
> that Jesus is the Christ, the Son of God;
> and that believing ye might have LIFE
> through His name." [6]

1. His HUMAN NATURE

Prophetic Forecast:

Genesis 3:15 — After the serpent tempted Eve in the Garden of Eden, the Lord God told Satan: "I will put enmity between thee and the woman, and between thy seed and her Seed [Christ]; it shall bruise thy head, and thou shalt bruise His heel."

Satan did bruise Christ's heel when His feet were nailed to the cross. In calling Jesus the "Seed" of "the WOMAN," God indicated that His Promised One would come as the offspring of a HUMAN BEING, not as an angel or other creature from outer space. This verse, the first of many regarding the Messiah, teaches that while He would be truly God, He'd also be truly MAN.

Isaiah 49:1, RSV — "The Lord called Me from the WOMB, from the body of My MOTHER He named My name."

Historic Fulfillment:

Matthew 24:27, 30, *etc.* — "The Son of man"
1 Timothy 2:5 — "The man Christ Jesus"
1 Timothy 3:16 — "God was manifest in the flesh."
John 1:14 — "The Word was made flesh."
Galatians 4:4 — "God sent forth His Son, made of a woman."

The promised One came NOT as some monstrous alien from outer space—like a "Man from Mars" in science fiction—but as a humble Babe, a human being, the most truly human ever born, on whom we can pattern our lives. To reveal Himself to the creatures He loved, the King of heaven stooped low to take our nature. His divinity was veiled with humanity, the invisible glory in the visible human form.

2. To Be a MALE Child

Prophetic Forecast:

Isaiah 9:6 — "For unto us a Child is born, unto us a Son is given: and the government shall be upon His shoulder: and His name shall be called Wonderful, Counsellor, The Mighty God, The Everlasting Father, The Prince of Peace."

Historic Fulfillment:

Matthew 1:21 — "She [Mary] shall bring forth a Son, and thou shalt call His name JESUS: for He shall save His people from their sins."

John 3:16 — "For God so loved the world, that He gave His only begotten Son, that whosoever believeth in Him should not perish, but have everlasting life."

3. To Be Born a JEW

Prophetic Forecast:

Genesis 22:15 & 18 — "And the angel of the Lord called unto Abraham . . . in thy Seed shall all the nations of the earth be blessed."[7]

The Messiah's race is clearly specified. He was to be born a Jew—not an Egyptian nor a Chinese—for Abraham, "the father of the faithful," was the progenitor of the Jewish people.

Historic Fulfillment:

John 4:9, NKJV — The woman at the well asked Christ, "'How is it that You, being a Jew, ask a drink from me, a Samaritan woman?' For Jews have no dealings with Samaritans."

Matthew 1:1 — "Jesus Christ, the Son of David, the son of Abraham."

Galatians 3:14 & 16, NKJV — "That the blessing of Abraham might come upon the Gentiles in Jesus Christ. . . . Now to Abraham and his Seed were the promises made. He [God] does not say, 'And to seeds,' as of many, but as of One, 'And to your Seed,' who is Christ."

4. From the Lineage of DAVID

Prophetic Forecast:

Isaiah 9:6-7 — "For unto us a Child is born, unto us a Son is given: and the government shall be upon His shoulder: and His name shall be called . . . The Prince of Peace. Of the increase of His government and peace there shall be no end, upon the throne of David."

Jeremiah 23:5-6 — "Behold, the days come, saith the Lord, that I will raise unto David a righteous Branch, and a King shall reign and prosper, and shall execute judgment and justice in the earth. . . . And this is His name whereby He shall be called, The Lord Our Righteousness."

Historic Fulfillment:

Matthew 20:30 — "And, behold, two blind men sitting by the wayside, when they heard that Jesus passed by, cried out, saying, Have mercy on us, O Lord, Thou Son of David." [8]

Acts 13:23, NIV — "From this man's ["David" verse 22] descendants God has brought to Israel the Savior Jesus, as He promised."

Romans 1:3 — "His Son Jesus Christ our Lord . . . was made of the seed of David, according to the flesh."

Revelation 22:16 — "I Jesus . . . am . . . the offspring of David."

The human ancestry of Jesus goes through the line of David, as seen in His genealogy recorded in Scripture. See Matthew 1:6 and Luke 3:31.

5. PLACE OF BIRTH

Prophetic Forecast:

Micah 5:2, NKJV — "But you, BETHLEHEM Ephrathah, though you are LITTLE among the thousands of Judah, yet out of you shall come forth to Me the One to be Ruler in Israel, whose goings forth are from of old, from everlasting. "

Today at Christmas we sing "O Little Town of Bethlehem"—though perhaps we're only dimly aware of the song's full significance. This remarkable prophecy pinpointed the Messiah's birthplace more than seven hundred years before that joyous Event took place!

Historic Fulfillment:

Matthew 2:1 — "Jesus was born in Bethlehem of Judea." [9]

It's thrilling to see how God arranged matters to have Jesus born in Bethlehem even though Joseph and Mary lived in Nazareth! Consider the following Providential happenings:

Luke 2:1-6, 11 — "It came to pass in those days, that there went out a decree from Caesar Augustus, that all the world should be taxed. . . . And all went to be taxed, every one into his own city. And Joseph also went up from Galilee, out of the city of Nazareth, unto the city of David, which is called Bethlehem; (because he was of the house and lineage of David:) To be taxed with Mary his espoused wife, being great with child. And so it was, that, while they were there, the days were accomplished that she should be delivered. . . . For unto you is born this day in the city of David a Saviour, which is Christ the Lord."

Truly, as poet William Cowper put it,

"God moves in a mysterious way, His wonders to perform." [10]

This prediction of the Messiah's birthplace was a very important prophecy known to all of Israel. In fact, some who were reluctant to accept Jesus as the Messiah even used this point against Him because Jesus spent much of His ministry in the northern province of Galilee, and they—ignorant of where He was born—assumed He was a Galilean. Please note John 7:41-42, NRSV: "Others said, 'This is the Messiah.' But some asked, 'Surely the Messiah does not come from *Galilee,* does he? Has not the Scripture said that the Messiah is descended from David and comes from *Bethlehem,* the village where David lived?'"

We should realize also that God in this prophecy really narrowed down the pool of prospects for the Messiah. For Bethlehem was a "little" town, not a huge population center like New York, London, or Tokyo.

6. TIME OF BIRTH

Prophetic Forecast:

Daniel 9:21-26 — The angel Gabriel gave Daniel this important message from heaven: "Know therefore and understand, that from the going forth of the commandment to restore and to build Jerusalem unto the Messiah the prince shall be seven weeks, and threescore and two weeks." [11]

To explain all the ramifications of this time prophecy would be a study in itself, [12] but suffice it to say, it's possible to prove BY MATHEMATICS that Jesus is the Messiah (by counting from the decree to restore and rebuild Jerusalem to His anointing by the Holy Spirit at His baptism). Christ's contemporaries understood this time prophecy and were indeed expecting and looking for the Messiah in His day, even asking John the Baptist if he were the Promised One. [13]

Historic Fulfillment:

Mark 1:15 — When Jesus began His ministry, John the Baptist told the people, "The time is fulfilled, and the kingdom of God is at hand."

Galatians 4:4, NKJV — "When the fullness of the time had come, God sent forth His Son."

7. VIRGIN BIRTH

Prophetic Forecast:

Isaiah 7:14 — "The Lord Himself shall give you a sign; Behold, a VIRGIN shall conceive and bear a Son."

Historic Fulfillment:

Luke 1:26-35, NKJV — "The angel Gabriel was sent by God to a city of Galilee named Nazareth, to a VIRGIN betrothed to a man whose name was Joseph, of the house of David. The virgin's name was Mary. . . . The angel said to her, . . . 'Behold, you will conceive in your womb and bring forth a Son.' . . . Then Mary said to the angel, 'How can this be, since I do not know a man?' And the angel answered and said to her, 'The Holy Spirit will come upon you, and the power of the Highest will overshadow you; therefore, also, that Holy One who is to be born will be called the Son of God.'"

Matthew 1:18-25, NIV — "This is how the birth of Jesus Christ came about: His mother Mary was pledged to be married to Joseph, but BEFORE they came together, she was found to be with child through the Holy Spirit. Because Joseph her husband was a righteous man and did not want to expose her to public disgrace, he had in mind to divorce her quietly. But after he had considered this, an angel of the Lord appeared to him in a dream and said, 'Joseph son of David, do not be afraid to take Mary home as your wife, because what is conceived in her is from the Holy Spirit.' . . . When Joseph woke up, he did what the angel of the Lord had commanded him and took Mary home as his wife. But he had no union with her UNTIL she gave birth to a Son . . . Jesus."[14]

The virgin birth of Christ was something truly unique—a miraculous occurrence! That's why the gospel song says that Jesus came by "Special Delivery, wrapped up in love."

8. Given Royal GIFTS

Prophetic Forecast:

Psalm 72:10, 11, 15 — "The kings of Tarshish and of the isles shall bring PRESENTS: the kings of Sheba and Seba shall offer GIFTS. Yea, all kings shall fall down before Him: all nations shall serve Him. . . . And to Him shall be given of the GOLD of Sheba."

Isaiah 60:3 & 6 — "And the Gentiles shall come to Thy light, and kings to the brightness of Thy rising. . . . The multitude of camels shall cover thee, the dromedaries of Midian and Ephah; all they from Sheba shall come; they shall bring GOLD and INCENSE."

Historic Fulfillment:

Matthew 2:1-2 & 11, NIV — "After Jesus was born in Bethlehem . . . Magi from the east came to Jerusalem and asked, 'Where is the one who has been born King of the Jews? We saw His star in the east and have come to worship Him.' . . . They saw the Child with His mother Mary, and they bowed down and worshipped Him. Then they opened their treasures and presented Him with GIFTS of GOLD and of INCENSE and of MYRRH."

9. FLIGHT into EGYPT

Prophetic Forecast:

Hosea 11:1 — "When Israel was a child, then I loved him, and called My Son out of Egypt." [15]

Historic Fulfillment:

Matthew 2:13-21, NKJV — "Behold, an angel of the Lord appeared to Joseph in a dream, saying, 'Arise, take the young Child and His mother, flee to Egypt, and stay there until I bring you word; for Herod will seek the young Child to destroy Him.' When he arose, he took the young Child and His mother by night and departed for Egypt, and was there until the death of Herod, that it might be fulfilled which was spoken by the Lord through the prophet, saying, 'Out of Egypt I called My Son.' . . . But when Herod was dead, behold, an angel of the Lord appeared in a dream to Joseph in Egypt, saying, 'Arise, take the young Child and His mother, and go to the land of Israel, for those who sought the young Child's life are dead.' "

10. HEROD's SLAUGHTER of CHILDREN

Prophetic Forecast:

Jeremiah 31:15, NIV — "This is what the Lord says: 'A voice is heard in Ramah, mourning and great weeping, RACHEL WEEPING FOR HER CHILDREN and refusing to be comforted, BECAUSE HER CHILDREN ARE NO MORE.' "

Historic Fulfillment:

Matthew 2:1, 7-12, 16-18, NIV — "During the time of King Herod, Magi from the east came to Jerusalem. . . . Then Herod called the Magi secretly . . . and said, 'Go and make a careful search for the Child. As soon as you find Him, report to me, so that I too may go and worship Him.' After they had heard the king, they went on their way, and . . . having been warned in a dream not to go back to Herod, they returned to their country by another route. When Herod realized that he had been outwitted by the Magi, he was furious, and he gave orders to KILL all the boys in Bethlehem and its vicinity who were two years old and under, in accordance with the time he had learned from the Magi. Then what was said through the prophet Jeremiah was FULFILLED: 'A voice is heard in Ramah, weeping and great mourning, Rachel weeping for her children and refusing to be comforted, because they are no more.' "

Revelation 12:1-4 says Satan—as a "dragon," identified in Revelation 12:9—stood ready to devour the Child as soon as He was born. King Herod allowed himself to be used as Satan's tool in this cruel attempt.

11. Heralding **FORERUNNER**

Prophetic Forecast:

Isaiah 40:3, NKJV — "The voice of one crying in the wilderness: 'Prepare the way of the Lord; make straight in the desert a highway for our God.'"

Malachi 3:1 — "Behold, I will send My messenger, and he shall prepare the way before Me . . . saith the Lord of hosts."

Luke 1:17 — Before John the Baptist was born as a miracle baby, the angel Gabriel prophesied to Zacharias, his elderly father, that "he [John the Baptist] shall go before Him [the Messiah] . . . to make ready a people prepared for the Lord."

Historic Fulfillment:

Matthew 3:1-3, NKJV — "In those days John the Baptist came preaching in the wilderness of Judea, and saying, 'Repent, for the kingdom of heaven is at hand!' For this is he who was spoken of by the prophet Isaiah, saying: 'The voice of one crying in the wilderness: "Prepare the way of the Lord; make His paths straight."'"

Matthew 11:10-11, NIV — Jesus Himself said, concerning John the Baptist: "This is the one about whom it is written: 'I will send My messenger ahead of You, who will prepare Your way before You.'"

John 1:19, 22-23, NASB — "This is the witness of John [the Baptist], when the Jews sent to him priests and Levites from Jerusalem to ask him, 'Who are you? . . . What do you say about yourself?' He said, 'I am a voice of one crying in the wilderness, "Make straight the way of the Lord," as Isaiah the prophet said.'"

12. Anointed by the **HOLY SPIRIT**

Prophetic Forecast:

Isaiah 11:1-2 — "There shall come forth a rod out of the stem of Jesse [the father of David], and a Branch shall grow out of his roots: And the Spirit of the Lord shall rest upon Him."

Isaiah 42:1 — "Behold My Servant, whom I uphold; Mine Elect, in whom My soul delighteth; I have put My Spirit upon Him: He shall bring forth judgment to the Gentiles."

Isaiah 61:1-2 — "The Spirit of the Lord God is upon Me; because the Lord hath anointed Me to preach good tidings unto the meek, He hath sent Me to bind up the brokenhearted, to proclaim liberty to the captives, and the opening of the prison to them that are bound; to proclaim the acceptable year of the Lord."

Historic Fulfillment:

Matthew 3:16-17, NKJV — "When He had been baptized, Jesus came up immediately from the water; and behold, the heavens were opened to Him, and He saw the Spirit of God descending like a dove and alighting upon Him. And suddenly a voice came from heaven, saying, 'This is My beloved Son, in whom I am well pleased.'"

Luke 4:14-21 — "And Jesus returned in the power of the Spirit into Galilee: . . . and, as His custom was, He went into the synagogue on the Sabbath day, and stood up for to read. And there was delivered unto Him the book of the prophet Esaias [Isaiah]. And when He had opened the book, He found the place where it was written, The Spirit of the Lord is upon Me, because He hath anointed Me to preach the gospel to the poor; He hath sent Me to heal the brokenhearted, to preach deliverance to the captives, and recovering of sight to the blind, to set at liberty them that are bruised, To preach the acceptable year of the Lord. And He closed the book, and He gave it again to the minister, and sat down. And the eyes of all them that were in the synagogue were fastened on Him. And He began to say unto them, This day is this Scripture FULFILLED in your ears."

Acts 10:38, NKJV — At His baptism, "God anointed Jesus of Nazareth with the Holy Spirit and with power. . . ."

13. To OPEN BLIND EYES

Prophetic Forecast:

Isaiah 42:6-7 — "I the Lord have called Thee . . . for a Light to the Gentiles; to open the blind eyes. . . ."

Historic Fulfillment:

Mark 10:46-52, NKJV — "Blind Bartimaeus . . . sat by the road begging. And when he heard that it was Jesus of Nazareth, he began to cry out and say, 'Jesus, Son of David, have mercy on me!' . . . So Jesus answered and said to him, 'What do you want Me to do for you?' The blind man said to Him, 'Rabboni, that I may receive my sight.' Then Jesus said to him, 'Go your way; your faith has made you well.' And immediately he received his sight and followed Jesus on the road."

Christ's ministry of miracles is so well known that there's danger we might take it for granted. But in John 9:32 we read: "Since the world began was it not heard that any man opened the eyes of one born blind." Read all the ninth chapter of John's Gospel for a dramatic account of Jesus performing that very miracle—among many.

14. REJECTED BY MEN

Prophetic Forecast:

Isaiah 53:3 — "He is despised and rejected of men; a Man of sorrows, and acquainted with grief: and we hid as it were our faces from Him; He was despised, and we esteemed Him not."

Historic Fulfillment:

John 1:10-11 — "He was in the world, and the world was made by Him, and the world knew Him not. He came unto His own, and His own received Him not."

John 7:5 & 48, NASB — "Not even His brothers were believing in Him. . . . No one of the rulers or Pharisees has believed in Him."

These verses show that not only Pharisees and rulers rejected Jesus but even His own "brothers"—members of His own household—refused to believe in Him as the Messiah until after His resurrection.

15. TRIUMPHAL ENTRY

Prophetic Forecast:

Zechariah 9:9, NKJV — "Rejoice greatly, O daughter of Zion! Shout, O daughter of Jerusalem! Behold, your King[16] is coming to you; He is just and having salvation, lowly and riding on a donkey, a colt, the foal of a donkey."

Historic Fulfillment:

Matthew 21:1-9, NKJV — "When they drew near Jerusalem . . . then Jesus sent two disciples, saying to them, 'Go into the village . . . and immediately you will find a DONKEY tied, and a COLT with her. Loose them and bring them to Me. And if anyone says anything to you, you shall say, "The Lord has need of them," and immediately he will send them.' . . . So the disciples went and did as Jesus commanded them. They brought the donkey and the colt, laid their clothes on them, and set Him on them. And a very great multitude spread their clothes on the road; others cut down branches from the [palm] trees and spread them on the road . . . saying: 'Hosanna to the Son of David! Blessed is He who comes in the name of the Lord! Hosanna in the highest!' "[17]

16. BETRAYAL BY A FRIEND

Prophetic Forecast:

Psalm 41:9, NKJV — "Even my own familiar friend in whom I trusted, who ate my bread, has lifted up his heel against me."

Historic Fulfillment:

John 13:18-26, NKJV — "Jesus . . . was troubled in spirit . . . and said, 'Most
assuredly, I say to you, one of you will betray Me.' . . . One of His
disciples . . . said to Him, 'Lord, who is it?' Jesus answered, 'It is he to
whom I shall give a piece of bread when I have dipped it.' And having
dipped the bread, He gave it to Judas Iscariot."

Judas was one of the trusted inner circle—the Twelve who knew Christ best.
As a "familiar friend," he betrayed Jesus with a kiss. [18]

17. THE TRAITOR'S FEE

Prophetic Forecast:

Zechariah 11:12, NKJV — "I said to them, 'If it is agreeable to you, give me
my wages; and if not, refrain.' So they weighed out for my wages thirty
pieces of silver."

Historic Fulfillment:

Matthew 26:14-16, NKJV — "Then one of the twelve, called Judas Iscariot,
went to the chief priests and said, 'What are you willing to give me if I
deliver Him to you?' And they counted out to him thirty pieces of silver.
So from that time he sought opportunity to betray Him."

18. PURCHASE OF POTTER'S FIELD

Prophetic Forecast:

Zechariah 11:13, NKJV — "I took the thirty pieces of silver and threw them
into the house of the Lord for the potter."

Historic Fulfillment:

Matthew 27:3-7, NKJV — "Then Judas, His betrayer, seeing that He had
been condemned, was remorseful and brought back the thirty pieces of
silver to the chief priests and elders, saying, 'I have sinned by betraying
innocent blood.' And they said, 'What is that to us? You see to it!' Then
he threw down the pieces of silver in the temple and departed, and went
and hanged himself. But the chief priests took the silver pieces and said,
'It is not lawful to put them into the treasury, because they are the price
of blood [blood money].' And they consulted together and bought with
them the POTTER'S FIELD, to bury strangers in."

Acts 1:16-19, NKJV — Judas's blood money "purchased a field with the wages
of iniquity. . . . And it became known to all those dwelling in Jerusalem;
so that field is called in their own language, *Akel Dama,* that is, Field of
Blood."

How marvelously specific is Bible prophecy! In the last three prophecies alone, we find the exact fulfillment of the following SEVEN POINTS:

1. Jesus would be **BETRAYED**
2. By a **FRIEND** (not an avowed *enemy*)
3. For **THIRTY** (neither *more* nor *fewer*) pieces
4. Of **SILVER** (not *gold*)
5. Which would be **THROWN DOWN** (not *placed*)
6. In the **HOUSE** of the **LORD** (not *elsewhere*).
7. The **MONEY** would then be used to **BUY** the **POTTER'S FIELD** (not *something else*).[19]

In so vital a matter as Jesus' divinity, we cannot plead ignorance. For God gives us the facts we need to draw intelligent conclusions. We have a multitude of Prophetic Forecasts with corresponding Historical Fulfillments for both Christ AND Antichrist (see Chapter 19, below).

19. FORSAKEN by Disciples

Prophetic Forecast:

Zechariah 13:7. NKJV — "'Awake, O sword, against My Shepherd, against the Man who is My Companion,' says the Lord of hosts. 'Strike the Shepherd, and the sheep will be scattered.'"

Historic Fulfillment:

Matthew 26:31 & 56, NKJV — Jesus said to His disciples: "'All of you will be made to stumble because of Me this night, for it is written: "I will strike the Shepherd, and the sheep of the flock will be scattered.". . . All this was done that the Scriptures of the prophets might be fulfilled.' Then all the disciples forsook Him and fled." [20]

20. Accused by FALSE WITNESSES

Prophetic Forecast:

Psalm 35:11 — "False witnesses did rise up; they laid to My charge things that I knew not."

Psalm 27:12 — "False witnesses are risen up against Me, and such as breathe out cruelty."

Psalm 109:2 — "The mouth of the wicked and the mouth of the deceitful are opened against Me: they have spoken against Me with a lying tongue."

Historic Fulfillment:

Mark 14:55-59, NKJV — "The chief priests and all the council sought testimony against Jesus to put Him to death, but found none. For many bore false witness against Him, but their testimonies did not agree. Then some rose up and bore false witness against Him. . . . But not even then did their testimony agree."

21. SILENT Under Accusation

Prophetic Forecast:

Isaiah 53:7, NKJV — "He was oppressed and He was afflicted, yet He opened not His mouth; He was led as a lamb to the slaughter, and as a sheep before its shearers is silent, so He opened not His mouth."

Historic Fulfillment:

Matthew 26:63 — During His trial, "Jesus held His peace."

Matthew 27:12-14, NKJV — "While He was being accused by the chief priests and elders, He answered nothing. Then Pilate said to Him, 'Do You not hear how many things they testify against You?' But He answered him not one word, so that the governor marveled greatly." [21]

22. BEATEN & SPAT Upon

Prophetic Forecast:

Isaiah 50:6, NIV — "I offered My back to those who beat Me, My cheeks to those who pulled out My beard; I did not hide My face from mocking and spitting."

Isaiah 53:5 — "He was wounded for our transgressions, He was bruised for our iniquities: the chastisement of our peace was upon Him; and with His stripes we are healed."

Historic Fulfillment:

Matthew 26:67, NIV — "They spat in his face and struck Him with their fists. Others slapped Him."

John 19:1, NRSV — "Then Pilate took Jesus and had Him flogged."

Luke 22:63-64, NKJV — "The men who held Jesus mocked Him and beat Him. And having blindfolded Him, they struck Him on the face and asked Him, saying, 'Prophesy! Who is the one who struck You?'" [22]

23. NAILED to a Cross

Prophetic Forecast:

Psalm 22:16 — "They pierced My hands and My feet."

Isaiah 49:16 — "Behold, I have graven thee upon the palms of My hands."

Zechariah 12:10 — "They shall look upon Me whom they have pierced, and they shall mourn for Him." [23]

Zechariah 13:6 — "And one shall say unto Him, What are these wounds in

Thine hands? Then He shall answer, Those with which I was wounded in the house of My friends."

John 3:14 — Jesus said: "As Moses lifted up the serpent in the wilderness, [24] even so must the Son of man be lifted up."

John 8:28, NIV — "Jesus said, 'When you have lifted up the Son of Man, then you will know that I am the one I claim to be.'"

John 12:32 — "And I, if I be lifted up from the earth, will draw all men unto Me. This He said, signifying what death He should die."

When Jesus prophesied, repeatedly, that He would be "lifted up," He was predicting His own crucifixion.

Historic Fulfillment:

Matthew 27:35, Mark 15:25, Luke 23:33, John 19:18 — "They crucified Him." [25]

24. Numbered with TRANSGRESSORS

Prophetic Forecast:

Isaiah 53:12 — "He was numbered with the transgressors."

Historic Fulfillment:

Mark 15:27-28, NKJV — "With Him they also crucified two robbers, one on His right and the other on His left. So the Scripture was fulfilled which says, 'And He was numbered with the transgressors.'" [26]

25. Garments DIVIDED

Prophetic Forecast:

Psalm 22:18 — "They part My garments among them, and cast lots upon My vesture."

Historic Fulfillment:

John 19:23-24 — "Then the soldiers, when they had crucified Jesus, took His garments, and made four parts, to every soldier a part; and also His coat: now the coat was without seam, woven from the top throughout. They said therefore among themselves, Let us not rend it, but cast lots for it, whose it shall be: that the Scripture might be fulfilled, which saith, They parted My raiment among them, and for My vesture they did cast lots. These things therefore the soldiers did."

This twofold prediction was remarkably fulfilled: Heathen soldiers did just as holy Scripture foretold, parting or dividing up some of His garments and casting lots for the other! This proves again that EVERY Old Testament prophecy concerning the Messiah met its EXACT fulfillment in Jesus Christ. You've just read the record of the Apostle John—see also Matthew 27:35, Mark 15:24, and Luke 23:34. As Paul said, "In the mouth of two or three witnesses shall every word be established."—2 Corinthians 13:1 (compare Deuteronomy 17:6).

26. MOCKED & RIDICULED

Prophetic Forecast:

Psalm 22:7-8 — "All they that see Me laugh Me to scorn: they shoot out the lip, they shake the head, saying, He trusted on the Lord that He would deliver Him: let Him deliver Him, seeing He delighted in Him."

Historic Fulfillment:

Matthew 27:39-43 — "They that passed by reviled Him, wagging their heads, and saying, . . . He saved others, Himself He cannot save. If He be the King of Israel, let Him now come down from the cross, and we will believe Him. He trusted in God; let Him deliver Him now, if He will have Him."

27. PRAYED FOR PERSECUTORS

Prophetic Forecast:

Isaiah 53:12 — "He . . . made intercession for the transgressors."

Historic Fulfillment:

Luke 23:34 — "Then said Jesus, Father, forgive them; for they know not what they do."

Here Jesus practiced what He preached in His Sermon on the Mount: "Pray for them who spitefully use you and persecute you." [27]

28. OFFERED GALL & VINEGAR

Prophetic Forecast:

Psalm 69:21 — "They gave Me also gall for My meat; and in My thirst they gave Me vinegar to drink."

Historic Fulfillment:

Matthew 27:34 — "They gave Him vinegar to drink mingled with gall: and when He had tasted thereof, He would not drink." [28]

29. LONELY & FORSAKEN

Prophetic Forecast:

Psalm 22:1 — "My God, My God, why hast Thou forsaken Me?"

Historic Fulfillment:

Mark 15:34, NKJV — "And at the ninth hour Jesus cried out with a loud voice, saying, 'Eloi, Eloi, lama sabachthani?' which is translated, 'My God, My God, why have You forsaken Me?'"

30. EARTHQUAKE Followed Anguished Cry

Prophetic Forecast:

Psalm 18:6-7, RSV — "In My distress I called upon the Lord; to my God I cried for help. From His temple He heard My voice, and My cry to Him reached His ears. Then the earth reeled and rocked; the foundations also of the mountains trembled and quaked, because He was angry."

Historic Fulfillment:

Matthew 27:46, 50-54, NKJV — "Jesus cried out again with a loud voice, and yielded up His spirit [and died] . . . and the earth quaked, and the rocks were split. . . . So when the centurion and those with him, who were guarding Jesus, saw the earthquake and the things that had happened, they feared greatly, saying, 'Truly this was the Son of God!'"

31. DARKNESS Covered the Land

Prophetic Forecast:

Amos 8:9-10, NKJV — "'In that day . . . I will make the sun go down AT NOON, and I will darken the earth in broad daylight. . . . I will make it like mourning for an only Son.'"

Historic Fulfillment:

Matthew 27:45 — "From the sixth hour there was DARKNESS over all the land unto the ninth hour."

"The sixth hour" by Jewish reckoning was NOON. Jesus hung upon the cross for three hours—from noon till 3 p.m. on the day we call "Good Friday"— but the sun itself refused to look upon the awful scene!

32. His Side PIERCED

Prophetic Forecast:

Zechariah 12:10 — "They shall look upon Me whom they have pierced, and they shall mourn for Him, as one mourneth for His only Son."
(Please see footnote #23.)

Historic Fulfillment:

John 19:34-37 — "One of the soldiers with a spear pierced His side, and forthwith came there out blood and water. . . . These things were done, that the Scripture should be fulfilled, . . . They shall look on Him whom they pierced."

John 20:24-27 — "But Thomas, one of the twelve, . . . said unto them, Except I shall see in His hands the print of the nails, and put my finger into the print of the nails, and thrust my hand into His side, I will not believe. . . . Then saith He [Jesus] to Thomas, Reach hither thy finger, and behold My hands; and reach hither thy hand, and thrust it into My side: and be not faithless, but believing."

33. "CUT OFF" FROM LIFE

Prophetic Forecast:

Daniel 9:26, NASB — "After the sixty-two weeks [29] the Messiah will be CUT OFF. . . ."

Isaiah 53:8 & 12 — "He was CUT OFF out of the land of the living. . . . He hath poured out His soul unto DEATH."

Historic Fulfillment:

Matthew 27:50, NRSV — "Jesus . . . breathed His last."

Acts 2:22-23, RSV — "Jesus of Nazareth . . . you crucified and killed."

34. DIED TO SAVE OTHERS

Prophetic Forecast:

Daniel 9:26 — "Messiah [shall] be cut off, but NOT for Himself."

Isaiah 53:4-12 — "Surely He hath borne OUR griefs, and carried OUR sorrows. . . . He was wounded for OUR transgressions, He was bruised for OUR iniquities: the chastisement of OUR peace was upon Him; and with His stripes WE are healed. All WE like sheep have gone astray; WE have turned every one to his own way; and the Lord hath laid on HIM the iniquity of US ALL. . . . For the transgression of my people was He stricken. . . . My righteous Servant [shall] justify MANY; for He shall bear THEIR iniquities. . . . He bare the sin of MANY."

Historic Fulfillment:

Matthew 20:28 — "The Son of man came . . . to give His life a ransom for MANY."

Romans 5:6-8 — "Christ died for the ungodly. . . . While we were yet sinners, Christ died for US."

1 Peter 2:21 & 24; 3:18 — "Christ also suffered for US. . . . Who His own self bare OUR sins in His own body on the tree . . . the Just for the unjust, that He might bring us to God."

1 John 2:2 — "He is the propitiation for OUR sins: and not for ours only, but also for the sins of the WHOLE WORLD."

A beautiful statement on this subject—God's chosen method of redeeming the lost race of mankind—is from *The Desire of Ages*, an inspiring biography of our Savior by E. G. White:

"Christ was treated as we deserve, that we might be treated as He deserves. He was condemned for our sins, in which He had no share, that we might be justified by His righteousness, in which we had no share. He suffered the death which was ours, that we might receive the life which was His. 'With His stripes we are healed.'"[30]

35. NO BONE BROKEN

Prophetic Forecast:

Psalm 34:20, RSV — "He keeps all his bones; not one of them is broken."

Historic Fulfillment:

John 19:31-36, NKJV — "Therefore, because it was the Preparation Day,[31] that the bodies should not remain on the cross on the Sabbath (for that Sabbath was a high day), the Jews asked Pilate that their legs might be broken, and that they might be taken away. Then the soldiers came and broke the legs of the first and of the other who was crucified with Him. But when they came to Jesus and saw that He was already dead, THEY DID NOT BREAK HIS LEGS. . . . And he who has seen has testified, and his testimony is true; and he knows that he is telling the truth, so that you may believe. For these things were done that the Scripture should be fulfilled, 'Not one of His bones shall be broken.'"

The import of this prophecy and fulfillment may not be apparent at first, but in His great sacrifice Jesus typified the Passover lamb. That's why John the Baptist pointed to Jesus and proclaimed, "Behold the Lamb of God, which taketh away the sin of the world."[32] And Paul says: "Christ our Passover is sacrificed for us."[33] God had clearly told His people in regard to the Passover lamb: "neither shall ye break a bone thereof."[34] Thus it was important that the soldiers did not break Jesus' legs—He is our Passover offered "once for all."[35] *In every detail, Christ FITS the Divine Blueprint!*

36. Buried in RICH MAN'S TOMB

Prophetic Forecast:

Isaiah 53:9 — "He made His grave . . . with the rich in His death."

Historic Fulfillment:

Matthew 27:57-60 — "When the even was come, there came a rich man of Arimathea, named Joseph, who also himself was Jesus' disciple: He went to Pilate, and begged the body of Jesus. Then Pilate commanded the body to be delivered. And when Joseph had taken the body, he wrapped it in a clean linen cloth, and laid it in his own new tomb."[36]

37. COULD NOT BE HELD IN TOMB

Prophetic Forecast:

Psalm 16:10 — "Thou wilt not leave My soul in hell; neither wilt Thou suffer Thine Holy One to see corruption."

"Hell" here is from the Hebrew *sheol* and simply means the *grave*—see any Bible dictionary. "Corruption" refers to the rotting decomposition of a dead body in the grave over the course of time.

Historic Fulfillment:

Acts 2:31-32, NIV — "Seeing what was ahead, he [the Psalmist David] spoke of the resurrection of the Christ, that He was not abandoned to the grave, nor did His body see decay. God has raised this Jesus to life, and we are all witnesses of the fact."

38. AROSE ON THE THIRD DAY

Prophetic Forecast:

Matthew 17:22-23, NIV — Jesus said: "The Son of man is going to be betrayed into the hands of men. They will kill Him, and on the THIRD day He will be raised to life." [37]

John 2:18-21, NKJV— The Jews asked, "'What sign do You show to us. . . ?' Jesus answered and said to them, 'Destroy this temple, and in three days I will raise it up.' Then the Jews said, 'It has taken forty-six years to build this temple, and will You raise it up in three days?' But He was speaking of the temple of His body." [38]

Historic Fulfillment:

Luke 24:6, 34, 46 — "He is not here, but is risen. . . . The Lord is risen indeed. . . . Thus it behoved Christ to suffer, and to rise from the dead the third day."

Christ not only foretold the FACT of His resurrection but also specified the length of TIME He would be in the grave! His enemies, remembering His prediction, even took precautions against it [39]—but their efforts proved futile. Our next chapter will closely examine Christ's marvelous Resurrection.

39. ASCENDED TO HIS FATHER

Prophetic Forecast:

Psalm 68:18 — "Thou hast ascended on high, Thou hast led captivity captive: Thou hast received gifts for men."

Psalm 110:1, NKJV — "The Lord said to my Lord, 'Sit at My right hand, till I make Your enemies Your footstool.'" (The two divine Beings here designated "Lord" are God the Father and God the Son.)

Psalm 24:7-10, NKJV — These verses describe, with adoring praise, Christ's triumphant re-entry into heaven:

> "Lift up your heads, O you gates!
> And be lifted up, you everlasting doors!
> And the King of glory shall come in.
> Who is this King of glory?
> The Lord strong and mighty,
> The Lord mighty in battle.
> Lift up your heads, O you gates!
> And lift them up, you everlasting doors!
> And the King of glory shall come in.
> Who is this King of glory?
> The Lord of hosts,
> He is the King of glory."

Historic Fulfillment:

Luke 24:51 — "And it came to pass, while He blessed them [the disciples], He was parted from them, and carried up into heaven."

Acts 1:9 — "And when He had spoken these things, while they [the disciples] beheld, He was taken up; and a cloud received Him out of their sight."

Mark 16:19, NKJV — "After the Lord had spoken to them, He was received up into heaven, and sat down at the right hand of God."

Acts 2:32-35, NKJV — "This Jesus God has raised up . . . being exalted to the right hand of God. . . . For David did not ascend into the heavens, but he says himself: 'The Lord said to my Lord, "Sit at My right hand, till I make Your enemies Your footstool." ' "

Acts 7:55-56, NKJV — Stephen, the first Christian martyr, sealed his testimony with his own blood: "But he, being full of the Holy Spirit, gazed into heaven and saw the glory of God, and Jesus standing at the right hand of God, and said, 'Look! I see the heavens opened and the Son of Man standing at the right hand of God!' "

Romans 8:34, NIV — "Christ Jesus, who died—more than that, who was raised to life—is at the right hand of God and is also interceding for us."

Ephesians 1:20. NRSV — "God put this power to work in Christ when He raised him from the dead and seated Him at His right hand in the heavenly places."

Ephesians 4:8-10 — "He ascended up on high."

Hebrews 1:3 — Jesus, after He had "purged our sins, sat down on the right hand of the Majesty on high."

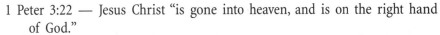

1 Peter 3:22 — Jesus Christ "is gone into heaven, and is on the right hand of God."

Revelation 12:5 — The promised "Man child . . . was caught up unto God, and to His throne."

THE CREDENTIALS OF CHRIST ARE CONVINCING

Jesus tells us: "Search the Scriptures; for in them ye think ye have eternal life: and they are they which testify of Me." [40] The "Scriptures" He refers to are the Old Testament—the only part of the Bible written at that time.

The prophecies pointing to the Messiah are all A MATTER OF RECORD. They were published to the world long ago in the Old Testament. And when we read about the life and experience of Jesus Christ in the New Testament, we find that He fits those divine prophecies precisely. Either Jesus IS the Son of God, or there's no such thing as Messianic prophecy!

Those who reject Jesus as the Son of God may claim He deliberately set out to fulfill prophecy—for example, He rode the donkey into Jerusalem on purpose because the Scripture predicted that. But this objection seems plausible only until we realize that MOST prophecies concerning the Messiah were TOTALLY BEYOND HUMAN CONTROL, such as His place of birth, His time of birth, His race and family heritage, details of His betrayal, the manner of His death and burial, and so on. Remember also that more than FOUR HUNDRED YEARS elapsed between the last book of the Old Testament and the first book of the New Testament, so no collusion between writers was possible.

Jesus warned that many impostors would come, saying, "I am Christ." [41] And some have come claiming to be the Messiah! But the true Christ, or Messiah, had to be born in Bethlehem, had to begin His earthly ministry in A.D. 27, and had to be crucified in A.D. 31. [42] We've seen that Jesus' birth in Bethlehem was a miracle in itself, since His family lived in Nazareth. And both sacred and secular history record that He appeared on the scene at the exact time predicted.

We could possibly find one or two of these prophecies fulfilled in someone else's life—but not ALL of them! One or two prophecies fulfilled in a person's life would hardly convince anyone to accept that individual as the divine Son of God, the Savior of mankind. But the CUMULATIVE EFFECT of fulfilling ALL of them in specific detail is overwhelmingly persuasive! These multiple strands of fulfilled prophecy, bound together like the wires of a great cable, make a bond of evidence no power on earth can break.

✦ ✦ ✦

CONCLUSION

I trust this study has strengthened your faith. You've been exposed to dozens of Bible facts about the Son of God, facts that help you believe in Him with all your *mind* as well as with all your *heart*. You've been brought face to face with Truth—an encounter that could be your own "rendezvous with destiny."

Intelligent people are willing to believe in God and His Son, but they demand credible reasons for their faith. Fortunately, the abundant evidence for Christ's divinity makes our decision to accept Him as Lord and Savior an easy one. These prophecies gave much information about Jesus in advance of His coming so we might not only recognize HIM as the Messiah but also have increased faith in the BIBLE as the inspired Word of God. Christianity's documented credibility proves that the believer has made no mistake—

Jesus truly IS the Son of God.

In closing this chapter, remember Jesus' experience when He confronted a man possessed by demons who "cried out with a loud voice, saying, 'Let us alone! What have we to do with You, Jesus of Nazareth? Did You come to destroy us? I know who You are—the Holy One of God!'"[43] "Unclean spirits, whenever they saw Him, fell down before Him and cried out, saying, 'You are the Son of God'"![44] And greedy exorcists, trying to profit by casting out demons in the names of Jesus and Paul, were confronted by a demon who said, "Jesus I know, and Paul I know; but who are you?"[45]

Did you get that? Even evil spirits—demons—recognize our Lord as "the Holy One of God!" One went on record as saying, "Jesus I know." Friend, do YOU know Him?

❧

Notes to Chapter 7

1. Acts 9:20 & 22, NKJV.
2. Acts 18:28.
3. Acts 17:2-3, NKJV.
4. John 1:45.
5. Luke 24:25 & 27.
6. John 20:31.
7. God's promise to Abraham was repeated for emphasis in such verses as Genesis 12:3, 18:18, 26:4, and 28:14.
8. See also Matthew 15:22; Luke 18:35-39; John 7:42; 2 Timothy 2:8. The genealogy of Jesus is recorded in Matthew 1:1-16 and in Luke 3:23-38—note especially Matthew 1:1 & 6 and Luke 3:31, showing the link to David.
9. Read Matthew 2, verses 1-6.
10. From "Light Shining Out of Darkness," in Cowper's *Olney Hymns* (1779).
11. The specific verse quoted here is Daniel 9:25.
12. See *Appendix C: The Seventy Weeks of Daniel 9*, at the back of this book.
13. See Luke 3:15-16 and John 1:19-27.
14. Paul was inspired to write Galatians 4:4 — "When the fulness of the time was come, God sent forth His Son, made of a woman"—NOT "a woman and a man"— because God was His Father through the agency of the Holy Spirit. See Matthew 1:18-20 and Luke 1:35.
15. Interestingly enough, this verse from Hosea has a double application, as seen from the following: First, when the children of Israel were slaves to Pharaoh, God called them out of Egypt in the great Exodus led and recorded by Moses (Exodus 4:22-23). Secondly, Joseph and Mary fled into Egypt with the Holy Child to escape the murderous designs of Herod. After Herod had died, God through an angel "called His Son out of Egypt." Under inspiration, gospel writer Matthew recognized in Jesus' experience the historical fulfillment of this prophecy.
16. "Pilate had a notice prepared and fastened to the cross. It read: JESUS OF NAZA-RETH, THE KING OF THE JEWS. . . . The chief priests of the Jews protested to Pilate, 'Do not write "The King of the Jews," but that this man CLAIMED to be king of the Jews.' Pilate answered, 'What I have written, I have written.'" — John 19:19-22, NIV.
17. Compare Luke 19:29-38.
18. See Matthew 26:21-25, 46-50 and Mark 14:10, 17-22, 44-45.
19. See Josh McDowell, *Evidence That Demands a Verdict* (San Bernardino, California: Here's Life Publishers, c. 1979), Volume I, p. 159.
20. Compare Mark 14:27 & 50 and John 16:32.
21. Compare Acts 8:26-35.
22. Compare Matthew 27:26 & 30 and Mark 14:65 & 15:19.
23. On this verse, Biblical scholar Matthew Henry (1662-1714) comments: "He [Christ] is spoken of as One whom WE have pierced. . . . It is true of all of us as sinners, WE have pierced Christ, inasmuch as OUR sins were the cause of His death. . . .

Those who truly repent of their sins look upon Christ as one whom THEY have pierced. . . . It makes them MOURN." — *Matthew Henry's Commentary on the Whole Bible* (Hendrickson Publishers, © 1992), p. 1590, on Zechariah 12:10.

24. When God's sinful people were attacked by poisonous serpents in the wilderness, "Moses made a serpent of bronze, and *put it upon a pole;* and whenever a serpent bit someone, that person would look at the serpent of bronze and live." — Numbers 21:9, NRSV.

25. "Doubting" Thomas refused to believe eye-witness reports of Christ's resurrection, saying, "Except I shall see in His hands the print of the nails, and put my finger into the print of the nails, . . . I will not believe." With loving patience, the risen Lord allowed Thomas personally to examine and touch those wounds (John 20:24-27). Many victims of crucifixion were simply tied to crosses rather than nailed and then left to die a lingering death from starvation and thirst. But Jesus' hands and feet were indeed "pierced" when He was nailed to Calvary's cross.

26. See also Matthew 27:38 and Luke 23:33.

27. Matthew 5:44 & Luke 6:28, NKJV.

28. See also Matthew 27:48 and John 19:28-29.

29. A definite, verifiable period of time explained in *Appendix C*, p. 779.

30. E. G. White, *The Desire of Ages* (Boise, Idaho: Pacific Press Publishing Association, c. 1940), p. 25.

31. "The preparation" means Friday, the sixth day of the week, used by God's faithful people to prepare for the Sabbath by finishing all work, cleaning up, *etc.* Mark 15:42 defines it as "the preparation, that is, the day before the Sabbath." Christ was crucified, you'll recall, on the day we call "Good Friday"—a "preparation day" to Sabbath observers.

32. John 1:29.

33. 1 Corinthians 5:7.

34. Exodus 12:43 & 46 and Numbers 9:12.

35. Hebrews 10:10.

36. Compare Mark 15:43-46, Luke 23:50-53, and John 19:38-42.

37. See also Matthew 16:21. Jesus spent part of Friday, all of Saturday, and part of Sunday dead in the tomb—making three days, for Jewish culture reckoned time INCLUSIVELY. The Internal Revenue System also reckons time that way: If my wife gives birth to a child at 11:59 P.M. on December 31st, we can claim that child as a dependent for the whole preceding year!

38. The apostle Paul makes clear in such verses as 1 Corinthians 5:16-17 & 6:19 and 2 Corinthians 6:16 that our body is "the temple of God."

39. See Matthew 27:62-66.

40. John 5:39.

41. Matthew 24:5.

42. See *Appendix C, The Seventy Weeks of Daniel 9*, p. 779, in this volume.

43. Luke 4:33-34, NKJV (and Mark 1:23-24).

44. Mark 3:11. See also Mark 5:1-9 and Luke 4:41.

45. Acts 19:13-15, NKJV.

~

CHAPTER EIGHT

THE RESURRECTION OF CHRIST: MYTH OR MIRACLE?

T HE CREDIBILITY OF CHRISTIANITY stands or falls with the resurrection of Jesus Christ. For the resurrection is not merely one Christian doctrine among many—it's the great fundamental which is absolutely vital and essential. Faith in the resurrection is the very keystone in the arch of Christian faith, and when it's removed, all the rest inevitably crumbles into ruin.[1] Had there been no resurrection, there would have been no Christian Church! The movement Jesus started would have come to a literal dead end with the execution of the carpenter-teacher.

So through the centuries the resurrection has been the storm center of the attack upon the Christian faith: DISPROVE the resurrection, and you DISPOSE of Christianity. As Paul put it, "If Christ be not risen, then is our preaching vain, and your faith is also vain."[2] And Christ Himself deliberately staked His whole claim to men's belief upon His resurrection: When asked for a sign of His divinity, He pointed to His resurrection as His single and sufficient credential.[3]

HOAX OR HISTORY?

The resurrection of Jesus Christ is either the greatest miracle or the greatest delusion history records. If it's true, then it's the Supreme Fact of history, and failure to adjust one's life to its implications means irreparable loss. If it's not true, if Christ has not risen, then Christianity is all a fraud—a heartless hoax foisted on the minds of men.

The meaning of the resurrection may be a theological matter, but the fact of the resurrection is a historical one.[4] For "Christianity is a historical religion. It claims that God has taken the risk of involving Himself in human history, and the facts are there for you to examine with the utmost rigor. They'll withstand any amount of critical investigation." [5]

The witness of history gives clear, abundant evidence in this case. William Lyon Phelps, distinguished professor at Yale for more than forty years and author of some twenty volumes, asserted that "The historical evidence for the resurrection is stronger than for any other miracle anywhere narrated." [6] And the evidence is conclusive.

Professor Thomas Arnold, for fourteen years headmaster of Rugby School in England, author of the three-volume *History of Rome*, appointed to the chair of Modern History at Oxford, was certainly well acquainted with the value of evidence in determining historical facts. This great scholar declared: "The evidence for our Lord's life and death and resurrection may be, and often has been, shown to be satisfactory; it is good according to the common rules for distinguishing good evidence from bad. Thousands and tens of thousands of persons have gone through it piece by piece. . . . I myself have done it many times over, . . . and I know of no one fact in the history of mankind which is proved by better and fuller evidence of every sort, to the understanding of a fair inquirer, than the great sign which God hath given us that Christ died and rose again from the dead." [7]

Agreeing with Arnold is John Singleton Copley, better known as Lord Lyndhurst and recognized as one of the great legal minds in British history. He was Solicitor-General of the British government in 1819, attorney-general of Great Britain in 1824, three times Lord Chancellor of England, and elected in 1846 High Steward of Cambridge University—thus holding in one lifetime the highest offices possible for a judge in Great Britain. When Lord Lyndhurst died, a document found in his desk, in his own handwriting, gave an account of his Christian faith, declaring: "I know pretty well what evidence is; and I tell you, such evidence as that for the Resurrection has never broken down yet." [8]

Let's examine and thoroughly sift this evidence by considering the arguments critics put forth as theoretical alternatives to the fact of Christ's resurrection. The subject is one that will repay very careful study.

I. THE FABRICATION THEORY

Some unbelievers try to dismiss the whole story of the resurrection by branding it all a fabrication, a deliberate lie concocted by the disciples. But few intelligent critics go that far—for good reason. Consider the following:

Does a LIE have power to transform lives? If not, how can we account for the remarkable change that took place in the disciples? In the first place, they were SAD. "Almost every home has mourned the loss of some dear one in death. Where real love exists, the weary hours, days, and weeks drag by slowly, with the wound seemingly not healing. Here was One, dearly loved, deeply mourned over, and greatly missed. Yet only three days after His death (some 36 hours), His closest friends had cast off all sorrow and were greatly rejoicing. A broken heart is not that easily cheered, unless there has been a resurrection."[9]

Secondly, the disciples were FEARFUL of their personal safety. Authorities were so violently hostile that anyone connected with Jesus was very apprehensive. The disciples fled in obvious panic and for the most part hid behind locked doors. Yet they soon preached so boldly that neither prison, persecution, nor threat of death could silence them.

- What changed the cowardice of *Peter*, "cringing under the taunt of a maid in the court of the high priests and denying with a curse that he knew 'this man of whom ye speak'"?[10] What changed his crippling fear into missionary zeal almost overnight?

- Consider *James*, the brother of Jesus. He was outside the original circle of apostles and their friends. He had few, if any, illusions concerning his own brother. During Christ's life, the attitude of James was cold and even hostile—the record says plainly that he did not believe in Jesus.[11] Yet he became a dominant figure in the Christian movement at Jerusalem, and Paul calls him one of the "pillars" of the church.[12] How do we account for the amazing change that took place in James? The simple answer is that the living Lord had appeared to him.[13]

- Take *Thomas*, the doubter whose name has become a byword for skepticism. Till he saw Jesus with his own eyes after the resurrection, he refused to believe even the testimony of his friends, the other disciples.[14] But Thomas, too, made a complete about-face after seeing his Lord risen from the grave.

- *Paul*, also, was miraculously changed. At first he had no intention of ever believing in the resurrection and eagerly persecuted the "fanatics" who did. But Saul, the proud, aggressive persecutor was suddenly changed into Paul, the apostle of the Lord. On the road to Damascus he had the shock of his life. He started for Damascus determined to stamp out Christianity—he arrived there an utterly shaken and repentant man. He began by being the outstanding figure on ONE side of the controversy and ended by becoming the outstanding figure on the OTHER. Why should a man of this tough breed be uprooted in an instant from his most cherished beliefs and swept into the camp of his most hated enemies?[15] What *was* the discovery that so staggered Paul on the road to Damascus? The only adequate cause for such a total reversal was that he had SEEN the resurrected Lord.[16]

The remarkable transformation of the disciples is perhaps the greatest evidence of all for the resurrection. Not only were all the disciples changed in a very short time from utter dejection to triumphant joy, but their faith was SUSTAINED throughout a life of devotion that ended in a martyr's death.

The first law of human nature is self-preservation. Yet this theory asks us to believe that the disciples would give their lives for what they KNEW to be false! If these men consciously told falsehoods, they must have had some motive for doing so. What was the motive? It was not to gain popularity, for their message was supremely displeasing to many. It was not to make money, for the disciples were practically penniless till the day they died. These people all had little to gain and much to lose by talking, but talk they did!

The most convincing testimony anyone can give for the truth of a statement is to suffer rather than deny it. The disciples didn't need to suffer— they could have escaped persecution simply by abstaining from preaching Christ and His resurrection. But prison, torture, and death couldn't alter their conviction that Jesus was alive. To their last breath they continued to teach the resurrection of Christ.

They could do no more than SEAL their testimony with their BLOOD. This the disciples did: Within three decades most of them perished violently for their adherence to the resurrection story. They suffered the supreme penalty for their convictions in the manner of that barbaric age—James in Jerusalem itself, Peter and Paul in Rome. If the resurrection had been a lie, surely one of the conspirators, in disillusionment or agony, would have divulged the secret. The fact that they remained steadfast even in the face of execution stamps the fabrication theory itself a falsehood.

Not only would men not die to uphold a mere lie, but the character of the converted disciples was such that they would not lie under any circumstances. "They gave the world the highest moral and ethical teaching it has ever known; and they lived it—as even their opponents were forced to admit."[17]

Is it credible that men could concoct such a fraud as the resurrection story and then continually lie while teaching converts to "lie not one to another,"[18] warning that liars will find their place at last in the lake of fire?

Is it credible that these men made it their lifework to propagate a LIE and then succeeded in turning multitudes of wicked people to lives of virtue and honesty?

"To have persisted in so gross a falsehood, after it was known to them, was not only to encounter, for life, all the evils man could inflict from WITH-OUT, but to endure also the pangs of INWARD and conscious guilt; with no hope of future peace, no testimony of a good conscience, . . . no hope of happiness in this life or in the world to come. . . . If then their testimony was not TRUE, there was no possible motive for its fabrication."[19]

Some critics try to make a case for the fabrication theory by pointing to slight discrepancies in certain details of the gospel story. It's true that there are a few minor differences among the four accounts written by the gospel writers, such as the fact that Matthew says the women who came back to the tomb to anoint Jesus' body encountered an angel who told them that Christ has risen, whereas Mark says it was a young man, Luke says two men, and John says two angels. It's reasonable to assume that the angels took human form so these friends of Jesus wouldn't be frightened. That's why Luke reported two "men" and John reported two "angels." Slight discrepancies on minor points in fact constitute a strong argument for the VALIDITY of the Scripture accounts. Eyewitnesses may be suspected of collaboration and collusion if their accounts are identical in every detail because no two people see the same thing in exactly the same way.

For instance, the assassination of John F. Kennedy has been treated differently by every author who has dealt with the subject. Some see a conspiracy while others see a lone fanatic causing the death of the President, and so on. All these reports leave some question as to the precise way in which the President was shot, but they don't leave a shred of doubt about the historical fact that the President was indeed shot. Future archaeologists finding a shelf of twentieth-century books on JFK's death will be all the more convinced that it really occurred by the very fact that people with different points of view all agreed that he had been shot.

The Gospels may be compared to four windows through which we look into a room from four different angles. The four views of Christ's life may appear contradictory on the surface, but really these brief records complement and supplement each other in a most harmonious way. If all the writers gave identical word-for-word reports, critics could say we don't have four reports but only one—and then they'd ask, "How can we trust only one witness?" But the Gospel writers make no pretense of agreeing, even though Mark's Gospel, the earliest version of what happened, was accessible to both Matthew and Luke when they wrote, and all three of those Gospels were common property when John produced his work. If this fundamental doctrine of the church were mere fabrication, care would have been taken to have all accounts of it in strict agreement.[20]

The resurrection story rings true also because of these points:

- How can we explain that awkward interval of seven weeks between the resurrection and its first public proclamation? No fabricator of false evidence would so arrange the story. The only adequate explanation of this interval is provided by the records themselves: The disciples spent the first forty days in intermittent fellowship with their risen Lord. After His Ascension to heaven, they waited the next ten days, as Christ had commanded, for the Holy Spirit who was to fill them with power.[21]

- Also, the Gospel records tell the unflattering truth about Peter's denial of Christ during the Lord's trial. Peter was a major leader in proclaiming the resurrection story, yet many of the facts recorded about him are the type which conspirators would not have reported, much less invented. (Who would have invented that story of Peter and the other disciples falling asleep when needed in the gravest hour of their Master's peril?[22]) The only explanation for such humiliating facts to appear in pro-Christian documents, written by Peter's friends, is that they were reporting the absolute truth.

- Another fact to remember is that the disciples proclaimed Christ's resurrection at a time when many people were still alive who KNEW about the events reported, "for this thing was not done in a corner."[23] No one could now publish a biography of Ronald Reagan full of anecdotes that were quite untrue—they'd be contradicted at once. (That's why Reagan's recent fictionized biography, *Dutch,* by Edmund Morris, caused such an uproar.) But when Peter gave his sermon on the Day of Pentecost, we find no refutation given by the Jewish leaders to his bold proclamation of Christ's resurrection. Even years later, when Paul wrote, many men were alive who knew all the facts and who, if Paul's account were false, could have refuted him with ease.

But "the SILENCE of the Jews speaks louder than the VOICE of the Christians"[24] and is as eloquent a proof of the resurrection as the apostles' witness. We must account for not only the enthusiasm of Jesus' friends but the paralysis of His foes. The best that the enemies of Christ could do in response to the preaching was to sneer or laugh it off or threaten the disciples with arrest or death if they did not remain silent. But why didn't they deny the tomb was empty? Because they knew it was empty. And why didn't they produce the body of Christ and silence the disciples once and for all? Because there no longer was a dead body to produce. Christ had risen a triumphant Conqueror over death, and the disciples were telling the truth.

One last point overlooked by the fabrication theory is the great fact of the Christian Church: To what does it owe its origin and existence? The church did not just HAPPEN—it had a definite cause. If the disciples' experience with their Lord had ended with His death on the cross, the Christian Church would not have come into existence.[25]

Yet consider the success of the early church: In Jerusalem the resurrection was preached within a few minutes' walk of Jesus' empty tomb, and not only were THOUSANDS converted in a single day[26] but "a great company of the PRIESTS were obedient to the faith."[27] Peter and the others were announcing an almost incredible thing to an unbelieving crowd, but instead of being laughed into silence, they won the crowd over. These disciples were themselves Jews, with centuries of privileged pedigree behind them, yet they threw it all away and became Christians. The whole system of Judaism was rocked to its foundations by this preaching.[28] And the believers did not remain in Judea—they "turned the world upside down."[29] They spread their new teaching so far and wide that even some "of Caesar's household"[30] became Christians.

Think of it: Those few despised Jews, without worldly power or prestige, went into all provinces of the Roman Empire, to men of other races and religions, and persuaded them to believe—not by scores, or hundreds, or thousands, but literally and ultimately by millions. They persuaded Roman citizens to believe when to believe meant suffering ridicule, persecution, and even death in the arena.[31] The full power of the Empire was against them. Yet the Christian Church did emerge! How can anyone say that the whole new direction given the course of history by those few men in first-century Palestine is founded on a lie? No, my friend, these facts prove the resurrection story to be more than the happy ending to a fairy tale. The fabrication theory has had to be abandoned because it cannot bear close scrutiny.

II. THE HALLUCINATION THEORY

In order to avoid some of the difficulties inherent in the fabrication theory, a few critics have proposed the hallucination theory. This says that the disciples were perfectly sincere in their belief that Christ had risen from the dead because of hallucinations caused by a fervent religious experience. They weren't lying—they were simply deceived and deluded.

However, modern medicine has shown that even psychological phenomena obey certain laws and may be subjected to certain tests. Let's examine the validity of the hallucination theory.[32]

In the first place, it's been found that, just as some persons make better subjects for hypnosis than others, only certain types of persons are likely to suffer from hallucinations.[33] Normally, psychiatrists find that persons prone to hallucinations are "high-strung," highly imaginative, and very nervous. A critic may point to Christ's reported appearance to Mary Magdalene and dismiss it as the hallucination of a distraught, hysterical woman. But remember that Christ appeared to all sorts of people! Aside from the women, there were Peter, the impetuous fisherman; Thomas, the miserable skeptic; Matthew, the hard-headed tax collector; the rest of the Twelve, who knew Him so well; James, His incredulous brother; and other disciples. It's impossible to dismiss these revelations of the Lord as mere hallucinations of deranged minds.[34]

Another well-established fact about hallucinations is that they're highly individualistic in nature. A drunkard may think he sees snakes, but they're all in his own mind. One individual may hallucinate and believe he's Napoleon, but it's rare to find many people from very different backgrounds all suffering from the same delusion. A whole asylum of insane patients may have hallucinations at the same time, but the hallucinations will all be different. Yet here we have the same phenomena reported by otherwise rational fishermen, tax collectors, close relatives, and on one occasion a crowd of over five hundred people at once![35] If this theory were correct, we would have in this collective hallucination something new in the annals of psychiatry!

A third difficulty with this theory is that hallucinations tend to recur over a long period of time with some degree of regularity, either increasing or decreasing in frequency as time goes by.[36] Someone who suffers from obsessions continues to suffer from them. But the phenomena we're considering occurred during a short period of forty days and then dramatically ceased. None of the people involved ever claimed to have experienced a later repetition.[37] If the appearances of the risen Lord were hallucinations, why did they stop so abruptly? Believers know that the Lord ascended to heaven after forty days. But critics who reject Christ's resurrection also reject His ascension and thus cannot account for the abrupt ending of His appearances. The hallucination theory is inconsistent with the fact that the appearances ended so suddenly.

However, some may suggest that the appearances were not hallucinations—perhaps they were optical illusions or supernatural visions of some sort. The following objections preclude this possibility:

- How could a "vision" roll away the heavy stone from the tomb?

- Another problem with the vision hypothesis is that it presupposes a miracle to get rid of a miracle. For the only objection to the fact of Christ's bodily resurrection is that it's a miracle and violates natural law, which skeptics won't accept. But a supernatural vision is a miracle, too, and also violates natural law—so what's the point? This hypothesis is a solution which doesn't solve, an explanation which doesn't explain.[38]

- The vision theory also fails to do justice to the empty tomb. Many counter-arguments studiously avoid reference to the empty tomb, but obviously if those who preached the resurrection had merely been deluded by "visions" or hallucinations, the foes of Christ would have effectively silenced them by producing Jesus' body.

- Furthermore, the vision theory overlooks some very pertinent facts of the Gospel accounts. For when Christ appeared to His disciples, they actually thought they WERE seeing a vision or that He was just a spirit. He convinced them He had a material body with "flesh and bones" by letting them TOUCH Him and by EATING in their presence.[39] So the testimony of the apostles does not depend on glimpsing a fleeting apparition. It rests instead on firm sensory experiences during prolonged interviews: They SAW Him, HEARD Him, TOUCHED Him. What more evidence could they want?

A final fact which lays to rest the hallucination theory is this: Most, if not all, hallucinations concern an expected event—meditated upon and desired by the recipient for a long time. For instance, a lonely mother may so fervently LONG for the return of her runaway son that she actually believes she sees him. In other words, hallucinations require an anticipating spirit of hopeful expectancy which makes the wish become father of the thought.[40] To have an experience like this, one first intensely WANTS to believe he envisions something and then attaches reality to his imagination. But in the disciples' case, we find nothing of this "wish fulfillment." Overwhelming evidence shows they were not expecting Christ to rise again. Though Christ Himself anticipated His death and resurrection, and plainly predicted it to His disciples and others, the Gospel writers frankly admit that such predictions really didn't penetrate their minds till the resurrection was an accomplished fact.[41]

When the women trudged through dark streets that early morning to anoint Christ's body more properly than they had during His hurried burial, they weren't expecting Him to be alive. Instead, they were puzzling over a practical problem: "Who shall roll us away the stone from the door of the sepulchre? . . . for it was very great."[42] Even the empty tomb did not cause the women to believe, for Mary Magdalene simply thought His dead body had been stolen: "They have taken away my Lord, and I know not where they have laid Him."[43] Also, she failed to recognize Christ during the first few moments He appeared to her.[44] When these first witnesses to Christ's post-resurrection appearances ran to tell the other disciples, they couldn't believe it.[45] It seemed too good to be true.

The resurrected Lord scolded some of His followers for being "slow of heart to believe."[46] The ones to whom He spoke these words were so far from expecting Christ to be alive they didn't even recognize Him at first.[47] They didn't expect to see a dead man walking around any more than we would. They were skeptical because they failed to comprehend Jesus' many promises that He would rise again.[48] No, the disciples weren't expecting the resurrection or even sentimentalizing over its possibility. Therefore, the appearances of the risen Christ were NOT hallucinations caused by wish-fulfillment regarding things the disciples were hoping for, yearning for, and expecting.

III. THE DISCIPLES STOLE THE BODY

Critics realize that if the tomb is empty, it must be the result of either a human or divine act. Since they reject the divine in this case, some have formulated the theory that the disciples stole the body. In fact, this theory is older than any other, having been invented by the Jewish leaders early that resurrection morning. Here's the record: When the Roman soldiers guarding Jesus' tomb witnessed His miraculous resurrection, they ran "into the city, and showed the Chief Priests all the things that were done."[49]

Note that the Chief Priests "never questioned the report of the guards. They did not themselves go out to see if the tomb was empty, because they KNEW it was empty. The guards would never have come back with such a story as this, unless they were reporting actual, indisputable occurrences."[50] The message of Christ's resurrection was delivered to the Jewish authorities by their OWN witnesses, "the soldiers they themselves had posted, the most unimpeachable witnesses possible."[51] They accepted the soldiers' testimony because they knew the guards had no reason to lie.

Instead of questioning the veracity of the guards, they decided to bribe them. "When they were assembled with the elders, and had taken counsel, they gave large money unto the soldiers, saying, Say ye, His disciples came by night, and stole Him away while we slept. And if this come to the governor's ears, we will persuade him, and secure you. So they took the money, and did as they were taught: and this saying is commonly reported among the Jews until this day." [52]

So the Roman soldiers sold their integrity for a bribe. They went in before the priests carrying *the greatest message ever given the world;* they went out burdened with a bag of *money.* Although those who wished this lie to be true accepted it, [53] we cannot—for the following reasons:

✓ MORALLY & ETHICALLY Impossible

The disciples *WOULD NOT* perform this deed even if they could, for this theory reduces the followers of Christ to the level of common grave robbers—body snatchers—who would desecrate the grave of their beloved Master. But why would they do such a thing? What would they want with a dead body? What could they do with it—except perhaps destroy it or hide it so it could never be found again?

But assuming that the disciples did sink so low as to snatch Christ's body from the tomb with the object of fabricating a story of His resurrection, this theory ignores the fact that the apostles would not LIE (with the exception of Judas, who was already dead, or Peter before he was converted [54]). The moral codes of some pagan religions permitted lying. But the stern, strict virtues of Christianity demand clean hearts and pure lives. As pointed out above, it's inconceivable that these eleven apostles would ALL agree to enter into such a vile conspiracy as this. No wonder few even among skeptics hold this theory today.

✓ PSYCHOLOGICALLY Impossible

Even if the early Christians did feel that "the end justifies the means" and compromised their consciences to such an extent that they did decide to rob the grave and lie about the pretended resurrection—they still wouldn't be so foolish as to DIE for a lie! Is it reasonable to suppose that none of them ever admitted the deception even under torture or at martyrdom? This point was established earlier.

Furthermore, the disciples weren't even THINKING about any resurrection! They were in no mood to plan a commando raid such as the theft of the body would entail. Sorrow lay like a lead weight on their hearts and made them as inanimate as the corpse they were supposed to have stolen. Steal the body to promote belief in the resurrection? Why would they promote a belief they THEMSELVES didn't have? [55] Utterly disheartened, their hopes dashed by Christ's death, they were anxious only to run away, hide, and forget the whole affair.

And not just the depression of the disciples counteracts this theory but also their timidity—frail and fearful creatures, they fled as soon as they saw Him taken into custody.[56] For instance, Peter, seemingly the most courageous, trembled at the voice of a servant girl and three times denied that he even knew Christ. Would they have jeopardized themselves by undertaking so perilous an enterprise on behalf of a man who apparently had cruelly imposed on their trust?[57] We know these eleven men pretty well, and until they actually spent time with their resurrected Lord, there was no trace of a daring ringleader among them with the imagination to plan a *coup* like that and carry it through without detection.

✓ PHYSICALLY IMPOSSIBLE

Moreover, the disciples *COULD NOT* perform this deed even if they wanted to. For even if we grant that these overwrought, harassed people had the originality and daring to conceive such a plan, they never could have carried it out because of the GUARDS at the tomb. At least four points should be noted about these guards.

1. The guards were trained Roman soldiers from the legion at Jerusalem. One critic thought they were Jewish temple police because of Pilate's reply when Jewish leaders requested a guard to watch Christ's tomb: He said, "Ye have a watch: go your way, make it as sure as ye can."[58] This was construed to mean, "You have guards of your own." But most authorities make plain that what Pilate meant was "You want a guard detachment to watch the tomb?—you have it." His prompt consent showed no reluctance to grant their wish. Two facts—that the Chief Priests needed Pilate's authorization[59] and that the guards feared his punishment[60]— prove those guards were NOT Jewish temple police but Roman soldiers under the Roman governor's authority. The iron discipline of trained Roman legionnaires is what enabled Imperial Rome to sweep the world with its power.

2. The guards were heavily armed, as were all Roman soldiers. As far as weaponry goes, the Roman soldier carried the famous Roman PIKE (a spear over 6 feet long with a sharp iron head, similar to a javelin), a large SHIELD, a SWORD (this was a thrusting rather than a slashing weapon, nearly 3 feet long), and a DAGGER (worn at the left side of his belt). In addition, he wore a breast-plate and helmet for protection in battle. In short, the Roman soldier was strictly disciplined and extremely well equipped. The picture he presented was that of a human fighting machine.

3. The guards at the tomb must have been strong enough numerically to do the job. When Pilate told the priests to "make it as sure as ye can," he was giving them *carte blanche* to secure the tomb against any eventuality—demonstrations, riots, vandalism, body snatching, *etc.* Some scholars estimate the number of guards at as high as one hundred soldiers (a squad under the command of a centurion).

4. Whatever the number of soldiers in the squad detailed to guard Jesus' tomb, we can be sure they were awake. "Punishment in the Roman army was severe in comparison with that in modern armies."[61] One authority mentions no less than eighteen offenses punishable by death, and declares that "fear of punishments produced faultless attention to duty."[62] It was death for a Roman sentinel to sleep at his post, so it's unthinkable that the whole guard, without exception, would fall asleep at once—especially with authorities so anxious that the grave remain undisturbed. One soldier might drop off to sleep briefly while on duty, but a whole squad? Never! "Soldiers cold-blooded enough to gamble over a dying victim's cloak [63] are not the kind to be hoodwinked by timid Galileans or to jeopardize their Roman necks by sleeping on their post."[64] Besides, even if the guards HAD all fallen asleep, how could a group of grave robbers roll back a huge, heavy stone so noiselessly as to awaken no one???

For a few fearful, defenseless disciples to overpower heavily armed, well-trained Roman soldiers, break the Roman seal affixed to the heavy stone over the door to the tomb and then escape unharmed while carrying a dead body would indeed be a MISSION IMPOSSIBLE!

And two other facets of this trumped-up story don't ring true. Remember that the Jewish leaders told the guards to say they were "sleeping" while the disciples stole away the body of Christ. But if they were asleep, how could they know who stole the body or what had happened to it? "What judge would listen if you said that while you were asleep, your neighbor broke in and stole your TV set? Who knows what goes on while he's asleep? Testimony like this would be laughed out of any court."[65] The story is obviously false in any event: If the soldiers were awake, they wouldn't allow anyone to steal the body; if they were asleep, they wouldn't know what had happened.

The final point that refutes this theory also lends great credibility to the whole resurrection story. We've already referred to the silent witness of the empty tomb. However, the tomb WASN'T really empty! Inside was another silent but eloquent witness: the GRAVECLOTHES. You see, God sent a dazzling, powerful angel at the proper moment to roll away the boulder from Christ's tomb.[66] He removed the enormous stone as we would a pebble. "His appearance was like lightning, and his clothes were white as snow. The guards were so afraid of him that they shook and became like dead men."[67] Angelic hands unbound the wrappings from Jesus' body. But the graveclothes (the napkin which bound the head and the linen cloths which shrouded the body) were not thrown carelessly aside—they were carefully folded, each in a place by itself. This is what Peter and John noticed when they first ran to the tomb.[68]

Also, when the disciples buried Jesus, they added to the wrapped linen clothes about 100 pounds of "a mixture of myrrh and aloes . . . as the manner of the Jews is to bury."[69] Aloes is a fragrant wood pounded to dust; myrrh is an aromatic gum. This combination made the graveclothes adhere and cling to the body, so they could not be removed quickly. Therefore, the disciples would never have stolen the body NAKED, dishonoring it and losing time stripping it, giving the terrible guards a chance to awake and seize them.[70] Robbers would never remove the graveclothes—fear of detection would make them act as quickly as possible. And they certainly wouldn't take time to arrange them neatly! Criminals don't leave looted, vandalized premises in a neat and tidy condition. On the contrary, disorder and disarray are a prowler's earmarks.[71] So the graveclothes constitute a remarkable piece of evidence. In fact, when John followed Peter into the tomb, the Record says "he saw, and believed."[72] What did he see that made him believe? It wasn't just the ABSENCE of the body but the PRESENCE of the neatly-placed graveclothes!

IV. ENEMIES OF CHRIST TOOK HIS BODY

We've just seen that the lie about the disciples stealing the body won't fool anyone. So some critics say: Suppose, then, that the chief priests or the Roman authorities moved the body to prevent possible veneration of the tomb—to keep it from becoming a shrine and place of pilgrimage. Though this may sound plausible at first, it poses too many problems to be a theory we can accept. Note the following points:

In the first place, what we've just said about the graveclothes applies to this theory as well: No grave-robber would carefully remove and fold the wrappings. He'd simply take the body, graveclothes and all.

If the body really were removed by mortal hands, quite a few people would need to be involved: Several men would be needed to move away the stone and to carry the body, presumably a considerable distance, to a new hiding place. And the Roman guards would all have to be in collusion with this scheme. So isn't it strange that with the passing of time not one of the many persons involved ever "talked" and divulged the secret? In our day we've seen that John Dean told all he knew about the Watergate cover-up even though he went to jail briefly himself for his part in it. It's unbelievable that not a single witness or party to this supposed conspiracy ever told what really happened, even on his deathbed, especially in a matter of such intense interest at the time!

Thirdly, the Jewish leaders and Pilate had no real motive for such a scheme. There's no evidence that any of Christ's enemies wanted to have His body removed. At long last, they had Jesus where they wanted Him—dead and buried. They were interested only in keeping Him there, which is why they had the squad of soldiers assigned to guard His tomb. As for Pilate, it would've been to the governor's advantage to keep the body in its grave. His main interest was to keep things under control. If he had removed the body, it's incredible that he wouldn't have informed the chief priests so they could produce Christ's corpse when confronted with the preaching of His resurrection.

Besides all this, any claim that Jesus had on people's belief would have been forfeited after three days if He had not risen. For Christ often asserted not merely that He'd arise from the dead but that He would arise within three days.[73] The Jewish leaders' request for the guard shows they were aware of Christ's claim—it was that claim which aroused their concern. So instead of bothering to move Jesus' body, all they had to do was guard it carefully till the three days were past. Thus this theory dies for lack of motive.

But just for the sake of argument, suppose we grant the possibility that Christ's foes moved His body for some reason we can't fathom. Remember that within seven short weeks Jerusalem was seething with the preaching of the resurrection. The Jewish leaders had reason to worry—the Scriptures say "they feared the people, lest they should have been stoned" for sentencing a righteous Man to death.[74] They arrested the apostles and told them, "Behold, ye have filled Jerusalem with your doctrine, and intend to bring this man's blood upon us."[75] In this extremity, why didn't they simply produce the body of Jesus? They could have nipped in the bud any Christian movement by saying, "Wait! We moved the body—Christ didn't rise from the dead." They could have shown exactly where His body was buried and called as witnesses those who had helped move it. As a last resort, they could have recovered the corpse, put it on a cart, and triumphantly wheeled it through the streets of Jerusalem.[76] The fact that they did none of these things demolishes this theory.

V. JOSEPH OF ARIMATHEA REMOVED THE BODY

Another theory says Joseph of Arimathea moved the body to a more suitable resting place. In this connection we must understand that critics and believers look upon Joseph in two different ways, which we should consider briefly:

Critics say he was a pious Jew and respected member of the Sanhedrin. But then he surely would have produced the body when the Jewish leaders needed it to refute the resurrection story.

Also, Joseph couldn't have undertaken the grisly task of moving the body alone, so some of his helpers might have divulged his secret. And it's unlikely that he'd act without prior knowledge of the authorities. Dr. Wilbur Smith makes the point that "the problem of the Roman soldiers still faces us. When they were paid to watch that tomb, they were not told to make an exception of Joseph. . . . They would no more have allowed Joseph to take out that body than they would have allowed one of the [other] disciples to do so." [77]

Finally, what motive could he possibly have had? If a so-called "more suitable" tomb were really available to Joseph, why hadn't he used it for Jesus' body in the first place?

Christ believers, on the other hand, accept the Bible statements that Joseph of Arimathea was a secret disciple of Jesus.[78] Neither he nor Nicodemus[79] had openly accepted the Savior while He was living. They knew such a step would exclude them from the Sanhedrin (the "supreme court" of the Jews, of which they were members), and they hoped to protect Him by their influence in its councils.

The fact that Joseph loved Jesus is evident from the fact that he took His body down from the cross with his own hands[80] "and laid it in his own new tomb."[81] The impression given is of a man compelled to seize the last fleeting opportunity to align himself with the cause of Jesus before it was too late. Would he incur the contempt of his old associates, the deep hostility of the Priesthood, and the disgrace of following a discredited, crucified prophet—only to remove the body 36 hours later and lose the glorious consolation of having his revered leader rest in his own tomb? He surely had no finer tomb in which to place Jesus' body than the one reserved for himself.

Also, if for some unknown reason he had wanted to move Christ's remains, he chose a strange time of day to perform a perfectly legitimate operation which could have been done much more easily during daylight hours. (If this theory is correct, he as a Jew would have had to act between the close of the Sabbath and the first crack of dawn—when the women arrived at the tomb to find it already empty.)

Joseph of Arimathea, an "honourable . . . good . . . just" man,[82] certainly would have informed his fellow disciples of his action in moving the body—so they could NOT have preached that Christ rose from the dead without deceiving people with deliberate lies, as discussed above.

This theory also fails to explain Christ's appearances to many people after His resurrection. (Please see *Appendix D* at the back of this book for a list of *Christ's Post-Resurrection Appearances*.)

Finally, this theory fails to account for the fact that no tomb supposed to contain the remains of Jesus ever became a shrine or object of veneration. This is inconceivable if Jesus really were buried elsewhere than in the vacant tomb. Yet no trace exists of anyone paying homage at the shrine of Jesus Christ, as Moslems make pilgrimages to Mohammed's tomb at Medina. Wouldn't Mary, His mother, ever wish to spend a few quiet moments at that site? Not only she, but also Peter and John and many others would feel the call of a sanctuary that held the remains of the Great Teacher.[83] If Christ's followers really knew their Lord were buried somewhere, isn't it strange that His grave didn't become a place of reverence and pilgrimage?

VI. THE WOMEN WENT TO THE WRONG TOMB

In 1907 Prof. Kirsopp Lake, D. D., a liberal New Testament scholar and professor at the University of Chicago, wrote a book [84] proposing the theory that the women simply made a mistake identifying the grave in the dim light of the early dawn. Lake doubts that the women could be certain which grave held Jesus' body, since he says Jerusalem's neighborhood is full of rock tombs, so it wouldn't be easy to tell one from another. He also feels that instead of being close to the tomb at the moment of burial, the women were more likely watching from a distance. If so, they would have had limited power to distinguish between one rock tomb and another close to it. Lake suggests that, on reaching an unexpectedly open tomb, they encountered a young man—possibly the gardener—who, recognizing their errand, tried to tell them they'd come to the wrong place. "He is not here," he said. "See the place where they laid Him." Then he probably pointed to the next tomb. But the women, frightened at the detection of their errand, fled without waiting for the young man to finish his statement and thus explain their mistake. Lake also asks us to believe that the women didn't tell the apostles this stupendous news for seven weeks, whereupon they started at once to preach it on the Day of Pentecost.

This novel supposition—that the women went to the wrong tomb—leaves several important questions unanswered:

- Is it likely that all three of the women who had so lovingly and coura-
geously attended to the last rites of Jesus on Friday afternoon would
mistake the location of His tomb a mere 36 hours later? Would any
rational person forget so quickly the place where a dear loved one was
laid to rest? While it's possible for anyone to make a mistake, in this
case it's most unlikely—for at least two reasons: (1) The women knew
they had to return to finish the task of proper burial. Planning to return
early Sunday morning, they'd logically seek out landmarks to remember,
as we seek location markers to recall where we parked our car in a
crowded parking lot. (2) Why should a tomb be so confusing and difficult to identify, since it was located in a private garden,[85] not a public
cemetery?

- Can it be argued that Peter and John also went to the wrong tomb? It's
inconceivable that both Peter and John would succumb to the SAME
mistake. Certainly Joseph of Arimathea, who owned the tomb, would
have solved the problem by correctly identifying it for them![86]

- Can we believe that neither the women nor the disciples ever went back
to the tomb to be sure that the right tomb was really empty? Isn't it
likely they would "double check" on such an important matter?

Prof. Lake blames the supposed mistake on the early morning darkness.
But if it was so dark that the women accidentally went to the wrong tomb,
it's quite improbable that the "gardener" would have been at work. And if it
was late enough and light enough for him to be at work, it's improbable that
the women would have made a mistake. The early hour poses a problem for
those who hold this theory.

Also, if this theory is true, why didn't the priests produce the young
"gardener" and explode the whole delusion by securing his testimony as
evidence that the women went to the wrong tomb?[87] The young man was
not the gardener—he was an angel from heaven.

Furthermore, how does this theory account for the many appearances
the living Christ made to others besides the women?

To make his theory more plausible, Professor Lake deliberately misquoted
the angel's words to the women by leaving out the key words "He is risen"
from the middle of his statement. The true quotation reads: "Do not be afraid,
for I know that you seek Jesus who was crucified. He is not here; for *He is
risen*, as He said. Come, see the place where the Lord lay. And go quickly
and tell His disciples that *He is risen from the dead. . . .*"[88] The impulse to
theorize may be strong, but arbitrarily ignoring part of the evidence is a
questionable practice for scholars or anyone else seeking truth.

One further point will dispose of this theory completely: IF the resurrection story arose because the women went to the wrong tomb, why didn't the priests go to the RIGHT tomb and produce the body?

VII. THE SWOON THEORY

Stated as fairly as possible, this final theory asserts that Christ did not actually die on the cross but simply swooned—fainted away—from pain, shock, and loss of blood. He was believed to be dead by all, since medical knowledge was limited at that time. Taken down from the cross in a state of swoon, He was placed in the tomb by those who mistakenly believed Him to be dead. The cool temperature of the grave revived Him enough so that eventually He was able to come forth from the tomb. His ignorant disciples couldn't believe this was a mere resuscitation—they insisted it was a miraculous resurrection from the dead.[89]

This theory ignores several vital facts. First of all, it wasn't until the end of the seventeenth century that a skeptic named Venturini first propounded this theory, and he overlooks the fact that all early historical accounts are emphatic about the fact that Christ died. There's clear evidence that even the Jewish leaders, the ENEMIES of Jesus, believed He was dead. For we read that they went to Pilate, saying, "Sir, we remember that that deceiver said, while He was YET ALIVE, After three days I will rise again"[90]—and they asked to have guards placed at the tomb.

Among all the insinuations levelled against Christianity since the beginning, no whisper has ever been heard that Jesus didn't die.[91] Testimony is positive and unanimous that He died a martyr's death.

Furthermore, Roman soldiers were familiar with evidences of death and with the sight of death following crucifixion. They knew a dead man when they saw one. Their commanding officer certified Jesus' death to the governor, Pontius Pilate,[92] who seemed surprised at the report that Christ was dead already.[93] Pilate verified this point by direct questioning of the centurion before giving permission for the disposal of the body.[94] If Pilate himself was sufficiently convinced by the centurion's assurance of Christ's death, perhaps we can accept his certification also.

The record is clear that "when they [the soldiers] came to Jesus, [they] saw that He was dead already. . . . But one of the soldiers with a spear pierced His side, and forthwith came there out BLOOD and WATER."[95] In other words, they knew He was dead, but just to make doubly sure they pierced His heart with a spear. There's no indication the body made any movement when the lance penetrated. But the point I wish to make is well expressed by British writer Michael Green:

"Had Jesus been alive when the spear pierced His side, strong spurts of blood would have emerged with every heartbeat. Instead, the observer noticed semi-solid dark red clot seeping out, distinct and separate from the accompanying watery serum. This is evidence of massive clotting of the blood in the main arteries, and is exceptionally strong medical proof of death. It is all the more impressive because the evangelist [the apostle John] could not possibly have realized its significance to a pathologist. The 'blood and water' from the spear-thrust is proof positive that Jesus was already dead." [96]

Samuel Houghton, M.D., the great physiologist from the University of Dublin, comments on this very point: "The importance of this is obvious. It shows that the narrative in St. John XIX could never have been invented; that the facts recorded must have been seen by an eye-witness; and that the eye-witness was so astonished that he apparently thought the phenomenon miraculous." [97]

✓ PHYSICALLY Impossible

The swoon theory also completely ignores the deadly character of the wounds inflicted upon Jesus. First of all, He was beaten with a brutal instrument called a *flagrum* which uses sharp pieces of bone and metal to lacerate flesh as it lashes the victim. The Hebrews limited by law the number of strokes to forty, but the Romans set no such limitation, so the victim was at the mercy of his scourgers. Early historians describe the horrible nature of the Roman scourging as almost equivalent to capital punishment, for the sufferer's veins were laid bare and sometimes the very muscles, sinews, and bowels of the victim were open to exposure.[98] And Christ's scourging may even have surpassed the severity of a normal one, judging by the vile mood of the soldiers who beat Jesus with their fists as they mocked and spat upon Him. [99]

Furthermore, crucifixion was an excruciatingly painful death, in which every nerve throbbed with incessant anguish. The lacerated veins and tendons, the loss of strength from the ebbing away of blood, the hopelessness of human aid when it was most needed—all these took their toll on the victim's utterly collapsed constitution. If Jesus WERE still alive when placed in the tomb, He would have been bleeding from FIVE gaping wounds, one caused by the spear which formed a hole large enough for a hand to enter.[100] Then He was placed on the cold slab of a tomb in April without food or water or medical attention or human help of any kind. To think this would revive Him instead of finishing His flickering life is to believe the impossible.[101]

Then, too, there's the problem of the stone which sealed the mouth of the tomb. Matthew speaks of this rock as "a great stone."[102] Mark says, "It was very great."[103] No doubt such stones were so large and consequently of such tremendous weight that several men were required to move them. The three women knew their combined strength couldn't move it.[104] Yet this theory asks us to believe that Jesus, greatly weakened by loss of blood and suffering terribly from his wounds, single-handedly performed the superhuman feat of moving that enormous stone!

Next, what about the guards? It's absurd to suppose that Jesus, staggering half-dead out of the tomb, could have fought off the Roman guards and made good His escape even if He had somehow managed to move away the stone.

Late in the afternoon on the day of the resurrection, two disciples were on their way to Emmaus, a small town seven miles from Jerusalem. They hadn't gone very far when they were joined by Christ (whom they failed to recognize at first because of their dejected mood). The Record tells us that Jesus walked the distance with them.[105] Are we to believe that Jesus, on feet which had been pierced through and through only two days before, walked without difficulty those miles between Emmaus and Jerusalem?? Are these the actions of a man who had just been taken down half-dead from the cross and laid in a grave in a state of complete exhaustion?

The swoon theory would have us believe that simply the cool restfulness of the tomb revived and invigorated the unconscious Lord. Yet one who has fainted away is ordinarily revived NOT by being shut up in a cave but by being brought out into the fresh air.

Even if Jesus were not dead and happened to regain consciousness in the sealed tomb, how could He manage—alone—to free Himself from the constricting graveclothes wrapped over His hands and arms as well as the rest of His body? This would be an escape act worthy of Houdini himself! Yet suppose we grant that it were accomplished:

If a merely human Jesus had recovered from a swoon, he would NOT have left the tomb without the graveclothes, for modesty would have prevented him from going forth NAKED. But if the Son of God rose in an immortal body, clothed with power from on high, clothes were superfluous, and the stately majesty of deity could have taken the time to fold the napkin which loving hands had wrapped around His head.[106]

✓ PSYCHOLOGICALLY Impossible

We've just seen that removal of the heavy stone and other considerations make the swoon theory a PHYSICAL impossibility. Be aware also of the PSYCHOLOGICAL impossibility inherent in this hypothesis. How could someone who crept half-dead out of a tomb, needing bandaging, strengthening, and tender care, give the disciples the impression that He was the Lord and Conqueror over death and the grave? The pitiful picture given couldn't possibly change their sorrow into enthusiasm or elevate their reverence into worship.[107]

A further psychological impossibility in the swoon theory, since it eliminates the whole Ascension narrative, is that it must "account for the sudden cessation of Christ's appearances by supposing that He withdrew Himself completely, to live and die in absolute seclusion."[108] He must have retired to some solitary retreat unknown even to closest friends. At the very time His church was rising around Him—while it was torn by controversies, exposed to trials, and placed in circumstances making it most dependent on His aid—He was absent from it to spend the rest of His days in solitude. And then at last He must have died—no one can say where, when, or how![109]

✓ MORALLY & ETHICALLY Impossible

Finally, we must face the MORAL and ETHICAL impossibility that Christ would be party to a colossal lie. For "IF Jesus had only swooned, He could not, without injury to His character, allow anyone to believe He'd been dead."[110] Remaining silent, He would have been a liar and deceiver of the worst kind. The swoon theory makes the Lord of truth the author of error.

CONCLUSION

We've analyzed the seven major theories offered as alternatives to the fact of Christ's resurrection. We've examined:

1. The **FABRICATION** Theory
2. The **HALLUCINATION** Theory
3. The **DISCIPLES** Stole the Body
4. **ENEMIES** of Christ Took His Body
5. **JOSEPH of ARIMATHEA** Removed the Body
6. The Women Went to the **WRONG TOMB**
7. The **SWOON** Theory

We've seen that these theories lack credibility. A point that needs stressing is that evidence must be considered as a WHOLE. It's comparatively easy to find an alternate explanation for one or another of the different strands of testimony. But such explanations are worthless unless they fit the other facts as well. A number of different theories, each of which might conceivably fit part of the evidence, can provide no alternative to the ONE explanation which fits the whole.[111]

We've seen that in an age which calls for evidence, the Christian can intellectually defend his belief. The critic, on the other hand, must abandon these theories when shown that they're impossible. As the great detective Sherlock Holmes wisely told Dr. Watson, "When you have eliminated the impossible, whatever remains, however improbable, MUST be the truth."[112]

Yes, the resurrection is the truth—the very stubbornness of the facts themselves force us to that conclusion. Both the MISSION and MESSAGE of Christ would have counted for nothing had He not risen from the dead. The grave in the garden is empty—we've seen the irresistible logic of that fact. But the resurrection never becomes a fact of EXPERIENCE till the risen Christ LIVES in the heart of the believer. The most important thing about the resurrection is not an empty tomb in Palestine two thousand years ago, but the risen Lord today, whom we can meet and know for ourselves. Belief in Christ takes more than a mere acknowledgment of evidence. Pilate heard that Jesus arose—it troubled him till the day he died, but it didn't save him. You see, *conviction* is not the same as *COMMITMENT!*

The resurrection of Christ is not a myth but a miracle. Buddha's tomb is occupied. Confucius's tomb is occupied. Mohammed's tomb is occupied. But Jesus' tomb is EMPTY! Mountains piled upon mountains over His grave could not have prevented His coming forth. And this fact matters to US, for it seals the certainty of *our own* future resurrection. Christ triumphantly declares: "I am the Resurrection, and the Life: he that believeth in Me, though he were dead, yet shall he live."[113] To every faithful follower, Jesus says: "Because I live, YE shall live also. . . . I am He that liveth, and was dead; and, behold, I am alive for evermore, Amen."[114]

It's paradoxically true that the GRAVE of Christ became the BIRTHPLACE of Christianity because Jesus rose again. The Church today rests on the solid rock of its risen Savior. Reason leads us to this FINAL VERDICT: The stupendous miracle of Christ's Resurrection really happened. When Jesus died upon the Cross, that mighty heart of love was *stilled* by death. But praise the Lord, *it beats once again* for us! The great and glorious Truth is—"The Lord is risen indeed"![115]

Notes to Chapter 8

1. Paraphrased from Henry P. Liddon, *Sermons* (New York: The Contemporary Pulpit Library, 1888), p. 73.
2. 1 Corinthians 15:14.
3. Matthew 12:38-40 & John 2:18-21. B. B. Warfield's statement along these lines is quoted in J. N. D. Anderson, *Christianity: The Witness of History* (Tyndale Press, 1970), p. 103.
4. This thought was first expressed by Wilbur M. Smith in his excellent book *Therefore, Stand* (Boston: W. A. Wilde Co., 1945), p. 386.
5. Michael Green, *Man Alive!* (Downers Grove, Illinois: Inter-Varsity Press, 1968), p. 61.
6. William Lyon Phelps, *Human Nature and the Gospel*, pp. 131-132.
7. Thomas Arnold, *Sermons on the Christian Life—Its Hopes, Its Fears, and Its Close,* 6th edition (London, 1859), p. 324.
8. John Singleton Copley (Lord Lyndhurst), quoted in Wilbur M. Smith, *Therefore, Stand* (Boston: W. A. Wilde Co., 1945), pp. 425 & 584.
9. Leslie G. Storz, "Many Infallible Proofs," *Review and Herald* Magazine (April 4, 1968), p. 6.
10. Albert Roper, *Did Jesus Rise from the Dead?* (Grand Rapids: Zondervan Publishing House, 1965), p. 50. See Matthew 26:69-75, Mark 14:66-72, Luke 22:54-62, and John 18:25-27.
11. Matthew 13:55-58, Mark 6:3-6, and John 7:5.
12. Galatians 1:19 and 2:9.
13. 1 Corinthians 15:7.
14. John 20:24-29.
15. Paraphrased from Frank Morison, *Who Moved the Stone?* (Downers Grove, Illinois: Inter-Varsity Press, 1967), pp. 142-143.
16. See Acts 7:58 – 8:4 and 9:1-31.
17. J. N. D. Anderson, *The Evidence for the Resurrection* (Downers Grove, Illinois: Inter-Varsity Press, c. 1966), p. 8.
18. Colossians 3:9. See also Revelation 21:8 & 27, and 22:15.
19. This statement comes from the pen of Simon Greenleaf (1783-1853), famous Royall Professor of Law at Harvard University who succeeded Justice Joseph Story as the Dane Professor of Law in the same University upon Story's death in 1846. The *Dictionary of American Biography* states that "To the efforts of Story and Greenleaf is to be ascribed the rise of the Harvard Law School to its eminent position among the legal schools in the United States." Greenleaf produced a famous work entitled *A Treatise on the Law of Evidence* (1842), still considered the greatest single authority on evidence in the entire literature of legal procedure. In 1846, while Professor of Law at Harvard, this brilliant jurist wrote a volume entitled *Testimony of the Evangelists, Examined by the Rules of Evidence Administered in Courts of Justice.* Our quotation was taken from pages 29-30 of that book, a reprint of which was published in 1965 by Baker Book House, Grand Rapids, Michigan.

20. Compare Alfred Edersheim, *The Life and Times of Jesus the Messiah* (Grand Rapids: William B. Eerdmans Publishing Co., 1962), Volume II, p. 628.

21. Acts 1:3-9.

22. See the Bible references in footnote #10, above, and also Matthew 26:36-46, Mark 14:32-42, and Luke 22:39-46.

23. Acts 26:26.

24. Josh McDowell, *Evidence That Demands a Verdict* (San Bernardino, Calif.: Here's Life Publishers, Inc., 1979), Volume I, p. 225. This book is an excellent resource.

25. This point is made by H. D. A. Major in *The Mission and Message of Jesus* (New York: 1938), p. 213, and by Paul E. Little in *Know Why You Believe* (Wheaton, Illinois: Scripture Press Publications, 1967), p. 62.

26. Acts 2:41 & 47 and 4:4.

27. Acts 6:7.

28. Paraphrased from Michael Green, *Man Alive!* (Downers Grove, Illinois: Inter-Varsity Press, 1968), p. 48—a very valuable book.

29. Acts 17:6.

30. Philippians 4:22.

31. See Hebrews 11:35-38 for a catalog of the hardships and trials suffered by the early Christians. One graffiti scribbler with a sick sense of humor was thinking of the wholesale slaughter of believers in the Roman arena when he wrote on the wall this box score: "LIONS 92, CHRISTIANS 0."

32. For much of this material on the hallucination theory, the author is indebted to McDowell, *Evidence That Demands a Verdict,* pp. 247-255; Anderson, *Evidence for the Resurrection,* pp. 20-23; and Green, *Man Alive!* pp. 46-47.

33. Paul William Peru, *Outline of Psychiatric Case-Study* (New York: Paul B. Hoeger, Inc., 1939), pp. 97-99.

34. Paraphrased from John R. W. Stott, *Basic Christianity* (Downers Grove, Illinois: Inter-Varsity Press, 1971), p. 57.

35. 1 Corinthians 15:6. For a chart of Christ's post-resurrection appearances, see *Appendix D,* page 791.

36. Peru, *loc. cit.*

37. Christ did appear to Saul/Paul at a later date, but the circumstances on that occasion were altogether exceptional. See Acts 9:1-31.

38. See Albert Roper, *Did Jesus Rise from the Dead?* (Grand Rapids: Zondervan Publishing House, 1965), p. 34.

39. Luke 24:36-43. See also John 20:24-29, which shows that only a tangible, physical body would satisfy the skepticism of Doubting Thomas.

40. Peru, *loc cit.*

41. When Jesus foretold His death and resurrection to His disciples, "they understood none of these things." Luke 18:31-34. See also Matthew 16:21 and John 20:9.

42. Mark 16:3-4.

43. John 20:13.

44. John 20:14-16.

45. Mark 16:11-14 and Luke 24:8-11.

46. Luke 24:25. See also Mark 16:14.

47. Luke 24:15-16 & 30-31.

48. For instance, when Jesus warned His disciples "that they should tell no man what things they had seen, till the Son of Man were risen from the dead . . . they kept that saying within themselves, questioning one with another what the rising of the dead should mean." Mark 9:9-10.

49. Matthew 28:11.

50. Wilbur M. Smith, *Therefore, Stand* (Boston: W. A. Wilde Co., 1945), pp. 375-376.

51. R. C. H. Lenski, *The Interpretation of St. Matthew's Gospel* (Columbus, Ohio: The Wartburg Press, 1943), p. 1161.

52. Matthew 28:12-15.

53. Evidently the Jewish rulers themselves did not believe what they instructed and bribed the soldiers to say. If they did, why weren't the disciples at once ARRESTED and QUESTIONED? The act imputed to them was a serious offense against authority. Why were they never PUNISHED for their crime? Nowhere is it intimated that the rulers even attempted to substantiate their charge. See Richard W. Dickinson, *The Resurrection of Jesus Christ Historically and Logically Viewed* (Philadelphia: 1865), pp. 31-32.

54. See Luke 22:31-34.

55. Paraphrased from A. B. Bruce, *The Training of the Twelve* (Grand Rapids: Kregel Publications, 1971) p. 494.

56. Mark 14:50.

57. Paraphrased from Samuel Fallow, editor, *The Popular and Critical Bible Encyclopedia and Scriptural Dictionary* (Chicago: The Howard Severance Co., 1908), Volume III, p. 1452.

58. Matthew 27:65.

59. Matthew 27:62-64.

60. Matthew 28:14.

61. George Currie, *The Military Discipline of the Romans from the Founding of the City to the Close of the Republic* (Abstract of his thesis published at Indiana University, 1928), p. 33.

62. *Ibid.*, p. 42.

63. Matthew 27:35, Mark 15:24, and John 19:23-24.

64. Albert Roper, *Did Jesus Rise from the Dead?* (Grand Rapids: Zondervan Publishing House, 1965), p. 33.

65. Paul E. Little, *Know Why You Believe* (Wheaton, Illinois: Scripture Press Publications, Inc., 1967), p. 64.

66. Matthew 28:2.

67. Matthew 28:3-4, NIV.

68. John 20:3-7.

69. John 19:39-40. Verse 40 says, "Then took they the body of Jesus, and wound it in linen clothes with the spices. . . ." But the practice of the time was also to anoint the body with a semiliquid unguent such as spikenard. The head and hair were also anointed with this unguent. But when our Lord's body was hurriedly prepared for

burial on Friday afternoon, sunset was fast approaching and with it the sacred hours of the Sabbath. So the body was simply wrapped with the linen using the myrrh and aloes. Then on Sunday morning the women were seeking to repair this omission as far as they could by bringing spikenard or some other costly unguent to complete the anointing. See also Luke 23:53 – 24:1.

70. See John Chrysostom, Archbishop of Constantinople in the 4th century, *Homilies on the Gospel of Saint Matthew*, in *A Select Library of the Nicene and Post-Nicene Fathers of the Christian Church*, edited by Philip Schaff (New York: The Christian Literature Company, 1888), Volume X, p. 530.

71. Paraphrased from Albert Roper, *Did Jesus Rise from the Dead?* (Grand Rapids: Zondervan Publishing House, 1965), p. 36.

72. John 20:8.

73. Matt. 16:21, 17:22-23, Mark 9:31, Luke 9:22, and John 2:19-21.

74. Acts 5:26.

75. Acts 5:28.

76. Paraphrased from Josh McDowell, *Evidence That Demands a Verdict* (San Bernardino, California: Here's Life Publishers, Inc., 1979), Volume I, p. 246.

77. Wilbur M. Smith, *Therefore, Stand* (Boston: W. A. Wilde Co., 1945), p. 380.

78. Matthew 27:57, John 19:38 and 12:42.

79. John 3:1-6, 7:50, and 19:39.

80. Luke 23:50-53.

81. Matthew 27:60.

82. Mark 15:43 & Luke 23:50.

83. Attorney Frank Morison raises these points in his excellent book *Who Moved the Stone?* (Downers Grove, Illinois: Inter-Varsity Press, 1967), p. 137.

84. Kirsopp Lake, *The Historical Evidence for the Resurrection of Jesus* (New York: Putnam, 1912), pp. 250-253.

85. John 19:41.

86. Paul E. Little, *Know Why You Believe* (Wheaton, Illinois: Scripture Press Publications, Inc., 1967), p. 65.

87. See Frank Morison, *Who Moved the Stone?* pp. 97-102.

88. Matthew 28:5-7, NKJV. Please note that the angel commanded the women to announce Jesus' RESURRECTION. See also Mark 16:6-7 and Luke 24:5-7.

89. Paraphrased from J. N. D. Anderson, *Christianity: The Witness of History* (Tyndale Press, c. 1970), p. 7.

90. Matthew 27:63.

91. Basic to Christian thought is the doctrine that Christ, the Son of God, died on the Cross to pay the penalty for our sins. His death, as a divine sacrifice, provides the basis of our salvation when we accept Jesus as our Savior. Groups or individuals who deny this Bible teaching cannot be considered Christian. Yet Mary Baker Eddy, the woman who founded the religion called "Christian Science," wrote this about Christ's condition between His crucifixion and resurrection: "His disciples believed Jesus to be dead while He was hidden in the sepulchre, whereas He was ALIVE." — *Science and Health with Key to the Scriptures* (Boston: Trustees under the Will of

Mary Baker G. Eddy, 1875 & 1934), p. 44. She makes this amazing statement on her own authority alone, giving no sources, ancient or modern, nor offering any Scriptural evidence. (Again with no evidence to support her statement, Mrs. Eddy also denies the doctrine of the Holy Trinity—Father, Son, and Holy Spirit as three Persons in one: p. 515 of her book.) Professor Smith is bold to say: "Let us remember that the one who, herself, said that death was something unreal, in fact, that there was no death, is held in the chains of death in a burial plot outside of Boston, where her grave is visited by many of her deceived followers each year. I refer to Mrs. Mary Baker Eddy." —Wilbur M. Smith, *Therefore, Stand* (Boston: W. A. Wilde Co., 1945), p. 385.

92. Paraphrased from Michael Green, *Man Alive!* (Downers Grove, Illinois: Inter-Varsity Press, 1968), pp. 32-33.

93. Mark 15:44.

94. Mark 15:43-45.

95. John 19:33-34.

96. Michael Green. *Man Alive!* (Downers Grove, Illinois: Inter-Varsity Press, 1968), p. 33.

97. Samuel Houghton, quoted in Frederick Charles Cook. *Commentary on the Holy Bible* (London: John Murray, 1878), p. 350. The Apostle testified: "He who has seen has borne witness, and his witness is true; and he knows that he is telling the truth, so that you also may believe." John 19:35, NASB. Also, a major medical publication recently addressed the issue of Christ's death when three experts conducted a post-mortem review and concluded that "interpretations based on the assumption that Jesus did not die on the cross appear to be at odds with modern medical knowledge." See William D. Edwards, M.D. (Mayo Clinic pathologist), *et al.*, "On the Physical Death of Jesus Christ," *Journal of the American Medical Association* (March 21, 1986), Volume 255, pp. 1455-1463.

98. John P. Mattingly, *Crucifixion: Its Origin and Application to Christ* (unpublished Master of Theology thesis, Dallas Theological Seminary, May 1961), pp. 21, 33, and 73.

99. Matthew 26:67-68, Mark 14:65, and Luke 22:63-65.

100. John 20:27.

101. See J. N. D. Anderson, "The Resurrection of Jesus Christ," *Christianity Today* (March 29, 1968), p. 7.

102. Matthew 27:60.

103. Mark 16:4.

104. Mark 16:3.

105. Luke 24:13-35 and Mark 16:12.

106. Floyd E. Hamilton, *The Basis of Christian Faith: A Modern Defense of the Christian Religion*, Third Revised Edition (New York: Harper & Brothers, 1946), p. 304.

107. These thoughts are paraphrased from a skeptic who didn't believe at all in Christ's resurrection but who nonetheless repudiates the fanciful idea of the swoon theory, David Friedrich Strauss, in his book *The Life of Jesus for the People*, English translation, 2nd edition (London: Williams and Norgate, 1879), Volume I, p. 412.

108. E. H. Day, *On the Evidence for the Resurrection* (London: Society for Promoting Christian Knowledge, 1906), p. 50.

109. Paraphrased from William Milligan, *The Resurrection of Our Lord* (New York: The Macmillan Company, 1927), p. 79.

110. E. Le Camus, *The Life of Christ* (New York: The Cathedral Library Association, 1908), Volume III, p. 485.

111. Paraphrased from British attorney J. N. D. Anderson in "A Dialogue on Christ's Resurrection," *Christianity Today* (April 12, 1968), p. 105.

112. Sherlock Holmes, in Arthur Conan Doyle, *The Sign of Four.*

113. John 11:25.

114. John 14:19 and Revelation 1:18. Don't be caught DEAD—without Jesus.

115. Luke 24:34.

Jesus asks: "But who do YOU say that I am?"

—MATTHEW 16:15, NKJV

Chapter Nine

~

Life's Greatest Question

ONE SUMMER, a little girl who never went to church attended vacation Bible school in her neighborhood. She rushed home the first day and breathlessly told her mother: "Know what, Mom? Jesus is a real Person, not just a swear word!"

To many, Jesus Christ is nothing but a convenient cuss-word, yet He was a real Person. But what else was He? Was He really the divine Son of God? That's the crucial question.

Sometimes Jesus asked embarrassing questions. Once He asked the Pharisees, "What think ye of Christ? Whose Son is He?"[1] And He asked His disciples, "Whom do men say that I the Son of man am?"[2] Hearing that some thought He was simply one of the prophets, Jesus pressed His followers for a more personal answer to THE GREATEST QUESTION EVER ASKED: "But whom say YE that I am?"[3]

Thoughtful people today puzzle over this same vital question. They ponder the matter and still ask: "Wasn't Jesus just a very good man and a great teacher—a 'son of God' in the same sense that we're all children of God?"

This chapter will give reasons why Christians believe Jesus was much more than human—much more, even, than the greatest man who ever lived. Jesus was and is God in the fullest sense of that term, the divine Son of God who "thought it not robbery to be equal with God,"[4] and the Second Member of the Holy Trinity. First, let's examine some Scripture statements which are quite clear and consistent:

TESTIMONY OF GOD THE FATHER:

- "This is My beloved Son, in whom I am well pleased." [5]

TESTIMONY OF THE ANGEL GABRIEL:

- "He shall be . . . called the Son of the Highest." [6]

- "He shall save His people from their sins." [7]

TESTIMONY OF JOHN THE BAPTIST:

- "Behold the Lamb of God, which taketh away the sin
  of the world. . . . This is the Son of God." [8]

TESTIMONY OF JUDAS, HIS BETRAYER:

- "I have sinned in that I have betrayed the innocent blood." [9]

TESTIMONY OF DEMONS AS UNCLEAN SPIRITS:

- "I know who You are—the Holy One of God!" [10]

- "You are the Son of God." [11]

TESTIMONY OF THE ROMAN COMMANDER:

- "Truly this Man was the Son of God." [12]

TESTIMONY OF THE APOSTLE PETER:

- "Salvation is found in no one else, for there is no other name
  under heaven given to men, by which we must be saved." [13]

TESTIMONY OF THE APOSTLE PAUL:

- "We have a great High Priest, that is passed into the heavens,
  Jesus the Son of God." [14]

TESTIMONY OF THE APOSTLE JOHN:

- "These are written, that ye might believe that Jesus is
  the Christ, the Son of God; and that believing
  ye might have life through His name." [15]

TESTIMONY OF CHRIST HIMSELF:

- "I am the Way, the Truth, and the Life:
  no man cometh unto the Father, but by Me." [16]

- "I am the Door: by Me if any man enter in,
  he shall be saved." [17]

- "I am the Resurrection, and the Life: he that believeth
  in Me, though he were dead, yet shall he live." [18]

- "I am the Light of the world." [19]

- "I am the living Bread which cometh down from heaven:
  If any man eat of this bread, he shall live forever." [20]

- "I came down from heaven, not to do mine own will,
  but the will of Him that sent Me." [21]

- "I am from above. . . . I am not of this world. . . . If ye
  believe NOT that I am He, ye shall DIE in your sins." [22]

- "For God so loved the world, that He gave His only begotten
  Son, that whosoever believeth in Him should not perish,
  but have everlasting life." [23]

- "The High Priest questioned Him, 'Are you the Christ,
  the Son of the Blessed One?' Jesus said, 'I am.'" [24]

- "The woman said, 'I know that Messiah . . . is coming.
  When He comes, He will explain everything to us.'
  Then Jesus declared, 'I who speak to you am He.'" [25]

- After healing the man born blind, Jesus asked him,
  "'Do you believe in the Son of God?' He answered and said,
  'Who is He, Lord, that I may believe in Him?'
  And Jesus said to him, 'You have both seen Him and it is He
  who is talking with you.' Then he said, 'Lord, I believe!'
  And he worshiped Him." [26]

THE STUPENDOUS CLAIMS OF CHRIST

Christ did make astonishing claims about Himself. No wonder the Pharisees were incensed to hear such enormous claims coming from the lips of this humble carpenter of Nazareth! But the claims of Jesus weren't those of a mere human teacher.

No other religious teacher made such claims about himself. For example, consider GAUTAMA BUDDHA (563-483 B.C.), the founder of Buddhism, a religion which has influenced perhaps half the human race. Men called him Buddha, "the enlightened one." He believed that he had a marvelous doctrine to offer men, but he never sanctioned or encouraged anyone to worship him.

He urged his followers not to think of him but rather to concentrate on his teaching.

CONFUCIUS (551-479 B.C.), the first and greatest of Chinese philosophers, with charming humility declared: "How dare I lay claim to holiness or love? A man of endless craving, who never tires of teaching, I might be called, but nothing more."[27]

Finally, MOHAMMED (A.D. 570-632), the Arabian prophet of the sixth century A.D. and founder of Islam, laid claim to no special significance for himself. He said he was just a man like other men. An old tradition has him say: "Praise me not as Jesus the son of Mary is praised."

In sharp contrast to the attitude of those great religious leaders, however, stand the astounding claims of CHRIST, who declared with supreme confidence: "All power is given unto Me in heaven and in earth."[28] Yet many today ignore those claims and prefer to think of Him simply as a dedicated, serious young man with a great concern for people. In some cases those who consider Jesus as nothing more than "a good man, a great teacher" pride themselves on their reasoning ability and the cool logic of their intellects, and they sometimes look down upon the believer in Christ as being emotional rather than coolly logical. But let's scrutinize their position and see how logical it really is.

Remember that in no uncertain terms, Jesus claimed to be the Son of God. But if He was not what He claimed to be, He was a blasphemous LIAR— the greatest hypocrite the world has ever seen and worthy of no honor whatsoever. Consider the strong statements of Christ quoted above in relation to the words of a modern writer, C. S. Lewis. In his stimulating little book *Mere Christianity,* the late Mr. Lewis examines Christ's claim to divinity:

> "One part of the claim tends to slip past us unnoticed because we've heard it so often that we no longer see what it amounts to. I mean the claim to FORGIVE SINS: any sins. Now unless the speaker is God, this is really so preposterous as to be comic. We can all understand how a man forgives offenses against himself. You tread on my toe and I forgive you, you steal my money and I forgive you. But what should we make of a man, himself unrobbed and untrodden on, who announces that he forgave you for treading on other men's toes and stealing other men's money? Asinine fatuity is the kindest description we should give of his conduct. Yet this is what Jesus did. He told people that their sins were forgiven,[29] and never waited to consult all the other people whom their sins had undoubtedly injured. He unhesitatingly behaved as if He was the party chiefly concerned, the person chiefly offended in all offenses. This makes sense only if He really was the God whose laws are broken and whose love is wounded in every sin. In the

mouth of any speaker who is not God, these words imply a silliness and conceit unrivalled by any other character in history.

"Yet (and this is the strange, significant thing) even His enemies, when they read the Gospels, do not usually get the impression of silliness and conceit. Still less do unprejudiced readers. Christ says that He is 'humble and meek' [30] and we believe Him; not noticing that, if He were merely a man, humility and meekness are the very last characteristics we could attribute to some of His sayings.

"I am trying here to prevent anyone saying the really foolish thing that people often say about Him: 'I'm ready to accept Jesus as a great moral teacher, but I don't accept His claim to be God.' That is the one thing we must NOT say. A man who was merely a man and said the sort of things Jesus said would NOT be a great moral teacher. He would either be a lunatic—on a level with the man who says he is a poached egg—or else he would be the Devil of Hell. You must make your choice. Either this man was, and is, the Son of God: or else a madman or something worse. You can shut Him up for a fool, you can spit at Him and kill Him as a demon; or you can fall at His feet and call Him Lord and God. But let's not come with any patronizing nonsense about His being a great human teacher. He has not left that open to us. He did not intend to." [31]

Yet a friend of mine, a very successful dentist, once argued: "Jesus was simply an effective leader who realized that no one would follow him unless he appeared strong, confident, and extraordinarily resourceful. So when he made those extravagant claims, he knowingly and deliberately stretched the truth—but he did it for a good cause."

In other words, my friend felt that Jesus believed the end justifies the means. Hitler was that kind of leader, and we give him the contempt that kind of leadership deserves. And if Christ were the same kind of leader—a "great moral teacher" who departed from strict adherence to truth if and when it suited His purpose—then He would deserve no more respect than unscrupulous men like Hitler.

In thinking of Jesus as a leader, bear in mind what His mission, His purpose was. Christ was not concerned about breaking the yoke of Roman bondage. If that were His objective, He was singularly unsuccessful, for all His disciples lived and died under Roman rule. He was not a political reformer—as He Himself put it: "My kingdom is not of this world." [32]

No, Christ's mission clearly was a spiritual one—His goal: to teach men the truth about God and to save men from their sins. Is it reasonable, then, to think He'd resort to the sin of lying to accomplish His purpose? Those who believe this theory about Christ are willing enough to impute good motives to His telling lies but unwilling to accept Him as the divine Son of God.

If the whole fabric of Christ's ministry was merely a web of well-intentioned falsehood, this theory still places Him in the class of LIAR, for a lie is a lie regardless of motive.

JESUS CHRIST: DECEIVER or DIVINE?

Taking into account the lofty claims of Christ, certain implications become clear. To say that "Jesus was a good man but not the divine Son of God" is not open to us as a valid option—simply because good men don't lie! Let's cross this option off our list, as I have below:

> ~~GOOD MAN~~
> ● ~~a great teacher~~
> ● ~~a wise philosopher~~
> ● ~~a kind humanitarian~~

We're left, then, with only three possibilities when we consider Christ. He was either:

(1) A **madman**—a lunatic babbling insane claims born of delusions of grandeur, who unintentionally deceived people, *or*

(2) A **bad man**—a charlatan and impostor who deliberately tried to deceive people, *or*

(3) A **God-man**—the divine Son who honestly was what He demonstrated Himself to be, bringing eternal salvation to all who accept and follow Him.

We can graphically show these three options below: [33]

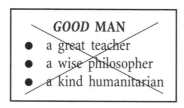

MADMAN	*BAD* MAN	*GOD*-MAN
● demented	● a charlatan	● the Lord
● deluded	● a phony	● the Savior
● deranged	● an impostor	● the Son of God

So make your choice—LUNATIC, LIAR, or LORD—what think ye of Christ? It's difficult to judge Him insane, for His teachings have the authentic ring of truth and rank among the most noble utterances in history. And it would be strange indeed if He were simply a bad man telling lies—

He'd certainly be a fool to die for His claims to divinity if they were only fabrications, for they were what led to His crucifixion. The only alternative left for us to accept is that Jesus Christ is exactly what he claimed to be— the divine Son of the living God!

You see, Jesus didn't leave an equivocal middle road open to us. On the contrary, He declared: "He that is not with Me is against Me." [34] And "I know your works: you are neither cold nor hot. Would that you were cold or hot! So, because you are lukewarm, and neither cold nor hot, I will spew you out of My mouth." [35]

But He did leave us an open invitation to receive Him: "Behold, I stand at the door, and knock: if any man hear My voice, and open the door, I will come in to him, and will sup with him, and he with Me." [36]

At this point some may respond, "Suppose that you've overcome my reluctance to accept Jesus—to regard Him as something more than just a good man. Suppose I accept the logic of what you've said thus far. I still don't see why this is such a *vital* question for anyone."

The vital nature of your decision for Christ is easily seen by examining three vital Scriptural facts:

A. **The PENALTY** – "The wages of sin is DEATH." [37] "The soul that sinneth, it shall DIE." [38] Just as God warned Adam and Eve very clearly what the penalty for disobedience would be, [39] He wants us also to understand the fatal consequences of sin.

B. **The PEOPLE INVOLVED** – "ALL have sinned, and come short of the glory of God." [40] "There is NONE righteous, no, not one." [41] This universal truth includes me—and you—and everyone else in this world of sin. And in consequence of *A*, above, it means that we're all condemned to death.

C. **The REMEDY** – "He was wounded for OUR transgressions . . . and the Lord hath laid on HIM the iniquity of us all." [42] "Christ also hath once suffered for sins, the JUST for the UNJUST, that He might bring us to God." [43] God's problem was to show mercy while still maintaining justice. He couldn't excuse man without condoning sin. And He couldn't abolish His Law without undermining the very foundation of Heaven's government. But He could die in man's place, and He did. He showed His love for man, met the demands of a broken law, and paid sin's penalty in one majestic Sacrifice.

Those texts are just a "mini-course" in the science of salvation, but—like it or not—they certainly affect our eternal destiny.

CONSIDER CALVARY

When Jesus died, "PARDON" was written across the sins of the whole human family—though we must individually accept the pardon God so graciously provides. When Jesus died, the basis of our salvation became clear—what had been the SIN issue became the SON issue, for He signed the emancipation papers of the race with His own blood.

While this is not the place to go into a detailed analysis of God's great plan of salvation, we should understand that since "The wages of sin is death," Jesus died in our place as the sacrificial Lamb of God, the divine Substitute. We must individually come to the point where we can say, "I caused the death of Christ. He climbed the hill called Calvary for me. Those nails were mine. Because of my sins, my hand held that hammer. I pierced His sinless flesh and caused His blessed blood to flow. Christ died the death that was mine."

God's invitation still remains open: "whosoever" will receive Him may do so. Said Jesus: "Whosoever therefore shall confess Me before men, him will I confess also before My Father which is in heaven. BUT whosoever shall deny Me before men, him will I also deny before My Father which is in heaven." [44]

The Apostle Paul warns of that future day when even the wicked will acknowledge Christ as Lord and Master—though such an act will then be too late to save them: "For we shall ALL stand before the judgment seat of Christ. . . . That at the name of Jesus every knee should bow . . . and every tongue confess that Jesus Christ is Lord, to the glory of God the Father." [45]

How is it with you, my friend? "What think ye of Christ?" Don't wait till it's too late and then acknowledge Christ as Lord. Prepare now to respond as Peter did when Jesus asked him *LIFE'S GREATEST QUESTION:* "Simon Peter answered and said, Thou art the Christ, the Son of the living God. And Jesus answered and said unto him, Blessed art thou, Simon Barjona: for flesh and blood hath not revealed it unto thee, but My Father which is in heaven." [46]

⌒

Notes to Chapter 9

1. Matthew 22:42.
2. Matthew 16:13.
3. Matthew 16:15.
4. Philippians 2:6.
5. A Voice from heaven proclaimed these words on two occasions, recorded in Matthew 3:17 & 17:5. Compare Isaiah 42:1, Matthew 12:18, Mark 1:11 & 9:7, Luke 3:22 & 9:35, and 2 Peter 1:16-18.
6. Luke 1:32.
7. Matthew 1:21.
8. John 1:29 & 34.
9. Matthew 27:4.
10. Luke 4:33-34, NKJV (and Mark 1:23-24).
11. Mark 3:11.
12. Mark 15:39 (and Matthew 27:54).
13. Acts 4:12, NIV.
14. Hebrews 4:14. Though some question whether Paul wrote the Book of Hebrews, the present writer agrees with the many who have no doubt of Paul's authorship.
15. John 20:31.
16. John 14:6.
17. John 10:9.
18. John 11:25.
19. John 8:12 & 9:5.
20. John 6:51.
21. John 6:38.
22. John 8:23-24.
23. John 3:16.
24. Mark 14:61-62, NEB.
25. John 4:25-26, NIV.
26. John 9:35-38, NKJV.
27. *The Sayings of Confucius*, translated by Leonard A. Lyall, Third Edition (New York: Longmans, Green and Company, 1935), p. 35.
28. Matthew 28:18.
29. Matthew 9:2, Luke 7:48-50, *etc.*
30. See Matthew 11:29.
31. C. S. Lewis, *Mere Christianity*, Revised Edition (New York, The Macmillan Company, 1960), pp. 55-56.
32. John 18:36.
33. Further discussion of this "trilemma" may be found in Josh McDowell, *Evidence That Demands a Verdict* (San Bernardino, Calif.: Here's Life Publishers, 1979), Volume I, pp. 103-107.
34. Matthew 12:30.

35. Revelation 3:15-16, RSV.
36. Revelation 3:20.
37. Romans 6:23.
38. Ezekiel 18:4 & 20.
39. Genesis 2:16-17 & 3:3 — "Thou shalt surely DIE."
40. Romans 3:23.
41. Romans 3:10.
42. Isaiah 53:5-6.
43. 1 Peter 3:18.
44. Matthew 10:32-33.
45. Romans 14:10, and Philippians 2:10-11, RSV.
46. Matthew 16:16-17.

✦ ✦ ✦

MYSTERY #4
State of the Dead

What happens when a man dies?
Are the dead really dead?—or alive
somewhere else? Will the wicked
be punished by burning forever?

"I will show thee
that which is noted in
the Scripture of Truth."
—Daniel 10:21

~

CHAPTER TEN

SOLVING THE MYSTERY OF DEATH: PART I.

BENJAMIN FRANKLIN said it: "In this world nothing is certain but death and taxes." How true that is! Every last one of us has "a rendezvous with Death"[1] because death is life's common denominator. It doesn't matter who we are—rich or poor, black or white, male or female—as far as this world goes, the Road of Life we travel has a dead end.

But though death is the one universal experience shared by all, we know very little about it. Perhaps that's why it holds great fascination. No one who's walked this earth can deny wondering what awaits him in "the great beyond." Even Henry Ward Beecher, perhaps the most famous American clergyman of the nineteenth century, said in his last, dying words: "Now comes the mystery." Let's face it: Death is the ultimate mystery, the final question mark. No one really knows what happens when we die.

Many opinions are voiced. Much speculation is heard. Stop a dozen people on the street and you'll hear many different ideas expressed on the mystery we call death. One will say: "When a man dies, that's it—there's no hereafter, no nothin'. Death is THE END. Period."

Another, who doesn't feel that death puts a period to life, says: "No! You're wrong. You never really die. Death is like a door we pass through to a whole new existence.[2] After you die, you're more alive than you've ever been before!"

A third will say: "Well, I think it's true that you're still alive, still conscious, after you die. But where you go depends on how you've lived. Good people go straight to heaven—bad ones go straight to hell—for all eternity."

Someone else may say: "I think death is just a sleep, so it's nothing to fear. We take a deep, dreamless sleep in the grave until the resurrection."

Other opinions are usually variations on the thoughts expressed above. But that's all they are—mere opinions—for no one really knows, and death remains the great unknowable, life's most perplexing puzzle.

Any human being without divine help who tries to philosophize and theorize about death's enigma is like . . .

> a blind man . . .
>> in a pitch-dark room . . .
>>> looking for a black cat . . .
>>>> that isn't there!

But note that I said "without divine help." Some people seek help from spirit mediums, séances, and the like. Others accept the "pop" theology offered by Broadway and Hollywood, whose characters in *Our Town* and *Heaven Can Wait* are perfectly conscious and very much alive after death.

So where can we get the real help we need? Where can we turn for answers to this final riddle? Well, the only Source that even pretends to give an authoritative answer is God's Book, which was written not by men but by the supernatural power of the Holy Spirit. [3] So let's not waste time on man's idle speculation and guesswork—let's solve the mystery of death by consulting Him who has CONQUERED death. By using inspired information from the Word of God, we can fit the puzzle pieces together.

Puzzle Piece #1:
God ALONE Is Immortal

We'd best begin by defining our terms: *MORTAL* means "subject to death" or "destined to die." *IMMORTAL* means "exempt from liability to die," "undying" or "imperishable."

It's fashionable today, in many popular churches, to speak of "the immortal soul." Fashionable, yes—but Scriptural? No. So much pulpit pounding is done in the attempt to impress congregations that they're "immortal" and possess "immortal souls"—that it may surprise many to learn that, according to the Bible, ONLY GOD is immortal or has immortality.

Strong's Exhaustive Concordance is perhaps THE standard reference used for word study in the Holy Scriptures, since it systematically lists every single word used in the Authorized King James Version of the Bible. But *Strong's* knows nothing of the phrase "immortal soul." Instead, it shows us that the word *immortal* is used ONLY ONCE in the entire Bible, and then it applies not to man but to "the only wise GOD." [4]

Furthermore, in the same epistle, the inspired theologian Paul explicitly declares that "God . . . the King of kings and Lord of lords . . . ALONE is immortal"—"ALONE possesses immortality." [5]

Not everything in life—or even in the Bible—is as plain as that. The primary fact we must nail down on the authority of the Word of God is that the Lord alone is immortal. Turn to those texts and read them with your own eyes in your own Bible! When the Bible plainly declares that God alone is immortal, that "[He] ONLY hath immortality," we needn't waste our time trying to find Scripture verses that say MAN now is immortal or has an immortal soul—for we won't find them. God's Holy Spirit never contradicts Himself!

PUZZLE PIECE #2:

MAN IS "MORTAL"—SUBJECT TO DEATH

Instead of finding contradictory statements attributing immortality to man, we find clear evidence from God's Word that our Creator MADE us as mortal creatures subject to death. Note the following Scriptures:

- "The LORD God commanded the man [Adam], saying, 'From any tree of the Garden [of Eden] you may eat freely; but from the tree of the knowledge of good and evil you shall *not* eat, for in the day that you eat from it you shall surely DIE.'" [6]

- And Eve knew that "God has said, 'You shall not eat from it or touch it, lest you DIE.'" [7]

- God had no intention of creating *immortal sinners,* so after Adam and Eve fell into sin, "The Lord God said, 'The man . . . must not be allowed to reach out his hand and take also from the Tree of Life and eat, and live for ever.' So the Lord God banished him from the Garden of Eden to work the ground from which he had been taken. After He drove the man out, He placed on the east side of the Garden of Eden cherubim [angels] and a flaming sword flashing back and forth to guard the way to the Tree of Life." [8]

Thus we see that even Adam—strong and fresh from the Creator's hand— was NOT naturally, inherently immortal but was dependent upon the Tree of Life in order to "live forever." Otherwise this prohibition and banishment would have been meaningless. Now ask yourself, how much *more* dependent is poor sinful man today? Bold and brazen indeed is he who insists that the human race today, with its long history of debilitating sin, is born with innate immortality!

- The Word of God declares that man is "mortal": "Shall MORTAL man be more just than God?" [9]

- The Bible does say that man can BECOME immortal, and God encourages us to "SEEK for glory and honour and IMMORTALITY, eternal life." [10] But if we're ALREADY immortal by nature, why would God tell us to "seek" it? We don't have to seek something we already have.

- Paul urges us to "Fight the good fight of faith, lay hold on eternal life." [11] Again, why "fight" to "lay hold" on something IF we already possess it?

- With perfect consistency, Paul explains that we mortals are NOT immortal NOW but will be changed to that status when Jesus comes: "For this corruptible must PUT ON incorruption, and this MORTAL must PUT ON immortality. So when this corruptible shall have put on incorruption, and this mortal shall have PUT ON immortality, then shall be brought to pass the saying that is written, Death is swallowed up in victory. O death, where is thy sting? O grave, where is thy victory?" [12] We wouldn't need to "put on" immortality if we already had it! Man's mortality is a dead certainty.

- The bad news/good news is: "The wages of sin is DEATH, but the GIFT of God is eternal life through Jesus Christ our Lord." [13]

- Jesus says: "Behold, I come quickly; and My reward is WITH Me, to give every man according as his work shall be." [14]

We poor children of the dust may like to pride ourselves with delusions of grandeur and innate immortality, but the Bible is quite clear: The second fact we can nail down with certainty is that MAN is MORTAL by nature but may conditionally, if faithful, attain immortality as a gift of God's grace when Jesus returns with His rewards.

Before proceeding any further, however, let's establish one important fact at the very outset: ALL Christians believe in a life after death. There's no argument on this point. [15] The Bible question, "If a man die, shall he live again?" [16] is answered in ringing tones of affirmation by all who believe in Jesus. The difference of opinion arises on *WHEN* the dead will live again and on the very *NATURE* of man himself. The issue is between a belief in CONDITIONAL immortality versus a belief in INNATE or natural immortality.

Believers in CONDITIONAL immortality assert that man is a mortal creature but can attain immortality on *condition* of faith in Christ and that he receives it only at the resurrection when Christ returns. Believers in IN-NATE immortality hold that man has an imperishable soul and therefore already does possess immortality which is inherently his, a part of his very nature.

Obviously, these two philosophies are mutually exclusive and cannot both be true: Either immortality is the gift of God, a gift reserved for believers and conferred when Christ returns, *OR* man is innately immortal. One of these teachings is in accord with Bible truth, and one is in harmony with Satan's first lie to mankind. Let's see which is which.

PUZZLE PIECE #3:
SATAN'S **LIVING LIE** ABOUT DEATH

Long before the rise of Christianity, ancient pagan religions taught that the soul is immortal. This is one of the basic tenets of Hinduism with its teaching of reincarnation. It's also written in Egypt's *Book of the Dead* and carved on statuary in that land. The pagan Greeks built a whole philosophy on the age-old belief that the soul does not die but lives on independent of the body. Plato was their leading philosophic writer, and basic in both his and Socrates' teachings was this belief that the soul of man can never die.[17]

But the origin of today's misunderstanding about death goes back beyond the heathen philosophies of India or Egypt or Greece. It started in the Garden of Eden, when *Satan preached the first sermon on the immortality of the soul*—a sermon only five words long. God had warned Adam and Eve that if they ate of the forbidden fruit they would "SURELY die."[18] Satan, speaking through the serpent to Eve, directly contradicted God Himself by saying: "You surely shall *NOT* die!"[19]

In other words: "You won't die—you're immortal!" But people have been dying ever since that statement was made. It was a lie, the first lie ever told in this world, by the one Jesus called "the father of [lies]."[20]

Satan's first sermon succeeded so well, he's been preaching it ever since. And he still succeeds—his ancient lie in various forms has been handed down from one era to another—so that today "that old serpent, called the Devil, and Satan . . . deceiveth the WHOLE WORLD."[21] Almost the whole world is deceived by Satan's lie about the immortal nature of man—not just pagan religions but even some Christians!

At times when this subject is discussed, someone may ask: "What difference does it make, anyway, what we believe about death?" The difference, my friend, is whether we believe GOD—or the DEVIL! Adam and Eve believed the Devil, and they brought death upon themselves and all their posterity. Ideas have consequences: Because our first parents bought the Devil's lie that "You surely shall *NOT* die!"—this planet became the CEMETERY of the Universe where EVERYONE dies!

So far, three of our puzzle pieces have snapped neatly together:

1. God—and **God only**—is immortal.
2. **Man is mortal** but may attain immortality as a gift.
3. The **idea** of innate immortality originated not with God but with **Satan** himself.

PUZZLE PIECE #4:
GOD CALLS DEATH A "SLEEP"

God, the only One who knows everything—including what death is like— tells us over and over again in both the Old and New Testament that death is a "sleep." Note these consistent statements:

- Writing under inspiration, the Psalmist David prayed to God lest he "SLEEP the SLEEP of death." [22]

- "Now shall I SLEEP in the dust; and thou shalt seek me in the morning, but I shall not be." [23]

- "Them that SLEEP in the dust of the earth shall AWAKE, some to everlasting life, and some to shame and everlasting contempt." [24]

- "Now the days of David drew nigh that he should DIE. . . . So David SLEPT with his fathers, and was buried." [25]

- Miracles occurred when Jesus died on the cross: "The earth quaked, and the rocks were split, and the graves were opened; and many bodies of the saints who had fallen ASLEEP were raised; and coming out of the graves after His resurrection, they went into the holy city and appeared to many ." [26]

- "AWAKE, thou that SLEEPEST, and arise from the dead." [27]

- When Stephen was stoned to death as the first Christian martyr, the Bible says, "he fell ASLEEP." [28]

These are but a few of many examples from such diverse Bible writers as David and Job, Matthew and Paul, and others who consistently speak of death as a "sleep." But let's close this discussion with an example from our Lord's own lips. One day Jesus received news that His friend Lazarus was very sick. After waiting two days before going to Lazarus, Jesus said:

- "'Our friend Lazarus has fallen ASLEEP; but I go, that I may AWAKEN him out of SLEEP.' The disciples therefore [knowing how helpful bed-rest is to sick people] said to Him, 'Lord, if he has fallen asleep, he will recover.' Now Jesus had spoken of his DEATH, but they thought that He was speaking of literal sleep. Then Jesus therefore said to them plainly, 'Lazarus is DEAD.'" [29]

The words of the Master Himself should settle the matter beyond all debate.

Speaking of death as a sleep is an appropriate, beautiful metaphor.[30] But when the Word of God uses that term so consistently, it becomes more than a convenient euphemism for an unpleasant subject. For all who take the Bible seriously, it becomes FACT. And death itself becomes nothing to fear: It's comforting to realize that just as drowsy slumber comes at the end of day, so death's quiet, restful sleep comes at the end of life.[31]

Puzzle Piece #5:
The Dead Sleep UNTIL the RESURRECTION

The Psalmist says, "As for me, I will behold Thy face in righteousness: I shall be satisfied, when I AWAKE, with Thy likeness."[32] You see, David didn't expect to go to heaven immediately when he died. If he had, he would have seen God's face during all these intervening centuries. But a correct understanding of God's plan made him look forward to seeing His Redeemer at the still-future resurrection, when he and all other saints will "awake" at the same time.

None of the other Bible writers believed that *death* is the time of reward, either. We've already noted that Jesus said: "Behold, I COME quickly; and My reward is WITH Me, to give every man according as his work shall be."[33] "For the Son of man shall COME . . . and THEN He shall reward every man according to his works."[34]

Peter reinforces the fact that *David did not go to heaven when he died*: "Men and brethren, let me speak freely unto you of the patriarch David, that he is both DEAD and BURIED, and his sepulchre is with us unto this day. . . . For David is NOT ascended into the heavens"![35]

Could language be clearer than that? These lines are from Peter's Pentecost sermon, but clergymen intent on teaching man's innate immortality seldom quote them. Instead, such preachers argue: "Of course David's BODY is dead and buried—we never said his body is ascended into heaven, but his soul IS." However, this explanation is less than convincing to all who note that Peter spoke not of "David's body" but of "David," the man himself. Christ resurrects the WHOLE person.

All dead believers from all time shall awake and arise at the same fateful moment—when Jesus returns: "Thy dead men shall live, TOGETHER WITH my dead body shall they arise. AWAKE and sing, ye that dwell in dust: . . . and the earth shall cast out the dead. . . . For, behold, the Lord cometh out of His place to punish the inhabitants of the earth for their iniquity." [36]

God gives us the promise of eternal life, but we don't receive that wonderful gift at the moment we die. I repeat: God does not receive us into His presence ONE by ONE as we individually die. No, we're all going to be resurrected and taken to heaven TOGETHER—Peter and Paul and John, David and Daniel and Job, and you and I—together!

This is called God's "better" plan: "These all [the faithful dead], having obtained a good report through faith, received NOT the promises [eternal life, heaven]: God having provided some BETTER thing for us, that they WITHOUT US should NOT be made perfect." [37]

"Man lieth down, and riseth not: TILL the heavens be no more,[38] they shall not AWAKE, nor be raised out of their SLEEP." [39]

"As in Adam all die, even so in Christ shall all be made ALIVE. But every man in his own order: Christ the first-fruits; afterward they that are Christ's at His COMING." [40]

Paul says plainly: "If the dead RISE NOT, . . . then they which are fallen asleep in Christ are PERISHED." [41] Now ask yourself, why would dead Christians be "perished" if they're already consciously enjoying heaven's bliss? Why do we need the resurrection if dead believers are already alive up in heaven? [42] Those who answer, "We need the resurrection because our bodies are dead in the grave but our souls are alive in heaven" must supply the much-needed PROOF that souls are alive after death. The word "perished" sounds as if the opposite is true: Without resurrection there'd be NO future life of any kind for the believer.

Faithful Job asks: "If a man die, shall he live again? all the days of my appointed time will I wait,[43] till my CHANGE come. Thou shalt CALL, and I will answer Thee." [44] Job's "change" from mortal to immortal will take place "at the last trump" when Jesus returns in glory. Paul says: "Behold, I show you a mystery; we shall *not all* SLEEP [the sleep of *death* before Jesus comes —some will be *alive* to see that dazzling sight!], but we shall all be CHANGED, in a moment, in the twinkling of an eye, at the last trump: for the trumpet shall sound, and the dead shall be raised incorruptible, and we shall be CHANGED." [45]

In the passage quoted to begin the paragraph above, Job's inspired pen wrote that God will "CALL" His sleeping saints back to life. Note how Paul describes the same event: "This we say to you by the word of the Lord, that we who are alive and remain until the coming of the Lord will by no means precede those who are asleep [or dead]. For the Lord Himself will descend from heaven with a SHOUT, with the voice of an archangel, and with the trumpet of God. And the DEAD in Christ will rise first. Then we who are ALIVE and remain shall be caught up together with them in the clouds to meet the Lord in the air. And thus we shall always be with the Lord. Therefore comfort one another with these words." [46] Here Paul comforts believers with the doctrine of the RESURRECTION. He didn't comfort them with the notion that the dead are already in heaven because they have immortal souls, for he didn't believe that.

Job mentioned the Lord's resurrecting "call," and Paul mentions His lifegiving "shout." Jesus Himself explains further when He says, "Marvel not at this: for the hour is coming, in the which all that are in the graves shall hear His voice, and shall come forth; they that have done good, unto the resurrection of life; and they that have done evil, unto the resurrection of damnation." [47] Please note that when the dead "hear His voice, and . . . come forth," they do not come down from heaven or up from hell—for that's not where they are! Where are they? Jesus says they're "in the GRAVES."

Can you recall when you were little and your family went to spend the day over at Grandma's or some other relative's house? You'd burn up so much energy running around, as kids do, that you soon grew tired and maybe a little cranky. So Mom put you to sleep on Grandma's bed while the grownups continued to chat and visit. Then, when it was time to leave, Dad would gently shake you and say, "Wake up, Sleepy-head, it's time to go home." That's how it'll be when Jesus comes, only much more thrilling—like a father calling, "Wake up—it's time to go HOME!"

Condemned to death in a Roman prison, Paul stated in the last letter he ever wrote: "I am now ready to be offered, and the time of my departure is at hand. I have fought a good fight, I have finished my course, I have kept the faith: HENCEFORTH there is LAID UP for me a crown of righteousness, which the Lord, the righteous Judge, shall give me AT THAT DAY: and NOT to ME ONLY, but unto ALL THEM ALSO that love His APPEARING." [48] No one needs an advanced degree in theology to understand what Paul is saying here. He knew he'd receive his "crown" not when he died a martyr's death but in the future—"at that day" of the Lord's "appearing." And he knew, too, that "all" the redeemed will receive theirs on the same glorious day. We don't go to heaven when we die but sleep in the grave till Jesus comes to resurrect us.

In closing our discussion of this puzzle piece, let's recall that after Lazarus died, his sisters Mary and Martha were weeping and mourning for him.

"Lord," Martha said to Jesus, "if You had been here, my brother would not have died." Then "Jesus said to her, 'Your brother will rise again.'"[49] He did not say, "Don't cry, Martha. Your brother is up in heaven right now." That would have been the appropriate thing to say to comfort her—IF it had been true, but it wasn't! Instead, Jesus promised her that Lazarus would indeed "rise again."

And her reply was also illuminating. "Martha answered, 'I know he will rise again in the RESURRECTION at the LAST DAY.'" Mary and Martha and Lazarus were among the faithful few who had been privileged to learn Bible truth from the lips of the Master Himself, so she knew nothing about man's theory that dead believers are ushered into heaven the moment they die. Instead, she remembered Christ's teaching that sleeping saints will be raised to life "at the last day"—when Christ returns in glory!

Finally, four times in one chapter Jesus repeats, for emphasis, His teaching that He will "raise up" His sleeping saints "at the LAST DAY," when He returns in glory. Please note:

✓ John 6:39, NIV—"I shall . . . raise them up at the LAST DAY."

✓ John 6:40, NIV—"I will raise him up at the LAST DAY."

✓ John 6:44, NIV—"I will raise him up at the LAST DAY."

✓ John 6:54, NIV—"I will raise him up at the LAST DAY."

That's when ALL believers come to life and go to heaven together—not one by one when they individually die!

Puzzle Piece #6:
The Dead Are NOT CONSCIOUS

We know already that the Bible calls death a sleep. But what kind of sleep is it? A sleep plagued by nightmares—or filled with pleasant dreams? Or maybe a deep, dreamless sleep, oblivious to the passing of time, so morning seems to come the moment after we place our head on the pillow?

The Bible clearly teaches that the latter is true, for God's Word declares that the dead are not conscious. Here are verses unequivocal in their meaning:

● "The living know that they shall die: but the dead KNOW NOT ANYTHING. . . . Also their love, and their hatred, and their envy, is now PERISHED."[50] Advocates for innate immortality admit that the body dies but argue that the real man, his mind and personality—his soul—can never die. Yet this verse speaks of a man's MIND, not his body. A man's

BRAIN dies with the rest of his body. *Intellectually,* "the dead know not anything." *Emotionally,* their love, hatred, and envy are "perished." [51]

- When a man dies, "his breath goeth forth, he returneth to his earth; in that very day HIS THOUGHTS PERISH." [52] No one can misinterpret that verse without being guilty of theological vandalism. Obviously God is using strong language to indicate absolutely NO MENTAL ACTIVITY. If the dead man's "thoughts perish," then he's not conscious of any thoughts and is therefore not conscious, period.

- "Whatsoever, thy hand findeth to do, do it with thy might; for there is no . . . KNOWLEDGE, nor WISDOM, in the grave, whither thou goest." [53] Those who contend that only one's body goes into the grave will find no comfort in this verse, for it does not say "in the grave, whither thy body goest" but "whither THOU goest." Again, no mental activity or consciousness is ascribed to the dead.

- "The dead PRAISE NOT the Lord, neither any that go down into silence." [54] But they would praise God devoutly and fervently—IF they were conscious!

- "O Lord, . . . in death there is NO REMEMBRANCE of Thee: in the grave who shall give Thee thanks?" [55] If the righteous dead were really conscious and taken to heaven at death, they wouldn't need to remember God—they'd see Him face to face. But that's not true. The dead are not conscious: "there is no remembrance" even of God!

- "The grave cannot praise Thee, death can not celebrate Thee: they that go down into the pit cannot hope for Thy truth. The LIVING, the living, HE shall praise Thee, as I do this day." [56]

- "While I live will I praise the Lord: I will sing praises unto my God while I have any being." [57] The idea here is that after we die, we not only cannot praise the Lord, but we don't even have "any BEING."

- The Bible calls the grave, where the dead abide, "the land of forgetfulness," [58] a very appropriate name for the place where inhabitants "know not anything," where one's "thoughts perish," where "there's NO remembrance" and NO "praise" and NO "thanks" even of God. Forgetfulness, indeed!

TWISTED THINKING

The false teaching that man is conscious after death has become so widespread that some men's thinking has become twisted. They know that if they fall down and hit their head they may become unconscious and not know anything. But they think that if they hit their head a little harder, they'd DIE and then know everything!

Preachers who spread the popular but unscriptural teaching that the dead are alive and conscious in "the great beyond," lead their listeners to believe that dead persons "are looking down on us right now! They see us. Why, they know what we're doing every day of our lives."

But if the dead are still consciously awake and aware of what's going on in this world and can WATCH us, it poses a problem: A young lady said that after her cousin was killed in the war, she was nervous and embarrassed about undressing or bathing. People whose opinion she respected told her that the dead are still perfectly conscious and looking down on us. Her cousin had been only a few years older than she, and the thought that he could WATCH her even though he was dead made her uncomfortable!

However, that's not the way things are. The Bible soundly refutes the idea that the dead are not really dead but are simply alive somewhere else. And it refutes the idea that the dead are conscious and watching what happens in this world. Your Bible says that when a man dies, even "his SONS come to honour, and he knoweth it NOT; and they are brought low, but he perceiveth it NOT of them." [59] Obviously, if a dead man were conscious of what's going on here on Planet Earth and able to watch from the vantage point of heaven, he'd be most interested in and concerned about those he loves—his own flesh and blood. But God's Word says he doesn't know what happens even to "his SONS"! Their successes and failures alike are not perceived by him.

God's way is always the best way, and that's certainly the case here. If our beloved dead could look down from heaven and watch the world going from bad to worse, watch our trials and tragedies, perhaps with sickness and suffering—with no opportunity to intervene—it could be mental torture worse than the torments of hell. But that's not God's plan. The dead simply rest in deep, dreamless sleep until the resurrection. And the passage of TIME—be it centuries or seconds—seems but a moment because, to them, TIME STANDS STILL. "The dead know not anything" of what happens to us or others alive today.

Further proof that death is a state of complete oblivion and total unconsciousness is seen in the fact that the Bible records cases of dead people who DID come back to life. What did they know, what could they tell us of that unique and wonderful experience? Nothing—absolutely *not one thing!* When Jesus' friend Lazarus died, the Master miraculously resurrected him. "When Jesus came, He found that [Lazarus] had lain in the grave four days already." [60] His body had begun to decompose: when Jesus ordered the stone to be taken away from the grave, Lazarus' sister cautioned, "Lord, by this time he stinketh: for he hath been dead four days." [61]

Think of it! Four glorious days to spend amid the beauties of heaven! Surely Lazarus would have much to tell about the dazzling experience IF he had really gone to heaven and IF he had even been conscious. If that miracle happened today, Lazarus would be overwhelmed by reporters, hounded by talk-show hosts to describe his experience in great depth, and his book would be an instant best-seller. Instead, Lazarus was strangely silent. He had no message from beyond the grave. Not a single word is recorded in Scripture about even ONE thing he'd seen or heard during those four days. His reaction is incredible if he were conscious and aware of his after-death experience—but it's exactly what we'd expect from one who had slept an unconscious, dreamless sleep. [62]

The silent reaction of Lazarus is not unique. Your Bible records SEVEN instances of dead people brought back to life—besides Jesus' own resurrection. Below are the seven miracles of triumph over death:

DEAD PERSON	RAISED BY	REFERENCE
The widow's son	Elijah	1 Kings 17:17-24
The Shunammite's son	Elisha	2 Kings 4:18-37
The widow's son at Nain	Jesus	Luke 7:11-17
The daughter of Jairus	Jesus	Luke 8:41-42, 49-56
Lazarus	Jesus	John 11:1-45, 12:1, 9
Tabitha / Dorcas	Peter	Acts 9:36-42
Eutychus	Paul	Acts 20:9-12

Check out these Scriptures for yourself. You'll find that NONE of those favored individuals said as much as a single syllable about their remarkable experience! But this is what I love about Bible truth: How consistent it is! Advocates for man's natural immortality must wish desperately for proof on their side of the case. Instead, the puzzle pieces keep fitting together to form the picture presented here.

THREE MORE BIBLE FACTS we've established from God's Word are:

4. Jesus and inspired Bible writers call death a very deep "**SLEEP**."

5. The dead sleep in the grave **till RESURRECTED** at Christ's Return.

6. The dead are **UNconscious**—totally unaware of all that happens.

PUZZLE PIECE #7:

"SOUL" IS A KEY WORD

Paul said, "I pray God your whole spirit and soul and body be preserved blameless unto the coming of our Lord Jesus Christ." [63] Three components are mentioned here: spirit, soul, and body. We all know what the body is, since it's visible and tangible. But what can we learn about those two mysterious entities, the soul and the spirit?

BIRD'S-EYE VIEW of the BIBLE WORD SOUL		
OLD TESTAMENT **HEBREW** WORD	NEW TESTAMENT **GREEK** WORD	BASIC **MEANING**
nephesh	*psuche*	**person being life creature**
"NEFF-esh"	"psoo-KAY"	

Let's consider the Bible word *soul*. How was Adam created? "The Lord God formed man of the dust of the ground, and breathed into his nostrils the breath of life; and man BECAME a living soul." [64] Carefully note what the Bible says—and, just as important, what it does NOT say. It says, "Man BECAME a living soul." It does not say, "Man HAS a soul," as if the man is one thing and the soul is a separate something he possesses. Man does not HAVE a soul. Man IS a soul, a living creature, a person.

In fact, the most accurate definition of the word *soul* is "person, being, life, or creature." Modern versions of the Bible recognize this and translate "a living soul" of Genesis 2:7 more clearly for us. Note the following examples:

"a living BEING"	–	New King James Version
"a living BEING"	–	New American Standard Bible
"a living BEING"	–	New American Catholic Edition
"a living BEING"	–	New International Version
"a living BEING"	–	Revised Standard Version
"a living PERSON"	–	The Living Bible

Once again, observe that Man does not HAVE a person or a soul. Man IS a person or a being or a soul. So it's theologically correct to say: "That poor *soul* is struggling along on a fixed income," meaning "That unfortunate person." A person is a soul. You are a soul. [65]

But someone may say: "Wait a minute—I don't want to get caught up in WORDS. Just answer me one thing: Our physical bodies die, but our SOULS can never, ever die, can they?"

Well, God says that they can and do: "The SOUL that sinneth, it shall DIE."[66] Why did the Holy Spirit inspire Ezekiel to write those words (twice in one chapter!) if the pagan Greeks were right in asserting that the soul of man is "imperishable"? You can understand why preachers who insist that "we have an IMMORTAL soul" don't like to quote this verse.

But God simply uses the word "soul" in the way we've just learned: A soul is a person, and if a person sins, he or she will die. Quoted in the paragraph above is the King James Version of Ezekiel 18:4, but note some modern translations of that verse:

- **"The PERSON** who sins is the one who **will die."**
    —Today's English Version
- "It is for a man's own sins that **HE will die."**
    —The Living Bible
- **"The SOUL** who sins **will die."**
    —New American Standard Bible (a footnote
    on *soul* says "**PERSON**")

Joshua 10:28, 30, 32, 35, 37, 39 and 11:11 all say "souls" were "destroyed" "with the edge of the sword"! This means "persons" were slain—not some invisible "essence" which a sword could not harm.

The Bible word *soul* may also mean "LIFE."[67] For instance, Jesus taught that "whosoever will save his LIFE shall lose it: and whosoever will lose his LIFE for My sake shall find it. For what is a man profited, if he shall gain the whole world, and lose his own SOUL? or what shall a man give in exchange for his SOUL?"[68] In recording this passage, Matthew wrote the Greek word *psuche* four times, but the King James translators twice rendered it "life" and twice "soul." You can see for yourself that the two words are interchangeable. And you can see, further, that "life" is not something naturally and irrevocably ours—we CAN lose it, for we're NOT inherently immortal.

When Peter says Noah's Ark saved "eight souls,"[69] he means eight persons or eight lives, and modern translations render it so.

Did you know that the Bible word "soul" applies not only to men but also to animals? The very same Hebrew words translated "living soul" (*nephesh chayyah: nephesh* meaning "soul" or "creature" and *chayyah* meaning "living") and applied to MAN in Genesis 2:7 are translated "living creature" and applied to ANIMALS in many instances, such as the following:

- "God created great whales, and every living creature [living soul]." [70]
- "God said, Let the earth bring forth the living creature [living soul] after his kind, cattle," *etc.* [71]
- "And out of the ground the Lord God formed every beast of the field, and every fowl of the air; and brought them unto Adam to see what he would call them: and whatsoever Adam called every living creature [living soul], that was the name thereof." [72]

In the New Testament, the Greek word *psuche* is used the same way: John saw one of the Seven Last Plagues poured out "upon the SEA; and it became as the blood of a dead man: and every living soul [the fish and other sea creatures] died in the sea." [73]

These Bible facts show that while man IS elevated above the beasts, it's not on the basis of any unscriptural fictions regarding the SOUL, for animals are "souls" or "creatures," too. The thing that elevates man above the level of beasts is that he alone in all Creation was made in the "image" or "likeness" of God. [74] What does this mean? It means that between man and beast at least FIVE distinctions can be made, as follows:

1. Man was created with an INTELLECT, with powers of REASON far above those of the beast.

2. Man was created with the capacity to WORSHIP, which none of the lower animals possess.

3. Man was created with the ability to use LANGUAGE far above the simple growls and grunts, the whines and whimpers of mere beasts.

4. Man was created with a MORAL NATURE, a CONSCIENCE sensitive to right and wrong, which is something completely foreign to beasts of the field. This last distinction gives rise to a fifth:

5. Man will answer at a FINAL JUDGMENT day for all his deeds. The beasts will not.

We could mention other distinctions, such as the RESURRECTION which man alone is promised. But the point is: the Bible makes NO distinction between man and beast on the basis of what some call "man's immortal soul." No one dares to say ANIMALS have immortal souls! The Bible tries to correct misconceptions and misunderstandings on this point as follows:

- "That which befalleth the sons of men befalleth beasts; even one thing [death] befalleth them: as the one dieth, so dieth the other; yea, they have all one breath; so that a man hath no pre-eminence above a beast: for all is vanity. All go unto one place; [75] all are of the dust, and all turn to dust again. Who knoweth the spirit of man that goeth upward, and the spirit of the beast that goeth downward to the earth?" [76]

That last sentence is an unfortunate translation which sometimes misleads people. Modern versions make Solomon's thought more clear:

- "WHO KNOWS whether the spirit of man goes upward and the spirit of the beast goes down to the earth?" —RSV

- "WHO KNOWS if the spirit of man rises upward and if the spirit of the animal goes down into the earth?" —NIV

- "WHO CAN PROVE that the spirit of man goes upward and the spirit of animals goes downward into dust?" —TLB

- "HOW CAN ANYONE BE SURE that a man's spirit goes upward while an animal's spirit goes down into the ground?" —TEV

The passage quoted above says that animals and man "have all one BREATH" and translates "breath" from the Hebrew word *ruach* which is often translated "spirit"—for *spirit* and *breath* are synonymous. In fact, the New American Standard Bible renders that final line as follows: "WHO KNOWS that the BREATH of man ascends upward and the BREATH of the beast descends downward to the earth?" So let's turn to the word *spirit*.

PUZZLE PIECE #8:
"SPIRIT" IS A KEY WORD

Let's consider the word *spirit* as used in the Bible. Its basic root meaning is "breath," seen in such words as "reSPIRation." "Spirit" is an English translation of the Latin *spiritus*, which of course is not found in the original Bible manuscripts at all. Instead, the New Testament used the Greek word *pneuma*, which gives us words like *pneumonia,* a disease that obstructs *breath* and re*spir*ation. PNEUMATIC balloon tires are blown up with "breath" or compressed *air*.

BIRD'S-EYE VIEW
of the BIBLE WORD **SPIRIT**

OLD TESTAMENT **HEBREW** WORD	NEW TESTAMENT **GREEK** WORD	BASIC **MEANING**
ruach	*pneuma*	**breath** **ghost** [77]
"ROO-akh"	"pNOO-mah"	**wind**

Remember that when God first made Adam, He used two components: "the DUST of the ground" and "the BREATH of life." [78] When our Creator combined those two elements, "man became a living soul"—a living, breathing person.

The miraculous process just described is called CREATION; the opposite process is called DEATH. Note how the Bible describes these two processes and also how the parallel structure in the very same verse shows the terms "spirit" and "breath" to be synonymous, equivalent terms:

- "Thou sendest forth Thy SPIRIT, they are created. . . .
  Thou taketh away their BREATH, they die,
  and return to their dust." [79]

- "The SPIRIT of God hath made me, and
  the BREATH of the Almighty hath given me life." [80]

- "If He should gather to Himself His SPIRIT and
  His BREATH, all flesh would perish together,
  and man would return to dust." [81]

Keep in mind two obvious facts about our breath or spirit:

✓ First, our breath / spirit does NOT EXIST apart from our body
  —take away our body and lungs, and we stop breathing.

✓ Second, our breath / spirit is NOT the CONSCIOUS part of us
  that THINKS—our brain does that.

Advocates for natural immortality reluctant to accept these basic facts need to remember WHERE God's spirit IS in each of us. I am alive "all the while my BREATH is in me, and the SPIRIT of God is in my NOSTRILS." [82] That's where our Creator placed it in the beginning: "The Lord God formed man . . . and breathed into his NOSTRILS the BREATH of life." [83]

What happens when a man dies? Read the wise man Solomon's inspired description: "Man goeth to his long home [the grave], and the mourners go about the streets. . . . Then shall the DUST return to the earth as it was: and the SPIRIT [BREATH] shall return unto God who gave it." [84]

At least THREE POINTS should be observed about this verse:

1. There's no implication that man's BREATH or SPIRIT is man's personality or "essence"—"the man himself." On the contrary, the Bible here uses the NEUTER pronoun "IT." Remember that when Jesus died, He committed His spirit (*pneuma*) into His Father's hands. [85] IF the body were a mere shell and the spirit "the real man," how strange that "three days" later Christ explicitly declared: "**I am NOT YET** ascended to My Father." [86] Those who teach that the spirit is a person's "very essence" contradict

Christ and claim He had ascended to His Father on Friday afternoon! However, we must take Christ at His word and conclude that the spirit (*pneuma*) which leaves the body at death is NOT "the real man." [87]

2. Also, there's NO implication that man's breath or spirit is a CONSCIOUS entity. Since Solomon says the DUST returns to earth "as it WAS," we can assume that the breath or spirit returns to God the same "as it was" before, also. Adam's breath was not conscious before God created him by breathing into his nostrils, so why should we assume that it's conscious after death? No Bible student believes in pre-existence of the human soul or person before life on earth—that concept was voiced by Plato and accepted by pagan religions of the East. [88]

3. Finally, this Biblical description of death provides no comfort to those holding the traditional view of conscious, immortal souls. For it makes NO distinction between GOOD and BAD men. It says the spirits of ALL the dead go back to God at the moment of death—everyone from the Apostle Paul to Adolf Hitler. If the traditional view were true, then this verse would put even Judas himself consciously, joyously, actually in the presence of God! But Universalism is a heresy few Christians can accept.

To close this discussion of man's spirit / breath, let's look at the opposite but complementary processes of CREATION and DEATH as if they were MATHEMATICAL EQUATIONS. [89] Please note:

> **DUST** *plus* **BREATH / SPIRIT** *equals* **LIFE,**
> a LIVING soul / creature.
>
> **DUST** *minus* **BREATH / SPIRIT** *equals* **DEATH,**
> a DEAD soul / creature.

The soul, then, is the combination of body and breath. It's the resultant life, the whole being. That's how the Bible teaches it. A good analogy is:

> **LIGHT BULB** *plus* **ELECTRIC CURRENT** *equals* **LIGHT**
> DUST / BODY   +   BREATH / SPIRIT   =   LIFE / SOUL

That combination brings about the resultant LIGHT. Take away EITHER the bulb OR the current, and the light is gone. Where did the light go? It didn't "go" anywhere. It simply ceased to exist. [90] And exactly the same thing happens to the soul when a man dies. The soul or person doesn't "go" anywhere—he simply ceases to exist as a conscious personality until the resurrection at Christ's Second Coming.

We've examined the Bible and found not only that it speaks of the dead as NOT being conscious but also that the words "soul" and "spirit" give NO evidence of or support for natural, innate immortality. Two more important pieces fit into our puzzle!

PUZZLE PIECE #9:

PAUL *VERSUS* PLATO

Ralph Waldo Emerson was right when he said, "Thoughts rule the world."[91] Always and forever, the battle is for man's MIND. Different schools of thought contend for supremacy: competing ideas are discussed, issues are debated, conclusions are drawn. And from the arena of ideas emerge results that change civilization and determine destinies.

Two of the foremost spokesmen for ideas were the apostle Paul and the Greek philosopher Plato. Both were brilliant thinkers. Both loved wisdom and sought Truth. Both left legacies for all future generations. But there the similarities end, for their ideas were diametrically opposed to each other.

Paul was the prime spokesman of the Judæo-Christian heritage, hand-picked by God to give the world His heaven-inspired message. Plato, on the other hand, was steeped in the pagan traditions and heathen philosophies of Greece. But let's make one thing clear: The Devil always MIXES good with evil. He knows from long experience that people will swallow his half-truths and sly lies if he sugar-coats them with good, wise, worthwhile ideas. He even quotes Scripture when it suits his diabolical purpose.[92] So Greek civilization—and Plato's ideas—were NOT all bad. Greek art and architecture are among mankind's timeless treasures. And even today, we cherish the concept of democracy which Greece invented and gave to the world.

But when we come to Plato's ideas on the nature of man, on the state of the dead and immortality—when we measure those ideas against the standard of God's Word—we must conclude that they come from ANOTHER source of inspiration.

The ideas Plato wrote in his *Dialogues* he ascribed to his friend Socrates.[93] Socrates, who taught by the oral method of questions and answers, died leaving nothing in writing, so Plato's pen preserved the ideas of both philosophers. Socrates clearly believed that his concept of death was inspired. He spoke of "the FAMILIAR ORACLE within me" and told how he followed the promptings of this oracle in his daily decisions of life.[94] Yet God commands: "A man also or a woman that hath a FAMILIAR SPIRIT, or that is a wizard, shall surely be put to death," [95] for He knows the so-called "familiar spirit" is that of a demon.

When Socrates was facing death, he said, "I may and must pray to the gods to prosper my journey from this to that other world," [96] he was not referring to the one Creator God we know and worship. He meant the *many pagan gods* of polytheistic Greece. Obviously, neither Socrates nor Plato qualify as teachers of CHRISTIAN doctrine!

Plato's grave errors about death and immortality fall under three headings. He thought that:

1. Man is a **dualistic** being, comprised of body and soul.

2. Death is a **friend** that liberates the soul.

3. The soul is **immortal and imperishable**.

Examine these Platonic ideas yourself and make up your own mind.

1. Plato's first error divides man into a distinct dichotomy, or dualism, of BODY and SOUL. Note the following points:

   a. Leading his students with a series of questions, he asks: "Is not one part of us BODY, and the rest of us SOUL?"[97] (Then he elicits the response that the body is "the seen" while the soul is "not seen.")

   b. Plato, whose philosophy was extremely ANTI-physical and ANTI-material, asserts that the soul "is engrossed by the corporeal," burdened by "the continual association and constant care of the BODY. . . . And this, my friend, may be conceived to be that HEAVY, WEIGHTY, EARTHY element of sight by which such a soul is DEPRESSED and DRAGGED DOWN again into the visible world."[98]

We've already seen how the Bible teaches the UNITY of man: Man does not HAVE a soul as a separate entity he possesses—man IS a soul, a unified person, a living being. The soul has no existence apart from the body. The whole man—body and soul—dies. And the whole man—body and soul—is resurrected on the last day. The false dualism fostered by Plato led him to depreciate the body as of little consequence, it being simply a mortal husk or outer shell. This is in common with HEATHEN religions that punish the body to "earn points" in the spiritual realm.

Christian teaching, in sharp contrast with all this, does not regard the material world as EVIL! The Bible teaches that all things—including the body—were created by God and were described as "*good . . . very* good." [99] Paul, instead of discounting and disparaging the body as Plato does, teaches us to honor and care for it as "the temple of God." [100]

2. Plato's second error seems to follow logically from his first, teaching that death is a FRIEND to be welcomed with joy, for death liberates the soul from its body prison. Consider the following:

a. "Those of us who think that death is evil are in error."[101]

b. "Will he [who is about to die] not depart with JOY? Surely, he will, my friend, if he be a true philosopher. For . . . there only, and nowhere else, he can find wisdom in her purity. And if this be true, he would be very absurd, as I was saying, if he were to fear death."[102]

c. "True philosophers . . . have always been enemies of the body, and wanting to have the soul alone, . . . REJOICING . . . to be rid of the company of their enemy."[103]

d. Plato inquires, "[Isn't death] the release of the soul from the chains of the body? . . . And what is that which is termed death, but this very separation and RELEASE of the soul from the body?"[104]

e. Plato would have us believe death is an achievement, an accomplishment to be desired: "Being dead is the ATTAINMENT of this separation [of soul and body] when the soul exists in herself."[105]

f. If death is such a friend, such an attainment, one may wonder whether SUICIDE may not be a good idea—to hurry things along. Such an inquiry was expressed: "Why, when a man is better dead, he is not permitted to be his own benefactor, but must wait for the hand of another." The only reply given to this apparent inconsistency is: "There is a doctrine uttered in secret that a man is a prisoner who has no right to open the door of his prison and run away; this is a great mystery which I do not quite understand."[106]

These ideas crept into the Church when Greeks and Romans "converted" to Christianity but still clung to their pagan beliefs. Ignorant of the Scriptures, people eventually accepted these teachings as Biblical, and the Church carried them to all the world. The once pure Christian faith combined Scripture and man-made traditions. Satan, twisting every truth in Scripture, led men to call evil good and good evil.

But God says, "Woe unto them that call evil good, and good evil; that put darkness for light, and light for darkness; that put bitter for sweet, and sweet for bitter!"[107] Perhaps Satan's most successful perversion of truth is this unscriptural doctrine of the "immortal soul" which transforms DEATH—the very CURSE God gave for sin—into a BLESSING, a portal to paradise!

The teaching of Plato that death is a FRIEND directly contradicts the inspired testimony of Paul, who calls death our ENEMY. The Apostle declares that Death is a terrible Intruder: "The last ENEMY that shall be destroyed is DEATH."[108]

3. Plato's third error is his claim that our soul is IMMORTAL and IMPER-ISHABLE—an echo of the Devil's lie that reverberates all the way from Eden! Read his explicit but unbiblical statements:

a. The philosopher's students are cleverly led to conclude that, inde-pendent of our bodies, "our souls EXIST in the world below . . . and that the souls of the dead are in existence."[109]

b. But the pagan philosopher goes even further when he asserts that "Our souls must have existed BEFORE they were in the form of man—without bodies, and must have had intelligence. . . . Our souls must have had a PRIOR existence. . . . Our souls must have existed BEFORE we were born."[110]

c. "The soul," says Plato, "is in the very likeness of the divine, and IMMORTAL . . . INDISSOLUBLE."[111] Those who agree with Plato sometimes reason thus: "I think Plato is right. We ARE 'in the very likeness of the divine,' for even the Bible says, 'God created man in His own image.'[112] And since God is immortal, if we're created in His image, we must be immortal, too!"

But the problem with this line of reasoning is that we have no valid reason to single out immortality as the only attribute of God. Our great Creator is not only immortal or never-dying. He's also omnip-otent or almighty, omniscient or all-knowing, and omnipresent or everywhere at once! Who among us is so bold as to claim THOSE attributes for puny man?

d. Plato, on no higher authority than his own reason, dares to say: "When the man is dead the soul dies NOT with him."[113]

e. By using mental gymnastics involving such opposites as odd and even numbers or heat and cold—concepts hardly analogous to the opposites of death and immortality!—Plato leads his willing student along a chain of reasoning which concludes: "Then the soul is IM-MORTAL? *Yes, he said.* And may we say that this is PROVEN? *Yes, abundantly proven.*"[114]

f. Finally, Plato triumphantly declares: "Beyond question, the soul is IMMORTAL and IMPERISHABLE, and our souls will truly exist in another world!"[115]

This chapter as a whole has already refuted this unsupported Greek concept, but note the contrast: PLATO argued for natural, innate immortality and knew nothing about the resurrection God has promised.[116] On the other hand, New Testament scholar F. F. Bruce writes, "PAUL could NOT contemplate immortality apart from resurrection; for him a body of some kind was essential to personality. Our traditional thinking about the 'never-dying soul' which owes so much to our Græco-Roman heritage, makes it difficult to appreciate Paul's point of view."[117] That's the problem: we've been "brainwashed" by ideas that Paul and Peter—and Jesus—never taught!

Condemned to death, Socrates said, "The hour of departure has arrived, and we go our ways—I to die, and you to live. Which is better God only knows."[118] Exactly! Socrates didn't know. Plato didn't know. Only God knows, and He lovingly told us about it in the sacred pages of His Book. So think it through: Are we actually expected to take Plato's WORD for it that the DEAD are ALIVE?—especially when his theories are refuted at every point by God's Word? One verse of Scripture outweighs a whole book of pagan philosophy.

SOCRATES' question about "which is better"—life or death—echoes the Devil's lie in Eden and implies death is a beneficial experience,[119] whereas God teaches that death was a PUNISHMENT for SIN. PAUL says: "By one man [Adam] sin entered the world, and death by sin; and so death passed upon all men, for that all have sinned."[120] Preachers who speak of "immortal souls" are echoing PLATO, who taught that very thing, not PAUL, who taught that only God has immortality. Thus they unwittingly perpetuate the Devil's legacy of lies.

But not quite all theologians have been seduced by Greek philosophy. Prominent among New Testament scholars is Oscar Cullmann, who served for decades on the theological faculty of the University of Basel in Switzerland. Among the books he wrote was one whose title sharply focuses the issue to be faced here. He called it *Immortality of the Soul or Resurrection of the Dead?* In that book Cullmann observes "how widespread is the MISTAKE of attributing to primitive Christianity the Greek belief in the immortality of the soul."[121]

Professor Cullmann further states:

"If we were to ask an ordinary Christian today (whether well-read Protestant or Catholic, or not) what he conceived to be the New Testament teaching concerning the fate of man after death, with few exceptions we should get the answer: 'The immortality of the soul.' Yet this widely-accepted idea is one of the greatest MISUNDERSTANDINGS of Christianity."[122]

Chalk one up for PAUL as opposed to PLATO! Though the world as a whole has sold out to the Devil, God still has His champions for Truth.

PUZZLE PIECE #10:
THE WAGES OF SIN = DEATH

If we go back to the beginning of the story and the root of the problem, we find God has a most instructive lesson to teach us. So let's go back to Adam and Eve, when Death first entered the picture. God, who does nothing without good reason, imposed death as a consequence of and punishment for the sin of disobedience. Read how God dealt with the crisis of Man's Fall into sin when Adam and Eve disobeyed:

> "The Lord God said, 'The man [Adam] . . . must not be allowed to reach out his hand and take also from the Tree of Life and eat, and live for ever.' So the Lord God banished him from the Garden of Eden to work the ground from which he had been taken. After He drove the man out, He placed on the east side of the Garden of Eden cherubim [angels] and a flaming sword flashing back and forth to guard the way to the Tree of Life." [123]

Please note this obvious fact: God's deliberate act of purposely SEPA-RATING Adam and Eve from the Tree of Life to insure He wouldn't have immortal sinners on His hands PROVES that man was not inherently, natu-rally immortal BEFORE his fall into sin—or such action by God would have been useless.

Now ask yourself: IF man was NOT immortal even before his sin, is it reasonable to assume he IS immortal after sin entered his life?

If man were inherently immortal, what NEED was there for any Tree of Life? It doesn't help for advocates of natural immortality to argue that "The Tree of Life served only to keep their BODIES alive." For it wasn't just Adam's body that sinned: it was more than his hand and teeth that sinned when he took the forbidden fruit and bit into it—it was also his mind and heart and will, his innermost being, that rebelled against his God and Maker. The WHOLE MAN sinned, so the WHOLE MAN died—not just his body.

You probably learned about this tragic event as a little child. But Plato, living in a pagan culture and ignorant of sacred Scripture, inevitably left this vital fact out of his thinking. Sadly enough, religious teachers today who spread the myth of man's immortal soul should know better than to substi-tute HUMAN REASONING for DIVINE REVELATION, which says, "The wages of sin is DEATH." [124]

PUZZLE PIECE #11:
GOD FORBIDS SPIRITUALISM

First let's define a few terms: *Spiritualism*, also often called *spiritism*, is "the belief that the dead SURVIVE as spirits that can COMMUNICATE with the living, especially with the help of a third party, called a MEDIUM." [125] The spiritualistic medium between our world of the living and the presumed world of the spirits of the dead is a WITCH. The definition of *witch* is "a woman supposedly having supernatural power by a compact with evil spirits." [126] The medium herself is on familiar terms with a particular spirit from the "other world." This particular spirit is called her "FAMILIAR SPIRIT" and serves as her contact or link with "the great beyond." The meeting at which a group of spiritualists try to communicate with spirits of the dead is called a SÉANCE.

Second, let's understand that God is absolutely and unalterably OPPOSED to séances, to witches or anyone else with a familiar spirit, and to spiritualism in general. He says in no uncertain terms:

- "Thou shalt not suffer [permit or allow] a witch to **LIVE**." [127]

- "Let no one be found among you . . . who is a MEDIUM or SPIRITIST or who CONSULTS THE DEAD. Anyone who does these things is DETESTABLE to the Lord." [128]

- "Do not turn to mediums or seek out spiritists, for you will be defiled by them. I am the Lord your God." [129]

- "When men tell you to consult mediums and spiritists, who whisper and mutter, should not a people enquire of their GOD? Why consult the DEAD on behalf of the living?" [130]

- "The soul that turneth after such as have familiar spirits, . . . I will even set My face against that soul, and will cut him off from among his people." [131]

- "A man also or woman that hath a familiar spirit, or that is a wizard, shall surely be put to DEATH." [132]

Now, with this background of facts established, we're ready for a BIG QUESTION. Ask yourself: WHY should God issue such vehement, damning prohibitions against those who might put us in touch with the dead and make it a capital offense—demanding their death?

WHY does God forbid us to consult with our departed loved ones, if they're alive and can talk to us? WHY is His prohibition in this regard so strong and absolute as to be utterly non-negotiable? God is our loving heavenly Father. Of Him we read: "No good thing will He withhold from them that walk uprightly." [133] WHY, then, does He withhold from us any contact with our beloved dead?

So much comfort and wisdom could be gained if we could talk, even briefly, with a loving parent who now dwells in the very presence of God!

If the dead are conscious in the great beyond, WHY should we not consult

- great intellectuals like Edison and Einstein,
- great statesmen like Lincoln and Churchill,
- great spiritual leaders like Moses and Paul?

WHY should God mind or care?

The reason is as the Bible says: God knows that the supposed spirits of the DEAD are really spirits of the ENEMY—devils and demons! He knows our beloved dead are unconsciously sleeping and "know not anything" until awakened at the resurrection. But Satan's legions, with diabolical cunning, pose very effectively, very convincingly, as our departed loved ones—if we allow ourselves to be deceived. They don't appear as spooks and specters or ghosts and ghouls. No, they can impersonate every detail of a dead person, copying little mannerisms like the tilt of the head, and imitating the sound of the voice even better than professional mimics.

Deadly Deceptions!

A grieving widow may be easy prey for the wiles of spirit mediums who would have her believe they really can contact her dead husband. She sees an apparition that looks just like the husband she misses so much. She hears his unique voice mentioning things known only to the two of them. She doesn't realize that demons, like our guardian angels, watch us as we grow up and know every intimate detail of our lives. So it's childishly simple for devilish spirits to give VERY convincing evidence at a séance.

A minister I know tells of visiting just such a widow and helping her study the plain statements from God's Word that her dead husband dreamlessly sleeps until the resurrection when Jesus will call him forth from the grave. But she said that she still sees her husband, that he stands in her bedroom and talks with her almost every night. Here's a case in which God's Word runs counter to the evidence of one's own senses! If she accepts what her eyes see, who is it standing in her bedroom? Her husband. If she accepts what her ears hear, who is it talking with her? Her husband. BUT if she accepts the infallible Word of God, who is it posing as her dear, departed husband? A demon from hell!

God warns His people about this danger through His servant Paul: "I am afraid that just as Eve was deceived by the serpent's cunning, your minds may somehow be led astray. . . . And no wonder, for Satan himself masquerades as an angel of light."[134] Our only safety lies in avoiding the occult and testing everything by the sure Word of God.[135]

You may recall that King David lost his first son born to Bathsheba when it died in infancy. While the child was sick, David prayed for him and grieved for his illness. But after the baby died, David washed himself and ceased mourning, explaining, "While the child was yet alive, I fasted and wept. . . . But now he is dead, wherefore should I fast? Can I bring him back again? I shall go to him, but he shall not return to me." [136]

How true that is! The dead cannot return to earth—even to their loved ones. God wants us to know these things so we won't be deceived by DEVILS posing as spirits of the dead. Deceptions of this kind are almost overpowering if we believe the communications are coming from someone we love and respect—coming from Paradise, in fact. Subtle suggestions whispered in darkness may not seem to erode our faith—at first. But once lying spirits gain our confidence, we believe them in spite of all the Bible says to the contrary, and our faith is unknowingly transferred from God to Satan. No wonder God is so incensed and so much in earnest to protect us from the menace of spiritualism!

This puzzle piece shows that the dead are DEAD! They're unconsciously asleep and awaiting the call of the Lifegiver. Therefore God has good reason to forbid any dabbling with spiritualism—He wants to protect us from contact with demons impersonating deceased loved ones!

Puzzle Piece #12:
What About NEAR-DEATH Experiences and OUT-of-BODY Experiences?

A strange new phenomenon began to sweep the country in the decade of the 1970's: Startling reports were heard from people who supposedly travelled outside their bodies or who experienced "life after death"—and lived to tell about it!

Those "near-death experiences" (NDE's) and "out-of-body experiences" (OBE's) reported in tabloid newspapers like the *National Enquirer* and in New Age books on the occult became hot topics. Thanatology—the study of death and dying, from the Greek word *thanatos*, meaning "death"—became big business. The floodgates were opened when Raymond A. Moody, Jr., published a best-selling book called *Life After Life* in which he reports interviews with fifty persons who told of "dying" and coming back to life. [137] Soon many were writing best-selling books and conducting seminars touting "Actual case histories which reveal there is life after death." [138]

The NDE's seem to have certain common elements in all or mostly all cases, namely: the "dying" person seems to leave his or her physical body, goes through a dark tunnel, is met by others who have deceased before, feels drawn to a "BEING of LIGHT" of unearthly brilliance, goes through an extraordinarily rapid review of the highlights of his life, is told he must come back to life back here—which he does very reluctantly because he desperately wants never to leave the presence of the being of light! With a few variations, that's a near-death-experience.

But those who know what GOD says about death in the pages of His Word won't be deceived by this popular craze. The whole phenomenon will quickly seem far less impressive when seen from the perspective of FOUR IMPORTANT POINTS. Let's examine them now . . .

A. OBJECTIVE SCIENTISTS—OR BIASED SPIRITUALISTS?

Satan knows that if he's to have any success in deceiving the world about death in an age when science is the world's highest authority, then he must first try to persuade the scientist.

Raymond Moody, shortly after publishing *Life After Life*, completed his medical studies and became a psychiatrist. The Foreword of that book was written by Swiss-born Elisabeth Kubler-Ross, herself another psychiatrist who has written extensively in this area. Together Moody and the late Kubler-Ross spearheaded interest in the whole area of death and dying. They gained fame and fortune as THANATOLOGISTS, capitalizing and feeding upon people's natural interest and curiosity about death and the hereafter.

Though both have the highly-respected letters of "M.D." after their names, readers of their books are immediately impressed with the fact that the data they've compiled is merely anecdotal rather than scientific. The experiences and stories making up their research could just as well have been gathered and published by any trained reporter or researcher, since there's little hint of the professional medical doctor on the pages.

Instead of displaying the cool detachment and professional objectivity of the scientist in his search for Truth, Moody makes clear at the outset that his book "reflects the background, opinions, and prejudices of its author. . . . I cannot claim total objectivity on that basis, since my emotions have become involved in this subject." [139]

Though he professes ignorance of "the vast literature on paranormal and OCCULT phenomena," he adds that "a wider acquaintance with it might have increased my understanding of the events I have studied. In fact, I now intend to look more closely at some of these writings." [140] When he does, he'll see that his writings, as well as those of Kubler-Ross, closely parallel OCCULT literature which is, without exception, spiritualistic and anti-Biblical.

One person who has first-hand knowledge of Raymond Moody's interest in spiritualism and the occult is Tal Brooke, founder of the most helpful

SPIRITUAL COUNTERFEITS PROJECT, a Berkeley-based research group and Christian think-tank which exposes charlatanism. It happens that . . .

"Tal Brooke was coincidentally a friend and fellow student of Moody at the University of Virginia. At the time Brooke was an avid and omnivorous student of esoteric philosophies, whether Eastern-religious, occult or psychic. This was a fascination which Moody shared, and this common interest was, in fact, a major basis for their companionship. Brooke (who became a Christian in India in 1971) relates that Moody claimed he regularly conversed with a SPIRIT BEING (which he defined as 'God') who manifested primarily as a voice in his head." [141]

But Moody is not the only psychiatrist/thanatologist who talks with the spirits! The *Yoga Journal* enthusiastically reported the appearance of Dr. Kubler-Ross as a speaker at a holistic health conference (holistic medicine often seeks to integrate occult healing techniques into medical practice). Before a large audience of doctors, nurses, and other medical professionals, she openly revealed her occultic leanings, saying:

"Last night, I was visited by Salem, my SPIRIT guide, and two of his companions, Anka and Willie. They were with us until three o'clock in the morning. We talked, laughed and sang together. They spoke and touched me with the most incredible love and tenderness imaginable. This was the highlight of my life. . . . It was totally apparent to me that this beautiful experience had occurred when and how it did, so that it would be heard with this assemblage." [142]

Also, an extensive article in the professional journal *Human Behavior* is illuminating. Contributing editor Ann Nietzke interviewed Kubler-Ross to discover why the noted psychiatrist believes "beyond the shadow of a doubt" in life after death, since her findings, along with those of other thantologists, are not conclusive evidence of the afterlife. [143] The editor found Kubler-Ross's belief emerges more out of her own personal biases and bizarre "out-of-body" experiences than from solid scientific data.

In the interview, Kubler-Ross vividly described her OBE's as "voyages" out of space and time, traveling at the speed of light. In addition to these bizarre trips, she told the editor about her "spiritual guides." Says Nietzke: "In September, 1976, she first witnessed the PHYSICAL MATERIALIZATION of SPIRITUAL BEINGS who now appear to her often and serve as her personal guides." [144]

All this is pure spiritualism, which looks upon death not as the "enemy" depicted in the Bible but—incredibly—as GROWTH! Kubler-Ross even produced a book entitled *Death: The Final Stage of Growth*. That book shows her acceptance of the heathen idea of REINCARNATION:

"The work with dying patients has also helped me to find my own religious identity, to know that there is life after death and to know that we will be reborn (*i.e.,* REINCARNATED) again one day in order to complete the tasks we have not been able to or willing to complete in this lifetime." [145]

So though both Moody and Kubler-Ross are trained psychiatrists, we should be aware of their spiritualistic sympathies—and a possible hidden agenda in that regard. Frankly, it's difficult to believe in the objectivity of a "scientist" who casually reports visits from a "spirit guide." By the way, another medical doctor who dabbled in these things was Sir Arthur Conan Doyle (1859-1930), author of the popular Sherlock Holmes mysteries. But his scientific training did not protect him from devilish delusions. *Encyclopedia Britannica* says: "Educated at Edinburgh University, he practised medicine until 1891. . . . In 1917, Sir Arthur declared himself a SPIRITUALIST and the rest of his life was dedicated to the propagation of his faith." [146]

Just as Doyle's immense prestige as a popular writer greatly increased the influence he had in promoting spiritualism, no doubt the medical degrees held by Moody and Kubler-Ross enhanced and furthered their influence in doing the same.

B.   Precisely **WHEN** Is Death?

On such an important matter as this, we need to know for certain if those people who tell of the next world really did DIE. We may well ask, Were any of those people who reported an NDE really dead?

Moody himself frankly admits: "The definition of 'death' is by no means settled, even among professionals in the field of medicine. Criteria of death vary not only between laymen and physicians, but also among physicians and from hospital to hospital." [147]

Moody then goes on to consider what being "dead" means by examining three helpful definitions, as follows:

1. "DEATH" AS THE ABSENCE OF CLINICALLY DETECTABLE VITAL SIGNS.

2. "DEATH" AS THE ABSENCE OF BRAIN-WAVE ACTIVITY.

3. "DEATH" AS AN IRREVERSIBLE LOSS OF VITAL FUNCTIONS. [148]

Let's examine each of these definitions in turn: The FIRST one is what we call "clinical death," with no detectable pulse, no respiration, no heartbeat. For centuries, when your heart stopped you died, and there was nothing to be done. But an interesting invention of our times is the term "cardiac arrest." With advanced medical technology, doctors found ways to get your tired ticker started again. So now when your heart stops you're not dead—you're suffering a "cardiac arrest," implying that your condition is temporary and with immediate attention ("Code Blue!") it can be alleviated.

Likewise, in the old days when you stopped breathing, that was it! But now a respirator machine breathes for us when we can't manage on our own. These new systems of preserving life—like artificial heart-lung machines—have created strange situations. Patients may be "clinically dead" but biologically alive. They're simultaneously dead and alive, depending on your definition. They breathe, eat, and eliminate; their blood circulates healthfully. They may be in a coma and unable to communicate, but they still function in ways that living people function. Though damaged beyond repair, they're kept alive around the clock by machines. It seems that it's getting harder to die.

Therefore, it's important to realize, first, that CLINICAL death doesn't always equal ACTUAL death, and, second, that the people reporting "life after death" experiences tend to have been merely "clinically dead" and may never have really died at all. They may even have been pronounced dead, but since they're still with us, it seems reasonable to assume that they were not dead. Though critically disabled, they were obviously not beyond resuscitation.[149]

Now, turning to the SECOND definition above, the electroencephalograph (EEG) is a machine which records the brain's minute electrical waves. Recently, the trend has been to base actual death on the absence of electrical activity in the brain, as determined by "flat" EEG readings.

But Moody admits that NONE of his interviewees had EEG readings done on them. He explains: "Obviously, in all of the cases of resuscitation which I have dealt with, there was an extreme clinical emergency. There was no time to set up an EEG; the clinicians were rightly concerned about doing what they could to get their patient back."[150]

Moody also discounts, quite justifiably, any absolute dependence on EEG readings as an infallible indicator of death—for at least two reasons. (1) "Setting up an EEG machine is a very complicated and technical task, and it is fairly common for even an experienced technician to have to work with it for some time to get correct readings, even under optimum conditions. In an emergency, with its accompanying confusion, there would probably be an increased likelihood of mistakes." And (2) "Flat EEG tracings have been obtained in persons who were later resuscitated. Overdoses of drugs which depress the central nervous system, as well as hypothermia (low body temperature) have both resulted in this phenomenon."[151]

In fact, flat EEG readings in those cases have gone on for 24 hours in patients who then completely recovered![152]

"One could consider that after 5 minutes of a flat EEG reading, meaningful life is extinct. Some biologists accept a shorter time—as short as one minute—as proof of death, while others adhere to the 24 or 48 hour time limits." [153]

Obviously, we'd all prefer a practitioner who opts for the longest time limit before writing us off, for horrible things can happen to people not quite dead. To avert real catastrophe, the National Academy of Medicine in France chose the 48-hour flat EEG reading for certifying death in the case of transplant donors. [154]

With this much uncertainty and leeway involved even with the technique of diagnosing death by the electroencephalograph method, and since "the specifics of determining death may even vary from one physician to the next," [155] for our purposes here we must ask for a more definite standard.

And that brings us to Moody's THIRD definition of death. We know that medical records are replete with cases of people in comas, having definitive signs of death registered on their charts, simply waking up after weeks or months of "CLINICAL death." [156] Therefore,

> "we must add the term 'irreversible' to the failure of vital signs. This is simply because what has appeared to be an utter failure of body functions can be reversed with the new machines. Blood pressure has dropped off the scale, persuading doctors that the patient was deceased, only to reappear when the appropriate mechanical procedure was applied. Heart failure, respiratory failure, dilation of the pupils, decrease in body temperature—all these common signs of physiological death have at one time or another yielded resuscitation. The patients were apparently alive through it all." [157]

However, Moody flatly admits that by this third definition, the one with the "irreversible" qualifier, ". . . NONE of my cases would qualify, since they all involved resuscitation." [158] Yet it remains the best definition, since it leaves no room for error. ALL the NDE reports have come from people who might have died clinically but have not experienced biological or irreversible death.

Therefore, NDE's do not prove anything about life after DEATH. Near-death-experiences are just that—experiences of people who have been NEAR death, not of those who have really died. The very expression—"*near*-death-experience," a term coined by Moody himself [159]—says as much. But those who promote reports of NDE's emphasize "death" and conveniently overlook "near."

Even the most fervent proponents of NDE's admit that their interviewees were not truly dead but only "close to death." Take, for example, the cover story in the *Reader's Digest* Magazine entitled "Life After Death: The Growing

Evidence." Despite the sensationalized title, readers actually find spread over five pages repeated expressions like the following disclaimers:

- "new group of people who had come CLOSE to death"
- "which occurred when they were CLOSE to death"
- "case histories of 2300 people who came CLOSE to death"
- "120 cases in which patients had CLOSE brushes with death"
- "those who have been CLOSE to actual physical death" [160]

Moody himself uses expressions like this and even puts quotation marks around the words "died" and "death" in regard to those reporting their NDE, showing that their so-called "death" was not as certain or as genuine as some naively suppose:

- "came very CLOSE to physical death"
- "circumstances surrounding CLOSE calls with death"
- "while he was 'dead'"
- "anything at all about their 'deaths'"
- "persons who have 'died'" [161]

Obviously, a person who is close to death is going through a very emotional time, and we know that emotional biochemical reactions can create vivid "realities" for the mind. This has been illustrated in the use of certain drugs in which images or lights are seen. The effect on the brain is REAL— therefore, the experience is real to the individual. But those who try to extrapolate from these *near*-death-experiences a theology on the state of the *dead* are going too far!

With more truth than humor, those having NDE's could say—as Mark Twain observed—"Reports of my death have been greatly exaggerated"! [162]

C. OBE's ARE OFTEN INDUCED BY DRUGS

Many *out-of-body-experiences* are reported by persons who are not dying or even close to death. Dr. Kubler-Ross herself reported having them years before she died. Believers in the authenticity of both NDE's and OBE's make strong claims, such as: "What is the spiritual purpose of NDE/OBE? NDE/OBE serve as witnesses that PROVE consciousness exists outside of the body." [163]

But there's nothing mystical or mysterious about experiencing travel while the body stays put. As a matter of fact, you or I or anyone else may have similar experiences every night without leaving the body at all! We call them d-r-e-a-m-s. Even while wide awake, many of us daydream in our imagination about faraway places and adventures. And the close similarity of dreams and OBE's is frankly admitted in occultic literature: "Indeed, all dreams could be called OBE's in that in them we experience events and places quite apart from the real location and activity of our bodies. So, we are saying that OBE's may be a kind of dream." [164]

Quite significant is the fact that such literature also admits that surveys studying the phenomenon show the overwhelming majority of OBE's—over 85 percent—occur while the person is resting, sleeping, or dreaming. A smaller percentage occur while the person is DRUGGED or MEDICATED. Since dreams are so common they prove nothing out of the ordinary, I'll focus here on OBE's induced by DRUGS.

Anyone familiar with psychedelic literature is immediately impressed with the similarities between the illusions experienced in the HALLUCINOGENIC drug state and those described in both NDE's and OBE's. Almost every aspect of these experiences is matched by accounts in drug literature. This is not to suggest that the persons reporting them were on drugs, for most of them were not. The point is, altered psychochemistry can create illusory experiences that are similar in many respects. [165]

For example, Timothy Leary, one-time lecturer at Harvard and LSD guru to the drug-oriented generation of the sixties and seventies, now deceased, had a psychedelic experience after ingesting some special mushrooms he purchased on a visit to Cuernavaca, Mexico. He recounts what followed:

> "I realized I had died, that I, Timothy Leary, the Timothy Leary game, was gone. I could look back and see my body on the bed. I relived my life, and re-experienced many events I had forgotten." [166]

But of course he was mistaken, wasn't he? He hadn't "died" at all. He had merely suffered a self-induced psychedelic hallucination. Even in this brief account we recognize several elements common to many NDE's and OBE's:

    (1) The feeling that "I had DIED."
    (2) The REMOTE VIEWING—"I could look back. . . ."
    (3) The feeling of being OUT OF one's body—
               ". . . and see my body on the bed."
    (4) The REVIEW of one's life—"I relived my life."

Psychiatrists know that persons under the influence of psychedelic, hallucinogenic drugs like LSD frequently report such feelings as: "My body is no longer my own," "I feel like I'm a bystander watching myself," "I feel as if I have no body." One individual described this depersonalization in colorful terms: "I feel like I'm blended with the universe." [167]

Some experimenting with drugs reported feelings of overwhelming love. Jane Dunlap, on LSD, writes:

"As I watched, love which I had felt overpoweringly throughout the day multiplied until I seemed to be experiencing the sum total of love in the soul of every person who lives. . . . It was unbelievable that so much love had lain hidden within myself or could exist in any human being." [168]

After the drug experience, she continued: "I feel that I am less critical and considerably more tolerant, sympathetic, forgiving, and understanding"— again an ECHO of many experiences reported by Moody and Kubler-Ross. [169]

To conclude this discussion of the hallucinogenic impact of drugs and chemicals, let me quote Professor Jack Provonsha, M.D., Ph.D.:

"There is one kind of chemical effect that Moody's subjects may have experienced. It is known that CARBON DIOXIDE can produce central nervous effects similar to those of hallucinogens. L. J. Meduna reports that almost all the effects of hallucinogens can be produced by *carbon-dioxide narcosis.*[170] . . . And, of course, CO_2 build-up WOULD be a major consequence of the impairment of circulation during the dying process.

"Could it be, then, that the anecdotes collected by Moody in *Life After Life,* purporting to be descriptions of life beyond the grave, are but the effects of psychochemicals such as CO_2 on *still-living* brain cells during the dying process? Could it be that what is being remembered after resuscitation is the dying process and not death itself?" [171]

D. SALVATION FOR **ALL**—BELIEFS DON'T MATTER!

According to the NDE reports, all people—good and bad, atheists and Christians—arrive in the same place![172] We know God offers salvation from death only as a part of salvation from sin. But salvation from sin is totally absent in the stories of those who reported their experiences to Dr. Moody. Those who relate their NDE would have us believe that life after death is not tied to one's relationship to Christ or to the nature of one's religious experience. All persons—religious or non-religious, converted or unconverted—are equally welcomed by the "being of light." [173]

No FINAL JUDGMENT, it seems, awaits us after death—according to those going through a near-death-experience. Instead, Moody says: "They found, much to their amazement, that even when their most apparently awful and sinful deeds were made manifest before the being of light, the being responded not with anger and rage, but rather only with understanding, and even with HUMOR." [174]

Moody reports the effect of near-death-experiences in these words: "So, in most cases, the reward-punishment model of the afterlife is ABANDONED and DISAVOWED"[175] by those who have gone through such an experience. No matter that God's Word plainly teaches the idea of reward and punishment, the idea that there's a heaven to win and a hell to shun. Their NDE causes them to "abandon and disavow" all that.

Therefore, careful investigation shows that these accounts do not harmonize with the Bible. In fact, they boldly contradict some of its plainest statements! So we must conclude that they're from some other source than the God of heaven.

Christians know that "the religion of the resuscitated" is dangerous and deceptive by preaching, as it does, that death leads to a higher degree of consciousness for all people regardless of their allegiance or beliefs. Those undergoing a near-death-experience would be far less eager to embrace the "BEING of LIGHT" if they knew that the inspired Apostle Paul warns us: "Satan himself masquerades as an angel of LIGHT." [176]

The topic of death is one often ruled more by the heart and emotions than by the mind and intellect. In the end, each one believes what he WANTS to believe. If the Devil and his teachings on the occult have captured some of us, then our feelings will win out over the clearest teachings of Scripture. So I pray we may have the faith and fortitude to submerge our feelings and take God at His Word. For this topic is a good one to illustrate the saying:

> If one believes, no proof is needed.
> If one won't believe, no proof is enough.

CONCLUSION

This piece of the puzzle fits in perfectly with all the others, helping to fill in the complete Biblical picture. That picture clears up the mystery of death, for it shows that:

- God alone is immortal, while mortal man may be given immortality on condition of faith in his Redeemer.

- Death is a deep, dreamless sleep from which we'll awaken at the resurrection.

- Man is not conscious in death, for the Bible words *soul* and *spirit* give no support to the concept of a never-dying entity existing apart from the body.

- Plato's idea of a naturally immortal soul is foreign to God's Word and irreconcilable to its plainest pronouncements— having originated with the Archenemy of God.

Though the devil's doctrine[177] of natural immortality has become quite widespread, many other thinking people through the ages have protested against it. One such was William E. Gladstone, keen Bible student and four-time Prime Minister of Great Britain, who wrote:

> "The doctrine of *natural*, as distinguished from *Christian*, immortality . . . crept into the Church, by a BACK DOOR. . . . When arguments are offered for the purely natural immortality of the soul, they are rarely, if ever, derived from Scripture. . . . The natural immortality of the soul is a doctrine wholly unknown to the Holy Scriptures, and standing on no higher plane than that of . . . philosophical opinion . . . of philosophical speculations disguised as truths of Divine Revelation." [178]

The Bible of Christianity teaches one thing about death—every pagan religion teaches quite another. Heathenism consistently teaches man's natural immortality. The Hindu idea of REINCARNATION is based on the false doctrine of "man's immortal soul" which has also given birth to such unscriptural concepts as PURGATORY and LIMBO.

Each of us must CHOOSE what he believes
about the state of the dead.
We can choose to believe either

CHRISTIANITY or PAGANISM,

PAUL or PLATO,

GOD or the DEVIL.

On the weight of Bible evidence presented here,
WHICH do YOU choose?

ᔕ᷈

Notes to Chapter 10

1. Poet Alan Seeger (1888-1916) was killed in World War I after writing:
   "I have a rendezvous with Death
   At some disputed barricade. . . .
   I shall not fail that rendezvous."

2. The famous prayer of Saint Francis of Assisi, so often quoted for the inspiration it contains, closes with the words:
   "It is in DYING that we are BORN to eternal LIFE."

3. "All Scripture is given by inspiration of God. . . . Holy men of God spoke as they were moved by the Holy Spirit." 2 Timothy 3:16 and 2 Peter 1:21, NKJV.

4. 1 Timothy 1:17. Despite the strong current of popular theology and the official stance of his own church, one Roman Catholic scholar at St. Ambrose College observed: "There is no such phrase in Scripture as 'immortal soul' or 'immortality of the soul' or its equivalent; there is only the PROMISE of immortality."—Father Joseph E. Kokjohn, "A HELL of a Question," *Commonweal* (January 15, 1971), p. 368.

5. 1 Timothy 6:15-16, NIV & NASB. The KJV says: "The King of kings, and Lord of lords . . . ONLY hath immortality."

6. Genesis 2:16-17, NASB.

7. Genesis 3:3, NASB. Note that Eve presumptuously added her own words, "or touch it," to God's.

8. Genesis 3:22-24, NIV. More is said on this in "Puzzle Piece #10," p. 271.

9. Job 4:17. Man's BODY is neither "just" nor unjust, so this text speaks of the "MAN" himself, the whole man, who is said to be "mortal."

10. Romans 2:7. Dr. William Temple, late Archbishop of Canterbury, wrote: "Man is not immortal by NATURE or by RIGHT, but he is CAPABLE of immortality and there is offered to him resurrection from the dead and life eternal IF he will receive it from God and on God's terms." Furthermore, "Eternal life is always the gift of God," and not the "natural property of human nature."—*Nature, Man and God* (London: Macmillan Co., Limited, 1953), pp. 472 & 464.

11. 1 Timothy 6:12.

12. 1 Corinthians 15:53-55.

13 Romans 6:23.

14. Revelation 22:12.

15. A sign on an office wall says: "Those who believe the dead never come to life should be here at quitting time."

16. Job 14:14.

17. Later, those pagan ideas infiltrated Christian thinking as a result of men attempting "to interpret and explain Scripture in terms derived primarily from Plato" and were "inherited from Athens, not Jerusalem." —Father Joseph E. Kokjohn, "A HELL of a Question," *Commonweal* (January 15, 1971), p. 368. See "Puzzle Piece #9: Paul *versus* Plato," on pages 266-270.

18. Genesis 2:15-17 and 3:1-3.
19. Genesis 3:4, NASB.
20. John 8:44.
21. Revelation 12:9.
22. Psalm 13:3.
23. Job 7:21.
24. Daniel 12:2.
25. 1 Kings 2:1 & 10.
26. Matthew 27:51-53, NKJV.
27. Ephesians 5:14. Interestingly enough, we call a burial ground a "cemetery"—from the Greek *koimeterion*, a "SLEEPING place."
28. Acts 7:60.
29. John 11:11-14, NASB. Furthermore, the Lord used the very same expression—speaking of death as a "sleep"—in regard to the daughter of Jairus, whom He miraculously raised from the dead. See Matthew 9:24, Mark 5:39, and Luke 8:52.
30. Poet John Donne's famous sonnet "Death, Be Not Proud" ends in these lines, using the same metaphor:
    "One short sleep past, we wake eternally,
    And Death shall be no more: Death, thou shalt die."
31. Psychiatrists know that death holds a terror for many people. But "men fear death as children fear the dark"—because it is unknown. Once we know the truth about death, that it's simply a sleep, its horror is dispelled.
32. Psalm 17:15.
33. Revelation 22:12. And Isaiah 40:10 says, "Behold, the Lord God will come. . . . Behold, His reward is with Him."
34. Matthew 16:27.
35. Acts 2:29 & 34. David did not go to heaven when he died, but it seems that he will be among the saved. Though he yielded to temptation and sinned, he was forgiven after he deeply repented. God numbers David among the heroes of faith and calls him "a man after My own heart" (Psalm 51, Hebrews 11:32-34, Acts 13:22, NKJV).
36. Isaiah 26:19-21.
37. Hebrews 11:39-40. See also verse 13.
38. A reference to the fact that, when Jesus returns, great upheavals of nature will occur. Not only will there be a tremendous earthquake and devastating hail (Revelation 16:18-21) but also we'll see "heaven departed as a scroll when it is rolled together" (Revelation 6:14), as if God's hand pulls aside the curtain and the sky opens up!
39. Job 14:10-12.
40. 1 Corinthians 15:22-23.
41. 1 Corinthians 15:16-18.
42. In the same chapter, Paul again emphasizes the absolute necessity of the resurrection, asking what advantage is anything in life, even heroic efforts, "IF the dead RISE NOT?" 1 Corinthians 15:32. But who would need the resurrection IF the dead were already praising God up in heaven?

43. WHERE will I "wait"? Job answers his own inspired question: "If I wait, the GRAVE is mine house: I have made my bed in the darkness." Job 17:13.

44. Job 14:14-15.

45. 1 Corinthians 15:51-55. ALL the saints, those who have died and those who remain alive, "shall all be changed" into immortal, incorruptible beings.

46. 1 Thessalonians 4:15-18.

47. John 5:28-29.

48. 2 Timothy 4:6-8.

49. John 11:21-24, NIV.

50. Ecclesiastes 9:5-6.

51. In Ecclesiastes 9:6 the Today's English Version, published by the American Bible Society, says: "Their loves, their hates, their passions, all died with them."

52. Psalm 146:4.

53. Ecclesiastes 9:10.

54. Psalm 115:17.

55. Psalm 6:5.

56. Isaiah 38:18-19.

57. Psalm 146:2.

58. Psalm 88:12 (read verses 10-12).

59. Job 14:21.

60. John 11:17.

61. John 11:39.

62. Something else to consider is this: If Lazarus had really been in heaven amid the indescribable glories of Paradise, would Jesus be doing His friend a FAVOR to bring him back to this wretched, sin-cursed planet?

63. 1 Thessalonians 5:23.

64. Genesis 2:7.

65. PEOPLE can *touch* things or *eat* things, but a non-material "essence"—as some people describe a soul—cannot perform those actions. Yet God says: "If a soul TOUCH any unclean thing, . . . he also shall be unclean, and guilty. . . . The soul which hath TOUCHED any such shall be unclean . . . unless he WASH his FLESH with water." And "The soul that EATETH it shall be cut off from his people. . . . Every soul that EATETH that which died of itself . . . he shall both wash his CLOTHES, and bathe himself in water." Leviticus 5:2, 22:6, 7:18-25, 17:12 & 15. So you see that SOULS are PEOPLE who not only "touch" and "eat" things, they also have "flesh" and "clothes" which must be washed!

66. Ezekiel 18:4—repeated for emphasis in verse 20.

67. Psalm 22:20 says, "Deliver my soul [*nephesh*, life] from the sword." (If a soul were our non-material "essence," a sword couldn't hurt it.) Ezekiel 22:27 speaks of the wicked who "destroy souls [*nephesh*, lives], to get dishonest gain." In Psalm 31:13 David says: "They took counsel together against me, they devised to take away my LIFE [*nephesh*, soul]." In Jeremiah 38:16 the words "soul" and "life" are BOTH translated from the SAME Hebrew word, *nephesh*. The meanings are interchangeable.

68. Matthew 16:25-26. Similarly translated in Mark 8:35-37.

69. 1 Peter 3:20.

70. Genesis 1:21.

71. Genesis 1:24.

72. Genesis 2:19.

73. Revelation 16:3. This verse shows (a) that the word "soul" may apply to sea creatures we call marine life as well as to man, and (b) that a "living soul" may DIE— an inconceivable concept IF the soul were immortal. Furthermore, note the repeated statements about a "living" creature or soul: The adjective *living* would be superfluous and redundant if *nephesh* or *psuche* meant by itself an immortal, never-dying entity. But inspired Bible writers deliberately added the adjective "living."

74. This fact is repeated several times in Scripture. See Genesis 1:26, 1:27 (twice in this one verse), 5:1, 9:6, 1 Corinthians 11:7.

75. "All" creatures—men and animals, good and bad—"go unto ONE place": the GRAVE. At the time of death, man goes NOT to *heaven* or *hell* or *purgatory* or *limbo* or some unknown *"spirit world."* He goes into the GRAVE, like the animals, where as a child of God he awaits the Judgment and the call of the Lifegiver.

76. Ecclesiastes 3:19-21.

77. "Ghost" and "spirit" are equivalent terms, the only difference being that "spirit" comes from the Latin *spiritus* while "ghost" comes from the German *geist*. (A *poltergeist* is a noisy spirit or mischievous ghost, and *zeitgeist* means the spirit of the age or times.) When we die, we "give up the ghost" or "breathe our last." See Matthew 27:50, Mark 15:37, Luke 23:46, and John 19:30 in different versions.

78. Genesis 2:7. This "breath of life" is more than just AIR. It's the life-giving power of God! Emergency rooms don't have it. When we *die*, or "breathe our last" and *expire*, God takes this life-giving power back to Himself. See Ecclesiastes 12:7.

79. Psalm 104:30 & 29.

80. Job 33:4.

81. Job 34:14-15, NKJV. Note the equivalence of "spirit" and "breath." For instance, Isaiah 42:5 says God "giveth BREATH unto the people . . . and SPIRIT to them that walk" the earth.

82. Job 27:3.

83. Genesis 2:7. This breath / spirit from God is our source of life. James 2:26 says, "The *body* without the *spirit* [the NEB & the margin of KJV say *"breath"*] is dead."

84. Ecclesiastes 12:5 & 7.

85. Luke 23:46.

86. John 20:17.

87. See D. E. Mansell, "The Nature of Man," in *Doctrinal Discussions* (Washington, D.C.: Review and Herald Publishing Association, 1962), pp. 195-196.

88. Latter-day Saints (Mormons) do teach the idea of man's existence before birth, but of course make no claim to get that doctrine from the Holy Bible.

89. Based on Genesis 2:7 for CREATION and Ecclesiastes 12:7 for DEATH.

90. Another helpful analogy may be to picture some carefully measured BOARDS which, when NAILED together, form a neat BOX. But if we disassemble the box, all we're left with is a pile of boards and a handful of nails. Where did the box go? It didn't "go"

anywhere—it simply ceased to exist. For it's the COMBINATION of boards and nails which creates the BOX. And it's the COMBINATION of body and spirit which creates the SOUL.

91. Ralph Waldo Emerson, "Progress of Culture," *Phi Beta Kappa* Address, July 18, 1867.

92. For instance, Satan quoted holy Scripture to Christ during the temptation in the wilderness. See Matthew 4:1-11, especially verse 6, taken from Psalm 91:11-12.

93. This fact makes it difficult to tell which ideas Plato presents were really those of Socrates, or Plato's own, or a combination of the two. That's why Plato's "picture has been suspected on the ground that Plato used Socrates as a 'mouthpiece' for speculations of his own." *Encyclopedia Britannica* (1967 edition), volume 20, p. 819, article "Socrates."

94. *The Works of Plato*, translated by Benjamin Jowett (New York: Tudor Publishing Company), *Dialogues of Plato: Apology*, section 40, p. 131.

95. Leviticus 20:27. See also 1 Chronicles 10:13, Isaiah 19:3, *etc.*, and "Puzzle Piece #11," below.

96. *Dialogues of Plato: Phaedo*, section 117, p. 270.

97. *Dialogues of Plato: Phaedo*, section 79, p. 217.

98. *Dialogues of Plato: Phaedo*, section 81, p. 220.

99. Genesis 1:4, 10, 12, 18, 21, 25, 31—repeated throughout Creation Week!

100. See such texts as 1 Corinthians 3:16-17, 6:19-20, 2 Corinthians 6:16, & Romans 12:1. A Christian, therefore, will be HEALTH CONSCIOUS not just for selfish physical reasons but for sublime religious reasons.

101. *Dialogues of Plato: Apology*, section 40, p. 132.

102. *Dialogues of Plato: Phaedo,* section 68, p. 200.

103. *Dialogues of Plato: Phaedo*, section 68, p. 199.

104. *Dialogues of Plato: Phaedo*, section 67, p. 199.

105. *Dialogues of Plato: Phaedo*, section 64, p. 194.

106. *Dialogues of Plato: Phaedo*, section 62, p. 191.

107. Isaiah 5:20.

108. 1 Corinthians 15:26.

109. *Dialogues of Plato: Phaedo*, sections 71-72, pp. 205-206.

110. *Dialogues of Plato: Phaedo*, section 76, p. 213.

111. *Dialogues of Plato: Phaedo*, section 80, p. 218.

112. Genesis 1:27.

113. *Dialogues of Plato: Phaedo*, section 88, p. 230.

114. *Dialogues of Plato: Phaedo*, section 105, p. 225.

115. *Dialogues of Plato: Phaedo*, section 107, p. 257.

116. "The idea of a resurrection of the body is contrary to Platonic principles. The entire scheme is to get rid of the body and all its functions, not to save it. . . . The body [says Plato] is an impediment, a hindrance, and the prison of the soul; heaven is reached only in a bodiless condition, in which the soul is free from every taint of the body. The doctrine of IMMORTALITY reached its highest point in Plato, and all subsequent writers who dealt with the future life followed in his footsteps."—Calvin Klopp Staudt, *The Idea of the Resurrection in the Ante-Nicene*

Period (Chicago: 1909), pp. 66-67.

117. F. F. Bruce, *Paul—Apostle of the Heart Set Free* (Grand Rapids, Mich.: William B. Eerdmans, 1978), p. 311.

118. *Dialogues of Plato: Apology,* section 42, p. 134. Man's Maker is best able to inform us on the nature of His creation and the truth about death.

119. Part of the Serpent's lie to Eve was that "your eyes shall be OPENED, and ye shall be as GODS, knowing good and evil." Genesis 3:5.

120. Romans 5:12.

121. Oscar Cullmann, *Immortality of the Soul or Resurrection of the Dead?* (New York: Macmillan, 1958), p. 6.

122. *Ibid.,* p. 15.

123. Genesis 3:22-24, NIV.

124. Romans 6:23.

125. *Webster's New World Dictionary of the American Language,* College Edition (New York: The World Publishing Company, c. 1964), p. 1406, entry "spiritualism."

126. *Ibid.,* p. 1679, entry "witch."

127. Exodus 22:18.

128. Deuteronomy 18:10-12, NIV.

129. Leviticus 19:31, NIV.

130. Isaiah 8:19, NIV.

131. Leviticus 20:6. Note again that "soul" means "person."

132. Leviticus 20:27. A wizard is a male witch.

133. Psalm 84:11.

134. 2 Corinthians 11:3 & 14, NIV.

135. Isaiah 8:20 points us *away* from lying spirits and *"to* the law and to the testimony: if they speak not according to THIS word [the Bible], it is because there is *no light* in them."

136. 2 Samuel 12:22-23. This Bible truth is reinforced by such texts as Job 7:9-10, which says: "He that goeth down to the grave shall come up no more. He shall return no more to his house, neither shall his place know him any more."

137. Raymond A. Moody, Jr., *Life After Life* (New York: Bantam Books, 1976). *Two thirds* of Moody's original cases were *secondhand* reports, or hearsay. But since it's difficult to trust testimony that says, "I knew a man who . . ." when dealing with so remarkable a subject as life after death, these were deleted from the published collection. And many of the remaining 50 were not involved with certifiable death at all. Pages 16-17.

138. Quoted from the cover of Moody's paperback book, *Life After Life.*

139. Moody, *Life After Life,* p. 3.

140. Moody, *Life After Life,* pp. 3-4.

141. Brooks Alexander and Mark Albrecht, "Thanatology: Death and Dying," *SCP Journal,* (Volume 1:1, 1977). Spiritual Counterfeits Project, P. O. Box 4308, Berkeley, CA 94704. Internet address: scp@dnai.com

142. Lennie Kronisch, *Yoga Journal* (September–October 1976), "Elisabeth Kubler-Ross, Messenger of Love," pp. 18-20.

143. Kubler-Ross has asserted in positive tones: "I know beyond a shadow of a doubt

that there IS life after death." Also, she has publicly stated that "death really does not exist."—Kenneth L. Woodward, "There Is Life After Death," *McCall's* (August, 1976), p. 97.

144. Ann Nietzke, "The Miracle of Elisabeth Kubler-Ross," *Human Behavior* (September, 1977), pp. 18-27.

145. Elisabeth Kubler-Ross, *Death: The Final Stage of Growth* (Engelwood Cliffs, New Jersey: Prentice-Hall, 1979), p. 119.

146. *Encyclopedia Britannica* (Chicago: Encyclopedia Britannica, Inc. © 1967) Volume 7, pp. 619-620, and Britannica CD 98 Standard Edition © 1994-1998, article "Doyle, Sir Arthur Conan."

147. Moody, *Life After Life*, p. 147.

148. *Ibid.*, pp. 147-150.

149. For much of this material the author gratefully acknowledges his indebtedness to John Weldon and Zola Levitt and their excellent book, *Is There Life After Death?* (Irvine, CA: Harvest House Publishers, 1977), pp. 30-39.

150. Moody, *Life After Life*, p. 148.

151. *Ibid.*, p. 149.

152. David Hendin, *Death As a Fact of Life* (New York: Warner, 1974), pp. 29 & 32.

153. *Ibid.*, pp. 28-29.

154. John Weldon and Zola Levitt, *Is There Life After Death?* p. 38, citing Hendin, *Death As a Fact of Life*, pp. 28-29.

155. Hendin, *Death As a Fact of Life*, p. 39.

156. *Ibid.*, p. 34.

157. Weldon and Levitt, *Is There Life After Death?* p. 37.

158. Moody, *Life After Life*, p. 150.

159. *Ibid.*, p. 14.

160. Mary Ann O'Roark, "Life After Death: The Growing Evidence," *Reader's Digest* Magazine (August, 1981), pp. 51-55. Condensed from *McCall's* Magazine (March, 1981).

161. Moody, *Life After Life*, pp. 16, 21, 14, 24-25, 96, *etc.*

162. Mark Twain, in a cable from Europe to the Associated Press.

163. Paula Thomas and Penny Warren, "Out-of-Body and Near-Death Experiences," presented at the PLIM 1997 Retreat in White Cloud, Michigan (Power Latent in Man, © 1977), not paged. Internet address: http://www.plim.org/OBE97.html

164. Lynne Levitan and Stephen LaBerge, "Other Worlds: Out-of-Body Experiences and Lucid Dreams" (NightLight volume 3.2, The Lucidity Institute, 1991), not paged. Internet address: http://www.lucidity.com/NL32.OBEandLD.html

165. Jack W. Provonsha, "Life After Life?" *Ministry* Magazine (July, 1977), pp. 21-22. Dr. Provonsha, M.D. and Ph.D., served as professor of the Philosophy of Religion and Christian Ethics at Loma Linda University in Loma Linda, California, where he helped train doctors to grapple with the ethical problems involved in death and dying. He's a recognized authority on the effects of *hallucinogenic* drugs—that is, drugs that induce hallucinations.

166. Timothy Leary, quoted in John Kohler, "The Dangerous Magic of LSD," *Saturday*

Evening Post (November 2, 1963), pp. 31-32.

167. G. D. Klee, "Lysergic Acid Diethyamide (LSD-25) and Ego Functions," *Archives of General Psychiatry* (May, 1963), p. 463.

168. Jane Dunlap, *Exploring Inner Space* (New York: Harcourt, Brace, and World, Inc., 1961), pp. 184-185.

169. *Ibid.,* p. 202.

170. L. J. Meduna, "The Effect of Carbon Dioxide Upon the Functioning of the Human Brain," in L. J. Meduna, editor, *Carbon Dioxide Therapy,* second edition (Springfield, Illinois: Charles C. Thomas, 1958), p. 40.

171. Provonsha, "Life After Life?" p. 22.

172. A very, very rare NDE or OBE—representing less than one-tenth of one percent of all those reported—may describe a descent into hell. But NO such report is included in Moody's celebrated book *Life After Life*—or in most of the other New Age books on the afterlife.

173. For instance, typical of many who reported a near-death-experience was Virginia Falce, who admitted: "I wasn't a churchgoer—I didn't believe in it." Quoted in Mary Ann O'Roark, "Life After Death: The Growing Evidence," *Reader's Digest* Magazine (August, 1981), p. 51. Condensed from *McCall's* Magazine (March, 1981).

174. Moody, *Life After Life,* pp. 97-98.

175. *Ibid.,* p. 97.

176. 2 Corinthians 11:14, NIV and The Amplified Bible.

177. "The Spirit speaketh expressly, that in the latter times some shall depart from the faith, giving heed to seducing spirits, and doctrines of DEVILS."—1 Timothy 4:1. Surely one of those doctrines is the one that came from the serpent's mouth in Eden.

178. William Ewart Gladstone, educated at Eton College and Oxford University, served as Member of Parliament, Master of the Mint, President of the Board of Trade, Chancellor of the Exchequer, and Prime Minister during most of the reign of Queen Victoria. Despite devoting himself chiefly to the affairs of state, Gladstone was also a theologian in his own right. The above quotations are from his significant, 370-page treatise, *Studies Subsidiary to the Works of Bishop Butler* (Oxford: The Clarendon Press, 1896), pp. 195-198.

◆ ◆ ◆

~

CHAPTER ELEVEN

SOLVING THE MYSTERY OF DEATH: PART II.

THE PRECEDING CHAPTER attempted to give the reader a Biblical foundation for solving death's intriguing mystery. We found that the Word of God speaks clearly and consistently on the subject. Yet there are admittedly a few passages which may seem problematical—at least at first glance. Those passages are the ones which may arise during a study of this kind, prompting an honest inquirer to ask: "What about *the Thief on the Cross* or *the Rich Man and Lazarus?*"

Such passages somehow appear to contradict the clear teaching of Scripture on this vital subject and so may raise *"Yes, but . . ." questions* in people's minds. In order to lay to rest any possible objection or concern about what we've learned thus far, we must address a handful of pertinent passages—six to be exact.

PUZZLE PIECE #13:
THE RICH MAN & LAZARUS

The picture in our puzzle is taking shape in a very definite way, but there are still a few pieces that don't seem to fit in. We need to examine them very carefully—from every angle—then perhaps we'll find that they DO fit, after all. One of these is the story of the Rich Man and Lazarus.[1] Let's read it:

"There was a certain rich man who was clothed in purple and fine linen and fared sumptuously every day. But there was a certain beggar named Lazarus, full of sores, who was laid at his gate, desiring to be fed with the crumbs which fell from the rich man's table. Moreover the dogs came and licked his sores. So it was that the beggar died, and was carried by the angels to Abraham's bosom. The rich man also died and was buried. And being in torments in Hades ["hell" in the King James Version], he lifted up his eyes and saw Abraham afar off, and Lazarus in his bosom. Then he cried and said, 'Father Abraham, have mercy on me, and send Lazarus that he may dip the tip of his finger in water and cool my tongue; for I am tormented in this flame.' But Abraham said, 'Son, remember that in your lifetime you received your good things, and likewise Lazarus evil things; but now he is comforted and you are tormented. And besides all this, between us and you there is a great gulf fixed, so that those who want to pass from here to you cannot, nor can those from there pass to us.' Then he said, 'I beg you therefore, father, that you would send him to my father's house, for I have five brothers, that he may testify to them, lest they also come to this place of torment.' Abraham said to him, 'They have Moses and the prophets; let them hear them.' And he said, 'No, father Abraham; but if one goes to them from the dead, they will repent.' But he said to him, 'If they do not hear Moses and the prophets, neither will they be persuaded though one rise from the dead.'" [2]

At first glance, this puzzle piece doesn't seem to fit in with the rest of the picture, for it has people talking after they're dead. But the Bible, as we've seen, presents a clear and consistent picture of the state of the dead. Keeping in mind the principle that the Word of God NEVER CONTRADICTS itself, how can we explain this apparent contradiction?

The problem resolves itself instantly when we determine one thing, and that is: What do we have here in the story of the Rich Man and Lazarus?

Is this story

1. A LITERAL account about real men and actual events?

Or is it

2. A PARABLE—a story told to teach a moral lesson?

A Bible parable is defined as "a heavenly story with an earthly meaning." The story may teach vitally important truths while not being literally true itself. Those who wish to defend the Bible sometimes have difficulty accepting the fact that parables may be figurative, fictional stories. Yet we can honor the Bible as the inspired Word of God without insisting on taking every word literally.

Proof of that is seen in our Lord's magnificent use of figurative language. He said, "Ye are the SALT of the earth" and "I am the DOOR"[3] without meaning an actual mineral or a wooden door. And Jesus often used parables to teach great lessons. The Master Teacher would place a simple story along-side a profound truth, and the profound was illumined by the simple.

Commenting on the story in question, Bloomfield in his *Greek Testament* said: "The best Commentators, both ancient and modern, with reason consider it as a parable."[4] "With REASON," he says. Let's examine some of those reasons right now.

NOT LITERAL BUT A PARABLE

✓ 1. Jesus Always Used Parables in Addressing Crowds

The Bible declares that Jesus not only used parables but that parables were in fact the ONE teaching device He used exclusively in teaching the people: "Jesus spoke all these things to the crowd in parables; He did not say anything to them without using a parable."[5] We may wonder why this is true. Even His "disciples came and said to Him, 'Why do You speak to them in parables?' He answered and said to them, 'Because it has been given to you to know the mysteries of the kingdom of heaven, but to them it has not been given. . . . Therefore I speak to them in parables, because seeing they do not see, and hearing they do not hear, nor do they understand.'"[6]

You see, Jesus knew He had many enemies who'd gladly cut short His ministry if they could. He could speak freely and openly with His disciples in private, but the crowds who thronged to hear Him contained both honest inquirers and enemy spies. So Jesus carefully veiled His meaning in parables which gave a lesson to the honest folk but allowed His enemies no opportunity to catch Him in His words. We read:

- "The chief priests . . . watched Him, and sent SPIES who pretended to be righteous, that they might SEIZE on His words, in order to deliver Him to the power and the authority of the governor."[7]

- "They send unto Him certain of the Pharisees . . . to CATCH Him in His words."[8]

- "Then went the Pharisees, and took counsel how they might ENTANGLE Him in His talk."[9]

During the Cold War, if you and I were behind the Iron Curtain, with KGB secret police listening to every word we say, just waiting to arrest us, we'd quickly learn to speak in parables, too! Warfare often demands use of such devices as camouflage and codes, so Jesus wisely encoded His messages and camouflaged His meaning in parables. On the occasion in question, we know that Pharisees were in the crowd, for the story of the Rich Man and Lazarus is introduced with the words: "The Pharisees . . . heard all these things." [10] These Scriptural facts lead us to conclude that Jesus here was speaking a parable.

✓ 2. PHYSICAL BODILY PARTS ARE MENTIONED

This story says nothing about "immortal souls" leaving the body at death. Instead, the rich man after he died had "EYES" and a "TONGUE"—that is, very real bodily parts. He wanted dead Lazarus to "dip the tip of his FINGER in water." We wonder how much real water a spirit finger could apply to a spirit tongue. And what good are tongues, fingers, and eyes to disembodied spirits? IF this narrative is to be taken literally, then at death both good and bad men do not soar away as intangible spirits, but go to their respective rewards in real bodies with physical bodily parts. Yet HOW COULD they go there bodily, since their bodies lie buried in the grave? This evidence alone leads the candid investigator to conclude that here we have a fictional parable, not a literal story. [11]

✓ 3. HELL IS NOT A SUBURB OF HEAVEN

Again, if this were a literal account, an actual picture of the geography of heaven and hell, then the homes of the saved and the damned are forever so close to each other that one can both see and speak across the gulf—an unthinkable situation, to say the least. Think of HEARING the sufferers' cries continually ascending—would such a heaven be a pleasant place to spend eternity? None but demons could enjoy such an atmosphere! And what kind of heaven would it be if the redeemed could SEE their unsaved friends and loved ones writhing in the tormenting flames of hell? No, saints and sinners will NOT eternally carry on conversation! Heaven and hell are NOT side by side, nor in sight and hearing of each other. Insisting that this story is literally true becomes absurd.

✓ 4. ABRAHAM'S BOSOM MUST BE GIGANTIC

How could Abraham be LARGE enough to carry Lazarus actually in his bosom? How could he possibly carry all the saved? Surely we must conclude that Abraham's "BOSOM"—another bodily part—cannot be taken literally, as no human, whether saint or sinner, has a breast large enough to contain all the saved. Also, note that Lazarus was carried "into ABRAHAM'S bosom," not into the presence of GOD, where dead saints are supposed to be. This immediately gives us a clue that Christ was speaking from the Pharisees' point of view: ABRAHAM is the most important character in this drama, and that corresponds to *Jewish* belief, not *Christian* teaching.

But Jesus had just told the parable of "The Unjust Steward" driving home His point that "You cannot serve both God and Money." [12] Yet "The Pharisees, who were lovers of money. . . scoffed at Him." [13] Then Jesus, the Master Teacher, turned to the Pharisees and compelled their attention by the story of the rich man and Lazarus, built on their OWN belief which they could not mock. Jesus loved even the Pharisees who sneered at His teaching, so He met them on their own ground and presented from their own standpoint the lesson He wanted to impress on their hearts. [14]

The phrase "Abraham's bosom" in this passage—found nowhere else in Scripture—is clearly NOT to be taken literally. Let's honestly ask ourselves: "Can we really believe that all the saints are even now gathered in Abraham's bosom? If they are, in whose bosom does Abraham rest?" [15] And if "Abraham's bosom" is figurative, then "Abraham" here cannot logically be literal, for it would be supremely incongruous to have Abraham literal but his bosom figurative!

✓ 5. JOSEPHUS DOCUMENTS CONTEMPORARY JEWISH BELIEF

Fortunately for our investigation, the great Jewish historian Josephus left on record a "Discourse to the Greeks Concerning Hades," which illuminates Jesus' story of "The Rich Man & Lazarus." Flavius Josephus was a contemporary but never a follower of Jesus. His writings constitute the most comprehensive Jewish history of that century. For information on the times and teachings of the Jews in the era of Christ and the apostles, Josephus is unsurpassed. A zealous and devout Pharisee himself, Josephus recorded the Pharisees' beliefs regarding the afterlife. Many of those beliefs were NOT Biblical. Pagan ideas had infiltrated their religion just as they have ours today. Though the Jews were custodians of God's Word, they had rejected much of it just as they rejected Christ when He came as their Messiah. Josephus wrote that Hades is "a subterraneous region" of "perpetual darkness" where the lost are dragged "into the neighborhood of hell itself." But the saved are guided "unto a region of light" where "the countenances of the fathers . . . always smile upon them. . . . This place we call THE BOSOM OF ABRAHAM." Though the wicked damned can "SEE the place of [the saved] . . . a CHAOS deep and large is FIXED between them," so that no one can, "if he were bold enough to attempt it, pass over it." [16]

Thus by consulting the writings of Josephus we find that the Pharisees believed in a condition of departed souls after death which echoes and exactly coincides with the condition described in the parable of the rich man and Lazarus, even to the naming of "Abraham's bosom" (mentioned in no other place in Scripture), the torment of the wicked by the flames of hell, the great gulf fixed and impassable between the righteous and wicked, the two abodes within sight of each other, and this whole situation existing inside this earth, where the Pharisees believed souls went when people died.

Jesus caught the Pharisees' attention, met them on their own ground, and then put on the lips of "Abraham" the message that would surely haunt them if they did not repent: "If they hear not Moses and the prophets [that is, if they don't believe the Scriptures], neither will they be persuaded, though one rose from the dead." [17] Those words proved true in the history of the Jews: Christ's crowning miracle was raising the REAL Lazarus of Bethany to life after he'd been dead four days, yet they refused to believe, [18] "though one rose from the dead." Even when Christ's own miraculous resurrection rocked the whole area of Jerusalem, they refused to believe, "though one rose from the dead." In order to teach important truths to unreceptive learners, Jesus framed His parable through people's pre-conceived opinions—but that doesn't mean He endorsed those opinions, any more than He endorsed the crafty, dishonest practices of "The Unjust Steward" when He told that parable. [19]

✓ 6. The Story Has PRAYERS to the HUMAN!

The prayer, "Father Abraham, have MERCY on me," reflects the trust some mistakenly put in the human. Was Jesus actually teaching that we should pray to a fellow mortal? "Father Abraham" is addressed as if he were God, with Lazarus at his beck and call. But God alone can grant mercy. No other name but the precious name of Jesus can save us. [20] Abraham, Peter, and the Virgin Mary were all good people, but they cannot save us. They can't even HEAR us, for they're dead.

Yet the pagan philosophy of "man's immortal soul" has led to the worship of saints, leading sincere believers to pray to other human beings (Catholicism), to theories on the pre-existence of the soul (Mormonism), to reincarnation (Hinduism), to spiritualism, eternal torment (see the next chapter), purgatory or limbo, and other theological fictions based on the Devil's lie in Eden. If this story depicts things as they truly ARE after death, then every other part of Scripture describing death is false.

✦　✦　✦

✓ 7. The Bible Is NOT ALWAYS LITERAL

The written Word of God we call the Bible, like the living, incarnate Word we call Jesus, is unequivocally true and is the divine Source of all truth. But God and His inspired spokesmen do not limit themselves to a narrow, literal mode of discourse. We gain much comfort when we read that "The Lord is my SHEPHERD," [21] for that figure of speech contains material for many a sermon. A fictitious parable may teach a vital, valuable lesson, but its details are not to be taken literally.

For example, the Bible records a parable which says that trees TALKED to each other! Please note: "The *trees* went forth . . . to anoint a king over them; and they said unto the *olive tree*, Reign thou over us. But the olive tree said unto them, . . . And the trees said to the *fig tree*, Come thou, and reign over us. But the fig tree said unto them, . . . Then said the trees unto the *vine*, Come thou, and reign over us. And the vine said unto them, . . . Then said the trees unto the *bramble*, Come thou, and reign over us. And the bramble said unto the trees, If in truth ye anoint me king over you, then come and put your trust in my shadow. . . ." [22] We have no difficulty recognizing this as a parable, for we know trees cannot talk—and they don't have kings!

Again, when the Holy Spirit revealed to the prophet Nathan the sin of King David's adultery with Bathsheba and the subsequent murder of Bathsheba's husband, Nathan used an intriguing parable to lead David to pronounce sentence unwittingly on himself, saying:

> "'There were two men in a certain town, one rich and the other poor. The rich man had a very large number of sheep and cattle, but the poor man had nothing except one little ewe lamb that he had bought. He raised it, and it grew up with him and his children. It shared his food, drank from his cup and even slept in his arms. It was like a daughter to him. Now a traveller came to the rich man, but the rich man refrained from taking one of his own sheep or cattle to prepare a meal for the traveller who had come to him. Instead, he took the ewe lamb that belonged to the poor man and prepared it for the one who had come to him.' David burned with anger against the man and said to Nathan, 'As surely as the LORD lives, the man who did this deserves to die! He must pay for that lamb four times over, because he did such a thing and had no pity.' Then Nathan said to David, 'You are the man!'" [23]

No one insists that Nathan's parable be taken literally. But the story of "The Rich Man & Lazarus"—despite the difficulties outlined here—is clung to by those seeking support for teaching that man's soul exists apart from the body, support which cannot be found elsewhere in Scripture. Insisting that this story is literal, they set great value upon it as the chief pillar supporting the dogma of man's natural immortality. But many points of evidence show this story to be no more literal than other Bible parables.

✓ 8. THIS STORY IS ONE OF A SERIES OF PARABLES

The CONTEXT of this story shows Jesus presenting parable after parable to the Jewish multitude. The story of "The Rich Man and Lazarus" is the last in an unbroken series of parables addressed primarily to the Pharisees and recorded by Luke. Go back to the beginning of the preceding chapter—Luke 15—and we find that Christ began His discourse in response to the Pharisees' ridicule: "Then all the tax collectors and the sinners drew near to Him to hear Him. And the Pharisees and scribes murmured, saying, 'This man receives sinners, and eats with them.' So He spoke this parable unto them, saying . . ." [24] Five wonderful parables followed:

| A SERIES of PARABLES ||
Reference	Parable
Luke 15:4-7	"The Lost Sheep"
Luke 15:8-10	"The Lost Coin"
Luke 15:11-32	"The Prodigal Son"
Luke 16:1-13	"The Unjust Steward"
Luke 16:19-31	"The Rich Man & Lazarus"

It's interesting to note that all of the last three parables have opening lines which are strikingly similar. *The Prodigal Son* begins: "A certain man had two sons." *The Unjust Steward* begins: "There was a certain rich man." And *The Rich Man & Lazarus* begins with *exactly* the same words: "There was a certain rich man"!

✓ 9. PARABLES ARE NOT ALWAYS LABELLED

Some claim that because Jesus did not say this story was a parable, it should be taken literally. However, that's a weak position, because Jesus and Gospel-writer Luke did not always label a parable as such. Proof of this is seen in the case of *"The Prodigal Son,"* a story universally recognized and classified as a parable, though it simply begins: "A certain man had two sons."

Incidentally, the story of that wasteful lad is sometimes called "The Lost Son" just as that of the rich man and Lazarus is sometimes called the great parable of "The Lost Opportunity," in line with Jesus' parables of "The Lost Sheep" and "The Lost Coin." Furthermore, other parables are not labelled as such in the Bible: Jotham's parable of the trees talking or Nathan's parable to King David are not LABELLED as parables—but that's exactly what they are. And that's exactly what the story of the Rich Man and Lazarus is.

✓ 10. THE TIMING IS FICTITIOUS

Just as many details in this story are clearly fictitious, so also is the timing involved in the narrative. The sequence of events in "The Rich Man & Lazarus" conflicts with the Bible truth that the Judgment is yet FUTURE. Paul, speaking years after Jesus' ascension to heaven, says plainly that God "has appointed a day on which He will judge the world."[25] And Peter says, "The Lord knoweth how to . . . RESERVE the unjust unto the day of Judgment TO BE punished."[26] How then could the rich man and Lazarus—and Abraham—already have received their rewards or punishment prior to the Judgment, which the Bible teaches was still future in Paul's and Peter's day?

Now consider this Bible fact: In the New Testament Book of Hebrews, Chapter 11, God says Abraham, like all the patriarchs, has not YET received the promise of eternal life but is awaiting the resurrection at Christ's Return. When the Book of Hebrews was written—several decades after Luke penned this parable as part of his Gospel, Abraham was not alive—and he's still not alive! God states plainly that Abraham and the other patriarchs "all died in faith, NOT having received the promises" of heaven and eternal life.[27] The faithful suffered persecution and even torture "that they might obtain a better RESURRECTION"[28]—and the resurrection has not occurred even to this day!

The chapter concludes by repeating that NONE of the faithful had received their reward YET: "These all, having obtained a good report through faith, received NOT the promise: God having provided some BETTER thing for us, that THEY without US should NOT be made perfect."[29] Here we have an echo of Isaiah 26:19 — "Thy dead men shall live, TOGETHER WITH my dead body shall they arise." So if Abraham "received not the promise" but awaits the "resurrection" that will "make perfect" ALL God's sleeping saints at the same time, who dares to say he's already alive?

In conclusion, we've seen that too many problems confront those who insist on taking this story as literal. When taken literally, the story collapses under the weight of its own inconsistencies.[30] We've turned this story inside out and found at least TEN good reasons why Jesus' account of "The Rich Man & Lazarus" is a parable, not an actual happening. After looking at these ten points, those who still insist this parable is a literal picture of life after death do so not because of the evidence but in spite of it! And those who understand the consistent Bible teaching on this subject have no trouble fitting this parable into the overall picture of our puzzle.

PUZZLE PIECE #14:

THE **THIEF** ON THE **CROSS**

Like "The Parable of the Rich Man & Lazarus," Christ's promise to the thief on the cross at first glance seems to contradict the many other clear statements of inspired Scripture on the subject of death. But whenever we encounter an apparent contradiction in the Bible, we immediately realize that something is wrong—wrong NOT with the Word of God but with our limited understanding or with the translation or something else. As we investigate the problem here to determine exactly what's wrong, you'll find a good name for this investigation is:

"THE **CASE** OF THE **MISPLACED COMMA**."

Let's go back 2000 years and get the picture in our mind's eye: Jesus was hanging on the cross between two thieves who were also crucified. One thief is unrepentant, but the other speaks a few words to our Lord:

> "He said unto Jesus, Lord, remember me when Thou comest into Thy kingdom. And Jesus said unto him, Verily I say unto thee, Today shalt thou be with Me in paradise."[31]

PUNCTUATION **NOT** INSPIRED

The first point to be made is that the PUNCTUATION of the Bible is NOT inspired. It was not added till about the time of the Reformation—A.D. 1500 or so. Note too, that in the text as copied above, capitals were added to pronouns pertaining to Jesus so you can tell which "thou" pertains to whom, but otherwise it appears as in the King James Version—without any QUOTATION MARKS around the words spoken by the thief or by Jesus. Those were added in still later versions.

```
THISISWHATANCIENTGREEKLO
OKEDLIKEOFCOURSEITISNTGR
EEKITSENGLISH
```

You see, those who added the commas and other punctuation marks to the Scriptures had no help from the Greek manuscript Luke wrote, because Greek was written all in CAPITAL letters, with no breaks between sentences,

WITHNOBREAKSEVENBETWEENWORDS

—to save on costly parchments. Naturally, when punctuation marks were added, they were placed so as to conform to the theology of the one who put them in. Translators used their best judgment in inserting punctuation, but they were certainly not inspired. Therefore we needn't be governed by marks translators added only four hundred years ago to find the intent of inspired writers nineteen hundred years ago.

Changing a comma often makes a great difference in meaning. For example, Hebrews 10:12 says, "But this Man [Jesus], after He had offered one sacrifice for sins for ever, sat down on the right hand of God." If the comma were wrongly placed after "sins," the passage would say Jesus "for ever sat down on the right hand of God" and thus will NEVER return to this world. But when we rightly place the comma after "for ever," the passage says Christ sat down after offering Himself as the final, once-for-all-time Sacrifice. This is a completely different meaning, just as we'd have a completely different meaning if translators—who in general did such excellent work—had placed the comma in Luke 23:43 after "today" instead of after "thee." The two choices look like this:

KING JAMES VERSION

"Verily I say unto thee,
Today shalt thou be with Me in paradise."

CORRECT PUNCTUATION

"Verily I say unto thee today,
Thou shalt be with Me in paradise." [32]

"Today" is an adverb of TIME, telling WHEN something happens.
It may modify the verb "be"
and tell when the thief would be with Jesus in paradise.
— OR —
It may modify the verb "say"
and emphasize when Jesus spoke those words to the thief.

There are TWO very clear, very BIBLICAL reasons why we know beyond any doubt that "today" must modify "say" and that therefore the comma was misplaced by the translators. Let's look at those two reasons.

✓ REASON #1: JESUS DID NOT GO TO HEAVEN THAT DAY

Christ did not go to Paradise that Friday of the crucifixion. How do we know for sure? Well, the term "Paradise" in the Bible means "heaven"—where God is—as shown by such verses as the following:

"A man . . . was caught up to the third HEAVEN. . . .
This man . . . was caught up to PARADISE." [33]

Furthermore, by comparing two texts of Scripture, namely . . .

"The TREE OF LIFE . . . is in the midst of the PARADISE of God" [34]

and

"He showed me a pure river . . .
proceeding from the throne of God. . . .
On either side of the river, was the TREE OF LIFE," [35]

we see that PARADISE is where "the THRONE OF GOD" is.

Therefore, if Christ had gone to Paradise that Friday afternoon, He would have gone into the very presence of God. But Christ Himself, on Sunday morning, told Mary Magdalene as she fell at His feet to worship Him, "Touch Me not; for I am *not yet ascended* to My Father." [36]

Are we therefore placed in the unenviable position of trying to decide whether to believe EITHER —

(1) Christ's promise to the thief on Friday afternoon

— OR —

(2) His statement to Mary on Sunday morning?

No! Christ did NOT contradict Himself. The fault lies in the misplaced comma.

✓ REASON #2: THE THIEF DID NOT DIE THAT DAY

Unquestionably, the thief did not die on the day Jesus gave him the promise. He didn't expect to die that day. He didn't expect Jesus to die that day, either. He knew that death by crucifixion was a long, slow process often taking several days. You'll recall the astonishment of Pilate, later that afternoon, when he learned that Jesus was already dead. The Bible says, "Pilate marveled that He was already dead." [37]

The Bible day ends at sundown, and the Jews didn't want the men to hang on the crosses that particular Sabbath, for it was the Passover weekend and a "high day." [38] Therefore, they had the soldiers break the legs of the thieves so they could not escape after they were taken down from the cross—but they did NOT break the legs of Jesus, because "He was dead already." [39]

Preachers who teach the immortal soul theory are aware of the problems posed by these facts, yet they WANT to believe that the thief died that day. So they tell their congregation that the thieves did die that day—from having their legs broken! Skiers or victims of car accidents have had both legs broken, but does this injury prove fatal? Criminals are executed by such means as beheading, hanging, firing squad, electrocution, gas chamber—but WHO has ever been condemned to death by leg breaking?!?

A broken leg wouldn't KILL the thieves. It would merely render them immobile so they couldn't escape. You see, the Jews didn't want the men to remain on their crosses during that high holy day, but they would let them lie on the ground till that day was past and then tie them on their crosses again till death came from lack of food and water. The Jews didn't want the thieves to escape, but they couldn't throw them back in prison because these condemned men had hung on a cross and were considered "cursed." We read: "CURSED is every one that hangeth on a tree" or a cross. [40] Criminals were always crucified outside the city. Therefore "Jesus also suffered *outside the city* gate." [41] And Stephen, the first Christian martyr, was stoned to death outside the city. [42] Since bringing a cursed individual within their city gates would contaminate or defile Jerusalem, and since their only prison was inside the city, the Jews had to take other measures to make sure the thieves could not escape.

Realizing that it's ridiculous to claim that breaking leg bones would kill the thieves, the preachers say their legs were broken "to hasten their death." This contention may have some validity, since victims nailed or tied to a cross found their lungs constricted unless they supported themselves with their legs, so breaking their legs made breathing more difficult. But we already know that Jesus did not meet the thief in heaven that Friday, for He did not ascend to His Father till some time after encountering Mary Magdalene on Sunday.

It's true that the Jews had to work fast to remove the thieves from the crosses, just as Jesus' followers had to give their Lord a hurried burial, for the Bible day ENDED at sundown. Listen: IF those Roman soldiers really wanted to hasten a condemned person's DEATH, they knew from training and experience how to do it. They could have pierced the thieves' side the same way they did Christ's. [43] Jabbing the spear into the thieves' hearts certainly would've "hastened their deaths." But they did not.

That day, Good Friday, was soon to end at sundown. So the thieves were left outside the city miserably alive with broken legs.

Now—keeping these two valid Biblical reasons in mind—we must answer this question:

How could a DEAD Christ meet a LIVING thief
in heaven
when NEITHER of them went there
that day???

The answer, of course, is that He didn't. Jesus had no intention of doing so when He made His promise. And the thief didn't even *ask* Jesus to take him to glory *that* day. The same Holy Spirit who revealed Christ's divinity to the thief also gave him the right question to ask. He asked to be a part of Christ's kingdom when He COMES—when He *comes* in His kingdom, not when He *goes* to the grave in His death or even when He *goes* back to heaven in His ascension. This was the same hope that Paul had,[44] and Job,[45] and all the Bible writers. The thief knew it wouldn't happen on that same day— that's why he said, "REMEMBER me."

And Jesus' response met the thief's request EXACTLY. The thief was primarily concerned with not when he would reach Paradise, but whether he'd have a place in Christ's kingdom—not *when* but *whether*. Jesus' majestic answer assured him that however undeserving he might feel, or however impossible it might appear for the dying Jesus to bring His promise to pass, he WOULD assuredly BE there!

Think of the trying circumstances under which Jesus spoke those words. Think of the significance of that word "today." Incredibly enough, Jesus boldly made this promise:

> TODAY, as His ministry was ending in agony and shame,
> TODAY, as His claim to be the Son of God appeared false,
> TODAY, as His own disciples had forsaken Him,
> TODAY, in this His darkest hour, before that mocking mob,
> TODAY, amid all these forlorn prospects and blasted hopes.

The crucified Christ calmly turned to the repentant thief and majestically declared: "Verily I say unto thee today, thou SHALT be with Me in Paradise."

Christ still hasn't come in His kingdom. That's why Christians everywhere are still praying "Thy kingdom come," as He taught us. But the promise to the thief on the cross is sure and certain—he SHALL be with Christ and all the redeemed in Paradise. Moving the comma to its proper place makes the whole passage harmonious—not only with itself but with all the rest of Scripture teaching on the state of the dead.

Another puzzle piece fits neatly into place as we close our investigation of "The Case of the Misplaced Comma." Case dismissed!

PUZZLE PIECE #15:
"THE SPIRITS IN PRISON"

Let's read this passage from the Bible:

"For Christ also suffered once for sins, the Just for the unjust, that He might bring us to God, being put to death in the flesh but made alive by the Spirit, by whom also He went and preached to the spirits in prison, who formerly were disobedient, when once the Divine longsuffering waited in the days of Noah, while the ark was being prepared, in which a few, that is, eight souls [eight *persons* or *lives*], were saved through water." [46]

Those who teach the immortality of the soul claim THREE THINGS about this passage from the pen of Peter, namely:

A. That Peter here must refer to disembodied spirits of people who lived before the Flood, the antediluvians.

B. That these disembodied spirits must have been conscious or else Christ would not have gone to preach to them. Therefore, they say, here is Scriptural proof that the dead are conscious.

C. That the time when Christ supposedly carried out this preaching mission was during the three days His body was in the tomb.

But suppositions such as these can never be made to harmonize with the clear, consistent teaching of the rest of Scripture on the state of the dead. Careful examination shows that all three of the above claims are absolutely wrong. Any confusion caused by this text can be cleared up by answering a few basic questions:

QUESTION #1 — WHEN WAS THIS PREACHING DONE?

The Scripture says it was "in the days of Noah, while the Ark was a preparing." It was "WHEN once the long-suffering of God waited in the days of Noah"—not thousands of years later in hell!

QUESTION #2 — HOW WAS THIS PREACHING DONE?

Quite plainly we read, "by the Spirit." The passage says that Christ was "put to death in the flesh, but quickened [made alive] by the Spirit: BY

WHICH also He went and preached unto the spirits in prison." That is, by the ministry of Noah, who preached for 120 years while he worked on the Ark. Noah was Christ's representative. Christ, by His Spirit, preached through Noah. In the very same letter Peter wrote of "the prophets" like Noah and states that "the Spirit of Christ . . . was in them." [47] And Peter himself calls Noah "a preacher of righteousness." [48] Noah, filled with the Holy Spirit, was Christ's spokesman preaching to the doomed antediluvians. [49]

QUESTION #3 — WHY WAS THIS PREACHING DONE?

There are MANY implications to such an astonishing theory that has our Lord preaching to disembodied spirits in Hell or Hades or some other intermediate place. What message could He bring them? Would He offer them a second chance even after death? If so, WHY single out that particular generation—why not give a second chance to ALL the many millions of dead? Is Peter teaching that God plays favorites? Is he teaching the doctrine of purgatory? No, Scripture makes plain that death seals our fate and there is no second chance: "It is appointed unto men ONCE to die, and after this the JUDGMENT." [50] Most Christians rightly reject the unscriptural teachings of purgatory and a supposed "second chance."

The purpose of this preaching was NOT to offer a second chance to disembodied spirits of dead sinners but to warn the wicked living in Noah's day to repent. The very chapter telling of God's plan to destroy the earth with a flood says: "My Spirit shall NOT ALWAYS strive [or plead] with man, . . . yet his days shall be an hundred and twenty years." [51] In other words, God's Spirit patiently preached through Noah, "a preacher of righteousness," waiting 120 years before finally destroying those who would not listen.

QUESTION #4 — MUST "SPIRITS" MEAN
DISEMBODIED SPIRITS OF THE DEAD?

By no means. When Moses called God "the God of the spirits of all flesh," he certainly referred to men in the FLESH, NOT men in a disembodied state, for Moses was praying for a leader among the living to take his place! [52] Peter's word translated "spirits" is from the Greek *pneumata* plural of *pneuma*, meaning "wind," "breath," or "spirit." Breath is a conspicuous characteristic of living beings, and by the figure of speech called synecdoche, a characteristic *part* of something stands for the *whole*. [53] Thus *pneuma* (breath or spirit) stands for the whole "person." [54] Accordingly, these *"spirits"* can be considered living human beings who were certainly as real as the "eight *souls*" in verse 20 of this same passage.

QUESTION #5 — TO WHAT DOES
THE "PRISON HOUSE" REFER?

Those who teach the unscriptural doctrines of purgatory, or a second chance, or the immortal soul tell us that—in their opinion—the metaphorical term "prison" refers to the prison house of DEATH. But Christians must honor God's Word above men's opinions. And several Scripture verses teach us that it is the prison house of SIN.

For instance, in Luke 4:17-21 Jesus read to the congregation from Isaiah 61:1-2, proclaiming "LIBERTY to the CAPTIVES, the opening of the PRISON to them that are BOUND." Then Jesus told His listeners: "This day is this scripture fulfilled in your ears." He was addressing sinners, not dead people!

Furthermore, when Jesus preached that "the truth shall make you FREE," [55] He was addressing living sinners, not dead people or disembodied spirits.

God called Jesus to be "a light to the Gentiles, to open blind eyes, to bring out PRISONERS from the PRISON, those who sit in darkness from the PRISON house." [56] Now Gentiles may be sinners, with eyes spiritually *blinded* by the *darkness* of disbelief. They may be held by the *chains* of evil habits in SIN'S PRISON HOUSE, but they're not DEAD. If they WERE dead prisoners of sin, there'd be no hope for them and no need of preaching.

When Christ quoted Isaiah in Luke's Gospel as mentioned above, He said, "The Spirit of the Lord is upon Me." Evidently the Spirit's work in Noah's day was the same as in Christ's—preaching to prisoners of sin, offering them a way of ESCAPE. How securely the prison house of sin held those who "were DISOBEDIENT. . . in the days of Noah" is evident from the fact that only eight persons escaped from it and survived the Flood. [57]

That Peter himself intended "prison" to mean the prison house of SIN, not DEATH, is seen from his own statement about those "who LIVE in error" and contrasts "LIBERTY" with the "BONDAGE" of those who "are SLAVES of corruption." [58] No one but Christ can set men free from the evil habits and desires with which Satan shackles them.

QUESTION #6 — WAS JESUS ALIVE OR DEAD
DURING HIS TIME IN THE TOMB?

The Bible itself has cleared up any misconceptions caused by this verse from Peter, but one last question should be answered: That Sabbath day after the Crucifixion, while Jesus lay quietly resting in the tomb, was He alive or dead?

Obviously, He was dead—since He was not resurrected till the first day of the week. Some try to sidestep this problem by assuming that Christ's spirit remained alive even though His body died. But Christ Himself said: "I am He that liveth, and was DEAD; and, behold, I am alive for evermore." [59] He didn't say, "My *body* was dead"—He said, "*I* was dead."

Our whole chance for salvation depends on whether or not Christ actually DIED. If Christ did not really die—body, soul, and spirit—then you and I must still pay the penalty for our sins, and He's not our Savior. But we must never get the idea that Jesus Christ is not our Savior or that He did not pay the full penalty for our sins by dying on the cross. [60] Christians who accept the Lord's atoning death have grave doubts about interpretations which have Christ prematurely alive and preaching to disembodied spirits in hellfire while He was in the tomb.

We've answered SIX relevant questions and found no support for the immortal soul theory which teaches consciousness after death. The Bible answer to any one of them is enough to render that theory invalid, but collectively their cumulative evidence is enough to demolish it. Rightly understood, this puzzle piece from Peter is in full accord with all other Scripture teaching, so it fits very nicely into God's overall picture.

PUZZLE PIECE #16:
SAUL & THE WITCH OF ENDOR

Although the Israelites were a theocracy, a favored nation led by God Himself who fought their battles for them, the time came when they felt this wasn't good enough for them. Rejecting God, they asked to have a regular king so they could be "like all the nations." [61] Saul, a handsome young man who stood head and shoulders taller than other people, was chosen to be king. [62] God knew Israel's desire for a human king was unwise and would cause them to trust more in human strength and less in divine power, but He let the people have their own way and poured out His blessings upon the new king. However, Saul's presumptuous disregard of God's will proved he could not be trusted with royal power. [63]

Those who accept the theory of "man's immortal soul" point with pride to the account of King Saul's visit to the witch of Endor. [64] For after all, the passage begins by saying that the prophet "Samuel was DEAD . . . and BURIED," yet the wicked king had a witch apparently conjure up Samuel's spirit who then gave him supernatural insight into the future. Champions of the conscious state of the dead feel that here we have a puzzle piece that could never fit in with the plain Bible statement that "THE DEAD KNOW NOT ANYTHING." [65]

Here is an apparent contradiction—yet God's Word never contradicts itself. So let's ask ourselves: Is this passage really Bible proof that spirits of the dead are conscious beings and that it's possible to communicate with those spirits?

Though answers to those questions may differ, one thing we can all agree on is that here we have the record of a SUPERNATURAL occurrence. However, God is not the only source of supernatural phenomena. Satan and his demons are supernatural beings who also succeed in "working miracles" [66] "with all power and signs and lying wonders." [67] But "we are not ignorant of his schemes," for God warns us that "Satan disguises himself as an angel of light." [68] If our Archenemy can disguise himself as a friendly, dazzling angel, it's no trick at all for him or his cohorts to impersonate Samuel. The manifestation of Samuel's spirit was either real or apparent, so—on the basis of the evidence—all we need to determine is,

- Was it GENUINE—that is, produced by God?

or

- Was it a clever COUNTERFEIT staged by Satan?

Since this passage is the one solitary instance in the Bible of the supposed communication with the dead, or necromancy, [69] it's worthy of close attention. As we examine the whole account, SEVEN FACTS stand out:

FACT #1 — GOD HIMSELF WOULD NO LONGER COMMUNICATE WITH SAUL

As Israel's first king, Saul led a nation favored by direct communication with God. But Saul grew so disobedient that he rarely sought advice from the Lord and refused to follow it when it was given. Now Saul's fortunes had fallen so low that he desperately wanted God to tell him what to do, because "the Philistines gathered their armies together for warfare, to fight with Israel." [70]

However, the Record clearly states that King Saul had departed so far from God that the Lord would not answer him: "When Saul inquired of the Lord, the Lord answered him NOT, neither by dreams, nor by Urim, nor by prophets." [71] The Lord never turns away a soul who comes to Him humbly and sincerely. Why, then, did He turn Saul away unanswered? By his own acts the king had rejected the methods of inquiring of God: He despised the counsel of God's prophet Samuel; he exiled God's chosen one, David; he killed God's priests. [72] Even now, Saul did not turn to God with humility and repentance. He wanted deliverance from his foes, not pardon for his sins. Having forsaken God, Saul's heart trembled with fear [73] when he saw the mighty Philistine armies. Earlier, God had told him by the prophet Samuel that the kingdom would be taken away from him as punishment for his failure to obey.[74] But Saul made no serious attempts to seek God's counsel—the Record says he "inquired not of the Lord."[75] Instead, the proud monarch cut himself off from God and determined to seek help from *another* supernatural source.

Fact #2 — SAMUEL Would
No Longer Communicate with Saul

King Saul pursued such a disobedient course that not only God but even Samuel, God's prophet, would have nothing further to do with him. The Divine Record states that "Samuel came no more to see Saul until the day of his [Samuel's] death."[76] So Saul could not inquire of Samuel, who, even before his death, had stopped giving any counsel. Greatly irritated by heaven's silence, Saul desperately tried to FORCE a reply!

Fact #3 — Saul Was on FORBIDDEN Ground

Saul ordered his servants to find a witch who could contact the spirit world,[77] so he might obtain the information that God withheld! This was his LAST STEP in disobedience to God. Saul knew he was stepping over the line onto Satan's territory. He KNEW that God strongly prohibited consulting with familiar spirits, witchcraft, sorcery, and spiritism.[78] Earlier, Saul himself as king had even "put away those that had familiar spirits, and the wizards, out of the land."[79] Yet despite that prohibition he sought to practice what God forbids.

In order to practice her unholy arts, the woman of Endor had made a pact with Satan. As a witch, she agreed to follow Satan in all things, and Satan agreed to perform wonders and miracles for her, revealing the most secret things, if she would yield herself unreservedly to be controlled by his Satanic majesty. This she had done.

King Saul made his visit to the witch "by night" to be under cover of darkness. Furthermore, "Saul DISGUISED himself, and put on other raiment,"[80] because he knew the witch would never practice her forbidden art before the very king who had outlawed it. The picture is one of people who both know they're doing something wrong!

Would God HONOR the request for information from one engaged in the very occult practices He had forbidden? Such a view is not only incredible but inconsistent with the entire body of Scripture. It's absurd to suppose that God, who had refused to speak to Saul through a *living* prophet, would then speak through a *dead* prophet and send Samuel from the so-called world of spirits in response to the devilish incantations of a WITCH!

Fact #4 — Saul Saw NOTHING But Was Deceived

Furthermore, Saul was DECEIVED: The "spirit" was not the good man of God we call Samuel—it was a demon from Satan's legions. Saul himself saw nothing. He had to ask the witch, "'What did YOU see?' And the woman said to Saul, 'I saw a spirit ascending out of the earth.' So he said to her, 'What is his form?' And she said, 'an old man is coming up, and he is covered with a mantle.' And Saul perceived that it was Samuel." [81]

Having told the witch to "Bring me up Samuel," Saul naturally jumped to the conclusion that the spirit she claimed to see was that of Samuel. Saul saw nothing but had to content himself with asking what the witch saw.

Fact #5 — The Pretended Prophet ACCEPTED WORSHIP!

In an attitude of reverent worship, Saul "stooped with his face to the ground, and bowed himself" before the spirit. [82] If it really had been Samuel's spirit, it would NEVER have received Saul's worship. Neither Samuel nor an ANGEL from God would have consented to receive such worship. [83] But EVIL angels—devilish spirits—would eagerly welcome it. [84]

Though the Bible states that "Samuel said," [85] when we know the prophet was already dead, we must not interpret this to mean it was actually Samuel who spoke. The writer simply describes events as they appeared, which is normal narrative technique. The Bible also speaks of the sun rising and setting, [86] and so do we. Yet no one is deceived or confused by the fact that we speak simply of appearances. Actually the sun does not rise or set; the earth simply revolves. And actually it was not God's holy prophet who came forth at the witch's incantation. Satan couldn't present the real Samuel, but he did present a counterfeit that served his deceptive purpose. If Satan can impersonate "an angel of light," [87] he could easily imitate Samuel's voice.

We can verify who was speaking by noting that the spirit dared to tell Saul: "The Lord . . . is become THINE ENEMY." [88] Those words identify their author as Satan, who always depicts God as man's enemy. No true believer would ever say such a thing about God, whose very essence is love. [89] God had not become Saul's enemy. Even though Saul had sinned, God still loved him and wanted to save him. But the lying spirit, posing as a voice from heaven, impersonated the dead Samuel and taunted Saul with God's decision to "rent [rip or tear] the kingdom out of thine hand," [90] which is simply a direct quotation from 1 Samuel 15:28. Satan succeeded in completely discouraging Saul, leading him on to ruin. Several days later Saul—like Judas—took his own life. [91]

The message which the spirit impostor gave Saul contained nothing new, with the exception of predicting Israel's deliverance into Philistine hands, and "TOMORROW shalt thou and THY SONS be with me [that is, dead]." [92] But the first part of this prediction was only what Satan might safely judge would happen with a strong enemy facing a demoralized king, and the latter part was a falsehood.

In the first place, there's no proof at all that Saul died the next day. On the contrary, the Record shows his death was several days later. [93] In the second place, only three of Saul's sons died in that battle against the Philistines. [94] Those three do not include other sons of Saul, such as *Ishui*, [95] *Ishbosheth*, [96] and two others who lived for long years after this till they were hanged by the Gibeonites. [97] Far from bringing Saul heavenly insight, the spirit's demoralizing message was filled with falsehood.

FACT #6 — "SAMUEL" CAME FROM THE WRONG DIRECTION

Those who believe in man's "immortal soul" claim that at the moment of death good people go up to heaven and bad people go down to hell. Samuel was definitely in the "good" class: He was faithful his entire life, serving the Lord ever since his mother took him to the Temple as a small lad. [98] Therefore, advocates of natural immortality assume that he immediately went to heaven when he died.

Many Christians believe that redeemed souls are now up in heaven, in the presence of the Lord. But the apparition seen by the witch came UP out of the EARTH. Could that have been Samuel's immortal soul or conscious spirit? Are redeemed souls down in the earth? Note the Bible expressions used in Saul's meeting with the witch:

> "Bring him UP, whom I shall name unto thee."
> "Whom shall I bring UP unto thee?"
> "Bring me UP Samuel."
> "ASCENDING out of the EARTH"
> "An old man cometh UP."
> "to bring me UP" [99]

Those expressions are exactly how the Bible describes *a witch's familiar spirit*: "Thou shalt be brought DOWN, and shalt speak out of the GROUND, and thy speech shall be LOW out of the DUST, and thy voice shall be, as of one that hath a *familiar spirit*, out of the GROUND, and thy speech shall WHISPER out of the DUST." [100] This evidence shows that "Samuel's ghost" was not a saint from heaven's glory but a demon from Satan's legions.

The demonic spirit impersonating Samuel pretended to be "disturbed" [101] by Saul. This seems to teach that redeemed saints, after departing this world, are still under the control of sinful mortals on this earth and are compelled to obey them. IF this spirit medium had power to force Samuel to come back to earth and talk to Saul after Samuel had refused to have anything more to do with him while he was alive, IF every witch has the dead so completely in her power that she can compel them to give information to whoever may pay her for it, then even the redeemed dead are truly to be pitied! Death must be miserable if even the saints are at any moment liable to be called from glory at the bidding of any witch or wizard who chooses to hold a séance. [102]

Fact #7 — The REASON for Saul's Death

Finally, any reader who still believes . . .

A. it really WAS Samuel and not a demon who was "brought up"

—and—

B. communicating with spirits of the dead is ALL RIGHT

will be quickly UNDECEIVED if he considers the REASONS for Saul's DEATH. God sets forth those reasons quite frankly:

> "Saul DIED for his transgression which he committed against the Lord, even against the word of the Lord, which he kept not, and also for asking counsel of one that had a familiar spirit, to inquire of it." [103]

Saul was cut off from life for attending a séance and inquiring of the spirits. So here's another reason why it could NOT have been the spirit of Samuel sent by the Lord, for this would charge God with approving and even taking part in the wickedness which cost Saul his life!

The seven foregoing facts—individually and collectively—show that Saul's forbidden visit to the witch of Endor does not prove Samuel to be alive and conscious. It proves only that God means what He says when he warns us against dabbling in the occult. [104] This puzzle piece teaches that the prophet Samuel was—and still is—asleep in his grave. The "spirit" was a demon.

Puzzle Piece #17:
ABSENT from the BODY,
PRESENT with the LORD

Personally, I would never criticize the Bible. I believe people should give it the respect it deserves as the inspired Word of God. But the Apostle Peter was bold enough to criticize the writings of "our dear brother Paul" by saying: "His letters contain some things that are HARD to understand, which ignorant and unstable people distort, as they do the other Scriptures, to their own destruction." [105]

"Some Things HARD to Be Understood"

There are a few Scriptures from the pen of Paul which may have called forth the above criticism from his fellow apostle. One of these is **2 CORINTHIANS 5:8**, which speaks of being "willing to be absent from the body, and to be present with the Lord."

Teachers of the immortal-soul theory often use this verse hoping it may provide some support for their ideas of "the immortal soul," consciousness in death, and that believers go immediately to heaven when they die. We'll see that it teaches no such thing. It would indeed be "hard to understand" if Paul *were* teaching those things in this verse, for he'd thereby contradict everything else he and other Bible writers taught on the subject of death!

♦ Paul NEVER Taught "the Immortal Soul"

First of all, we can be sure that the Holy Spirit does NOT contradict Himself—and neither does the inspired Apostle Paul. That great servant of God wrote more than one fourth of the New Testament—fourteen of its twenty-seven parts were penned by him—and he NEVER taught the immortality of the soul. Paul is the only writer in the entire Bible who even uses the words "immortal" and "immortality," yet in not one instance does he anywhere apply these terms to people—either righteous or wicked—prior to their resurrection from the dead. Likewise, in not one instance does he apply these terms to men's souls, either before or after death. Instead, Paul says it's "the King eternal . . . the only wise God" who is "immortal." [106] Indeed, he plainly states that God ALONE possesses immortality, speaking of "the King of kings, and Lord of lords; Who ONLY hath immortality." [107]

Paul further declares that we should "SEEK for . . . immortality," since we don't have it now. [108] In the resurrection of the righteous at Christ's Second Coming, we believers—being mere mortals—"MUST PUT ON immortality." [109] Thus Paul agreed with the Bible concept that mankind is mortal or subject to death: in Job 4:17 we read, "Shall MORTAL man be more just than God?" As shown in Part One of this study on death in Chapter 10, the *theological fiction* that man's soul is naturally "immortal" was invented by the Greeks and other pagans, but Paul gave no support to that idea.

♦ Paul NEVER Taught Consciousness in Death

Secondly, neither did the Apostle support the man-made idea of consciousness in death. Instead, he taught that death is a "sleep." Please note: In 1 Corinthians 15:51 Paul says, "We shall not all sleep [die], but we shall all be changed" when Jesus returns to raise the dead. And in 1 Thessalonians

4:14 Paul speaks of believers who have died as "those also which sleep in Jesus." In this Paul is in agreement with the inspired statements of others, like Jesus: "Our friend Lazarus SLEEPETH. . . . Lazarus is DEAD" [110] and like David: "Lighten mine eyes, lest I sleep the sleep of death." [111] God's Word makes clear that this sleep is an UNconscious, dreamless sleep: "The living know that they shall die, but the dead know not anything." [112] When a man dies, "he returneth to his earth; in that very day his thoughts PERISH." [113]

◆ Paul NEVER Taught Death Is the Doorway to Life

Thirdly, Paul called death an ENEMY[114]—not a portal to Paradise! He did not believe or teach that dead believers go to heaven immediately when they die. His "blessed hope" focused on the resurrection that will take place at the "glorious appearing of our great God and Savior Jesus Christ." [115] He unequivocally stated: "If the dead rise not, . . . then they also which are fallen asleep in Christ are perished." [116] If dead believers go directly into Christ's presence when they die, why would they be "perished" if they didn't "rise" in the resurrection? They wouldn't need to "rise" if they were already enjoying the bliss of heaven!

The fact is, Paul taught us Christians to look to "the Coming of the Lord" and the RESURRECTION of believers that will then take place: "For this we say to you by the word of the Lord, that we which are alive and remain unto *the Coming of the Lord* shall not prevent [precede] them which are asleep [dead]. For the Lord Himself shall descend from heaven with a shout, with the voice of the archangel, and with the trump of God: and the dead in Christ shall rise first: then we which are alive and remain shall be caught up together with them in the clouds, to meet the Lord in the air: and so [in this way] shall we ever be with the Lord." [117]

Now with this background in mind, we're prepared to turn to the text in question.

2 Corinthians 5:1-9

This passage from the pen of Paul is much discussed—and much misunderstood. Let's simply READ it in the New King James Version:

> "For we know that if our earthly house, this tent, is destroyed, we have a building from God, a house not made with hands, eternal in the heavens. For in this we groan, earnestly desiring to be clothed with our habitation which is from heaven, if indeed, having been clothed, we shall not be found naked. For we who are in this tent groan, being burdened, not because we want to be unclothed, but further clothed, that mortality may be swallowed up by life. Now He who has prepared

us for this very thing is God, who also has given us the Spirit as a guarantee. So we are always confident, knowing that while we are at home in the body we are absent from the Lord. For we walk by faith, not by sight. We are confident, yes, well pleased rather to be absent from the body and to be present with the Lord. Therefore we make it our aim, whether present or absent, to be well pleasing to Him."

First, let's see what the text does NOT say, and then we'll see what it DOES say. It does NOT say anything about being "absent from the body and present with the Lord *in a spirit form when I die.*" If I think it says that, then I'm reading into the text something that isn't there. That's an interpretation of the text, but it's not what the text says. It does not say (1) I would be present with the Lord *in a spirit form,* and it does not say (2) I would be present with the Lord *immediately when I die.* That much is clear at the very outset.

A VERSE-BY-VERSE EXAMINATION

Now let's see what the text actually DOES say. Many simply focus on the single verse of **2 Corinthians 5:8** divorced from its context, but we need to go back to the beginning of the chapter to get the whole picture. Let's examine the passage of **2 Corinthians 5:1-9** and determine its precise meaning verse by verse. I'll use the New King James Version here, but we'll consider other translations as we go along.

Verse 1: "For we know that if our EARTHLY HOUSE, this tent, is destroyed, we have a BUILDING from God, a house not made with hands, ETERNAL in the heavens." How many "houses" does verse 1 mention? Two. Where are those houses? One's in heaven; the other's on earth. The house on earth is said to be a "tabernacle" in the KJV. Most modern versions—like the NKJV, NASB, NIV, RSV, and the NRSV—call it a "tent." The other house is not called an earthly "tent," which is temporary, but is "a BUILDING from God, a house not made with hands, ETERNAL in the heavens." So we'll see as we proceed that Paul is using an illustration contrasting two houses—an earthly house and a heavenly house—to stand for our temporary earthly body in contrast to our everlasting house or body "not made with hands, eternal in the heavens."

Verse 2: "For in THIS [in this what? in this house, in this earthly tent of flesh, in this physical mortal body] we groan, earnestly desiring to be clothed with our habitation which is from heaven." Now notice what the DESIRE is: I am in an earthly body that's a tentlike structure, that is temporary. The body that God will give me is eternal. I groan for that, I desire that—the glorious body He's preparing for me.

Verse 3: "if indeed, having been CLOTHED, we shall not be found NAKED." What does "clothed" mean? It means—as Paul just said in verse 2—'to be CLOTHED with our habitation [or body] which is from heaven" and not having an earthly, mortal body. What does it mean to be "naked"? It means to have *neither* an earthly *nor* a heavenly body—it means to be dead. Paul says, I want to be "clothed" with my body from heaven.

Verse 4: "**For we who are in this tent** [this temporary, earthly tent of flesh] **groan, being burdened, NOT because we want to be unclothed** [dead]**, but further clothed, that mortality** [this mortal being] **may be swallowed up by life** [immortal life in a new 'building from God']." Paul says my great longing is not that I would be UNCLOTHED, or dead, but that I might be CLOTHED UPON by my body from heaven, and that this MORTAL existence might be swallowed up by IMMORTALITY which is from heaven.

Verse 5: "**Now He who has prepared us for this very thing is God, who also has given us the Spirit as a guarantee.**" In other words, God has planned that we be clothed by immortality, planned that we not have a mortal body. "Who also has given us the Spirit as a guarantee." The King James Version uses the word "earnest"—which means "pledge" or "guarantee"—of His Spirit. The pledge of the Holy Spirit living within my heart is a glorious promise that mortality will fade into insignificance as I'm clothed with my immortal body from heaven. The current manifestation of the Spirit in my life is a glorious indication—a virtual guarantee—that Christ will clothe me with immortality. In fact, Paul explains that "if the Spirit of Him who raised Jesus from the dead dwells in you, He who raised Christ from the dead will also give life to your mortal bodies through His Spirit who dwells in you." [118]

Verse 6: "**So we are always confident, knowing that while we are at home in the body we are absent from the Lord.**" Here Paul says "we are at home in the body," just as he's been saying we're living in our earthly tent. And while we're at home in this tentlike structure, we're absent from the Lord—we're not in God's presence—because we're not yet clothed with our immortal body. In our mortal body we could never endure the presence of God. It's only as we're clothed with our immortal body that we will be in the presence of God. So Paul says very plainly in verse 6, "So we are always confident, knowing that while we are at home in the body we are absent from the Lord." At home in this mortal body, we're absent from the Lord because we do not yet have our immortal body.

Verse 7: "**For we walk by faith, not by sight.**" It is by faith that I look forward to being clothed by my immortal body that comes from heaven; it's by faith that I look forward to Christ's Return and the glorious resurrection; it's by faith that I sense God is preparing a body for me that will be immortal. This whole passage, from beginning to end, is written in the spirit of the resurrection.

Verse 8: "**We are confident, yes, well pleased rather to be absent from the body and to be present with the Lord.**" Absent from *what* body? From this *mortal* body. Paul says, I *want* to be absent from this mortal body and present with the Lord. Present with the Lord HOW? In my *immortal* body. He's been contrasting two bodies, and he says, My great desire is to be absent from this mortal body and present with the Lord in my *immortal* body, the building God has for me in heaven.

Verse 9: "**Therefore we make it our aim, whether present** [that is, present with the Lord in my immortal body] **or absent** [from the Lord in my mortal body]**, to be well pleasing to Him.**" That's the crucial thing—to be accepted by God and pleasing to Him in this life and in the life to come.

● ● ●

This important passage must be understood from the standpoint of TWO VITAL PERSPECTIVES that answer TWO CRUCIAL QUESTIONS:

HOW would Paul be present with the Lord?

— and —

WHEN would he be present with the Lord?

If we answer these two questions, we'll have the truth Paul wanted to teach.

QUESTION #1 – PRESENT WITH THE LORD—HOW?

Paul's point in 2 Corinthians 5 is that there are two BUILDINGS—an *earthly* and a *heavenly*—which symbolize two BODIES—a *mortal* and an *immortal.* Now if we really seek the truth, we can't hopscotch around the facts. Here is ONE FACT all must admit regardless of their theological leanings: At no point in this entire passage does Paul even once mention man's "soul" or "spirit"—he's not talking about that at all. Instead, he is dramatically contrasting two BODIES:

1. the earthly, temporary, perishable body
   subject to decay, disease, and death   – *and* –
2. the heavenly, eternal, glorious, immortal body
   given by God when Christ returns.

Just a few verses before this passage—in **2 Corinthians 4:16**—the pen of Paul traced these words: "our outer man is *decaying*" NASB, "our outward man is *perishing*" NKJV, referring to our fleshly, mortal body. He continues that same thought in **2 Corinthians 5:1**, where he says "our earthly house," this temporary tent, will some day be "destroyed"—the KJV says "dissolved"—

by death and decay. But then he points us to our heavenly hope for a new, immortal body that never grows old.

Therefore, since the Apostle was crying out from the depths of his heart to be free from his mortal body and to be clothed with his immortal body from heaven, and since the text offers NO support for the idea of a conscious "immortal spirit," we can answer this first question as follows:

- The expression **"absent from the body"** means absent from the MORTAL body with its earthly infirmities—in which Paul would "groan, being burdened."

- The expression **"present with the Lord"** means present in the glorious IMMORTAL body—with which Paul was "earnestly desiring to be clothed" or "clothed upon"—KJV.

The Bible will explain itself if we'll only let it. Now let's consider our second question.

QUESTION #2 – PRESENT WITH THE LORD—WHEN?

To that question this passage itself definitely rules out answers like "at death" or "when we die." For Paul explicitly states in plain words that he did NOT desire to be "unclothed," which signifies the condition of DEATH! Please note various translations of 2 Corinthians 5:4 —

"NOT for that we would be unclothed"	– KJV
"NOT because we want to be unclothed"	– NKJV
"NOT that we would be unclothed"	– RSV
"we do NOT want to be unclothed"	– NASB
"we do NOT wish to be unclothed"	– NIV
"we wish NOT to be unclothed"	– NRSV

On the other hand, 2 Corinthians 5:8 states that he WAS "well pleased" to be "present with the Lord." Therefore, if the "unclothed" or "naked" (verse 3) state of death is what Paul did NOT desire, and the state of being "present with the Lord" is what he DID desire, we safely conclude that those two states are *mututally exclusive*. Thus Paul teaches that **in DEATH the Christian is NOT present with the Lord.** [119] This is a very important point which is often overlooked.

The only way to understand *from the context* WHEN the change from mortal to immortal will take place—and thus when we'll be "present with the Lord"—is to look carefully at what Paul says in verse 4 of this passage: "For we who are in this tent GROAN, being burdened, NOT because we want to be UNCLOTHED [dead], but FURTHER CLOTHED, *that mortality may be swallowed up by life.*" He's talking about a time—a glorious moment—when we'll see the *swallowing up of mortality,* the *swallowing up of earthliness,* being *clothed upon* by our immortal body from heaven.

Go back to the very important chapter of 1 Corinthians 15 and note that Paul brings out that very same thought. In 1 Corinthians 15:49 he brings out the same two contrasts as he does in 2 Corinthians 5, about the EARTHLY and the HEAVENLY: "As we have borne the image of the earthy [our earthly mortal body], we shall also bear the image of the heavenly [our glorious immortal body]." Paul is just furthering that theme in 2 Corinthians 5, knowing that the believers at Corinth already have the background from his first letter to them.

In the next verse, 1 Corinthians 15:50, Paul tells us "flesh and blood cannot inherit the kingdom of God," meaning that our present earthly bodies are not fit for heaven. So these mortal bodies must be CHANGED, and Inspiration tells us when that change will come, when we can expect to be "clothed" by our new immortal bodies. In 1 Corinthians 15:51-54 Paul writes:

> "Behold, I shew you a mystery; We shall not all sleep [that is, we shall not all die and sleep the sleep of death before Jesus returns], but we shall all be CHANGED, in a moment, in the twinkling of an eye, at the last trump: for the trumpet shall sound, and the dead shall be raised incorruptible, and we shall be CHANGED. For this corruptible must put on incorruption, and this mortal must put on immortality. So WHEN this corruptible shall have put on incorruption, and this mortal shall have put on immortality, THEN shall be brought to pass the saying that is written, Death is swallowed up in victory."

That last line, a perfect parallel to 2 Corinthians 5:4, echoes Paul's hope to be "clothed, that mortality might be SWALLOWED UP of life." One speaks of "DEATH . . . swallowed up." The other one speaks of "MORTALITY . . . swallowed up." And when does this happen? The preceding verses in 1 Corinthians 15 tell us that it's *when Christ shall come with trumpet sound to resurrect the dead.* For all who accept the Bible, these verses answer the second question as to WHEN we shall be "present with the Lord."

DEATH IS MORE THAN JUST DYING

One other aspect of this passage should be brought out: We must understand Paul's meaning when he spoke of the STATE of death, which he calls the *dissolution* of this earthly house—"dissolved," 2 Corinthians 5:1, KJV. Many would have it mean a momentary act, the act of dying, which they like to think of as the departure of the soul from the body. This is a grave error. See CHART #1, on the next page.

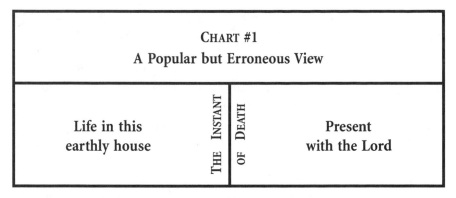

From the fact that it takes a long period of time for one's mortal body of flesh and bones to be "dissolved," we know that Paul looks here at the whole STATE of death and dissolution, not merely its beginning. DYING is merely entering upon the state of death. But the whole range of DEATH from its beginning to its end is what Paul refers to here. The state of death *begins* with the act of dying, *continues* perhaps for centuries, and *ends* only at the resurrection. The state of death is not a *point* in time. It covers the *whole period* of time during which the body lies in the grave. The reign of death is an *unbroken* reign during the entire period, from the act of dying to the act of resurrection.

It's not the MOMENT when a man dies Paul is thinking of here. Rather, it's the whole PERIOD of time during which he's dead—"unclothed," "naked," the earthly house of his mortal body "destroyed" or "dissolved." See CHART #2, below.

CHART #2		
Paul Actually Depicts THREE Consecutive STATES		
This present earthly LIFE	The period of DEATH	The future state of IMMORTALITY

The momentary act of dying, far from being the whole of death, is only the entrance of death upon our experience. The earthly house of this tent is "dissolved," over the course of time, and continues in this state of dissolution until the Lord wakes us from sleep at His promised Return. Paul includes the WHOLE INTERMEDIATE STATE in the dissolution of this earthly house.[120] For a more detailed overview, see CHART #3 on pages 326-327.

When we die, our "earthly house" or mortal body is "dissolved" or "destroyed," as various translations render 2 Corinthians 5:1, by the corrupting process of rotting in the grave. Nevertheless, because "we have a building from God, a house not made with hands, eternal in the heavens . . . [we are] earnestly desiring to be CLOTHED with our habitation which is from heaven. . . . CLOTHED [he repeats], that MORTALITY might be swallowed up by LIFE." —2 Corinthians 5:1, 2, 4, NKJV.

Paul makes it plain that his being "present with the Lord" is not AT death, or IN death, or DURING the period of death, but AFTER death at the glorious *resurrection* when Christ shall appear and we're clothed in a new eternal body, mortality being swallowed up by life.

We see this by noting how remarkably PARALLEL Paul's thoughts in this passage of 2 Corinthians 5:1-9 are to Romans 8:22-23, where he says:

> "The whole creation groaneth and travaileth in pain together until now. And not only they, but ourselves also, which have the firstfruits of the Spirit, even we ourselves groan within ourselves, waiting for the adoption, to wit, the redemption of our body."

Please note:

2 Corinthians 5:1-9	**Romans 8:22-23**
● "We groan"	● "We . . . groan within ourselves"
● "Earnest of the Spirit"	● "Firstfruits of the Spirit"
● "Earnestly desiring"	● "Waiting for"
● "Clothed upon" by our immortal body	● "Redemption of our body"

These passages are almost "twins," but the most pertinent parallel is the last one, which shows that Paul looked forward to "the redemption of our body" when he and all believers will be "clothed upon, that mortality might be swallowed up of life." Another text from Paul which speaks of "waiting for . . . the redemption of our BODY" is this: "Our citizenship is in heaven, from which we also eagerly wait for the Savior, the Lord Jesus Christ, who will transform our lowly BODY that it may be conformed to His glorious BODY."[121] And WHEN will this be? At His Coming, as all agree.

Paul is not dealing here with an experience that takes place at death. His being "present with the Lord" awaits the resurrection day. How beautifully this agrees with his own inspired statement that at the RESURRECTION when the "dead in Christ" are raised, we're caught up "to meet the Lord" and "so shall we ever be with the Lord."[122]

One last thought: That little word *SO*, just quoted above, means "in this way" or "by this means." The Apostle says, "so"—in this way, by this means— "shall we ever be with the Lord." When he thus describes the way and means by which we go to be with the Lord, he precludes every other means. We CANNOT go to be with the Lord by means of an immortal spirit when we die, if—as Paul declares here—we go to Him by means of the visible Coming of Christ, the resurrection of the dead, and the change or translation of the living.[123]

Finally, 2 Corinthians 5:1-9 may possibly be one of Paul's passages Peter called "hard to understand, which ignorant and unstable people distort, as they do the other Scriptures, to their own destruction." But we can say, in conclusion, that this puzzle piece is seen to be an additional *confirmation* of God's teaching regarding the nature of man—not at all a *contradiction* of it. The notion that we're instantly "present with the Lord" at the moment of death is a teaching that exists only in the minds of those who proclaim it, and certainly not in the black ink of Scripture.

PUZZLE PIECE #18:
PAUL'S "DESIRE TO DEPART,
AND TO BE WITH CHRIST"

This text from Paul could possibly be another of those which prompted the Apostle Peter to criticize the writings of "our dear brother Paul" by saying: "His letters contain some things that are hard to understand, which ignorant and unstable people distort, as they do the other Scriptures, to their own destruction."[124]

Let's look at the passage of Scripture in **Philippians 1:20-24**:

> "According to my earnest expectation and my hope, that in nothing I shall be ashamed, but that with all boldness, as always, so now also Christ shall be magnified in my body, whether it be by life, or by death. For to me to live is Christ, and to die is gain. But if I live in the flesh, this is the fruit of my labour: yet what I shall choose I wot [know] not. For I am in a strait betwixt [that is, I am in a dilemma between] two, having a desire to depart, and to be with Christ; which is far better: Nevertheless to abide in the flesh is more needful for you."

Teachers of the immortal-soul theory like to focus on verse 23 where Paul says he has "a desire to depart, and to be with Christ," claiming this

CHART #3 — 2 Corinthians 5:1-9

Here Paul portrays & analyzes **three consecutive states** or **conditions** for believers:
(numbers below refer to <u>verses</u> in 2 Corinthians 5, from KJV or NKJV)

The Present State of **This Mortal Life**	The Intermediate State of **Death**	The Future State of **Immortality**
On Earth	*In the Grave*	*In Heaven*
our earthly house - 1 at home in the body - 6	dissolved *or* destroyed - 1	our house *or* habitation which is from heaven - 2 a building of God, a house not made with hands, eternal in the heavens - 1
this tabernacle *or* tent - 1		
clothed - 3	unclothed - 4 naked - 3	clothed upon - 2

——— The Act of Dying: ———

——— The Act of Resurrecting: ———

Eternal

Longed for with intense desire

earnestly desiring to be clothed upon with our house which is from heaven - 2

present with the Lord - 7

mortality . . . swallowed up by life - 4

—— "in a **MOMENT**, in the twinkling of an eye" 1 Corinthians 15:52 ——

Temporary

Not to be desired

we do *not* want/wish to be unclothed - 4 NASB, NIV

—— one breathes his last at the **MOMENT** of death ——

Temporary

Not to be desired

in this we *groan* - 2

we . . . in this tent do *groan*, being *burdened* - 4

willing rather to be absent from the body - 8

mortality - 4

means his departure is at the moment of death as a disembodied spirit, to enter immediately into the presence of Christ. They often use this verse hoping it may provide some support for their ideas of "the immortal soul," of consciousness in death, and that believers go immediately to heaven when they die. But that's not at all what Paul SAYS—or what the passage means.

It's obvious that Paul's passage in **2 Corinthians 5** about being "absent from the body and present with the Lord" (just dealt with above) and this passage in Philippians mutually explain each other. Assuming that the reader has read my analysis of 2 Corinthians 5:8, I won't take time or space here to substantiate important points such as the fact that Paul—in ALL his extensive New Testament writings—

> ➤ never taught "the immortal soul,"
>> ➤ never taught consciousness in death,
>>> ➤ never taught that death is the doorway to life,
>>> and—in this present passage of **Philippians 1:20-24**—
>>>> ➤ never even MENTIONS man's "soul" or "spirit."

A VERSE-BY-VERSE EXAMINATION

IF we're clear in our minds that this passage does NOT say Paul would be "present with the Lord *as a disembodied spirit,*" then we're ready to see what the text actually DOES say by examining the whole passage and determining its precise meaning. I'll use the King James Version here, but other versions are fine, too.

Verse 20: "**According to my earnest expectation and my hope, that in nothing I shall be ashamed, but that with all boldness, as always, so now also Christ shall be magnified in my body, whether it be by life, or by death.**" I want you to see that Paul is speaking about TWO THINGS: What are they? LIVING and DYING. He's speaking about the implications of his life and his death, and he wants Christ to be magnified whether he lives OR dies.

Verse 21: "**For to me to live is Christ, and to die is gain.**" Paul says "to me," emphasizing this is his own outlook, which differs from that of most men, who selfishly cling to life and dread death. His plans, his hopes, his every aspiration, were all centered in Christ. But what did Paul mean when he said "to die is gain"? WHY did he say death was but a gain for him? Did he mean death was a gain because he'd wing his way to heaven as a disembodied spirit when he dies? Or are there other reasons which would make him count death as a gain? Do you know WHERE and under what CIRCUMSTANCES Paul was when he wrote this letter? He was in PRISON in

Rome. But even before that, his life was no bed of roses. Paul's own description of his labors is uncomplaining but tragic:

> "We are hard pressed on every side, yet not crushed; we are perplexed, but not in despair; persecuted, but not forsaken; struck down, but not destroyed. . . . In labors more abundant, in stripes above measure, in prisons more frequently, in deaths often. From the Jews five times I received forty stripes minus one. Three times I was beaten with rods; once I was stoned; three times I was shipwrecked; a night and a day I have been in the deep; in journeys often, in perils of waters, in perils of robbers, in perils of my own countrymen, in perils of the Gentiles, in perils in the city, in perils in the wilderness, in perils in the sea, in perils among false brethren; in weariness and toil, in sleeplessness often, in hunger and thirst, in fastings often, in cold and nakedness—besides the other things, what comes upon me daily: my deep concern for all the churches." [125]

We can only read this catalog of calamities and exclaim, "*No wonder! Of course* Paul or anyone else would welcome death as 'gain' after a hard life like that!" It *would* be "gain" for Paul to be safely tucked away in the grave—never again to be tempted by Satan, never again to be shipwrecked, never again to suffer the bondage of a Roman prison, never again to face an angry mob, never again to be beaten or stoned!

Yet the apostle's attitude toward death was not that of a pessimist who says, "Life is not worth living" or that of a holy man wearied from exhausting labors and anxious to be finished with trials and persecutions. No, his thoughts were unselfish and under the control of his Master—Paul was considering death only if "Christ shall be magnified" by it (verse 20). The death of a righteous man as a martyr who seals his testimony with his own blood can be a powerful affirmation of the faith. This Paul was willing to do if his Lord thought it best. In fact, he later did do it without flinching. His death was not like that of one who dies without hope. But note that in this short but powerful verse we again see Paul's focus on two alternatives: "to live . . . and to die."

Verse 22: "But if I live in the flesh, this is the fruit of my labour: yet what I shall choose I wot [know] **not."** On the other hand, Paul says, if I remain "in the flesh"—if I live and labor for the church—I'll see results, I'll see "fruit," I'll see souls won to Christ. But, he says, I'm still not sure which of these two alternatives—living or dying—would be best to choose.

Verse 23: "For I am in a strait betwixt two, having a desire to depart, and to be with Christ; which is far better." Paul says, I'm torn between these two choices—living and dying—and can't decide, though I have a DESIRE to depart from this life, "AND [here Paul introduces a THIRD possible option] to be with Christ; which is far better." Far better than what? Far better than EITHER *living* OR *dying*.

PAUL COULD DESIRE A GLORIOUS **THIRD** OPTION

We must grant Paul the freedom to desire a third possibility—a third thing which appealed to him much more that the other two. NOT life, NOT death, but an eager leap over all else "to be with Christ" either by *translation* without seeing death or by *resurrection* when awakened by Christ, the Life-giver. Paul is "thinking out loud," so to speak, as he records his letter to those at Philippi. It's just as we ourselves say:

- "I don't know if I want a *Ford* or a *Chevy*
    —or a *Rolls Royce*, which is far better!"
- "I can't decide if I want a *chocolate* or *vanilla* ice cream cone
    —or a *banana split*, which is far better!"
- "I'm not sure if I want to work as a *school crossing-guard*
  or a *part-time janitor*
    —or a *renowned brain surgeon*, which is far better!
- "I can't decide if my favorite display of color in nature is
  a *bright red rose* or a *fresh green meadow*
    —or a *dazzling rainbow*, which is far better!"
- "I am in a strait betwixt two: to *live* or to *die*
    —or to *be with Christ by being translated
  without seeing death*, which is far better!"

Paul was determined to magnify Christ whether he lived or died. If he lived, he would actively promote the cause of Christ. If he died, his becoming a sacrifice on the altar of Truth would still be gain to the cause of Christ.

So, between living in the flesh and dying as a martyr, without being sure which would gain the most advantage to the gospel, he was "in a strait betwixt [these] two." A third thing appealed to him much more. That third thing was clearly not either of the former two indifferent things. The third thing, he says, was "far better." Better than life, better than death. This third choice was "to be with the Lord" in heaven.

TWO AVENUES TO HEAVEN

There are two ways that a faithful believer may be taken to heaven to be with the Lord—one is very special, and the other is more general though no less miraculous. The special way would be by TRANSLATION of the body without ever seeing death. Only a favored few have ever been granted such a special honor. One such was the faithful patriarch ENOCH—of him we read: "All the days of Enoch were three hundred sixty and five years: And Enoch walked with God: and he was not; for God took him. . . . By faith Enoch was translated that he should not see death; and was not found, because God had translated him: for before his translation he had this testimony, that he pleased God." [126]

Another mortal favored in this wonderful way was the great prophet ELIJAH—of him we read that he turned over his mantle of authority to his successor, Elisha, and "Elijah said to Elisha, 'Tell me, what can I do for you before I am taken from you?' 'Let me inherit a double portion of your spirit,' Elisha replied. 'You have asked a difficult thing,' Elijah said, 'yet if you see me when I am taken from you, it will be yours—otherwise not.' As they were walking along and talking together, suddenly a chariot of fire and horses of fire appeared and separated the two of them, and Elijah went up to heaven in a whirlwind." [127] These examples show that translation without seeing death is a rare but not unheard-of event.

The apostle Paul had many marvelous evidences of the Lord's power and favor, so it's by no means out of the question that he might have been favored by being translated also. But suppose he did not have translation in mind when he wrote Philippians 1:23. The other way to be taken to heaven to be with the Lord, more general though still quite miraculous, is for dead believers to be RESURRECTED and raptured away when Jesus returns.

The word Paul uses—depart—"having a desire to depart, and to be with Christ; which is far better," is generally taken to mean to die, to depart from this life. He uses another form of the same Greek word—translated departure—in the last letter he ever wrote, right before his execution. Except that there, in 2 Timothy 4:6-8, he's much more explicit about the TIME FRAME of "departing" or dying and "henceforth . . . [receiving his] crown . . . at that day" of Christ's future "appearing." Please note:

> "I am now ready to be offered [as a martyr to my faith], and the time of my DEPARTURE [my death by execution] is at hand. I have fought a good fight, I have finished my course, I have kept the faith: Henceforth [not now, when I die, but henceforth, at some future time] there is laid up [God has a "layaway plan" that reserves our rewards] for me a crown of righteousness, which the Lord, the righteous Judge, shall give me at THAT DAY [the glorious day of Christ's Return]: and not to me only, but unto all them also that love His APPEARING [when Christ appears at His Return]."

We need not be concerned with whether Paul, in his third option of being with Christ, envisioned the avenue of TRANSLATION OR RESURRECTION.

Perhaps he himself didn't care. For both of those miraculous means would be equally effective in ushering him into the divine presence of Christ, in whose "presence is fullness of joy; at [whose] right hand are pleasures forevermore." [128] Since the unconscious sleep of death gives no perception of time—as when we pass a dreamless night sleeping soundly—the resurrection morn would seem to Paul like the very next moment, even though 2000 years had passed by without his knowing it!

As it turned out, RESURRECTION was the avenue God chose for Paul, because death was his fate, as we know. But we must be clear enough in our minds to understand, and honest enough in our hearts to admit, that the apostle did not mean—or say—that if he died he would go immediately "to be with Christ."

Paul himself has told us often enough—and explicitly enough—WHEN the Christian goes "to be with Christ." Note the following many examples:

- It's at "the redemption of our body."—Romans 8:23.
- It's at "the day of the Lord Jesus."—1 Corinthians 5:5.
- It's at "the last trump" when "death is swallowed up in victory." —1 Corinthians 15:51-55.
- It's when we're "clothed upon with our house . . . from heaven" and "mortality . . . [is] swallowed up of life."—2 Corinthians 5:2-4.
- It's "when Christ, who is our life, shall appear."—Colossians 3:4.
- It's when "the Lord Himself shall descend from heaven with a shout . . . and the dead in Christ shall rise."—1 Thessalonians 4:16.
- It's at "the coming of our Lord Jesus Christ."—2 Thessalonians 2:1.
- It's "at that day . . . [of Christ's] appearing."—2 Timothy 4:8.

"Yet Paul, in ONE instance, without stopping to explain, uses the expression, 'to depart, and to be with Christ,' whereupon his words are seized upon by religious teachers as unanswerable evidence that at death the spirit enters at once into the presence of its Redeemer." [129]

Separated Events MAY Be Coupled

If any are still concerned that Paul mentioned departing in death and being with Christ almost in the same breath, we must remember that Bible writers sometimes couple together events that are separated by a long span of time. The Bible rarely goes into detail but sets forth the really important points of God's dealing with man along the course of centuries.

For example, Isaiah 61:1-2 contains a prophecy of the work Christ would do at His first advent. In Luke 4:17-19 is the account of Christ's reading this prophecy to the people, and informing them: "This day is this scripture fulfilled in your ears" Luke 4:21. But a close examination reveals that Christ did not read ALL the prophecy from Isaiah, though apparently it's one connected statement. In fact, He stopped at a *comma* in the middle of Isaiah 61:2! He ended with the phrase: "To proclaim the acceptable year of the Lord." But the very next phrase in the sentence—on the other side of the comma—is: "and *the day of vengeance* of our God." He did not read this, because it was not yet to be fulfilled. This passage in Isaiah does not even suggest that a LONG period of time intervenes between this phrase and the ones preceding. But other Bible passages show this fact clearly, and by examining all those other passages we learn how to understand a brief, compressed prophecy like that of Isaiah 61.

Another example of separated events being placed together is the prophecy of the Second Advent in 2 Peter 3:1-13. If no other Bible passage was compared to this one, we might easily reach the conclusion that the Second Advent of Christ results immediately in the destruction of this earth by fire. Yet when we compare 2 Peter 3 with Revelation 20, we learn that a thousand-year period intervenes between the Second Advent and the fiery destruction of this earth. [130] Peter was giving only a brief summary of the outstanding events impending. He passed immediately from the great fact of the Second Advent over to the next great act in the drama of God's dealing with this earth, its destruction by fire. But with Peter's prophecy, as with Isaiah's, there's no confusion if we follow the Bible plan of comparing scripture with scripture to fill in the details. [131]

Now if PETER could place in one sentence—2 Peter 3:10—two great events separated by a thousand years, and if ISAIAH could couple in another sentence—Isaiah 61:2—two mighty events separated by a vast period of time, why should it be thought strange if PAUL followed this practice, and coupled together in one sentence—Philippians 1:23—the sad event of dying with the glorious event of being "with Christ" at the Second Advent? As we've just seen, the mere fact of coupling together two events does not necessarily mean that those two events are immediately sequential—especially when other statements made elsewhere in Scripture clearly show that those two events are separated by an intervening period of time.

Here in this text Paul is not giving a doctrinal explanation of what happens at death. He's simply expressing his "desire" to depart this present troubled existence AND to be with Christ—without reference to a lapse of time that occurs between those two events.

Paul's DILEMMA Is a Good CLUE

Recall, for a moment, the apostle's tantalizing dilemma of the twin alternatives—*living* or *dying*—which tor mented him with such indecision. He says, with all-too-human vacillation: "What shall I choose? I do not know! I am TORN between the two." Philippians 1:22-23, NIV. So evenly balanced were the influences drawing him in both directions that he hardly knew which course he would take, were it up to him as a matter of choice.

Now IF the apostle really believed that DEATH was a portal to paradise which would transport him instantly into the presence of Christ, he would have HAD no dilemma over which to choose. If that were the case, inasmuch as he desired above all else "to be with Christ," that being "far better" than all else, his choice would have been death. If death would have done THAT for him, his uncertainty would have vanished. [132]

But he *knew* that death would not do that. He knew that "the dead know not anything," [133] and that, consequently, being dead, he would not be with Christ. It is IMPOSSIBLE to think that Paul believed the righteous go "to be with the Lord" at death. Why? Because Paul wrote much on the subject of being with Christ, and his words consistently prove the very opposite. Take, for example, this passage from 1 Thessalonians 4:13-18 and consider its implications:

> "I would not have you to be ignorant, brethren, concerning them which are asleep [dead, sleeping the sleep of death], that ye sorrow not, even as others which have no hope. . . . For the Lord Himself shall descend from heaven . . . and the dead in Christ shall rise first: Then we which are alive and remain shall be caught up TOGETHER with them in the clouds, to meet the Lord in the air: and so shall we ever be with the Lord. Wherefore comfort one another with these words."

Here the inspired apostle specifically tells the Thessalonian believers that the righteous, both the living and those raised from the dead, go "together" [134] to "be with the Lord" at the Second Advent. He declared that he was writing them so that they would not be "IGNORANT." Now please get this point—it is incredible that he would leave them in ignorance that their loved ones go to be with Christ at death, IF he believed that. In fact, he told them the very opposite—that the dead do NOT go to be with the Lord at death, but await the resurrection. If he believed that we go to be with the Lord the moment we die, he would have said so, especially when he was writing specifically to "comfort" them. Instead, he urged them to find their "comfort" in a future event—the resurrection. [135]

This puzzle piece of Philippians 1:23 is found to be not quite so "hard to understand" as it may at first seem. And it certainly does not contradict the Bible's clear teaching on the state of man in death.

CONCLUSION

We've analyzed six additional puzzle pieces which cause some Christians concern in this area of death and immortality. We've found no valid cause for alarm, for the Bible never contradicts itself. Advocates for the immortal soul theory are mistaken when they think they find evidence in these texts supporting their position. In fact, these pieces fit the picture in perfect harmony with all other Scriptural teachings!

The Bible was written not for theological scholars but for ordinary folks like you and me. Usually we don't need to analyze obscure texts to find hidden meanings in cryptic messages. All we need is common sense. For instance, Jesus spoke plainly about these things. Near the close of His ministry He told His disciples—not in a parable, but directly and privately, with no Pharisees or other spies around:

> "I go [to heaven] to prepare a place for you. And if I go and prepare a place for you, I will COME AGAIN, and RECEIVE you to Myself; that where I am, there you may be also." [136]

Consider those words of Christ very carefully. The popular teaching that believers are present with the Lord whenever they happen to die is wrong. But it takes a verse as plain and explicit as this to show just *how* wrong that teaching is. Let's examine the "immortal soul" theory in the light of the Master's words, for the words of Christ Himself should settle the matter beyond all dispute:

1. When Jesus says that He will come again and RECEIVE His disciples to Himself, it clearly implies that they are NOT to be with Him BEFORE that time!

2. IF we believers went to heaven at the moment of death, WE would be going to HIM. Yet Jesus' declaration proves that WE won't GO to Him—HE will COME to US to achieve that grand reunion!

3. There's something terribly wrong with a theory that puts each believer in heaven when he dies—with Jesus receiving each one INDIVIDUALLY at that time—because the Lord says He'll "receive" us ALL at once when He comes again!

4. This theory also makes a mockery of Christ's promise to return to this earth to take us home with Him: Who needs to make a RETURN TRIP to get his loved ones if they're already with him?

Besides all this, the idea of "man's immortal soul," originating with Satan and perpetuated by pagan philosophy, DOES AWAY with three of the most fundamental Christian doctrines:

- The **Second Coming** of Jesus
- The **Final Judgment** of Mankind
- The **Resurrection** of the Dead

WHAT NEED would there be of those divine events if people, both wicked and righteous, go to their reward at the moment of death? How ridiculous to go through the mockery of a "judgment" of those already judged! Imagine calling each sinner up from the flaming pit of hell or a believer down from the glories of heaven to check the records and see if he'd been sent to the right place! Such a judgment would be an empty charade.

WHY should we believe in CONDITIONAL immortality rather than IN-NATE, UNconditional immortality? Because every true Bible doctrine has CHRIST as its center. And conditional immortality puts Christ in His proper place in the scheme of things—squarely in the center of each doctrine. For example:

- The doctrine of the *Second Coming* puts Christ at the center in His role as **RESCUER** from this lost and dying planet.
- The doctrine of the *Final Judgment* puts Christ at the center in His dual role as both **JUDGE** and **ADVOCATE**. [137]
- The doctrine of the *Resurrection* puts Christ at the center in His role as **LIFEGIVER**.

Conditional immortality keeps Christ in the center of all three of these vital doctrines, whereas innate, unconditional immortality nullifies any need for those great events, causing them to lose their Christian significance.

In closing, we see that all of these eighteen puzzle pieces don't just happen to fit—they lock snugly together forming the clear Bible picture of death painted by God Himself. We recognize that death was never a part of God's original plan for His creation. It was an *intruder,* an *enemy* that injected itself into the scheme of things after Adam and Eve disobeyed God and fell into sin. But we see, too, that this enemy of God and man will finally be forever destroyed. God's way and God's will shall ultimately triumph. So we can close this chapter with the comforting thought that "Father knows best."

⌒

Notes to Chapter 11

1. The "Lazarus" of this story is not the same one who was Jesus' friend that He raised from the dead. In those days, Lazarus happened to be a common name among the Jews—just as Tom, Dick, and Harry are common names today.
2. Luke 16:19-31, NKJV.
3. See Matthew 5:13 and John 10:9.
4. Eminent scholars such as Whitby, Doddridge, Lightfoot, Bloomfield, Gill, Edersheim, John Wesley, and others considered it a parable.
5. Matthew 13:34, NIV.
6. Matthew 13:10-13, NKJV.
7. Luke 20:19-20, NKJV.
8. Mark 12:13.
9. Matthew 22:15.
10. Luke 16:14.
11. Bodily parts make it impossible to interpret this passage literally, so some say it's partly figurative and partly literal. But since the Bible account is a UNIT, it must be considered EITHER a literal, historical episode OR a figurative parable. Who can decide which portions are literal without being guilty of manufacturing evidence?
12. Luke 16:1-13, NIV.
13. Luke 16:14, NIV.
14. That lesson teaches a number of things of great importance. Jesus may have wished to teach truths like the following:
    A. RICHES ARE NO PASSPORT TO HEAVEN. In Jesus' day riches were so highly regarded as a sign of God's favor while poverty was considered a sign of God's curse, that when the disciples heard Jesus say, "It is easier for a camel to go through the eye of a needle, than for a rich man to enter into the kingdom of God. . . . They were exceedingly amazed, saying, WHO then can be saved?"—Matthew 19:23-25. Even the disciples felt that if a rich man couldn't be saved, it's useless for the rest of us to try. To correct this widespread misconception, Jesus taught this parable to the "covetous" Pharisees, with the rich man LOST and the poor beggar SAVED. Jesus wanted to teach "the truth that no matter how rich a man might be, he could still be lost eternally, and no matter how poor a man might be, he still had a chance for the heavenly country, and so He depicted the extreme cases of the rich man and Lazarus."—Charles T. Everson, *The Rich Man and Lazarus* (Nashville, Tennessee: Southern Publishing Association, 1935), p. 7.
    B. WE DECIDE OUR ETERNAL DESTINY IN THIS LIFE. Our own daily decisions determine where we spend eternity. If self-indulgent choices fix "a great gulf" between us and God, that is our fate. There's no second chance, no future probation. We may accept salvation NOW, but when death comes, it's forever too late.
15. Dennis Crews, *The Rich Man and Lazarus* (Frederick, Maryland: Amazing Facts, Inc., 1986), p. 11.
16. Flavius Josephus, *The Works of Flavius Josephus*, translated by William Whiston (Auburn and Buffalo, New York: John E. Beardsley, no date), "Discourse to the Greeks Concerning Hades," Paragraphs 1, 2, 3, 4.

17. Luke 16:31.
18. Instead of believing, they wanted to KILL Lazarus! See John 12:9-11.
19. Luke 16:1-13. Here Jesus taught that even a wicked person makes provision to assure his EARTHLY future, and how much MORE important it is that a child of God should assure his HEAVENLY future!
20. Acts 4:12.
21. Psalm 23:1.
22. Judges 9:7-15. Note that a similar passage is found in 2 Kings 14:9— "The *thistle* that was in Lebanon sent to the *cedar* that was in Lebanon, saying, Give thy daughter to my son to wife. . ."!
23. 2 Samuel 12:1-7, NIV.
24. Luke 15:1-3, NKJV. The Pharisees' words, intended as an insult, were really a compliment for our gracious Lord!
25. Acts 17:31, NKJV.
26. 2 Peter 2:9.
27. Hebrews 11:8 & 13.
28. Hebrews 11:35.
29. Hebrews 11:39-40.
30. The only substantiated point made by those who take this parable literally is that Jesus used a specific name—Lazarus—here, which is not the case in His other parables. But that argument in no way proves that a name like Lazarus—a name as common as "Joe" or "Bob" in our culture today—could NOT be used in a parable just as well as in a historical account. Besides, a name is a useful label to identify and differentiate a character when MORE THAN ONE PERSON is found in a story, as is the case here.
31. Luke 23:42-43.
32. Lest any complain that I took undue liberty in reversing the order of the pronoun in "shalt thou be," I should point out that Greek, like the Latin languages, has the pronouns (I, you/thou, he/she/it, we, they) COMBINED in the one-word verb form. English separates the pronoun from the verb. In Greek, therefore, "thou shalt be" is identical to "shalt thou be," being synthesized in the very same word.
33. 2 Corinthians 12:2-4, NIV. The first heaven is the ATMOSPHERIC heaven, where we breathe the air and the birds fly. The second heaven is the STARRY heaven, where planets orbit and stars shine. The third heaven is the DIVINE heaven, where angels dwell and our Lord abides. Paul shows here that "the third heaven" where God lives is synonymous with "Paradise."
34. Revelation 2:7.
35. Revelation 22:1-2, NKJV.
36. John 20:17.
37. Mark 15:44, NKJV.
38. John 19:31.
39. John 19:31-33.
40. Galatians 3:13. Compare Deuteronomy 21:22-23.
41. Hebrews 13:12, NIV.
42. Acts 7:58.

43. John 19:33-34. Jesus "was dead already," but the spear thrust made the soldiers doubly sure of that fact.

44. 2 Timothy 4:8. Paul knew his "crown" was "laid up" for him, to be bestowed by the Lord "at that day . . . [of] His appearing."

45. Job 19:25-27. Job knew he would see his Redeemer when the resurrection restores his decomposed body "at the latter day."

46. 1 Peter 3:18-20, NKJV.

47. 1 Peter 1:10-11.

48. 2 Peter 2:5.

49. Another text that's similarly misconstrued is 1 Peter 4:6 – "For this cause was the gospel preached also to them that are dead, that they might be judged. . . ." This doesn't mean dead people really do have the gospel preached to them. Read it carefully: "For this cause WAS [past tense] the gospel preached to them that ARE [present tense] dead." The gospel was preached to them while they were alive, but after hearing the gospel, they died. Death eternally closes each case.

50. Hebrews 9:27.

51. Genesis 6:3.

52. Numbers 27:15-17, NKJV. "Moses spoke to the Lord, saying: 'Let the Lord, the God of the SPIRITS of all FLESH, set a MAN over the congregation . . . who may lead them.'"

53. We use synecdoche ("sin-EK-duh-key") in everyday expressions: Seeing a friend in a new suit, we say, "Nice *threads!*" using the principle of PART for the WHOLE. Or meeting an old acquaintance, we say, "Five long *winters* have past since I've seen you!" using *winters* for *years* under synecdoche's PART-for-WHOLE principle. Jesus used the same figure of speech in "the Lord's Prayer" when He asked God to "Give us this day our daily *bread*," meaning *food* in general.

54. The Apostle Paul uses synecdoche in this very way, speaking of PART of a person when meaning the WHOLE person. For instance, if we compare his benedictions, it's clear that "*your spirit*" means "*you*":
    "The grace of our Lord Jesus Christ be with *your spirit.*"—Galatians 6:18.
    "The grace of our Lord Jesus Christ be with *you* all."—Philippians 4:23.

55. John 8:32.

56. Isaiah 42:1, 6-7, NKJV.

57. See Genesis 6:5-13, 7:13, and 1 Peter 3:20.

58. 2 Peter 2:18-19, NKJV. And Proverbs 5:22, NKJV, says: "His own *iniquities entrap* the wicked man, and he is *caught* in the *cords* of his *sin.*"

59. Revelation 1:18.

60. The only Christian denomination that openly denies the atoning death of Christ is Christian Science. (Please see footnote #91 on pages 231-232, in Chapter 8, above.) Consistency forces such a position, however, since Christian Science denies death in general as well as other negative "thoughts" such as sin, sickness, *etc.*

61. 1 Samuel 8:4-22.

62. 1 Samuel 9:2 and 10:23-24.

63. For instance, note Saul's self-justifying lies in 1 Samuel 15:2-28.

64. Recorded in 1 Samuel 28:3-25.

65. Ecclesiastes 9:5.

66. Revelation 16:14.

67. 2 Thessalonians 2:9.

68. 2 Corinthians 2:11 and 11:14, NASB.

69. Interestingly enough, the unabridged dictionary defines *necromancy* as "revealing the future by PRETENDED communication with the spirits of the dead." *Webster's New International Dictionary,* Second Edition Unabridged (Springfield, Mass.: G. & C. Merriam Company, Publishers, © 1950), p. 1635.

70. 1 Samuel 28:1.

71. 1 Samuel 28:6.

72. See 1 Samuel 22:17-19.

73. 1 Samuel 28:5.

74. 1 Samuel 15:28.

75. See 1 Chronicles 10:13-14.

76. 1 Samuel 15:35.

77. 1 Samuel 28:7.

78. See Exodus 22:18, Leviticus 19:31 & 20:27, Deuteronomy 18:9-12, *etc.*

79. 1 Samuel 28:3. Stern measures had to be taken to stamp out the bewitching influence of the occult. People were so deluded, Psalm 106:37 says: "they sacrificed their sons and their daughters unto DEVILS"! The "familiar spirits" contacted are NOT spirits of the dead but are in reality demons, the messengers of Satan.

80. 1 Samuel 28:8.

81. 1 Samuel 28:13-14, NKJV.

82. 1 Samuel 28:14.

83. Bible proof is seen in these three examples: "As Peter was coming in, Cornelius met him and fell down at his [Peter's] feet and worshiped him. But Peter lifted him up, saying, *'Stand up;* I myself am also a man.'"—Acts 10:25-26, NKJV. The Revelator wrote: "And I [John] fell at his [the angel's] feet to worship him. But he said to me, 'See that you *do not do that!* I am your fellow servant. . . . Worship God!'"—Revelation 19:10, NKJV. Again he wrote, of another occasion: "I, John, saw and heard these things. And when I heard and saw, I fell down to worship before the feet of the angel who showed me these things. Then he said to me, 'See that you *do not do that.* For I am your fellow servant. . . . Worship God.'"—Revelation 22:8-9, NKJV.

84. Worship was the main thing Satan sought in tempting Christ: "All the kingdoms of the world, and the glory of them . . . will I give Thee, if Thou wilt *fall down and worship me.*" Matthew 4:8-9.

85. 1 Samuel 28:15-16.

86. "The sun also RISES, and the sun GOES DOWN, and hastens to the place where it AROSE." Ecclesiastes 1:5, NKJV. Many similar texts may be cited, such as Psalm 50:1 & 113:3, Malachi 1:11, Matthew 5:45, *etc.*

87. 2 Corinthians 11:14.

88. 1 Samuel 28:16.

89. "God IS love." 1 John 4:8 & 16.

90. 1 Samuel 28:17.

91. 1 Samuel 31:4. Saul, oppressed by the horror of *despair,* could not inspire his army with *courage.* Having *separated himself* from the Lord, he could not lead Israel to *look to God* as their Helper. The words of doom from hell's messenger crushed all physical and moral hope from Saul.

92. 1 Samuel 28:19.

93. 1 Samuel 29:10-11, 30:1 & 17, 31:1-6 show that *at least THREE DAYS intervened,* and probably more.

94. 1 Samuel 31:2 & 6.

95. 1 Samuel 14:49.

96. 2 Samuel 2:8-12.

97. 2 Samuel 21:8-9.

98. The brief story of Hannah, the barren wife who became Samuel's mother and who gave her son to the Lord's service, is full of human interest. You'll find it in the first chapter of the First Book of Samuel.

99. 1 Samuel 28:8, 11, 13, 14, 15.

100. Isaiah 29:4.

101. 1 Samuel 28:15, in all modern versions. KJV says "disquieted."

102. For many of the ideas expressed here, the writer is greatly indebted to the late Carlyle B. Haynes and his most helpful book *Life, Death, and Immortality* (Nashville, Tenn.: Southern Publishing Association, c. 1952), pp. 195-201.

103. 1 Chronicles 10:13.

104. Those who lose a loved one in death may be tempted to try to contact the dead. British writer Rudyard Kipling knew this, and his poem "En-Dor"—about King Saul's visit to the witch—*opens* with these lines:
    "The road to En-dor is easy to tread
        For Mother or yearning Wife."
    However, the poem *ends* like this:
    "Oh, the road to En-dor is the oldest road
        And the craziest road of all!
    Straight it runs to the Witch's abode,
        As it did in the days of Saul,
    And nothing has changed of the SORROW in store
    For such as go down on the road to En-dor!"
    We can never gain happiness by indulging in what God forbids.
    Poem quoted from *Rudyard Kipling's VERSE,* Definitive Edition (Garden City, New York: Doubleday and Company, Inc., © 1940), pp. 363-364.

105. 2 Peter 3:15-16, NIV.

106. 1 Timothy 1:17.

107. 1 Timothy 6:16.

108. Romans 2:7.

109. 1 Corinthians 15:53.

110. John 11:11-14.

111. Psalm 13:3.

112. Ecclesiastes 9:5.

113. Psalm 146:4.

114. In 1 Corinthians 15:26 Paul says, "The last enemy that shall be destroyed is death."
115. Titus 2:13, NKJV.
116. 1 Corinthians 15:16-18.
117. 1 Thessalonians 4:15-17.
118. Romans 8:11, NKJV.
119. This incisive reasoning is from Uriah Smith, *Here and Hereafter* (Washington, D.C.: Review and Herald Publishing Association, 1897; Reprint Edition by Amazing Facts, Roseville, CA: 1977), p. 202.
120. This line of reasoning is taken from Carlyle B. Haynes, *Life, Death, and Immortality* (Nashville, TN: Southern Publishing Association, © 1952), pp. 265-274.
121. Philippians 3:20-21, NKJV. The KJV says "our vile body."
122. 1 Thessalonians 4:17. For the insights in the last three paragraphs the writer is indebted to Francis D. Nichol, *Answers to Objections* (Washington, D.C.: Review and Herald Publishing Assn., © 1952), pp. 332-336.
123. Uriah Smith, *Here and Hereafter,* p. 212.
124. 2 Peter 3:15-16, NIV.
125. 2 Corinthians 4:8-9 and 11:23-28, NKJV. And in the very chapter at hand—Philippians 1:13, 14, & 16—Paul refers to "my bonds . . . my bonds . . . my bonds."
126. Genesis 5:23-24 and Hebrews 11:5.
127. 2 Kings 2:9-11, NIV.
128. Psalms 16:11, NKJV.
129. Uriah Smith, *Here and Hereafter,* pp. 206-207.
130. See Chapter 18 on "The Millennium," below.
131. The Bible plan of study is for us to gather ALL that God's Word has to say on a given subject, searching its pages everywhere for His complete Truth and gathering it together: "Whom shall He teach knowledge? and whom shall He make to understand doctrine? . . . Precept must be upon precept, precept upon precept; line upon line, line upon line; HERE a little, and THERE a little. . . . But the word of the Lord was unto them precept upon precept, precept upon precept; line upon line, line upon line; HERE a little, and THERE a little." —Isaiah 28:9-10 & 13.
132. Carlyle B. Haynes, *Life, Death, and Immortality*, p. 278.
133. Ecclesiastes 9:5.
134. Please see "Puzzle Piece #5," pages 253-256, above, for Bible texts which prove we don't go to heaven one-by-one when we die but all together when Jesus returns.
135. Francis D. Nichol, *Answers to Objections,* pp. 345-346.
136. See John 14:2-3, NASB.
137. John 5:22 & 27, Acts 10:42, 1 John 2:1.

~

CHAPTER TWELVE

ETERNAL TORMENT:
A BURNING ISSUE

A BURNING QUESTION in many minds is that of the nature and degree of the punishment of the wicked. People wonder about these because a popular teaching in the world today says that those who die unsaved will burn in the flames of hell through all eternity—yet our own innate sense of mercy and justice recoils at such a prospect. Perhaps we should begin by defining our terms.

WHAT "ETERNAL TORMENT" MEANS

The Roman Catholic Church teaches this about hell: "Hell is the place and state of ETERNAL punishment. . . ."[1] Again, "Hell may be defined as the place and state in which the devils and such human beings as die in enmity with God suffer ETERNAL torments."[2]

But the Catholic Church is not alone in teaching this dreaded doctrine—this teaching is heard from many Protestant pulpits as well. Listen to Puritan preacher Jonathan Edwards:

"The God that holds you over the pit of hell, much as one holds a spider or some loathsome insect over the fire, abhors you, and is dreadfully provoked: His wrath towards you burns like fire; He looks upon you as worthy of nothing else, but to be cast into the fire; He is of purer eyes than to bear to have you in His sight; you are ten thousand times more abominable in His eyes than the most hateful venomous serpent is in ours. . . . O sinner! Consider the fearful danger you are in: 'tis a great furnace of wrath, a wide and bottomless pit, full of the fire of wrath. . . . 'Tis EVERLASTING wrath. It would be dreadful to suffer this fierceness and wrath of Almighty God one moment; but you must suffer it through all eternity: there will be NO END to this exquisite horrible misery. . . . You must wear out long ages, millions and millions of ages, in wrestling with this almighty merciless vengeance; and then when you have done so, you will know that all is but a point to what remains. So that your punishment will indeed be INFINITE." [3]

Talk about a horror story! Edwards loved to dwell upon the ghastly suffering of an endless hell. Note these terrifying words in another of his sermons describing the wicked in the roaring flames of hell:

". . . vast waves or billows of fire continually rolling over their heads, of which they shall FOREVER be full of quick sense within and without: their heads, their eyes, their tongues, their hands, their feet, their loins, and their vitals shall forever be full of a glowing, melting fire, fierce enough to melt the very rocks and elements; and they shall also ETER-NALLY be full of the most quick and lively sense to feel the torments; not for two ages, nor for a hundred years, nor for ten thousand of MILLIONS of ages, one after another, but forever and ever, without any end at all, and never, never to be delivered." [4]

Sad to say, many others besides Jonathan Edwards preached this appalling doctrine. Baptist preacher Charles Spurgeon, master of language that he was, put it this way:

"In fire exactly like that which we have on earth, thy body will lie, asbestos-like, FOREVER UNCONSUMED . . . all thy veins roads for the hot feet of pain to travel on, every nerve a string on which the devil shall ever play his diabolical tune of Hell's Unutterable Lament." [5]

But the limits of blasphemy are not yet reached. The following quotation turns the God of love into a monster who *takes delight* in the woes of the lost!

"God, who is of purer eyes than to behold iniquity, cannot look [upon sinners] but with utter detestation. His face shall be red in His anger, His eyes shall not pity, nor His soul spare for their crying. The day of vengeance is in His heart. It is what His heart is set upon. He will DELIGHT in it. He will tread that rebel crew in His anger, and trample them in His fury." [6]

And the *Works of Samuel Hopkins, D.D.*, pages 457-458, declare that the burning of the wicked throughout eternity will constitute the light of heaven; and if hell is brought to an end, heaven would be in darkness! Men go to such lengths when lost in the mazes of their own speculation. But thank God, this dreaded doctrine of eternal torment is not a BIBLE concept! Revelation 21:23 says the heavenly city will have "no need of the sun, neither of the moon, to shine in it: for the glory of God did lighten it, and the Lamb is the light thereof."

AN ASSAULT ON THE CHARACTER OF GOD

This false teaching of endless suffering in perpetual pain, is so fiendish that most of us cannot believe it. Hideous cruelty beyond that of any earthly tyrant is ascribed to God by such a doctrine. Our minds revolt against such a caricature of God in His alleged fiendishness.

If the Devil wanted to blacken God's character and destroy belief in His love and justice, he'd want a doctrine like this to give children nightmares and drive adults to unbelief. And if they still believed, they'd serve God out of fear. Even Satanic acts would look good in comparison.

No feat of mental gymnastics can reconcile the picture of a God of LOVE, MERCY, HOLINESS, and JUSTICE with a theory that attacks all those divine attributes. Henry Constable, canon of the cathedral at Cork, Ireland, shows how this doctrine contradicts every attribute of God, when he asks:

> "Is it the part of LOVE to inflict eternal pain if it can be helped?
> . . . Is it the part of MERCY never to be satisfied with the misery of others? . . . Is it essential to HOLINESS to keep evil forever in existence?
> . . . Can JUSTICE be satisfied only with everlasting agonies?" [7]

Probably no other doctrine in the Christian faith has produced more atheists than this one. You may have heard of Robert Ingersoll, perhaps the most famous (or infamous!) agnostic ever seen in America. Did you know Ingersoll's father was a Christian minister? Young Bob, who would have made a tremendous speaker and minister for God himself, heard the doctrine of eternal torment being preached and said, "If God is like *that,* I hate Him." Ingersoll became an infidel and a leading spokesman against God in America. And English poet Percy Shelley wrote: "God is a vengeful, pitiless, and almighty fiend." These are just two examples showing the effects of this slanderous teaching.

Such a grotesque doctrine is another phase of the Devil's war against God, the war that broke out in heaven and was transferred to this earth, as we're told in Revelation 12:7-9. Throughout this great controversy, Satan has attacked the character of God. He not only led many angels to join his diabolical rebellion by causing them to doubt the wisdom of God and the justice of His divine government, but he also caused our first parents to fall by leading them to doubt God's truthfulness, directly contradicting the Creator with the lie that "Ye shall not surely die." [8]

Satan wants to paint God as a sadistic monster who plunges his victims into endless, agonizing misery. But the facts are that God the Father and our Lord Jesus Christ will NEVER do anything unjust or unmerciful. Please note these Scriptures:

- "God is LOVE." —1 John 4:8 & 16.
- "The Lord [is] MERCIFUL and GRACIOUS . . . FORGIVING." —Exodus 34:5-7.
- "The Lord God [solemnly swears], I have NO PLEASURE in the death of the wicked." —Ezekiel 33:11.
- "Shall not the Judge of all the earth DO RIGHT?" —Genesis 18:25

That's the kind of God we worship. But in studying this whole question, I learned a new word, the word "indefeasible." Advocates of the immortal soul claim man has "*indefeasible* immortality." What does that mean? Well, "indefeasible" means "That which CANNOT be undone or made void." In other words, they believe not only that God made man with a so-called immortal soul[9] but that, having made him so, God cannot undo this act or change man back to a mortal creature. Like the mad scientist who created a Frankenstein monster, God is left with a creature He CANNOT destroy. They feel this is true because BY DEFINITION our soul is: *inherently* immortal, *innately* immortal, *indefeasibly* immortal. Consequently, they teach that man's soul by its very nature is imperishable and indestructible.

This theory about man's immortal nature made the corollary doctrine of eternal torment necessary, for if God can create life but cannot destroy it, His only recourse is to cast rebellious creatures into a lake of fire where, because they're immortal, they must burn forever. Yet reason tells us: if God created all things out of nothing, then He can reduce all things back to nothing—or Omnipotence has ceased to be omnipotent.

But let's examine this theory and the dilemma it poses. This doctrine drives us to one of two alternatives, and neither is acceptable.[10]

1. If we say that the wicked MUST live forever because man has an immortal soul that God Himself is powerless to destroy, then we have an extremely LIMITED God, a God not worthy of worship, for He created us, bungled the job, and lost control.

2. The other alternative is even more objectionable in misrepresenting God's character. It is this: If we admit that God IS all powerful, that He CAN destroy those He's created but CHOOSES to keep them miraculously alive, then it follows that He WILLFULLY will burn, scorch, and sizzle His disobedient creatures FOREVER as punishment for the crimes of one short lifetime. Talk about "cruel and unusual punishment"! It's doubtful that even the most vindictive man would wish such cruelty on his worst enemy. The God of this second alternative inspires only fear and hate, not love, for He's a sadist of the first magnitude.

It's time we cleared the good name of God of these false charges by examining what the Bible teaches about the destiny of the wicked. A theory so appalling needs to be sustained by evidence proportionately strong, yet the Bible does not corroborate it. In the first place,

Hell Is Not Burning NOW

Jesus plainly taught that a sinner goes into hell not as a mere spirit but with his BODY, saying: "If your right hand causes you to sin, cut it off and throw it away. It is better for you to lose one part of your BODY than for your whole BODY to go into hell." [11] But a dead person's body is in the grave and will remain there till the resurrection. Therefore hell cannot be burning now.

As we learned in Chapter 10, the Bible clearly teaches that at death man goes to neither heaven nor hell, but into the grave, to await the resurrection at Jesus' Return. In harmony with this are Peter's words: "The Lord knoweth how to deliver the godly out of temptations, and to RESERVE the unjust unto the day of judgment to be punished." [12] Note the expressions "reserve," "the day of judgment," and "to be punished," for they prove no punishment is going on now in some place of torment.

The prophet Job taught the same truth: "Do you not know ... the wicked are RESERVED for the day of doom; they shall be brought out [resurrected] on the day of wrath." [13] The fact is, *hell hasn't happened yet*. Just as the wicked are not burning now, being "reserved for the day of doom," so the righteous are not in heaven now, their "inheritance incorruptible" being "RESERVED in heaven." [14]

Not even the devils are burning now. Jude 6 declares: "The angels [who became devils] which kept not their first estate, but left their own habitation, He hath RESERVED in everlasting chains under darkness, unto the judgment of the great day." And Peter says: "God spared not the angels that sinned, but cast them down to hell, [15] and delivered them into chains of darkness, to be RESERVED unto judgment." [16]

So the punishment of Satan and his demons is "reserved" till some future time. Evidently the devils themselves understand this, for when Jesus met two demon-possessed men, the devils "cried out, saying, What have we to do with Thee, Jesus, Thou Son of God? Art Thou come hither to torment us BEFORE the TIME?" [17]

Besides, IF Satan and his devils were confined to a place of burning now, who'd carry on their evil work? Satan's punishment is "reserved . . . unto the judgment of the great day," for he's not yet judged. Redeemed saints will even take part in his trial: "Know ye not that WE shall judge angels [fallen angels like Lucifer]?" [18]

JUSTICE Demands
That Hell Is Not Burning NOW

Not only does Scripture prove that punishment is yet future, as we've just seen, but justice also demands that it be so. For the false theory of eternal torment, teaching that the wicked go immediately to a burning hell at the moment of death, charges God with infinitely more UNFAIRNESS than is within the power of sinful mankind to practice. How? Because a sinner of the first century—like Cain, who killed his brother Abel—would already be burning for SIX THOUSAND YEARS. Therefore a twentieth-century sinner—like Hitler, who was responsible for slaying *millions*—would have a six-thousand-year *lighter* sentence! Where's the justice in that?

God's "STRANGE Act"

I'm glad we can clear away the many misconceptions about hell. But make no mistake: Hell and hell-fire are real, literal, and HOT! There IS a heaven to win and a hell to shun. There WILL be excruciating *physical pain* as well as unbearable *mental anguish* from realizing what one has lost. (Spanish writer Calderón de la Barca said, "The loss of heaven is the greatest pain in hell.") But though there's an act of final destruction, even that destruction is an act of LOVE, like shooting a horse that has a broken leg. Lives of rebellion have unfitted the wicked for heaven. Its purity and peace would be torture for them, and they'd long to flee from that holy place. They'll welcome destruction itself in order to be hidden from the face of Him who died to redeem them. [19] The destiny of the wicked is fixed by their own choice.

It's in mercy to the universe that God destroys sin and sinner. God will destroy Satan and his followers to make the universe safe for those wise enough to trust and follow their Creator. Sinners will die, but not at the hands of an angry God. Rather, it's more like seriously ill patients who refuse life-saving help from a kindly physician.

God's done all He could to save each rebellious individual, but in the end He respects each one's own freedom of choice. Reluctantly, like a parent who hates to punish a beloved child, God goes about His strange work of destruction—strange because for *Him* it's completely out of character. Note how our loving heavenly Father describes it: "The Lord shall rise up . . . He shall be wroth . . . that He may do His work, His STRANGE work; and bring to pass His act, His STRANGE act." [20]

Opposed to the theology of men who teach endless torment is another extreme—some believe that God is too good to punish the wicked at all. But between these two extremes is the Bible picture of a God of both mercy and justice. The word *gospel* means "good news"—and God's just and merciful punishment is part of His good news.

THERE WILL BE DEGREES OF PUNISHMENT

God is a God of infinite justice. Paul speaks of "the righteous judgment of God, who will render to every man according to his deeds." [21] God keeps careful record books: "And I saw the dead, small and great, stand before God; and the books were opened . . . and the dead were judged out of those things which were written in the books, according to their works. . . . They were judged every man according to their works." [22] The word "according" implies varying degrees of punishment.

Jesus Himself explicitly teaches that there will be individual degrees of punishment. He says: "That servant who knows his master's will and does not get ready or does not do what his master wants will be beaten with MANY blows. But the one who does not know and does things deserving punishment will be beaten with FEW blows." [23]

So it's clear that some will burn briefly before dying, while others will burn longer. Probably Satan will burn longest of all, for he not only committed the most evil but also had the best opportunity in heaven to KNOW "his master's will."

Our loving God is so fair, so just, that in the judgment He even takes into account our place of BIRTH and the attendant opportunities that involves. He declares: "I will make mention of Rahab and Babylon to them that know Me: behold, Philistia, and Tyre, with Ethiopia; this man was born THERE. And of Zion it shall be said, This man was born in her. . . . The Lord shall COUNT, when He writeth up the people, that this man was born THERE." [24]

Justice demands different degrees of punishment, but this would hardly be possible if all sinners were thrown into the same lake of fire and burned throughout all eternity.

The Wicked Will Finally Be DESTROYED

Even though the unsaved will be punished in varying degrees, apparently for different lengths of time before dying, all will finally be destroyed—utterly, completely annihilated. The Bible is extremely explicit on this. Paul, for instance, gives positive testimony when he says: "The wages of sin is DEATH" [25]—*not* eternal LIFE in unending torture! And James says plainly, "Sin, when it is finished, bringeth forth DEATH." [26]

But someone may ask, "Maybe these texts simply refer to the death of the body. The soul of man could never be destroyed, could it?" That's a good question which Christ Himself answered when He warned us to "Fear Him who is able to destroy both soul and body in hell." [27] So obviously the soul can be destroyed.

Contrary to popular belief, the soul is neither immortal nor a conscious entity that can exist apart from the body. The word "soul" in the New Testament comes from the Greek word *psuche* (pronounced "psoo-KAY"), which simply means "life" or "living being" or "living creature." For instance, in Matthew 16:25-26 the Greek word *psuche* appears four times, but it's translated twice as "life" and twice as "soul," showing that the two terms are interchangeable. Here's how that text reads: "For whosoever will save his LIFE [*psuche*] shall lose it: and whosoever will lose his LIFE [*psuche*] for My sake shall find it. For what is a man profited, if he shall gain the whole world, and lose his own SOUL [*psuche*]? or what shall a man give in exchange for his SOUL [*psuche*]?" [28]

The whole man sins, so the whole man dies. His entire being, his life, his body, are all DESTROYED. "The candle of the wicked shall be put out," says the wise man Solomon. [29]

Ezekiel plainly declares: "The SOUL that sinneth, it shall DIE." [30] Then a few verses later the prophet repeats this, for good emphasis: "The SOUL that sinneth, it shall DIE." [31] The infallible Word of God ought to settle the matter. No support can be found there for the immortal-soul theory.

Furthermore, everlasting hell-fire punishment is inconsistent with the teaching of Jesus. In the most familiar verse in all the Bible, John 3:16, Jesus said that whoever believed in Him would "have everlasting life" and whoever did not would "perish." The word *perish*—a correct translation of the Greek—means to *cease to exist* and describes an END to the punishment rather than eternal torment.

Dr. Richard Weymouth, the first to translate the New Testament into modern English and esteemed the most accomplished Greek scholar of his day, strongly declared:

"My mind fails to conceive a grosser *misrepresentation* of language than when five or six of the strongest words which the Greek tongue possesses, signifying to DESTROY or DESTRUCTION, are translated to mean 'maintaining an everlasting but wretched existence.' To translate *black* as *white* is nothing compared to this." [32]

Note how clearly the Bible describes the utter destruction of the wicked, specifically how all the wicked will be "destroyed together"—not burning one by one as they happen to die: "And the destruction of the transgressors and of the sinners shall be TOGETHER, and they that forsake the Lord shall be CONSUMED. . . . The strong shall be as *tow*, [33] and the maker of it as a spark, and they shall both burn TOGETHER, and none shall quench them. . . . The transgressors shall be destroyed TOGETHER." [34]

The psalmist David uses unmistakable language: "For yet a little while, and the wicked shall not BE: yea, thou shalt diligently consider his place, and it shall not BE. . . . But the wicked shall PERISH, and the enemies of the Lord shall be as the *fat* of lambs: [35] they shall CONSUME; into smoke shall they consume away." [36]

The final chapter of the Old Testament vividly describes the sinner's fate: "For, behold, the day cometh, that shall BURN as an OVEN: and all the proud, yea, all that do wickedly, shall be *stubble*; [37] and the day that cometh shall burn them UP, saith the Lord of hosts, that it shall leave them neither root nor branch. . . . And ye shall tread down the wicked; for they shall be ASHES under the soles of your feet in the day that I shall do this, saith the Lord of hosts." [38]

When the pen of Inspiration says that the day of God's judgment will not just "burn them" but will "burn them UP," it means total destruction by flames—as does the plain word "ashes."

FEAR Is an UNWORTHY Motive

Believers in eternal torment object to the teaching that the Bible says complete destruction awaits the sinner. They believe mere annihilation isn't scary enough to be a deterrent to sin. They think sinners won't repent of wrong-doing if convinced they won't burn eternally in the flames of hell.

But fear is a poor motive for intelligent beings. A wife threatened by her bullying husband may yield to his wishes. But threats won't make her *love* him more than she did before. Instead, she'll tend to *hate* him. Those who become "religious" because they fear hell and fear God are actually FARTHER from salvation than they were before.

Our loving Savior never intended to scare people into heaven. True religion is more than a mere "fire escape." Besides, we know that most men have remained impenitent even under the preaching of eternal torment. The natural tendency of that theory is to make men infidels instead of Christians. Most people, if made to believe that *that* is what Scripture teaches, will reject the Bible altogether.

It's love, not fear, that converts a soul. It's love, caught in one glimpse of the Savior dying on the cross, that melts the hard heart. Understanding God's love leads to genuine conversion and saves more people in the eternal kingdom than believing the doctrine of eternal torture. In heaven the redeemed won't slink around like cowed beasts, afraid of their master's lash, but will love and praise God sevenfold, "saying with a loud voice, *worthy is the Lamb that was slain* to receive POWER, and RICHES, and WISDOM, and STRENGTH, and HONOR, and GLORY, and BLESSING."[39]

The Bible teaches: "There is no fear in love; but perfect love casteth out fear: because fear hath torment. He that feareth is not made perfect in love."[40]

"EVERLASTING DESTRUCTION"

Psalm 92:7 declares that "The wicked . . . shall be DESTROYED FOR EVER." And because the sinner's destruction is so complete—God says the wicked "shall be as though they had not BEEN"[41]—the Bible uses such words as "eternal," "everlasting," and "forever and ever" in connection with the fate of the wicked. These expressions show that the overthrow of the wicked is a complete overthrow, that there'll never be any hope of recovery from their fate, for it is eternal. Their *torment* is not eternal. Their *grief* and *anguish* are not eternal. But their *destruction* IS eternal.

The apostle Paul explicitly stated this thought of the complete destruction of the wicked: "Who shall be punished with everlasting DESTRUCTION."[42] And Jesus said: "These shall go away into everlasting punishment."[43] However, note carefully that "everlasting punishMENT" is NOT *endless punishING*. This isn't "playing with words"—the very same principle applies to such vital Bible subjects as the following:

> Hebrews 5:9 teaches
>> not an ongoing PROCESS of ENDLESS SAVING
>> but a final RESULT of "ETERNAL SALVATION."
> Hebrews 6:2 teaches
>> not an ongoing PROCESS of ENDLESS JUDGING
>> but a final RESULT of "ETERNAL JUDGMENT."
> Hebrews 9:12 teaches
>> not an ongoing PROCESS of ENDLESS REDEEMING
>> but a final RESULT of "ETERNAL REDEMPTION."

2 Thessalonians 1:9 teaches

     not an ongoing PROCESS of ENDLESS DESTROYING

     but a final RESULT of "EVERLASTING DESTRUCTION."

And Matthew 25:46 teaches

     not an ongoing PROCESS of ENDLESS PUNISH**ING**

     but a final RESULT of "EVERLASTING PUNISH**MENT**."

We must not confuse the *process* with the *product*. The "eternal" or "everlasting" pertains to the RESULT, not the PROCESS.

Furthermore, there's no dispute at all concerning the *length* or *duration* of the "punishment"—we've just read Jesus' words that it will be "everlasting." The only question is, What will that punishment BE? If the punishment for sin is *torment*, then there's no question but that the torment will be eternal. If, however, the punishment for sin is *death*, then the death will be "everlasting." And no Bible reader disputes the fact that "the wages of sin is DEATH."[44]

"ETERNAL FIRE"

But what about the "everlasting fire" spoken of by Jesus in Matthew 25:41? The words "everlasting" and "eternal" are synonymous, and in the New Testament both come from the same Greek word. In fact, verse 46 of Matthew 25 contains both words, each translated from the same original Greek word, *aionios*. Remember, the Bible explains itself, if we only let it. We can understand what Jesus meant here if we compare Scripture with Scripture, so let's look at some examples . . .

Jude 7 says that "Sodom and Gomorrah . . . are set forth for an EXAMPLE, suffering the vengeance of ETERNAL FIRE." Here's a Biblical "example" of what hell's everlasting fire will be. God says Sodom and Gomorrah were destroyed by "eternal fire"—but are those cities burning today, burning forever? Of course not! The fire did its destructive work and then WENT OUT thousands of years ago—2000 years, even, before Jude was inspired to write this verse in the First Century A.D.!

The Apostle Peter corroborates this when he speaks of God "turning the cities of Sodom and Gomorrah into ASHES, condemned them to destruction, making them an EXAMPLE to those who afterward would live ungodly."[45] And evidently it does not take long for "eternal fire" to reduce whatever it attacks to mere "ashes," for Jesus said that "the SAME DAY that Lot went out of Sodom it rained fire and brimstone from heaven, and DESTROYED them all."[46] Then Jeremiah tells us that "Sodom . . . was overthrown as in a MOMENT."[47] Here again, "eternal" means an everlasting RESULT, not an endless PROCESS.

Note what Dr. William Temple, late Archbishop of Canterbury, Primate of Great Britain, says about this "everlasting [*aeonian*] fire":

> "One thing we can say with confidence: everlasting torment is to be *ruled out*. If men had not imported the Greek and unbiblical notion [from Plato], of the natural indestruction of the individual soul, and then read the New Testament with that already in their minds, they would have drawn from it a belief, not in everlasting torment, but in ANNIHILATION. It is the FIRE that is called *aeonian*, not the LIFE cast into it." [48]

Dr. Temple added: "Are there not, however, many passages which speak of the endless torment of the lost? No; as far as my knowledge goes there is none at all. . . . After all, annihilation IS an everlasting punishment though it is not unending torment." [49]

"UNQUENCHABLE FIRE"

Another adjective the Bible uses to describe hell-fire is "unquenchable." Jesus warns that the fire which punishes the wicked "never shall be quenched." [50] Is that true? Will hell-fire never be quenched? You'd better believe it! But let's understand what that means: to *quench* a fire means to *put it out*. A fire that shall never be quenched is not one that shall never GO out but one that cannot be PUT out. In 1871 the Great Chicago Fire destroyed that city. If we describe that fire by saying the flames could not be quenched, would you conclude that Chicago was still burning? No, you'd simply understand that the fire raged till it devoured everything within reach and then died down.

The Bible says even Jerusalem was burned with a fire that could "not be quenched." God warned the ancient Jews: "But if ye will not hearken unto Me . . . then I will kindle a fire in the gates thereof, and it shall devour the palaces of Jerusalem, and it shall NOT be QUENCHED." [51] The literal fulfillment of this prophecy came when the Babylonians put the torch to Jerusalem. [52] But is that fire still burning? Are those Jewish "palaces" ever burning, yet never quite consumed? No, but this unquenchable fire brought the city to destruction and ashes, just as hell-fire will bring the wicked to destruction and ashes. The fire which destroys the wicked MUST of necessity be UNQUENCHABLE, for if it were not, the wicked would put it out.

WORM DIETH NOT?

Some believe that Mark 9:43-48 proves the truth of the doctrine of eternal torment, for there Jesus warns the wicked against being cast into hell,

"Where their worm dieth not, and the fire is not quenched." The last part of this text poses no problem, since we've just seen what "unquenchable fire" means. So let's focus on the first part which says, "their worm dieth not."

Understand first of all that "their worm" is not a soul but only a MAG-GOT, feeding upon a dead body and not inhabiting a living one. Jesus' words echo those of the prophet Isaiah, who says the redeemed "shall go forth, and look upon the carcases [dead bodies] of the men that have transgressed against Me: for their worm shall not die, neither shall their fire be quenched." [53] The picture is again that of maggots preying on *dead bodies.*

The worm—a gnawing, carrion-eating destroyer—causes no suffering to the insensible carcass but simply hastens the disappearance of dead bodies. The worm and fire together, as agents of destruction, actually indicate the utter impossibility of eternal life in torment. This awesome warning stands for dissolution, disintegration, and final disappearance. So this text does NOT support the theory of eternal conscious suffering of the living damned. The work of the "worm" and "fire" is ETERNAL in RESULTS but not in process or duration.

Jesus is unmistakably alluding to the ghastly scenes of the ancient Valley of Hinnom, a ravine south of Jerusalem, just outside the city wall. It was a place of fire and destruction used as a vast refuse pit. All that was worthless was cast into the Gehenna fires: refuse, animal carcasses, even corpses of criminals so wicked as to be judged unworthy of burial. Here fires were kept burning to consume the corruption, and worms preyed upon the putrefying flesh. Whatever the fire failed to consume along the outer edges of the pit, the worms would devour.

The Valley of Hinnom in Hebrew is *Ge Hinnom*, which Greek transliter-ates into *Gehenna*, the term for "hell" Christ used here. Jesus, the Master Teacher, knew His listeners were familiar with this place where refuse was burned up, having seen it with their own eyes. So in using *Gehenna* to des-ignate the final fires of God's destructive judgments, He achieved instant communication.

But in so doing He offered no support to the doctrine of eternal tor-ment. For the ancient fire of Gehenna was not a fire into which living per-sons were cast, to be kept alive under torture, but one into which corpses were cast to be consumed. Any part remaining unburned was devoured by worms, so nothing was left. Bible scholar Dr. Richard Weymouth tells us:

> "*Gehenna of Fire* Or 'Hell.' The severest punishment inflicted by the Jews upon any criminal. The CORPSE (after the man had been stoned to death) was thrown out into the Valley of Hinnom (*Ge Hinnom)* and was DEVOURED by the worm or the flame." [54]

As a place of burning, especially for the punishment of the wicked, *Gehenna* fits our idea of Hell—except that *Gehenna* is not presently burning but simply symbolizes the coming "lake of fire" mentioned in Revelation.

Instead of supporting the theory of "eternal torment of the damned," Christ again portrayed the doom of the wicked as destruction. The "worm," like the "unquenchable fire," is a symbol of DEATH and DESTRUCTION.

HOW LONG IS "FOREVER"?

Now let's consider the word "forever." The pen of Inspiration says the wicked will be "cast into the lake of fire . . . and shall be tormented day and night for ever and ever." [55] What's the explanation? How do we know from that very chapter of Revelation 20 that "for ever and ever" in verse 10 does not mean "without end"? Because verse 9 says, "And fire . . . DEVOURED them," and because verse 14 says, "The lake of fire . . . is the second DEATH." The Bible never contradicts itself. It consistently describes the end of the wicked as ultimate destruction. For instance, Psalm 21:9 says of God's enemies that "The fire shall DEVOUR them" in the KJV, NKJV, NASB. The RSV and NIV say "CONSUME them"—both expressions are as powerful as one can use to signify destruction or annihilation.

Now, in regard to the word *forever,* English readers must remember that the Hebrew and Greek words (*olam* and *aionios*) translated "forever" in the Bible are *idioms* which don't always mean what we think they mean.

Let's ask the BIBLE itself what it means by "forever"—let's apply the acid test of USAGE to find the Bible meaning of this word. Exodus 21:6 describes the custom followed if a man was willing to be the slave of another man for the rest of his life: "His master shall bore his ear through with an awl; and he shall serve him FOR EVER." But how long is "for ever" in this case? Another translation says: "for the rest of his life." That's as long as he could serve him, of course. But it SAYS "for ever"! "For ever" in this case just means as long as he lives.

And what about Samuel? His mother dedicated him to the Lord. She was barren of children, so she promised that if the Lord would give her a son, she'd let him serve God all his life. As soon as the boy was weaned, she brought him to the Temple, "that he may . . . there abide FOREVER." [56] How could that be? The context itself explains: "As long as he lives, he is given to the Lord." [57] After all, Samuel could serve the Lord only as long as he lived. Here again, the word "forever" means for the rest of a man's life.

Paul, writing to Philemon regarding the return of his runaway servant Onesimus, said: "Thou shouldest receive him FOREVER." [58] What does that mean? Obviously, Philemon could receive Onesimus back only as long as either one of them lived. So "forever" here means as long as life lasts.

Commenting on this verse of Philemon 15, that scholarly reference, *The Cambridge Bible for Schools and Colleges*, says that *forever* in Biblical usage "tends to mark duration as long as the NATURE of the SUBJECT allows."

Thus the time involved depends upon the subject to which the word *forever* or *everlasting* is applied. When used to describe God or the gift of life that God gives, it naturally means "without an end, eternal." Applied to something transitory, such as mortal man, it means a relatively short period of time—the lifetime of that person. Please remember these simple words of Scripture: "He that hath the Son hath life; and he that hath NOT the Son of God hath NOT life." [59] For example, "No MURDERER hath eternal life abiding in him." [60] Could God make it plainer than that?

We often use the word *forever* in the same way ourselves. For instance, when we receive a gift or award, we often say: "I'll treasure it forever!" What does this really mean? As long as I live. And the idea of "forever" meaning duration limited by the SUBJECT to which it applies is reflected in some of our other English usage. For example, we speak of . . .

- a "tall" MAN and think of **six** feet,
- a "tall" TREE and think of **sixty** feet,
- a "tall" MOUNTAIN and think of **six thousand** feet!

But we use the same word "tall" in each case.

The Bible applies the same principle to its use of the word "forever." At least 56 times the Bible uses the word "forever" for things that have already come to an end. [61] The familiar expression "for ever and ever" means literally "to the ages of the ages" and is an idiomatic expression meaning "to the end of the age," "to the end of life," or "to the end of any particular experience." And that's exactly how it's used in the Bible.

SMOKE ASCENDS FOREVER?

Speaking of the fate of those who worship the Beast and receive his Mark, Revelation 14:11 says, "the smoke of their torment ascendeth up for ever and ever: and they have no rest day nor night." It's true that no night's rest will interrupt the suffering of the wicked: it will continue until they're annihilated. But those who claim this passage teaches eternal torment overlook the fact that it does NOT say their TORMENT will continue forever—rather, it is the "smoke" of their torment that drifts on endlessly.

The psalmist wrote, "The wicked . . . shall CONSUME; into SMOKE shall they CONSUME away." [62] The New King James Version says, "into SMOKE they shall VANISH away." That this is not endless burning is evident from the fact that the same expression is used concerning mystical "Babylon," called "the great whore": "And her smoke rose up for ever and ever." [63] This means complete and total destruction, for God says: "She shall be utterly burned with fire . . . and shall be found no more at all." [64]

Bible scholars know that this phrase about "smoke rising up for ever and ever" is derived from Isaiah 34:10. A look at the context in Isaiah 34 disproves any contention about endless burning. Isaiah predicted that "The sword of the Lord" would fall upon the idolatrous city of Bozrah, twenty miles southeast of the Dead Sea. God's curse on Bozrah says, "The land thereof shall become burning pitch. It shall not be quenched night nor day; the SMOKE thereof SHALL GO UP FOR EVER: from generation to generation it shall lie waste; . . . the cormorant [pelican] and the bittern shall possess it. . . . And thorns shall come up in her palaces, nettles and brambles in the fortresses thereof. . . . The wild beasts of the desert shall also meet with the wild beasts of the island . . . there." [65]

Thus God's Word in Isaiah proves that fire which makes smoke ascend "for ever and ever" does NOT *BURN* forever. If it did, how could thorns, nettles, and brambles grow up and wild animals take possession of Bozrah?

God repeats that city's fate: "I have sworn by Myself, saith the Lord, that Bozrah shall become a desolation, a reproach, a waste, and a curse; and all the cities thereof shall be perpetual wastes." [66] This same destiny befalls the wicked: when they're burned up as Bozrah was, their complete annihilation will last through all eternity.

PLACE OF PUNISHMENT WILL BE ON EARTH

It's fitting that the sinner will be punished on this earth, for it's here that the sins were committed. Revelation 20:9 says the resurrected wicked "went up on the breadth of the EARTH . . . and fire came down . . . and DEVOURED them." Also, describing Satan's doom, God says, "I will bring forth a fire . . . it shall DEVOUR thee, and I will bring thee to ASHES upon the EARTH in the sight of all them that shall behold thee . . . and never shalt thou BE any more." [67]

That's why Peter describes hell-fire by saying "The elements shall melt with fervent heat, the EARTH also and the works that are therein shall be BURNED UP. . . . Nevertheless we, according to His promise, look for new heavens and a NEW EARTH, wherein dwelleth righteousness." [68]

Therefore, since the Bible teaches

    (1) that the PLACE of hell-fire punishment is this EARTH,
             and
    (2) that God's people "shall INHERIT the earth";[69]
             it follows
    (3) that the burning MUST come to an END.

It does come to an end—the fire does its work and then goes out so completely that there's not even a "coal" left to warm at: The wicked "shall be as stubble; the fire shall burn them; they shall not deliver themselves from the power of the flame: there shall not be a coal to warm at, nor fire to sit before it."[70]

GOD WILL HAVE A CLEAN UNIVERSE

Thus the Bible describes the utter extinction of evil from its last and only stronghold in the universe. But the theory of eternal torment would not have it so. Instead, according to that teaching, sin and sinners would be perpetuated, living forever, hating, cursing, raising rebel hands in pain against the God of everlasting love. In that scenario, Christ's victory would never be complete, for He doesn't destroy evil—He only segregates it. The continuance of such a dark spot would forever blight God's universe.

Besides, how can there be a Paradise for any while there's unending torment for some? Each damned soul was born into the world as a mother's child, and Paradise cannot be Paradise for her if her child is in such a hell.[71]

No, it will not be so. God has no use for sin. There won't be a place in the universe where sin and sinners survive, even in a state of torture. Hell will have an ending.

You see, the doctrine of eternal torment WEAKENS the power and glory of the gospel in two ways:

    (1) by denying Christ His ultimate triumph
         in finally DESTROYING sin, and
    (2) by denying Christ His chief glory
         in BESTOWING life eternal upon the saved,[72]

for IF man were inherently, indefeasibly immortal by nature, what man—saint or sinner—would need God for life itself? But God alone is the Lifegiver, the Dispenser of immortality. Immortal-soulism is immortality WITHOUT a Savior.[73]

BIBLE SCHOLARS RECONSIDER THEIR TEACHING

In recent years many leading Bible scholars, including mainstream evangelicals and other prominent Protestant teachers and writers, have written in favor of annihilation.

"These scholars, who support the Bible and reject the more liberal interpretations of Scripture, have stated that they do not believe the more traditional views about hell [that is, eternal torment]. Most of them confess a belief in a punishment for the wicked that ends in annihilation." [74]

One of those influential writers was the British John Stott, who affirmed his belief in the annihilation of sinners in his 1988 book *Essentials: A Liberal-Evangelical Dialogue*. Stott said that it was "with great reluctance and a heavy heart" that he approached the subject of hell because he did not wish to cause division in the ranks of evangelicals. But he went on to state his belief that "*Scripture points in the direction of annihilation,* and that 'eternal conscious torment' is a tradition which has to yield to the authority of Scripture." Stott pleads for a frank dialogue on the subject among evangelicals "on the basis of SCRIPTURE." [75]

Another Briton is Anglican writer John Wenham, whose book, *The Goodness of God,* [76] was the first to be published by an evangelical publishing house in Britain that contradicted traditional ideas about hell. More recently, Wenham wrote a chapter included in the book *Universalism and the Doctrine of Hell,* a report on the Fourth Edinburgh Conference on Christian Dogmatics. Wenham gives a good account of the debate among evangelicals and adds: "I feel that the time has come when I must declare my mind honestly. I believe that endless torment is a HIDEOUS and UNSCRIPTURAL doctrine which has been a terrible burden on the mind of the church and a terrible blot on her presentation of the gospel. I should indeed be happy, if, before I die, I could help in sweeping it away." [77]

American evangelicals, too, have found a wealth of Bible evidence against eternal torment and in favor of annihilation. In 1982 Edward Fudge published a significant work, *The Fire That Consumes*. What is significant about the book is that it was written by an active member of America's Evangelical Theological Society and was, furthermore, an Alternate Selection of Evangelical Book Club. In the Preface to his book, Fudge writes:

> "The fact that final punishment will indeed be final—irreversible and without restoration or remedy forever—came as no surprise. The Bible clearly warns of destruction and punishment which are eternal, even as it speaks of everlasting life. What took my breath [away] more than once was the fact that Scripture so consistently and emphatically

teaches the nature of that everlasting punishment to be utter EXTINC-TION into OBLIVION forever. It was disappointing to realize the extent to which traditionalist authors have passed by the other side of Biblical passages unfavorable to their position." [78]

In 1992 another prominent American evangelical scholar deserted the traditional view of conscious eternal torment. Clark Pinnock, in *Four Views on Hell,* writes:

> "The Bible uses the language of *death* and *destruction,* of *ruin* and *perishing,* when it speaks of the fate of the impenitent wicked. It uses the imagery of fire that CONSUMES whatever is thrown into it; linking together images of fire and destruction suggests annihilation. . . . Al-though there are many good reasons for questioning the traditional view of the nature of hell, the most important reason is the fact that *the Bible does not teach it.* Contrary to the loud claims of the traditional-ists, it is NOT a Biblical doctrine." [79]

As the debate over hell heats up, Peter Toon observes: "In conservative circles, there is a seeming reluctance to espouse publicly a doctrine of hell, and where it is held, there is a seeming tendency towards a doctrine of hell as ANNIHILATION. . . . CONDITIONAL immortality appears to be gaining accep-tance in evangelical orthodox circles." [80] So we see an increasing number of evangelicals abandoning tradition and adopting the Scriptural view.

Jesus PAID the Penalty

We've looked at Scripture evidence, examined this question from every angle, and discovered that the Bible presents an air-tight case refuting the false idea of eternal tor ment. However, there's still one last argument against that damnable doctrine, an argument which will clinch our case, and that is the substitutionary sacrifice of Christ.

Basic to Christianity is the concept of Jesus dying in the sinner's place. This teaching is at the heart of God's plan of salvation and is accepted by every Christian. The Bible is full of the idea that Christ bore our sins—both Old and New Testaments consistently teach this. For example, Isaiah 53:6 says: "The Lord hath laid on Him the iniquity of us all." And 1 Peter 2:24, NASB, states that Jesus, our divine Substitute, "bore our sins in His body on the cross."

As our divine Substitute, Christ had to suffer the penalty to which fallen man was sentenced at the beginning. [81] If that penalty is endless suffering in the flames of hell, then the Savior must have known that and accepted it as His fate. In that case, Jesus must suffer that penalty before we can go free.

But in fact, the Lord would be FOREVER paying that penalty and never satisfying its claims. Either Christ took the full punishment for sin, or even forgiven sinners will have to take it themselves.

But thank God that the wages of sin is DEATH. Jesus paid those wages in full. He suffered our punishment and paid our penalty—but He did NOT "burn forever." *Calvary forever settles the question.* The death of Christ on the cross is all-sufficient for our deliverance—we are truly redeemed! Christ did NOT taste eternal torment, but the Scriptures declare that He did "taste DEATH for every man." [82] What a wonderful Savior! Let's praise Him for paying the full penalty for our sins by His atoning death on the cross.

CONCLUSION

Friends, hell was never intended for you and me. Jesus says it will be "prepared for the Devil and his angels." [83] If we go there it won't be God's fault—rather it will be in spite of God's love and Calvary's cross. Only one thing can cause us to go to hell, and that is unforgiven sin.

No one will be lost just because he fell into the trap of sin. No one will go to hell because he stole, killed, or committed adultery. He'll go to hell because he refused to turn to Christ for deliverance from those sins. The greatest sin of all is to spurn salvation, and the most unanswerable question of all is: "How shall we escape if we neglect so great salvation?" [84] Let's NOT neglect salvation by refusing the way of escape God so lovingly provides!

〜

Notes to Chapter 12

1. Donald Attwater, editor, *A Catholic Dictionary*, 3rd edition (New York: The Macmillan Company, 1962), p. 226, article "Hell."

2. William E. Addis and Thomas Arnold, *A Catholic Dictionary*, 2nd edition (London: Kegan Paul, Trench and Company, 1884), p. 395, article "Hell."

3. Jonathan Edwards, "Sinners in the Hands of an Angry God," in Bradley, Beatty, and Long, editors, *The American Tradition in Literature*, Revised (New York: W. W. Norton & Company, Inc., 1962), Volume II, pp. 115-119. Edwards delivered this infamous sermon on July 8, 1741, at Enfield, Connecticut.

4. Jonathan Edwards, *Sermons*, Volume VII, p. 166.

5. C. H. Spurgeon, Sermon preached on February 17, 1856, "The Resurrection of the Dead," in *The New Park Street Pulpit* ([republished] Grand Rapids: Zondervan Publishing House, 1964), Volume II, pp. 104-105.

6. Sermon by Reverend William Davidson, quoted in Carlyle B. Haynes, *Life Death, and Immortality* (Nashville: Southern Publishing Association, 1952), p. 340.

7. Henry Constable, *Duration and Nature of Future Punishment*, 6th edition (London: Edward Hobbs, 1886), p. 166, quoted in Edward Fudge, *The Fire That Consumes* (Houston: Providential Press, 1982), p. 431.

8. Genesis 3:4 (contradicting Genesis 2:16-17 & 3:3).

9. If man really *were* inherently immortal, it would have been pointless for God to WARN Adam and Eve about DEATH, as he did in Genesis 2:16-17 & 3:3. God's warning would have been an empty threat!

10. See Elizabeth Cooper, "Clearing God's Name," *Review & Herald* Magazine (December 5, 1974), p. 5.

11. Matthew 5:30, NIV.

12. 2 Peter 2:9.

13. Job 21:29-30, NKJV.

14. 1 Peter 1:4.

15. The word *hell* here is translated from the Greek word "Tartaros" which means simply "a dark abyss." This is the only use of *Tartaros* in the entire Bible, and nothing in this Greek word even implies a place of fire or burning. Like Jude 6, quoted above, this verse speaks not of fire but of "chains of darkness" and says judgment is "reserved" or FUTURE.

16. 2 Peter 2:4.

17. Matthew 8:29.

18. 1 Corinthians 6:3.

19. At Christ's Second Coming the wicked will call "to the mountains and rocks, FALL on us, and HIDE us from the face of Him that sitteth on the throne." See Revelation 6:15-17.

20. Isaiah 28:21.

21. Romans 2:6.

22. Revelation 20:12 & 13.

23. Luke 12:47-48, NIV. Other statements of Jesus, such as those found in Matthew 11:20-24 and Luke 20:45-47, prove that there will be degrees of punishment, asserting that especially wicked sinners "shall receive GREATER damnation."
24. Psalm 87:4-6.
25. Romans 6:23.
26. James 1:15.
27. Matthew 10:28, NKJV.
28. Chapter 10, "Solving the Mystery of Death, Part I," clarifies the Bible terms "soul" and "spirit." See pages 260-270, above.
29. Proverbs 24:20.
30. Ezekiel 18:4.
31. Ezekiel 18:20.
32. Richard Francis Weymouth, quoted in Edward White, *Life in Christ,* 3rd edition, revised and enlarged (London: Elliot, 1878), p. 365. Dr. Weymouth was headmaster of Mill Hill School and the translator of *New Testament in Modern Speech* (Boston: The Pilgrim Press, 1902).
33. "Tow" is the coarse, broken fibers of hemp or flax, before spinning, which burns very quickly.
34. Isaiah 1:28 & 31; Psalm 37:38.
35. Like a grease fire on the stove, nothing burns as readily as "fat," which water cannot extinguish—it keeps burning till it's "consumed."
36. Psalm 37:10 & 20.
37. "Stubble" is short stubs or stumps of grain, left after the harvest, which burns very fast.
38. Malachi 4:1-3.
39. Revelation 5:12.
40. 1 John 4:18.
41. Obadiah 16.
42. 2 Thessalonians 1:9. In Philippians 3:18-19, Paul speaks of "the enemies of the cross of Christ, whose END is DESTRUCTION"—not eternal burning. Likewise, in Matthew 7:13-14, Jesus speaks of the "broad" and "narrow" ways and contrasts "life" with "DESTRUCTION"—not with eternal burning.
43. Matthew 25:46.
44. Romans 6:23.
45. 2 Peter 2:6, NKJV.
46. Luke 17:29.
47. Lamentations 4:6.
48. William Temple, Archbishop of Canterbury, *Christian Faith and Life* (London: SCM Press Ltd., 1954), p. 81 (from a 1931 address at Oxford's University Church).
49. William Temple, *Nature, Man and God* (London: Macmillan Co., Limited, 1953), p. 464 (from his lectures at Glasgow University, 1932-34).
50. Mark 9:43-45.
51. Jeremiah 17:27. See also Jeremiah 7:20.
52. 2 Chronicles 36:19-21.

53. Isaiah 66:24. See also verses 15-17 and 22-23.

54. Richard Francis Weymouth, *New Testament in Modern Speech*, 3rd edition (Boston: The Pilgrim Press, 1902), Matthew 5:22, note 12.

55. Revelation 20:10 (see also verse 15).

56. 1 Samuel 1:22.

57. 1 Samuel 1:28, NRSV.

58. Philemon 15.

59. 1 John 5:12.

60. 1 John 3:15.

61. A Catholic professor at St. Ambrose College explains, "As for the frequently used word *eternal*, its meaning is often the same as that in many secular writings—a period of long duration, NOT necessarily time without end."—Father Joseph E. Kokjohn, "A HELL of a Question," *Commonweal* (January 15, 1971), p. 368.

62. Psalm 37:20.

63. Revelation 17:1, 5, 18; 19:3.

64. Revelation 18:8 & 21.

65. Isaiah 34:6, 9-14.

66. Jeremiah 49:13.

67. Ezekiel 28:18, 19.

68. 2 Peter 3:10 & 13.

69. Psalm 37:9 and Matthew 5:5. Proverbs 11:31 states that "the righteous shall be recompensed in the EARTH: much more the wicked and the sinner."

70. Isaiah 47:14.

71. Paraphrased from Dr. William Temple, Archbishop of Canterbury, in "The Idea of Immortality in Relation to Religion and Ethics," *The Congregational Quarterly* (January, 1932), Volume X, p. 11.

72. The Bible clearly promises eternal life to one group of people and eternal death to another group. If the latter suffered ENDLESS torture, then both groups would have eternal life, though one wouldn't enjoy it.

73. Any doctrine which teaches that unrepentant sinners are immortal clearly contradicts such New Testament texts as John 3:16; 1 John 3:15; 1 John 5:11-12, and many others. Such a teaching, therefore, must originate from *some source other* than the divine Author of the Bible.

74. Brian P. Phillips, "Annihilation or Endless Torment?" *Ministry* Magazine (August, 1996), p. 15.

75. John R. W. Stott, *Essentials: A Liberal-Evangelical Dialogue* (London: Hodder & Stoughton, 1988), pp. 306-326.

76. John W. Wenham, *The Goodness of God* (London: InterVarsity Press, 1974).

77. John W. Wenham in *Universalism and the Doctrine of Hell*, edited by N. M. S. Cameron (Grand Rapids, MI: Baker Book House, 1992), p. 190.

78. Edward William Fudge, *The Fire That Consumes: A Biblical and Historical Study of Final Punishment* (Houston: Providential Press, 1982), p. xiii.

79. Clark H. Pinnock in *Four Views on Hell*, edited by William V. Crockett (Grand Rapids, MI: Zondervan Publishing House, 1992), pp. 145-146.

80. Peter Toon, *Heaven and Hell* (Nashville: Thomas Nelson, 1986), pp. 174, 176.

81. Simple justice demands that the penalty for a transgression be explicitly stated in advance, so all may clearly understand what's involved. Therefore God, at the very outset, made plain the penalty for sin. Genesis 2:17 says He declared in the Garden of Eden that the sinner "shall surely DIE"—*not burn forever.* In this connection Christian philosopher John Locke presents an incisive observation: "By *death,* some men understand *endless torments in hell fire;* but it seems a strange way of understanding a law, which requires the plainest and directest of words, that by *death* should be meant eternal *life* in misery. Can any one be supposed to intend by a law which says, "For felony thou shalt surely DIE," not that he should *lose his life,* but *be kept alive* in exquisite and *perpetual torments?* And would any one think himself fairly dealt with that was so used?"—John Locke, *The Reasonableness of Christianity,* in Richard Watson, *A Collection of Theological Tracts in Six Volumes* (London: J. Nichols, 1785), Volume 6, p. 3.

82. Hebrews 2:9.

83. Matthew 25:41.

84. Hebrews 2:3.

MYSTERY #5
Day of Worship

Why do most Christians worship on Sunday
while many others observe the seventh day?
Which day IS the Christian Sabbath?

"...make it PLAIN...."

—HABAKKUK 2:2

CHAPTER THIRTEEN

~

WHEN GOD SAID "REMEMBER"—
AND THE WHOLE WORLD
FORGOT

We live in an age of stress. The hectic pace of modern life produces tension, ulcers, and "burn-out." Our "pressure cooker" society is strewn with the psychological wreckage of people suffering from the wear and tear of daily living and subjected to the stress and strain of over-crowded schedules, deadlines, and traffic jams.

The workaholic, with his "Type A" personality, is becoming more and more common. Our materialistic society drives people to succeed at any price, regardless of the toll it takes on their mental and physical health or on their relationships with others. We eat fast, live fast, and spend our energy on pursuits that fail to satisfy. Exhausted by the frantic pace of our hectic lives, we're tempted to pop a few pills or other stimulants when we feel we can't afford to slow down. Even vacations take on the grueling tempo of today's "rat-race." Someone has said, "These days, if you want to *relax,* you really have to *work* at it."

God knew it would be this way. He knew our physical frame, having made it, and He foresaw our need for rest. He knew our personalities, often triggered by greed or ambition, and He realized that if left to ourselves we'd find no time for spiritual things of lasting value—no time for fellowship with Him.

A GIFT FROM EDEN

That's why God, in His wonderful wisdom and infinite love, gave us a gift that only He could give—a gift of TIME. Time to relax and unwind after a busy week. Time for physical rest and spiritual refreshment. Time for fellowship with our loved ones and with our Creator. The Sabbath is part of the *Prescription* given mankind by the *divine Physician*. The healing power of the Sabbath gives God's rest for man's restlessness.[1] It can free our minds from the cares of yesterday and the problems of tomorrow. It can re-charge our "spiritual batteries" and energize our souls as nothing else can.

Yes, the Sabbath is a HEAVENLY idea! Next time you say: "Thank God it's Friday," reflect on the fact that it was indeed God who gave us the weekend wrapped in the Sabbath—back in Eden at Creation Week.

> *God's holy Sabbath comes,*
> > *Offering calm and tranquil rest.*
> *But the world rushes on,*
> > *Knowing not the refreshing peace*
> *Our God would give.*

DON'T LET PREJUDICE ROB YOU

Too often Christians dispose of the Bible Sabbath with the prejudice-filled remark, "It's Jewish." How short-sighted! All the early Christians—the apostles and the Lord Himself—were Jewish. Can we dispose of these people for the sake of prejudice? Most of the Bible was written in the Hebrew language and clothed in Jewish imagery. The "Holy Land" itself is Jewish. Can we throw all this overboard to satisfy the whims of prejudice?

Satan has many weapons in his arsenal, like envy, lust, greed. But prejudice is one of the most devilish attitudes of all. Prejudice is a poison he pours over anything he doesn't want us to like or examine closely—a poison made up of equal parts of pride and hatred.

And the Devil succeeds in poisoning the minds of many, even among supposedly loving Christians, who should know better. So some people have a very negative reaction to anything connected with the Jews—anything they consider "Jewish." Hitler and the Nazis who followed him in his madness persecuted the Jews mercilessly. But they paid an ironic price for their course of action: One Jew who left Germany before the war to escape persecution was a young physicist named Albert Einstein. He later became the key figure in leading President Franklin D. Roosevelt to develop the atomic bomb which helped America emerge victorious. How fateful it would have been for the world if he had remained to help the Nazis build the bomb!

What if America had been prejudiced against Jews and had slammed the door in the face of that immigrant named Einstein? Anti-Semitism on that occasion could have cost a fearful price—a price that Love never needs to pay. Oh, friend, can you or I afford to close our minds before all the facts are in? Let's realize that the Old Testament Jews were the chosen people of God in those days, and when they were faithful, they followed the Lord's direction in all things, including the Sabbath.

Don't let prejudice rob you of all the truth and light God may shed on your path!

The Sabbath Is Actually CHRISTIAN

Still, someone may say, "Wait a minute! I'm as unprejudiced and liberal as anyone. I have nothing against the Jews. When I say that the Sabbath is Jewish, it has nothing to do with prejudice. I'm simply stating a fact: The seventh-day Sabbath IS Jewish, that's all. It was MADE for the Jew, and it has nothing whatever to do with Christians today. So, what's wrong with saying that?"

The thing that's wrong with it is this: It's absolutely not true!

Examine the facts: Your Bible says God gave the Sabbath as a blessing to Adam and Eve on the seventh day of Creation Week, long before there were any Jews or Egyptians or Chinese or any other race or nationality.[2] What is Jewish about the creation of the world? Remember, Abraham was the first Jew, and he lived approximately 2000 B.C. Therefore, if we hold to a 6000-year period of earth's history, we see that the seventh-day Sabbath was instituted and kept some two thousand years BEFORE the first Jew existed!

Satan's argument that God intended only Old Testament Jews to observe the Sabbath has gained such strength that many Christians refer to God's Sabbath as the "Jewish Sabbath." But no such expression is found in the Bible. The seventh day is called "the Sabbath of the LORD,"[3] but never "the Sabbath of the JEWS." Luke, a Gentile writer of the New Testament, often referred to specifically Jewish things. He wrote of:

- "the NATION of the Jews" .... Acts 10:22
- "the LAND of the Jews" .... Acts 10:39
- "the PEOPLE of the Jews" .... Acts 12:11
- "the SYNAGOGUE of the Jews" .... Acts 14:1.

But though he mentioned the Sabbath repeatedly, Luke never called it "the Sabbath of the Jews"—nor did any other Bible writer.

Christ Himself never implied that the Sabbath was made exclusively for Jews. Instead, He clearly taught that "the Sabbath was made for MAN," [4] using *man* in the generic sense, meaning all mankind. After all, as Timothy Dwight, President of Yale University, observed: "It was no more necessary for a Jew to rest after the labor of six days was ended, than for any other man. It was no more necessary for a Jew to commemorate the perfections of God, displayed in the works of creation." [5] The Jews kept God's holy day not because the Sabbath was just for them but because they were the only people faithful to the true God in Old Testament times.

Our Creator gave His holy day to Adam and Eve back in Eden at the same time He gave them the institution of MARRIAGE. No one foolishly claims marriage is "just for the Jews"! The twin institutions of God's holy Sabbath and holy matrimony are like two roses plucked from the Garden of Eden—one is no more "Jewish" than the other. Both have been fiendishly attacked by Satan. [6]

But just proving that the seventh-day Sabbath is not Jewish does not automatically prove that it's Christian. Let's go to the Bible to provide that proof right now.

CHRIST Is the CREATOR

If someone asked me as a young Christian, "How did the world come into being?" my reply always was "God created it." I thought this was a good answer, and it was—as far as it went. But the word *God* is not too specific when we remember that the holy Trinity is composed of three divine Persons: God the Father, God the Son, and God the Holy Spirit. So years ago when pressed to be more specific in my answer to how all things came to be, I'd say, "They were created by God the Father."

That's because I hadn't yet learned the Bible truth that God the Father gave His dear Son the honor of being the active Agent in the great work of Creation. This fact is easily demonstrated, first of all, by Genesis 1:26, which reads: "And God said, Let US make man in OUR image, after OUR likeness." The PLURAL pronouns used here show that the divine Being we call GOD was speaking to Someone as an equal, Someone already in His image and likeness.

The Bible identifies this divine Being as Jesus, the only-begotten Son: "In the beginning was the Word, and the Word was WITH God, and the Word WAS God. The same was in the beginning WITH God. . . . And the Word was MADE FLESH, and dwelt among us . . . the ONLY BEGOTTEN of the Father. . . ." [7]

In unmistakable terms, God's Word tells us that CHRIST was the CREATOR. Note the following texts:

- **John 1:3 & 10**—"ALL THINGS were made by Him [that is, by Christ, the incarnate Word], and without Him was not any thing made that was made. . . . He was in the world, and the WORLD was made by Him, and the world knew Him not."

- **Colossians 1:16**—"By Him [that is, by Christ, the "dear Son" of verse 13] were ALL THINGS created, that are in heaven, and that are in earth, visible and invisible. . . : ALL THINGS were created by Him and for Him."

- **Hebrews 1:1-2, 8-10**—"God . . . hath in these last days spoken unto us by His Son, . . . by whom also He made the WORLDS. . . . Unto the Son He saith, . . . the heavens are the works of Thine hands."

Verses such as these clearly establish that God the Father gave Jesus the honor of being our Creator. How thrilling to realize that the humble Carpenter who walked the hills of Galilee was also the Almighty Creator who made not only those very hills but even this entire world—and "ALL things"! How sublime for Christians to recognize that the One they call Savior is also their Creator! Those who already feel indebted to Christ by virtue of His sacrificial act of Redemption will find their love and appreciation enhanced when they acknowledge also His earlier act of divine Creation!

Therefore, we see that the seventh-day Sabbath is in fact CHRISTIAN, for it was Christ who made this world, made Adam and Eve, and also made the Sabbath for man. [8] It was Christ who spent the first Sabbath with our first parents at the end of Creation Week in Eden. But there's even more Bible evidence which proves the Sabbath to be Christian.

CHRIST IS ALSO OUR LAWGIVER

When the Bible says, "The Lord is our JUDGE, the Lord is our LAWGIVER, the Lord is our KING; He will SAVE us," [9] we know that "the Lord" it refers to is *Christ*, because:

- "He will SAVE us" implies our Savior, Jesus Christ

- "our KING" denotes Christ, for "Christ" means "king" or "Messiah" or "anointed One"—as kings are anointed

- "our JUDGE" also refers to Christ, "For the Father judgeth no man, but hath committed all judgment unto the Son." [10]

Thus in three different ways this verse confirms that Jesus Christ is "our LAWGIVER."

But Scripture makes even more clear that the same Lord who died on the *hill called Calvary* also came down on the *mountain called Sinai* to give us His Ten Commandments. Note how Nehemiah describes the Lord leading His people in their miraculous Exodus from Egypt after they'd served Pharaoh as slaves for centuries:

> "You divided the sea [the Red Sea, between Egypt and the Sinai Peninsula] before them, so that they went through the midst of the sea on the dry land; and their persecutors [Pharaoh's pursuing army] You threw into the deep, as a stone into the mighty waters. Moreover You led them by day with a CLOUDY pillar [not only to guide them over the trackless sand but also to shade them from the blazing heat of the desert sun], and by night with a pillar of FIRE [not only to illuminate their encampment but also] to give them light on the road which they should travel. **You came down also on Mount Sinai**, and spoke with them from heaven, and gave them just ordinances and true laws, good statutes and commandments. **You made known to them Your holy Sabbath,**[11] and commanded them precepts, statutes and laws, by the hand of Moses Your servant. You gave them bread from heaven [called "manna"] for their hunger, and brought them water out of **the ROCK** for their thirst." [12]

As we'll see in a moment, this passage is pregnant with meaning. Who is this divine Being that accompanied His people in their exodus from Egypt? When Old Testament writers use the word "Lord" or "God," does it refer to God the FATHER, God the SON, or God the HOLY SPIRIT? After all, the doctrine of the Trinity teaches that there are three Persons in the Godhead, all three of whom are divine Deities. (Someone has said, in regard to the Holy Trinity, that "God" is the FAMILY name.) We've already learned that the One called "God" in the first verse of the Bible—"In the beginning GOD created the heaven and the earth"—was none other than Jesus Christ, our CREATOR and SAVIOR.

But who is the "Lord" who went with His liberated people in their wilderness wanderings, shading them with cloud by day and lighting their camp with fire by night, feeding them and giving cool water to drink? Which member of the Godhead came down on Mt. Sinai and gave His Law of Ten Commandments and made known once again His blessed day of rest and worship?

Paul, the great Apostle to the Gentiles, declares it was JESUS. Paul's inspired words remind us how our spiritual forefathers in their exodus passed through the Red Sea, wandered under the cloud, ate the manna God provided, and drank the water that gushed forth from the ROCK: "They drank of that spiritual Rock that followed them: and that Rock WAS CHRIST."[13]

There you have it. Comparing Paul's words with Nehemiah's quoted above reveals from Scripture that the Lord who followed His people and fulfilled their needs was Christ! The Lord we sing about as the "Rock of Ages" is the Lord who spoke the Law from Sinai—Christ. The Lord who blessed the Sabbath at Creation is the same One who re-introduced it to His people after their captivity—Christ Himself.

Once we realize that Christ was the CREATOR who rested on that first Sabbath, that Christ was the LAWGIVER who proclaimed His Ten Commandment Law from Mt. Sinai, it changes our attitude toward His holy day. We understand as never before that the seventh-day Sabbath, far from being "Jewish," is actually CHRISTIAN—a living memorial of Christ's wondrous Creation.

WHY KEEP THE 7TH-DAY SABBATH?

At this point, knowing as we do a little more about the true Christian nature of the Lord's Day than the average person, we may even feel it's impertinent to ask the question, "Why should we keep the seventh-day Sabbath?" But let's address that question anyway, for the sake of exploring this matter thoroughly. The words of Jesus provide the best reason—for those Christians who demand reasons before obeying the One they call Lord. Christ said, "It is written, Man shall not live by bread alone, but by EVERY WORD that PROCEEDETH out of the MOUTH OF GOD."[14] The Ten Commandments did proceed out of the mouth of God. The Bible says He not only wrote them with His own finger on two tablets of stone but also spoke them in thunderous tones atop Mt. Sinai.[15]

Some people give "lip service" to God's Law. Some even try to obey as many as NINE of those eternal principles. But only those who observe all TEN—including the seventh-day Sabbath—are following Christ's admonition to "live . . . by EVERY WORD that proceedeth out of the mouth of God."

Sunday-keepers may well be asked the counterpart question, "Why do you go to church on the first day of the week when the Lord Himself specifically commands us to keep holy the seventh day?" The stock answer to such a query usually mentions the resurrection of Christ as having occurred on the first day of the week.

But it's the glorious FACT of Christ's resurrection that's all-important, not the incidental TIME of its occurrence. Proof of this is seen when we realize that, in addition to His resurrection, the sacrificial death of Christ on the cross is another monumental event that makes possible our salvation—but nowhere in Scripture does God command us to "keep FRIDAY holy" in honor of the CRUCIFIXION or to observe Sunday each week in honor of the RESURRECTION.[16]

BAPTISM: A MEMORIAL OF BOTH GREAT EVENTS

God had no need to institute the observance of DAYS to commemorate Christ's crucifixion and resurrection, because He chose instead to use the ceremony of baptism to be a beautiful memorial of both those marvelous events. Paul teaches plainly that BAPTISM is a fitting symbol of each Christian's act of:

- DYING to his old sinful way of life—
    just as Christ died on the cross,

- BURYING his sins in the watery grave of baptism—
    just as Christ was buried in the tomb,

- RISING AGAIN out of the water to walk a new life—
    just as Christ arose in His triumphant resurrection.

Let's grasp the Bible truth given by Paul that baptism by immersion—not the weekly observance of days—is the divinely-appointed memorial of Christ's DEATH, BURIAL, and RESURRECTION. The Apostle asks:

> "Know ye not, that so many of us as were baptized into Jesus Christ were baptized into His DEATH? Therefore we are BURIED with Him by baptism into DEATH: that like as Christ was RAISED UP from the dead by the glory of the Father, even so we also should walk in newness of life. For if we have been planted together in the likeness of His DEATH, we shall be also in the likeness of His RESURRECTION: Knowing this, that our old man is CRUCIFIED with Him, that the body of sin might be destroyed, that henceforth we should not serve sin."[17]

Naturally, we see God's wisdom in instituting such a perfectly fitting memorial of His Son's death and resurrection—but this is seen only in the baptism of believing adults by IMMERSION as taught in the Bible. That's what the very word "baptism" means: to immerse in, to dip or "dunk" under water. Rather than several modes of baptism, God offers only *one*. Ephesians 4:5 says there is "One Lord, one faith, *one* baptism." The so-called baptism of uninstructed infants by SPRINKLING—as changed by man—can offer no such parallels to the monumental acts of Christ in achieving our salvation. But Bible baptism does commemorate Christ's death and resurrection.

A Great Many Things Have Gotten *TWISTED*

Unfortunately, the purity of the early Christian church did not survive the Dark Ages. Satan saw to that in his merciless attacks on doctrinal truth. Many teachings foreign to the apostles crept in. True doctrines of Jesus were betrayed by those willing to compromise. The Bible method of baptism is not the only practice which has been corrupted through the centuries and accepted by many religious leaders. Another casualty in the war between Christ and Satan has been the Bible-designated day of worship.

Has the Sabbath been changed? No, not by God—but it's obvious that a change has taken place when we see that the day our Maker set aside at Creation Week is not now the day the world at large observes. It's vital to realize that this change was *never divinely approved.*

Remember when President Reagan fired the striking air-traffic-controllers? Or when President Bush sent the troops to fight in Desert Storm? As Chief Executive, they each had the power to do it. With the proverbial stroke of the pen, presidents and prime ministers can change things. But **NO** man or monarch has the authority to change the Law of God!

BURDEN of PROOF?

Since God Himself reminds us to "REMEMBER the Sabbath day," in the very wording of the Fourth Commandment, no reason or excuse is needed by those showing loyalty to their Creator by honoring the day He's told us to honor.

The burden of proof is not on those who follow the plain, explicit teaching of God's Word. They're under no obligation to prove that the day of worship was never really changed.

However, those who contend that God made such a change—not only abolishing the Bible Sabbath but also sanctifying Sunday in its place—must bear the burden of proof. In this case it's a heavy burden indeed!

The mistaken sanctity of Sunday and false teaching abolishing the Sabbath of the Lord are scandals the Christian conscience can no longer endure.

A Matter of LOVE & LOYALTY

Some Christians are so firmly committed to the wonderful One they call Lord and Master that they remain fiercely loyal to His Word. Their hearts delight in demonstrating unswerving loyalty to Him even when the majority are misled by unscriptural traditions.

Jesus cherishes this loyal commitment. He says: "IF ye LOVE ME, keep My commandments. . . . He that hath My commandments, and keepeth them, he it is that LOVETH Me." [18] And we know that when Jesus speaks of "My" commandments, it embraces the Ten Commandments, including the Sabbath of the Fourth Commandment, since those were all written by the finger and proclaimed by the voice of Christ Himself.

Critics of those who keep the seventh-day Sabbath claim that such observance of God's Law is an attempt to work one's way to heaven, and they hurl the charge of "legalism." On the contrary, those who obey in a spirit of love are not legalists but loyalists. They know no higher honor than to obey the King who redeemed them. Motivated only by love, they obey not in order TO BE saved but because they already HAVE BEEN saved. It's their natural response to Him who loved them enough to die in their place.

The Crux of the Matter

Satan is called "the great deceiver" because he fools people. He deceived even holy angels in the courts of heaven and persuaded them to join him in his rebellion against God. The Devil is a master of falsehood whom Jesus called "the father" of lies and lying. [19] "Satan . . . deceiveth the whole world." [20] That same old Devil stands ready to fool you and me today, if we let him.

Remember that Lucifer rebelled against God's authority, His government, His Law. Because Lucifer wanted to be "like the most High," [21] wanted to make himself God, he finally reached the point where he could not bring himself to submit to God—after all, to obey God is to admit His supremacy, and pride drove Lucifer to want to be supreme himself.

So in his rebellion, the thrust of Satan's attacks has always been aimed at the focal point of God's authority, His government, His Law:

- In HEAVEN, Lucifer led many of his fellow angels to disobey God— he wanted them to obey *him* instead and follow in his rebellion.

- In the GARDEN OF EDEN, he led Adam and Eve to disobey God.

- In TODAY'S WORLD, he still attacks loyal obedience to God.

American poet Robert Frost once wrote that his choice for the epitaph on his own gravestone would be:

"I had a lover's quarrel with the world."

Isn't that the way we all feel sometimes? In my own case, I know I love the people, all the people, for whom Christ died—I long to enjoy heaven with them. But my "lover's quarrel" is over the fact that people often ignore a clear "Thus saith the Lord" in the Bible and instead follow what their clergyman tells them!

After all, they feel justified in following the expert, the man supposed to be an authority in religious matters. But we must beware of what we're told—even by popular preachers. We must check out every statement for ourselves in the Bible. Josh Billings was right when he said:

"It's better to know NOTHING than to know what AIN'T SO."

Do I mean to imply that the world at large "knows" something that's not true? I certainly do. I mean more than to imply it: I mean to come right out and state flatly that, even though most Christians supposedly "know" that Sunday is the correct day of worship according to the Bible, such knowledge is based on a misconception, a false teaching that simply "ain't so."

Need I point out that the day of worship, that special time which marks our appointment with God, is spelled out explicitly in the Fourth Commandment of God's holy Law—the Law that's always been the special object of Satan's hatred? If the Devil can deceive us into thinking we're good Christians while disobeying God by observing the wrong day, he's well satisfied. He doesn't care HOW he gets us to fall into sin, just so we fall! God says very clearly: "Whosoever committeth sin transgresseth also the Law: for *sin IS the trangression of the Law*." [22] With that divine definition in mind, we see that it doesn't matter which Commandment we break. We don't have to be mass murderers to be guilty of sin.

Is God PARTICULAR?

Someone may say, "I don't think it matters. I don't think it makes any difference on which day we worship." But let's be very careful here, because this involves our RELATIONSHIP with GOD: He's the Lord—our Creator—and we're His creatures. And when it comes to your salvation and mine, our relationship with the Lord is a matter of LIFE or DEATH.

Even on a merely human level, relationships are important. Suppose my boss explains very carefully, *"This* is the way I'd like it to be done," and I say, "Well, I don't think it *matters.* I don't think it makes any *difference* how we do it." What do you suppose my boss would think of my attitude?

A clear example that God IS particular is seen in the experience of Cain and Abel, the first sons of Adam and Eve. Note the contrast in attitude: Abel had a spirit of loyalty to God, whereas Cain harbored feelings of rebellion. God had told Adam and Eve to confess their sins over the sacrificial offering of a lamb, which pointed forward in faith to the sacrificial death of Christ, "the Lamb of God, which taketh away the sins of the world." [23] "Abel was a keeper of sheep, but Cain was a tiller of the ground." [24] So Cain reasoned in his own mind that God would accept his offering of "the fruit of the ground" instead of the sheep, even though "without the shedding of blood there is no forgiveness of sins." [25] When God accepted Abel's lamb and rejected Cain's fruit, Cain angrily slew his brother and became the first murderer.

This experience shows that God is indeed particular: Even though both brothers erected their altars alike, and each brought an offering, only one acted in accordance with the Lord's directions. If we deliberately disregard the Lord's direct and explicit command, is it FAITH or PRESUMPTION to expect God's acceptance? In all ages there have been those like Cain who claimed a right to God's favor even while disobeying His commands. But the Scriptures declare that he who professes to know God "and keepeth not His commandments, is a LIAR, and the truth is not in him." [26]

Attitudes are important, for they reflect outwardly what we're like inwardly. Like it or not, our attitudes put our HEART on display. Secret thoughts and inner feelings are betrayed by outward attitudes. So let's carefully examine our own hearts and pray that God will give us the right attitude—a submissive heart and obedient spirit.

When someone asks, "What's wrong with keeping one day—any day— in seven?" he's not asking you or me, he's questioning God. He doesn't really want to know OUR opinion, for we have no authority in these matters. GOD'S opinion is the only one that counts.

When a man asks, "What's WRONG with keeping holy any day in seven?" he should consider his attitude and weigh his motive in asking God that question. Is he asking simply because he's unwilling to do what God says? Is he trying to justify a spirit of rebellion—the same spirit that motivated Satan, the original rebel?

Or is he sincerely asking God to enlighten him because he lacks information and doesn't understand His Command? If that's the case, God will lovingly explain all he needs to know to remove the doubts and questions from his mind.

Let's imagine several things the Lord might say to such an inquirer. He could point out that He gave the first Sabbath at the end of Creation Week to commemorate His divine act of creating the world. Was the Sabbath simply "one day in seven" in the FIRST week? Of course not. It was specifically the *seventh* day, set aside after God "finished" His great works of Creation. [27]

Your Bible says: "*THE* seventh day," never "*A* seventh day" or "one day in seven." The idea that man can pick any day of the seven stems from the attitude which puts MAN "in the driver's seat"—even when it comes to worshipping his Maker. If we succumb to this attitude, then God is no longer the

One who makes the rules, and we may worship Him WHEN we please, IF we please, and HOW we please—IF we have the time!

The very phrase "the SEVENTH day" shows that a particular day is meant, not just one day in seven. If we told a friend that we lived in "the seventh house" on a certain block, what would we think if he began at the first house on the block and knocked on each door till he came to the seventh, explaining at each front door that he was trying to find an old friend who had told him he lived in the seventh house on the block, and of course that meant he lived in ANY ONE of the seven houses? What would we think—and what would our neighbors think of the friends we had?

If I had seven ladies lined up in a row and the seventh happened to be my wife, would it make any difference which one I walked up to and kissed? (If you knew my wife, you'd know it would make a difference!) Why is it all right for me to show this kind of affection toward only one of the seven? The first one may be much closer and handier, but only with the seventh am I to have a special kind of relationship, for once upon a time this lady and I were SET APART for one another in a very special way. And that's exactly what happened back there on the seventh day of Creation Week: God set aside a SPECIFIC day for a special relationship between that day and man.

The Divine Record states that when He made the first Sabbath,

1. God RESTED on the seventh day,
2. God BLESSED the seventh day, and
3. God SANCTIFIED the seventh day. [28]

"Sanctified" means "SET APART for a special, HOLY purpose." That's what God says He did to the seventh-day Sabbath at creation. No other day was made holy or set aside for a holy purpose. Later, when God wrote the Ten Commandments, He said: "Remember the Sabbath day, to KEEP it holy." [29] If we choose to disregard the Lord's command and worship on some other day, the real question is, Can we get a blessing from a day God never blessed? Can we *keep* holy a day that was never *made* holy?

Finally, the suggestion that Christians should "keep EVERY day" is sometimes made by those who use this as an excuse for not observing the Sabbath of the Bible. But can we really honor the Lord by disobeying Him? Heaven knows we must work to support ourselves financially, so we surely can't rest every day. The Fourth Commandment itself demands that we not be lazy idlers: "Six days shalt thou LABOR, and do all thy work: But the seventh day is the Sabbath of the Lord thy God: in it thou shalt NOT do any work." [30] Those who claim to "keep" every day often observe none. It's true that we should worship and seek God every day—but this, rather than being a substitute for Sabbath observance, is just normal Christian living.

A friend once asked comedian W. C. Fields why he was reading the Bible so diligently. Fields replied, "I'm looking for loop-holes!" We can assume he was joking, but let's be sure we're not guilty of "looking for loop-holes" in our reading of God's Word. Let's take God at His word and accept the Bible just as it reads. God SAYS what He means and MEANS what He says. Genuine faith won't put a question mark where God has put a period. We won't *want* to do that when we realize that our heavenly "Father knows best!"

WHICH DAY IS THE SEVENTH DAY?

At this point a devoted Christian may say, "All right, I see now as never before God's teaching that we should keep the seventh day as the Sabbath. But there's still a practical problem in my mind: How can we tell which day IS the seventh day? The calendar may be so mixed up by this time that the day which originally was the seventh now falls on Tuesday—for all we know."

That's a fair question that deserves an honest answer. Fortunately, there are at least three ways by which we can tell that Saturday is the seventh day: HISTORICALLY, LINGUISTICALLY, and BIBLICALLY.

First of all, we have the **HISTORIC** evidence from faithful Jews that the weekly cycle of seven days has never been changed. Orthodox Jews—from that majestic day when God delivered the Ten Commandments to Moses till the present—have observed the Sabbath from sundown Friday until sundown Saturday. Week after week, year after year, century after century, the seven-day sequence has brought the return of God's holy day. This historic fact alone is enough to establish the certain identity of the Bible Sabbath.

There's no possibility that faithful Jews were confused on this point because Jesus, as the all-knowing Lord and Master of Time, would have corrected them in their day of worship—just as He unhesitatingly did in many other respects. So we know the Sabbath was accurately the seventh-day when Jesus walked the earth.

Another historic fact is that the ONLY calendar change in the Christian Era occurred in October 1582 when Pope Gregory XIII reformed the Julian calendar by REMOVING TEN DAYS in order to synchronize the calendar with the seasons and the heavenly bodies. (England waited until 1752 to make a similar change.) But this change affected only the DATES of the month, not the DAYS of the week. In other words, Thursday, October 4th, was followed immediately by Friday, October 15th, so that the correction of ten days modified the normal sequence of DATES but left the order of DAYS intact. See the facsimile calendar on the next page:

1582	OCTOBER				1582	
SUN	MON	TUE	WED	THU	FRI	SAT
	1	*2*	*3*	*4*	15	16
17	18	19	20	21	22	23
24	25	26	27	28	29	30
31						

HOW THE CALENDAR WAS CHANGED

All authorities—astronomers, encyclopedias, chronologists—agree that the unbroken continuity of the days of the week have come down in regular succession from the earliest times. Thus the Gregorian calendar posed no problem for either orthodox Jews or Christian believers who faithfully observed the Sabbath.

Second, let's consider the **LINGUISTIC** evidence. Language is an important part of any culture, having its roots deep in antiquity. What can LANGUAGE teach us about this matter? Well, linguistic evidence proves that the day we now call Saturday IS the seventh day—the true Sabbath of the Lord—and proves also that no calendar change has affected in any way the order of the days of the week.

For example, consider GREEK, the language in which the New Testament was written. The Jews called the day preceding the Sabbath "the preparation" day because they'd use it to prepare for God's holy day, finishing up their work, cleaning house, *etc.* So the Bible speaks of "the Preparation Day, that is, the day before the Sabbath." [31] The Greek word for "preparation"—the sixth day of the week—is *paraskeue.* And 2000 years later the day called

"Friday" in the English calendar is called *Paraskeue* ("Preparation") in the Greek calendar still today, just as it was in New Testament manuscripts.

Or take GERMAN for another example. If you look at a calendar printed in the German language, you'll see that the day we call "Wednesday" is called *Mittwoch*. That word *Mittwoch* means "mid-week," and Wednesday IS the day in the middle of the week—thus proving linguistically that no mix-up of the days of the week has taken place.

A third example could be SPANISH, a language somewhat popular even in parts of the United States today. So many of us know that the Spanish word for "Saturday"—the seventh day—is *Sábado*, which means *Sabbath*. Again the message is clear: The order of the days has NOT been changed.

Some years ago the late Dr. William Mead Jones of London published a "Chart of the Week," giving the designation of days of the week in different languages. This chart shows definitely that the seven-day period, or week, was known from the most ancient times, and that at least 108 languages designate the seventh day as the Sabbath. Consider the table below:

LANGUAGE	WORD for 7th DAY or "SATURDAY"	MEANING
GREEK	Sabbaton	Sabbath
LATIN	Sabbatum	Sabbath
SPANISH	Sábado	Sabbath
PORTUGUESE	Sabbado	Sabbath
ITALIAN	Sabbato	Sabbath
FRENCH	Samedi	Sabbath day
GERMAN	Samstag	Sabbath
PRUSSIAN	Sabatico	Sabbath
RUSSIAN	Subbota	Sabbath
POLISH	Sobota	Sabbath
HEBREW	Shabbath	Sabbath
AFGHAN	Shamba	Sabbath
HINDUSTANI	Shamba	Sabbath
PERSIAN	Shambin	Sabbath
ARABIC	Assabt	The Sabbath
TURKISH	Yomessabt	Day Sabbath
MALAY	Ari-Sabtu	Day Sabbath
ABYSSINIAN	Sanbat	Sabbath

Thus an examination of language in this connection is very revealing, for it conclusively shows that different peoples, in widely-scattered parts of the world, still call Saturday—the seventh day—"the Sabbath."

Third, **BIBLICAL** evidence clearly pinpoints the day Christ honored as the Sabbath as the day that comes *between Friday and Sunday*. "And Jesus cried out with a loud voice, and breathed His last. . . . It was the Preparation Day, that is, the day BEFORE the Sabbath." [32] Did you get that? The Record says Jesus *died* on "the day **before** the Sabbath." All Christians and anyone else familiar with the Crucifixion account know that Jesus died on a **Friday**—we call it "Good Friday." So *Friday* is the day *before* the Sabbath.

A few verses further we read: "And when the Sabbath was PAST . . . very early in the morning the first day of the week," [33] the women who loved the Lord came with spices to anoint His body. This tells us plainly that "the Sabbath is *past*" when "the first day of the week" arrives. Jesus *arose* on the first day of the week we call Easter **Sunday**. Any schoolboy examining these texts will see at a glance that the Sabbath is the day falling BETWEEN Friday and Sunday, making Saturday the seventh day of the week at the time of Christ.

IF the calendar had become mixed up before the time of Christ so that the day observed by God's people as the Sabbath were incorrect, then Jesus surely would have known the error and pointed it out. Christ, the Creator who gave the first Sabbath and who called Himself "Lord . . . of the Sabbath," [34] unflinchingly corrected other faulty practices of the Jews. But there was no need for any correction. The seventh-day Sabbath was and is the proper day of worship, for God has permitted no tampering with the weekly cycle either before or since Christ's day. No mix-up has occurred: Friday and Sunday still flank the seventh-day Sabbath of the Lord.

Thus the Living Bible paraphrase is correct in rendering *Sabbath* as "Saturday" in Luke 4:16, which tells how Jesus began His ministry by going to the place of worship and publicly reading from the Scriptures. The question of which day is the seventh is laid to rest. Abundant, convincing evidence from HISTORY, from LANGUAGE, and from the BIBLE itself demonstrates that there need be no confusion.

But Satan doesn't give up easily. He doesn't want us to see the truth about God's requirements. In this matter of the Sabbath commandment, for instance, one of his pet arguments, is, "Why don't all churches worship on the seventh day if it is right? Why don't more of the leading churchmen, the popular ministers, observe that day rather than Sunday? Surely they can't all be wrong." Thus the arch-deceiver seeks to attract attention to MAN instead of GOD.

Remember: The religious establishment in Jesus' day was not willing to follow God, either. Incredibly enough, it was the religious leaders—the chief priests themselves—who conspired with Judas against our Lord! Satan successfully used the majority at that time to crucify Christ.

Is the MAJORITY Always RIGHT?

Is Truth determined by popular vote? We in a democratic society are taught from infancy to accept "majority rule," but the voice of Reason tells us that there are limits to the valid application of that rule. If mere numbers were an evidence of success, then Satan might claim the prize; for in this world his followers are greatly in the majority. If the majority is right in matters of religion, then Christianity must be wrong, for paganism in its varied forms outnumbers Christianity. If the majority is right in the field of science, then Creationists must be wrong, for Evolutionists outnumber those who believe in divine creation.

The majority once believed that this round world was flat, but that didn't make it so. Majority vote can never decide some issues. Popular opinion has absolutely no bearing on ultimate Truth. But the ruts of conformity run deep, and the Devil knows many will bow to "the tyranny of the crowd." Satan exploited this human weakness even in Jesus' day. The Bible says,

> "Many even of the rulers believed in Him, but because of the Pharisees [the most influential religious sect] they were not confessing Him, lest they should be put out of the synagogue; for they loved the approval of men rather than the approval of God"! [35]

When people were being swayed to follow Christ, His opponents would use the Devil's argument, "Have any of the rulers or of the Pharisees believed on Him?" [36] So today opponents of God's Sabbath ask, "Have any popular preachers stopped worshipping on Sunday and begun to observe the seventh day?" When someone resorts to this argument and asks, "How can all the world be wrong?" explain patiently but firmly that most of the world has been wrong most of the time.

God's faithful people have always been in the minority, but RIGHT makes MIGHT: "If God be for us, WHO can be against us?" [37] Note these inspiring examples:

Noah was very much in the minority when he built the Ark that saved only eight dear souls. He ranked so low on the popularity poll that only his immediate family accepted his unpopular message—but Noah was right and the world that perished was wrong! [38]

Gideon and his small band of followers were an insignificant minority when they marched against the Midianites—but God led them to vanquish an army of tens of thousands! [39]

Elijah was a lonesome minority when he stood alone on Mt. Carmel to confront 850 prophets of the false god Baal—but God caused Elijah to triumph over them all! [40]

The three Hebrews—Shadrach, Meshach, and Abednego—were a conspicuous minority when they refused to go along with the crowd and bow down to the king's golden image in spite of a fiery furnace that threatened to make things pretty hot for nonconformists—but the Lord was with them in their trial by fire! [41]

The majority wasn't right in those days, and it wasn't right when Jesus "came unto His own, and His own received Him not." [42] So you see, you're not necessarily on the right road just because it's a well-beaten path. In fact, Jesus taught quite the opposite when He said: "Heaven can be entered only through the narrow gate! The highway to hell is broad, and its gate is wide enough for all the multitudes who choose its easy way. But the Gateway to Life is small, and the road is narrow, and only a few ever find it." [43]

I'd rather go to heaven alone than to hell in a crowd, wouldn't you? It's better to be with a few who are right than with many who are wrong. Christ's own words in the Ten Commandments tell us to "Remember the Sabbath day, to keep it holy." [44] Yet virtually the whole world, suffering a chronic case of spiritual amnesia, has forgotten. He must have known this would happen, because for this particular Commandment He deliberately used that word *"Remember . . . ,"* which still echoes down the corridors of time to the searching ears of those willing to listen to their Lord.

One pastor I know, who turned his back on riches and worldliness to seek truth and meaning in life, became a faithful minister and evangelist for the Lord. When he learned the Sabbath truth, he was puzzled that so many ministers—who seem to know the Bible—were so zealous in observing Sunday. Note this illuminating exchange:

> "Surely my Sunday-keeping friends had good reasons for their beliefs. I decided to ask ten ministers, but when I did I received *eleven* answers.
>
> "One minister said, 'The law has been done away with. We don't have to keep the Sabbath.'
>
> "'Oh,' I said, 'does that mean we don't have to keep the Ten Commandments?'

"'Oh, no. We keep the other nine,' he admitted.

"'Do you mean the one we're supposed to *forget* is the one GOD said to *remember*? That doesn't make sense!'" [45]

Truth, you see, is not always popular—but it's always right. When the majority is in the wrong, pray that you'll be in God's faithful minority, the faithful few who aren't afraid to march to the beat of a different drum. As the renowned Christian philosopher John Locke declared:

"An ERROR is not the better for being common, nor TRUTH the worse for having lain neglected: and if it were put to the vote anywhere in the world, I doubt . . . whether truth would have the majority." [46]

NONE IS SO BLIND
AS HE WHO WILL NOT SEE

Let me warn you right now: You mustn't be surprised if your own pastor—your personal minister—does not see the truth of God's seventh-day Sabbath. Why not? Because God Himself forewarned that some pastors and priests who pretend to serve Him will depart from His Word and refuse to see the clear light of His Sabbath truth:

- "Her PRIESTS have violated My Law, and have profaned Mine holy things: they have put no difference between the holy and the profane, neither have they showed difference between the unclean and the clean, and have HID their EYES from my Sabbaths, and I am profaned among them." [47]

- "The PRIEST'S lips should keep knowledge, and they [the people] should seek the Law at his mouth: for he is the messenger of the Lord of hosts. But ye [corrupt, unfaithful priests] are departed out of the way; ye have caused many to STUMBLE at the Law. . . . Ye have not kept My ways, but have been PARTIAL in the Law." [48]

- "Woe be unto the PASTORS that destroy and scatter the sheep of My pasture! saith the Lord. Therefore thus saith the Lord God of Israel against the pastors that feed My people; Ye have scattered My flock, and driven them away, and have not visited them: behold, I will visit upon you the evil of your doings, saith the Lord." [49]

- "My people hath been lost sheep: their SHEPHERDS have caused them to go astray, . . . they have forgotten their RESTINGplace." [50]

These indictments are terribly true today. Ezekiel's expression "HID their eyes from My Sabbaths" means purposely turning away, as we hide our eyes from the sun. I know pastors who close their eyes to plain Bible evidence and stubbornly declare, "I can't see it." Jesus urgently warned about *the BLIND leading the blind!* [51] The Jews in His day were led by the blind, and—like the tragic followers of Jim Jones and the Heaven's Gate suicide cult—many are being led by the blind today. We must study for ourselves and make up our own minds in the light of Bible evidence!

Sabbath-Keepers Are in GOOD COMPANY

The mature Christian is willing to stand alone. He doesn't bow to group pressure. But though his faith is not dependent upon numbers, he may find it comforting to know that—viewed in the proper perspective—he's never really in a minority. Though it may appear that faithful, loyal Christians are an absurd minority in this present evil world, they're really always in the majority.

You see, from God's point of view, His faithful children are part of His universal family in heaven and earth, joined to those unnumbered heavenly beings who have never fallen into sin. Human language cannot express, nor finite brains conceive, the mind-boggling infinitude of God's heavenly kingdom—but the Bible writers try to convey what God has shown them. John the Revelator says, "I heard the voice of MANY angels round about the throne . . . and the number of them was *ten thousand TIMES ten thousand, and thousands of thousands.*" [52]

A marvelous incident revealing God's universal majority is recorded about the prophet Elisha and his servant, who once were surrounded by a hostile army of overwhelming force:

> "And when the servant of the man of God arose early and went out, there was an army, surrounding the city with horses and chariots. And his servant said to him, 'Alas, my master! What shall we do?' So he answered, 'Do not fear, for those who are with US are more than those who are with THEM.' And Elisha prayed, and said, 'Lord, I pray, *open his eyes* that he may see.' Then the Lord opened the eyes of the young man, and he saw. And behold, the mountain was FULL of horses and chariots of fire [innumerable *angel armies*] all around Elisha." [53]

So Wendell Phillips was quite correct when he gave this inspired and inspiring thought: "**ONE on God's side is a MAJORITY.**" The one who honors God by loyally keeping His day of rest and worship is obviously in good company, for *ALL the faithful of the entire Bible* observed the seventh-day Sabbath according to God's Word!

Beginning with Adam and Eve, call the roll of God's people—Noah, Abraham, Moses, David, Daniel, ALL the great heroes of the Old Testament—

and you'll find them to be faithful Sabbath-keepers. The same is equally true of New Testament heroes, as seen below.

JESUS Kept the Sabbath

Centuries before Christ's birth as the Son of man, Inspiration foretold His attitude toward the Law of God. In one of the prophecies of the Messiah He said, "I DELIGHT to do Thy will, O My God; Thy Law is within My heart."[54]

Jesus is our Example in all things. We can safely follow the divine pattern set by Him. And that pattern includes Sabbath-keeping. Six days a week we'd find the little carpenter shop where He and Joseph labored buzzing with activity. But on Saturday we'd find it—CLOSED! Two thousand years ago in the humble village of Nazareth, Jesus would be ready for the Sabbath when it came at the end of each week: tools were carefully put away, shavings were swept from the floor. He would join the people as they all walked toward a conspicuous building in the center of town. The carpenter's Son would even participate in the worship service, as the Record shows:

> "And He came to Nazareth, where He had been brought up: and, as HIS CUSTOM was, He went into the synagogue on the Sabbath day, and stood up for to read."[55]

Why did He close His shop—why did He worship so faithfully on this special day that it became "His custom"? Was He simply conforming to the traditions of His culture, merely following the Jewish crowd in which He found Himself? Hardly! Our Lord was neither an opportunist nor a legalist. Christ repeatedly rebuked the Jewish leaders who had heaped man-made restrictions on His Law.[56] The uninspired, unscriptural traditions of the Jews had turned what *God* designed to be a *blessing* into a burden no one could bear.

Some would suggest that Christ kept the Sabbath only because He found Himself in a Jewish culture. But is this true? Such reasoning carries us to the logical conclusion that Christ would have adopted pagan habits in a pagan culture, but that's absurd and blasphemous. Our Lord was NOT a mere conformist, bowing to the expediency of "When in Rome, do as the Romans do." On the contrary, many see Christ as a courageous Revolutionary from heaven—and His followers were described as those who "*turned the world upside down*"![57]

When the Pharisees were outraged that Jesus repeatedly healed on the Sabbath, the Lord fearlessly rebuked their hypocrisy and taught that "It is lawful to do good on the Sabbath"[58]—men should never rest from doing good. God's Law had become encumbered and encrusted with regulations never found in the Ten Commandments, and Jesus made no pretense of following *those* man-made rules. But Jesus could truthfully say: "I have KEPT My Father's commandments." [59] And that includes the Sabbath.

Jesus' FOLLOWERS Kept the Sabbath
Even AFTER the Crucifixion & Resurrection

The Bible shows that not only Jesus honored the Sabbath by His personal example, but His closest followers—those who knew Him best—did also. The Bible confirms that His followers observed the Sabbath even after His crucifixion:

> "It was Preparation Day [Friday], and the Sabbath was about to begin. The women who had come with Jesus from Galilee followed Joseph and saw the tomb and how His body was laid in it. Then they went home and prepared spices and perfumes. But they rested on the Sabbath in obedience to the commandment." [60]

Several important points can be gained from this text. In the first place, these women were from the inner circle of Christ's disciples—if Jesus had had any instruction, any plans about changing the day of rest, He surely would have shared those plans with His closest followers.

Secondly, it's obvious that our Lord had given NO such instruction, for this verse tells us that these women—even after Christ's crucifixion—"rested on the Sabbath in obedience to the commandment"! Which commandment? The Fourth Commandment, of course, regarding Sabbath observance. God's moral law was never nailed to the Cross. [61]

Furthermore, the apostles faithfully kept the Sabbath of God many years AFTER Jesus' resurrection and ascension to heaven. For example, consider the practice of Paul, the great "apostle to the Gentiles." He was hand-picked by God to minister specifically to the Gentile—or non-Jewish—world. The Lord told Paul, "I have set you to be a light for the Gentiles." [62] And Paul himself, after being so soundly rejected by the Jewish brethren he loved, declared: "Lo, we turn to the Gentiles." [63]

When Paul spoke of "the prophets which are read every Sabbath day," [64] he was calling the seventh day the "Sabbath" more than a decade and half AFTER Jesus' death and resurrection. And Paul, as a faithful Christian and leader of Christians, kept the Sabbath every week. We read: "Paul and his company . . . came to ANTIOCH . . . went into the synagogue on the Sabbath day," and took advantage of the opportunity to preach the gospel. [65]

The next few verses are especially revealing:

"And when the Jews were gone out of the synagogue, the GENTILES besought that these words might be preached to them the next Sabbath. . . . And the next Sabbath day came almost the WHOLE CITY together to hear the Word of God." [66]

Do you see what this means? These Scriptures provide positive proof:

    (1) that Paul was observing the seventh-day Sabbath and

    (2) that he was not keeping Sunday in a religious way.

For if his practice had been to worship on Sunday, he would have told the Gentile inquirers, "Look, you don't have to wait till next Sabbath to hear me preach. I'm holding worship services tomorrow, on the first day of the week."

But Paul told them no such thing—though this would have been a golden opportunity to put in a good word for Sunday sacredness IF the Lord had wanted to change the day of worship. Your Bible says it was "the next Sabbath day" that the whole city gathered "to hear the Word of God"! Bible facts like these speak more loudly than anything men may say, don't you think?

Furthermore, "they came to THESSALONICA, where there was a synagogue of the Jews: And Paul, as his MANNER was, went in unto them, and three Sabbath days reasoned with them out of the Scriptures, . . . and some of them believed, . . . and of the Greeks [Gentiles] a great multitude." [67] A devout Christian, Paul felt it a privilege to follow His Lord's example in all things: Just as Christ kept the Sabbath "as His CUSTOM was," Paul kept the Sabbath "as his MANNER was." [68] Both obeyed all of God's commandments and provide us a good example.

"After these things Paul . . . came to CORINTH. . . . And he reasoned in the synagogue EVERY Sabbath, and persuaded the Jews AND the Greeks. . . . And he continued there a year and six months, teaching the Word of God among them." [69] Remember that Paul was a self-supporting missionary and worked to cover his own expenses. Verse 3 says he "wrought"—or worked— as a tentmaker for his trade. But he didn't work on Sabbath. The Divine Record says that Paul religiously kept "*every* Sabbath." And since he stayed there "a year and six months," we have here a record of Paul keeping the seventh-day Sabbath for **78** consecutive weeks in Corinth alone!

Some try to argue that "The only reason Paul went to the house of worship on God's holy day was so that he'd have a chance to reach the Jews." But we've already seen that Paul understood his calling as being uniquely "the Apostle to the Gentiles." Besides, Paul kept the Sabbath whether or NOT there was a Jewish synagogue in town. We've already seen examples of Paul's Sabbath-keeping in cities like Antioch, Thessalonica, and Corinth. But take the example of "PHILIPPI, which is the foremost city of that part of Macedonia, a [Roman] colony. And we [Paul and Luke] were staying in that city for some days. And on the Sabbath day we went out of the city to the riverside, where prayer was customarily made; and we sat down and spoke to the women who met there." [70]

Here, you see, was a Roman colony, a Gentile city with no Jewish synagogue. Thus if Paul's only motive in keeping the seventh day had really been to meet with Jews, as some would have us believe, then he could have skipped this Sabbath and worked on his tents. But he didn't. God says that Paul found a quiet spot where he could worship outside the city, a place where prayer was customarily made. There, before the day was over, he baptized a Gentile woman and her family. [71] Paul kept the Christian Sabbath by doing God's work, not his own.

Jesus Himself clinches the case for us that His followers *were* keeping the Sabbath—and were *supposed* to keep it—long AFTER the Cross. Please note:

Christ foretold the destruction of Jerusalem nearly forty years before it happened, declaring that the city would be so completely devastated that even the buildings of the Temple would be demolished, with not one huge stone left standing upon another. [72] This prophecy itself is tremendously impressive, since it deals with events that were to take place long after the Lord's crucifixion, resurrection, and ascension to heaven.

He warned His disciples that when they saw armies drawing near, they must immediately "flee into the mountains." Then, in a most significant statement, He added, "But pray ye that your flight be not in the winter, neither on the Sabbath day." [73]

Why pray this? Because it would be a hardship to flee in winter. And the fear, commotion, and travel involved in fleeing would be inappropriate on the Sabbath day. Christ's followers were to pray they might be able to keep the Sabbath as a day of rest and worship, because His holy day would STILL be just as sacred then as it was when He spoke these words on the Mount of Olives.

Thus Christ gave no hint that His Sabbath would be abolished or changed, even when He discussed it in connection with an event to happen far in the future!

So forceful is this statement from the Lord's own lips that it hits a nerve in some people, so they try to weaken it by claiming that Christ said it only because He knew the city gates would be closed on the Sabbath, making it difficult or impossible for Christians to flee on that day. The Devil hopes this argument will sound plausible enough to be accepted, but the FACTS contradict it.

1. In the first place, Christ, who knows the end from the beginning, knew that the Jews would go out through the opened city gates to battle the Romans even on the Sabbath, as recorded by the contemporary Jewish historian Josephus. [74]

2. Secondly, Jesus warned even those "in the field," [75] "those outside the city," [76] or "out in the country" [77] to pray as He told them—yet no gates or walls would hinder their flight from those areas.

3. Finally, the command to flee is addressed to "them which be in Judea." [78] The land of the Jews called the province of Judea was not surrounded by walls and gates! Yet Christians in all Judea were to pray that their flight would not be on the Sabbath day! Could Christ have given clearer evidence that He viewed the Sabbath as different from other days? [79]

WHAT WAS "NAILED TO THE CROSS"?

A passage often MISUSED [80] by some to prove that the seventh-day Sabbath was abolished, "nailed to the cross" by the dying Savior, is **Colossians 2:14-17**, which speaks of Christ . . .

> "Blotting out the handwriting of ordinances that was against us, which was contrary to us, and took it out of the way, nailing it to His cross. . . . Let no man therefore judge you in meat, or in drink, or in respect of an holyday, or of the new moon, or of the sabbath days: which are a shadow of things to come; but the body is of Christ."

Though a quick glance at this passage leads one to think that here indeed is Bible evidence that Christ did do away with the Sabbath, careful analysis shows that Paul was clearly referring to the CEREMONIAL laws of the Old Testament and NOT to the seventh-day Sabbath at all. The following Bible reasons will appeal to any unprejudiced reader:

REASON #1

First of all, Paul says that Christ succeeded in "blotting out" something, "nailing it to His cross." What was that something? It was "the handwriting of **ORDINANCES**." This statement echoes Paul's words in Ephesians 2:15, where he says that Christ "ABOLISHED in His flesh the enmity, even the law of commandments contained in ORDINANCES."

So if we can identify "the law of commandments contained in ORDINANCES," we'll know what was abolished, blotted out, and nailed to the cross. The Bible makes that identification for us, so we needn't take the mere word of any man on this matter.

For example, the Lord gave careful instructions for the Passover ceremony: His people were to kill a male lamb, roast it and eat it, but sprinkle its blood upon the door posts of their houses. [81] God says:

> "Now the blood shall be a sign for you on the houses where you are. And when I see the blood, I will PASS OVER you; and the plague shall not be on you to destroy you when I strike the land of Egypt. So this day shall be to you a memorial. . . . You shall keep it as a feast by an everlasting ORDINANCE. . . . You shall observe the Feast of Unleavened Bread, . . . you shall observe this day throughout your generations as an everlasting ORDINANCE. . . . You shall observe this thing as an ORDINANCE for you and your sons forever. . . . This is the ORDINANCE of the Passover." [82]

God further describes the lamb which His people were to sacrifice:

> "They shall leave none of it until morning, nor break one of its bones. According to all the ORDINANCES of the Passover they shall keep it. . . . And if a stranger dwells among you, and would keep the Lord's Passover, he must do so according to the RITE of the Passover and according to its CEREMONY; you shall have one ORDINANCE, both for the stranger and the native of the land." [83]

You can see from this statement that those ordinances had to do with RITES and CEREMONIES. The Bible says, "The FIRST covenant had . . . ORDINANCES of divine service." [84] For the word *ordinances,* the margin of the King James Version says "ceremonies," showing that this was part of the CEREMONIAL law—not God's MORAL Law of Ten Commandments. It speaks of those regulations "which stood only in MEATS and DRINKS, and divers[e] washings, and carnal ORDINANCES, imposed on them until the time of reformation. But Christ being come . . ." [85] Here again, on the word *ordinances,* the King James Version margin says "rites or ceremonies."

So "ordinances" refers to rites, rituals, and ceremonies governing divine worship service, like "the ordinances of the altar." [86] Obviously, the entire CEREMONIAL law, with its ordinances of the Passover, *etc.,* was abolished when Jesus, the true "Lamb of God," [87] was sacrificed on the cross. Paul himself says that Christians need not observe that ritual, "For even *Christ our Passover* is sacrificed for us." [88] It is those RITES and CEREMONIES, therefore, that Paul means were "nailed to the cross."

REASON #2

Secondly, notice that Colossians 2:14 says it was "the **HANDWRITING** of ordinances" which was "blotted out." Here's another clear point of identification pointing inescapably to the ceremonial law. An important distinction must be made between the Moral Law of Ten Commandments and the ceremonial law of ordinances and rituals. [89] God Himself engraved the Moral Law on two tables of STONE with His own finger:

> "He gave unto Moses, when He had made an end of communing with Him upon Mt. Sinai, two tables of testimony, tables of STONE, written with the finger of GOD. . . . And the tables were the work of God, and the writing was the writing of God, graven upon the tables." [90]

In contrast to the *Moral* Law of Ten Commandments, which God Himself engraved on stone, is God's *ceremonial* law of ordinances, which Moses wrote by hand in a BOOK:

> "MOSES wrote down this law. . . . After Moses finished writing in a BOOK the words of this law from beginning to end, he gave this command to the Levites who carried the ark of the covenant of the LORD: 'Take this BOOK of the law and place it *beside* the ark.'" [91]

Did you notice another distinction between the Ten Commandments and the book of ordinances? The verse above informs us that Moses' handwritten "book of the law" of ordinances was put "BESIDE the ark," into a holder or bracket on the side of the ark. But God told Moses to put the sacred tables of the Ten Commandments INTO the ark itself:

> "The Lord said unto me, . . . I will write on the tables . . . and thou shalt put them IN the ark. . . . And I [Moses]. . . put the tables IN the ark." [92] "And he [Moses] took and put the testimony [margin: "tables of the Law"] INTO the ark." [93] "There was nothing IN the ark save the two tables of stone, which Moses put there at Horeb [Sinai]." [94]

The TEN COMMANDMENTS are UNIVERSAL and PERMANENT, applying to all mankind for all time. They were engraved by God's finger in stone. The ORDINANCES, on the other hand, were of LIMITED and TEMPORARY application, pointing forward as they did to Christ. They were handwritten by Moses in a book—they were the "handwriting of ordinances" which Paul says were "blotted out" when Christ died on Calvary's cross.

One last thought: It would be an embarrassing, illogical slip called a mixed metaphor to say that anything engraved in STONE could be *"blotted out"*—any more than it could be *"nailed* to the cross"! A brilliant writer like Paul would hardly be guilty of such an error. But the *parchments penned by Moses* in recording God's ordinances could be both BLOTTED OUT and NAILED in beautiful word-pictures from an inspired writer.

REASON #3

Thirdly, note that Colossians 2:14 says this "handwriting of ordinances" which Christ took away "was **AGAINST** us . . . **CONTRARY TO** us."

That's exactly how Moses referred to his handwritten book of ceremonial laws, when he said to the Levite priests: "Take this Book of the Law and place it beside the ark of the covenant of the LORD your God. There it will remain as a witness AGAINST you." [95]

But that's NOT the way God refers to His Ten Commandments—they were never "AGAINST" us but were given "FOR our GOOD," as we read: "The Lord commanded us to do all these statutes, to fear the Lord our God, FOR our GOOD always, that He might preserve us alive, as it is at this day." [96]

God in His infinite wisdom knows what is for our good, just as loving parents tell their children not to play with matches or with evil companions. "Father knows best," even on a human level. That's why Paul, speaking of the Ten Commandments, says: "The law is holy, and the commandment HOLY, and JUST, and GOOD." [97]

God's holy law of Ten Commandments is like a wall of protection, guarding us from the evil in this world. Just as the commandment against adultery keeps our marriage pure and protects us from the evils of divorce and disease, so each of the other nine commandments protects us from deadly evils. Though Satan craftily whispers that "They're restrictive . . . cramping your style . . . AGAINST you . . . ," they're really totally FOR us—"for our GOOD always"!

REASON #4

In the fourth place, Colossians 2:16 clearly reveals that Paul in this passage is dealing with CEREMONIAL laws, not moral principles, when he speaks of "**MEAT**, or . . . **DRINK**."

The Bible says it was the first covenant that had "ORDINANCES of divine service . . . which stood only in MEATS and DRINKS, and divers washings, and carnal ORDINANCES, imposed on them." [98]

You see, all the different convocations or FEASTS of the Lord had very specific "meat offerings" and "drink offerings" spelled out in Moses' "handwriting of ordinances." For example, "The fourteenth day of the first month is the Passover of the Lord. And in the fifteenth day of this month is the FEAST: seven days shall unleavened bread be eaten." [99] Other details of the week-long convocation are given, particularly specifying the "MEAT offering" and "DRINK offering." [100]

Moses then discusses other convocations, such as "the day of the firstfruits," the Feast of Trumpets, and other feasts or festivals, [101] again mentioning the specific MEAT and DRINK offerings. These ceremonial "MEAT offerings" and "DRINK offerings" played so large a part in Israel's worship rites that they're referred to more than 100 times in the Old Testament. In the two chapters listed below alone, we find the following MULTIPLE references to meat and/or drink offerings:

NUMBERS 28 – verses 5, 7, 8, 9, 10, 13, 14, 15, 20, 24, 26, 28, 31.
NUMBERS 29 – verses 3, 6, 9, 11, 14, 16, 18, 19, 21, 22, 24, 25, 27, 28, 30, 31, 33, 34, 37, 38, and 39. Verse 39 says, "These things shall ye do unto the Lord in your set FEASTS."

"These things" pertaining to MEAT and DRINK obviously are *ceremonial* and have nothing to do with God's *moral* law of Ten Commandments, which doesn't even mention them. So when Paul told Christians at Colossi: "Let no man therefore judge you in MEAT, or in DRINK," he referred to false Judaizing teachers who mistakenly insisted on the binding claims of the Jewish CEREMONIAL system.

REASON #5

Colossians 2:16 says also, "Let no man therefore judge you . . . in respect of an **holyday**, or of the **new moon**, or of the **sabbath days**." To what was Paul referring? Consider the following:

HOLYDAY – The ceremonial ordinances that Moses wrote contained commandments for observing various holy days—Passover, Pentecost, the Feast of Unleavened Bread, the Feast of Tabernacles, the Day of Atonement.

NEW MOON – In the Jewish economy, one of the ordinances required the observance of the FIRST DAY of each month, or NEW MOON day. God told His people to fashion two silver trumpets and to blow them on various occasions (for assembling the congregation, for alarm, for going into battle, *etc.*). And He said: "Also at your times of rejoicing—your appointed feasts and NEW MOON festivals—you are to sound the trumpets . . . before your God."[102] God also commanded: "On the FIRST of every month, present to the Lord a burnt offering of two young bulls, one ram and seven male lambs. . . . This is the monthly burnt offering to be made at each NEW MOON during the year." [103]

SABBATH DAYS – Besides THE Sabbath, that is, the weekly seventh-day Sabbath of the Fourth Commandment, the CEREMONIAL law commanded several other "sabbath days." These were ANNUAL sabbaths which could fall on any given day of the week (Monday, Tuesday, Thursday, *etc.*), just as our annual holidays like Valentine's Day or the Fourth of July fall on a different day of the week each year.

The PLURAL form used here could indicate that Paul had these ceremonial "sabbath days" in mind rather than THE seventh-day "Sabbath of the Lord" given in the Ten Commandments,[104] but this is not conclusive. What we do know is that in connection with the various annual feasts/festivals were certain *ceremonial rest days or sabbaths* listed in Leviticus 23. Note the clear distinction your Bible makes between "THE Sabbath of the Lord," designated by the *definite* article *the,* and the ANNUAL rest days, designated by the *indefinite* article—"A sabbath."

God begins Leviticus 23 by emphasizing the weekly, holy Sabbath of the Decalogue: "And the Lord spake unto Moses, saying, . . . Six days shall work be done: but the seventh day is THE Sabbath of rest, an holy convocation; ye shall do no work therein: it is THE Sabbath of the LORD in all your dwellings." [105]

Then, for the rest of Leviticus 23, He turns to the CEREMONIAL ordinances: "These are the FEASTS of the Lord, even holy convocations, which ye shall proclaim in their seasons." [106] Annual feasts are listed:

- "the Lord's Passover" .... verse 5

- "the Feast of Unleavened Bread" ...... verse 6

- "fifty days"—Pentecost .... verses 15-16

- "Day of Atonement"—*Yom Kippur* .... verse 27

- "the Feast of Tabernacles" .... verse 34

Each of these annual sacred feasts had rest days which were ANNUAL sabbaths—distinct from the WEEKLY seventh-day Sabbath—which could fall on ANY day of the week. [107] Of those annual rest days Moses specifically wrote: "Ye shall do no servile work therein." [108]

But those CEREMONIAL sabbaths, the Bible says, were "BESIDE THE Sabbaths of the Lord," or "in ADDITION to the regular Sabbaths." [109] In stark contrast to the weekly Sabbath which God calls "THE Sabbath of the Lord," the annual rest days were simply called "A sabbath . . . A sabbath of rest . . . A sabbath . . . A sabbath." [110]

So Paul's reminder to the Colossians that the earlier observance of "holydays, new moons, and sabbath days" was abolished does NOT mean that any part of God's moral law of Ten Commandments was cancelled.

REASON #6

Colossians 2:17 closes this passage by saying that those things Paul was discussing "are a **SHADOW** of **things to COME**; but the **BODY** is of Christ."

This final statement clinches our case that Paul was clearly and consistently referring to that law of *rites* and *ceremonies* which FORESHADOWED and pointed forward to the good "things to come" of the gospel. All the blood shed by every sacrificial lamb pointed forward to "the Lamb of God [Jesus] who takes away the sin of the world." [111]

The writer of the Book of Hebrews makes this fact very clear when he says, in almost the same language used in the Colossian passage,

> "For the [ceremonial] law, having a **SHADOW of** the good **things to COME**, and not the very image of the things, can never with these same SACRIFICES, which they offer continually year by year, make those who approach perfect. . . . For it is not possible that the blood of bulls and goats could take away sins. Therefore, when He came into the world, He said, . . . 'A **BODY** You have prepared for Me.' . . . We have been sanctified through the offering of the **BODY** of Jesus Christ once for all." [112]

This makes clear that the animal sacrifices which they offered **foreshadowed** the offering of the **BODY** of Christ on the cross. Those ceremonial ordinances pointed FORWARD to "the good things to COME" in the form of Jesus. But this phrase could not possibly describe the seventh-day Sabbath, for that memorial points not FORWARD to Christ's death on the cross but BACKWARD to Creation Week in honor of Jesus Christ, our Creator. [113]

And God's last call to a dying world, the Three Angels' Messages of Revelation,[114] also admonishes us to worship God as CREATOR: "Worship Him that MADE heaven, and earth, and the sea, and the fountains of waters." [115]

We've analyzed this passage, illuminating it by the spotlight of Scripture. We see at least six sound reasons why this passage from Paul cannot be used to support the teaching that God's Sabbath of the Fourth Commandment is no longer to be obeyed by Christians.

Several of the world's most respected Bible scholars have reached this very same conclusion. Witness a few samples:

- Adam Clarke, a Methodist, said: "There is NO intimation here that the *Sabbath* was done away, or that its moral use was superseded, by the introduction of Christianity. . . . *Remember the Sabbath day, to keep it holy,* is a command of perpetual obligation, and can never be superseded but by the final termination of time." [116]

- Dwight L. Moody, founder of Chicago's Moody Bible Institute, stated: "The [Ten] Commandments did not originate with Moses, nor were they done away with when the Mosaic Law was fulfilled in Christ, and many of its CEREMONIES and regulations abolished. . . . I honestly believe that this commandment [the Fourth Commandment of the Sabbath] is just as binding today as it ever was. I have talked with men who have said it has been abrogated, but they have never been able to point to any place in the Bible where God repealed it. When Christ was on earth, He did nothing to set it aside; He freed it from the traces under which the scribes and Pharisees had put it, and gave it its true place. . . . The Sabbath was binding in EDEN, and it has been in force ever since. . . . How can men claim that this one Commandment has been done away with when they will admit that the other nine are still binding?" [117]

- The classic commentary by Jamieson, Fausset, and Brown noted that the *annual ceremonial* sabbaths "of the day of atonement and feast of tabernacles have come to an end with the Jewish services to which they belonged," but "the *weekly* Sabbath rests on a more permanent foundation, having been instituted in Paradise to commemorate the completion of creation in six days." [118]

- Noted Presbyterian commentator Albert Barnes speaks for many honest theologians when he declares: "There is NO evidence from this passage that he [Paul] would teach that there was no obligation to observe any holy time, for there is not the slightest reason to believe that he meant to teach that one of the Ten Commandments had ceased to be binding on mankind. . . . He had his eye on the great number of days which were observed by the Hebrews as *festivals,* as a part of the *ceremonial* and typical law, and NOT to the *moral* law, or the Ten Commandments. No part of the moral law—no one of the Ten Commandments—could be spoken of as 'a shadow' of good things to come.' These Commandments are, from the nature of moral law, of PERPETUAL and UNIVERSAL application." [119]

One last point should be enough to settle the question of Colossians 2:16-17. We should realize that IF Paul had intended to announce that the seventh-day Sabbath was no longer of any consequence, surely this news would have created quite a stir, not merely in Colossae but in other cities. The argument from silence is not a strong argument, but as copies of Paul's letter were certainly made, and these copies were taken to other churches and read, the SHOCK of the believers in learning that Christ's death on the cross abolished the Sabbath would have been so great that the ensuing discussions would have been recorded—as were those regarding circumcision, idol worship, fornication, and other matters (see Acts 15).

But Paul's letter was NOT a bombshell. It sent NO shock waves through the community of believers. People apparently understood that Paul was speaking of *Jewish* rituals and festivals involving meat and drink, annual ceremonial sabbaths, and special days governed by the new moon—NOT abolishing the weekly Sabbath of God's Ten Commandments. [120]

The Sabbath Was NEVER Changed

Some people believe that Christ abolished God's Law because that's what they've been TOLD. Preachers, priests, and pastors tell people many unscriptural things like that. But the truth about God's holy day will be found in God's holy Book. In His magnificent "Sermon on the Mount," Jesus said very plainly:

> "Think not that I am come to *destroy* the Law, or the prophets: I am NOT come to destroy, but to fulfill. For verily I say unto you, Till heaven and earth pass, *one jot* or *one tittle* shall in no wise pass from the law, till ALL be fulfilled. Whosoever therefore shall break ONE of these least commandments, and shall teach men so, he shall be called the least in the kingdom of heaven: but whosoever shall do and teach them shall be called great in the kingdom of heaven." [121]

"THINK NOT," says Jesus, "that I am come to destroy the Law." In other words, don't even *think* it, let alone *teach* it to others as a doctrine. A "jot" or a "tittle" in Hebrew writing is like the crossing of a "t" or dotting of an "i" in English. And Jesus says that not even this much shall be expunged from His Law "till heaven and earth pass" away! I haven't noticed heaven and earth passing away yet, have you?

But some religious teachers so completely oppose God's Law (the technical term for their attitude is "antinomian"—from the Greek *anti* meaning "against" + *nomos* meaning "law") that they desperately grasp at the word "fulfill" in Jesus' words quoted above and tell us that when Jesus fulfilled the Law He abolished it! But that's not what the word *fulfill* means. Christ came to *fill* the Law *full* of meaning by faithfully KEEPING it—the Savior acting as Substitute for all of us who slip and fall so many times.

Those who claim that "fulfill" means to *destroy* presume to put these words into Christ's mouth: "I came not to destroy [the Law] but to *destroy* [it]"! But that distortion of meaning should not deceive us. We don't cancel traffic laws by fulfilling them. We don't cancel a contract by fulfilling our part of the agreement—instead, we validate it. And that's what the Savior did in every act of His obedient life. At Jesus' baptism, when John the Baptist humbly hesitated to "wash away the sins" of the Sinless One, Jesus encouraged him by saying, "Thus it becometh us to *fulfill* all righteousness." [122] Was Jesus suggesting that all righteousness be *abolished*? No—He was validating the act of baptism for us all.

If *fulfill* means to nullify or abolish, then we nullify and abolish the law of Christ if we bear another man's burdens, for Paul says: "Bear ye another's burdens, and so *fulfill* the law of Christ." [123] Jesus KNEW some would mistake and misinterpret His words, so in His immortal Sermon on the Mount He emphatically and explicitly stated: "I am NOT come to destroy."

Our precious Lord had ample opportunity to state that the Sabbath was done away with, or that it was just for Jews to observe, or to voice any of the other arguments some men put forth against the Sabbath—but He did not. As we would expect, He never said *anything* against the Law or the Sabbath He Himself had given.

No LAW, No SIN

If it were *true* that Jesus abolished the Ten Commandments by His death on the cross, then it would be all right not only to break the rule of Sabbath observance, it would ALSO be perfectly all right to lie, to steal, to commit adultery, and all the rest. In fact, if there were no Law, there could be no such thing as SIN, for the Law of God is what *defines* sin. "Whosoever committeth sin transgresseth also the Law: for sin IS the transgression of the Law." [124] As King "Saul said unto Samuel, I have sinned: for I have transgressed the commandment of the Lord." [125]

The Bible makes plain that "where NO LAW is, there is NO TRANSGRESSION," for "SIN is not imputed when there is NO LAW." [126] So if the antinomian argument is true—if in fact God's Law has been abolished—then we have **NO SIN** and therefore **NO NEED of a Savior.** Few of us need three guesses to name the author of such a diabolical doctrine!

The function of God's Law is to point out sin in our lives—it creates a conscious awareness of sin. "I had *not known* sin, but by the Law," Paul says, "for by the Law is the knowledge of sin." [127] The Ten Commandments spell out God's standard and show us how He wants us to live. When we break that standard, we're driven to the Savior for forgiveness and salvation. But we'd NEED no forgiveness IF there were no Law to break.

CHRIST'S DEATH PROVES
GOD'S LAW IS STILL IN EFFECT

The sacrificial death of Christ is not only the greatest demonstration to the universe of God's LOVE, it's also the clearest evidence that God's Law is still very much in force on Planet Earth. As a matter of fact, if God had intended to abolish His Law, Jesus need not have died. You see, God says that "sin is the transgression of [His] law" and "the wages of sin is DEATH." [128]

So when mankind broke God's Law and sinned, God had only three alternatives:

1. He could make MAN pay the penalty of the broken Law and execute him. But then God would have to kill the whole human race, "For ALL have sinned, and come short of the glory of God." [129]

2. Or He could ABOLISH His Law, the instrument which defines sin for mankind, so that by lowering His standard and watering down His requirements He could make it possible for man to avoid sin and hence its penalty. But that would undermine the government of the entire universe, for who in heaven would want to live next door to a liar, idolator, or murderer? Besides, God's laws are not arbitrary requirements, like eating meat on Fridays, which can easily be changed. The eternal principles of God's Law are a virtual *transcript* of His *character* and can never be changed. [130] As long as God is God, it will be wrong to lie and kill. As long as God is honored as the Creator of heaven and earth, it will be wrong to bow down to lesser gods of wood or stone or to forget the day He told us to "Remember . . . "—the Sabbath memorial of Creation, the "birthday" of the world.

3. Or He could provide a SUBSTITUTIONARY death by offering the dear Son Himself to pay the price for sinful man and meet the demands of the broken Law. This solution—the only one of the three that allows God to exercise both His JUSTICE and His MERCY, the only one that allows God to save fallen man and keep His Law intact—is the one adopted by the infinitely wise God.

Finite men may think it would have been much easier, in a way, simply for God to have changed His Law. Easier, perhaps, but at the price of sacrificing the integrity of God's government, His authority, and the future security of the universe! We see the wisdom of God's loving choice. But we see also that IF God could conscientiously have lowered His standard and changed His Law, Jesus would NOT have NEEDED to die. This simple but sublime fact is the strongest argument that *God did NOT abolish His divine Law!*

POPULAR ATTACKS ON GOD'S LAW

Yet Satan persists in attacking God's Law and our allegiance to it. We must be alert and prepared to counter the Devil's arguments, "Lest Satan should get an advantage of us: for we are not ignorant of his devices." [131] Let's examine four of his most popular attacks currently in vogue.

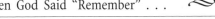

1. **Satan** says: "Forget about God's Law. All you need is to **have FAITH**."
   Your **Bible** says: "Do we then make void the Law through faith? God
   forbid: yea, we ESTABLISH the Law." [132] In other words, having faith
   does not annul God's Law. Just the opposite is true—only faithful believers will obey and establish the Law in their hearts, while unbelievers
   laugh at God's requirements.

2. **Satan** says: "Don't worry about God's Law. All you need is to **PRAY**."
   Your **Bible** says: "He that turneth away his ear from hearing the Law,
   even his PRAYER shall be ABOMINATION." [133] That's strong language,
   but those are God's words, not mine.

3. **Satan** says: "You don't have to keep God's Law—just **BELIEVE IN GOD**."
   Your **Bible** says: "Thou believest that there is one God; thou doest well:
   the DEVILS also believe, and tremble." [134] The devils *know* God is real—
   they lived with Him for eons of time before being expelled from
   heaven. [135] But they rebelled against His government and refused to love
   and obey Him. Are we any better than the devils if our belief is mere
   intellectual assent without commitment shown by loving obedience?

4. **Satan** says: "God's Law is unimportant. The vital thing is to **LOVE GOD**."
   Your **Bible** says: "This IS the love of God, that we KEEP His commandments: and His commandments are not grievous." [136] Jesus Himself says:
   "IF you love Me, KEEP My commandments. . . . He who has My commandments and keeps them, it is HE who loves Me." [137] Evidently the
   primary way God expects us to show our love for Him is by faithful
   obedience to His commands, which He says "are not grievous" or bur-
   densome.

The Devil, you see, is quite willing to resort to GOOD things like FAITH,
PRAYER, and LOVE to achieve his ultimate goal of undermining God's
government. He's even willing to focus our attention on a good thing like
Christ's resurrection if, by so doing, he can lead us to break God's Law on
the Sabbath. But whether his sly insinuations are WHISPERED in our ear or
SHOUTED from a pulpit, we must not forget our allegiance to our Creator /
Savior—and what His Book, the Bible, says about these things.

The Lord's discerning eye sees we lack that allegiance when we refuse to
obey His Ten Commandments—even if we engage in other seemingly
religious activities. "Behold, to OBEY is better than sacrifice." [138] *The TEST of
DISCIPLESHIP* is obedience, not lip service. Jesus says plainly: "Not every
one that SAITH unto Me, Lord, Lord, shall enter into the kingdom of heaven;
but he that DOETH the will of My Father which is in heaven. Many shall say

unto Me in that day [of Judgment], Lord, Lord, have we not prophesied in Thy name? and in Thy name have cast out devils? and in Thy name done many wonderful works? And then I will profess unto them, *I never knew you: Depart from Me, ye that work iniquity."* [139]

Those people—please note—had been at least nominal Christians. They called Christ "Lord," even though He says they didn't really do His will. But they never surrendered to Him as Lord and Master of their lives. They had never really been His disciples, His obedient followers. And so He utters the sad words that reflect the choice they made.

"But," someone may ask, "don't you think God is present with those who worship Him on Sunday?"

Well, if we want the right answer, we must ask the right question. And this is not the right question. Why not? Because the question is not: Is GOD good? Is HE loving? Is HE present with His people—good or bad—on *any* given day of the week? It's not GOD'S devotion or conduct which is at issue. It's OUR devotion and conduct which are subject to judgment. So we must ask instead:

- Did God make His command CLEAR as to the day of His choice?

- Are we WILLING to obey what God tells us to do?

- And if we're NOT willing, isn't it presumptuous to expect God's presence and blessing when we willingly, knowingly disobey the One we say is our Lord?

Is Law OPPOSED to Grace?

Some religious teachers boldly tell us that grace does away with God's Law and that anyone who is saved by grace need no longer obey the Law of God—or, as they often call it, "the law of Moses." They go so far as to claim that Christians are living under "the new dispensation" of grace, so the moral Law of Ten Commandments is utterly abolished and no longer binding. Wow! No wonder we see such lawlessness everywhere today!

The Bible text they use in teaching such an antinomian philosophy is Romans 6:14, in which Paul says: "Sin shall not have dominion over you: for *ye are not under the law, but under grace."* This wonderful text has a comforting message for all forgiven sinners, but it does NOT mean we have a license to sin!

The problem lies in the ambiguity of the phrase "under the Law," which has two possible meanings. We must distinguish between:

> "under [the **JURISDICTION** of] the Law"
> and
> "under [the **CONDEMNATION** of] the Law"

To be "under the JURISDICTION of the Law" means we're subject to the law and must obey it. Everyone in this country is under the jurisdiction of the laws of the United States. A person living in California is under the jurisdiction of the laws of that state, but he would not be subject to the laws of New York or Oklahoma.

On the other hand, "under the Law" may also mean to be "under the CONDEMNATION of the Law." When we *break* the Law, we as sinners fall under its condemnation and must *pay its penalty*. God's Word says, "Sin is the transgression of the Law," and the penalty or "wages of sin is DEATH." [140]

But this is where GRACE comes in.

The grace of God operates to FREE repentant sinners from the CONDEMNATION of the Law. Since Jesus died in the sinner's place, the death penalty is paid for all who accept Him as their Savior. Every sin they've ever committed is forgiven. At that moment they have a clean record on the Books of Heaven because they enjoy "the remission of sins that are PAST." [141] But they're still under the JURISDICTION of God's Law and may not break it without incurring sins in the FUTURE.

Happily, however, the good news of the gospel is that God's grace operates in BOTH areas in the lives of believers: not only to *cover* PAST sins by cancelling the condemnation of the Law but also to *prevent* FUTURE sins by helping us cope with the jurisdiction of the Law!

When we confront the jurisdiction of the Law and are tempted to sin, divine grace can empower us and strengthen us to resist and overcome the temptation. God promises that "We may obtain mercy, and GRACE to HELP in time of need." [142] Let's face it: We need more than just *forgiveness* for the PAST. We need *help* in our PRESENT time of need. I'd rather have help when I'm IN trouble than forgiveness after I've been in trouble, wouldn't you?

Christians who continue sinning after coming to Christ—either through human weakness or because they've bought the Devil's lie that God's Law was abolished—painfully *wound* Christ anew with every misdeed and bring reproach on the name "Christian." God says, "They crucify to themselves the Son of God afresh, and put Him to open shame." [143]

But God's ideal for His children is much higher than this. He wants to give us MORE than forgiveness for sin—He wants to give us VICTORY *OVER* sin! He wants to give us not just *PARDON for the past* but *POWER for the present* and future! He wants us to live so close to Christ that by His grace we'll live above whatever temptations the Devil may throw at us. Then Paul's words will be perpetually true in our lives: "There is therefore now NO CONDEMNATION to them which are in Christ Jesus, who walk not after the flesh, but after the Spirit." [144]

Thank God He doesn't run His universe in such a way as to give sinners a license to commit future sins! Would we feel safe even in heaven with those who felt they could sin with impunity? The libertine who claims he's free to break God's commandments is not living "under grace"—he's living in DISgrace! It's obvious that if there were no longer any Law in effect, no standard of righteousness, there could be no sin—just as no one could accuse us of breaking the rules in a game or sport if there were no rules. And if it were really true, as some claim, that grace did away with the JURISDICTION of God's Law, then we'd have no further NEED of grace.

But the great apostle Paul felt the constant, daily need of God's grace. "I die DAILY," says Paul, but "nevertheless I live; yet not I, but Christ liveth in me: and the life I now live in the flesh I live by the faith of the Son of God, who loved me, and gave Himself for me." [145] Paul's secret of victorious living is to die every day to his own selfish desires and weaknesses. But this would hardly be necessary IF the possibility of sinning against an ever-present Law did not exist.

Paul himself shows that such a possibility does exist, for in the very next verse after saying "Ye are not under the Law, but under grace," he asks: "What then? Shall we SIN, because we are not under the law, but under grace? God forbid"![146] Sin is still possible, for we're still under the Law's jurisdiction.

Moreover, the great God of the universe has a divine sense of justice, and in the day of judgment none will accuse Him of "CHANGING the RULES in the middle of the game." It's not true that men before the Cross had to keep the Ten Commandments whereas those of us living this side of Calvary are free from that obligation. God has no "double standard." Just as all men in all time will be JUDGED by the same divine standard of God's Law, so all men in all time will be and have been saved by GRACE through faith. Those living before the Cross had faith that sacrificing the innocent lamb would save them, and we living after the Cross have faith that Christ's great sacrifice will save us.

Grace is not a "new kid on the block," an afterthought of God, available only in the so-called "new dispensation." Paul, speaking of the very entrance of sin into the world by the disobedience of Adam and Eve, says: "Where sin abounded, GRACE did much more abound." [147] "For the GRACE of God that bringeth salvation hath appeared to ALL men." [148]

So it's not a question of *law OR grace.* It's a case of *law AND grace!* For law and grace, far from being antithetical rivals, are really complementary friends. Like husband and wife, they go together. Just one last point in this connection: The Law CANNOT SAVE us—it can only condemn us. We're SAVED only through the GRACE of God, but the Law serves to point out our sin and thus drives us to the arms of the loving Savior who offers His grace and forgiveness for our sin.

A simple analogy may illustrate the reciprocal, complementary functions of law and grace: Think of God's Law as a MIRROR [149] that reveals DIRT on our face (or SIN in our life) when we hold it up and look into it. [150] A perfect mirror cannot declare that a mechanic's face, smeared with grease and dirt, is clean. It's just as impossible for a violated Law to testify that its transgressor is guiltless. The Law cannot *save* us from our *sin* any more than we can *wash* our *face* with the mirror to remove the dirt it reveals! No, to wash our face (and cleanse our sin) we must use the SOAP of God's GRACE—and that will do the job!

You know, to *smash* the mirror wouldn't clean the mechanic's face, and neither can man's attempt to do away with the Law cleanse him from the stain of sin or pay the penalty for his transgression. We need not despise God's Law, for it is what tells us we need the Savior. Both Law *and* grace are needed, and when rightly understood they work in perfect harmony.

THE TWO COVENANTS

Some people—even ministers, who should know better—say, "Only the Old Covenant required obedience to the law of Ten Commandments. Today we live under the New Covenant and don't need to worry about law anymore." Bless their hearts, if people say *THAT,* they don't have the foggiest idea what the New Covenant is! For we'll see that God's Law is the basis of BOTH the Old and New Covenants.

A "covenant" is an agreement between two parties, but it's much more than a routine, casual contract. It's a solemn, even a sacred, exchange of pledges and promises such as bride and groom make to each other in the wedding ceremony. The Bible speaks of two covenants, the Old and the New.

The OLD COVENANT was made between God and Israel at Mount Sinai and was based upon the people's promise to keep the Ten Commandments. The people, not realizing their own weakness and sinful nature, quickly promised: "ALL that the Lord hath said, will we DO, and be obedient."[151] But within days they broke that promise as they danced around the golden calf, proving sinful man's inability to keep God's Law in his own strength.

Speaking of the NEW COVENANT, God says that Jesus is the

"Mediator of a better covenant, which was established on BETTER PROMISES. For if that first covenant had been faultless, then no place would have been sought for a second. Because finding fault with THEM [the people and their promises], He says: 'Behold, the days are coming,' says the Lord, 'when I will make a New Covenant with the house of Israel and with the house of Judah—not according to the [Old] covenant that I made with their fathers in the day when I took them by the hand to lead them out of the land of Egypt; because they did not continue in My covenant, and I disregarded them,' says the Lord."[152]

Some erroneously suppose that the Old Covenant was the moral Law, the Ten Commandments, and that when the New Covenant was ratified, the law was annulled and set aside. But the Old Covenant was NOT the Ten Commandment Law. It was, like all covenants, an agreement—in this case an agreement between God and the people regarding the keeping of His Law. It was ABOUT the keeping of the Ten Commandment Law, but it was NOT the Law itself. The Law was only the *subject* of the contract or agreement. (If I sign a contract agreeing to buy your house, we both know that *your house* is NOT the *contract.* Your house is simply the *subject* of our contract or agreement. And tearing up the contract will *not* destroy your house!)

God Himself explained His New Covenant in unmistakable terms:

"For THIS is the covenant that I will make with the house of Israel after those days, saith the Lord; I WILL PUT MY LAWS INTO THEIR MIND, AND WRITE THEM IN THEIR HEARTS: and I will be to them a God, and they shall be to Me a people."[153]

The New Testament writer here was quoting Jeremiah 31:31-33, which is cited below.

The sinner certainly *needs* a new heart, with God's Law inscribed within! At the risk of contradicting the *Guinness Book of World Records,* I must say that Dr. Christiaan Barnard was not the first to make a successful HEART TRANSPLANT—God was. Note these verses:

- **Jeremiah 24:7** – "I will give them an heart to know Me, that I am the Lord: and they shall be My people, and I will be their God."

- **Ezekiel 11:19-20** – "I will give them one heart, and I will put a new spirit within you; and I will take the STONY heart OUT of their flesh, and I will give them an heart of FLESH: That they may WALK in My statutes, and KEEP Mine ordinances, and DO them: and they shall be My people, and I will be their God."

- **Ezekiel 36:26-27** – "A new heart also will I give you, and a new spirit will I put within you: and I will take away the STONY heart out of your flesh, and I will give you an heart of FLESH. And I will put My Spirit within you, and cause you to WALK in My statutes, and ye shall KEEP My judgments, and DO them."

- **Jeremiah 31:31-33** – "Behold, the days come, saith the Lord, that I will make a New Covenant with the house of Israel, and with the house of Judah: Not according to the [Old] covenant that I made with their fathers in the day that I took them by the hand to bring them out of the land of Egypt; which My covenant they brake although I was an husband unto them, saith the Lord. But THIS shall be the [New] covenant that I will make with the house of Israel; after those days, saith the Lord, I will put MY LAW in their inward parts, and WRITE it in their HEARTS; and will be their God, and they shall be My people."

The Old Covenant's weakness was its PROMISES. Man's side of the agreement was weak in that he could not do what he'd promised to do. He hadn't learned that without God's strength he could do nothing.

The New Covenant's strength is being "established upon BETTER promises." [154] WHY are the promises of the New Covenant better than those of the Old? Because CHRIST makes them all! God's side of the agreement stands as before. But man's side is changed. Now instead of boldly declaring, "I will do," man feels his utter helplessness and turns to Jesus for strength. And Jesus promises us: "I will do FOR you and THROUGH you. By My Spirit, I will put My laws into your *mind*, and on your *heart* also will I write them."

This great truth is beautifully set forth in this inspired prayer: "Now the God of peace, that brought forth again from the dead our Lord Jesus, that great Shepherd of the sheep, through the blood of *the everlasting covenant,* make you perfect in every good work to do His will, WORKING IN YOU that which is wellpleasing in His sight, through Jesus Christ; to whom be glory for ever and ever. Amen." [155]

So the New Covenant brings in a mighty Helper to aid us in obeying God's commands. This Helper is the Spirit of God, "the Holy Ghost, whom God hath given to them that OBEY Him." [156] Only those ignorant of what the New Covenant really is would suggest that it doesn't require obedience to God's Law, for it explicitly mentions writing that Law on our very hearts!

Notice how Paul, the great "Apostle to the Gentiles," puts it in writing in one of his epistles or letters to Christian believers:

"You yourselves are our letter, written on our hearts, known and read by everybody. You show that you are a letter from Christ, the result of our ministry, written NOT with INK but with the Spirit of the Living God, not on tablets of STONE [the *Old* Covenant] but on tablets of human HEARTS [the *New* Covenant]." [157]

When Sunday Came Three Days TOO LATE

It's interesting to note that this New Covenant is also referred to as a *will* or *testament*—in fact, as the Last Will and Testament of Jesus Christ. The Bible sets forth this legal principle regarding wills:

"In the case of a will it is necessary to prove that the person who made it has DIED, for a will means nothing while the person who made it is alive: it goes into effect only after his death." [158]

Jesus' will went into effect when He died on the cross.

Now for an IMPORTANT QUESTION: Since Christ's death ratified the New Covenant, could it be changed afterward? Read the Bible answer in different translations of Galatians 3:15.

● *King James Version* — "Though it be but a man's covenant, yet if it be confirmed, no man disannulleth, or addeth thereto."

● *Revised Standard Version* — "No one annuls even a man's will, or adds to it, once it has been ratified."

● *New English Bible* — "When a man's will and testament has been duly executed, no one else can set it aside or add a codicil."

● *New Revised Standard Version* — "Once a person's will has been ratified, no one adds to it or annuls it."

● *New American Standard Bible* — "Even though it is only a man's covenant, yet when it has been ratified, no one sets it aside or adds conditions to it."

In other words, a will can be changed any number of times while the one who made it, the testator, is alive. But his death forever seals his last will and testament. When Jesus Christ's death at Calvary confirmed and ratified His New Covenant, it still contained God's promise to write His Law in the hearts of His people. That Law still contained the Fourth Commandment which reads: "Remember the Sabbath day, to keep it holy. Six days shalt thou labour, and do all thy work: But THE SEVENTH DAY IS THE SABBATH of the Lord thy God." [159] So the Law of God stood with just that wording when Jesus expired upon the cross.

Everything that Jesus taught—His entire legacy of baptism, the Lord's Supper, *etc.*—had to be placed in His will before He died. It's extremely interesting that the Lord's Supper was instituted by Christ before His death rather than some time during the forty days He spent with His disciples after His resurrection. Interesting, I say, because that ceremony is a MEMORIAL service: Jesus said, "This do in REMEMBRANCE of Me." [160] What does this memorial service show? "As often as ye eat this bread, and drink this cup, ye do show the Lord's DEATH." [161]

We never have a *memorial* service for an event BEFORE that event occurs, but Christ DID—for if He had waited till after His death and resurrection it would've been too late to be part of His will. Jesus didn't hesitate to command observance of His death, even though it hadn't taken place yet. Just as easily He could've commanded Sunday observance of His future resurrection and made it a New Covenant requirement. But He did not!

If, as the Bible teaches, a man's will CANNOT be changed AFTER His death, could the Sabbath be changed after the death of Christ—even five minutes after His death? No! It's a criminal offense to tamper with a man's will after his death. So SUNDAY came just THREE DAYS TOO LATE to be included in the New Covenant, the last will and testament of Jesus Christ.

Remember that neither Christ nor His apostles had anything to do with observing Sunday as a "Christian Sabbath." Right up to the cross, and after, we find the disciples resting on "the Sabbath day according to the Commandment." [162] Therefore, the Sabbath was obviously not changed *before* the cross, and any attempt to change it *afterwards* must be regarded as a criminal offense, as treason against God's throne and kingdom.

THE TEST OF TIME: A MORAL ISSUE?

Someone may say, "I do want to be honest about my relationship with God, but I honestly don't see how the Sabbath is a MORAL issue. The other Ten Commandments have a basis in morality—it makes a definite difference whether or not we lie, steal, or murder. But what possible difference can the day on which we worship make?"

Those who voice this candid question may be surprised to learn that, in a very fundamental way, the Fourth Commandment regarding the Sabbath is the most moral of all!

Morality always has to do with God, who gave us our moral nature in the first place. Morality is the quality of our response to God and to the creatures He's made. So instinctively we sense that it's morally wrong to set up other gods between us and our Creator or to take His name in vain. We innately understand that it's wrong to lie to or steal from a fellow human being. And we won't steal another man's wife by committing adultery with her, if we follow the "Golden Rule" of morality.

Because we see the sense of those commands of God, we obey them. But the Sabbath command seems so arbitrary. There seems to be no reason for it. REST appeals to us, but a particular TIME for rest does not. Why should we keep the seventh day when the first or any other day seems just as good? Herein lies the real TEST of our morality: To obey our Maker just because He SAYS so, even when we see no good reason for it!

You see, when we keep *only* those commands we happen to AGREE with, we're obeying ourselves, not God. So the Fourth Commandment is better adapted than any of the other Ten Commandments, of which we see the reason, to *test* our morality and obedience to God. An effective barometer of our spirituality, it's the only command of the Ten we can flagrantly break, over and over again, and still be accepted in good society. It's a "respectable sin"! ONLY God's expressed preference for the seventh day—and His own example regarding it—distinguishes it from the other six days. Only those seeking to do exactly as God says will feel any concern about obedience in this matter.

A parallel situation from the Garden of Eden is illuminating: There wasn't anything wrong with the tree that God asked Adam and Eve not to touch—it wasn't booby-trapped or poisonous or anything. God simply used the tree as a *test* or *sign* that Adam and Eve would obey Him. They might have reasoned, "I don't see anything wrong with this tree! And I see no reason not to eat its fruit, either!"—no reason, except that God SAID not to.

In the same way, God says, "Hallow My Sabbaths; and they shall be a SIGN between Me and you, that ye may know that *I am the Lord* your God." [163] The word *Lord* denotes RULER, as in "lord and master," to whom we give unquestioning obedience. The seventh-day Sabbath is "a sign" used by God to show whether we obey Him because **He is our Lord** or only because we *happen to agree* with what He asks. [164]

In the final analysis, our highest morality is simply to obey God with no IF's, AND's, or BUT's. On the other hand, we can hardly call ourselves "moral" if we do only those things we personally agree with, for in so doing we—like self-indulgent hedonists—obey only our own inclinations and not the commands of God.

Are you ready at this point, having gained a new understanding of the Sabbath Christ gave, to follow God's command and remember the day which most of the world has forgotten?

THE SABBATH ON THE NEW EARTH

God's original plan for mankind was tragically disrupted by sin. But that beautiful original plan will be consummated when Christ comes to save His faithful people and "make all things new." [165] The Bible's two final chapters paint a magnificent picture of the New Earth.

The "gospel prophet" Isaiah offers heavenly insight into the coming of the Lord with fire to slay and consume the wicked. [166] The redeemed, on the other hand, face a future of fellowship with the Lord they love:

> "For as the new heavens and the NEW EARTH, which I will make, shall remain before Me, saith the Lord, so shall your seed and your name remain. And it shall come to pass, that, from one new moon to another, and from one SABBATH to another, shall all flesh come to WORSHIP before Me, saith the Lord." [167]

God made the Sabbath in the perfect paradise of Eden, BEFORE sin entered. And AFTER sin and sinners are eradicated from the universe, God will restore all things to those He died to redeem—including Sabbath worship. The seventh-day Sabbath of God, far from being abolished, actually spans the history of man from *Paradise Lost* to *Paradise Regained*. If we're going to keep the Sabbath in the *hereafter* of God's wonderful New Earth, I want to begin keeping it *here and now*—don't you?

Notes to Chapter 13

1. See Samuele Bacchiocchi, *Divine Rest for Human Restlessness* (Berrien Springs, Michigan: Biblical Perspectives, 1980). 319 pages.
2. Genesis 2:1-3.
3. Exodus 20:10.
4. Mark 2:27. The word "man" in this text is the Greek *anthropos* and means "ALL mankind, irrespective of nationality or sex." It's the same Greek word translated "man" in John 1:9, which refers to "EVERY man that cometh into the world."
5. Timothy Dwight, *Theology Explained & Defended* (Middleton, Conn.: Printed by Clark and Lyman, 1818), Volume III, p. 225.
6. "The Sabbath idea is as old as creation itself."—Gordon J. Wenham, *Word Biblical Commentary*, D. A. Hubbard & G. W. Barker, editors (Waco: TX: Word Books, © 1987), Volume 1, p. 36.
7. John 1:1, 2 & 14. Genesis 1:2 shows that the Holy Spirit also was present at the creation of the world: "And the Spirit of God moved upon the face of the waters." Thus we find evidence for the Holy Trinity on the very first page of the Bible.
8. Since "the Sabbath was made for man" and since "all things were made by Him [Christ]; and without Him was not any thing made that was made," we know that *Christ made the Sabbath.* Mark 2:27 and John 1:3.
9. Isaiah 33:22.
10. John 5:22. This Bible teaching is reinforced in John 5:27 and Acts 10:42 & 17:31.
11. God's people had lost track of His holy day during their centuries-long bondage in Egypt, when as slaves they'd been forced to work seven days a week.
12. Nehemiah 9:11-15, NKJV.
13. 1 Corinthians 10:1-4.
14. Matthew 4:4.
15. Exodus 31:18 and 20:1.
16. In Chapter 14 we'll carefully study "Sunday in the Bible."
17. Romans 6:3-6.
18. John 14:15 & 21.
19. John 8:44.
20. Revelation 12:9.
21. Isaiah 14:12-14.
22. 1 John 3:4.
23. John 1:29.
24. Genesis 4:2.
25. Hebrews 9:22, RSV.
26. 1 John 2:4.
27. Genesis 2:1-3.
28. Genesis 2:1-3.
29. Exodus 20:8.
30. Exodus 20:9-10.

31. Mark 15:42, NKJV. See also texts such as John 19:31.

32. Mark 15:37 & 42, NKJV.

33. Mark 16:1-2.

34. Matthew 12:8, Mark 2:28, and Luke 6:5. "Christ's claim to the title of Lord of the Sabbath was and is a VALID one. His authority for saying that the Sabbath is His day—the Lord's day—rests upon the fact that He, as God and Creator, *made it* by resting on it, blessing it, and setting it apart as holy *in the beginning* when this world was created."—Robert L. Odom, *Sabbath and Sunday in Early Christianity* (Washington, D.C.: Review and Herald Publishing Association, c. 1977), p. 20.

35. John 12:42-43, NASB.

36. John 7:48.

37. Romans 8:31.

38. Genesis 6 & 7.

39. Judges 6:11 – 8:10.

40. 1 Kings 18:17-40.

41. Daniel 3.

42. John 1:11.

43. Matthew 7:13-14, The Living Bible.

44. Exodus 20:8.

45. Doug Batchelor, *The Richest Caveman: The Doug Batchelor Story*, as told to Marie Tooker (Roseville, CA: Amazing Facts, 1991), p. 87.

46. John Locke, *An Essay Concerning Human Understanding*, Book iv, chapter iii, section vi, note, p. 465.

47. Ezekiel 22:26.

48. Malachi 2:7-9. "Partial" here refers to ministers who teach that PART of God's Law is still in effect—like the commands against murder or lying—but PART is abolished and no longer binding—like the commandment specifying the seventh day. The text further says that "many"—in fact, *untold millions*—"stumble at the Law," because preachers leave the truth literally *untold!*

49. Jeremiah 23:1-2.

50. Jeremiah 50:6.

51. Matthew 15:14.

52. Revelation 5:11.

53. 2 Kings 6:15-17, NKJV. Read the whole context in verses 8-23.

54. Psalms 40:8, NASB. The fact that this is a Messianic prophecy is seen by comparing Psalm 40:6-7 with Hebrews 10:5-7.

55. Luke 4:16.

56. In regard to the Sabbath alone, some 600 *halakah,* or man-made requirements, smothered the day with legalistic rabbinical burdens.

57. Acts 17:6.

58. Matthew 12:12, NKJV.

59. John 15:10.

60. Luke 23:54-56, NIV.

61. Please see "What Was Nailed to the Cross?" on pages 394-402.

62. Acts 13:47, RSV.
63. Acts 13:46.
64. Acts 13:27.
65. Acts 13:13-14 are quoted. Paul's preaching goes through verse 41.
66. Acts 13:42-44.
67. Acts 17:1-4.
68. The phrase "as his manner was" in Acts 17:2 is in Greek identical with that rendered "as His custom was" in Luke 4:16. The practice of Paul, as Christ's faithful apostle, was just like that of His Master.
69. Acts 18:1, 4, 11.
70. Acts 16:12-13, NKJV.
71. Acts 16:14-15.
72. See Matthew 24:1-2, 15-19 and Luke 21:20-21.
73. Matthew 24:20.
74. Josephus, *Jewish Wars,* Book 2, Chapter 19.
75. Matthew 24:18.
76. Luke 21:21, The Living Bible.
77. Luke 21:21, Revised Standard Version, Amplified Bible, New English Bible.
78. Matthew 24:16 and Luke 21:21.
79. For insights expressed on this passage of Scripture, the writer is indebted to Francis D. Nichol, *Answers to Objections* (Washington, D. C., Review and Herald Publishing Association, c. 1952), p. 163.
80. This passage could well qualify as one written by "our dear brother Paul . . . which ignorant and unstable people DISTORT, as they do the other Scriptures, to their own *destruction.*" 2 Peter 3:15-16, NIV.
81. Exodus 12:1-7.
82. Exodus 12:13, 14, 17, 24, and 43, NKJV.
83. Numbers 9:12-14, NKJV.
84. Hebrews 9:1.
85. Hebrews 9:10-11.
86. Outlined in Ezekiel 43:18-27.
87. John 1:29.
88. 1 Corinthians 5:7.
89. Please see *Appendix F, "The Two Laws: A Study in Contrasts,"* at the back of this book for pages full of distinctive differences.
90. Exodus 31:18 and 32:16. See also Exodus 24:12, 34:1, Deuteronomy 4:13 and 5:22.
91. Deuteronomy 31:9, 24-26, NIV.
92. Deuteronomy 10:1-5.
93. Exodus 40:20.
94. 1 Kings 8:9. See also Hebrews 9:4.
95. Deuteronomy 31:26, NIV.
96. Deuteronomy 6:24.
97. Romans 7:12. The seventh verse identifies this "law" as God's moral law of Ten Commandments.

98. Hebrews 9:1 & 10. In Ezekiel 45:17 we read: "It shall be the prince's part to give burnt offerings, and MEAT offerings, and DRINK offerings, in the FEASTS, and *in the new moons, and in the sabbaths*. . . . He shall prepare the sin offering, and the MEAT offering, and the burnt offering, and the peace offerings, to make reconciliation for the house of Israel." All this was obviously part of the CEREMONIAL law.

99. Numbers 28:16-17.

100. Numbers 28:20 and 24.

101. Numbers 28:26, 29:1, *etc.*

102. Numbers 10:1-10—verse 10 quoted, NIV.

103. Numbers 28:11 & 14, NIV.

104. Exodus 20:10.

105. Leviticus 23:1-3.

106. Leviticus 23:4.

107. By way of illustration, do you happen to know what DAY of the week your birthday, or New Year's Eve, or Halloween will fall on, say, five years from now?

108. See Leviticus 23:7, 8, 21, 25, and 35.

109. Leviticus 23:38, Today's English Version. Almost all modern translations say "besides" or "in addition to" for the word "beside" in the King James Version.

110. Leviticus 23:24, 32, and 39. See also Leviticus 16:31.

111. John 1:29, NKJV.

112. Hebrews 10:1-5 and 10, NKJV.

113. See such texts as Exodus 20:11; Genesis 2:1-3; John 1:1-3, 10, 14, Colossians 1:13-16; and Hebrews 1:1-2.

114. See Revelation 14:6-12.

115. Revelation 14:7.

116. Adam Clarke, *The New Testament of Our Lord and Saviour Jesus Christ* (New York, Abingdon-Cokesbury Press, no date), Volume 2, p. 524, on Colossians 2:16.

117. D[wight] L. Moody, *D. L. Moody On the Ten Commandments* (Chicago: Moody Press, 1977 edition), pp. 14, 47-48.

118. Robert Jamieson, A. R. Fausset, and David Brown, *Commentary Critical and Explanatory on the Whole Bible* (Grand Rapids, Michigan: no date), p. 378.

119. Albert Barnes, *Notes, Explanatory and Practical, on the Epistles of Paul to the Ephesians, Philippians, and Colossians* (New York: Harper, 1851), pp. 306-307, on Colossians 2:16.

120. Kenneth H. Wood, "The 'Sabbath Days' of Colossians 2:16-17" in *The Sabbath in Scripture and History,* Kenneth A. Strand, editor (Washington, D.C.: Review and Herald Publishing Association, c. 1982), p. 340.

121. Matthew 5:17-19.

122. Matthew 3:15.

123. Galatians 6:2.

124. 1 John 3:4.

125. 1 Samuel 15:24.

126. Romans 4:15 and 5:13.

127. Romans 7:7 and 3:20.

128. 1 John 3:4 and Romans 6:23.
129. Romans 3:23.
130. Please see *Appendix G, "God's Law Reflects His Character,"* at the back of this book.
131. 2 Corinthians 2:11.
132. Romans 3:31.
133. Proverbs 28:9.
134. James 2:19.
135. Revelation 12:7-9.
136. 1 John 5:3.
137. John 14:15 & 21, NKJV.
138. 1 Samuel 15:22. The context (verses 1-23) is illuminating.
139. Matthew 7:21-23.
140. 1 John 3:4 and Romans 6:23.
141. Romans 3:25.
142. Hebrews 4:16.
143. Hebrews 6:6.
144. Romans 8:1.
145. 1 Corinthians 15:31 and Galatians 2:20.
146. Romans 6:15.
147. Romans 5:20.
148. Titus 2:11.
149. James 1:25. See James 1:22-25 and 2:10-12. For insight into this Biblical analogy, the writer is indebted to the late Allen Walker and his book *The Law and the Sabbath* (Roseville, CA: Amazing Facts, c. 1985), p. 14.
150. Romans 7:7 asserts this function: "I had not known sin, but by the Law."
151. Exodus 24:7.
152. Hebrews 8:6-9, NKJV.
153. Hebrews 8:10.
154. Hebrews 8:6.
155. Hebrews 13:20-21.
156. Acts 5:32.
157. 2 Corinthians 3:2-3, NIV.
158. Hebrews 9:16-17, Today's English Version.
159. Exodus 20:8-10.
160. 1 Corinthians 11:24, and repeated in verse 25.
161. 1 Corinthians 11:26. For the insight here expressed, the writer is indebted to Joe Crews' booklet *Why the Old Covenant Failed* (Roseville, CA: Amazing Facts, Incorporated, c. 1980), p. 22.
162. Luke 23:56.
163. Ezekiel 20:20.
164. That's why the Sabbath is perhaps the best indicator of our spiritual experience. "As the Christian takes heed of the Sabbath day and keeps it holy, he does so *purely in answer to God's command,* and *simply because God is his Creator.* Thus, the Sabbath command comes nearer to being a true measure of spirituality than

any other of the commandments. . . . To be willing on the Sabbath day to withdraw from the tyranny of the *world of things* to meet the Lord of heaven and earth in the quiet of our souls *means to love God with all our hearts, souls, minds, and bodies."*—Raoul Dederen, "Reflections on a Theology of the Sabbath," in *The Sabbath in Scripture and History,* Kenneth A. Strand, editor (Washington, D.C.: Review and Herald Publishing Association, c. 1982), p. 302.

165. Revelation 21:5.
166. Isaiah 66:15-17.
167. Isaiah 66:22-23.

✦ ✦ ✦

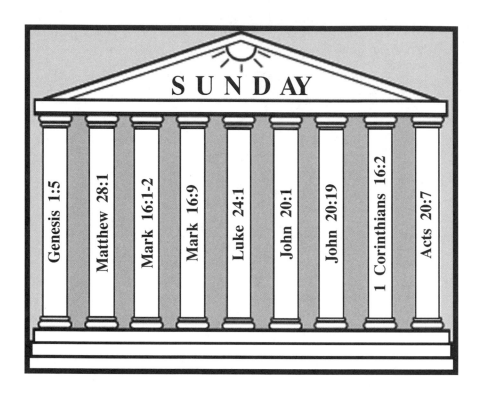

The columns of the temple, from left to right, read:

- Genesis 1:5
- Matthew 28:1
- Mark 16:1-2
- Mark 16:9
- Luke 24:1
- John 20:1
- John 20:19
- 1 Corinthians 16:2
- Acts 20:7

The pediment reads: **SUNDAY**

THE TEMPLE OF SUNDAY

~

CHAPTER FOURTEEN

EVERYTHING YOU ALWAYS WANTED TO KNOW ABOUT SUNDAY IN THE BIBLE

SUNDAY has attained such a time-honored, special status in our culture that we naturally assume its claim to fame is authentic. That's why a scholarly detective's modest proposal to investigate Sunday in an attempt to discover how legitimate its standing really is may seem somewhat shocking. But I propose that we examine Sunday under the searching eye of Scripture to see if its status as a day of Christian worship is theologically sound. Since the Bible is the rule of faith for most Christians, those who take the Bible as their guide must find within its sacred pages documented evidence for their beliefs. When we put Sunday to the test of Scripture, what do we find?

SUNDAY IS **NOT** A **SACRED** DAY

Your Bible includes Sunday among "the six WORKING days" as opposed to "the SABBATH," the day when "the people of the land shall WORSHIP." [1] It may come as a surprise to some, but nowhere does the Word of God speak of the sanctity of Sunday. As a matter of fact, the entire Bible—from Genesis to Revelation—mentions Sunday only NINE times! Let's briefly examine these few references.

"Your Days Are **NUMBERED** . . . "

The name "Sunday" appears not at all in the Bible, since no day of the week except the Sabbath was given any name. All the other six days were designated by numbers: the first day, the second day, *etc.*[2] The Old Testament mentions "the first day" only once,[3] in connection with Creation, as the Record simply tells what God did on each day of Creation Week. "The first day" was one of the six working days of our Creator, just as He prescribes it to be for us.

Since there's nothing in that single Old Testament verse to confer sacredness on Sunday, we must look to the eight references in the New Testament if we're to find a "Thus saith the Lord" making Sunday holy. Five of these references are as follows:

✓ Matthew 28:1

"In the end of the Sabbath, as it began to dawn toward the first day of the week, came Mary Magdalene and the other Mary to see the sepulchre."

✓ Mark 16:1-2

"When the Sabbath was past, Mary Magdalene, and Mary the mother of James, and Salome, had brought sweet spices, that they might come and anoint Him. And very early in the morning the first day of the week, they came unto the sepulchre at the rising of the sun."

✓ Mark 16:9

"Now when Jesus was risen early the first day of the week, He appeared first to Mary Magdalene, out of whom He had cast seven devils."

✓ Luke 24:1

"Now upon the first day of the week, very early in the morning, they came unto the sepulchre, bringing the spices which they had prepared, and certain others with them."

✓ John 20:1

"The first day of the week cometh Mary Magdalene early, when it was yet dark, unto the sepulchre, and seeth the stone taken away from the sepulchre."

These five passages mention "the first day of the week" but give no indication that Sunday should be regarded as holy. You'll recall that the women who loved the Lord gave Him a hasty burial on Good Friday but were unable, due to lack of time, to prepare His precious body the way they desired. So "they went home and prepared spices and perfumes. But they RESTED on the Sabbath in OBEDIENCE to the COMMANDMENT."[4] Yet as soon as dawn brought sufficient light for them to see well enough to continue the sad work of burying their Lord, they returned to the tomb to finish their labor of love.

They did NOT look upon Sunday as the resurrection day, for they thought Jesus was still dead. Puzzled by the practical problem of how to move the massive stone which sealed our Lord's tomb, "They were saying to one another, 'Who will roll away the stone for us from the door of the tomb?'"[5]

These five verses, which simply record the sad return of the women to the tomb, fail to provide any evidence of Sunday sacredness. Thus we're left with ONLY THREE Bible verses in which the first day of the week is even mentioned. If we're to find Scriptural proof that Sunday is the holy day on which God wants Christians to worship, we must find it in these three remaining verses.

Let's examine these texts under the MICROSCOPE of God's Word and see if the idea of Sunday sacredness can stand up under the scrutiny of Scripture.

✓ John 20:19

The first of these three remaining texts reads:

> "Then the same day at evening, being the first day of the week, when the doors were shut where the disciples were assembled for fear of the Jews, came Jesus and stood in the midst, and saith unto them, Peace be unto you."

Advocates for Sunday use this verse, but they really need better evidence than this. For John doesn't even HINT that this was a meeting celebrating Christ's triumph over death and honoring His resurrection. Instead, the Scripture quite plainly states that "the disciples were assembled for FEAR of the Jews."[6]

The disciples were afraid, all right. They'd seen what the Jews and Romans had done to their Leader; and when He died, their hope had died with Him. Now the frightened disciples were HIDING OUT behind closed doors "for FEAR of the Jews." This was certainly NOT a resurrection celebration!

A second fact proves conclusively that this was not a special gathering to honor Sunday as the day Christ rose from the dead: The disciples DID NOT BELIEVE Christ had risen from the dead. It wasn't just "Doubting Thomas" who was incredulous at first. Virtually all the disciples refused to believe

Christ had arisen even when TOLD that glorious news by eyewitnesses! Note what the Bible says:

- The women who found the stone rolled away and the tomb empty "told these things to the apostles. And their words seemed to them like idle tales, and they did NOT believe them." [7]

- After the Lord "appeared first to Mary Magdalene, . . . she went and told those who had been with Him, as they mourned and wept. And when they heard that He was alive and had been seen by her, they did NOT believe." [8]

- Two believers who met but didn't at first recognize their resurrected Lord on the road to Emmaus rushed back with the news that they'd seen Jesus alive and told that momentous fact to the assembled disciples. [9] The Record says: "These returned and reported it to the rest; but they did NOT believe them either." [10]

- "Later," when Jesus Himself appeared in their midst, "He rebuked them for their lack of faith and their stubborn REFUSAL to believe those who had seen Him after He had risen." [11]

- In fact, *even when Jesus did appear,* the fearful disciples REFUSED to believe it was really their living Lord in His resurrected body, "But they were terrified and affrighted, and supposed that they had seen a spirit" or ghost. [12]

Therefore, this meeting was held by frightened disciples who absolutely did not believe that the Lord had risen from the dead. In the light of these facts, no one can claim that this first-day meeting was a religious one and an example for us to follow in our worship.

Let's move on to our next text to see if it offers any Bible backing to the claims for Sunday.

✓ 1 Corinthians 16:2

Paul wrote the believers at Corinth: "Upon the first day of the week let every one of you lay by him in store, as the Lord hath prospered, that there be no gatherings when I come."

Some religious teachers use this verse as proof that we should go to church on Sunday. But this text doesn't even mention a meeting or assembly of any kind! The word "gatherings" here refers to the gathering or saving up of money offerings, not to the gathering of people.

In this verse the apostle was simply encouraging systematic giving by believers rather than spur-of-the-moment, impulse giving. He was telling individual members in all the churches to PLAN their giving in advance. Time was precious to the busy apostle, and the time he could spend visiting each of the many churches in different locations was limited. He didn't want members to have to leave an important, inspiring meeting in order to rush home and figure out what to give when he finally did visit.

Paul didn't say he would arrive on a Sunday. There was no way to tell when he might arrive—it could be on a Tuesday or Friday or any other day. He simply says, Plan your offering in advance and have it ready, "so that there will be no need for collections WHEN I come." [13]

What should be done "upon the first day of the week"? Paul says, Figure out how much you've made, how much "the Lord hath prospered" you in the preceding week, and set aside what you can for a donation. You see, it wouldn't be proper spiritual activity for a businessman to do his bookkeeping on God's holy Sabbath and figure his profit and loss then. And Friday, the preparation day, was always so busy winding up business and closing up shop, getting ready to spend the next day exclusively with the Lord, that Paul knew the average person would have no time to do it then.

But on the first day of the week, when the Sabbath is past and it's back to "business as usual," Paul urges us to put the Lord's work first and check over the books from the preceding week, putting aside what we can for the cause of God systematically. What we *shouldn't do* on the Sabbath and have *no time to do* on the preparation day Paul tells us to do "upon the first day of the week."

And where should this offering be placed? Should it be taken to church on the first day of the week and collected? Not at all. Instead, it should be kept at home with each individual giver. Paul doesn't speak collectively of the church in an assembled gathering. He speaks singularly to each individual: "Let every ONE of you *lay by* HIM *in store*, as God hath prospered HIM." Please note the singular pronouns. Modern English versions translate this verse even more clearly:

New International Version
"EACH ONE of you should SET ASIDE a sum of money . . . saving it up, so that *when I come* no collections will have to be made."

Today's English Version
"EACH of you must PUT ASIDE some money . . . and save it up, so there will be no need to collect money *when I come.*"

Amplified Bible

"Let EVERYONE of you (personally) PUT ASIDE something and save it up . . . so that no collections will need to be taken after I come."

New American Standard Bible

"Let EACH ONE of you PUT ASIDE and save": here a footnote tells us, "Literally, put by HIMSELF."

New English Bible

"EACH of you is to PUT ASIDE and keep by HIM a sum."

Revised Standard Version

"EACH of you is to PUT something ASIDE and STORE IT UP."

Store it up where? The Spanish Bible *(Santa Biblia)* says, *"en su propia casa,"* which means "in his own HOUSE" or "at HOME." A Catholic version says: "Let EACH ONE of you put aside at HOME and lay up whatever he has a mind to, so that the collections may not have to be made after I have come."—*New American Catholic Edition of The Holy Bible.*

Therefore, since Paul is not talking about a Sunday church meeting or any other kind of meeting, preachers who resort to using this text to prove Sunday sacredness are guilty of one of two things:

1. Either they DON'T KNOW what it really means—a bad position for teachers to be in.
2. Or they DO KNOW but use it anyway, hoping to fool others who don't understand its meaning.

Since they're either IGNORANT or DECEPTIVE, their word should not be taken as "gospel."

✓ Acts 20:7

Now we come to the very last Bible text mentioning the first day of the week. Many advocates for Sunday observance, realizing the weakness of the other Bible texts we've just examined, "put all their eggs in one basket," so to speak, and in desperation try to find in this lone verse the proof they need for Sunday sacredness. Let's read it:

"And upon the first day of the week, when the disciples came to-gether to break bread, Paul preached unto them, ready to depart on the morrow; and continued his speech until midnight." [14]

We won't be confused by religious teachers who tell us this text proves the sacredness of Sunday if we remember two definite points:

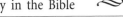

A. PREACHING DOES NOT MAKE A DAY HOLY. It's true that Paul "preached" to those present. But if preaching makes a day holy, then *every* day was made holy, for the Bible says: "DAILY in the Temple, and in every house, they CEASED NOT to teach and PREACH Jesus Christ."[15] In that First Century, the Holy Spirit was poured out in such full measure that the church was "on fire" with zeal. Enthusiastic Christians like Paul lost no opportunity to speak a word for the Lord. When a great apostle like Peter or Paul arrived in town, believers there would urge him to preach and to feed their faith—whatever day it happened to be! So we shouldn't marvel that the early disciples would PREACH "DAILY."

B. COMMUNION SUPPER DOES NOT MAKE A DAY HOLY. Sunday advocates point to the part of this verse that says, "the disciples came together to break bread," and claim that this proves our day of worship was transferred from Sabbath to Sunday because they feel this refers to a communion service partaking of the Lord's Supper. But that assumption is completely unwarranted—for four very good reasons.

1. In the first place, we're not at all sure that this verse refers to the communion of the Lord's Supper. The assertion that the expression "breaking bread" always refers to the Lord's Supper is open to question because that phrase was quite common among Jews and other ancient people with reference to ordinary meals. For instance, the very same Bible book of Acts makes it sound as if "breaking bread" simply means EATING. Please note this passage about Paul's shipwreck on Malta:

"And as day was about to dawn, Paul implored them all to take food, saying, 'Today is the fourteenth day you have waited and continued without food, and eaten nothing. Therefore I urge you to take nourishment, for this is for your survival, since not a hair will fall from the head of any of you.' And when he had said these things, he took BREAD and gave thanks to God in the presence of them all; and when he had BROKEN IT he began to eat. Then they were all encouraged, and also took food themselves."[16]

Even in the Old Testament, your Bible says: "The young children ask for bread, but no one breaks it for them."[17] The common expression "breaking bread" is there—but the idea of the Lord's Supper is not.

2. Secondly, there's good evidence for concluding that "breaking bread" in this particular instance simply refers to eating a meal. Consider such points as the following:

a. The Record states that when Paul "had broken bread, and EATEN," he continued to preach "a long while, even till break of day"![18] The word *eaten* strongly implies eating a meal to satisfy hunger rather than observing the ceremonial Lord's Supper.

b. The breaking of bread took place after midnight, which appears strange if the purpose of the gathering was to celebrate the Lord's Supper. [19]

c. Verse 11 speaks only of PAUL as eating bread, not the entire congregation.

d. There's no mention of a *cup*—symbolizing Jesus' blood—nor of any *prayers.* [20]

3. Thirdly, even if it were true that the expression "to break bread" here means to eat the Lord's Supper, it's a gigantic, unwarranted leap to jump to the conclusion that celebrating Communion makes a day holy or changes one of the Ten Commandments! Remember, the Lord Himself instituted the FIRST Lord's Supper with His disciples in the Upper Room on a Thursday night.[21] But no one suggests that Christians today should keep Thursday as their day of worship!

4. Finally, IF (1) "breaking bread" means partaking of the Lord's Supper, and IF (2) celebrating the Lord's Supper means making a day holy, then, again, the early Christians made EVERY day holy. For your Bible says that "they, continuing DAILY with one accord in the Temple, and BREAKING BREAD from house to house," [22] went about the work of the Lord. The theory that taking communion supper makes a day holy is reduced to absurdity.

A FAREWELL MEETING

So Acts 20:7 gives little evidence that the meeting was held in celebration of Sunday as a resurrection memorial. Actually, the context makes very clear that this was a farewell meeting for Paul in that city of Troas: we read that he was "ready to depart on the morrow" (or in the morning). God's Word says that when Paul said farewell to believers from those various churches, "they all wept sore, and fell on Paul's neck, and kissed him, sorrowing most of all . . . that they should see his face no more." [23]

Thus the question becomes, What was the PURPOSE of this meeting? Was it to commemorate the resurrection on the first day of the week? Or was it to give Paul a chance to encourage and bid farewell to believers there, knowing—through the Holy Spirit—that he'd never again return as he had in the past and "that they should see his face no more" as the Scripture tells us?

The evidence seems to favor the latter, especially when the mention of the first day of the week seems to be inserted quite incidentally among OTHER details of TIME. Please note that the single chapter in question includes more than a dozen references to time:

> Acts 20:3 – Paul "abode THREE MONTHS" in Greece
>
> Acts 20:6 – He "came . . . to Troas in FIVE DAYS"
>
> Acts 20:6 – "where we abode SEVEN DAYS"
>
> Acts 20:7 – "upon the FIRST DAY of the week"
>
> Acts 20:7 – "ready to depart ON THE MORROW"
>
> Acts 20:7 – "continued his speech UNTIL MIDNIGHT"
>
> Acts 20:11 – "talked . . . even TILL BREAK OF DAY"
>
> Acts 20:15 – "THE NEXT DAY . . . Chios"
>
> Acts 20:15 – "THE NEXT DAY . . . Samos"
>
> Acts 20:15 – "THE NEXT DAY . . . Mitylene"
>
> Acts 20:16 – "to be at Jerusalem THE DAY OF PENTECOST"
>
> Acts 20:29 – "AFTER MY DEPARTING shall . . . wolves enter in"
>
> Acts 20:31 – "by the space of THREE YEARS"

Remember that the writer of the Book of Acts was Dr. Luke, "the beloved physician,"[24] who, with his scientific mind, no doubt wanted to make his historical record of the early church as clear and accurate as possible. Thus we see in this very passage MANY references to time. Luke, it seems, mentioned "the first day of the week" simply because he included it along with many other chronological details. At any rate, IF the pen of Inspiration wished to tell faithful believers to transfer their worship from Sabbath to Sunday, a definite **"Thus saith the Lord"** would be needed. But God did not inspire Luke or any other Bible writer to write that.

THE NIGHT EUTYCHUS **DROPPED OUT** OF THE CHURCH

On the occasion in question, Luke tells us this was an unusually long, protracted meeting.[25] Note that Paul "continued his speech until midnight . . . and talked a long while, even till break of day."[26] Well, in consequence of all this, note what happened . . .

> "Seated in a window was a young man named Eutychus, who was sinking into a deep sleep as Paul talked on and on. When he was sound asleep, he FELL to the GROUND from the third story and was picked

up DEAD. Paul went down, threw himself on the young man and put his arms around him. 'Don't be alarmed,' he said. 'He's alive!' . . . The people took the young man home alive and were greatly comforted." [27]

Since Acts 20:7 is not so strong a verse as Sunday advocates wish, they sometimes ask, "If Luke didn't intend to stress this meeting as an important example of Sunday-keeping, why did he even INCLUDE it in the Sacred Record at all? There were many other days in Paul's life which aren't included!" The answer, I believe, lies in the experience of Eutychus. Even though both Paul's preaching and the breaking of bread were everyday occurrences and nothing out of the ordinary, the raising of a dead person to life WAS noteworthy, and it was to record this MIRACLE that the Troas meeting was included.

THIS MEETING WAS ON **SATURDAY NIGHT!**

One last aspect of this passage remains to be explored, and that's the specific time of its occurrence. Dr. Luke is quite explicit in his account, but the import of his language may easily slip past our modern minds. We know, of course, that this meeting took place at NIGHT: Paul preached until MID-NIGHT and beyond, "and there were MANY LIGHTS in the upper chamber, where they were gathered together." [28] But how many of us realize that this meeting was NOT what we'd call "a Sunday meeting" at all—for it was held on Saturday night!

This fact is corroborated by several modern versions of the Bible that translate "upon the first day of the week" as follows:

> "On the SATURDAY NIGHT"—New English Bible
> "On the SATURDAY NIGHT"—Revised English Bible
> "On SATURDAY EVENING"—Today's English Version
> "On SATURDAY NIGHT"—The Living Bible, footnote
> "On the SATURDAY EVENING"—The Jerusalem Bible,
> footnote (Catholic)

The explanation for this is simple: The Bible day begins at sunset and ends with the following sunset, so that the dark part or nighttime hours precede the light part or daytime hours. God made this plain at the very outset when the days of Creation Week began with each succeeding sun-down, so that *evening comes first:* "The EVENING and the morning were the first day. . . . And the EVENING and the morning were the second day," [29] and so on. Accordingly, God instructed His people: "From evening until evening you shall keep your Sabbath." [30] Early man in ancient times didn't have—or need—a watch to tell when each day began or ended; he'd simply watch the sun go down.

The man-made system, beginning each day at midnight, came much later, in Roman times. Such a system may be convenient for dating business transactions in commercial countries. But the fact remains, as the *Encyclopedia Britannica* observes: "In Israel the day began at evening." [31] Even today, in connection with important holidays, God's reckoning of time persists: Christmas Eve precedes Christmas Day, New Year's Eve precedes New Year's Day, and Halloween is named "All Hallows' Eve" because it precedes All Saints' Day. In the same way, the Sabbath's *Eve* always precedes the daytime portion.

We read that "upon the first day of the week, . . . Paul preached unto them . . . until MIDNIGHT. And there were many LIGHTS in the upper chamber." [32] This is speaking of the DARK PART or evening portion of the "first day" of the week. The *seventh-day Sabbath* begins at evening on Friday night and ends at sundown on Saturday night, at which time the *first day* begins. So the DARK part or EVENING portion of the first day of the week is what we today call "Saturday night." [33]

The EXAMPLE of Paul & Luke on SUNDAY

When daybreak came and Paul said farewell to his fellow Christians at Troas, he had a long journey ahead of him that Sunday. He departed and traveled on foot a distance of nearly TWENTY MILES to Assos, where he had arranged for the ship to meet him. That's quite a long walk—especially so if Paul intended to keep Sunday holy and honor it as a day consecrated to his Lord.

Luke and the others traveling with Paul were also involved in rather heavy labor during these supposedly sacred hours. They were working hard taking the ship around the peninsula to Assos while Paul was holding this all-night farewell meeting at Troas. Remember that when Paul started the meeting, he had plans "to depart on the morrow." [34] This journey, like most of Paul's missionary journeys around the Mediterranean region, involved travel by ship. So while Paul was still speaking to the group gathered at Troas, "We [that is, Luke and the others except Paul] went AHEAD to the ship and set sail for Assos, intending to take Paul on board there; for he had made this arrangement, intending to go by land himself. When he met us in Assos, we took him on board." [35]

"He had made this arrangement" means Paul gave them the orders to work on Sunday. Therefore, both Paul and Luke, in spending the day traveling over land and sea, hardly set the best example for Christians to keep Sunday holy.

(The MAP on the next page gives you some idea of this.)

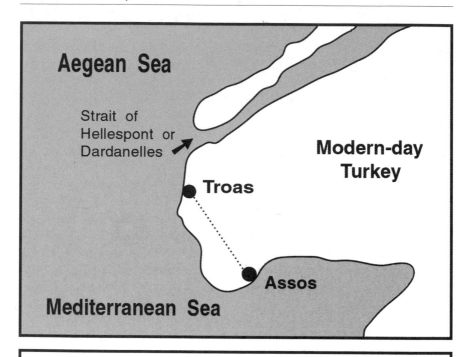

MAP OF PAUL'S SUNDAY JOURNEY IN ACTS 20

Thus this text, like all the rest, offers NO evidence of Sunday-keeping. The fact of the matter is simply that these texts supposedly sanctifying Sunday observance do not stand up under scrutiny. The temple of Sunday is supported by nothing but *man-made pillars of tradition.*

TRADITION DOESN'T COUNT

Religious teachers who promote the observance of Sunday point with pride to its "long tradition" as the Christian day of worship. But mere tradition is not safe for you or me to follow. We've seen that, though the custom of Sunday-keeping has a long tradition behind it, there is NO *"Thus saith the Lord"* behind the practice.

The Lord Jesus Christ made it quite clear that man's traditions carry no weight with God when He asked, "Why do ye also transgress the commandment of God by your tradition? . . . Thus have ye made the commandment of God of none effect by your tradition. . . . But IN VAIN do they worship Me, teaching for doctrines the commandments of MEN"! [36]

Mark similarly records Jesus' words: "In vain they worship Me, teaching as DOCTRINES the commandments of MEN. For laying aside the COM-

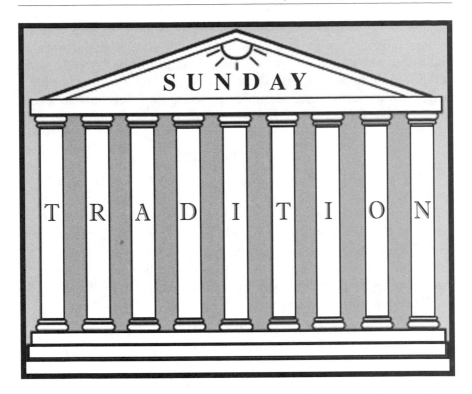

MANDMENT of GOD, you hold the TRADITION of men. . . . All too well you reject the COMMANDMENT of GOD, that you may keep your TRADITION . . . making the Word of God of no effect through your TRADITION." [37]

Adolf Hitler was a master of propaganda, and one of the most successful devices of his Nazi regime was "the BIG LIE technique," which says: "If you tell a lie

LONG enough,

LOUD enough,

OFTEN enough,

it becomes the truth."

That's one reason why the long tradition of Sunday-keeping has successfully "brain-washed" so many people. Human nature being what it is, the longer a man is wrong, the surer he is he's right. A tradition that's unbiblical and untrue is like a bad habit, and the longer we have it, the harder it seems to break. But if a practice is wrong, mere age won't make it right. In fact, the older it is, the more shameful it becomes. As Cyprian said: "CUSTOM is often the ANTIQUITY of ERROR."

Besides, if tradition alone counts for anything, we'd best keep the seventh-day Sabbath, for it was designated by God at CREATION and has behind it three times as many centuries of faithful observance as does Sunday-keeping. Unfortunately, the holy Sabbath is one of those Bible doctrines we find hidden beneath the dust of man-made Tradition! Recognizing the world of difference between the COMMANDMENTS of GOD and the TRADITIONS of MEN, Peter, when imprisoned and beaten for preaching Christ against the wishes of Jewish authorities, boldly answered: "We ought to obey God rather than men."[38]

DID PAUL TELL ALL?

Since absolutely NO explicit evidence is found for Sunday sacredness, some may wonder: "Perhaps God told Paul that the Sabbath was changed, and he knew this in his own mind, but he didn't teach it to the people— maybe because he felt they weren't ready for it." This weak "argument from silence" is an unsupported assumption, but let's consider it anyway.

Could it be possible that the Apostle to the Gentiles failed to reveal all that God told him about the day of worship and other things? No, absolutely not. Three times Paul says plainly:

- "I kept back NOTHING that was profitable. . . ."
- "I have not shunned to declare unto you
  ALL the counsel of God."
- "I have showed you ALL things."[39]

This means that nothing has been concealed from us by either God or Paul that is necessary for our salvation. Paul "kept back nothing"—yet he never said a word about the sanctity of Sunday.

WHICH DAY IS "THE LORD'S DAY"?

Abraham Lincoln, you'll recall, tried many cases as a lawyer in Illinois before he was elected President. In one of those cases, Lincoln asked a rather strange question while cross-examining a witness. "If we call a cow's tail a leg," he asked, "how many legs does a cow have?"

"Well," the witness replied, "if we call a cow's tail a leg, then I'd say a cow has five legs."

"Wrong!" snapped Lincoln. "A cow still has only four legs, because CALL-ING a tail a leg doesn't MAKE it a leg."

And calling a day holy, doesn't make it holy. Only God can make a day or anything else holy. Yet enthusiasts for Sunday holiness, with no warrant from the Bible, habitually call that day "the Lord's Day." But is Sunday really "the Lord's Day"?

God's Word uses the phrase "the Lord's Day" only ONCE, when the Apostle John says, "I was in the Spirit on the Lord's day, and heard behind me a great voice, as of a trumpet." [40] But as you can see, that solitary reference gives no hint as to which day of the week is designated by that special title. The text simply lets us know that the Lord HAS a day which He calls His own, but we must look elsewhere to determine which day that is.

Rather than simply accept what any man says or what any church teaches, let's allow the Bible to be its own interpreter. Even a few texts may suffice to clarify this point. For instance, in Isaiah the Lord Himself calls "the SAB-BATH . . . MY holy DAY . . . the holy of the Lord, honourable, . . . for the mouth of the LORD hath spoken it." [41]

Little logic is required to see that:

A. John says the Lord HAS a day He calls His own:
   He calls it "the Lord's Day." *And*

B. Isaiah records the Lord's own words calling the
   Sabbath "MY holy day." *Therefore,*

C. the Sabbath is "the Lord's Day."

Other texts substantiate this clear conclusion. In the Old Testament we read that the Sabbath was the only day the LORD "blessed . . . and sancti-fied," [42] and many other passages tell us that "the seventh day is the Sabbath of the LORD thy God." [43] In the New Testament we read Jesus' own words that "the Son of man is LORD even of the Sabbath day." [44]

The Sabbath is the Lord's Day—it's the only period of time with which the Lord Jesus ever identified Himself. On the other hand, careful study of God's Word reveals that Christ never said ANYTHING about the first day, either as a holy day or otherwise.

The Holy Scriptures give no sacred title to the first day of the week. Consider, for example, John 20:1 or John 20:19, studied near the beginning of this chapter. Those New Testament texts were written many years after our Lord's resurrection—and written, incidentally, by the same John who wrote Revelation 1:10, the verse now under question. However, in those texts John did NOT call SUNDAY "the Lord's Day," which is strange if that's what he be-lieved and wanted to teach. He called it simply "the first day of the week." Men may mistakenly CALL Sunday "the Lord's Day," but that doesn't make it so. [45]

CONCLUSION

We've examined the Scriptural evidence. We've found that the Bible blows away every excuse we ever had for observing Sunday as the holy Sabbath. [46] The only objective Standard we have by which to TEST doctrine is the Holy

Bible. Organized religion recognizes that fact and loudly professes to follow the Scriptures as the divine Source of all teaching. So when a teacher or preacher pretends to teach what the Bible says, we need to check out his message to see for ourselves how closely it measures up to the Word of God. A hymn by a pastor I greatly admire[47] says it quite well:

> *"Is Sunday in the Bible, my brother?*
> *Is it on its pages fair?*
> *If it's there, believe it,*
> *If it's there, receive it,*
> *But be sure that you can find it there."*

A friend of mine recently retired from her career as a lab technician. She spent her lifetime peering through a microscope doing blood counts, *etc.,* and she shared with me an insight gained from her long experience.

"It's absolutely amazing," she said, "that everything that comes from GOD looks more and more perfect the closer we look at it. We see order and beauty of design even on the microscopic level—it's really remarkable! But that's in sharp contrast to everything made by MAN. For instance, a new razor blade with its finely-honed edge appears perfect to the naked eye. But place it under a high-powered microscope for a closer look, and we see raggedness and imperfections. The more closely we examine it, the more glaring the flaws appear."

Why do I mention this? I do so because I see in her remarks a striking analogy between material things and spiritual truths: The truths that come from God are simple yet beautiful and logical. They will bear any amount of examination and not suffer. Dissect them, investigate them, scrutinize them to the "Nth" degree—and they appear only more perfect because TRUTH LOSES NOTHING BY INVESTIGATION. But the uninspired, erroneous ideas that come from the minds of men are not like that. The closer we examine man-made doctrines, the more imperfect they appear. Penetrating investigation reveals inconsistencies, logical fallacies, and downright deception.

In the last two chapters, you've made a close investigation of the Sabbath and Sunday from a Biblical perspective. Under penetrating analysis, one looks *better and better* the more you examine it, and the other looks *worse and worse.* Does that fact tell you anything about their origins?

We must not trifle with truth. We must not "play games" with God. We must not pray for Him to reveal His truth to us and then reject it when He answers that prayer. Sunday may be the popular day of worship, but popularity is not the measure used by God. The most popular minister in the world can't sweep the Bible under the rug or ignore the Ten Commandments. On this issue every single person will have to decide one way or the other. But remember, when it comes to decisions, YOURS is the one that counts! May God guide you as you draw your own conclusion in this vital matter.

Notes to Chapter 14

1. Ezekiel 46:1-3.
2. Sometimes the sixth day of the week was called "the preparation" or "the preparation day" since that's the day we are to prepare for the Sabbath by cleaning house and closing up shop. See Mark 15:42, John 19:42, *etc.*
3. Genesis 1:5.
4. Luke 23:56, NIV.
5. Mark 16:3, RSV.
6. John 20:19. The word translated "fear" is the Greek *phobos*, from which we get our "–phobia" words naming different kinds of fear.
7. Luke 24:10-11, NKJV.
8. Mark 16:9-11, NKJV.
9. See Luke 24:13-35.
10. Mark 16:12-13, NIV.
11. Mark 16:14, NIV.
12. Luke 24:37.
13. 1 Corinthians 16:2, Phillips translation.
14. Acts 20:7.
15. Acts 5:42.
16. Acts 27:33-36, NKJV.
17. Lamentations 4:4, NKJV.
18. Acts 20:11.
19. The narrative also shows that the meal—ceremonial *or* ordinary—was eaten between midnight and dawn! Please note:
    > Acts 20:7 – "Paul preached . . . **until midnight**."
    > Acts 20:8 – "And there were **many lights** in the upper chamber."
    > Acts 20:9 – "Paul was **long** preaching."

    Here it was, after midnight, and the breaking of bread had **not yet** taken place. Then, **after** Eutychus had fallen to his death and been miraculously restored to life, we read:
    > Acts 20:11 – "When he [Paul] therefore was come up again [to the upper chamber], and had **broken bread, and eaten**, and talked a LONG while, **even till break of day**, so he departed."

    Can anyone seriously contend that this example sets the pattern for congregational worship today?
20. Walter F. Specht, "Sunday in the New Testament," in *The Sabbath in Scripture and History,* Kenneth A. Strand, editor (Washington, D.C.: c. 1982), p. 123.
21. Christ and His disciples ate the Lord's Supper—the Last Supper—on the Thursday night preceding His crucifixion on Good Friday. See Matthew 26:20-30, Mark 14:12-26, and Luke 22:7-23.
22. Acts 2:46. Nowhere does the Bible specify Sunday or *any other* prescribed time for celebrating the Lord's Supper. Paul, in outlining the ordinance of communion in 1 Corinthians 11:23-29, simply says "**as often** as ye eat this bread, and drink this cup,

ye do show the Lord's death till He come." Verse 26 (quoting Jesus' words "**as oft**" from verse 25). So the Lord's Supper may be celebrated any day— or every day— at the option of the church.

23. Acts 20:37-38.
24. Colossians 4:14.
25. This fact is yet another that contradicts the idea that here we have the pattern for future congregational worship.
26. Acts 20:7 & 11.
27. Acts 20:9-12, NIV.
28. Acts 20:8.
29. Genesis 1:5, 8, 13, 19, 23, 31.
30. Leviticus 23:32, NASB.
31. *Encyclopedia Britannica* (1967 edition), Volume 4, p. 612, article "Calendar."
32. Acts 20:7-8.
33. It doesn't help Sunday advocates to say, "Well, we don't know but perhaps Luke used the new Roman way of reckoning time from midnight to midnight." Exactly— we DON'T know. Without evidence, such an assumption lacks proof, and a sound legal principle asserts:

> "That which is DECLARED without proof
> may also be DENIED without proof."

Besides, if that were the case, then this meeting on the *dark* part of the *first* day of the week would have taken place on what we now call Sunday night, and the all-important "breaking of bread" would have occurred on MONDAY MORNING, since it took place after midnight!
34. Acts 20:7.
35. Acts 20:13-14, NRSV. See Allen Walker, *The Law and the Sabbath* (Roseville, California: Amazing Facts, Incorporated, c. 1985), p. 121.
36. Matthew 15:3, 6, 9.
37. Mark 7:7-9, & 13, NKJV.
38. Acts 5:29. See Acts 5:18 and 40.
39. Acts 20—the very chapter under discussion!—verses 20, 27, and 35.
40. Revelation 1:10.
41. Isaiah 58:13-14.
42. Genesis 2:3.
43. Exodus 20:10, Leviticus 23:3, Deuteronomy 5:14, *etc.*
44. Matthew 12:8, Mark 2:28, and Luke 6:5.
45. A line from Gilbert and Sullivan's *H. M. S. Pinafore* comes to mind:

> "Things are seldom what they seem,
> Skim milk masquerades as cream."

46. Regarding the idea that we should observe Sunday in honor of Christ's resurrection, see "Baptism: A Memorial of Both Great Events," pages 376-377, above.
47. The late James William McComas, Ph.D.

"BUY the TRUTH, and SELL it NOT; also wisdom, and instruction, and understanding."
—PROVERBS 23:23

MYSTERY #6
Final Events/The Future

~

What does the future hold?
Is there any way of knowing
what's next on the world's agenda?

"The REVELATION of . . .
things which must
shortly come to pass."
—Revelation 1:1

~

CHAPTER FIFTEEN

HISTORY TOLD IN ADVANCE

A LL OF US would like to know the future—or at least we THINK we would! In Bible times the disobedient consulted seers, soothsayers, witches, astrologers, so-called "wise men"—anyone who might predict future events. Today people read horoscopes, visit palm-readers, consult fortune-tellers, hold seances, and use Ouija boards, all for the same reason—to know the future.

The future is, and always has been, a mystery. It's hard for us to predict—"What we anticipate seldom occurs; what we least expected generally happens." [1] Man's predictions go wrong so often that someone has described the weather bureau as "a NON-PROPHET agency." Paul Harwitz facetiously made a double-edged point: "A top-secret government study indicates that we'd be no worse off if we let the economists predict the weather and the meteorologists predict the economy."

Even so-called psychics have a very LOW batting average: For instance, it seems that the late Jeane Dixon was 100% right—less than 10% of the time. Man-made predictions are notoriously UNdependable! Consider stock-market forecasts, the outcome of a political election, or even a horse race. What will men's and women's fashions look like a year or two from now? No one in the present moment can peer even twenty-four hours into the future, let alone tell what'll happen on some distant day.

On a purely human level, it's ANYBODY'S GUESS what the future holds. Anyone who could tell what's in store because he knew—really KNEW—the future would become the greatest leader the world has ever seen. But man's vision is limited to the horizon of today, and tomorrow is shrouded in mystery. Human prognostications are based on clumsy guesswork—and when occasionally such predictions prove partially true, it's just a lucky coincidence.

God REVEALS Secrets

The Securities & Exchange Commission has outlawed "insider" trading schemes on Wall Street—it's obviously unfair to allow stock manipulation by those privileged to have inside information. But students of prophecy have INSIDE INFORMATION on the future from God Himself. Fortunately, God's future plans are NOT classified as "TOP SECRET," for He's divulged them in advance through His prophets, those chosen servants to whom and through whom God speaks. We read:

> "Surely the Lord God does nothing,
> > without revealing His secret
> > to His servants the prophets." [2]
> When God was going to destroy the world through a flood,
> > He revealed His secret to NOAH. [3]
> When God was about to destroy Sodom and Gomorrah,
> > He revealed His secret to ABRAHAM and LOT. [4]
> When God was about to destroy the wicked city of Nineveh,
> > He revealed His secret to JONAH. [5]
> When God sent His Son as Savior, He revealed His secret
> > to JOHN THE BAPTIST and others. [6]

Countless other examples could be given, for "The SECRET things belong unto the Lord our God: but those things which are REVEALED belong unto us and to our children forever. . . ." [7] Though some things remain "secret," Bible prophecy reveals much of the future.

PROPHECY: God's ACID TEST

Predictive prophecy is the acid test of divinity. Fulfilled prophecy gives authority and authenticity to the Bible and stamps the Word of God as divine. The other supposedly sacred books—the Koran of the Muslims, the Bhagavad-Gita of the Hindus, the writings of Confucius—do not stress prophecy and make no claim to predict the future. But the Bible does. In fact, God stakes his reputation on His ability to forecast the future. Here are a few of His claims:

● "I am God, and there is none like Me, declaring the END from the BEGINNING, and from ancient times the things that are not yet done." [8]

- God challenges the false gods of the people to prophesy: "Bring in your idols to tell us what is going to happen. . . . Declare to us the things to come, tell us what the future holds, so we may know that you [heathen images] are gods." [9]

- God reminds His people: "I foretold the former things long ago, My mouth announced them and I made them known; then suddenly I acted, and they came to pass. For I knew how stubborn you were. . . . Therefore I told you these things long ago; before they happened I announced them to you so that you could not say, 'My idols did them; my wooden image and metal god ordained them.'" [10]

- "I alone am the Lord your God. No other god may share My glory; I will not let idols share My praise. The things I have predicted have now come true. Now I will tell you of new things even before they begin to happen." [11]

"THE GUIDING LIGHT OF PROPHECY"

The inspired Apostle Peter was an eye-witness of our Lord's glory on the Mount of Transfiguration and heard first-hand the voice of God from heaven declaring "This is My beloved Son, in Whom I am well pleased." [12] He asserts with confidence: "We have not followed cunningly devised fables, . . . but were eyewitnesses of His majesty. . . . And this voice which came from heaven we heard, when we were with Him in the holy mount." Yet even in the face of this sublime experience, Peter immediately adds: "We have also a more sure word of PROPHECY; whereunto ye do well that ye take heed, as unto a LIGHT that shineth in a dark place." [13]

God's "word of prophecy" is "more sure" than what? Peter says it's MORE SURE than even his own senses of sight and hearing!

Someone has said that "History is prophecy read backwards," and the two certainly are reciprocal in nature. Bible prophecy and human history are like TWO SIDES of the SAME COIN. Read in this light, history takes on an exciting new meaning: Ceasing to be an unending revolution of the wheels of fortune and fate, history takes on divine dimensions. Seeing God's hand on the helm of history gives assurance in a chaotic world. Yet most people, neglecting the study of God's Word, don't know this comforting fact.

PAGAN PROPHETS FALL SHORT

Delphi was an ancient Greek town where the celebrated oracle of Apollo supposedly foretold the fortunes of those who consulted her. Going into a trance, the prophetess would utter words which were thought to be uttered by Apollo. "The prestige of the oracle . . . ensured a steady stream of visitors from all parts of the Greek world. People came from abroad also." [14] Even kings made long trips to Delphi to question the oracle.

But the "catch" was that the Delphic oracle didn't really know the future. So she'd purposely clothe her prognostications in ambiguous language to give them a double meaning. *Encyclopedia Britannica* tells of "numerous cases in which the response was couched in language so obscure, vague or ambiguous as to leave room for different interpretations. Thus there would be a sufficient explanation if events did not agree with the meaning the inquirer had attached to the reply given him." [15]

Herodotus, the "Father of History," reported the following example of this Delphic deception: When Croesus, King of Lydia, consulted the oracle as to whether or not he should fight the Persians, he was told that *"By crossing the River Halys, Croesus will destroy a mighty power."* Thinking this meant he would conquer the Persians, he did cross the river, and he did destroy a mighty power—his own!

Again, when King Pyrrhus sought advice on a similar military venture, the oracle at Delphi made this cryptic reply so the prophecy would appear to come true *no matter who triumphed:*

> "I declare thee, O Pyrrhus,
> the Roman to be able to conquer."

Many human prophecies are like those of the Delphic oracle. False prophets "hedge their bets" and resort to evasive wording, but God's predictions are definite and distinct. Bible prophets didn't peddle vague and general predictions that could be adjusted to fit any outcome. Events predicted in the Bible have taken place with clocklike precision and amazing accuracy! Bible prophecy is better than a crystal ball, for SPECULATION by man is no match for REVELATION by God, who knows the future even better than we know the past.

Shakespeare was right when he said:

> "All the world's a stage,
> And all the men and women merely players.
> They have their exits and their entrances;
> And one man in his time plays many parts." [16]

As history's GREAT DRAMA unfolds, our eyes focus so often on the human actors that we fail to see God's part in the whole production. The Lord of history is a backstage God [17] who gives each individual freedom of choice, but He's still "working in the wings" directing the larger affairs of this world.

History in that sense becomes His story—though we certainly can't blame the man-made sordidness, wars, and tragedies on Him.

ANCIENT Manuscripts
Reveal FUTURE Events

Casually we use the expression—"in the foreseeable future"—forgetting that there's no such thing! Life is always uncertain, complicated by uncontrollable events and unforeseeable circumstances, so we don't know what the future holds. But God does. He sees the end from the beginning and holds the future in the hollow of His hand. One writer describes God's providential care in this way:

> "Above the distractions of the earth He sits enthroned;
> all things are open to His divine survey;
> and from His great and calm eternity
> He orders that which His providence sees best." [18]

Numerous examples of God's divine intervention could be cited from the inspired pages of His Word, but let's look at only three:

- **Tyre,**
- **Egypt,** and
- **Babylon.**

I. TYRE'S Doom Declared

Tyre was found in what we today call modern Lebanon, fifty miles south of bombed-out Beirut. *Encyclopedia Britannica* says the present small village (called "Sur" in Arabic) has a population of less than 17,000 and "is of no particular significance." [19]

But ancient Tyre, or Tyrus, was a different story. Authorities tell us that "Tyre was the chief stronghold of ancient Phoenicia, and one of the *greatest* cities of the ancient world." [20] The Phoenicians were among the earliest sea-going peoples of the world. They were great sailors, great navigators, great traders. They knew every corner of the Mediterranean Sea a thousand years before Christ was born. When Israel's King Solomon built a navy, "Hiram the King of Tyre" lent him workers who were "shipmen that had knowledge of the sea." [21]

Tyre was a booming, bustling seaport on the eastern Mediterranean shore and was the leading Phoenician city. Carthage, in North Africa, became a powerful rival of Rome, yet Carthage was only a colony of Tyre.

A magnificent city with a fine harbor, Tyre became the "New York" of Asia, the great mart of the Mediterranean world. Ships from all nations anchored in her harbor. Their passengers bartered in her streets for African ivory, Oriental silk, Egyptian linen, exotic perfumes, flocks, and slaves. The Bible called it "Tyre, the CROWNING city, whose merchants are princes, whose traffickers are the honourable of the earth." [22]

Thus Tyre was truly a great city of the ancient world. But it was an enemy of God. For instance, Jezebel, the wicked queen of Israel, was from Tyre, being the daughter of the king of Tyre. She, along with her equally wicked husband, King Ahab, introduced pagan Baal worship among God's people in Israel. [23]

So this proud, rich, evil city was to suffer a severe change of fortune. God pronounced a message of doom through His spokesman, Ezekiel. That prophetic message is worth studying in detail.

First of all, God boldly foretold even the NAME of Tyre's invader: "Thus saith the Lord God; Behold, I will bring upon Tyrus Nebuchadrezzar [24] king of Babylon, . . . with horses, and with chariots, and with horsemen, and companies, and much people. He shall slay with the sword thy daughters in the field: and he shall make a fort against thee. . . . And he shall set engines of war against thy WALLS, and with his axes he shall break down thy TOWERS. By reason of the abundance of his horses their dust shall cover thee: thy walls shall shake at the noise of the horsemen, and of the wheels, and of the chariots, when he shall enter into thy GATES, as men enter into a city wherein is made a breach. With the hoofs of his horses shall he tread down all thy streets: he shall slay thy people by the sword, and thy strong garrisons shall go down to the ground." [25]

Babylon was master of the land as Tyre was mistress of the sea. Soon after Ezekiel's prediction, Babylonian armies under King Nebuchadnezzar surrounded and laid siege to Tyre. Yet it was not an easy victory: the siege lasted thirteen years! [26] When the city finally fell, Nebuchadnezzar destroyed it completely. But the conquerors found that many of Tyre's inhabitants, realizing they could hold out no longer, had already evacuated the city, fleeing to a nearby offshore island and taking with them their treasures. There on the island, beyond reach of Nebuchadnezzar's landlocked troops, who were without ships, survivors proceeded to build a new city, a second Tyre.

What kept Nebuchadnezzar at his seemingly hopeless task for five years, ten years, and more? Heaven had proclaimed he would enter the city, and enter it he did! Tyre was destroyed by the very conqueror named in divine prophecy. Babylon's armies destroyed the walls of the city and broke down her towers exactly as God had said.

Furthermore, "Thus saith the Lord God; Behold, I am against thee, O Tyrus, and will cause MANY NATIONS to come up against thee, as the sea causeth his WAVES to come up." [27]

This second point really makes two things clear. First, that more than one nation would punish Tyre for its wickedness, for God would "cause many nations" to fulfill His will. Second, those nations would war against the city successively rather than in a united attack, for God said they'd come against Tyre as the sea causes its waves to come.

History verifies God's prophetic word: In 585 B.C. BABYLON under Nebuchadnezzar attacked and destroyed old Tyre. That ancient city was never rebuilt. In 332 B.C. GREECE under Alexander the Great attacked and destroyed new Tyre. That island city was rebuilt on a smaller scale. In A.D. 1291 the MUSLIMS attacked new Tyre and finally destroyed the city.

This list does not include other successive conquests such as that by the SELEUCIDS in 198 B.C. and the ROMANS in 68 B.C. Truly, "many nations" came up against Tyre, "as the sea causeth his waves to come up."

THE MARVELOUS PRECISION OF PROPHECY!

But there's more to the story, because there's more to the prophecy. God declared further in regard to Tyre: "I will also scrape her DUST from her, and make her like the top of a rock. It shall be a place for the spreading of nets in the midst of the sea: for I have spoken it, saith the Lord God. . . . [For emphasis, God repeats this dire prophecy.] And they shall break down thy walls, and destroy thy pleasant houses: and they shall lay thy STONES and thy TIMBER and thy DUST in the midst of the water. . . . And I will make thee like the top of a rock: thou shalt be a place to spread nets upon . . . for I the Lord have spoken it, saith the Lord God." [28]

Here we have one of the most unique and specific prophecies in God's wonderful Book. Its astounding fulfillment is absolutely uncanny!

When Nebuchadnezzar's victory was complete, he left—but he also left the rubble of the once-proud city lying as mute evidence of the destructive battle. The people of Tyre made no attempt to rebuild on the old site. They were engaged in building a new city on the nearby island. Time passed. Months lengthened into years, years into decades, decades into centuries. The prophet Ezekiel lay dead in his grave, his body turned to dust, his prophecy only partially fulfilled. Debris of the demolished city still lay everywhere, providing the only remnant of ancient Tyre.

Remember, God had dared to predict that not only the STONES and TIMBER but even the DUST of Tyre would be "scraped" into the midst of the

SEA, leaving the ancient city completely barren, "like the top of a rock." How could that happen? Who would even care enough to bother scraping such a desolate site clean? What strange set of circumstances could possibly fulfill the details of the Lord's decree?

For *two and a half centuries,* God's prophecy waited. Still the ruins of the old city remained, challenging prophetic accuracy. Then in 332 B.C.   Alexander the Great strode onto the scene leading his invincible Greek armies. Young Alexander had just defeated the Persians at the Battle of Issus and was marching south to Egypt. But when Alexander reached the vicinity of Tyre, the Tyrians resisted and refused to admit him to their island city. Standing on the shore, the Greeks saw half a mile of water surging between them and the city they'd come to take.

Alexander, the man of action, the military genius, determined to conquer the city and destroy it—but how? He decided to build a CAUSEWAY across the channel of water separating the old ruined city from the new and to attack the island city directly. In doing so, Alexander unwittingly fulfilled Ezekiel's prophecy in a dramatic vindication of the ancient Scriptures. His workmen took the walls, towers, ruined houses and palaces of ancient Tyre, and cast these into the water, building a solid causeway two hundred feet wide out to the island. So great was the demand for material that they tore down the TIMBER, lifted the STONES, and literally *scraped* the very DUST from the site, laying these in the sea exactly as God had said!

Alexander captured Tyre's stronghold in the sea and burned the new city to the ground, thus fulfilling this word of the prophet Zechariah: "Tyre has built herself a stronghold; she has heaped up silver like dust, and gold like the dirt of the streets. But the Lord will take away her possessions and destroy her power on the sea, and she will be consumed by fire." [29]

Encyclopedia Britannica makes two assertions worth noting:

1. "As a general Alexander is among the greatest the world has known."
2. "The storming of Tyre in July 332 was Alexander's GREATEST military achievement." [30]

God used Nebuchadnezzar to fulfill one part of Ezekiel's prophecy and Alexander the Great to fulfill another part! Over the centuries sand and silt have washed in upon both sides of Alexander's causeway, accumulating to such an extent that what was once an ISLAND is now a PENINSULA and appears to be part of the mainland.

The simplified map on the next page shows what it was like after Alexander finished his remarkable work:

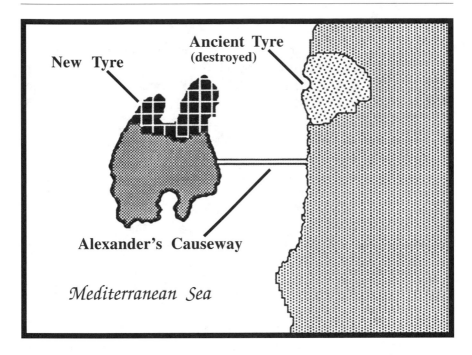

So the prophecy was remarkably fulfilled. The renowned old city of Tyre was made "like the top of a rock . . . a place to spread nets upon." [31] Many eyewitnesses, including Volney, the French skeptic, tell of visiting this spot and observing fishermen drying their nets on the rocky shore, just as the prophet said they would. [32]

Nothing is located on the deserted site where grand old Tyre once flourished. Many cities destroyed in the past *have* been rebuilt. For instance, Jerusalem was rebuilt twice after being completely destroyed. Rome rose again after Nero watched it burn. And on the peninsula where new Tyre, the island city, once stood, we find the little Muslim village of Sur. But of old Tyre, that once great city, God said: "Thou shalt be built no more. . . . I shall make thee a desolate city, like the cities that are not inhabited . . . , that thou be not inhabited. . . . Thou shalt BE no more." [33]

Because ancient Tyre, with all its building material, was scraped into the ocean, archaeologists cannot with certainty find the exact spot where that city stood. What an amazing fulfillment of the prophecy, "Though thou shalt be sought for, yet shalt thou never be found again, saith the Lord God." [34]

In 1860 French historian Ernest Renan traveled to Lebanon on an archaeological expedition to study Phoenician inscriptions. As an eyewitness, he stated: "I do not think any great city that played, through the centuries, a role of the first order has LEFT FEWER TRACES than Tyre." [35]

II. EGYPT'S Fate Foretold

As we turn to God's prophecies concerning Egypt, bear in mind that King Nebuchadnezzar, the instrument of God's will against Tyre, failed to profit from his service in that long, thirteen-year campaign. For the people of Tyre had moved their treasures to the offshore island which the Babylonians, lacking ships, could not plunder.

So the God of divine justice, who is eminently fair, gave Ezekiel the following promise and prophecy:

> "The word of the Lord came to me, saying, 'Son of man, Nebuchadnezzar king of Babylon caused his army to labor strenuously against Tyre; . . . yet neither he nor his army received wages from Tyre, for the labor which they expended on it. Therefore thus says the Lord God: "Surely I will GIVE the land of Egypt to Nebuchadnezzar king of Babylon; he shall take away her wealth, carry off her spoil, and remove her pillage; and that will be the wages for his army. I have given him the land of Egypt for his labor, because they worked for Me,'" says the Lord God." [36]

Fulfillment of this prophecy not only (1) rewarded those who worked for God against Tyre but also (2) punished the arrogant Pharaoh of Egypt. Note what Ezekiel says:

> "The word of the Lord came to me, saying, 'Son of man, set your face against Pharaoh king of Egypt, and prophesy against him, and against all Egypt. Speak, and say, "Thus says the Lord God: 'Behold, I am against you, O Pharaoh king of Egypt, . . . who has said, "My River [the Nile] is my own; *I have made it.*"'. . . Therefore thus says the Lord God: 'Surely I will bring a sword upon you. . . . And the land of Egypt shall become desolate and waste; then they will know that I am the Lord, because he said, "The River is mine, and I have made it."'. . . Therefore thus says the Lord God: 'Surely I am against Pharaoh king of Egypt, and will break his arms, . . . and I will make the sword fall out of his hand. . . . I will strengthen the arms of the king of Babylon and put My sword in his hand; but I will break Pharaoh's arms. . . . They shall know that I am the Lord, when I put My sword into the hand of the king of Babylon and he stretches it out against the land of Egypt.'" [37]

This Pharaoh, called Hophra in the Bible and Apries by the Greeks, reigned from 588-569 B.C. during the 26th Dynasty—the FINAL dynasty of Egyptian kings. According to Herodotus, Hophra/Apries boasted with blasphemy that not even God could defeat him. [38] God calls him by name in Jeremiah 44:30 – "Thus says the Lord: 'Behold, I will give Pharaoh Hophra king of Egypt into the hand of his enemies and into the hand of those who seek his life.'"

Exactly as God had foretold, Nebuchadnezzar's armies swept into Egypt. And Hophra was assassinated by one of his own generals. But here's another part of God's prophecy against Egypt I haven't told you—a part which remains true till this very day.

"A LOWLY KINGDOM . . . "

The Lord of time who controls the future had some words for Egypt— the land of pomp and pride, the land of glorified polytheism, the land that worshipped the sun and the crocodile: Through Ezekiel He told the once mighty Egyptians that "They shall be a LOWLY kingdom. It shall be the LOWLIEST of kingdoms; it shall never again exalt itself above the nations, for I will DIMINISH them so that they will not rule over the nations anymore. . . . I will make the land WASTE, and all that is in it, by the hand of ALIENS. I, the Lord, have spoken." [39]

There, in as few words as capsule comment will allow, is the entire subsequent history of a nation that was once among the richest and most powerful on earth. Every student of history recalls that Egypt has indeed been "the LOWLIEST of kingdoms" from that hour to this. It has been ruled "by the hand of ALIENS," dominated in turn by the Persians, the Greeks, the Romans, the Byzantine Greeks, the Saracens, the Turks, the French, and the British.

Egypt truly is "a LOWLY kingdom" of departed glory. But it *still exists* as a nation. In the course of time other large nations as well as smaller kingdoms have disappeared. Assyria was conquered and absorbed. Babylon has crumbled into dust. Even the mighty Roman Empire is no more. HOW DID THE PROPHET KNOW that Egypt wouldn't pass away? After all, Egypt is very OLD. When Old Testament prophets like Isaiah, Jeremiah, and Ezekiel lived, Egypt was *even then so ancient* that she boasted an unbroken line of kings longer than that of any other nation. When the city of Rome was founded, Egypt was already two thousand years old! WHO TOLD EZEKIEL that Egypt would (1) still *remain*—but only as (2) a *lowly* kingdom (3) largely under *foreign* domination, in a land (4) that would be made *waste*?

The proud, prosperous nation of Egypt was once the granary of the world, supplying grain and linen to other lands. "It is probable that in predynastic and dynastic times the Egyptian landscape was very different from that of today. . . . Twelve branches of the Nile were said to flow through it [the delta] in ancient times." [40] But God said, "I will make the rivers dry, . . . and I will make the land waste. [The plural "rivers" describes the Nile with its former branches and network of canals.] . . . And the river shall be wasted and dried up."[41] Egypt was dependent upon the Nile for its very existence. Whenever the Nile was too low to flow into irrigation canals, economic disaster followed. A very low Nile would leave the whole irrigation system completely dry. Judge for yourself to what degree God's dire prophecy was fulfilled: Today, says *Encyclopedia Britannica*, "Windblown sand dunes and stony and sandy plains comprise approximately 90% of Egypt's land."[42]

By the way, in addition to the preceding general prediction for Egypt as a whole, God gave a separate prediction for the specific city of Memphis, Egypt's ancient capital. "This is what the Sovereign Lord says: I will destroy the idols and put an end to the images in Memphis."[43] In all other cities of Egypt, tourists today see idols and images in abundance—but NOT in what was once the great city of Memphis.

Though time did not destroy the idols and images of other Egyptian cities equally old, of Memphis the *Encyclopedia Britannica* says, "In modern times hardly anything is left of the great city. Excavations carried out over half a century by [archaeologist] Flinders Petrie, the University of Pennsylvania, the Egyptian Antiquities service and others have recovered scant remains."[44]

Egyptologist Amelia B. Edwards records her amazement: "This is all that remains of Memphis, eldest of cities: a few rubbish heaps, a dozen or so of broken statues, and a name! . . . WHERE are the stately ruins that even in the Middle Ages extended over a space estimated at half a day's journey in every direction? One can hardly believe that a great city EVER flourished on this spot or can hardly understand how it should have been effaced so utterly."[45]

World Book Encyclopedia explains, "The city was the seat of government for the early Pharaohs. Memphis fell into ruins after the Arab conquest of Egypt, and the stones of its buildings were carted away to build the newer city of Cairo."[46]

With these facts, History testifies to the Bible's truth.

III. BABYLON'S DEATH DECREED

Babylon, one of the most famous cities of the ancient world, was the magnificent capital of the powerful Babylonian Empire. Located in the land of Chaldea or Mesopotamia, it was situated about sixty miles south of modern Baghdad in what today is southern Iraq.

Never had the world seen such a city. Babylon was dependent for supplies on no foreign country: Its rich soil, part of the famous Fertile Crescent in the valley of the Tigris and Euphrates Rivers, yielded huge harvests. The legendary "Hanging Gardens of Babylon," arranged in successive terraces, were one of the Seven Wonders of the world. Babylon's temples and palaces were among the most splendid buildings of antiquity, and the Euphrates River flowed through the city.

Babylon's fortifications were virtually impregnable. The city was laid out in a rectangle surrounded by two sets of walls reinforced at regular intervals with towers. The inner wall was protected by a moat. Fields between the walls could provide food for the city if enemies besieged it. The massive walls were strong enough and wide enough to drive chariots atop them. *Encyclopedia Britannica* states that the outer walls were twenty-three feet wide [47]—easily enough room for three or four chariots to ride abreast and pass each other!

So the mighty city of Babylon had little to fear from man. But its pagan religion was very offensive to God.

King Hammurabi gave Babylon political conquests and his famous code of laws. "It was, however, as a RELIGIOUS center that the city attracted both power and prestige, and from the time of Hammurabi onward an established priesthood fostered the cult of MARDUK there." [48]

According to Babylon's false religion, Marduk was "the chief god of the city of Babylon and the national god of Babylonia. (As such he was eventually called simply Bel, 'lord.')" [49] Astrology originated in this region, as did the WORSHIP of heavenly bodies, especially the SUN. Marduk, "the greatest of all Babylonian gods . . . was the chief SUN GOD." [50]

It was here that man tried the first "do-it-yourself" salvation. After the Flood of Noah's day, the people tried to build the infamous TOWER OF BABEL to save themselves in case another flood came and even to "reach unto heaven" on their own. [51] God frustrated their impudent efforts by confusing their language, but archaeologists have uncovered the ruins of more than one ziggurat in the area. (A *ziggurat* is a temple tower in the form of a terraced pyramid with each story smaller than the one below it.)

Britannica says: "The best known [ziggurat] is the seven-staged tower of Babel at Babylon." [52] This monumental building was described by ancient Greek historian Herodotus: "One of his remarks about the ziggurat, popularly known as the 'tower of Babel,' bears the authentic imprint of an eyewitness: 'when one is about half-way up, one finds a resting-place and seats, where persons are wont to sit some time on their way to the summit.'" [53]

At the summit was built a sacred temple. "There the shrine of the chief god [the sun god Bel Marduk] was placed. The great ziggurat in Babylon was about six hundred feet [sixty stories] high, built on a base sixty feet high." [54] Babel, the ancient site of this tower and pagan temple, gave its name to the city of Babylon.

Against this background of paganized society devoted to false religion, God foretold Babylon's doom. His prophet Isaiah warned that "Babylon, the glory of kingdoms, the beauty of the Chaldees' excellency, shall be as when God overthrew Sodom and Gomorrah." [55]

Right here I'd like you to notice two fascinating things. First, at the very time God made this prediction in Isaiah's day, Babylon was emerging as *the greatest nation in existence*—which makes any word of its doom all the more incredible and remarkable.

Secondly, we know that sometimes an UNWILLING witness is worth more than a willing one. If God used only His own people to prove the fulfillment of prophecy, it might be said that they worked and schemed to make it look that way. So God uses heathen nations who oppose Him to be His unwilling witnesses in proving He is the only true God. We've already seen God use this principle in the cases of Tyre and Egypt. Now let's examine His predictions about Babylon.

Ever Meet a **BABYLONIAN**?

I have met Egyptians, Chinese, and Jews. I've met Persians, who are now called Iranians. But I've never met a Babylonian, have you? For centuries no one's ever seen a native of Babylonia because "There *ain't* no such animal!"

Boldly, God declared Babylon "shall NEVER be inhabited, neither shall it be DWELT IN from generation to generation." [56] Sometimes people say, "It all depends on the interpretation you give a text." But there's no room for "interpretation" in this text—it's a plain, explicit statement. That mighty metropolis, once filled with countless homes and teeming crowds thronging its marketplaces, is no more. Archaeologists who occasionally visit Babylon's deserted site hear no human voice break the silence. The sun-baked clay is desolate and uninhabited but for a lonely lizard who scurries over a rock.

HOW DID THE PROPHET KNOW that "Babylon shall become HEAPS, a dwelling-place for dragons [or lizards], an astonishment . . . without an inhabitant"? [57] WHO TOLD HIM that the city, once richly fertile, would become "desolate, a dry and desert land, a land where no one lives, through which no man travels"? [58] It could be no one but the omniscient God!

Yet there's more to the prophecy. God also says: "Neither shall the Arabian pitch tent there; neither shall the shepherds make their fold there." [59] The Arabs, a nomadic people at the height of Babylonian glory, still wander about with their camels just as they did then, but the Babylonians are all gone—you'll never meet one. God knew that today there wouldn't be a Babylonian in existence, but the Arabs would continue on indefinitely. As you drive along from Baghdad to Babylon, the land is flat in all directions, and you'll see Arab tents scattered here and there. But Babylon is a pile of rubbish, and superstitious Arabs cannot be induced to spend even one night there.

Furthermore, "They shall not take of thee a stone for a corner, nor a stone for foundations; but thou shalt be desolate for ever, saith the Lord." [60] We know that Alexander used the ruins of TYRE to build his causeway, and the Egyptians used the ruins of MEMPHIS to build Cairo, but God said that the immense amount of building material left in Babylon's ruins would NOT be so used. Babylon was built of sun-dried bricks, and it would've been simple to use those sturdy bricks to rebuild the city, but no one's ever done this. Other cities have been destroyed and rebuilt time after time. But God said Babylon would be desolate forever. HOW DID JEREMIAH KNOW that the Arabs would prefer to continue living in TENTS rather than make use of all that wonderful building material? God told him.

God foretold also, "Chaldea [a synonym for Babylon, which was located in the land of Chaldea] shall be a spoil. . . . Open her storehouses. . . . A sword is upon her treasures; and they shall be robbed." [61] Babylon was repeatedly robbed by wave after wave of looters and vandals who swept over the city pillaging and plundering her treasures. Cyrus took huge treasures when he captured Babylon. Xerxes is said to have taken 150 million dollars in gold alone. From those ruins, Alexander the Great gave the equivalent of $50 to each of his soldiers.

Then came the Romans. Of the Roman plunder, historian Gibbon says: "Though much of the treasure had been removed, . . . the remaining wealth appears to have exceeded their hopes and even to have satiated their avarice." [62] God foretold of Babylon: "All that spoil her shall be *satisfied*." [63] Gibbon says they were *satiated*. How literally is God's prophecy fulfilled!

If you could see how Babylon looks today, you'd understand at once that God's expression "Babylon shall become HEAPS" [64] is uncannily descriptive. The place is not recognizable as a city. What rubble and ruins there are lie buried. There's not much to see except what the prophet saw in vision and recorded so faithfully. Everywhere are seen mounds of baked clay, in heaps.

The reason for this is that, after Babylon finally fell, treasure-seekers dug for plunder, turning over the ground as they searched. A pioneer archaeologist, Britain's Sir Austen Henry Layard, found this condition at Babylon in 1845: "Shapeless HEAPS of rubbish cover for many an acre the face of the land." [65] Through the centuries so many robber bands have dug about the ruins searching for treasures buried there, that Babylon today is literally just "heaps" of debris and nothing more!

Though the Great Wall of China still stands in good repair and fine condition after millenniums of war and weather, "Thus saith the Lord of hosts; The broad walls of Babylon shall be UTTERLY BROKEN"[66]—and they certainly were!

DIVINE FOREKNOWLEDGE!

Any who've read this far should be so impressed with the omniscience of the all-knowing God as to have faith in His Word because it directs such impressive light onto the future. However, if you still have doubts, let me ask you this:

- Would it help if God foretold the SPECIFIC NATION that would conquer Babylon?

- Would it help if God foretold the VERY MEANS by which Babylon's invader would breach those impregnable walls?

- Would it help if God named the CONQUEROR of Babylon more than a hundred years BEFORE he was born?

After all, divine foreknowledge like this would be absolute proof that God is God, affixing a seal to His divinity that none can counterfeit.

Incredibly enough, God DID specify in advance the nation that would destroy Babylon: "Make the arrows bright! Gather the shields! The Lord has raised up the spirit of the kings of the MEDES. For His plan is against Babylon to destroy it. . . . Prepare against her [Babylon] the nations, with the kings of the Medes." [67]

God spoke through the prophet Isaiah as well as Jeremiah: "Behold, I will stir up the Medes against them [the Babylonians]." [68] This prophecy is all the more striking when we realize that in Isaiah's time the chief enemy of Babylon was the might of militant Assyria, whereas the Medes, while known as a people, were scarcely a united nation. And the Persians, who later conquered the Medes and formed the dual empire of Medo-Persia, were at that time an even more insignificant power.

Amazing ACCURACY

But God is even more specific, naming both the MAN and the MEANS by which Babylon would be conquered centuries before that proud city fell without a fight!

A striking example of HISTORY TOLD IN ADVANCE is heaven's predictions about CYRUS THE GREAT. The work of Cyrus was outlined long in advance by

God's prophet Isaiah, who was born in the first half of the eighth century before Christ, about the year 760 B.C. And Cyrus was born early in the sixth century about 599 B.C.—more than *a century and a half later.* He conquered Babylon in 539 B.C. Any reliable reference book will substantiate these dates. So *Isaiah prophesied and was dead and buried before Cyrus was even born.*

A bit of background may be helpful here: Some time earlier, Babylon under Nebuchadnezzar had been used by God to punish His rebellious people after many warnings and calls for repentance. Jerusalem had been conquered, the Temple destroyed, and all surviving Jews taken in chains to Babylon where they remained in captivity.

When Cyrus came on the scene as the skillful Persian leader, he wanted to capture Babylon—but how could he? It was the city that could never be taken by the means of warfare then known. No soldier could climb the high, strong walls surrounding it without being detected. And it was useless to lay siege to the city, since there was always enough food grown within its walls to feed everyone. It even had its own water supply, for the River Euphrates ran into the city and emerged from the other side, passing under the walls. Huge two-leaved gates of brass barred all entrance from the river bed to the city itself.

Cyrus resolved to make the channel of the river his highway into his enemy's stronghold. Learning of an approaching annual festival lasting several days in which the whole city would be given to mirth and revelry, Cyrus fixed on the last night of the prolonged party to execute his plan. At a given hour, his soldiers diverted the river into a large artificial lake so they could silently creep along the empty river bed under the outer walls. Providentially, the Babylonians' drunken revelry made for careless security, and the river gates were left open and unprotected.

The soldiers of Cyrus fell upon the royal guards in the palace of the king and easily overcame them. Miraculously, the invincible city fell without a fight. That is the record of history. [69] This is what Isaiah wrote many years before, as the inspired penman of God . . .

> "That saith of CYRUS, He is My shepherd, and shall perform all My pleasure: even saying to Jerusalem, Thou shalt be built; and to the Temple, Thy foundation shall be laid. Thus saith the Lord to His anointed, to Cyrus, whose right hand I have holden, to subdue nations before him; and I will loose the loins of kings, to open before him the two leaved gates; and the GATES shall NOT be SHUT; I will go before thee, and make the crooked places straight: I will break in pieces the gates of brass, and cut in sunder the bars of iron: And I will give thee the treasures of darkness, and hidden riches of secret places, that thou

mayest know that I, the Lord, which call thee by name, am the God of Israel. For Jacob My servant's sake, and Israel mine elect, I have even called thee by thy name: I have surnamed thee, though thou hast not known Me; I am the Lord, and there is none else, there is no God beside Me: I girded thee, though thou hast not known Me. . . . I have raised him up in righteousness, and I will direct his ways: he shall build My city, and he shall let go My captives, not for price or reward, saith the Lord of hosts." [70]

Please note the following prophetic points about Cyrus:

1 – NAMED more than a century before he was born
2 – Would have NATIONS FALL before him
3 – Would find GATES OPENED before him
4 – Would be from those who had NOT KNOWN the Lord
5 – Would RELEASE God's captive people
6 – Would order the REBUILDING of Jerusalem
      and especially the Temple there.

Mere human wisdom or lucky guesswork could never produce such precise predictions!

History records that CYRUS THE GREAT, founder of the Persian Empire, reigned from 559 to 530 B.C. when he was killed in battle. "Cyrus was an outstanding soldier and statesman . . . and left behind him a reputation for justice and clemency." [71] For instance, when he conquered the Median kingdom, he did not subjugate the people but made them part of a joint Medo-Persian empire. History records that the Medes were made subject to the Persians, but "in the new empire they retained a prominent position; in honour and war they stood next to the Persians . . . and many noble Medes were employed as officials, satraps, and generals." [72]

In fact, Cyrus sent DARIUS THE MEDE to head his attack on Babylon. But, as we said above, the Babylonians were not alarmed—no weapons made were a match for Babylon's walls! In fact, Babylonian ruler Belshazzar and his court carelessly feasted in a drunken orgy, using the sacred vessels taken from God's Temple in Jerusalem to drink toasts to their pagan gods. But during that feast a heavenly hand inscribed cryptic *handwriting on the wall* of the king's palace. [73]

A small detail of the prophecy concerning Cyrus may have escaped our attention when we read it on the preceding page. God said, "I will loose the loins of kings." And when Belshazzar and his guests saw the disembodied hand mysteriously writing on the wall, he was absolutely terrified. As drunk as he was, "his thoughts troubled him, so that the joints of his LOINS were

LOOSED, and *his knees smote one against the other*" [74]—the king was so scared, his knees were knocking together!

At that moment, unknown to the frightened king, Darius and his men were making their way through the city gates left open (Greek historian Herodotus, writing from the 5th century B.C., relates that on the night the city fell, its gates were not closed) by careless guards who also had been drinking. In a surprise attack, the invaders proceeded through the darkness killing all they met on the way. Upon reaching the royal palace, they killed the king that very night.

God predicted even the drunken FEAST that became the prelude to their deaths. "In their heat I will make their feasts, and I will make them drunken, that they may rejoice, and sleep a perpetual sleep, and not wake, saith the Lord. . . . And I will make drunk her princes, and her wise men, her captains, and her rulers, and her mighty men: and they shall sleep a perpetual sleep, and not wake, saith the King, whose name is the Lord of hosts." [75]

One last point should be made clear: Though Cyrus captured Babylon exactly as God said he would, the Medes and Persians did not destroy the city but made it their capital. Regarding the vanquished NATION, *Britannica* says with a note of finality: "This is the end of the history of Babylonia." [76] The final ruin of the CITY proper came centuries later, many hundreds of years after Isaiah's and Jeremiah's prophecies were written.

Jewish historian Josephus reported that Cyrus was shown God's predictions regarding himself shortly after Babylon's fall. [77] So profound an effect did God's prophetic Word have on the monarch that we read: "The Lord moved the heart of Cyrus king of Persia to make a proclamation throughout his realm and to put it in writing: 'This is what Cyrus king of Persia says: The Lord, the God of heaven, has given me all the kingdoms of the earth and He has appointed me to build a Temple for Him at Jerusalem in Judah.'" [78] Furthermore, all the Jews captive in Babylon who wished to return to their native land were free to do so.

Secular sources corroborate this marvelous fulfillment of prophecy. For instance, *Encyclopedia Britannica* states that Cyrus "in 538 B.C. authorized the return to Palestine of the Jews deported by Nebuchadrezzar and made arrangements for the rebuilding of the Temple in Jerusalem." [79]

As we look back in history, we see that both EGYPT and BABYLON, in their turn, held God's people captive as slaves in their respective lands. [80] And both were punished by God in a remarkable way.

✦ ✦ ✦

WHO TOLD THE PROPHETS?
HOW DID THEY KNOW?

Fulfilled Prophecy is a fascinating mystery. For instance, Jesus boldly predicted that Christianity would NOT die! [81] Since even the mighty Roman Empire has long since crumbled into dust, how did He know that Christianity would not be superseded by some other moral system—IF there's no such thing as divinely-inspired prophecy?

In all ages and by all possible means, man has endeavored to unlock the future—but his attempts to predict have been a disastrous failure. God alone can declare the end from the beginning. Considering these things, can we believe that those who wrote the Bible were poor deluded fanatics who made some lucky guesses? Or are they what they claimed to be—inspired prophets of God? Even if there were no OTHER reason for believing the Bible has God for its Author, its fulfilled prophecies provide convincing evidence!

Today, of course, from our vantage point, we can SEE the precise, supernatural fulfillment of all these remarkable prophecies. So we can say with assurance that the Bible is true beyond a shadow of a doubt. In fact, this is the prime purpose of predictive prophecy—to build our faith in God's Word. Note Jesus' words: "I have told you BEFORE it come to pass, that, WHEN it come to pass, ye might BELIEVE." [82]

Therefore, no student of prophecy is a skeptic. The witness of fulfilled Bible prophecy is unquestionably one of the strongest proofs of the TRUTH of the Christian faith, providing an unanswerable argument for unbelievers. The unimpeachable testimony of events themselves provides proof positive that the Bible is the inspired Word of God.

So far we've looked at examples of God's foreknowledge applied to the specific cities or nations of TYRE, EGYPT, and BABYLON. But Bible prophecy goes further than that: On a broad canvas, with one amazing stroke of His brush, God paints the whole panorama of history! Let's examine the future as seen through the inspired eyes of the prophet Daniel.

THE PROPHETIC PANORAMA
OF DANIEL – CHAPTER *Two*

The Book of Daniel, as no other in the Bible, pictures the rise and fall of WORLD EMPIRES. If we want to know where we are in the stream of time, we must study the prophecies of Daniel.

The Master Himself told us to do just that: Jesus specifically urged His followers to "UNDERSTAND" the book of "Daniel the prophet." [83] Here, then, is the only book of the Bible about which Christ gave this special admonition, giving not only an invitation to read but a promise to understand Daniel's vital prophecies.

Young Daniel was actually a prisoner of war in a foreign land when God gave him this marvelous glimpse into the future. Along with other surviving Jews, he was carried away captive by King Nebuchadnezzar to the heathen courts of Babylon. But the Lord was with Daniel even in adversity. Few have been as faithful to God as this young Hebrew slave. And few have been as favored by God with revelations of the future.

> "The story of the decline and fall of the Roman Empire was first written, not by Edward Gibbon the skeptic in the eighteenth century of the Christian era, but by Daniel the prophet in the sixth century B.C. And Gibbon the skeptic used six large volumes in telling us in detail how accurate were the predictions of Daniel the prophet. . . . Gibbon's *Decline and Fall of the Roman Empire* is but an unwitting commentary on the uncanny accuracy of Daniel." [84]

The second chapter of Daniel's book has fittingly been called "the ABC of Bible prophecy" because it's both easy to understand and basic to our understanding of parallel prophecies in later chapters of the same book.

This second chapter tells of King Nebuchadnezzar's 2500–year–old dream. The dream God gave this Babylonian monarch was actually a PROPHECY giving "a bird's-eye-view" of history from Daniel's time till our own day and beyond. This prophecy is still being fulfilled twenty-five hundred years later! And it concerns YOUR future.

THE FORGOTTEN DREAM

King Nebuchadnezzar awoke one night greatly disturbed by a dream he could neither understand nor remember. He called on his counsellors, but the so-called "wise" men of Babylon had to admit their ignorance. "The magicians, and the astrologers, and the sorcerers . . . [said to the king] tell thy servants the dream, and we will show the interpretation." [85]

Obviously, they'd be glad to make up some plausible interpretation for the dream, as they had in the past, if the king would only tell them what the dream was. But the king, having forgotten what he had dreamed, could recall only that it "troubled" him. Furious from suspecting his wise men were frauds, Nebuchadnezzar threatened to cut them in pieces if they did not show him the dream and correctly interpret it for him.

But Daniel, who'd been brought to the king's palace to be groomed for leadership, was also one of the wise men of Nebuchadnezzar's court. Learning of the death decree, Daniel asked for more time so he could pray to God for a revelation of the dream. "Then was the secret revealed unto Daniel in a night vision." [86]

Going in before Nebuchadnezzar, Daniel was asked if he could really make known the forgotten dream. The young prophet took no honor to himself and humbly replied that no mortal could unlock the king's secret. "But," said Daniel, giving all glory to God, "there is a God in heaven that revealeth secrets, and maketh known to the king Nebuchadnezzar what shall be in the latter days." [87]

Daniel told the king that his dream was really a prophecy about "what would come to pass HEREAFTER: and He that revealeth secrets maketh known to thee what shall come to pass." [88] Then the prophet recalled for Nebuchadnezzar exactly what he had dreamed:

> "You looked, O king, and there before you stood a large statue—an enormous, dazzling statue, awesome in appearance. The HEAD of the statue was made of pure GOLD, its CHEST and ARMS of SILVER, its BELLY and THIGHS of BRONZE, [89] its LEGS of IRON, its FEET partly of IRON and partly of baked CLAY. While you were watching, a rock was cut out, but not by human hands. It struck the statue on its feet of iron and clay and smashed them. Then the iron, the clay, the bronze, the silver and the gold were broken to pieces. . . . The wind swept them away without leaving a trace. But the rock that struck the statue became a huge mountain and filled the whole earth." [90]

Having told the king his dream, Daniel proceeded to explain its meaning. Inspired by God, the prophet declared that Nebuchadnezzar was the "head of gold" in the dream. Since Daniel identified the other parts of the image as representing KINGDOMS, it's evident that the head of gold symbolized Nebuchadnezzar's kingdom, Babylon. In this and later chapters the terms "king" and "kingdom" are used interchangeably—for example, compare Daniel 7:17 and 23.

The HEAD of GOLD fittingly represented **Babylon**, "the golden city." [91] Jeremiah called the city "a golden cup . . . abundant in treasures." [92] Ancient historian Herodotus reported on Babylon's lavish use of solid gold, especially in its temples, describing a great golden image of Bel Marduk seated on a golden throne before a golden table and a golden altar. [93] The Greek poet Aeschylus (died 456 B.C.) similarly wrote of Babylon as "teeming with gold." [94]

But Babylon's glory was short-lived. For "after" it, Daniel continues the sequence, "another kingdom inferior to" Nebuchadnezzar's, represented by the CHEST and ARMS of SILVER, would conquer and supplant the golden kingdom. This was the kingdom of the **Medes and the Persians**. As silver is inferior to gold, the Medo-Persian Empire was inferior to the Babylonian.

Though the new kingdom covered more territory, it never equalled its predecessor in splendor and magnificence. The Medo-Persian conquerors adopted the Babylonian culture, for their own was far less developed.

Bible proof that the second kingdom of silver represents Medo-Persia is found in Daniel's account of the feast of Belshazzar, Babylon's last king. The prophet told the trembling ruler: "God hath numbered thy kingdom and finished it," and it was henceforth "given to the Medes and Persians." [95]

The third power, represented by the image's MID-SECTION of BRONZE, was the Macedonian **Greeks** led by Alexander the Great. That young military genius beat the Persians in several battles, finally routing them completely at the Battle of Arbela in 331 B.C. The bronze metal of the king's dream fittingly applies to Greece, for the Greeks were experts in molding bronze. Earlier armies were clothed in soft attire, but brazen armor distinguished the Greek warriors. Wearing bronze breastplates and helmets, they carried bronze shields and swords.

One authority states that in passing from the third to the fourth kingdom "we are actually passing from a bronze to an iron age. To the Roman poets bronze weapons spoke of the olden time." [96]

"The fourth kingdom," said Daniel, "shall be as strong as IRON," represented by the statue's IRON LEGS. "As iron breaks in pieces and shatters everything . . . that kingdom will break in pieces and crush all the others." [97] The iron monarchy of **Rome** conquered Alexander's homeland at the Battle of Pydna in 168 B.C. By 30 B.C. Egypt was subjugated, and Rome completed her conquest of the Mediterranean world. So inescapably did the prophetic portrayal correspond to its historical fulfillment that the great historian Edward Gibbon, though not a Christian or a Bible believer himself, wittingly or unwittingly used Scriptural language when he wrote: "The images of GOLD, or SILVER, or BRASS, that might serve to represent the nations and their kings, were successively broken by the IRON monarchy of ROME." [98]

Just as legs form the longest part of the body, Rome had the longest reign of any of the other world powers. For more than 600 years Rome was invincible, her banners waving from the British Isles to the Arabian Gulf, from the North Sea to the Sahara Desert, from the Atlantic to the Euphrates.

But Daniel, under divine inspiration, foretold the BREAK-UP of the mighty Roman Empire. When he came to the feet and toes in his explanation, Daniel predicted: "The kingdom shall be DIVIDED."

History verifies Daniel's words. During the fourth and fifth centuries A.D., Rome suffered invasions from barbarian tribes like the Goths and Huns. Attacked from without and decaying from within, Rome was divided into independent kingdoms that later became the nations of modern Europe. True to God's Word, those nations to this day remain "divided"—adjacent but separate—*like the toes of the foot.*

At least two profound lessons may be drawn from the prophecy and interpretation of Nebuchadnezzar's dream. *First,* we again see that God unerringly knows the future. No human foresight could predict that there'd be four—and only four—world powers from Daniel's day to ours. After all, Babylon was followed by Medo-Persia, Medo-Persia was conquered by Greece, and the Greek Empire was succeeded by Rome. Human logic would conclude that Rome itself would be overcome and followed by successive world-dominating empires. But no: God had prescribed four world powers and four only—and so it was.

GOD HIMSELF HAS SPOKEN: NO REVIVED ROMAN EMPIRE!

Second—and this lesson escapes the notice of many Bible students who look for a "revived Roman Empire" in the future—God said those nations of Western Europe, "the feet and toes, part of potter's clay, and part of iron, . . . shall be DIVIDED. . . . They shall NOT cleave [or adhere] one to another, even as iron is not mixed with clay." [99]

Heaven knows man has TRIED to weld those iron-clay nations into a superstate. CHARLEMAGNE tried about A.D. 800; CHARLES THE FIFTH, about 1500; NAPOLEON BONAPARTE, about 1800. KAISER WILHELM II's attempt led to World War I, and ADOLPH HITLER's led to World War II. But all failed miserably. [100] "All the king's horses and all the king's men couldn't put [Rome] together again." God's seven words still stand regarding the nations: "They SHALL NOT cleave one to another."

Not only have military leaders and dictators like those mentioned above failed. So have the LEAGUE OF NATIONS and the UNITED NATIONS, which, despite good intentions, degenerated into mere debating societies. True unity has not been achieved by either armies of war or organizations of peace. Some Christians overlook God's message in Daniel 2 and expect a rebirth of the old Roman Empire, pinning their hopes on the European Common Market. But prophecy's verdict comes ringing down the corridor of time leaving the nations still divided by different MONETARY systems. Though efforts are being made to introduce a single currency—called the "euro," today's traveler copes with the British *pound,* Danish *kroner,* Dutch *guilder,* French *franc,* German *mark,* Greek *drachma,* Italian *lira,* Spanish *peseta,* and Swedish *krona.* Understandably, American travelers carrying U.S. *dollars* feel a little confused.

Even if monetary unification is achieved, the problem of different LAN-GUAGES still remains in the polyglot nations that were once the monolithic Roman Empire. In addition to all this, each nation brings to the mix many cultural differences plus a historical heritage loaded with proud nationalistic feelings which aren't easily erased. Thus the European Common Market faces an impossible task from both a practical and a Scriptural standpoint.

Daniel foresaw that man would try to unify the divided empire even through INTERMARRIAGE. Daniel 2:43 specifically says of those divided nations: "They shall mingle themselves with the SEED of MEN." In just one example, Henry the Eighth's first wife, Catherine of Aragon, was the eldest daughter of Ferdinand and Isabella of Spain. In another case, England's Queen Victoria married Germany's Prince Albert. Politically motivated, the ruling heads of many European nations intermarried to such a degree that Queen Victoria was called "the grandmother of Europe." But again man's efforts were doomed to failure. Suspicion, intrigue, and war followed to maintain the division God predicted: "They shall NOT cleave one to another."

So what's next on the agenda for the world? Well, finally Daniel prophesied: "In the days of these kings [the nations of modern Europe] shall the God of heaven set up a kingdom which shall never be destroyed."[101] We now live "in the days of these kings." Chronologically we find ourselves NOT in the head of gold or chest and arms of silver, not in the belly and hips of bronze or even in the legs of iron. We're living in the statue's feet and toes—in the very toeNAILS!—of the last days when God says His everlasting kingdom will be set up.

Daniel assures us we can have complete confidence in this prophecy: "The dream is CERTAIN and the interpretation thereof SURE."

THE PROPHETIC PANORAMA
OF DANIEL – CHAPTER *SEVEN*

One of the most vital and comprehensive prophecies in all the Bible is found in Daniel, Chapter 7. As if to underline the great lessons presented in Daniel 2, God gave an "instant replay" in Chapter 7. Using the principle of repetition in teaching, the Master Teacher goes over the same ground more than once when something is of supreme importance. (Witness the way Christ's life story is told over and over again in the four gospels.)

In Daniel 7, however, a prophetic dream was experienced not by the pagan king but by Daniel himself. Instead of a metallic image, Daniel saw four beasts arise from the sea. Let's read it together:

"Daniel had a dream and visions of his head while on his bed. . . . Behold, the four winds of heaven were stirring up the Great Sea. And FOUR GREAT BEASTS came up from the sea, each different from the other. The first was like a LION, and had eagle's wings. I watched till its wings were plucked off; and it was lifted up from the earth and made to stand on two feet like a man, and a man's heart was given to it." [102]

Symbolic prophecy—God's "sign-language"—is easily understood if we let the Bible be its own interpreter. God tells us plainly: "These great beasts, which are four, are four kings, which shall arise. . . . The fourth beast shall be the fourth kingdom upon earth." [103] So these beasts are not four individual kings but rather four successive kingdoms or world empires.

This first beast, the LION, clearly depicts the BABYLONIAN EMPIRE. The lion was a symbol quite common in ancient Babylon. One of the few artifacts still to be seen among the utter ruin of the city is a huge, monumental lion weighing several tons. Also, archeologists who uncovered the Babylonian ruins found that the broken walls had been decorated by colored tiles depicting countless lions in relief sculpture. Many of those beautiful lions have been restored and are on display in the museum at East Berlin.

The prophet Jeremiah, warning Israel that God will punish their backsliding unfaithfulness by sending Babylonian armies, uses the lion as a symbol: "The LION is come up from his thicket, and the destroyer of the Gentiles is on his way; he is gone forth from his place to make thy land desolate." [104] "Israel is a hunted sheep driven away by LIONS. First the king of Assyria devoured him, and now at last Nebuchadnezzar king of Babylon has gnawed his bones. . . . The king of Babylon . . . [is] like a LION." [105]

The eagle's wings on the lion denote speed of conquest. Speaking of the Chaldeans or Babylonians, God says they are "swifter than the leopards, . . . and their horsemen . . . fly as the eagle that hasteth to eat." [106] Describing the "lion" that will destroy Israel, God says, "His chariots shall be as a whirlwind: his horses are swifter than eagles." [107]

But a change comes—the lion heart is taken away, and "a man's heart," timorous and afraid, replaces it. Jeremiah predicted: "The mighty men of Babylon have ceased fighting, they have remained in their strongholds; their might has failed, they became like women." [108] In Nebuchadnezzar's day, mighty Babylon stood against the world—and won! But during the closing years of its history, the nation became weak and effeminate through indulgence in luxury. When Cyrus and Darius laid siege to the city, Belshazzar's troops chose not to fight but "remained in their strongholds"—within the supposed security of those massive walls.

To continue Daniel's dream, we see "suddenly another beast, a second, like a BEAR. It was raised up on one side, and had three ribs in its mouth between its teeth. And they said thus to it: 'Arise, devour much flesh!'"[109]

The BEAR represents the new empire of MEDO-PERSIA which succeeded Babylon. This kingdom was composed of two nationalities, the Medes and the Persians, but the Persians became dominant. Thus the bear "was raised up on one side." In this twin merged empire we see a perfect parallel to the *two* silver arms in Daniel 2 and the *two* ram's horns in Daniel 8:

> "I lifted up mine eyes, and saw . . . a ram which had two horns: and the two horns were high; but one was HIGHER than the other, and the higher came up last. . . . The ram . . . having two horns are the kings of Media and Persia."[110]

The three ribs in the bear's mouth symbolize Babylon, Egypt, and Lydia,[111] the three principal kingdoms conquered by Medo-Persia. So the command "Arise, devour much flesh" is fitting for a power whose rapacious assaults were so widespread.

Daniel say, "After that, I looked, and there before me was another beast, one that looked like a LEOPARD. And on its back it had four wings like those of a bird. This beast had four heads, and it was given authority to rule."[112]

The third world power, GREECE, is represented here by a LEOPARD. If wings upon the Babylonian lion signified rapidity of conquest, they'd signify the same here. The leopard is naturally a swift beast, but it must have wings added to symbolize the exceptionally rapid rise of this nation. The two wings the lion had were not sufficient here—the leopard must have four, denoting the conquests of Alexander the Great which were unmatched for suddenness and rapidity. Cambridge historian Sir W. W. Tarn states that "His [Alexander's] speed of movement was extraordinary."[113] In less than eight years Alexander marched his armies more than 50,000 miles, covering enormous distances over unknown country. Never defeated, Alexander died while still a young man, having conquered all of the world he had seen.

Daniel further describes the leopard as having "four heads." When Alexander died without leaving an heir, the Grecian Empire was torn by civil war until his four leading generals carved up the kingdom among themselves. One general, CASSANDER, took the west including Macedonia and Athens. LYSIMACHUS took the north with Thrace and part of Asia Minor. SELEUCUS took the east with most of Syria, Mesopotamia, and Persia, while PTOLEMY took the south including Palestine and Egypt.

Skeptics who discount prophecy must admit that more than mere coincidence is found here in Daniel's dream. With no real successor to Alexander available, why didn't the huge empire simply disintegrate into countless petty fragments—why into just *four* parts and no more? The leopard beast's "four heads" were indeed significant. But these divisions weakened the empire and opened the way for the rising power of Rome.

Daniel continues, "After this I saw in the night visions, and behold a fourth beast, dreadful and terrible, and strong exceedingly; and it had great IRON teeth: it devoured and brake in pieces, and stamped the residue with the feet of it; and it was diverse from all the beasts before it; and it had ten horns." [114]

The first beast was like a LION; the second, a BEAR; and the third, a LEOPARD. But the fourth beast Daniel saw in his dream—or nightmare— was almost indescribable. So "diverse from all the beasts before it," it was unlike anything the prophet had ever seen before. The other beasts—the lion, bear, and leopard—were ferocious. But Daniel emphasizes the horror of this "dreadful and terrible" beast, stressing its voracious aggressiveness.

ROME, "the fourth world power [to] rule the earth," [115] fits these dream symbols in every respect. It was "strong exceedingly." Its Roman legions "devoured and brake in pieces" all who stood in their way. And its "great iron teeth" echo the great iron legs of the huge statue in Nebuchadnezzar's dream.

Also, as that statue had TEN TOES, Daniel is careful to state that this fourth beast or kingdom "had TEN HORNS." When the prophet became "grieved" and "troubled" by the visions, he asked to know "the truth of all this." [116] Then a celestial voice explained that "The ten horns out of this kingdom are ten kings [117] that shall arise." [118]

Does this prophetic fact with its divine interpretation also meet its fulfillment in Rome? Indeed it does! The Roman Empire declined in power and finally fell in A.D. 476, only to be divided into TEN SMALLER KINGDOMS we know today as Italy, Germany, France, England, Spain, *etc.*

Through the centuries many have marvelled at the prophetic precision of Daniel's vision. For instance, Martin Luther speaks for countless other theologians when he says: "The first kingdom is the Assyrian [119] or BABYLONIAN kingdom; the second, the MEDO-PERSIAN; the third, the great kingdom of Alexander and the GREEKS; and the fourth, the ROMAN EMPIRE. In this the whole world agrees, and history supports it fully in detail." [120]

How did Daniel, a prophet who lived about 625 to 535 B.C., know these things which happened so many centuries later—and are still happening in our time? How can we explain his uncanny accuracy except by divine foresight revealed by a supernatural Source?

Comparison of Daniel's Symbolic Visions

Daniel 7		Daniel 2
LION	BABYLON	GOLD
BEAR	PERSIA	SILVER
LEOPARD	GREECE	BRASS
FIERCE BEAST	ROME	IRON
LITTLE HORN	DIVIDED KINGDOMS	IRON AND CLAY
JUDGMENT	CHRIST'S KINGDOM	STONE

Much more is found in this marvelous chapter of Daniel's book than space permits us to include here, such as a preview of the solemn judgment scene in heaven and the mysterious "Little Horn" that arises among the ten-horn nations of Western Europe. This "Little Horn," a blasphemous and persecuting power which symbolizes the Antichrist, will be dealt with in detail when we arrive at Mystery #7 – The MARK of the BEAST: "Chapter 19 – Antichrist Unmasked."

CONCLUSION

These prophecies—and many others like them—affirm and validate your Bible. They make us realize that God has acted in human history. So history, as mentioned above, becomes HIS story—not man's or "a tale told by an idiot . . . signifying nothing."[121]

Our human hindsight is always "20-20," but among us poor mortals the future is always shrouded in mystery. Tony Hulman, the late owner of the Indianapolis Motor Speedway, was asked who he thought would win the classic 500-mile race that year. With wisdom and restraint, he replied: "I don't know. That's why we run the darn thing." Man-made prognostications are worth little, for the future is predictably UNpredictable!

But the Bible speaks more certainly of the future that any historian ever spoke of the past, with all his records before him. The Bible chronicles the future as if it were past, with the sure, luminous strokes of infinite knowledge. For God doesn't coyly play hide-and-seek with us. He shares His mind regarding the future. No speculation. No foggy predictions. No your-guess-is-as-good-as-mine.

When we see God's explicit prophecies so remarkably fulfilled time after time, we realize that "He knew it all along!" Yes, God knows all about tomorrow—He holds it in His hand. For the Lord we serve is God of the PAST, the PRESENT, *and* the FUTURE!

That's why Justin Martyr, the great scholar who was converted from paganism by the evidence of prophecy, said: "To DECLARE a thing should come to pass long before it is in being, and to BRING it to pass, this or nothing is the work of God."

Of course, a really stubborn skeptic may still say, "Well, prophecy doesn't actually prove the Bible is true."

Listen—perhaps prophecy doesn't prove the Bible is the Word of God. But I'll tell you this: Prophecy could certainly prove that it is NOT the Word of God. If just a few prophecies—if just one prophecy—FAILED to come true as predicted in the Bible, it could not be the Word of Almighty God!

But every prophecy has been literally fulfilled at God's appointed time. And the literal fulfillment of Bible prophecies in the past vouches for the fulfillment of the remaining ones.

Prophecy may be written on dusty parchments with mere words, but it's fulfilled in the real world of actual events. At the moment of fulfillment, PROPHECY becomes REALITY! And fulfilled prophecy stamps the Word of God as divine. The prophecies of the Bible give the clearest and most convincing evidence that that Book is the inspired revelation of the all-knowing God!

Notes to Chapter 15

1. British Prime Minister Benjamin Disraeli.
2. Amos 3:7, RSV.
3. See Genesis 6.
4. See Genesis 18 & 19.
5. See Jonah 3:1-10.
6. See John 1:19-34.
7. See Deuteronomy 29:29.
8. Isaiah 46:9-10.
9. Isaiah 41:21-23, NIV.
10. Isaiah 48:3-5, NIV.
11. Isaiah 42:8-9, TEV.
12. 2 Peter 1:16-18.
13. 2 Peter 1:19.
14. *Encyclopedia Britannica* (1967 edition), Volume 16, p. 1015, article "Oracle."
15. *Ibid.,* p. 1014.
16. William Shakespeare, *As You Like It,* Act II, Scene 7, lines 139-142.
17. James Russell Lowell wrote: "Behind the dim unknown,
    Standeth God within the shadow, keeping watch above His own."
    —"The Present Crisis," 1844.
18. E. G. White, *The Ministry of Healing* (Boise, Idaho: Pacific Press Publishing Association, c. 1942), p. 417.
19. *Encyclopedia Britannica* (1967 edition), Volume 22, p. 452, article "Tyre."
20. *World Book Encyclopedia* (1955 edition), Volume 16, p. 8239, article "Tyre."
21. 1 Kings 9:11, 26-27.
22. Isaiah 23:8.
23. *Encyclopedia Britannica* (1967 edition), Volume 22, p. 452, article "Tyre."
24. This famous king's name is a Hebrew version of the Babylonian form and is spelled in English as both Nebuchad**r**ezzar and Nebuchad**n**ezzar.
25. Ezekiel 26:7-11.
26. From 585 to 573 B.C. *Encyclopedia Britannica* (1967 edition), Volume 22, p. 452, article "Tyre."
27. Ezekiel 26:3.
28. Ezekiel 26:4-5 and 12-14.
29. Zechariah 9:3-4, NIV.
30. *Encyclopedia Britannica* (1967 edition), Volume 1, pp. 573 and 576, article "Alexander."
31. Ezekiel 26:4-5, 14.
32. The French rationalist traveled in Syria and Egypt, December 1782–April 1785. See Constantin François Chasseboeuf, Comte de Volney, *Voyage en Syrie et en Egypte,* published in 2 volumes in 1787, edited by J. Gaulmier (1959), Volume 2, p. 212.
33. Ezekiel 26:14, 19-21.
34. Ezekiel 26:21.

35. Ernest Renan, *Mission de Phénicie* (1864-74), quoted in Wallace B. Fleming, *The History of Tyre*, Volume 10 of Columbia University Oriental Studies (New York: Columbia University Press, c. 1915), p. x, footnote.

36. Ezekiel 29:17-20, NKJV.

37. Ezekiel 29:1-9 and 30:22-25, NKJV.

38. Herodotus, *History*, Book ii, 170.

39. Ezekiel 29:14-15 and 30:12, NKJV.

40. *Encyclopedia Britannica* (1967 edition), Volume 8, p. 41, article "Egypt."

41. Ezekiel 30:12 and Isaiah 19:5.

42. *Encyclopedia Britannica* (1967 edition), Volume 8, Plate II, facing p. 61, article "Egypt."

43. Ezekiel 30:13, NIV. The King James Version uses the Hebrew name "Noph" for the Greek name, "Memphis."

44. *Encyclopedia Britannica* (1967 edition), Volume 15, p. 140, article "Memphis."

45. Amelia B. Edwards, *A Thousand Miles Up the Nile* (Philadelphia: David McKay, no date), pp. 97-99.

46. *World Book Encyclopedia* (1955 edition), Volume 5, p. 2224, article "Egypt."

47. Max Mallowan, *Encyclopedia Britannica* (1967 edition), Volume 2, p. 950, article "Babylon." Professor Mallowan (husband of mystery writer Agatha Christie) taught at the University of London and was Vice-Chairman of the British School of Archaeology in Iraq.

48. *Ibid.*, p. 949.

49. *Encyclopedia Britannica* (1967 edition), Volume 14, p. 859, article "Marduk."

50. *World Book Encyclopedia* (1955 edition), Volume 11, p. 4802, article "Marduk."

51. Genesis 11:4. God had already pledged His solemn word that a flood would never again destroy the world. Genesis 9:8-17.

52. *Encyclopedia Britannica* (1967 edition), Volume 23, p. 970, article "Ziggurat."

53. Mallowan, *Encyclopedia Britannica, op. cit.*, Volume 2, p. 950.

54. *World Book Encyclopedia* (1955 edition), Volume 1, p. 370, article "Architecture."

55. Isaiah 13:19.

56. Isaiah 13:20. Compare Jeremiah 50:39.

57. Jeremiah 51:37.

58. Jeremiah 51:43, NIV.

59. Isaiah 13:20.

60. Jeremiah 51:26.

61. Jeremiah 50:10, 26, 37.

62. Edward Gibbon, *The History of the Decline and Fall of the Roman Empire*, Volume IV, p. 480.

63. Jeremiah 50:10.

64. Jeremiah 51:37.

65. Austen Henry Layard, *Discoveries Among the Ruins of Nineveh and Babylon* (New York: Harper, 1856), chapter 21, p. 413.

66. Jeremiah 51:58.

67. Jeremiah 51:11 & 28, NKJV.

68. Isaiah 13:17.
69. Herodotus, *The History of Herodotus,* translated by Henry Cary (London: G. Bell and Sons, 1917), pp. 67-71; George Rawlinson, *The Seven Great Monarchies of the Ancient Eastern World* (New York: John B. Alden, 1885), Volume II, pp. 254-259; Humphrey Prideaux, *The Old and New Testament Connected in the History of the Jews and Neighboring Nations* (New York: Harper and Brothers, 1842), Volume I, pp. 136-137.
70. Isaiah 44:28 and 45:1-5 & 13.
71. *Encyclopedia Britannica* (1967 edition), volume 6, p. 960, article "Cyrus."
72. Encyclopedia Britannica (1967 edition), volume 15, p. 68, article "Media."
73. Daniel 5:1-5.
74. Daniel 5:6—but please read the whole remarkable chapter!
75. Jeremiah 51:39 & 57.
76. *Encyclopedia Britannica* (1967 edition), volume 2, p. 968, article "Babylonia and Assyria."
77. Flavius Josephus, *Antiquities* xi. 1.2., translated by Ralph Marcus (Cambridge, Mass.: Harvard University Press, 1958), Volume 6, pp. 315-317. Probably the one who showed Isaiah's words to Cyrus was the prophet Daniel, who enjoyed a position of influence in Babylon under NEBUCHADNEZZAR (Daniel 2:48), BELSHAZZAR (Daniel 5:16-17), and DARIUS (6:1-2). Daniel was now advanced in years, but we know he lived to see CYRUS reign (Daniel 1:21), and his recent miraculous deliverance from the lions' den may have been used by God to create a favorable impression upon the king's mind.
78. Ezra 1:1-2, NIV. See also Ezra 1:3-4 and 6:3-5.
79. *Encyclopedia Britannica* (1967 edition), Volume 6, p. 960, article "Cyrus."
80. See Exodus 1:8 to 14:31 and 2 Kings 24:10-16.
81. Matthew 16:18 – "Upon this rock I will build My church; and the gates of hell shall not prevail against it."
82. John 14:29. See also John 13:19.
83. Matthew 24:15 and Mark 13:14.
84. Earl Albert Rowell, *Prophecy Speaks* (Hagerstown, Maryland: Review and Herald Publishing Association, 1933), pp. 43 & 47.
85. Daniel 2:2-4.
86. Daniel 2:19.
87. Daniel 2:28.
88. Daniel 2:29.
89. The term "brass" in the King James Version is more correctly translated "bronze."
90. Daniel 2:31-35, NIV.
91. Isaiah 14:4.
92. Jeremiah 51:7 & 13.
93. Herodotus, *Histories,* book i, 178-183; translated by A. D. Godley (Cambridge, Mass.: Harvard University Press, 1946), Volume 1, pp. 227-229.
94. Aeschylus, *The Persians,* line 52, in Loeb Classical Library, *Aeschylus,* Volume 1, p. 115.
95. Daniel 5:26 & 28.

96. Charles Boutflower, *In and Around the Book of Daniel* (London: The Macmillan Company, 1923), p. 31.

97. Daniel 2:40, NKJV.

98. Edward Gibbon, *The History of the Decline and Fall of the Roman Empire,* edited by J. B. Bury (London: Methuen & Co., 1898), Volume 4, general observations at the end of Chapter 38, p. 161.

99. Daniel 2:41-43. They "will not remain united, any more than iron mixes with clay." —Daniel 2:43, NIV. "They will not adhere to one another, even as iron does not combine with pottery."—Daniel 2:43, NASB.

100. Winston Churchill obviously recognized God's hand in history when he declared: "Any man must have a blind soul who cannot see that some great purpose and design is being worked out here below." (Address to the U. S. Congress, December 26, 1941.)

101. Daniel 2:44.

102. Daniel 7:1-4, NKJV.

103. Daniel 7:17 & 23. The Living Bible says the fourth beast "is the fourth WORLD POWER that will rule the earth."

104. Jeremiah 4:7. This "lion" is identified as "the king of Babylon" in Jeremiah 20:4-5, 21:1-10 and many similar verses.

105. Jeremiah 50:17 & 43-44, RSV.

106. Habakkuk 1:6-8.

107. Jeremiah 4:13.

108. Jeremiah 51:30, NKJV.

109. Daniel 7:5, NKJV.

110. Daniel 8:3 & 20.

111. Lydia was an ancient country of Asia Minor located where Turkey lies today. Its last ruler, the fabulously wealthy King Croesus, was defeated by the Persian armies of Cyrus.

112. Daniel 7:6, NIV.

113. Sir William Woodthorpe Tarn, "Alexander: The Conquest of the Far East," Chapter 13 in *The Cambridge Ancient History* (Cambridge, England: Cambridge University Press, 1927), Volume 6, p. 425.

114. Daniel 7:7.

115. Daniel 7:23, The Living Bible.

116. Daniel 7:15 & 16.

117. Or kingdoms, comparing Daniel 7:17 & 23.

118. Daniel 7:24.

119. The Babylonians had conquered and absorbed the Assyrian Empire prior to Nebuchadnezzar's dream and the beginning of Daniel's book.

120. Translated from the German of Martin Luther, *Dr. Martin Luthers Sammtliche Schriften,* edited by Johann Georg Walch, 23 volumes published in 25 (St. Louis: Concordia Publishing House, 1881-1910), Volume 6, column 898.

121. William Shakespeare, *Macbeth,* Act V, Scene v, lines 26-28.

Jesus said:
"The SUN will be
darkened . . . and
the STARS will fall
from heaven."
—MATTHEW 24:29, RSV

~

CHAPTER SIXTEEN

SIGNS OF CHRIST'S COMING

IN THE

SUN, MOON, & STARS

MOST OF THE SIGNS of Jesus' Second Coming need no documentation. We know all too well the fulfillment of Peter's words which say: "There shall come in the last days SCOFFERS, walking after their own lusts, and saying, Where is the promise of His coming?"[1] We know the Lord's prophecy about "wars and rumors of war"[2] is abundantly fulfilled whenever the latest news reaches us. And in the social world we see the CRIME and MORAL DECAY predicted by Paul as signs of "the last days."[3]

In the scientific world, we see the fulfillment of Daniel 12:4, which speaks of "the TIME of the END" when "many shall run to and fro, and knowledge shall be increased." Note what Norman Cousins, editor of the *Saturday Review of Literature*, has to say:

> "A wheel turned no faster in Hannibal's time than it did in George Washington's. It took just as long to cultivate a wheat field in Egypt in 5000 B.C. as it did anywhere at the turn of the nineteenth century. ... The speed of technological change was almost as slow as that of life itself. Then, suddenly, with the utilization of steam and electricity, more changes were made in technology in two generations than in all the thousands of years of previous human history put together. Wheels and machines turned so fast that man could cover more distances in one day than he used to be able to do in a lifetime."[4]

In other words, NOAH in Bible days of old and NOAH WEBSTER of dictionary fame were each bound to the same slow speed of horseback or sailboat while traveling by land or sea. Then, as the curtain began to rise on "the TIME of the END," tremendous changes began to take place. The difference between the world of the Bible patriarch ABRAHAM and that of ABRAHAM LINCOLN is LESS than that of the world of Lincoln's day and our own! It's been said that ninety per cent of all the scientists who ever lived are living today.

So we know we're living in an age of an "explosion" of knowledge just as we know we're living in an age of FAMINE, when experts tell us that half the world goes to bed hungry each night, fulfilling Jesus' prediction of "famines" as a sign of His Second Coming. [5]

So this chapter won't be a "rehash" of things you already know. Rather, it will give you the documentation needed to prove that the Bible signs in the PHYSICAL world—the darkening of the sun, the falling of the stars, and the great earthquake—have already taken place precisely as divine prophecy said they would. You'll find this documentary evidence quite convincing.

I. The **DARKENING** of the **SUN** – 1780

Bible writers in both the Old and New Testament speak of signs in the sun, moon, and stars as divinely foreshadowing Christ's Second Coming. Jesus Himself gave a daring prophecy which told the TIME when men might look for these signs in the heavens. He says, "Immediately AFTER the tribulation of those days shall the sun be darkened." [6] He was referring to the great tribulation of the Dark Ages, a period of 1260 years, during which countless thousands of the true followers of Christ were tortured on the rack, burned at the stake, and otherwise abused, tormented, and massacred. It was that tribulation which drove our forefathers to this new land of freedom in search of religious liberty. As the famous Christian hymn says:

> "Faith of our fathers! living still
> In spite of dungeon, fire, and sword,
> O how our hearts beat high with joy
> Whene'er we hear that glorious word.
> Our fathers, chained in prisons dark,
> Were still in heart and conscience free;
> How sweet would be their children's fate,
> If they, like them, could die for Thee!"

Revelation foretells this persecution in which the "dragon . . . that old serpent, called the Devil, and Satan . . . persecuted the woman," with the *woman* being a symbol of the church.[7] This persecution would last for "a thousand two hundred and threescore days."[8] We'll study this time period and its computation later when we make the identification of the Antichrist Beast.[9] Suffice it to say for now that this period of the Dark Ages—when learning and liberty were at low ebb, when tribulation and persecution of God's saints were the order of the day—was to last for 1260 years, from A.D. 538 to 1798.

But Jesus said that those days would bring such "GREAT tribulation" that, "unless those days were shortened, no flesh would be saved; but for the elect's sake those days WILL be shortened."[10] And God's Word explains: "The earth HELPED the woman."[11] How could the "earth" help the persecuted church? By opening up a new continent—a whole new land of opportunity which Columbus was led to discover in 1492[12] and where the Pilgrims landed in 1620. Settlement was slow at first, but as years went by, more and more believers made their pilgrimage to these shores in search of religious freedom. By the time the Founding Fathers of this country signed the Declaration of Independence in 1776, the persecution of the Old World was a thing of the past, "the tribulation of those days" (which was to have lasted till 1798) had been quite effectively "shortened."

TIME SCOPE Prophetically PINPOINTED

As we read in Matthew's account above, Jesus prophesied: "Immediately AFTER the tribulation of those days shall the sun be darkened." Gospel writer Mark uses words even more specific: "But IN those days, AFTER that tribulation, the sun shall be darkened."[13] Here the possibilities of variation are narrowed to an exact order of events. "In those days" means within the prophetic period of 1260 days which was to close in 1798. "AFTER that tribulation" means after 1776 or so, when persecution had ended. This neatly narrows down the time scope for the darkening of the sun, pinpointing the period from, say, 1776 to 1798.

So, if this particular prophecy was fulfilled, we'd expect to find a miraculous DARKENING of the sun recorded in history. And, if our calculations are correct, we'd expect to find it somewhere between 1776 and 1798. Did such an event occur? The testimony of History is clear and unequivocal that it did! On **May 19, 1780**, over a large area of the earth's surface, the LIGHT of day suddenly and mysteriously turned into the BLACKNESS of midnight.

This was the famous "DARK DAY" of which Noah Webster wrote in his dictionary:

"So called on account of a remarkable darkness on that day extending over all New England. . . . Birds sang their evening songs, disappeared, and became silent; fowls went to roost; cattle sought the barnyard; and candles were lighted in houses. . . . The true cause of this remarkable phenomenon is not known."—entry "Dark Day." [14]

Dr. Samuel Tenney (1748-1816), who was a physician and patriot surgeon in the Revolutionary War, was an eyewitness of this divine sign. Read his account:

"The darkness of the following evening was probably as gross as ever has been observed since the Almighty fiat gave birth to light. It wanted only palpability to render it as extraordinary as that which overspread the land of Egypt in the days of Moses.[15] . . . I could not help conceiving at the time, that if *every luminous body in the universe* had been shrouded in impenetrable shades, or struck out of existence, the darkness could not have been more complete. A sheet of white paper held within a few inches of the eyes was equally invisible with the blackest velvet." [16]

The italicized words above agree completely with the prophetic words of JOEL in the Old Testament: "The sun and the moon shall be dark, and the stars shall withdraw their shining." [17] ISAIAH also agrees: "Behold, the day of the Lord cometh. . . . For the stars of heaven and the constellations thereof shall not give their light: the sun shall be darkened in his going forth, and the moon shall not cause her light to shine. And I will punish the world for their evil, and the wicked for their iniquity." [18]

Note especially the words above from Isaiah which say that "the sun shall be darkened in his *going forth*," meaning in the *morning* hours, while the sun is *still rising* toward the zenith it reaches at noon.

MODERN JOURNALS RECOGNIZE FULFILLMENT

Magazines from recent decades confirm that this is exactly how it happened on that remarkable day, as witness the following examples:

Consider first an article in *The American Mercury* Magazine, whose founder and long-time editor was H. L. Mencken. In April, 1943, an article appeared entitled "DARK DAY IN NEW ENGLAND." It begins . . .

"They speak of it as the Dark Day, they whose forebears lived through the soul-stirring experience in 1780, echoes of which have come down through so many New England generations. It was a day on which countless thousands turned fearful eyes toward a sunless sky, nameless terror clutched at their throats. What awful portent was this? What grim visitation was at hand? . . . DARKNESS invaded the Northeast without warning on Friday, the nineteenth of May . . . *about ten in the morning* and spread swiftly. . . . People spoke in hushed voices. They lighted candles in the houses, and as *the blackness grew deeper toward NOON* great numbers of them fell upon their knees at home or in the churches and sent up fervent prayers." [19]

Another modern-day publication which may be cited is *Coronet* Magazine, which has ceased publication but which you may recall was the same handy size as *Reader's Digest*. In the May, 1946, issue an article appeared entitled "AMERICA'S FIRST BLACK FRIDAY" (an allusion to the disastrous day the stock market crashed in 1929, popularly referred to as "Black Friday"). It begins:

> "Inhabitants of New England had no suspicion of a coming ordeal as *the sun rose bright and warm* on the morning of May 19, 1780. . . . There was little warning that this day would be the original "Black Friday" of American history. . . . Suddenly, *about 10 o'clock,* a haze formed in the sky. . . . New Englanders expected a storm, then a hurricane. The darkness deepened, lights appeared in windows, dinners [noontime dinners] were eaten by candlelight, schools were dismissed. Along town streets torches appeared, and in the rural districts the chickens went to roost and cows gathered at the barns. *By 1 o'clock in the afternoon* the outer limits of the ebon [ebony, or black] area had been reached. . . ." [20]

These articles, contemporary with our own times, prove that not only did the darkening of the sun occur as Jesus said it would but that the sun was indeed "darkened *in his going forth,*" as prophesied by Isaiah. Moreover, the Old Testament prophet AMOS corroborates this. Please note:

> "And it shall come to pass in that day, saith the Lord God, that I will cause the sun to go down at NOON, and I will darken the earth in the clear day." [21] The Revised Standard Version translates that last line: "and darken the earth in BROAD DAYLIGHT."

The revelation of this fulfillment of prophecy may come as a surprise to most of us. A reasonable reaction might be, "Who ever heard of the so-called 'Dark Day'? Why isn't it mentioned in history class? Why weren't we taught about it in school?"

Well, we weren't taught about the dark day of 1780 in our school classes because the schools of today are not in harmony with God. They're too busy teaching the theory of evolution and other humanistic philosophy to point us to fulfilled prophecy. Let's face it: the schools of this world do little to prepare us for the world to come. And, sadly enough, even many clergy in the churches do not know or teach these things.

"NOT Caused by an ECLIPSE"

Another reasonable question is whether or not this remarkable phenomenon could have been caused by an *eclipse* of the sun. This question is answered by R. M. Devens in his book *OUR FIRST CENTURY: 1776-1876.* Chapter 4, entitled "The Wonderful Dark Day—1780," declares:

> "That this darkness was NOT caused by an eclipse, is manifest by the various positions of the planetary bodies at that time; for the moon was more than one hundred and fifty degrees from the sun all that day, and, according to the accurate calculations made by the most celebrated astronomers, there could not, in the order of nature, be any transit of Venus or Mercury upon the disc of the sun that year." [22]

Furthermore, astronomers tell us that total eclipses of the sun are of quite brief duration, never lasting more than a very few *minutes*, whereas the spectacular darkness of May 19, 1780, lasted many *hours*.

A WEALTH of Witnesses Testify

Corroborating testimony, as we've seen already, comes from many sources—NOT from sensational supermarket tabloids but from eyewitnesses who are credible and trustworthy. For example, Timothy Dwight, president of Yale from 1795 to 1817, had this to say:

> "The 19th of May, 1780, was a remarkable dark day. . . . The legislature of Connecticut was then in session at Hartford. A very general opinion prevailed, that the day of judgment was at hand. The House of Representatives, being unable to transact their business [because of the unnatural darkness], adjourned. A proposal to adjourn the Council was under consideration. When the opinion of Colonel [Abraham] Davenport was asked, he answered, 'I am against an adjournment. The day of judgment is either approaching, or it is not. If it is not, there is no cause for an adjournment: if it is, I choose to be found doing my duty. I wish therefore that candles may be brought." [23]

This very incident was immortalized in a poem by one of America's outstanding writers. Here are a few lines from "ABRAHAM DAVENPORT" by the Quaker poet, John Greenleaf Whittier:

> "'Twas on a May-day of the far old year
> Seventeen hundred eighty, that there fell
> Over the bloom and sweet life of the Spring,
> Over the fresh earth and the heaven of NOON,
> A horror of great darkness. . . .

Birds ceased to sing, and all the barn-yard fowls
Roosted; the cattle at the pasture bars
Lowed, and looked homeward; bats on leathern wings
Flitted abroad; the sounds of labor died;
Men prayed, and women wept; all ears grew sharp
To hear the doom-blast of the trumpet shatter
The BLACK sky. . . .

Meanwhile in the old State House, dim as ghosts,
Sat the lawgivers of Connecticut,
Trembling beneath their legislative robes.
"It is the Lord's Great Day! Let us adjourn,"
Some said; and then as if with one accord,
All eyes were turned to ABRAHAM DAVENPORT.
He rose, slow cleaving with his steady voice
The intolerable hush. "This well may be
The Day of Judgment which the world awaits;
But be it so or not, I only know
My present duty, and my Lord's command
To occupy till He come.[24] So at the post
Where He hath set me in His providence,
I choose, for one, to meet Him face to face—
No faithless servant frightened from my task,
But ready when the Lord of the harvest calls;
And therefore, with all reverence, I would say,
Let God do His work, we will see to ours.
Bring in the CANDLES." And they brought them in. . . .

And there he stands in memory to this day,
Erect, self-poised, a rugged face, half seen
Against the background of UNNATURAL DARK,
A witness to the ages as they pass,
That simple duty hath no place for fear." [25]

MOON APPEARED "AS BLOOD"

Closely connected with the **darkening of the sun** is the prophecy regarding the **moon**. In at least three Bible passages we read that the moon at this time took on a reddish, coppery appearance, as of blood. For instance, JOEL was inspired to tell us that "The *sun* shall be turned into *darkness*, and the *moon* into *blood*, before the great and terrible day of the Lord come." [26]

The Apostle PETER quoted this text in his sermon on the Day of Pentecost, as recorded in Acts 2:20. And JOHN the Revelator wrote: "The *sun* became *black* as sackcloth of hair, and the *moon* became as *blood*." [27]

This was fulfilled on the night following the Dark Day. Notwithstanding the fact that the moon gave no light and was not seen during most of the hours of that strange night, when it *did* appear, it had the reddish-copper color of blood! One witness described the supernatural happenings of the Dark Day and then discusses

> "the moon's turning to blood. . . . It did take place between 2 o'clock and day break in the morning of the same night after which the sun was darkened, which was said to appear as a clotter of blood [a blood-clot]; and it is the more probable, as that night, before the moon appeared, was as dark, in proportion, as the day, and of course would give the moon an extraordinary appearance—not suffering the moon to give her light. The next in course, it seems, is the falling of the stars from heaven." [28]

The *Coronet* Magazine article mentioned above describes the moon like this:

> "Midnight came—and passed. Thousands of square miles under the black blight, white faces and fear-filled eyes were dimly visible in the flickering of candles and torches. . . . Suddenly there were shouts. Thousands of eyes turned skyward: BLOOD-RED and dim, the moon appeared. Now, again, there was hope. Tears of joy flowed freely. It was 1 o'clock on the morning of May 20." [29]

Before we close our discussion of the Lord's prophecy, let's consider two legitimate questions: First, why was this miraculous phenomenon seen in North America but not worldwide? We must remember that Bible prophecy is always given only as it concerns *the people of God*. As we know, the Lord gave countless prophecies about His people Israel and their surrounding neighbors. But why did He give no prophecies concerning China, Japan, or Antarctica? Because His people never went there and had no dealings with those people or lands. When persecution arose in the period of the great tribulation, God opened *this new continent* as a land of freedom for His faithful people. Therefore God showed His great signs here in the North Anerican haven of refuge where His people had fled to escape religious tyranny.

Second, why does it seem that reports of the Dark Day were concentrated in eastern Canada and New England and not more widespread? The answer is that the written reports would naturally be concentrated where the population was centered. *U.S. News & World Report* printed a map showing the United States' CENTER of POPULATION for each decade that the census was taken, beginning with 1790.

The *U.S. News & World Report* article,[30] using official data supplied by the U. S. Department of Commerce, states that "After nearly two centuries of westward movement, the center of U. S. population has FINALLY crossed the Mississippi River." The map shows the 1980 population center very near St. Louis, which is still nowhere near the *geographical* center! The article adds: "The first census, in 1790, put the center *east* of Baltimore"—which would be virtually *on the coast* of the Eastern seaboard! Thus, when the Dark Day dawned in 1780, there may have been a few frontiersmen and Indians farther west who witnessed the miracle and talked about it, but the preserved records had to come from the literate, populated parts of our land— that is, from the East Coast—which in fact is the case. See the **MAP** on the next page. ➡️

So May 19, 1780, stands in history as "The Dark Day." Since the time of Moses [31] no period of darkness of equal density, extent, and duration, has ever been recorded. Eyewitness descriptions of this event faithfully echo the inspired words recorded by Bible prophets.

Unbelievers, of course, may still refuse to accept the evidence, abundant as it is, just as they refuse to accept the existence of God or the authenticity of the Bible. But one thing is sure: Science cannot explain this remarkable event. We read:

> "In an age when the term 'philosophy' was often used to denote science, or natural philosophy, Sir William Herschel, the British astronomer, dismissed the subject by saying: 'The Dark Day in Northern America was one of those wonderful phenomena which will always be read of with interest, but which philosophy is at a LOSS to explain.'" [32]

But you and I know what caused it—or rather WHO caused it. You and I are told to "SEEK HIM that . . . maketh the day dark with night. . . . The LORD is His name." [33]

II. THE FALLING OF THE STARS – 1833

Jesus very clearly pointed out, in definite prophetic sequence, certain celestial signs. After the sign of the Dark Day and the moon withholding her light, there was to be another. Said Christ: "And the STARS shall FALL from heaven." [34] How could the stars fall? The fixed stars, of course, are steadfast and unmovable to provide man a fixed point by which to navigate. So what could Jesus have meant? He was talking about METEORS which rush into our atmosphere and give the appearance that the heavens are crashing

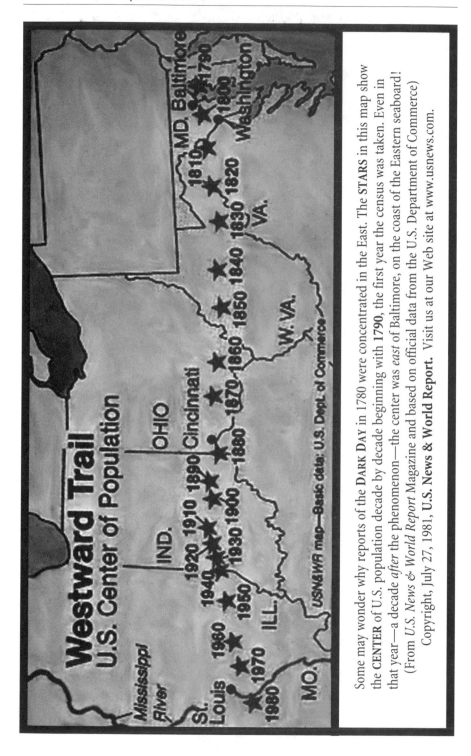

Westward Trail
U.S. Center of Population

Some may wonder why reports of the **DARK DAY** in 1780 were concentrated in the East. The **STARS** in this map show the **CENTER** of U.S. population decade by decade beginning with **1790**, the first year the census was taken. Even in that year—a decade *after* the phenomenon—the center was *east* of Baltimore, on the coast of the Eastern seaboard! (From *U.S. News & World Report* Magazine and based on official data from the U.S. Department of Commerce) Copyright, July 27, 1981, **U.S. News & World Report.** Visit us at our Web site at www.usnews.com.

USN&WR map—Basic data: U.S. Dept. of Commerce

earthward. Even today, we ourselves refer to meteors as "SHOOTING STARS" or "FALLING STARS."

We're forced to realize that Jesus could not possibly have meant real, literal stars when we read John's parallel prophecy saying that "the stars of heaven FELL UNTO THE EARTH." [35] Obviously, such an event could never literally take place without destroying our world. We know this because stars are not only tremendously hot (since each star is also a sun) but also enormously huge. For instance, our SUN is a star, and it has a diameter more than one hundred times that of our earth and constitutes more than 99 percent of the mass of our entire solar system! Yet though the sun appears as the largest and brightest of the stars visible to the naked eye, it's classified as a dwarf and "is actually among the smallest and faintest . . . much smaller than many stars, some having a diameter 800 times that of the sun." [36] A collision between earth and even a *single* star would be much worse than a basketball crashing into a sphere the size of this capital "O"! Our planet would be completely destroyed if we ever were star struck—no pun intended.

Therefore, a literal fulfillment of this prophecy—with actual stars—would not mean a "sign" that Jesus soon will come; instead it would mean absolute annihilation of the earth itself. This fact was understood as long ago as 1697, when Dr. Thomas Burnett (1635-1715), an Anglican clergyman, discussed this prophetic sign of stars falling in these words:

> "We are sure, from the nature of the thing, that this cannot be understood of either fix'd Stars or Planets; for if either of these should tumble from the Skies, and reach the Earth, they would break it all in pieces, or swallow it up, as the Sea does a sinking ship. . . . It is necessary therefore by these Stars to understand either fiery Meteors falling from the middle Region of the Air, or Comets and Blazing Stars. No doubt there will be all sorts of fiery Meteors at that time; and amongst others, those that are call'd Falling Stars; which, tho' they are not considerable singly, yet if they were MULTIPLIED in great numbers, falling, as the Prophet says, as figs from the fig-tree, they would make an astonishing sight." [37]

History records that this sign did appear, that this prophecy was fulfilled, in the great meteoric shower of **November 13, 1833**. In the *New York Journal of Commerce* newspaper of November 14, 1833, appeared a long article regarding this wonderful phenomenon, containing this statement:

> "No philosopher or scholar has told or recorded an event, I suppose, like that of yesterday morning. A prophet eighteen hundred years ago foretold it exactly, if we will be at the trouble of understanding STARS FALLING to mean FALLING STARS, . . . in the only sense in which it is possible to be literally true." [38]

AWE-inspiring SPECTACLE!

Eyewitness accounts abound which testify to the majesty of this breath-taking display. For instance, FREDERICK DOUGLASS (1817-1895) was the "Martin Luther King" of his day. This noted Negro leader and orator was born a slave but escaped, obtained an education, became a journalist and was appointed U. S. Minister to Haiti. In 1833 Douglass was only sixteen and still a slave, but Chapter 14 of his autobiography records the unforgettably awesome falling of the stars:

> "I went to St. Michaels to live in March, 1833. I know the year, because it was . . . the year of that strange phenomenon when the heavens seemed about to part with their starry train. I witnessed this gorgeous spectacle, and was awe-struck. The air seemed FILLED with bright descending messengers from the sky. It was about daybreak when I saw this sublime scene. I was not without the suggestion, at the moment, that it might be the harbinger of the coming of the Son of Man, and in my then state of mind I was prepared to hail Him as my friend and deliverer. I had read that the 'stars shall fall from heaven,' *and they were now falling."* [39]

Another eyewitness of the spectacle, a Mr. Clarkson, the agricultural editor of the *Iowa State Register*, after reading a statement that modern fireworks surpass even the glory of falling stars, wrote in his newspaper the following reaction:

> "The writer of that sentence did not witness the glorious meteoric shower of November, 1833, when the display was so much superior to any artistic display of fireworks that neither language nor any element in nature can furnish comparisons. . . . The awful grandeur of the display on the night of the thirteenth of November, 1833, which made the stoutest heart stand in awe, and the most defiant infidel quake with fear, is never to be compared with the most brilliant fireworks. Those who witnessed the meteoric shower named saw the greatest display that men will ever see until the day that Peter speaks of when the heavens, being on fire, shall be dissolved, and the elements shall melt with fervent heat. [40] The agricultural editor of the *Register* was out alone with a team and a load of lumber all night on that never-to-be-forgotten night. And he cannot now consent to hear of human fireworks being superior to that most grand and sublime spectacle ever before or since beheld by man. Patent fireworks are no nearer this wonderful phenomenon than a *lightning bug* is equal to the *sun*." [41]

✦ ✦ ✦

ASTRONOMERS Corroborate Phenomenon

Scientists as well as laymen were impressed by the dazzling display. The noted contemporary observer, Denison Olmsted, professor of astronomy at Yale, had this to say on the unparalleled extent of the star shower:

> "The attention of astronomers was particularly directed to the extraordinary shower of METEORS which occurred on the 13th of November, 1833. I had the good fortune to witness these grand celestial fireworks . . . an exhibition of the phenomenon called SHOOTING STARS. . . . The extent of the shower of 1833 was such as to cover no inconsiderable part of the earth's surface, from the middle of the Atlantic on the east to the Pacific on the west; and from the northern coast of South America to undefined regions among the British possessions on the north, the exhibition was visible, and everywhere presented nearly the same appearance. . . . Probably no celestial phenomenon has ever occurred in this country, since its first settlement, which was viewed with so much admiration and delight by one class of spectators, or with so much astonishment and fear by another class. For some time after the occurrence, the 'meteoric phenomenon' was the principal topic of conversation in every circle." [42]

Corroboration of the fact that this prophetic sign was seen across all North America to the Pacific Coast is found in California historian Robert G. Cleland, who reports on the journals of frontier trapper Joseph Reddeford Walker:

> "The great meteoric shower of the night of November 12-13, 1833, which terrorized thousands of people even in the thickly populated parts of the United States and convinced the credulous multitude that the end of the world had come, found Walker's company camped in the lonely expanse of the *San Joaquin Valley,* and for hours "the air appeared to be completely thickened with meteors falling toward the earth." Some of the meteors exploded in the air and others were dashed to pieces on the ground. Frightened by the noise and dazzling light, the horses tried repeatedly to stampede; and until Walker explained the nature of the phenomenon, some of the superstitious trappers were probably as panic-stricken as the frantic horses.
> "The morning after the meteor display the company broke camp and traveled on till it came to an arm of *San Francisco Bay.* A day and a half later the party crossed the Coast Range Mountains and reached *the shores of the Pacific.*" [43]

✦ ✦ ✦

The INCREDIBLE INTENSITY of the Display

The intensity of this celestial sign was even more remarkable than its extensive nature. Let's see what Fletcher G. Watson has to say on the subject. Professor Watson is a leading expert on meteors and an astronomer at Harvard Observatory. Chapter 7 of his book *Between the Planets* is entitled "Meteor Showers" and begins with these words:

> "A magnificent display of shooting stars startled the inhabitants of the Americas on November 12, 1833. Beginning before midnight, the meteors increased in frequency until at dawn they were as thick as SNOW FLAKES. A single observer often saw TWENTY appear *within a second*. . . . Many superstitious people thought this marked the end of the world and, as bells tolled, they prepared for the future. Next day all was serene, but a new branch of astronomy, the study of meteors, had been founded." [44]

Watson's estimate is no exaggeration. British astronomer A. C. B. Lovell has written a thick book entitled *Meteor Astronomy*, devoted exclusively to that branch of science. "Table 132" in that book shows that the "Hourly Rate" of the meteors seen on the night of November 12, 1833, was a phenomenal "**10,000?**"— far surpassing that of any other such occurrence! [45]

And Canadian astrophysicist Peter Mackenzie Millman says the number of "Meteors per hour" was "**60,000**"! Dr. Millman declares that "more than a BILLION shooting stars appeared over the United States and Canada alone." [46]

Professor Olmsted of Yale says the dazzling meteor shower was so extremely intense that "The flashes of light, although less intense than lightning, were so BRIGHT as to awaken people in their beds." [47] He adds that in Missouri the brilliance of these countless meteors was so great that common-sized print could be read without much difficulty. [48]

Stars RADIATED "from a POINT"

One last fact about this marvelous falling of the stars is of vital importance and must not be overlooked. That is this: the shower of "falling stars" or meteors, as vast as it was, seemed to come or emanate from A SINGLE POINT in the heavens. Note these quotations:

> "To form some idea of the phenomenon, the reader may imagine a constant stream of fire balls, resembling sky rockets, radiating in all directions from a POINT in the heavens, a few degrees south-east of the zenith, and following the arch of the sky towards the horizon . . . from the radiating POINT." [49]

W. J. Fisher, lecturer on astronomy at Harvard Observatory as well as instructor of physics at Cornell and professor at University of New Hampshire, reports that "All the observers saw that the meteors darted away from a single POINT in the sky [in the constellation Leo]; the meteors 'were like the ribs of a gigantic umbrella.'" [50]

And professor A. C. B. Lovell informs us that "The great shower in November 1833 was the first occasion on which it became evident that the meteors were apparently radiating from a POINT." [51]

FULFILLED the Prediction PRECISELY

The import of this remarkable fact may escape us unless we realize that this is just the way John the Revelator described this portentous event eighteen centuries earlier! Please read it with me:

> "And the stars of heaven fell unto the earth, even as a FIG TREE casteth her untimely figs, when she is SHAKEN of a mighty wind." [52]

You see, if we shook a fig tree, it would drop its ripe fruit. But that fruit would not drop straight down. No, as we shook the trunk and branches, the figs would be *flung out* from the common center to the left and right in all directions. However, they would seem to emanate *from a single point,* from the branches of a single tree. So John gave quite an accurate pen-picture of what would happen!

Dr. Henry Dana Ward, well-known Episcopal minister of New York, witnessed the stars falling like snow flakes and wrote immediately to the editor of the *New York Journal of Commerce:*

> "Truly, 'the stars of heaven fell unto the earth, even as a fig tree casteth her untimely figs, when she is shaken by a mighty wind.' Rev. 6:13. This language of the prophet has always been received as metaphorical. Yesterday it was literally fulfilled. The ancients understood by *aster* in Greek, and *stella* in Latin, the smaller lights of heaven [as opposed to the larger lights we call the sun and moon]. The refinement of modern astronomy has made the distinction between *stars* of heaven, and *meteors* of heaven. Therefore, the idea of the prophet, as it is expressed in the original Greek, was literally fulfilled in the phenomenon of yesterday, though no man before yesterday had conceived to be possible that it should be fulfilled.

> "And HOW did they fall? . . . Were I to hunt through nature for a simile, I could not find one so apt to illustrate the appearance of the heavens as that which St. John uses in the prophecy, before quoted. 'It *rained fire!*' says one—Another, 'it was like a *shower* of *fire*.' Another, 'it was like the large flakes of *falling snow,* before a storm, or large drops of rain before a shower.'

"I admit the fitness of these for common accuracy; but they come far short of the accuracy of the figure [of speech] used by the prophet. 'The stars of heaven fell unto the earth'; they were not sheets, or flakes, or drops of fire; but they WERE what the world understands by the name of 'Falling Stars'; and one speaking to his fellow in the midst of the scene, would say, 'See how the stars fall,' and he who heard would not pause to correct the astronomy of the speaker, any more than he would reply, 'The sun does not move,' to one who told him, 'The sun is rising.'

"The stars fell 'Even as a fig tree casteth her untimely figs, when she is shaken of a mighty wind.' Here is the EXACTNESS of the prophet. The falling stars did not come, as if from *several* trees shaken, but from *one:* those which appeared in the east fell toward the East; those which appeared in the north fell toward the North; those which appeared in the west fell toward the West, and those which appeared in the south (for I went out of my residence into the Park), fell toward the South; and they fell, not as the *ripe* fruit falls. Far from it. But they flew, they were CAST, like the *unripe* fruit, which at first refuses to leave the branch; and, when it does break its hold, flies swiftly, straight off, descending; and in the multitude falling some cross the track of others, as they are thrown with more or less force." [53]

Jesus Himself told us of certain CELESTIAL SIGNS—in the sun, moon, and stars—and now we know that each of these was most assuredly seen. Our Lord's prophecy hasn't failed—it is we who have failed to discern the signs of the times!

III. THE GREAT EARTHQUAKE – 1755

Chronologically, the FIRST sign prophesied by John the Revelator was a tremendous earthquake. Notice the sequence of predicted events as recorded in the Inspired Volume: "And I beheld when He had opened the sixth seal, and, lo, there was (1) a GREAT EARTHQUAKE; and (2) the sun became black as sackcloth of hair, and (3) the moon became as blood; and (4) the stars of heaven fell unto the earth. . . ." [54]

Right here our study becomes as fascinating as a detective mystery. For if we're on the right track—if this indeed is Bible truth—we should find a notable earthquake, "a GREAT earthquake," which occurred BEFORE the darkening of the sun in 1780.

Now, in regard to earthquakes as a prophetic sign of Christ's Second Advent, two things must be kept in mind. First, Jesus warned us that MANY "earthquakes in various places" [55] would be a sign of His Coming. This prediction is certainly fulfilled today, as we live in an age of very high seismic activity. Second, the Bible describes the end of the Seven Last Plagues as the world's WORST earthquake of all time, accompanied by colossal hail. That will happen right before Jesus comes in glory. [56]

But IF the prophetic sequence of Revelation 6:12-13 was fulfilled, the question for our purposes here is: DID an outstanding earthquake, a particularly devastating earthquake, occur prior to 1780 when the sun was darkened? The answer is, it certainly did—on **November 1, 1755**. It's called "the LISBON earthquake" because the epicenter was near that great European city —but its effects were unbelievably widespread.

"THE GREATEST EARTHQUAKE ON RECORD"

Most authorities consider the 1755 Lisbon earthquake the greatest one to occur so far, as the following quotations point out:

- "Probably the most famous of all earthquakes is that which destroyed Lisbon on November 1, 1755. . . . [German scientist] Alexander von Humboldt stated that the total area shaken was FOUR TIMES that of Europe." [57]

- In *Nelson's Encyclopedia* we read: "The Lisbon earthquake, which occurred on November 1, 1755, was the most NOTABLE earthquake of history." [58]

- G. A. Eiby, geophysicist at the Seismological Observatory at Wellington, New Zealand, states in his book *About Earthquakes:* "By far the MOST SPECTACULAR earthquake of earlier times was that of Lisbon, in 1755. This has some claim to be regarded as the GREATEST earthquake on record. If it is possible to believe reports, the felt area, which was certainly more than 700 miles in radius, extended from the Azores to Italy, and from England to North Africa. . . . The damage to Lisbon itself was very great. . . . Great numbers of people were in the churches, for it was All Saints' Day, and the time of the first Mass." [59]

Dr. Eiby goes on to explain that, although the famous Richter scale registers as high as 9 or more, no quake can actually shake that hard, because the bedrock which is shaken will split or crack before that point is reached, thus releasing the energy causing the quake. He says:

> "The UPPER LIMIT of magnitude, set by the strength of the rock, is round about 8.6. Any earthquake of magnitude 8 or more is a very great one indeed. The famous Lisbon earthquake of 1755, the California earthquake in 1906, and the Assam earthquake of 1950 all had magnitude of MORE than 8. . . . Anything much above 7 is a major disaster." [60]

TIDAL WAVES MULTIPLIED DEATHS

Besides the shaking of the land itself which is felt by man, two other results of earthquakes are TSUNAMI (huge tidal waves in the *ocean)* and SEICHES (wave movements in *ponds* and *lakes)*. Note what the *Encyclopedia Britannica* says:

> "On November 1, 1755, Lisbon, Portugal, was destroyed by a GREAT earthquake which occurred at 9:40 in the morning. The source was probably situated some distance off the coast. The principal shock was felt strongly for about *six minutes.* The violent shaking demolished all large public buildings and about 12,000 dwellings. November 1st being All Saints' Day, a large portion of the population was in the churches, most of which were destroyed with great loss of life. *The total number of persons killed in Lisbon alone was estimated to be at least 60,000,* including those who perished by drowning and in the fire that burned for *six days* following the shock. Damage was severe in Fes, Morocco [the entire village of eight or ten thousand inhabitants was swallowed up], and some damage was reported in Algiers, 700 miles to the east. The earthquake generated a *TSUNAMI* which produced waves 60 feet high at Cadiz, Spain, and 40 feet high at Lisbon. They [the tidal waves] traveled on to Martinique, a distance of 3,740 miles, in ten hours and there rose to a height of 12 feet." [61]

This last fact illustrates the great force generated by the amazing speed of *tsunamis,* for if the tidal wave which crossed the Atlantic Ocean to Martinique traveled *3,740 miles in ten hours,* it must have had an average velocity of **374 miles per hour**—faster than that of some airplanes!

EFFECTS FELT OVER **WIDESPREAD** AREA

In addition to these overwhelming tidal waves on the ocean, this great earthquake generated SEICHES which were tremendously widespread. One authority states: "The most famous of ALL earthquake-generated seiches occurred after a very LARGE shock in Portugal in 1755. It set bodies of water into oscillation all over western and northern Europe. Various lakes in Scotland, Switzerland, and Scandinavia began to oscillate." [62]

So the convulsions of the earth pervaded an extent of not less than FOUR MILLION square miles! It was in Spain and Portugal that the shock manifested its most extreme violence, but in Africa the shock was almost as severe as in Europe. Estimates declare that *ninety thousand persons* lost their lives on that fatal day.

With no exaggeration, then, one book calls this titanic earthquake "The CALAMITY of the CENTURY." Read the account:

"It was All Saints' Day in Lisbon, Portugal—Saturday, November 1, 1755—and the people were crowded into temples and cathedrals. At nine-thirty A.M. rose a rumbling noise that sounded like heavy traffic on an adjacent street. Buildings trembled, and fear was struck in the hearts of the people.

"Then there was quiet. But only for a moment.

"A second shock came, lasting two full minutes. This brought down roofs, walls, façades, churches, homes, and shops in a roar of destruction and death. Then a third tremor quickly followed, after which a suffocating cloud of dust settled like fog over the city.

". . . Fires broke out. Aftershocks kept slamming again and again into the stricken city, and marble churches swayed like ships on the sea." [63]

Collier's Encyclopedia sums it up neatly by saying that the Lisbon earthquake was "probably the MOST VIOLENT in historic time." [64]

This milestone of Bible prophecy was fulfilled, then, in 1755, when there occurred the most terrible—the most catastrophic—earthquake ever recorded.

CONCLUSION

We've examined the evidence. We've seen the documentation. Is it possible that we can look a FACT in the face and still not recognize it? Did all these events *just happen* by mere chance? Never! Jesus foretold these remarkable signs. More than that, He even foretold their exact SEQUENCE or order. He said the great earthquake would come first. Then He said the sun and moon would be darkened. Then He listed the falling of the stars as the final event in this sequence. Had these things been accidental, the stars might well have fallen first. *These marvelous events not only HAPPENED, but they happened in the precise Biblical ORDER predicted by Jesus Himself!*

His Second Coming is sure. May we be ready for that great day is my prayer.

⁓

Notes to Chapter 16

1. 2 Peter 3:3-4. Please see *Appendix H* at the back of this volume for an overview of widespread signs of Christ's Return in the *social, political, economic, religious,* and *scientific* worlds. This chapter will focus on signs in the *physical* world.
2. Matthew 24:6.
3. 2 Timothy 3:1-5.
4. Norman Cousins, *Modern Man Is Obsolete* (New York: Viking Press, 1945), pp. 15-16.
5. Matthew 24:7.
6. Matthew 24:29.
7. Revelation 12:9 & 13. For "woman" as a symbol of God's people, the church, see 2 Corinthians 11:2, Matthew 9:15, Revelation 19:7-9, *etc.*, and Chapter 19, "Clue G," pages 601-604.
8. Revelation 12:6.
9. Please see Chapter 19, "Clue U," pages 678-686.
10. Matthew 24:21-22, NKJV.
11. Revelation 12:16.
12. See facts on Columbus in Chapter 19, below, pages 710-711, footnote #194.
13. Mark 13:24. Please note that although this period of "great tribulation" spoken of by Jesus lies in the past, as careful Bible students we must be aware that troublous times still lie ahead. For instance, "the Mark of the Beast" is a future event, along with "the Seven Last Plagues," which are to be poured out on those who receive that Mark. See Revelation 13:16-18 and 14:9-10 and 15:1, as well as Chapters 19 & 20.
14. Noah Webster, *An American Dictionary of the English Language* (Springfield, Mass.: G. & C. Merriam, 1869), entry "Dark Day."
15. See Exodus 10:21-23. On that occasion, the miraculous darkness *was palpable*—it was "darkness which may be FELT."
16. Samuel Tenney, *Collections of the Massachusetts Historical Society,* Volume 1, 1792 (Boston: Belknap and Hall, 1792), pp. 97-98.
17. Joel 2:10—repeated in Joel 3:15.
18. Isaiah 13:9-11.
19. John Nicholas Beffel, "Dark Day in New England," *The American Mercury* Magazine (April, 1943), pp. 481-485.
20. Vincent H. Gaddis, "America's First Black Friday," *Coronet* Magazine (May, 1946), pp. 87-89.
21. Amos 8:9.
22. R. M. Devens, *OUR FIRST CENTURY: 1776-1876,* Chapter 4, "The Wonderful Dark Day—1780," (Springfield, Mass.: C. A. Nichols & Co., 1876), p. 95.
23. Timothy Dwight, quoted in *Connecticut Historical Collections,* compiled by John Warner Barber, Second edition (New Haven: Durrie & Peck and J. W. Barber, 1830), p. 403.

24. See Luke 19:11-13.

25. John Greenleaf Whittier, "Abraham Davenport," in his *Complete Poetical Works,* Cambridge edition (Boston: Houghton Mifflin Company, 1894), p. 260.

26. Joel 2:31.

27. Revelation 6:12.

28. Benjamin Gorton, *A View of Spiritual, or Antitypical Babylon* (Troy, N.Y.: Published by Benjamin Gorton, 1808), p. 73.

29. Vincent H. Gaddis, "America's First Black Friday," *Coronet* Magazine (May, 1946), p. 88.

30. *U.S. News & World Report* Magazine, "Westward Trail: U. S. Center of Population" (July 27, 1981), p. 6.

31. Exodus 10:21-23, NKJV, tells us: "The Lord said to Moses, 'Stretch out your hand toward heaven, that there may be DARKNESS over the land of Egypt [where the pagan Egyptians worshiped the SUN and the MOON], darkness which may even be felt.' So Moses stretched out his hand toward heaven, and there was thick darkness in all the land of Egypt three days. They did not see one another; nor did anyone rise from his place for three days. But all the children of Israel had LIGHT in their dwellings."

32. Sir William Herschel, quoted in J. N. Beffel, "Dark Day in New England," *The American Mercury* Magazine (April, 1943), p. 484.

33. Amos 5:8.

34. Matthew 24:29.

35. Revelation 6:13.

36. *Encyclopedia Britannica* (1967 edition), Volume 21, p. 414, article "Sun."

37. Thomas Burnet, *The Theory of the Earth* (London, 1697), Book 3, Volume 2, pp. 98-99.

38. *New York Journal of Commerce* (November 14, 1833), p. 2.

39. Written by Himself: *LIFE AND TIMES OF FREDERICK DOUGLASS: His Early Life as a Slave, His Escape from Bondage, and His Complete History,* With a New Introduction by Raymond W. Logan, Reprinted from the revised edition of 1892 (New York: Collier Books, 1962), pp. 103-104. (Original edition, 1855.)

40. See 2 Peter 3:12.

41. *Iowa State Register,* July 12, 1889.

42. Professor Denison Olmsted, in *The American Journal of Science and Arts,* Volume XXV (1834), pp. 363-364.

43. Robert G. Cleland, *This Reckless Breed of Men: The Trappers and Fur Traders of the Southwest* (New York: Alfred A. Knopf, Inc., 1952), pp. 292-293.

44. Fletcher G. Watson, *Between the Planets,* Revised Edition (Cambridge, Mass.: Harvard University Press, 1956), p. 95.

45. A. C. B. Lovell, *Meteor Astronomy* (London: Oxford University at the Clarendon Press, 1954), p. 339, "Table 132."

46. Peter Mackenzie Millman, "The Falling of the Stars," *The Telescope* Magazine (May-June, 1940), pp. 57 & 60.

47. Denison Olmsted, "Observations on the Meteors of November 13th, 1833," *The American Journal of Science and Arts,* Volume XXV (1834), p. 365.

48. *Ibid.,* p. 382.

49. *Ibid.,* p. 363.

50. Willard James Fisher, "The Ancient Leonids," *The Telescope* Magazine (October, 1934), p. 80.

51. A. C. B. Lovell, *Meteor Astronomy* (London: Oxford University at the Clarendon Press, 1954), p. 340.

52. Revelation 6:13.

53. Dr. Henry Dana Ward, Letter to the Editor of the *New York Journal of Commerce* (November 15, 1833), p. 2.

54. Revelation 6:12-13.

55. Matthew 24:7, NKJV.

56. See Revelation 16:17-21.

57. Perry Byerly, *Encyclopedia Britannica* (1961 edition), Volume 7, p. 848, article "Earthquakes."

58. *Nelson's Encyclopedia,* Volume 4, p. 205.

59. G. A. Eiby, *About Earthquakes* (New York: Harper, 1957), pp. 141-142.

60. *Ibid.,* p. 96. To put things in proper perspective, the 1906 earthquake in San Francisco, mentioned here and considered the worst one in this country, killed only 452 people. Whereas in the 1755 disaster at Lisbon, "the city was devastated by one of the GREATEST earthquakes EVER recorded. . . . It is believed that 30,000 lives were lost, and more than 9,000 buildings were destroyed."—Britannica CD 98 Standard Edition © 1994-1998, Enylopedia Britannica, Inc., article "Lisbon Earthquake."

61. Hugo Benioff (Professor of Seismology at Caltech), *Encyclopedia Britannica* (1967 edition), Volume 7, pp. 856-857, article "Earthquake."

62. John H. Hodgson (Chief, Division of Seismology Dominion Observatory, Ottawa, Canada), *Earthquakes and Earth Structure* (Englewood Cliffs, New Jersey: Prentice-Hall, 1964), p. 53.

63. Ann and Myron Sutton, *Nature on the Rampage; A Natural History of the Elements* (Philadelphia: J. B. Lippincott Company, 1962), p. 219.

64. *Collier's Encyclopedia* (1966 edition), Volume 8, p. 258.

✦ ✦ ✦

~

CHAPTER SEVENTEEN

TRUTH on TRIAL:
The Secret Rapture

EVIDENCE from the Word of God:
What Does the Bible Teach About
Christ's Second Coming?

"**G**OOD MORNING, LADIES AND GENTLEMEN. As the prosecuting attorney on this case I want to thank you personally for serving on this panel of jurors. Now that you've been sworn in, you twelve people will bear a heavy responsibility to determine the truth of an important matter. We don't expect you to be experts on the Bible or anything else, but we do expect you to listen carefully and to weigh evidence impartially, without prejudice.

"Let me now begin my opening statement by asking you a question: What would you think of an accountant who can't balance the books, a beauty contestant who looks repulsively ugly, a surgeon who faints at the sight of blood? Ridiculous, you say? Yes, but no more ridiculous than preachers who don't teach according to the Bible!

CAVEAT EMPTOR—THAT'S LATIN FOR 'LET THE BUYER BEWARE'

"Consumer advocates like Ralph Nader and David Horowitz have raised our consciousness as to our rights in today's marketplace. But what about the concepts we 'buy' in the Marketplace of Ideas? People are victimized in many different ways. And being 'sold a bill of goods'—deceived by those we trust—is often worse than being short-changed at the cash register.

"It's easy for preachers to claim to speak in God's name and to claim His authority, but that's not always 'truth in advertising.' If you've been taught the Secret Rapture[1] doctrine, you have a right to ask for Scriptural evidence of its validity. You have a right to demand proof that it's true, according to the Bible. You have a right to know whether the Secret Rapture theory was taught by Jesus and the Bible writers—or was it born centuries later?

"On this as well as any other theological question, we want more than the mere assumptions of men. We want the clear, explicit teaching of the Word of God. The question is not 'What do MEN *think?*' but 'What does the BIBLE *say?*' because in this area our only safe authority is God's holy Word.

"LET THE RECORD SHOW THAT . . . "

"This doctrine of the Secret Rapture is not a single, simple problem— it has as many facets as an octopus has legs! Investigating it is like opening a kind of Pandora's box, for there's not just ONE fallacy but a whole SET of interlocking errors, each of which must be exposed.

"But let's not make this case too complicated. In the final analysis the question is extremely simple: The doctrine of the Secret Rapture either IS in harmony with the Bible—or it's NOT. There are no two ways about it.

"Unfortunately, when this theory is discussed, it seems hard to 'nail down' because people often give Answer XYZ when they're asked Question ABC. So to keep this trial on track, let's focus step-by-step on EIGHT KEY ISSUES, listed in Exhibit 'A' [reproduced on the next page]:

"Note that all eight of these issues are based on ASSUMPTIONS which NEED Scriptural support. Too often those assumptions go unchallenged— with too many questions never asked, too many assertions never tested. Secret Rapture teaching has become so widespread that many otherwise careful Christians uncritically accept it as an article of faith.

"A few years ago a little old lady named Clara Peller electrified a fast-food commercial by demanding, 'Where's the BEEF?' And in the marketplace of ideas, we consumers must demand more than the mere fluff of opinion, conjecture, and speculation. We, too, should demand 'Where's the BEEF?' to back men's claims—where's the Bible evidence needed for proof? Religious teachers who advocate a theory like this need more authority than the 'un-named source' proverbial in journalism. They need to *beef up* their claims with a 'Thus saith the Lord,' citing chapter and verse.

"So let's sift the evidence with all the thoroughness of Scotland Yard or the FBI as we examine these issues. If we dare to compare each point against the divine Standard of the Bible, we'll soon see where the truth lies.

Exhibit "A"
CRUCIAL ISSUES
Involved in the ASSUMPTIONS
of the Secret Rapture Theory

1. Advocates for the theory ASSUME that the Rapture of the Church by Christ goes unnoticed by the unsaved multitude, so they teach that it must be **SILENT**.

2. For the same reason, teachers of the Secret Rapture ASSUME that it must be **INVISIBLE**.

3. Secret Rapturists ASSUME that Christ's Rapture of the Church **leaves the wicked ALIVE**.

4. Advocates for the theory ASSUME that God **MUST remove** the righteous **to protect them** from the Tribulation.

5. Rapturists ASSUME Christ's Return will be in **TWO STAGES**: first the Rapture, which will be secret—unseen and unheard—then the actual Coming, which will be glorious.

6. They ASSUME, further, that these two supposed stages of Christ's Second Coming will be **SEVEN YEARS APART**.

7. Teachers of the theory ASSUME Christ's Rapture of the Church will take place **BEFORE** the revelation of **Antichrist**, who then brings about the period called the Tribulation.

8. Advocates for the theory ASSUME that the wicked, who are "left behind" by the Rapture, will then have another opportunity, a **SECOND CHANCE**, to be converted and to make their commitment to Christ.

"WILL THE WITNESS PLEASE TAKE THE STAND?"

"At this point we call as witnesses some of the great men of the Bible—the Gospel writers, the Apostles Paul and Peter, the Psalmist David, and others—from Old Testament prophets to John the Revelator—including the Lord Jesus Himself. As each one steps into the witness box to testify, we can rest assured that his testimony is true and that it will help us learn 'the truth, the whole truth, and nothing but the truth' on this important matter.

ISSUE #1:
Is the Rapture SILENT?

"Your Honor, the people call as our first witness the great Apostle PAUL."

The courtroom is hushed as the illustrious servant of God takes his place on the witness stand and is asked to respond to this question of Issue #1. Paul looks squarely at the jury and testifies in clear, ringing tones from 1 Thessalonians 4:15-17, NKJV—"This we say to you by the Word of the Lord, that we who are alive and remain until the coming of the Lord will by no means precede those who are asleep [or dead, sleeping the sleep of death]. For the Lord Himself will descend from heaven with a SHOUT, with the VOICE of an archangel, and with the TRUMPET of God. And the dead in Christ will rise first. Then we who are alive and remain shall be caught up together with them in the clouds to meet the Lord in the air. And thus we shall always be with the Lord."

"Thank you, Paul. You've cited for us the main verse in the entire Bible describing the rapture or gathering of the saints. But far from being silent, it's probably the noisiest verse in Scripture! It's very difficult to find a secret coming of Christ in this verse. The word 'voice' here is from the Greek word *phone,* from which we get the word *telephone.* Who ever heard of an inaudible 'phone' being put into a home or place of business? No one would hear it when it rings! We may be sure the 'phone' of the archangel WILL be heard by all when it 'rings' up there in the clouds so loudly as to wake the dead! No, ladies and gentlemen, a *phone* is not silent. A *voice* is not silent. A *shout* is not silent. Neither is a *trumpet.* [2]

"Those who teach the Secret Rapture theory paint a picture of the Rapture as if it were an isolated event happening all by itself and even going unnoticed by people at large who continue going about their daily duties! Such teachers need to remember that the Rapture of God's living saints takes place at the RESURRECTION of all the dead saints who ever lived. In fact, this general gathering of ALL God's faithful children has the bodily resurrection of DEAD believers PRECEDE the Rapture of His LIVING saints! And the resurrection, you know, is accompanied by the glorious, cataclysmic Coming of the Son of God. [3]

"This most important fact is overlooked by advocates for the Secret Rapture theory. In the testimony Paul just gave, note his use of repetition for the sake of clarity or emphasis:

Verse 15 – The living believers shall 'NOT PRECEDE' [4] the dead.

Verse 16 – The dead believers shall 'RISE FIRST'—before the living faithful are gathered and raptured away.

"Just imagine the shouts of joy and thundering chorus of praise that will issue from the immortal throats of all those redeemed! They certainly won't be silent. Paul, have you anything to add?"

The Apostle testifies further from 1 Corinthians 15:51-53, describing the rapture as very audible—"Behold, I show you a mystery; we shall not all sleep, but we shall all be changed, in a moment, in the twinkling of an eye, at the last TRUMP: for the TRUMPET shall SOUND, and the dead shall be raised incorruptible, and we shall be changed. For this corruptible must put on incorruption, and this mortal must put on immortality."

"Thank you, Paul. Remember that a trumpet is noisy, producing the loudest, most penetrating sound of all musical instruments!"

Next, the witness DAVID takes the stand and declares from Psalms 50:3-5—"Our God shall come, and shall NOT keep SILENCE: a fire shall devour before Him, and it shall be very TEMPESTUOUS round about Him. He shall CALL to the heavens from above, and to the earth, that He may judge His people. GATHER my saints together unto Me; those that have made a covenant with Me by sacrifice."

"Thank you, David. Not only will our God 'call' and 'not keep silence' when He comes to 'gather' His saints, but they themselves will also shout loud praises as they rise in their immortal bodies, asking, 'O Death, where is thy sting? O Grave, where is thy victory?'[5]

"At this time we want the Lord's own testimony. Your Honor, the people call the LORD JESUS CHRIST to the stand.

"Let me say, Lord—and I know I speak for all of us here—how honored we are by Your presence. It's the duty of this court to seek the truth, but I reverently believe we are graced by the presence of One who *is* the Truth. Now, Jesus, what do *You* say about how *silent* or *noisy* it will be when You gather Your saints and rapture them away?"

With commanding dignity, the Master replies from Matthew 24:31, saying, "[I] shall send [My] angels with a GREAT SOUND of a TRUMPET, and they shall GATHER together [My] elect[6] from the four winds, from one end of heaven to the other."

"Thank You for Your testimony, Jesus. You may be excused. But in rebuttal, advocates for the silent nature of the Rapture would question the Lord about His words in Revelation 16:15, NKJV—'Behold, I am coming as a THIEF. Blessed is he who watches, and keeps his garments, lest he walk naked and they see his shame.'

"This text, ladies and gentlemen, is one of the few used by supporters of the Secret Rapture to promote their theory—for they can't find many Scriptures in their favor. They think it means that Jesus will return silently, secretly, the way a thief surreptitiously goes about his dishonorable work. But is that what the Bible really teaches? Let's look at similar texts and let the Bible explain itself.

"For this purpose, Your Honor, we call again the Apostle PAUL to the stand. Now, Paul, you've just testified from 1 Thessalonians 4:15-17, giving your classic description of Christ's glorious rapture of the saints. I believe if you'll read the next few verses which immediately follow in chapter 5, we can clear up any confusion."

Nodding in agreement, Paul then asserts 1 Thessalonians 5:1-4, NKJV— "But concerning the TIMES and the SEASONS, brethren, you have no need that I should write to you. For you yourselves know perfectly that the DAY of the Lord so comes as a THIEF in the night. . . . But you, brethren, are not in darkness, that this DAY should overtake you as a THIEF."

"Thank you. Please note what Paul's testimony makes marvelously clear: It's not the Lord who comes as a thief—it's the DAY of the Lord, the TIME of His Return, that sneaks up and surprises those who fail to watch. Paul explicitly states in verse 1 that this passage deals with 'the times and the seasons.' He's discussing here not the MANNER but the TIME of Christ's Return. He's giving insight into WHEN Christ will return, not HOW. There's no reason in logic or Scripture for Jesus to come for His people in the manner of a sneak thief.

"If you told me that 'The father of the bride was state boxing champ,' should I understand that the BRIDE was good with her fists?!? Or is 'the bride' simply the object of the preposition 'of' to identify which 'father' you mean? The real subject of the sentence is 'father,' not 'bride'! Again, if I say, 'The captain of the team got drunk and missed the game,' do I mean the whole team did that—or just the captain?

"Exactly the same sentence structure is seen in Paul's words, 'The DAY of the Lord so cometh as a thief in the night.' Rules of elementary grammar dictate that the subject of the sentence is 'day,' not 'Lord'! And the words 'of the Lord' are simply a prepositional phrase used to identify which 'day' is meant."

Now the Apostle PETER steps into the witness box to share 2 Peter 3:10— "The DAY of the Lord will come as a THIEF in the night."

"Here Peter agrees with Paul in saying that it's the DAY of the Lord which comes as unexpectedly as a thief to most people. But the event itself, when it happens, will be anything but secret! In fact, Peter's text eloquently disproves the quietness of the thief concept. It says: 'But the day of the Lord will come as a thief in the night; in the which the heavens shall pass away with a GREAT NOISE.'

"When the Japanese attacked Pearl Harbor and propelled us into World War II, we were not expecting it. So December 7th, 1941, the 'day of infamy,' did sneak upon us as a thief. But the attack itself was anything but secret—it was like 'the shot heard round the world.' In the same way, Jesus said the TIME of His return is top secret: 'Of that day and hour knoweth no man, no, not the angels of heaven, but My Father only.'[7] But the momentous, awesome EVENT itself will be breathtaking beyond all belief, a cataclysmic climax to human history that will be of dazzling majesty and unimaginable glory!!

"Now, Ladies & Gentlemen of the Jury,

having carefully weighed the evidence, please ask yourself, Do I AGREE or DISAGREE with this statement: 'The rapture will be **SILENT**'?

ISSUE #2:
Is the Rapture **INVISIBLE**?

"Your Honor, the prosecution calls to the stand the LORD JESUS CHRIST."

Jesus, in answer to this question of Issue #2, testifies from Mark 13:26-27—"Then shall they SEE the Son of man coming in the clouds with GREAT POWER and GLORY. And then shall He send His angels, and shall GATHER together His elect from the four winds, from the uttermost part of the earth to the uttermost part of heaven."

"Let the record show that Christ Himself teaches that when He comes in glory to 'gather' His people in the Rapture, He'll be seen. Now Jesus, this gathering of your saints sounds like a most spectacular event when You say it's accompanied 'with great power and glory'! Is there anything You could add to describe the awesome drama of Your majestic Return?"

The Lord looks squarely at the jury and in ringing tones quotes Matthew 24:27, NASB—"For just as the LIGHTNING comes from the east, and FLASHES even to the west, so shall the Coming of the Son of Man be."

"I see—and we'll all see it, too! For is anything more noticeable than a blazing flash of lightning on a dark night? Could Jesus use language more vivid than this to describe a VISIBLE return?

"But, Lord, You know that defenders of the Secret Rapture theory claim the the world at large will go on as usual after You take Your church away—as if no one even sees that happen! When confronted by Bible texts describing how openly public and glorious Your Coming will be, they claim that 'Maybe the SAINTS who are raptured away will see the Lord, but to the WICKED He'll be invisible!' Can You please clarify this for the court?"

Jesus then reviews His words in Matthew 24:30-31—"Then shall APPEAR the sign of the Son of man in heaven: and then shall all the tribes of the earth MOURN, and they shall SEE the Son of man coming in the clouds of heaven with POWER and GREAT GLORY. And He shall send His angels . . . and they shall GATHER together His elect."

"Those who 'mourn,' of course, are the wicked. Yet Jesus says plainly that the wicked will 'see' Him coming to 'gather' His people in the Rapture, and they will 'mourn' at their loss and impending doom. Obviously, the wicked will be EYE-WITNESSES to this spectacular event!

"Thank You, Jesus, for Your testimony." Next, the Apostle JOHN is a corroborating witness in Revelation 1:7—"Behold, He cometh with clouds; and EVERY EYE shall SEE Him, and they also which pierced Him: and all kindreds of the earth shall WAIL because of Him."

"Thank you, John. 'Every eye shall see Him' includes ALL the living—righteous and wicked alike! So we needn't think that only the righteous see Jesus, while the wicked are oblivious to the whole thing. When the *wicked* see Christ coming, they 'shall WAIL because of Him.'

"This pointed testimony from such unimpeachable witnesses is most impressive. We know that the Almighty Lord of heaven and earth will return, not as the helpless Babe who once lay in a manger, but as King of kings and Lord of lords! When He comes with millions of bright and shining angels, I'm sure words like *glorious* and *breathtaking* will seem totally inadequate to describe the awesome scene. In the face of all this, it seems that to teach that the most dazzling, cataclysmic Event in the history of the world will be secret or invisible is to contradict Scripture Truth.

"Now, Ladies & Gentlemen of the Jury,

having carefully weighed the evidence, please ask yourself, Do I AGREE or DISAGREE with this statement: 'The rapture will be **INVISIBLE**'?

ISSUE #3:
DOES THE RAPTURE LEAVE THE **WICKED ALIVE?**

"This question is a simple one when we realize that there are no two ways about it: When Jesus returns, the wicked are either left alive or they are not—one or the other. Our first witness is Paul, the Apostle to the Gentiles. I ask you, PAUL, as the servant of the Lord, what is your inspired answer to this question?"

In unmistakable words, Paul now speaks from 2 Thessalonians 2:8 of the lawless wicked, "whom the Lord shall CONSUME with the spirit of His mouth, and shall DESTROY with the BRIGHTNESS of His COMING."

"Oh, my!—'consume' and 'destroy.' That's clear enough, so thank you, Paul. Your Honor, the people call JESUS CHRIST as our next witness. Now will

You please tell the court whether or not the wicked will be left ALIVE when You return in Your Second Coming?"

The Master replies plainly in Luke 17:26-30, NKJV—"As it was in the days of Noah, so it will be also in the days of the Son of Man: They ate, they drank, they married wives, they were given in marriage, until the day that Noah entered the ark, and the FLOOD came and DESTROYED them ALL. Likewise as it was also in the days of Lot: They ate, they drank, they bought, they sold, they planted, they built; but on the day that Lot went out of Sodom it rained fire and brimstone from heaven and DESTROYED them ALL. Even so will it be in the day when the Son of Man is REVEALED."

"Ladies and gentlemen, Christ's word 'revealed' here proves again that His Return is not secret. The Lord will be 'revealed,' not 'concealed.' The key examples given are the worldwide Flood and the destruction of Sodom and Gomorrah. In both cases, Noah's and Lot's experiences prove that the Lord's Coming will be audible, visible—and destructive to the wicked!"

Jesus continues His testimony from Luke 17:34-36, NKJV—"I tell you, in that night there will be two men in one bed: the one will be TAKEN and the other will be LEFT. Two women will be grinding [grain] together: the one will be TAKEN and the other LEFT. Two men will be in the field: the one will be TAKEN and the other LEFT."

"Thank You, Jesus. This passage You just read is again one of the few texts used by Rapturists to prove their case. They say, 'The Lord says the saints are "taken" to heaven, but the wicked are "left" behind to face the Antichrist and the tribulation he brings.'

"But they neglect to read the NEXT verse! They not only OVERLOOK the question asked by the disciples, who knew the righteous would be taken to heaven but wondered where the wicked would be left, but they also SKIP the Lord's answer: 'They. . .said unto Him, Where, Lord? And He said unto them, Wheresoever the BODY is, thither will the EAGLES be gathered together.'

"The word translated 'eagles' in the King James Version really means *buzzards* or *vultures,* which feed on the dead bodies of the slain wicked. And the word 'body' here means *dead* body or *corpse.* Modern English Bibles translate the passage that way. If we look up Luke 17:37 in . . .

The New Testament in Modern English (Phillips)
The Good News Bible, Today's English Version
The New American Standard Bible
The New International Version
The New English Bible
The Amplified Bible
The Living Bible
we find that they all say: 'VULTURES' for *eagles.*

"If we look up that same text in . . .
The New Testament in Modern English (Phillips)
The Good News Bible, Today's English Version
The New International Version
The Amplified Bible
we find they all say: 'DEAD body' for *body*.

The New English Bible says, 'CORPSE.' And the parallel passage in Matthew 24:28 says 'CARCASE' even in the King James Version.

"So believers are 'taken' up in the rapture when Jesus appears, and the wicked are 'left.' But they're NOT left ALIVE! Ministers who try to mislead us into thinking this text supports the secret rapture theory do so at the price of doing violence to the plain teaching of Scripture, and I wouldn't want to be in their shoes in the Judgment.

"Jesus here is teaching this about His return: At the same time the righteous are 'taken,' the wicked are destroyed just as surely as were the wicked in the days of Noah and Lot. All over the earth, their unburied bodies are 'left' dead for vultures to feed upon.

"Your Honor, to clarify this point even further, the people call JOHN, the Revelator, to the stand. Now, John, we know that in the chapter you wrote called Revelation 19 you vividly depict Christ's Return under the twin metaphors of joyous Bridegroom and conquering Hero. Would you please describe for the court what will happen when Jesus returns to claim His bride, the church?"

John therefore testifies from Revelation 19:7-9—"The marriage of the Lamb is come, and His wife hath made herself ready. And to her was granted that she should be arrayed in fine linen, clean and white: for the fine linen is the righteousness of saints. . . . Blessed are they which are called unto the marriage supper of the Lamb . . ."

"—Excuse me for interrupting, John, but please allow me to give a bit of background as a foundation for the point I'd like you to make: Because there are two classes of people in the world, righteous and wicked, there are two suppers spoken of in this chapter. One is the wedding banquet enjoyed by those who have committed themselves to Christ as a bride commits herself to the bridegroom. The other is the alternate supper of doom in which the slain wicked provide a feast for vultures.

"To the wicked, Jesus appears not as He did in His First Advent, a humble Carpenter, but—as you yourself have put it, John—as conquering King upon 'a white horse. . . . And the [angel] armies which were in heaven followed Him upon white horses. . . . And He hath on His vesture and on His thigh a name written, KING OF KINGS, AND LORD OF LORDS.'[8]

"Since the wicked cannot stand in the presence of a holy God, they'll be struck dead at Christ's coming, as Paul testified to begin our investigation of this issue.

"Now John, please describe the vision God gave you of how an angel then invites the vultures to feast upon their dead flesh."

John continues his testimony from Revelation 19:17-18—"An angel . . . cried with a loud voice, saying to all the fowls that fly in the midst of heaven, Come and gather yourselves together unto the supper of the great God; that ye may eat the flesh . . . of ALL men, both free and bond, both small and great."

"Thank you, John, for confirming Jesus' point about the vultures. Now can you give us an inspired preview of the plight of the wicked?"

This time John quotes Revelation 6:15-17—"The kings of the earth, and the great men, and the rich men, and the chief captains, and the mighty men, and every bondman, and every free man, hid themselves in the dens and in the rocks of the mountains; and said to the mountains and rocks, FALL on us, and HIDE US from the face of Him that sitteth on the throne, and from the wrath of the Lamb: for the great day of His wrath is come; and who shall be able to stand?"

"The answer to that tragic question is, No one—none of the wicked will be able to stand in the presence of a holy God, and they instinctively realize this. They try to hide themselves, even calling for the rocks and mountains to fall on them. But—as Paul testified a moment ago—they're struck dead 'by the brightness of His coming.' You may step down, John.

"For our next witness, Your Honor, the people call the Old Testament prophet JEREMIAH."

Jeremiah gives his confirming testimony from Jeremiah 25:33—"The SLAIN of the Lord shall be at that day from one end of the earth even unto the other end of the earth: they shall not be LAMENTED, neither GATH-ERED, nor BURIED; they shall be DUNG [excrement or manure] upon the ground."

"Did we hear you correctly, Jeremiah? Did you say 'the slain of the Lord . . . shall not be lamented, neither gathered, nor buried?' Surely even Mafia gangsters are LAMENTED by someone—surely their criminal friends or at least their mother would lament their passing. And even the wholesale bod-ies of those killed in warfare are GATHERED and BURIED, simply for reasons of sanitation and public health. So how can your statement possibly be true? It's true, ladies and gentlemen, because all the righteous are raptured away 'to meet the Lord in the air,'[9] and all the wicked are struck dead by 'the brightness of His coming.'[10] So there's no one LEFT to lament, gather, or bury the wicked dead!

"Jeremiah, what else can you tell us from the inspired insight God has given you?"

The faithful prophet now quotes a part of his divine vision from Jeremiah 4:23-27—"I beheld, and, lo, there was NO MAN, and all the birds of the heavens were fled . . . and all the CITIES thereof were BROKEN DOWN at the presence of the Lord, and by His fierce anger."

"Excuse me for interrupting again, Jeremiah. But how could it be true that there was 'no man'? My honorable opponents might contend that your vision was of the earth before the creation of Adam on the sixth day of that first week—and thus 'no man' was seen. But let me point out that you mentioned 'cities . . . broken down at the presence of the Lord, and by His fierce anger.' Yet during Creation Week, cities did not exist, and God had no reason to feel anger!

"Your vision, Jeremiah, confirms the testimony given by John and Jesus, who preceded you as witnesses. You can truly say: 'There was no man' because the righteous are all in heaven, and the wicked are all dead, their bodies rotting as 'dung upon the ground.'

"Thank you for your testimony. Your Honor, the people now call ISAIAH, another Old Testament prophet, to the stand. Can you, Isaiah, corroborate what Jeremiah has told us?"

The aged prophet composes himself as he gazes into the distance and sees again with the eye of Inspiration his vision of Isaiah 26:21—"Behold, the Lord cometh out of His place to PUNISH the inhabitants of the earth for their INIQUITY: the earth . . . shall no more COVER her slain."

"Well, Isaiah, if the earth won't cover her slain, it's plain that the wicked not only won't survive—they won't even be buried, as Jeremiah testified. Have you anything to add which may be pertinent?"

The prophet pauses thoughtfully, then he quotes Isaiah 24:1 & 3—"Behold, the Lord maketh the earth EMPTY, and maketh it waste, and turneth it upside down, and scattereth abroad the inhabitants thereof. . . . The land shall be utterly EMPTIED, and utterly spoiled: for the Lord hath spoken this word."

"Thank you, Isaiah. You obviously confirm Jeremiah's vision of seeing 'no man' on earth when you call the land 'utterly emptied'!

"At this time, Your Honor, I'd like to request the Court Reporter to read back part of Paul's testimony when he quoted 1 Thessalonians 5:1-4, NKJV. We looked at this passage earlier when considering Issue #1, but I'd like to have the part I've highlighted read aloud."

The Court Reporter reads that Paul told believers: "You yourselves know perfectly that the day of the Lord so cometh as a thief in the night. For when they [the wicked] say, 'Peace and safety!' then sudden DESTRUCTION comes upon them, as labor pains upon a pregnant woman. And they shall NOT ESCAPE."

"Thank you—that's far enough. Thus, ladies and gentlemen, you see that in the same passage of 1 Thessalonians 4 & 5 Paul not only explains what will happen to the living and dead RIGHTEOUS when the Lord returns, he also tells us that the living WICKED will face 'sudden DESTRUCTION. . . . And they shall not escape'!

"Let the record show that the sworn testimony of these witnesses hardly fits into the Secret Rapture scheme which leaves the wicked alive. On the contrary, the wicked, lying dead all over the earth, won't even be buried. But this theory is a prime example of Bible truth buried in a theological grave.

"Now, Ladies & Gentlemen of the Jury,
having carefully weighed the evidence, please ask yourself, Do I AGREE or DISAGREE with this statement: 'The rapture will leave the wicked **ALIVE**'?

ISSUE #4:
MUST GOD **REMOVE** THE RIGHTEOUS?

"All Bible students know that God warns of a time of trouble or tribulation coming upon the world near the end time.[11] There's no disagreement on that fact. But some believe that Christ comes for His church BEFORE the tribulation—they are called Pre-Tribulationists. Others believe Christ comes AFTER the tribulation to rescue His people and to put an end to the trouble— they are called Post-Tribulationists.

"Supporters of the Secret Rapture theory are Pre-Tribulationists. They claim not only that Christ WILL come before the time of trouble but that He MUST come and take His people out of the world in order to protect them. However, I intend to show this court Bible evidence proving beyond the shadow of a doubt that such a teaching is wrong and not in harmony with Scripture.

"To begin our case, Your Honor, the prosecution again calls the Apostle JOHN to the stand. We all know that much of the trouble and tribulation of the last days before Christ's return will be from the Seven Last Plagues. But let's establish who receives those plagues. Let me ask you first this question, John: What punishment will be given to those willing to receive the Mark of the Beast?"

Solemnly, John answers from Revelation 14:9-10, NKJV—"If anyone worships the Beast and his image, and receives his Mark on his forehead or on his hand, he himself shall also drink of the wine of the wrath of God, which is poured out full strength into the cup of His indignation."

"I see: They will drink of 'the wrath of God.' Can you tell us, John, where this wrath is found—what it is that contains it?"

The Revelator replies from Revelation 15:1 & 16:1-2—". . . the seven last plagues; for IN THEM is filled up the wrath of God. . . . And I heard a great voice out of the temple saying to the seven angels [having the seven last plagues], Go your ways, and pour out the vials of the wrath of God upon the earth. And the first [angel] went, and poured out his vial . . . upon the men which had the Mark of the Beast, and upon them which worshipped his image."

"Well, then, we see that the Seven Last Plagues are brought by God upon the wicked who receive the Mark of the Beast. Since these plagues contain 'the wrath of God,' they're a punishment for those who rebel against God, NOT for God's people. The faithful saints may suffer the wrath of man but never the wrath of God. Paul tells us Christians clearly in 1 Thessalonians 5:9—'God hath not appointed US to wrath, but to obtain salvation by our Lord Jesus Christ.'

"Thank you, John. Let's turn now to the Old Testament for an instructive example. When we study the Ten Plagues sent to punish Egypt for Pharaoh's refusal to let God's people go, we learn that the FIRST THREE PLAGUES were experienced by ALL in the land, but the LAST SEVEN PLAGUES were *not* upon God's people. Please note the table, Exhibit 'B' [reproduced on the next page]:

"We call to the stand the Patriarch MOSES to confirm this important point. Moses, would you please tell the court, if you can recall, the words God had you speak to Pharaoh when the Fourth Plague was about to fall?"

Without hesitation, Moses recalled Exodus 8:20-24, NKJV—"The LORD said to [me], . . . 'Stand before Pharaoh . . . [and] say to him, "Thus says the LORD: Let My people go, that they may serve Me. Or else, if you will not let My people go, behold, I will send swarms of flies on you and your servants, on your people and into your houses. The houses of the EGYPTIANS shall be full of swarms of flies, and also the ground on which they stand. And in that day I will SET APART the land of Goshen, in which MY PEOPLE dwell, that NO swarms of flies shall be there, in order that you may know that I am the LORD in the midst of the land. *I will make a difference between My people and your people.* Tomorrow this sign shall be."' And the LORD did so. Thick swarms of flies came into the house of Pharaoh, into his servants' houses, and into all the land of Egypt. The land was corrupted because of the swarms of flies."

EXHIBIT "B" — THE TEN PLAGUES OF EGYPT

SCRIPTURE TEXT		NATURE OF PLAGUE
Exodus 7:19-21	1.	Nile **waters turned to blood**
Exodus 8:1-6	2.	Plague of **frogs**
Exodus 8:16-19	3.	Plague of **lice**

But **the LAST SEVEN PLAGUES fell
ONLY on the Egyptians**—
they were *not* suffered by God's people!

Exodus 8:20-24	4.	Swarms of **flies**
Exodus 9:1-7	5.	Plague of **livestock disease**
Exodus 9:8-11	6.	Plague of **boils**
Exodus 9:18 & 22-26	7.	Plague of **hail**
Exodus 10:12-15	8.	Plague of **locusts**
Exodus 10:21-23	9.	Plague of **darkness**
Exodus 11:1-7 and 12:13, 29-30	10.	**Death of the firstborn**

"That's marvelous, Moses—how the Lord watches over His own! Could you give one more example?"

Moses then repeated details about the Ninth Plague, from Exodus 10:21-23, NKJV—"Then the LORD said to [me], 'Stretch out your hand toward heaven, that there may be darkness over the land of Egypt, darkness which may even be FELT.' So [I] stretched out [my] hand toward heaven, and there was THICK darkness in all the land of Egypt three days. They did not see one another; nor did anyone rise from his place for three days. But all the children of Israel HAD light in THEIR dwellings"!

"Thank you, Moses! Your testimony from the history of God's people proves our point that the Lord didn't NEED to take His people out of Egypt in order to protect them from those terrible plagues! He took them out AFTER the plagues were over. Neither will God need to rapture away His church to protect it from the Seven Last Plagues. He will rapture His faithful people AFTER those plagues are finished. God's people may to some extent be AFFECTED by the Plagues, but they'll never be AFFLICTED by them.

"One last question: could you please tell the court the promise God gives His people going through tribulation in the end times?"

With a kind smile, Moses replies from Deuteronomy 4:30-31—"When thou art in TRIBULATION, and all these things are come upon thee, even in the LATTER DAYS, if thou turn to the Lord thy God, and shalt be obedient unto His voice; (for the Lord thy God is a merciful God;) He will NOT forsake thee, neither DESTROY thee. . . ."

"Thank you, Moses—you may step down. So Moses testifies that as believers go through the 'Tribulation . . . in the latter days,' they'll be under God's 'merciful' protection. The Antichrist/Beast may trouble the Church, but God is the One who brings the plagues upon the wicked—and He certainly won't subject His faithful children to that danger and destruction! God will be with His people and 'not forsake' them in the latter-day tribulation.

"Now we call to the stand the Psalmist DAVID, who I think has something to say on this subject. David, could you add a thought to build on the testimony of Moses and John?"

David shares an encouraging passage from Psalm 91:7-10—"A THOUSAND shall fall at thy side, and TEN thousand at thy right hand; but it shall NOT come nigh thee. Only with thine eyes shalt thou behold and see the reward of the WICKED. . . . There shall no evil befall thee, neither shall any PLAGUE come nigh THY dwelling."

"Excellent, David. You're in complete harmony with the others.

"Now let me quickly share with you, ladies and gentlemen of the jury, THREE CLASSIC EXAMPLES along this line in Exhibit 'C':

Exhibit "C"

- **Genesis 6-8.** God preserved and protected *Noah and his family* in the MIDST of the Flood. He didn't need to take them to heaven to save them.

- **Daniel 3**. God preserved and protected *the three Hebrew children* (Shadrach, Meshach, and Abednego) WITHOUT REMOVING them from the fiery furnace. Instead, He was with them in their ordeal, so that not a hair of their heads was singed, nor did they have so much as the smell of smoke upon them!—Daniel 3:27. Our God is just the same today: He will preserve and protect us, but He doesn't need to REMOVE us from this world to do it.

- **Daniel 6**. God preserved and protected *Daniel in the lions' den* WITHOUT REMOVING him from that place of danger. God has a thousand ways to protect us that we know nothing about. He can give the lions "lockjaw" or perform any miracle needed to preserve faithful Daniel or His people today. We need not assume that the church MUST be raptured before the tribulation in order to be safe, for God's people are surely safe in His hands.

"Ignoring such beautiful Biblical examples, my worthy opponents often quote Revelation 3:10 to try to prove that the righteous will be taken out of the world before the tribulation: 'Because thou has KEPT the WORD of My patience, I will also KEEP THEE FROM the hour of temptation, which shall come upon all the world, to try them that dwell upon the earth.'

"It's immediately obvious that this text does not speak of the righteous LEAVING this world at all! Those who insist on such meaning are forced to assume the very point which must be proved. Furthermore, Jesus completely clarified the meaning by something He said in prayer to His Father which sounds very similar: 'They have KEPT Thy WORD. . . . I pray NOT that Thou shouldest take them OUT of the world, but that Thou shouldest KEEP THEM FROM the evil.'[12] If those who 'kept the word' can be 'kept from the evil' of the world WITHOUT being taken out of the world, why assume a special Coming and pre-tribulation Rapture is required for those who 'kept the word' to be 'kept from the hour of temptation'? Whatever else may be taught in Revelation 3:10, it's clear that no extra Coming of Christ is indicated.

"Revelation 4:1 is also used by some to teach the Secret Rapture: 'After this I [John] looked, and, behold, a door was opened in heaven: and the first voice which I heard was as it were of a trumpet talking with ME; which said, Come up hither, and I will show THEE things which must be hereafter.'

"Some try to interpret the open door and the voice calling, 'Come up hither' to symbolize the Rapture of the Church. But the voice was addressed to John, NOT to the Church! Secret Rapture teachers claim the Rapture occurs between chapters three and four of Revelation, yet John passes over it in silence leaving his readers to assume it has taken place. If we interpret Scripture by assumption, we can find anything we want in the Word of God simply by assuming it's there!

"As we've just seen, Exhibit 'C' provides impressive examples of God's protective care for His faithful people during tribulation. Those were all from the Old Testament, but careful Bible scholars know that the New Testament teaches the same thing! Believers in the Secret Rapture Theory say that Christians won't go through the Tribulation, but if they took a Bible concordance and looked up the word "tribulation," they'd be shocked to learn that almost every reference describes *the suffering of believers!* Please note:

- John 16:33 — Jesus told His followers, "In the world ye shall have *tribulation.*"

- Acts 14:22 — Paul told his early Christian converts, "We must *through* much *tribulation* enter the kingdom of God." Remember that Noah, Daniel, and the three Hebrew children were not saved *from* tribulation but were brought "through" it by God!

- 2 Thessalonians 1:4 — Paul praised the church at Thessalonica "for your patience and faith in all your persecutions and *tribulations* that ye endure."

- Revelation 1:9 — In exile on the lonely Island of Patmos, the Apostle John called himself "your brother and companion in *tribulation.*"

- Revelation 2:9 — Jesus told His church at Smyrna, "I know thy works, and *tribulation.*"

"In the light of these Scriptures, the idea of Christians escaping tribulation seems like fantasy and illusion. Besides, even in the *Left Behind* series of books that teach the Rapture theory, there *are* Christians (called "the Tribulation Force") who *do* go through "the Tribulation"![13]

"At this time, Your Honor, the people call to the stand JESUS CHRIST. Let the record show that the Master's parable of the wheat and the tares (or weeds) is too long to quote here, being found in Matthew 13:24-30 and 36-43, but I request that each juror read it carefully, with all the attention it deserves.

"Now, Jesus, will You please summarize that parable for the court?"

The Lord's melodious voice repeats Matthew 13:37-39—"He that soweth the good seed is the Son of Man; the field is the world; the GOOD seed are the children of the kingdom; but the TARES are the children of the WICKED one; the enemy that sowed them is the DEVIL; the HARVEST is the END of the world; and the reapers are the ANGELS."

"Thank You, Jesus. You've given the meaning so clearly as to prevent all misunderstanding. Here we have the two groups of people—saved and unsaved—at the time of the Rapture, when God's angels will 'reap' the earth. Now here's the question: Are the good people of the church spirited away in a Secret Rapture seven years before the end of the world to escape the tribulation that must be endured by the bad people? Is that Your teaching in this parable, Jesus?"

Jesus decisively shakes His head and replies from Matthew 13:30 & 40— "Let BOTH grow TOGETHER until the harvest . . . [when] the tares are gathered and burned in the fire; so shall it be in the end of this world."

"Thank You! This parable teaches that the separation called the Rapture is made at the 'harvest.' And 'the harvest is the END of the world.' Since 'both grow together until the harvest'—the end—those who teach a Rapture seven years earlier contradict this plain teaching of the Lord.

"Yet C. I. Scofield, who was one of the main teachers responsible for spreading the Secret Rapture doctrine, attempts to do this in his *Scofield Reference Bible* when he says, 'The gathering of the tares into bundles for burning does NOT imply IMMEDIATE judgment.'[14] But Jesus didn't say the tares are *merely gathered.* He said plainly, 'the tares are GATHERED and BURNED in the fire.'[15]

"Also, Scofield says in the same note that 'The tares are set apart for burning, but FIRST the **wheat** is gathered into the barn.' However, Scripture has Jesus saying: 'Gather ye together FIRST the **tares**'[16]—the exact opposite! Such direct contradiction of the plain Word of God makes me suspicious of this teaching. What do you say?

"Now, Ladies & Gentlemen of the Jury,
having carefully weighed the evidence, please ask yourself, Do I AGREE or DISAGREE with this statement: 'God will **REMOVE** the righteous before the tribulation in order to protect them from it'?

ISSUE #5:
Is Jesus Coming in **TWO STAGES?**

"English poet Lord Alfred Tennyson was in perfect harmony with Scripture truth when he wrote of the Second Advent in these terms:

> 'One God, one law, one element,
> And ONE far-off divine event
> To which the whole creation moves.'
> *—In Memoriam*

"Since the Bible consistently describes Christ's Return as the climax of the ages, a single, indivisible Event, the burden of proof rests heavily on those who try to teach the contrary. No proof whatever is required to sustain a belief in the Second Coming as ONE event—that's the most natural way to interpret the clear passages dealing with it.

"As a matter of fact, such passages were so interpreted by great theologians and common students of the Bible for century upon century of the Christian era. The Secret Rapture teaching, with its idea of splitting Christ's Return into two stages, is a recent innovation, a 'Johnny-Come-Lately' theory of only the last 150 years or so.[17] Before we abandon the time-honored Bible interpretation for this two-stage innovation, we need explicit assertions from the Word of God—not mere inferences resting on no higher authority than human teaching. Where is the Bible proof we need for the two-stage theory?

"In an attempt to provide this sorely-needed proof, advocates of the Secret Rapture resort to the obscurity of the Greek language—obscure at least to us who feel 'It's Greek to me!'[18] Let's look at the New Testament vocabulary used to describe the Second Advent:

Exhibit "D"
The *GREEKS* Had a WORD for It:

	Word		Meaning
1.	*parousia*	=	coming, arrival, presence
2.	*apokalupsis*	=	revelation, unveiling, appearing
3.	*epiphaneia*	=	brightness, manifestation of glory

"Teachers of the Secret Rapture theory tell us: 'The TWO phases of Christ's second coming are clearly distinguished in the Greek. When we look at the original words, the *parousia* is His coming FOR His saints in the Secret Rapture. The *apokalupsis* or *epiphaneia* is His coming WITH His saints in glory.'

"But these terms do NOT indicate two separate events! Instead, they're used interchangeably in such a way as to show there's only ONE Second Coming of Christ—not two! Note just a few examples:

"**1.** *Parousia,* Secret Rapture teachers would have us believe, denotes a SECRET coming or presence. But is this true? Not at all. For example, in 1 Thessalonians 4:15-17 Paul described 'the coming *[parousia]* of the Lord' in very noisy terms: a 'shout,' *etc.,* resurrects the faithful dead and all believers are raptured to meet the Lord in the air.

"And Matthew 24:27 likens 'the coming *[parousia]* of the Son of man' to glorious visible LIGHTNING shining from one horizon to the other! The 39th verse of the same chapter says the *parousia* will be like the destruction of Noah's day—not secret at all!

"Furthermore, 2 Thessalonians 2:8 speaks of the Antichrist 'whom the Lord shall . . . DESTROY with the brightness of His coming *[parousia].*' This verse locates Christ's coming at the END of the Tribulation, describing the *parousia* as taking place after Antichrist's reign, not as an escape rapture before his reign begins.

"**2.** *Apokalupsis* obviously means a 'revelation' or open 'appearing,' so Rapturists generally apply this word only to what they call the glorious 'second phase' of Christ's Coming. But 1 Peter 1:13 speaks of 'the grace that is to be brought unto you at the revelation *[apokalupsis]* of Jesus Christ.' Yet believers wouldn't have to wait for that grace till Christ's glorious revelation IF they'd been raptured earlier in the supposed first phase of His Coming!

"Likewise, in verse 7, Peter spoke of Christians being victorious, so 'That the trial of your faith . . . might be found unto praise and honour and glory at the appearing *[apokalupsis]* of Jesus Christ.' But Secret Rapture theorists teach that Christians will be taken to heaven, away from all trials, in the so-called first phase of Christ's Coming years before His revelation in glory.

"MATTHEW 24:37 says that as the days of Noah were, 'so shall also the coming *[parousia]* of the Son of man be.' LUKE'S account of the same passage says as the days of Noah were, 'Even thus shall it be in the day when the Son of man is revealed *[apokalupsis]*.' Luke 17:26 & 30. This shows that Christ's coming *[parousia]* and revelation *[apokalupsis]* are THE SAME EVENT!

"**3.** *Epiphaneia* is another of these Greek words that creates problems for the Secret Rapture theory. This word denotes a glorious manifestation of dazzling brightness. Titus 2:13 speaks of Christians 'Looking for that blessed hope, and the glorious appearing *[epiphaneia]* of the great God and our Saviour Jesus Christ.'

"This verse says our blessed hope is Christ's glorious appearing. But Rapturists teach this is NOT our hope. According to them, we're waiting not for His glorious 'appearing' *(epiphaneia)* but for the rapture at His invisible 'coming' *(parousia).*

"One further example may suffice: 2 Thessalonians 2:8 uses BOTH words in ONE text! It tells how the Lord shall destroy the wicked Man of Sin by the 'brightness *[epiphaneia]* of His coming *[parousia]*.'

"To sum up, we can say that Greek vocabulary offers no comfort to advocates of the Secret Rapture theory, for obviously no distinction can be made between the *parousia,* the *apocalypse,* and the *epiphany* of our Lord. They are one and the same event.

"Now let's examine another one of the few texts used by advocates of the Secret Rapture theory. It's Jude 14, which says: 'And Enoch also, the seventh from Adam, prophesied of these, saying, Behold, the Lord cometh WITH ten thousands of His SAINTS.'

"This text is sometimes used in an attempt to prove that Christ's Second Coming really has two stages. For Rapturists say, 'Surely He has to come FOR His saints before He can come WITH them—isn't that right?' It may seem so, at first glance. But not only would such an assumption contradict all the explicit declarations of God's Word we've already examined, it would be only that—an ASSUMPTION based upon a questionable interpretation of the word 'saints.'

"The word translated 'saints' here is the Greek *hagios,* which simply means 'holy' or 'holy ones.' It's applied to anything sacred, consecrated, blameless, pure, religious, *etc.* Though it may refer to people, it often refers to 'holy ANGELS,' as, for instance, in Mark 8:38, which speaks of 'the Son of man . . . when He cometh in the glory of His Father WITH the holy ANGELS.'

"This parallel passage in Mark no doubt expresses what Jude had in mind, for Matthew 25:31 also says: 'When the Son of man shall come in His glory, and ALL the holy ANGELS WITH Him, then shall He sit upon the throne of His glory.' Yes, He'll come with all His angels, His innumerable angels—so many that from a distance it appears Jesus is riding on a cloud. Remember, the angels will be the 'reapers' in earth's 'harvest.' If I were an angel, I wouldn't want to be left behind on this excursion all heaven is longing for, would you?

"Any seeker after truth willing to accept Biblical evidence will be impressed with Deuteronomy 33:2—a passage perfectly parallel to the one in question. Please note the striking similarity . . .

Jude 14 says:

'The Lord cometh with ten thousands of His saints.'

Deuteronomy 33:2 says:

'The Lord came from Sinai . . . **with ten thousands of saints**: from His right hand went a fiery Law for them' This tells of God giving His Law of Ten Commandments to Moses on Mt. Sinai accompanied by hosts of holy angels. We can be sure 'ten thousands of saints' here means ANGELS, not human saints, as Christ had not yet had even His First Advent, so there had been no resurrection.

"Along the same line, in Daniel 4:13 & 23 the prophet speaks of 'a watcher and a HOLY ONE coming down from heaven.' This 'holy one' was of course an angel messenger.

"In fact, many modern Bible translations render the word 'saints' of Jude 14 also as 'holy ones.' The New American Standard Bible, The Living Bible, The Amplified Bible, The Twentieth Century New Testament, The Phillips Translation, and The New International Version all do. Furthermore, Today's English Version of the Good News Bible and The New English Bible come right out and say, 'holy ANGELS.' *The Pulpit Commentary* says: 'The "ten thousands of His saints" is better rendered "ten thousands of His holy ones." . . . For the "holy ones" here intended are the ANGELS.' [19]

"All great teachings of the Bible are supported by clear, explicit, unequivocal statements of Scripture—but such is not the case with this theory. Instead of clear, EXPLICIT texts which unequivocally prove their point, advocates of the Secret Rapture must resort to texts like Jude 14 which they *interpret* according to their theory. They'll read Jude 14, for example, and tell us, 'This has *GOT* to mean SUCH and SUCH,' using human logic, not divine revelation. Their interpretative teaching is resoundingly refuted by clear statements of Scripture diametrically opposed to such theoretical interpretations.

"A good text to close this discussion and clinch this point is 1 Thessalonians 3:13, which says: 'To the end He may stablish your hearts unblameable in holiness before God, even our Father, at the coming of our Lord Jesus Christ WITH all His SAINTS.'

"Even though the expression '*with* all His saints' leads Rapturists to place this text at the supposed *second phase* of Christ's Return, note this important fact: Paul is here writing to fellow Christians in Thessalonica, and through them he's addressing the entire church. WHY should he pray to God to establish believers' 'hearts *unblameable* . . . at the coming of our Lord Jesus Christ WITH all His saints' IF they'd been raptured years earlier when the Lord came 'FOR His saints'???

"The only logical answer is: This text refers to the one and only Second Coming of Christ when He comes in glory 'WITH all His holy ANGELS.' The supposed distinction between 'for' and 'with' His saints is a verbal smokescreen thrown up by desperate men in an attempt to save a bankrupt theory.

"Now, Ladies & Gentlemen of the Jury,

having carefully weighed the evidence, please ask yourself, Do I AGREE or DISAGREE with this statement: 'Christ's Coming will be in TWO separate and distinct stages'?

ISSUE #6:
SEVEN YEARS APART?

"Secret Rapture teachers claim that the supposed 'two phases' of Christ Second Coming will take place seven years apart. Of course, we shouldn't be expected to address that claim until they prove Issue #5. For unless they demonstrate from Scripture that there ARE indeed two separate stages to Christ's Return, it's pointless to argue a time span of any length whatever between them. But let's take a moment anyway to examine their claim in the light of the Bible.

The Secret Rapture assumes that:
    A. the Rapture takes place seven years BEFORE
         the end time, and that
    B. life goes on for unbelievers AFTER
         Jesus secretly takes His church to heaven.

"Watch those assumptions self-destruct before your very eyes as we bring to light what the Word of God teaches. Your Honor, the people call to the stand the LORD JESUS CHRIST.

"Now, Jesus, as You know, there are religious teachers who proclaim that You will come to resurrect all dead believers and rapture away the church seven years before the end—that is, *seven years before the last day of earth's history*. Does Your testimony confirm or deny such teaching?"

With a look of patient love but firm conviction, Jesus testifies from John 6:39, 40, 44, & 54, NIV—"This is the will of Him who sent Me, that I shall lose none of all that He has given Me, but raise them up at the LAST DAY. For My Father's will is that everyone who looks to the Son and believes in Him shall have eternal life, and I will raise him up at the LAST DAY. . . . No one can come to Me unless the Father who sent Me draws him, and I will raise him up at the LAST DAY. . . . Whoever eats My flesh and drinks My blood has eternal life, and I will raise him up at the LAST DAY."

"Thank You, Jesus, for that powerful statement! Did you get that, ladies and gentlemen? Here from the Lord's own lips is a most significant fact—repeated for emphasis *four times in one chapter!*—that He will raise up His faithful dead at the LAST day, NOT seven years before!

"To continue, Jesus, would You please tell the court to what You would compare Your Second Coming?"

Jesus answers from Luke 17:28-30—"[My Coming shall be] as it was in the days of Lot; they did eat, they drank, they bought, they sold, they planted, they builded; but the SAME DAY that Lot went out of Sodom it rained fire and brimstone from heaven, and destroyed them all."

"So Your testimony does not say that Lot, the believer, went out of Sodom and then seven years later fiery destruction fell upon unbelievers! No, it says those two things happened 'the SAME DAY.'

"You know, ladies and gentlemen, sometimes we tell a person who over-reacts, 'Relax! It's not the end of the world!' Well, according to this theory, the Secret Rapture is not the end of the world, either. I mention this because a further assumption made by Secret Rapture theorists is that when God's Church is taken from the earth, *the Holy Spirit is also withdrawn*—seven years before the end of the world.

"But Jesus, would You recall for us now Your closing words to Your disciples after instructing them to carry on God's work by teaching people and baptizing them into Your church?"

Jesus then shared this encouraging promise from Matthew 28:20—"Lo, I am with you alway[s], even UNTO the END of the world."

"Very good, Jesus. Ladies and gentlemen, after Christ ascended back to heaven, the only way He could be with His people was through His Spirit. And through His Spirit, He promises to be with them here ALWAYS. This promise proves that BOTH believers AND the Holy Spirit will remain here 'even unto the end of the world' and NOT be removed seven years before!

"You can see that the Secret Rapture theory itself is just the tip of the iceberg. Beneath it lies a whole package of other assumptions—NONE of which is backed by the Bible!

"The question may well be asked: 'WHERE does rapture theology get the idea of the seven-year period which supposedly intervenes between the two stages of Christ's Second Coming?' The answer is, from their unique interpretation of Daniel 9:24-27, the momentous message God sent to Daniel by the angel Gabriel. However, that message had to do with Christ's FIRST Coming as 'the Messiah the Prince,' not His SECOND Coming at the end of the world! More is said on that great prophecy of Daniel in *Appendix C* at the back of this book, but perhaps you can already see what a colossal Biblical blunder they've made in promoting this doctrine.

"Now, Ladies & Gentlemen of the Jury,

having carefully weighed the evidence, please ask yourself, Do I AGREE or DISAGREE with this statement: 'The two supposed stages of Christ's Second Coming will be SEVEN YEARS APART'?

ISSUE #7:
WILL THE RAPTURE PRECEDE THE COMING OF ANTICHRIST?

"The Pre-Tribulation scheme of things in the Secret Rapture theory has the church being gathered away to heaven BEFORE the Antichrist is revealed. Please note the chart in Exhibit 'E'—which is based on the 'Pre-Tribulation' chart in Hal Lindsey's book *The Rapture*.[20] Note that, as the chart clearly shows, Rapturists teach this order of events:

> FIRST we believers are gathered and raptured away.
> THEN the Antichrist—that Man of Sin—is revealed.

"Keeping that sequence in mind, let's call to the stand <u>the Apostle PAUL</u>. I think you're too modest to say so yourself, Paul, but I believe we can all consider you an expert witness on this subject! What can you say to put us straight on the order of events in the Last Days?"

Paul seems almost excitedly eager to testify, as he repeats 2 Thessalonians 2:1-3—"We beseech you, brethren, by the COMING of our Lord Jesus Christ, and by our GATHERING together unto Him. . . . Let no man deceive you by any means: for THAT DAY [the day of the Lord's coming and our gathering together unto Him] shall NOT come, except there be a falling away FIRST, and that MAN of SIN be REVEALED, the son of perdition."

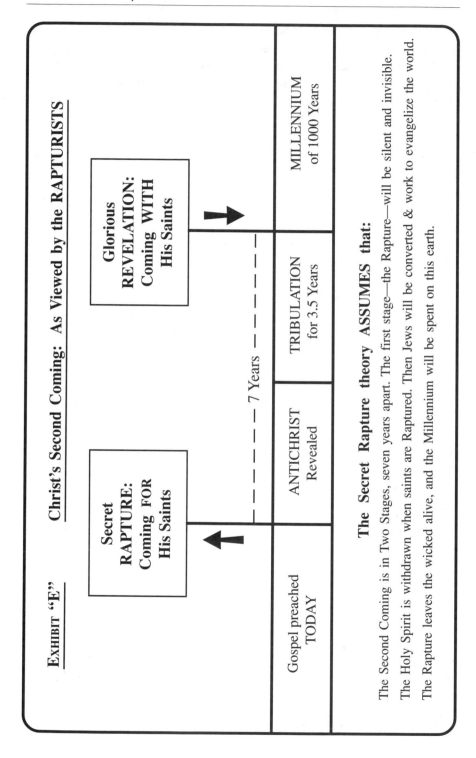

EXHIBIT "E"   Christ's Second Coming: As Viewed by the RAPTURISTS

Secret
RAPTURE:
Coming FOR
His Saints

Glorious
REVELATION:
Coming WITH
His Saints

7 Years

| Gospel preached TODAY | ANTICHRIST Revealed | TRIBULATION for 3.5 Years | MILLENNIUM of 1000 Years |

The Secret Rapture theory ASSUMES that:

The Second Coming is in Two Stages, seven years apart. The first stage—the Rapture—will be silent and invisible.

The Holy Spirit is withdrawn when saints are Raptured. Then Jews will be converted & work to evangelize the world.

The Rapture leaves the wicked alive, and the Millennium will be spent on this earth.

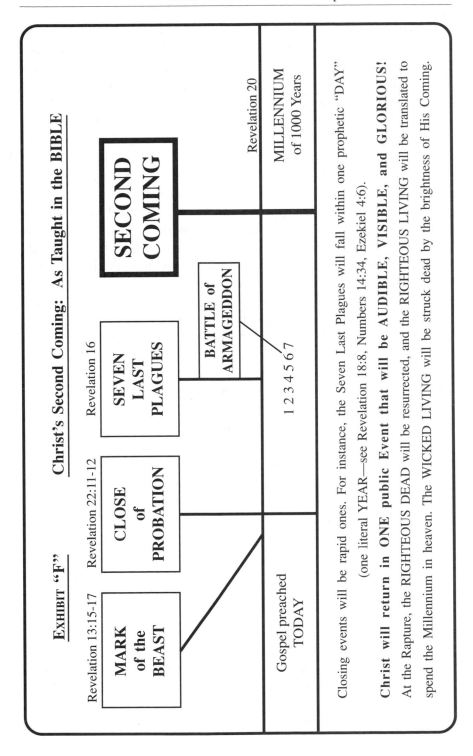

EXHIBIT "F"   Christ's Second Coming: As Taught in the BIBLE

Revelation 13:15-17   Revelation 22:11-12   Revelation 16

MARK of the BEAST

CLOSE of PROBATION

SEVEN LAST PLAGUES

BATTLE of ARMAGEDDON

SECOND COMING

Revelation 20

MILLENNIUM of 1000 Years

Gospel preached TODAY

1 2 3 4 5 6 7

Closing events will be rapid ones. For instance, the Seven Last Plagues will fall within one prophetic "DAY" (one literal YEAR—see Revelation 18:8, Numbers 14:34, Ezekiel 4:6).

Christ will return in ONE public Event that will be AUDIBLE, VISIBLE, and GLORIOUS!

At the Rapture, the RIGHTEOUS DEAD will be resurrected, and the RIGHTEOUS LIVING will be translated to spend the Millennium in heaven. The WICKED LIVING will be struck dead by the brightness of His Coming.

"Well, Paul, that's very clear. You may step down. Paul states under oath that the Rapture or 'gathering' of the saints will take place only AFTER that 'Man of Sin' is revealed, NOT before. And note, ladies and gentlemen, our witness is careful to warn 'Let no man *deceive* you' on the timetable of events regarding the Rapture and the Antichrist.

"In fact, Paul and Daniel and John write as though Christians NEED to be warned against the deceptions of Antichrist—which would be unnecessary if they were raptured away before the Beast comes along!

"For our last witness on this issue, Your Honor, the people call the Apostle JOHN, the Revelator who wrote about the Millennium—that thousand-year period the redeemed of all ages will spend with Christ [which is explored in our next chapter]. Now we know that when Christ comes to rapture away His church, the Christian dead will be raised in the resurrection of the righteous. John, would you please tell the court whether or not those resurrected had to defend their faith against the Antichrist?"

John quotes for us Revelation 20:4-6, NIV—"I saw thrones on which were seated . . . those who had been beheaded because of their testimony for Jesus and because of the Word of God. They had NOT worshipped the Beast or his image and had NOT received his Mark on their foreheads or their hands. They came to life and reigned with Christ for a THOUSAND YEARS. (The rest of the dead [the wicked] did not come to life until the thousand years were ended.) This is the FIRST resurrection. Blessed and holy are those who have part in the FIRST resurrection. The second death has no power over them, but they will be priests of God and of Christ and will reign with Him for a THOUSAND YEARS."

"Thank you, John, for that illuminating testimony! Now, ladies and gentlemen, let's carefully analyze what we've just heard:

- ✓ There are two resurrections, 1000 years apart.
- ✓ 'Blessed and holy are those [that is, the righteous redeemed] who have part in the FIRST resurrection.'
- ✓ 'The rest of the dead [those who are NOT "blessed and holy"— that is, the wicked] did not come to life until the thousand years were ended.'
- ✓ The Millennium is the thousand-year period between those two resurrections. Now follow closely:
- ✓ John's testimony here says that some of those who in the first resurrection 'came to life and reigned with Christ a thousand years' are those who 'had NOT worshipped the BEAST' we call Antichrist, and who 'had NOT received his MARK.'

"How completely this demolishes the theory's interpretation! For its advocates claim that Antichrist arises and gives his Mark only after the first resurrection and rapture.

"I recently heard a radio preacher express this belief: 'I don't expect to be here when the Antichrist Beast is enforcing his Mark upon people. I expect to go up in the Rapture and be in heaven during the great tribulation time.'

"Yet we've just heard unimpeachable testimony that some of those who come up in 'the first resurrection' and who 'live and reign with Christ a thousand years' have already refused to worship the Beast or receive his Mark! Thus the Antichrist must have already been carrying on his oppressive work before 'the first resurrection,' which takes place at the Rapture of God's people.

"Now, Ladies & Gentlemen of the Jury,
having carefully weighed the evidence, please ask yourself, Do I AGREE or DISAGREE with this statement: 'The Rapture will take place BEFORE ANTICHRIST is revealed'?

ISSUE #8:
WILL UNBELIEVERS HAVE A SECOND CHANCE?

"Another assumption among many made by the theory is that the period of seven years following the Rapture is a time of great evangelism despite persecution by the Antichrist. Since the faithful Christians are all gone, this evangelism will be conducted by the Jews—who are all converted—even without the aid of the absent Holy Spirit! [21]

"Many who subscribe to the Secret Rapture theory are reluctant to admit that that doctrine provides a 'second chance' for the wicked, but the practical effect of such a teaching does just that. After all, if unbelievers who have no use for Christ or His religion discover some day that all Christians have suddenly disappeared from the face of the earth, it could have a sobering effect on their attitude and lead them to reconsider. And according to the theory, they'll have seven years to change their minds!

"If their Christian friends today tell them about a mysterious seven-year period of evangelism following the Rapture after which Jesus will return again, many will be tempted to postpone accepting Him NOW in favor of that future time.

"Even though its assumptions are not Biblically supported, an unbeliever who's taught the whole package of Secret Rapture theology could find quite appealing the idea that one is NOT irrevocably lost even if he's uncommitted to Christ when the saints are raptured. Although persecution by the Beast may break out, an unbeliever may well reason, 'I'm man enough to take it!' Herein lies the deadly danger of Secret Rapture theology.

"Let's examine Bible evidence on the impossibility of a second chance. Your Honor, the prosecution calls <u>our LORD JESUS CHRIST</u> to the stand.

"Let's recall for a moment now, Jesus, Your famous parable of the Bridegroom whose arrival was delayed while ten bridesmaids or virgins impatiently waited. Five of these virgins were 'wise' believers who faithfully looked for the Bridegroom to come. But five were 'foolish' and unprepared—they allowed their lamps [22] to go out for lack of oil. So they left their place of waiting to go buy more oil. Please tell us what happened while they were gone on that emergency shopping trip."

In sober tones, Jesus replied from Matthew 25:10—"While they went to buy, the Bridegroom came; and they that were READY went in with Him to the marriage: and the door was SHUT."

"Amen! This parable clearly teaches that when Christ, 'the Bridegroom' comes to claim His bride, the Church, some people like the five foolish virgins won't be 'ready.' But does this parable give any comfort to those who need a second chance? Decidedly not. It says with a note of finality: 'The door was SHUT.'

"Jesus, would You share with us the next few verses so we can determine whether or not You teach a second chance at salvation?"

The Master then testifies from Matthew 25:11-13, NKJV—"Afterward the [five foolish] virgins came also, saying, 'Lord, Lord, OPEN to us!' But He answered and said, 'Assuredly, I say to you, I do not know you.' Watch therefore, for you know neither the day nor the hour in which the Son of Man is coming."

"One is reminded that when the Flood came in Noah's day, possibly many wicked people who had spurned God's invitation to enter the Ark rushed to it in a belated attempt to force open the door and seek safety. But they had made their decision, and it was too late. No human hand had closed that door on the family of Noah, for we read that 'The Lord shut him in.' [23] There was no second chance that time, and Jesus has testified it will be just that way when He returns. [24]

"Finally, Jesus, on the last page of the last chapter of the last book of the Bible, You speak of the Close of Probation, when every person will already have made that irrevocable decision that forever seals his fate. We know, Lord, that You are loving and patient, but there comes a time when You can wait no longer. Please tell the court what You must then declare."

With awful solemnity, Jesus pronounces the fateful words of Revelation 22:11-12, NKJV—"He who is unjust, let him be unjust still; he who is filthy, let him be filthy still; he who is righteous, let him be righteous still; he who is holy, let him be holy still. And behold, I am coming quickly, and My reward is with Me, to give every one according to his work."

"This pronouncement precedes Jesus' Coming to 'reward' His 'holy' and 'righteous' people with 'the gift of . . . eternal life' and to give those who are 'unjust' and 'filthy' *their* just 'reward' also—'the wages of sin [which] is DEATH.'[25] When every destiny is decided, *probation closes on that decision*, and Christ returns to reap the earth accordingly. No second chance is seen in the theology of Jesus.[26]

"Besides these clear teachings of Jesus that leave no room for a second chance at salvation, Issue #3 above—as to whether the Rapture leaves the wicked alive—showed conclusively that after Jesus comes for His saints there'll be no wicked LEFT to be converted!

"Now, Ladies & Gentlemen of the Jury,
having carefully weighed the evidence, please ask yourself, Do I AGREE or DISAGREE with this statement: 'The wicked who miss the Rapture will still have another opportunity, a SECOND CHANCE, to be saved'?

CONCLUSION

"Let me sum up my case, ladies and gentlemen of the jury, by reminding you that sometimes a person will come face to face with Truth on a subject like this and still say: 'Well, of course that's all very interesting. But after all, both those who accept and those who reject the Secret Rapture doctrine all agree that the Lord WILL return soon. So what DIFFERENCE does it make what a person believes or a church teaches on this point?'

"It makes a GREAT DEAL of difference, because the teaching of the Secret Rapture is both deceptive and dangerous. It's DECEPTIVE because it's not in harmony with the Word of God—the clear testimony of Scripture we've examined proves that fact beyond all argument. And it's DANGEROUS because of the supposed 'second chance' it holds out to the uncommitted heart. Satan, a keen student of human psychology, knows how natural it is for man to put things off. By teaching a second chance at salvation, the Rapture doctrine offers a hope that is unfounded. Commitment to Christ loses its urgency, and some—in a false and fatal sense of security—delay the only decision that saves.

"It's true that many great men have embraced the doctrine of the Secret Rapture. But '*Great men are not ALWAYS wise*.'[27] They're as liable to make mistakes as all the rest of us are. May we follow not men—however great—but the humble Carpenter of Galilee and His teachings in the Book of books.

"In arguing this case and bringing it to the Court of Public Opinion, we're not making a mountain out of a molehill. The Secret Rapture theory is very widespread. Thousands of books have been printed teaching this erroneous doctrine. It's heard from countless pulpits every Sunday. Millions of trusting people have been exposed to it. Now, since the evidence shows it to be untrue—a fabrication of fiction, we can't just pass it off as a misunderstanding of no importance! It's vital that people know the facts.

"Fraud is fraud wherever we find it. A pickpocket who steals our wallet is no worse than those who rob our minds of truth! So consumer protection must extend to the Marketplace of Ideas, or we're at the mercy of any pious-sounding preacher who claims to teach the Word of God.

"All true ministers of God will go by the Book—the Good Book, that is! Preachers may weave engrossing tales about the Secret Rapture or some other doctrine, but without Bible backing, their opinions are worth nothing. For instance, actress Shirley MacLaine can stand up before crowds all over this country and tell them she is God [28]—which is as outrageous and incredible a statement as you'll hear outside insane asylums! Declarations like that are absolutely worthless, having no foundation in Scripture, no Bible backing.

"To be valid, any teaching on the Rapture must be based on the Bible—for the Book that tells us Jesus WILL return is the same Book that tells us HOW He'll return. Notions that go beyond what God says in His Word must be considered un-Scriptural and unsafe. The Achilles' heel of Secret Rapture theory is its lack of Bible backing.

"Let me ask in all sincerity: Is Truth itself 'an endangered species?' Are we so brain-washed by today's religious establishment that our minds are closed by intellectual *rigor mortis?* If you're willing to be persuaded by the facts, you've been impressed by the one-sided nature of the evidence in this case on the most public Event of all ages! On the other side of the case is a wealth of unsupported assumptions—what those in legal circles call 'assuming facts not in evidence'—something no judge in any courtroom can allow. Teachers of the Secret Rapture theory have left us with too many questions unanswered. And with too many "answers" unquestioned.

"Folks, there's nothing wrong with holding companies responsible for products they sell—or ministers responsible for doctrines they teach. Please don't think I feel those who teach the Secret Rapture theory are malicious or evil. They certainly are not! They're simply passing on, in good faith, what they themselves have been taught as the Truth. But if doctors don't treat their patients properly, they may be found guilty of *malpractice.* If lawyers are unscrupulous, they may be *disbarred*. And if ministers mislead their flock, their errors should be *exposed* for the sake of the people. We depend on doctors, lawyers, and rocket scientists to deliver 'the right stuff.' In the case of Christian ministers, the 'right stuff' is Bible truth.

"So think of this case as TRUTH ON TRIAL—simply weighing a concept in the scales of reason to determine its Scriptural validity—an objective, fact-finding search for Truth. Many a battle in the war on Truth has been waged against God's Word. Satan's battle for man's mind is a most *UNCIVIL WAR*, a no-holds-barred conflict using outright lies, half-truths, and misleading myths to deceive us so we won't be ready to go with Jesus when He comes to take us to heaven.

"You've heard the testimony and weighed the evidence. Now you must render a FINAL VERDICT. The word 'verdict' comes from the Latin *vere dictum,* meaning 'true saying.' If you've freed your mind from any preconceptions you may have had on this case, you'll render a fair verdict that will be, in the eyes of God, a 'true saying.'

"If the weight of Bible evidence leads you to conclude that . . .
  ✓ the Rapture is *neither* silent *nor* invisible,
  ✓ it does *not* leave any humans *alive* on Planet Earth,
  ✓ it occurs at the *single* glorious event of Christ's Return,
  ✓ it does *not* precede the coming of Antichrist,
  ✓ it affords *no* second opportunity to choose salvation . . .
then your decision is indeed an easy one!

"THANK YOU for serving on this jury."

Now the JUDGE of all the earth solemnly charges: "Ladies and Gentlemen of the Jury, please ask yourself, in the presence of these witnesses, Do I AGREE or DISAGREE with this statement: 'The doctrine of the Secret Rapture is a true Bible teaching'"?

Notes to Chapter 17

1. The word *rapture* means to be "carried away." It comes from the same Latin root as *rape,* for the rapist may carry away the victim in order to perpetrate that crime. We may be "enraptured" or "carried away" by beautiful music, joy, or ecstasy. And the Bible certainly teaches that the Church WILL be raptured away to heaven when Christ returns—there's no question about that. The question is, Will the rapture be stealthily SECRET or gloriously PUBLIC?

2. Incidentally, the folklore of popular theology may have the word *trumpet* allude to "Gabriel blowing his horn." But "the trumpet of God" may refer instead to the Lord's own VOICE. Each voice is so unique and hard to describe that Bible writers may have found it difficult to portray in human language a voice so clear yet so blastingly loud that it was trumpet-like. But John the Revelator says, "The first VOICE I heard was as it were of a TRUMPET talking with me." Revelation 4:1. See also Revelation 1:10.

3. Many verses teach this truth. For example: "The Son of Man will come in the glory of His Father with His angels, and then He will reward each according to his works."—Matthew 16:27, NKJV. "When the Son of Man comes in His glory, and all the holy angels with Him, then He will sit on the throne of His glory. All the nations will be gathered before Him, and He will separate them one from another, as a shepherd divides his sheep from the goats."—Matthew 25:31-32, NKJV. *Etc.*

4. Modern versions all say "precede" (or some similar word) for the King James Version's "prevent" in 1 Thessalonians 4:15. Just as the crew of a sinking ship order "Women and children first" into the lifeboats, God clearly spells out the order here.

5. 1 Corinthians 15:55.

6. Secret Rapture teachers seize upon the word *elect* and insist it refers only to Jews as the chosen people of God. They teach that Jews WILL see Christ return in a glorious second phase of His Second Coming (see Issue #5). But "elect" simply means "chosen" and is not restricted to Jews. Peter, writing to Christians in general but primarily to Gentile Christians (former idolaters, guilty of "abominable idolatries" according to 1 Peter 4:3), says: "You are a CHOSEN generation, a royal priesthood, a holy nation, His own special people . . . who once were not a people but are NOW the people of God."—1 Peter 2:9-10, NKJV. The elect in any age are simply those chosen by God to be His people. The Lord Jesus, in a passage clearly addressed to Christians, said: "Ye have not chosen Me, but I have CHOSEN you."—John 15:16.

7. Matthew 24:36.

8. Revelation 19:11-16.

9. 1 Thessalonians 4:17.

10. 2 Thessalonians 2:8.

11. See Daniel 12:1-2, NKJV—"At that time . . . there shall be a TIME of TROUBLE, such as never was since there was a nation, even to that time. And at that time your people shall be delivered, every one who is found written in the book. And many of those who sleep in the dust of the earth shall awake, some to everlasting life, some to shame and everlasting contempt." Much of this trouble is caused by the Antichrist/Beast—see Revelation 13:11-18. Much of it is caused by the Seven Last Plagues—see Revelation 15:5 *through* 16:21.

12. John 17:6 & 15.
13. For this insight I'm indebted to Steve Wohlberg, *The LEFT BEHIND Deception* (Coldwater, Michigan: Remnant Publications, c. 2001), pp. 26-27.
14. C. I. Scofield, *The Scofield Reference Bible* (New York: Oxford University Press, c. 1945), p. 1016, footnote 1.
15. Matthew 13:40.
16. Matthew 13:30.
17. The theory of the pre-tribulation Rapture was invented by John Nelson Darby, a member of the Plymouth Brethren, in 1830. The idea evolved slowly, piece by piece. Another member of the Brethren and contemporary of Darby, Samuel P. Tregelles, tells us that the *secret* aspect of the Rapture was added when a woman named Margaret Macdonald received the revelation while ecstatically speaking in tongues: "I am not aware that there was any definite teaching that there would be a Secret Rapture of the Church at a *secret* coming, until this was given forth as an 'utterance' in Mr. [Edward] Irving's Church, from what was there received as being the voice of the Spirit. . . . It was from that supposed revelation that the modern doctrine and the modern phraseology respecting it arose. It came NOT from Holy Scripture, but from that which falsely pretended to be the Spirit of God."—Samuel P. Tregelles, *The Hope of Christ's Second Coming* (London: Samuel Bagster and Sons, 1864), p. 35, quoted in Dave MacPherson, *The Incredible Cover-up: The True Story of the Pre-Trib Rapture* (Plainfield, New Jersey: Logos International, 1975), p. 7. The Secret Rapture is so secret that the church never heard of it for 1800 years!
18. William Shakespeare, *Julius Caesar,* Act I, Scene ii, line 288.
19. *The Pulpit Commentary,* Volume 22, p. 12, commenting on Jude 14.
20. Hal Lindsey, *The Rapture: Truth or Consequences* (New York: Bantam Books, c. 1983), p. 25.
21. Please see *Appendix I, "Is Israel Still God's Chosen People?"* at the back of this book.
22. Evidently their "lamps" symbolize the Bible, for Psalm 119:105 says, "Thy WORD is a lamp unto my feet, and a light unto my path."
23. Genesis 7:16.
24. See Luke 17:26-27 & 30, as well as Matthew 24:37-39.
25. Romans 6:23—"The wages of sin is death; but the gift of God is eternal life through Jesus Christ our Lord."
26. To counteract the terrible urgency about salvation taught by the Lord, Satan teaches that men have a second chance. For the DEAD, he teaches a second chance called *Purgatory* and *prayers for the dead,* which are refuted by Hebrews 9:27—"It is appointed unto men once to die, but after this the Judgment." For the LIVING, he teaches the devilish doctrine of a second chance for the lost even after believers are raptured away!
27. Job 32:9.
28. Shirley MacLaine, quoted in Cover Story "New Age Harmonies," *TIME* Magazine (December 7, 1987), p. 64. Also Shirley MacLaine, quoted in Nina Easton, "Shirley MacLaine's Mysticism for the Masses," *Los Angeles Times* Magazine (September 6, 1987), p. 34.

✦   ✦   ✦

"Then shall they SEE the Son of man coming in POWER and great GLORY."
—MARK 13:26

~

CHAPTER EIGHTEEN

THE MILLENNIUM:

GOD'S PRELUDE TO ETERNITY—

HIS TIMETABLE OF FINAL EVENTS

EVER DAYDREAM about "the perfect vacation"? Instead of being cut short by practical demands, it would be long enough for you really to rest, recuperate, and enjoy yourself—maybe a thousand years would do the trick! And it would be in some beautiful place, with breathtaking scenery, invigorating air, and delightful climate—maybe Heaven would fill the bill!

That's exactly what God has in mind for each one of us—a trip to Paradise to spend one thousand glorious years with Him and the angels in Heaven! And that's where the Millennium comes in.

Fascinating is how most people describe this illuminating subject, for the Bible Millennium reveals the SCHEDULE God plans to use when He brings down the curtain on the drama of this world's history.

The Lord who loves us is willing to divulge His plans so we'll know what to expect. He knows that "forewarned is forearmed." He also wants to give us hope, "for we are saved by hope." [1] Dark days ahead could discourage God's people and drive them to despair. But that needn't happen to us if we heed God's Word.

Did you ever turn to the back of a book you're reading "to see how it's gonna end"? I can assure you that I've read the back of the Book—and WE WIN! It certainly does give us hope to know we're on the winning side.

But God is more specific than that. Beyond the general fact that Christ will triumph over Satan and his followers, the Bible shares with us a few particulars about how the end will come, how earth's history will be consummated, and how Time's transition to Eternity will take place. These specific facts all revolve around, or are included in, the subject of the Bible Millennium.

A DEFINITION

The term *millennium* itself is not found in the Bible but is derived from two Latin words: *mille* meaning "thousand" and *annus* meaning "year." Therefore, *millennium* means a period of "one thousand years"—and that expression IS found in the Bible six times, in six different but consecutive verses of Revelation 20, at the back of your Book.[2]

In the religious world today, a major difference of opinion revolves around the question of WHERE Jesus spends the Millennium—is it on this earth or up in heaven? It's clear enough where the resurrected saints are—they're with Jesus, for the Bible says, "they lived and reigned with Christ a thousand years. . . . They shall be priests of God and of Christ, and shall reign with Him a thousand years."[3]

But where Jesus is during this time, we're not directly told. The common teaching heard from most pulpits and published in most theological books and magazines, is that Jesus' Millennial reign will take place on earth.

Yet this is merely assumed by those who teach it. The verses quoted above do not explicitly place Jesus and the saints either in heaven or on earth during the thousand years, so how can we be sure? Are there any clues to help solve this mystery?

Yes, there are. In fact, God's Word gives definite evidence supporting the view that resurrected saints spend the Millennium with Jesus in heaven, not on earth. Scriptural clues clearly place the saints in heaven and demolish any theories about an earthly Millennial reign—at least for those who base their beliefs on the Bible.

God's Word answers the question of where the Millennium will be spent as simply as ABC! Please follow closely this chain of evidence as we examine it link by link:

A. John speaks of those "who had not worshiped the Beast or his Image, and had not received his mark on their foreheads or on their hands . . . lived and reigned with Christ for a thousand years."[4]

B. John speaks of this same group: "I saw something like a sea of glass mingled with fire, and those who have the victory over the Beast, over his Image and over his mark and over the number of his name, standing on the sea of glass." [5]

C. John pin-points the location of "the sea of glass" for us: "I looked, and behold, a door standing open in heaven. . . . And behold, a throne set in heaven, and One sat on the throne. . . . Before the throne there was a sea of glass, like crystal." [6]

Therefore, if the saints are standing on the sea of glass—which is in heaven before the throne of God—they must be in HEAVEN and not on earth. The Bible explains itself if we let it.

Heaven knows God's Word covers many subjects—major last-day events alone number more than a dozen! So Inspiration has included the Millennium and its surrounding details to help us "sort it all out."

The Millennium ushers in God's great Kingdom of glory. It's a period of time coming at the end of this world's history and lying at the threshold of the eternal ages. So we may think of it as GOD'S PRELUDE TO ETERNITY.

But it's even more than that. So many vital events cluster around the Millennium that it may also be thought of as GOD'S TIMETABLE OF FINAL EVENTS. The Bible states that "For everything there is a season, and a time for every matter under heaven." [7] So we'd expect God—the God of order— to have the culmination of all things as neatly organized and scheduled as everything else He ordains. And He does, as we shall see.

Let's consider Final Events under three headings: Events *before, during,* and *after* the Millennium.

EVENTS BEFORE THE MILLENNIUM

Let's look first at the LAST-DAY EVENTS God says will happen just before this thousand-year period begins.

Some events the Bible speaks of can be seen occurring right now. For instance, God's Word declares that "this gospel of the kingdom shall be preached in all the world for a witness unto all nations; and then shall the end come." [8] That divine directive is being carried out this very moment— even as you read this book.

The cataclysmic Event which triggers or inaugurates the Millennial period is Christ's glorious Return to this rebel planet. [9] That Return has been heralded by many "signs" which precede and foreshadow it, [10] but Scripture mentions three other events which still must precede the Return of Christ and the Millennium:

EVENT #1 – THE MARK OF THE BEAST

EVENT #2 – THE CLOSE OF PROBATION

EVENT #3 – THE SEVEN LAST PLAGUES

Let's see why we can be sure of the order of those three last-day events. The Mark of the Beast is dealt with in some detail under Mystery #7 of this volume,[11] so we'll focus now only on its place in the stream of Time and on the sequence of events. Please see pages 550-551 for the **CHART** which lists fifteen end-time events.   ➡

The Mark of the Beast sets off a chain-reaction of events which culminates in the end of the world as we now know it. How do we know this is true? How do we know, for instance, that the Seven Last Plagues follow and don't precede the Mark of the Beast? Because God says the Seven Last Plagues fall on those who accept that Mark and come as a consequence of and punishment for receiving the Mark of the Beast. Note the divine decree:

> "If any man worship the Beast and his Image, and receive his Mark in his forehead, or in his hand, the same shall drink of the wine of the wrath of God, which is poured out without mixture into the cup of His indignation." [12]

What *is* "the wrath of God" in this context? The Bible explains that it is "the SEVEN LAST PLAGUES, for IN THEM is filled up the wrath of God." [13]

In vision, John watched as "seven angels came out of the Temple [in Heaven], having the Seven Plagues, . . . seven golden vials [14] full of the wrath of God. . . . And I [John] heard a great voice out of the Temple saying to the seven angels, Go your ways, and pour out the vials of the wrath of God upon the earth." [15] The angels then pour out the Seven Last Plagues.

Therefore, if "the wrath of God" contained in the Seven Last Plagues is the Biblically–specified punishment for any who receive the Mark of the Beast,[16] then the giving of that Mark must precede the falling of those Plagues.

Next, note that the CLOSE OF PROBATION for all mankind is stated by Christ in these solemn words:

> "The time is at hand. He who is unjust, let him be unjust still; he who is filthy, let him be filthy still; he who is righteous, let him be righteous still; he who is holy, let him be holy still. And behold, I am coming quickly, and My reward is with Me, to give to every one according to his work." [17]

Each one's character is fixed, each one's fate is sealed when Jesus pronounces those solemn words in Heaven. Obviously, then, this Closing of

Probation cannot take place before man is called upon to choose between the Mark of the Beast and the Seal of God, for it's that very choice that shows our allegiance to God or Satan. FIRST the alternatives are offered and the choice is made. THEN each one's fate is sealed by Probation's Close.

One may wonder if perhaps the Seven Last Plagues should, like the Mark of the Beast, precede the Close of Probation. This may seem possible till we realize that God evidently has more than one purpose in sending those Plagues: they punish, yes—but they also reveal character. Let me explain.

In His infinite wisdom, God allowed Satan to reveal his true character as the fiendish monster that he is. One may ask, "Why didn't God destroy Lucifer the moment he sinned?" Because although God was never deceived by the Devil's lies, He knew that others were fooled by the subtle insinuations. If He had snuffed out Lucifer's life at once, many holy angels who had listened to Lucifer would say, "You see? Lucifer tried to tell us God was a tyrant, and look what happened to him! It seems that Lucifer was right."

The best way—perhaps the only way—to remove any doubt from every mind in the Universe was to let the Devil show his true colors. This way was painful and costly, costing the death of God's dear Son. But Satan had to be allowed to reveal his character.

In the same way, if Probation eternally closes after each soul chooses for or against the Beast and his Mark—without a way to demonstrate the characters of those unredeemed—then some free moral agent in the Universe could ask, "Wasn't God too hasty in closing the door to further change, further opportunity for salvation? For all we know, many poor damned mortals simply followed the path of least resistance, but if given half a chance, they'd gladly reverse their decision and join God's side. I love God, but I must question His wisdom and justice in this one instance."

The true sequence of events precludes any such misunderstanding: After the Beast's Mark is placed upon all not loyal to God, Probation closes on each fateful decision, and the Seven Last Plagues fall on those who chose to disobey the Lord. Those terrible punishments would cause any honest soul to repent, to fall on his knees, acknowledge his sins, and beg for forgiveness. But what does the Record say? Please note:

> When the fourth angel poured out his Plague, "men were scorched with great fire, and BLASPHEMED the name of God, . . . and they REPENTED NOT." Again, when "the fifth angel poured out his vial . . . they gnawed their tongues for pain, and BLASPHEMED the God of heaven because of their pains and their sores, and REPENTED NOT of their deeds."[18]

That's proof positive that God's Closing of Probation was not prematur—the wicked reveal their true unredeemable characters, showing that not a single additional soul would repent and come to Christ. Their unrepentant, remorseless reaction is like that of Jimmie Wayne Jeffers, who was executed in Arizona for murdering his ex-girlfriend. The Associated Press reported that Jeffers "unleashed a stream of obscenities and [made an obscene gesture to the executioner] moments before being executed. . . . His middle finger was still extended when he died Wednesday night." [19]

Thus these three last-day events follow a prescribed and certain sequence, bringing us to the fourth great Happening in the series, the Second Coming of Christ, like this:

EVENT #1 – THE MARK OF THE BEAST

EVENT #2 – THE CLOSE OF PROBATION

EVENT #3 – THE SEVEN LAST PLAGUES

EVENT #4 – THE RETURN OF CHRIST

Jesus' glorious, awe-inspiring Return was seen by John in vision and recorded in these words: "I saw heaven opened, and behold a white horse; and He that sat upon him . . . is called The Word of God . . . , KING OF KINGS, AND LORD OF LORDS." [20]

The description of Christ's triumphant Return with the angel armies of heaven is preceded by these cryptic words: "He hath judged the great whore, which did corrupt the earth with her fornication, and hath avenged the blood of His servants at her hand." [21]

Symbols like "the great whore" and "that great city Babylon" are used in Revelation and explained below under Mystery #7 in this book. But the point to be made here is that the Second Coming directly follows the seventh and final Plague. This fact is seen from the following:

While Chapter 16 of Revelation tells about the SEVEN LAST PLAGUES and Chapter 19 describes the SECOND COMING, Chapters 17 and 18 are parenthetically inserted to elaborate on the deeds and doom of the great whore.

John says one of the angels with the Seven Last Plagues told him, "Come hither; I will show unto thee the judgment of the great whore." [22] This judgment is NOT a separate event apart from the Plagues, for the seventh Plague was directed against the woman God calls "the great whore." [23]

No other prophetic event separates the Seven Last Plagues from Christ's Second Coming, for when "the seventh angel poured out his vial into the air . . . there came a great voice out of the Temple of heaven, from the throne, saying, It is done." [24] That voice from the throne carries a note of finality, reminiscent of Christ's last words from the cross: "It is finished." [25]

It's beyond the scope of this chapter to dwell on describing the Second Coming. Besides, no human pen can portray that scene, no mortal mind can conceive its splendor. Instead, we'll concentrate on placing in their proper order three events that accompany the Lord's Return.

EVENT #5 – THE RIGHTEOUS DEAD ARE RESURRECTED

In that breathtaking instant when Christ comes with His retinue of holy angels in dazzling glory, the graves open and the righteous dead come up clothed with immortality. "In a moment, in the twinkling of an eye, . . . the dead shall be raised incorruptible, and we shall be changed. For . . . this mortal must put on immortality." [26]

With a voice that penetrates the ear of the dead, Christ calls His sleeping saints to rise, imbued with eternal life. All blemishes gone, all defects and deformities left in the grave, they arise with unspeakable joy in newness of life—imbued with the freshness and vigor of eternal youth.

The Apostle John speaks of the faithful dead who "had not worshipped the Beast, neither his Image, neither had received his Mark upon their foreheads, or in their hands; and they lived and reigned with Christ a thousand years. . . . This is the FIRST resurrection. BLESSED and HOLY is he that hath part in the first resurrection: on such the second death hath no power, but they shall be priests of God and of Christ, and shall reign with Him a thousand years." [27]

Here God teaches at least TWO VITAL FACTS:

1. By enumerating this "the first resurrection," He lets us know there must be a second one.

2. By specifying that only the dead who were faithful to God are raised in the first resurrection ("Blessed and holy is he that hath part in the first resurrection") He lets us know that all the REST of the dead—those NOT faithful, the UN-blessed and UNholy—are raised at some later time.

John explicitly verifies these facts in a parenthetical remark inserted in verse 5, saying: "(The rest of the dead"—that is, those NOT blessed and holy— "did not come to life UNTIL the thousand years were ENDED.)" [28]

Let's see what we've learned so far:

First of all, if the faithful dead are raised in "the first resurrection" and "reign with Christ a thousand years," then they must be resurrected at the beginning of the thousand-year period. This means the Millennium BEGINS with "the First Resurrection."

Secondly, if as we've just read "the rest of the dead"—the wicked—are not raised "until the thousand years were ended," then it means the Millennium ENDS with "the Second Resurrection."

Thus the Millennium is bounded at either end by the "first" and "second" resurrections of the righteous and wicked, respectively. We may graphically depict these facts like this:

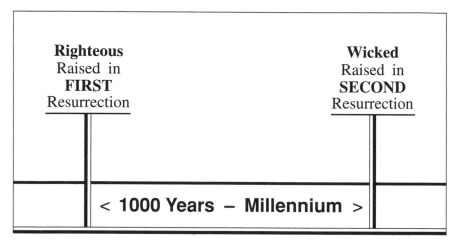

Righteous
Raised in
FIRST
Resurrection

Wicked
Raised in
SECOND
Resurrection

< 1000 Years – Millennium >

The fact that there are TWO separate and distinct resurrections—one for the righteous and one for the wicked—comes as no surprise to Bible students familiar with the many implicit and explicit clues to that effect which are sprinkled throughout God's Word.

For instance, the God who created the orderly, clocklike precision of the Universe also inspired Paul to write: "Let all things be done decently and in order. . . . As in Adam all die, even so in Christ shall all be made alive. But every man in his own ORDER: Christ the firstfruits; afterward they that are Christ's at His coming." [29]

This passage teaches that God's plan for resurrecting man is UNIVERSAL in operation: Just as truly as "ALL die, . . . ALL [shall] be made alive." But not all will be raised at the same time—Paul says there's an "order" to God's plan, and events shall occur on His schedule, according to His timetable.

What is the "order" this text brings to light? It says the initial resurrection was that of "Christ the firstfruits." Paul repeats this thought: "Now is Christ risen from the dead, and become the firstfruits of them that slept [the sleep of death]." [30] Luke echoes this order: "Christ . . . should be the first that should rise from the dead." [31] And John calls Jesus Christ "the first begotten of the dead." [32]

We may wonder how Christ can be "first" when the Bible records a few others raised earlier than Christ. (See list in box on page 259.) Two facts provide the answer: (1) Those others listed were not raised to immortality as Christ was—they all died again. Therefore, Christ's miraculous resurrection to immortal, everlasting life was indeed FIRST in being unique, in a class by itself. (2) Although Christ's resurrection was not numerically first, it was first in pre–eminence and importance, "first" in the same sense the President's wife is "First Lady." Praise the Lord, His glorious resurrection provides the sole basis and assurance for resurrecting all mankind.

So Christ's resurrection, the initial one, set the pattern. But when it comes to resurrecting mankind, Paul explains in 1 Corinthians 15:23, quoted above, that only "they that are CHRIST'S [shall be made alive] at His Coming." Unbelievers, however, will be raised later.

In Heaven's eyes—in the Final Judgment, at least—there'll be only two classes: righteous and wicked, pardoned and punished, saved and lost. There is no middle ground. The Judgment is a simple "Pass / Fail" proposition: we're either counted with the righteous or numbered with the wicked. And God plans TWO resurrections, one for each of those two classes. Note the clear contrasts between the two:

● A major difference is the TIME when each resurrection occurs.
The resurrection for *believers* in Christ
takes place "at His COMING." [33]
The other, for "the *rest* of the dead,"
takes place at the *end* of the Millennium,
when "the thousand years were FINISHED." [34]

● A second major difference is the TERMINOLOGY the Bible applies.
One, "the FIRST resurrection," [35] is also called
the "BETTER resurrection," [36]
"the resurrection of the RIGHTEOUS," [37] and
"the resurrection of LIFE" as opposed to the other,
"the resurrection of DAMNATION." [38]

● A third major difference is the CLASS of people raised in each.
Those who have a part in the *first* resurrection are
"BLESSED and HOLY," [39]
"the children of GOD," [40]
"the dead IN CHRIST," [41]
"they that are CHRIST'S," [42]
"they that have done GOOD" as opposed to

"they that have done EVIL," [43]
"the JUST" as opposed to
the "UNJUST," [44]
those who awake "to everlasting LIFE" as opposed to
those who awake "to everlasting SHAME
and CONTEMPT." [45]

Thus the Millennium is bounded by two separate resurrections for two very different groups of people.

The righteous who are alive when Christ comes praise God as they recognize friends torn from them by death! They see holy angels gather resurrected saints from watery graves, from the lowest recesses of the deepest mines, from long-forgotten unmarked graves. From four corners of the earth, they see awakened saints lifted on mighty angel wings to the Prince of Life waiting in the sky.[46] But the living righteous haven't long to wait themselves, for more than one great event occurs when Jesus returns. Not only are the righteous dead resurrected, but—

EVENT #6 – THE RIGHTEOUS LIVING ARE CAUGHT UP TO MEET THE LORD IN THE AIR

These two breathtaking miracles happen very closely in time, but they do occur in the sequence listed, as Paul assures us: "The Lord Himself shall descend from heaven with a shout, with the voice of the archangel, and with the trump of God: and [1] the dead in Christ shall rise FIRST: THEN [2] we which are alive and remain shall be caught up together *with them* in the clouds, to meet the Lord in the air: and so shall we ever be with the Lord." [47]

What a grand reunion that will be! Loved ones cruelly separated by death are reunited, never to part again! Little children who had died are joyfully carried by holy angels to their mothers' arms!

Then, in the company of the Savior and the angelic host, the redeemed of all ages ascend together to the City of God through stellar space. With songs of gladness on their lips and with hearts overflowing with unutterable love, they praise the One who ransomed them from death.

Thus the earth is reaped of all the faithful in that great Harvest. [48] But what about those who are not faithful? What happens to the wicked who are living when Christ returns?

EVENT #7 – THE WICKED LIVING ARE STRUCK DEAD

When Jesus Returns the righteous shall welcome Him with unutterable joy: "It will be said on that day, 'Lo, this is our God; we have waited for Him, that He might save us. This is the Lord; we have waited for Him; let us be glad and rejoice in His salvation.'" [49]

But their reaction is in sharp contrast to that of unbelievers, who realize it's now forever too late for salvation. They tragically exclaim: "The harvest is past, the summer is ended, and we are not saved!" [50] When the wicked see Christ coming in glory, they "wail" and "mourn." [51] A deep sense of guilt fills them with terror. They cry for the very rocks and mountains to "FALL on us and HIDE us from the face of Him who sits on the throne and from the wrath of the Lamb! For the great day of His wrath has come, and who is able to stand?" [52]

Sad but true are the Lord's words: "I called, and you refused; I stretched out My hand, and no one paid attention; and you neglected all My counsel, and did not want My reproof." [53]

But the instincts of God's enemies are right: wicked man cannot live in the presence of the holy God. "For our God is a consuming fire." [54] So every single one is slain among the wicked, "whom the Lord shall CONSUME with the spirit of His mouth, and shall DESTROY with the brightness of His coming." [55]

We don't understand it—can't comprehend it, really—but God's holy nature, His glory, cannot help but consume SIN. The two simply cannot co-exist.

The Bible consistently draws the same picture for us: the wicked are slain when Jesus returns. The Master Himself told us His Coming will be "as it was in the days of Noah" when the Flood overwhelmed the wicked "and DESTROYED them ALL." [56]

Chapter 19 of Revelation depicts Christ coming as a Conqueror on a white horse to claim His bride, the church. But the wicked "were slain with the sword of Him that sat upon the horse, which sword proceeded out of His mouth: and all the fowls were filled with their flesh." [57]

That last statement about fowls like buzzards and vultures feasting on dead flesh of the wicked clearly means that God's enemies go unburied. The angel called "to all the fowls that fly in the midst of heaven, Come and gather yourselves together unto the supper of the great God; that ye may eat the flesh of kings, and the flesh of captains, and the flesh of mighty men, and the flesh of horses, and of them that sit on them, and the flesh of all men, both bond and free, both great and small." [58]

The prophetic significance of the dead lying unburied will be explained under Event #8, which is discussed following the CHART that appears on the next two pages.

THE BIBLE MILLENNIUM: God's Timetable of Final Events

1000 Years Between Resurrections

BEFORE the Millennium

1. **Mark of the Beast is given**
   Revelation 13:16-17; 14:9-11

2. **Probation closes**
   Revelation 22:11-12

3. **Seven Last Plagues fall**
   Revelation 15:1, 8; 16:1-17

4. **Second Coming of Christ**
   Matthew 24:30-31; 25:31, etc.

5. **Righteous dead are resurrected**
   1 Thessalonians 4:16
   Revelation 20:6
   Luke 14:14
   Isaiah 26:19

FIRST RESURRECTION

DURING the Millennium

8. **On EARTH: Satan is "bound"**
   with no one left to tempt
   Revelation 20:1-3
   Jeremiah 4:25-27; 25:33
   Isaiah 24:1, 3, 22; 26:21

9. **In HEAVEN: Saints assist**
   in the Judgment
   Revelation 20:4
   Luke 22:30
   1 Corinthians 6:2-3
   Jude 6

SECOND RESURRECTION

AFTER the Millennium

10. **Wicked are resurrected,**
    so Satan is loosed
    Revelation 20:3, 5a, 7

11. **Holy City descends from**
    God out of heaven
    Revelation 21:2 & 10; 3:12

12. **Wicked surround Holy City**
    Revelation 20:7-9

13. **Wicked are judged before**
    the "Great White Throne"
    Revelation 20:11-13
    Isaiah 45:23
    Romans 14:10-12
    Philippians 2:10-11

BEFORE the Millennium	DURING the Millennium	AFTER the Millennium
6. Righteous living are caught up to the Lord in the air *1 Thessalonians 4:17* **7. Wicked living are struck dead** *2 Thessalonians 1:7-9; 2:8* *Isaiah 13:9; 26:21; 66:15-16*	FIRST RESURRECTION Earth is "EMPTY" Wicked are ALL dead Righteous are ALL in heaven SECOND RESURRECTION	**14. Wicked are destroyed by fire** *Revelation 20:9, 14, 15; 21:8* **15. Earth is cleansed by fire and made new** *2 Peter 3:10-13* *Revelation 21:1 & 5* *Matthew 5:5 & Psalm 37:11* *Isaiah 65:17, 21-25; 66:22-23*
END of the WORLD	**1000 YEARS (MILLENNIUM)**	**NEW EARTH & ETERNITY**

EVENTS DURING THE MILLENNIUM

So far we've looked at seven remarkable events which precede the Millennium. But what takes place during that thousand-year period? Let's turn our attention now to Millennial events first on earth, then in heaven.

EVENT #8 – ON EARTH: SATAN IS "BOUND"
WITH NO ONE LEFT TO TEMPT

John the Revelator opens his Millennial chapter with these words:

> "I saw an angel come down from heaven, having the key of the bottomless pit and a great chain in his hand. And he laid hold on the dragon, that old serpent, which is the Devil, and Satan, and bound him a thousand years, and cast him into the bottomless pit, and shut him up, and set a seal upon him, that he should deceive the nations no more, till the thousand years should be fulfilled: and after that he must be loosed a little season. . . . When the thousand years are expired, Satan shall be loosed out of his prison." [59]

What does this mean? Well, this passage snaps into sharp focus if we clarify two key terms: (1) the "great chain" which binds Satan and (2) "the bottomless pit" which forms the "prison" where he spends the thousand years. Can these things be LITERAL?

The Devil is real and literal enough. Jesus Himself said: "I beheld Satan as lightning fall from heaven." [60] But the dazzling angel Lucifer, who made himself into the Devil called Satan, is a supernatural being. As Paul put it: "We wrestle NOT against flesh and blood, but against principalities, against powers, against the rulers of the darkness of this world, against spiritual wickedness in high places." [61]

Simple reason tells us that no actual, literal "chain" or "pit" or "prison" could secure a supernatural being. More importantly, sacred Scripture tells us the same thing. You may recall Christ's experience one day after sailing across the Sea of Galilee:

> "Then they came to the other side of the sea, to the country of the Gadarenes. And when He had come out of the boat, immediately there met Him out of the tombs a man with an unclean spirit [a devil or demon], who had his dwelling among the tombs; and no one could bind him, not even with chains, because he had often been bound with shackles and chains. And the CHAINS had been *pulled apart* by him, and the SHACKLES *broken in pieces;* neither could anyone tame him." [62]

Now ask yourself, if a devil-possessed MAN could easily break asunder a chain with superhuman strength, is it likely that the prince of devils himself could be bound with one? So what kind of "chain" is it that God uses to effectively bind Satan?

It's a chain of CIRCUMSTANCES which binds the Devil more securely than any literal chain ever forged. Note the circumstances in which Satan finds himself at this point in the stream of Time: In the first place, all the righteous—who were unwilling to listen to him, anyway—have been taken to heaven. And all the wicked have been struck dead. Thus the entire earth is de-populated with NO ONE LEFT for Satan to tempt!

This unique situation was foreseen and depicted by Old Testament prophets. Jeremiah declares: "The SLAIN of the Lord shall be at that day from one end of earth even unto the other end of the earth: they shall not be *lamented,* neither *gathered,* nor *buried;* they shall be DUNG upon the ground." [63]

Usually when people die, they're *lamented* by survivors who care. Dead bodies are always *gathered* from the site of an accident or other tragedy. And of course they're *buried* out of respect and for sanitary reasons. So why does Inspiration say NONE of these things will be true in the day of this worldwide, wholesale slaughter? Simply because there are no survivors around to do any of these things! All the righteous are raptured to heaven at the Second Coming, and all the wicked perish, to the very last man.

Isaiah echoes the thought with this promise to believers: "Thy dead men shall live, together with my dead body shall they arise. Awake and sing, ye that dwell in dust: . . . for, behold, the Lord cometh out of His place to punish the inhabitants of the earth for their iniquity: the earth . . . shall NO MORE COVER her slain." [64]

"Behold, the Lord maketh the earth EMPTY. . . . The land shall be utterly EMPTIED, and utterly spoiled: for the Lord hath spoken this word." [65] We see, then, how very effective this chain of circumstances is!

To illustrate, imagine for a moment a man who's in deep trouble. He thinks of someone he can call on for help—a friend in a position of influence. But when he goes to this friend, the regrettable reply is, "I'd like to help—I really would. But with circumstances the way they are, my hands are tied, and there's absolutely nothing I can do."

As the disappointed man looks at his friend's hands, he sees no actual ropes or cords, but he knows only too well that intangible circumstances can often be more restricting than any literal bonds. And that's the case here: Satan is securely bound—"chained," if you will—by circumstances beyond his control. We can only marvel at the beauty of God's perfect plan!

But what is meant by "the BOTTOMLESS PIT"? Well, the Greek word translated "bottomless pit" is *abussos* from which we get our English word *abyss*. In fact, modern Bible versions like the New International Version, the Amplified Bible, the New English Bible, the New American Standard Bible, Today's English Version, and others translate "bottomless pit" in Revelation 20:1 as 'abyss." *Abussos* is exactly the same word which the Greek translation of the Old Testament [66] uses in Genesis 1:2, where it says "the earth was WITHOUT FORM, and VOID."

The prophet Jeremiah directed divine light on this question when, centuries ago, he looked down the corridor of time with the eye of Inspiration and testified:

> "I beheld the earth, and, lo, it was WITHOUT FORM, and VOID; and the heavens, and they had no light. I beheld the mountains, and, lo, they trembled, and all the hills moved lightly. I beheld, and, lo, there was NO MAN, and all the birds of the heavens were fled. I beheld, and, lo, the fruitful place was a wilderness, and all the CITIES thereof were broken down at the presence of the Lord, and by His FIERCE ANGER. For thus hath the Lord said, The whole land shall be desolate; yet will I not make a full end." [67]

We know Jeremiah wrote this vision around 620 B.C. But what period of earth's history was he seeing when he wrote, "Lo, there was NO MAN"? At first glance, we might think it was *at the start of Creation Week,* because (1) "there was no man" before God formed Adam, the first man, and because (2) Jeremiah said "the earth . . . was without form, and void," which was also true at that time.

But although those two clues fit that time period, we immediately realize that God placed a third and a fourth clue in this prophetic passage which do NOT fit: Jeremiah says: (3) the Lord felt "fierce anger"—an unreasonable and ungodly attitude at the beginning of Creation Week—and (4) "all the CITIES . . . were broken down." This vision couldn't possibly be of the beginning of Creation Week, for man didn't build cities before he was even created!

The only other time in human history when prophecy could describe the earth as having "no man" is during the Millennium while the earth is de-populated of all living people—"empty," as we read before. At that time "all the cities" WILL be "broken down," completely levelled from the devastation of the final one of the Seven Last Plagues. For that last plague brings the most terrific EARTHQUAKE ever to destroy the earth and pulverizing "HAIL out of heaven, every stone about the weight of a talent" or about 66 pounds! [68]

Thus God reduces this wicked world to its original state of chaos. Once again, says Jeremiah, there is "no man," for the righteous are all in heaven and the wicked are all dead. Once again, he says, the earth is "without form, and void," for the Seven Last Plagues have broken down the cities and destroyed all traces of civilization. In this state of absolute devastation and chaos, the earth itself is "the bottomless pit" where Satan and his demon cohorts will be helplessly confined for the Millennium.

You know how parents will give a troublesome youngster "Time out!" so he can settle down and think over his actions? Well, the Millennium is Satan's "time out"—*big time!* Alone on Planet Earth, the devils have a thousand years to think over what they've lost themselves and what they've cost others. Everywhere the land is strewn with dead bodies—unburied bodies—decaying, rotting, stinking. Satan will have more than enough time to contemplate the results of rebellion: small comfort to him *then* to sing "I Did It My Way"!

The demon host is in virtual "solitary confinement" with not a single human being to deceive and lead astray. With no one to tempt, the original "rebel without a cause" will find time hanging heavy on his hands. Satan will find himself securely held by a chain of circumstances that not even his supernatural power can break. Confined to "the bottomless pit" of this "empty" world for a thousand years, Satan and his devils will be forced to wander through the wasteland of broken cities beholding the tragic results of sin.

Now let's look at the other event that takes place during the Millennium and see what the redeemed saints are doing up in heaven.

EVENT #9 – IN HEAVEN:
SAINTS ASSIST IN THE JUDGMENT

Speaking of the saints who "lived and reigned with Christ a thousand years," John says, "I saw thrones, and they sat upon them, and JUDGMENT was given unto them." [69]

Jesus had touched upon this earlier when He promised His disciples they would "sit on thrones JUDGING the twelve tribes of Israel." [70]

And Paul asks, "Do ye not know that the saints shall JUDGE the world? . . . Know ye not that we shall JUDGE angels?" [71] The "angels" are those fallen angels who exercised their free choice to indulge evil and follow Lucifer in his rebellion.

One may wonder exactly what such "judgment" involves. Close reflection shows that mankind has already been judged when Christ returns, for all are instantly divided into two classes. When Jesus says, "I come quickly; and My reward is with Me," [72] it's obvious that the decision regarding who gets which reward has already been made at the time of His Coming.

Yes, God's judgment of all mankind separating saint and sinner, righteous and wicked, sheep and goats, HAS already been made and settled forever in heaven before Christ comes. What need, then, of any further "judgment" by the saints?

The answer lies in the fact that even in human legal proceedings, a case is not disposed of in a flash. There are several stages to the whole PROCESS, as follows:

- There is first of all the investigation of all pertinent facts
    we call a TRIAL.
- Then there is the rendering of a decision
    we call a VERDICT.
- Then there is often an assessment of the verdict
    we call a JUDICIAL REVIEW.
- Then there is finally a carrying out of the verdict
    we call the EXECUTION of the sentence.

Apparently the same process holds true in the Final Judgment of mankind, with similar stages. You could say that the first two steps take place in heaven before Jesus returns: STEP ONE, any investigation or "trial" must precede STEP TWO when Christ announces His "verdict" that each morally filthy or holy person can stay that way.[73] And we'll see that STEP FOUR, the "execution" of the final death sentence against the wicked will take place after the thousand years are finished.

But STEP THREE is where the redeemed saints come into the picture during their thousand-year stay in heaven. That's when God allows them the privilege of conducting a "judicial review" of the cases of the wicked who lie dead on earth. This review is no sham, no mere "window dressing." You see, God knows that because some people are not saved, they'll be missed by the saints—yet He wants no heavy hearts in heaven. So God will allow any questions to be asked about His decision as to why some are not saved in heaven, such as:

??? "How come Aunt Martha isn't here? She always seemed
        like such a good person—a real Christian."
??? "Where's Grandfather? If any man was a saint,
        he certainly was!"
??? "Yes, and how about Pastor Jones and Father Brown?
        God made a mistake if they're not here!"

Questions like these, God knows, may quite naturally arise even in the hearts and minds of committed believers. Then an angel will lead the inquirers to heaven's Record Books, now lying open to examination, and sadly reveal the unforgiven sins—sins not blotted out, unknown to the world, unknown even to close friends and loved ones.

You see, our God is too wise to allow even a trace of a ghost of a hint of a shadow of a doubt to linger in anyone's mind about His justice. That's what started the great controversy between God and Satan in the courts of heaven millenniums ago. Doubts and insinuations and subtle aspersions were cast on the character of God by Lucifer, causing some to question God's wisdom, justice, and righteousness. He's certainly not going to allow this tragedy to repeat itself—we won't have to go through the affliction caused by Satan again. God promises: "Affliction shall not rise up the second time." [74]

How can God be so sure in a Universe He gives free will? Because He wants every question answered, every doubt resolved, every lingering insinuation put to rest. The judicial review by the saints will do that—no tiny seed of doubt will remain in any mind to germinate and grow into a future crop of rebellion. Here, in this "judgment" or judicial review by a jury of our peers, God is satisfying finite minds that His infinite wisdom has been just and right all along.

Though the wicked from all ages suffered the first death common to all men, God will not destroy them in the Lake of Fire until this review of His judgment is completed. In other words, the God of love and infinite wisdom makes sure that Event 14 on your Chart will not take place until Event 9 has been thoroughly completed.

So the Bible makes plain how the thousand years pass, both on earth and in heaven during the Millennium. And that brings us to the END of that monumental period of 1000 years.

EVENTS AFTER THE MILLENNIUM

We've come to the third and final section of our study, the one dealing with events which follow the thousand years.

EVENT #10 – THE WICKED ARE RESURRECTED, SO SATAN IS LOOSED

The fact of a separate resurrection for the wicked was established above, but let's note three brief points.

A. Just as the wicked seem to outnumber God's people in each generation, this second group will be larger than that raised in the First Resurrection. "They will be as numerous as the sand of the seashore." [75] The number of wicked is virtually beyond computation, for their group includes ALL the unsaved from the foundation of the world.

B. The wicked show marked contrasts to the righteous raised a thousand years earlier. The righteous were raised rejuvenated with immortal youth and unfading beauty. But the wicked are raised still bearing traces of disease and death, for God's gracious promises to His people don't apply to them. [76]

C. The wicked being raised to life means Satan is loosed once again. John watched as an angel "laid hold on . . . Satan, and bound him a thousand years, and cast him into the bottomless pit . . . till the thousand years should be fulfilled: and after that he must be LOOSED a little season. . . . And when the thousand years are expired, Satan shall be LOOSED out of his prison." [77] His confinement resulted from God's acts of removing the righteous to heaven and slaying the living wicked. His release will result from God's act of resurrecting all the wicked, which again provides Satan with subjects on whom to practice his deceptions.

Event #11 – The HOLY CITY DESCENDS
from God out of Heaven

A thousand years before, the redeemed ascended with Jesus to the celestial City of God, which is New Jerusalem. [78] At that time the Savior opened wide the pearly gates and welcomed to His kingdom those who kept the truth. Now the Millennium is past, and they watch as that majestic metropolis—in breathtaking beauty and magnificent splendor—comes down from heaven to this earth. Outside the City but accompanying it, Jesus descends, followed by His ransomed saints and a train of heavenly angels. Says the prophet Zechariah: "Then the Lord, my God, will come, and all the holy ones with Him!" [79]

You may recall that at Christ's Second Coming, His feet did not touch the earth, but this time (which may be called Christ's Third Coming) His feet DO—in the very spot, appropriately enough, where His nail-pierced feet left this world at the time of His ascension! [80] For Zechariah says further: "On that day His feet will stand on the Mount of Olives, east of Jerusalem, and the Mount of Olives will be SPLIT in two from east to west, forming a great valley, with half of the mountain moving north and half moving south." [81]

On this divinely excavated plain or valley the Holy City comes to rest, completely covering the site of old Jerusalem, for the heavenly City is incomparably larger. Measuring twelve thousand furlongs around its square walls (since a furlong is an eighth of a mile), the colossal City will be 375 MILES on each side! Containing 140,625 square miles, it will cover an area larger than Pennsylvania, Virginia, and several smaller states combined! And since it's not only huge but CUBE-shaped—"the length and the breadth and the height of it are equal," [82] BILLIONS of people could live in the City.

The Revelator says, "I John saw the Holy City, New Jerusalem, coming down from God out of heaven, prepared as a bride adorned for her husband." [83] It's clear that John's description here of the City's descent is not in strict chronological order [84] among the other details he mentions, for he repeats it later in the chapter, telling us who gave him this vision: "There came to me one of the seven angels which had the seven vials full of the Seven Last Plagues, and talked with me, saying, Come hither, I will show thee . . . the holy Jerusalem, descending out of heaven from God." [85]

EVENT #12 – THE **WICKED SURROUND** THE HOLY CITY

Picture if you can the situation at this time: Satan sees the magnificent City of God, and through its translucent walls he sees the redeemed beyond his reach. But he also sees the multitude of the resurrected wicked ready to do his bidding. Not only is this the largest army ever marshalled, but within its ranks are found the greatest warlords of all time.

With the wicked restored to life, Satan is "loosed out of his prison, and shall go out to deceive the nations which are in the four quarters of the earth, Gog and Magog, [86] to gather them together to BATTLE: the NUMBER of whom is *as the sand of the sea*. And they went up on the breadth of the earth, and compassed the camp of the saints about, and the beloved City." [87]

The fact that "the beloved City" is surrounded by the wicked shows clearly that it has descended from heaven, though its actual descent is not described by John till eight verses later.

Urged on by the Devil, the wicked gaze with covetous eyes upon the dazzling riches of the New Jerusalem. Among unnumbered millions raised from the dead "are kings and generals who conquered nations, valiant men who never lost a battle, proud, ambitious warriors whose approach made kingdoms tremble. In death these experienced no change. . . . They come up from the grave . . . actuated by the same desire to conquer that ruled them when they fell." [88]

Leaders like Hitler and Attila the Hun rally to the Devil's call. He declares that the army within the City is small in comparison with theirs and convinces them that with the strength and numbers on their side they're well able to overcome any resistance. Some time may elapse as they lay their plans and prepare for battle, but at last the combined forces of all ages—such an army as the world has never seen—advance on "the camp of the saints" within "the beloved City." Satan leads the attack, and his evil angels unite their forces with the wicked warriors.

As we contemplate the scene from the comfort of our easy chairs, the wicked may seem incredibly foolish—and they are—but no more foolish than sinners have always been. And the wicked, in the final folly of this attack, prove again they have NO real change of heart.

Event #13 – The Wicked are Judged
Before the GREAT WHITE THRONE

Catholics and Protestants don't often meet at the same confessional. But here they will—in an event that is truly unique! Catholics and Protestants, Jews and Gentiles, atheists and believers—in fact, the WHOLE family of Adam will then meet together *for the first and last time ever* to confess that Jesus Christ is Lord.

The assault on the Holy City is unexpectedly interrupted. In the very midst of their onslaught the wicked see KING JESUS appear in full view of His enemies, lifted far up above the City. On a great white throne sits the Son of God, radiant with glory and power and majesty no language can describe. The awesome scene arrests the advance of Satan's army as every eye is magnetically drawn to the solemn splendor.

The jeering jests have ceased. Lying lips are hushed into silence. Those who derided His claim to be the Son of God are now totally speechless, struck dumb by His awesome might and majesty. The lawless multitude stand in open-mouthed awe, overwhelmed by His piercing gaze and the overpowering glory of His presence.

As Heaven's Record Books[89] are opened, the annals of evil trace each unforgiven sin as if written in letters of fire. A grand drama on a majestic stage, the awful spectacle will appear exactly as it happened—no fictional soap opera, but the ultimate real-life tragedy. Each actor recalls the part he performed. The *deeds* and *words,* even the *thoughts* and *motives* of the wicked are brought to light with damning clarity.

Painfully conscious of every sin they ever committed, aware of just how far their feet strayed from the path of rectitude, the wicked recall the warnings they rejected, the appeals they spurned. Once more they see the opportunities God opened to them but vividly recall how they despised the Cross and the things of God.

The wicked see what they forfeited by their life of rebellion, but they also see the justice of their exclusion from heaven. In their heart of hearts they realize God has dealt fairly with them—they can blame no one but themselves for their fate. Recognizing that God is just, they bend their knees and bow their heads.[90] But their acknowledgment of Him who is King of kings is tragically tardy. Forever too late is their reluctant recognition of the One who died to save them.

But make no mistake: the wicked come forth from their graves as they entered them, with the same enmity to Christ and the same spirit of rebellion. Their selfish hearts were never subject to God's Kingdom, never willing to follow and obey Him. Even now, it's not love that inspires their words—it's no contrite confession from renewed hearts that we hear. Only circumstances now are such that the wicked can no longer reject reality. The force of truth alone urges the words from unwilling lips.

So no new probation is offered to remedy the defects of their past, for nothing would be gained by this. A lifetime of transgression has molded their character and fixed their destiny. "The whole wicked world stand arraigned at the bar of God on the charge of high treason against the Government of Heaven. They have none to plead their cause;[91] they are without excuse; and the sentence of eternal death is pronounced against them."[92]

Some may wonder about the purpose of the Great White Throne Judgment. It's just another part of the process to VINDICATE God's character and government. God wants every mind in the Universe, *including the wicked,* to recognize His Judgment as just and righteous. Even from the foundation of the world, Christ knew exactly why He couldn't save the unrepentant wicked. The redeemed saints understood it after examining Heaven's Books in their judicial review. But the wicked themselves see it clearly as it's brought home to them before the Great White Throne. Then even *their* rebellious minds see that God is JUST.

That's why the redeemed shall sing in praise to God, "Your just judgments—Your righteous sentences and deeds—have been made known and displayed."[93] God wants to reveal His judgments to the entire Universe so ALL will see the justice and wisdom of His ways. And that's the loving purpose of both the Judicial Review and the Great White Throne Judgment.

As Christ looks down from the Great White Throne with the penetrating eyes of Supreme Judge, He deals only with the sins of the WICKED. The sins of the righteous were cleansed by Jesus' blood long ago. Their records are clear and clean, with each sin stamped "PARDONED" in Heaven's Books.[94] But the plight of the wicked who never confessed their sins or asked God to forgive them is quite different. Persian poet Omar Khayyám said of their fateful records:

> *"The Moving Finger writes; and, having writ,*
> *Moves on: not all your Piety nor Wit*
> *Shall lure it back to cancel half a Line,*
> *Nor all your Tears wash out a Word of it."*[95]

As we might expect, the two classes are not treated the same in the Judgment: "He that believeth on Him [Jesus Christ] is NOT condemned: but he that believeth not is condemned already, because he hath not believed in the name of the only begotten Son of God." [96]

Note the contrast in the two classes: "Some men's sins [those of the righteous] are open beforehand, going BEFORE to judgment; and some men [the wicked] they follow AFTER." [97] Faithful believers openly confess their sins and lay them at the foot of the Cross. When a person professes to be a Christian, a child of God, his case is one of those "going BEFORE to judgment," as we just read. Since he claims forgiveness on the basis of Christ's great Sacrifice, the only thing to be determined by Heaven's tribunal is whether or not his repentance is genuine and his Christian experience is real. If he's a true believer and not a hypocrite, he's judged safe to save. His sins are blotted out [98] from his record "beforehand"—BEFORE Probation closes and BEFORE Jesus returns.

But with no time limit or "statute of limitations" in the heavenly courts, the sins of the wicked "follow after" them, even till the day of reckoning before the Great White Throne.

Peter says, "Judgment must BEGIN at the house of God: and if it first begin at US, what shall the end be of them that obey not the gospel of God?" [99] So judgment begins by deciding the cases of professed believers before Probation's close. It ends by judging unbelievers at the Great White Throne when the thousand years are finished.

EVENT #14 – THE WICKED ARE **DESTROYED** BY FIRE

We read that after the wicked "were judged, each one according to his works, . . . anyone not found written in the Book of Life was cast into the Lake of Fire. . . . He who overcomes shall inherit all things, and I will be his God and he shall be My son. But the cowardly, unbelieving, abominable, murderers, sexually immoral, sorcerers, idolaters, and all liars shall have their part in the lake which burns with fire and brimstone, which is the second DEATH." [100]

The wicked are still apparently in the same position as when their attack on the Holy City was arrested by the Great White Throne Judgment. Then, the Record says, "Fire came down from God out of heaven and DEVOURED them." [101]

In this fateful event God finally executes the sentence of eternal death against the wicked. The day has finally come which was predicted at the very end of the Old Testament: "For, behold, the day cometh, that shall BURN as an OVEN; and all the proud, yea, and all that do wickedly, shall be stubble: and the day that cometh shall burn them UP, saith the Lord of hosts, that it shall leave them neither root nor branch. . . . They shall be ASHES." [102]

That fate also includes Satan, who certainly is among "all the proud . . . and all that do wickedly." Also, when the prophet says the fires shall leave "neither root nor branch," he alludes to the Devil. Just as Jesus told His followers, "I am the VINE, ye are the branches," [103] Satan is the ROOT of sin, and his followers are the branches. Neither shall be left, for Satan also shall be destroyed.

Speaking of the Devil's destruction, God says, "Thou hast been in Eden, the Garden of God [as the serpent tempting Eve]. . . . Thou art the anointed cherub [as Lucifer in heaven before his rebellion]. . . . Thou wast perfect in thy ways from the day that thou wast created, till iniquity was found in thee. . . . Thou hast sinned. . . . Therefore will I bring forth a fire from the midst of thee, it shall DEVOUR thee, and I will bring thee to ASHES upon the earth in the sight of all that behold thee. . . . And never shalt thou BE any more." [104]

EVENT #15 – THE EARTH IS CLEANSED BY FIRE AND MADE NEW

Now we come to the final event in God's Prelude to Eternity. Sin and sinners are no more. And the same fire that destroys the wicked also cleanses the earth. Peter saw that . . .

> "the heavens [the atmospheric heavens with all polluted air] shall pass away with a great noise, and the ELEMENTS shall MELT with fervent heat, the earth also and the works that are therein shall be burned up. Seeing then that all these things shall be DISSOLVED, what manner of persons ought ye to be in all holy conversation and godliness, looking for and hasting unto the coming of the day of God, wherein the heavens being on fire shall be dissolved, and the elements shall melt with fervent heat? Nevertheless we, according to His promise, look for new heavens and a New Earth, wherein dwelleth righteousness." [105]

The flames of course don't harm the Holy City or the saints inside it. In Noah's day, when the floodwaters were at their height, the earth appeared like a boundless LAKE of WATER. When God finally purifies the earth, it will appear like a boundless LAKE of FIRE. But just as God preserved the Ark amid the devastating Flood, because it contained eight faithful persons, He'll preserve the New Jerusalem, containing the faithful of all ages. Though the whole earth, except where the City rests, will be wrapped in a sea of liquid fire, God preserves the City as He did the Ark—by a miracle of Almighty power.

That the saints within the City are preserved unharmed amid the devouring elements, Isaiah testifies: "'Who among us shall dwell with the devouring fire? Who among us shall dwell with everlasting burnings?' He who walks righteously and speaks uprightly, . . . who gestures with his hands, refusing bribes, who stops his ears from hearing of bloodshed, and shuts his eyes from seeing evil." [106]

The flames purify the earth, destroying all that is undesirable like weeds and disease germs. The AIDS virus, for instance, won't rear its ugly head in the New Earth.

More than that, God promises to renovate this old earth. "He that sat upon the throne said, Behold, I make all things new." [107] Note that He did not say, "I make all new things"—He's not going to junk this old world, throw it away, and make a completely different new one. Instead, He plans to renew this earth, the site of Christ's triumph over death and Satan, and will re-create it anew from the purified elements of the old. It is this earth which the Bible says is the heritage of the saved: "the meek shall inherit the earth." [108] But our Creator will make it over so completely that John could say, "I saw a new heaven and a New Earth: for the first heaven and the first earth were passed away; and there was no more sea." [109]

So unspeakably marvelous will be the delights in the Earth Made New that we cannot conceive them even in our wildest imagination: "It is written: 'Eye has not seen, nor ear heard, nor have entered into the heart of man the things which God has prepared for those who love Him.'" [110]

So no one knows the many wonderful things that will be in the hereafter, but we're told some of the things that WON'T be there, for "God shall wipe away all TEARS from their eyes; and there shall be no more DEATH, neither SORROW, nor CRYING, neither shall there be any more PAIN: for the former things are passed away." [111]

CONCLUSION

In closing, let me say that we've surveyed fifteen events which close this world's history and usher in Eternity. We've found that the Bible teaches, in several ways, that the righteous redeemed will spend the thousand years of the Millennium not on EARTH but in HEAVEN. Other clues further establishing that fact are seen in these two Scriptures:

1. Jesus promised, "In My Father's house are many mansions; if it were not so, I would have told you. I GO to prepare a place for you. And if I go and prepare a place for you, I will come again and RECEIVE YOU to Myself; that WHERE I AM, there YOU may be also. And WHERE I go

you know [that is, to heaven], and the way you know."[112] He did NOT say: "YOU will receive ME, down here, that where YOU are, there *I* may be also." In other words, just before the thousand years Jesus will return, receive us, and take us back where He was going—to heaven.

2. In contrast to this, just after the thousand years God will come down on the earth-made-new to dwell with the redeemed. John says: "I heard a loud voice from heaven saying, 'Behold, the tabernacle of God is WITH MEN, and He will dwell WITH THEM, and they shall be His people. God Himself will be WITH THEM and be their God.'"[113] Three times in one verse, God emphatically repeats this new state of things!

Therefore we see that . . .

● At the BEGINNING of the Millennium, Jesus will take us to be with HIM, in heaven.
● At the END of the Millennium, God will come down to be with US, on the New Earth.

Suffice it to say that God Himself will be here, dwelling with us. And we can rest assured that, as David said, "In Thy presence is fullness of joy; at Thy right hand are pleasures for evermore"![114]

Finally, we see that FOUR GROUPS of people have been accounted for:

1 – The RIGHTEOUS DEAD
2 – The RIGHTEOUS LIVING
3 – The WICKED LIVING
4 – The WICKED DEAD

Any study attempting to explore and explain the Millennium must cover all four groups. God's plan accounts for every type of person—good or evil, living or dead.

The Bible not only presents that plan but it truly presents "History told in advance." In other chapters, we see literally dozens[115] of Scripture predictions precisely fulfilled to the letter, and as American orator Patrick Henry said: "I know of no way of judging the future but by the past."[116] The fact that all those FORMER predictions came true in the past assures us that all these LAST-DAY events will come to pass in the future. This chapter has given us a prophetic preview of end-time events. We have nothing to fear for the Future except as we forget how the Lord has led His people in the Past.

Notes to Chapter 18

1. Romans 8:24.
2. Revelation 20:2-7.
3. Revelation 20:4 & 6.
4. Revelation 20:4, NKJV.
5. Revelation 15:2, NKJV.
6. Revelation 4:1-6, NKJV.
7. Ecclesiastes 3:1, RSV. God inspired Paul to write: "Let all things be done decently and in order."—1 Corinthians 14:40.
8. Matthew 24:14.
9. His majestic Return will be anything but "secret," as we saw in Chapter 17, "Truth on Trial: The Secret Rapture."
10. See Chapter 16, "Signs of Christ's Coming in the Sun, Moon, and Stars," and *Appendix H* at the back of this book.
11. See Chapter 19, "Antichrist Unmasked: The Beast Power Revealed," and Chapter 20, "The Mark of the Beast."
12. Revelation 14:9-10.
13. Revelation 15:1.
14. For the word *vials,* most modern versions say *bowls.* The Living Bible says *flasks.*
15. Revelation 15:6-7 & 16:1.
16. Further proof that this is the case is seen in Revelation 16:2—"So the first [angel] went and poured out his bowl . . . upon the men who had the Mark of the Beast and those who worshipped his Image."
17. Revelation 22:10-12, NKJV.
18. Revelation 16:8-11.
19. "Killer Makes Obscene Gesture to Executioner," *Los Angeles Times* (September 15, 1995), Section A, p. 28.
20. Revelation 19:11-16.
21. Revelation 19:2.
22. Revelation 17:1.
23. Carefully compare Revelation 16:19 & 17:18.
24. Revelation 16:17.
25. John 19:30.
26. 1 Corinthians 15:52-53.
27. Revelation 20:4-6.
28. Revelation 20:5, NIV.
29. 1 Corinthians 14:40 and 15:22-23.
30. 1 Corinthians 15:20.
31. Acts 26:23.
32. Revelation 1:5.
33. 1 Corinthians 15:23 (& 1 Thessalonians 4:16).
34. Revelation 20:5.

35. Revelation 20:6.
36. Hebrews 11:35.
37. Luke 14:14, NIV, NASB.
38. John 5:29.
39. Revelation 20:6.
40. Luke 20:36.
41. 1 Thessalonians 4:16.
42. 1 Corinthians 15:23.
43. John 5:29.
44. Acts 24:15.
45. Daniel 12:2.
46. Matthew 24:31 says: "He shall send His angels with a great sound of a trumpet, and they shall gather together His elect from the four winds, from one end of heaven to the other."
47. 1 Thessalonians 4:16-17. It's worth noting that the righteous "meet the Lord in the AIR," for *Christ does not touch the earth* at His Second Coming.
48. In Matthew 13:39 Jesus teaches—"The *harvest* is the end of the world; and the *reapers* are the angels."
49. Isaiah 25:9, RSV.
50. Jeremiah 8:20, NKJV.
51. Revelation 1:7 and Matthew 24:30-31.
52. Revelation 6:15-17, NKJV.
53. Proverbs 1:24-25, NASB.
54. Hebrews 12:29.
55. 2 Thessalonians 2:8. Though the living wicked are all struck dead, this is just the first death common to all men, not "the second death" or final destruction in "the lake of fire" (Revelation 20:14-15), which takes place after the Millennium.
56. Luke 17:26-27, NKJV.
57. Revelation 19:7, 11-16, and 21. This "sword"—obviously figurative, since it proceeds "out of His mouth"—may simply be His inspired WORD, for the Bible is described as "sharper than any two-edged sword."—Hebrews 4:12. And Ephesians 6:17 speaks of "the sword of the Spirit, which is the Word of God."
58. Revelation 19:17-18.
59. Revelation 20:1-3 and 7.
60. Luke 10:18.
61. Ephesians 6:12.
62. Mark 5:1-4, NKJV.
63. Jeremiah 25:33.
64. Isaiah 26:19-21.
65. Isaiah 24:1-3.
66. Known as the Septuagint (pronounced "SEP-too-uh-jint"), this earliest translation of the Old Testament from the original Hebrew into Greek, made in the 3rd century B.C., derives its name from the 70 (or rather 72) scholars who did the work of translation.
67. Jeremiah 4:23-27.

68. Revelation 16:18 and 21. Incidentally, this last verse says that those on whom the Plagues fall "blasphemed God," revealing their utter, undying contempt for Him—even at the END of the Seven Last Plagues!
69. Revelation 20:4.
70. Luke 22:30.
71. 1 Corinthians 6:2-3.
72. Revelation 22:12.
73. Revelation 22:11.
74. Nahum 1:9.
75. Revelation 20:8, Phillips translation.
76. Promises, for instance, like these: "Behold, your God . . . will come and *save* you. Then the eyes of the *blind* shall be opened, and the ears of the *deaf* shall be unstopped. Then the *lame* shall leap like a deer, and the tongue of the *dumb* sing." Isaiah 35:4-6, NKJV.
77. Revelation 20:2-3 and 7.
78. See Revelation 3:12, 21:2 & 10.
79. Zechariah 14:5, NASB, RSV, NIV. For "holy ones," the KJV and NKJV read "saints."
80. Acts 1:9-12. Jesus ascended to heaven "from the Mount called Olivet" or Mount of Olives.
81. Zechariah 14:4, NIV.
82. Revelation 21:16.
83. Revelation 21:2.
84. Please see *Appendix J, "Is the Bible Written in Chronological Order?"*
85. Revelation 21:9-10.
86. Dr. C. Mervyn Maxwell explains: "The symbolic terms 'Gog' and 'Magog' are adapted from the names of ancient Israel's northern enemies in Ezekiel 38:2. Here they stand for ALL of God's enemies—northern, southern, eastern, and western—all of the unsaved nations of all the world's generations." *God Cares* (Boise, Idaho: Pacific Press Publishing Association, c. 1985), Volume 2, p. 500.
87. Revelation 20:7-9.
88. E. G. White, *The Great Controversy* (Boise, Idaho: Pacific Press Publishing Association, c. 1950), p. 664.
89. The patriarch Job understood about Heaven's Record Books, which witness either for or against us: "Behold, my *witness* is in heaven, and my *record* is on high."—Job 16:19.
90. Fulfilling Romans 14:10-12—"We shall all stand before the judgment seat of Christ. For it is written, As I live, saith the Lord, every knee shall bow to Me, and every tongue shall confess to God. So then every one of us shall give account of himself to God." Compare Philippians 2:10-11.
91. The righteous have always had Jesus—who has never lost a case—as their Defense Attorney in Heaven's Supreme Court: "If any man sin, we have an Advocate with the Father, Jesus Christ the righteous."—1 John 2:1. But the wicked, having refused His services, have no one.
92. E. G. White, *The Great Controversy* (Boise, Idaho: Pacific Press Publishing Association, c. 1950), p. 668.

93. Revelation 15:4, The Amplified Bible.
94. "As far as the East is from the West, so far hath He removed our transgressions from us."—Psalm 103:12. "Who is a God like unto Thee, that pardoneth iniquity . . . ? Thou wilt cast all their sins into the depths of the sea."—Micah 7:18-19.
95. Omar Khayyám, *The Rubáiyát,* translated by Edward Fitzgerald, Stanza 71.
96. John 3:18. And Romans 8:1 says, "There is therefore now no condemnation to them which are in Christ Jesus."
97. 1 Timothy 5:24.
98. The Lord assures us, "I, even I, am He that BLOTTETH OUT thy transgressions . . . and will not remember thy sins. . . . I have BLOTTED OUT . . . thy transgressions, and . . . thy sins." Isaiah 43:25 and 44:22. See also Acts 3:19 and Psalm 51:1-2 & 9.
99. 1 Peter 4:17.
100. Revelation 20:13-15 and 21:7-8, NKJV. Everyone is either "born twice to die once, or born once to die twice." Christians—born twice by experiencing conversion's new birth—die only once (unless alive when Jesus returns). But unsaved sinners, never being born again, die "the second death" after being resurrected with the wicked.
101. Revelation 20:9.
102. Malachi 4:1-3. For more on the fate of the wicked, see Chapter 12, "Eternal Torment: A Burning Issue."
103. John 15:5.
104. Ezekiel 28:13-19.
105. 2 Peter 3:10-13.
106. Isaiah 33:14-15, NKJV. The "everlasting burnings" need not be considered longer in duration than the "eternal fire" of Sodom and Gomorrah. See Jude 7 and Chapter 12, "Eternal Torment: A Burning Issue."
107. Revelation 21:5.
108. Psalm 37:11 and Matthew 5:5.
109. Revelation 21:1. Why is "no more sea" a good thing? The seven seas today cover about *seventy-five per cent of the earth* with UNDRINKABLE salt water. They also act as divisive BARRIERS separating loved ones.
110. 1 Corinthians 2:9, NKJV. Compare Isaiah 64:4.
111. Revelation 21:4.
112. John 14:2-4, NKJV.
113. Revelation 21:3, NKJV.
114. Psalm 16:11.
115. For instance, see Chapter 7, "Jesus Meets Every Test"; Chapter 15, "History Told in Advance"; and Chapter 19, "Antichrist Unmasked: The Beast Power Revealed."
116. Patrick Henry, in his famous speech, "Give Me Liberty or Give Me Death."

"Life without God
can be HELL."
—BUMPER STICKER

Mystery #7
Mark of the Beast

How can we identify the Antichrist / Beast?
What is meant by "the Mark of the Beast"?
Is there any way we can avoid that Mark?

"Cry aloud, spare not,
lift up thy voice like a trumpet,
and show My people. . . ."
—Isaiah 58:1

ANTICHRIST UNMASKED

INTRODUCTION: THE BEAST POWER IDENTIFIED— REVELATION REVEALS THE ANTICHRIST!

ORIGIN & EARLY HISTORY OF THE BEAST POWER

A. Its PLACE of origin was foretold.

B. Its TIME of origin was foretold.

C. It would uproot THREE kings or kingdoms.

D. It would be a "GREAT CITY."

RELIGIOUS NATURE OF THE BEAST POWER

E. It would be UNLIKE the first ten kingdoms.

F. It would be a RELIGIOUS power that is "worshipped."

G. It would be a CHURCH, a "woman."

H. It would be, in God's eyes, a CORRUPT church, a "whore."

I. It would be a church built on "SEVEN HILLS."

J. It would be a large, WORLDWIDE church.

K. It would use a LANGUAGE difficult for most to understand.

L. It would be a RICH church.

M. It would be clothed in "PURPLE & SCARLET."

N. Its leader would be a religious figure enthroned IN the church.

O. It would be identified by a mysterious NUMBER: 666.

ACTIONS & CHARACTER OF THE BEAST POWER

P. It would have "a mouth speaking GREAT THINGS."

Q. It would be a RELIGIOUS power dominating the CIVIL powers.

R. It would be a PERSECUTING power.

S. It would be guilty of BLASPHEMY against God.

T. It would attempt to CHANGE the Law of God.

LATER HISTORY OF THE BEAST POWER

U. Its period of supremacy would be of SPECIFIC DURATION.

V. It would receive a "DEADLY WOUND."

W. Its "deadly wound" would be "HEALED."

CONCLUSION: What was *foretold* has been *fulfilled!*

~

CHAPTER NINETEEN

ANTICHRIST UNMASKED: THE BEAST POWER IDENTIFIED

By Way of INTRODUCTION...

WINSTON CHURCHILL once said of Russia: "It is a riddle wrapped in a mystery inside an enigma." The identity of the Beast presents the same kind of puzzle to many minds, even among Bible students. But this chapter should sweep away the confusion. God's Word offers a multitude of clues which make this mystery a theological thriller!

GOD'S WOEFUL WARNING

God is a God of love. Nevertheless, the most fearfully threatening words in all the Bible were uttered by an angel in this awesome warning from God Himself:

> "If any man worship the Beast and his image, and receive his Mark in his forehead, or in his hand, the same shall drink of the wine of the wrath of God, which is poured out without mixture into the cup of His indignation; and he shall be tormented with fire and brimstone in the presence of the holy angels, and in the presence of the Lamb." [1]

Though men may differ as to what the Mark of the Beast is, all must agree that the consequences of receiving the Mark will be the most terrible punishment ever inflicted. Unfortunately, the average person has scarcely heard about this urgent subject. He hasn't the faintest idea about the Beast or his Mark, though his very destiny hangs on this issue. Others who have heard something about the Beast power believe no one can know who the Beast is or what his Mark is. They believe these things constitute a puzzle man can never hope to solve because their preachers comfort them in their ignorance by saying, "Don't worry about the Beast. It's too complicated to understand. As long as you love the Lord, you'll be all right."

Listen! With such terrible punishment threatened, would God leave us in doubt as to who the Beast is and what his Mark is? Would He warn us about the fearful danger of this Beast—a danger so deadly it means LIFE or DEATH—and then keep its identity a secret? [2] Would He say, "You'll be cast into the fire if you have the Mark, but I won't tell you what it is—it's just too bad if you have it"?

No, God isn't like that. He warns of danger He wants us to avoid. He knows we can be safe from the Beast only if we know who the Beast is. We can be free from his Mark only if we know what the Mark is. Since ignorance on this matter is folly, we can and must identify the Beast beyond a shadow of a doubt. Thank God, revelation REVEALS the real Antichrist!

AN AMAZING EXPOSÉ

In the 1970's the entire country was abuzz over a scandal called "Watergate." Bob Woodward and Carl Bernstein, investigative reporters for the *Washington Post,* exposed many hidden facts which implicated the White House itself. This took courage, but they did it.

How about you? Would you be as willing to alert the world on some vital matter? What if, during the days of Queen Victoria, you knew the true identity of the criminal called Jack the Ripper? Or what if today you had a cure—a sure cure—for cancer? Would you tell others and let the world know? Or would you keep it to yourself?

Without exaggeration, the subject at hand is every bit as important. We're talking about the FUTURE of the WORLD, for the Mark of the Beast will affect all mankind! God urgently WARNS us that "the image of the Beast should both speak and cause as many as would not worship the image of the Beast to be KILLED. And he causes all, both small and great, rich and poor, free and slave, to receive a Mark on their right hand, or on their foreheads, and that no man may buy or sell except one who has the Mark or the name of the Beast, or the number of his name." [3] Therefore, we must ask some tough questions—and expect to get answers.

The term "beast" here is not derogatory. In the Bible it simply refers to an ANIMAL depicting an earthly power—a kingdom or nation—in prophecy. Political cartoonists use the same symbols today in their cartoons: the Russian BEAR, British LION, or American EAGLE, the Republican ELEPHANT or Democratic DONKEY, *etc.* In chapters 7 and 8 of the Book of Daniel, God uses "beasts" to symbolize earthly powers, and to interpret Daniel's prophecy is simply to identify those powers. [4]

SUPER SLEUTH

Do you enjoy the challenge of following clues wherever they lead in order to solve a mystery? I think you'll find, as I did, that this investigation is a fascinating exercise in detective work! When a criminal investigator has the fingerprints of the murderer he's seeking and finally finds the one whose prints match perfectly, he knows he's identified the killer. When we, in our investigation, find the power that perfectly matches all the Bible clues, we'll know we've correctly identified the Beast.

Sherlock Holmes, Inspector Jacques Clouseau, and Lieutenant Columbo are all fascinating detectives—fictional ones from literature, movies, and television. But this present mystery—worthy of our most penetrating powers of deduction—is anything but fictional! It's real, it affects each one of us, and it could be called the greatest mystery of all time!

But truth is stranger than fiction. A fictional detective must be satisfied with just a few clues leading to the identification of the culprit. Often he has only a few scraps of evidence—a single fingerprint, a torn photograph, the thinnest thread on which to hang a conviction. In this real-life mystery, however, God gives a wealth of clues, an abundance of evidence. Just as God gave many prophetic signs to identify CHRIST,[5] so He gives many clear signs to identify ANTIchrist. In fact, He gives the Biblical detective twenty-three very definite leads substantiated by the testimony of History. There's so much evidence of such high quality that you can call this "an open and shut case."

THE TESTIMONY OF HISTORY

Samuel Taylor Coleridge was right when he said, "If men could learn from history, what lessons it might teach us!" One lesson history teaches us is to trust Bible prophecy, for today's history verifies and validates age-old prophecy.

History is prophecy's chief interpreter, for prophecy is history written in advance. As ages roll by, the foretold becomes the fulfilled. What Daniel, Paul, and John predicted, history verifies with centuries of unerring testimony, and the Record of the Past is there for all to read.

In our investigation, History walks onto the scene of action and makes the identification for us, pointing an unmistakable finger at the culprit called the Beast power. We won't need to resort to guess-work or speculation, for God's Word and the historian's pen validate our conclusions. In fact, if you know anything about history—the collective memory of mankind—you'll be able to make the identification yourself, without needing help from me or anyone else. Since the clues are clear, our search is sure, for the clues are the damning fingerprints of the Antichrist/Beast, giving us positive identification of this mysterious power.

When it comes to clues, the secret lies in knowing where to look. Our clues are found in ancient manuscripts. God entrusted this vital information to three Bible writers: The prophet DANIEL in the Old Testament and the apostles PAUL and JOHN in the New Testament. Thus three distinct lines of evidence paint a composite portrait depicting the rise, character, deeds, and doom of Antichrist. From them we learn "the nature of the Beast." No one of these three is complete in itself. Only by combining their separate features will we see the complete picture, just as we can't derive a perfect portrait of Christ from one Gospel alone. Our conclusions can be safely based on these MULTIPLE fulfillments of Bible prophecy.[6]

A SHOCKING Revelation

For many, studying this subject in the Bible is like reading the SMALL PRINT in a contract—they never knew it was there before. And many have a "blind spot" when it comes to a fault in a loved one—they just can't see it. So we must open our eyes to what God would teach us in His Word. Devoted Catholics, especially, must approach this vital subject with an objective attitude and pray that God's Holy Spirit will enlighten them according to His will. When we want to know the truth, we can't be DEAF, DUMB, and BLIND to the evidence.

These findings and conclusions are not new. It's a matter of historical fact that, for CENTURIES, church reformers, scholars, and theologians have found the Papacy—the Papal system of the Roman Catholic Church—to be the clear and incontrovertible fulfillment of the prophesied "Beast" power. To some people, perhaps to some of you, this comes as a surprise. But it's really the old, time-honored position of Bible scholars throughout history. Call the roll of the most illustrious men in the Protestant Reformation over the centuries—Martin Luther (LUTHERAN), John Calvin and John Knox (PRESBYTERIAN), Adam Clarke (METHODIST), Roger Williams (BAPTIST), or their contemporaries—and without exception those great leaders understood that the prophecies of Antichrist applied to the Papacy.

Many great men besides theologians came to the same conclusion. SIR ISAAC NEWTON, for instance, the outstanding scientific genius of his age, stated this in his *Observations Upon the Prophecies of Daniel, and the Apocalypse of St. John.*[7] And England's KING JAMES I, who sponsored the English translation of the Bible, openly identified the Pope as the prophesied Beast power and contended that Rome was the "Seat" of Antichrist. He wrote these facts in a forceful warning to all the rulers of Christendom.[8] Centuries later, when Pope John Paul II announced plans to visit England in 1982, *The Wall Street Journal*—a non-religious, conservative newspaper—headlined a front-page article: "Pope's Coming Visit Riles Some Britons . . . He is Viewed as the Antichrist."[9]

So we're in good company: Far from being on the radical fringe of theology, the conclusions presented here are clearly in the mainstream of Protestant thought. Yet to a large extent this prophetic message was allowed to die. Today, the identity of the Antichrist/Beast as taught by all the Reformers is Christianity's best-kept SECRET! For the last century or so, the dust-covered evidence has lain dormant. But now you hold in your hands, in documented form, the long-neglected and largely unknown evidence concerning the prophetic faith of our spiritual forefathers.

This very evidence helped launch the Protestant Reformation—which was BUILT upon the identification of the Papacy as Antichrist—not only in Germany, but in Switzerland, Scandinavia, the Low Countries, Great Britain, and France. You'll see the accuracy of this position as we examine Bible specifications pinpointing the Antichrist/Beast, which point unquestionably to the Pope and his power as exercised in the Roman Catholic Church.

Some may ask, "Are you saying that the Roman Catholic Pope is the Antichrist?" Please understand that I'm not saying anything. I'm simply showing what the *BIBLE* says and examining the testimony of History along with it. But most investigators find that the historical facts of the Papacy correspond perfectly to the Biblical data on Antichrist.

Some may wonder if it's right to delve into these things—if it's right to point a finger and declare, "You are the Beast referred to in Scripture!" If you feel this way, I understand your sensitive feelings and your reluctance to indulge in what may seem like name-calling. I understand, because it's not pleasant for me to discuss the subject, either. Since it touches some long-cherished beliefs, it's a difficult lesson to teach. But our minds may be set at ease if we remember two things:

First, remember that this is a matter of Life or Death—we're dealing with the most solemn warning given in all the Bible. A matter-of-fact frankness may be tolerated, and welcomed, when the issues are as VITAL as this.

We MUST understand who the Beast is and what his Mark is, so we can avoid the awful condemnation awaiting those who receive that Mark.

Second, remember this: God placed these identifying marks in Scripture because He WANTS you to know these things. In any life-and-death matter like this, you have a God-given right to know—there's too much at stake not to! Jesus promised, "Ye shall know the truth, and the truth shall make you free." [10]

"With MALICE Toward NONE . . . "

These pages are written with malice toward none, with charity and enlightenment for all. Please understand that we're talking not about our Roman Catholic friends or any other PEOPLE in this study—we're talking about a SYSTEM. We're dealing not with personalities but with teachings and practices perpetuated by that system—the religious institution of the Papacy.

We're not implying that the Pope himself is personally corrupt or wicked. The Bible says, "Satan . . . deceiveth the whole world," [11] and that includes the Roman Catholic Church and its leaders. So the Pope may be quite sincere in following what he's been taught. It's possible to be sincere yet deceived. The PERSON of the Pope is one thing—the OFFICE of the Pope is quite another.

As we investigate this question, bear in mind that when Catholic writers use the word *church*, they refer primarily to the Papal hierarchy—the Pope, the cardinals, the archbishops and bishops—not to the lay members as a body. Strictly speaking, individual Catholics belong TO "the Church," as subjects; they're not a part OF it in the Protestant sense and *have no vote or voice* in its councils. We'll use the term *church* in the Catholic, not the Protestant, sense.

If the evidence seems damning to the hierarchy of the Roman Catholic Church, individual members of that church needn't feel embarrassed or personally guilty any more than Republicans felt personal guilt when Watergate revelations came to light or Democrats felt personal shame for the Clinton scandals. The truth *should* come out—people *should* be informed. For Christians to learn these things and realize their truth is simply to say that they're wiser today than they were yesterday.

I want to say right now, as lovingly as I can, that I believe Roman Catholics simply do not know the truths revealed in this book. The wonderful Catholic people as I know them are entirely sincere in their beliefs and devout in their worship. These comments and conclusions have nothing to do with any individual Catholic, from the Pope on down to his humblest parishioner, and they're offered in the spirit of Christ as a warning against delusion—not as a malicious attack. The spirit of Christ leaves no room for prejudice or bigotry of any kind or in any degree. My task in presenting this study is simply one of "speaking the truth in love," as Paul puts it.[12]

Other books have tried to cover this subject. This one UNcovers it. When you finish this investigation, you will have proved to yourself who the Antichrist Beast is—you won't have to guess. So let's do some detective work. Let's begin our investigation and see what clues we can find to solve the mystery of the Antichrist!

CLUE "A"

ITS PLACE OF ORIGIN WAS FORETOLD—IT WOULD ARISE AMONG THE NATIONS OF WESTERN EUROPE (THAT IS, AMONG THE TEN DIVISIONS OF THE ROMAN EMPIRE).

Your BIBLE says:

1. **Daniel 7:7-8, RSV**—"After this I saw in the night visions, and behold, a fourth beast, terrible and dreadful and exceedingly strong; and it had great IRON teeth: it devoured and broke in pieces, and stamped the residue with its feet. It was different from all the beasts that were before it; and it had TEN HORNS. I considered the horns, and behold, there came up AMONG THEM *another* horn, a *little* one, . . . and behold, in this horn were eyes like the eyes of a man, and a mouth speaking great things."

2. **Daniel 7:8, 24**—"AMONG them," that is, among "the ten horns" which verse 24 says are "ten kings" or kingdoms—the ten political divisions of the ROMAN EMPIRE, which became the modern nations of WESTERN EUROPE. Thus we needn't look for the Beast power to arise in North or South America, Africa, Asia, or Australia. Daniel pinpoints its location as within the divided Roman Empire—that is, somewhere within the nations of Italy, Germany, England, France, Spain, Portugal, Switzerland, *etc.* (Please see pages 464-474, above, for background on Daniel 2 & 7.)

3. **Daniel 2:41-42**—Daniel's vision of a great metal image speaks of the ten "toes" into which the Roman feet of the image were divided after its break-up as an empire. Whether represented by ten HORNS or ten TOES, the ten divisions are the modern nations of Western Europe.

CHART: A Bird's-Eye-View of Pertinent Prophecies

Scripture passages pertaining to the Antichrist / Beast are relatively few in number, collectively comprising barely six full chapters. Yet they are DYNAMITE!—containing virtually all vital clues to unlock the mystery of the Beast. Those passages, from three Bible writers, are listed below:

Bible Writer:	Prophet Daniel	Apostle Paul	Apostle John
REFERENCES from the Bible:	Daniel 7:1-26	2 Thessalonians 2:1-8	1 John 2:18, 22; 4:3 2 John 7 Revelation 13:1-18 Revelation 14:9-10 Revelation 17:1-18 Revelation 18:1-24
TITLES applied to this Wicked Power:	"LITTLE HORN"	"that MAN of SIN" "SON of PERDITION" "MYSTERY of INIQUITY" "that WICKED"	"ANTICHRIST" "the BEAST" "MOTHER of HARLOTS" "BABYLON" "that GREAT CITY"

Comments on the Preceding CHART

Just as criminals often use **aliases**, the Devil himself is known in Scripture by several different names. For example, he's also called "Lucifer" and "Satan" and "the prince of this world."[13] In the same way, the Bible refers to the mysterious **Antichrist / Beast** by *more than ONE* symbolic title, as the *bottom half* of the *above chart* shows. You'll see, as you proceed through the clues presented in this chapter, that these titles refer to the same power and are synonymous. However, since the first clue starts out by considering the "Little Horn" power, let's note how God reveals it to be the SAME as the "Beast." The Bible shows several *obvious parallels*, as follows:

The "LITTLE HORN" of Daniel 7	The "BEAST" of Revelation 13
• "a mouth speaking great things"[14] • arose among "ten horns"[15] • "made war with the saints, and prevailed against them"[16]	• "a mouth speaking great things"[17] • had "ten horns"[18] • "to make war with the saints, and to overcome them"[19]

13. Isaiah 14:12, Luke 10:18, John 12:31.
14. Daniel 7:8, 20.
15. Daniel 7:7-8, 20, 24.
16. Daniel 7:21. Verse 25 says the Little Horn would "**WEAR OUT the saints.**"

17. Revelation 13:5.
18. Revelation 13:1.
19. Revelation 13:7.

4. Revelation 13:1-2—"And I stood upon the sand of the sea, and saw a BEAST rise up out of the sea, having seven heads and TEN HORNS. . . . And the Beast which I saw was like unto a leopard, and his feet were as the feet of a bear, and his mouth as the mouth of a lion: and the DRAGON gave him his power, and his SEAT, and great authority." To understand the Bible statement that "the dragon gave . . . his seat" to the Beast, we must know who the DRAGON is and what is meant by the word *seat*. Fortunately, the preceding chapter, **Revelation 12**, deciphers this cryptic statement for us.

First, Revelation 12:3 speaks of "a great red DRAGON, having seven heads and TEN HORNS"—just as the Beast has in chapter 13. Then Revelation 12:9 declares "the DRAGON" to be "that old serpent, called the Devil, and Satan." Thus Satan himself is always the great antichrist or "dragon," as this text expressly states.

But the Devil works through human agents. Just as Christian people are the Lord's feet and lips to take the Lord's message to the world, it is people—wicked people, if you will—who do the Devil's dirty work. So even though "the dragon" is primarily Satan, in a secondary sense "the dragon" is clearly seen to be pagan Rome. For Revelation 12:4, NKJV says, "the dragon stood before the woman who was ready to give birth, to DEVOUR her Child as soon as it was born." Who was this Child that faced mortal danger as soon as it was born? Well, Revelation 12:5 describes Him as "a Man Child, who was to rule all nations with a rod of iron," who according to Revelation 19:15-16 can be none other than Jesus Christ Himself. Furthermore, Revelation 12:5 says this "Child was caught up unto God, and to His throne," and Mark 16:19 and John 20:17 show this to be Jesus, who after His resurrection ascended to God and His throne.

The second chapter of Matthew shows that just such an attempt as John the Revelator describes WAS made to destroy the Baby Jesus. But that attempt was made not by the Devil incarnate—it was made by King Herod. You see, as we said above, Satan, like God, works through human agents. And pagan Rome—the Rome of the Caesars in the form of Herod, its king in Palestine—was the Devil's human agent in his attempt to kill Christ as soon as He was born. Not only that, but pagan Rome did Satan's dirty work once again in our Lord's Crucifixion:

- A ROMAN governor, Pilate, condemned Christ to die.
- A ROMAN executioner nailed Him to the cruel cross.
- A ROMAN seal was affixed to His tomb.
- A ROMAN squad of soldiers guarded His tomb.

5. Now back to our clue: **Revelation 13:2** says, "the DRAGON gave him
. . . HIS seat." The points above help identify "the dragon" as the pagan
Roman empire of the Caesars. The Greek word here translated "seat" is
thronos, or "throne." The throne of the Caesars was located in the imperial city of ROME, pinpointing the geographical location—the birthplace—
of the Beast.

HISTORY testifies:

Chapters 2 and 7 of Daniel bring to light all world history in very small
scope: both the FOUR METALS of the image in the king's dream (gold, silver,
brass, and iron) and the FOUR BEASTS (lion, bear, leopard, and "terrible"
beast) represent the four world empires of Babylon, Medo-Persia, Greece, and
ROME, respectively. [20]

Universal agreement exists that the fourth beast represents Rome. As
Martin Luther put it: "What Daniel says concerning the beast with ten horns,
this we must understand to be spoken of the Roman Empire." [21]

Hippolytus, a church writer and bishop of Porto, near Rome, who died
about A. D. 235, shows that Daniel's prophecies were understood even in the
days of the Roman Empire:

> "The *golden head* of the image, and the *lioness,* denoted the BABY-
> LONIANS; the *shoulders and arms of silver,* and the *bear,* represented the
> PERSIANS AND MEDES; the *belly and thighs of brass,* and the *leopard,*
> meant the GREEKS, who held sovereignty from Alexander's time; the *legs
> of iron,* and the *beast dreadful and terrible,* expressed the ROMANS, who
> hold the sovereignty at present; the *toes of the feet* which were part *clay*
> and part *iron,* and the *ten horns* were emblems of the [ten] kingdoms
> that are to rise; the other *Little Horn* that grows up among them meant
> the ANTICHRIST in their midst. . . . Rejoice, blessed Daniel! thou has not
> been in error: all these things have come to pass. After this again thou
> hast told me of the beast dreadful and terrible. 'It had iron teeth and
> claws of brass: it devoured and brake in pieces, and stamped the resi-
> due with the feet of it.' Already the iron [Rome] rules; already it sub-
> dues and breaks all in pieces; already it brings all the unwilling into
> subjection; already we see these things ourselves. Now we glorify God,
> being instructed by thee." [22]

As this whole shocking story unfolds, we'll see more and more clearly
that the Papacy is a prime suspect. Even the very name "ROMAN Catholic
Church" places it at "the scene of the crime." Let's quickly look at three
quotes from eminent historians:

- "The mighty Catholic Church was little more than the Roman Empire baptized. . . . The very CAPITAL of the old Empire became the capital of the Christian Empire. . . . Even the Roman language [Latin] has remained the official language of the Roman Catholic Church down through the ages. . . . *Out of the ruins of political Rome* arose the great moral Empire in the giant form of the Roman Church." [23]

- "The Roman Church pushed itself into the place of the Roman World-Empire, of which it is the actual continuation. . . . The Pope, who calls himself 'King' and 'Pontifex Maximus,' is Caesar's successor." [24]

- "The Bishop of Rome had become a temporal prince, so that the philosopher Hobbes could truthfully say of the Papacy that it was 'the ghost of the Roman Empire, crowned and seated on the grave thereof.'" [25]

So on such an important matter as the Beast's PLACE of origin, God doesn't resort to an indefinite location like "East of the Sun and West of the Moon." Not at all. Instead, He clearly pinpoints the place in prophecy. And when we must hunt through a whole ATLAS of places in this wide world, it's good that God helps us narrow it down!

CLUE "B"
ITS TIME OF ORIGIN WAS FORETOLD—IT WOULD ARISE "AFTER" THE BREAK-UP OF THE ROMAN EMPIRE INTO TEN KINGDOMS.

Your BIBLE says:
1. **2 Thessalonians 2:7**—The apostle Paul, writing in A. D. 51, declared: "The mystery of iniquity doth ALREADY work: only he who NOW *letteth* WILL *let*, UNTIL he be taken out of the way." The word "let" is Old English and means *prevent, hinder,* or *restrain.* Please note:

    a. In **Isaiah 43:13** God says, "I will work, and who shall LET Me?"— in other words, "who shall STOP Me?"

    b. In tennis, a "LET ball" is one *interfered with* or *prevented* from going into play by striking the net or other *hindrance* and is played over.

    c. The New International Version puts Paul's verse into modern English as follows: "The secret power of lawlessness is ALREADY at work; but the one who NOW holds it back will continue to do so TILL he is taken out of the way."

In this verse we see that "let" obviously refers to Caesar; for as long as there was a Caesar on the throne of the Roman Empire, he would PRE-VENT the Beast or any other rival within his realm from coming to power. Therefore, the rise of the Beast power is chronologically pinpointed: It must be after the fall of the last Roman emperor, who was "taken out of the way" in A. D. 476. Paul's statement that he who holds back the Beast power will restrain it only "TILL he is taken out of the way," means the Beast would assume power shortly after Rome fell in A. D. 476.

2. **Daniel 7:24**—Five hundred years before Paul, the prophet Daniel was inspired to write his corroborating prophecy that the Beast power "shall rise AFTER them" that is, after the *ten horns* or kingdoms had arisen. Rome's power as a unified empire declined until, by A. D. 476, it was divided into the ten smaller kingdoms of Western Europe. So to fit DANIEL'S prophecy, as well as PAUL'S, the Beast had to rise to power some time after A. D. 476.

HISTORY testifies:

History records that Romulus Augustulus, the last Roman Emperor, fell from power in A. D. 476 after a brief reign of just one year. History further records that in A. D. 533 the Bishop of Rome was elevated to a position of universal dominance by JUSTINIAN, the great Byzantine Emperor who ruled at Constantinople. You see, after barbarian tribes had brought about the down-fall of the Roman Empire, Justinian became the most powerful man in Europe. His greatest contribution to civilization—his work of most lasting importance—was to unify Roman law into one code, the Justinian code. Note what we read in his

> "One Hundred and Thirty-First New Constitution. Chapter II. Con-cerning the Precedence of Patriarchs. . . . We order that the Most Holy Pope of ancient Rome shall hold the FIRST rank of ALL the Pontiffs, but the Most Blessed Archbishop of Constantinople, or New Rome, shall occupy the second place after the Holy Apostolic See of ancient Rome, which shall TAKE PRECEDENCE over ALL other sees." [26] (Note: The word *see* refers to the area of authority or jurisdiction of a bishop.)

Justinian's monumental decree of A. D. 533, elevating the Pope to su-premacy, was one that certainly SHAPED HISTORY! Thus the Papacy rose to power at a TIME which fits the prophecy precisely:

● It arose shortly "after" the Roman Empire broke up into ten smaller kingdoms. [27]

- That is, it arose shortly after the restraining Caesars were "taken out of the way" when the last Roman emperor fell.

The FALLACY of FUTURISM

In order to "clinch the case" for the facts outlined above, let's look at the alternate interpretation known as FUTURISM, which surprisingly claims that the Antichrist has not yet appeared but will arise some time in the future, soon after the Secret Rapture. [28]

First of all, as pointed out in Issue #7 of Chapter 17, above, Futurism's teaching that the Antichrist/Beast is NOT revealed till after Jesus comes to gather His saints and rapture away His church is diametrically opposed to God's Word. In 2 Thessalonians 2:1-3, Paul says:

> "Now we beseech you, brethren, by the COMING of our Lord Jesus Christ, and by our GATHERING together unto Him [speaking of the Rapture of God's people]. . . . Let no man deceive you by any means: for that day [the day of Christ's "Coming . . . and . . . our GATHERING" in the Rapture] shall NOT come except there come a falling away FIRST, and that Man of Sin be REVEALED, the son of perdition."

Thus the Futurist timetable directly contradicts God's divine schedule for closing events: Futurists teach that the church is raptured first and then the Beast is revealed and rises to power, but God says that Man of Sin is revealed first and then the saints are gathered home to heaven.

Secondly, though both Daniel and Paul pointed to the supreme manifestation of Antichrist as still in the future, the early Christians understood it would be NOT SO FAR in the DISTANT future as some interpreters today would push it. For instance, Paul's key verse of 2 Thessalonians 2:7 tells us that "The secret power of lawlessness is ALREADY at work," though it was being restrained by a rival power. [29] And John, a contemporary and fellow apostle with Paul, assured believers in his day that "EVEN NOW are there many antichrists" [30] and "that spirit of antichrist . . . EVEN NOW ALREADY is it in the world." [31] Even in apostolic days, then, seeds were sown for Antichrist's growth *in embryo*, but he'd come to full fruition and power only after Rome fell.

Thirdly, since Futurism schedules Antichrist far in the future, of necessity it grafts a huge GAP into the prophetic time scheme. But the idea of a great gap of centuries intervening before the rise of the Antichrist Beast violates the precedents of prophecy. Please note: The twin prophecies in Daniel chapters 2 and 7 predict the rise and fall of the four great world empires of Babylon, Medo-Persia, Greece, and Rome. Was there a GAP between any of them? Of course not! Victor followed vanquished with no historical break. Next, the disintegration of the fourth empire, pagan Rome, was likewise followed—without a gap—by the rise of ten smaller kingdoms. Then the prophetic sequence spotlights the Little Horn / Antichrist power in the early Middle Ages, similarly with NO HINT of a gap, arising after Rome's breakup. These prophecies show a continuous sequence of unfolding history, so any who teach a FUTURISTIC Antichrist arising after a great GAP of centuries bear a heavy burden of proof to substantiate their theory.

Therefore, any interpretation of the Beast power that falls for the fallacy of Futurism misses the mark. But let's examine that theory a bit further.

As mentioned before, every leader of the Christian church over the centuries—Martin Luther of the Lutheran Church, John Calvin of the Presbyterian Church, John Wesley of the Methodist Church, Roger Williams of the Baptist Church, and others virtually without exception—accepted the time-honored position of this book on the Bible teaching concerning the Beast.

Even the Roman Catholic Bible, the Douay Version, makes this admission in a footnote on 2 Thessalonians 2:3—"The ROMAN EMPIRE . . . was first to be destroyed, before the coming of Antichrist." And the *Catholic Encyclopedia* says: "The impediment is the ROMAN EMPIRE; the main event impeded is the 'man of sin.'" [32]

But Futurists can't accept Caesar as the obvious restraining force that delayed the Beast's rise, because so many centuries have past since the preventive power of Caesar was removed that even Futurists realize this makes their theory ridiculous! Instead, Futurists insist the restraining power who hinders the Beast is the Holy Spirit, Who they say will be withdrawn from the earth at the time of the Secret Rapture. However, there are several reasons why this restraining power is not the Holy Spirit but Caesar, the pagan Roman emperor. Please note:

a. In the first place, Paul carefully ENCODES his meaning in the cryptic phrase "*he* who now restrains" because he could not boldly and openly state that CAESAR "will be taken out of the way" without needlessly exposing his ministry to danger. If he were to "name names" and refer directly to Caesar as one who'd be "removed," he'd appear as a traitor to the Empire and would provoke more persecution on the Church. So he veiled his meaning in language which is understandable but not provocative.

b. No doubt Paul spoke plainly to his Thessalonian friends when he was with them *in person*. In fact, in the preceding verses he even reminds them of his words regarding the Beast: "Do you not remember that when I was still with you I told you this? And YOU KNOW what is restraining him now so that he may be revealed in his time." [33] Paul's written words were carefully chosen to avoid political complications should his letter fall into enemy hands. It's as if he wrote his Thessalonian readers, "For obvious reasons, I can't be more explicit in this letter, but just recall what I told you in person about the restraining power of ROME being taken out of the way, and you'll understand what I'm saying!" Christians of Paul's day familiar with his teaching would readily understand, of course, yet Roman authorities could not accuse Paul of treason.

    c. On the other hand, IF Paul really WERE referring to the Holy Spirit, there'd be no reason not to come right out and openly say so, for he and the other apostles often wrote of God's Holy Spirit! Therefore when Paul spoke of someone who would restrain "until he be taken out of the way," we cannot assume he implied the Holy Spirit would be removed.

    d. The powerful restraining force was that of Caesar, who, as Emperor, was supreme monarch of the then-known world. Can you imagine Caesar allowing the Beast to come to power while he was on the imperial throne? Not on your life! No rival to Caesar would be tolerated—in Papal form or any other.

    e. But the Bible speaks of God as the almighty One who "REMOVETH kings, and setteth up kings." [34] Clearly, then, God could remove Caesar and his restraining power when the time came for the Beast to march onto the stage of action. Historian Edward Gibbon's monumental work, *The Decline and Fall of the Roman Empire,* details how this came to pass, and the interpretation of Caesar as the restraining power harmonizes perfectly with both Scripture and history.

Another alternative explanation Futurists sometimes suggest is that CHRISTIANS are the restraining force that keeps the Beast from coming to power! Could this possibly be true? Absolutely not, for three reasons:

    1. Instead of the saints being able to dominate the Beast and keep him in check, the Bible says the saints themselves were unmercifully persecuted by the Beast power. [35]

Sometimes, when those holding this theory see the difficulty of the overwhelming persecution the Bible mentions, they assert that converted JEWS are the persecuted saints. Here, to "prove" their theory, they resort to a teaching which itself is in need of proof!

    2. The theory that Christians could restrain the Beast does not meet the demands of the text, for it's obvious that Paul is not speaking of MORAL influence. Moral influence is already too late in the case of the Beast—he's

the Devil's agent. The Bible is talking about effective practical force. Christians could no more stop the Beast than the Jews could stop Hitler from putting them into gas ovens. But Caesar, as undisputed Emperor, could and would stop any rival from coming to power.

3. Finally, if Paul had really meant that Christians would restrain the dreaded Beast until they're "taken out of the way" in the Rapture, he'd have no need to use coded, cryptic language. Paul constantly spoke of Christians and never had to speak in riddles on that account!

These three reasons refute the interpretation that Christians are the restraining force but leave intact the idea that Caesar had to be removed before the Beast could arise.

The Papacy simply COULD NOT come to power till the Caesars of Rome were "taken out of the way" with the crumbling of the Roman Empire. But it did arise soon "after" Rome fell, thus fitting this chronological clue. Obviously, those who look for the Beast to appear in the FUTURE don't have a CLUE as to who the Beast is!

CLUE "C"
IT WOULD UPROOT **THREE** KINGS OR KINGDOMS.

Your BIBLE says:

1. **Daniel 7:8**—As Daniel considered the ten horns, "there came up among them another Little Horn, before whom there were THREE of the first horns PLUCKED UP by the ROOTS."

2. **Daniel 7:20**—The Little Horn, "before whom THREE FELL."

3. **Daniel 7:24**—The Little Horn "shall SUBDUE THREE kings."

HISTORY testifies:

First of all, let's get the whole picture by examining the historical background of these verses. Remember that through the prophet Daniel, God foretold the breakup of the Roman Empire into ten "toes" or "horns."[36] The TEN HORNS of the Fourth Beast in Daniel 7 represent the TEN KINGDOMS into which Rome was divided when barbarian tribes carved up the empire.[37] They are:

✦ ✦ ✦

- Anglo-Saxons: *England*
- Alamanni: *Germany*
- Burgundians: *Switzerland*
- Franks: *France*
- Lombards: *Italy*
- Suevi: *Portugal*
- Visigoths: *Spain*

- **Heruli**
- **Vandals**
- **Ostrogoths**

After the Roman Empire crumbled in A. D. 476, the Papacy began to assert its power and sovereignty. Most of the barbarian nations into which the Roman Empire split accepted the Catholic faith. But Papal ambitions were hindered by three Arian powers: the HERULI, the VANDALS, and the OSTROGOTHS. [38] In the list above, note that *no modern names* are given these three, for as Daniel had predicted they were "plucked up by the roots" and no longer exist.

Seven of the ten kingdoms survive to this day, grown into modern nations on the map of Europe. But while those seven are significant twentieth-century powers, the other three have disappeared from the stage of history just as God foretold. The prophecy was so remarkably fulfilled that no one but historians ever heard of the Heruli and Ostrogoths! And the only vestige left of the Vandals is the name we give those who wreck and ruin things, as the Vandals pillaged and plundered.

Let's review for a moment how this came about by journeying back in time to the late fifth century: The HERULI occupied Italy, the VANDALS dominated North Africa from the city of Carthage, and the OSTROGOTHS [39] settled near the Danube in what is modern Yugoslavia and Bulgaria. These Arian powers were a thorn in the side of the Papacy because Arians everywhere bitterly opposed the teachings and claims of the Papal hierarchy. But Prophecy declared that the Little Horn symbolizing the Papacy would rise to supreme power and in reaching this position would "subdue three kings." Did that happen? History answers, "Yes!"

1. THE HERULI

It was the barbarian Germanic tribe called the Heruli that invaded Italy and struck the final blow in what we call "the fall of the Roman Empire." [40] In 476 their leader ODOACER removed the last Roman Emperor, Romulus Augustulus, and proclaimed himself king. But the fact that the Heruli were powerful Arians posed some problems for the Pope. Obviously the spread of Arianism would check the onward march of Catholicism. Possession of Italy and its renowned capital by people of Arian persuasion would be fatal to the supremacy of a Catholic bishop.

But the Pope had a friend and ally in Zeno, the Byzantine Emperor who reigned at Constantinople. Zeno, too, was concerned about the Heruli who had overthrown the Roman Emperor. At the same time, Zeno became fearful of the Arian Ostrogoths who, encamped near Constantinople, were becoming increasingly restless. When Theodoric, king of the Ostrogoths, wrote to Zeno complaining that it was impossible for him to restrain his men within the impoverished province they occupied and asking Zeno's permission to lead them to a more favorable region they might conquer and possess, Zeno gave him permission to march against Odoacer and take possession of Italy.

By this clever move, Zeno accomplished two things: Not only would the Ostrogoths be occupied in military engagements far away and so be removed as a potential threat to Constantinople, but also—no matter which tribe won the contest in Italy, the Heruli or the Ostrogoths—there'd be one less Arian tribe for the Pope and Zeno to contend with. After five years of fighting, the Ostrogoths fulfilled their mission and in 493 destroyed the Heruli, who then disappeared from history. [41]

In this way the Catholic Emperor Zeno eliminated one of the three Arian "horns." But the conquest of the Heruli by the Ostrogoths failed to solve the Pope's problems, for it meant Italy was still occupied by an Arian power. As Cardinal Newman put it: "Odoacer [king of the Heruli] was sinking before Theodoric [king of the Ostrogoths], and the Pope was exchanging one Arian master for another." [42]

2. THE VANDALS

Another Germanic barbarian tribe were the Vandals, who maintained a kingdom in North Africa from A. D. 429 to 534, with Carthage as their capital. In 455 the Vandals sacked Rome, storming through the city, plundering, raping, destroying. The term "vandalism" became proverbial for ruthless, malicious destruction.

Since the Vandals, as Arians, opposed the Papacy, something had to be done to remove both them and the Arian Ostrogoths occupying Italy. In 527 Justinian ascended the throne to become Byzantine Emperor in Constantinople. Deeply committed to religious affairs, the Catholic Justinian elevated the bishop of Rome to be the "HEAD of ALL the holy churches" in A. D. 533, as mentioned in Clue "B" above. But that edict could not go into practical effect, as both Pope and Emperor well knew, until the Arian enemies were removed.

To accomplish that, in 533 Justinian commissioned his finest general, Belisarius, to sail with a large army from Constantinople to North Africa and destroy the Vandals. This he succeeded in doing in 534. The *Encyclopedia Britannica* says of the Vandals:

> "They were utterly defeated by Belisarius. . . . Thus, in one campaigning season the Vandal kingdom was definitively destroyed. The harsh measures taken by Justinian in restoring Roman rule in Africa led practically to the disappearance of the Vandals and their Arianism. The churches were restored to the Catholics. . . . Thereafter the Vandals played no further part in history." [43]

The second of the three Arian "horns" had been "plucked up by the roots."

3. THE OSTROGOTHS

So far, so good. But the third Arian power, the Ostrogoths, still occupied Italy and the city of Rome and dominated the Catholic Pope. Therefore, "Justinian declared war [against them] in 535, the year after Belisarius had completed the overthrow of the Vandals in Africa." [44] From his position in Africa, Belisarius obeyed orders to turn north with a fleet against the Arian Ostrogoths in Italy. He invaded Sicily in 535 and in 536 took Naples. In December 536 he marched unopposed into Rome with a mere 5,000 men. When the Ostrogoths counterattacked by surrounding Rome with 150,000 men, [45] General Belisarius was virtually made a prisoner inside the city he hoped to liberate.

However, Belisarius triumphed when "reinforcements were sent and he was able to rout the enemy," [46] driving the Goths from Rome once and for all in March, 538. Pockets of resistance held out here and there in Italy for a number of years till the Catholic general Narses annihilated all but a few of the Ostrogoths. Even for the survivors, laments the *Shorter Cambridge Medieval History,* "nothing remained but to die." [47] Their epitaph reads: "The Ostrogoths thereafter had NO national existence." [48]

When the Ostrogoths disappeared as a great and powerful people, the last of the three Arian "horns" of Daniel 7:8 had passed away. The crucial military event that lay behind this fact was the calamitous defeat of Ostrogothic Rome in 538 when, says Thomas Hodgkin in *Italy and Her Invaders,* Catholic soldiers "dug the grave of the Gothic monarchy." [49] English historian George Finlay states that "With the conquest of Rome by Belisarius . . . commences the history of the Middle Ages." [50] And of course the period known as the Middle Ages is, roughly speaking, the age of the Papacy.

Three "horns," then, were "plucked up by the roots" and disappeared from history. The HERULI were conquered in 493, the VANDALS were destroyed in 534, and the OSTROGOTHS were driven from Rome in 538. History leaves no room for doubt that the Papacy—Daniel's "Little Horn"—through its allies engineered these acts of conquest.

This fact is admitted by a loyal Italian son of the Roman Church, Niccolo Machiavelli, who says: "Nearly all the wars which the northern barbarians carried on in Italy, it may be remarked, were occasioned by the PONTIFFS; and the hordes with which the country was inundated, were generally called in by them." [51]

We've examined the evidence and found the facts quite clear regarding the three conquered kings. A fascinating sidelight is this: Though the Pope's triple crown officially symbolizes his supposed triple kingship,[52] it's interesting to note that in former days crowns of conquered kings were placed on the head of their conqueror.[53] How fitting, therefore, that the Pope wears a triple crown!

CLUE "D"
IT WOULD BE A "GREAT CITY"
WITH THE MYSTICAL NAME "BABYLON."

Your BIBLE says:

1. **Revelation 17:18**—"that GREAT CITY, which REIGNETH OVER the kings of the earth."

2. **Revelation 18:18**—"What city is like unto this GREAT CITY!"

3. **Revelation 17:5**—"Mystery, BABYLON the great."

4. **Revelation 18:2**—"BABYLON the great is fallen, is fallen, and is become the habitation of devils, and the hold of every foul spirit."

5. **Revelation 14:8**—"BABYLON is fallen, is fallen, that GREAT CITY."

6. **Revelation 18:10**—"Alas, alas, that GREAT CITY BABYLON, that mighty city!"

7. **Revelation 18:16 &19**—"Alas, alas, that GREAT CITY . . . !"

8. **Revelation 18:21**—"Thus with violence shall that GREAT CITY BABYLON be thrown down, and shall be found no more at all."

✦ ✦ ✦

HISTORY testifies:

History tells us that when John wrote, "Babylon is fallen, is fallen, that great city. . . . Babylon the great is fallen, is fallen," [54] he could not have been referring to the literal historical city of Babylon. Ancient Babylon had *already* fallen centuries before and lay in utter ruins, completely uninhabited, as God had predicted in His curse on that wicked city/empire. [55] The apostle John was as well aware of this fact as anyone else when he wrote the Book of Revelation in the First Century.

The apostle Peter, too, could not have been referring to literal Babylon when he wrote that "The church that is at Babylon . . . saluteth you," [56] for there was no church or any other human institution in the desolate ruins of ancient Babylon. Obviously, therefore, the name "Babylon" here must have a different meaning—a symbolic meaning—and it does! It symbolically represents the city of ROME, as we shall see.

"A TALE OF TWO CITIES" — BABYLON & ROME

Charles Dickens' historical novel about the French Revolution concerned Paris and London. But let's focus now on the twin cities of BABYLON and ROME. It's easy to see why Jews and early Christians used "Babylon" as a code-word or nickname for Rome. For as we examine LITERAL Babylon of ancient times and FIGURATIVE "Babylon" or Rome, we find a remarkable series of historic parallels. Note the following comparisons:

1. BABYLON was the dominant warring power of its day.
   ROME was the dominant warring power of its own era.
2. BABYLON was God's predicted instrument of punishment on His people, just as ROME was later. [57]
3. BABYLON conquered Israel. Centuries later, ROME also conquered Israel.
4. BABYLON destroyed the first Jerusalem Temple— ROME destroyed the second.
5. Each carried sacred vessels from the Jewish Temple back to BABYLON in the East and ROME in the West. [58]
6. BABYLON completely destroyed the city of Jerusalem. ROME, too, completely destroyed and devastated the city of Jerusalem.
7. BABYLON carried away surviving Jews into captivity: ROME likewise carried away many Jews into captivity. [59]
8. ROME was like BABYLON not just historically and militarily but religiously. Ancient BABYLON began the practice of astrology with its

pagan worship of the sun, moon, and stars. This nature worship "worshipped and served the creature more than the Creator." [60] ROME was just as confused in its religious practices:

> "Of all the pagan religions practiced by the civilized peoples of the past it can be said that none was less endowed with ethical and spiritual principles than the Roman religion. The religion of the Latins . . . was little more than a form of *nature worship* or a rudimentary anthropomorphism." [61]

No Jews or Christians living in John's day could fail to see the obvious parallels. For ROME was BABYLON all over again. No wonder they regarded Rome this way. When they saw Rome so closely follow Babylon's footsteps, they probably thought, *"Here we go again!"* As Babylon's "carbon copy," Rome provides a perfect example of History repeating itself!

With this background we can appreciate the force of the statement by Dr. William Smith in the "Babylon" entry of his *Dictionary of the Bible:*

> "BABYLON, in the Apocalypse [that is, the Book of Revelation], is the symbolic name by which ROME is denoted. Rev. 14:8; 17:18. The power of ROME was regarded by the later Jews as was that of BABYLON by their forefathers."

Any who seek an alternative interpretation find it hard to suggest another CITY to match the Babylon/Rome combination. Ancient powers like Assyria, Persia, Egypt, and Greece were kingdoms or nations, NOT cities. None of them could be designated "that great city" as could both Babylon and Rome.

Roman Catholic writers also acknowledge this. For example, Cardinal Gibbons, the famed late archbishop of Baltimore, declared: "'BABYLON,' from which Peter addresses his first epistle, is understood by learned annotators, Protestant and Catholic, to refer to ROME." [62]

Manuel de Lacunza (1731-1801), himself a Jesuit Catholic priest, wrote fearlessly on Antichrist and maintained that Peter's term "Babylon" is not literal BABYLON on the Euphrates but ROME on the Tiber. [63]

And the Roman Catholic Bible itself, the Douay Version, makes this footnote comment on the word "BABYLON" in 1 Peter 5:13—"Figuratively, ROME." Another Catholic version, the Confraternity of Christian Doctrine translation, says in a footnote on Revelation 14:8—"BABYLON: in Jewish and Christian circles, BABYLON was a symbol for ROME."

As for persecution of God's people, what ancient Babylon did to literal Israel (the Jews), spiritual Babylon did—and will yet do—to spiritual Israel (the Christian church).

"What's in a Name?"

The very name, "ROMAN Catholic Church," pinpoints the fact that the Papacy fits this clue. The imperial city of Rome was in fact "the great city" John describes in Revelation 17:18: "that GREAT CITY, which REIGNETH OVER the kings of the earth." Remember that

1. John wrote this verse using the present tense, and
2. the Empire emanating from the city of Rome in John's day was a great world power. Luke 2:1 proves this: "There went out a decree from Caesar Augustus, that all the WORLD should be taxed."

Thomas Cranmer (1489-1556), as Archbishop of Canterbury, was the highest-ranking clergyman in England. Through study of God's Word, he became convinced that the Pope is the prophesied Antichrist of Scripture. And he had the courage of his convictions. When Catholic Queen Mary came to the throne of England, she was called "Bloody Mary" for her cruel persecution of Protestants, and Archbishop Cranmer was burned ALIVE at the stake as a martyr.

Note Cranmer's insight into this text—Revelation 17:18—"'The woman which thou sawest is that GREAT CITY which REIGNETH OVER the kings of the earth.' Now what other city reigned at that time, or at any time since, over the Christian kings of the earth, but only Rome? Whereof it followeth Rome to be the seat of Antichrist, and the Pope to be the very Antichrist himself. I could prove the same by many other scriptures, old writers, and strong reasons." [64]

Archbishop Cranmer did not make these claims lightly but sealed his words with his life, even when facing a most painful death.

CLUE "E"

It would be UNLIKE the first ten kingdoms. That is, it would be "diverse" or different from the other nations of modern Europe.

Your BIBLE says:

1. **Daniel 7:7**—The terrible fourth beast "was DIVERSE from all the beasts that were before it."

2. **Daniel 7:19, RSV**—"Then I desired to know the truth concerning the fourth beast, which was DIFFERENT from all the rest."

3. **Daniel 7:23**—"The fourth beast shall be the fourth kingdom upon earth [The Living Bible says, "This fourth animal . . . is the fourth WORLD POWER that will rule the earth"], which shall be DIVERSE from all kingdoms."

4. **Daniel 7:24**—"He [the Little Horn] shall be DIVERSE from the first." That is, the "Little Horn" would be different from the first ten horns or kingdoms. [65]

HISTORY testifies:

History tells us that Rome was "the fourth world power" spoken of by Daniel, following Babylon, Medo-Persia, and Greece (see Chapter 15, above). History further tells us that PAGAN ROME, with its vast Empire, was succeeded by PAPAL ROME, with its far-flung influence.

God, through Daniel, exhibited the four great world empires under successive images of fierce animals: the first three resembling a lion, a bear, and a leopard. The fourth beast—denoting PAGAN Rome—was not only UNLIKE the other three, but was so different from anything else in the animal world that Daniel could hardly describe it.[66] Then we're told that the "Little Horn"— denoting PAPAL Rome—would be UNLIKE the other horns. Let's examine this "Little Horn" now to see what makes it "different."

1. The first ten horns were the ten divisions of the Roman Empire, which became the modern nations of Western Europe. Those were and are all POLITICAL in nature. This new "Little Horn" would be different or "diverse" in that it proved to be a RELIGIOUS power or at least a hybrid, being part religious and part political—a religio-political entity.

The Papacy DIFFERS from all other purely political powers, for it is BOTH religious AND political. It is religious, of course, being the spiritual head of the Roman Catholic Church. But it's also a political entity, issuing its own Vatican postage stamps, maintaining its own troops (the Pope's Swiss Guard), and exchanging ambassadors on a formal basis with most governments of the world. The Papacy is, therefore, a combination CHURCH/STATE power, uniquely different from all other nations—thus fulfilling the prophecy and fitting the clue.

2. The place of the Papacy in world affairs is obvious to all: The Pope, a *religious* leader, speaks out on *political* questions with all the authority of a head of state. The recent appointment of a full United States ambassador to the head of the Roman Catholic Church underscores again the religio-political nature of the Papacy, a power DIFFERENT from all other kingdoms or nations the world has seen before or since its rise.

Vatican
Postage
Stamps

The diplomatic relations which the Papacy had during the Dark Ages, and which have recently been restored, cause the Pope and his ambassadors to feel perfectly at home as they negotiate with the world's civil rulers. Yet we never read of Jesus or the apostles courting the favor of the Caesars of Rome. Christ and His followers were not politicians interested in earthly governments, and were they on earth today, royal palaces would be strange places to them. It's ironic that the leader of the world's most POLITICALLY-involved church claims to be the vicar of Christ, when Jesus said: "My kingdom is NOT of this world." [67]

3. Prophecy details the fact that this Beast power depicted by the Little Horn DIFFERS from the other kingdoms mentioned, though in some ways it resembles them: It was a horn, but with eyes and a mouth.[68] It would be a kingdom like the rest, but its king would be a Pope, a religious overseer clothed in priestly robes. This kingdom would differ from all predecessors because it would claim religious as well as civil authority, governing men's SOULS as well as their BODIES.

It seems clear, therefore, that here we have "a different kind of animal"— a political / ecclesiastical HYBRID!

CLUE "F"

IT WOULD BE A **RELIGIOUS** POWER

THAT WOULD BE "WORSHIPPED."

Here truth becomes "stranger than fiction." To realize that this diabolical Beast power, the Antichrist, would disguise himself in religious garb and actually be worshipped by millions all over the world is almost incredible, but—

Your BIBLE says:

1. **2 Thessalonians 2:3-4**—"That man of sin . . . exalteth himself above all that is called God, or that is WORSHIPPED."

2. **Revelation 13:3-4**—"All the world . . . WORSHIPPED the Beast."

3. **Revelation 13:8**—"All that dwell upon the earth shall WORSHIP him, whose names are NOT written in the Book of Life."

4. **Revelation 13:12**—"He . . . causeth the earth and them which dwell therein to WORSHIP the . . . Beast."

5. **Revelation 13:15**—"The Image of the Beast should both speak, and cause that as many as would *NOT* WORSHIP the Beast should be KILLED."

6. **Revelation 20:4**—This verse speaks of martyrs, "them that were beheaded for the witness of Jesus, and for the Word of God, and which had *NOT* WORSHIPPED the Beast, neither his image, neither had received his Mark upon their foreheads, or in their hands."

7. **Revelation 14:9-10**—God solemnly declares: "If any man WORSHIP the Beast and his image, and receive his Mark in his forehead, or in his hand, the same shall drink of the wine of the wrath of God, which is poured out without mixture into the cup of His indignation."

8. **Revelation 16:2**—The Seven Last Plagues are "poured out . . . upon the men which had the Mark of the Beast, and upon them which WORSHIPPED his image."

9. **Revelation 19:20**—"The false prophet . . . deceived them that had received the Mark of the Beast, and them that WORSHIPPED his image."

HISTORY testifies:

In the past some have misinterpreted the Bible clues and taught that the Beast was a political entity—a leader like Hitler or an ideology like Communism. But they were wrong—both Hitler and Communism have passed away without fulfilling these prophecies. Lest we mistake the Antichrist for some POLITICAL tyrant who opposes God, the apostles Paul and John both identify him as a RELIGIOUS power who is the object of WORSHIP. The pen of Inspiration depicts "that man of sin" as one who exalts himself as a god to be worshipped. [69]

No one familiar with the Papacy could fail to see how closely it fulfills this amazing prophecy. Consider this question:

HOW Is Worship SHOWN?

By its very nature, worship is such an intensely personal experience that it's impossible to observe or explain except through outward manifestations. Worshipping, like thinking, is an inward, subjective experience. That's why we cannot understand the essence of a person's worship any more than we can read his mind. But we can often tell something about a person's thoughts and mental processes by observing his actions—the things he SAYS and DOES.

Observe the outward manifestations of those who recognize the Pope as being at the pinnacle of the Roman Catholic hierarchy. How do they SPEAK about him? How do they ACT around him? They call him "Holy Father"—a title belonging to God alone.[70] Cardinal Bellarmine, one of the more illustrious princes of the Church, declared: "All names which in the Scriptures are applied to CHRIST, by virtue of which it is established that He is over the church, all the same names are applied to the POPE."[71] History records that the bishop of Rome, by assuming the titles of Holy Father, Universal Father, His Holiness, Sovereign Pontiff, Vicar of Christ, and Lord God the Pope, fulfills this prophecy and fits the clue.

But devout Roman Catholics not only refer to the Pope with exalted titles, they treat him with a respect that's elevated to reverence. They bow before him, fall on their knees before him, kneel at his feet to kiss his ring, *etc.* The author has in his possession many photographs from the media showing people—priests and laymen alike—bowing before or falling absolutely prostrate at the feet of the Pope in adulation, adoration, or worship. There are many churches within the Christian communion, but in no other instance do we find that the head—the earthly leader or president—of the church is bowed down to and, presumably, worshipped.

In contrast to this, PETER—supposedly the first Pope, according to Catholic teaching—did NOT accept worship from a fellow mortal when Cornelius fell down at Peter's feet:

> "As Peter was coming in, Cornelius met him, and fell down at his feet, and worshipped him. But Peter took him up, saying, STAND UP; I myself also am a MAN."[72]

Similarly, the apostle JOHN, so dazzled by the awe-inspiring angel God had sent, said, "I fell at his feet to worship him [the angel]. But he said to me, 'See that you do not do that! I am your fellow servant. . . . Worship God!'"[73] And on another occasion, John said, "I fell down to worship before the feet of the angel who showed me these things. Then he said to me, 'See that you do not do that. For I am your fellow servant. . . . Worship God.'" [74]

Note that on both these occasions the ANGEL, as a humble "fellow servant" of God, corrected John and refused to accept his worship. The angel told John to worship God alone. Now, if even this mighty ANGEL refused to allow men to bow down to or worship him, how can a mere man like the Pope allow people everywhere to bow down to him?

At this point some very devoted, very sincere Catholics may object by saying, "No matter what some people think, we do not 'worship' the Pope." Fortunately, we need not worry about what people think—but we should be concerned about what God thinks and what He says in His Word. And the Bible does equate certain actions with worship. Both Peter's and John's experiences quoted above show that falling down at a person's feet implies worship.

And how did God look upon Baal worship? Baal (pronounced "BAY-uhl") was a pagan god of nature whose worship was quite popular in Old Testament times. At one point God's prophet Elijah was so discouraged he sat down and cried, "I alone am left"—thinking he was the last person remaining faithful to God. But the Lord corrected him: "Yet I have reserved seven thousand in Israel, all whose KNEES have not BOWED to Baal, and every MOUTH that has not KISSED him." [75]

Thus in Heaven's Book, at least, those who show devotion to the Pope by bowing the knee and kissing his ring, are implying an inner worship by their outward actions, even though this may not be intended on their part.

Perhaps we shouldn't belabor the point, for more evidence will be seen along these lines, especially when we consider Clues "G," "N," "P," and "S." But whether or not one agrees that the Pope precisely fulfills this prophecy because he "exalteth himself above all that is called God, or that is worshipped," we can see that in this clue the Holy Spirit makes plain that the Antichrist must be a RELIGIOUS power—for he concerns himself with and accepts the "worship" of the people.

CLUE "G"
IT WOULD BE A CHURCH.

Your BIBLE says:

The Bible symbol of a WOMAN always represents a CHURCH. And the relationship between Christ and His church is symbolized by MARRIAGE. Christ is the "Bridegroom." His church is the "woman" who becomes His "bride."

Both Old and New Testaments give striking examples, as seen below:

1. **Isaiah 54:5-6**—"Thy Maker is thine HUSBAND, the Lord of hosts is His name. . . . For the Lord hath called thee as a WOMAN . . . and a WIFE of youth." Here is introduced the thought that the woman, the church, is the Lord's bride.

2. **Isaiah 62:5**—"As the BRIDEGROOM rejoiceth over the BRIDE, so shall thy God rejoice over thee."

3. **Jeremiah 3:14**—God says, "I am MARRIED unto you."

4. **Jeremiah 6:2**—"I have likened the daughter of Zion to a comely and delicate WOMAN." (In Isaiah 51:16 God says: "Zion, thou art My people.")

5. **Hosea 2:19-20**—"I will BETROTH thee unto Me forever; yea, I will BETROTH thee unto Me in righteousness: . . . I will even BETROTH thee unto Me in faithfulness."

6. **Matthew 9:14-15**—Christ clearly referred to Himself as "the Bridegroom." Please note: "Then came to Him the disciples of John [the Baptist], saying, Why do we and the Pharisees fast oft, but Thy disciples fast not? And Jesus said unto them, Can the children of the bridechamber mourn, as long as the Bridegroom is with them? but the days will come, when the Bridegroom shall be taken from them, and then shall they fast." Incidentally, John the Baptist's inspired statement that he is "the friend of the Bridegroom"—John 3:29—makes no sense to those who fail to recognize Christ as the Husband of His bride, the church.

7. **2 Corinthians 11:2**—"I am jealous over you with godly jealousy: for I have ESPOUSED you to one HUSBAND, that I may present you as a CHASTE VIRGIN to Christ."

8. **Revelation 19:7-9**—"The MARRIAGE of the Lamb is come, and His WIFE hath made herself ready." This chapter describes the awesome Second Coming of Christ, the Lamb of God. But His church, His bride, has nothing to fear, for she "hath made herself ready" for "the marriage supper of the Lamb."

9. **Revelation 17:3, 4, 6, 7, 9, 18**—John saw a "WOMAN" seated on a "beast." As we've just seen, God uses the symbol of a WOMAN to represent a CHURCH in both the Old and New Testaments.

Everything in the clue may be clear so far, but an important connection remains to be established between this "WOMAN" sitting upon a "beast" in Revelation 17 and the BEAST in Revelation 13.

The beast the woman sits on in Revelation 17:3 has *three features:*
- "full of NAMES OF BLASPHEMY"
- "having SEVEN HEADS"
- "and TEN HORNS."

The Beast of Revelation 13:1 exhibits *the same three features:*
- "upon his heads the NAME OF BLASPHEMY" [76]
- "having SEVEN HEADS"
- "and TEN HORNS."

As you read the many Bible clues presented in these pages, you'll see more clearly that the Beast power of Revelation 13 represents the Papacy. And since, as we just noted above, the beast ridden by the woman in Revelation 17 is the same as the Beast in Revelation 13, both depict the Papacy.

But a question may arise: How could this *beast* of Revelation 17 represent the Papacy IF the *woman* riding it also represents the same? Many scholars have answered this question by pointing out that in Revelation 13 no distinction is made between the religious and the political aspects of the Papacy. Here in Revelation 17 that distinction is now made—the *Beast* representing POLITICAL power and the *woman* representing RELIGIOUS power, as a woman always symbolizes a church.

HISTORY testifies:

Though at first glance we may be shocked to consider the prospect of Satan working within professedly Christian churches, this clue may, instead of shocking us, serve to confirm a hunch many of us have had all along: That there's something terribly WRONG with the world, and it even includes our churches!

If you are shocked to find this clue pointing to a church, remember that in a good mystery, it's always the one you LEAST expect—like a whodunit in which "The butler did it." The Devil uses careful disguises, or else he could deceive very few.

This is one clue which obviously needs no documentation or proof: The term "woman" points to a church, and the Papacy is the ruling power of a church. What's amazing, however, is that the Antichrist/Beast power should be found within the professedly Christian church! Yet isn't that just the diabolical strategy we'd expect Satan to use? He knows that, to some people's minds, that's an unbeatable alibi. But is it, really? We all know that Judas, for instance, served the Devil very well from within Christ's inner circle.

In the early centuries, Satan attacked God's church from without, by pagan persecution. But his efforts back-fired when the church continued to grow—historian Tertullian observed: "The blood of martyrs is the seed of the Church." Therefore . . .

> "Satan is not fighting churches; he is joining them. He does more harm by sowing tares [weeds] than by pulling up wheat. He accomplishes more by imitation than by outright opposition." [77]

So the Devil changed his tactics to the familiar "If you can't beat 'em, join 'em" technique. Just as Ku Klux Klan groups deceitfully use the Cross of Christ as a symbol of lynching, bigotry, and hatred, Satan began working from within God's church through compromise and corruption. Sad to say, his efforts here have met with brilliant success.

Thus we see that the Beast would be a religious power working as a CHURCH.

CLUE "H"
IT WOULD BE, IN GOD'S EYES,
A CORRUPT CHURCH.

Your BIBLE says:

As shown by the preceding clue, a woman in prophecy always represents a church. If the "woman" is described as pure, she represents a pure, undefiled church. If, however, the "woman" is described as corrupt, she represents a corrupt, impure church.

When Israel turned away from God because she allowed other gods and false religions to seduce her, it was likened to *violation of the marriage vow*. God symbolized it as *spiritual adultery*. It made Him very unhappy. Note what He says in the following verses:

1. **Jeremiah 3:1, 8**—"Thou hast played the HARLOT with many lovers; yet return again to Me, saith the Lord. . . . For all the causes whereby backsliding Israel committed ADULTERY I had put her away, and given her a bill of DIVORCE; yet her treacherous sister Judah feared not, but went and played the HARLOT also."

2. **Jeremiah 3:20**—"As a wife treacherously DEPARTETH FROM her husband, so have ye dealt treacherously with Me, O house of Israel, saith the Lord."

3. **Jeremiah 31:32**—God says His chosen people broke His covenant, "although I was an HUSBAND unto them, saith the Lord."

4. **Ezekiel 16:28, 32**—"Thou hast played the WHORE . . . yea, thou hast played the HARLOT . . . as a wife that committeth ADULTERY, which taketh strangers instead of her husband!"

5. **Ezekiel 23:1-49**—Again Ezekiel devotes an entire chapter to the SPIRI-TUAL ADULTERY of God's people: "Aholibah" is specifically identified as "Jerusalem" (verse 4). The "WHOREDOMS" repeatedly spoken of (13 times in this chapter alone!) are figurative and not necessarily literal, for God makes a spiritual application: "with their IDOLS have they committed adultery. . . . They have defiled My sanctuary . . . and have profaned My Sabbaths" (verses 37-38).

6. **Hosea 1:2**—"For the land hath committed great WHOREDOM, departing from the Lord."

7. **Hosea 3:1**—God strangely requested His prophet Hosea to marry "an ADULTERESS, according to the love of the Lord toward the children of ISRAEL, who look to other gods."

8. **Hosea 4:12**—"My people . . . have gone a WHORING from under their God."

9. **Hosea 9:1**—"O Israel . . . thou hast gone a WHORING from thy God."

The NEW TESTAMENT uses similar language to address nominal Christians who seek the friendship of the world above the favor of God.

10. **James 4:4**—"Ye ADULTERERS and ADULTERESSES, know ye not that the friendship of the world is enmity with God? whosoever therefore will be a friend of the world is the enemy of God."

The Book of Revelation emphatically and repeatedly represents Babylon as an IMPURE woman.

11. **Revelation 17:1**—"the great WHORE"—HARLOT in modern versions

12. **Revelation 17:15**—"the WHORE"

13. **Revelation 17:16**—"the WHORE"

14. **Revelation 18:5**—"HER SINS have reached unto heaven, and God hath remembered HER INIQUITIES."

15. **Revelation 19:2**—"the great WHORE, which did corrupt the earth with HER FORNICATION."

HISTORY testifies:

God makes it plain: this "woman" symbolizing a church is corrupt and wicked, guilty of spiritual adultery. Any church that departs from the plain truths of God's Word to adulterate and contaminate "the faith once delivered to the saints"[78] is unfaithful, to say the least.

That the Papacy has unflinchingly, unblushingly borrowed practices from polluted pagan sources is a fact confirmed by history. It's beyond the scope of this book to trace the pagan roots of such practices as IDOL adoration (bowing down to IMAGES), the ROSARY, celebrating our Lord's birth on DECEMBER 25 (right after the winter solstice of the SUN), the festival of EASTER (with its fertility symbols of colored eggs and bunny rabbits), SUNDAY worship, and other man-made traditions which have no basis whatsoever in Scripture.[79] When a church's doctrines and practices are little more than "baptized paganism," she is no longer the pure "bride of Christ."

Honest critics even within the Roman Catholic Church have applied this prophecy to the Church of Rome. The Italian writer Dante did so in his classic *Divine Comedy* [80] two centuries before the rise of the Protestant Reformation. According to a leading German Catholic theologian and professor of church history, *The Divine Comedy* was "the boldest, most unsparing, most incisive, denunciatory song that has ever been composed." [81]

Dante, a faithful Catholic and loyal son of the Church, nevertheless poured his indignation into his masterpiece, consigning Popes to the hottest hell for their misdeeds. [82] He declared:

> "The Church of Rome,
> Mixing two governments that ill assort, [83]
> Hath miss'd her footing, fallen into the mire,
> And there herself the burden much defiled." [84]

Dante deplored the fact that the pastors or shepherds of God's flock were transformed into wolves and that religious teachers had laid aside the Gospel, thinking more on the Vatican than on Nazareth. [85]

> "In shepherd's clothing, greedy wolves below
> Range wide o'er all the pastures. Arm of God!
> Why longer sleep'st Thou? Cahorsines and Gascons
> Prepare to quaff our blood." [86]

Reverence for the keys of Peter restrains Dante from using still stronger language concerning Papal corruption and the greed or avarice of the church:

> "If reverence of the keys restrain'd me not,
> Which thou in happier time didst hold, I yet
> *Severer speech* might use. Your *avarice*
> O'ercasts the world with mourning, under foot
> Treading the good, and raising bad men up. . . .
> Of *gold* and *silver* ye have made your god." [87]

Dante sadly felt—and stated in writing—that, as things then stood, his church was "a shameless whore" or "harlot" who "mingled kisses" with earthly kings.[88] Boldly, Dante asserted that the Pope had USURPED God's place on earth![89]

Another Italian member of the Roman Catholic Church was a Dominican priest named GIROLAMO SAVONAROLA, a preaching friar who fearlessly dared to raise his voice against the corruption he saw everywhere in his church.

Encyclopedia Britannica states that Savonarola became a leader in Florence, "the most civilized city in Italy,"[90] which had also been the city of Dante a century and a half before. "He introduced a democratic government, the best the city ever had. . . . The results he obtained were amazing." But at that time the "Pope was the corrupt Alexander VI." Savonarola "appeared to refer to the Pope's scandalous private life, and the latter took offense at this. A college of theologians found nothing to criticize in what the friar had said," so he continued his sermons. "As Savonarola's authority grew, the Pope tried to win him over by offering him a cardinal's hat," but the offer was refused.

Finally "Savonarola was taken like a common criminal. . . . After examination by a commission of his worst enemies and after SAVAGE TORTURE, it was yet necessary to falsify the record of the inquiry if he were to be charged with any crimes. But his fate was sealed." Savonarola's voice was silenced in 1498 when he was HANGED and BURNED.

The writer of the *Encyclopedia Britannica* article, an Italian scholar holding a department chair at the University of Florence, asserts that "Savonarola's quarrel was with the CORRUPTION of the clergy, of whom [Pope] Alexander VI was merely the most scandalous example."

The shocking story unfolds. . . .

"COME OUT OF HER, MY PEOPLE"

Jesus said, "Ye shall know the truth, and the truth shall make you free."[91] I have many close friends and relatives in the Roman Catholic Church. Because I love them, I want them to know the truth as God's Word presents it. The simple, straightforward facts should be known by all people, but most of all by Catholics, since they are most intimately touched by the system described as the Beast.

It's not easy or pleasant to re-evaluate something so personal as one's religion. It's devastating to re-appraise the beliefs of a lifetime. But we mustn't fall into the trap of blindly refusing to examine the facts and spurning the lessons the Savior would teach.

God's loving voice calls, "Come OUT of her, MY people."[92] But we may be torn between heeding God's call and strong cultural traditions. We may wonder, "How can so many people be wrong?"—forgetting that the Papacy grew strong in times when the masses COULD NOT READ.

Also, family background creates pressure. We may think, "If this religion was good enough for my grandfather, it's good enough for me." But our ancestors were not encouraged to study the Bible for themselves. They were taught that ONLY PRIESTS could understand and interpret Scripture. They did what priests and Pope told them to do—not knowing there was no "Thus saith the Lord" behind it. Many even among Protestants are too busy, too lazy, or too disinterested to read and study God's Word. Our forefathers lived up to the light they knew, but most never learned the Bible truths you're learning.

You see, if people were never willing to accept new light, new lessons, new principles, a cannibal would never be converted, Mary Magdalene would have continued life as a miserable prostitute, and the great apostle Paul would have remained a Jew zealously persecuting the early Church.

Friend, do you hear God's loving voice calling *you* as you read these words today?

CLUE "I"
IT WOULD BE A CHURCH BUILT ON
SEVEN HILLS OR MOUNTAINS.

Your BIBLE says:

Revelation 17:3-9—John the Revelator "saw a woman sit upon a scarlet-coloured beast, full of names of blasphemy, having SEVEN HEADS and ten horns. . . . And the angel said unto me, Wherefore didst thou marvel? I will tell thee the mystery of the woman, and of the beast that carrieth her, which hath seven heads and ten horns. . . . And here is the mind which hath wisdom. The seven heads are SEVEN MOUNTAINS, on which the woman SITTETH."

The Greek word translated "mountains" here in the King James Version means to *rise* or *rear*, as any land that's lifted above the plain. It may be translated either "hill" or "mountain." For instance, the King James Version renders it "hill" in Matthew 5:14—"A city that is set on an HILL cannot be hid." Modern Bible versions translate the word that way in Revelation 17:9. Please note:

"Now think hard: His seven heads represent a certain CITY built on SEVEN HILLS where this WOMAN has her residence."[93]

Thus God gives divine insight to help us identify this "woman," this church.

HISTORY testifies:

Ancient Rome is proverbial as "THE CITY BUILT ON SEVEN HILLS."

1. "The seven hills on which ROME was first built have long been famous," states *World Book Encyclopedia.*[94] The article goes on to name the hills, such as the PALATINE HILL (where most early Roman *palaces* were built), the CAPITOLINE HILL (site of the *Capitol*), and five others.

2. Under the entry "seven-hilled," *Webster's* large unabridged dictionary says: "as, the Seven-hilled City, that is, ROME, Italy." Under the entry "seven hills" we read: "A group of seven hills; especially [capitalized], the seven hills upon and about which was built the city of ROME."[95] Illustrating the entry is a MAP with the seven hills and their names sketched in. (Reproduced on the next page.)

3. In the Milestones of History Series, editor S. G. F. Brandon states simply: "ROME was founded . . . on the group of SEVEN HILLS above the Tiber [River]."[96]

4. The late Mario Lanza was a gifted singer of the caliber of Enrico Caruso, in whose movie biography he starred. But another MGM film he starred in was significantly titled: *The SEVEN HILLS of ROME*—so this clue is no mystery even to Hollywood!

5. John Cotton (1564-1652), learned Puritan minister of Plymouth and Boston, had no trouble making the identification from God's clue: "The seven heads are seven Mountaines *[sic]* on which the Woman sitteth, which are the mountaines of the City of ROME: it is built upon seven hills."[97]

6. Timothy Dwight was an educator, Congregational minister, and writer who from 1795 till his death in 1817 was college president of Yale. Note his straightforward acceptance of the fact that the prophecy points to Rome: "From the angel interpreter we know, that the seven heads are the SEVEN MOUNTAINS of ROME, the great city which at that time reigned with undivided empire over the kingdoms of the earth; and that the ten horns are the ten kingdoms, into which that empire was finally divided."[98]

< from the *Merriam-Webster Dictionary*, Unabridged >

sev′en–hilled′ (66), *adj.* Having or comprising seven hills; as, the **Seven–hilled City**, that is, Rome, Italy.
seven hills. A group of seven hills; esp. [*cap.*], the seven hills upon and about which was built the city of Rome. According to tradition, the original city of Romulus was built upon the *Palatine* hill (later the site of the palaces of the Caesars), though later he united with his settlement those upon the *Capitoline* and *Quirinal*. The *Caelian* was said to have been added by Tullus Hostilius; the *Aventine*, by Ancus Martius; the *Esquiline* and *Viminal*, by Servius Tullius, who built a wall (the *Servian Wall*) around the whole group. The Capitoline hill (originally called the *Satur-*

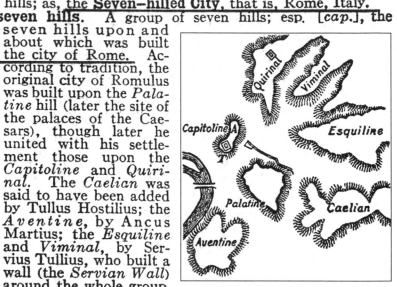

The Seven Hills of Rome. *A* Arx; *T* Tarpeian Rock.

nian) anciently comprised two peaks, the *Capitolium*, which was earlier known as the *Tarpeian rock*, and the *Arx*. In early times the hills, which are of volcanic origin, were very abrupt.

Eleven years later Dwight also wrote, again while president of Yale, that the "seven heads" were "in allusion to the SEVEN HILLS on which ROME was built." [99]

7. More examples could be given, but let's close with a statement from Dr. William Smith's *Dictionary of the Bible:* "ROME, the famous capital of the ancient world, is situated on the Tiber [River] at a distance of about 15 miles from its mouth. The 'SEVEN HILLS,' Revelation 17:9, which formed the nucleus of the ancient city, stand on the left bank." [100]

As we investigate this whole subject by following leads found in the Bible, we stand in awe as we realize that the God who loves each of us has given a multitude of very specific clues—even CONCRETE clues like this about Rome's famous "seven hills." Many people are not aware of these vital matters. No doubt few of our Catholic friends know these things. But God wants us to be enlightened. He wants us to exercise an intelligent faith and follow Him with our minds and our eyes wide open.

CLUE "J"
IT WOULD BE A *LARGE, WORLDWIDE* CHURCH.

Your BIBLE says:

1. **Revelation 17:1**—"I will show unto thee the judgment of the great whore that sitteth upon MANY WATERS."

2. **Revelation 17:15**—"The WATERS which thou sawest, where the whore sitteth, are PEOPLES, and MULTITUDES, and NATIONS, and TONGUES."

   These two verses, Revelation 17:1 & 15, show—through symbols interpreted by the Bible itself—that "many waters" means many "peoples . . . and nations." When God makes plain that MANY peoples and nations are involved, we understand He means a large, world-wide church.

3. **Revelation 14:8**—"She made ALL nations drink" of her wine.

4. **Revelation 18:3**—"ALL nations have drunk" of her wine.

5. **Revelation 18:23**—By her "sorceries were ALL nations deceived."

6. **Revelation 13:3-4**—"ALL the WORLD wondered after the Beast . . . and they worshipped the Beast."

7. **Revelation 13:8**—"ALL that dwell upon the earth shall worship him, whose names are NOT written in the Book of Life."

HISTORY testifies:

It's a matter of record that the GLOBAL expanse of the Roman Catholic Church fits this particular clue:

1. It has by far the LARGEST membership of any other Christian church on earth.

2. It is WORLDWIDE in its work and influence—unlike many smaller churches.

3. Its very *name*, "Catholic," means UNIVERSAL.

In point after point, clue after clue, we see the Beast power's portrait sketched by an Inspired hand. Again we find that another piece of the puzzle snaps into place!

CLUE "K"
IT WOULD USE A *LANGUAGE*
DIFFICULT FOR MOST TO UNDERSTAND.

Your BIBLE says:

1. **Daniel 8:23**—"A KING of FIERCE countenance, and understanding DARK SENTENCES, shall stand up." Here Daniel is quoting the verse below:

2. **Deuteronomy 28:48-50**—To punish His disobedient people, "The Lord shall . . . put a yoke of IRON upon thy neck. . . . The Lord shall bring a nation against thee from FAR, from the end of the earth, as swift as the eagle flieth; a nation whose TONGUE thou shalt NOT understand; a NATION of FIERCE countenance."

HISTORY testifies:

The verses quoted above enable any student of Scripture and history to recognize the following facts:

1. ROME was that warlike *"nation* of fierce countenance."

2. ROME was the *nation* God sent "from far, from the end of the earth."

3. CAESAR was that *"king* of fierce countenance."

4. CAESAR was the *king* "understanding [Latin's] dark sentences."

5. LATIN was the Roman "tongue thou [God's people] shalt not understand."

These verses clearly depict the ROMANS coming "far" from the western Mediterranean, which—when Moses wrote Deuteronomy in the 13th century Before Christ—was truly at "the end of the earth." ROME'S fierce legions came speaking their new, strange tongue—LATIN.

Centuries after the widespread conquests by Alexander the Great, in the time of Christ and the apostles, GREEK was the almost universal language of Western civilization. Greek spread throughout the world and became so widely known and deeply rooted that the Romans could not suppress it. Even in Italy, where Latin was the mother tongue, educated people, especially, used Greek as a second language. Matthew, Mark, Luke, and John—Peter and

Paul—James and Jude—all wrote the Bible's New Testament in Greek. But the fiercely warring legions of ROME spoke the strange language of LATIN few could understand.

EVIDENCE Too CLEAR to Be Misunderstood

But the Bible is even more explicit. The prophetic Book of Daniel, corroborated by the pages of history, offers evidence beyond all dispute. Let no one say this clue is "just a matter of interpretation," for man's ideas and interpretations needn't enter the picture. We'll let the Bible be its *own* interpreter. Let's look at the eighth chapter of Daniel's remarkable book (quoted below) and see what heavenly insight it offers.

Daniel 8:1-25 (verse numbers in parentheses)

"In the third year of the reign of [Babylon's] King Belshazzar a vision appeared unto me, even unto me Daniel. . . . (2) I saw in a vision . . . (3) a RAM which had two horns: and the two horns were high; but one was higher than the other, and the higher came up last. (4) I saw the RAM pushing westward, and northward, and southward; so that no beasts might stand before him, neither was there any that could deliver out of his hand; but he did according to his will, and became great. (5) And as I was considering, behold, an HE-GOAT came from the WEST on the face of the whole earth, and touched not the ground: and the GOAT had a notable horn between his eyes. . . . (7) And I saw him come close unto the RAM, and he . . . smote the RAM, and brake his two horns: and there was no power in the ram to stand before him, but he cast him to the ground, and stamped upon him: and there was none that could deliver the RAM out of his hand. (8) Therefore the HE-GOAT waxed very great: and when he was strong, the great horn was broken; and for it came up four notable ones toward the four winds of heaven. . . . (16) And I heard a man's voice . . . which called, and said, GABRIEL, make this man to understand the vision. (17) So he came near where I stood. . . . (19) And he said, Behold, I shall make thee know what shall be. . . . 20) The RAM which thou sawest having two horns are the kings of MEDIA and PERSIA. (21) And the rough GOAT is the king of GRECIA: and the great horn that is between his eyes is the FIRST KING. (22) Now that being broken, whereas four stood up for it, four kingdoms shall stand up out of the nation, but not in his power. (23) And in the LATTER TIME of their kingdom . . . a king of FIERCE countenance, and understanding DARK sentences, shall stand up. . . . (25) He shall also stand up against the Prince of princes."

Here the angel Gabriel gives Daniel the historical sequence, even "naming names" so there may be no mistake. Since prophecy and history are two sides of the same coin, let's see how Daniel's prophetic words were historically fulfilled:

1. In verse 20 Gabriel says the RAM represents the MEDO-PERSIAN Empire.

2. In verse 4 God says, "no beasts [kingdoms] might stand before him [the RAM], neither was there any that could deliver out of his hand." History records that Medo-Persia, the RAM, conquered even the mighty Babylonian Empire.

3. Scripture depicts the Medo-Persian Empire, a joint or dual power:

   a. by the breast and TWO ARMS of silver in the IMAGE of Nebuchadnezzar's dream (Daniel 2:32),

   b. by the BEAR RAISED UP on ONE side in Daniel's dream (Daniel 7:5), and

   c. by the RAM'S two horns of UNEQUAL length in Daniel's vision (Daniel 8:3, 20). Since history records that the PERSIANS became STRONGER than the MEDES, the one-sided, unequal symbolism is appropriate.

4. In verse 3 God says "the HIGHER [of the two horns] came up LAST." History records that though it rose LATER than Media, Persia became the dominant power. The Medes, however, were treated not as inferiors or as a subjugated people but as confederates in a joint empire.

5. In verse 21 the angel says the GOAT represents the GREEK Empire. History records that Greece conquered and succeeded the Medo-Persians.

6. In verse 5 God says the Grecian "HE-GOAT came from the WEST" to attack the Medo-Persian RAM. Greece, of course, was west of the Persian Empire.

7. In verse 21 Gabriel says "*the great* horn" of the goat represents the Greeks' "first king." History tells us—in the very same words—that this was Alexander *the Great!*

8. Verse 5 says that the "HE-GOAT . . . touched not the ground." This description of great swiftness depicts the astonishing speed of Alexander's conquests. In the parallel prophecy of Daniel 7:6, the Greek Empire is symbolized by "a leopard, which had upon the back of it FOUR WINGS." Though the leopard itself is a swift creature, its natural speed seems

inadequate to describe the amazing rapidity of Alexander's conquests. Daniel's symbolic dream showed the animal with wings added to it, not two but four, denoting superlative speed. That symbol fittingly describes the lightning speed with which Alexander and his Macedonians in less than a decade took possession of the largest empire the world had yet known. There's no other example in ancient times of such rapid troop movements on so large and successful a scale. Ancient Greek biographer Plutarch wrote: "Alexander . . . was sweeping swiftly through the world like a shooting star." [101]

9.　Verses 5 & 8 say that the Grecian "HE-GOAT came from the west on the face of the WHOLE EARTH. . . . Therefore the HE-GOAT waxed VERY GREAT." History records that Greece was a great world empire. Though the Medo-Persian Empire was great, larger than the mighty Babylonian expansion, it pushed toward three points of the compass—verse 4 says, "I saw the RAM pushing westward, and northward, and southward"— thus falling short of the world conquest to all four points by Greece and Rome.

10.　In verse 8 God says, "the HE-GOAT waxed very great: and when he was STRONG, the great horn was BROKEN." In most cases, a king's power is broken when he is WEAK, but Inspiration says in the case of the great horn representing Alexander it would happen "when he was strong." Alexander the Great died a young man of only 33. He did not die in battle but was "broken" in the prime of life at the very HEIGHT of his powers.

11.　In verses 8 & 22 the angel says that when "the great horn was broken," it was replaced by "four horns" or "four kingdoms." This symbolism is obviously parallel to the "four heads" of the leopard beast representing Greece in Daniel 7:6. History records that when Alexander died leaving no heir to the throne, Greece was divided among his FOUR GENERALS: Ptolemy (in Egypt), Cassander (in Macedonia), Lysimachus (in Thrace), and Seleucus (in Syria).

12.　Verse 22 says these divisions of Alexander's Empire would continue for a time, "but NOT in his [Alexander's] power." History records that after Alexander's death, Greece did not continue to expand but declined till these divisions were swallowed by the Roman Empire.

13.　In verse 23 Gabriel said, "in the LATTER TIME of their kingdom," that is, toward the end of the divided Grecian Empire, "a king of FIERCE countenance . . . shall stand up." History records that Rome arose and conquered Greece, thus becoming the next world empire. The chronological sequence contained in this one verse alone is enough to identify Rome as the "king of fierce countenance."

14. Verse 25 predicts this "king of fierce countenance" would even "stand up against the Prince of princes." History records that Jesus, "the Prince of princes," was condemned by a ROMAN governor, Pilate. Executed under ROMAN jurisdiction, ROMAN hands nailed Christ to the cross, a ROMAN spear pierced His side, and a ROMAN seal sealed His tomb, which was guarded by ROMAN soldiers.

The chronology of Daniel's 8th chapter proves this clue to be factual beyond all dispute. It mentions by name the world powers of MEDO-PERSIA and GREECE and says, "in the LATTER TIME of their kingdom" shall this power arise. We all know ROME was the next world power on the stage of history.

15. In verse 23 Gabriel said that this Roman "king of fierce countenance, and understanding DARK sentences, shall stand up." Deuteronomy 28:49-50 also speaks of this "nation whose TONGUE thou shalt NOT understand; a nation of fierce countenance." History records that Caesar and his Roman legions spoke the new, difficult language of LATIN.

Latin was the official language of both PAGAN Rome, the world empire at that time, and also of PAPAL Rome, its successor. Today Latin is a dead language not spoken by people in any nation. (How many of us would understand *e pluribus unum, tempus fugit,* and *ipso facto* if we hadn't heard them countless times?) But remarkably enough Latin has been and still remains the OFFICIAL language of the Papacy. It's used whenever the Pope makes an *ex cathedra* pronouncement and is most often used by bishops and priests in the mass and other ceremonies. They are, incidentally, the ONLY ones today actually speaking Latin as an audible tongue.

Oh, how wonderful is God's holy Word! The divine prediction made more than thirty centuries ago has come true with unerring accuracy!

CLUE "L"
IT WOULD BE *A RICH CHURCH.*

Your BIBLE says:

1. **Revelation 17:4**—God makes plain that this church would be a rich one when He describes this symbolic wicked woman—the corrupt church—as being "decked with GOLD and PRECIOUS STONES and PEARLS."

2. **Revelation 18:16**—"decked with GOLD, and PRECIOUS STONES, and PEARLS!"

3. **Revelation 17:4**—"having a GOLDEN cup in her hand."

HISTORY testifies:

Lift this clue from the pages of God's Word and take it out into the world to search for the fulfillment of this divine prediction. Ask the first hundred people you meet, "Which church is the richest in material wealth?" The answer is common knowledge: Without question, the Roman Catholic Church has always been the RICHEST church on earth.

To appraise the REAL ESTATE owned by the Church around the circle of the earth would be a titanic task and would result in staggering figures—if the total could even be determined. Its magnificent cathedrals, countless churches, hospitals, parochial schools, colleges and universities, as well as other commercial enterprises such as the major hotels in Italy, Washington's Watergate Hotel, *etc.*—are, collectively and literally, worth many BILLIONS of dollars today.

For example, the Roman Catholic archdiocese of Los Angeles alone is tremendously rich. "Today the archdiocese's wealth is an estimated $1 BILLION, including one of the nation's largest parochial school systems and 23 hospitals." [102]

Its ART TREASURES also, not only in the Vatican but throughout the world, are worth a king's ransom. Priceless masterpieces accumulated over centuries—a wealth of paintings and sculptures by such inspired artists as Michelangelo, Raphael, Caravaggio, and others—comprise a fabulous fortune almost beyond estimate.

> "The Vatican is RICH in assets. A ranking cardinal recently estimated the Vatican's assets at $560 million, but this figure apparently did not include two of the church's chief financial supports, the *Patrimony of the Holy See* and the *Institute for Religious Works*. They are the equivalents, respectively, of an investment portfolio and a bank, and some outside observers have estimated their value at $2 billion to $3 billion." [103]

Perhaps no one knows the total worldwide budget and annual income from the faithful of such a colossal church, but they would be enormous. *TIME* Magazine carried an article titled "THE GREAT VATICAN BANK MYSTERY: A Tale of Two Deaths, Twelve Investigations and Missing Millions." The opening words of that article are intriguing:

"Two suicides, both of which could conceivably be murder. As much as $1.2 billion in unsecured loans. The failure of Italy's huge Banco Ambrosiano, which has left more than 200 international financial institutions holding the bag for millions in loans. A scandal that has threatened the stability of the entire international banking system. . . . Even if these were the only ingredients, the story would still be intriguing enough for a Robert Ludlum thriller. But an added element is making the scandal that has rocked the world of international finance one of the most compelling real-life mysteries of the century: the involvement of the *Instituto per le Opere de Religione* (I. O. R.) [Institute for Religious Works], better known as the Vatican Bank." [104]

The press later reported that the Vatican Bank settled out of court by agreeing "to pay $250 million to Ambrosiano creditors." [105] The Vatican made clear that this payment of a quarter of a BILLION dollars was only "a voluntary contribution" and no admission of responsibility for the bank's collapse.

Any institution—church or otherwise—that can afford to pay a "contribution" of a quarter of a BILLION dollars in a CASH settlement is indeed a RICH one!

CLUE "M"

IT WOULD BE CLOTHED IN
"PURPLE AND SCARLET."

Your BIBLE says:

1. **Revelation 17:4**—"The woman was arrayed in PURPLE and SCARLET colour."

2. **Revelation 18:16**—"clothed in . . . PURPLE, and SCARLET"

HISTORY testifies:

Do we dare expect this wicked church, this "whore" [106] in God's eyes, to show her TRUE COLORS, when this clue is so explicitly stated in Scripture? Could the Beast be so bold and brazen as even to array itself in purple and scarlet, knowing that doing so invites identification as the Antichrist? Could be! For here we have another case of fact being stranger than fiction.

Since the regular parish priest ordinarily wears a black suit for everyday attire and the Pope often travels in white robes, we may not recall that the ceremonial colors of the Roman Catholic hierarchy are SCARLET and PURPLE. But that fact is so much a matter of record that just a few examples will serve to refresh our memories.

The large unabridged *Webster's* dictionary gives this very pertinent information under the entry for the noun "cardinal" (reproduced on next page):

> "Roman Catholic Church. One of the ecclesiastical princes who constitute the Pope's council, or the college of cardinals, and who are appointed by the Pope. . . . The cardinals take precedence of all dignitaries except the Pope. The principal parts of a cardinal's costume are a RED cassock, a rochet, a short PURPLE mantle, and a RED hat. . . ."[107]

Each "prince of the church" called a cardinal dresses in scarlet robes and wears a hat in "CARDINAL RED"—a vivid scarlet. (Even the American bird of SCARLET plumage is called a "cardinal." Once, on the popular game show *Jeopardy* the ANSWER in the category of BIRDS was "This bird was named for Roman Catholic officials whose bright red robes its plumage resembles." The correct QUESTION was "What is a cardinal?")

LIFE Magazine for July 5, 1963, devoted not only its cover but also some double-page spreads (see especially pages 24-25) to beautiful full-color photographs showing the installation of Pope Paul VI. These photos take us inside the Sistine Chapel as the cardinals pay homage to the newly elected Pope, a view rarely afforded outsiders. The colors of the brilliant Kodachromes are overwhelmingly SCARLET and PURPLE! Please note:

The sublime scenes show each of the seventy cardinals approaching the new Pope one by one to *kneel before him* and *kiss his ring*. As they await their turns, they're seated on thrones lining the two side walls. Set up before each seated cardinal is a small individual table, draped to the floor in PURPLE. Set up behind each one is an individual PURPLE backdrop canopy. The brilliant red of SCARLET robes and hats contrasts vividly against the deep purple seen in each cardinal's table, draped in luxurious purple, as well as in the purple backdrop canopies behind each seated "prince of the church." As each cardinal's colors are repeated seventy times side by side, the scene becomes an ocean of SCARLET and PURPLE!

If we're unaware of this Biblical clue, the historical evidence escapes our attention. For instance, a news article in the *Los Angeles Times* reported from Vatican City that Pope John Paul II installed eighteen new cardinals. Buried in the mass of details are these two sentences:

> "There were representatives of all five continents among the 18 CRIMSON-cassocked churchmen who *knelt before the pontiff* while he placed the RED zucchetto (skullcap) and biretta (tri-cornered pillbox hat), their new symbols of office, on each man's head. . . . The smiling Pope, dressed in white vestments with a PURPLE cape . . . , nodded approvingly."[108]

The Papal hierarchy, wittingly or unwittingly, fits this clue precisely. Yet what is so remarkable about this clue is that except for army uniforms (like the BLUE and GRAY of the Civil War) few organizations can be identified by color. The list grows even smaller when it comes to churches! Yet prophecy states that "the woman"—the church—is to be "arrayed in PURPLE and SCARLET colour." I challenge anyone to apply this prophetic fulfillment to any other church organization on earth.

The purple and scarlet colors used by the Roman Catholic Church in its official ceremonies constitute important PHYSICAL evidence. Clues like this one and that of the Seven Hills of Rome constitute something REAL, something TANGIBLE we can see with our own eyes and touch with our own hands. They may sometimes be forgotten by the careless or overlooked by the uninformed—but they're not easily painted over. Stripped of all pageantry and poetry and sentimentalism, the stark reality of the Papacy is seen in the light of history to be a perfect fulfillment of prophecy.

< from the *Merriam-Webster Dictionary*, Unabridged >

3. Of or pertaining to a cardinal or the cardinals.
4. Of a cardinal-red color. See CARDINAL RED.
Syn. — See RADICAL.
car′di·nal (kär′dĭ·năl; -n'l), *n*. [F. *cardinal* and ML. *cardinalis* (ecclesiae Romanae); cf. It. *cardinale*. See CARDINAL, *adj*.] **1.** *R. C. Ch.* One of the ecclesiastical princes who constitute the Pope's council, or the college of cardinals, and who are appointed by the Pope. Since the time of Sixtus V, their number can never exceed 70 (6 of episcopal rank, 50 priests, 14 deacons), and the number of cardinal priests and deacons is seldom full. When the papal chair is vacant a pope is elected by the college of cardinals. See POPE. The cardinals take precedence of all dignitaries except the Pope. The principal parts of a cardinal's costume are a red cassock, a rochet, a short purple mantle, and a red hat with a small crown and broad brim, with cord and tassels of a special pattern hanging from it. The cardinal's hat is placed on the head of the candidate by the Pope and is then laid aside until the obsequies, when it is placed on the catafalque of

Thus God gives us in Scripture another telltale sign by which to identify the Antichrist Beast. Taken by itself, it may not mean much. But in conjunction with all the other incriminating evidence, it's an impressive clue to all who are not color blind.

CLUE "N"

ITS LEADER WOULD BE AN ACTIVE RELIGIOUS FIGURE ENTHRONED *IN THE CHURCH.*

Your BIBLE says:
2 Thessalonians 2:3-4—"that man of sin . . . sitteth IN the temple of God"!

HISTORY testifies:

The fulfillment of this clue is another case of FACT being stranger than FICTION! After all, to take this clue at face value and to look for Antichrist among the leaders of the church is to "Think the Unthinkable"—for surely the church is the very LAST place we'd expect to find the archenemy of God's people.

But Satan's strategy has always been one of camouflage, deception, and disguise. The Apostle Paul warned that Satan disguises himself as a dazzling angel. We are warned of . . .

> "false apostles, deceitful workers, disguising themselves as apostles of Christ. And no wonder! Even Satan disguises himself as an angel of light. So it is not strange if HIS MINISTERS ALSO disguise themselves as ministers of righteousness." [109]

Never underestimate our enemy, the Devil. He's had millenniums of experience in deceiving humans. He knew that to succeed in establishing an outpost for his agents here on Planet Earth, he must supply them with a plausible alibi, a perfect "cover" for their work.

What better cover could there be than to infiltrate the CHURCH and work from within? This would automatically accomplish two great objectives:

    (1) It would not only make the Antichrist / Beast power
        less likely to be SUSPECTED, but
    (2) it would also place that power in a better POSITION
        to tamper with and corrupt God's true religion.

An illustrative example of such a "cover"—though in a different situation—came to light in a *TIME* Magazine article on the tragic death of actor Rock Hudson. The writer of the article "The Double Life of an AIDS Victim" points out the all-American image of the romantic star, adored by millions of women and admired by millions of men. "Yet in one of those plot twists that any screenwriter would have rejected as too improbable to consider, in the last weeks of his life Hudson became perhaps the most famous homosexual in the world." [110]

Here in the annals of Antichrist, we encounter another "one of those plot twists that any screenwriter would have rejected as too improbable to consider"! It would be like foreign spies infiltrating the upper levels of government—including the White House itself. A VILLAIN is dangerous enough. Even more dangerous is a villain in DISGUISE.

English clergyman Christopher Wordsworth, M.A., D.D., (1774-1846) was the youngest brother of English poet William Wordsworth. He became chaplain to the Archbishop of Canterbury and later Master of Trinity College at Cambridge University. Wordsworth gives words worth quoting when he comments on the inspired appropriateness of the name "Mystery" [111] given to the Antichrist Whore. He says,

> It was NO Mystery when HEATHEN Rome persecuted the Church. But a Christian Church, calling herself the Mother of Christendom, and yet drunken with the blood of saints [112]—IS a Mystery. A Christian Church boasting herself to be the Bride, and yet being the Harlot; styling herself Zion, and being Babylon—IS a Mystery. It's a Mystery when she says to all, "Come unto me," and the voice from heaven cries, "Come OUT of her, My people." [113] It's a Mystery that she who boasts herself the city of Saints, becomes the habitation of devils; [114] that she who claims to be Infallible should corrupt the earth; [115] that a self-named "Mother of Churches" should be called by the Holy Spirit the "Mother of Harlots and Abominations." [116] All this is truly a great MYSTERY.

> Nineteen Centuries have passed since the Holy Spirit prophesied that this Mystery would be revealed in that City which was then Queen of the Earth, the City on Seven Hills—the City of Rome.

> "The Mystery was then dark, dark as midnight. Man's eye could not pierce the gloom. The fulfillment of the prophecy seemed improbable—almost impossible. Age after age rolled away. By degrees, the mists which hung over it became less thick. The clouds began to break. Some features of the dark Mystery began to appear, dimly at first, then more clearly, like Mountains at daybreak. Then the form of the Mystery became more and more distinct. The Seven Hills, and the Woman sitting upon them, became more and more visible. Her voice was heard. Strange sounds of blasphemy were uttered by her. Then they became louder and louder. And the golden chalice in her hand, her scarlet attire, her pearls and jewels were seen glittering in the Sun. Kings and Nations were displayed prostrate at her feet, and drinking her cup. Saints were

slain by her sword, and she exulted over them. And now the prophecy became clear, clear as noon-day; and we tremble at the sight, while we read the inscription, emblazoned in large letters, 'MYSTERY, BABYLON THE GREAT,' written by the hand of St. John, guided by the Holy Spirit of God, on the forehead of the CHURCH of ROME." [117]

One may be excused if the mind rebels at the surprise and shock this clue embodies. But God's Word is sure, no matter how surprising it may seem. We can trust it—even when it says we're to look for Antichrist not OUTside but INside the church, sitting in the very temple of God.

A CHURCH Is A TEMPLE

Yet some are troubled by the word "temple," which they take to mean a presently non-existent Jewish temple at Jerusalem.

Only an extreme literalist would insist that "temple" must refer only to a Jewish and not to a Christian place of worship. Such narrow insistence would negate Paul's warning (in 2 Thessalonians 2:3-4) for the CHRISTIAN world and apply it only to JEWS. But no one will deny the fact that Paul was writing to Christians.

Any contention that "temple" is Jewish and has no place in the Christian world evaporates when we realize that Paul WAS in fact addressing CHRISTIANS when he gave this inspired message from God:

"Know ye not that YE are the TEMPLE of God, and that the Spirit of God dwelleth in you? If any man defile the TEMPLE of God, him shall God destroy; for the TEMPLE of God is holy, which TEMPLE YE are. . . . What? know ye not that YOUR BODY is the TEMPLE of the Holy Ghost which is in you, which ye have of God, and ye are not your own? . . . For YE are the TEMPLE of the living God; as God hath said, I will dwell in them, and walk in them; and I will be their God, and they shall be My people." [118]

From a practical point of view, there's really NO distinction to be made among such terms as

TEMPLE,
TABERNACLE,
SYNAGOGUE,
SANCTUARY,
CHURCH,
CATHEDRAL,

as they all have one thing in common: They ALL are called "the house of God," the place of worship.

The position set forth in this book is that of virtually every non-Catholic scholar since the Reformation. For instance, the famous "Westminister Confession of Faith" (1648) gives the official doctrinal statement of the Presbyterian Church. In its original form it read: "There is no other Head of the Church but the Lord Jesus Christ, nor can the Pope of Rome in any sense be Head thereof, but is that ANTICHRIST, that man of sin and son of perdition, that exalteth himself IN the Church. . . ."[119]

JESUIT PRIEST Manuel Lacunza, of Chile and Italy, wrote *La Venida del Mesias en Gloria y Magestad* ("The Coming of the Messiah in Glory and Majesty") under the pen name Juan Josafat Ben-Ezra, a Christian Hebrew. Lacunza's book, produced almost under the shadows of the Vatican, aroused immediate interest and admiration and had an amazing circulation all the way "from Havana to Cape Horn." It was translated from Spanish into Latin and then Italian.

Commenting on Paul's prophecy of "that Man of Sin . . . [who] as God sitteth in the temple of God," Lacunza said this:

"THE TEMPLE OF GOD whereof St. Paul speaketh, is nothing else than THE CHURCH OF CHRIST, is nothing else than the congregation of all the faithful, is nothing else than these believers united in one, who, as St. Peter saith, 'as lively stones are built up a spiritual TEMPLE.'[120] And this is the TEMPLE of God, where the man of sin, the son of iniquity shall formally sit, publicly showing himself, and freely operating therein, as if he were God: 'showing himself that he is God.'"[121]

Thus writes a Jesuit himself with telling logic. Those who object that "temple" cannot mean "church" are merely playing with words. They offer not a reason but a mere excuse for refusing to accept the prophecy at face value.

Note what Timothy Dwight, president of Yale, said about this clue:

"This description the clergy and especially the Popes of the Romish church have, for many ages, literally verified. They have seated themselves IN the church, or TEMPLE of God, and showed that they WERE God, by assuming powers which belong only to God."[122]

THE GREEKS HAD A WORD FOR IT:
THE PREFIX "ANTI–"

Some may wonder how we can look for the Beast or Antichrist within the church itself, for doesn't *anti–* mean "against"? After all, if this power is against Christ, how could he be IN the Christian church? That's a logical question, but it overlooks the fact that the prefix "anti–" has more than one possible meaning. *Against* is only one possible meaning, as anti-aircraft guns are fired *against* enemy planes and anti-freeze acts *against* freezing conditions in a car radiator.

But in the past a very common use of *anti–* was with the meaning "instead," "instead of," "in place of," "for," "replacement," "simulating," "pretended," or "substituting for." A good historical English dictionary or Greek/English dictionary will bear out this definition.[123]

That's the meaning of "anti–" in the word *antichrist*—not one who is openly AGAINST Christ but one who claims to TAKE THE PLACE OF Christ, to act in His stead, to SPEAK FOR Christ and be a vicarious SUBSTITUTE FOR Him in His absence from this earth. Paul's inspired description is fitting and meaningful: "that man of sin . . . sitteth in the temple of God, showing himself that he is God."

Thus the name "Antichrist" signifies not an avowed antagonist of Christ but one professing to be VICE–Christ, a vicar or substitute who presumes to occupy the place and fulfill the functions of Christ.

The Papacy fits—and in its claims to *stand in the place* of Christ *admits* that it fits—the DICTIONARY DEFINITION of the term "antichrist."

A DEEPER LESSON

But there's another even deeper lesson to be learned from the term "antichrist." The Scriptures actually use that word or title only four times, in 1 John 2:18 & 22; 4:3; 2 John 7. In the latter two verses John gives—twice—an inspired definition of Antichrist. He says it's anyone "that does not confess that Jesus Christ has come in the FLESH."

Our first thought may be, "Well, you'll never find anyone in the Christian church who denies that Jesus has come in the flesh. The Incarnation[124] of God in man is one of our basic teachings."

True Christians everywhere accept the truth of such verses as the following:

- Hebrews 2:14-17—"As the children are partakers of flesh and blood, He [Christ] also Himself likewise took part of the SAME. . . . He took NOT on Him the nature of ANGELS; but He took on Him the seed of Abraham. . . . In all things it behooved Him to be made LIKE unto His brethren."

- Philippians 2:7—The Bible repeatedly makes clear that Jesus "was made in the likeness of MEN."

- Romans 8:3—Here Paul speaks of "God sending His own Son in the likeness of sinful FLESH."

One may argue that "While the Antichrist denies the Incarnation—denies that 'Christ is come in the flesh'—the Pope does not deny this. Therefore he cannot be the Antichrist." This argument has seemed so logical that some Protestants have given up the Protestant doctrine that the Papacy is Antichrist and have ceased to protest.

However, that argument is based on a misunderstanding caused by overlooking one word in the text. Antichrist was not to deny that Christ had come in flesh, but was to deny that He had come "in THE flesh," in the same KIND of flesh, as the human race He came to save. On this vital difference hinges the real truth of the gospel. Did Christ come *all the way down* to make contact with the fallen race, or only part way, so we must have saints, popes, and priests intercede for us with a Christ who is *too far removed* from fallen humanity and its needs to make direct contact with the individual sinner?

Right here lies the great divide that parts Protestantism from Roman Catholicism.

The gospel of Christ teaches that man has separated himself from God through sin. Only through Christ, our Mediator, can man be rescued and brought again into connection with the Source of purity and power. But to become such a connecting link, Christ had to partake of both the DIVINITY of God and the HUMANITY of man—His divine arm encircling God and his human arm embracing man, thus connecting both in His own Person. Jesus Christ was both truly GOD and truly MAN, embodying a union of the human with the divine in order to lift man from his degradation.

Because it was fallen MAN that was to be rescued from sin, Christ condescended to take OUR nature upon Himself—NOT some HIGHER kind of flesh. Hebrews 2:14-17 says: "Forasmuch then as the children are partakers of flesh and blood, He [Christ] also Himself likewise took part of the SAME. . . . He took NOT on Him the nature of ANGELS; but He took on Him the seed of Abraham. Wherefore in ALL things it behoved Him to be made LIKE unto His brethren." This text is so worded that it cannot be misunderstood. Christ "took part of the SAME" flesh and blood as ours. He came in "the" flesh. To deny this is to adopt the spirit of Antichrist.[125] To bridge the gulf made by sin, Christ must be one with the FATHER in divinity and one with MAN in humanity, thus again linking earth with heaven.

God revealed this truth to Jacob in a dream, showing him a LADDER reaching from earth to heaven.[126] Jacob, feeling guilty, feared that his sins had cut him off from heaven. But the mystic Ladder, connecting heaven and earth, represented Jesus.[127] Unbelieving modernism has tried to cut off the

UPPER part of this ladder by denying Christ's divinity. The Roman Catholic Church cuts off the LOWER rungs by teaching that the Virgin Mary was born without sin—consequently Christ took upon Himself not OUR kind of flesh and blood, but HOLY flesh, so far ABOVE us that He doesn't make contact with fallen humanity. For this reason the poor sinner cannot come directly to Him, they say, but must come through Mary, saints, popes, and priests, who will mediate for him. This dogma[128] of MARY'S supposed "Immaculate Conception" opened the floodgate for all the idolatry of the Catholic Church.

A MISCONCEPTION!

Many misunderstand this dogma and assume it refers to the Virgin Birth of Christ. But it really refers to Mary's own birth[129] and has nothing to do with the Virgin Birth of Jesus. The Pope's actual wording of the Immaculate Conception dogma in 1847 officially "holds the BLESSED VIRGIN MARY to have been, from the first instant of her conception, by a singular grace and privilege of Almighty God, . . . preserved free from all stain of original sin."[130]

This Papal dogma declares the mother of Jesus absolutely free from all implication in the Fall of Adam and its consequences. It makes Mary an EXCEPTION from the universality of original sin. And side by side with this doctrine there developed the doctrine that Mary did not commit sin at any time during her life. Catholics gave her the attribute of impeccability, which means that she COULD NOT sin, that her nature was such that it was IMPOSSIBLE for her to sin! Of course, this contradicts the explicit Bible teaching that "ALL have sinned, and come short of the glory of God."[131]

Every human being was born to parents who were subject to sin and who in turn had been born to similar sinful parents. The psalmist David spoke for all of us when he said: "Behold, I was shapen in iniquity; and in sin did my mother conceive me."[132] But this Papal dogma makes Christ different in that respect and sets Him as a breed apart. We know that God through the Holy Spirit was the heavenly Father of our blessed Lord. We know, further, that Jesus never committed even one sin, though He was terribly tempted by Satan.[133]

Yet He took on humanity through His mother, Mary. Certainly she was a very special girl for God to give her the unspeakable honor of bearing "His only begotten Son." But the question is: Was she human in all respects as we are, including the taint of sin we inherited from Adam and Eve? Or was she "a cut above" in that respect, unique from other flesh-and-blood mortals?

No, Mary was fully human. We read, "Mary said: 'My soul magnifies the Lord, and my spirit has rejoiced in God my SAVIOR.'"[134] Note Mary's words, "my Savior." None but sinners need a Savior, for no punishment can justly be inflicted on an innocent person. In those words Mary confessed she was a sinner in need of a Savior.

The dogma of Mary's Immaculate Conception, like other distinctive doctrines of the Roman system, completely lacks any Scriptural support. The Bible says, "There is . . . ONE Mediator between God and men, the MAN Christ Jesus." [135] Jesus WAS a man, a part of mankind, as surely as He was God Almighty. The Bible repeatedly makes clear that Jesus "was made in the likeness of MEN." [136] Inspiration speaks of "God sending His own Son in the likeness of sinful FLESH." [137]

THE GENEALOGY OF CHRIST

The human genealogy of Jesus Christ is recorded for all the world to see in the first chapter of the Gospel of Matthew, and it's very interesting. Genealogies often are boring—with all their "begats"—but here God has a beautiful lesson for us!

As we read through Matthew 1:1-17, two unusual things stand out. First, WOMEN are not usually included in Bible genealogies, but here we find four women mentioned—besides His mother Mary! Second, most of us never mention unsavory ancestors with TARNISHED reputations who happen to be in our background, but the Lord doesn't hesitate!

Please note the following four "black sheep" in Christ's family tree as they're listed in the King James Version:

1. Matthew 1:3 – THAMAR — She was Tamar who was driven to become PREGNANT by Judah, her father-in-law. See Genesis 38:1-26.

2. Matthew 1:5 – RACHAB — She was the HARLOT Rahab of Jericho. See Joshua 2:1-22 and 6:1-25. See also Hebrews 11:31.

3. Matthew 1:5 – RUTH — Although she was a good woman herself, some members of society might have judged her harshly because of her ancestors. She was descended from Moab, who was born as the product of INCEST. See Ruth 1:4 and Genesis 19, especially verses 30-37.

4. Matthew 1:6 – BATHSHEBA ("the wife of Urias") — She was the wife of Uriah for whom King David lustfully committed the sins of ADULTERY and MURDER. See 2 Samuel 11:1 to 12:14.

Jesus loves sinners, like these four women, and like you and me. He was willing to be numbered among them, to call them His own, and to die for them.

Our wonderful Savior was fully God—and fully man. There was a REAL union of FLESH and SPIRIT, of DIVINITY and HUMANITY in Christ. Obviously, the God of the Universe could have chosen human ancestors with lily-white reputations and impeccable backgrounds for the lineage of His Son—but He didn't. So perhaps we should let Christ be as HUMAN as He intended to be.

(Early Christianity had to fight against false doctrine which taught that MATTER was EVIL and the spirit good. It taught that Christ was born without any participation of MATTER and had only an apparent, ethereal "body." Look up GNOSTICISM and DOCETISM in a good encyclopedia.)

The Scriptures depict the cosmic controversy between Christ and Satan under the twin symbols of two great mysteries:

"the Mystery of INIQUITY"—MAN making himself God,[138]

and

"the Mystery of GODLINESS"—GOD making Himself man.[139]

Therefore:

- because Papal doctrine DENIES the Incarnation of Jesus "in the flesh" of HUMANITY, and

- because the Pope FITS the meaning of "anti–" as "in place of," and

- because the Roman Pontiff sits enthroned IN the purported church of God,

we recognize here another clue identifying the Papacy as Antichrist.

CLUE "O"

IT WOULD BE IDENTIFIED BY
A MYSTERIOUS NUMBER: 666.

Your BIBLE says:

1. **Revelation 13:17**—Dictatorial laws will be passed "that no man might buy or sell, save he that had the Mark, or the name of the Beast, or the NUMBER of his NAME."

2. **Revelation 13:18**—John the Revelator offers us this inspired clue: "Here is wisdom. Let him that hath understanding count the NUMBER of the Beast: for it is the number of a MAN; and his number is Six hundred threescore and six [666]."

3. **Revelation 13:18, New English Bible** says: "Here is the key; and anyone who has intelligence may work out the number of the Beast. The num-

ber represents a man's NAME, and the NUMERICAL value of the LET-TERS is six hundred and sixty-six."

4. Note *The Living Bible* on **Revelation 13:18**—"Here is a puzzle that calls for careful thought to solve it. Let those who are able, interpret this CODE: the NUMERICAL values of the LETTERS in his NAME add to 666!"

HISTORY testifies:

This mysterious clue is like a secret code, but God wants us to understand it. That's why He put this "classified information" into His Book of Revelation. In fact, He even challenges us to "count the number of the Beast." Let's accept God's challenge and decipher this cryptic number!

THE POPE'S OFFICIAL TITLE

To check the possibility that the Papacy may fit this clue as closely as it has the others we've considered, let's note what Catholic translators of the Douay Version of the Bible say about this mystic number. The Douay Bible, called "the most venerable English version printed under Catholic auspices," has the following comment on Revelation 13:18 in a special footnote on that verse: "*Six hundred sixty-six.* The NUMERAL letters of his NAME shall make up this number."

Of course, individual Popes over the years have had many names, such as John, Paul, John Paul, Gregory, *etc.* But what is the *official* title used by the Papacy which, like an umbrella, covers the whole dynasty of Popes? Several titles are used, such as "Holy Father" and "Roman Pontiff," but the main one—the one on which the other titles are based—is "VICAR OF THE SON OF GOD," along with its variations, "Vicar of Christ," "Vicar of Jesus Christ," and "Vicar of God." That official title in Latin is "VICARIUS FILII DEI" (pronounced "vigh-KAIR-ee-uss FILL-ee-eye DEE-eye").

We needn't be Latin scholars to understand this Papal title. *Dei* means "God" and is found in English words like *deity* and *deified* (don't spell the latter backwards!). *Filii* is Latin for "son." In English, *filial* love is love of a son for his parent. An *affiliated* organization is one taken in or adopted as a son or member of the parent company. *Vicarius* is Latin for "substitute." In English, a "vicarious experience" is a substitute for the real thing. For instance, if you can't really climb Mount Everest or be a master spy, you can have that experience *vicariously* by reading a book about it. In England a "vicar" of a church is a substitute clergyman who fills in for the regular minister when the latter is away. Our term "vice" as in "vice-President" comes from the same Latin root, *vicis,* and means a deputy who substitutes for the President at ceremonial functions, *etc.* Literally translated, then, the title *Vicarius Filii Dei* means "vicar of the Son of God." Thus the Pope claims to stand in the place of Jesus as His substitute since the latter has returned to heaven.

This title, *Vicarius Filii Dei,* or some equivalent form of it, has appeared so frequently in Roman Catholic literature and rituals for CENTURIES, that it scarcely seems necessary to add other proof of its validity and importance. The title appeared as early as A. D. 752 in a document historically known as the "Donation of Constantine." Though this document later proved to be a forgery, the so-called Donation of Constantine was used as valid by at least ten Popes over a period of seven centuries to establish the supremacy of the bishops of Rome.[140]

We find the exalted title *Vicarius Filii Dei* used officially in Roman Catholic canon law from medieval times down to the present. In the earliest collection of canon law we read:

> "*Beatus Petrus in terris* **Vicarius Filii Dei** *esse videtur constitutus.*"—
> "*Decretum Gratiani,*" *prima pars, dist. xcvi.* The English translation reads:
> "Blessed Peter is seen to have been constituted **Vicar of the Son of God** on the earth."—"Decretum of Gratian," part 1, div. 96.[141]

This title is not only found repeatedly in the publications of the Roman Church, but it's also inscribed on the Pope's crown. In the weekly Catholic magazine, *Our Sunday Visitor,* a reader asks the question: "What are the letters supposed to be in the Pope's crown, and what do they signify, if anything?" The answer is: "The letters inscribed in the Pope's miter are these: *Vicarius Filii Dei,* which is the Latin for VICAR OF THE SON OF GOD."[142] This title is also used in the coronation ceremonies of each newly-crowned Pope.

LATIN: THE CHURCH'S OFFICIAL LANGUAGE

Latin was not only the official language of **Rome** during its days as the ruling world empire—it's also the official language of the Roman Catholic Church itself. For example, whenever the Pope speaks *ex cathedra,* he speaks in Latin, and until recently the Catholic mass was always said in Latin. Wherever the church of Rome goes, the use of Latin goes with it. Consequently, the Latin language would naturally be used in computing the number 666. Latin's ALPHABET LETTERS have NUMERIC VALUES in ROMAN numerals.

ROMAN CHURCH—ROMAN NUMERALS

In ancient times, before Arabic numerals came into use, certain letters of the alphabet did double duty as numbers. Roman numerals were used by the ancient Romans for computation and are still used today to number the face of *clocks* and *watches*, to list the main points in *outlines*, to number the *preliminary* pages of books, to number *chapters* and *volumes* of books, and for inscriptions of *dates* on monuments and public buildings.

Now let's use this background information to make sense out of our clue. Revelation 13:17-18 says quite plainly that "the number of the BEAST . . . is the number of a MAN." More specifically, it's "the number of his NAME." Still more to the point, a footnote comment in a Catholic Bible says: "Verse 18. *Six hundred sixty-six*. The NUMERAL LETTERS of his NAME shall make up this number."[143] So let's investigate the possibility that the Pope's name, his official title, fits this clue. Let's count the Roman "numeral letters of his name," *Vicarius Filii Dei.*

COUNTING THE BEAST'S NUMBER!

Meet Mr. 666, whose numerical code-name, like that of Agent 007, has become intriguingly popular in recent decades:

V	5	
I	1	
C	100	
A	0	(not used as a numeral)
R	0	(not used as a numeral)
I	1	
U	5	(formerly the same as V)
S	0	(not used as a numeral)
F	0	(not used as a numeral
I	1	
L	50	
I	1	
I	1	
D	500	
E	0	(not used as a numeral)
I	1	

Total   =   666

As you can see, this convincing computation totals 666 exactly—no more, no less.

"U" Was Formerly "V"

Some may inquire why the letter "U" in the calculation above is counted like the letter "V" and given the Roman numeral value of 5. A critic may complain that this is forcing things to come out to the preconceived total. But that's a groundless complaint, for the fact is that the letter "V" was the same as "U" until recent centuries.

The Romans wrote the letter "V" for both *U* and *V* sounds, just as today we still write the letter "C" for both *K* and *S* sounds in words like *calculate* and *certainty*. Later, Medieval scholars began writing "U" for a vowel and "V" for a consonant. Encyclopedias confirm this fact. For instance, under articles for the letter "V" we read:

> "The history of this letter is IDENTICAL with that of *U*, from which it was not differentiated till the 15th to 17th century. . . . The pointed form V became identified with the consonant, the rounded form with the vowel." [144]

> "V is the twenty-second letter of our alphabet. Its history is the SAME as that of the letter *U*. . . . During the 1400's to 1600's, the rounded form *U* came to be used only to represent the vowel, and the pointed form *V* only to represent the consonant." [145]

Besides this documentation, think of our letter "W." It looks like two letter V's written together. But when we pronounce its name, we call it a "double-*you*"—not a "double-*vee*"! And sometimes a building has its name engraved above the entrance, like this:

PVBLIC LIBRARY.

Those things are a throwback to the days when U and V were identical.

Just a **REMARKABLE COINCIDENCE?**

Some try to blunt the force of this striking fulfillment by pointing out that other names may also add up to 666. That may be, but remember: This computation is ONLY ONE of many God-given clues, and when considered in connection with them, it IS significant. It certainly adds weight and strength to the LONG LIST of other identifying points found in Scripture.

✦   ✦   ✦

CLUE "P"

THE BEAST POWER WOULD BOAST SO OUTRAGEOUSLY AND MAKE SUCH UNPARALLELED CLAIMS THAT IT COULD ONLY BE SAID TO VOICE "GREAT WORDS" AND "VERY GREAT THINGS."

Your BIBLE says:

1. **Daniel 7:8**—The "Little Horn" had "a mouth speaking GREAT things."

   Modern translations render Daniel's *Aramaic* phrase as follows:

The Living Bible	"a bragging mouth"
New King James Version	"pompous words"
Today's English Version	"boasting proudly"
New American Standard Bible	"great boasts"
New International Version	"spoke boastfully"

In the same chapter, with no worry about overdoing it or boring his readers, the prophet Daniel REPEATS that thought over and over again!

2. **Daniel 7:11**—Daniel was fascinated because of "the GREAT words which the Horn spake."

3. **Daniel 7:20**—The "Horn . . . had . . . a mouth that spake VERY great things."

4. **Daniel 7:25**—"He shall speak GREAT words against the most High."

5. **Revelation 13:5**—The Beast had "a mouth speaking GREAT things."

   Modern translations render Revelation's *Greek* phrase as follows:

Today's English Version	"proud claims"
New International Version	"proud words"
New American Standard Bible	"arrogant words"
Revised Standard Version	"haughty . . . words"

HISTORY testifies:

The pages of the past bear mute but shocking testimony to the fact that the Papacy fits this clue. Men seated on the Papal throne have made such outrageous claims that it's absolutely incredible! Let's sample a few of these enormously arrogant statements.

GREAT WORDS *CIRCA* 889:

The 9th Century Pope Stephanus V unflinchingly proclaimed these "great words": "The Popes, like Jesus, are CONCEIVED through the overshadowing of the HOLY GHOST. All Popes are a certain species of MAN-GODS, for the purpose of being the better able to conduct the functions of MEDIATOR between God and mankind. ALL powers in HEAVEN, as well as on earth, are given to them." [146]

GREAT WORDS IN 1073:

A man named Hildebrand rose to the Papal throne and was Pope under the name of Gregory VII from 1073 to 1085. He issued 27 propositions known as the "Dictates of Hildebrand" or *Dictatus Papae* ("Dictates of the Pope"). Among them are the following:

"2. That the Roman Pontiff alone is justly called universal."

"9. That all princes should KISS the FEET of the Pope alone."

"12. That it is lawful for him to DEPOSE EMPERORS."

"18. That his sentence is NOT to be reviewed by ANY one; while he alone can review the decisions of all others."

"19. That he can be judged by no one."

"22. That the Roman Church never erred; nor will it, according to Scripture, ever err."

"27. That he can absolve subjects from their allegiance to unrighteous rulers." [147]

These arrogant assertions of Gregory VII seem sufficient in themselves to fulfill this prophecy on behalf of the Papacy, but more examples will be seen when we examine further Bible evidence—especially Clues S and T, below.

GREAT WORDS IN 1302:

Pope Boniface VIII, who reigned from 1294-1303, stated: "We, moreover, proclaim, declare, and pronounce that it is altogether necessary to SALVATION for every human being to be SUBJECT to the Roman Pontiff." [148]

GREAT WORDS IN 1342:

"All the popes of the last six centuries have worn the triple tiara. . . . [When a new Pope is crowned,] the triple tiara is placed on the candidate's head with the words: 'Receive the tiara adorned with THREE CROWNS and KNOW that thou art . . .

FATHER of princes and kings,
RULER of the world,
VICAR of our Saviour Jesus Christ.'"[149]

GREAT WORDS IN 1512:

Addressing the Roman Pontiff in a speech at the Fifth Lateran Council, Catholic Archbishop Christopher Marcellus told the Pope: "Thou art the shepherd, thou art the physician, thou art the director, thou art the husband-man; finally, **thou art another GOD on earth**."[150] And the Pope did not rebuke him for making such a blasphemous statement!

GREAT WORDS IN 1619:

Cardinal Bellarmine audaciously declared: "All names which in the Scriptures are applied to CHRIST, by virtue of which it is established that He is over the church, all the SAME names are applied to the Pope."[151]

GREAT WORDS IN 1746:

In 1746 Lucius Ferraris, an Italian Catholic professor and canonist, wrote a monumental book which has remained influential for more than two centuries. The *Catholic Encyclopedia* praises Ferraris's work as "a veritable encyclopedia of religious knowledge" and states it "will EVER REMAIN a precious mine of information."[152] Here's a small sample:

"The Pope is of so great dignity and so exalted that he is not a mere man, but as it were GOD, and the vicar of God. . . .

"He is likewise the DIVINE monarch and supreme emperor, and KING of kings.[153]

"Hence the Pope is crowned with a triple crown, as KING of HEAVEN and of earth and of the lower regions.

"Moreover the superiority and the power of the Roman Pontiff by no means pertain only to heavenly things, to earthly things, and to things under the earth, but are even over ANGELS, than whom he is greater.

"So that if it were possible that the ANGELS might err in the faith, or might think contrary to the faith, they could be judged and excommunicated by the Pope.

"For he is of so great dignity and power that he forms one and the same tribunal with Christ. . . .

"The Pope is as it were GOD ON EARTH, sole sovereign of the faithful of Christ, chief KING OF KINGS, having plenitude of power, to whom has been entrusted by the omnipotent God DIRECTION not only of the EARTHLY but also of the HEAVENLY kingdom."[154]

GREAT WORDS IN 1870:

In 1870 the lofty decree of Papal INFALLIBILITY was proclaimed as an official dogma of the Roman Catholic Church.[155] So besides all the other boastful words quoted above, the Pope even has INFALLIBILITY as part of his "claim to fame." This indeed makes him unique—and makes our identification of this clue all the more sure.

GREAT WORDS IN 1890:

Pope Leo XIII asserted that "the supreme teacher in the Church is the Roman Pontiff. Union of minds, therefore, requires . . . COMPLETE SUBMISSION and OBEDIENCE of will to the Church and to the Roman Pontiff, AS TO GOD HIMSELF." [156]

The Bible clue speaks of a "MOUTH speaking great things." The Pope is the mouth—the official mouthpiece or spokesman—for the Papal system. You can see that when we measure the Papacy in the "Great Words" Department, the needle goes completely off the scale!

GREAT WORDS IN 1894:

Pope Leo XIII boldly declared: "We [that is, we Popes] hold upon this earth the place of GOD ALMIGHTY." [157]

GREAT WORDS TODAY:

Despite Jesus' command: "Call no man your FATHER upon earth: for One is your Father, which is in heaven," [158] the Roman hierarchy not only teaches the people to call each priest "Father," but it also calls its leader the "Pope," a title derived from the Latin *papa*, meaning "father." We see the root word *papa* more clearly in words like "papal" and "papacy."

Furthermore, despite the fact that Scripture declares: "There is NONE righteous, no, not one. . . . ALL have sinned, and come short of the glory of God" [159]—still today we see the Pope answering to such titles as "HOLY FATHER," "MOST HOLY FATHER," and "HIS HOLINESS"!

Such unbelievably arrogant, impudent, insolent Papal claims bring to mind these wise words from Shakespeare:

> "But man, proud man,
> Dressed in a little brief authority, . . .
> Plays such fantastic tricks before high heaven
> As make the angels weep." [160]

MARTIN LUTHER, the great Reformer of Germany and founder of the Lutheran Church, said this in regard to Daniel's and John's prophecies about the Beast's "great words":

> "Here the POPE is clearly pictured, who in all his decrees shouts impudently that all churches and thrones will be judged by him, but HE cannot be judged by anyone. . . . As the SUN is superior to the MOON, so the Pope [he says] is superior to the emperor." [161]

JOHN KNOX, guiding light of the Reformation in Scotland and leader of the Presbyterian Church, discussed the "great words" predicted in Daniel and cited the Pope's haughty claims as fulfillment.

> "If these and many other, easy to be shown in his own Canon Law, be not GREAT and BLASPHEMOUS words, such as NEVER mortal men spake before, let the world judge. . . . Let very Papists themselves judge." [162]

ADAM CLARKE, author of the famous Methodist commentary on the Bible, makes this comment on the "great words" of Daniel 7:

> "To none can this apply so well or so fully as to the Popes of Rome. They have assumed infallibility, which belongs only to God. They profess to forgive sins, which belongs only to God. They profess to open and shut heaven, which belongs only to God. They profess to be higher than all the kings of the earth, which belongs only to God. And they go beyond God in pretending to loose whole nations from their oath of allegiance to their kings, when such kings do not please them." [163]

THOMAS CRANMER, England's Archbishop of Canterbury, later burned alive at the stake under the persecutions of Catholic Queen Mary (often called "Bloody Mary," a nickname earned after the fate of nearly 300 victims who perished at the stake created a revulsion), said that the Pope's boastful words made him "more insolent than LUCIFER." [164] Indeed, the arrogant assertions of equality with God and of universal jurisdiction even over heavenly inhabitants are strangely reminiscent of Lucifer's boast, "I will be like the most High." [165]

These impudent Papal claims to DIVINE dignity and authority exactly match God's prophetic specifications. Could we imagine a more precise fulfillment? No other responsible organization has ever made such claims. In fact, what more COULD a man claim? Antichrist has once again identified himself.

✦ ✦ ✦

CLUE "Q"
NOT ONLY WOULD IT PRESUME POWERS OVER OTHER KINGS AND KINGDOMS, BUT IT WOULD BE SPECIFICALLY A RELIGIOUS POWER *DOMINATING* THE CIVIL POWER.

Your BIBLE says:

1. **Daniel 7:20**—Daniel saw the Little Horn "whose look was MORE STOUT than his fellows." This was a "LITTLE Horn," but Daniel said it paradoxically . . .

> "was STRONGER than the others"
> > —The Living Bible
>
> "seemed GREATER than its fellows"
> > —Revised Standard Version
>
> "looked MORE IMPOSING than the others"
> > —New International Version
>
> "was MORE TERRIFYING than any of the others"
> > —Today's English Version

to quote modern Bible versions.

2. **Revelation 13:7**—"POWER was given him [the Beast] OVER all kindreds, and tongues, and nations."

3. **Revelation 17:3**—"I saw a WOMAN SIT UPON a scarlet coloured BEAST."

4. **Revelation 17:7**—"I will tell thee the mystery of the WOMAN, and of the BEAST that CARRIETH HER. . . ."

5. As Clue "G" already established, a "woman" in prophecy symbolizes a church, and a "beast" represents a political power.[166] So if God's Word depicts the woman as RIDING the beast, it means that a *church* would DOMINATE and CONTROL the *civil* power of the *state*.

6. **Revelation 17:18**—"the WOMAN . . . REIGNETH OVER the KINGS of the earth."

HISTORY testifies:

Did the Pope fulfill this prophecy, according to History? Did he assume a posture, a look, "more stout than his fellows," as the prophet said? History confirms that he did, in the areas of both church and state.

CONTROL of the CHURCH

Bishops of the early Christian church were found presiding in ALL size-able cities, such as Jerusalem, Alexandria, Constantinople, Antioch, Rome, Athens, *etc.* But the Bishop of Rome was not satisfied to be just another bishop among many, for his ambition was to be more than just one among equals. His original sin was PRIDE—a desire to be GREATER than his fellow bishops. Unfortunately, he achieved his ambition to such an extent that for centuries he was—and even today considers himself to be—ABSOLUTE RULER of the Christian church!

DOMINATION of the STATE

But the ambitious heart of prideful man is not easily satisfied. Even though supreme in the Church, the Pope yearned to exercise political power. The period of Papal supremacy which began in A.D. 538 gave the Roman Pontiff dominion over the civil State as well, so that as time progressed and his influence grew, the Pope actually DICTATED to the kings of Europe! After that date, you see, the removal of the last vestiges of Imperial Roman power and the defeat of the three Arian kingdoms left the bishop of Rome in a perfect position to fill the "power vacuum" existing at that time in history. [167]

The Pope became "larger than life." His dominance of the CHURCH gave him unrivalled authority over the other bishops. His dominance of the STATE gave him power over kings as well. The reigning Pope, at any given time during the period of Papal supremacy, wielded MORE POWER than anyone else could hope to have in several lifetimes!

Very wisely, the Constitution of the United State separates the powers of the three branches of our federal government. But the Papacy combines ALL in one, vesting legislative, executive, and judicial power in one man. Under the despotism of the Papacy's absolute dictatorship, there was NO REFUGE and NO APPEAL from the Pope's decree. His word was law—his decision, immutable. He was a monarch without peer, as two examples may illustrate.

Example One:
England's KING JOHN

Innocent III, who was Pope from 1198 to 1216, declared: "As the SUN and MOON are placed in the firmament, the greater as the light of day and the lesser of the night, so there are two powers on earth, the greater the PONTIFICAL and the lesser the ROYAL." Proving this was no empty claim, Innocent III exercised his tyrannical power against King John of England.

Their dispute was over the Pope's appointment of Stephen Langton as Archbishop of Canterbury, England's highest church office. King John resented this appointment. *Encyclopedia Britannica* says: "This [appointment by the Pope], it could be argued, violated the then established convention on these matters. . . . John, with some justification, chose to regard this election as an invasion of his established rights and refused to recognize Langton."[168] And even though John—the same King John who signed the *Magna Carta*—had some problems with the English barons, *Britannica* adds: "The baronage, however, were heartily behind John in the struggle" with the Pope.

But all this was to no avail, for in November 1209 Innocent III EXCOM-MUNICATED John from the Roman Catholic Church and in 1212 DEPOSED him as England's king, so that NO Catholic citizen could thereafter in good conscience be subject to him.

Pandulph, Cardinal of Milan and the Pope's official ambassador in this matter, delivers these words to the monarch in Shakespeare's play *King John:*

> "Thou shalt stand cursed and excommunicate:
> And BLESSED shall he be that doth revolt
> From his allegiance to an heretic;
> And MERITORIOUS shall that hand be called,
> That takes away by any secret course
> Thy hateful life."[169]

Thus forced to capitulate, in 1213 John submitted and GRANTED "to our lord the Pope Innocent and his Catholic successors, the whole realm of ENGLAND and the whole realm of IRELAND with all their rights and appurte-nances" and promised to PAY AN ANNUAL TRIBUTE to the Roman Church of "1000 marks sterling" to atone for his supposed "sin" of defying the Pope.[170]

Encyclopedia Britannica points out that this Pope—Innocent III—wasn't even ordained a *priest* until more than a month *after* being elected *Pope* and states:

> "Innocent III's very EXALTED conception of the role of the Papacy in the Christian world and his success at making this conception a reality . . . [resulted in] unprecedented splendour and majesty for the glorification of the Papal office. At the same time the political constel-lations within Christendom during his pontificate allowed the Pope to exercise spiritual authority not only in the inner precincts of the CHURCH but also in all vital POLITICAL questions of the day."[171]

Thus History testifies that the Papacy exerted an awesome influence so forceful and far-reaching that it actually deposed this royal ruler, the King of England himself, until he submitted to the POLITICAL power of the Roman CHURCH![172]

EXAMPLE TWO:

GERMANY'S HENRY THE FOURTH

Another example of the CHURCH dominating the STATE was Pope Gregory VII's humiliation of Henry IV of Germany. You'll recall from Clue "P" that Gregory VII was the Pope who proclaimed his "Dictates of Hildebrand" which declared "That all princes should *kiss* the *feet* of the Pope alone" and other great words.

For presuming to disregard the Pope's authority, Henry IV was EXCOMMUNICATED from the church and DEPOSED as king (February 21, 1076). Terrified by the subsequent desertion and threats of his own princes, who were encouraged in rebellion against him by the Papal mandate, Henry felt compelled to seek his peace with Rome. In company with his wife and a faithful servant he CROSSED THE ALPS IN MID-WINTER to meet the Pope at Canossa in northern Italy.

> "Henry's crossing of Mont Cenis in one of the severest winters recorded in the Middle Ages was extremely hazardous and arduous. When he arrived at Canossa he was faced with the even harder task of obtaining absolution from the Pope. Gregory hesitated to absolve and even to receive the king, who nevertheless ON THREE SUCCESSIVE DAYS came to the castle and stood before the gate in the garb and attitude of a penitent." [173]

And there, in the severe cold of winter, with UNCOVERED HEAD AND NAKED FEET, this monarch awaited the Pope's permission to come into his presence. Read, in the Pope's own words,

> "how King Henry came to Italy to do penance. . . . We learned that the king was approaching. Now before he entered Italy he had sent to us and had offered to make complete satisfaction for his fault, promising to reform and henceforth to obey us [174] in all things, provided we would give him our absolution and blessing. We hesitated for some time, taking occasion in the course of the negotiations to reprove him sharply for his former sins. Finally he came in person to Canossa. . . . Once arrived, he presented himself at the gate of the castle, BAREFOOT and clad only in WRETCHED woollen garments, beseeching us with tears to grant him absolution and forgiveness. This he continued to do FOR THREE DAYS, until all those about us were moved to compassion at his plight and interceded for him with tears and prayers. Indeed, they marvelled at our hardness of heart, some even complaining that our action savored rather of heartless tyranny than of chastening severity. At length his persistent declarations of repentance and the supplications of all who were there with us overcame our reluctance." [175]

A relatively recent work, *Documents of German History,* adds this thought on the struggle between the Pope and Henry IV, Emperor of Germany:

> "For three days and three NIGHTS Henry stood outside the castle, stripped clear of all his regalia, 'wretched, BAREFOOTED, and clad in wool,' waiting for the forgiveness of the Pope. The spectacle of the mightiest king in Christendom humbling himself in this sensational fashion was one to amaze the whole Christian world—king, lord, and peasant alike." [176]

But making and unmaking kings was the pastime of Pontiffs. Oliver Wendell Holmes, Sr., observed: "The Pope put his foot on the neck of kings."

French Catholic priest and theologian Joseph Turmel wrote of how *papal Rome of the Church* survived and succeeded *pagan Rome of the Caesars* when the latter Empire declined and crumbled:

> "What is to become of the Church? Are its days numbered, and is the Empire to bring it down as its companion into an open tomb? No, the Church will not descend into the tomb. It will survive the Empire. . . . At length a second empire will arise, and of this empire the POPE will be the master—more than this, he will be the master of Europe. He will dictate his orders to KINGS who will obey them." [177]

Historian Carl Conrad Eckhardt explains:

> "Under the Roman Empire the Popes had NO temporal [civil or secular] powers. But when the Roman Empire had disintegrated and its place had been taken by a number of rude, barbarous kingdoms, the Roman Catholic Church not only became independent of the states in RELIGIOUS affairs but DOMINATED SECULAR affairs as well. . . . Under the weak political system of feudalism, the well-organized, unified, and centralized Church, with the Pope at its head, was not only independent in ECCLESIASTICAL affairs but also CONTROLLED CIVIL affairs." [178]

A. C. Flick, professor of European history, declares:

> "The Papal theory . . . made the Pope alone God's representative on earth and . . . culminated with Boniface VIII, at the jubilee of 1300 when, seated on the throne of Constantine, girded with the imperial sword, wearing a crown, and waving a sceptre, he shouted to the throng of loyal pilgrims: 'I am Caesar—I am Emperor.'" [179]

Gullible masses often naively presume that "the King can do no wrong." But English historian LORD ACTON deplored and feared the tendency of powerful men to become corrupt. Though a faithful Roman Catholic himself, he saw this tendency even in the Pope. In a letter to Bishop Mandell Creighton, Acton wisely declared:

"I cannot accept your canon that we are to judge Pope and King unlike other men, with a favorable presumption that they did no wrong. If there is any presumption it is the other way, against the holders of power, increasing as the power increases. . . . POWER TENDS TO CORRUPT, AND ABSOLUTE POWER CORRUPTS ABSOLUTELY." [180]

Thus Lord Acton warned against the overmastering temptations of almost limitless power. *Encyclopedia Britannica* says of Lord Acton, called the "Apostle of Liberty" and philosopher of freedom, "He had a hatred of the Papal temporal [civil] power and an outraged sense of the many instances of its MISUSE in history." [181]

In the 1870 Roman Catholic crisis over the dogma of Papal infallibility, Acton vociferously opposed it, as did his teacher Döllinger. Ignaz von Döllinger was Catholic professor of canon law and church history at Munich, president of the Bavarian Royal Academy of Sciences, and later rector of Munich University. Professor Döllinger stated unequivocally: "As a Christian, as a theologian, as a historian, as a citizen, I CANNOT accept this doctrine." [182] So the Pope excommunicated him.

"What the Papacy aimed at was not simply to be a temporal power by reason of sovereignty over a little Italian state, but to exercise a universal sovereignty over ALL sovereigns by reason of the spiritual office of the Pope, who was to be the MASTER and arbiter of all other temporal authorities." [183]

The inspired insight God gave John depicts the "woman"—the church— SEATED UPON and RIDING the "beast"—the civil power, [184] by which she is upheld, and which she controls and guides to her own ends, as a rider controls the animal he sits upon. It is clearly a church-state power, a religio-political entity—but the CHURCH is in control. The pages of history bear record that earthly monarchs became mere vassals of the Roman Pontiff. Kings and princes of Europe swore allegiance to him as their overlord. Rome once more was mistress of the world.

CLUE "R"
IT WOULD BE A PERSECUTING POWER
AGAINST THE SAINTS OF GOD.

Your BIBLE says:
1. **Daniel 7:21**—The Little Horn "MADE WAR with the saints, and PREVAILED against them."

2. **Revelation 13:7**—Power was given the Beast "to MAKE WAR with the saints, and to OVERCOME them."

3. **Daniel 7:25**—The Little Horn "shall WEAR OUT the saints of the most High."

4. **Revelation 17:6**—"I saw the woman DRUNKEN with the BLOOD of saints, and with the BLOOD of the MARTYRS of Jesus."

5. **Revelation 18:24**—"In her was found the BLOOD . . . of saints."

6. **Revelation 19:2**—"He hath judged the great whore, which did corrupt the earth with her fornication, and hath avenged the BLOOD of His servants at her hand."

HISTORY testifies:

Let's make clear, first of all, what we mean by "persecution" in this investigation. We don't mean a mere MENTAL attitude like *prejudice*. We don't even mean ACTS of *intolerance* like prohibitions that curb or outlaw the practice of another religion. Those things are all bad enough, but what we mean here is persecution that touches one's BODY in a very *painful* way: cold-blooded TORTURE and MURDER! The Bible clues speak of "war" and "blood" and "martyrs."

Because this is not a pretty picture, we may prefer God would spare us the pain of examining any evidence of persecution. It's a shocking story that should send a chill down the spine of every thinking person. History's pages are stained with the blood of bitter persecution. Man's inhumanity to man is well documented. But some of us forget that much of the very worst persecution involving wholesale torture and death has been done in the name of GOD! TORTURE is TORTURE, and TERROR is TERROR—even if practiced by so-called holy men and resorted to by a CHURCH! The Papacy ironically perpetrated awful atrocities under the cloak of RELIGION!

A Witch Hunt for "HERETICS"

The archives of this chapter of history contain a secret dark as death—the death of countless Christians faithful to God! Countless lives were wiped out for no other crime than "heresy"—that is, for daring to believe something contrary to the teachings of the Roman Church.[185] Those who held opposing views became unwilling actors in a tragic drama staged by the Papal Inquisition.

Christ, the embodiment of Truth, could have struck dead all mankind for being in error—but He did not. On the other hand, no one can accuse the Papacy of being unduly tolerant of religious views it judged "heretical." Think of it: MURDER and TORTURE of the innocent. MARTYRDOM of men and women whose only crime was being faithful to God rather than compromise their conscience to follow misguided men.

Many heroes of the Reformation gave their lives for the truths they preached.[186] For instance, WILLIAM TYNDALE translated the Word of God into English so beautiful and stately that it later remained largely unchanged when the King James committee did their work on the Holy Scriptures. Since his work was too good to improve upon, at least 90 per cent of the King James Version may be attributed to Tyndale.

But for his "crime" of putting the Bible into the language of the people, Tyndale was hunted by priests and had to leave England, never to see his beloved country again. On the Continent, however, he was subsequently captured—the bishops who'd burned some of his Bibles now resolved that HE must be burned. After suffering in a cold dungeon sixteen months, he was taken from prison Friday, October 6, 1536. First he was strangled, and then he was burned at the stake. But his work for God lives on.

In the face of this cruel persecution from a totalitarian regime, we see the enormous personal risk taken by Martin Luther and his fellow Reformers in daring to protest against the abuses of the Pope.

Protestants automatically were treated as heretics:

> "Another *auto de la fe*[187] was held on the 22nd of July, 1587, at which George Gaspar, a tailor, twenty-four years old, a native of London, was BURNT in person, for refusing to abjure the Lutheran religion in which he had been born and bred. He stabbed himself the night before, but was STILL ALIVE when his sentence was executed."[188]

The poor man's only crime was following the Protestant religion he'd been taught from birth. His misfortune was multiplied many times in the tragic experience of countless other sincere Christians.

Some who separated from the Roman Catholic Church even before the Reformation were the WALDENSES, who fled to the mountains of Piedmont in northern Italy. In 1655 Catholics conducted a violent persecution of the Waldenses, hunting them down like animals and hurling them over the cliffs. In outraged protest, JOHN MILTON, the blind English poet who penned the Biblical epic *Paradise Lost*, wrote the following sonnet, "ON THE LATE MASSACRE IN PIEDMONT":

"Avenge, O Lord, Thy slaughtered saints, whose bones
Lie scattered on the Alpine mountains cold;
Even them who kept Thy truth so pure of old
When all our fathers worshipped stocks and stones,[189]
FORGET NOT: in Thy book record their groans
Who were Thy sheep, and in their ancient fold
Slain by the bloody Piedmontese, that rolled
Mother with infant down the rocks. Their moans
The vales redoubled to the hills, and they
To heaven. Their martyred blood and ashes sow[190]
O'er all the Italian fields, where still doth sway
The triple tyrant;[191] that from these may grow
A hundredfold, who, having learnt Thy way,
Early may flee the Babylonian woe."[192]

Revelation 12 symbolizes God's true church as a pure "woman" PERSE-CUTED by the "serpent" or "dragon" symbolizing Satan.[193] But just as God opened the Red Sea when His people were fleeing from Pharaoh's armies, so He opened a way of escape for His saints persecuted in Europe. Revelation 12:16 says: "The earth HELPED the woman and the earth opened her mouth, and the earth swallowed up the flood which the dragon cast out of his mouth."

HOW did God have "the earth" HELP "the woman"? By providing America as a haven of refuge! Until God opened this New World through Christopher Columbus[194] there was NOWHERE to RUN, NO PLACE to HIDE. Like the Jews caught in Hitler's holocaust, faithful believers were hunted, persecuted, and slaughtered on a wholesale basis. That's why the Pilgrims came over on the *Mayflower*. That's why the Puritans and countless other persecuted Christians fled comfortable homes in Europe, braved an ocean voyage in rickety ships, and came to the cold unknown of this "land of liberty." Their noble motive was to flee persecution and seek religious freedom.[195]

Just as Revelation 12 speaks of the TRUE church as a pure woman, Revelation 17 speaks of the FALSE church as a corrupt woman. Verse 6 says this corrupt woman or CHURCH would be "drunken with the blood of saints, and with the blood of the martyrs of Jesus." This point we MUST NOT MISS: God says His saints, the true Christian believers, would be persecuted *not* by any worldly power but by a CHURCH, a corrupt church. This fact consequently rules out Hitler's terrible Holocaust of the Jews, or political terrorism, or other instances of atrocities. Incredibly enough, we must look for a CHURCH that persecuted God's faithful people!

THE ROMAN CATHOLIC INQUISITION

What can be said about the Inquisition that won't sound like an exaggeration? Heaven knows this old earth is soaked in blood and tears, but in a world that's seen much tyranny and terror, the NIGHTMARE of the INQUISITION still stands alone. The tragic enormity of it all cannot be fully comprehended, but three points should be made:

(1)　Its persecution was systematically ORGANIZED and planned, with officers being appointed, records being kept, *etc.*

(2)　Its persecution was extremely WIDESPREAD, being virtually universal against those considered enemies of the Church.

(3)　It was a concerted effort over a PROLONGED period of time!

The strangely ironic name Rome gave to its iniquitous Inquisition was "the HOLY OFFICE"!!! Note the definition:

> "The Inquisition or the 'Holy Office' is the name of the spiritual court of the Roman Catholic Church for the DETECTION and PUNISHMENT of those whose OPINIONS DIFFER from the doctrines of the Church." [196]

Since the Inquisitors were in total control, it was easy to sustain a conviction against the hapless victim on a charge of "heresy" or, say, "sorcery." French Catholic priest and scholar E. Vacandard says this about the latter charge:

> "It is impossible to estimate the number of sorcerers condemned. Louis of Paramo triumphantly declared that in a century and a half the Holy Office sent to the stake over thirty thousand. Of course we must take such round numbers with a grain of salt, as they are always greatly exaggerated. But the fact remains that the condemnations for sorcery were *so numerous* as to stagger belief." [197]

GALILEO, the Italian astronomer and physicist, was one of the fortunate few who escaped with his life after offending the Roman Church. *Encyclopedia Britannica* states: "Galileo was tried by the Inquisition in Rome, ordered to **recant** and forced to spend the last eight years of his life under house arrest." [198] Even though Galileo was RIGHT about the earth going around the sun, he was forced to renounce that belief by the terrible Inquisition.

That was in Italy. What about Spain? Historian Paul J. Hauben answers: "The Spanish Inquisition has been called many things, from the resolute defender of Catholicism to the earliest version of the NAZI GESTAPO." [199]

And Dr. Cecil Roth of Oxford asserts that . . .

> "No OTHER organization for religious persecution has EVER equalled the Spanish Inquisition in intensity, scope or efficiency of operation. In

1478 Pope Sixtus IV issued the fatal Bull [papal order] empowering the Spanish sovereigns to set up tribunals to extirpate heresy within their realms, and from then until its abolishment in 1834, the Inquisition pursued a career of blood whose goal was no less than the destruction of every person who was not a sincere Roman Catholic Christian. First and foremost this meant Jews, but the Holy Office later expanded its range of victims to include Protestants, mystics, and non-conformists of every sort." [200]

But the agony of the Papal Inquisition was not limited to Spain and Italy. Far from it. British preacher and writer H. Grattan Guinness says: "EVERY Catholic country . . . had its Inquisition. . . . It has been calculated that the Popes of Rome have, directly or indirectly, slain . . . FIFTY MILLIONS of men and women who refused to be parties to Romish idolatries, who held to the Bible as the Word of God." [201]

John Lothrop Motley, American historian and diplomat who served as U.S. minister to Austria and Great Britain, declared:

> "Upon February 16, 1568, a sentence of the Holy Office condemned ALL the inhabitants of the NETHERLANDS to death as heretics. From this universal doom only a few persons, especially named, were excepted. A proclamation of the king, dated ten days later, confirmed this decree of the Inquisition, and ordered it to be carried into instant execution, without regard to age, sex, or condition. This is probably the most concise death warrant that was ever framed. Three MILLIONS of people— men, women, and children—were sentenced to the scaffold in three lines [of print]." [202]

Little of the Inquisition's DARK HORROR has come to public light, even though the historical facts are well-documented. Today the subject is shockingly neglected by schools and colleges. Desiring to be tolerant to all religions, educators feel any fact incriminating to a church is "inadmissible evidence." But HUMANITY, as the injured party, has a right to expose the perpetrator of these crimes by revealing the truth. The Roman Catholic Inquisition was not just a dusty footnote in history—it was a living nightmare in the lives of millions!

Let me stress that though the Inquisition sounds like something out of a bad horror movie, it was REAL. The Inquisitional Palace at Cartagena, Spain, can be seen today where it still stands in amazingly good repair. The church's reign of terror included incarceration in horrible dungeons, coercion through unspeakable torture, and death by the sword or being burned alive at the stake.

The St. Bartholomew's Day MASSACRE

The massacre of St. Bartholomew's Day was a horrible BLOODBATH of premeditated persecution against Huguenots, the Protestants of France. It began at the pre-arranged signal of the tolling of church bells in Paris shortly before dawn of St. Bartholomew's Day, August 24, 1572. Thousands of MEN, WOMEN, and CHILDREN were killed in their beds on that fateful morning. *Encyclopedia Britannica* states:

> "The homes and shops of Huguenots were pillaged, and their occupants brutally murdered, many of their bodies being thrown into the Seine. On August 25 the government ordered the killings to stop, but the bloodthirsty mob would not listen. . . . Meanwhile the massacre spread to the provinces of France in a sporadic and haphazard way, continuing till the first week in October. Some towns, notably Rouen, Lyons, Bourges, Orleans, Bordeaux, and Toulouse, were scenes of CARNAGE." [203]

Though no precise assessment can be given of the number of victims throughout France, the encyclopedia states that one contemporary "put the number as high as 70,000."

Notorious in American history is the infamous "Saint Valentine's Day Massacre," resulting from gangland warfare in Chicago. But only SEVEN lives were lost in that execution-style massacre—and those were the lives of murderous gangsters. In contrast, the St. Bartholomew's Day Massacre claimed TEN THOUSAND TIMES more lives, and those were the lives of innocent Christians. That was a crime of infinitely greater magnitude than the other, yet few people today could correctly answer a "Trivial Pursuit" question about it.

The Massacre of St. Bartholomew's Day was such a deliberate, bloodthirsty act that we'd expect the world universally to condemn it. But what was the reaction of the POPE reigning at that time to this wholesale persecution of Protestant believers? Was it horror and disgust? Sorrow and pity? No, History testifies that "The Papacy was jubilant and had a MEDAL struck to celebrate the event." [204] And Catholic historian Lord Acton admits:

> "[Pope] Gregory XIII exclaimed that the massacre was more agreeable to him than fifty victories of Lepanto. [205] . . . On the 8th of September the Pope went in procession to the French Church of St. Lewis, where three-and-thirty Cardinals attended at a mass of THANKSGIVING. On the 11th he proclaimed a JUBILEE. . . . Before a month had passed Vasari [206] was summoned from Florence to decorate the hall of kings [in the Vatican] with PAINTINGS of the massacre. The work was pronounced his masterpiece; and the shameful scene may still be traced upon the wall, where, for three centuries, it has insulted every Pontiff that entered the Sistine Chapel." [207]

PAPAL MEDAL: Pope Gregory XIII celebrates St. Bartholomew's Massacre
REVERSE SIDE: "Slaughter of the Huguenots *(Ugonottorum Strages)* 1572"

Rome then sent Cardinal Orsini as Papal ambassador to the French court of Charles IX and his mother, Catherine de Medici. Lord Acton writes that Cardinal Orsini . . .

> "desired, for the glory of God and the good of France, that the Huguenots should be EXTIRPATED [pulled up by the roots] utterly. . . . When Catherine knew that the Pope was NOT YET satisfied, . . . she exclaimed that she WONDERED at such designs. . . . To Charles, who had done so much, it seemed unreasonable that he should be asked for more. He represented to Orsini that it was impossible to eradicate ALL the remnants of a faction which had been so strong. He had put SEVENTY THOUSAND Huguenots to the sword; and if he had shown compassion to the rest, it was in order that they might become good Catholics." [208]

Commenting on "The hidden thoughts which the Court of Rome betrayed by its conduct on this memorable occasion," Lord Acton points out how Pope Gregory XIII was NOT as BAD as the preceding Pontiff, Pius V.

> "The predecessor of Gregory had been Inquisitor-General.[209] . . . Men were hanged and quartered almost daily at Rome; and Pius declared that he would release a culprit guilty of a hundred MURDERS rather than one obstinate heretic. . . . [As for Huguenots,] He required that they should be pursued to the death, that not one should be spared under any pretence, that all prisoners should suffer death. . . . When he sanctioned the murder of Elizabeth[210] he proposed that it should be done in execution of HIS sentence against her. It became usual with those who meditated assassination or regicide on the plea of religion to look upon the representatives of Rome as their natural advisers." [211]

Sometimes when a life is taken, the killing is judged as justifiable homicide if there were extenuating circumstances such as self defense, *etc.* But that wasn't the case with the St. Bartholomew's Day Massacre. Naturally those who perpetrated such an atrocity concluded it was "justifiable homicide" when their supposedly all-wise leader praised and rewarded them for it. But these homicides were not justifiable at all. They were cruel and bloody mass murders. Simply put, the goal was GENOCIDE of the Huguenots.

Lord Acton was a scholar and a Christian of such integrity that, though a devout Catholic himself, he declared:

> "A time came when the Catholics, having long relied on force, were compelled to appeal to opinion. That which had been defiantly acknowledged and defended [that is, the St. Bartholomew's Day Massacre] required to be ingeniously explained away. The same motive which had justified the murder now prompted the lie. Men shrank from the conviction that the rulers and restorers of their Church had been murderers and abetters of murder, and that so much infamy had been coupled with so much zeal. They feared to say that the most monstrous of crimes had been solemnly APPROVED at Rome, lest they should devote the Papacy to the execration of mankind. A swarm of facts were invented to meet the difficulty: The victims were insignificant in number; they were slain for no reason connected with religion; . . . the medal is fictitious; . . . the Pope rejoiced only when he heard that it was over. These things were repeated so often that they have been sometimes believed. . . . Such things will cease to be written when men perceive that TRUTH is the only merit that gives dignity and worth to history." [212]

Rome's Own Candid ADMISSION

The Papacy can't whitewash what it did to millions during those centuries of the Dark Ages. Usually it doesn't even try. Instead, quite often the Roman Catholic Church boldly admits resorting to violence and persecution.

From a Roman Catholic source we have this admission:

> "The church HAS persecuted. Only a tyro [a beginner] in church history will deny that. . . . Protestants were persecuted in France and Spain with the full approval of the church authorities. We have always defended the persecution of the Huguenots, and the Spanish Inquisition. . . . *When she thinks it good to use physical force, she will use it. . . .* But will the Catholic Church give bond that she will NOT persecute at all? Will she guarantee absolute freedom and equality of all churches and all faiths? The Catholic Church gives NO BONDS for her good behavior." [213]

A Catholic cardinal who was professor of history and vicar-general of the *Institut Catholique* in Paris points out how the Church used CIVIL power to carry out her will:

> "The Catholic Church . . . has, and she loudly proclaims she has, a 'horror of blood.' [That is, she dislikes shedding blood personally.] Nevertheless when confronted by heresy she does not content herself with persuasion; arguments of an intellectual and moral order appear to her insufficient and she has recourse to FORCE, to CORPORAL punishment, to TORTURE. She creates tribunals like the Inquisition, she calls the laws of the STATE to her aid, if necessary she encourages a crusade, or a religious war and all her 'horror of blood' practically culminates into urging the SECULAR power to shed it, which proceeding is almost more odious—for it is less frank—than shedding it herself. Especially did she act thus in the sixteenth century with regard to Protestants. NOT CONTENT to reform morally, to preach by example, to convert people by eloquent and holy missionaries, she LIT in Italy, in the Low Countries, and above all in Spain the funeral piles of the Inquisition. In France under Francis I and Henry II, in England under Mary Tudor, she TORTURED the heretics." [214]

Martin Luther's recognition of the fact that the Roman Church usually condemned the victim and then turned him over to the State for execution[215] was questioned and corrected by another cardinal:

> "'The church,' says Luther, . . . 'has never burned a heretic.' . . . I reply that this argument proves not the opinion, but the ignorance or impudence of Luther. Since almost INFINITE numbers WERE either burned or otherwise killed, Luther either did not know it, and was therefore ignorant, or if he was not ignorant, he is convicted of impudence and falsehood; for that heretics were OFTEN burned by the church may be proved if we adduce a few from many examples." [216]

Here's a telling quote from a Roman Catholic priest published in a Catholic journal:

> "The MAFIA knows about power. If you betray the 'code,' you are in for a very intimate introduction to the bottom of the Hudson River, or wherever. Yet, I have often thought we in the church have made the Mafia look like small change."[217]

THE WORLD'S GREATEST PERSECUTOR

When it came to religious persecution during the Dark Ages, the Roman Catholic Church was not an innocent bystander. Quite the contrary. The Papacy, being guilty of HIGH CRIMES against humanity, deserves status as a

WORLD-CLASS champion in the role of persecutor and wins hands down against all competitors! No one disputes that fact—far too much PAINFUL EVIDENCE substantiates it.

Irish theologian Charles H. H. Wright states:

> "PAGAN persecutions were bad, but the number of sufferers by those terrible outbreaks of heathen fury was far below the number of those who suffered at the hands of the CHURCH of Rome throughout the long centuries during which she ruled the Western world." [218]

H. Grattan Guinness adds: "We recognize Papal Rome by . . . her strange and terrible inebriation with the blood of saints and martyrs. . . . Papal Rome through long centuries has held the pre-eminence as the persecutor of those faithful to the teachings of the gospel of Christ." [219]

Only God knows the full BODY COUNT of victims from the ongoing slaughter, but MILLIONS were martyred for their faith during those dark centuries. J. A. Wylie stated it well when he said: "The NOON of the Papacy was the MIDNIGHT of the world." [220]

The painful truth is, persecution was virtually a way of life for the church in those days. Persecution was "Standard Operating Procedure" for the church, its *modus operandi*. Pope Innocent III enunciated this principle as a matter of Papal policy: "Use against heretics the SPIRITUAL sword of excommunication, and if this does not prove effective, use the MATERIAL sword." [221]

What makes it all the more shocking is the fact that we're not talking about ATTILA the HUN! We're talking about ruthless crimes committed by a church in the name of God and vigorously carried on under the cloak of religion! A Church that has the police power of the State behind it is ARMED and DANGEROUS! During the long nightmare of the Dark Ages, under the despotism of the Papacy's absolute dictatorship, there was no refuge and no appeal. Therefore, the world witnessed the spectacle of nothing less than the murder of millions! Far from being impersonal statistics, these figures shriek in pain—as did the people they represent.

Papal persecution was truly a tale of terror. The merciless massacres, the cruel carnage of pitiless torture, the barbarities worse than those of savages seem all the more infernal when inflicted at the command of the ministers of a gospel of love! In Germany, the procedure called for the instruments of torture to be BLESSED by a PRIEST before being used on the victim.

LEGAL TORTURE!

The *New Catholic Encyclopedia* admits that "the use of torture as a means of obtaining a confession or other testimony in a judicial inquiry" was made LEGAL by the Pope's official approval:

"In 1252 [Pope] Innocent IV sanctioned the infliction of TORTURE by the civil authorities upon heretics, and torture later came to have a recognized place in the procedure of the inquisitorial courts." [222]

The Church used some of the most DIABOLICAL methods of torture ever devised. Much of it is too painful to print, but two shall be mentioned just to give the reader some inkling of what happened.

(1) **STRAPPADO** was a common form of torture to force the victim to confess and to name alleged accomplices. His hands were tied behind his back with a rope attached to a pulley which then hoisted him in the air. The prisoner was kept hanging for a considerable time while being questioned. Often heavy weights were attached to his feet to pull his shoulders from their sockets without leaving visible marks of rough treatment.

(2) **SQUASSATION** was really a more severe form of *strappado*, for heavy lead weights were always attached to the feet, after which the prisoner was raised all the way to the high ceiling, till his bound hands touched the pulley. If his answers seemed unsatisfactory to his inquisitors, the pulley rope was suddenly slackened and he was allowed to DROP almost—but not quite—to the floor. The jerking shock he received from the sudden stop of his fall completely dislocated his shoulders and other limbs. More than three applications ("severe torture") usually caused death. Philip Limborch, in his *History of the Inquisition,* [223] left a detailed description of many modes of torture used in the infamous and inhuman Inquisition.

The actual candid history of the Papacy shows that, as frightful as the Antichrist/Beast prophecies are, they do NOT exaggerate!

Relics of the Inquisition are seen even in our own legal system. For instance, (1) the principle of SEPARATION of church and state was favored by Founding Fathers who recalled the tragic times when the civil power executed the decrees of the Roman Church. And (2) the FIFTH AMENDMENT of our Constitution was framed by legal minds who remembered prisoners being forced by unspeakable torture to testify against themselves.

A QUESTION OF **GUILT**

It's difficult even for those most sympathetic with the Papacy to attempt to justify the unjustifiable. "If, as [Roman Catholic historian] Lord Acton wrote: 'The principle of the Inquisition is murderous,' then no man in cold blood can justify what our forefathers did, without becoming an accomplice after the fact." [224]

Apologists for the Roman Catholic Church try to condone this butchering of believers by saying other churches have persecuted also. But this lame excuse pales before the fact that no other church—no other organization of any kind, including the Holocaust of Jews by Hitler's Nazi regime—ever persecuted MORE lives for so LONG a period of time as has the Church of Rome. [225]

Historian William E. H. Lecky puts that excuse into proper perspective in these words:

> "She [the Roman Church] persecuted to the FULL EXTENT of the power of her clergy, and that power was VERY GREAT. The persecution of which every Protestant Church was guilty, was measured by the same rule, but clerical influence in Protestant countries was comparatively weak. The Protestant persecutions were never so sanguinary [bloody] as those of the Catholics." [226]

Historian Lecky continues:

> "That the Church of Rome has shed MORE innocent blood than ANY OTHER institution that has ever existed among mankind, will be questioned by no Protestant who has a competent knowledge of history. The memorials, indeed, of many of her persecutions are now so scanty that it is impossible to form a complete conception of the multitude of her victims, and it is quite certain that no powers of imagination can adequately realize their sufferings. Llorente, who had free access to the archives of the SPANISH Inquisition assures us that by that tribunal alone more than 31,000 persons were burnt, [227] and more than 290,000 condemned to punishments less severe than death. The number of those who were put to death in the Netherlands alone, in the reign of Charles V, has been estimated by a very high authority at 50,000 and at least half as many perished under his son. And when to these memorial instances we add the innumerable less conspicuous executions that took place, . . . the most callous nature must recoil from the spectacle.
>
> "These atrocities were not perpetrated in the brief paroxysms of a reign of terror, or by the hand of obscure sectaries, but were inflicted by a triumphant Church, with every circumstance of solemnity and deliberation. Nor did the victims perish by a BRIEF and PAINLESS death, but by one which was carefully selected as among the most poignant that man can suffer. They were usually BURNT ALIVE. They were burnt alive not infrequently by a slow fire. They were burnt alive after their constancy had been tried by the most excruciating agonies that minds fertile in torture could devise. This was the physical torment inflicted on those who dared to exercise their reason in the pursuit of truth; but what language can describe, and what imagination can conceive, the mental suffering that accompanied it? . . . Recollect those frightful massacres, perhaps the most fearful the world has ever seen: the massacre of the Albigenses which a Pope had instigated, or the massacre of St.

Bartholomew for which a Pope returned solemn thanks to Heaven. . . . When we consider all these things, it can surely be no exaggeration to say that the Church of Rome has inflicted a greater amount of unmerited suffering than any other religion that has ever existed." [228]

Nazi war criminals were tried and executed for "crimes against humanity." The Popes guilty of wholesale persecution of God's people will be brought before a Higher Court, a heavenly tribunal.

Seeing Is Believing

Many are unaware of these facts because they've never been shown them before. That's the way Satan likes it. But seeing is believing, and once they open their Bibles and see these crystal-clear clues, once they check the record of history and see prophecy's remarkable fulfillment, their minds are enlightened and they can begin to believe.

Regarding this clue, Presbyterian scholar Albert Barnes, in his classic commentary on the Bible, asks:

> "Can anyone doubt that this is true of the Papacy? The Inquisition, the 'persecutions of the Waldenses,' the ravages of the Duke of Alva, the fires of Smithfield, the tortures at Goa—indeed, the whole history of the Papacy may be appealed to in proof that this is applicable to that power. If anything could have 'worn out the saints of the Most High'— could have cut them off from the earth so that evangelical religion would have become extinct, it would have been the persecutions of the Papal power. In the year 1208, a crusade was proclaimed by Pope Innocent III against the Waldenses and Albigenses, in which a MILLION of men perished. From the beginning of the order of the Jesuits, in the year 1540, to 1580, nine hundred thousand were destroyed. One hundred and fifty thousand perished by the Inquisition in thirty years. In the Low Countries fifty thousand persons were hanged, beheaded, burned, and buried alive, for the crime of heresy, within the space of thirty-eight years from the edict of Charles V against the Protestants, to the peace of Chateau Cambreses in 1559. Eighteen thousand suffered by the hand of the executioner in the space of five years and a half during the administration of the Duke of Alva. Indeed, the slightest acquaintance with the history of the Papacy will convince anyone that what is here said of 'making war with the saints' and 'wearing out the saints of the Most High' is strictly applicable to that power, and will certainly describe its history." [229]

Some very vital HISTORY LESSONS have been forgotten. Yet we owe it to the silent dead to speak the tragic truth. True, these facts make *grim reading*, but they're not fairy tales. They serve as powerful evidence, constituting another piece of the puzzle identifying the Antichrist / Beast. Once again we see that these Biblical clues are not "blind alleys" leading nowhere. They're inspired leads pointing unanimously and inexorably in one direction.

POSTSCRIPT:

The Bible and history have just presented a very sobering message. Even more sobering is the thought that, in the future, history will REPEAT itself! For prophecy foretells with terrible exactitude that the Last Days just before Jesus returns will be a time of trouble and persecution for God's people. [230] The Antichrist/Beast power will issue a death decree against all who refuse to accept his Mark of authority. [231]

Force, compulsion, coercion—all are foreign to the God of Heaven and to the practice of a religion of love. Everyone realizes this in his heart. Yet the Papacy, in its official pronouncements, insists that the Church cannot afford to be tolerant of any ideas or teachings but her own. For instance, Pope Leo XIII attacked the American system of a free democracy in his encyclical letter on "The Christian Constitution of States" in which he said:

> "The unrestrained freedom of THINKING and of openly making known one's thoughts is NOT inherent in the rights of citizens, and is by no means to be reckoned worthy of favor and support." [232]

And Pope Pius IX published a "Syllabus of Errors" listing propositions which he pronounced as ERRONEOUS. For instance, he branded FALSE the beliefs that:

- "Every man is FREE to embrace and profess that religion which, guided by the light of reason, he shall consider true."
- "The Church has NOT the power of using force."
- "The Church ought to be SEPARATED from the State, and the State from the Church." [233]

J. B. Bury, Irish historian who served as regius professor of modern history at Cambridge University, explains the "thesis/hypothesis" idea embodied in the Pope's "Syllabus of Errors":

> "The *Syllabus* is concerned with *thesis*, the laying down of principles, which are of absolute validity, and WOULD PREVAIL in an ideal society when the Church possessed the power of enforcing its authority, as it did to such a vast extent in the Middle Ages. But in modern times the Church in practice has to deal with *hypothesis*, *i.e.*, it has to determine its actions to meet certain given conditions which it CANNOT control; it has to compromise and conciliate its theoretical principles, up to a certain point, with actual circumstances. This it has had to do

in the interests of self-preservation. . . . But notwithstanding this un-willing and necessary condescension, the Papacy never abandoned the theoretical principles which are the logical consequence of its claim to independent sovran *[sic]* authority, superior to the civil authority; they remain in the background as the ideal, like a utopia, which the Church would realize if it could." [234]

These facts give us cause for concern. In many countries today the Pa-pacy lacks the power to impose its will by force. But if circumstances change—? Persecution slumbers at present, not because Rome has had a change of heart, but because the spirit of religious freedom in the world makes that method unwise. The Church would lose more than it could ex-pect to gain. It's true that some Catholic leaders now speak in favor of reli-gious liberty—according to their definition of the term. But given the right circumstances, any future Pope could instantly revive persecution by a stroke of the pen.

Thomas Babington Macaulay, English writer and statesman, expresses well the deplorable attitude at the root of persecution:

"The doctrine which, from the very first origin of religious dissen-sions, has been held by all bigots of all sects, when condensed into a few words, and stripped of rhetorical disguise, is simply this: *I* am in the right, and *you* are in the wrong. When you are the stronger you ought to TOLERATE me; for it is your duty to tolerate truth. But when I am the stronger, I shall PERSECUTE you; for it is my duty to persecute error." [235]

CLUE "S"
IT WOULD BE A BLASPHEMOUS POWER.

Your BIBLE says:

1. **Daniel 7:25**—"He [the Little Horn power] shall speak great words AGAINST the most High."

2. **2 Thessalonians 2:3 & 4**—"The Man of Sin . . . EXALTETH HIMSELF above all that is called God, or that is worshipped; so that he AS God sitteth in the temple of God showing himself that he IS God."

3. **Revelation 13:1**—The Beast had "upon his heads the name of BLAS-PHEMY."

4. **Revelation 13:5**—"And there was given unto him [the Beast] a *mouth* speaking . . . BLASPHEMIES."

5. **Revelation 13:6**—The Beast "opened his mouth in BLASPHEMY against God, to BLASPHEME His name."

6. **Revelation 17:3**—John saw the wicked "woman sit upon a scarlet coloured Beast, full of names of BLASPHEMY."

HISTORY testifies:

The divine wisdom found in God's Word tells us that the Antichrist/ Beast would be a BLASPHEMOUS power.

Here we have another helpful point of identification. First of all, let's understand the Bible meaning of "blasphemy," for the same Bible that warns about the Beast being guilty of blasphemy also clearly defines that sin for us.

For instance, blasphemy occurs only in the realm of religion. As a result, we know that the Beast, though a political power in some respects, would also deal in religion. And in the realm of religion, blasphemy was perhaps the WORST of crimes. It was punishable by the supreme penalty of DEATH. Our Lord Jesus was accused of blasphemy on two occasions. Let's examine those to determine what the Bible calls "blasphemy."

BIBLE EXAMPLE #1

Jesus told a man who was paralyzed, "'Man, your sins are forgiven you.' And the scribes and the Pharisees began to reason, saying, 'Who is this who speaks *blasphemies?* Who can FORGIVE SINS but GOD alone?'" [236] It IS blasphemy for a mere man to presume to forgive sins! The Jews were right in saying that only God can do that. For a man to make such claims would constitute blasphemy, but Jesus was not a blasphemer, because He really was, and is, GOD.

BIBLE EXAMPLE #2

When Jesus said "I and My Father are ONE," the Jews took up stones to stone Him to death. [237] Our Lord reminded them that He had done many good works and asked for which of those works they would stone Him. "The Jews answered Him, saying, 'For a good work we do not stone You, but for BLASPHEMY, and because You, being a Man, make Yourself GOD.'" [238]

In other words, when a man represents himself to be God or in the position of God, that is blasphemy. But though it's blasphemous for a MAN to pretend to be God, the Lord Jesus Christ was never guilty of that sin because He's truly God in the flesh. He's "Immanuel, God with us." [239]

Now that we've laid the foundation for understanding specifically what the Word of God calls blasphemy, we're prepared to search the real world for persons or institutions guilty of "CERTIFIED BIBLICAL BLASPHEMY." Objective investigation leads to the same conclusion: The Catholic Church has two distinctive doctrines which the Bible calls blasphemy. One is its claim to have the power to FORGIVE SINS. The other is attributing to the Pope the office of GOD on earth. We'll examine each of these in turn.

First of all, the Roman Catholic Church claims that the power of FORGIVENESS or absolution is vested in HER HUMAN PRIESTS:

> "Seek where you will, through heaven and earth, and you will find but one created being who *can* forgive the sinner, who can free him from the chains of hell, that extraordinary being is the priest, the Catholic priest. 'Who can forgive sins except God?' was the question which the Pharisees sneeringly asked. 'Who can forgive sins?' is the question which the Pharisees of the present day also ask, and I answer there IS a man on earth that CAN forgive sins and that man is the Catholic priest. Yes, beloved brethren, the priest not only declares that the sinner is forgiven, but he REALLY FORGIVES him. The priest raises his hand, he pronounces the word of absolution, and in an instant, quick as a flash of light, the chains of hell are burst asunder, and the sinner becomes a child of God. So great is the power of the priest that the judgments of HEAVEN ITSELF are subject to his decision." [240]

In reality, however, when a priest raises his hand over the penitent and dares to pronounce the words, "I absolve thee," he himself is GUILTY of blasphemy! Furthermore, in the Roman Catholic priesthood a multitude of human mediators are substituted for Christ, whom the Bible calls the "ONE Mediator between God and man." [241]

The Vatican not only intends to keep its priestly army of mediators interposed between the repentant sinner and the forgiving God, it even insists that sinners CANNOT approach God for forgiveness but MUST go through a Roman Catholic priest! Proof of this fact is seen in a recent news item announcing "an authoritative Papal statement" under the headline:

✦ ✦ ✦

"NO FORGIVENESS 'DIRECTLY FROM GOD,' POPE SAYS."

The 138-page document—issued in Latin, Italian, German, French, Spanish, Portuguese, English, and Polish—notes that "the sacrament of reconciliation and penance, informally known as CONFESSION—an obligation of all Catholics . . . has fallen increasingly into disuse, especially in the industrial countries." The Papal exhortation may be summarized in the following capsule comment from the *Los Angeles Times* article: "VATICAN CITY—Rebutting a belief widely shared by Protestants and a growing number of Roman Catholics, Pope John Paul II on Tuesday DISMISSED the 'widespread idea that one can obtain forgiveness DIRECTLY from GOD' and exhorted Catholics to confess more often to their PRIESTS." [242]

Surely the Pope has read Old and New Testament texts like these:

- "Thou art a God READY to pardon, gracious and merciful, slow to anger, and of great kindness." [243]

- The Psalmist DAVID approached God DIRECTLY rather than obliquely through a priest when he prayed: "For Thy name's sake, O Lord, PARDON mine iniquity; for it is great. . . . FORGIVE all my sins." [244]

- ISAIAH, the "gospel prophet," wrote: "Let the wicked forsake his way, and the unrighteous man his thoughts: and let him return unto the Lord, and He will have MERCY upon him; and to our God, for He will ABUNDANTLY PARDON." [245]

- DANIEL prayed DIRECTLY to God: "O my God, incline Thine ear, and hear. . . . O Lord, hear; O Lord, FORGIVE; O Lord, hearken"—and we know God did hear him, for He dispatched the angel Gabriel in instant response to that prayer. [246]

- The MASTER HIMSELF taught us, in the Lord's Prayer, to approach God DIRECTLY and ask "Our Father . . . [to] FORGIVE us our debts, as we forgive our debtors." [247]

Now, turning to our second Bible example, we must deal with the blasphemous claim of any man to be God or to stand in the place of God. An INSANE or DIABOLICAL man may claim to be God or Christ, but any Bible student knows at once it's either a delusion or a blasphemous lie.

In the 1930's, the late Reverend M. J. Divine (better known as "FATHER DIVINE") began his Peace Mission Movement and claimed to be God. [248]

In the 1970's, the Reverend JIM JONES, with his Peoples' Church of Jonestown in Guiana, South America, claimed to be God. But the idea that any MAN should be called God is DANGEROUS and should be held at arm's length.

A Jesuit priest, however, writes this:

> "'Thou art a priest forever,' says the ordaining bishop, 'set apart to offer up gifts and sacrifices for sins.' . . . In the eyes of God and His heavenly court he is no longer a man, a sinful child of Adam, but an *alter Christus,* 'another Christ.'
>
> "'Did I meet an angel and a priest,' said St. Francis of Assisi, 'I would salute the PRIEST before the ANGEL.'
>
> "'Thou art a priest forever,' is written on his soul. Forever a priest of the Most High with POWER OVER the Almighty." [249]

Yet when holy orders are conferred upon the mortal man called a priest and he assumes the title of *alter Christus*—another Christ—it is then that the guilt of BLASPHEMY is registered against him and those who ordain him.

Catholic theologian ALPHONSUS DE LIGUORI exerted tremendous influence over doctrine in the Roman Church. *Encyclopedia Britannica* says, "Liguori wrote extensively. By 1953 his works had gone through about 18,000 editions and had been translated into 60 languages." [250] He was canonized as a SAINT in 1839 and further honored in 1871 when the Pope declared him a DOCTOR (that is, a "teacher," from the same root as "doctrine") of the Church. Here's a sample of what Liguori wrote—and what his Church teaches:

> "With regard to the POWER of priests over the real body of Jesus Christ, . . . we find that *in obedience* to the words of His priests—*HOC EST CORPUS MEUM* [This is My body]—*God Himself* descends on the altar, that He comes *whenever* they call Him, and *as often* as they call Him, and places Himself in their hands, even though they should be His enemies [?]. And after having come, He remains, entirely at their disposal; they move Him as they please, from one place to another; they may, if they wish, shut Him up in the tabernacle, or expose Him on the altar, or carry Him outside the church; they may, if they choose, eat His flesh, and give Him for the food of others. . . .
>
> "Thus the priest may, in a certain manner, be called the CREATOR of his Creator, since by saying the words of consecration, he creates, as it were, Jesus in the sacrament, by giving Him sacramental existence, and produces Him as a victim to be offered to the eternal Father. . . .
>
> "'The power of the priest,' says St. Bernardine of Sienna, 'is the power of the DIVINE Person; for the transubstantiation of the bread requires as much power as the creation of the world.' . . .
>
> "The priest holds the PLACE of the SAVIOR HIMSELF, when, by saying 'Ego te absolvo,' he absolves from sin. . . . To pardon a single sin

requires all the omnipotence of God. The Jew justly said: *Who can forgive sins but God alone?* But what only GOD can do by His omnipotence, the PRIEST can also do by saying *'Ego te absolvo a peccatis tuis'* ["I absolve you from your sins"]. . . . [Pope] Innocent III has written: 'Indeed, it is not too much to say that in view of the sublimity of their offices the priests are so many GODS.' "[251]

Agreeing with the blasphemous thought that Roman Catholic priests are "so many GODS" is this official *Catechism* of the Church:

"Bishops and priests being, as they are, God's interpreters and ambassadors, empowered in His name to teach mankind the divine law and the rules of conduct, and holding, as they do, His PLACE on earth, it is evident that no nobler function than theirs can be imagined. Justly, therefore, are they called not only Angels, but even GODS, because of the fact that they exercise in our midst the POWER and the prerogatives of the immortal GOD." [252]

The Roman Catholic publication *Western Watchman* makes this assertion by priest David S. Phelan:

"I never invite an angel down from heaven to hear mass here. This is not the place for angels. The only person in heaven I ever ask to come down here is Jesus Christ, and Him I COMMAND to come down. He HAS to come when I bid Him. I took bread in my fingers this morning and said: 'This is the body and blood of Jesus Christ,' and He had to come down. This is one of the things He must do. He MUST come down every time I say mass at my bidding. . . . I do it in obedience, reverence, homage, and adoration, but I do it, and when I do it, Christ MUST obey." [253]

Thus this church, through her priesthood, fits into the prophetic picture.

BOLD, **BRAZEN,** *BLASPHEMOUS!*

But it's not the priesthood alone which fulfills this clue pointing to blasphemy. At the head of the Church, in the Papacy, we find a power, an institution that scales the heights and plumbs the depths of the prideful sin called BLASPHEMY!

For instance, the Pope is quite commonly called "the HOLY FATHER"— appropriating the very title we use to refer to GOD Himself! And this is true even despite the fact that Jesus explicitly tells us: "Call no man your FATHER upon earth: for One is your Father, which is in heaven." [254] And the Lord says, "You shall call ME, 'My Father.' "[255] As for being "holy," the man-made vote which makes a man the Pope doesn't confer on him a visible halo of light, and even official Catholic sources are forced to admit by the facts themselves that *some* popes have been embarrassingly, flagrantly, notoriously WICKED.

Let's consider some other blasphemous claims and statements regarding the Pope:

> "The Pope is of so great dignity and so exalted that he is *not* a mere man, but as it were GOD, and the vicar of God. . . . Hence the Pope is crowned with a triple crown, as KING of HEAVEN and of earth and of the lower regions. . . . The Pope is as it were GOD on earth, . . . chief KING of kings, . . . to whom has been entrusted by the omnipotent God direction . . . of the HEAVENLY kingdom." [256]

> "All names which in the Scriptures are applied to CHRIST, by virtue of which it is established that He is over all the church, all the SAME names are applied to the Pope." [257]

> "For thou art the shepherd, thou art the physician, thou art the director, thou art the husbandman; finally, thou art another GOD on earth." [258]

Pope Leo XIII urged "complete submission and obedience of will to the Church and to the Roman Pontiff, as to GOD HIMSELF"![259] The same proud Pontiff also boasted: "We [the Popes] hold upon this earth the place of GOD Almighty." [260]

Of Lucifer's blasphemous, diabolical pride, God says:

> "How thou art fallen from heaven,
> O Lucifer, son of the morning! . . .
> For thou hast said in thine heart,
> *I* will ascend into heaven,
> *I* will exalt *MY* throne above the stars of God:
> *I* will sit also upon the mount of the congregation, . . .
> *I* will ascend above the heights of the clouds;
> ***I* will be like the Most High**." [261]

After reading that, it's easy to GUESS WHO is behind any ambition to take the place of the Most High God!

Aware of how the Papal hierarchy assumes prerogatives that belong only to God, Adam Clarke, three times Methodist conference president, wrote:

> "To none can this [prophetic clue] apply so well or so fully as to the Popes of Rome. They have assumed INFALLIBILITY, which belongs only to God. They profess to FORGIVE SINS, which belongs only to God. They profess to open and shut heaven, which belongs only to God. They profess to be HIGHER than all the kings of the earth, which belongs only to God. And they go beyond God in pretending to loose whole nations from their oath of allegiance to their kings, when such

kings do not please them! And they go against God when they give INDULGENCES for sin. This is the WORST of all blasphemies!" [262]

Here's a "quick quiz" for you—

The Roman Catholic Papacy is guilty of BLASPHEMY because of:

A. Claiming to be God.

B. Presuming to forgive sins. (See *Appendix K,* below.)

C. Tampering with God's Law. (See the *next* clue.)

D. All of the above.

You probably were able to choose the correct answer—"D. ALL of the above." History indicts the Papacy as guilty of *all three* statements above, which makes it guilty of the sin of BLASPHEMY as well.

CLUE "T"

IT WOULD EVEN *ATTEMPT TO* CHANGE THE LAW OF GOD!

Your Bible says:

1. **Daniel 7:25**—"And he [the Little horn power] shall . . . think to CHANGE times and laws."

   These must be DIVINE laws, because MAN-MADE laws are changed every day and would not be worthy of note in Bible prophecy. Therefore, this text must warn about a change in the LAW OF GOD.

2. **Daniel 7:25**—The Revised Standard Version says he "shall think to change times and THE law"—that is, THE Law of God.

Since the two preceding statements in this verse in Daniel (7:25) declare what the Little Horn would do against the MOST HIGH ("he shall speak great words against the MOST HIGH, and shall wear out the saints of the MOST HIGH"), we must conclude that it is also the "times and the law" of the MOST HIGH which the Little Horn would attempt to change.

In the final analysis this must be only an ATTEMPTED change in God's Law rather than an ACTUAL change, since no mere man or even the Devil himself could really change God's Law. Thus the text says that the Little Horn power would "THINK to change the law," meaning he would INTEND to change it and TRY to change it without actually changing it.

It's a wise man who knows his own limitations. For instance, I can't pull myself up by my own boot-straps. And poet James Weldon Johnson told the truth when he wrote, "Your arm's too short to box with God"—and, we may add, it's too short to touch or tamper with the divine Law of God. That's out of our reach. Since it's beyond any man's power to add to or subtract from God's holy Law, it's pure presumption and blasphemy for anyone even to THINK he could do so. But Daniel's text here says that the Little Horn power DID "think" to change God's Law.

HISTORY testifies:

Did the Devil really suppose he could change God's Ten Commandments and no one would be the wiser—that no one would notice? We wouldn't think so, would we? For the Law God wrote with His own finger on tables of stone is very clear and specific.

Yet in the dim and distant past, in the days when Christianity compromised with paganism, such changes were relatively easy to slip past the people. Bible manuscripts were slowly, laboriously copied by hand, not printed on high-speed presses, and so were very expensive. Therefore, precious copies of the Bible were extremely rare, found only in monasteries, libraries, or chained to the wall of a church.

And what few Bibles did exist were not translated into the common language of the people but were written only in the original languages of Hebrew or Greek, or possibly translated into Latin. In addition to these problems, the average person couldn't read, anyway. So he depended on what the Church told him to be true—and that's where his troubles began.

Fortunately, the important question of "Who changed the Law of God?" is NOT an unsolvable whodunit. We can discover the answer perfectly well, for the guilty party has boldly ADMITTED the deed. We find that when it comes to the attempted change of God's Law, the Roman Catholic Church was not an innocent bystander!

A good law we have in this country provides that no one can be forced to testify against himself. And if we accused the Catholic Church of attempting to change the holy Law of God,[263] she wouldn't need to be forced to testify against herself because she willingly admits the deed. See for yourself what Roman Catholic authorities say about making those attempted changes in God's Law. They unblushingly admit it. In fact, they BOAST about it in great words like these:

> "The Pope is of so great authority and power that he can **modify**, explain, or interpret even DIVINE laws. . . . Petrus de Ancharano [died 1416] very clearly asserts this in *Consil.* 373, no. 3 verso: 'The Pope can modify DIVINE law, since his power is not of man, but of God, and he acts in the PLACE of GOD upon earth.'"[264]

No one, of course, can re-write the Bible. And Roman Catholic versions of the Bible, such as the Douay or the Jerusalem Bible, are just as valid as any other version of God's Word. Our Catholic friends can find ALL Scriptural teachings in their Bibles that are found in any other.

But in their CATECHISMS—the official teaching manuals of the Roman Catholic Church—it's another story. Few people read the Bible anyway, even among Protestants—many find it a formidable Book. So the fact that all the original Ten Commandments may be found in Catholic Bibles doesn't really matter. Faithful, practicing Catholics are TAUGHT by the questions and answers found in the catechism. And in the catechism, the Law of God has been drastically ALTERED: In the brief scope of the Ten Commandments, covering only 15 verses in the Bible, there are THREE distinct, definite changes. [265]

ALTERATION NUMBER ONE:
Deleting the SECOND Commandment

As the Papacy grew in power, it did not hesitate to tamper with the Law of God. Finding the Second Commandment out of harmony with its use of images, the Papal Beast did away with it altogether, for that Commandment forbids us to bow down to images. Any who minimize the importance of this divine Command must have forgotten the inspiring story of Shadrach, Meshach, and Abednego. [266] Their tremendous courage would not have been needed if God had never commanded us NOT to bow down to images!

We see idols and images—statues of Mary and other saints—set up in every single institution of the Roman Catholic Church: every school, every hospital, every cathedral. Yet God HATES statue images! He explicitly says so in Deuteronomy 16:22—"Neither shalt thou set thee up any image; [267] which the Lord thy God HATETH." And in His Second Commandment, God forbids us to make them or bow down to them.

Let me speak with love and understanding to my Roman Catholic friends: I know how you feel about the practice of using images in your worship. You've told me, "Oh, I don't worship the image—I don't believe the image is God. I just believe the image represents God." But that's precisely the thing the Second Commandment forbids! The Second Commandment doesn't say, "Don't make the image the god." It says, "Don't worship God through the image."

Exodus 20:4-6 says: "Thou shalt not make unto thee any graven image, or any LIKENESS of any thing that is in HEAVEN. . . ." In other words, the image is a likeness—a representation—of something in heaven that you worship *through* the image. But God is saying, "Don't make any likeness of anything that's in heaven above or in the earth beneath or in the water under the earth. Don't BOW DOWN to them or serve them." Yet the Church of Rome not only dared to delete that command but also, through its practice, teaches men and women to break it.

ALTERATION NUMBER TWO:
SPLITTING THE TENTH COMMANDMENT

Just as one lie often leads to another, one sin often makes another necessary. Catholic leaders who eliminated God's command banning images faced the problem of being left with only NINE Commandments. Since it's impossible to teach the "Ten Commandments" with only nine, they DIVIDED the Tenth Commandment to retain the ten in number if not in fact.

However, this stratagem was a deception, an attempt at a cover-up. Why? Because while Catholic catechisms deceptively appear to retain all ten in number, they do not. They don't teach the Second Commandment at all, and splitting God's Tenth Commandment was a transparent TRICK to FOOL people in this regard. The Catholic Church has TWO Commandments against coveting, whereas Paul speaks of it six times in the *singular* as only one "commandment." [268]

ALTERATION NUMBER THREE:
CHANGING THE "TIMES" OF THE FOURTH COMMANDMENT

The Beast was also to "change times." But the only Commandment that has to do with TIME is the Fourth, which commands us to keep holy the seventh day, on which God rested at Creation. [269]

Who would dare to lay hands on Jehovah's Law and change His holy Sabbath, without any warrant of Scripture? All Protestant denominations disclaim any part in this audacious crime. But the Roman Catholic Church BOASTS of having made this change and even points to it as an evidence of its authority to act in God's place on earth! (Please bear in mind, as you read the official Catholic claims which follow, that the Roman Catholic DOUAY VERSION of the Bible gives this identifying warning about the Little Horn power in Daniel 7:25—"He shall THINK himself ABLE to change times and laws.")

♦ CATHOLIC CLAIMS

"*Question*—Have you any other way of proving that the [Catholic] Church has power to institute festivals of precept?

The LAW of GOD: As GIVEN by God*

I
Thou shalt have no other gods before Me.

II
Thou shalt not make unto thee any graven image, or any likeness of any thing that is in heaven above, or that is in the earth beneath, or that is in the water under the earth: thou shalt not bow down thyself to them, nor serve them: for I the Lord thy God am a jealous God, visiting the iniquity of the fathers upon the children unto the third and fourth generation of them that hate Me; and showing mercy unto thousands of them that love Me, and keep My commandments.

III
Thou shalt not take the name of the Lord thy God in vain; for the Lord will not hold him guiltless that taketh His name in vain.

IV
Remember the Sabbath day to keep it holy. Six days shalt thou labour, and do all thy work: but the seventh day is the Sabbath of the Lord thy God: in it thou shalt not do any work, thou, nor thy son, nor thy daughter, thy manservant, nor thy maidservant, nor thy cattle, nor thy stranger that is within thy gates: for in six days the Lord made heaven and earth, the sea, and all that in them is, and rested the seventh day: wherefore the Lord blessed the Sabbath day, and hallowed it.

V
Honour thy father and thy mother: that thy days may be long upon the land which the Lord thy God giveth thee.

VI
Thou shalt not kill.

VII
Thou shalt not commit adultery.

VIII
Thou shalt not steal.

IX
Thou shalt not bear false witness against thy neighbour.

X
Thou shalt not covet thy neighbour's house, thou shalt not covet thy neighbour's wife, nor his manservant, nor his maidservant, nor his ox, nor his ass, nor any thing that is thy neighbour's.

* As recorded in Exodus 20:3-17.

The LAW of GOD: As CHANGED by Man*

I

Thou shalt have no other gods before Me.

II

Thou shalt not take the name of the Lord thy God in vain.

III

Remember that thou keep holy the Sabbath day.

IV

Honor thy father and thy mother.

V

Thou shalt not kill.

VI

Thou shalt not commit adultery.

VII

Thou shalt not steal.

VIII

Thou shalt not bear false witness against thy neighbor.

IX

Thou shalt not covet thy neighbor's wife.

X

Thou shalt not covet thy neighbor's goods.

* As taught over the centuries by many Catholic catechisms.

"*Answer*—Had she not such power, she could not have done that in which all modern religionists agree with her;—she could not have SUBSTITUTED the observance of Sunday the first day of the week, for the observance of Saturday the seventh day, a change for which there is NO Scriptural authority"![270]

* * *

"*Question*—How do you prove that the [Catholic] Church has power to command Feasts and Holy-days?

"*Answer*—By this very act of CHANGING the Sabbath into the Sunday, which is admitted by Protestants, and therefore they contradict themselves by keeping Sunday so strictly, and breaking most other Feasts commanded by the same Church.

"*Question*—How do you prove that?

"*Answer*—Because by keeping Sunday they acknowledge the POWER of the [Catholic] Church to ordain Feasts and to command them under sin, and by not keeping the remainder, equally commanded by her, they deny in fact the same power."[271]

* * *

"The Catholic Church for over one thousand years before the existence of a Protestant, by virtue of her Divine mission CHANGED the day from Saturday to Sunday. . . . But the Protestant says: How can I receive the teachings of an apostate Church? How, we ask, have you managed to receive her teaching all your life, in direct opposition to your recognized teacher, the Bible, on the Sabbath question? . . . The Protestant world at its birth found the Christian Sabbath [supposedly Sunday] too firmly entrenched to run counter to its existence; it was therefore placed under the necessity of acquiescing in the arrangement, thus implying the [Roman] Church's right to CHANGE the day, for over 300 years. The Christian Sabbath is therefore to this day the acknowledged offspring of the Catholic Church, as Spouse of the Holy Ghost, without a word of remonstrance from the Protestant world."[272]

* * *

"It was the Catholic Church which, by the authority of Jesus Christ, has TRANSFERRED this rest to the Sunday in remembrance of the resurrection of our Lord. Thus the observance of Sunday by the Protestants is an homage they pay, in spite of themselves, to the authority of the [Catholic] Church."[273]

* * *

"*Question*—Which is the Sabbath day?

"*Answer*—Saturday is the Sabbath day.

"*Question*—Why do we observe Sunday instead of Saturday?

"*Answer*—We observe Sunday instead of Saturday because the Catholic Church, in the Council of Laodicea (A.D. 336), TRANSFERRED the solemnity from Saturday to Sunday." [274]

* * *

Father William Gildea, Rector of St. James Catholic Church in London, tells us that "The [Catholic] Church . . . took the pagan Sunday and made it the Christian Sunday. . . . And thus the PAGAN Sunday, dedicated to BALDER,[275] became the Christian Sunday, sacred to Jesus."[276]

* * *

Finally, Father John O'Brien, of the University of Notre Dame, puts it very clearly: "Since Saturday, not Sunday, is specified in the Bible, isn't it curious that non-Catholics who profess to take their religion directly from the Bible and not from the Church, observe Sunday instead of Saturday? Yes, of course, it is inconsistent; but this change was made about fifteen centuries before Protestantism was born, and by that time the custom was universally observed. They have continued the custom, even though it rests upon the authority of the Catholic Church and NOT upon an explicit text in the Bible." [277]

♦ PROTESTANT ADMISSIONS

While Catholics claim responsibility for the change of the Sabbath, promi-nent Protestants—from Reformation times onward—ADMIT that the change was NOT by Scriptural authority or apostolic act, but by human churchly action. Thus:

The LUTHERAN CHURCH, in the AUGSBURG CONFESSION of 1530, declared: "They [the Catholic hierarchy] allege the CHANGE of the Sabbath into the Lord's Day, contrary, as it seemeth, to the Decalogue; and they have no example more in their mouths than the change of the Sabbath. They will needs have the [Roman] Church's power to be very great, because it hath DISPENSED with a precept of the Decalogue." [278]

* * *

The DISCIPLES OF CHRIST CHURCH states: "Either the Law remains in all its force, to the utmost extent of its literal requirements, or it is passed away with the Jewish ceremonies. If it yet exist[s], let us observe it according to Law. And if it does not exist, let us abandon a mock observance of another day for it.

"'But,' some say, 'it was CHANGED from the seventh to the first day.' Where? when? and by whom? No man can tell. No, it NEVER was changed, nor COULD it be, unless CREATION was to be gone through again: for the reason assigned must be changed before the observance, or respect to the reason, can be changed!! It is all old wives' fables to talk of the change of the Sabbath from the seventh to the first day. IF it be changed, it was that august personage changed it who changes times and laws *ex officio*—I think his name is DOCTOR ANTICHRIST." [279]

* * *

German church historian AUGUSTUS NEANDER, in *The History of the Christian Religion and Church,* asserts: "The festival of Sunday, like all other festivals, was always only a HUMAN ordinance, and it was FAR from the intentions of the apostles to establish a Divine command in this respect, far from them, and from the early apostolic Church, to transfer the laws of the Sabbath to Sunday." [280]

* * *

And WILLIAM E. GLADSTONE, "the greatest British statesman of the 19th century and four times Prime Minister" [281] of Great Britain, observed: "The seventh day of the week has been DEPOSED from its title to obligatory religious observance, and its prerogative has been carried over to the first, under NO direct precept of Scripture."[282]

* * *

You'll recall that when God made the Sabbath for man, He blessed the seventh day and sanctified it, setting it apart for a holy purpose. Could any man CANCEL that act of God? Of course not! Remember Balaam's words: "He hath BLESSED, and I cannot reverse it." [283]

The attempted change was not one of mere names or numbers. It was a basic change of meaning, a change of authority, a change of experience. You see, true *worship* is to acknowledge the "worthship" of God. [284] If God is *worthy* of worship, He's worthy of your TIME. If someone is not worthy, you don't have TIME for him. Substituting the Papal Sunday for the Bible Sabbath was a change from a God-given HOLY DAY to a man-made HOLIDAY!

♦ CONSTANTINE the Great

It is true that the Roman Emperor Constantine made the first Sunday law in A.D. 321. Constantine the Great, as he was called, lived from 272 to 337 and is often regarded as Rome's first "Christian" emperor. However, many scholars have found reason to doubt the genuineness of Constantine's supposed conversion.

> "By birth and early training, Constantine was a pagan. His father, Constantius, was a devotee of the Sun God and Constantine who followed his monotheistic example accepted at first Hercules and later the Sun God as his protective deity. . . . When in 321 A.D., he declared Sunday a general holiday he had in mind both Christians and pagans, for while the former celebrated it as 'the Lord's Day,' the latter could regard it as the 'day of the Sun-god.' . . . Constantine only received Christian baptism on his deathbed." [285]

The story goes that Constantine was converted in 313 when, as *Encyclopedia Britannica* explains:

> "he saw a cross of light superimposed on the sun. . . . He also made Sunday a public holiday according to Christian practice, although *he emphasized its sacredness to the SUN.* . . . His religious beliefs, though sincere, were perhaps vague. For instance, for some years after his conversion he continued to issue coins in honour of 'the Unconquered Sun *[Sol Invictus]*.' He may at first have believed, as his vision might suggest, that CHRIST and the SUN were both aspects of 'the Highest Divinity.' " [286]

But there was no mention of CHRIST when Constantine passed the first piece of Sunday legislation on the 7th day of March, A.D. 321. In passing that law, the once-pagan emperor was thinking of the SUN, not the SON! Here's the exact text of that brief law:

> "On the venerable Day of the SUN let the magistrates and people residing in cities REST, and let all workshops be CLOSED. In the country, however, persons engaged in agriculture may freely and lawfully continue their pursuits; because it often happens that another day is not so suitable for grain-sowing or for vine-planting; lest by neglecting the proper moment for such operations the bounty of heaven should be lost." [287]

Constantine's decree—the first Sunday law of which we have any record—was made more than two centuries AFTER all the apostles were dead and buried. Walter Woodburn Hyde, professor of Latin, Greek, and ancient history in several American universities, establishes the fact that this is the "grand-daddy" of all Sunday laws, saying:

> "This is the 'parent' Sunday law making it a day of rest and release from labor. For from this day to the present there have been decrees about the observance of Sunday which have profoundly influenced European and American society. When the CHURCH became a part of STATE under the Christian emperors, Sunday was enforced by civil statutes and later, when the Empire was past, the Church in the hands of the Papacy enforced it by ecclesiastical, and also influenced it by civil, enactments." [288]

> "This legislation by Constantine probably bore *no relation to Christianity*; it appears, on the contrary, that the emperor, in his capacity of Pontifex Maximus, was only adding the day of the SUN, the WORSHIP of which was then firmly established in the Roman Empire, to the other ferial days of the sacred [pagan] calendar. . . .
>
> "What began, however, as a PAGAN ordinance, ended as a CHRISTIAN regulation"! [289]

How, we may ask, did Sunday observance end as a seemingly "Christian" regulation? Because Constantine's pagan CIVIL legislation was ratified by and incorporated into the CATHOLIC CHURCH—first by the Council of Laodicea and later by countless ecclesiastical councils, synods, and Papal pronouncements. Around the middle of the fourth century, the Council of Laodicea made a TWO-PRONGED attack on Christians loyal to the seventh-day Sabbath of the Lord. It ordered:

> "Christians shall not Judaize and be IDLE on Saturday [the word translated "Saturday" is "Sabbath" in the original], but shall WORK on that day; but the Lord's day [supposedly Sunday] they shall especially honour, and, as being Christians, shall, if possible, do no work on that day. If, however, they are found Judaizing, they shall be shut out from Christ." [290]

MANY DOCTRINAL CHANGES

If we held "AN INQUEST INTO THE DEATH OF TRUE RELIGION," the solemn facts of the case would indict that Power which undermined truth after truth given by Christ. Some of those corrupted teachings are as follows:

- the substitution of the supposed immortal soul for the Biblical state of the dead [291]

- the sprinkling of infants instead of baptizing instructed adult believers by immersion

- the supposed forgiveness of sins by priests instead of forgiveness by the "one Mediator," Christ [292]

- the man-made sanctity of Sunday in place of the seventh-day Sabbath of the Bible. [293]

In the battle for truth, these changes in doctrine are like visible scars. They're tangible evidence we can point to and say, "This Church has departed from 'the faith which was once delivered unto the saints.'"[294] In fact, even in the days of Edward Gibbon (1737-1794), the English historian whose pen gave us the classic *Decline and Fall of the Roman Empire*, that departure was so marked that he was moved to write:

> "The sublime and simple theology of the primitive Christians was gradually corrupted: and the MONARCHY of heaven, already clouded by metaphysical subtleties, was degraded by the introduction of a popular mythology, which tended to restore the reign of *polytheism* [because of praying to *countless* dead saints]. . . . If the Christian apostles, St. PETER or St. PAUL, could return to the Vatican, they might possibly inquire into the name of the Deity who is worshipped with such MYSTERIOUS rites in that magnificent temple [that is, St. Peter's basilica]: at Oxford or Geneva, they would experience less surprise [at the Protestant forms of worship]; but it might still be incumbent on them to peruse the catechism of the church, and to study the orthodox commentators on their own writings and the words of their Master." [295]

The CHURCH'S Responsibility

Just as the doctrinal corruptions named above may be charged to the Roman Church, so may the CHANGE of GOD'S LAW. Such changes were wholly within the hands of that powerful church to prevent. For obvious reasons, the change of God's Law must have been "an INSIDE job." After all, only some institution with access to the Law, the one charged with protecting and promoting the Law, could possibly effect such a change. It would be impossible for any secular man, be he ruler or commoner, to make such a change as long as the CHURCH stood firm to maintain and observe and teach the Law as originally given by God.

Understand, first of all, what the church IS and what its FUNCTION is in this fallen world. This rebel planet we call Earth was sold out because of Adam and Eve's disobedience, and Satan became "the prince of this world." [296] Thus God's church, made up of people loyal to Him, is an OUTPOST of Heaven in "enemy-held territory." As such, it's the only repository of God's Law and Word, committed to preserve His truth against all onslaughts of the enemy.

So it follows that if the teachings of the Bible or the Law of God were changed or corrupted, we can lay the responsibility squarely at the door of the church. During those long centuries of the early Christian era, the Roman Catholic Church was not as it is today, one church among many competing for allegiance. It was the ONLY church in Christendom. There were small pockets of resistance—a few independent groups like the Waldenses— but until the Protestant Reformation of the sixteenth century, Catholicism was "the only game in town," the only church for the millions of Christians. This fact is significant, for it means that if something happened to God's Law since apostolic days, the one church that was the only repository of that Law MUST be responsible.

In conclusion, therefore, we recognize that laying violent hands on God's holy Law is a most SERIOUS OFFENSE. But we're justified in charging the Roman Catholic Church with this crime against Heaven's government for two valid reasons:

1. The Roman Catholic Church is the ONLY institution that COULD have done it.

2. The Roman Catholic Church ADMITS doing it!

CLUE "U"
ITS PERIOD OF SUPREMACY WOULD BE OF SPECIFIC DURATION: 1260 YEARS.

Your Bible says:

1. **Daniel 7:25**—"the saints of the most High . . . shall be given into his hand [that is, into the hand of the Little Horn power] until a TIME and TIMES and the DIVIDING of time." At first glance this seems like a very cryptic clue, but we can decipher it if we put on our thinking caps and closely follow point by point:

   a. A "time" in Bible terminology means a YEAR. [297]

   b. "Times" here means specifically TWO years. [298]

   c. The word translated "dividing" may also be translated "HALF," adding up to a total of three-and-a-half prophetic years.

   Thus modern Bible versions translate Daniel 7:25 as follows:

   ● Revised Standard Version says, "they shall be given into his hand for a TIME, TWO times, and HALF a time."

- The New International Version and the New American Standard Version each says in a footnote, "for a YEAR, TWO years, and HALF a year."

- The Living Bible and Today's English Version say, "for THREE and a HALF years."

2. A second important point is that ancient calendars had 360 days to a year. For instance, in the EGYPTIAN calendar "Twelve nominal months of 30 days each gave 360 days. . . ." Similarly, in the HINDU calendar "the duration of the civil year seems to have been estimated at 360 days, or 12 months of 30 days. . . ." Again, for the ASSYRIAN calendar "the year attested in the Kültepe texts of the 19th century B. C. had 360 days. . . ." [299] The HEBREWS of Bible times, too, had twelve months of thirty days each. [300] So three-and-a-half years would contain 1260 days, thus:

3 & 1/2 YEARS X 360 DAYS = 1260 DAYS.

3. In SYMBOLIC PROPHECY, each prophetic "DAY" stands for an actual YEAR. Just as architects use a scale value of "1 quarter-inch equals 1 foot" on their blueprints, and cartographers use a scale of "1 inch equals 100 miles" on their maps, God uses a scale value of "1 day equals 1 year" in symbolic time prophecies. In Numbers 14:34 we read: "each day for a year"—applying the Bible principle of counting a day for a year—"even forty days . . . even forty years." Again in Ezekiel 4:6 God says, "I have appointed thee each day for a year." On this basis, 1260 prophetic DAYS equal 1260 actual YEARS—so we understand Daniel's prophecy: It teaches that the Little Horn's period of dominance over the saints of God would last 1260 years.

4. Revelation 12:6—"And the WOMAN" (referring to God's CHURCH, as we learned in Clue "G," above) "FLED into the wilderness . . . a THOUSAND TWO HUNDRED and THREESCORE days." During the Dark Ages, while the Bible was virtually a closed Book, God's church had to flee persecution and go underground, so to speak, for a period of 1260 prophetic days or 1260 actual years.

5. Revelation 12:14—Here again we read that "the WOMAN" had to "FLY into the wilderness . . . where she is nourished for a TIME, and TIMES, and HALF a time, from the face of the SERPENT." The Living Bible and Today's English Version say, "for THREE and a HALF years."

6. Revelation 13:5—"and power was given unto him [the Beast] to continue **FORTY and TWO months.**" At 30 days to a month, this time period *again* equals precisely 1260 days, thus:

$$42 \text{ MONTHS } \times 30 \text{ DAYS } = 1260 \text{ PROPHETIC DAYS}$$
or
1260 ACTUAL YEARS.

God won't waste our time on anything as vague as "the twelfth of Never."

HISTORY testifies:

IF the Beast power described by Inspiration is the Papacy, then we should expect to find in history a 1260-year period of Papal supremacy—and that's exactly what we DO find!

Here again the facts of history testify to the unerring accuracy of prophecy, because the Little Horn/Beast power did continue dominant for exactly 1260 years—from A.D. 538 to 1798, as we see from the following:

Three of the ten horns (or kings or kingdoms) were to be "plucked up" by the Little Horn power.[301] These three were the Heruli in Italy (conquered in A.D. 493), the Vandals in North Africa (destroyed in A.D. 534), and the Ostrogoths in Italy (driven from Rome in A.D. 538). Those conquests left the Pope in undisputed control, and after many years of conflict he found himself without rival in Rome.

Actually, Emperor Justinian (reigning from Constantinople in the East, since Constantine had moved the capital from Rome to Constantinople) issued his imperial letter elevating the bishop of Rome to be the "Head of ALL the holy churches" in A.D. 533. But there were PROBLEMS—apparently not even an emperor can always change things by a mere stroke of his pen. At that time the Goths—Arian Ostrogoths—were ruling Italy. Justinian's decree laid the legal foundation for Papal supremacy, but from a practical point of view it couldn't actually go into effect until the heretical Arian powers were removed. So Justinian sent his armies, under General Belisarius, first into North Africa against the Arian Vandals, conquering them in A.D. 534. Then Belisarius and a second army sent by Justinian moved into Italy and succeeded in driving the Goths from Rome in March, 538. Only then, when Ostrogothic control was removed, could the Roman Pontiff be free to exercise his jurisdiction.

Thus the period of Papal dominance BEGAN in the year **538**. Adding 1260 years to 538 brings us to **1798**. Did anything happen in that year to bring the period of Papal supremacy to an end? History answers with a resounding "YES!" For in 1798 Napoleon's general entered Rome and took the Pope captive. The Pontiff was dethroned, imprisoned, and exiled in France, where he soon died. We'll take a closer look at this world-shaking event in our next clue (Clue "V"), but please don't miss the significant TIMING of this historical event: God's great prophetic clock—which keeps perfect time— had set the year 1798 as the end of Papal supremacy, and when the hour struck, the mighty Papal ruler, at whose displeasure kings had so long trembled, went "into captivity" [302] as the Bible had predicted, and his government was abolished.

Justinian's decree of A.D. 533—implemented in 538 with the overthrow of the Ostrogoths—was one that certainly SHAPED HISTORY! Twelve hundred and sixty years later, the triumphal march of Napoleon's armies across Europe provided another milestone along the stream of time. EXACTLY 1260 years! "Like the stars in the vast circuit of their appointed path, God's purposes know no haste and no delay." [303] To borrow Paul's words in Galatians 4:4, "When the fullness of the TIME was come," God rang down the curtain on the Beast—or at least on that act of the tragic drama featuring his dominance of God's people.

Rome's **Counter-Reformation**

Fearless men like Martin Luther tried to reform the church they believed the Papacy had deformed. The Protestant Reformation was a great WAR waged over Bible truth. The Reformers risked their lives, fighting to point out the forgotten teachings contained in God's Book. Some of them were put to death, being burned at the stake, but the people listened and learned. Throughout Europe, impressive declarations by voice and pen that the Papacy is the Antichrist of prophecy gained so great a hold on men's minds that it was a crisis of major proportions.

As long as men took the Bible just as it reads, especially the books of Daniel and Revelation, the Papacy was vulnerable to identification as the Beast. Identifying Antichrist as the Papacy through multiple evidences proved so embarrassing, so damning, that Rome, like a wounded giant, sought defense measures. The incriminating finger of prophecy—pointed by Daniel, Paul, and John—must be diverted, but how? The COUNTER Reformation of the Roman Catholic Church was a COUNTER ATTACK on the efforts of men like Luther to warn and reform the church. This Papal reaction took many forms, such as the following:

1. Establishing (in 1559) the INDEX, a list of prohibited books condemned by Rome. Absolute censorship of reformers' ideas was very strict. [304] Writing or printing, buying or selling, possessing or reading any book on the Papal Index was a grave offense—the consequences were sometimes literally *grave*. Often author and publisher of an offensive book were chained together and burned at the stake, with the flames being kindled by lighting pages from the book.

2. Establishing the militant Order of JESUITS, a so-called holy militia, with Ignatius Loyola as its first general. This spiritual army had as its mission the defense of the Papacy. Formed by Pope Paul III in 1540 under his Papal order *Regimini Militanti Ecclesiae,* the Jesuits entrenched themselves in universities as influential teachers in every land.

3. Both of the above measures became powerful weapons in the arsenal of militant Catholicism (along with the INQUISITION, mentioned above in Clue R, dealing with merciless persecution). But the specific thrust of the Counter Reformation we must now consider was its effort to find NEW WAYS to INTERPRET the prophecies of Scripture which proved so incriminating. What could be done?

Rome's answer came from two Spanish Jesuits: FRANCISCO RIBERA from Salamanca and LUIS DE ALCAZAR from Seville. These men, determined to locate Antichrist at some point in time where he could NOT be identified as the Papacy, devised two entirely different interpretations of prophecy. About 1590 Ribera introduced his **FUTURIST** counter-interpretation which teaches that Antichrist is not in the world now but will some day appear as a single individual who will rebuild the Jerusalem Temple, abolish the Christian religion, deny Christ, be received by the Jews, pretend to be God, and conquer the world—all in the brief space of three-and-a-half literal years! Then in 1614 Alcazar's **PRETERIST** theory was published which pushes Antichrist not into the future but far into the past.[305] To divert suspicion from the Papacy they served, Alcazar and Ribera were willing to lead us down the blind alleys of Preterism and Futurism.

Obviously, these two Jesuit theories are conflicting and contradictory, relegating God's prophecies of the Beast to either the DISTANT PAST or the REMOTE FUTURE, far away from the uncomfortable facts of Papal history as it unfolded from 538 to 1798. Rarely does one church organization promote two such INCONSISTENT systems of Biblical interpretation, for if these prophecies were fulfilled in early Roman history, then Futurism is wrong; and if Futurism's assumptions are right, then Preterism is wrong. The theories are so entirely opposite that one nullifies the other! But Papal Rome is not embarrassed by this inconsistency as long as these interpretations serve their purpose of confusing people who study the prophetic clues.

Both Preterism and Futurism are relatively new theories, being advanced around 1600 or so. Compared to the time-honored Historical system of interpretation, each is a "Johnny-Come-Lately." Preterism never gained much popularity, and Futurism was virtually unknown in America until 1830 or later. For almost three centuries, Futurism was confined to Romanists, but early in the nineteenth century it sprang forth afresh, even among Protestants.

The tragedy of modern Protestantism accepting this foul legacy from Rome is expressed by Bible scholar Joseph Tanner:

> "It is a matter for deep regret that those who hold and advocate the Futurist system at the present day, Protestants as they are for the most part, are thus really playing into the hands of ROME, and helping to SCREEN the Papacy from DETECTION as the Antichrist. It has been well said that 'Futurism tends to obliterate the BRAND put by the Holy Spirit upon Popery.'" [306]

But sad to say, Futurism, conceived and brought forth as a child of the Papacy, has in the last century been adopted and nurtured by Protestants!

FALLACIES OF FUTURISM

Several facts show Futurism to be patently false:

First of all, the Futurist theory was not arrived at in the normal way of Bible study. Instead, it was deliberately designed by Ribera to relieve the pressure of the virtually unanimous identification of Antichrist as the Papacy. It's one thing to mine the quarry of Scripture and bring forth gems of Truth, following wherever the Spirit leads. It's quite another to set out intentionally to invent a scheme and then try to make Scripture appear to support that preconceived plan. This transparent attempt to lift the stigma brought by prophecy and history is a questionable basis for Bible doctrine, to say the least!

Secondly, Futurist theory IGNORES or DENIES such clear clues as the Seven Hills, the scarlet and purple apparel, the tampering with God's Law, *etc.,* which were predicted by Scripture and confirmed by History. "None is so blind as he who will not see."

Thirdly, Futurists abandon the tested Year/Day principle and the Historical system of interpreting prophecy for an unreasonable insistence on literal time periods. They selectively ABANDON that principle when it appears to incriminate the Pope as Antichrist. Yet they ACCEPT that principle for other time prophecies. For instance, Futurists do apply the Year/Day principle to the 70-week prophecy of Daniel 9:24-27, making it 490 YEARS instead of 490 literal DAYS, thus:

70 weeks X 7 days = 490 prophetic days or actual years. [307]

Christian scholars unanimously agree that these seventy weeks pertain to the 490 years leading to the Messiah's First Advent. For if the 70-week prophecy pointing to the Messiah had been a mere 490 DAYS rather than 490 YEARS, *how could the following momentous events have taken place?*

1. The Jewish people had to be released from captivity in Babylon.

2. They had to travel back—on foot—around the Fertile Crescent to Jerusalem, which lay in ruins. The trip alone would take months.

3. They had to rebuild the Temple, and the entire city, and the city wall. Could all that be done in LESS than a year and a half?

4. The human gestation period of the Messiah would take 270 days alone, more than half of the brief 490 days! And Jesus would have been born about 456 years BEFORE CHRIST—but was He? Of course not.

5. Not only was the Messiah to be born during this prophetic time period, but He was to live His life, complete His ministry, and die a sacrificial death on the cross. No one—not even a Futurist—teaches that these events were completed within a mere 490 days!

That's why EVERY Bible scholar, Catholic or Protestant, Futurist or Historical, applies the Year/Day principle to the 70-week prophecy of Daniel 9.

But then the Futurists inconsistently refuse to apply that same symbolic principle to the period of 1260 prophetic day/years and insist on taking them literally! We'd expect to find literal time in a literal prophecy, but symbolic time obviously belongs with symbolic prophecy like this (which uses symbols like "beasts" and "horns" and a "woman" named "Mystery, Babylon"). By imposing LITERAL time on SYMBOLIC prophecy, Futurism makes calculation meaningless.

Their refusal to apply the Bible's own Year/Day principle might be more excusable IF the 1260-year period did not meet the pragmatic test of HISTORIC FULFILLMENT. Since its divine fulfillment is so strikingly obvious, the unwillingness of Futurists to accept it is puzzling. The proven HISTORICAL FULFILLMENT of the 1260-day prophecy of the Beast is impressive, and the chronology of the 70-week prophecy of Daniel 9:24-27 is so persuasive that it not only helps prove the divinity of Christ, it also proves the validity of the Year/Day principle. The ACID TEST is: The Year/Day principle works!

A *fourth* fallacy of Futurist theory is the idea that the Beast power will be a SINGLE individual person—a so-called "Future Fuehrer." But how could the Antichrist be a single individual? The Year/Day principle of symbolic Bible prophecy tells us that the 3 and 1/2 times, or 42 months, or 1260 days were really a period of 1260 YEARS—quite a long time for ONE MAN to live. Rather than being a single individual, it was a DYNASTY, a whole succession of Papal leaders who over the centuries reigned as the Beast power.

John Calvin, founder of the Presbyterian Church, unflinchingly declared that the Papal system was the Antichrist prophesied by Scripture. Calvin also demolishes the notion that Antichrist would be just one man by citing 2 Thessalonians 2:1-8, where Paul says that:

> "even in HIS days [Paul's days] 'the mystery of iniquity' did 'already work' in *secret,* what it was afterwards to effect in a more *public* manner, he gives us to understand that this calamity was neither to be INTRODUCED by ONE man, nor to TERMINATE with ONE man." [308]

In every land, Reformers understood Antichrist to be a corrupt ecclesiastical system, not an individual. For example, John Knox, fearless leader of the Reformation in Scotland, emphatically declared that:

> "This 'man of sin,' or Antichrist, was NOT to be restrained to the person of any ONE MAN only, no more than by the Fourth Beast [representing pagan Rome in Daniel 7], was to be understood the person of any ONE EMPEROR." [309]

A *fifth* and final fallacy is that literal DAYS don't give enough time for the many events portrayed in Revelation chapters 13 through 19 to occur.

Note what Joseph Mede, or Mead (1586-1638), professor of Greek at Cambridge University, says about this fallacy:

> "Our adversaries [310] would have them literally understood for three single years and a half, as though it were an HISTORY and not a PROPHECY: but besides the use of prophecy to reckon days for years, I think it would trouble any man to conceive how so many things as should be performed in this time, should be done in three single years and a half. . . . Peoples, and multitudes of nations, and tongues to serve and obey him. To make war with the Saints and overcome them. To cause all that dwell upon the earth to worship him. Babylon to ride the Beast so long, that all nations shall drink of the wine of her fornication, the Kings of the earth commit fornication with her. . . . Methinks all this should ask much more than three years work, or four either. . . . Therefore, three years and a half . . . cannot be taken HISTORICALLY, it must be taken PROPHETICALLY, every day for a year." [311]

How foolish to short-circuit the Year-Day principle and insist on interpreting the time units as literal days! Literal days fail to give a time period adequate for and commensurate with the MAGNITUDE of the events portrayed. As the visions embrace titanic rather than trifling themes, so the time periods symbolize long rather than limited eras. Finally, we must consider the fact that these time periods are found in the midst of symbolic prophecy—therefore their measurement of time is not literal but symbolic.

In summary, we see that Futurism fails as a valid Bible doctrine for several good reasons:

1. It was arrived at DEDUCTIVELY, to support a cause, rather than inductively by impartial scholars.

2. It IGNORES the numerous clues presented by prophecy and the wealth of evidence presented by history.

3. It ABANDONS, on an inconsistent selective basis, the classic Year/Day principle.

4. It insists that Antichrist will be a SINGLE INDIVIDUAL—despite the fact that no one could live for 1260 years.

5. It fails to provide enough TIME—allowing a mere 42 months for the Beast to accomplish the titanic deeds ascribed to him.

This Papal contention teaches men to look for a fictitious Antichrist in the FUTURE while overlooking the PAST and PRESENT reality at Rome.

TIME WILL TELL

The answer to some questions must be, "Only time will tell," because we must wait to see what the outcome will be. For many centuries, this clue lay in that category. Earlier Christians had to take a "wait-and-see" attitude toward this 1260-year clue. But today we can look back on this prophecy like "Monday-morning quarterbacks." Father Time steps into the witness box and testifies that God's prediction was precisely fulfilled.

SEVEN times,[312] in both Old and New Testaments, God foretold that the Beast's dominating power would continue more than twelve centuries, for 1260 years, to be exact. No one but the Lord gave these prophetic forecasts —and no one but the Pope fulfills them.

CLUE "V"
THE BEAST WOULD RECEIVE A
"DEADLY WOUND."

Your Bible says:

1. **Revelation 13:3**—Of the Beast, John says: "I saw one of his heads *as it were* WOUNDED to DEATH; . . . his DEADLY WOUND. . . ."

2. **Revelation 13:10**—"He that leadeth into captivity shall GO into CAPTIVITY: he that killeth with the sword must be killed with the SWORD."

3. **Revelation 13:12**—The Beast had a "DEADLY WOUND."

4. **Revelation 13:14**—"The Beast . . . had the WOUND by a SWORD."

HISTORY testifies:

Bible prophecy foretold not only the rise of the Papacy but also its downfall. And history faithfully records both. From the Scriptural clues listed above, we can deduce at least four facts:

    A. The Beast would clearly receive a wound.

    B. That wound would appear to be serious or even mortal—a "deadly wound." The Beast would seem "as it *were* wounded to death."

    C. His wound would be inflicted by military might—"by a sword"—rather than by some natural calamity.

    D. The Beast would be taken prisoner by an enemy—he would be forced to "go into captivity."

Furthermore, we can deduce from Scripture within very narrow limits the time frame WHEN this wound would occur. Since Clues B, C, and U demonstrate that the 1260 years of Papal supremacy began in A.D. 538, it's an easy matter to find their close. Adding 1260 years to 538 brings us to 1798. Therefore, if we've given the right application to this prophecy, history must record an event in 1798 that would appear like a death stroke to the Papacy. Turning to history, we find that when the hour struck on God's prophetic clock, just such an event was recorded!

As the allotted period of 1260 years of Papal supremacy neared its end, political events were shaping up for its collapse.

> "We should recognize that something subtler and deeper than any shift in world political power was operating against the Church in the eighteenth century. This was the growth of . . . the enlarged sense of the omni-competence of the State to control all aspects of a country's life including its religion. . . . The exalted and new notion which the eighteenth century entertained of the functions of the State was bound to lead into conflict with the claims of the Church. . . . It followed that he [Louis XIV of France] would resent much more keenly any interference from Rome. . . . The position of the Papacy, and with it the vitality and influence of the spiritual power, DECLINED ominously." [313]

> "She [the Church] had resisted the outward assault of the Protestant Reformation to be sapped by the Revolution which had its seat in

Catholic countries [like France], and extensively prevailed in the Church herself. The spirit of opposition to the Holy See grew in energy, and the opposition to its system and ideas spread still more widely." [314]

"Rome had not hitherto been confronted without prior consultation, with anything like this entire reorganization of the French Church, this turning of the hierarchy of her authority upside down, this spoliation [plundering] presented as a *fait accompli* [accomplished fact]. It was more than even Pius VI, an elderly and conciliatory Pontiff, whose reign came at the conclusion of a long period of DECLINE in the power and prestige of Rome, was prepared to accept. . . . In the eighteenth century the authority, throughout Europe, of the Holy See had SUNK lower than at any time since the confused years before the advent of Hildebrand in the eleventh century." [315]

So the SUN of Papal power was now SETTING. But the singular event which actually fulfilled prophecy in wounding the Beast was precipitated, ironically enough, by France—France, the first daughter of the Church! For the ancient Franks were the first of the barbarian tribes to embrace Christianity by converting to Roman Catholicism when Clovis, their King, "was baptized, with more than 3,000 of his warriors," in A.D. 496. [316]

The French Revolution of 1789 was the extreme reaction of the people not only against the selfish nobility of royal government but also against the corrupt practices of Papal religion. Stepping onto the stage of history at this time was a new actor with a major role to play: NAPOLEON BONAPARTE. With rapid strides, Napoleon, one of the most powerful generals in history, began to change the face of Europe. The moment had come for the Papal head of the Beast to be "as it were wounded to death." [317] The Pope, who had for centuries driven God's people "into captivity," was himself forced to "go into captivity," as the prophet declared. [318]

THE SWORD OF BERTHIER

Napoleon sent his aide, General Berthier, on this mission into Italy. *Encyclopedia Britannica* says that Louis Alexandre Berthier, "the first of Napoleon's marshals, chief of staff in the Grande Armee . . . was the perfect assistant to Napoleon." [319] Though it's hard to say what his influence was, Napoleon himself declared Berthier to be "the man who has served me longest and has never failed me." [320]

ROME was taken by the French on February 10, 1798; the Roman Republic was proclaimed on the fifteenth; and on the night of the twentieth, POPE PIUS VI was hurried off "into captivity," where he soon died at Valence, France, in 1799. Napoleon had previously ordered that no new Pope was to be elected in his place. Father Joseph Rickaby, a Jesuit priest, writes:

"When, in 1797, Pope Pius VI fell grievously ill, Napoleon gave orders that in the event of his death NO SUCCESSOR should be elected to his office, and that the Papacy should be DISCONTINUED.

"But the Pope recovered. The peace was soon broken; Berthier entered Rome on the 10th [of] February 1798, and proclaimed a republic. The aged Pontiff refused to violate his oath by recognizing it, and was hurried from prison to prison in France. Broken with fatigue and sorrows, he died . . . [on the 29th of] August 1799, in the French fortress of Valence, aged 82 years. No wonder that half Europe thought Napoleon's veto would be obeyed, and that with the POPE the PAPACY was dead."[321]

German historian Leopold von Ranke similarly says: It "now seemed that the Papal power had been brought to a final close."[322]

George Trevor, Canon of York, explains:

"The object of the French Directory [the executive body of French government from 1795 to 1799] was the destruction of the Pontifical government, as the irreconcilable enemy of the republic. . . . The aged Pope [Pius VI] was summoned to surrender the temporal government; on his refusal, he was dragged from the altar. . . . His rings were torn from his fingers, and finally, after declaring the temporal power abolished, the victors carried the Pope PRISONER into Tuscany, whence he never returned (1798).

"The Papal States, converted into the Roman Republic, were declared to be in perpetual alliance with France, but the French general was the real master of Rome. . . . The territorial possessions of the clergy and monks were declared national property, and their former owners cast into prison. The Papacy was EXTINCT: not a vestige of its existence remained; and among all the Roman Catholic powers not a finger was stirred in its defence. The Eternal City had no longer prince or Pontiff; its bishop was a dying CAPTIVE in foreign lands; and the decree was already announced that no successor would be allowed in his place."[323]

John Adolphus, English lawyer and historian, gives the following account of 1798:

"Berthier advanced to the city [of Rome] by forced marches; summoned the castle of St. Angelo, allowing only four hours for its evacuation by the Papal troops; the convicts were set at liberty; the gates of the city secured by the French; the Pope, all the cardinals except three, and the whole people of Rome, made prisoners at discretion. . . .

"Shortly afterwards, Berthier made his triumphal entry into Rome; and a tree of liberty being planted on the capitol, . . . a proclamation was issued, declaring . . . a free and independent republic, under the special protection of the French army. A provisional government was acknowledged, as established by the sovereign people; and every other temporal authority emanating from the Pope was suppressed, nor was he any longer to exercise ANY function. . . .

"As a refinement in the art of insult, the day selected for planting the tree of liberty and deposing the Pontiff was the [twenty-third] anniversary of his accession to the sovereignty; and while he was, according to custom, celebrating divine service in the Sistine chapel and receiving the congratulations of the cardinals, Haller, the commissary-general of the French army, and Cervoni, abruptly rushed in, and announced the termination of his authority. . . .

"The Pope remained, after the abrogation of his authority, a prisoner in his own palace. The French first seized on it as a barracks, and in less than a week confined him to his own rooms, putting the seal of confiscation on all his effects. Even the furniture of his apartments was at length contemplated with a greedy eye, and the unfortunate Pontiff was removed from Rome to Sienna. . . .

"[A footnote in this source adds:] He was removed, according to the caprice or policy of his persecutors, at all hours in the night and day, to many cities in Italy, where he was exhibited in chains, and at length confined in a fortress at the top of the Alps, where, under the French government, it was sometimes customary to send regiments by way of punishment. In the course of the ensuing year it was deemed necessary to remove him to Valence, where he terminated his days amid the horrors of neglect and insult." [324]

It's true that the French Revolution, with its horrible "Reign of Terror" and unbridled excesses of infidelity, can give no one cause to rejoice. But Adolphus adds:

"The downfall of the Papal government, by whatever means effected, excited perhaps less sympathy than that of any other in Europe: the errors, the oppressions, the tyranny of [Papal] Rome over the whole Christian world, were remembered with bitterness; many rejoiced, through religious antipathy, in the overthrow of a church which they considered as idolatrous, though attended with the immediate triumph of infidelity; and many saw in these events the accomplishment of PROPHECIES, and the exhibition of signs promised in the most mystical parts of the Holy Scriptures." [325]

So the Pope's arrest and dethronement made dramatic news. Many Protestants recognized the fulfillment of prophecy and felt that the event confirmed the truths they had proclaimed. The result was a great spiritual awakening in Europe, in the Middle East, in India, in North and South America, even as far away as the new land of Australia.

For instance, theologian David Simpson, who lived during those world-shaking events as a contemporary eye-witness, impressively wrote:

"Is it not extremely remarkable, and a powerful confirmation of the truth of Scripture prophecy, that just 1260 years ago from the present 1798, in the very beginning of the year 538, Belisarius put an end to the empire of the Goths at Rome, leaving no power therein but the Bishop of that Metropolis?

"Read these things in the prophetic Scriptures; compare them coolly with the present state of Europe, and then, I say again, deny the truth of Divine Revelation, if you can. Open your eyes, and behold these things accomplishing in the face of the whole world. This thing was not done in a corner." [326]

Indeed, not! Far from being done in a corner, the prophecy concerning the wounding of the Beast was FULFILLED before the eyes of the whole world!

DIVINE JUSTICE

"In the Sistine Chapel of the Vatican, the ante-hall to which has a fresco painted by Papal order commemorative of the Protestant massacre on St. Bartholomew's Day,[327] (might not the scene have served as a memento of God's retributive justice?) there, while seated on his throne, and receiving the gratulations of his cardinals on the anniversary of his election to the Popedom, he was arrested by the French military, the ring of his marriage with the Church Catholic torn from his finger, his palace rifled, and himself carried prisoner into France, only to die there in exile shortly after." [328]

Arthur R. Pennington, Fellow of the Royal Historical Society, says of this event:

"One day the Pope was sitting on his throne in a chapel of the Vatican, surrounded by his cardinals who had assembled for the purpose of offering him their congratulations on his elevation to his high dignity. On a sudden, the shouts of an angry multitude penetrated to the conclave, intermingled with the strokes of axes and hammers on the doors. Very soon a band of soldiers burst into the hall, who tore away from his finger his pontifical ring, and hurried him off, a PRISONER, through a hall, the walls of which were adorned with a fresco, representing the armed satellites of the Papacy, on St. Bartholomew's Day, as *bathing their swords in the blood of unoffending women and helpless children*. Thus it might seem as if he were to be reminded that the same God who visits the iniquities of the fathers upon the children unto the third and fourth generation, had made him the victim of His retributive justice for a deed of ATROCITY which had long been crying aloud to Him for vengeance." [329]

The sword of Berthier "as it were wounded to death" the great Papal power. The Pope was arrested and forced to "go into captivity" where he died in disgrace as a prisoner in exile. The properties of the Church were confiscated. The French Directory government decreed that there would never be another Bishop of Rome. For all practical purposes, and by all outward appearance, the Papacy was dead. All this not only **happened**, but it happened **in the very year of 1798**, *precisely* according to the prophetic timetable. God's Word is sure, and His purposes know no haste and no delay.

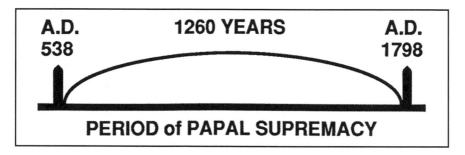

Thus the events of history fit exactly into the mold of prophecy, demonstrating the truth of Peter's words: "We have the word of the prophets made more certain, and you will do well to pay attention to it, as to a light shining in a dark place, until the day dawns." [330]

But prophecy ALSO foretold that this "deadly wound" would be HEALED, and that the world would once more briefly follow the Papal power! Our final divine clue will consider that remarkable—almost incredible—prophecy.

CLUE "W"
THE BEAST'S "DEADLY WOUND"
WOULD BE "HEALED."

Your Bible says:

1. **Revelation 13:3**—"And I saw one of his heads as it were wounded to death; and his deadly WOUND was HEALED: and all the world wondered after the Beast."

2. **Revelation 13:12**—"The first Beast, whose deadly WOUND was HEALED."

3. **Revelation 13:14**—"The Beast, which had the WOUND by a sword, and DID LIVE."

HISTORY testifies:

The preceding clue shows that God's prediction of the Beast's "deadly wound" was fulfilled in a marvelous way. However, that clue of the deadly wound—and all the others, for that matter—would be of no consequence to us today IF the Papacy had remained dead and passed out of existence! But God said the wound must be "HEALED." Is that what happened in the REAL world of HISTORY?

Of course we all know that the Papal institution which received that deadly wound in 1798 is "alive and well" today and working in Rome with business as usual. We not only READ about it in the Bible—we also SEE it thriving in the world around us.

When that "deadly wound" was inflicted and the decree went forth that no successor to the dying Pope would be allowed on the throne of the Vatican, it appeared that the Papacy was extinct. But He who sees the end from the beginning declared through John the Revelator that this "deadly wound" would be healed and all the world would again wonder after the Beast.

This predicted resurgence of power has been fulfilled in an astonishing revival of Papal influence. In some respects the priest-king of Rome has been elevated to new heights of spiritual power and greatness. The prophet Daniel, also, indicated that his sovereignty would continue in some form until the time of the final judgment and the setting up of God's eternal kingdom:

> "I beheld, and the same [Little] Horn made war with the saints, and prevailed against them: UNTIL the Ancient of days came; and the time came that the saints possessed the kingdom. . . . But the judgment shall sit, and they shall take away his dominion, to consume and destroy it unto the end." [331]

Note how German theologian Christian G. Thube, another contemporary witness, warned in 1799 that the events of the preceding year—astounding though they were—constituted only a WOUND that would be HEALED:

> "The Beast has received a deadly wound, Revelation 13:12. It received the wound by the sword, verse 14.
>
> "This was fulfilled by the French who with the sword banished the Pope and his cardinals from Rome, dissolving the Papal States and erecting a so-called Roman Republic. . . .
>
> "The deadly wound will be HEALED, but whether it will take a short or long time we do not know; nor do we understand now in which manner and by which process it will come to pass." [332]

When Pope Pius VI died in French captivity, without a successor in sight, the outlook for the future of the Papacy seemed dark indeed. As the world crossed the threshold of the nineteenth century, the Papacy was extinct.

English historian and essayist Thomas Babington Macaulay expressed it this way:

> "[The Pope] was carried away CAPTIVE by the unbelievers. He died a PRISONER in their hands; and even the honours of sepulture were long withheld from his remains [that is, for a while his body was left unburied].
>
> "It is not strange that, in the year 1799, even sagacious observers should have thought that, at length, the hour of the Church of Rome was come. . . .
>
> "But the END was not yet. Again doomed to death, the milk-white hind[333] was still fated NOT to die."[334]

✓ A HEALING Treaty with NAPOLEON

Fellow of the Royal Historical Society Arthur R. Pennington explains how this came about:

> "Many of the men in those days [of 1798] imagined that the dominion of the Pope had come to an END, and that the knell of the temporal power was then sounding among the nations. This supposition, however, proved to be erroneous. The French republicans were very anxious that Rome should not have another Pope. But as the reverses of the revolutionary armies had left Southern Italy to its ancient masters, the cardinals were able to proceed to an election at Venice. They elected, on March 14th, 1800, Barnabas Chiaromonti, who assumed the name of Pius VII.
>
> "The first transaction of this Pope was a negotiation with the government of France, of which Napoleon Bonaparte was the First Consul.
> . . .
>
> "He [Napoleon] felt that, as the large majority of the inhabitants of France knew no other form of faith than Romanism, it must become the established religion of the country. Accordingly we find that he now began negotiations with the Pope, which issued in a CONCORDAT in July, 1801, whereby the Roman Catholic religion was once more established in France."[335]

But Carnegie Fellow and English Catholic Edward E. Y. Hales emphasizes: "It is important to remember how desperate was the position from which the Concordat with Napoleon saved the Catholic Church."[336]

We must not suppose that this Concordat immediately restored full powers and authority on the resurrected Papacy. Far from it. The Papacy was re-established but with much less of its former power. As a matter of fact, Hales continues:

"In publishing the Concordat, in April 1802, the First Consul [Napoleon] published alongside it, without any previous consultation with Rome, what were called the "Organic Articles," designed to regulate the administration of the Church in France. His excuse was that he was only publishing the police regulations which the Concordat had allowed him to make for the maintenance of public order, but a glance at the articles in question shows . . . that he was, in fact, concerned to SUBJECT the Church, even in matters evidently spiritual, to the control of the State." [337]

One may wonder why Napoleon reversed his stand on the Papacy and agreed to the Concordat at all, thus becoming the unique instrument not only to WOUND the Papacy but also to effect its HEALING. The answer is purely pragmatic:

"Bonaparte was determined to enlist the clergy on the side of his regime. . . . The concordat not only gave Bonaparte the support of the clergy and their congregations, it also deprived the royalists of their chief argument and ally against his regime." [338]

Naturally, negotiations with the French government were difficult for the newly elected Pope, and he had to make many concessions in exchange for the right to exist. Among those concessions were the following:
The Pope had to agree to—

1. Waive the claim that Catholicism be recognized as
the state religion.
2. Give his official blessing to the liquidation of the
pre-Revolutionary church in France.
3. Renounce the ecclesiastical property that had been
secularized.
4. Call on the surviving bishops to resign their sees. [339]

These and other concessions were quite stringent, but they won from Napoleon the all-important right of SURVIVAL for the Papacy.

✓ A HEALING Treaty with MUSSOLINI

The 1801 Concordat with Napoleon was important, but of equal importance was the 1929 Concordat signed by BENITO MUSSOLINI, Premier of Italy. You see, following the "deadly wound" which brought captivity and death in exile to the Pope, other Popes were elected—but Papal power remained at a low ebb. A century later, on February 11, 1929, the famous treaty signed by Mussolini and Cardinal Gasparri again made the Pope one of the sovereigns of the earth.

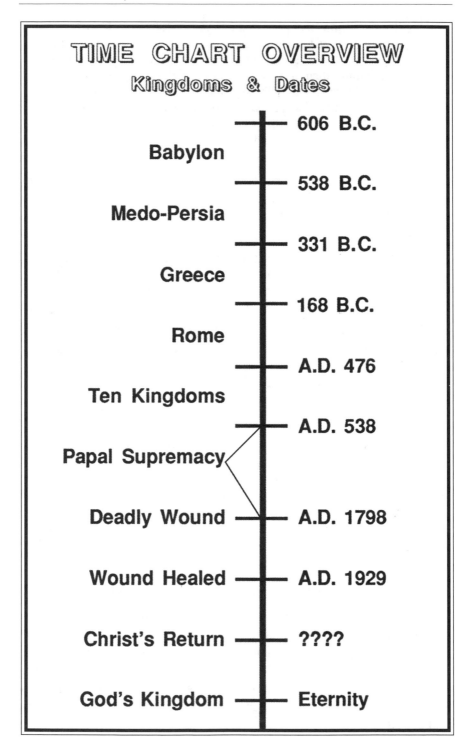

TIME CHART OVERVIEW
Kingdoms & Dates

606 B.C.

Babylon

538 B.C.

Medo-Persia

331 B.C.

Greece

168 B.C.

Rome

A.D. 476

Ten Kingdoms

A.D. 538

Papal Supremacy

Deadly Wound — A.D. 1798

Wound Healed — A.D. 1929

Christ's Return — ????

God's Kingdom — Eternity

On Tuesday, February 12, 1929, the following story made *front-page news* around the world:

[Headlines:] **MUSSOLINI AND GASPARRI SIGN HISTORIC ROMAN PACT ... *HEAL WOUND* OF MANY YEARS ...**

"Rome, Feb. 11 (AP)—The Roman question tonight was a thing of the past and the Vatican was at peace with Italy. The formal accomplishment of this today was the exchange of signatures in the historic Palace of St. John Lateran by two noteworthy plenipotentiaries, Cardinal Gasparri for Pope Pius XI and Premier Mussolini for King Victor Emmanuel III.

"In affixing the autographs to the memorable document, HEALING the WOUND which has festered since 1870,[340] extreme cordiality was displayed on both sides. . . ."[341]

This 1929 Concordat, often called the LATERAN TREATY, was more favorable to the Papacy than the earlier one had been. It not only gave the Pope sovereign status as ruler over Vatican City, but a financial clause "arranged for Italy to PAY nearly 2,000,000,000 [two BILLION] lire either in cash or consolidated stock as compensation for church properties seized in 1870."[342]

Even the most casual observer is compelled to recognize the rapidly growing influence and prestige of the Roman Pontiff. In 1929, when the Pope was once again hailed as a king, only fourteen nations had representatives at the Vatican. Today most countries of the world have ambassadorial representatives at Vatican City. The recent appointment of a United States ambassador to the Vatican is only one of many evidences of the reviving power of the Papacy. Millions look to the Papal power as the greatest POLITICAL influence today. Today's newspaper headlines attest to the Papacy's incredible influence in world affairs. The Pope's *every word, every move, every deed* is published to the ends of the earth in glowing press releases and network TV news. As I write this, the latest issue of *TIME* Magazine sits on my desk: the cover picture shows Pope John II on his trip to the Holy Land, and eleven full pages—crammed with pictures—make up a "Special Report."

"The media have a love affair with the Catholic Church. Look at your newspapers, magazines and television sets. The Catholic Church has replaced mainline Protestantism as the nation's most newsworthy religious force. . . . Curiously, the growth of the media during the 20th Century, and especially the advent of television, has made the PAPACY stronger than it has ever been during the preceding 1,900 years. . . . Never has the Papal office been so magnified in power."[343]

The Beast's mortal wound has certainly "healed" very well. The Antichrist of these last days is simply the Papacy restored to power. The startling survival of the Papacy after receiving its "deadly wound" in 1798 is LIVING PROOF that it FULFILLS this prophecy!

✦ ✦ ✦

CONCLUSION TO THE CLUES

An old saying states that "All roads lead to Rome." And we've just seen that all CLUES POINT to Rome, identifying the Roman Papacy as Antichrist. So overwhelming is the evidence against the Papacy that it fits not just a few clues like A–E–I–O–U or P–D–Q but "ALL of the above." The striking similarity between prophetic blueprint and historic fact cannot be denied. As we survey the centuries, we find only ONE power in all history that fits the divine description. These twenty-three points of identification all meet in one great reality: the Papacy is the Beast.

Thousands of years ago, word-pictures from Daniel, Paul, and John accurately depicted "that Man of Sin."[344] An inspired hand sketched the Antichrist/Beast on the incriminating pages of prophecy. Someone has said, "If the Pope is not Antichrist, he's had bad luck to be so like him." For the Biblical predictions of the Beast and the historical record of the Papacy are a MIRROR IMAGE of each other—the Papacy is precisely what the Bible said Antichrist would be. The many prophecies, all fulfilled with terrible exactness in the Papal power, provide a powerful argument that the Scriptures are the Word of God!

If other investigators can take these same clues and show us better conclusions, I'd welcome any light they can share. God's church and I would both be indebted to them for it. But the chance of some other power fitting all these clues is LESS than ZERO! I wish, for the sake of my Catholic friends, I could show from Bible prophecy that Antichrist was someone other than the Papacy. It's painful to destroy the illusions and faith that sincere, loving, God-fearing people have in their Church. It hurts me because I know it hurts them to have their religious beliefs shattered and exposed as untrue.

But we must remember that *God knows the heart,* and He knows how devoutly His dear ones in the Catholic Church have worshipped and served Him. That's why He lovingly calls His faithful people out of the false religious system called Babylon, saying: "COME OUT of her, MY people, that ye be not partakers of her SINS, and that ye receive not of her PLAGUES."[345] Is it unreasonable for God to expect us to divorce ourselves from a false system He must destroy? He doesn't want us to be deceived any longer.

What was FORETOLD has been FULFILLED. So the manhunt is over. Revelation reveals the Antichrist, unmasking and exposing him, and the Mystery of the Beast is solved.

But is that all there is to it? Since the mystery is solved, do we simply mark it "Case Closed" and go on about our business? No! This new knowledge carries with it a responsibility to warn God's people to "Come out" of "Babylon." We must acknowledge publicly what we know privately about these things.

Our next chapter, on the IMAGE of the Beast and MARK of the Beast, is one you'll find most fascinating!

⁓

"And the murderer is . . . THE BUTLER! Yes, the butler . . . who, I'm convinced, first gored the Colonel to death before trampling him to smithereens."

"The Far Side" cartoon panel by Gary Larson is reprinted by permission of Chronicle Features, San Francisco.

Notes to Chapter 19

1. Revelation 14:9-10.
2. Your Bible says, "Surely the Lord God does nothing, unless He reveals His secret to His servants the prophets."—Amos 3:7, NKJV.
3. Revelation 13:15-17, NKJV.
4. See Daniel 7:3, 17, and 23. Sometimes the Bible makes the identification of the symbols for us, as in Daniel 8:3, 5, 20, and 21.
5. For instance, when the angel said, "This shall be a SIGN unto you; Ye shall find the Babe . . . lying in a manger," he gave a clear, UNIQUE sign: Not many babies are born in a stable, where mangers are found. See Luke 2:12 and Chapter 7, "Jesus Meets Every Test," pages 181-204, above.
6. For an overview, see the "CHART: A Bird's-Eye-View of Pertinent Prophecies" on pages 580-581 following this chapter's Introduction.
7. Sir Isaac Newton, *Observations Upon the Prophecies of Daniel, and the Apocalypse of St. John* (London: J. Darby and T. Browne, 1733), p. 75.
8. James I reigned as monarch of Great Britain from 1603 to 1625. See *A Paraphrase Upon the Revelation of the Apostle S. John* and *A Premonition to All Most Mightie Monarchs, Kings, Free Princes, and States of Christendome,* in *The Workes of the Most High and Mightie Prince, James, . . . King of Great Britaine,* edited by James [Mountague], Bishop of Winton (London: Robert Barker and John Bill, 1616), pp. 39, 287-292, and 308-310.
9. *The Wall Street Journal* (Monday, April 19, 1982), Part I, p. 1.
10. John 8:32. And God says in Hosea 4:6, "My people are destroyed for lack of knowledge"—knowledge they *could* have gained but didn't.
11. Revelation 12:9.
12. Ephesians 4:15.
13. Isaiah 14:12, Luke 10:18, John 12:31.
14. Daniel 7:8 & 20.
15. Daniel 7:7-8, 20, 24.
16. Daniel 7:21. Verse 25 says the Little Horn would "WEAR OUT the saints."
17. Revelation 13:5.
18. Revelation 13:1.
19. Revelation 13:7.
20. See pages 464-474 of Chapter 15, "History Told in Advance," above, dealing with Daniel 2 & 7.
21. Martin Luther, *The Table Talk of Martin Luther,* translated and edited by William Hazlitt (London: H. G. Bohn, 1857), p. 327.
22. Hippolytus, *Treatise on Christ and Antichrist,* sections 28, 32, 33, translated in *Ante-Nicene Fathers,* Volume 5, p. 210.
23. Alexander Clarence Flick, Ph. D., Litt. D. (1869-1942); professor of European history at Syracuse University, in *The Rise of the Mediæval Church,* (reprint; New York: Burt Franklin, 1959), pp. 148-150.

24. Adolf von Harnack (1851-1930); professor of church history at University of Berlin, in *What Is Christianity?* translated by Thomas Bailey Saunders, 2nd edition, revised (New York: Putnam, 1901), p. 270. A new edition of this book is now available (Philadelphia: Fortress Press, 1986, 301 pages).

25. Walter Woodburn Hyde, A. M., Ph. D., Litt. D. (1871-1966); professor of Latin, Greek, and ancient history in several American universities, in *Paganism to Christianity in the Roman Empire*, (Philadelphia: University of Pennsylvania Press, © 1946), p. 7.

26. Justinian, *The Civil Laws*, translated by S. P. Scott (Cincinnati: The Central Trust Company, © 1932), Volume 17, p. 125.

27. Daniel 2:41-43 and Daniel 7:24, respectively.

28. For more on the theory of Futurism and its *origin*, see Clue "U," pages 682-686.

29. 2 Thessalonians 2:7, NIV.

30. 1 John 2:18.

31. 1 John 4:3.

32. *The Catholic Encyclopedia*, edited by Charles G. Herbermann and others (New York: Robert Appleton Company, 1907-1914), Volume I, p. 560, article "Antichrist."

33. 2 Thessalonians 2:5-6, RSV.

34. Daniel 2:21.

35. For more on the Beast's persecution of God's saints, see Clue "R," pages 644-659.

36. Daniel 2:41-43 and 7:7 & 24—also Chapter 15, pages 468-472, above.

37. Daniel 7:24 says plainly: "The ten horns out of this kingdom [Rome] are ten kings that shall arise. . . ." Here KINGS means KINGDOMS: "These great beasts, which are four, are four KINGS. . . . The fourth beast shall be the fourth KINGDOM" Daniel 7:17 & 23.

38. Arians were followers of Arius, a heretic who limited the divinity of Christ by saying He was a CREATED being NOT truly equal to the Father.

39. The Ostrogoths were *eastern* Goths, as distinguished from the Visigoths or *western* Goths, who centered in Spain.

40. The author is indebted to C. Mervyn Maxwell, *God Cares: The Message of Daniel*, Volume 1 (Boise, Idaho: Pacific Press Publishing Association, © 1981). Dr. Maxwell's excellent treatment of Daniel—and of Revelation, in Volume 2 (1985)—are among the most penetrating and up-to-date studies available today.

41. *Encyclopedia Britannica* says of the Heruli: "Nothing is heard of them after the early 6th century [the early 500's]." (1967 edition), Volume 11, p. 458, article "Heruli."

42. Cardinal John Henry Newman, *An Essay on the Development of Christian Doctrine*, Part II (London: 1878), p. 320.

43. *Encyclopedia Britannica* (1967 edition), Volume 22, p. 881, article "Vandals."

44. *Encyclopedia Britannica* (1967 edition), Volume 10, p. 607, article "Ostrogoths."

45. Procopius, *History of the Wars*, translated by H. B. Dewing, The Loeb Classical Library (Cambridge, Mass.: Harvard University Press, 1961), (Book V, chapter xvi, line 11), Volume 3, p. 161. Procopius was the Byzantine historian who followed Justinian's armies and served as private secretary to Belisarius.

46. *Encyclopedia Britannica* (1967 edition), Volume 3, p. 438, article "Belisarius."

47. C. W. Previte-Orton, *The Shorter Cambridge Medieval History*, 2 volumes (Cambridge, England: The University Press, 1953), Volume 1, p. 192.

48. *Encyclopedia Britannica* (1967 edition), Volume 10, p. 607, article "Ostrogoths."

49. Thomas Hodgkin, *Italy and Her Invaders*, second edition, 8 volumes (Oxford: Clarendon Press, 1885-1899), Volume 4, p. 250.

50. George Finlay, *Greece Under the Romans* (Edinburgh and London: William Blackwood and Sons, 1844), p. 295.

51. Niccolo Machiavelli, *The History of Florence*, Harper Torchbooks (New York: Harper & Row, Publishers, 1960), p. 13.

52. Official Catholic sources claim: "The Pope is crowned with a triple crown, as king of HEAVEN[!] and of EARTH and of the LOWER REGIONS *[infernorum]*." Lucius Ferraris, *Prompta Bibliotheca* (Venice, Italy: Gaspar Storti, 1772), Volume 6, p. 26, article 2 "Papa."

53. For instance, the Bible says: "David . . . went to Rabbah, and fought against it, and took it. And he took their king's crown from off his head, . . . and it was set on David's head."—2 Samuel 12:29-30.

54. Emphatically repeated in Revelation 14:8 and 18:2.

55. See Jeremiah 50:23-24, 35, 40 and pages 456-463 in Chapter 15, above.

56. 1 Peter 5:13.

57. See Jeremiah 21:7, Daniel 8:23, and Deuteronomy 28:49-50.

58. Daniel 5:2-5 records how BABYLONIAN King Belshazzar desecrated the sacred "golden and silver vessels . . . that were taken out of the Temple of the house of God which was at Jerusalem." And the relief sculpture on the great Arch of Titus in Rome graphically depicts ROMAN legions carrying home in triumph the sacred seven-branched candlestick and other plundered items from the Jerusalem Temple.

59. In his drama *Julius Caesar*, Shakespeare wrote of the Roman emperor:
    "He hath brought MANY CAPTIVES home to Rome,
    Whose ransoms did the general coffers fill."
    —Act III, scene ii, lines 93-94.

60. Romans 1:25.

61. Guilio Giannelli, editor, *The World of Ancient Rome* (New York: Putnam, 1967), p. 175. "Anthropomorphism" refers to the pagan concept of deities in human form, like Jupiter, Mars, Venus, and others.

62. Cardinal James Gibbons, *The Faith of Our Fathers*, One Hundred and Tenth Revised Edition (Baltimore: P. J. Kenedy & Sons, Printers to the Holy See, 1917), p. 87.

63. [Manuel Lacunza], *The Coming of Messiah in Glory and Majesty*, by Juan Josaphat Ben-Ezra (pseudonym), translated from the Spanish [*La Venida del Mesias*], with a preliminary discourse by Edward Irving (London: L. B. Seeley and Son, 1827), Volume 2, p. 65. For thirty years Lacunza engaged in the most profound study of the Scriptures, but could not get ecclesiastical permission to publish his book. It was still unpublished when he was found dead in 1801, on the bank of the river near Imola, Italy, where he resided. Later printed in both Spanish and English, it greatly stirred the two continents of both Europe and South America. Lacunza was a clarion voice from the Catholic Church, and numerous priests accepted his views.

64. Thomas Cranmer, *The Works of Thomas Cranmer*, edited by John Edmund Cox, 2 volumes (Cambridge, England: The University Press, 1844-46), Volume 2, p. 63.

65. Modern versions say the "Little Horn" which came up after the first ten horns would be "DIFFERENT from the earlier ones" or "former ones" or "previous ones"— as the New International Version, Revised Standard Version, and New American Standard Version put it.

66. Daniel 7:7, 8, 19.

67. John 18:36.

68. Daniel 7:8 & 20.

69. 2 Thessalonians 2:3-4.

70. Christ commanded, "Call no man your Father on earth: for One is your Father, which is in heaven."—Matthew 23:9. Jesus used the term "HOLY FATHER" when praying in John 17:11, but He used it to refer to His HEAVENLY Father, the almighty God of the universe! Any mere mortal who accepts such a title is guilty of the sin of blasphemy. See Clue "S," pages 659-666.

71. Cardinal Robert Bellarmine, *On the Authority of Councils* (1619 edition), Volume II, Book 2, Chapter 17, p. 266.

72. Acts 10:25-26.

73. Revelation 19:10, NKJV.

74. Revelation 22:8-9, NKJV.

75. 1 Kings 19:14 & 18, NKJV.

76. The *margin* in the King James Version of the Bible corrects this translation to read "*names* of blasphemy," making it identical to the description in Revelation 17:3. Modern translations such as The Amplified Bible, The Living Bible, New American Standard Bible, Today's English Version – Good News Bible, The New Testament in Modern English – Phillips translation, and the New International Version all translate this verse so as to let us know that *several* "names of blasphemy" are involved.

77. Vance Havner, quoted in *Current Thoughts and Trends* (October, 1998), p. 24.

78. See Jude 3.

79. The creeping compromise and ultimate corruption of the Church has already been thoroughly documented by Alexander Hislop in his classic work *The Two Babylons, or The Papal Worship* (Neptune, NJ: Loizeaux Brothers, Second American Edition, 1959), 351 pages.

80. Dante Alighieri (1265-1321), was the greatest Italian poet and one of the greatest writers of all time. See *The Divine Comedy of Dante Alighieri; Hell, Purgatory, Paradise*, translated by Henry F. Cary (New York: P. F. Collier & Son, 1909), The Harvard Classics, Volume 20.

81. Johann J. Ignaz von Döllinger, *Studies in European History*, translated by Margaret Warre (London: J. Murray, 1890), pp. 85-86.

82. Specific Popes mentioned as languishing in the flames are Linus, Cletus, Sextus, Pius, Callixtus, Urban, Boniface VIII, and Nicholas III. See *Divine Comedy*, "Hell," Canto XIX, pp. 78-79 and "Paradise," Canto XXVII, p. 400. Besides these Popes in particular, Dante mentions "both Popes and Cardinals" in general over whom avarice or greed maintains absolute dominion. "Hell," Canto VII, p. 30.

83. The "two governments that ill assort" are CHURCH and STATE.
84. Dante, *Divine Comedy,* "Purgatory," Canto XVI, p. 211.
85. Dante, *Divine Comedy,* "Paradise," Canto IX, p. 324.
86. Dante, *Divine Comedy,* "Paradise," Canto XXVII, p. 400. A footnote there explains "Cahorsines and Gascons" as Dante's allusion to Pope John XXII, a native of Cahors, and Pope Clement V, a Gascon.
87. Dante, *Divine Comedy,* "Hell," Canto XIX, p. 80.
88. Dante, *Divine Comedy,* "Purgatory," Canto XXXII, p. 279.
89. Dante, *Divine Comedy,* "Paradise," Canto XXVII, p. 399.
90. All quotations in this paragraph and the two following are from the Marchese Roberto Ridolfi, *Encyclopedia Britannica* (1967 edition), Volume 19, p. 1114, article "Savonarola, Girolamo."
91. John 8:32.
92. Revelation 18:4.
93. Revelation 17:9, The Living Bible. Other modern versions of the Bible which translate it as "SEVEN HILLS" are: Today's English Version (Good News Bible), The Amplified Bible, New Testament in Modern English (Phillips Translation), Revised Standard Version, New International Version, *etc.*
94. *World Book Encyclopedia* (1955 edition), Volume 14, p. 7013, article "Rome."
95. *Webster's New International Dictionary,* Second Edition, Unabridged (Springfield, Massachusetts: G. & C. Merriam Company, 1950), p. 2294, entries "seven-hilled" and "seven hills."
96. S. G. F. Brandon, editor, Milestones of History Series, in *Ancient Empires* (New York: Newsweek Books, 1973), p. 102.
97. John Cotton, *An Exposition Upon the Thirteenth Chapter of the Revelation* (London: Printed for Livewel Chapman, 1655), p. 9.
98. Timothy Dwight, *A Discourse on Some Events of the Last Century* (New Haven: Ezra Read, 1801), p. 35.
99. Dwight, *A Discourse in Two Parts* (New Haven: Howe & Deforest, 1812), p. 9.
100. William Smith, *Dictionary of the Bible* (Chicago, John C. Winston Company, © 1884), p. 569, entry "Rome."
101. Plutarch, *Moralia,* "On the Fortune of the Romans," 326.13; translated by Frank Cole Babbitt (Cambridge, Mass.: Harvard University Press, 1936), Volume 4, p. 377.
102. Bob Baker, "Monsignor Hawkes Dies; Ex-Financial Chief of Archdiocese," *Los Angeles Times,* September 23, 1985, Metro Section, p. 1.
103. Don A. Schanche, "John Paul II," *Los Angeles Times* Magazine, September 13, 1987, p. 11.
104. "The Great Vatican Bank Mystery," *TIME* Magazine (September 12, 1982), p. 24.
105. *Los Angeles Times* (May 27, 1984), Section I, p. 14. How ironic that the leader of the world's RICHEST church claims to be the successor of Peter, a man who had *neither silver nor gold.* See Acts 3:6.
106. Revelation 17:1, 15, 16 and 19:2. The worst name a woman can be called is a "whore."

107. *Webster's New International Dictionary,* Second Edition, Unabridged (Springfield, Massachusetts: G. & C. Merriam Company, © 1950), p. 404, entry "cardinal."

108. Don A. Schanche, "John Paul Installs 18 New Cardinals," *Los Angeles Times* (February 3, 1983), Part I, p. 5.

109. 2 Corinthians 11:13-15, NRSV.

110. Gerald Clarke, "The Double Life of an AIDS Victim," *TIME* Magazine (October 14, 1985), p. 106.

111. Revelation 17:5.

112. Revelation 17:6. See Clue "R," pages 644-659, on persecution.

113. Revelation 18:4.

114. Revelation 18:2.

115. Revelation 19:2.

116. Revelation 17:5.

117. This paragraph and the two preceding ones were paraphrased and quoted from Christopher Wordsworth, *Union with Rome,* (London: Longmans, 1909), pp. 61-63.

118. 1 Corinthians 3:16-17; 6:19; 2 Corinthians 6:16.

119. Westminster Confession of Faith, section 6 of chapter 25, quoted in Philip Schaff, *The Creeds of Christendom,* 4th edition revised (New York: Harper, 1919), Volume 3, pp. 658-659. This very statement was adopted and repeated at Boston in 1680 by Increase Mather, Congregational pastor and illustrious president of HARVARD. Mather, the first Doctor of Divinity in America, presided as moderator over a synod of Massachusetts churches which adopted this view by formal vote. See *Confession of Faith Owned and Consented Unto by the Elders and Messengers of the Churches Assembled at Boston in New England, May 12, 1680. Being the Second Session of That Synod* (Boston: John Foster, 1680), chapter 26, article 4, p. 55. As you can see, this was the commonly accepted colonial American position.

120. 1 Peter 2:5—"As living stones . . . let yourselves be used in building the spiritual TEMPLE. . . ." Today's English Version.

121. [Manuel Lacunza], *The Coming of the Messiah in Glory and Majesty,* by Juan Josafat Ben-Ezra, . . . translated from the Spanish *[La Venida del Mesias en Gloria y Magestad],* with a preliminary discourse by Edward Irving (London: L. B. Seeley and Son, 1827). 2 Volumes. Volume 1, p. 262.

122. Timothy Dwight, *A Sermon, Preached at Northampton* (Hartford, Connecticut: Nathaniel Patten, 1781), p. 27.

123. A quick glance at authoritative reference works like the monumental *Oxford English Dictionary* on the prefix *anti–* will verify the meanings stated above. Further verification is found in Greek sources, such as the *Dictionary of the Greek Testament* found in James Strong, *Strong's Exhaustive Concordance* (Grand Rapids, Mich.: Associated Publishers, no date); Liddell & Scott, *Greek-English Lexicon,* Abridged Twenty-Sixth Edition (New York: Follett Publishing Company, 1956); and J. T. Pring, *Oxford Dictionary of Modern Greek* (Oxford: The Clarendon Press, 1965).

124. The word *incarnation* literally means "in the flesh," from the Latin word meaning *flesh,* just as "chili con *carne*" is *chili with meat* or flesh food. When capitalized, the word "Incarnation" refers to Christ's human birth.

125. See 1 John 4:3 and 2 John 7.

126. Genesis 28:12.

127. John 1:51.

128. "A DOGMA is a doctrine laid down with authority," says *Webster's New International Dictionary,* Second Edition, Unabridged (Springfield, Mass.: Merriam-Webster, Inc., © 1950), p. 763, entry "doctrine." When the Pope enunciates a dogma, it MUST be accepted by the Church as true and unquestionable. Denial of a dogma is considered heresy.

129. *Encyclopedia Britannica* defines this dogma as the belief that "Mary, God's Virgin Mother, by a special divine privilege . . . was preserved free from all stain of original sin in the first instant of her conception." Father J. B. Carol, *Encyclopedia Britannica* (1967 edition), Volume 11, p. 1101, article "Immaculate Conception."

130. Pope Pius IX, translated in Philip Schaff, *The Creeds of Christendom* (New York: Harper, 1919), Volume 2, pp. 211-212.

131. Romans 3:23.

132. Psalm 51:5.

133. Hebrews 4:15 affirms that Jesus "was in all points tempted like as we are, yet without sin."

134. Luke 1:46-47, NKJV.

135. 1 Timothy 2:5.

136. Philippians 2:7.

137. Romans 8:3.

138. The chapter containing this Scriptural clue declares: "That man of sin . . . exalteth himself above all that is called God, or that is worshipped; so that he as God sitteth IN the temple of God, showing himself that he IS God. . . . The Mystery of INIQUITY doth already work."—2 Thessalonians 2:3-7.

139. 1 Timothy 3:16 says: "Great is the Mystery of GODLINESS: GOD was manifest in the FLESH. . . ."

140. Written by someone else who signed the name of Constantine the Great to give it his weight of authority, "The Donation of Constantine [is] . . . the most famous FORGERY in European History," says historian Christopher B. Coleman on page 1 of his *Treatise of Lorenzo Valla on the Donation of Constantine* (New Haven: Yale University Press, © 1922). Note also the following: "In 1440 Laurentius Valla proved conclusively that the Constantine document was a pious fraud and that it had been written several centuries AFTER Constantine's time. Valla's argument was never answered and his conclusion is not now disputed."—Paul Hutchinson and Winfred Ernest Garrison, *20 Centuries of Christianity: A Concise History,* 1st edition (New York: Harcourt, Brace and World, © 1959), p. 71. Valla, who died in 1457, served as papal secretary and escaped being burned at the stake only when the King of Naples interceded.

141. Translated by Christopher B. Coleman, in *The Treatise of Lorenzo Valla on the Donation of Constantine* (New Haven: Yale University Press, © 1922), p. 13.

142. *Our Sunday Visitor,* April 18, 1915, Volume 4, p. 3.

143. Rheims (Douay) Version of the New Testament, Revised by Dr. Challoner (New

York: C. Wildermann, Co., Inc., Publishers to the Holy See, 1937), p. 621, footnote on Revelation 13:18.

144. *Encyclopedia Britannica* (1967 edition), Volume 22, p. 832, article "V."

145. *World Book Encyclopedia* (1955 edition), Volume 17, p. 8417, article "V."

146. Pope Stephanus V, quoted in George Seldes, compiler, *The Great Quotations* (New York: Lyle Stuart, 1960), p. 661.

147. Pope Gregory VII, *Dictatus Papae* ("Dictates of the Pope," sometimes called the Dictates of Hildebrand), Latin text in Karl Hofmann, *Der "Dictatus Papae" Gregors VII* (Paderborn, Germany: Ferdinand Schoningh, 1933), p. 11. Reproduced in part in *Encyclopedia Britannica* (1967 edition), Volume 17, p. 251, article "Papacy."

148. Pope Boniface VIII, from his Papal Bull *Unam Sanctum,* 1302, in *Translations and Reprints from the Original Sources of European History,* Volume 3 (Philadelphia: University of Pennsylvania Press, 189-), No. 6, p. 23. Also found in Anne Fremantle, editor, *The Papal Encyclicals in Their Historical Context* (New York: Putnam, 1956), p. 74.

149. Paul Hutchinson and Winfred Ernest Garrison, *20 Centuries of Christianity: A Concise History,* 1st edition (New York: Harcourt, Brace and World, © 1959), p. 120.

150. Archbishop Christopher Marcellus, "Oration to the Pope in the Fifth Lateran Council," Session IV (1512), in J. D. Mansi, editor, *Sacrorum Conciliorum Nova et Amplissima Collectio,* Reprint of the 1901 edition, 53 volumes in 59 (Graz, Austria: Akademische Druck- und Verlag- sanstalt, 1960-61), Volume 32, column 761. Latin. Also in Labbe and Cossart's *History of the Councils* (1672), Volume XIV, column 109. Marcellus was a Roman Catholic priest and the archbishop of Corcyra.

151. Cardinal Robert Bellarmine, *On the Authority of Councils* (1619 edition), Volume II, book 2, chapter 17, p. 266.

152. *Catholic Encyclopedia* (New York: Robert Appleton Co., 1909), Volume VI, p. 48, article "Ferraris." This reference shows that Ferraris's statements—astounding as they are—have the official approval and sanction of the Roman Catholic hierarchy!

153. The Lord JESUS is the only One the Bible calls "KING of kings." It never applies that term to any mere man. See Revelation 17:14 & 19:16.

154. Lucius Ferraris, "Papa," article 2 in his *Prompta Bibliotheca* ("Handy Library"), Volume 6 (Venice, Italy: Gaspar Storti, 1772), pp. 26-29. Latin. Reprinted (Rome: Press of the Propaganda, 1899).

155. *Encyclopedia Britannica* (1967 edition), Volume 12, p. 216, article "Infallibility."

156. Pope Leo XIII, Encyclical Letter "On the Chief Duties of Christians as Citizens," dated January 10, 1890, translated in *The Great Encyclical Letters of Pope Leo XIII* (New York: Benziger, 1903), p. 193.

157. Pope Leo XIII, Encyclical Letter "The Reunion of Christendom," dated June 20, 1894, translated in *The Great Encyclical Letters of Pope Leo XIII* (New York: Benziger, 1903), p. 304.

158. Matthew 23:9. Jesus obviously uses the word in its SPIRITUAL sense and is not referring to our physical or biological father.

159. Romans 3:10 & 23.

160. William Shakespeare, *Measure for Measure,* Act II, Scene ii, Lines 117-122.

161. Martin Luther, *Dr. Martin Luthers Sammtliche Schriften,* edited by Johann Georg Walch (St. Louis: Concordia Publishing House, 1881-1910), Volume 6, column 917.

162. John Knox, *The Historie of the Reformatioun of Religioun Within the Realm of Scotland* (Edinburgh: Robert Fleming and Company, 1732), Book 1, p. 77.

163. Adam Clarke, *The Holy Bible, With a Commentary and Critical Notes. The Old Testament* (New York: Lane and Scott, 1850), Volume IV, p. 596.

164. Thomas Cranmer, *The Works of Thomas Cranmer,* 2 Volumes (Cambridge: The University Press, 1844-46), Volume 2, p. 222.

165. Isaiah 14:14 (see verses 12-15).

166. Daniel 7:23 says, "The fourth BEAST shall be the fourth KINGDOM." For example, in Daniel 8:20-21, RAM = MEDO-PERSIA, and GOAT = GREECE.

167. The removal of the three Arian kingdoms is discussed in Clue "C," pages 589-593.

168. *Encyclopedia Britannica* (1967 edition), Volume 13, p. 24, article "John, king of England."

169. William Shakespeare, *King John,* Act III, Scene i, Lines 173-179. Those latter words were no idle threat, for later when the real John took refuge in a monastery he was POISONED by a MONK acting as his protective "taster," who died of poison himself for the sake of destroying the king. See Act V, Scene vi, Lines 23-30.

170. King John of England, "Declaration of Submission," Latin, translated in *Documents of the Christian Church,* Henry Bettenson, editor (New York: Oxford University Press, 1957), pp. 231-232.

171. *Encyclopedia Britannica* (1967 edition), Volume 12, p. 262, article "Innocent III."

172. A later Pope, Innocent IV, who reigned from 1243 to 1254, dared to ask: "Is not the KING OF ENGLAND our vassal, or I should rather say our SLAVE?"—Innocent IV, quoted in Matthew Paris, *English History: From the Year 1235 to 1273,* translated by J. A. Giles (London: Henry G. Bohn, 1852-1854), 3 Volumes. Volume 1, p. 38.

173. *Encyclopedia Britannica* (1967 edition), Volume 10, p. 910, article "Gregory VII."

174. For the royal "we," "us," and "our" read "I," "me," and "my."

175. "Letter of Gregory VII to the German Princes concerning the Penance of Henry IV at Canossa, *circa* January 28, 1077," in *A Source Book for Mediaeval History,* Oliver J. Thatcher and Edgar Holmes McNeal, editors (New York: Charles Scribner's Sons, © 1905 [copyright renewed 1933 by Oliver J. Thatcher]), pp. 158-159.

176. Louis L. Snyder, editor, *Documents of German History* (New Brunswick, N.J.: Rutgers University Press, © 1958), p. 33.

177. [Joseph Turmel], *The Latin Church in the Middle Ages,* by Andre Lagarde [pseudonym] (New York: Scribner, 1915), p. vi.

178. Carl Conrad Eckhardt, *The Papacy and World Affairs* (Chicago: The University of Chicago Press, © 1937), p. 1.

179. Alexander Clarence Flick, *The Rise of the Mediaeval Church* (reprint; New York: Burt Franklin, [1959]), p. 413.

180. John Emerich Edward Dalberg Acton (Lord Acton), in *Historical Essays and Studies,* J. N. Figgis and R. V. Laurence, editors ([facsimile edition, Essay Index Reprint Service] Ayer Co., Publishers, 1907). Letter dated April 5, 1887. *Many cite his oft-quoted closing sentence without knowing it originally referred to the Papacy.*

181. *Encyclopedia Britannica* (1967 edition), Volume 1, p. 112, article "Acton."

182. Johann Josef Ignaz von Döllinger, quoted in *Encyclopedia Britannica* (1967 edition), Volume 7, p. 560, article "Döllinger."

183. Paul Hutchinson and Winfred Ernest Garrison, *20 Centuries of Christianity: A Concise History,* 1st edition (New York: Harcourt, Brace and World, Inc., © 1959), p. 120.

184. The beasts in chapters 13 and 17 of Revelation are essentially the SAME—both having *seven heads* and *ten horns* inscribed with the names of *blasphemy* (Revelation 13:1 and 17:3)—and both depict the Papacy. But how could the BEAST of chapter 17 represent the Papacy if the WOMAN riding it also represents the same? The answer is: *God gave John further details in the later chapter.* As mentioned earlier, chapter 13 makes NO distinction between the RELIGIOUS and POLITICAL aspects of the Papacy. But chapter 17 does make that distinction: the beast symbolizing POLITICAL power and the woman, RELIGIOUS power—just as a beast and a woman represent these two aspects throughout Scripture.

185. Please note carefully that "heresy," defined by the Papal hierarchy, is as follows: "Heresy (from the Greek word *hairesis,* 'choice'): DECIDING FOR ONESELF what one shall believe and practise."—*New Catholic Dictionary* (New York: Universal Knowledge Foundation [a Roman Catholic institution], 1929), p. 440, entry "Heresy."

186. Foxe's famous *Book of Martyrs* offers many stirring examples of such heroes of faith. See John Foxe, *The Acts and Monuments of John Foxe: A New and Complete Edition,* 8 Volumes, edited by the Rev. Stephen Reed Cattley (London: R. B. Seeley and W. Burnside, 1841); also his *Book of Martyrs,* a condensation of *Acts and Monuments.*

187. Execution by BURNING ALIVE. The usual term, *auto da fe,* is defined in *Webster's New World Dictionary,* College Edition (New York: The World Publishing Company, 1964), as "literally, act of the faith; 1. in the Inquisition, the ceremony connected with trying and sentencing a heretic. 2. the execution by the secular power of the sentence thus passed; hence, 3. the public BURNING of a heretic."

188. W. de Gray Birch, "Catalogue of Original MSS. [Manuscripts] of the Inquisition in the Canary Islands" (1903), Volume I, Introduction, p. xx; quoted in G. G. Coulton, *The Death-Penalty for Heresy* (Medieval Studies, No. 18. London: Simpkin, Marshall, Hamilton, Kent, and Co., Ltd., 1924), p. 52.

189. Stone statues, when England was a Catholic country—the Puritan view of Catholic worship.

190. A reference to the BLOOD of the martyrs as "the SEED of the Church," with an allusion to the Parable of the Sower, Matthew 13:3-23.

191. The Pope, alluding to his triple tiara.

192. The Puritans applied to the Roman Catholic Church God's denunciation of Babylon in Revelation 17 and 18. See especially Revelation 18:1-4.

193. Revelation 12:1, 9, 13.

194. Columbus was a deeply religious man who devoutly believed God was leading him. His own diaries establish the fact that he considered himself an instrument in

God's hands, and his convictions regarding exploration were based on Scripture. *Encyclopedia Britannica* says: "It is a fact that Columbus discovered America by PROPHECY rather than by astronomy." (1967 Edition). Volume 6, p. 111, article "Columbus, Christopher."

195. President Ronald Reagan, in an address on November 25, 1982, confessed his conviction that "I have always believed that this anointed land was SET APART in an uncommon way, that a DIVINE PLAN placed this great continent here between the oceans to be found by people from every corner of the Earth who had a special love of faith and freedom." Quoted by Kenneth L. Woodward in "How the Bible Made America," *Newsweek* Magazine (December 27, 1982), p. 44.

196. Karl Benrath, "Inquisition," in *The New Schaff-Herzog Encyclopedia of Religious Knowledge* (New York: Funk & Wagnalls Company, © 1910), Volume 6, p. 1.

197. Elphege Vacandard, *The Inquisition*, translated from the 2nd Edition by Bertrand L. Conway (New York: Longmans, 1908), p. 201.

198. *Encyclopedia Britannica* (1967 edition), Volume 9, p. 1088, article "Galileo Galilei."

199. Paul J. Hauben, editor, *The Spanish Inquisition*, Major Issues in History Series (New York: Wiley, 1969), p. 1.

200. Cecil Roth, *The Spanish Inquisition* (New York: Norton, 1964), Back Cover.

201. Henry Grattan Guinness, *The Approaching End of the Age Viewed in the Light of History, Prophecy, and Science*, 2nd Edition (London: Hodder and Stoughton, 1879), p. 212.

202. John Lothrop Motley, *The Rise of the Dutch Republic* (New York: A. L. Burt, no date), Volume 1, p. 626.

203. *Encyclopedia Britannica* (1967 edition), Volume 19, p. 892, article "Saint Bartholomew's Day, Massacre of."

204. *Ibid.*

205. The Battle of Lepanto had been a recent naval victory over the Turks on October 7, 1571.

206. Italian painter Giorgio Vasari (1511-1574).

207. John Emerich Edward Dalberg, Lord Acton, *The History of Freedom and Other Essays*, Edited with an Introduction by J. N. Figgis and R. V. Laurence (Freeport, N. Y.: Books for Libraries Press, 1967), p. 134-135.

208. Lord Acton, *History of Freedom*, p. 137.

209. That is, he was the chief officer in charge of the terrible tribunal called the Inquisition. *Encyclopedia Britannica* states that Pius V was "a former Inquisitor of GREAT SEVERITY." (1967 edition), Volume 17, p. 261, article "Papacy."

210. Queen Elizabeth I of England—her proposed murder was sanctioned in correspondence from Pope Pius V to King Phillip II of Spain, who later (in 1588) sent the Spanish Armada against Elizabeth in an abortive attempt to extend his realm and make England Catholic.

211. Lord Acton, *History of Freedom*, pp. 138-139.

212. *Ibid.*, pp. 148-149.

213. *The Western Watchman* (St. Louis: Western Watchman Publishing Co. [Roman Catholic]), December 24, 1908.

214. Cardinal Henri Marie Alfred Baudrillart, *The Catholic Church, the Renaissance and Protestantism*, translated by Mrs. Philip Gibbs (London: Kegan Paul, Trench, Trubner & Co., Ltd., 1908), pp. 182-183.

215. Just as the Jews turned Jesus and Paul over to Roman governors—the difference being that the Jews did not control the government of the Roman Empire, whereas the Papacy to a large degree DID control the civil powers, as seen in Clue "Q," pages 639-644, above.

216. Cardinal Robert Bellarmine, *Disputationes de Controversiis Christianae Fidei* ("Disputations Concerning Controversies of the Christian Faith"), Latin (Colonia Agrippina [Cologne]: Hierati Frates, 1628), Volume 1, p. 388.

217. Father James S. O'Leary, *National Catholic Reporter,* March 1, 1985.

218. Charles Henry Hamilton Wright, *Daniel and His Prophecies* (London: Williams and Norgate, 1906), p. 167.

219. Henry Grattan Guinness, *History Unveiling Prophecy* (London and Edinburgh: Fleming H. Revell Company, 1905). The American edition was entitled *Key to the Apocalypse,* pp. 89-90.

220. J. A. Wylie, *The History of Protestantism* (London: Cassell and Company, Limited, 1899), Volume I, p. 16.

221. Pope Innocent III, quoted in George Seldes, compiler, *The Great Quotations* (New York: Lyle Stuart, © 1960), p. 353.

222. *New Catholic Encyclopedia* (New York: McGraw-Hill Book Company, © 1967), Volume 14, p. 208, article "TORTURE."

223. Philip Limborch (1633-1712), *The History of the Inquisition,* originally published in Latin in 1692, translated into English by Samuel Chandler (London, J. Gray, 1731), two Volumes in one.

224. G. G. Coulton, *Inquisition and Liberty* (Boston: Beacon Press, 1959), p. 118.

225. Even the cruel emperors of pagan Rome did not kill as many Christians. One authority, W. H. C. Frend, calculates a maximum of 3500 died under the persecution by Emperor Diocletian and only "hundreds" under that by the Emperor Decius. Since all other persecution was only spotty, local, and occasional during the period under study, he concludes that between Pentecost and the end of persecution under pagan Rome the total number of martyrdoms did not exceed 5000. See W. H. C. Frend, *Martyrdom and Persecution in the Early Church: A Study of a Conflict from the Maccabees to Donatus* (New York: New York University Press, 1967), pp. 308-394.

226. William Edward Hartpole Lecky, *History of the Rise and Influence of the Spirit of Rationalism in Europe* (reprint; New York: Braziller, 1955), Volume 2, p. 46. Dr. Lecky (1838-1903) was an Irish historian and essayist, member of Parliament, member of the British Academy and the French Institute.

227. Llorente was the Catholic priest who served as general secretary of the Spanish Inquisition and wrote its history. His figures show that 31,912 persons perished in the FLAMES, and about TEN TIMES that many were condemned to other severe penances. Don Juan Antonio Llorente, *The History of the Inquisition of Spain* (London: George B. Whittaker, 1827), p. 583.

228. Lecky, *op. cit.,* Volume 2, pp. 40-45.

229. Albert Barnes, *Notes: Critical, Illustrative, and Practical, on the Book of Daniel* (New York: Leavitt and Allen, 1859), p. 328, comment on Daniel 7:25.

230. Daniel 12:1 warns: "At that time . . . there shall be a TIME of TROUBLE, such as never was since there was a nation even to that same time: and at that time Thy people shall be delivered, every one that shall be found written in the book [God's Book of Life—Revelation 20:12 & 15]."

231. See Revelation 13:15-16 and Chapter 20, below, on the Image and the Mark of the Beast.

232. Pope Leo XIII, "The Christian Constitution of States," in *The Great Encyclical Letters of Pope Leo XIII,* third edition (New York: Benziger, 1903), p. 126.

233. Pope Pius IX, "Syllabus of Errors," translated in *Dogmatic Canons and Decrees* (New York: Devin-Adair Company, © 1912), pp. 191, 194, 202. Errors #15, #24, and #55.

234. John Bagnell Bury, *History of the Papacy in the 19th Century,* edited by R. H. Murray (London: Macmillan, 1930), pp. 42-43.

235. Thomas Babington Macaulay, "Sir James Mackintosh," in his *Critical and Historical Essays* (London: Longmans, 1865), Volume 1, pp. 333-334.

236. Luke 5:20-21, NKJV. See also Matthew 9:2-3 and Mark 2:5-7.

237. John 10:30-31.

238. John 10:33, NKJV. Compare Matthew 26:63-66 and Mark 14:61-64.

239. See Isaiah 7:14 and Matthew 1:23.

240. Michael Muller, *The Catholic Priest* (Baltimore: Kreuzer Bros., 1876), pp. 78-79.

241. 1 Timothy 2:5.

242. Don A. Schanche, *Times* Staff Writer, "No Forgiveness 'Directly From God,' Pope Says," Los Angeles *Times,* Wednesday, December 12, 1984, Part I, p. 11.

243. Nehemiah 9:17.

244. Psalm 25:11 & 18.

245. Isaiah 55:7.

246. Daniel 9:18-23.

247. Matthew 6:12.

248. See Walter Martin, *The Kingdom of the Cults,* Revised Edition (Minneapolis: Bethany Fellowship, Inc., 1977), Chapter 8, "The Reign of Father Divine," pp. 213-221.

249. William Doyle, S. J., *Shall I Be a Priest?* 16th edition (Dublin, Ireland: Office of the *Irish Messenger,* 1936), p. 8.

250. *Encyclopedia Britannica* (1967 edition), Volume 14, p. 23, article "Liguori, Saint Alfonso Maria de."

251. Alphonsus de Liguori, *Dignity and Duties of the Priest* (Brooklyn, N.Y.: Redemptorist Fathers, 1927), pp. 26-36.

252. *Catechism of the Council of Trent for Parish Priests,* translated by John A. McHugh and Charles J. Callan (New York: Joseph F. Wagner, Inc., 1958), p. 318.

253. Roman Catholic priest David S. Phelan, *The Western Watchman* (St. Louis: Western Watchman Publishing Company), June 10, 1915.

254. Matthew 23:9.

255. Jeremiah 3:19, NKJV.

256. Lucius Ferraris, "Papa," article 2 in his *Prompta Bibliotheca* ("Handy Library"), Volume 6 (Venice, Italy: Gaspar Storti, 1772), pp. 26-29. Latin. Reprinted (Rome: Press of the Propaganda, 1899).

257. Cardinal Robert Bellarmine, *On the Authority of Councils* (1619 edition), Volume II, book 2, chapter 17, p. 266.

258. Archbishop Christopher Marcellus, "Oration to the Pope in the Fifth Lateran Council," Session IV (1512), in J. D. Mansi, editor, *Sacrorum Conciliorum Nova et Amplissa Collectio*, Reprint of the 1901 edition, 53 volumes, in 59 (Graz, Austria: Akademische Druck- und Verlag- sanstalt,1960-61), Volume 32, column 761. Latin. Also in Labbe and Cossart's *History of the Councils* (1672), Volume XIV, column 109. Marcellus was a Roman Catholic priest and the archbishop of Corcyra.

259. Pope Leo XIII, Encyclical Letter "On the Chief Duties of Christians as Citizens," dated January 10, 1890, translated in *The Great Encyclical Letters of Pope Leo XIII* (New York: Benziger, 1903), p. 193.

260. Pope Leo XIII, in an encyclical letter dated June 20, 1894, translated in *The Great Encyclical Letters of Pope Leo XIII* (New York: Benziger, 1903), p. 304.

261. Isaiah 14:12-14—SIX personal pronouns express Lucifer's self-centered pride!

262. Adam Clarke, *Commentary on the Bible,* Abridged by Ralph Earle, (Grand Rapids, Mich.: Baker Book House, 1967), One-volume Edition, p. 699, note on Daniel 7:25. Clarke's *Commentary* has long been considered among the most perceptive ever published. The book jacket remarks that "Adam Clarke's monumental commentary on the Bible has been a standard reference work for over a century and . . . has won for the author the accolade, 'Prince of Commentators.'"

263. "The Law is HOLY, and the commandment holy, and just, and good." Romans 7:12.

264. Lucius Ferraris, "Papa," article 2 in his *Prompta Bibliotheca* ("Handy Library") (Venice, Italy: Gaspar Storti, 1772), Volume 6, p. 29. Latin. Reprinted (Rome: Press of the Propaganda, 1899).

265. See pages 670-671 for a helpful comparison of God's Ten Commandments as recorded in Exodus 20:3-17 and as CHANGED and recorded in Father Peter Geiermann, C.S.S.R., *The Convert's Catechism of Catholic Doctrine,* 1957 edition (St. Louis: B. Herder Book Co., © 1930), pp. 37-38.

266. Daniel, Chapter 3, records the thrilling account of how these three heroic children of God refused to bow down to "the golden image" set up by Babylon's King Nebuchadnezzar—and how God honored their faithfulness! Let it inspire you as you read it.

267. The margin or footnote says: *"statue or pillar."*

268. See Romans 7:7-13.

269. See Exodus 20:8-11 and Genesis 2:1-3.

270. Father Stephen Keenan, *A Doctrinal Catechism*, 3rd American edition, revised, (New York: P. J. Kenedy, 1876), p. 174.

271. Daniel Ferris, *Manual of Christian Doctrine: or, Catholic Belief and Practice* (Dublin: M. H. Gill & Son, Ltd., 1916), pp. 67-68. This work is an updated version of Henry

Tu(r)berville's *An Abridgment of the Christian Doctrine* (known also as the Douay Catechism) of 1649.

272. *The Christian Sabbath* (Baltimore: The Catholic Mirror, 1893), pp. 29-31. This pamphlet is mostly a reprint of four editorials in *The Catholic Mirror* (Baltimore), September 2, 9, 16, and 23, 1893.

273. Louis Gaston de Segur, *Plain Talk About the Protestantism of To-day* (Boston: Patrick Donahoe, 1899), p. 225. Segur (1820-1881) was a French Catholic prelate and official at Rome.

274. Father Peter Geiermann, C.S.S.R., *The Convert's Catechism of Catholic Doctrine*, 1957 edition (St. Louis: B. Herder Book Co., © 1930), p. 50. This work received the "apostolic blessing" of Pope Pius X on January 25, 1910.

275. "Balder was the god of the SUN . . . in Norse mythology." *World Book Encyclopedia* (1955 edition), Volume 2, p. 610, article "Balder."

276. Father William L. Gildea, *Catholic World* (New York), March 1894, p. 809.

277. John A. O'Brien, Ph. D., LL. D., *The Faith of Millions: The Credentials of the Catholic Religion*, Ninth Edition, Revised and Enlarged (Huntington, Indiana: Our Sunday Visitor, © 1938), p. 473.

278. *The Augsburg Confession* (1530), part 2, article 7, "Of Ecclesiastical Power," translated in Philip Schaff, *The Creeds of Christendom* (New York: Harper, 1919), Volume 3, p. 64.

279. Alexander Campbell, "Address to the Readers of *The Christian Baptist*, No. III," *The Christian Baptist* (February 2, 1824), p. 1 (in reprint of 1848, 7 volumes in one, p. 44). Campbell (1788-1866) was the founder of the Disciples of Christ Church and founder and president of Bethany College.

280. Augustus Neander, *The History of the Christian Religion and Church*, translated by Henry John Rose (Philadelphia: James M. Campbell & Co., 1843), p. 186. Neander (1789-1850) was professor of church history in Berlin from 1813.

281. *Encyclopedia Britannica* (1967 edition), Volume 10, p. 442, article, "Gladstone, William Ewart."

282. William Ewart Gladstone, *Later Gleanings* (Salem, N.Y.: Ayer Company Publishers, Essay Index Reprint Service [reprint of 1897 edition], 1972), p. 342.

283. Numbers 23:20.

284. Etymologically, the basic meaning of the word *worship* IS *worthship* or *worthyness*.

285. Arthur E. R. Boak, *A History of Rome to 565 A.D.*, 4th edition, (New York: The Macmillan Company, © 1955), pp. 432-433. For many years Dr. Boak was professor of ancient history at the University of Michigan.

286. *Encyclopedia Britannica* (1967 Edition), Vol. 6, pp. 385-386, article "Constantine."

287. Constantine, *Codex Justinianus*, lib. 3, tit. 12, 3: translated in Philip Schaff, *History of the Christian Church*, 5th edition. (New York: Scribner, 1902), Volume 3, p. 380, note 1.

288. Walter Woodburn Hyde, *Paganism to Christianity in the Roman Empire* (Philadelphia: University of Pennsylvania Press, © 1946), p. 261.

289. Hutton Webster, *Rest Days* (New York: The Macmillan Company, © 1916), pp.

122-123, 270. Dr. Webster was an American historian, professor of social anthropology at the University of Nebraska, and professor emeritus of sociology at Stamford University.

290. Council of Laodicea, canon 29, translated in Charles Joseph Hefele, *A History of the Christian Councils*, translated and edited by H. N. Oxenham (Edinburgh: T. and T. Clark, 1896), Volume 2, p. 316. PLEASE NOTE that though the Church here tries to stigmatize the Sabbath with Jewish overtones by using the word "Judaizing," this law in itself provides GOOD EVIDENCE that Christians were still faithfully observing God's true Sabbath centuries after the Crucifixion and Resurrection!

291. See Chapters 10 & 11, above, on "Solving the Mystery of Death."

292. 1 Timothy 2:5.

293. See Chapters 13 & 14, above, on the Sabbath and Sunday.

294. Jude 3.

295. Edward Gibbon, *The History of the Decline and Fall of the Roman Empire*, edited by J. B. Bury, 2nd edition (London: Methuen & Co., 1901), chapter 28, Volume 3, p. 214, and chapter 50, Volume 5, p. 394.

296. Jesus called Satan "the prince of this world" repeatedly, in John 12:31, 14:30, and 16:11.

297. In Daniel 4:16, 23, 25, 32 we read of "seven TIMES" referring to the seven YEARS when King Nebuchadnezzar was driven out to dwell with beasts of the field. The King James Version says "times," but modern translations like Today's English Version, New International Version, The Living Bible, and the New American Standard Bible all say "years" either in a footnote or in the text itself. A "time" was an ancient way of expressing a year.

298. The word translated "times" is *not* an ordinary *plural* (which could mean several) but a *dual.* Both Hebrew and Aramaic, the languages used by Daniel, had ordinary PLURALS, but they also had a special grammatical form for DUALS, used only for TWO—no more, no less, such as two eyes, two ears, two children, or in this case two years, just as we in English speak of "a pair (of gloves)" or "a couple."

299. *Encyclopedia Britannica* (1967 Edition) Volume 4, pp. 620, 621, and 623 for Egyptian, Hindu, and Assyrian, respectively, article "Calendar."

300. We know the Bible reckoned a month as thirty days from the following details concerning the Flood of Noah's day: "In the SECOND month, the *seventeenth day* of the month . . . the windows of heaven were opened. . . . And the waters prevailed upon the earth *an hundred and fifty days.* . . . And after the end of the hundred and fifty days the waters were abated. And the ark rested in the SEVENTH month, on the *seventeenth day* of the month, upon the mountains of Ararat." Genesis 7:11 & 24, 8:3-4. Thus *a five-month period stretched 150 days,* showing thirty days to a month.

301. As we learned in Clue "C," pages 589-593, above. See Daniel 7:8, 20, 24.

302. Revelation 13:10.

303. E. G. White, *The Desire of Ages* (Boise, Idaho: Pacific Press Publishing Association, © 1940), p. 32.

304. Said patriot George Mason in his Virginia Bill of Rights, "Freedom of the press is

one of the great bulwarks of liberty, and can never be restrained but by DESPOTIC governments." Though Mason never held high office, "few men did more to determine the original shape of American political institutions."—*Encyclopedia Britannica* (1967 edition), Volume 14, p. 1014, article "Mason, George." Censorship, being undemocratic and un-American, was found in places like Communist Russia, a CLOSED society that waged war against IDEAS. Ironically, Communists called their leading newspaper *Pravda,* meaning "Truth," yet they censored all media and jammed the radio broadcasts beamed to their people by the Free World. They erected "DO NOT ENTER" signs against ideas at their borders. The Roman Catholic Church has often resorted to the same tyranny, denying the FREEDOM to READ "forbidden" books and silencing dissidents—even by execution. Still today, when we should be able to ventilate a subject in the free air of open discussion, some people would suppress any ideas with which they disagree. Like the Berlin Wall of the past, their attitude makes us wonder what they're afraid of, for *Truth loses nothing by investigation.* A totalitarian state or military dictatorship suppresses ideas, but Christ told us to "Prove all things" (1 Thessalonians 5:21), and His church should be devoted to the search for Truth wherever it's found.

305. Most Preterists teach that Antichrist was a dim figure from the past named Antiochus IV, commonly known as Antiochus Epiphanes (pronounced "an TEE uh kuss uh PIFF uh nees"), a minor Roman ruler who governed the area later known as Syria from 175 to 164 B.C. Preterist interpretation applies the prophecies of the Little Horn power to Antiochus Epiphanes and makes him "the abomination of desolation" prophesied in Daniel 9:24-27 because he desecrated the Jewish Temple in 168 B.C. If space permitted, MANY facts could be brought forth to refute the Preterist interpretation, but just one statement from the lips of Christ may suffice to prove that Antiochus DOES NOT FIT the prophetic chronology. In Matthew 24:15-16 Jesus warned His disciples: "When ye therefore see the abomination of desolation, spoken of by Daniel the prophet . . . FLEE into the mountains." If the Master used the FUTURE tense to warn His followers of a FUTURE danger (the destruction of the Temple and Jerusalem by the Romans), then Preterist interpreters are wrong to apply those Scriptures to Antiochus or anyone else far in the PAST.

306. Joseph Tanner, *Daniel and the Revelation* (London: Hodder and Stoughton, 1898), p. 17.

307. See also *Appendix C: "The Seventy Weeks of Daniel 9,"* at the back of this book.

308. John Calvin, *Institutes of the Christian Religion,* 7th American edition revised (Philadelphia: Presbyterian Board of Christian Education, 1936), Volume 2, p. 411.

309. John Knox, *The Historie of the Reformatioun of Religioun Within the Realm of Scotland* (Edinburgh: Robert Fleming and Company, 1732), Book 1, p. 76. Spelling in the quoted words has been modernized.

310. Catholics, for when Mede wrote, no Protestant accepted Futurism.

311. Joseph Mede, *The Apostasy of the Latter Times* (London: Samuel Man, 1644), pp. 72-73.

312. The SEVEN REFERENCES to the 1260 Days:

Apparently because of its vital importance, the 1260-day period is mentioned SEVEN times in Daniel and Revelation—twice by Daniel and five times by John. The period is expressed in different but equivalent ways: three times as 3 & 1/2 TIMES, twice as 42 MONTHS, and twice as 1260 DAYS. With beautiful harmony, these texts describe a single period differently but always with the same duration! Note the following table:

1. Daniel 7:25 .... 3 & 1/2 times
2. Daniel 12:7 .... 3 & 1/2 times
3. Revelation 11:2 .... 42 months
4. Revelation 11:3 .... 1260 days
5. Revelation 12:6 .... 1260 days
6. Revelation 12:14 .... 3 & 1/2 times
7. Revelation 13:5 .... 42 months

313. Edward Elton Young Hales, *The Catholic Church in the Modern World* (Garden City, N. Y.: Hanover House, 1958), pp. 25-26. Hales is an English Catholic who won honors in history at Oxford and was awarded a Carnegie Fellowship in the U.S.

314. John Emerich Edward Dalberg, Lord Acton, *Lord Acton on the States of the Church* (reprint; Portsmouth, R.I.: F. E. Lally, 1940), p. 26. Like Hales in the preceding footnote, Lord Acton was an English Catholic and a very distinguished historian.

315. Hales, *The Catholic Church in the Modern World*, pp. 37-38, 52.

316. *Encyclopedia Britannica* (1967 edition), Volume 5, p. 952, article "Clovis."

317. Revelation 13:3.

318. Revelation 13:10.

319. *Encyclopedia Britannica* (1967 edition), Volume 3, p. 534, article "Berthier, Louis Alexandre."

320. Napoleon Bonaparte, quoted in *Encyclopedia Britannica* (1967 edition), Volume 3, p. 535, article "Berthier, Louis Alexandre."

321. Joseph Rickaby, S. J., "The Modern Papacy," in *Lectures on the History of Religions* (London: Catholic Truth Society, 1910; St. Louis: B. Herder, 1911), Volume 3, lecture 24, p. 1.

322. Leopold von Ranke, *The History of the Popes* (London: Henry G. Bohn, 1853), Volume 2, p. 459. Of this illustrious scholar, *Encyclopedia Britannica* says his peers considered him "almost the COLUMBUS of modern history." (1967 edition), Volume 18, p. 1163, article "Ranke, Leopold von."

323. George Trevor, *Rome: From the Fall of the Western Empire* (London: The Religious Tract Society, 1868), pp. 439-440.

324. John Adolphus, *The History of France from 1790-1802* (London: George Kearsley, 1803), Volume 2, pp. 364-369.

325. *Ibid.*, Volume 2, p. 379.

326. David Simpson, *A Plea for Religion and the Sacred Writings* (London: Printed for J. Mawman, 1802), p. 166.

327. Please see the whole context surrounding footnote 206 on page 650, above.

328. Edward B. Elliott, *Horae Apocalypticae* (London: Seeley, Burnside, and Seeley, 1862), Volume 3, p. 401.

329. Arthur Robert Pennington, *Epochs of the Papacy* (London: George Bell and Sons, 1881), pp. 449-450. The closing words quoted from Pennington allude to Revelation 6:9-10, where John writes of "them that were SLAIN for the Word of God, and for the testimony which they held. And they cried with a loud voice, saying, How long, O Lord, holy and true, dost Thou not judge and AVENGE OUR BLOOD on them that dwell on the earth?"

330. 2 Peter 1:19, NIV.

331. Daniel 7:21-22, 26. Revelation 19:7-20 agrees that the Beast CONTINUES till the time of the Second Advent.

332. Christian Gottlob Thube, *Anleitung zum richtigen Verstande der Offenbarung Johannis* (Guidance to the Right Understanding of the Revelation of John), (Schwerin und Wismar, Germany: Bodmer, 1799), pp. 123-124.

333. An allusion to John Dryden's poem "The Hind and the Panther," an allegorical beast-fable in which the poet uses a white female deer or hind as a symbol of the Roman Church.

334. Thomas Babington Macaulay, "Ranke's History of the Popes" (first published 1840), in his *Critical and Historical Essays* (London: Longmans, 1865), Volume 2, pp. 147-148.

335. Arthur Robert Pennington, *Epochs of the Papacy* (London: George Bell and Sons, 1881), pp. 450 and 452.

336. Edward Elton Young Hales, *The Catholic Church in the Modern World* (Garden City, N.Y.: Hanover House, 1958), p. 60.

337. *Ibid.*, pp. 60-61.

338. *Encyclopedia Britannica* (1967 edition), Volume 9, p. 734, article "France."

339. *Encyclopedia Britannica* (1967 edition), Volume 17, p. 266, article "Papacy."

340. In 1870 the Papacy received another set-back when the nation of Italy was united under GARIBALDI'S revolution. At that time, the Roman Catholic Church was stripped of even her lands, leaving the Pope a virtual prisoner in the Vatican. This Concordat of 1929 restored a part of those lands.

341. *San Francisco Chronicle* (Tuesday, February 12, 1929), Part I, pp. 1 and 2. The lengthy news report was carried over the wires of the Associated Press to every major news outlet.

342. *Encyclopedia Britannica* (1967 edition), Volume 12, p. 781, article "Italy." This sum was equivalent to many, many millions of dollars and was especially valuable when the Depression arrived soon thereafter and money became extremely scarce. Obviously, this settlement went far toward healing the wound financially.

343. Editorial by Michael Novak (visiting professor at the University of Notre Dame) "Pope Will Lead Way Into 21st Century" *Los Angeles Times* (September 8, 1987) Part II, p. 5.

344. 2 Thessalonians 2:3-4.

345. Revelation 18:2 & 4.

◆   ◆   ◆

"He causeth ALL, both
small and great,
rich and poor,
free and bond,
to receive a MARK
in their right hand,
or in their foreheads."

—REVELATION 13:16

CHAPTER TWENTY

❧

THE MARK
OF THE BEAST

O**UR PRECEDING CHAPTER** de-mystifies the puzzle of the Beast's identity. The prophecies of God and the history of man unite in testifying against the Papacy as the Antichrist. After examining clue after clue in the Bible, we're forced to say: "Guilty on all counts." The evidence requires us to identify the Beast as the Papacy.

Now that we know who the Beast is, we need to learn what his Mark is. In order to understand what the Bible teaches about the Mark of the Beast, however, we must first understand two other closely related elements:

(1) The IMAGE of the BEAST—the political agent
that implements the Mark
(2) The SEAL of GOD—the Christian counterpart
of the Mark of the Beast.

Let's consider each of these in turn.

PART I. — THE MYSTERIOUS **IMAGE** OF THE BEAST

To warn us further of the danger to come, God gave John a vision involving the "image of the Beast" which the aged apostle recorded for us in Revelation 13:11-17. After discussing at some length the Antichrist Beast, John says he saw "ANOTHER beast," a second symbolic creature, who made "an image" of the first Beast and then made the whole world "worship the first Beast" already identified as the Antichrist. As we examine this vital passage, let's clearly establish two facts:

(1) the IDENTITY of this second beast power, and
(2) the MEANING of the expression, "to make an IMAGE of the Beast."

THE UNITED STATES IN PROPHECY!

Prepare for a surprise as we identify the second beast John saw in vision. You'll discover that it's none other than the United States of America. While you may be shocked to see our beloved country brought into the terrible context of this chapter, you shouldn't be surprised to find such an important world power as the United States mentioned in God's Word.

Why? Ask yourself, Is it reasonable that the Bible would remain silent about the most powerful nation this world has ever seen? Down through history, God's Word speaks of the Egyptians, Assyrians, Babylonians, the Medes and Persians, the Greek Empire of Alexander the Great, the Roman Empire and its subsequent break-up into the nations of modern Europe. Every kingdom, nation, and world power that has touched God's people has been prophetically foretold in its pages.

Is it reasonable, then, to suppose that the richest, most influential world power of the 20th century would be excluded from Scripture? No, it would be strange if God, seeing the end from the beginning, failed to give a place in prophecy to the nation He used not only as the greatest haven of refuge for the oppressed, but also as the foremost nation in the world for spreading the gospel!

Let's examine the evidence from the Bible and history. In Revelation 13:11 John tells us: "I beheld ANOTHER beast coming up out of the earth. . . ." As we study the clues given in this prophecy, we'll discover that the United States—and the United States alone—fits every detail, as the following facts prove:

CLUE #1:
IT IS DEPICTED AS A POLITICAL POWER

The term "beast" is the Bible symbol of a kingdom or nation. Daniel 7:23 equates "beast" with "kingdom." The Living Bible renders *kingdom* in that verse as a "world power." Therefore, the second "beast" John sees in Revelation 13 can refer only to a political government or nation, and thus can fittingly describe the United States.

CLUE #2:

IT AROSE IN THE RIGHT PLACE

It arose "out of the EARTH," that is, in an UNpopulated area of the world. We know this because Revelation 17:15 explains that "WATERS" as a Bible symbol "are *peoples,* and *multitudes,* and *nations,* and *tongues.*"

Thus when John says in Revelation 13:1, "I stood upon the sand of the sea, and saw a beast [the Antichrist Beast] rise up out of the SEA," we understand that this first beast arose out of a POPULATED area, from among the organized nations of the world. And of course the Antichrist did arise from Rome itself.

But John sees this second beast of Revelation 13, depicting the United States of America, arising "out of the EARTH," not the sea. The Amplified Bible makes it plain by saying, "I saw another beast rising up out of the LAND [itself]." Absence of water denotes scarcity of people. So it could not arise among the crowded nationalities of the Old World—in the great sea of humanity, that turbulent sea of "peoples, and multitudes, and nations, and tongues." And quite fittingly, the United States did arise out of new, previously UNOCCUPIED territory.

The wilderness of this vast American continent—unpopulated but for a few scattered Indian tribes—marvelously fits the Bible description of unpopulated, "dry" ground and fulfills this prophecy in a remarkable way. This great continent, kept hidden by God in a small world, became the cradle for our new-born nation.

Clue "U" in our preceding chapter established the dates 538 to 1798 for beginning and ending the 1260-year period of Papal supremacy. During this period God's true church, symbolized by a "woman," was persecuted and "fled into the wilderness . . . a thousand two hundred and threescore days [years]."[1] But toward the end of this time, Revelation 12:16 says, "the earth HELPED the woman, and the earth opened her mouth, and swallowed up the flood" of pilgrims who fled to the New World to escape the peril and persecution of Papal-dominated Europe. The flame of freedom burned brightly in their souls! This land of liberty became a haven of refuge, a sanctuary for saints oppressed for their faith, and they recognized it as such.[2]

Truly—and providentially—"the earth HELPED the woman." How remarkable is fulfilled prophecy!

✦ ✦ ✦

CLUE #3:
IT AROSE AT THE RIGHT TIME

God gives enough facts to place the prophecy in its proper TIME FRAME. Reading Revelation 13:10-11, we see that this second beast was arising or "coming up" around the time that the Beast (the Papacy) was led "into captivity," having received its deadly wound.

When was this? Well, we know that the Pope died in exile after being taken "into captivity" by Napoleon's general in 1798. As we scan the horizon of history we discover only ONE world power "coming up" in 1798—the United States of America.

The American colonies began their struggle for independence in 1775. In 1776, they declared themselves a free and independent nation. In 1777, delegates from the thirteen original States adopted the Articles of Confederation. In 1783, the Revolutionary War closed in a peace treaty with Great Britain. In 1787, the Constitution was framed; and in March of 1789, it was ratified and went into effect. George Washington served as our first President until 1797. Thus we come to the pivotal year 1798, when this nation is introduced in prophecy—"coming up" at the RIGHT TIME!

Also, the government symbolized by this second beast is introduced in the early part of its career, that is, while still a youthful power. John says, "I beheld another beast coming up out of the earth; and he had two horns like a lamb." Why doesn't John simply say, "He had two horns"? Why does he add "like a *lamb*"? Obviously, he wants to emphasize not only this second beast's innocent and harmless character but also its youthful nature. For a lamb's horns are horns that have barely begun to grow.

Not only the lamblike horns but the phrase "coming up" must signify that this political power was newly organized and just then ARISING. With our gaze still fixed on the year 1798, we again ask: What notable power was at that time coming into prominence, but still in its youth? There's only one answer: the new nation of the United States!

In 1754 John Wesley, founder of the Methodist Church, said of this prophetic beast: "He has not yet come, though he cannot be far off. For he is to appear at the end of the forty-two months of the first beast [which ended in 1798]." [3] In looking for a nation to arise in a very short time, Wesley was correct.

CLUE #4:
IT IS A DEMOCRACY

The perceptive student of Scripture will note that the Antichrist Beast in Revelation 13:1 had ten horns with "TEN CROWNS." Those multiple crowns represent "the crowned heads of Europe" (England, France, Germany, Italy, Portugal, Spain, *etc.*). By way of strong contrast, the second beast had NO crowns on his lamblike horns. Since a crown is the fitting symbol of a monarchy, the notable absence of crowns in this case clearly indicates a democratic government vesting its power in the hands of the PEOPLE—not in any ruling king.

Revelation reveals the form of government the United States has always had, and this constitutes another strong link in the chain of evidence that this prophecy denotes our own country of the United States of America. Had the second beast in John's vision been depicted wearing a crown, no one could maintain that the prophecy represented the U.S.A., for we've never had a king. In fact, early American patriots, applauding our "experiment in democracy," were proud to point out that on this side of the Atlantic we have "a Church without a Pope, a State without a King!"

But this is not the most conclusive proof that the new nation symbolized here is DEMOCRATIC in government. A democracy, by definition, is "government of the people, by the people, for the people." Revelation 13:14 makes plain that this power says to the PEOPLE "that THEY should make an image to the Beast, which had the wound by the sword, and did live." Thus it has a democratic form of government rather than an absolute monarchy or dictatorship. A dictator or powerful king can say "Off with his head!" or pass laws without asking anyone's permission. But the President of the United States cannot act unilaterally and autocratically. He must ask the PEOPLE in CONGRESS to make and pass a law.

So when the prophet depicts the second beast as "saying to THEM that dwell on the earth, that THEY should make an image to the Beast," God clearly foretells a form of government in which the legislative power rests with the PEOPLE.

CLUE #5:
IT IS A **POWER** OF **WORLDWIDE** INFLUENCE

When Revelation 13:12 states that this power "causeth the EARTH and them which dwell therein to worship the first Beast, whose deadly wound was healed," we begin to understand the vast leadership role played by this prophetic power. A century ago scoffers could well doubt how the United States could possibly be said to wield such influence. However, America has become more than a mere footnote in history. In recent decades, especially since World War II, the United States has enjoyed prestige and power on a worldwide scale, both economically and politically. Despite our detractors, despite momentary fluctuations in our fortunes, the United States is unquestionably in a position of great international influence and leadership.

And the Revelator tells us that this influential world power—the United States—shall take the lead in worshipping the Beast and that the whole world will follow that lead. Scripture says the Mark of the Beast will finally become so widespread as to be universal—a GLOBAL spiritual tyranny.

Perhaps moves toward regimented religion will be made in a time of trouble. Multitudes are easily led in times of economic emergency or military crisis. When panic sets in, principles are easily lost or compromised. We needn't doubt that what the Bible says will happen—will happen.

The point to remember here is that the second beast of Revelation 13 must be capable of exerting worldwide influence, and the United States today is—by any standard—a leader among nations, a superpower.

CLUE #6:
IT IS A POWER THAT WORKS WONDERS

We live in an age of wonders, though we often take that fact for granted. The list of *American* inventors who have contributed to these modern miracles is impressive, so let me name just a few. In the field of transportation, Robert Fulton, the Wright Brothers, and Henry Ford were Americans who gave us the steamboat, the airplane, and the mass-produced automobile. Thomas Edison invented the phonograph and the electric light, while Charles Goodyear learned how to vulcanize rubber; Samuel F. B. Morse invented the telegraph, Alexander Graham Bell invented the telephone, and they were all Americans. American doctor Jonas Salk conquered polio with his vaccine. Americans were also the first to develop television, transistors, and the Xerox machine— as well as to fly solo across the Atlantic and to land men on the moon.

Talk about doing wonders! That's exactly what Revelation 13:13 does— speaking of this same power, the two-horned beast—it says: "And he doeth great WONDERS, so that he maketh FIRE come down from heaven on the earth in the sight of men." Could this refer to the gigantic mushroom cloud and ball of fire rising up to heaven from the atomic bomb developed by the United States? Of course it could. Can we conceive of a more awesome wonder—or ask John's words of 2000 years ago to describe more vividly an atomic blast?

As John gazed down the corridor of Time with the prophetic eye of Inspiration and saw the atomic fireball, he tried his best to express in human language what he "beheld." Imagine God revealing the future many centuries ago not to John but to *you* or *me:* Could we describe a nuclear explosion any better, especially with the handicap of the non-scientific vocabulary of that day?

In the providence of God, the United States was the nation that unlocked the secrets of the atom and performed this "great wonder," ushering in the Atomic Age. That fact no one can argue. The additional fact that today the United States remains a major nuclear power gives our country, from a military standpoint, great respect and influence. Unfortunately, that same fact may help explain John's prediction that our once lamblike nation will some day speak "as a DRAGON." [4]

NOTE TO THE READER: Let me say that the four paragraphs above give a plausible interpretation of Revelation 13:13 about *signs* or *wonders* and *fire coming down from heaven*. This interpretation seems to me both reasonable and credible, since it's supported by history. But since I'm not a prophet, I have no quarrel with those who advance some other explanation. One alternative view [5] is that *fire coming down from heaven* as a *sign* and *wonder* could be a repetition of the Mt. Carmel test—from 1 Kings 18:16-40—to prove WHO is GOD. But this time it's a misleading sign manifested NOT by the true God but by Satan's power, since it's brought about on behalf of the two-horned beast, the United States.

I must say that this alternative view has much to recommend it. First, consider that Satan, as a supernatural being, can work miracles: God's Word speaks of "the working of Satan, with all power, SIGNS, and lying WONDERS, and with all unrighteous deception among those who perish, because they did not receive the love of the truth, that they might be saved." [6] Second, consider that the Devil would be well pleased to exercise his demonic power on behalf of the two-horned beast—the United States—when the task is to persuade people to accept the Mark of the Beast. For these reasons, I certainly do accept this interpretation along with the first one stated above. They are dual fulfillments—one past, one yet future—of this point in the prophecy.

Now let's sum up what we've learned. So far, we've established that the second beast John saw is identified by not just one or two clues but by SIX very specific points:

> ✓ It must be a **nation**
> ✓ that arose in territory **sparsely populated**
> ✓ around the year **1798**. Furthermore,
> ✓ this nation must be a **democracy**
> ✓ that exercises **worldwide influence**
> ✓ and works **great wonders**.

These half-dozen points unmistakably identify the second beast as the UNITED STATES—no one could reasonably apply ALL these prophetic clues to any other nation.

How I wish we could stop right here in our study, for so far the prophecy paints a positive picture of our great country, a picture of which all patriotic Americans can be proud. But sad to say, the picture will change, as we shall now see.

Revelation 13:14-15 speaks about this second beast—the United States—making "an image to the Beast" or "image of the Beast." So let's turn to the task of understanding the Bible phrase, "to make an IMAGE of the Beast."

WHAT IS MEANT BY "AN IMAGE"?

An IMAGE of anything is something that looks like or resembles it. If a little boy looks just like his dad, we say, "He's the spittin' image of his father." The Revelator tells us that this Image would be just like the Papal power—that is, it would be just like "the first Beast, whose deadly wound was healed . . . the Beast, which had the wound by the sword, and did live." [7]

The Image of the Beast won't be a literal image like a statue or idol. Instead, it will be a reverberating echo of the first Beast. It will be almost an exact replica—a REPEAT PERFORMANCE of what the world suffered centuries ago during the Dark Ages. To learn what the "image" will be like, we must first recall what the Papal Beast was like, especially during the heyday of its power.

The Papacy was a CHURCH clothed with CIVIL power—an ecclesiastical body having absolute authority to threaten and punish all dissenters with confiscation of goods, imprisonment, torture, and death. It was a UNION of Church and State. So what would be an "image" of the Papacy? It will be another ecclesiastical establishment clothed with civil power—in other words, a MODERN-DAY union of Church and State.

How could such an image be formed in the United States? Consider this: God warns that just before Christ returns, "There shall be a time of TROUBLE, such as never was." [8] We all know that the "Christian lobby" in Washington has already grown strong. Let a crisis come—"a time of trouble" like worldwide economic depression or nuclear war—and hear the voices cry: "This is a judgment from God because we've wandered so far from His ways! We've GOT to get back to God! Let's make this a CHRISTIAN nation. This is our last chance!"

✦ ✦ ✦

"There Oughtta Be a LAW!"

And well-meaning Americans—whether laymen, ministers, or legislators—will seek a POLITICAL solution to a SPIRITUAL problem. They will compromise the Bill of Rights under the guise of preserving public morality. They will band together to pass LAWS forcing people to do by civil power what the church has FAILED to do by persuasive preaching and teaching—to change men's hearts under the influence of God's Holy Spirit.

Those who believe "The end justifies the means" will see no problem in this, for Christianizing our nation and improving society's moral and spiritual health is the same goal God's church has always had. The tragedy is, our nation—"the cradle of Liberty"—will "speak like a dragon" and adopt tactics of force and coercion used by the Antichrist, tactics resurrected from the Dark Ages and condemned by the God who never uses force.

When the early church became corrupted by adopting pagan rites and customs, she lost the Spirit and power of God. Then in order to control people's consciences, she sought the support of civil power. The result was the Papacy, a church that controlled the power of the state and employed it to further her own ends, especially to punish "heresy." In order for the United States to form an "image" of the Beast, the religious power must once again so control the civil government that the strong arm of the STATE will be employed by the CHURCH to accomplish her own ends.

History shows that whenever the church obtains civil power, she employs it to punish dissent from her doctrines and restrict liberty of conscience. A sample of Papal philosophy is seen in this quotation on "Human Liberty" from Pope Leo XIII: "It is quite UNLAWFUL to demand, to defend, or to grant unconditional FREEDOM of THOUGHT, of speech, of writing, or of WORSHIP, as if these were so many rights given by nature to man." [9]

Revelation 13:12 declares that the United States will exercise the same power as the Papacy: "He exerciseth all the power of the first Beast before him." The first Beast was Papal Rome, and during the centuries of its supremacy, the Papacy was dictatorial and very intolerant—especially in matters of religion. It persecuted any and all who disagreed with its dogmatic teachings, and used the civil arm—the POLICE power of the State—to carry out its commands and enforce its edicts.

We've just read that the two-horned beast (the United States) will do the same thing, exercising the same power as the first Beast. Historians know that persecution—the use of deadly force—is as American as the Salem witch trials, Indian massacres, and John Wilkes Booth. Those understandably reluctant to accept this fact, who say, "It CAN'T happen here!" need to remember Thomas Jefferson's wisely prophetic words: "The spirit of the times may alter, WILL alter. Our rulers will become corrupt, our people careless. A single zealot may commence persecution, and better men be his victims." [10]

"And Justice for ALL"?

True, our country's strong federal Constitution expressly guarantees freedom of religion. But those who put blind trust in the Constitution or any other man-made laws will be surprised how quickly things can change in an hour of crisis. It wouldn't take corrupt leaders who bend the law to their own ends, as in the Watergate affair. It wouldn't take some dictator posing as a super-hero, as in Hitler's Germany. All it would take is PEOPLE willing to enforce religion by civil power. And already we see people seeking to legislate morality.

Recent decades have seen many examples of Jefferson's "single zealot." There was Jerry Falwell leading his "Moral Majority" to influence voters, tipping the balance in elections. There's Pat Robertson and the Christian Coalition, doing the same thing. Organized religion's lobbying power can exert tremendous pressure on legislators dealing with touchy issues. Chuck Colson, who survived a prison term for Watergate offenses to become a powerful voice for the Christian Right, warns about *power,* warns about *mixing* politics and religion in his book *Kingdoms in Conflict.* About those who'd use political power to play God, Colson says: "Not since the Crusades have religious passions and prejudices posed such a threat" [11] to shake our world and shape our future.

In no way do I wish to reflect upon the character of those endeavoring to legislate morality. They're good men of high moral standing, sincerely concerned with this nation's welfare and honestly trying to remove evils they see rampant in society.

But they're good men misled into doing things against which God utters a solemn warning. We regret to see Protestant America actively fulfilling this prophetic picture. For even well-meaning men may be wrong—remember that Paul vigorously persecuted the early church thinking he was right.

Let him who doubts the possibility of Church-State union reflect a moment on our government's growing tendency to ENTANGLE itself in religious issues. On the one hand, Pat Robertson, Jerry Falwell, and other RELIGIOUS leaders are talking more and more about POLITICS, seeking government control of abortion and other moral issues. On the other hand, Ronald Reagan was just one of several POLITICAL leaders talking more and more about RELIGION, calling for state-prescribed prayer in public schools and sending an ambassador to the Vatican. And all this is happening in America today!

THE BATTERED WALL OF SEPARATION

Thomas Jefferson—one of the Founding Fathers of our new nation, who served as the writer of the immortal, magnificent words of the Declaration of Independence, as our Minister to France, as George Washington's Secretary of State, as John Adams' Vice President, and as our country's third President—stated that our Constitution built a "WALL of SEPARATION between church and state." [12]

Jefferson's church-state separation is not understood or appreciated by everyone today—but it was by the LORD JESUS, who enunciated that principle Himself. Christ obviously agreed with Jefferson on the vital need for separation when He urged upon us this clear distinction:

"Render to CAESAR the things that are Caesar's,
and to GOD the things that are God's." [13]

This means, of course, that each of these two realms has its own province, and we shouldn't have to answer to "Caesar"—the government—for spiritual things, which exclusively "are God's."

Jefferson also made such statements as these:

- "We hold these truths to be self-evident—that all men . . . are endowed by their Creator with certain unalienable rights; that among these are life, LIBERTY [which must include RELIGIOUS liberty], and the pursuit of happiness." [14]

- "The God who gave us life, gave us LIBERTY at the same time." [15]

- "Error of opinion may be tolerated where reason is LEFT FREE to combat it." [16]

- In a letter to Rabbi Mordecai M. Noah, this same great American deplored the religious persecution against Jews, writing: "Your sect by its sufferings has furnished a remarkable PROOF of the universal spirit of religious intolerance. . . . Our laws have applied the only antidote to the vice. . . . But more remains to be done; for although we are free by the law, we are not so in practice; public opinion erects itself into an Inquisition, and exercises its office with as much fanaticism as fans the flames of an *auto da fe*." [17]

Jefferson's home state was Virginia, and though he improved its LEGAL system and system of public EDUCATION, his most outstanding contribution was the STATUTE OF RELIGIOUS FREEDOM. Of it we read:

"Even more important [than legal and educational reforms] were bills designed to secure religious toleration, disestablish the Anglican Church, and forever SEPARATE church and state in Virginia. Here Jefferson met hostility not only from Anglican interests, but also from other denominations which feared that a separation of church and state would lead to a loosening of all religious ties. But in 1779 the Anglican Church was disestablished. In 1786, after a struggle which Jefferson described as 'the severest contest in which I have ever been engaged,' the assembly passed the famous STATUTE OF RELIGIOUS LIBERTY. This triumph Jefferson counted so important that he directed it to be commemorated on his tombstone—along with the Declaration of Independence and the founding of the University of Virginia." [18]

As we quote just one part of his Statute, judge for yourself how well Jefferson understood human nature and how his thoughts blend both common sense and uncommon wisdom. It says we are:

"Well aware that the impious presumption of legislators and rulers, civil as well as ecclesiastical, who, being themselves but FALLIBLE and UNINSPIRED men, have assumed dominion over the FAITH of others, setting up their OWN opinions and modes of thinking as the ONLY true and infallible, and as such endeavoring to IMPOSE them on others, hath established and maintained false religions over the greatest part of the world and through all time." [19]

Encyclopedia Britannica adds this:

"Although Americans had largely abandoned the gross forms of persecution common a few generations earlier, the toleration they practiced was limited and erratic. In some states, as in Virginia, a single church was established; others restricted public office to Protestants; some required belief in specific doctrines. . . . The Virginia Statute constituted a complete break with the traditional relationship between church and state. It prohibited support of any religion by public taxation and forbade all civil disabilities imposed on citizens because of religious belief or the lack of it. Jefferson regarded the statute as partial fulfillment of his celebrated vow:

'I have sworn upon the altar of God
eternal hostility against every form of TYRANNY
over the MIND of man.'" [20]

Half a century ago, Supreme Court Justice Hugo Black reminded us that "In the words of Jefferson, the [Constitution's] clause against establishment [of religion] was intended to erect a 'WALL of SEPARATION' between church and state"—adding strongly that this wall "must be kept HIGH and IMPREGNABLE." [21]

But today, incredibly enough, leaders of the Religious Right want to tear down the time-honored "wall of separation between church and state" erected by our Founding Fathers. Even more menacing is the stance taken in recent decades by members of the UNITED STATES SUPREME COURT—the very ones who should PROTECT us from religious persecution! Read just a few shocking statements:

- Chief Justice Warren Burger said that "the line of separation, far from being a 'wall,' is a blurred, indistinct and variable barrier." [22]

- Justice Antonin Scalia called religious liberty a "LUXURY" we can no longer afford. [23]

- Chief Justice William Rehnquist declared: "The 'wall of separation between church and state' is a metaphor based on bad history, a metaphor which has proved useless as a guide in judging. It should be frankly and explicitly ABANDONED." [24]

This trend in judicial thinking is frightening when we realize, as some-one has said, that "The Constitution IS what the Supreme Court SAYS it is." For the Supreme Court is the final arbiter of our precious Bill of Rights, painstakingly hammered out and ratified over 200 years ago. Those rights are at the mercy of whatever a 5-4 majority happens to think at any given moment!

And not just judges and right-wing legislators, but many MINISTERS are all too willing to have church observances enforced by civil authority. For instance, in the May 7, 1976, issue of *Christianity Today,* editor Harold Lindsell entitled an article, "The Lord's Day and Natural Resources." He proposed, for the sake of conserving energy, that "ALL businesses, including gasoline stations and restaurants, should CLOSE every Sunday."

Lindsell expressed his conviction that such a move would accord both with the natural laws that govern man's well-being and with the "will of God for all men." Sensing that people are "highly unlikely" to observe Sunday as a rest day through VOLUNTARY action alone, he further suggested that the only way to accomplish the dual objectives of Sunday observance and energy conservation would be "by force of legislative fiat [an arbitrary order or decree] through the duly elected officials of the people."

So it seems that certain clergy, having failed themselves to instill religion in society, now want POLICE to do it. They want their religion made the state religion. Yet as British writer Oscar Wilde observed, "You can't make people good by Act of Parliament." [25] It's not that easy! Even almighty God, in His infinite wisdom, does not use force.

Ours Is a Land of Religious PLURALISM

The United States is called "a melting pot" because of the diversity of peoples who have crowded our shores. But Americans are a mixture not only of different *cultures* and *nationalities,* a blend not just of different *races* and *ethnic* backgrounds; it's a mixture also of many different *faiths* and *religions.* America is "ONE nation, indivisible," but it's a nation widely diversified and pluralistic. Those who wish to squeeze everyone into one mold, who wish to impose their brand of Christianity on all, would do well to remember that—like it or not—Americans come in many religious varieties: We have Jews & Gentiles, Christians & Muslims, Catholics & Protestants, believers & atheists. Even among Protestant Christian believers, not all interpret the Bible the same way.

That's fine in a land of liberty where there's freedom for each to worship God according to the dictates of his own conscience—or not to worship at all, if that's his choice. In the realm of religion, God alone is the Judge, not the civil magistrate in the courthouse or the preacher in the pulpit. But this would change overnight if we surrender to those who demand conformity to religious dogma enforced by man-made laws. Those people—the Religious Right and others—dream of making our country a Christian nation, but they want to do it by force of law. When their plan is put into action, their DREAM will become our NIGHTMARE!

Popular Christian writer C. S. Lewis wisely said: "Of all tyrannies, a tyranny sincerely exercised for the GOOD of its victims may be the most oppressive. . . . Those who torment us for our own good will torment us without end, for they do so with the approval of their own conscience." [26] That's why Christ warns us that: "A time is coming when anyone who KILLS you will think he is offering a service to God." [27]

If we examine Christ's words, we see He's telling us that PERSECUTION will arise NOT from atheistic pagans but from well-meaning "religious" people who want to serve God! Such people, with the best of intentions, will promote the metamorphosis of the "lamb" into the "dragon." Perhaps that's why Edward Albee, three-time Pulitzer Prize-winning playwright, calls them "the *religious right,* an organization that is neither religious nor right."

Therefore, their plan to implement the Mark of the Beast, like the Road to Hell, "is paved with good intentions." But we can't legislate salvation, for FORCE is foreign to real religion, which is "an affair of the heart." Compulsion is as far removed from worship as RAPE is from LOVE. The church, as the "bride" of Christ, goes to Him willingly. Coercion injected into a relationship—whether by the rape of a girl or the shotgun wedding of a young man—makes a most unhappy union! But the Image of the Beast wants us to have "government *of* the church-state, *by* the church-state, *for* the church-state" in a return to SPIRITUAL TYRANNY.

As Harvard philosopher George Santayana said, "Those who cannot remember the past are condemned to repeat it." [28] Are we doomed to lose our freedom because of a poor memory? Unfortunately, history WILL repeat itself in an agonizing ECHO of the cruel Dark Ages, and we'll see again the adulterous connection between Church and State! When Church and State combine to force you and me to worship according to *their* dictates, they form an unholy alliance and become "partners in crime"—a crime against humanity.

Freedom CAN Be Forfeited

As the farmer said, "We never miss the water till the well runs dry." And we who take our freedom for granted won't miss religious liberty until we LOSE it! The average American places a childlike trust in our democratic institutions and the men who run them. But those who are experienced in administrative affairs don't retain such illusions. Thomas Jefferson warned: "Eternal vigilance is the price of liberty." And a recent Past President of the United Nations General Assembly voiced this opinion: "If fools and folly rule the world, the end of man in our time may come as a rude shock, but it will no longer come as a complete surprise." [29]

Freedom is FRAGILE! It fractures easily in times of crisis. Who knows what extremes we'd be driven to in an emergency? (Ask the Japanese-American CITIZENS rounded up during World War II and placed in our version of concentration camps. Ask them how much their "Constitutional rights" were respected.) Tragedy triggers a willingness in man to justify drastic actions he'd not normally take. George Orwell outlined coercive measures taken by the State in his fictional novel *1984,* but the acts threatening individual freedom and religious liberty predicted in the Bible won't be fiction. This isn't science fiction or a fairy tale we're discussing—it's the Biblical blueprint of the future!

The Christian exiles who fled to America sought refuge from both royal oppression and priestly intolerance. America did not disappoint them. Its two lamblike horns represent the twin principles of CIVIL and RELIGIOUS liberty, a *separation* of church and state, a *division* of governmental and ecclesiastical power. It's painful to contemplate our nation, devoted to such noble principles of freedom, descending to the role of persecutor. But we must be guided by the inspired outline prophecy so plainly gives us, and that outline—in Revelation 13:11—says the beast with lamblike horns "spoke like a DRAGON."

A nation or a nation's government "speaks" through its LAWS—the only OFFICIAL "speaking" of a nation is the action of its legislative and judicial authorities. Since the United States is unquestionably the nation denoted by the symbol that will speak "like a dragon," it follows that it will enact oppressive LAWS against religious freedom to become a persecuting power.

A Russian diplomat in England sarcastically asked a defector from Communist Russia, "What's the matter—don't you love your country?" Fearlessly, the refugee defector answered, "Yes, I DO love my country—very much. It's the GOVERNMENT I hate." God says a time will come, even in our beloved country, when the government will intolerantly speak "as a dragon." [30]

This is still a free country, but it won't be when these prophecies on the Image and Mark of the Beast are fulfilled, involving coercion, force, economic boycott, even a death decree! It will be a new edition of the Spanish Inquisition—an American edition at first, but it quickly will spread WORLD-WIDE.

Next, let's focus on . . .

THE SEAL OF GOD

VERSUS

THE MARK OF THE BEAST

History's awful final chapter remains to be written, but God's remarkable Book of Revelation portrays much of what we can expect in the climax of the ages. Though it sounds like something out of *Star Wars,* it's still terribly true that from the dawn of this world's history, the entire Universe has been involved in a GREAT CONTROVERSY—a COSMIC CONFLICT between the forces of Good and Evil. Revelation 12:7 tells us: "There was WAR in HEAVEN"!

Without dwelling on details, let me point out the dichotomy that exists between the two opposing sides in this controversy.

ON THE ONE SIDE:	ON THE OTHER:
Christ	Satan
Good	Evil
Angels	Demons
Truth	Error
Divine Creation	Atheistic Evolution
Loyal Obedience	Disobedient Rebellion
The Seal of God	The Mark of the Beast
The Saved	The Lost

Just as the great controversy has two sides and only two, so in the last days there'll be just two classes of people on this planet. We all face one choice with only two options: To follow God or the Devil—and GOD'S SEAL or the BEAST'S MARK is the SIGN of loyalty to one or the other.

So it's imperative that we know without a doubt what the Seal of God and the Mark of the Beast are. The Seal of God is the complementary counterpart of the Mark of the Beast. Like two sides of the same coin, they're similar but opposed to each other. "Heads" and "tails" superficially seem much alike, but really they're exclusive opposites. Everyone living in the last days will receive either one OR the other—everyone will have either GOD'S SEAL or the BEAST'S MARK. God warns that only those sealed by his Spirit will be saved and rewarded with eternal life, while those with the Mark of the Beast will not only suffer terribly from the Seven Last Plagues but will be ultimately destroyed.

Let's begin by examining the Seal of God before identifying the Mark of the Beast because we'll understand the latter much better if we first understand the former.

PART II. — THE SEAL OF GOD

In Bible days a SEAL was a device having a raised design (like a signet ring) that could be stamped on clay or wax and leave an impression in order to SIGN legal documents, thereby authenticating royal commands and validating laws, as an official signature does today. Several texts illustrate this:

1. 1 Kings 21:8 – Queen Jezebel "wrote letters in [King] Ahab's name, and SEALED them with his SEAL." An official order in the king's name must be duly "signed, sealed, and delivered."

2. Esther 3:10-12, NKJV – "The king took his signet ring from his hand and . . . in the name of king Ahasuerus it was written, and SEALED with the king's SIGNET RING." In ancient times, kings who couldn't write even their own names employed learned men called "scribes" as secretaries and signified their royal approval by sealing documents with their signet rings.

3. Esther 8:8, NKJV – "Write a decree . . . in the king's name, and SEAL it with the king's signet ring; for whatever is written in the king's name and SEALED with the king's signet ring *no one can revoke*."

4. Daniel 6:8 – "Now, O king, establish the decree, and SIGN the writing, that *it may not be changed. . . .*"

Please note: A comparison of those last two texts shows that the Bible uses SIGN and SEAL as synonymous terms. Kings in ancient times would SEAL their documents with a signet ring, just as we SIGN ours today with a signature.

Revelation 7:1-3 says: "And after these things I saw four angels standing on the four corners of the earth, holding the four winds of the earth, that the wind should not blow on the earth, nor on the sea, nor on any tree. And I saw another angel ascending from the east having the SEAL of the living God: and he cried with a loud voice to the four angels, to whom it was given to hurt the earth and the sea, saying, Hurt not the earth, neither the sea, nor the trees, till we have SEALED the servants of our God in their foreheads."

Thus the Bible makes plain that God does have a "SEAL." But what IS "the seal of the living God," and where do we find it? Well, the idea of LAW is inseparable from a seal, as the four examples above show. When a law was passed, the king would seal the legal document with his signet ring to make it official. And the following texts show that God will SEAL His divine LAW in the minds of His disciples:

1. Isaiah 8:16 – God says, "SEAL the LAW among My disciples."

2. Hebrews 8:10 & 10:16 – In both verses, God says: "I will put My LAWS . . . in their MINDS."

3. Revelation 7:3 – Angels hold the winds of strife "till we [angels] have SEALED the servants of our God in their FOREHEADS."

This sealing work is accomplished not only by angels but by God's Holy Spirit, and it involves our obeying God's statutes or laws.

1. Ephesians 4:30 – "Grieve not the Holy Spirit of God, whereby ye are SEALED unto the day of redemption."

2. Acts 5:32, NKJV – ". . . the Holy Spirit, whom God has given to them that OBEY Him."

3. Ezekiel 36:26-27 – "And I will put My Spirit within you, and cause you to WALK in My STATUTES."

Therefore, we know that God has a seal having to do with His law, which His angels and Holy Spirit want to place in our minds or foreheads. But let's get more specific: Remember that an official seal or authoritative signature always contains THREE ELEMENTS:

A. The NAME of the law-giver.
B. His OFFICE or TITLE—his right to rule.
C. The TERRITORY which he rules—his jurisdictional area.

For example:

Person's Name	George Washington
Official Title	President
Area of Jurisdiction	United States

or

Person's Name	Winston Churchill
Official Title	Prime Minister
Area of Jurisdiction	United Kingdom

Keeping in mind these three elements of an official seal, we see that *God's seal or signature is found in His Law, specifically in the Fourth Commandment.* For as we read that Commandment in Exodus 20:8-11, we find it contains all of the three following elements:

A. The NAME of the Law-Giver:

Exodus 20:11 identifies the Law-giver as "The LORD."
And texts like . . .
    Isaiah 42:8—"I am the LORD: that is My name"
    Jeremiah 16:21—"My name is The LORD"
    Exodus 15:3 & Amos 5:8—"The LORD is His name"
clearly show that Jehovah's NAME is "the LORD."

B. His TITLE:

God's unique title is "CREATOR" or "MAKER," for Exodus 20:11 majestically declares: "The Lord MADE . . ."!

C. The TERRITORY over which He rules:

Exodus 20:11 says that the Lord's area of jurisdiction embraces "HEAVEN and EARTH."

NOTE: Just as the seals of earthly rulers are found in connection with their laws, so we find the Seal of the living God in His Law of Ten Commandments. The Lord—writing with His own finger—formally SIGNED and SEALED His divine Law!

THE SABBATH IS GOD'S SEAL

The Seal and signature of God is found in the heart of His Law—in the Fourth Commandment. Only the Sabbath command, of all the Ten, contains both the NAME and the TITLE of the Law-Giver. It uniquely identifies Him as CREATOR of heaven and earth, authenticating His claim to obedience and worship above all other gods.

Aside from the Sabbath command, nothing in the Decalogue shows by whose authority the Law was given. The last five Commandments don't contain God's name at all. The first three and the Fifth contain the words "God" and "Lord," but we cannot tell from those words WHO is meant, for there are many deities to which such names are applied. As the apostle says, there are "gods many and lords many." [31]

A pagan worshipper of stone images could say, "The IDOL before which I kneel is my god, and these commands are *his* precepts." A heathen worshipper of the heavenly bodies could say, "The dazzling SUN is my god, and I worship him according to this law which *he* gave." A miserly atheist who worships money could happily obey, saying, "I'm happy to have no other god before my six-figure BANK ACCOUNT!" Without the Seal of God's Fourth Commandment, no one could tell which deity is meant or who gave the Law.

But the Sabbath command identifies God as CREATOR, and it is this great fact which constitutes God's power and authority. "For all the gods of the nations are idols: but the Lord MADE the heavens." [32] The Lord, the only true God, is our rightful Ruler because He is our Creator, and His Seal means this law cannot be applied to FALSE "gods that have NOT made the heavens and the earth." [33] Abraham Lincoln and John F. Kennedy had authority not because of their *personal* names but because they held the OFFICE and TITLE of President. God has the right to expect obedience from all His creatures because He is the CREATOR of all—that's His divine office and title. God's Seal and signature in the Sabbath command make it the one Commandment that tells us who it is that claims obedience from all men everywhere, the *one* Commandment that tells us WHY *we should obey the other nine.*

In fact, God repeatedly and explicitly tells us that His "SIGN" or Seal IS the Sabbath:

1. First of all, God says observing His Sabbath is the SIGN we recognize Him as our CREATOR. Exodus 31:16-17 says: "The Sabbath . . . is a SIGN . . . for ever: for in six days the Lord MADE heaven and earth, and on the seventh day He rested." [34]

2. Secondly, God says keeping His Sabbath is the SIGN we accept Him as our SANCTIFIER. Exodus 31:13 says: "Verily My Sabbaths ye shall KEEP: for it is a SIGN between Me and you throughout your generations; that ye may know that I am the Lord that doth SANCTIFY you."

3. God says in Ezekiel 20:12—"Moreover also I gave them My Sabbaths, to be a SIGN between Me and them, that they might know that I am the Lord that SANCTIFY them."

4. Again, in Ezekiel 20:20 God urges: "Hallow My Sabbaths; and they shall be a SIGN between Me and you, that ye may know that I am the LORD your GOD."

All this is even more significant when we realize that the words "sign" and "seal" are synonymous in the Bible. For instance, Romans 4:11 states that Abraham "received the SIGN of circumcision, a SEAL of the righteousness of the faith which he had. . . ."

Thus the seventh-day Sabbath of the Fourth Commandment, the SEAL of God's Law, is plainly declared His "SIGN"—in fact, a double sign of Christ as both Creator and Sanctifier. Those sanctified by the "new covenant" relationship of having God's Law written in their hearts and minds [35] acknowledge His authority by obeying ALL of the Ten Commandments, including the seventh-day Sabbath. All the other Commandments may be observed ethically even by those opposed to organized religion. But for those willing to submit to God's Lordship, the Sabbath becomes the outward sign of an inward character—a sign of sanctification honoring our Creator.

Now that we have some understanding of the *Image of the Beast* and the *Seal of God,* we can proceed to the crucial question: What is the *Mark of the Beast?*

PART III. — THE MARK OF THE BEAST

We've learned that the *second* beast John saw, the two-horned beast representing America, will lead the world in worshipping Antichrist, "the *first* Beast, whose deadly wound was healed." [36] But the United States will do more than that. Paradoxically, *Protestant* America will promote and enforce the MARK of the *Papal* Beast! Of the two-horned beast that follows in Rome's footsteps by forming a UNION of Church & State, John says: "He causeth ALL, both small and great, rich and poor, free and bond, to receive a mark in their right hand, or in their foreheads." [37]

Most people, at some time or other, have heard about the Mark of the Beast and wonder exactly what it will be. Perhaps you've heard stories— stories about a gigantic super-computer in Belgium called "the Beast." Or about the number 666 being invisibly "tattooed" by a laser on our hands or foreheads. Or about a miniaturized computer chip being implanted under the skin of our hands or foreheads.

But all those speculations get us nowhere. Those imaginings all focus NOT on the Mark itself but on possible ways in which it may be IMPLEMENTED, which is quite irrelevant. If you're condemned to be executed by a firing squad at dawn, it doesn't help much to speculate whether .30 caliber or .45 caliber bullets will be used. Such thinking is majoring in minors.

It may well be that computerized lists WILL be used by authorities who impose and enforce the Mark of the Beast. But who cares about that? What we want to know and must understand is exactly WHAT the Mark IS so we can avoid it!

PENALTIES Are SEVERE

Human nature being what it is, almost every person has a price. Almost every person will violate his conscience if pushed beyond a certain point: to avoid embarrassment or scandal; to gain power, prestige, or money; or to preserve health, wealth, or life. Most people, though they're unaware of it, act from the security-at-any-cost philosophy. As long as they don't have to violate any principle to live a prosperous, happy life they might think themselves good moral people or even Christians. But when the chips are down, many people's principles evaporate like drops of water on a hot tin roof. Judas sold Jesus for thirty pieces of silver, Esau sold his birthright for a bowl of lentils, and David sold his integrity for a beautiful woman.

The two-horned beast KNOWS this, so severe penalties are threatened against all who refuse that Mark of the Beast. John predicts an ECONOMIC BOYCOTT: "that no man might BUY or SELL, save he that had the Mark. . . ." [38] Imagine what this would mean: A businessman would be forced out of business, thus losing his livelihood. A mother couldn't buy milk for her baby or food for herself. Stringent measures like these seem strong enough to force all into line.

But John goes even further and predicts the DEATH DECREE: "as many as would not worship the image of the Beast should be KILLED." [39] Evidently the authorities mean business and consider any violation of their edict a very serious offense.

We know that the "image" of the beast will be a "carbon copy" of the Antichrist's Church/State union that supported church doctrine by force of LAW. What we need to know is, Which dogma or doctrine will that be? What will be the Mark of the Beast?

Prepare for another shock, for you'll discover that when the Mark of the Beast is finally given, it will be the PAPAL SUNDAY! Many reasons for this conclusion may be given, but consider the Mark of the Beast in the light of the following facts:

✦ ✦ ✦

FACT #1:
THE MARK MUST BE A RELIGIOUS DOGMA

The warnings against the Mark of the Beast are given by God Himself, the center and focus of everything *religious*. They are recorded in the Bible, a *religious* Book. The Beast, whose Mark it is, is "worshipped" [40] as a *religious* power. Since the whole context is religious, we can safely conclude that the Mark itself will be some kind of RELIGIOUS dogma.

Further, it will be a religious dogma enforced by law. The church will seek the strong arm of the state to enforce her edicts, bringing about a union of civil and religious power. The MARK of the Beast will be implemented and enforced by the IMAGE of the Beast.

It will be a CIVIL law, but it will be specifically one that coerces the CONSCIENCE—a direct descendant of the oppressive church-state union that drove pilgrims to our shores seeking RELIGIOUS freedom.

FACT #2:
THE MARK MUST CONFLICT WITH GOD'S LAW

The Apostle Paul reveals one of Antichrist's main characteristics to be a LAWLESS attitude, emphatically describing him as:

2 THESSALONIANS 2:3 & 7-9 [41]

"the man of LAWLESSNESS"
"the mystery of LAWLESSNESS"
"the LAWLESS one (the Antichrist)"
"the LAWLESS one, the Antichrist"

Thus Paul's inspired pen makes clear that the Beast's main thrust is one of lawlessness—an attack on the Lawgiver through His Law.

Now note carefully that the doctrine chosen as the Mark of the Beast must be one that CONFLICTS with the Law of God. For the apostle Paul describes the Beast power, in the person of the Pope, as "that man of sin . . . who . . . EXALTETH himself ABOVE all that is called God, or that is worshipped." [42]

Ponder, for a moment, the question HOW he can exalt himself ABOVE God. He might institute any number of ceremonies or wield any degree of power—but as long as people observed GOD'S requirements over his, he would NOT be above God. Or he might even enact a law and teach people they were under AS GREAT an obligation to HIS law as to GOD'S Law—but then he'd make himself only EQUAL with God.

No, he must do more than this! He must make a law which CONFLICTS with God's Law. Then, by demanding obedience to his own law in preference to God's, he attempts to exalt himself ABOVE God. If he can cause people to adopt his change in God's Law in place of the original enactment, then he, the law changer, exalts himself ABOVE God, the Law Maker.

When this is done, what do we have? We have two laws demanding obedience—one, the divine Law God originally enacted to embody His will, the other, a REVISED EDITION of that Law, emanating from the Antichrist and expressing his will. *The Mark of the Beast will be the civil enforcement of a law which breaks God's Law.*

It's extremely pertinent that GOD PREDICTED an attempted change of His Law. As we learned earlier, Daniel states that the Beast power would "think to change the TIMES and the LAW." [43] At least three points should be noted about this verse:

1. First, this text must refer to DIVINE law, not human, for human laws are routinely changed every day, so a change in human law would not be a subject for prophecy.

2. Second, the expression "THINK to change" denotes only an attempted change in the Law God wrote in stone with His own finger, for no mere man could really change God's Law. But the Antichrist power deliberately *intended* to change it and *attempted* to change it.

3. Third, the word "TIMES" calls our attention specifically to the Fourth Commandment, since the Sabbath command is the only one of the Ten that deals with any element of TIME.

Daniel's prophecy does NOT say the Papal Beast would SET ASIDE God's Law and give one entirely different. He was only to attempt a CHANGE, so that the Law coming from God and the law coming from the Papacy are alike, except for the change the Papacy has made. The two laws have much in common, but please note that *none* of the precepts they have *in common* can distinguish a person as one who honors or worships either power in preference to the other. Thus if God's Law says, "Thou shalt not kill," and the law given by the Papacy says the same, no one can tell whether a person obeying *that* precept intends to obey God rather than the Pope or the Pope rather than God. BUT when a precept that's been CHANGED is the issue— such as Sabbath *versus* Sunday—then obeying one or the other clearly distinguishes the two classes of worshippers. Obedience to one or the other distinguishes those who acknowledge the supremacy of the papal authority from those who acknowledge the authority of God.

Remember that "Babylon," another name for the Papal Beast, is a false RELIGIOUS system opposed to God and His truth. The closing scenes of earth's history will involve conflict—but NOT a conflict between RELIGION and IRRELIGION, between those who are *religious* and those who are *not*. It will be instead a conflict between **TRUE** religion and **FALSE** religion—between the false Babylon, which God says "is fallen, is fallen," [44] and the true saints who "KEEP the Commandments of God, and the faith of Jesus." [45]

FACT #3:
THE MARK IS A COUNTERFEIT SABBATH

The Mark of the Beast is the spiritual counterpart of the Seal of God. Since God's Seal is His memorial of Creation, the seventh-day Sabbath, it follows that the Mark of the Beast is *another day of worship* opposed to the Sabbath. It will be SIMILAR but DIFFERENT.

God's Seal, the Sabbath, is like the Beast's Mark in that both are placed in the FOREHEADS [46] of those who receive them. This is significant, for psychologists who've succeeded in "mapping" the human brain tell us that different areas of the brain are associated with different functions (like vision, motor activity, coordination, *etc.*), but the FRONTAL lobe of the cerebrum—the "forehead"—is the place where the important functions of volition, will, and judgment are located. Thus the forehead signifies the mind's power to CHOOSE: We must make a decision in this matter. Some choose the Mark of the Beast because they sincerely but mistakenly BELIEVE Sunday to be the true Sabbath despite what the Bible teaches. They receive the Mark "in their FOREHEADS" because they really BELIEVE it in their MINDS.

Another class receives it "in their right hand," not because they care anything about Sunday or any other religious observance, for they are not religious people. But they're willing to go along with the crowd, willing to conform and obey the edict for the sake of convenience—not conviction. The HAND symbolizes *passive acceptance* of the enforced mark, which they complacently comply with simply for self preservation. They receive the Beast's "credit card" or "ration coupons" in their HANDS so they can "buy or sell" and not be killed by the Image of the Beast, or civil power.

Thus the Mark of the Beast may be received either in the forehead or in the hand. The Seal of God, however, is received ONLY in the forehead, NOT in the hand, because it must be intelligently and consciously chosen by an act of the will. All who receive the Seal of God BELIEVE in it. The God who gives the Seal knows our thoughts and motives and knows we obey out of love and loyalty to Him.

As we've already learned, God's protecting Seal is called a "sign." It's also called a "mark" in Ezekiel chapter 9, which tells of "six men . . . and every man [had] a slaughter weapon in his hand: and one man among them was clothed with linen, with a writer's inkhorn by his side." [47] To the heavenly being clothed with linen, who had the writer's inkhorn, God said, "Go through the midst of the city, through the midst of Jerusalem, and set a MARK upon the FOREHEADS of the men who sigh and that cry for all the abominations that be done in the midst thereof. And to the others He said . . . Go ye after him through the city, and smite: let not your eye spare, neither have ye pity: Slay utterly old and young, both maids, and little children, and women: but come not near any man upon whom is the MARK." [48]

Ezekiel's vision closely parallels those given John in Revelation. What John calls a "SEAL," [49] Ezekiel calls a "MARK." But note their similarities, for in BOTH cases the emblem is placed:

- By ANGELS
- In the FOREHEAD
- Of those LOYAL to God
- And SAVES them from destruction.

There's no indication that either the "seal" or "mark" is visible to human eyes: It seems to be seen only by God and His angels. But please note that the Bible uses all three words—"SEAL" and "SIGN" and "MARK"—interchangeably and synonymously. God has a mark that angels place on His faithful people, and the Beast has a mark he places on those in rebellion against heaven.

Here's an intriguing question: In Ezekiel's vision, what prompted God's wrath so that He would "slay" any who did not have His mark or seal? The prophet's preceding chapter answers that question, when he tells of being shown in vision "the GREAT abominations" the people committed. Then God showed him progressively "greater . . . GREATER . . . **GREATER** abominations than these." [50]

What abominations would God consider "greater"? Ezekiel tells us. He was shown "men, with their BACKS toward the Temple of the Lord, and their FACES toward the east; and they worshipped the SUN toward the east"! [51]

When the destruction described in Ezekiel chapter 9 follows, we see just how *abominable* sun worship is in the eyes of God. [52] Ancient people commonly worshipped the sun as their SUPREME deity, for it gave them LIGHT, and WARMTH, and FOOD by making their crops grow. But Paul says they "changed the truth of God into a lie, and worshipped and served the creature [53] more than the Creator." [54] Still today, misguided men have "changed the truth of God into a lie," and many have been led to worship on Sunday instead of on the day honoring our Creator, God's holy Sabbath.

Although both the Seal of God and the Mark of the Beast may be referred to as a "mark," the resemblance ends there. For one is a COUNTERFEIT of the other. The Roman Catholic Church, as a system of religion, offers many counterfeits. For example:

Instead of Bible baptism—*immersion* of *adult believers*—
    it offers SPRINKLING of *infants*.
Instead of the Bible concept of death as an unconscious sleep,[55]
    it teaches the so-called "IMMORTAL soul."
Instead of the authority of the Word of God, the Bible,
    it reveres the TRADITION of "church fathers."
Instead of Christ's once-and-for-all Sacrifice, [56]
    it REPEATEDLY performs "the *sacrifice* of the Mass."
Instead of God's holy Tithe to support the gospel, [57]
    it resorts to taxes, indulgences, and bingo games.
Instead of God's immutable, eternal Law,
    it claims to have CHANGED the Ten Commandments.[58]
Instead of God's seventh-day Sabbath,
    it teaches SUNDAY sacredness.[59]

The problem with a counterfeit is that it looks like the real thing. We wouldn't worry about phony $20 bills if they didn't look genuine—if they were printed in purple ink, for instance. A counterfeit is dangerous only when it looks so real that it FOOLS people. And Sunday seems almost like the real Sabbath of the Bible—it's the very next day to the seventh, so it can't be much closer in that respect. Satan's counterfeits so closely resemble the genuine that they deceive those willing to be deceived.

But don't let the counterfeit fool you. Keeping the genuine, seventh-day Sabbath is a SIGN . . .

- that you worship the TRUE God, the Creator. [60]
- that you recognize God's AUTHORITY in your life
    and willingly obey HIS authority, not man's. [61]
- that you're being SANCTIFIED by the Holy Spirit.[62]
- that you're living under the NEW COVENANT. [63]
- that you've found freedom from the power of SIN.[64]
- that you have a LOVE relationship with JESUS,
    the Lord who *made* you,

> who *spoke* the Law from Sinai and
> who *died* in your place
> to pay the *penalty* of that broken Law! [65]

But the Mark of the Beast is different. Just as observing the true Sabbath is a sign of CHRIST'S authority in the life, so observing the counterfeit day becomes a sign of ROME'S authority in your life. We certainly don't have God's authority for it. In fact, one of the best-kept secrets of the Christian world is that there's not a word in the Bible—from Genesis to Revelation—telling you to keep Sunday holy. Not a word!

Let's verify this by quoting from a few Roman Catholic sources:

The very first cardinal appointed by the Roman Catholic Church in the United States was CARDINAL JAMES GIBBONS, Archbishop of Baltimore. In a best-selling book he declares very candidly:

> "You may read the BIBLE from Genesis to Revelation, and you will NOT find a SINGLE LINE authorizing the sanctification of SUNDAY. The SCRIPTURES enforce the religious observance of SATURDAY, a day we [Catholics] NEVER sanctify." [66]

That thought is closely echoed in another popular book, this one by University of Notre Dame professor John A. O'Brien:

> "I have read the BIBLE from the first verse of Genesis to the last verse of Revelations [*sic*], and have found NO reference to the duty of sanctifying the SUNDAY. The day mentioned in the BIBLE is NOT the SUNDAY, the first day of the week but the SATURDAY, the last day of the week." [67]

Furthermore, an official Catholic catechism proudly stated:

"**Question**—Have you any other way of proving that the Church has power to institute festivals of precept?

"**Answer**—Had she not such power, she could not have done that in which all modern religionists agree with her;—she could not have substituted the observance of SUNDAY the first day of the week, for the observance of SATURDAY the seventh day, **a change for which there is NO SCRIPTURAL AUTHORITY**"! [68]

Note carefully that the controversy is over DAYS of WORSHIP: the true Sabbath made by God on the seventh day of Creation and the Papal Sunday instituted by man. The Catholic hierarchy doesn't mind admitting that "there is no Scriptural authority" for Sunday observance, because the Catholic Church bases its dogmas not only on SCRIPTURE but on its own TRADITION. And to a good Catholic, tradition is just as important as the Bible. They make no apology for this at all. On the contrary, they even boast (as in the preceding quote) of having POWER to substitute. But what enlightened person would choose a counterfeit substitute when he can have the genuine article?

FACT #4:
THE MARK MUST BE ACCEPTED BY THE MAJORITY

Obviously, the Mark is something accepted by both Protestants and Catholics, for the Record says: "He causeth ALL . . . to receive a Mark in their right hand, or in their foreheads." [69] The popular churches, even among Protestant denominations, have already accepted the Papal Sunday with no "protest."

Many people—perhaps the majority—see no problem in Sunday laws. In their minds, going to church on Sunday is "as American as apple pie and the red, white and blue." Therefore, they think Sunday legislation is "No big thing." To them it doesn't matter that God specifies ANOTHER day for rest and worship. To them it doesn't matter that enforcing RELIGIOUS LAWS would violate every principle of freedom for which our nation stands.

H. L. Mencken, the sage of Baltimore, sounded cynical when he said: "No one ever went broke underestimating the taste of the American people"— but he was right. Even more cynical comments could truthfully be made about the religious sophistication of our people: many are Biblical illiterates. So it's easy for a Jim Jones or Heaven's Gate suicide cult to lead them astray. They believe what they're told, and they're told that Sunday is "the Christian Sabbath" or "the Lord's Day" in spite of clear Bible evidence to the contrary. [70] "They have a zeal of God, but NOT according to KNOWLEDGE." [71]

Lincoln said, "You can fool *some* of the people *all* of the time. And you can fool *all* of the people *some* of the time. But you can't fool ALL of the people ALL of the time." Well, religious leaders have misled millions so that nearly all of the people are fooled as to the Biblical day of worship—and blindly accept the substitute Sabbath.

FACT #5:
SUNDAY IS THE ADMITTED MARK

The Roman Catholic Church herself claims that the act of changing the day of worship is a "MARK" of her authority. Please note:

> "Sunday is our MARK of authority. . . . The Church is ABOVE the Bible, and this transference of Sabbath observance is proof of that fact."
> —*Catholic Record,* September 1, 1923.

"**Question**—How do you prove that the [Catholic] Church has power to
command Feasts and Holy-days?

"**Answer**—By this very act of CHANGING the Sabbath into the Sunday,
which is admitted by Protestants, and therefore they contradict themselves by keeping Sunday so strictly, and breaking most other Feasts
commanded by the same Church.

"**Question**—How do you prove that?

"**Answer**—Because by keeping Sunday they ACKNOWLEDGE the POWER
of the [Catholic] Church. . . ." [72]

Catholics, you see, are very frank and open about this: They remind us
that those who keep Sunday are *acknowledging the power* of the Roman
Church. The problem is that Sunday is NOT an innocent "feast" or holiday
like Washington's Birthday. It's a man-made day of WORSHIP diametrically
opposed to a clear command of GOD!

Furthermore, Catholics claim that "The observance of Sunday by the
Protestants is an HOMAGE they pay, in spite of themselves, to the AUTHOR-
ITY of the [Catholic] Church." [73] They're right, of course. When people choose
to obey the Church rather than God in the matter of their day of worship,
that day does become the MARK of AUTHORITY of that Church.

The office of Cardinal Gibbons of Baltimore, one of the most illustrious
princes of the Roman Catholic Church, literally stated this in a letter answering an inquiry about the Church's change of the Bible's seventh-day Sabbath
to the Papal Sunday.

J. F. Snyder, of Bloomington, Illinois, wrote Cardinal Gibbons asking if
the Catholic Church claims the change of the Sabbath "as a mark of her
power." The Cardinal, through his Chancellor, gave the following reply:

> Of course the Catholic Church claims that the
> change was her act. It could not have been other-
> wise, as none in those days would have dreamed of
> doing anything in matters spiritual and ecclesias-
> tical and religious without her. And the act is a
> MARK of her ecclesiastical POWER and AUTHORITY in
> religious matters.
>
> (Signed) H. F. Thomas,
> Chancellor for the Cardinal
>
> Nov. 11, 1895

Finally, let me quote the words of Father Enright, former President of Redemptorist College:

> "The Bible says, remember that thou keep holy the Sabbath day. The Catholic Church says, No! By my divine power I ABOLISH the Sabbath day, and command you to keep holy the FIRST day of the week. And lo! The entire civilized world bows down in reverent obedience to the command of the holy Catholic Church."

FACT #6:
THE MARK IS AN ISSUE OF VITAL IMPORTANCE

Are we beginning now to see how much is at stake here? The issue involves far MORE than a matter of DAYS—it's a CHOICE of MASTERS! Paul says:

> "Surely you know that when you surrender yourselves as slaves to obey someone, you are in fact slaves of the MASTER you obey—either of SIN, which results in death, or of OBEDIENCE, which results in being put right with God." [74]

Jesus warned us that "No man can serve two masters: for either he will hate the one, and love the other; or else he will hold to the one, and despise the other." [75] When the test of a National Sunday Law comes, we'll be found on one side or the other: either obedient and loyal to God or disobedient and rebellious against Him.

There's a cosmic contest going on here—a great controversy. In God's closing Book of Revelation, the Bible contrasts those who worship the CREATOR with those who worship the BEAST:

Rev. 13:15 says, **WORSHIP the Beast or DIE.**	**Rev. 14:7** says, **WORSHIP God as CREATOR.** [76]

It's a battle for men's minds and souls, a life-and-death struggle for their allegiance—and it focuses on and revolves around . . . **WORSHIP**. Satan desperately wants worship—that's what he sought from Christ above everything else in the Temptation in the Wilderness:

> "The devil took Him [Christ] up on an exceedingly high mountain, and showed Him all the kingdoms of the world and their glory. And he said to Him, 'All these things I will give You if You will fall down and

WORSHIP me.' Then Jesus said to him, 'Away with you, Satan! For it is written, "You shall worship the LORD your GOD, and HIM ONLY you shall serve." ' " [77]

It seemed like such a little thing. All he asked was that Christ bow down to him for just a brief moment. In this case, too, it seems like such a little thing. And IF it were merely a matter of days—and IF days were all alike— it would be a little thing. But eternal consequences hang in the balance here!

EDEN REVISITED

Let's not be so blind as Eve was in the Garden of Eden. *At the beginning* of the great controversy between Christ and Satan on Planet Earth, God provided a SIMPLE TEST of loyalty. *At the end,* just before Jesus returns, He plans to provide *another* such test. There's nothing inherently sinful in Sunday, just as there was nothing poisonous in the fruit the Serpent offered. The issue then as now is obedience, loyalty, allegiance—in a word: **WORSHIP!**

Bible readers know the tragic story of Adam and Eve's first two children, Cain and Abel. [78] Angry jealousy drove Cain to kill his brother Abel when God accepted Abel's offering but rejected Cain's. Instead of bringing the God-ordained BLOOD sacrifice of a lamb, Cain stubbornly substituted "the FRUIT of the ground." Perhaps he reasoned, "An *offering* is an *offering,* and God won't mind." But God DID mind, and He did not accept Cain's substitute. And some may reason, "A *day* is a *day.* I don't think it makes any difference." They, like Cain, may be surprised to learn how BIG a difference a tiny act of worship can make when it shows our devotion to God—or the lack of it.

After Pentecost God told Peter and the other disciples to preach the gospel of Christ. But the Jewish leaders told them not to preach, or they'd be thrown into jail. "Then Peter and the other apostles answered and said: We ought to obey GOD rather than MEN." [79] Pray that you and I will fearlessly make the same response when faced with the coercion of the Mark of the Beast.

FACT #7:
THE MARK HAS NOT YET BEEN GIVEN

This is a very important point to understand. The Mark of the Beast has NOT been given to anyone yet. It's not true to say that Sunday-keepers have the Mark of the Beast or that all good people of past ages who kept Sunday had the Mark of the Beast.

The Bible makes clear that the Mark and worship of the Beast will be enforced by the IMAGE of the Beast, which we learned will be the United States in a governmental union of Church and State. But both the *forming of* the Image and *enforcement by* the Image have NOT YET come to pass. The receiving of the Mark of the Beast is a specific act which the Image of the Beast will compel. The Third Angel's Message[80] about the Mark of the Beast is a warning mercifully given in ADVANCE to prepare God's people for the coming danger—and the book you're now reading is part of that warning.

Our study of prophecy in PART I of this chapter showed that the United States will implement the Mark of the Beast by passing Sunday laws. What was once the "Land of Liberty" will become an ecclesiastical dictatorship. At that time there will be a revival of religious tyranny and persecution brought about by a union of Church and State. But *that hasn't happened yet:* the Image hasn't been formed, and the Mark hasn't been imposed on anyone.

Now some may ask, "If Sunday observance IS the Beast's Mark of authority, as the evidence seems to show, and over the years millions have religiously kept that day, then how can one say that the Mark hasn't been imposed on anyone?" Let's explain it this way: It's true that, strictly speaking, Sunday IS the wrong day of worship—it's a manufactured substitute without foundation in Scripture. But millions of sincere Christians—among whom I count some of my own dear loved ones—have gone to their graves devoutly believing Sunday to be appointed by their Lord. They were mistaken, being ignorant of the facts uncovered in this book. But since their devotion to the Lord they loved was real, and since *they lived up to every ray of light that shined upon their pathway,* it's safe to say that HAD the Holy Spirit made clear the truth of God's Sabbath, they WOULD have accepted and followed it.

God's divine sense of justice is seen in the following Scriptures:

- "Therefore to him that KNOWETH to do good, and doeth it NOT, to him it is sin. . . .
- "The times of this IGNORANCE God winked at [overlooked]; but now commandeth all men everywhere to repent. . . .
- "If ye were BLIND, ye should have no sin: but now ye say, We see; therefore your sin remaineth. . . .
- "If we sin WILLFULLY after that we have knowledge of the truth, there remaineth no more sacrifice for sins."[81]

God holds us responsible for what we know, and many faithful Christians of the past honestly did not know the truth about the Sabbath/Sunday issue. But when the Image of the Beast imposes the infamous Mark, no one will be able to claim ignorance, for it will be front-page news.

When the Sunday legislation constituting "the Mark of the Beast" is passed in this country, it won't be done quietly or "in a corner." On the contrary, the Sabbath/Sunday question will loom large not only in the pulpits of churches everywhere but as an issue of national interest and debate on a par with the Clinton impeachment hearings. It will be argued on the floor of Congress by aroused legislators who will "make a FEDERAL case out of it." Consequently, this matter will be brought to the forefront of attention and the issues made clear to every person in the land.

THEN we'll have a chance to choose. As poet James Russell Lowell put it,

> "Once to every man and nation
> Comes the moment to decide,
> In the strife of Truth with Falsehood,
> For the good or evil side." [82]

THEN if an enlightened citizen, with eyes wide open, knowingly decides for the sake of comfort, convenience, or expediency to honor the man-made counterfeit Sabbath—instead of remaining loyal to his Creator—he will have sold his own soul. It is then and only then that he receives "the Mark of the Beast."

Daniel 12:1 predicts "a time of trouble, such as never was." When that crisis comes, well-meaning but misguided men who place TRADITION above a "Thus saith the Lord" will react by promoting the Image of the Beast. Emotionalism will play a big part in the process. The majority of people will be swept along on a wave of mass hysteria. Those ignorant of what the Bible teaches will be easily coaxed aboard the Beast's bandwagon. They've relied on their ministers to guide them in spiritual matters rather than searching the Scriptures themselves to find whether or not a teaching is true. [83] They'll form the Image to the Beast and coerce others to join them.

At this point mankind will have reached the moment of supreme crisis. This is the FINAL ACT in the great drama of deception, and Satan knows "It's now or never." The Arch-deceiver is willing to pull out all the stops in an ultimate effort to tip the scales in his favor. In the past the Devil has introduced into mankind *false christs,* mere men like charlatan Jim Jones, convicted tax cheat Sun Myung Moon, and others who have been moderately successful at misleading multitudes. But now Satan may be willing to take things into his own diabolical hands, now he may feel he must act personally, and with telling effect!

CONSIDER THIS SCENARIO: Suppose Satan, no longer content with masquerading as "an angel of light," [84] *himself* pretends to be Christ! He could make it appear that Christ has come. In different parts of the world, he could show himself as a majestic being of dazzling brightness in unsurpassed glory. As people prostrate themselves before him, he lifts up his hands and pronounces a blessing upon them. His voice is soft but richly melodic—it sounds loving and heavenly.

Suppose he works demonic miracles,[85] healing diseases and appearing to raise the dead. Suppose a few of his devils also appear as physical manifestations of the Lord's apostles. Suppose, after Satan in the garb of Christ deceptively appears to restore a dead baby's life, his "apostles," with glowing smiles, carry it in triumph to the eager arms of its mother. Do you think that she or the crowd around her will refuse to believe anything—anything at all—that they say?

If the supposed apostles tell the multitude that some of their teachings were *not recorded correctly* in the Bible, would anyone in the mesmerized crowd dare to deny it? If Satan—as the masterful, loving Christ—claims to have CHANGED the Sabbath to Sunday, who would dare contradict him? The delusion would be overpowering.[86]

Revelation 13:14 warns that Satan "DECEIVETH them that dwell on the earth by the means of those MIRACLES which he had power to do." At this point, in a diabolical display reminiscent of Elijah's contest on Mt. Carmel, Satan as the false Christ exhibits his supernatural power, "even making FIRE come down from heaven to earth in the sight of men,"[87] to PROVE that HE is GOD!

The masses of humanity, seeing the great deceiver personate Christ so perfectly not only in person in various parts of the world but also over world-wide television—for this will be the biggest news story of all time—will agitate their legislators to pass Sunday laws. No matter what our Constitution says against laws establishing religion, law-makers will then be under tremendous pressure.

It's a cruel choice for those who want to remain faithful to God when government tries to force humanity to disobey Him! The Beast and his Image will command all to receive his Mark of authority.[88] On the other hand, God warns us NOT to receive that Mark.[89] What a moral dilemma! Worse than "Catch 22," it's truly a case of being damned if we *do* and damned if we *don't*.

Awesome indeed is the precious POWER of CHOICE, both in its responsibility and in its consequences! EVE made a choice—and sin was born. JUDAS made a choice—and betrayed the Lord who loved him. YOU and I face a choice—the challenge of showing loyal allegiance either to Christ, our Creator, or to the Antichrist/Beast. Pray that God gives us the courage to follow Him in this crisis.[90]

Yet it often takes the great darkness of a crisis to reveal genuine Christian character. In the daytime we look toward heaven but don't see the stars.

They are there, fixed in the firmament, but the eye cannot distinguish them. In the darkness of the night we behold their genuine luster. The deeper the night for God's people, the more brilliant the stars. May God help you and me to shine for Him.

Without overstating the case, it's a matter of LIFE and DEATH. The Image of the Beast threatens death to any who refuse the Mark. He "causeth the earth and them that dwell therein to worship the first Beast, whose deadly wound was healed. . . . And he causeth all, both small and great, rich and poor, free and bond, to receive a Mark in their right hand, or in their fore-heads." [91] That word *"causeth"*—repeated in those two verses—really denotes FORCE. Newer versions translate it in those verses as "compels," "made," "required," "forced."

While men attempt to force the man-made Sabbath upon us under threat of death, God warns that if we yield our allegiance from Him and obey the Beast as our master, we'll suffer the Seven Last Plagues and then burn in hell. [92] But our dilemma disappears and our choice becomes clear the moment we realize that *we'll never go wrong doing right.* The God who loves us will protect us when the plagues fall if we remain faithful to Him. [93] He promises us:

> "A thousand shall fall at thy side, and ten thousand at thy right hand; but it shall not come nigh thee. Only with thine eyes shalt thou behold and see the reward of the wicked. . . . There shall no evil befall thee, neither shall any PLAGUE come nigh thy dwelling." [94]

God pleads with us as a loving Father: "COME OUT of her [the Beast's fallen church—"Babylon"], MY people, that ye be not partakers of her sins, and that ye receive NOT of her plagues." [95]

Our heavenly Father has a thousand ways to provide for us and protect us, of which we know nothing. But one thing we do know: He will cast "the Beast . . . and them that worshipped his Image . . . into a Lake of Fire burning with brimstone." [96] So the choice which seems hard at first is really easy: The committed Christian confirms his decision that—sink or swim, live or die, come what may—he'll be faithful *no matter what!* When the crisis-hour comes, he steadfastly resolves: "As for me and my house, we will serve the Lord." [97]

The Mark of the Beast is that invisible profession of servitude and obedience called allegiance—allegiance to a false system of worship. But though that inner attitude cannot be seen, if you openly trample on God's Sabbath and accept a man-made substitute, the FACT that you have that Mark WILL be visible to all the world and all the universe. Paul says: "We

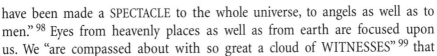

have been made a SPECTACLE to the whole universe, to angels as well as to men." [98] Eyes from heavenly places as well as from earth are focused upon us. We "are compassed about with so great a cloud of WITNESSES" [99] that our reaction—good or bad—to the enforced Mark will be visible everywhere!

CONCLUSION: Two CHOICES
LEAVE ONLY TWO CLASSES OF PEOPLE

The end-time crisis polarizes all humanity into TWO CAMPS—those who accept or reject the Mark of the Beast. The disobedient, who ignore God's warning, will be destroyed in the Lake of Fire. Those obedient to God, who trust His promises, will be protected not only from the Beast's death decree but also from the Seven Last Plagues. They will spend eternity with Jesus. [100]

The STAGE is SET for the LAST ACT in the great prophetic DRAMA! How will you decide? Is Sunday the holy day you thought it was—or is it "a Roman holiday" with roots in pagan sun worship? Will you be counted as one of God's obedient children and keep the seventh-day Sabbath according to God's command? Or will you honor a man-made "holy" day instead? In the very end of this world's history, the day one chooses to keep will reveal his response to truth. You will have to choose, but you must see that the ultimate issue is not a choice between DAYS but between God and the Devil. I pray that you'll make your decision now and be ready for that great Final Test.

That test is coming sooner than you think. Like a ticking time-bomb, there's an awesome urgency to this revelation. For, though the Mark of the Beast has not yet been given, it will surely be a world-wide issue soon.

God has granted you the privilege of examining some vital Scriptures. Hopefully you've learned something new. Heaven is watching to see just how much this means to you now. The angels are watching—the Father is watching—the Savior is watching. All heaven is watching to see what YOU will DO with your new discoveries. The decision is yours.

- "You are the God who SEES me."
  —Genesis 16:13, NIV
- "The EYES of the Lord run to and fro throughout the whole earth."
  —2 Chronicles 16:9
- "His EYES are on the ways of men; He sees their every step."
  —Job 34:21, NIV
- "All things are naked and open to the EYES of Him to whom
  we must give account."—Hebrews 4:13, NKJV

Notes to Chapter 20

1. Revelation 12:6. Compare verse 14 also.
2. God led Columbus to this land. Please see pages 706-707, footnote #194.
3. John Wesley, *Explanatory Notes Upon the New Testament* (reprint; London: The Epworth Press, 1952), p. 1010, comment on Revelation 13:11.
4. Revelation 13:11.
5. Norman R. Gulley, *Christ Our Refuge* (Boise, Idaho: Pacific Press Publishing Association, © 1996), p. 79. Also Norman Gulley, *Christ Is Coming* (Hagerstown, Maryland: Review & Herald Publishing Association, © 1998), p. 491.
6. 2 Thessalonians 2:9-10, NKJV. The Bible states that devils can work miracles in such texts as Revelation 16:14, which speaks of "the spirits of devils, working miracles." No mere illusions or amazing tricks are foretold here. Men are deceived by "those MIRACLES which [Satan and his agents] had POWER to DO," not which they pretend to do.—Revelation 13:14. See also page 755 in this chapter.
7. Revelation 13:12 & 14. Please see Clues "V" and "W" of Chapter 19 for an explanation of the deadly wound and its healing.
8. Daniel 12:1.
9. Pope Leo XIII, "Human Liberty," translated in *The Great Encyclical Letters of Pope Leo XIII,* 3rd edition (New York: Benziger, 1903), p. 161.
10. Thomas Jefferson, "Notes on Virginia," Query 17, *The Writings of Thomas Jefferson,* Volume VIII, p. 402.
11. Charles Colson, *Kingdoms in Conflict* (New York: William Morrow, 1987).
12. Thomas Jefferson, "Letter to the Danbury [Connecticut] Baptist Association," January 1, 1802.
13. Mark 12:17 (also Matthew 22:21 and Luke 20:25).
14. Thomas Jefferson, "The Declaration of Independence," July 4, 1776.
15. Thomas Jefferson, "Summary View of the Rights of British America," 1774.
16. Thomas Jefferson, "First Inaugural Address," March 4, 1801.
17. Thomas Jefferson, "Letter to Mordecai M. Noah, May 28, 1818," *Thomas Jefferson Papers,* Volume 213, p. 37988, in Manuscript Division, Library of Congress. *Auto da fe* is Portuguese for "act of the faith," the tragically ironic term applied to the act of BURNING heretics at the stake!
18. *World Book Encyclopedia* (Chicago: Field Enterprises, Inc., © 1955), Volume 9, p. 3999, article "Jefferson, Thomas."
19. Thomas Jefferson, "Virginia Statute of Religious Freedom," Item 5, quoted in Garry Wills, *Under God: Religion and American Politics* (New York: Simon and Schuster, © 1990), p. 364.
20. *Encyclopedia Britannica* (CD 98 Standard Edition © 1994-1998, Encyclopedia Britannica, Inc.), article "Thomas Jefferson."
21. U. S. Supreme Court Justice Hugo Black, in the 1947 case of *Everson v. Board of Education,* 330 U.S. 1 (1947), p. 16.
22. U. S. Supreme Court Chief Justice Warren Burger, in *Lemon v. Kurtzman,* 403 U.S. 602, 614 (1971).

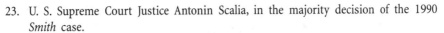

23. U. S. Supreme Court Justice Antonin Scalia, in the majority decision of the 1990 *Smith* case.

24. U. S. Supreme Court Chief Justice William Rehnquist, in the 1985 case of *Wallace v. Jaffree,* p. 2517.

25. Oscar Wilde, in his drama *A Woman of No Importance.*

26. C. S. Lewis, *God in the Dock: Essays on Theology and Ethics* (Grand Rapids, Michigan: Eerdmans, 1970).

27. John 16:2, NIV.

28. George Santayana, *The Life of Reason,* Revised One-Volume Edition (New York: Charles Scribner's Sons, 1953), p. 82.

29. Abdul Rahman Pazhwak, "The Nuclear Time Bomb," *Saturday Review of Literature,* December 9, 1967, front cover and p. 17.

30. Revelation 13:11.

31. 1 Corinthians 8:5.

32. Psalm 96:5.

33. Jeremiah 10:11. (The evidence that the Fourth Commandment contains the three elements of a SEAL—name, title, and territory—is already clear and compelling. An additional sidelight is the fact that the word "SABBAth" contains *abba*, the Aramaic word for "father" used for God in early Christian prayers—see Romans 8:15, Galatians 4:6, and our Lord's example in Mark 14:36. This may be mere coincidence, or it just may be that God ingeniously signed His name in the Sabbath.)

34. Lest some think that because these verses mention "the children of Israel" they don't apply to Christians today, remember Paul's teaching that in a spiritual sense we Christians ARE Israel: "If ye be *Christ's,* then are ye *Abraham's* seed, and heirs according to the promise," Galatians 3:29. Furthermore, by honoring our Creator we honor Christ, for He is the Creator who gave us the Sabbath, as we've already seen in Chapter 13, pages 372-373. Please see also *Appendix I* at the back of this book.

35. God says: "I will make a NEW covenant. . . . This is the covenant that I will make with the house of Israel after those days, saith the Lord; I will put My LAWS into their MIND, and write them in their HEARTS."—Hebrews 8:8-10. "This is the covenant that I will make with them after those days, saith the Lord, I will put My LAWS into their HEARTS, and in their MINDS will I write them."—Hebrews 10:16. ". . . written not with INK, but with the SPIRIT of the living God; not in tables of STONE, but in FLESHY tables of the HEART."—2 Corinthians 3:3. See also Jeremiah 31:31-33 and Ezekiel 36:26-27. Misguided men who teach that "The new covenant does away with God's Law" display a shocking ignorance of God's Word, and they in turn mislead others.

36. Revelation 13:12.

37. Revelation 13:16.

38. Revelation 13:17.

39. Revelation 13:15.

40. Revelation 13:4, 12, 15.

41. The version quoted here is the Amplified Bible, but the passage is similarly translated in other modern versions such as the New American Standard Bible, the New

International Version, the New King James Version, the Revised Standard Version, the New Revised Standard Version, *etc.*

42. 2 Thessalonians 2:3-4.

43. Daniel 7:25, RSV.

44. Revelation 14:8 and 18:2.

45. Revelation 14:12. Compare also Revelation 12:17, which speaks of God's "remnant" church (KJV) in the Last Days, those that "KEEP the Commandments of God and have the testimony of Jesus Christ."

46. Revelation 7:3 and 13:16.

47. Ezekiel 9:2. That this "man" was an ANGEL is evident from his being described emphatically and repeatedly (in Ezekiel 9:2, 3, 11 and 10:2, 6, 7) as one "clothed with linen," for that's how angels are clothed. Revelation 15:6 speaks of "the seven angels . . . clothed in pure and white linen."

48. Ezekiel 9:3-6.

49. Revelation 7:1-3.

50. Ezekiel 8:3-15.

51. Ezekiel 8:16.

52. Deuteronomy 4:2-24, NKJV says: "KEEP the commandments of the Lord your God. . . . The Lord spoke . . . Ten Commandments; and He wrote them on two tablets of stone. . . . Take careful heed to yourselves . . . lest you lift your eyes to heaven, and when you see the SUN, the moon, and the stars, all the host of heaven, you feel driven to worship THEM, and serve THEM. . . . For the Lord your God is a consuming fire, a jealous God."

53. The sun is just a "creature" or creation of God.

54. Romans 1:25.

55. See Chapters 10 & 11, "Solving the Mystery of Death."

56. Your Bible teaches that "Christ was offered ONCE to bear the sins of many."—Hebrews 9:28. See also Hebrews 9:25-26 and 10:10, 12 & 14 for more emphatic statements to this effect.

57. See, for instance, Malachi 3:8-11 and Genesis 28:20-22. Jesus, even in His sharp rebuke to the hypocritical Pharisees, endorsed the payment of tithe. See Matthew 23:23 and Luke 11:42.

58. See "Clue T" in Chapter 19, "Antichrist Unmasked: The Beast Power Revealed."

59. See Chapters 13 and 14, above, on the Sabbath and Sunday.

60. Exodus 20:8-11 and 31:17.

61. Matthew 15:3, 6, & 9.

62. Ezekiel 20:12 (& 20).

63. Hebrews 8:8-10.

64. 1 John 3:4.

65. John 14:15.

66. Cardinal James Gibbons, *The Faith of Our Fathers,* 110th Revised Edition (New York: P. J. Kenedy & Sons, Printers to the Holy See, 1917), pp. 72-73.

67. John A. O'Brien, *The Faith of Millions: The Credentials of the Catholic Religion* (Huntington, Indiana: Our Sunday Visitor, © 1938), p. 154.

68. Father Stephen Keenan, *A Doctrinal Catechism*, 3rd American edition, revised, New York: P. J. Kenedy & Sons, Printers to the Holy See, 1876), p. 174.

69. Revelation 13:16.

70. See Chapters 13 and 14, above, on the Sabbath and Sunday.

71. Romans 10:2.

72. Daniel Ferris, *Manual of Christian Doctrine: or, Catholic Belief and Practice* (Dublin: M. H. Gill & Son, Ltd., 1916), pp. 67-68. This work is an updated version of Henry Tu(r)berville's *An Abridgment of the Christian Doctrine* (also known as the Douay Catechism) of 1649.

73. Louis Gaston de Segur, *Plain Talk About the Protestantism of To-day* (Boston: Patrick Donahoe, 1899), p. 225. Segur (1820-81) was a French Catholic prelate and official at Rome.

74. Romans 6:16, TEV. Note how Paul, at the risk of appearing *legalistic,* contrasts "sin" and "obedience" as antithetical opposites.

75. Matthew 6:24.

76. Revelation 14:7 tells us to "Fear God, and give glory to Him; for the hour of His judgment is come: and worship Him that MADE HEAVEN, and EARTH, and the SEA, and the fountains of waters." This last-day call to "worship Him that MADE" all things—that is, the Creator—is an ECHO of the Sabbath Command in Exodus 20:11—"For in six days the Lord MADE HEAVEN and EARTH, the SEA, and all that in them is, and rested the seventh day: wherefore the Lord blessed the Sabbath day, and hallowed it."

77. Matthew 4:8-10, NKJV. (See verses 1-11.)

78. See Genesis 4:1-15.

79. Acts 5:29.

80. See Revelation 14:9-10.

81. James 4:17, Acts 17:30, John 9:41, and Hebrews 10:26.

82. James Russell Lowell, "The Present Crisis," stanza 5.

83. See Acts 17:10-11. Those in Berea didn't accept even what PAUL taught till they searched the Scriptures to see whether those things were true.

84. 2 Corinthians 11:14.

85. Revelation 16:14 speaks of "devils, working miracles."

86. But the people of God will not be misled—for two reasons. First, the TEACHINGS of this false Christ will *contradict* God's Word. Second, Satan is not permitted to counterfeit the MANNER of Christ's Return. When Jesus comes again, *His feet won't touch the earth:* the raptured saints will "meet the Lord in the AIR."—1 Thessalonians 4:17. This is why Christ warns that if people say, "'Look, He is in the desert!' do NOT go out; or 'Look, He is in the inner rooms!' do NOT believe it. For as the LIGHTNING comes from the east and flashes to the west, so also will the coming of the Son of Man be."—Matthew 24:26-27, NKJV. Only those who've been diligent students of the Bible will be shielded from miracle-working devils and the powerful delusion that takes the whole world captive.

87. Revelation 13:13, RSV. Please see 1 Kings 18:16-40 and pages 726-727, above. Warning of this whole deceptive scenario, Jesus plainly predicted: "FALSE Christs . . . will arise and will show great SIGNS and WONDERS, so as to mislead, if possible,

even the elect. Behold, I have told you in advance."—Matthew 24:24-25, NASB.

88. Revelation 13:15-17.

89. Revelation 14:9-11.

90. John F. Kennedy could not have known *how appropriate* to our present situation are these inspiring words from his *Inaugural Address*: "In the long history of the world, *only a few generations have been granted the role of preserving freedom in its hour of maximum danger.* I do not shrink from this responsibility—I welcome it. I do not believe that any of us would exchange places with any other people or any other generation. The energy, the faith, the devotion which we bring to this endeavor will light our country and all who serve it—and *the glow from that fire can truly light the world.* . . . Let us go forth . . . asking His blessing and His help, but knowing that *here on earth God's work must truly be our own."*

91. Revelation 13:12 & 16.

92. Revelation 14:9-11. (Revelation 15:1 identifies "the wrath of God.")

93. The Bible records *another* death decree against God's people. King Ahasuerus, better known as Xerxes, of the vast Medo-Persian Empire, was misled into signing a decree "to DESTROY, to KILL, and to cause to PERISH, all Jews, both young and old, little children and women, in one day." See Esther 3:12-13 and 4:7. But God providentially PROTECTED His faithful ones in the very face of the threat. The Bible tells of many other instances of God's miraculous protection of those faithful to Him. For example, Daniel 3 tells of the three Hebrew children ordered to bow down not to the Image of the Beast but to another "golden image" under threat of being thrown into the fiery furnace, yet God miraculously saved them. These examples reassure us that He's always in command. With good reason, Romans 8:31 asks: "If God be for us, who can be against us?"

94. Psalm 91:7-10. Read the whole 91st Psalm for comfort and assurance.

95. Revelation 18:4.

96. Revelation 19:20, 20:15.

97. Joshua 24:15.

98. 1 Corinthians 4:9, NIV. The word *spectacle* here is translated from the Greek *theatron,* which gives us our English word "theater." The "angels" referred to are the unfallen angels who remained loyal to God after Lucifer's rebellion. They make an intensely interested audience for a drama far more fascinating—and infinitely more important—than any soap opera!

99. Hebrews 12:1.

100. In 1977 C. C. Cribb wrote a book about these two classes of people. He titled it *"The Horrified and the Glorified."*

◆   ◆   ◆

Reference: page 150, footnote 138.

APPENDIX A

~

A PHYSICIAN'S VIEW

OF

EVOLUTION

MY SON,[1] A PROFESSOR OF MEDICINE (Board Certified in the fields of both Internal Medicine and Emergency Medicine) has often chatted with me about evolutionary claims. On one occasion he said:

"Those who dreamed up the idea of aimless, purposeless evolution were obviously NOT physicians, who know how complex and marvelous the human body really is—made up of many interdependent and interactive systems. We have the . . .

- central nervous system
- peripheral nervous system
- cardiovascular system
- respiratory system
- gastrointestinal system
- genitourinary system
- musculoskeletal system [2]

"Each one of these is a finely-tuned marvel of design and engineering. Yet ALL of them must function perfectly—at the SAME TIME, because a good renal [kidney] system won't do you any good if your lungs don't work. You see, in a hypothetical evolving prototype, any DEFECTS = DEATH. For instance—to give just a few examples:

✓ The human body must have a perfectly functioning CARDIO-VASCULAR SYSTEM to survive.

✓ BLOOD must be able to clot, for if it does not coagulate, you bleed to death.

✓ WOUNDS must be spontaneously able to heal and repair themselves. [3]

✓ RED BLOOD CELLS last only 120 days and must then be replaced. WHITE BLOOD CELLS—without which you'd die of infection—last only 10 days! HOW does the organism KNOW that these vital cells must be replaced in order to avoid death?

✓ Without a faultless REPRODUCTIVE system, the whole story ends."

✦ ✦ ✦

My son's insights helped me to understand why physicians, molecular biologists, and others familiar with the mind-boggling COMPLEXITY of the human machine—its many marvels all so perfectly engineered—see a Higher Intelligence behind it, not a blind and mindless evolution.

I asked him to jot down a few additional thoughts on evolution from the standpoint of a physician, and here they are . . .

PROBLEMS WITH EVOLUTIONARY THEORY:
ORIGINS-OF-LIFE ISSUES & ENGINEERING PROBLEMS

I. LIFE COMES ONLY FROM LIFE

The one inviolate universal law in all of biological science is that "life can come only from life." A living organism can originate only from another *living* organism; a living cell can originate only from another *living* cell. This is true one-hundred-per-cent of the time, with NO exceptions—ever. Thus we state the obvious when we observe that a human can be born only from another *live* human; a dog can be born only from another *live* dog; an amoeba can arise only from another *living* amoeba, and so on.

This fundamental law of biology is just as true at the CELLULAR level: a functioning hepatocyte (that is, a liver cell) can originate only from living hepatocyte lineage; a red blood cell only from red-blood-cell lineage; a staphylococcal bacterium can originate only from living staphylococcal parentage—and so on. Never has a living organism or cell claimed a *non-living aggregate of molecules* as its parent. Never has life appeared "out of nowhere."

Just for the sake of argument, let's concede that advanced life forms did indeed originate from lower life forms. Following the thread of evolutionary theory back hundreds of millions of years to the earliest forms of life we must inevitably arrive at the first cellular parents, the "Adam and Eve," of all life forms. It is at this critical point in evolutionary theory that the evolutionist is faced with an absolutely insurmountable hurdle: the evolutionist CANNOT account for the origin of the "first" living cell. You see, it's impossible for the evolutionist to produce the first living cell without violating the *universal law* of biology that "life comes only from life." Whatever its other major shortcomings—and they are many—the fatal blow to the theory of evolution is the fact that evolutionary theory cannot explain the ORIGIN of LIFE.

In contemplating the origin of the "first" living cell, the evolutionist sidesteps this universal law. The evolutionist unabashedly asserts that through some fancy chemical tap-dance routine a hodgepodge of carbon, nitrogen, hydrogen, phosphorus, and oxygen atoms were able to *spontaneously* form highly complex molecular structures that became the precursors of living cells.

Evolutionary theory remains entirely clueless, however, as to HOW these complex molecular structures were able to spontaneously form and as to what PROCESS transpired to convert these "cell precursors" into actual living cells. No one has ever been able to demonstrate in the laboratory how DNA could spontaneously form from a "soup" of carbon and other atoms. It's obvious that even a perfectly assembled cell with all of the molecular structures in place cannot *regain* that entity called "life" once it has died. It is equally impossible for a "cellular precursor" to *achieve* living status no matter how fancy the molecular tap-dance routine envisioned by the evolutionist.

Our planet abounds with life in all forms and varieties: plants and animals; procaryotes and eucaryotes;[4] macroscopic, microscopic, and submicroscopic; land-bound and marine based. We see broad ranges of life expectancy—from hundreds of years for some plants to only a few days for some insects. Yet in NO circumstance, despite all of the abundant varieties of life that surround us, do we observe the transformation from non-living "precursor" to living organism. Despite the abundance of carbon, nitrogen, phosphorus, hydrogen, and oxygen atoms on our planet, we NEVER see the spontaneous formation of the complex molecular structures essential to evolutionary theory.

Yet IF evolutionary theory is true, with such an abundance of life on our planet, the spontaneous formation of living cells and organisms from cellular "precursors" should be a COMMON occurrence, as natural and routine as algae growing in a swimming pool or toadstools growing in a meadow.

There is absolutely no scientific foundation to modern evolutionary theory and no credible basis to advance the theory within the scientific community.

II. COMPLEX STRUCTURE AND FUNCTION REQUIRE AN ENGINEER

Architectural structures and engineering marvels presuppose the existence of a designer, and the existence of the Golden Gate Bridge, the St. Louis Arch, or an advanced national highway system imply the handiwork of a gifted architect or engineer. Not even an evolutionist would suggest that the Golden Gate Bridge was formed when molten steel, gravel, sand, and concrete-mix were "shaken and stirred" in such a way as to produce the magnificent structure recognized the world over. Yet when it comes to the incredibly complex molecular biology of HUMAN BEINGS, evolutionists shamelessly assert that the formation of nucleic acids and their arrangement with great precision into specific sequences paired off in the form of DNA (which constitutes the human genome, or genetic pattern) WERE spontaneously occurring events!

When one recalls that the human genome has 80,000 separate genes arranged in 3 *BILLION* DNA molecule pairs arranged in *precise order,* the evolutionist's claim begins to look entirely ludicrous.[5] Compared to the complexity of LIFE, the Golden Gate Bridge is little more than a Tinker Toy set— mere child's play. Simply stated, it is mathematically impossible for RANDOM sequences of nucleic acids to serve any functional purpose whatsoever or to provide any meaningful genetic information.

Evolutionary theory teaches that living cells and living organisms have become more advanced and more complex along an evolutionary continuum. This theoretical "evolutionary continuum," which originated first with "simple" life forms and progressed to highly complex life forms, has a number of MAJOR ENGINEERING DEFECTS. In order for a particular organism to continue on down the evolutionary line, that organism must produce progeny capable of:

    (1) *living long enough* to reproduce, and

    (2) producing progeny that *can* reproduce.

Foremost among the engineering defects in the evolutionary schema is the prospect that any significant molecular DEFECT in the progeny along the evolutionary continuum would result in the TERMINATION of that line of progeny and extinguish that progeny's entire evolutionary line.

For the sake of brevity, I will use only one physiological system to illustrate how evolutionary theory cannot work: HEMATOPOIESIS [6] —although I could use virtually any system of the body to illustrate my point.

HEMATOPOIESIS

Humans have an elaborate hematological system whereby we produce several lines of blood cells. I will focus on the erythrocyte, or red blood cell (RBC) line. The purpose of the body's RBC's is to pick up *oxygen* molecules in the lungs for delivery to the distant tissues and organs throughout the body. After delivering oxygen to the body the RBC picks up *carbon dioxide*, a by-product of cellular metabolism, and returns to the lungs to *exchange* carbon dioxide for more oxygen molecules.

The average LIFE SPAN of an RBC is 120 days, and so RBC's must be produced continuously to keep up with natural RBC losses. It's vital that the number of RBC's be maintained within a very narrow range because if the RBC count is either too high or too low, DEATH will result. For example, if the RBC count is *too high,* the blood becomes very viscous and sludgy, resulting in blockage of the blood vessels going to the brain, kidneys, lungs, and so on. On the other hand, if the RBC count is *too low* because of bone-marrow failure or hemorrhage, the organs die from the lack of oxygen and nutrient supply necessary for survival.

The evolutionist postulates that at some point along the evolutionary continuum, as organisms became more advanced, they began to produce red blood cells. Let's consider the following questions:

1. How would the first RBC-producing organism KNOW HOW to produce a red blood cell in the first place?

2. RBC's consist of long chains of amino acids arranged in precise sequence (like the letters arranged in this sentence to spell out all words correctly); any deviation in even a *single* amino acid in the sequence results in a defective RBC. How did the organism KNOW the EXACT amino-acid sequence [7] necessary to form a red blood cell? (Remember that the first RBC-forming organism had *only one chance* to get the RBC amino-acid sequence right or it would have DIED immediately—there could be no second chance.)

3. How did that first RBC-producing organism KNOW that its RBC's would live only 120 days and that CONTINUOUS RBC production—within a very narrow window—was VITAL to its survival? (Remember, it had never seen an RBC before and it would have had *only one opportunity* to get

its RBC production *perfectly right* or it would have DIED—and the whole evolutionary chain must start back at "square one.")

Any defect in the hematological system and that first RBC-forming organism DIES, and all further progress along the evolutionary continuum stops in mid-stream and must begin anew. Please note:

- If that first organism *didn't know how* to make *perfect* hemoglobin, it would have DIED.

- If that first organism *didn't know* that it would be necessary to continuously *replace* its RBC's every 120 days, it would have DIED.

- If that first RBC-producing organism tried to replace *too many* RBC's, it would have DIED.

In short, the consequence of the organism's failure to anticipate its physiological requirements is its DEATH. It has no second chance. For evolution to succeed, the evolutionist must contemplate a *zero-defects* engineering system. No retrospective correction of physiological miscalculations is available to the organism.

Yet Darwinism would have us believe that a finely–engineered system as complex as HEMATOPOIESIS—along with many others that exist[8] among the *hundreds of trillions of cells* in our bodies—could arise by random mutation / natural selection, or even by chance. Obviously, this is one of the most DARING claims in the history of science! It's also one of the most unsubstantiated.

༄

Notes to Appendix A

1. Howard A. Peth, Jr., M.D., J.D.

2. You can see that the human body as a whole is a perfect example of the IRREDUC-IBLE COMPLEXITY we discussed above (in Chapter 4, "Evolution – Part II," pages 104-107). The body simply could NOT function if any one of these systems—and others not listed—was removed.

3. Among the many marvels of the body is the fact that it HEALS itself! Throughout our bodies, individual cells continually grow old and die. These cells must be re-placed—and the body performs this miracle! An evolutionist may casually remark: "That's how the body evolved—it fixes itself." But CARS don't fix themselves! BUILD-INGS don't fix themselves! It's only the things made by GOD that fix themselves. The body is constantly rebuilding itself, restoring itself, replenishing cells everywhere. The same God who created us also sustains us in many "small" miracles day by day.

4. Two fundamentally different types of cells. An oversimplified definition is that *procaryotes* are UNICELLULAR and *eucaryotes* are MULTICELLULAR. Also, eucaryotes have a second membrane, different from the cell membrane, which encloses the nucleus of the cell—and the procaryotes don't.

5. Recent front-page news reports announced that scientists have just determined the order of all 34 million chemical "letters" that spell out the genetic code for "a single human chromosome." If there are 34 million chemical letters on a *single* human chromosome, a little arithmetic tells us there are about 1.6 BILLION letters on all 46 chromosomes—*per cell!* All this mind-boggling compexity places the suggestion that "It evolved by pure chance" more in the realm of MYTH than science.

6. Hematopoiesis refers to the formation of blood in the body, from the Greek *hemato-* meaning "blood" + *poiesis* meaning "to create."

7. Amino acids are the complex building blocks of proteins. The proteins are made by chemically hooking together amino acids into a long chain. Typical protein chains have anywhere from about FIFTY to about a THOUSAND amino-acid links. And each position in the chain is occupied by one of TWENTY DIFFERENT amino acids. In this they're like words and sentences, which can come in different lengths but are made up from a set of just 26 letters. If a single letter on this page is missing or transposed, we have an unfortunate typographical error. But if a single amino acid is missing or incorrect in its chain, it's a defect which can be fatal.

8. Those aware of these things stand in awe and agree with Shakespeare's exclamatory assessment: "What a piece of work is a man!"—*Hamlet,* Act II, Scene ii, Line 314.

✦   ✦   ✦

"I am fearfully
and wonderfully made:
MARVELOUS
are Thy works."
—Psalm 139:14

Reference: page 177, footnote 27.

APPENDIX B

SCIENCE

AND THE

SCRIPTURES

T ODAY'S *EXPLOSION* OF KNOWLEDGE[1] renders many science textbooks out
of date within a decade. The Bible is NOT a textbook on science, but
it always tells the truth. And even though its pages were written many centuries ago, it contains remarkable insights into scientific principles which are
as valid as tomorrow's research reports. God's written Word and the Creator's
book of Nature are in perfect harmony, for they have the same Author. A few
examples may serve to illustrate that harmony. Let's consider several SCIEN-
TIFIC PRINCIPLES in the light of pertinent SCRIPTURE STATEMENTS.

1. ROUNDNESS OF THE EARTH,
OR THE CIRCUIT OF ITS ORBIT

Isaiah 40:22, NIV—"He [God] sits enthroned above the CIRCLE of the
earth." Many still thought the world to be FLAT as late as the time of Christopher Columbus (around A.D. 1500). Since Isaiah's book dates from 740
B.C., it's clear that God's inspiration put the prophet centuries ahead of his
time.

Luke 17:34-36, The Living Bible—"That NIGHT two men will be ASLEEP
in the same room, and one will be taken away, the other left. Two women
will be WORKING TOGETHER at household tasks; one will be taken, the
other left; and so it will be with men WORKING side by side IN THE FIELDS."

This passage implies a ROUND earth, for the instantaneous Event of Christ's Second Coming will find some retired for the night and others engaged in their daytime duties.

Psalm 103:12—"As far as the EAST is from the WEST, so far hath He removed our transgressions from us." The North and South Poles are a fixed distance apart, so a traveler going northward eventually reaches the North Pole. If he then continues in the same direction, he'll be traveling SOUTH-WARD. But this limitation is NOT true for one traveling eastward or westward. A person traveling eastward will *always* travel eastward, no matter how often he goes around the globe. The God who inspired this verse also created the earth, and He knew its shape was a SPHERE.

2. GRAVITATION:
THE EARTH HANGS ON NOTHING

Job 26:7—"He . . . hangeth the earth upon NOTHING." Today astronauts take pictures showing the earth suspended in space, but in ancient days men theorized that the earth rested on the back of a huge elephant or on the shoulders of Atlas.

3. THE MOON AS A
NON-LUMINOUS REFLECTIVE BODY

Job 25:5—"The MOON . . . SHINETH NOT." *1 Corinthians 15:41*—"There is one glory of the SUN, and another glory of the MOON." In other words, the moon and the sun give *different kinds of light*. The SUN is self-luminous, as are all STARS, whereas the MOON "shineth not," but lights the night-time skies with reflected light only.

4. INFINITE NUMBER OF STARS

Jeremiah 33:22—"The host of heaven [the STARS] CANNOT be NUM-BERED." [2] Down through the centuries, man thought he COULD count the stars, as his naked eye gazed through smogless skies at stars gleaming like diamonds against the black velvet of night. Not until Galileo invented the telescope in 1609, opening new vistas to astronomy, did we begin to realize the truth of the prophet's apparent exaggeration. Modern telescopes have increased the star count beyond human comprehension.

5. ATMOSPHERIC PRESSURE

Job 28:25—"To make the WEIGHT for the WINDS." Barometric pressure is a measure of the "weight" of air affecting a column of mercury in a barometer.

6. EVAPORATION

Psalm 135:7, NKJV and *Jeremiah 10:13, NKJV*—"He [God] causes the VAPORS to ASCEND from the ends of the earth."

7. HYDROLOGIC CYCLE

Ecclesiastes 1:7—"All the rivers run into the sea; yet the sea is NOT FULL; unto the place from whence the rivers come, thither they RETURN again." All rivers and streams DO flow down to the sea. Then the sea water evaporates, rising to form clouds. Wind blows the clouds back over the land, where they release the water in the form of rain. Then the cycle repeats itself.

8. CHEMICAL COMPOSITION OF OUR BODIES

Genesis 2:7—"The Lord God formed Adam of the DUST of the GROUND." *Genesis 3:13-19*—"And the Lord God said . . . unto Adam . . . DUST thou art." We now know that our bodies are composed of the same chemical elements found in the earth—CARBON, IRON, CALCIUM, PHOSPHORUS, *etc.* Poetic imagination gives the fanciful idea that little GIRLS originated from "Sugar and spice and all things nice" and little BOYS came from "Snips and snails and puppy-dog tails."[3] But God's penman for Genesis, Moses, didn't have to rely on unaided human reason, and his record of Creation is scientifically accurate.

9. PROTECTIVE EFFECT OF OUR EARTH'S ATMOSPHERE

Isaiah 40:22—"It is He [God] . . . that stretcheth out the [atmospheric] heavens as a CURTAIN." Today we know that the ozone in our atmosphere forms a thin but vital protective layer to shield us from harmful solar rays.[4] Furthermore, the wispy "curtain" of air in our atmosphere protects us from the impact of meteors by burning them up through friction. As the meteors enter the atmosphere at speeds of about 40 miles per second, they become incandescent from the heat generated by friction against the air particles. "In a 24-hour period about 1,000,000 meteors . . . may strike the earth's atmosphere,"[5] but—thank God—virtually all these "shooting stars," as we call them, BURN UP before hitting the ground!

✦ ✦ ✦

10. UNIFORMITARIANISM, A GEOLOGIC
PRINCIPLE POPULAR AMONG EVOLUTIONISTS

2 Peter 3:3-4, RSV—"SCOFFERS" sneeringly ask, "'Where is the promise of His [Christ's] Coming?' For ever since the fathers fell asleep, all things have continued as they were from the beginning of creation." Uniformitarianism rejects the idea of CATASTROPHISM with its Biblical worldwide FLOOD as an explanation for the world as we know it. It claims that the ordinary natural forces now at work—like erosion—are sufficient to account for all geologic forms. The Bible mentions this atheistic philosophy, but it's important to note that the words come from *unbelievers.*

11. ROCK EROSION

Job 14:19—"The WATERS WEAR the STONES." The action of running water not only erodes tremendous amounts of SOIL but also etches the hardest ROCK.

12. TRIANGULAR PRISM

Job 38:24—"By what way is the LIGHT PARTED . . . ?" Sir Isaac Newton's experiments with optics demonstrated that a prism can SEPARATE white light into its component colors.

13. STERILE MASK & QUARANTINE

Leviticus 13:45-46—"The leper . . . shall put a COVERING upon his UPPER LIP, and he shall cry, Unclean, unclean. . . . He shall dwell ALONE; without [outside] the camp shall his habitation be." Many valid public health measures are found in Moses' inspired writings.

14. STERILIZATION

Numbers 31:23, NKJV—"Everything that can endure fire, you shall PUT THROUGH THE FIRE, and it shall be CLEAN. . . . But all that CANNOT endure fire you shall put through WATER."

15. ANESTHESIA DURING SURGERY

Genesis 2:21—"The Lord God caused a DEEP SLEEP to fall upon Adam, and he slept: and He TOOK ONE OF HIS RIBS, and CLOSED UP THE FLESH instead thereof." Before anesthesia was discovered about a hundred years ago, skeptics would laugh at this inspired record, saying: "How ridiculous! As if anyone would remain ASLEEP while you tore out one of his ribs!" But today we accept such a procedure as routine.

16. VITAL NATURE OF THE BLOOD

Leviticus 17:11—"The LIFE of the flesh IS IN THE BLOOD." Science today knows the truth of this Bible statement, for it's the circulation of this vital fluid that carries both life-giving *oxygen* and *nourishment* to every part of our body. Yet when George Washington became sick with a bad sore throat and laryngitis, well-intentioned but ignorant men "bled" him, draining off considerable amounts of his blood. However, the treatment of that day only caused the patient to grow weaker: "He was bled four times . . . , his strength meanwhile rapidly SINKING."[6] Washington died that night.

17. ONE BLOOD FOR ALL MANKIND

Acts 17:26—God "hath made of ONE BLOOD all nations of men on all the face of the earth." In 1930 Karl Landsteiner won a Nobel Prize for discovering that human blood has four chief groups: O, A, B, and AB. But all blood groups occur among all races! The Bible is correct—the many races of men all have the same basic blood types and are of "one blood."

18. PSYCHOSOMATIC ILLNESS, PSYCHOSOMATIC MEDICINE

Proverbs 17:22—"A MERRY HEART doeth good like a MEDICINE: but a BROKEN SPIRIT drieth the BONES." *Proverbs 16:24*—"PLEASANT WORDS are . . . HEALTH to the BONES." The close relationship between physical and emotional health is understood more and more today.

19. VITAMIN "A" DEFICIENCY

Jeremiah 14:6—"Their EYES did FAIL, because there was NO GRASS." Lack of vitamin A, which is found in carrots and other vegetables as well as fish-liver oils, results in night blindness and "eventual complete blindness."[7]

20. RADIO-TV BROADCASTING

Job 38:35, RSV—"Can you send forth LIGHTNINGS, that they may GO, and SAY to you, 'Here we are?'"

21. AUTOMOBILES OF TODAY, WITH THEIR HEADLIGHTS

Nahum 2:3-4—"The CHARIOTS shall be with FLAMING TORCHES in the day of His preparation. . . . The CHARIOTS shall RAGE in the STREETS, they shall jostle one against another in the BROADWAYS: they shall seem like TORCHES, they shall RUN like the LIGHTNINGS."

22. Human FLIGHT

Isaiah 60:8—"Who are these that FLY as a CLOUD, and as the DOVES to their windows?" The prophet describes what he's seen by the eye of Inspiration.

23. Destruction by NUCLEAR FISSION

2 Peter 3:10-12—At the end of the world, "the heavens [the earth's atmosphere, the atmospheric heavens] shall pass away with a GREAT NOISE, and the ELEMENTS shall MELT with FERVENT HEAT, the EARTH also and the works that are therein shall be BURNED UP. . . . All these things shall be DISSOLVED, . . . the heavens being on fire shall be DISSOLVED, and the ELEMENTS shall MELT with FERVENT HEAT." For centuries, skeptics would ridicule religious persons who spoke about the final destruction of the world by fire, pointing out how difficult it usually was even to keep a good bonfire going, so it would be absolutely beyond the realm of possibility for the whole earth to be on fire or the "elements" to "melt with fervent heat"! But since the atomic age began a few decades ago, science itself is worrying about that very possibility. Today marchers in the nuclear disarmament movement fear that not only GOD but MAN could destroy the earth. *Revelation 11:18, TEV,* records heavenly voices saying: "The time has come to destroy those who DESTROY the EARTH!"

24. ATOMIC THEORY

Hebrews 11:3—"Through faith we understand that the worlds were framed by the word of God, so that things which are SEEN are NOT made of things which do APPEAR." Man NOW knows that all matter is composed of tiny molecules made up of even tinier atomic particles, so that something we see and touch—like a table or this book—is actually made of *invisible* ATOMS. But the question is, WHO TOLD the prophet?

The *Bible statements* quoted above were all recorded many, many centuries ago on the inspired pages of Holy Scripture. The *scientific principles* listed were established as scientific truths much later, in some cases rather recently. But individually and collectively, they DO confirm the Bible. As English astronomer SIR WILLIAM HERSCHEL (1738-1822) stated:

"All human discoveries seem to be made only for the purpose of CONFIRMING more and more strongly, the TRUTHS contained in the Sacred Scriptures."

Nature guards her secrets well. But slowly—as man's knowledge increases—SCIENCE is catching up with the BIBLE.

✦ ✦ ✦

Many great, eminent men of SCIENCE were also Bible-believing Christians and creationists, men who believed in the inspiration and authority of the Bible, as well as in the deity and saving work of Jesus Christ. Even a short list of those scientists must include the following:

JOSEPH LISTER ★ LOUIS PASTEUR ★ ISAAC NEWTON
JOHANN KEPLER ★ ROBERT BOYLE ★ GEORGES CUVIER
CHARLES BABBAGE ★ JAMES CLERK MAXWELL ★ MICHAEL FARADAY
LORD KELVIN ★ WILLIAM HERSCHEL ★ GREGOR MENDEL
LOUIS AGASSIZ ★ JAMES SIMPSON ★ LEONARDO DA VINCI
BLAISE PASCAL ★ JAMES JOULE ★ CAROLUS LINNEAUS
HUMPHREY DAVY ★ JOSEPH HENRY ★ RUDOLPH VIRCHOW
JOHN HERSCHEL ★ FRANCIS BACON ★ SAMUEL F. B. MORSE

—and others. Their achievements have been phenomenal.

〜

Notes to Appendix B

1. Daniel 12:4 tells us that in "the *time* of the *end* . . . KNOWLEDGE shall be INCREASED."
2. Verses like Genesis 22:17 and Hebrews 11:12 imply that the stars in the sky are as COUNTLESS as the INNUMERABLE grains of sand on the seashore! How did the Bible writers know? The omniscient God told them. Inspiration says, "He [God] counts the number of the stars; He calls them all by NAME. . . . His understanding is INFINITE." Psalm 147:4-5, NKJV.
3. British poet Robert Southey (1774-1843), "What All the World Is Made Of."
4. "The TOTAL amount of ozone in a vertical column above the earth's surface, if it were separated from the air with which it is mixed and brought to conditions of normal temperature and pressure, would form a gaseous column only a few MILLI-METERS high. . . . However, even this minute amount of ozone is sufficient to absorb ALL the solar energy in the ultraviolet . . . thus protecting life on the earth from a LETHAL excess of short-wave radiation." *Encyclopedia Britannica* (1967 edition), Volume 16, p. 1198, article "Ozone."
5. *Encyclopedia Britannica* (1967 edition), Volume 15, p. 270, article "Meteor."
6. *Encyclopedia Britannica* (1967 edition), Volume 23, p. 244, article "Washington, George."
7. *Encyclopedia Britannica* (1967 edition), Volume 23, p. 85, article "Vitamins."

References: p. 185, footnote 12; p. 526 middle; p. 683, footnote 307.

APPENDIX C

∾

THE

"SEVENTY WEEKS"

OF DANIEL 9

THE BOOK OF DANIEL is of tremendous importance because of its penetrating prophecies. The one in CHAPTER 9 is of special interest not only because it forecasts the time when the MESSIAH would arrive but also because of its prominent use in the theology of the SECRET RAPTURE (see Chapter 17 of this volume).

Let's look at this prophetic passage in DANIEL 9:24-27.

24   Seventy weeks are determined upon thy people and upon the holy city, to finish the transgression, and to make an end of sins, and to seal up the vision and prophecy, and to anoint the most Holy.

25   Know therefore and understand, that from the going forth of the commandment to restore and to build Jerusalem unto the Messiah the Prince shall be seven weeks, and threescore and two weeks: the street shall be built again, and the wall, even in troublous times.

26   And after threescore and two weeks shall Messiah be cut off, but not for Himself: and the people of the prince that shall come shall destroy the city and the sanctuary; and the end thereof shall be with a flood, and unto the end of the war desolations are determined.

27   And He shall confirm the covenant with many for one week: and in the midst of the week He shall cause the sacrifice and the oblation to cease. . . .

The obvious meaning of this passage is as follows:

A LINE-by-LINE Analysis

"**Seventy weeks**" = If we multiply 70 weeks X 7 days to a week, we get 490 prophetic days. And using the DAY-FOR-A-YEAR PRINCIPLE of Numbers 14:34 and Ezekiel 4:6 ("I have appointed thee each day for a year"), we get a time-period of 490 actual years.

This method of computing prophetic time is so widely recognized and accepted by scholars that it is seen directly in some Bible translations: for example, The Revised Standard Version and The Amplified Bible both say "Seventy weeks of YEARS" rather than weeks of DAYS. The Good News Bible, Today's English Version, says, "Seven times seventy YEARS," and The Living Bible says simply "490 YEARS."

But the greatest proof that this interpretation is correct is seen in the fact that it WORKS—historical fulfillments of time prophecies correspond exactly with this day-for-a-year mathematical computation, as you'll see below.

"**determined upon THY PEOPLE**" = Refers to Daniel's people, the JEWS. The 490 years were given to the Jews as one last chance—one final period of probation—after many failings.

"**thy holy city**" = JERUSALEM, which at this time lay in ruins.

"**to anoint the most Holy**" = Jesus was anointed by the Holy Spirit in the form of a dove at His baptism in A.D. 27.[1] In His first sermon Jesus said, "He hath anointed Me to preach the gospel. . . ."[2] (Some Bible scholars believe this phrase could refer to the anointing of the heavenly sanctuary prior to Christ's inauguration as High Priest.)

"**to make reconciliation for iniquity**" = Accomplished both by Jesus' death on the cross[3] and by His ministry as High Priest in heaven.[4]

"**from the going forth of the commandment to restore and to build Jerusalem**" = Jerusalem lay in ruins, having been destroyed by Babylonian armies under Nebuchadnezzar. But the three decrees successively issued by the great Persian kings CYRUS, DARIUS, and ARTAXERXES are matters of historical record and finally went into effect in the fall of 457 B.C.[5]

"**unto the Messiah the Prince**" = Jesus is the Messiah, as He Himself declared.[6] And because the name "Christ" means the same as "Messiah,"[7] every time we call Him "Jesus CHRIST," we acknowledge that He IS the Messiah.

This prediction is so momentous that God sent the angel GABRIEL himself to give it to Daniel.[8] It foretells with mathematical precision the time when King Jesus would come and begin His work in this world as the promised Messiah. The prophet Micah had already said the PLACE He was to be born was the "little town of Bethlehem" [9]—here Daniel gives us the TIME. "When the fulness of the TIME was come, God sent forth His Son, made of a woman." [10]

Shortly after His baptism "Jesus came into Galilee, preaching the gospel of the kingdom of God, and saying, "The TIME is fulfilled." [11] What time did He mean? Surely it was this prophetic time of which Daniel wrote that was to reach to "the Messiah the Prince." He had indeed come, and with His own lips He announced that the time had expired and His reign as Messiah had begun.

"shall be seven weeks, and threescore and two weeks" = Adding these fragmentary periods together, we get **7 + 60 + 2**, for a total of **69 weeks**. Then a further computation shows those *69 weeks X 7 days to a week* amounts to 483 prophetic days or 483 actual years, using the day-for-a-year principle. Please see the CHART on the next page.

MATHEMATICS Verifies Jesus' Messiahship

This year-day principle is verified by the fact that Jesus was *anointed* as Messiah by the Holy Spirit at His BAPTISM in the fall of A.D. 27, just as predicted! Note the arithmetic: 483 years *minus* 457 B.C. = A.D. 27. (In crossing from "B.C." to "A.D." one year must be ADDED because there never was a "zero" year, but A.D. 1 immediately followed B.C. 1.) Thus, in addition to other abundant evidence, MATHEMATICS proves the Messiah is Jesus.

Some may puzzle as to how Christ could begin His work in A.D. 27 when the Record says He was "about 30 years of age" when He started His public ministry.[12] This is because an error of about four years crept in when the Christian Era was first computed. That Christ was NOT born in A.D. 1 is evident from the fact that when He was born HEROD THE GREAT was still alive, and Herod died in 4 B.C.! [13]

Jesus did not assume His role as Messiah until He was anointed, and He was not anointed until His baptism.[14] Finally, Jesus was baptized "in the fifteenth year of the reign of Tiberius Cæsar," [15] which history records as A.D. 27—*the very year predicted centuries before!*

The prophecy points not to Jesus' BIRTH but to the beginning of His ministry. Just as holders of public office must reach a certain age before they qualify, priests were anointed at the age of thirty.[16] As noted above, in A.D. 27 Jesus reached that age, was anointed by the Holy Spirit, and began His ministry as the Messiah.

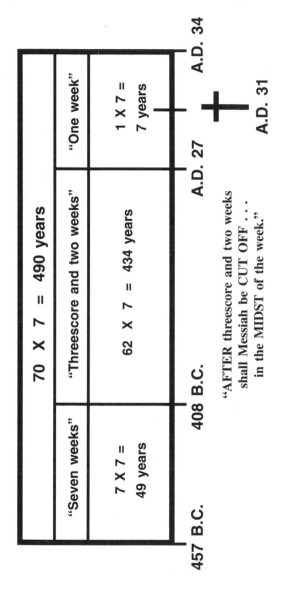

The "Seventy Weeks" of Daniel 9:24-27

70 X 7 = 490 years

"Seven weeks"

7 X 7 = 49 years

"Threescore and two weeks"

62 X 7 = 434 years

"One week"

1 X 7 = 7 years

457 B.C.

408 B.C.

A.D. 27

A.D. 31

A.D. 34

"AFTER threescore and two weeks shall Messiah be CUT OFF . . . in the MIDST of the week."

"Even forty days, each DAY for a YEAR, . . . even forty years."—Numbers 14:34.

"I have appointed thee each DAY for a YEAR."—Ezekiel 4:6.

THREE SUCCESSIVE PERIODS—IN ONE TIME PROPHECY

The CHART on the preceding page shows that the seventy weeks were subdivided into three smaller blocks of time:

- The FIRST time-block—"seven weeks"—was a 49-year period devoted to REBUILDING the city: "the street shall be built again, and the wall, even in troublous times."

- The SECOND time-block was a 62-week period of WAITING for the Messiah, making a total of 69 weeks before that great event.

- The THIRD time-block was a FINAL week—which in turn was divided in half—foretelling MESSIAH'S DEATH "in the *midst* of the week," as we'll now see.

"**And AFTER threescore and two weeks shall Messiah be CUT OFF**" = This tells us plainly that Messiah would be KILLED, or "cut off out of the land of the living." [17]

Note carefully that Jesus would be killed "after" the 69 weeks, not within that time period. Gabriel is telling us that Jesus would be put to death during the 70th or final week of this overall time prophecy.

"**but NOT for Himself**" = Jesus was put to death not because of any crime or sin He committed, since He never sinned. He was put to death as a Sacrifice for others.

"**And He shall confirm the covenant with many for ONE WEEK**" = This was the 70th and final week of probation for the Jewish people. Jesus, during His three-and-a-half-year public ministry, repeatedly offered God's chosen people, the Jews, every opportunity to accept the gospel. Then for three-and-a-half MORE years His apostles tried to evangelize the Jews before turning to the Gentiles.

"**in the MIDST of the week He shall cause the sacrifice and the oblation to cease**" = The midst of the week would be three-and-a-half years after Jesus' baptism in the fall of A.D. 27, bringing us to the spring of A.D. 31—the very time of the CRUCIFIXION!

DID He "cause the sacrifice and the oblation [a word meaning religious *offering*] to cease" at that very time? Yes! God had taught His people to offer ANIMAL sacrifices which FORESHADOWED the death of His Son, "the Lamb of God, which taketh away the sin of the world." [18] In the Temple, where the blood of the sacrificial offerings was applied, a magnificent veil or curtain of heavy material separated the Holy Place from the Most Holy Place. When Jesus breathed His last and died, providing the Supreme Sacrifice once and for all time, "the veil of the Temple was rent in twain [ripped in two] from the top to the bottom" by an unseen Hand,[19] signifying that God would no longer accept any sacrifice but Christ's. This happened at the EXACT time predicted—"in the midst of the week"!

GOD'S DIVINE FOREKNOWLEDGE!

We see, then, that Gabriel's prophecy foretold the date of the Cross precisely: three-and-a-half years "after" the 69 weeks brings us to "the MIDST" or MIDDLE of the 70th and final week, which was A.D. 31. Jesus, in His divine foreknowledge, knew not only HOW He would die[20] but WHEN. That's why He would often say, "My time is not yet come."[21] Then just prior to His betrayal and death He said, "My time is at hand"[22] and finally, "The hour is come."[23] This TIME ELEMENT is further proof that Jesus is the Son of God.

"to finish the transgression" = Gabriel told Daniel that his people, the Jews, had 70 weeks or 490 years of probationary time either to finish their transgression and become loyal children or else to fill their cup of iniquity to the full by rejecting God's Son. The Lord is patient, but Israel as a nation failed Him so many times! Gabriel brought this heavenly message just when Daniel had been "praying, and confessing my sin and the sin of my people Israel. . . . Yea, all Israel have TRANSGRESSED Thy Law. . . . We have SINNED against Thee. . . . We have REBELLED."[24] So God told Daniel, in answer to his prayer, that Israel would mercifully have *one last chance*. God would liberate them from their exile as prisoners in Babylon and Persia and help them rebuild the ruins of their homeland.

They would have 490 years to prove themselves, during which time the Messiah would come. But when Jesus did come and was so rudely rejected, He had to tell them:

> "You are sons of those who MURDERED the prophets. Fill up, then, the measure of your fathers' guilt. Serpents, brood of vipers! How can you escape the condemnation of hell? . . . O Jerusalem, Jerusalem, the one who KILLS the prophets and STONES those who are sent to her! How often I wanted to gather your children together, as a hen gathers her chicks under her wings, but you were not willing! See! Your house is left to you DESOLATE."[25]

Instead of accepting their Savior, the Jews cried, "Crucify Him! . . . Crucify Him! . . . His blood be on us, and on our children."[26] When Peter and John tried to preach Christ in Jerusalem, the Jews had them arrested and beaten.[27]

But the "last straw" was the stoning of Stephen. This fearless man of God, in the power of the Holy Spirit, reviewed the history of Israel with its

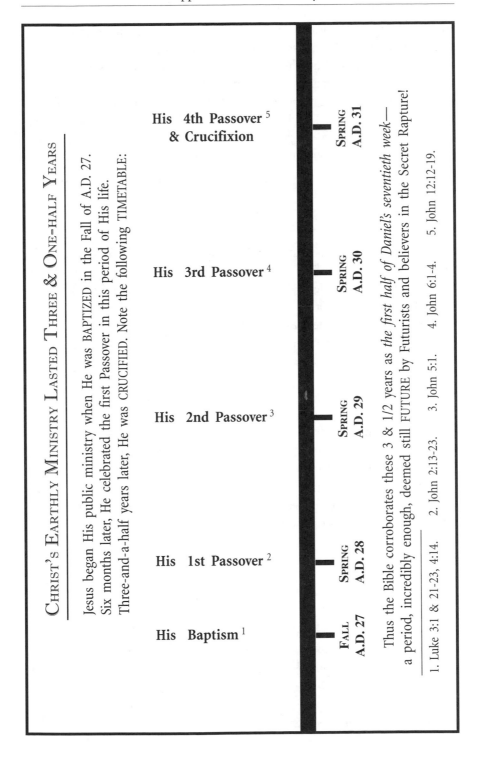

CHRIST'S EARTHLY MINISTRY LASTED THREE & ONE-HALF YEARS

Jesus began His public ministry when He was BAPTIZED in the Fall of A.D. 27. Six months later, He celebrated the first Passover in this period of His life. Three-and-a-half years later, He was CRUCIFIED. Note the following TIMETABLE:

His Baptism [1]
**FALL
A.D. 27**

His 1st Passover [2]
**SPRING
A.D. 28**

His 2nd Passover [3]
**SPRING
A.D. 29**

His 3rd Passover [4]
**SPRING
A.D. 30**

His 4th Passover [5]
& Crucifixion
**SPRING
A.D. 31**

Thus the Bible corroborates these 3 & 1/2 years as *the first half of Daniel's seventieth week*— a period, incredibly enough, deemed still FUTURE by Futurists and believers in the Secret Rapture!

1. Luke 3:1 & 21-23, 4:14.   2. John 2:13-23.   3. John 5:1.   4. John 6:1-4.   5. John 12:12-19.

tragic failings all the way from their ancestor Abraham to their becoming "betrayers and murderers," as he put it, of God's dear Son. [28]

When Stephen finished his powerful sermon, the Jews, instead of falling on their knees and repenting, dragged Stephen out of the city and mercilessly stoned him to death [29] to FINISH their TRANSGRESSION and fill their cup of sin to the full. This happened in A.D. 34—exactly three-and-a-half years after Jesus' death, to close not only the final 70th week but also to bring their allotted probation of 490 years to a bitter close.

> "Then Paul and Barnabas grew bold and said, 'It was necessary that the word of God should be spoken to you [Jews] first; but since you REJECT it, and judge yourselves UNWORTHY of everlasting life, behold, we turn to the GENTILES.'" [30]

"the people of the prince that shall come shall DESTROY the city and the sanctuary" = The "prince" here predicted was TITUS, the Roman general who destroyed Jerusalem in A.D. 70. This is obvious from many indisputable facts of history.

In the first place, he was a PRINCE, being the elder son of Emperor Vespasian of Rome. Titus himself later succeeded his father as Roman emperor—Vespasian following Nero and reigning from A.D. 69 to 79 and Titus reigning from A.D. 79 to 81.

Secondly, history records that his Roman soldiers, "the PEOPLE of the prince that shall come," DID destroy the city in one of the most terrible sieges of all time when the Jews refused to surrender. Historian Josephus records that more than a MILLION Jews perished from starvation and the fighting, and those not killed were sold into slavery.

Thirdly, in the conflict the "sanctuary" or Temple in Jerusalem also was destroyed as Gabriel predicted, but note the minute accuracy of this verse: Titus himself wished to preserve the Temple as a priceless ornament of the Roman Empire, but the ROMAN SOLDIERS, tasting victory after a long and frustrating siege, would not be restrained. Contrary to orders, they set the Temple on fire so it was completely destroyed. Therefore it was not Titus, the prince himself, who did this, but "the PEOPLE of the prince"—exactly as God said!

A few items like the golden candlesticks were saved from the flaming Temple and taken as plunder. To this very day, these can be seen commemorated in sculpture on Rome's well-preserved Arch of Titus (of the same pattern as the later *Arc de Triomphe* in Paris). Through the centuries, this monument has witnessed to the fact that Daniel's words were literally fulfilled concerning Jerusalem's "sanctuary."

Now that we've analyzed this important passage, you may well ask:
**"HOW can anyone find in these verses seven years
that apply to a FUTURE Secret Rapture?"**

How, indeed! But believe it or not some people do, because they were taught that these verses apply to Antichrist, who they believe will appear in the future. They take the final week, the 70th, AWAY from the overall time prophecy and project it into the FUTURE! There are several reasons why that teaching CANNOT be true, and here are a few of them:

FALLACIES OF FUTURISM REFUTED

1. The Antichrist can be easily identified as being already PRESENT in the stream of history, rather than yet to arise in the FUTURE. See Chapter 19 on "Antichrist Unmasked: The Beast Power Identified," above.

2. The 69 weeks were to reach "UNTO the Messiah the Prince." Then Messiah would be cut off "AFTER" 69 weeks (note that the word is not "in" but "after" 69 weeks)—that is, during the 70th week. Therefore, since the Crucifixion took place DURING the 70th week, the 70th week cannot possibly refer to a yet future period of time.

3. Futurists claim there's a GAP between the 69th and 70th weeks of Daniel's prophecy. But they *assume* this gap without a shred of Bible evidence! There was NO GAP between the first period (7 prophetic weeks or 49 actual years, devoted to rebuilding Jerusalem) and the second (62 more prophetic weeks, reaching to the Messiah the Prince). All agree that those first two periods followed in succession and ended when Jesus began His public ministry at His baptism. Since the first two periods passed WITHOUT a gap between, and since neither Daniel nor anyone else made any mention of a gap, it seems logical that the third period—the 70th week—would follow in sequence without a gap.

4. When Gabriel told Daniel that "Seventy weeks are determined" upon his people, the verb for "are determined" is actually singular, not plural, indicating that the whole period is viewed as a SINGLE block of time.

We should object to any interpretation that puts gaps into that seventy-week period. There can be no time gaps in TIME prophecies, for if we insert indefinite gaps, *there's no point in calculating the time at all!* What would we think of a yardstick that had a strip of ELASTIC inserted between the 35th and 36th inches? It could then be stretched to fit any measurement desired, but that would defeat the very purpose of a yardstick!

And what would we think if we had to travel 70 miles down a road and find the first 69 miles to be CONSECUTIVE miles but then encounter a sign telling us that the 70th or last mile is about 2000 miles down the road?!? Yet if this "gap theory" were correct, then the supposed gap of nearly 2000 years is already LONGER than the entire period originally prophesied!

5.   This passage deals with Christ's FIRST Advent, not with the Rapture or any other aspect of His SECOND Coming. There's no Biblical justification for saying that Daniel speaks in one breath of the First Advent and Crucifixion of Christ, then in the next breath jumps to the subject of the Second Coming. Nor is any Scriptural proof offered for this interpretation—it's simply assumed to be so.

6.   Furthermore, this passage deals primarily with JESUS—not with some "future Fuehrer," to use Hal Lindsey's term for the Antichrist. In fact, the prophecy points so unmistakably to the time of the MESSIAH'S COMING, and so directly foretold HIS DEATH, that in later centuries Jewish rabbis who did not accept Jesus DISCOURAGED its study and finally pronounced a CURSE on all who attempt to compute the time elements! [31]

The outstanding figure in this passage is Christ, not Antichrist! There's a world of difference in these two schools of thought: One says the 70th week is FUTURE—the other says it's FULFILLED! One says there's a HUGE GAP between the 69th and the 70th weeks—the other requires NO GAP. One says the 70th week pertains to ANTICHRIST—the other, to JESUS CHRIST!

7.   Futurists claim that "the people of the prince that shall come" refers to some future Antichrist who will build a new Jewish Temple in Jerusalem. But Daniel's prophecy teaches that "the people of the prince that shall come" will not BUILD anything. On the contrary, they shall DESTROY both the city and the Temple—as the Roman armies led by Titus did in A.D. 70!

As a matter of fact, when the Temple was aflame, the heat became so intense that large quantities of GOLD the building contained MELTED and ran down between the stones of the Temple. So later, stone after stone was thrown down and turned over and over by plunderers seeking the gold that had melted. As Jesus had said: "There shall not be left here one stone upon another, that shall not be thrown down." [32] The scenario that has a FUTURE Antichrist BUILD a new Jewish Temple also has him set up within the Temple a heathen idol to be worshipped. If this were so, the Antichrist would not then DESTROY the Temple—he'd PRESERVE it as a shrine of false religion! But all this is based on assumption and conjecture—and it doesn't fit the Bible blueprint at all.

8. Futurists who realize they cannot ignore history try to argue, "Of course we know that Jerusalem was destroyed in A.D. 70. 'The people of the prince' did that as a *partial* fulfillment of this prophecy. But the *real* fulfillment will occur when the prince himself comes as the FUTURE Antichrist."

This is a lame argument at best, for how much credence can we put in an interpretation that *separates* a PRINCE from his PEOPLE by two thousand years? In contrast to a gap theory that AMPUTATES the 70th week from the very time block that gives it its name, you can accept Daniel's prophecy just as it reads, with every detail falling into its proper place with a harmony that can only be divine!

In the face of all this evidence, we must conclude that those "seven years" Secret Rapturists talk about in their theological scheme are the result of a colossal misinterpretation!

The astounding prophecy of the Seventy Weeks
is one that Nostradamus MISSED!

Notes to Appendix C

1. Matthew 3:16-17, Mark 1:9-11, Luke 3:21-22, Acts 10:38.
2. Luke 4:18.
3. Romans 5:10.
4. Hebrews 2:17, 4:14-16, and 7:23-25.
5. The little book written by Ezra the scribe documents these three royal decrees. The decree of CYRUS is mentioned in Ezra 1:1-2 & 7-11; 5:13 & 17; and 6:3-4. That of DARIUS is mentioned in Ezra 6:1 & 6-13. That of ARTAXERXES is mentioned in Ezra 7:1-28. Since the first two decrees were impeded by neighboring force around Jerusalem—as shown in chapter 4 of Ezra—the work had to "cease." That's why *all three were needed,* and in fact all three are referred to as ONE "commandment" to achieve the same end in Ezra 6:14. The third and last of these decrees, the one which not only allowed work to resume but also *restored the Jews' civil government* in Jerusalem again with "magistrates and judges"(Ezra 7:25), went into effect "in the seventh year of the king" Artaxerxes' reign. That year was 457 B.C. — the key date which began the Seventy Week prophecy mentioned in Daniel 9:25.
6. John 4:25-26.
7. *Christ* is Greek and *Messiah* is Hebrew for "anointed one" or KING. Even today the crowned heads of Europe are ceremonially *anointed* with a few drops of oil upon assuming the throne. *Jesus* is Greek for "Savior" (Matthew 1:21), so the Lord's name "Jesus Christ" means "Savior King."
8. See Daniel 9:21-23.   9. Micah 5:2.
10. Galatians 4:4.   11. Mark 1:14-15.
12. Luke 3:23.
13. See Matthew 2:13-20. Encyclopedias confirm the date of Herod's death as 4 B.C.
14. Compare Acts 10:38 with Mark 1:9-11 and Luke 3:22.
15. Luke 3:1 and 3:22.
16. "Thirty years old and upward." See Numbers 4:3, 23, 30, 35, 39, 43, 47.
17. Isaiah 53:8.   18. John 1:29.
19. Matthew 27:50-51, Mark 15:37-38, Luke 23:45-46.
20. That is, on a cross: See Psalm 22:16 and John 12:32-33.
21. See, for example, John 2:4, 7:6, 7:8, 7:30, 8:20.
22. Matthew 26:18.   23. John 17:1 and Matthew 26:45.
24. Daniel 9:20, 11, 8-9.   25. Matthew 23:31-38, NKJV.
26. Mark 15:13-14 & Matthew 27:25.
27. Acts 5:17-18, 40.   28. Acts 7:52.
29. Acts 7:58.   30. Acts 13:46, NKJV.
31. See Talmud *Sanhedrin* 97b, Soncino edition, p. 659.
32. Matthew 24:2.

Reference: page 212, footnote 35.

APPENDIX D
POST-RESURRECTION APPEARANCES OF THE LIVING CHRIST

Scripture Text:	Christ Appeared to:	Location:
John 20:1,11-18; Mark 16:9	Mary Magdalene	At Christ's empty tomb
Matthew 28:1-10	The other women	Returning from the tomb
Luke 24:34; 1 Cor. 15:5	The apostle Simon Peter (Cephas)	Not specified
Luke 24:13-32; Mark 16:12	Cleopas and another disciple	On the road to Emmaus
John 20:19-25; Luke 24:36-43	The ten apostles, Thomas absent	In the Upper Room
John 20:26-29; Mark 16:14	The eleven apostles, Thomas present	In the Upper Room
John 21:1-14 (see John 6:1)	Seven of the disciples	At the Sea of Galilee/Tiberias
1 Corinthians 15:6	More than 500 brethren	Not specified
1 Corinthians 15:7	His brother James	Not specified
Matthew 28:16	The eleven apostles	On a mountain in Galilee
Acts 1:2-12; Luke 24:49-52	The eleven apostles, at the Ascension	Mount Olivet, near Bethany
Acts 9:1-6; 1 Cor. 9:1 & 15:8	Saul / The apostle Paul	On the road to Damascus
Revelation 1:9-19	John the Revelator	On the Island of Patmos

After His cruel death, Jesus "showed Himself ALIVE . . . by many infallible PROOFS . . . whereof we ALL are WITNESSES." —Acts 1:3, 2:32, 3:15.

"What is His name, and what is His SON'S name, if thou canst tell?"

—Proverbs 30:4

APPENDIX E

~

WHAT MAKES YOU THINK JESUS IS MICHAEL, THE ARCHANGEL?

ANY FAITHFUL CHRISTIAN finds the idea that Jesus is a mere angel utterly unacceptable. Our reaction to any such suggestion that dethrones our Lord is "No way!"—and properly so. The Jehovah's Witnesses, who do not accept the deity of Christ, sometimes use this teaching to detract from our estimation of the Lord Jesus as a full-fledged Member of the Holy Trinity. They claim that their identification of Christ as Michael lowers Him to the level of mere angels and "shows conclusively that he [Christ] is NOT EQUAL to Jehovah God." [1]

Still, there are a number of good reasons why many Bible scholars believe that the Personage known in Scripture as "Michael, the Archangel," CAN be identified as our Lord, Jesus Christ—

WITHOUT accepting the belittling conclusions of Jehovah's Witnesses,

WITHOUT making the Son of God an angel, and

WITHOUT detracting one iota from His divine deity as GOD in the fullest sense of that word. Let's examine these reasons point by point.

POINT #1

When the Son of God became incarnate by being born in the flesh through the Virgin Mary, He was given many appropriate names. A few of these are "Emmanuel,"[2] "Jesus,"[3] "the Lamb of God,"[4] "Christ,"[5] *etc.* Since we know Jesus pre-existed throughout the ages of eternity[6] long before coming as the Babe in Bethlehem, it's only natural to assume that He had SOME name before that time.[7] What WAS that name? The wise man Solomon, after asking us several questions about God, ends by inquiring: "What is His name, and what is His SON'S name, if thou canst tell?"[8] Before we're finished here, you'll find good reason to conclude that Christ's former name in heaven was "MICHAEL."

POINT #2

In Biblical times, names were looked upon as profoundly important. Nearly every name had a specific MEANING which was either immediately obvious or which became apparent upon translation. For instance, a few examples may serve to illustrate the fact that the letters "**EL**" in a name pertained specifically to GOD:

- ELIJAH means "my GOD is Jehovah."
- DANIEL means "judgment of GOD."
- GABRIEL means "man of GOD."

And the name MICHAEL means the One "who is like GOD." Absolutely no one is "like God" but God Himself. We know that Lucifer, in his devilish pride, said: "I will be like the Most High."[9] But he's doomed to disappointment, for no created being—even a dazzling angel like Lucifer—can ever be equal to his Creator.

Therefore, in the case of Michael, we see in the very NAME itself a potent clue which points unerringly to Christ and Christ alone, who is "like God" because He IS God.[10]

POINT #3

Some believe the term "archangel" couldn't refer to Christ because they think that would mean our Lord is a mere angel, a created being. And they'd be right—IF the Archangel were merely another angel, chosen from the ranks of the angelic host to serve in a position of authority. If that were the case, no Christian would dare to think that Christ could be the Archangel, for that would depose Him from His throne of deity and make the Creator simply a created being, although an exalted one.

But we must understand that the prefix "arch" comes from the Greek word meaning RULER, one who REIGNS over—as in our word *monarch*. We know that our heavenly Father, as God, rules or reigns over all faithful believers without being a human being Himself. By the same token, our Lord Jesus can assume the position of RULER over all angels without being an angel Himself. [11]

So in saying that Jesus is Michael, the Archangel, the Bible is simply calling Him the Supreme Commander or divine Leader of the angelic host, just as our United States President is called the official Commander-in-Chief of all our armed forces. That doesn't mean the President is a soldier, wearing a uniform. He's ABOVE all soldiers, sailors, airmen, or marines. He outranks them and rules them, according to the Constitution. According to the Bible— the Christian "Constitution"—Jesus Christ has the honor of being "Commander-in-Chief" or Lord over all the angelic forces of heaven. Serving in this capacity does not detract from His deity or make Him in any way a created being, as our next point proves.

POINT #4

Another example clinching the fact that Michael need not be an angel Himself in order to be their Ruler is seen in Genesis 1:28, when God gave MAN "dominion over" all creatures of the animal kingdom, whether fish, fowl, or animal.

"Dominion" means LORDSHIP or authority to rule. Thus God placed man in charge of His creation, so man would dominate or rule the animals as a LORD rules his subjects. If man can rule the animal kingdom WITHOUT being one of the animals, WHY insist that Christ can't be the Archangel without being one of the angels?

POINT #5

The Word of God makes all this very clear in Joshua 5:13-15, NKJV. Let's read it:

> "It came to pass, when Joshua was by Jericho, that he lifted his eyes and looked, and behold, a MAN stood opposite him with His sword drawn in His hand. And Joshua went to Him and said to Him, 'Are You for us or for our adversaries?' So He said, 'No, but as COMMANDER of the army of the Lord I have now come.' And Joshua fell on his face to the earth and WORSHIPED, and said to Him, 'What does my LORD say to His servant?' Then *the COMMANDER of the Lord's army* said to Joshua, 'Take your sandal off your foot, for the place where you stand is HOLY.' And Joshua did so."

Any Bible student will immediately recognize the divine Being visiting Joshua on this occasion as none other than the Lord Jesus Christ in His pre-incarnate state. At different times, the Lord appeared to others in the Old Testament, like Abraham[12] and Jacob.[13] On this occasion with Joshua—only two verses beyond the portion quoted above[14]—the Bible tells us plainly that it's "the LORD" who speaks with Joshua and tells him how to capture the city of Jericho without even fighting, because the walls would come tumbling down!

But let's analyze that quoted passage a bit further. We read that the heavenly Being assumed the form of "a Man" with his "sword drawn." When Joshua inquires, he's told that the Stranger is "Captain of the host of the Lord," as the King James Version puts it. The Living Bible says: "I am Commander-in-Chief of the Lord's army." This is just another way of saying "Archangel" or Ruler of the angel hosts.

Even though we know that this was the Archangel or Captain of the angel armies, we also know that this was NO MERE ANGEL. Two facts make this clear.

First, we read that then "Joshua fell on his face . . . and WORSHIPED" at the feet of this "Man." And the Stranger did not stop him from doing so, which certainly would have been the case IF Joshua had been worshipping an angel. We know this from Revelation 19:10, NIV, when John the Revelator fell down to worship an angel, the angel abruptly stopped him. Please note: "I [John] fell at his feet to worship him [the angel]. But he said to me, 'Do NOT do it! . . . Worship GOD!'" This same truth is repeated on another occasion in Revelation 22:8-9, NIV—"I [John] fell down to worship at the feet of the angel. . . . But he said to me, "Do NOT do it! . . . Worship GOD!"

Secondly, this divine Being not only accepts the worship of Joshua but also tells him to take off his shoes, "For the place where you stand is HOLY." Earlier, MOSES had the same experience when he met the Lord God—again, Jesus in His pre-incarnate state[15]—at the BURNING BUSH and was told: "Take your sandals off your feet, for the place where you stand is HOLY ground."[16]

We see, then, that the Leader of the heavenly armies is no mere angel—He's the divine LORD JESUS HIMSELF!

POINT #6

Other Scriptures which mention the name Michael lead us to understand He is a Very Special Person—He must be, in fact, a heavenly Being of ROYAL blood. For instance, God sent the angel Gabriel to give special messages to the prophet Daniel.[17] This angel messenger told Daniel that "Michael" is "the GREAT PRINCE who protects your people."[18]

A PRINCE is the SON of a KING, of course, and Jesus is the Son of God, the King of Heaven. Christians would call Him "the great Prince." The angel GABRIEL, in the very same book, calls "the Messiah, the PRINCE." [19] Now please note what we've learned from the pen of the same inspired writer, Daniel:

A. "MESSIAH" = "the Prince"

B. "MICHAEL" = "the great Prince"

C. Therefore, since "two things equal to the SAME thing are equal to EACH OTHER," the MESSIAH and MICHAEL are the same Person, JESUS CHRIST.

POINT #7

God's Word gives inspired insight into Lucifer's terrible rebellion against the government of God: "There was WAR in HEAVEN: MICHAEL and his angels fought against the dragon; and the dragon fought and his angels, and prevailed not; neither was their place found any more in heaven. And the great dragon was cast out, that old serpent, called the Devil, and Satan, which deceiveth the whole world: he was cast out into the earth, and his angels were cast out with him." [20]

Fortunately the Bible here clearly identifies "the dragon" as "that old serpent, called the Devil, and Satan"—so there's no question of the adversary's identity on that side of the controversy. And the various points considered above (the pre-incarnate Christ as "Commander-in-Chief of the Lord's army," [21] *etc.*) lead many to conclude that the great Leader on the other side was none other than Christ Himself. Thus MICHAEL / CHRIST fought against LUCIFER / SATAN—the two opposing generals leading armies of ANGELS and DEVILS in cosmic conflict.

POINT #8

Practically the only Bible verse quoted by those who deny that Jesus is Michael the Archangel is Jude 9, which says:

"MICHAEL THE ARCHANGEL, when contending with
the devil . . . said, THE LORD rebuke thee."

Objectors think this verse proves their point because Michael, rather than rebuking the devil Himself, says: "The LORD rebuke thee." They reason that the Archangel cannot be the Lord Jesus, for here He's calling someone ELSE "the Lord."

But instead of accepting any man's idea or any church's teaching, let the Bible be its OWN interpreter. We gain a clearer understanding of **JUDE 9** by comparing it with ZECHARIAH 3:2, where Jesus is again confronting Satan. We read:

"THE LORD said unto Satan, THE LORD rebuke thee,
O Satan."

This verse is *a perfect parallel* to Jude 9—almost a Xerox copy—except the names are changed: in one verse the speaker is called "MICHAEL THE ARCHANGEL" and in the other He's called "THE LORD."

In Zechariah's text
Jesus, referred to as "the Lord"—God the Son,
called on "the Lord" His heavenly Father to rebuke Satan.

In Jude's text
Jesus, referred to as "Michael the Archangel,"
called on "the Lord" His heavenly Father to rebuke the devil.

On both occasions, Christ knew it was pointless to argue with a closed mind. He knew it would do no good to bring "a railing accusation" [22] against the devil. He knew also that as Lord and Judge of all the universe, He WILL "rebuke" Satan some day by condemning him to the Lake of Fire. [23]

Another perfectly permissible interpretation of these two texts is to recognize that Christ was simply speaking of Himself when He said, "The Lord rebuke thee"—meaning "*I* rebuke thee." Grammatically, Jesus often referred to Himself in "the third person singular," saying things like: "When the SON OF MAN cometh, shall HE find faith on the earth?" [24] We all know He meant "When *I* come, shall *I* find faith?" And shall we foolishly conclude that Jesus is NOT the Son of God simply because in John 3:16 He referred to Himself in the third person singular, saying "whosoever believeth in HIM" rather than saying "in ME"?

The Bible itself, therefore, proves this objection groundless. But aside from providing evidence AGAINST the theory which says "Christ cannot be the same as Michael," Jude 9 provides strong evidence FOR the fact that He IS. Let's quote the part of the verse omitted before:

"Michael the Archangel, when contending with the devil
He DISPUTED about the BODY of Moses."

Remember that when Moses died, the Lord buried His faithful servant, but his grave was not known to men. [25] Jude now reveals that the DEAD BODY of Moses was the subject of dispute between Christ and Satan. From the fact that MOSES appeared with ELIJAH on the Mount of Transfiguration, [26] we may conclude that the Lord triumphed in the contest with the devil and raised Moses from his grave. These two—MOSES and ELIJAH—typify the TWO CLASSES of the redeemed of all ages when Christ returns in glory:

ELIJAH represents those believers ALIVE when Jesus comes,
who'll be translated without ever dying,[27]
and
MOSES represents those faithful believers who have DIED
but who'll then be raised from the dead.

When Jesus—the Prince of life—approached Moses' lonely grave, Satan was alarmed, for he claimed all who were in the grave as his captives and felt threatened by this invasion of his territory. "The accuser of the brethren"[28] boasted that even the leader of God's people, Moses, the faithful servant of God, had sinned[29] and become his prisoner. Christ refused to argue with Satan but then and there performed His work of breaking the devil's power and bringing the dead to life.

But here's the point: How do we KNOW it was Christ Himself and not a mere angel that contended with Satan over the resurrection of Moses' body? Because angels, like ourselves, are created beings and have no power to create life. Satan and his fallen angels are powerful supernatural beings who falsely APPEAR to raise the dead in spiritualistic seances and the like,[30] but they cannot really create life.

Although God empowered faithful men to resuscitate a dead person on a few occasions,[31] those miracles were NOT resurrections to a glorious, immortal life—the people who were raised, later died again. They were not taken bodily to heaven as Moses and Elijah were. Only Christ, the Lifegiver, can raise a dead person to eternal life. He is our only hope, not some angel.

The contention with Satan over "the BODY of Moses" could only be about RESURRECTING that body. This clearly implies Christ, since no angel could resurrect the dead! If we keep this fact in mind, we come again to the conclusion that the One who contended with Satan over Moses' body was a heavenly Being more powerful than any angel.

POINT #9

Jesus said, "Search the Scriptures."[32] And a good principle of Bible study says: "Precept must be upon precept, precept upon precept; line upon line, line upon line; HERE a little, and THERE a little."[33] We must compare a line here and a line there, in different books of the Bible, because no single writer of Old or New Testament had ALL of God's truth revealed to him.

God didn't choose to put all the information on a given subject into a single Bible chapter where we could learn all He would teach us about prayer, or baptism, or heaven, or any other subject. Each inspired writer was given a glimpse of the heavenly vision. But if we're to get the WHOLE truth, we must carefully SIFT through the Bible placing "line upon line," as we have in this book, and "comparing spiritual things with spiritual." [34]

Let's use this heaven-approved method of study right now for this question of Michael's identity. Let's place two inspired passages side by side and carefully compare them:

1. The Apostle Paul says dead believers are resurrected at "the voice of the ARCHANGEL." Please note:

"The Lord [Jesus] Himself shall descend from heaven with a shout, with *the voice of the Archangel*, . . . and the DEAD in Christ shall RISE." [35]

2. The Lord Jesus says dead believers are resurrected at the sound of HIS OWN voice. Please note:

"The DEAD shall hear *the voice of the Son of God:* and they that hear shall LIVE. . . . All that are in the GRAVES shall hear His voice, and shall COME FORTH . . . unto the resurrection." [36]

These parallel passages are speaking of the same EVENT and the same VOICE. Paul calls it "the voice of the ARCHANGEL," and Jesus calls it "the voice of the SON OF GOD." When Christ returns to call His faithful ones to life, every single angel in heaven will come with Him: "the Son of man shall come in His glory, and ALL the holy angels with Him" [37]—HE is their COMMANDER! There's no mystery here: JESUS, THE LIFEGIVER, is MICHAEL, THE ARCHANGEL.

These nine points clearly show that the identification of Jesus as Michael the Archangel is a valid one. Christians who accept this Bible-based teaching are not heretics who degrade Christ but faithful believers who love and honor their Lord.

∿

Notes to Appendix E

1. Official Jehovah's Witnesses publication *THE WATCHTOWER* (December 15, 1984), p. 29.
2. *Emmanuel* means "God with us," Matthew 1:23.
3. *Jesus* means "Savior," Matthew 1:21.
4. See John the Baptist's salutation in John 1:29.
5. *Christ* means "Messiah," "anointed One," or "King," John 1:41 & 4:25.
6. John 17:5 & 24, John 8:58, Micah 5:2, *etc.*
7. For instance, the Devil had the name "Lucifer" before rebelling against God and the name "Satan" afterward. See Isaiah 14:12 & Revelation 12:9. Other Bible examples of a name change after an important juncture in one's life are:
   Abram > Abraham; Sarai > Sarah; Jacob > Israel; Saul > Paul.
8. Proverbs 30:4.
9. Isaiah 14:14.
10. John 1:1 & 14 and countless other verses.
11. In the traditional Christmas carol "O Come, All Ye Faithful," we sing: "Come and behold Him, born the King of angels!" Christ is the KING of angels *without* being an angel Himself—just as a shepherd is the LEADER of the sheep *without* being a sheep himself.
12. See Genesis 18:1-33.
13. See Genesis 32:24-30.
14. Joshua 6:2.
15. Paul says plainly that CHRIST was the "Rock" that followed the Israelites in their wilderness wanderings. 1 Corinthians 10:1-4.
16. Exodus 3:1-5, NKJV.
17. See Daniel 8:16 & 9:21.
18. Daniel 12:1, NIV.
19. Daniel 9:25.
20. Revelation 12:7-9.
21. Joshua 5:14, The Living Bible.
22. Jude 9.
23. Revelation 20:10.
24. Luke 18:8.
25. Deuteronomy 34:5-6.
26. Matthew 17:1-9, Mark 9:2-10, Luke 9:28-36.
27. Elijah was taken to heaven without ever dying. 2 Kings 2:9-15.
28. Revelation 12:10. Satan is our accuser, but Christ is our Advocate or Defense Attorney in the Judgment. See 1 John 2:1.
29. Numbers 20:7-12. God told Moses merely to SPEAK to the rock in the wilderness in order to bring forth water. Instead, he lost his temper and STRUCK it—twice. Not only did he disobey, but the rock represented Christ. See 1 Corinthians 10:4.
30. When a dead person seems to appear to his loved ones, we instinctively feel an innate, God-given fear. This feeling of spooky danger would be out of place if we

really WERE in the presence of our beloved dead, but it's God's way of warning us that demons from Satan's legions impersonate those who sleep in the grave. "Spirits of devils [can work] miracles" (Revelation 16:14), even appearing to raise the dead! But in reality they cannot do so—God alone is the Lifegiver. See Chapters 10 & 11, "Solving the Mystery of Death," above, for more Bible facts on this subject.

31. ELISHA in 2 Kings 4:18-37, PETER in Acts 9:36-42, PAUL in Acts 20:9-12.
32. John 5:39.
33. Isaiah 28:10 (& 13).
34. 1 Corinthians 2:13.
35. 1 Thessalonians 4;16.
36. John 5:25-29.
37. Matthew 25:31.

Reference: pages 396 & 418, footnote 89.

APPENDIX F

The TWO LAWS—
A Study in CONTRASTS

MORAL LAW of GOD: The Ten Commandments	*CEREMONIAL* LAW of MOSES: The Law of Ordinances
1. Spoken by **God Himself** Exodus 20:1 & 22, Deuteronomy 4:12-13; 9:10	1. Spoken by **Moses** Exodus 24:3, 35:1, Leviticus 1:1-2
2. Written by **God, with His own finger** Exodus 24:12, 31:18, 32:16, 34:1, Deuteronomy 9:10	2. Written by **Moses** Exodus 24:4 & 34:27, Deuteronomy 31:9 & 24
3. On **tables of stone** Exodus 24:12, 31:18, 34:1	3. In **a book** Deuteronomy 31:24, 2 Chronicles 35:12
4. Handed by God, its writer, to **Moses** Exodus 31:18, 24:12, Deuteronomy 5:22, 9:10	4. Handed by Moses, its writer, to the priests, the **Levites** Deuteronomy 31:9 & 25-26
5. Placed by Moses **inside** the ark * Deuteronomy 10:2 & 5, 1 Kings 8:9	5. Placed by the Levites **beside** the ark Deutcronomy 31:24-26 (any modern translation)
6. Deals with **moral precepts**, our duty toward God and man Exodus 20:3-17, Matthew 19:17	6. Dealt with **ceremonies**, the ordinances and rituals of worship Parts of Exodus, Leviticus, Numbers, Deuteronomy
* *Not* Noah's Ark. This instead was a beautiful wooden chest covered inside and out with pure gold.	

MORAL LAW of GOD: The Ten Commandments	*CEREMONIAL* LAW of MOSES: The Law of Ordinances
7. **Reveals** sin to us, **defines** sin for us Romans 3:20, 7:7	7. Prescribed **rituals** & **offerings** for sin Leviticus (compare Leviticus 3:6-8 and John 1:29)
8. Breaking this law is **sin** even **today** 1 John 3:4	8. No sin in breaking these ordinances, which were "**abolished**" by Christ Ephesians 2:15, Romans 4:15
9. Christians to "keep the **whole** law" James 2:10-11, Matthew 5:19	9. Apostles "gave no such command- ment" to "be **circumcised**, and keep the law" Acts 15:24
10. We "shall be **judged**" by this law James 2:11-12, Eccl. 12:13-14, Romans 2:12	10. We are **not** to be judged by this law Colossians 2:16
11. Called the "law of **liberty**" James 1:25, 2:12	11. Called a "yoke of **bondage**"; Chris- tians who keep it lose their liberty Galatians 5:1-6
12. **Not destroyed** by Christ Matthew 5:17-18	12. **Abolished** by Christ's sacrifice Ephesians 2:15
13. Called "the **royal** law" James 2:8 & 11	13. Called "the law of commandments contained in **ordinances**" Ephesians 2:15
14. Is "**for** our good always" Deuteronomy 6:24, 10:13	14. Was "**against** us . . . contrary to us" Colossians 2:14, Deuteronomy 31:26
15. **Eternal**: "all . . . stand fast forever and ever" Psalm 111:7-8, Matthew 5:17-18	15. **Temporary**: "nailed to the cross" by Jesus' sacrifice Colossians 2:14
16. Deals with **eternal** principles of holy living, not with "things **to come**" It has **ALWAYS** been wrong to lie, to steal, to kill, to put false gods before the true God, *etc.*	16. "A **shadow** of things **to come**," these **temporary** ordinances *pointed forward* to the sacrifice of Christ's body Colossians 2:17, Hebrews 10:1-10; also compare Hebrews 8:1-5 with 9:1-14

MORAL LAW of GOD: The Ten Commandments	*CEREMONIAL* LAW of MOSES: The Law of Ordinances
17. Contains, as a memorial of Creation, the seventh-day "Sabbath **of the Lord thy God**" which the redeemed shall keep **even in the New Earth** Exodus 20:10, Isaiah 66:22-23	17. Contained, as a commemorative part of Jewish worship, several **yearly sabbaths** which were annual holy days that could fall on **any** day of the week Colossians 2:16-17, Leviticus 23:4-7 & 23-39
18. Is "**perfect**" Psalm 19:7	18. "Made **nothing** perfect" Hebrews 7:19, 9:9-10, 10:1
19. A "**spiritual**" law Romans 7:14 (see also verse 12)	19. "The law of a **carnal** commandment" and "**carnal ordinances**" Hebrews 7:16, 9:10
20. Is "**not grievous**" but a "**delight**" 1 John 5:3, Psalm 119:77, 143, 174, 40:8	20. Was a "**yoke**" we're not "able to **bear**" Acts 15:5 & 10
21. **Established** by FAITH in Christ Romans 3:31	21. **Taken "out of the way"** by Christ in giving His body as "the Lamb of God" Colossians 2:14, John 1:29, Mark 15:37-38
22. Called "the law **of the Lord**" & "the law **of God**" Psalm 1:2, 19:7, 119:1, Isaiah 5:24, Amos 2:4, Romans 7:22-25, 8:7	22. Called "the law **of Moses**" 2 Chronicles 23:18, 30:15-16, Ezra 3:2, Acts 13:39, 15:5, 1 Corinthians 9:9

The apostle Paul makes a clear Christian distinction between the abolished CEREMONIAL LAWS and God's eternal MORAL LAWS when he says: "CIRCUMCISION is nothing and UNCIRCUMCISION is nothing, but KEEPING the COMMANDMENTS of GOD is what matters." — 1 Corinthians 7:19, NKJV.

A Pertinent Quotation . . .

"The ritual or **CEREMONIAL** law, delivered by Moses to the children of Israel, containing all the injunctions and **ordinances** which related to the old sacrifices and service of the Temple, our Lord did indeed come to destroy, to dissolve, and utterly abolish. To this bear all the apostles witness. . . . This 'handwriting of ordinances our Lord *did* blot out, take away, and nail to His cross.' . . .

"But the **MORAL** law contained in the Ten Commandments, and enforced by the prophets, He did *not* take away. It was not the design of His coming to revoke any part of this. . . . The **MORAL** stands on an entirely different foundation from the **CEREMONIAL** or ritual law. . . . Every part of this [moral] law must remain in force upon ALL MANKIND, and in ALL AGES."

—**JOHN WESLEY,** founder of the METHODIST CHURCH, Sermon 25, "Upon Our Lord's Sermon on the Mount," *Sermons on Several Occasions,* Volume 1 (New York: B. Waugh and T. Mason, 1836), pp. 221-222.

The Jews, as God's chosen people, had *three distinct codes* by which to live. They were:

1. **CIVIL laws** to govern their everyday lives, imposing specific penalties in various legal matters (for example, see Exodus 21:12 to 22:24).

2. **CEREMONIAL laws** to regulate religious rites and sacrificial services of the Old Testament sanctuary (see Exodus 25:1 to 30:38).

3. **MORAL laws** to govern their spiritual relationships with God and man. The *first four* of the Ten Commandments teach our duty toward GOD (Exodus 20:3-11), and the *last six* teach our duty toward our fellow MAN (Exodus 20:12-17).

- Israel's national **CIVIL** laws came to an end, of course, when the nation came to an end, being destroyed by Rome. Therefore, when the modern state of Israel was set up in 1948, a new constitution and new civil laws had to be enacted. Geographically and politically, of course, the CIVIL laws of both ancient and modern Israel must be limited to the borders of that country alone and restricted to that government only.

- The **CEREMONIAL** laws came to an end when Christ, "the Lamb of God," died on the cross. At that moment an unseen hand tore in two the magnificent curtain in the Jewish Temple (Matthew 27:50-51, Mark 15:37-38, Luke 23:45-46). By this supernatural act of ripping the "veil" from top to bottom, God signified that the Old Testament ceremonies had come to a dramatic end.

- But the **MORAL** law of Ten Commandments is *universal* and *eternal*, given by God as the divine Standard for every person in every land and every age.

Opponents of God's Sabbath REFUSE TO DISTINGUISH between the moral and ceremonial laws, insisting that "They're all one body of law." So when they read that God abolished the ceremonial law, nailing it to the cross, they claim the moral law was likewise abolished. But we see MANY BIBLICAL DISTINCTIONS between the different codes of law.

Moses tells us in Deuteronomy 5:22 that when God spoke the Ten Commandments and wrote them on two tables of stone, "**He added no more.**" Thus the CEREMONIAL and CIVIL laws were in an entirely different class and cannot be added to God's MORAL law.

And God Himself clearly distinguishes between "all that I have commanded" and "all the law that My servant **Moses** commanded" by "ordinances" in Bible texts like 2 Kings 21:8 and 2 Chronicles 33:8.

GREAT THOUGHTS ON THE GREATEST BOOK

"The Bible is the Word of Life. I beg that you will read it and find this out for yourself. . . . You will find it full of real men and women, but also full of things you have wondered about and been troubled about all your life. . . . When you have read the Bible, you will know that it is the Word of God, because you will have found it the key to your own heart, your own happiness, and your own duty." —WOODROW WILSON

"It [the Bible] is the best gift God has given to man. All the good Saviour gave to the world is communicated through this Book. But for it we could not know right from wrong. All things most desirable for man's welfare, here and hereafter, are to be found portrayed in it." —ABRAHAM LINCOLN

"The Bible is worth all other books that have ever been printed." —PATRICK HENRY

"I believe a knowledge of the Bible without a college education more valuable than a college education without the Bible. Everyone who has a thorough knowledge of the Bible may truly be called educated, and no other learning or culture, no matter how extensive or elegant, can form a proper substitute." —WILLIAM LYON PHELPS, Professor at Yale

"The Bible is of vital importance in teaching freedom. Dictators fear the Bible—and for good reason. It inspired the *Magna Charta* and the *Declaration of Independence*." —LOWELL THOMAS, Journalist

"It is impossible to rightly govern the world without God and the Bible." —GEORGE WASHINGTON

"The Bible is the most wonderful Book in the world. The Bible! It is beautiful . . . because in my darkness the Bible makes me see the great Light." —HELEN KELLER, who was deaf and blind

"I have always said and always will say that the studious perusal of the Sacred Volume will make better citizens, better fathers, and better husbands . . . the Bible makes the best people in the world." —THOMAS JEFFERSON

The Bible, among all books, is the world's best seller. Translated into more languages than any other, it is the world's most treasured volume. As you can see from the few tributes quoted above, the Bible believer is in very GOOD COMPANY!

Appendix G

~

God's Law Reflects His Character

When Paul praises God's Law as being "HOLY, and JUST, and GOOD," [1] and the Psalmist David exclaims that "the Law of the Lord is PERFECT," [2] we learn from the Pen of Inspiration that God's moral Law of Ten Commandments is no mere checklist of rules! It's a TRANSCRIPT of God's character, reflecting its divine Author in every respect. Compare the attributes of GOD with inspired descriptions of HIS LAW:

GOD Is:	ATTRIBUTE	God's LAW Is:
1 Peter 1:16 Isaiah 6:3	< HOLY >	Romans 7:12
Revelation 15:3 Deuteronomy 32:4	< JUST >	Romans 7:12
Psalm 25:8 Luke 18:19	< GOOD >	Romans 7:12
Psalm 11:7	< RIGHTEOUS >	Psalm 119:172
1 John 4:8 & 16	< LOVE >	Matthew 22:36-40 Romans 13:8-10
Matthew 5:48	< PERFECT >	Psalm 19:7
Psalm 90:2	< EVERLASTING >	Psalm 111:7-8

God's Law of Ten Commandments is an expression of His thought, an embodiment of His very nature! As such, we should no more expect it to be changed than we'd expect GOD to change. We read:

- God says, "I am the Lord, I change NOT." [3]
- He is "the Father of lights, with whom is NO variableness, neither shadow of turning." [4]
- "Jesus Christ is the SAME yesterday, today, and forever." [5]

Famed Baptist preacher Charles H. Spurgeon says this about the Ten Commandments:

"The Law of God is a divine Law, holy, heavenly, perfect. Those who find fault with the Law, or in the least degree depreciate it, do not understand its design, and have no right idea of the Law itself. . . . The Law is one of the most sublime of God's works. There is not a Commandment too many; there is not one too few; but it is so incomparable, that its perfection is a proof of its divinity." [6]

Notes to Appendix G

1. Romans 7:12.
2. Psalm 19:7.
3. Malachi 3:6.
4. James 1:17.
5. Hebrews 13:8, NKJV.
6. Charles Haddon Spurgeon, *Sermons*, Second Series (New York: Sheldon, Blakeman & Co., 1857), Sermon 18, p. 280.

References: *page 500, footnote 1; and footnote 10 on pages 541 & 566.*

APPENDIX H

SIGNS SHOWING JESUS WILL RETURN SOON

SIGNS IN THE **RELIGIOUS** WORLD

Falling away from Bible truth — 1 Timothy 4:1; 2 Thessalonians 2:1-3
False prophets, false christs — Matthew 24:11 & 24
Scoffers at Second Coming — 2 Peter 3:3-4
Won't endure sound doctrine — 2 Timothy 4:3-4
Covetous false teachers — 2 Peter 2:1-3
Religious skepticism — Matthew 24:12-13, Luke 18:8
Gospel preached to all the world — Matthew 24:14

SIGNS IN THE **SOCIAL** WORLD

Craze for pleasure — 2 Timothy 3:1-5 (verse 4)
Increasing crime and evil — 2 Timothy 3:1-5 & 13
Divorce — Matthew 24:37-39 (compare Genesis 6:2)
Juvenile delinquency — 2 Timothy 3:1-5 (verse 2)
Foul, blasphemous speech — 2 Timothy 3:1-5 (verse 2)
People will be too busy — Luke 21:34, Matthew 24:37-39
Homosexuality and / or child abuse — 2 Timothy 3:3 [1]

SIGNS IN THE **POLITICAL** WORLD

Wars and rumors of wars — Matthew 24:6
Nations are angry — Revelation 11:18
Truce breakers, traitors — 2 Timothy 3:1-5 (verses 3 & 4)
Distress of nations, with perplexity — Luke 21:25-28
Great peace movements — 1 Thessalonians 5:1-4

SIGNS in the ECONOMIC World

Accumulation of wealth — James 5:1-8 (verses 1-3)
Capital / Labor troubles — James 5:1-8 (verse 4)
Famines — Matthew 24:7

SIGNS in the SCIENTIFIC World

Unparalleled travel — Daniel 12:4
Increase of knowledge — Daniel 12:4
Men have power to destroy the earth — Revelation 11:18

SIGNS in the PHYSICAL World

A great earthquake — Revelation 6:12
Sun darkened — Matthew 24:29
Moon turned to blood — Revelation 6:12
Stars fell to the earth — Revelation 6:13
Earthquakes in various places — Matthew 24:7

Most of these signs need no documentation, for observers of current events see fulfillment of them reported daily in the media. They are signs ripped from today's headlines. But for the last category above, the reader is directed to Chapter 16, above, which deals with the *celestial* "signs in the *sun, and in the moon, and in the stars*" foretold by Christ in Luke 21:25.[2] Jesus sums it up by saying: "When these things [these signs] begin to take place, look up and raise your heads, because your redemption is drawing near."[3]

Notes to Appendix H

1. The text says, "without natural affection."
2. Since Genesis 1:14 tells us, "God said, Let there be LIGHTS in the firmament of the heaven to divide the day from the night; and let them be for SIGNS," we shouldn't be too surprised at this divine skywriting! Looking for Jesus' soon Return is not a gloom-and-doom attitude but a positive point of view that looks for something far better than life as we know it in this old weary world.
3. Luke 21:28, RSV.

Reference: page 530, footnote 20.

APPENDIX I

~

IS ISRAEL STILL GOD'S CHOSEN PEOPLE?

Our study of the Secret Rapture theory in Chapter 17 revealed that doctrine to be based on a multitude of assumptions. Prominent among those assumptions is the idea that ALL the Jews will be converted and will then go forth to evangelize the world. This will happen, Rapturists believe, during the last half of the 7-year period following the Rapture and the REMOVAL of God's Holy Spirit.[1]

The main reasons given for this teaching is (1) that God made many PROMISES to His chosen people, Israel, and (2) that God's promises MUST come true. Rapturists believe some of those promises were not fulfilled in Israel's past experience, so they must be fulfilled in the future.

Let's briefly examine this assumption in the light of Scripture.

It's true that when God needed a missionary people to evangelize the world that had fallen into idolatry, He chose the Israelites. He placed them at "the crossroads of the world"—the strategic juncture or hub of three continents: Europe, Africa, and Asia. "Thus saith the Lord God; This is Jerusalem: I have set it in the MIDST of the nations and countries that are round about her."[2]

So there's no question that God chose Israel as His people. The question arises over whether or not, when they failed repeatedly not only to evangelize the WORLD but also to remain faithful THEMSELVES, God could rightfully reject the Jews as His chosen people and elect the Gentiles.

"IF" Is a BIG Word

A further question revolves around God's promises to His people. Those who feel the promises were not kept overlook the nature of CONDITIONAL promises. Suppose you say to me, "I'll give you two thousand dollars if you paint my house." But I don't paint it. Do you still have to pay me the money? Of course not! I failed to fulfill the conditions of the contract and deserve nothing.

The promises God made to His people were like that. DEUTERONOMY 28 is one of the best chapters in the Bible illustrating the fact that the promises and threatenings of God are alike CONDITIONAL. The BLESSINGS begin with verse 1, and they're beautiful. "It shall come to pass, IF thou shalt hearken diligently unto the voice of the Lord your God, to observe and to do all His commandments . . . all these BLESSINGS shall come upon thee, and overtake thee, IF thou shalt hearken unto the voice of the Lord thy God." There follows a list of blessings of every description, covering all aspects of life.

On the other hand, the CURSES begin with verse 15, and they're absolutely staggering. "But it shall come to pass, IF thou wilt not hearken unto the voice of the Lord thy God, to observe to do all His commandments . . . all these CURSES shall come upon thee, and overtake thee." There follows a list of curses, some detailed enough for us to recognize their fulfillment in history—such as the Jews' uprooting and dispersal from their homeland: "the Lord shall scatter thee among all people, from one end of the earth even unto the other." [3]

In each case God's promises or threatenings were dependent upon the CONDITION of obedience or disobedience, just as Adam and Eve's probation was. Those who expect God's promises to be fulfilled to unbelieving Israel now, nineteen centuries after the Jews' collective rejection of Jesus Christ, the Messiah, ignore the CONDITIONAL nature of those promises.

Promises KEPT!

But many careful Bible scholars believe God faithfully kept His promises. The Lord did indeed keep His promises to Abraham, "the father of the faithful." Let's look at just two of those promises: the ones regarding the number of his SEED and the extent of his LAND.

First of all, proponents of the theory say, "God told Abraham his seed would be as numerous as the stars in the sky and the sand by the seashore—even like the dust of the earth!" [4] They insist that that promise never came true.

However, the Bible explicitly states that this WAS true of the nation of Israel in King Solomon's time—and it uses the very words God earlier used in His covenant with Abraham!

● "Judah and Israel were many, as the SAND which is by the sea in multitude, eating and drinking, and making merry." [5]

● Solomon's father, King David, had tried to take a census of his people, "But David took not the number of them from twenty years and under: because the Lord had said He would increase Israel like to the STARS of the heavens." [6]

● Solomon prayed, "O Lord God, let Thy promise unto David my father be established: for Thou hast made me king over a people like the DUST of the earth in multitude." [7]

It would be unreasonable and unrealistic for us to insist that these statements be fulfilled literally rather than figuratively, for our little planet could not actually hold that many people. Besides, the New Testament confirms that this promise WAS fulfilled in the golden age of the Monarchy: "Therefore from one man, and him as good as dead, [8] were born as many as the STARS of the sky in multitude—innumerable as the SAND which is by the sea-shore." [9]

So God's promise regarding Abraham's SEED was marvelously fulfilled!

But proponents of the theory still argue that "God promised to give Abraham not only 'all the land of Canaan' [10] but all the LAND 'from the [Nile] River of Egypt unto the great river, the River Euphrates' [11] of Babylon—a land in possession of many nations." [12]

And God DID fulfill this promise! The Bible says plainly:

> "Solomon reigned over ALL the kingdoms from the River [Euphrates] unto the land of the Philistines, and unto the border of Egypt. . . . You are the Lord God, who chose Abram . . . and You made a covenant with him to give to his descendants the LAND of the Canaanites, Hittites, Amorites, Perizzites, Jebusites and Girgashites. YOU HAVE KEPT YOUR PROMISE because You are righteous." [13]

THE JEWISH NATION WAS FINALLY REJECTED

The history of Israel reveals a checkered career of spiritual highs and lows, a roller-coaster ride of ups and downs of faith. God, in an amazing display of undying love and infinite patience, wooed His erring children back to Him time and time again. The loving heavenly Father bore long with their many failings, but finally—as the One who carries the ultimate responsibility for evangelizing the world—He sadly turned from the Jews to the Gentiles.

Many Scriptures testify to this fact:

When the Jews rejected the gospel, "contradicting and blaspheming, they OPPOSED the things spoken by Paul. Then Paul and Barnabas grew bold and said, 'It was necessary that the word of God should be spoken to you [Jews] first; but since you REJECT IT, and judge yourselves UNWORTHY of everlasting life, behold, we turn to the GENTILES.' " [14]

Paul loved his Jewish brothers, but the Inspired Record says: "When they [the Jews] opposed him and blasphemed, he [Paul] shook his garments and said to them, 'Your blood be upon your own heads; I am clean. From now on I will go to the GENTILES.' " [15]

NOW THE CHURCH IS "SPIRITUAL ISRAEL"

From Adam and Eve on, God has always had His people, His faithful followers. The Christian church is actually the true continuation of God's people, or Israel.

When the Jews screamed, "We have no king but Cæsar"![16] they forfeited their place as God's chosen people. Israel's failure to carry out God's plan was a tragedy of infinite proportions. But what God intended to do for the world through ISRAEL, the chosen nation, He'll finally accomplish through HIS CHURCH.

Peter declared: "YOU are a chosen race, a royal priesthood, a holy nation, God's own people, that you may declare the wonderful deeds of Him who called you out of darkness into His marvelous light." [17] That Peter addressed those words to the CHRISTIAN CHURCH at large, most of whom were Gentiles, is clear from his very next verse: "Once you were no people but NOW you are God's people; once you had not received mercy but NOW you have received mercy."

Sadly, the words Peter wrote to the church were originally spoken to the Israelites by God Himself. [18] But they were preceded by that conditional word—"IF." Israel, having failed God so many times, was explicitly told by Jesus: "Therefore say I unto you [the Jews], The kingdom of God shall be TAKEN FROM YOU, and given to a nation bringing forth the fruits thereof." [19] Peter, in the words quoted above, simply identifies that new nation—the Christian church.

Not Jews in the FLESH but Abraham's children by FAITH are now the real Israel in God's sight.

✦ ✦ ✦

SCRIPTURE Speaks ELOQUENTLY on This Point

- **Galatians 3:7-16,** NKJV—"Therefore KNOW that only those who are of FAITH are sons of Abraham. And the Scripture, foreseeing that God would justify the GENTILES by faith, preached the gospel to Abraham beforehand, saying, 'In you ALL the nations shall be blessed.' So then those who are of FAITH are blessed WITH believing Abraham. . . . That the blessing of Abraham might come upon the GENTILES in Christ Jesus, that we might receive the promise of the Spirit through faith. Brethren, I speak in the manner of men: Though it is only a man's covenant, yet if it is confirmed, no one annuls or adds to it. Now to Abraham and his Seed were the promises made. He does NOT say, 'And to seeds,' as of *many,* but as of *one,* 'And to your SEED,' who is CHRIST."

- **Galatians 3:28-29**—"There is neither JEW nor GREEK, there is neither bond nor free, there is neither male nor female: for ye are all ONE in Christ Jesus. And if ye be CHRIST'S, then are ye ABRAHAM'S seed, and heirs according to the promise."[20]

- **Colossians 3:11**—"There is neither GREEK nor JEW, circumcision nor uncircumcision, . . . bond nor free: but Christ is all, and *in all.*"

- **Romans 2:28-29**—"For he is NOT a Jew which is one OUTWARDLY; neither is that circumcision, which is outward in the flesh: but he IS a Jew, which is one INWARDLY; and circumcision is that of the heart, in the spirit. . . ."

- **Matthew 22:1-10,** NKJV—Please read Jesus' whole parable: "The kingdom of heaven is like a certain KING who arranged a marriage for His SON, and sent out His servants to CALL those who were invited to the wedding; and they were NOT WILLING to come. . . . They made light of it and . . . SEIZED His servants . . . and KILLED them. . . . Then He said to His servants, 'The wedding is ready, but those who were invited [the Jews] were NOT WORTHY.'" So God invited others from the highways and byways to His marriage supper—the GENTILES.

- **Ephesians 3:6**—"The GENTILES should be FELLOW HEIRS, and of the same body, and partakers of His promise in Christ by the gospel."

- **Romans 8:14-17**—"As many as are led by the Spirit of God, they are the sons of God. For . . . ye have received the Spirit of ADOPTION. . . . The Spirit itself beareth witness . . . that WE are the children of God: And if children, then HEIRS of God, and joint heirs with Christ."

- **Acts 10:45,** NIV—"The circumcised believers [that is, Jewish converts to Christ] . . . were astonished that the gift of the Holy Spirit had been poured out even on the GENTILES."

- **1 Corinthians 12:13**—"By one Spirit are we ALL baptized into ONE body, whether we be JEWS or GENTILES, whether we be bond or free; and have been all made to drink into one Spirit."

- **Ephesians 2:11-19,** NKJV—"Remember that you, once GENTILES in the flesh . . . at that time you were without Christ, being ALIENS from the commonwealth of Israel and STRANGERS from the covenants of promise, having no hope and without God in the world. But NOW in Christ Jesus you who once were far off have been brought near by the blood of Christ. For He . . . has made both ONE, and has broken down the middle wall of separation. . . . For through Him we both have access by one Spirit to the Father. Now, therefore, you are no longer strangers and foreigners, but FELLOW CITIZENS with the saints and MEMBERS of the household of God."

- **Romans 9:6-8,** NRSV—"Not all Israelites TRULY BELONG to Israel, and not all of Abraham's children are his TRUE descendants. . . . This means that it is NOT the children of the FLESH who are the children of God, but the children of the PROMISE are counted as descendants."

Israel's forfeited future, by default, was inherited by the Christian church. LITERAL Israel of the flesh has become SPIRITUAL Israel of the church.

"GOD IS **NO RESPECTER** OF PERSONS"

The words in that heading above mean that "God does not play favorites." As modern Bible versions put it, "God shows no partiality." Note the following texts:

- **Acts 10:34-35**—"Peter . . . said, Of a truth I perceive that God is no respecter of persons: But in EVERY nation he that feareth Him, and worketh righteousness, is accepted with Him."

- **Romans 2:5-11,** NIV—God "will give to each person according to what he has done. . . . Trouble and distress for every human being who does EVIL: first for the JEW, then for the GENTILE; but glory, honour and peace for everyone who does GOOD: first for the JEW, then for the GENTILE. For God does not show favouritism."

- **Romans 3:29**—"Is He the God of the JEWS only? Is He not also of the GENTILES? Yes, of the GENTILES also."

- **Romans 10:12-13,** NIV—"There is NO DIFFERENCE between JEW and GENTILE—the same Lord is Lord of ALL and richly blesses ALL who call on Him, for, 'Everyone who calls on the name of the Lord will be saved.'"

Our heavenly Father has no priorities among His children. Many other texts repeat the same truth about God's impartiality, such as Deuteronomy 10:17, Ephesians 6:9, Colossians 3:25, and 1 Peter 1:17.

WILL "ALL ISRAEL" BE SAVED?

To try to prove their point, advocates of the Secret Rapture theory sometimes use ROMANS 11:26, which says: "And so all Israel shall be saved." Is that true? It certainly is! If the Bible says it, you'd better believe it!

Let's focus on that little word *so*—which is quite important in this sentence. The word "so" here does NOT express a *conclusion,* meaning "And THEREFORE all Israel shall be saved," as Rapturists wrongly interpret it. The Greek word *(houtos)* translated "so" expresses *manner,* meaning "And IN THIS WAY all Israel shall be saved."

Paul had just finished telling how some of Israel's "branches" were broken off from God's "olive tree" and the GENTILES were "grafted in" to take their place. [21] He even explained how the severed branches could be reunited with the parent stock, discussing the salvation of both LITERAL and SPIRITUAL Israel. Then he says: "And SO [in this way, by this manner] shall all Israel be saved." Thus "all Israel" represents the sum total of those saved—Jews and Gentiles—who together make up "all" of true Israel.

Paul is NOT teaching UNIVERSAL salvation for either Gentiles or Jews. This is clear when he expresses his fervent hope for his fellow Israelites that "by any means . . . SOME of them" might be saved. [22]

We must not try to LIMIT God's favor to the Jews alone. He says, "I will . . . be gracious to whom I will be gracious, and will show mercy on whom I will show mercy." [23] So the Lord is the almighty One who will choose—and if He decides to "graft in" the GENTILES, no one can stop Him.

CONCLUSION

Some Bible students believe the Jews' 1948 RETURN to PALESTINE, establishing the modern nation of Israel, is somehow an important sign. But the nation and people of Israel have NOT returned to Palestine in penitence and faith, in order to fulfill God's purposes for them.

The Jews were God's special people from Abraham to Christ whether they enjoyed political independence in PALESTINE, or suffered the bonds of slavery in EGYPT, or grieved in exile at BABYLON—for location is not of prime importance. They ceased to be God's people when they rejected that special relationship, crucified Christ, and persecuted the early Christians. The Israeli nation has returned to JERUSALEM—but not to CHRIST. Therefore the Jews as a people have not returned to their special relationship.

Individual Jews, of course—like individual Swedes or Chinese or Muslims or Hindus—can still become God's people by accepting Christ as their personal Savior. [24] No doubt in the closing proclamation of the gospel many Jews, like Saul of Tarsus, will by faith receive Christ as their Redeemer. We pray that this will be so. But unbelieving Jews have no "ticket to heaven" any more than other unbelievers.

No Biblical basis can be found for the notion that the nation of Israel as a whole will be converted. In fact, the weight of Scriptural evidence is much to the contrary.

Our relationship to God and status in heaven depends on our faith, not on the accident of birth. Thank God our salvation depends on GRACE—not RACE!

⌣

Notes to Appendix I

1. Proponents of that theory do not make clear what AGENCY succeeds in converting the Jews in a few short years if all Christians leave the earth in the Rapture and—as they teach—the Holy Spirit is withdrawn with them. Two thousand years have not been enough to do the job even with the earnest efforts of Christians like the apostle Paul and modern "Jews for Jesus" combined with the divine work of the Holy Spirit!

2. Ezekiel 5:5.

3. Deuteronomy 28:64. Compare Jeremiah 26:2-6. Further evidence of the fact that Israel did NOT enjoy God's unqualified, unconditional favor is seen in this curse upon His rebellious people: "I Myself will fight against you." Jeremiah 21:5. See also Deuteronomy 8:19 and Jeremiah 18:6-10.

4. Genesis 13:16, 15:5, and 22:17.

5. 1 Kings 4:20.

6. 1 Chronicles 27:23.

7. 2 Chronicles 1:9.

8. Abraham was 100 years old when his son Isaac was born! See Genesis 21:5 and Romans 4:19.

9. Hebrews 11:12 (see verses 8-12).

10. Genesis 17:8.

11. Genesis 15:18-21.

12. See Genesis 15:19-21.

13. 1 Kings 4:21 (compare 2 Chronicles 9:26) and Nehemiah 9:7-8, NIV. Israel DID possess the land, but they failed to keep it "for ever." It was forfeited because of disobedience. Obedience is a vital prerequisite for blessing under all circumstances, even when unexpressed. In Abraham's case obedience is particularly stressed: God hoped through Abraham to raise up a faithful people who would "KEEP the way of the Lord."—Genesis 18:19. After Abraham met his supreme test of faith when God commanded him to offer up his only son Isaac, the covenant was renewed to him, closing with the words: "*because* thou hast OBEYED My voice."—Genesis 22:18. Compare Genesis 26:5. For ideas on the last two pages the author is deeply indebted to Oswald T. Allis and his excellent book *Prophecy and the Church* (Nutley, New Jersey: Presbyterian and Reformed Publishing Company, 1974), pp. 33 & 57-58.

14. Acts 13:45-46, NKJV.

15. Acts 18:6, NKJV.

16. John 19:15.

17. 1 Peter 2:9, RSV.

18. See Exodus 19:5-6.

19. Matthew 21:43. Read the whole parable (beginning with verse 33) as well as the similar account in Isaiah 5:1-7, where it's explained that "The vineyard of the Lord is the house of ISRAEL."

20. An illuminating comment on this verse says: "In the Jewish form of morning prayer, which Paul must all his pre-Christian life have used, there is a thanksgiving in which the Jew thanks God that 'Thou hast not made me a GENTILE, a SLAVE, or a WOMAN.' Paul takes that prayer and REVERSES it. The old distinctions are gone . . . all are one in Christ."—William Barclay, *Galatians,* p. 35.
21. Romans 11:12-25.
22. Romans 11:14.
23. Exodus 33:19.
24. Acts 4:12 and Romans 11:23.

APPENDIX J

IS THE BIBLE WRITTEN IN CHRONOLOGICAL ORDER?

A QUESTION THAT SOMETIMES ARISES in the study of the Millennium is whether or not the Holy Scriptures are written in consistent time sequence—in chronological order. The answer is a simple one: Parts of the Bible are in chronological order, and other parts clearly are not.

In no way does it detract from the inspiration of God's Word to acknowledge that Bible writers did not always follow time order. There's nothing sacred about time order, space order, order of importance, or any other organizational pattern which serves simply as a tool for the writer. So it's pointless and foolish to insist that each passage in Scripture follows chronologically in strict time order from the preceding one.

LET ME REPEAT . . .

In the first place, such blind insistence ignores the principle of REPETITION, a common literary device often employed in the Bible and other writings. For instance, God gave us FOUR Gospels—Matthew, Mark, Luke, and John. Each Gospel writer presents basically the same story of Christ, covering largely the same events from his own point of view. One Gospel would have been enough, perhaps, but the repetition adds emphasis and further details.

Let me ask you a question: How MANY Saviors does the Bible tell us were born and crucified? One, you say? But we read about HIM in the Gospel of Matthew. What about the other books of Mark, Luke, and John? Are they talking about subsequent Redeemers or the same Lord and Master? The same One, of course! But that makes these four books repetitive, NOT consecutive.

God's repetition is also seen in the Books of Moses: Exodus, Leviticus, Numbers, and Deuteronomy repeat much of the same history of God's people. And the Bible's first two chapters, Genesis 1 and 2, give an "instant replay," repeating the story of the creation of Adam and Eve, adding interest by including more details.

Furthermore, God's successive visions to the prophet Daniel repeat the future history of the same world empires to follow Babylon: Medo-Persia, Greece, and Rome, in chapters 2 *and* 7 *and* 8 of the Book of Daniel.

And John the Revelator repeats his account of the majestic DESCENT of God's beloved city, the New Jerusalem, from heaven to earth in Revelation 21, verses 2 and 10. Obviously, all these cases of clear repetition rule out any insistence on strict chronological order.

COMMON SENSE ALSO RULES OUT CHRONOLOGICAL ORDER

But besides the Biblical use of repetition, there's other evidence which destroys the theory that God's Word must always be read, interpreted, and understood in a strictly chronological sense. Common sense must also be used. For instance, Acts 12:21-23, NKJV describes the death of proud King Herod, who allowed people to ascribe divinity to him:

> "Herod, arrayed in royal apparel, sat on his throne and gave an oration to them. And the people kept shouting, 'The voice of a GOD and not of a MAN!' Then immediately an angel of the Lord struck him, because he did not give glory to God. And he was EATEN BY WORMS and DIED."

Since parasites like tapeworms are not fatal and don't eat people, we conclude that Herod's worms were those which feed on dead bodies in the grave (see Job 19:26). To those who insist on strict time order, Acts 12:23 teaches that Herod's body was "eaten" by worms *before* he died—and that's putting the cart before the horse!

Look into the great prophetic book of DANIEL. There, chapter 5 begins by saying, "BELSHAZZAR the king made a great feast to a thousand of his lords, and drank wine before the thousands" (Daniel 5:1). Then we're told how that pagan king displeased God by drinking from the sacred "golden vessels that were taken out of the temple of the house of God which was at Jerusalem" (verse 3).

Viewing the terrifying "handwriting on the wall," the wicked king learns that he is "weighed in the balances, and . . . found wanting. . . . In that night was Belshazzar the king of the Chaldeans SLAIN. And DARIUS the Median took the kingdom, being about threescore and two years old" (Daniel 5:27-31). Chapter 6 then tells about the reign of the conquering king, DARIUS.

Then—though BELSHAZZAR was DEAD and BURIED and had been succeeded on the throne by DARIUS—chapter 7 begins with these amazing words: "In the FIRST year of BELSHAZZAR king of Babylon . . ."! Chapter 8:1 says: "In the THIRD year of the reign of king BELSHAZZAR . . ."! And chapter 9:1 begins: "In the FIRST year of DARIUS the son of Ahasuerus . . ."

These facts are graphically depicted below:

Daniel 5:1-31
BELSHAZZAR **slain** by DARIUS

Daniel 6
The **Reign** of King DARIUS

Daniel 7:1
The **first** year of King BELSHAZZAR

Daniel 8:1
The **third** year of King BELSHAZZAR

Daniel 9:1
The **first** year of King DARIUS

Obviously, chapters 5 through 9 of the Book of Daniel are NOT in chronological order!

Furthermore, take this statement from the Gospel of Mark: "King Herod . . . said, 'John the Baptist is risen from the dead. . . . This is John, whom I BEHEADED; he has been raised from the dead!'" (Mark 6:14 & 16, NKJV.) THEN the FOLLOWING verses (17-28) have John ALIVE and tell the whole story of how Herod came to behead him!

Another example is seen in the Book of Revelation, chapter 12. The first verses (1-6) tell about Jesus' Birth. THEN the FOLLOWING verses (7-9) tell about Satan's Fall and expulsion from heaven—which we know happened long before!

One last example may lay to rest the idea that every sentence in Scripture follows, step by step, in time sequence from the preceding one. In Revelation 1:7 John describes the Second Coming of Christ, yet this passage is a proleptic or parenthetic statement inserted early into his prophetic book which later describes many scenes which were to happen—and still are to happen—BEFORE Jesus returns!

In short, the idea that the Bible is in strict time order dies a quick death once we realize that Biblical passages such as the following are not in chronological sequence:

- **BOOKS** (the four Gospels are repetitive, not consecutive)

- **CHAPTERS** (in the Book of Daniel)

- **VERSES** (Revelation 21:2 and 10)

- **PARTS** of a single verse (Acts 12:23).

More examples could be cited, but these may suffice to show that God had no intention of sticking to strict chronological order when He supervised the writing of His holy Scriptures.

⟨∿⟩

Reference: pages 659-666.

APPENDIX K

~

CAN ROMAN CATHOLIC PRIESTS REALLY FORGIVE SINS?

I N CLUE "S" OF CHAPTER 19, revealing the BLASPHEMOUS character of the Antichrist/Beast, we saw that the men appointed as Catholic priests claim power which the Bible says belongs only to God—namely, the power to forgive sins.

We saw that they boldly, brazenly claim such power for themselves and that the Pope, furthermore, *denies* that sinners can obtain forgiveness directly from God but *must* go through a Roman Catholic priest!

Perceptive Christians have always questioned such outrageous, blasphemous claims. You'll recall C. S. Lewis's observation on Christ's . . .

> "claim to forgive sins: ANY sins. Now unless the speaker is God, this is really so preposterous as to be comic. We can all understand how a man forgives offenses against himself. You tread on my toe and I forgive you, you steal my money and I forgive you. But what should we make of a man, himself unrobbed and untrodden on, who announces that he forgave you for treading on other men's toes and stealing other men's money? Asinine fatuity is the kindest description we should give of his conduct. Yet this is what Jesus did. He told people that their sins were forgiven, and never waited to consult all the other people whom their sins had undoubtedly injured. He unhesitatingly behaved as if HE was the party chiefly concerned, the person chiefly offended in all

offenses. This makes sense only if He really was the God whose laws are broken and whose love is wounded in every sin. In the mouth of any speaker who is NOT God, these words imply a silliness and conceit unrivalled by any other character in history." [1]

But because so many good Catholics devoutly believe this power IS indeed vested in their priests because of one passage of Scripture, we must address that Bible text.

The CATHOLIC CONFESSIONAL Examined Briefly:

In addition to what was already established in Clue "S" of Chapter 19, above, let's dig a little deeper and see what we find.

A. – Rome's Claims REFUTED by SCRIPTURE

If the Pope tells us, "You cannot approach God directly for forgiveness," we answer, "We need not fear approaching God, our loving heavenly Father, in confession"—for we're promised:

- **1 John 1:9** — "If we confess our sins, He is faithful and just to FORGIVE us our sins, and to CLEANSE us from all unrighteousness."

If Rome tells us, "You need a priest to approach the holy God," we answer, "We HAVE a priest—a great High Priest—named Jesus the Son of God, who loves us and welcomes us as we come boldly to the throne of grace!"— for we read:

- **Hebrews 4:14-16,** NKJV — "Seeing then that we have a great HIGH PRIEST who has passed through the heavens, Jesus the Son of God, let us hold fast our confession. For we do not have a High Priest who cannot sympathize with our weaknesses, but was in all points tempted as we are, yet without sin. Let us therefore come BOLDLY to the throne of grace, that we may obtain mercy and find grace to help in time of need."

- **Luke 18:9-14** — When Christ told the parable of the Pharisee and the publican, His words were most instructive. The Pharisee was a self-righteous religionist, while the publican was a despised tax-collector. But please note: The publican had NO PRIEST, and he did NOT go to a confessional. All he did was to cry with bowed head, "God, be merciful to me a sinner." He went DIRECTLY to God. And Jesus said that "he went down to his house justified" or pardoned.

Former Catholic James G. McCarthy makes the point that Biblical confession is to GOD ALONE:

"When KING DAVID repented of his adultery, he confessed his sin directly to God. No priest. No ritual. No sacrament. Just a broken man owning up to his sin before his Maker. He later wrote of the incident in a psalm to God, saying: 'I acknowledged my sin to THEE, and my iniquity I did not hide; I said, "I will confess my transgressions to the LORD"; and Thou didst forgive the guilt of my sin.'"[2] Confession directly to God was also the experience of NEHEMIAH,[3] DANIEL,[4] and EZRA.[5] Ezra, though a Levitical priest himself, taught God's people to 'make confession to the LORD GOD of your fathers.'[6]"[7]

Sorely feeling the lack of any proof of divine origin for many of her teachings, and searching the Bible in vain for any Scriptural support, the Catholic Church often turns to "the Church Fathers"—Catholic leaders and theologians of the early Christian centuries—for the opinions of MEN. But even here she fails, at least in this case.

For not a word is found in the writings of the early church fathers about confessing sins to a priest or to anyone except God alone. The priestly confessional is not mentioned in the writings of such luminaries as AUGUSTINE, ORIGEN, NESTORIUS, TERTULLIAN, JEROME, CHRYSOSTOM, or ATHANASIUS. All of these and many others apparently lived and died without ever thinking of going to confession. Those writers give many rules about Christian living, but they never say a word about going to confession. Never were penitents forced to kneel to a *priest* and reveal to *him* all their evil thoughts, desires, and human frailties. No one other than GOD was thought to be worthy to hear confessions and grant forgiveness. It was not until 1215 that the Fourth Lateran Council under Pope Innocent III made private priestly confession compulsory.[8]

Like the Church Fathers who did not teach or promote this practice, there are those today who have their doubts. Dr. Joseph Zacchello tells of his experience as a Catholic priest before his conversion to Protestantism in these words:

"Where my doubts were really troubling me was inside the confessional box. People were coming to me, kneeling down in front of me, confessing their sins to me. And I, with a sign of the cross, was promising that I had the power to forgive their sins. I, a sinner, a man, was taking God's place, God's right, and that terrible voice was penetrating me saying, 'You are depriving God of His glory. If sinners want to obtain forgiveness of their sins they must go to God and not to you. It is God's law they have broken, not yours. To God, therefore, they must make confession; and to God alone they must pray for forgiveness. No man can forgive sins, but Jesus can and does forgive sins.'"[9]

B. – ONE Lone Text

So far in our examination of the Catholic confessional, we've seen a wealth of evidence against such a practice. In Clue "S" of Chapter 19 and in this Appendix so far, we've listed at least TEN Scripture passages—with more to come—which clearly refute Rome's claims. To be fair, however, I must point out one lone verse which seems at first glance to offer some support for the Catholic position:

● **John 20:23** — "Whose soever sins ye remit, they are remitted unto them; and whose soever sins ye retain, they are retained."

The Master here was speaking to His followers who were hiding out in the Upper Room "for fear of the Jews." [10] Ten of the apostles were present and some other disciples, presumably including a few women. In this text Christ gives no liberty or license for any man to pass judgment on others. In the Sermon of the Mount He explicitly forbade this—"JUDGE NOT," says the Lord, "that ye be not judged." [11] That is the exclusive prerogative of God.

But on the collective body of the church He places a responsibility for its individual members. Toward those who fall into sin, the church has a duty—to warn, to instruct, and if possible to restore. "Reprove, rebuke, exhort," the Lord says, "with all long-suffering and doctrine." [12] We must deal faithfully with wrongdoing in the spirit of Him who hates sin but loves sinners. Warn every endangered soul. Leave none to deceive themselves. Call sin by its right name. Declare what God has said in regard to lying, stealing, idolatry, and every other evil. Let them know that "Those who do such things shall not inherit the kingdom of God." [13] *If they persist in sin, the judgment we have pronounced from God's Word is pronounced upon them in heaven.* For in *choosing* to sin, they disown Christ. Therefore the church must show that she does not—cannot—approve of their deeds, or she herself dishonors her Lord. She must say about sin what GOD says about it. She must deal with it just as God directs, and her action is ratified in heaven.

But there's a brighter side to the picture. "Whose soever sins ye remit, they are remitted." Let this thought be kept uppermost. In working for sinners, all eyes must be directed to Christ. As shepherds, we must have a tender care for the flock of the Lord's pasture. Speak to the erring of our Savior's forgiving mercy. Encourage the sinner to repent and to believe in HIM who can pardon. All who repent have the assurance: "He will again have compassion on us; He will tread our iniquities under foot. Yes, Thou wilt cast all their sins into the depths of the sea." [14]

With grateful hearts, let the church accept the sinner's repentance. Lead the repenting one out of the darkness of his unbelief into God's light of faith and devotion. Place his trembling hand in the loving hand of Jesus. Such a remission, born of the Holy Spirit, is ratified in heaven.

Only in this sense has the church power to absolve the sinner. To NO man, to no BODY of men, is given power to free the soul from guilt. Christ charged His disciples to PREACH the remission of sins in His name among all nations. [15] But they themselves were not empowered to remove one stain of sin. Instead, they and we are to "know that the SON of MAN [Jesus Christ] has power on earth to forgive sins." [16] Rather than mere mortal men granting forgiveness, the Lord Himself says: "I, even I, am He who blots out your transgressions for My own sake; and I will not remember your sins." [17]

The disciples were to go forth as witnesses, preaching and proclaiming the forgiveness of sins through Jesus Christ. They were to be the LORD'S WITNESSES—NOT the SINNER'S CONFESSORS. And that's exactly what we find them doing in the Book of Acts. For example, Peter proclaimed Christ to Cornelius, saying, "everyone who believes in Him receives forgiveness of sins." [18] When the Holy Spirit came upon Cornelius and his household, Peter realized that his listeners had believed. He then proclaimed that they WERE forgiven and accepted by God, so he baptized them in the name of the Lord.

There were also occasions when the disciples found it necessary to proclaim the sins of some RETAINED. Simon the sorcerer was one such person. Simon heard the gospel, said that he believed, and was baptized. But shortly thereafter he revealed his true motive: He thought he could obtain, or even purchase with money, magical powers from the apostles! Peter told Simon he was still in his sins. [19] But note also that Peter—whom the Church of Rome claims was the first pope—offered to sinful Simon a remedy. Was that remedy to seek a priest for forgiveness? No. Was it for Simon to confess to Peter or some other apostle? No, not at all. Instead, Peter faithfully directed Simon to the only One who could provide a remedy, saying: "Repent of this wickedness and pray to the LORD. Perhaps HE will forgive you for having such a thought in your heart." [20]

The surrounding context of John 20:23, the verse in question, also shows that the disciples were to serve as WITNESSES, presenting the good news of God's forgiveness for all who believe in Christ. In the two verses immediately preceding this text, Jesus said to them: "As the Father has sent Me, I also send you"—that is, He sends them out into the world as witnesses or missionaries. And then He mentions their reception of the Holy Spirit, who gives divine power for witnessing.

Thus as Christ sent forth His disciples with the gospel commission to preach His gospel of forgiveness, He gave them a DECLARATIVE power by which they ANNOUNCED the gracious terms on which salvation is granted to sinful men. His words in John 20:23—

> "indicate a DECLARATIVE power only: the right to PROCLAIM in Christ's name and with His authority, that all who truly repent of sin and trust in Him for pardon and salvation, shall surely be forgiven and saved. But it is CHRIST alone, and not the minister, who forgives. According to Scripture, the minister is only a HERALD to ANNOUNCE what the KING will do, on condition of repentance and faith on the part of the sinner."[21]

One final but very IMPORTANT point supports the interpretation of John 20:21-23 as teaching that the disciples were to proclaim God's forgiveness as witnesses: John 20:23 uses *a very significant verb tense* in the original Greek. The Lord did NOT say, "If you forgive the sins of any, their sins WILL BE forgiven them." NOR did He actually say, "If you forgive the sins of any, their sins ARE forgiven them." What He said was, "If you forgive the sins of any, their sins HAVE BEEN forgiven them; if you retain the sins of any, they HAVE BEEN retained." Careful literal translations like that of the New American Standard Bible (NASB) record His words as such.[22]

Scholarly Bible students know the same thing is true in the familiar text of Ephesians 2:8, which reads in the King James Version: "For by grace ARE ye saved through faith." The word *are* is not too bad a translation—IF the reader understands it as saying, "By grace you *are* [already] saved through faith." But modern versions like the NKJV, NIV, RSV, NRSV, and the NASB unanimously agree in translating it: "For by grace you HAVE BEEN saved through faith."

Here in John 20:23 Jesus uses the GREEK PERFECT TENSE. Grammar scholars Dana and Mantey explain: "It implies a process, but views that process as having [already] reached its consummation and existing in a FINISHED state."[23] This means that the disciples, as part of their witnessing, had the authority to DECLARE forgiveness to those whom God had ALREADY forgiven.

Thus we find that Jesus gave to them—and to us, living today as His disciples—authority to preach the gospel of Jesus Christ and share God's good news. As people RESPOND to His message of salvation by believing, we have authority to tell them, "Your sins are forgiven because you believe in the name of Jesus Christ."

Conversely, when we preach the gospel and people REJECT it and turn their backs on the Lord, He gave us authority as His disciples to say, "You are still in your sins, and you'll be lost in your sins unless you repent."[24]

C. – ABUSES OF THE CONFESSIONAL

Let's conclude our discussion of the confessional, as administered by erring humans, in a look at the abuses which are automatically inherent in such a practice.

In the *first* place, even Rome has never claimed infallibility for its thousands of priests—whom we know often have to be disciplined or defrocked, since they're only human. Therefore we might ask how is it possible for a priest to judge an ANONYMOUS individual, whom he cannot even SEE clearly, based on a FEW MINUTES' discussion. Let's put it this way:

> HOW can one MAN—human, erring, and fallible— [25]
> look into the HEART of another and
> judge his hidden, often unconscious MOTIVES,
> measure the seriousness of his sin,
> the degree of his guilt, and
> the depth of his contrition,
> ALL of which are often impossible to ascertain,

so as to be truly able to assign what the Church calls the divine "satisfaction" for that sin? No wonder the question is asked, "Who can forgive sins but GOD ALONE?" [26]

In the *second* place, Roman Catholic priests who left the Church after many years experience have themselves admitted and exposed some of the abuses intrinsic to the confessional. Here are a few examples:

Father Charles Chiniquy, after spending twenty-five years as a Roman Catholic priest in Canada and the United States, renounced the priesthood and became a Presbyterian minister. The following paragraphs express his sense of humiliation and shame at having ever engaged in the processes of the confessional:

> "With a blush on my face, and regret in my heart, I confess before God and man, that I have been through the confessional plunged for twenty-five years in that bottomless sea of iniquity, in which the blind priests of Rome have to swim day and night.

> "I had to learn by heart the infamous questions which the Church of Rome forces every priest to learn. I had to put these impure, immoral questions to women and girls who were confessing their sins to me. Those questions, and the answers they elicit, are so debasing that only a man who has lost every sense of shame can put them to any woman.

"Yes, I was bound in conscience, to put them to the ears, the mind, the imagination, the memory, the heart and soul of women and girls, questions of such a nature, the direct and immediate tendency of which is to fill the minds and hearts of both priests and penitents with thoughts and temptations of such a degrading nature, that I do not know any words adequate to express them. Pagan antiquity has never seen any institution more polluting than the confessional. I have lived twenty-five years in the atmosphere of the confessional. I was degraded and polluted by the confessional just as all the priests of Rome are. It has required all the blood of the great Victim, who has died on Calvary for sinners, to purify me." [27]

Lucien Vinet, a former Canadian priest, discloses the TORTURE of the confessional in his autobiographical book, *I Was a Priest*:

"*Confession of a Young Girl.* We now have a shy Roman Catholic young girl, passing through the state of childhood to puberty, who is about to enter the confessional. She is naturally embarrassed and her state of mind is just what a sordid confessor wishes to explore. The priest will now hear from a young woman the most secret thoughts and desires of her soul. Her mind and soul are sacrificed on the altar of Romanism. Many embarrassing questions are asked according to the sins accused. . . . These shameful details of a confession are mentioned here to illustrate what is meant by the *torture* of confession. Roman Catholics know very well that what we disclose is the crude truth.

"*Confession of a Married Woman.* A married woman enters the confessional. She will tell a strange man secrets which she probably would not dare reveal to her husband. She is even bound to reveal certain secrets of her husband. In the Roman Church birth control of all varieties is a sin and must be confessed with all its circumstances. The husband might be of Protestant faith and his Roman Catholic wife will have to disclose to the priest the most intimate relations of their marital life. The priest will know more about the wife than the husband. There are no family secrets because Rome has required that hearts and souls shall be fully explored by priests. . . .

"Poor Roman Catholic women! We know well that your kind souls are tortured to death by this terrible Roman obligation of telling, not only your sins, but also the most intimate secrets of your married life. As an ex-priest we can tell you that these mental tortures imposed upon your souls are NOT a prescription of the Saviour of mankind to obtain forgiveness of your sins, but are pure inventions of men to keep your minds and hearts under the control of a system, the torturous Roman religious organization. We must admit that as a priest we had no power to forgive your sins. No priest has such powers." [28]

CONCLUSION

Roman Catholic priests audaciously claim the power to forgive sins. We have subjected this claim to the scrutiny of Scripture. In doing so, we've discovered at least seven important truths:

1. It is NOT NECESSARY to confess to priests, for the Bible gives clear examples uniformly teaching us to confess directly to God.

2. Neither the holy Scriptures nor the writings of fallible "church fathers" offer examples of sinners receiving forgiveness from someone ELSE in the place of God.

3. We don't need a HUMAN priest through whom we approach God, for we already have "a great High Priest"—Jesus Christ, the "ONE Mediator between God and men." [29]

4. It is BLASPHEMY for any mere mortal—a sinner like ourselves—to claim the power that rightfully belongs only to God. [30]

5. The text Rome uses in its attempt to claim this power, John 20:23, really gives Christians only the right to PROCLAIM God's forgiveness as WITNESSES to His saving grace as we spread the good news of His gospel.

6. The original GREEK of John 20:23, in its VERB construction, confirms the validity of point #5, above, and refutes the blasphemous assertions of those who would usurp the office of God.

7. The actual practice of the Catholic confessional—operated as it is in the hands of fallible men—is open to an infinite number of inherent abuses, abuses which are only natural to a man-made system.

✦ ✦ ✦

In closing, we must say that in the light of all these considerations, the Catholic confessional is a demonstrably unscriptural practice. Sadly enough, it's also a futile fraud perpetrated on sincere believers who deserve better.

Notes to Appendix K

1. Quoted at more length in Chapter 9, "Life's Greatest Question," pages 238-239.
2. Psalm 32:5, NASB.
3. Nehemiah 1:4-11.
4. Daniel 9:3-19.
5. Ezra 9:5–10:1.
6. Ezra 10:11.
7. James G. McCarthy, *The Gospel According to Rome* (Eugene, OR: Harvest House Publishers, © 1995), p. 80.
8. Loraine Boettner, *Roman Catholicism* (Grand Rapids, MI: Baker Book House, © 1962), p. 199.
9. Dr. Joseph Zacchello, quoted in Boettner, *Roman Catholicism,* p. 203.
10. John 20:19.
11. Matthew 7:1.
12. 2 Timothy 4:2.
13. Galatians 5:21, RSV.
14. Micah 7:19, NASB.
15. Luke 24:47.
16. Mark 2:10, NKJV.
17. Isaiah 43:25, NKJV.
18. Acts 10:43, NASB.
19. See Acts 8:9-23.
20. Acts 8:22, NIV.
21. Dr. Henry M. Woods, *Our Priceless Heritage* (Harrisburg, PA: The Evangelical Press, 1941), p. 118.
22. Bible scholar J. B. Phillips wrote the "Foreword" to *The Interlinear Greek-English New Testament,* a most helpful volume offering the 21st edition of Eberhard Nestle's reliable Greek text, based on the study and careful research of generations of scholars, interlaced with a literal English translation by Dr. Alfred Marshall giving word-for-word verbal equivalents. In his "Foreword," Phillips makes this pertinent comment: "I am glad, for example, to see that Dr. Marshall has not missed the peculiar Greek construction in Matthew 16:19, where Jesus tells Peter that 'what he binds on earth' will be 'what HAS BEEN bound' in Heaven. There is a WORLD of difference between *guaranteeing celestial endorsement* of the Apostle's actions and promising that his actions guided by the Holy Spirit *will be* in accordance with the Heavenly pattern!" *The Interlinear Greek-English New Testament: The Nestle Greek Text with a Literal English Translation* by The Reverend Alfred Marshall, D. Litt. (London: Samuel Bagster & Sons, Limited, 1960), p. iii.
23. H. E. Dana and Julius R. Mantey, *A Manual Grammar of the Greek New Testament* (Toronto: Macmillan Company, 1955), p. 200.
24. Ron Carlson and Ed Decker, *Fast Facts on False Teachings* (Eugene, OR: Harvest House Publishers, 1994), pp. 220-221.

25. Even the inspired apostle Paul and his missionary colleague Barnabas, when those in Lystra attempted to confer divine honors upon them, promptly refused, saying, "We also are men of like passions with you."—Acts 14:1.

26. Mark 2:7, NKJV.

27. Father Charles Chiniquy, *The Priest, the Woman, and the Confessional* (Toronto: The Gospel Witness), pp. 67-68, quoted in Boettner, *Roman Catholicism*, p. 213.

28. Lucien Vinet, *I Was a Priest*, pp. 62-67, quoted in Boettner, *Roman Catholicism*, p. 212.

29. See Hebrews 4:14-16 and 1 Timothy 2:5.

30. For a discussion on blasphemy in this regard, see "Clue S" in Chapter 19, pages 659-666.

"Put your hand in the hand
of the MAN who stilled the water,
Put your hand in the hand
of the MAN who calmed the sea,
. . . the MAN from Galilee!"
—GOSPEL SONG by Gene MacLellan

~

A Personal Note

from the Author

THANK YOU for reading this far! It's been like a journey, traveling together and talking. Along the way, we've considered many topics, probed cosmic questions, investigated puzzling mysteries.

But, my friend, it's *no mystery* that GOD LOVES YOU! His love for you is INFINITE—so strong that He gave His life for you. He's coming back soon, and He wants to take you home with Him forever. You can safely trust everything to the HAND that was NAILED to the CROSS.

Yet confusing voices fill the air, clamoring for attention. Infidels arrogantly declare, "God is dead," while atheists echo, "There is no God!"   Fire-and-brimstone preachers loudly proclaim, "God is love, and if you don't believe it, He'll burn you forever."

In our desperate search for meaning, we wander in this maze of confusion. We try to sort through the claims and counterclaims, try to seek ORDER out of the CHAOS in our modern world, try to solve the Mystery of Life.

Most people are hesitant and resistant at first, then defensive and perhaps evasive, till they finally reach the point where they simply say,

"Just tell me the TRUTH."

Then the still, small voice of the Spirit speaks in the pages of Holy Scripture, the Word of God, expressing His love, offering His grace, thundering His Truth. Can't you hear it?

Friend of mine, when God whispers your name, how do you respond? Won't you give your heart to Him just now, surrender your life to His love, and walk with Him forever? He longs to give you His divine gifts of hope and wisdom and salvation. ACCEPT THEM—and you'll never be the same!

As an instrument in God's hands, you can also help change things for the better. You can be a witness to the world—a world that doesn't know the things you've learned. You don't have to be a seminary professor or have a degree in theology in order to be used very effectively in God's great work. Remember the blind man whose sight Jesus miraculously restored? He said simply: "One thing I know, that, whereas I was blind, now I see." [1] He didn't argue. He didn't make fancy speeches. He simply gave his personal testimony—which is something no one else can refute.

That man had been physically blind from his birth when Jesus flooded his life with light. Millions still are spiritually blind, stumbling through life in the darkness of Satan's lies. You can enlighten them with the truth you've learned, leading them step-by-step out of darkness into God's marvelous light. Why do you suppose the Lord led you to this book? There are no accidents, no mere coincidences in life, my friend. "The Lord knows those who are His." [2]

A saving relationship with Christ is very personal—it's something you must experience first-hand, for yourself. That's why the Psalmist says: "Oh, TASTE and SEE that the Lord is GOOD." [3] But you cannot expect your Christian experience to be meaningful unless you feed regularly on God's Word. Once you do this, you'll develop a taste for it and become hungry when you go without it. You'll gain for yourself the UNcommon sense and wisdom its pages provide.

With Christ you have a high destiny, a glorious future, a bright tomorrow that will last through all eternity. But you also have a God-given responsibility, a mission to carry out, while this earth lasts. We—you and I—must warn a world that's perishing without a Savior. And we haven't much time left to do it.

You'll find your efforts—and your faith—ten times stronger if you ally yourself with others of like faith. In unity there is strength, as we all know. But when you join a church, be absolutely sure it's one that teaches "the TRUTH, the WHOLE truth, and nothing BUT the truth"! I pray that the Scripture guidelines found in this book will help you in your search.

Notes to Afterword

1. John 9:25.
2. 2 Timothy 2:19, NKJV.
3. Psalms 34:8, NKJV.

DIALOGUE

with Hart Research

TELL US WHAT
YOU THINK

YOUR OPINION MATTERS!

Don't miss this chance to express your views with the author, editors, and publisher of this book.

Your input will help us do a better job of creating books that are relevant to you—and of sharing the truth of God's good news!

HART RESEARCH CENTER

MAIL:	488 Industrial Way—A-1
	Fallbrook, CA 92028
E-MAIL:	mail@hartresearch.org
FAX:	(760) 728–0879
TELEPHONE:	(760) 723–8082
WEB PAGE:	www.hartresearch.org

Meet the Author . . .

Howard Peth was born in 1930 in Chicago, Illinois, where he grew up—except for two carefree years spent in Fort Worth, Texas. He's lived his adult life in Southern California. With degrees from both UCLA and USC, he spent forty-two enjoyable years in the stimulating arena of the classroom, thirty-one of them at Mt. San Antonio College in Walnut, California, serving also as department chairman.

Retiring recently to the San Diego area, Mr. Peth now spends much of his time writing and presenting screen-illustrated lectures. He and Diane, his wife of forty-seven years, have three grown children and six grandchildren.